Organization Theory
A Libertarian Perspective

KEVIN A. CARSON
Center for a Stateless Society

BOOKSURGE

BookSurge

ISBN 1-4392-2199-5

Carson, Kevin A.
Organization Theory: A Libertarian Perspective
Includes bibliographic references and index
1. Organizational behavior. 2. Management. 3. Industrial management—employee
participation. 4. Anarchism. I. Title

To my mother, Ruth Emma Rickert, and the memory of my father, Amos Morgan Carson, with love.

Contents

Preface

This book had it origins in a passage (the "Fiscal and Input Crises" section of Chapter Eight) of my last book, *Studies in Mutualist Political Economy*. If you read that passage (it's available online at Mutualist.Org), you'll get an idea of the perspective that led me to write this book. The radical thoughts on organizational pathologies in that passage, both my own and those of the writers I quoted, dovetailed with my experiences of bureaucratic irrationality and Pointy-Haired Bossism in a lifetime as a worker and consumer.

To get the rest of the questions on my perspective out of the way, I should mention that the wording of the subtitle ("A Libertarian Perspective") reflects a long process of indecision and changes, and is something I still find unsatisfactory. I vacillated between the adjectives "mutualist," "anarchist," "individualist anarchist," and "left-libertarian," not really satisfied with any of them because of their likely tendency to pigeonhole my work or scare away my target audience. I finally ended up (with some misgivings) with plain old "Libertarian." It's a term of considerable contention between the classical liberal and libertarian socialist camps. I don't mean the choice of term in a sense that would exclude either side. In fact, as an individualist in the tradition of Tucker and the rest of the Boston anarchists, I embrace *both* the free market libertarian and libertarian socialist camps. I chose "libertarian" precisely it was large and contained multitudes: it alone seemed sufficiently broad to encompass the readership I had in mind.

I write from the perspective of individualist anarchism, as set forth by William B. Greene and Benjamin Tucker among others, and as I attempted to update it for the twenty-first century in my last book. Here's how I described it in the Preface to that book:

> In the mid-nineteenth century, a vibrant native American school of anarchism, known as individualist anarchism, existed alongside the other varieties. Like most other contemporary socialist thought, it was based on a radical interpretation of Ricardian economics. The classical individualist anarchism of Josiah Warren, Benjamin Tucker and Lysander Spooner was both a socialist movement and a subcurrent of classical liberalism. It agreed with the rest of the socialist movement that labor was the source of exchange-value, and . . . entitled to its full product. Unlike the rest of the socialist movement, the individualist anarchists believed that the natural wage of labor in a free market was its product, and that economic exploitation could only take place when capitalists and landlords harnessed the power of the state in their interests. Thus, individualist anarchism was an alternative both to the increasing statism of the mainstream socialist movement, and to a classical liberal movement that was moving toward a mere apologetic for the power of big business.[1]

I belong to the general current of the Left so beautifully described by the editors of *Radical Technology* ("the 'recessive Left' of anarchists, utopians and visionaries, which tends only to manifest itself when dominant genes like Lenin or Harold Wilson are off doing something else"). As such, I tend to agree with the Greens and other left-wing decentralists on the evils to which they object in current society and on their general view of a good

---

1. Kevin A. Carson, *Studies in Mutualist Political Economy*. Self-published via Blitzprint (Fayetteville, Ark., 2004), p. 9.

society, while I agree with free market libertarians on their analysis of the cause of such evils and how to get from here to there. In short: green ends with libertarian means.

My analysis of the large organization is informed by the same principles as my study of the state capitalist economy, namely: 1) that the exercise of power creates conflict of interest, within the nominally "private" corporation as well as in the larger economy; 2) hierarchy, by separating authority from knowledge, leads to the same informational problems within an organization that Hayek described at the level of political economy; and 3) by externalizing effort and reward on different actors, authority creates fundamental incentive problems. The primary function of authority is to create privilege: the wielder of power is able to externalize the costs of his decisions on others, while appropriating the benefits for himself. The result, when the costs and benefits of action are not internalized by the same actors, is that particular forms of organization are adopted beyond Pareto-optimal levels, and self-reinforcing distortions in feedback lead to a series of synergetic instabilities and interventions of the sort Mises described at the level of the economy as a whole. In short: state capitalism, along with the large, pathological organizations it breeds, is unsustainable.

The central question of Part One is that of Ronald Coase: If markets are more efficient than hierarchy and planning, why are the latter so prevalent? Why do we find the phenomenon that Coase remarked on—islands of corporate central planning in an economy supposedly governed by the market? Coase's answer was that firm boundaries—the boundaries between market and hierarchy—are set at the point at which the transaction costs of market contracting surpass than those of administration and planning. The subject of Part One is the extent to which the state artificially shifts these boundaries upward, so that the size of the dominant organization is far larger than warranted by genuine considerations of efficiency.

Part Two (consisting of a single chapter, Four) considers the pathological effects of large size, centralization and hierarchy, on a systemic level, under the hegemony of the corporation and the centralized state. That is, it considers the effect of the predominance of the large, hierarchical organization, and of the professionalized and bureaucratic culture it spawns, on the character of society as a whole.

Part Three examines the effects of large size and hierarchy *within* the large organization. Chapters Five and Six are brief surveys of the literature on information and incentive problems within the large organization, both by conventional organization theorists and by radical thinkers like Robert Anton Wilson and Paul Goodman. Chapter Seven applies the Austrian critique of central planning to the corporation. Chapter Eight is a broad-ranging examination of the irrationality and authoritarianism of the large organization, and of the general pathologies of managerialism: in particular, it is a critique of the currently prevailing MBA model of downsizing human capital, stripping assets, and gutting long-term productive capabilities in order to game management bonuses and stock options. Chapter Nine is a study of the internal crisis of governability of the large corporation, and—based on conventional literature on incomplete contracting—applies an asymmetric warfare model to labor relations within the corporation. And Chapter Ten examines the broad range of management theory and reform gimmicks, which I argue either serve as a mere legitimizing ideology of lip-service, or amount to an attempt to incorporate libertarian and decentralist elements into the old framework of corporate hierarchy rather than making them the building blocks of a fundamentally new form of society.

Finally, Part Four—of which I am especially proud—surveys the range of technical and organizational alternatives that might prevail in a decentralist, cooperative, genuinely free market economy. Chapters Eleven and Twelve discuss the twin structural principles of a genuinely libertarian society: the abolition of privilege and its replacement by a genuinely free market governed by the unfettered operation of the cost principle. Chapter Thirteen discusses the most feasible process for dismantling the state and moving toward such a society, summed up by the Wobbly slogan "Building the structure of the new society within the shell of the old." Chapter Fourteen examines the technological building blocks of a decentralized economy (especially small-scale general-purpose production machinery, desktop production machinery, and community-supported agriculture) based on small-scale production for local markets. Chapters Fifteen and Sixteen, finally, examine the organizational building blocks of production (cooperatives, peer production, and the informal and household economies) and distribution.

This book, for better or worse, is an example of peer production. The chapters have all appeared as rough drafts online, and much of the material within them appeared before that as posts on my blog (*Mutualist Blog: Free Market Anti-Capitalism*). The final form of this book reflects the enormous amount of fruitful discussion in the comments at my blog, and the helpful questions and criticisms raised by my readers, and the insights I have gained from dialogue with other organization theory bloggers and writers. I've received invaluable help in identifying typos and other errors from readers (particularly Matthieu Gues) who have compiled painstaking errata lists from reading the online drafts. Both the pdf I submitted to the publisher and the beautiful cover design are the work of Gary Chartier. So in many ways this is a collaborative product, and I owe my readers a debt of gratitude.

I welcome questions and criticisms. I can be reached by email at <free.market.anticapitalist@gmail.com>.

Part One
State Capitalist Intervention
in the Market

A Critical Survey of Orthodox Views on Economy of Scale

H erbert Simon remarked that, to an observer from Mars, "the dominant feature of the [economic] landscape" would be, not the market, but large organizations.[1] Or as David Friedman put it, "The capitalist system of coordination by trade seems to be largely populated by indigestible lumps of socialism called corporations."[2] The dominance of that feature, those lumps, is the central theme of Part One: the ways in which the state intervenes in the market to promote the predominance of organizations that are excessively large (i.e., larger than the efficiency considerations of a free market would justify). In the process, it will be helpful to keep in mind questions raised by R.H. Coase seventy years ago:in their analysis of American industrial history, have tended to assume the superior efficiency of large-scale organization, and to accept "economies of scale" as a sufficient explanation for the rise of the large corporation from a supposedly "laissez-faire" economy. In the words of Randall Meyer,

> As D. H. Robertson points out, we find "islands of conscious power in this ocean of unconscious co-operation like lumps of butter coagulating in a pail of buttermilk." But in view of the fact that it is usually argued that co-ordination will be done by the price mechanism, why is such organization necessary? Why are there these "islands of conscious power"?[3]

What determines the boundaries between firm and market? Why is there any substitution of hierarchy for independent contracts at all, and, conversely, why is there not one big firm?

> The main reason why it is profitable to establish a firm would seem to be that there is a cost of using the price mechanism . . . . The costs of negotiating and concluding a separate contract for each exchange transaction which takes place on a market must also be taken into account . . . . It is true that contracts are not eliminated when there is a firm but they are greatly reduced. A factor of production (or the owner thereof) does not have to make a series of contracts with the factors with whom he is co-operating within the firm . . . . For this series of contracts is substituted one . . . .
> . . . . A firm becomes larger as additional transactions (which could be exchange transactions co-ordinated through the price mechanism) are organized by the entrepreneur and becomes smaller as he abandons the organization of such transactions. The question which arises is whether it is possible to study the forces which determine the size of the firm. Why does the entrepreneur not organize one less transaction or one more? . . . .

---

1. Herbert Simon, "Organizations and Markets," *Journal of Economic Perspectives* 5 (1991), p. 27.
2. David Friedman, *Hidden Order*, quoted in Matt McIntosh, "All In, Comrade," *Distributed Republic*, February 26, 2007 <http://www.distributedrepublic.com/distributedrepublic/comment/reply/4685>.
3. Ronald H. Coase, "The Nature of the Firm," *Economica* (November 1937), p. 388.

The answer is that the maximum boundary of the firm is determined by the point "where the costs of organizing an extra transaction within the firm are equal to the costs involved in carrying out the transaction in the open market . . ."

> . . . [Therefore], a firm will tend to expand until the costs of organizing an extra transaction within the firm will become equal to the costs of carrying out the same transaction by means of an exchange on the open market or the costs of organizing in another firm.[1]

In this chapter we will survey the conventional view of economy of scale, primarily as expounded by technocratic liberals like Alfred Chandler and John Kenneth Galbraith. We will examine its pathological implications for the organization of the political economy as a whole, along with its unstated assumptions and value judgments and its internal contradictions.

In Chapter Two, we will examine the available evidence on economy of scale, which shows not only that the dominant firm is many times larger than would be warranted by efficiency considerations, but that its size results in significant net inefficiency costs compared to the smaller firm. The obvious question arises, in response to this finding: if the large firm is less efficient, why does it exist?

The answer, found in Chapter Three, is that the state makes it artificially efficient by subsidizing its inefficiency costs and insulating it from competition, and thereby artificially shifts the boundary between market and hierarchy.

A. Cross-Ideological Affinity for Large-Scale Organization

Technocratic liberals, in their analysis of American industrial history, have tended to assume the superior efficiency of large-scale organization, and to accept "economies of scale" as a sufficient explanation for the rise of the large corporation from a supposedly "laissez-faire" economy. In the words of Randall Meyer,

> [The] problems of our times will require greater, bigger organizations than we have now, rather than smaller ones, for their solution . . . . [We must therefore] cast aside our outmoded notions of size and our fear of bigness.[2]

Of course this assumption is not limited to liberal managerialists. It is shared by both the vulgar Marxists (who see One Big Trust as the penultimate stage in the progressive development toward state socialism), and the vulgar Austrians (who equate capital-intensiveness or "roundaboutness" as such with superior productivity).

Among the Marxists, it can be found in the work of Marx and Engels themselves. In *The Communist Manifesto*, they identified the concentration of capital and the centralization of production, as such, with the progressive role of the bourgeoisie:

> The bourgeoisie keeps more and more doing away with the scattered state of the population, of the means of production, and of property. It has agglomerated population, centralised the means of production, and has concentrated property in a few hands . . . .
>
> The bourgeoisie, during its rule of scarce one hundred years, has created more massive and more colossal productive forces than have all preceding generations together. Subjection of Nature's forces to man, machinery, application of chemistry to industry and agriculture, steam-navigation, railways, electric telegraphs, clearing of whole continents for cultivation, canalisation of rivers, whole populations conjured out of the

1. *Ibid.*, p.

2. "The Role of Big Business in Achieving National Goals," in David Mermelstein, ed., *Economics: Mainstream Readings and Radical Critiques*. 3rd ed. (New York: Random House, 1975). Quoted in Walter Adams and James W. Brock. *The Bigness Complex: Industry, Labor and Government in the American Economy*. 2nd ed. (Stanford, Cal.: Stanford University Press, 2004), p. 64.

ground—what earlier century had even a presentiment that such productive forces slumbered in the lap of social labour?[1]

For the Marxists, economic centralization is a natural process that proceeds until the increasingly efficient system of large-scale production can no longer be contained by the "capitalist integument."

Engels took this tendency of Marxism even further, laying the groundwork for Lenin's later embrace of Taylorism[2]:

> If man . . . has subdued the forces of nature, the latter avenge themselves upon him by subjecting him, in so far as he employs them, to a veritable despotism independent of all social organisation. Wanting to abolish authority in large-scale industry is tantamount to wanting to abolish industry itself, to destroy the power loom in order to return to the spinning wheel . . . .
>
> We have thus seen that, on the one hand, a certain authority, no matter how delegated, and, on the other hand, a certain subordination, are things which, independently of all social organisation, are imposed upon us together with the material conditions under which we produce and make products circulate.
>
> We have seen, besides, that the material conditions of production and circulation inevitably develop with large-scale industry and large-scale agriculture, and increasingly tend to enlarge the scope of this authority.[3]

Lenin, like Engels, saw "state capitalist monopoly" as a progressive development, with the final progressive step being the expropriation of the ultra-efficient trusts by the workers' state: ". . . socialism is merely state-capitalist monopoly which is made to serve the interests of the whole people . . . ."[4]

On the right, the identification of large scale with efficiency is shared by some Austrian economists, who seem to think that capital-intensiveness (or "roundabout" production methods) involves unlimited, or almost unlimited efficiencies. The distinction originated with Böhm-Bawerk:

> That roundabout methods lead to greater results than direct methods is one of the most important and fundamental propositions in the whole theory of production. It must be emphatically stated that the only basis of this proposition is the experience of practical life. Economic theory does not and cannot show *a priori,* that it must be so; but the unanimous experience of all the technique of production says that it is so.[5]

The same assumption was restated, more forcefully, by Robert Murphy in his lecture "Capital and Interest":

> ★The more roundabout processes are, the more efficient and physically productive they are.

1. Karl Marx and Friedrich Engels, *Manifesto of the Communist Party.* Marx and Engels, *Collected Works,* vol. 6 (New York: International Publishers, 1976), pp. 448–449.

2. There is a legitimate question as to whether Taylor himself was a "Taylorist," in the vulgar sense. See Chris Nyland, "Taylorism and the Mutual Gains Strategy," *Industrial Relations* vol. 37 no. 4 (October 1998), pp. 519–542 (thanks to Eric Husman for the tip). Subsequent references to "Taylorism" in this book will reflect conventional usage, without necessarily implying any aspersion on the work of Taylor himself.

3. Friedrich Engels, "On Authority." Marx and Engels, *Collected Works,* vol. 23 (New York: International Publishers, 1988), pp. 422–425.

4. V.I. Lenin, *The Impending Catastrophe and How to Combat It.* V.I. Lenin, *Collected Works,* vol. 25 (Moscow: Progress Publishers, 1967), p. 358.

5. Eugen von Böhm-Bawerk, *The Positive Theory of Capital.* Translated by William Smart (London: Macmillan and Co., 1891), p. 20.

★The greater productivity of roundabout methods is why *Capital Accumulation* generates great wealth.[1]

Lew Rockwell charged that "many people today . . . long for a system of economics that prevailed in the Middle Ages."

> On the Left, we have the neo-Rousseauians who imagine that modern technology has a hopelessly corrupting effect, while many on the Right dream of a guild-dominated system of small craftsmen and home-based production. But these fantasies are not only unworkable; in reality, they are nothing short of lethal. Most of the world's population would die immediately if such a system were imposed.[2]

This howler indicates that he knows next to nothing about the technical possibilities of home-based and small shop production using modern power machinery, or about the greater productivity per acre of intensive small-scale agriculture (about both of which see the material below on Ralph Borsodi).

At the crudest extreme is George Reisman. A central theme in his work runs something like this: the way to increase the standard of living is to make the rich even richer, so they will undertake the capital accumulation that alone increases the productivity of labor, which will cause wages to rise.[3]

The irony is that the Austrians, who consider themselves such iconoclasts in savaging so much of the received wisdom of neoclassical economics and liberal managerialism, also accept without any critical awareness so many of its implicit assumptions. The Austrians are remarkably selective, to say the least, in their choices of which "conventional wisdom" to reject. But then consistency is not exactly the Austrians' strong suit. Their approach to deciding which parts of present-day reality to blame on the state, and which to credit to the wonders of the "free market," is (to say the least) somewhat arbitrary. The denizens of Lew Rockwell.Com and Mises.Org, when it comes to politics, resemble nothing so much as American Jacobites in their patronage of lost causes, standing athwart history and yelling "Stop!" on behalf of such might-have-beens as the Anti-Federalists and the southern secessionists. So it's somewhat jarring to see them turn on a dime and become ardently triumphalist enthusiasts for the sheer Hegelian "is-ness" of things when it comes to Wal-Mart and sweatshops. It's a bit odd to be so anti-Hamiltonian, and yet so fond of an economy founded on Hamiltonianism.

B. CHANDLER, GALBRAITH, AND PUSH DISTRIBUTION

But despite these parallels in other segments of the ideological spectrum, the apologetic for large-scale organization is a defining characteristic, especially, of twentieth century liberalism. Its roots can be traced back to the Progressive movement of the early twentieth century, which was the intellectual foundation for big government liberalism as it was known in the following decades. Progressivism took for granted that the twentieth century was to be the age of the large organization, and that the dominance of the giant corporation and the centralized government agency was a fact of nature. The only question was in whose interests such organizations would be managed. The Progressive movement, along

---

1. Robert Murphy, "Capital and Interest (Lecture 9 of 32)," posted by David Heinrich at Mises Economics Blog, June 11, 2004. <http://blog.mises.org/archives/002113.asp>; See also M. Northrup Buechner. "Roundaboutness and Productivity in Bohm-Bawerk" *Southern Economic Journal*, Vol. 56, No. 2 (Oct., 1989), pp. 499-510.

2. Lew Rockwell, "Imperialism: Enemy of Freedom," LewRockwell.Com, October 30, 2006. <http://www.lewrockwell.com/rockwell/bamboozle-bourgeoisie.html>

3. George Reisman, "For Society to Thrive, the Rich Must be Left Alone," Mises.Org, March 2, 2006 <http://mises.org/story/2073>.

with the twentieth century liberalism it sired, was personified by Herbert Croly, with his goal of achieving "Jeffersonian ends by Hamiltonian means." (Of course the Jeffersonianism of ends was largely spurious; as Roy Childs put it, liberal intellectuals historically have been "the 'running dogs' of big businessmen . . .")[1]

The first great apostle of economy of scale was Joseph Schumpeter, whose charism has since been passed down through the succession of J.K. Galbraith and Alfred Chandler. Schumpeter wrote at length on the giant oligopoly corporation as a progressive force for innovation:

> . . . . The theory of simple and discriminating monopoly teaches that, excepting a limiting case, monopoly price is higher and monopoly output smaller than competitive price and competitive output. This is true provided that the method and organization of production—and everything else—are exactly the same in both cases. Actually however there are superior methods available to the monopolist which either are not available at all to a crowd of competitors or are not available to them so readily: for there are advantages which, though not strictly unattainable on the competitive level of enterprise, are as a matter of fact secured only on the monopoly level, for instance, because monopolization may increase the sphere of influence of the better, and decrease the sphere of influence of the inferior, brains, or because the monopoly enjoys a disproportionately higher financial standing . . . .
>
> There cannot be any reasonable doubt that under the conditions of our epoch such superiority is as a matter of fact the outstanding feature of the typical large-scale unit of control . . . . These units may not only arise in the process of creative destruction . . . , but in many cases of decisive importance they provide the necessary form for the achievement.[2]

Schumpeter's most important disciple in these matters, of course, was John Kenneth Galbraith. Galbraith accepted, as an article of faith, that innovation came about through the large, capital-intensive organization:

> . . . a benign Providence . . . has made the modern industry of a few large firms an excellent instrument for inducing technical change. It is admirably equipped for financing technical development. Its organization provides strong incentives for undertaking development and for putting it into use . . . .
>
> . . . Technical development has long since become the preserve of the scientist and the engineer. Most of the cheap and simple inventions have . . . been made. Not only is development now sophisticated and costly but it must be on a sufficient scale so that successes and failures will in some small measure average out . . . .
>
> Because development is costly, it follows that it can be carried on only by a firm that has the resources which are associated with considerable size. Moreover, unless a firm has a substantial share of the market it has no strong incentive to undertake a large expenditure on development . . . .
>
> . . . [I]n the modern industry shared by a few large firms size and the rewards accruing to market power combine to insure that resources for research and technical development will be available. The power that enables the firm to have some influence on prices insures that the resulting gains will not be passed on to the public by imitators . . . before the outlay for development can be recouped . . . .
>
> The net of all this is that there must be some element of monopoly in an industry if it is to be progressive.[3]

In *The New Industrial State*, Galbraith wrote at much greater length about the connection between capital intensiveness and the "technostructure's" need for predictability and control:

1. Roy Childs, "Big Business and the Rise of American Statism" (1971), *Reason*, February and March 1971, reproduced at <http://praxeology.net/RC-BRS.htm>.

2. Joseph A. Schumpeter, *Capitalism, Socialism, and Democracy* (New York and London: Harper & Brothers Publishers, 1942), pp. 100-101.

3. John Kenneth Galbraith, *American Capitalism: The Concept of Countervailing Power* (Boston: Houghton Mifflin, 1962), pp. 86-88

. . . [Machines and sophisticated technology] require . . . heavy investment of capital. They are designed and guided by technically sophisticated men. They involve, also, a greatly increased lapse of time between any decision to produce and the emergence of a salable product.

From these changes come the need and the opportunity for the large organization. It alone can deploy the requisite capital; it alone can mobilize the requisite skills . . . . The large commitment of capital and organization well in advance of result requires that there be foresight and also that all feasible steps be taken to insure that what is foreseen will transpire.[1]

The need for planning . . . arises from the long period of time that elapses during the production process, the high investment that is involved and the inflexible commitment of that investment to the particular task.[2]

Planning exists because [the market] process has ceased to be reliable. Technology, with its companion commitment of time and capital, means that the needs of the consumer must be anticipated—by months or years . . . . [I]n addition to deciding what the consumer will want and will pay, the firm must make every feasible step to see that what it decides to produce is wanted by the consumer at a remunerative price . . . . It must exercise control over what is sold . . . . It must replace the market with planning.[3]

. . . The need to control consumer behavior is a requirement of planning. Planning, in turn, is made necessary by extensive use of advanced technology and capital and by the relative scale and complexity of organization. These produce goods efficiently; the result is a very large volume of production. As a further consequence, goods that are related only to elementary physical sensation—that merely prevent hunger, protect against cold, provide shelter, suppress pain—have come to comprise a small and diminishing part of all production. Most goods serve needs that are discovered to the individual not by the palpable discomfort that accompanies deprivation, but by some psychic response to their possession . . . .[4]

For Galbraith, the "accepted sequence" of consumer sovereignty (what Mises called "dollar democracy"), in which consumer demand determines what is produced, has been replaced by a "revised sequence" in which oligopoly corporations determine what is produced and then dispose of it by managing consumer behavior. In contemporary terms, the demand-pull economy is replaced by a supply-push model. As Michael Piore and Charles Sabel put it:

Mass production required large investments in highly specialized equipment and narrowly trained workers. In the language of manufacturing, these resources were "dedicated": suited to the manufacture of a particular product—often, in fact, to just one make or model. When the market for that particular product declined, the resources had no place to go. Mass production was therefore profitable only with markets that were large enough to absorb and enormous output of a single, standardized commodity, and stable enough to keep the resources involved in the production of that commodity continuously employed. Markets of this kind . . . did not occur naturally. They had to be created.[5]

Alfred Chandler, like Galbraith, was thoroughly sold on the greater efficiencies of the large corporation. He argued that the modern multi-unit enterprise arose when administrative coordination "permitted" greater efficiencies.[6] Its chief efficiency was a reduction in

1. John Kenneth Galbraith, *The New Industrial State* (New York: Signet Books, 1967), p. 16

2. *Ibid.*, p. 31.

3. *Ibid.*, pp. 34-35.

4. *Ibid.*, pp. 210-212.

5. Michael J. Piore and Charles F. Sabel, *The Second Industrial Divide: Possibilities for Prosperity* (New York: HarperCollins, 1984), p. 49.

6. Alfred D. Chandler, Jr., *The Visible Hand: The Managerial Revolution in American Business* (Cambridge and London: The Belknap Press of Harvard University Press, 1977), p. 6.

transaction costs: "internalizing," under administrative control, the activities that were previously conducted by free contract among a number of independent businesses.

> Such an internalization gave the enlarged enterprise many advantages. By routinizing the transactions between units, the costs of these transactions were lowered. By linking the administration of producing units with buying and distributing units, costs for information on markets and sources of supply were reduced. Of much greater significance, the internalization of many units permitted the flow of goods from one unit to another to be administratively coordinated. More effective scheduling of flows achieved a more intensive use of facilities and personnel employed in the processes of production and so increased productivity and reduced costs.[1]

In discussing the internal efficiencies achieved through large-scale production and internal hierarchy, Chandler's enthusiasm fairly jumps off the page:

> Organizationally, output was expanded through improved design of manufacturing or processing plants and by innovations in managerial practices and procedures required to synchronize flaws and supervise the work force. Increases in productivity also depend on the skills and abilities of the managers and the workers and the continuing improvement of their skills over time. Each of these factors or any combination of them helped to increase the speed and volume of the flow, or what some processors call the "throughput," of materials within a single plant or works . . . .
>
> Where the underlying technology of production permitted, increased throughput from technological innovation, improved organizational design, and perfected human skills led to a sharp decrease in the number of workers required to produce a specific unit of output. The ratio of capital to labor, materials to labor, energy to labor, and managers to labor for each unit of output became higher. Such high-volume industries soon became capital-intensive, energy-intensive, and manager-intensive.[2]

They achieved "economies of speed" from "greatly increasing the daily use of equipment and personnel."[3] (Of course, Chandler starts by assuming the need for a capital-intensive mode of production, which *then* requires "economies of speed" to reduce unit costs from the expensive capital assets).

This model of production resulted in the adoption of increasingly specialized, asset-specific production machinery:

> The large industrial enterprise continued to flourish when it used capital-intensive, energy-consuming, continuous or large-batch production technology to produce for mass markets.[4]

Chandler's account resembled, with his assumption of managerial capitalism as the only possible response to objective technological necessity, the transposition of the Whig theory of history to the industrial realm. As Yehouda Shenhav describes it,

> . . . [C]apitalists came to realize that they needed a much more systematic control mechanism for efficiency purposes . . . . The advent of the first integrated enterprises during the 1880s and 1890s "brought about" new problems, such as an increase in the volume of output, that "led" to the building of the first administrative systems . . . . To Chandler, "the appearance of managerial capitalism has been . . . an economic phenomenon", and not a political one . . . . Administrative systems were adopted as rational responses to problems of economic reality confronting capitalists. In Chandler's analysis, the development of systems had no reference to power, politics, and interests. Although Chandler was vague about agency ("led", "brought about"), he attributes the rise of

---

1. *Ibid.*, pp. 6–7.
2. *Ibid.*, p. 241.
3. *Ibid.*, p. 244.
4. *Ibid.*, p. 347.

business administration to employers' and managers' (alike) attempts to meet the strategic challenges facing them . . . .[1]

Chandler's Achilles Heel was his admission (although he did not recognize it as such) that achieving productive efficiencies through such "progressive" innovations required the preexistence of a high-volume, high-speed, high-turnover distribution system on a national scale.

> . . . [M]odern business enterprise appeared for the first time in history when the volume of economic activities reached a level that made administrative coordination more efficient and more profitable than market coordination.[2]
> . . . [The rise of administrative coordination first] occurred in only a few sectors or industries where technological innovation and market growth created high-speed and high-volume throughput.[3]

William Lazonick, a disciple of Chandler, described the process as obtaining "a large market share in order to transform the high fixed costs into low unit costs . . . ."[4]

The railroad and telegraph, "so essential to high-volume production and distribution," were in Chandler's view what made possible this steady flow of goods through the distribution pipeline.[5]

The primacy of such state-subsidized infrastructure is indicated by the very structure of Chandler's book. He begins with the railroads and telegraph system, themselves the first modern, multi-unit enterprises.[6] And in subsequent chapters, he recounts the successive evolution of a national wholesale network piggybacking on the centralized transportation system, followed by a national retail system, and only then by large-scale manufacturing for the national market. A national long-distance transportation system led to mass distribution, which in turn led to mass production.

> The coming of mass distribution and the rise of the modern mass marketers represented an organizational revolution made possible by the new speed and regularity of transportation and communication.[7]
> . . . The new methods of transportation and communication, by permitting a large and steady flow of raw materials into and finished products out of a factory, made possible unprecedented levels of production. The realization of this potential required, however, the invention of new machinery and processes.[8]

In other words, the so-called "internal economies of scale" in manufacturing could come about only when the offsetting *external diseconomies* of long-distance distribution were artificially nullified by corporate welfare.

From Chandler's perspective, of course, all the above simply means that the state's role in creating centralized infrastructure *facilitated* the introduction of organizational forms that were *inherently* more efficient.

But despite his touching faith, there is in fact no such thing as generic or immaculate "efficiency." One method or another is only more efficient *given* a particular package of input costs that determine which inputs are to be economized on. Subsidies are subject to what might be called The Law of Conservation of Costs: costs can be shifted, but they

1. Yehouda Shenhav, *Manufacturing Rationality: The Engineering Foundations of the Managerial Revolution* (Oxford and New York: Oxford University Press, 1999), p. 103.
2. Chandler, *The Visible Hand*, p. 8.
3. *Ibid.*, p. 11.
4. William Lazonick, *Business Organization and the Myth of the Market Economy* (Cambridge, 1991), pp. 198–226.
5. Chandler, *The Visible Hand*, p. 79.
6. *Ibid.*, pp. 79, 96–121.
7. *Ibid.*, p. 235.
8. *Ibid.*, p. 240.

cannot be destroyed. In other words, as the saying goes, There Ain't No Such Thing As A Free Lunch. The overall cost of a good from a giant factory two thousand miles away does not become less than that of a good from a small factory twenty miles away, just because part of the cost is collected by the IRS instead of by the retailer. If the total cost amounts to more than the product's worth, the product doesn't become a net social good because some items on the cost side of the ledger don't show up in retail price.

Chandler's version of history, turned rightside-up, can be restated thusly: transportation subsidies and internal improvements were primary in creating the low distribution costs and resulting artificially large market areas without which large scale production would have been impossible. *Given* the artificial inflation of this high-volume distribution system, and *given* the resulting artificial profitability of large organizations, hierarchy becomes necessary to manage those organizations. And *given* these artificial conditions, the pioneers of the multi-unit corporation did indeed come up with some great accomplishments. Their great feats of administrative innovation were a rational way of carrying out an inherently irrational task.

As Chandler himself admitted, the greater "efficiency" of national wholesale organizations lay in their "even more effective exploitation of the existing railroad and telegraph systems."[1] That is, they were more efficient parasites. But the "efficiencies" of a parasite are usually of a zero-sum nature.

Chandler also admitted, perhaps inadvertently, that the "more efficient" new production methods were adopted almost as an afterthought, *given* the artificially large market areas and subsidized distribution:

> . . . the nature of the market was more important than the methods of production in determining the size and defining the activities of the modern industrial corporation.[2]

Despite all this, Chandler—astonishingly—minimized the role of public policy in creating the system he so admires:

> The rise of modern business enterprise in American industry between the 1880s and World War I was little affected by public policy, capital markets, or entrepreneurial talents because it was part of a more fundamental economic development. Modern business enterprise . . . was the organizational response to fundamental changes in processes of production and distribution made possible by the availability of new sources of energy and by the increasing application of scientific knowledge to industrial technology. The coming of the railroad and telegraph and the perfection of new high-volume processes . . . made possible a historically unprecedented volume of production.[3]

Chandler's statement also reflects an unquestioned assumption that what Lewis Mumford called "paleotechnics" (i.e., the large-scale factory production of the coal and steam age—about which more in Part Four) were more efficient than the decentralized, small-scale production methods of Kropotkin and Borsodi. The possibility never occurs to him that massive state intervention, at the same time as it enabled the revolutions in corporate size and capital-intensiveness, might also have tipped the balance between alternative forms of production technology.

Despite all the state intervention up front to make the large corporation possible, state intervention was required *afterward* as well as before in order to keep the system running. These great corporate paragons of efficiency were unable to survive without the government guaranteeing an outlet for their overproduction, and protecting them from market competition.

1. *Ibid.*, p. 215.
2. *Ibid.*, p. 363.
3. *Ibid.*, p. 376.

The ruling elites of the corporate-state nexus perceived, as early as the depression of the 1890s, that overbuilt industry could not dispose of its output, operating at full capacity, without government help. This problem was first addressed through imperial adventure to secure foreign markets. The system, in Schumpeter's phrase, was "export-dependent monopoly capitalism." It gave rise to what W.A. Williams called "Open Door Empire," which was institutionalized in the Bretton Woods agencies of FDR and Truman, and remains the basis of U.S. foreign policy to the present day.[1]

Another approach to the problem of overproduction was mass advertising and consumer credit. Although somewhat less state-dependent than imperialism, it had a large state component. For one thing, the founders of the mass advertising and public relations industries were, in large part, also the founders of the science of "manufacturing consent" used to manipulate Anglo-American populations into support for St. Woodrow's crusade. For another, the state's own organs of propaganda (through the USDA, school home economics classes, etc.) put great emphasis on discrediting "old-fashioned" atavisms like home-baked bread and home-grown and -canned vegetables, and promoting in their place the "up-to-date" housewifely practice of heating stuff up out of cans from the market.[2] Jeffrey Kaplan described this, in a recent article, as the "gospel of consumption":

> [Industrialists] feared that the frugal habits maintained by most American families would be difficult to break. Perhaps even more threatening was the fact that the industrial capacity for turning out goods seemed to be increasing at a pace greater than people's sense that they needed them.
>
> It was this latter concern that led Charles Kettering, director of General Motors Research, to write a 1929 magazine article called "Keep the Consumer Dissatisfied." . . . Along with many of his corporate cohorts, he was defining a strategic shift for American industry—from fulfilling basic human needs to creating new ones.
>
> In a 1927 interview with the magazine *Nation's Business*, Secretary of Labor James J. Davis provided some numbers to illustrate a problem that the *New York Times* called "need saturation." Davis noted that "the textile mills of this country can produce all the cloth needed in six months' operation each year" and that 14 percent of the American shoe factories could produce a year's supply of footwear. The magazine went on to suggest, "It may be that the world's needs ultimately will be produced by three days' work a week."
>
> Business leaders were less than enthusiastic about the prospect of a society no longer centered on the production of goods. For them, the new "labor-saving" machinery presented not a vision of liberation but a threat to their position at the center of power. John E. Edgerton, president of the National Association of Manufacturers, typified their response when he declared: "Nothing . . . breeds radicalism more than unhappiness unless it is leisure."
>
> By the late 1920s, America's business and political elite had found a way to defuse the dual threat of stagnating economic growth and a radicalized working class in what one industrial consultant called "the gospel of consumption"—the notion that people could be convinced that however much they have, it isn't enough. President Herbert Hoover's 1929 Committee on Recent Economic Changes observed in glowing terms the results: "By advertising and other promotional devices . . . a measurable pull on production has been created which releases capital otherwise tied up." They celebrated the con-

---

1. Joseph Stromberg did an excellent job of integrating this thesis, generally identified with the historical revisionism of the New Left, into the theoretical framework of Mises and Rothbard, in "The Role of State Monopoly Capitalism in the American Empire" *Journal of Libertarian Studies* Volume 15, no. 3 (Summer 2001), pp. 57-93. Available online at <http://www.mises.org/journals/jls/15_3/15_3_3.pdf>.

2. This is the theme of Stuart Ewen, *Captains of Consciousness: Advertising and the Social Roots of Consumer Culture* (New York: McGraw-Hill, 1976).

ceptual breakthrough: "Economically we have a boundless field before us; that there are new wants which will make way endlessly for newer wants, as fast as they are satisfied."[1]

Chandler's model of "high-speed, high-throughput, turning high fixed costs into low unit costs," and Galbraith's "technostructure," absolutely require a "push" model of distribution. Here's how it was described by Paul Goodman:

> . . . in recent decades . . . the center of economic concern has gradually shifted from either providing goods for the consumer or gaining wealth for the enterpriser, to keeping the capital machines at work and running at full capacity; for the social arrangements have become so complicated that, unless the machines are running at full capacity, all wealth and subsistence are jeopardized, investment is withdrawn, men are unemployed. That is, when the system depends on all the machines running, unless *every* kind of good is produced and sold, it is also impossible to produce bread.[2]

The same imperative was at the root of the hypnopaedic socialization in Huxley's *Brave New World*: "ending is better than mending"; "the more stitches, the less riches." Or as GM designer Harley Earl said in the 1950s,

> My job is to hasten obsolescence. I've got it down to two years; now when I get it down to one year, I'll have a perfect score.[3]

Because of the imperative for overcapitalized industry to operate at full capacity, on round-the-clock shifts, in order to spread the cost of its expensive machinery over the greatest possible number of units of output, the imperative of ensuring consumption was equally great.

> Integration of mass production with mass distribution afforded an opportunity for manufacturers to lower costs and increase productivity through more effective administration of the processes of production and distribution and coordination of the flow of goods through them. Yet the first industrialists to integrate the two basic sets of processes did not do so to exploit such economies. They did so because existing marketers were unable to sell and distribute products in the volume they were produced.[4]

The older economy that the "push" distribution system replaced was one in which most foods and drugs were what we would today call "generic." Flour, cereal, and similar products were commonly sold in bulk and weighed and packaged by the grocer (the ratio had gone from roughly 95% bulk to 75% package goods during the twenty years before Borsodi wrote in 1927); the producers geared production to the level of demand that was relayed to them by the retailers' orders. Drugs, likewise, were typically compounded by the druggist on-premises to the physician's specifications, from generic components.[5]

Under the new "push" system, the producers appealed directly to the consumer through brand-name advertising, and relied on pressure on the grocer to create demand for what they chose to produce.

> It is possible to roughly classify a manufacturer as belonging either to those who "make" products to meet requirements of the market, or as belonging to those who "distribute" brands which they decide to make. The manufacturer in the first class relies upon the natural demand for his product to absorb his output. He relies upon competition among

1. Jeffrey Kaplan, "The Gospel of Consumption: And the better future we left behind," *Orion*, May/June 2008 <http://www.orionmagazine.org/index.php/articles/article/2962>.
2. Paul and Percival Goodman, *Communitas: Means of Livelihood and Ways of Life* (New York: Vintage Books, 1947, 1960), pp. 188-89.
3. Eric Rumble, "Toxic Shocker," *Up! Magazine*, January 1, 2007 <http://www.up-magazine.com/magazine/exclusives/Toxic_Shocker_3.shtml>.
4. Chandler, *The Visible Hand*, p. 287.
5. Ralph Borsodi, *The Distribution Age* (New York and London: D. Appleton and Company, 1929), pp. 217, 228.

wholesalers and retailers in maintaining attractive stocks to absorb his production. The manufacturer in the second class creates a demand for his brand and forces wholesalers and retailers to buy and "stock" it. In order to market what he has decided to manufacture, he figuratively has to make water run uphill.[1]

The problem was that the consumer, under the new regime of Efficiency, paid about four times as much for trademarked flour, sugar, etc., as he had paid for bulk goods under the old "inefficient" system.[2]

The advantage of brand specification, from the perspective of the producer, is that it "lifts a product out of competition":[3] "the prevalence of brand specification has all but destroyed the normal basis upon which true competitive prices can be established."[4] As Barry Stein described it, branding "convert[s] true commodities to apparent tailored goods, so as to avoid direct price competition in the marketplace."

> The distinctions introduced—elaborate packaging, exhortative advertising and promotion that asserts the presence of unmeasurable values, and irrelevant physical modification (colored toothpaste)—do not, in fact, render these competing products "different" in any substantive sense, but to the extent that consumers are convinced by these distinctions and treat them as if they were different, product loyalty is generated.[5]

Competition between identifiable producers of bulk goods enabled grocers to select the highest quality bulk goods, while providing them to customers at the lowest price. Brand specification, on the other hand, relieves the grocer of the responsibility for standing behind his merchandise and turns him into a mere stocker of shelves with the most-demanded brands.

The change, naturally, did not go unremarked by those profiting from it. For example, here's a bit of commentary from an advertising trade paper in 1925:

> In the statement to its stockholders issued recently by The American Sugar Refining Company, we find this statement:
> "Formerly, as is well known, household sugar was largely of bulk pricing. We have described the sale of package sugar and table syrup under the trade names of 'Domino' and 'Franklin' with such success that the volume of trade-mark packages now constitutes roundly one-half of our production that goes into households . . . ."
> These facts should be of vital interest to any executive who faces the problem of marketing a staple product that is hard to control because it is sold in bulk.
> Twenty years ago the sale of sugar in cardboard cartons under a brand name would have been unthinkable. Ten years hence this kind of history will have repeated itself in connection with many other staple commodities now sold in bulk . . . .[6]

The process went on, just as the paper predicted, until—decades later—the very idea of a return to price competition in the production of goods, instead of brand-name competition for market share, would strike manufacturers with horror. What Borsodi proposed, making "[c]ompetition . . . descend from the cloudy heights of sales appeals and braggadocio generally, to just one factor—price.,"[7] is the worst nightmare of the oligopoly manufacturer and the advertising industry:

> At the annual meeting of the U.S. Association of National Advertisers in 1988, Graham H. Phillips, the U.S. Chairman of Ogilvy & Mather, berated the assembled executives for

1. *Ibid.*, p. 110.
2. Quoted in *Ibid.*, pp. 160-61.
3. *Ibid.*, p. 162.
4. *Ibid.* pp. 216-17.
5. Barry Stein, *Size, Efficiency, and Community Enterprise* (Cambridge: Center for Community Economic Development, 1974), p. 79.
6. *Advertising and Selling Fortnightly*, February 25, 1925, in Borsodi, *The Distribution Age*, pp. 159-60.
7. Stuart Chase and F. J. Schlink, *The New Republic*, December 30, 1925, in *Ibid.*, p. 204.

stooping to participate in a "commodity workplace" rather than an image-based one. "I doubt that many of you would welcome a commodity marketplace in which one competed solely on price, promotion and trade deals, all of which can be easily duplicated by competition, leading to ever-decreasing profits, decay, and eventual bankruptcy." Others spoke of the importance of maintaining "conceptual value-added," which in effect means adding nothing but marketing. Stooping to compete on the basis of real value, the agencies ominously warned, would speed not just the death of the brand, but corporate death as well.[1]

The overall system, in short, was a "solution" in search of a problem. State subsidies and mercantilism gave rise to centralized, overcapitalized industry, which led to overproduction, which led to the need to find a way of creating demand for lots of crap that nobody wanted.

Government tried in a third way to solve the problem of overproduction: the increasing practice of directly purchasing the corporate economy's surplus output, through massive highway and civil aviation programs, the military-industrial complex, the prison-industrial complex, foreign aid, and so forth.

Parallel to these trends, the state also played a major role in cartelizing the economy, to protect the large corporation from the destructive effects of price competition. At first the effort was mainly private:

> American manufacturers began in the 1870s to take the initial step to growth by way of merger—that is, to set up nationwide associations to control price and production. They did so primarily as a response to the continuing price decline, which became increasingly impressive after the panic of 1873 ushered in a prolonged economic depression.[2]

The process was further accelerated by the Depression of the 1890s, with mergers and trusts being formed through the beginning of the next century in order to control price and output:

> the motive for merger changed. Many more were created to replace the association of small manufacturing firms as the instrument to maintain price and production schedules.[3]

Chandler's account of the trust movement ignores one central fact: the trusts were *less* efficient than their smaller competitors. They immediately began losing market share to less leveraged firms outside the trusts. The trust movement was an unqualified failure, as big business quickly recognized. Subsequent attempts to cartelize the economy, therefore, enlisted the state. As recounted by Gabriel Kolko,[4] the main force behind the Progressive Era regulatory agenda was big business itself, the goal being to restrict price and quality competition and to reestablish the trusts under the aegis of government.

As Richard Du Boff and Edward Herman point out,[5] Chandler's treatment of the managerial corporation as a passive response to objective technological necessity leaves out a good many relevant issues. "Government is treated as an exogenous force, not as part of a symbiotic relationship with private capital . . . ." Moreover, Chandler "effectively denies us the means by which we might assess the impact of the corporate system on the population at large and the social costs produced by the needs of that system." " . . . [T]here is no intimation that technology affords a potentially wide spectrum of choices . . . ."

1. Naomi Klein, *No Logo* (New York: Picador, 1999), p. 14.
2. Chandler, *The Visible Hand*, p. 316.
3. *Ibid.*, p. 331.
4. Gabriel Kolko, *The Triumph of Conservatism: A Reinterpretation of American History, 1900-1916* (New York: The Free Press, 1963).
5. Richard B. Du Boff and Edward S. Herman, "Alfred Chandler's New Business History: A Review," *Politics & Society* 10:1 (1980), pp. 87-110.

For example, Chandler notes Carnegie's concern almost exclusively with labor costs, but "does not discuss the implications for technological choices or the consequences for labor (wage rates, output requirements, unemployment)."

In almost every particular, Chandler's paean to the superior efficiency of the large, Sloanist corporation is laughably implausible. The managers of the large corporation are almost as inefficient and out of touch as those at Gosplan, and the large corporation itself almost as insulated from market pressures as the state-owned economy of the old USSR. It only survives because it's competing with two or three other large corporations in the same industry, all with senior management who are equally clueless products of identical MBA curricula, and all with the same sick organizational cultures.

Chandler's book on the tech industry[1] is a telling illustration of just what he meant by his pet notion of "organizational capability." For Chandler, "organizational capabilities" in the consumer electronics industry amounted to the artificial property rights by which the firm is able to exercise ownership rights over technology and over the skill and situational knowledge of its employees, and to prevent the transfer of technology and skill across corporate boundaries. Thus, his chapter on the history of the consumer electronics industry through the mid-20th century consists largely of what patents were held by which companies, and who subsequently bought them.

Galbraith and Chandler had things exactly backwards. The "technostructure" can survive because it is enabled to be *less* responsive to consumer demand. An oligopoly firm in a cartelized industry, in which massive, inefficient bureaucratic corporations share the same bureaucratic culture, is protected from competition. The "innovations" Chandler so prizes are made by a leadership completely out of touch with reality. These "innovations" succeed because they are determined by the organization for its own purposes, and the organization has the power to impose top-down "change" on a cartelized market, with little regard to consumer preferences, instead of responding flexibly to them. "Innovative strategies" are based, not on finding out what people want and providing it, but on inventing ever-bigger hammers and then forcing us to be nails. The large corporate organization is not more efficient at accomplishing goals received from outside; it is more efficient at accomplishing goals it sets for itself for its own purposes, and then using its power to adapt the rest of society to those goals.

The authoritarianism implicit in push distribution is borne out by Lazonick's circular understanding of "organizational success," as he discusses it in his survey of "innovative organizations" in Part III of his book. The centralized, managerialist technostructure is the best vehicle for "organizational success"—defined as what best suits the interests of the centralized, managerialist technostructure. And of course, such "organizational success" has little or nothing to do with what society outside that organization might decide, on its own initiative, that it wants. Indeed (as Galbraith argued), "organizational success" requires institutional mechanisms to prevent outside society from doing what it wants, in order to provide the levels of stability and predictable demand that the technostructure needs for its long planning horizons. These theories amount, in practice, to a circular argument that oligopoly capitalism is "successful" because it is most efficient at achieving the ends of oligopoly capitalism.

One of Lazonick's examples of "innovative organizations" is the railroad,[2] historically the first multi-unit corporation and the testing ground for administrative techniques which later became standard throughout the corporate economy. Nowhere in his discussion did he raise the question of whether a high-capacity national system of trunk lines was actually de-

1. Alfred D. Chandler, Jr., *Inventing the Electronic Century* (New York: The Free Press, 2001), pp. 13-49.
2. Lazonick, *Business Organization and the Myth of the Market Economy*, pp. 231-37.

sirable for society as a whole, or whether it increased net economic efficiency. With all costs internalized in a market price system, and without the distorting effects of cartelization and railroad subsidies, it might well have been a greater net efficiency to have Mumford's economy of small-scale neotechnic industry, with towns and villages loosely networked into diversified local economies by light rail and canals. Rather, Lazonick starts out with the technocratic *assumption* that a centralized national economy with a centralized transportation system is a Good Thing, and defines "efficiency" in terms of the administrative mechanisms necessary to make it possible without interference from the market. It was, no doubt, an "organizational success" in the sense of being a success *for the organization.* Our society, unfortunately, has no shortage of such "organizational successes."

Another example cited was Swift's engineering of a national mass market for fresh meat, shipped by refrigerator car. But if the costs of the subsidized railroads had been internalized in the price of the meat, rather than externalized on the taxpayer, local production might have been considerably more competitive.

Lazonick's reference to "*successful* capitalist development" raises the question 'successful' for whom? His "innovative organization" is no doubt "successful" for the people who make money off it—but not for those at whose expense they make money. It is only "success" if one posits the goals and values of the organization as those of society, and acquiesces in whatever organizational supports are necessary to impose those values on the rest of society.

His use of the expression "value-creating capabilities" seems to have very little to do with the normal understanding of the word "value" as finding out what people want and then producing it more efficiently than anyone else. According to his Galbraithian version of value, rather, the organization decides what it wants to produce based on the values and interests of its hierarchy, and then uses its organizational power to secure the stability and control it needs to carry out its self-determined goals without interference from the people who actually *buy* the stuff. This parallels Chandler's view of "organizational capabilities," which he seemed to identify with an organization's power over the external environment.

The beautiful picture Lazonick paints is no doubt gratifying to the shades of Bob McNamara and Albert Speer. To those already predisposed to such an aesthetic, Lazonick provides the reassurance that Ford's in his flivver, and all's well with the world. Nowhere, however, does he actually provide *evidence* to *demonstrate* that the large organization, using internal coordination and administrative incentives, is better able to improve product or process. Lazonick repeatedly *asserts* his a priori assumption of the superior efficiency of the large organization, without ever really being able to demonstrate *why.* He is stuck in an endless loop of explaining that the large, managerialist bureaucracy is more efficient because, well, it's large and managerial—in other words, *it just is.*

The "innovation" he celebrates means, in practice, 1) developing processes so capital-intensive and high-tech that, if all costs were fully internalized in the price of the goods produced, consumers would prefer simpler and cheaper models; or 2) developing products so complex and prone to breakdown that, if cartelized industry weren't able to protect its shared culture from outside competition, the consumer would prefer a more durable and user-friendly model. Cartelized, over-built industry deals with overproduction through planned obsolescence, and through engineering a mass-consumer culture, and succeeds because cartelization restricts the range of consumer choice.

Lazonick has one thing in his favor, in comparison to Chandler. While Chandler's body of work is an extended apologetic for Sloanism, Lazonick's preferred model of corporate managerialism is much closer to the Toyota model. Thus his emphasis on eliminating bottlenecks and increasing throughput. But his perverse identification of the efficiencies of the Toyota production system with *large size* takes things in precisely the opposite direction from H. Thomas Johnson, who (as we shall see in Chapter Fourteen) sees local economies on the Emilia-Romagna model as the ideal embodiment of Taichi Ohno's ideas).

The innovative products that emerge from Chandler's industrial model, all too often, are gold-plated turds: horribly designed products with proliferating features piled one atop another with no regard to the user's needs, ease of use, dependability or reparability. A good example is Microsoft Vista.[1]

Lazonick's version of "successful development" is a roaring success indeed, if we start with the assumption that society should be reengineered to desire what the technostructure wants to produce. Robin Marris described this approach quite well:

> The "bureaucratic" environment of the large corporation . . . is likely to divert emphasis from the character of the goods and services produced to the skill with which these activities are organized . . . . The concept of consumer need disappears, and the only question of interest . . . is whether a sufficient number of consumers, irrespective of their "real need" can be persuaded to buy [a proposed new product]."[2]

The marketing "innovations" Chandler trumpeted in *Scale and Scope*—in foods the techniques for "refining, distilling, milling, and processing"[3]—were actually expedients for ameliorating the inefficiencies imposed by large-scale production and long-distance distribution: refined white flour, inferior in taste and nutrition to fresh-milled local flour, but which would keep for long-term storage; gas-ripened rubber tomatoes and other vegetables grown for transportability rather than taste; etc. The standard American diet of refined white flour, hydrogenated oils, and high fructose corn syrup is in large part Chandler's legacy.

Lest I incur charges of rhetorical excess or facetiousness in referring to the "push" model as "find[ing] a way to create demand for lots of crap that nobody wanted," I will read Jeremy Weiland's caveat into the record:

> In the parts where you address the management of consumer demand according to institutional interests, you're not suggesting that consumer demand plays *no* role in the decisions about what to produce, right? I don't mean to be so blithe but that seems patently false . . . the issue is that consumer demand is moderated and channeled into demand for things that corporations decide they can produce most profitably given a rigid institutional structure. The way you frame the issue seems extreme . . . as if there is no role for consumer demand, rather than a substantially neutered and manipulated one. Even with demand management, PR, advertising, etc. it seems obvious to me that there are still instances of new choices introduced by competitors from outside the established oligopoly responding to demand. It's simply that these choices would be more plentiful without statist intervention, right? I'm concerned your argument is too sweeping and ignoring a much more fine and important point—that consumers aren't just lacking choices but are being manipulated subtly.

Precisely. When I say the corporate economy tries to create demand for lots of crap that nobody wants, it's just a colorful way of saying that consumer demand (in Weiland's well-crafted language) is "substantially neutered and manipulated," that it's "moderated and channeled into demand for things that corporations decide they can produce most profitably given a rigid institutional structure."

In the same vein, I'm familiar with defenses of advertising by Rothbard and other Austrians, and with their general theory of consumer sovereignty. Oddly enough, though,

---

1. Alan Cooper's *The Inmates are Running the Asylum: Why High-Tech Products Drive Us Crazy and How to Restore the Sanity* (Indianapolis: Sams, 1999) is an excellent survey of the tendency of American industry to produce gold-plated turds without regard to the user.

2. Quoted in Stein, *Size, Efficiency, and Community Enterprise*, p. 55.

3. Alfred Chandler, *Scale and Scope: The Dynamics of Industrial Capitalism* (Cambridge and London: The Belknap Press of Harvard University Press, 1990), p. 262.

these same people (quite rightly) make the most strenuous objections to the statist propaganda effects of the government schooling system in promoting a statist understanding of American history, inculcating support for the state's expansionist foreign policy, and the like. Now I would argue that if the human mind is vulnerable to the cumulative effects of propaganda in the case of state political propaganda, it's also vulnerable to similar effects of consumer propaganda.

No doubt the Austrians will acknowledge, as a general phenomenon, the cumulative sleeper effects of propaganda. After all, their own polemics at LewRockwell.Com and similar venues are full of references to the effect of public school indoctrination on American political culture over the past century. They will simply argue that the individual is capable, with an effort, of countering this effect, and that the responsibility lies with the individual of critically evaluating all communication meant to persuade. Their objection to the government schools' propaganda, presumably, is that the scales are further tilted in favor of the statist message, because the schools' propaganda operation is funded with tax money and backed with compulsory attendance laws, and therefore has an unfair advantage in crowding out competing messages with the help of the state.

I fully agree. I simply argue that the state-backed cartelization of industry into oligopoly markets, the creation and centralization of mass broadcast media through state action, and the use of the schools and other agencies of government propaganda to engineer a culture of mass consumption, are a similar (in kind, if not in degree) use of state power to tilt the playing field in favor of a particular message.

C. WILLIAMSON ON ASSET-SPECIFICITY

Williamson explains the choice of administrative over market coordination, where it occurs, in terms not of technological determinism but of asset-specificity ("the degree to which an asset can [or rather cannot] be redeployed to alternative uses and by alternative users without sacrifice of productive value."). Asset specificity results in "bilateral dependency" between parties whose assets are adapted to a specific transaction.[1] Ordinarily, Williamson argues, the transaction costs of internal administration tend to outweigh those of market contracting. Internal integration normally carries greater diseconomies, and provides incentives inferior to the high-powered incentives of the market. Hierarchy, therefore, is a necessary evil, and replaces the market only in those special circumstances where market contracting breaks down. Vertical integration is "rarely due to technological determinism but . . . more often explained by the fact that integration is the source of transaction cost economies."[2]

He writes elsewhere that vertical and lateral integration "are usefully thought of as organization forms of last resort, to be employed when all else fails." Markets, normally, are "a 'marvel' in adaptation . . . ."

> Given a disturbance for which prices serve as sufficient statistics, individual buyers and supplier can reposition autonomously. Appropriating, as they do, individual streams of net receipts, each party has a strong incentive to reduce costs and adapt efficiently. What I have referred to as high-powered incentives result when consequences are tightly linked to actions in this way . . . .
> Matters get more complicated when bilaterial dependency intrudes . . . . [B]ilateral dependency introduces an opportunity to realize gains through hierarchy. As compared with the market, the use of formal organization to orchestrate coordinated adaptation to

1. Oliver Williamson, "Comparative Economic Organization: The Analysis of Discrete Structural Alternatives," *Journal of Law, Economics, and Organization* IV:1 (1988), pp. 70-71.
2. Williamson, *The Economic Institutions of Capitalism: Firms, Markets, Relational Contracting* (New York: Free Press; London: Collier Macmillan, 1985), pp. 87-88.

unanticipated disturbances enjoys adaptive advantages as the condition of bilateral dependency progressively builds up. But these adaptation gains come at a cost. Not only
can related divisions within the firm make plausible claims that they are causally responsible for the gains . . . , but divisions that report losses can make plausible claims that others are culpable. There are many ways, moreover, in which the headquarters can use the
accounting system to effect strategic redistributions (through transfer pricing changes,
overhead assignments, inventory conventions, etc.), whatever the preferences of the parties. The upshot is that internal organization degrades incentive intensity, and added bureaucratic costs result . . . .[1]

Internal hierarchy becomes more efficient than market contracting under the special
conditions of asset specificity, or small-numbers bargaining situations:

> . . . the principal factor to which transaction cost economics appeals to explain vertical
> integration is asset specificity. Without it, market contracting between successive produc-
> tion stages ordinarily has good economizing properties.[2]
> . . . the governance costs of internal organization exceed those of market organiza-
> tion where asset specificity is slight.[3]

The situation in small-numbers bargaining is that of two scorpions in a bottle:

> Although it is always in the collective interest of autonomous parties to fill gaps, correct
> errors, and effect efficient realignments, it is also the case that the distribution of the re-
> sulting gains is indeterminate. Self-interested bargaining predictably obtains. Such bar-
> gaining is itself costly.[4]

In promoting asset specificity as his Rosetta Stone of hierarchy, Williamson proposes a
third alternative to the neoclassicals' emphasis on external monopoly power, and the radicals' emphasis on internal labor discipline. Hierarchy, he argues, is chosen as a way to
economize on transaction costs in cases of asset specificity or small-numbers bargaining. In
promoting this explanation *to the exclusion* of external power explanations, however, he
goes too far.

Williamson's thesis of the superiority of hierarchy over markets "only" in cases of asset specificity is in practical terms quite sweeping, since asset specificity must be the rule
rather than the exception if it is to explain the prevalence of hierarchy to the degree that
we observe. And in fact Williamson sticks to his guns, defending the real as the rational, in
arguing that the prevalence of the large corporate form and vertical integration as the result of superior efficiency at dealing with asset specificity problems.

> . . . it is no accident that hierarchy is ubiquitous within all organizations of any size . . . .
> In short, inveighing against hierarchy is rhetoric; both the logic of efficiency and the his-
> torical evidence disclose that nonhierarchical modes are mainly of ephemeral duration.[5]

The problem is that, in his appeal to "efficiency," Williamson simply removes the
problem of power by a single step, like the Hindu cosmologist adding a bigger turtle on
the bottom. "Efficiency" is determined by the nature of the environment to which the

1. Oliver Williamson, "Comparative Economic Organization: The Analysis of Discrete
Structural Alternatives," *Administrative Science Quarterly* 36/2 (June 1991), p. 279.
2. Williamson, *The Economic Institutions of Capitalism*, p. 90.
3. *Ibid.* pp. 131-32.
4. Williamson, "Comparative Economic Organization," p. 278.
5. Williamson, "The Organization of Work: A Comparative Institutional Assessment," *Journal
of Economic Behavior and Organization*, 1(1): 35, quoted in Geoffrey Hodgson, "Organizational Form
and Economic Evolution," in Ugo Pagano and Robert Rowthorn, eds., *Democracy and Efficiency in
the Economic Enterprise*, a study proposal for the World Institute for Development of Economic Research (WIDER) of the United Nations University (London and New York: Routledge, 1996).

firm is adapting; but what role did power play in structuring the environment itself? As Geoffrey Hodgson points out,

> Williamson ignores the important point that the selection of the "fitter" in evolution is not simply relative to the less successful but is dependent upon the general circumstances and environment in which selection takes place. The "fitter" are only fit in the context of a given environment.[1]

The structure of the environment, Hodgson suggests, is determined not only by state interventions which have made the large hierarchical organization artificially competitive against small ones, but by path dependency.[2] As we have seen, the state reduces the competitive costs of bureaucratic inefficiency, thereby shifting the point at which the transaction costs of hierarchy exceed those of contracting, and reducing the level of asset specificity required to invoke the advantages of hierarchy; and it promotes a predominant mode of production characterized by artificially high asset specificity. Thus, the state "selects" for hierarchy. Only when organization makes it possible to exert external power over the market and seek rents from the state, do the governance advantages of hierarchy outweigh the bureaucratic inefficiency costs.

Williamson might as well argue for the comparative efficiency of the state-owned and -managed enterprise, based on its prevalence in the old Soviet economy. And in practical terms, he makes the moral equivalent of just such an argument in defense of hierarchy:

> To be sure, this does not preclude the possibility that power is also operative. For example, entrenched interests may sometimes be able to delay organizational transformations. Power enthusiasts have not, however, demonstrated that significant organizational innovations—those in which large transaction cost savings are in prospect—are regularly defeated by established interests. There is abundant evidence to the contrary. Within the economic arena, therefore, if not more generally, I submit that organizational innovations for which nontrivial efficiency gains can be projected will find a way to subdue . . . opposed interests. Power is relegated to a secondary role in such a scheme of things.[3]

The main problem with this approach is that Williamson treats the "economic arena" as a given, as a more or less spontaneously arising environment that can be taken as a rough approximation of pure market forces. He ignores the extent to which his "efficiency" itself is a loaded concept, *defined in terms of* a general environment shaped by power. Specifically, he ignores the extent to which asset specificity and other agency problems "solved" by organization are themselves the results of power. The hierarchical firm is the most efficient "solution" to an artificial problem. Again:

> The efficiency hypothesis . . . is that . . . mistaken vertical integration can rarely be sustained, and that more efficient modes will eventually supplant less efficient modes—though entrenched power interests can sometimes delay the displacement.[4]

But what is "efficient" and what is "mistaken" is relative to a given environment, and the environment itself is structured by the exercise of corporate power at the level of the political regime.

The importance of asset-specificity in promoting internal hierarchy, by the way, is itself greatly exaggerated. As we have seen, Williamson argues that in general the high-powered incentives of the market are so spectacular that only an exceptional situation can

---

1. Geoffrey Hodgson, "Organizational Form and Economic Evolution," in Ugo Pagano and Robert Rowthorn, eds., *Democracy and Efficiency in the Economic Enterprise*, a study proposal for the World Institute for Development of Economic Research (WIDER) of the United Nations University (London and New York: Routledge, 1996), p. 100.

2. *Ibid.*, pp. 107-109.

3. Williamson, *The Economic Institutions of Capitalism*, pp. 124-125.

4. *Ibid.*, p. 236.

justify replacing them with the administrative incentives of a hierarchy. The agency costs of asset specificity and small-numbers bargaining must be quite extreme to override the market's presumptive superiority. I believe Williamson underestimates both the extent to which the state reduces the comparative costs of hierarchy (by subsidizing its costs, and by cartelizing markets so as to limit the competitive penalty for inefficiency), and the extent to which it artificially inflates the prevailing level of asset specificity. In so doing, it artificially shifts the Coasean boundary at which organizing a transaction by hierarchy becomes more efficient than doing so by market.

Williamson fully recognizes, in principle, that general-purpose production technology would result in less use of transaction-specific assets, and thus reduce the need for specialized governance structures.[1] But despite his many differences with Chandler and Lazonick, Williamson shares their Schumpeterian assumption that increased productivity and innovation result from asset specificity and capital-intensiveness. For all of them, the association of asset-specificity with improved technique is a given.

The possibility that such high-fixed cost, asset-specific forms of production are only more efficient *given* artificially increased market size and a "push" model for disposing of the overproduced output of the overbuilt facilities, seems to escape Williamson almost as totally as it does his adversaries. Without transportation subsidies to reduce distribution costs, and other state action to artificially increase the size of markets and the degree of division of labor, the most efficient form of production might be, rather, one resembling the decentralist vision of Kropotkin, Mumford, and Bookchin: small-scale production for local markets using far less specialized production technology. The specialization of assets and division of labor are dependent variables, determined by market size. Likewise, state subsidies to capital-intensiveness and firm size (depreciation allowances, R&D credits, subsidies to technical education, the interest deduction for corporate debt, etc.) tend to increase the specialization of assets. When multiple-purpose machinery predominates, and the opportunity costs of the next-best use are much lower, small numbers bargaining isn't much of an issue.

So in a sense, despite Williamson's denial, his theory of asset-specificity *is* a technological theory of firm boundaries: he simply ignores the degree to which asset-specificity itself reflects a choice between possible technologies.

In short, absent state interference to externalize the inefficiency costs of large scale on taxpayers, production technology would likely be far less asset-specific. The substitution of hierarchy for the market is, in large part, a solution to an artificial problem.

There are two separate problems with Williamson's asset specificity thesis. First, as we already saw above, the level of asset specificity at which the governance benefits of hierarchy exceed its costs is not fixed. It shifts, as the competitive costs of bureaucratic inefficiency are reduced by the state, so that the number of cases in which asset specificity is great enough to justify hierarchy is artificially increased. Second, the level of asset specificity itself is not fixed either. It shifts upward as the state promotes artificially large market areas and artificially high division of labor.

In conclusion: If we strip away all the starting assumptions of the technocratic apologists for unlimited economy of scale, and counterpose certain working hypotheses of our own, we come up with this rival model of economic organization: In a decentralized economy without subsidized transportation infrastructure, it is generally more economical to make short production runs for local markets, using multiple-purpose machinery. Given limited demand for any particular product, these short production runs are likely to be driven by demand-pull, with production being shifted to other goods when the current demand is met. Absent the push model of creating demand for predetermined outputs,

---

1. *Ibid.*, pp. 32, 34.

product design is more likely to be for durability and ease of repair, rather than planned obsolescence. Demand is likely to be further reduced by greater reliance on community repair and recycling centers, with even custom machining of replacement parts being more economical in some cases than the purchase of a new product. Product innovation, in a demand-pull economy, is also more likely to come about in the small shop or skunk works, with design organized on a peer-production basis. And process innovation is likely to be based on a series of incremental improvements, which (as Barry Stein argued in *Size, Efficiency, and Community Enterprise*) cumulatively often have a greater effect on productive efficiency than major generational leaps in production technology. Such incremental improvements are most likely to be generated by direct observation of the production process, which gives a natural advantage to the producers' cooperative. Without the subsidized waste and overhead costs of Rube Goldberg bureaucratic structures, without subsidized distance and energy consumption, and without state subsidies to parasitic consumption by rentier classes, such decentralized economies could quite plausibly provide a comparable standard of living with average work weeks of twenty hours or less.

This is, essentially, the vision of a free market cooperativist economy we intend to present in Part Four. But we're getting too far ahead of ourselves. We still have Part One to get through.

APPENDIX A
ECONOMY OF SCALE IN DEVELOPMENT ECONOMICS

E. F. Schumacher effectively demolished assumptions by technocratic liberals similar to those above, in the context of Third World development. He cited the argument of the neo-Keynesian Kaldor and others that

> The amount of available capital is given. Now, you may concentrate it on a small number of highly capitalised workplaces, or you may spread it thinly over a large number of cheap workplaces. If you do the latter, you obtain less total output than if you do the former.

He went on to quote directly Kaldor's assertion that "research has shown that the most modern machinery produces much more output per unit of capital invested than less sophisticated machinery which employs more people." And since the amount of capital is assumed to be fixed, this quantity sets "the limits on wages employment in any country at any given time." Kaldor's argument continues, at length:

> If we can employ only a limited number of people in wage labour, then let us employ them in the most productive way, so that they make the biggest possible contribution to the national output, because that will also give the quickest rate of economic growth. You should not go deliberately out of your way to reduce productivity in order to reduce the amount of capital per worker. This seems to me nonsense because you may find that by increasing capital per worker tenfold you increase the output per worker twentyfold. There is no question from every point of view of the superiority of the latest and more capitalistic technologies.[1]

Notice, right off, the implicit assumption that capital is to be invested in "wage labor," rather than (say) making self-employment or small-scale cooperative production more efficient. And notice his assumption that "we" are employing "them." Needless to say, even the most "liberal" of technocratic liberals views the recent centuries' history of primitive accumulation and top-down industrialization from the standpoint of the victor. The standpoint of "liberal" development economists is essentially that of the old colonial powers: Third World countries are seen mainly as sources of raw materials and other export goods, rather than in terms of domestic production for the internal market.[2]

And Kaldor's assumptions do, indeed, seem to govern the distribution of capital investment in the Third World. Colin Ward refers to the rationing of credit for small artisans who could benefit immensely from small power tools, and the diversion of investment funds to large-scale industry:

> Kenneth King, studying the multitude of small-scale producers in Nairobi, reminds us that the enterprising artisans do not use the improvised equipment from choice: 'Many would be anxious to obtain and use lathes if power were available, but the most popular brands now cost L3,000-L5,000. Although Western observers may admire the cheapness and ingenuity of the various Heath Robinson machines, their inventors regard them very differently. They know precisely what kind of Czechoslovakian centre-lath they would buy first, what it would cost, and why they cannot afford it.' He contrasts the millions of pounds worth of credit advanced for the high-technology plastics industry with the extraordinary difficulties experienced in raising any kind of credit in the artisan sector. 'It is not principally the technical dimension which constitutes the obstacle, but rather the

---

1. Quoted in E. F. Schumacher, *Small is Beautiful: Economics as if People Mattered* (New York, Hagerstown, San Francisco, London: Harper & Row, Publishers, 1973), p. 182.
2. *Ibid.*, p. 216.

lack of basic credit infrastructure, security of tenure in the urban areas, and a technology policy that would support the very small-scale entrepreneur.'[1]

Schumacher administered a well-deserved intellectual beating to Kaldor, pointing out that the quantity of available capital was not in fact static, and that bringing unemployed labor into productive use, even in labor-intensive forms of production, would increase the total pool of income from which investment capital might be saved.

> The output of an idle man is nil, whereas the output of even a poorly equipped man can be a positive contribution, and this contribution can be to "capital" as well as to "wages goods."[2]

And the idle (and starving) man might well welcome the opportunity to support himself in subsistence production, even if "poorly equipped," while he's waiting for a job to open up in one of those giant whiz-bang factories.

The question is whether investment capital is to be obtained through the traditional method of "primitive accumulation"—i.e., robbing the laboring classes of their small property and squeezing them dry—or by enabling labor to keep its full output, and cooperatively pool its own surplus income as an investment fund to increase its standard of living over time.

Schumacher also argued that the ratio of output to capital investment was irrelevant in itself, unless one addressed the most effective ratio of capital to labor in the context of large quantities of unused labor. The ratio of output to labor might be maximized with production methods that resulted in a less than optimum ratio of output to capital investment. The goal is not the maximum return on capital investment, but to enable labor to produce the maximum possible output to support itself.[3] And from the laborer's standpoint, the purpose of capital investment is to maximize consumption per unit of effort. On the other hand, the goal of capital investment, from the employer's point of view, is not necessarily to increase the return per unit of capital, but to substitute capital for labor power even when the total output is not thereby increased. The substitution of capital-intensive for labor intensive forms of production is often aimed, not at any abstract criterion of "efficiency," but at reducing the employer's dependence on wage labor.[4]

It also matters, I should add, where the "output" *goes*. It makes little difference to the dispossessed peasant how "efficient" industry is, if he is unemployed and therefore unable to buy its output at any price. On the other hand, if he is employed, even in more labor-intensive (and thus less "productive" by Kaldor's standard) industry, he will be able to buy a larger portion (infinitely larger, compared to zero) of the resulting output. The products of intermediate technology more than likely are not intended for the export market, but for local consumption by those who could not afford the output of "modern" industry in any case. By Kaldor's standards, Robinson Crusoe should have found it more "efficient" to starve on his desert island than to support himself by "obsolete" methods.

And even by the standards of Galbraithian technocracy, it turns out that centralized, capital-intensive industry is by no means as "productive" as the technocrats think. When reduced distribution costs are taken into consideration, and transportation subsidies do not artificially increase the division of labor past the point of diminishing returns, we find that small-scale production for local markets, using labor-intensive techniques or multi-purpose machinery, may actually be cheaper per unit of output. Schumacher pointed out that

> a considerable number of design studies and costings, made for specific products in specific districts, have universally demonstrated that the products of an intelligently chosen

1. Colin Ward, "Anarchism and the informal economy," *The Raven* No. 1 (1987), p. 32.
2. Schumacher, *Small is Beautiful*, pp. 182-83.
3. *Ibid.*, pp. 182-84.
4. *Ibid.*, p. 183.

intermediate technology could actually be cheaper than those of modern factories in the nearest big city.[1]

Another, related argument Schumacher demolished is that centralized, large-scale industry is necessary to make optimal use of a limited supply of entrepreneurial skill—supposedly quite scarce in the Third World. Like capital, so the argument goes, entrepreneurial skill should be concentrated in a few Stalinist blockbuster projects. Schumacher responded, quite sensibly, that no such thing as generic "entrepreneurial ability" existed outside the context of the specific form of technology being used.

> Men quite incapable of acting as entrepreneurs on the level of modern technology may nonetheless be fully capable of making a success of a small-scale enterprise set up on the basis of intermediate technology . . . .[2]

According to Schumacher, native development officials in the Third World mirror the assumptions of Western technocrats. The manager of an African textile mill, for example, explained that it was highly automated because

> African labour, unused to industrial work, would make mistakes, whereas automated machinery does not make mistakes. The quality standards demanded today . . . are such that my product must be perfect to be able to find a market."[3]

Anyone familiar with the rework and recall rates under Sloanism should keep the laughter to a minimum.

On the other hand, the capital-intensiveness of such production is an effective entry barrier such that production is dominated by a few blockbuster projects, likely funded with foreign aid money or World Bank loans. And the relatively small number of workers employed, concentrated in urban areas, means that the vast majority of the population will lack the purchasing power needed to buy the factory's output. Hence the manager's assumption, which he never stops for a minute to examine, that his "perfect" product is being produced for the demanding standards of the export market, or for a small urban luxury market of the comprador bourgeoisie. Were intermediate-scale production technology used, with local labor employed in much larger quantities, the more widely distributed purchasing power would likely result in a ready local market for goods produced to somewhat less exacting standards.

Elsewhere, Schumacher cited a discussion in a World Bank study of the prospects for industrial development of small and medium-sized towns. The study made short work of the issue, dismissing the possibility on the grounds that such localities "lack[ed] the basic infrastructure of transport and services," and that "[m]anagement and professional staff [were] unwilling to move from the major cities." As Schumacher crowed,

> the proposition, evidently, is to transplant into a small place the technology which has been developed in such a way *that it fits only a very large place.*[4]

More recently, the same dumbed-down dogmas of development economics have been recycled by Michael Strong of FLOW (and quickly circulated to a wider audience by John Tierney of the *New York Times*). Strong, commenting on the Nobel prize awarded Grameen Bank's Muhammad Yunus, wrote that there was

> a thatched-ceiling to poverty alleviation through micro-finance . . . . Poor, rural microentrepreneurs selling eggs to other poor rural peasants simply do not have access to the vast pipeline of wealth from the developed world.

1. *Ibid.*, pp. 185–86.
2. *Ibid.*, p. 185.
3. *Ibid.*, p. 194.
4. E. F. Schumacher, *Good Work* (New York, Hagerstown, San Fransisco, London: Harper & Row, 1979), p. 48.

The best route out of poverty, rather, was a job in a factory. Hence Wal-Mart, which gets some 70% of its goods from Chinese sweatshops, is the most effective anti-poverty organization in the world.[1]

Of course, Strong's argument is full of implicit assumptions that don't bear much looking into. For example, he falsely equates nominal income to access to use-value: he regurgitates statistics on how high the income of a sweatshop worker is compared to that of a subsistence farmer, without any indication that he is taking into account the extent of goods and services obtained by rural people outside the official money economy, through household and barter and other informal economies, that would require cash expenditures by urban workers. In a flourishing economy of small-scale farming and artisan production, with barter and other unmonetized forms of exchange, the vast majority of wealth consumed in the household might never even show up in income statistics.

He also mindlessly repeats a version of the "best available alternative" defense of sweatshops, arguing that peasants "choose" to go to the city for factory jobs—ignoring the issue of whether the state (in collusion with sweatshop employers) may be artificially restricting the range of alternatives for those in the rural economy. It's funny how sweatshop employers tend to gravitate to countries where peasants' independent access to the land is limited by latifundismo and modern-day enclosures, and the bargaining power of wage labor is weakened by the suppression of union organizing. It's also funny (ho ho ho) how much more likely workers are to "choose" sweatshop factory employment when their alternatives have been so limited.

Strong asks rhetorically whether the World Bank has helped anywhere near as many people as Wal-Mart and its sweatshops: a rather disingenuous question, given the importance of corporate welfare (er, "foreign aid") in making overseas factories artificially profitable (helping Wal-Mart and its sweatshops, in other words). If it weren't for subsidized transport for long-distance shipping, subsidized electrical utilities, and the like, we might be importing a lot less of our stuff from sweatshops in the Third World and producing a lot more of it in small factories where we live—and so might they.

Strong's assumptions about the preferability of factory to farm labor are equally unfounded. In fact, the literature of the Enclosure period in England is full of complaints by the owning classes as to how hard it was to get enough labor, or to get it on profitable terms, from people with independent access to the means of subsistence and production. In East Africa, for example, Britain had to resort to heroic efforts to deprive the native population of lands held under traditional tenure: the best fifth of land was expropriated for settlers, and a head tax used to force those remaining on the land into the wage economy to earn the money for taxes.

As P. M. Lawrence has argued, the just comparison of sweatshop factory employment is not to actually existing subsistence farming, but to subsistence farming as it might exist if the rules were not rigged by the state in the interests of sweatshop employers and landed oligarchs. Historically, he points out, subsistence farming has involved relatively modest labor time and comfortable levels of food consumption, when it has been able to function free of tribute to the tax-collector and feudal landlord.

> It is *not* true that wherever and whenever people were given the choice they chose urban life over agriculture. The Highland Clearances and Irish Evictions forced people into the cities. One natural experiment—Leverburgh—showed that when crofting remained an alternative, Scottish islanders stayed away from the factory in droves . . . .

1. Michael Strong, "Forget the World Bank, Try Wal-Mart," Tech Central Station, August 22, 2006. <http://www.nyu.edu/fas/institute/dri/Easterly/File/TCS%20Daily%20-%20Forget%20the%20World%20Bank,%20Try%20Wal-Mart.htm>; John Tierney, "Shopping for a Nobel," New York Times, October 17, 2006. <http://select.nytimes.com/2006/10/17/opinion/17tierney.html>.

Most rural people, if not oppressed by rents and/or taxes, were effectively free peasant proprietors; the comparison should be with those who stayed, not with those like the
ploughboy who left . . . . From what little we can reliably infer, unless someone is carrying an extra burden or being forced onto marginal land that yields with work, subsistence farming is a comfortable 20 hours per week . . . .

Because the countryside had more subsistence activity, wage and price levels were
generally lower there. This misled many people who only saw the size of the wages
without realising the cost of living . . . .[1]

. . . . subsistence farming is not harder work than factory work, only full time farming is; true subsistence farming is just not that intensive except when people are forced
onto really marginal land the way some evicted Irish were. Normally, subsistence farming involves occasional hard work and a lot of spare time for other activities (like making
cuckoo clocks in Black Forest winters, for cash sale when travel could resume). Working
your own land and then some to pay rent, tithes or taxes, now that does need more work
. . . . So the author is mistakenly comparing factory conditions with the artificial alternatives obtaining during industrialisation, instead of with the conditions that would have
obtained if it had not been for industrialisation . . . .[2]

The superior overall productivity of small-scale machine production, discussed earlier,
applies equally in the Third World. The logical first step toward machine manufacturing,
from the perspective of a local economy, might be along the lines Jane Jacobs described in
the development of the Japanese bicycle industry: the custom manufacture of replacement
parts, in small machine shops, to keep foreign-manufactured machinery in operation (see
Chapter Fourteen). This economy of village recycling/repair/remanufacture shops might
eventually evolve into small-scale manufacture of consumer goods, with general-purpose
machinery, from start to finish.

One practical barrier to dissemination of intermediate technology is that large
corporations cannot sell it at a price that covers their overhead costs from high
capitalization. A good example mentioned by Wakefield and Stafford is John Deere's refusal
to manufacture small, affordable tractors suitable for a Third World village. But small
manufacturers might find it more affordable.[3] In fact, their discussion of this possibility was
quite prescient. What was true of small manufacturers is even more true of peer production
networks, using small-scale production technology and open-source design (see, for example, the discussion of the Life-Trac light tractor and power source in Chapter Fifteen).

1. Lawrence's comment under Jeffrey Tucker, "Down with (parts of) the past!" Mises Blog,
November 11, 2005 <http://blog.mises.org/archives/004328.asp>.

2. Quoted in Kevin Carson, "Glenn Reynolds' Upside-Down Version of History," Mutualist
Blog, June 20, 2005 <http://mutualist.blogspot.com/2005/06/glenn-reynolds-upside-down-version-
of.html>.

3. *Ibid.*, p. 75.

A Literature Survey on
Economies of Scale

I must begin with a caveat. The data cited below on economies of scale reflects comparative performance in the existing economy, with the given structure of costs and returns. It ignores the extent to which the existing environment is itself the product of state subsidies and other interventions. The ideal size for efficiency in the existing economy refers to the size needed for maximizing profit *given* subsidized inputs, and *given* protected monopoly prices for outputs. The optimally sized firm, in other words, is optimal for maximizing profits in a distorted environment that rewards inefficiency.

This is indicated, in most cases, by the very methods used to determine the ideal size for economy of scale. According to F.M. Scherer,[1] the methods used to determine minimum efficient scale (MES) are the following:

1) Analyzing profitability as a function of size. This is problematic because it is hard to distinguish profitability resulting from internal efficiency from profitability resulting from monopoly or monopsony power. For example, a Johnson administration study found the average rate of profit to be 50% higher in concentrated industries.[2] Even in recessions, losses from the late fifties through the early seventies were relatively rare among the largest corporations. Only one of the top 200 industrials operated at a loss in the recession of 1957; and only seven and 34 of the Fortune 500 lost money, respectively, in the recessions of 1964 and 1970.[3] Oligopoly power permits administered pricing: in the 1960s, for example, General Motors targeted its prices to provide a 15–20% return after taxes, with costs estimated on the assumption that plants operated at only 60–70% capacity. U.S. Steel set prices to allow for a profit even when operating only two days a week. Bethlehem Steel's Chairman complained in 1971 that the company had to operate at 70% capacity to make a profit, compared to only 50% in 1966. (This also complicates the engineering approach described below, which estimates peak efficiency on the assumption that the different size plants being compared operate at 100% of capacity. The comparative "efficiency" estimates would differ somewhat if it were taken into account that the smaller plant can operate at full capacity, while the larger one cannot.)[4] An FTC study cited by the Nader Group estimated that oligopoly markup amounted to 25% of existing prices, where the four largest firms controlled 40% or more of an industry's sales.[5]

---

1. F.M. Scherer and David Ross, *Industrial Market Structure and Economic Performance.* 3rd ed (Boston: Houghton Mifflin Company, 1990) pp. 111–15.
2. Barry Stein. *Size, Efficiency, and Community Enterprise* (Cambridge: Center for Community Economic Development, 1974), p. 54
3. *Ibid.*, p. 55.
4. *Ibid.*, p. 56.
5. Mark J. Green, with Beverly C. Moore, Jr., and Bruce Wasserstein, *The Closed Enterprise System: Ralph Nader's Study Group Report on Antitrust Enforcement* (New York: Grossman Publishers, 1972), p. 14.

2) Statistical cost analysis, relating costs to volume of output. This method takes into account such complex variables as capacity utilization, age of capital stock, etc. The sheer amount of numbers crunching involved makes this approach quite intensive. The results are also potentially misleading, because detailed cost data are available disproportionately from regulated monopolies, whose rates are determined by a cost–plus markup.

3) The "survivor test," associated in particular with George Stigler. " . . . [F]irm or plant sizes that survive and contribute increasing fractions of an industry's output over time are assumed to be efficient; those that supply a declining share of output are deemed too large or too small." This approach measures "efficiency" in terms of the ability to thrive under a given set of conditions—the shortcomings of which approach should be obvious.

4) The engineering approach, based on engineers' technical knowledge of "alternative equipment and plant designs and the associated investment and operating costs," relies heavily on a complicated and labor-intensive series of interviews and questionnaires.

So when empirical studies of economy of scale find that the dominant plant or firm is far larger than the ideal for maximum efficiency, it is really an *a fortiori* argument: the dominant plant or firm size is above the maximum size for ideal efficiency *even* in an economy where subsidies make large size artificially profitable, and *even* where cartelization enables large firms to escape many of the competitive penalties for their large size. So even the "ideal" size for plant or firm, as determined by the empirical studies cited below, is it-self artificially large.

A. Economies of Firm Size

Assessments of economy of scale must distinguish between economies of plant size and economies of firm size. Economies of plant size result from purely technical considerations; as Barry Stein put it,

> some of the factors required for production are "lumpier" (that is, less divisible) than others. In principle, capital can be subdivided as finely as desired, but the same cannot be said for tools or people. In consequence, these resources can only be used efficiently when the scale of activity is large enough to employ them fully.[1]

If the smallest available widget machine costs $100,000 and turns out a thousand widgets a day at full capacity, a small firm cannot spend $10,000 for a machine to produce a hundred a day. And if it must be used along with other machines of different capacities, to minimize unit costs it is necessary to purchase the proper ratios of different kinds of machinery, and to maintain sufficient output that no individual machine has idle capacity.

Economies of plant size are real, at least, however much controversy there may be as to the precise point at which they level off. On the alleged economy of firm size, there is less agreement.

> It rests upon alleged efficiencies of management rather than technology. Efficiency, it is said, is enhanced by spreading administrative expertise and expenses over multiplant operations; by eliminating duplication of officials, services, and records systems; by providing sophisticated statistical, research, and other staff services that smaller firms cannot afford; by circumventing "transaction costs" by performing support activities in house rather than purchasing them from outsiders; by obtaining credit on more advantageous terms; by attracting more competent executives and mounting more effective marketing campaigns; and so forth.[2]

1. Stein, *Size, Efficiency, and Community Enterprise*, p. 1.
2. Walter Adams and James W. Brock. *The Bigness Complex: Industry, Labor and Government in the American Economy*. 2nd ed. (Stanford, Cal.: Stanford University Press, 2004)., pp. 30-31.

The savings from spreading administrative costs over more than one plant are doubt-less true, *ceteris paribus*. But as usual, *ceteris* is not *paribus*. Whatever savings result from administrative rationalization are probably offset by the bureaucratic inefficiencies resulting from added layers of administration, and from increased Hayekian problems of aggregating distributed information.

The advantages resulting from superior bargaining power in the credit market, from the power of a large-scale buyer to negotiate lower prices, and so forth, are also real. But as Adams and Brock point out, such advantages of superior bargaining power are not real operating efficiencies: unlike internal efficiencies, which result in real cost savings overall, they are zero-sum transactions that merely shift a portion of costs to those with less bargaining power.[1] Barry Stein made the same distinction in *Size, Efficiency, and Community Enterprise*:

> It is necessary . . . to distinguish between true social efficiency and simple power. Efficiency has been defined . . . as a measure of the extent to which social and individual needs are met for a given set of available resources. But large and well-established firms also have power, the ability to control the environment toward their own ends. To a considerable degree, organizations with power can be less efficient; at least, they can change the nature of the contest so that others, even if more truly efficient, are less able to compete. Thus, many of the gross measures of the relative efficiency of firms of different scale (such as overall profit, sales growth, or survival), may be indicative of the power of size, rather than the economic effect of scale . . . .
> And, in fact, there is evidence that, in concentrated industries, profits are higher than they would be otherwise.[2]

Joseph Schumpeter suggested, as we saw in the previous chapter, that large firm size, by insulating the corporation from risk, put it in a superior position to undertake expensive and long-term innovations. But as we shall see below, in the real world the large firm is far less innovative.

Economies of firm size are relatively insignificant compared to economies of plant size. Honda's main operating plants in Japan are about three times the average plant size for the American Big Three. But Honda as a firm, with only two major plants in Japan, is far smaller than either GM (28 plants) or Ford (23 plants). Not only does GM's larger size fail to provide any cost efficiencies compared to Honda; it is riddled with inefficiency. GM is significantly less efficient than either Ford or Chrysler, while all three American producers are far (24-38%) less efficient than Honda's North American operations.[3]

A 1956 study by Joe Bain found that the efficiencies of multiplant firms were "either negligible or totally absent" in six of twenty industries. In another six, unit cost economies accruing to multiplant firms were small but measurable, ranging from "slight" in cigarettes to 2-5% in steel. In the remaining eight, no estimates of multiplant firms' advantages were available.[4]

B. ECONOMIES OF PLANT SIZE

Cross-industry studies have found little evidence to back up the alleged efficiencies of large plant size. For example, a study by T.R. Saving covering the 1947-54 period found that in 64 of 91 manufacturing industries, the minimum efficient plant created 1% or less of industry value added.[5]

---

1. *Ibid.*, p. 31.
2. Barry Stein, *Size, Efficiency, and Community Enterprise*, pp. 52-54.
3. Adams and Brock, 2nd ed., pp. 31-32.
4. *Barriers to New Competition: Their Character and Consequences in Manufacturing Industries.* Third printing (Cambridge, MA: Harvard University Press, 1965), pp. 86-87.
5. Scherer and Ross, *Industrial Market Structure and Economic Performance*, p. 114.

Bain's 1956 study found that in eleven of twenty industries, the plants with the lowest unit production costs operated on average with an output of 2.5% or less of total national sales (with the individual outputs ranging from 0.02% to 2.5%); in fifteen industries, less than 7.5%; and in seventeen out of twenty, less than 10%.[1]

A 1975 study of 12 industries in seven industrialized nations, based on the engineering survey method, found that—with the exception of the refrigerator-freezer industry—the least-cost plant sizes were "quite small relative to the national market." The same study found a remarkably shallow cost curve for plants below optimal size: in half of the industries surveyed, a plant operating at one-third the optimal output suffered an increase in unit costs of under 5%.[2]

According to F. M. Scherer, the statistical cost analysis method of investigation typically shows that, "[w]ith few exceptions, the minimum efficient scale revealed in studies of U.S. manufacturing industries has been small relative to industry size." The most common finding has been "distinct economies of scale at relatively small plant sizes, a range of intermediate sizes over which unit costs did not differ appreciably, and (in a minority of cases) diseconomies of scale for very large plants."[3]

In the steel industry, for example, minimills have been cleaning the clocks of the old steel giants. According to Adams and Brock, minimills operating at infinitesimal fractions of the output of U.S. Steel and Bethlehem Steel had by 1998 achieved a 45% share of the U.S. market. They used electric furnaces to process scrap metal, and oriented their output toward local markets. Minimills produced wire rod and cold-rolled steel sheets 28% and 29% cheaper, respectively, than U.S. Steel. A minimill could produce steel bars with only thirty employees on average, compared to 130 even in a single plant of U.S. Steel.[4]

C. THE COMPARATIVE SIGNIFICANCE OF SCALE ECONOMIES AND ORGANIZATIONAL EFFICIENCY

Barry Stein suggested that whatever the increased costs resulting from below-optimum-size production facilities, they pale in comparison to the variations in cost resulting from greater or lesser efficiencies within facilities of *any* given size.

The normal neoclassical approach, according to Stein, is to treat the firm's internal functioning as a "black box":

> One of the characteristics of classical economists' view of business organization is a tendency to view firms as entities operating at near-optimal efficiency within whatever constraints size, industry, and the environment impose. The treatment of economies of scale and of other questions related to efficiency thus have generally focused on the allocative aspects; that is, the extent to which resources or factors of production have been optimally distributed to firms and establishments within the economic system. Within that framework, firms are assumed to operate on the frontier of their specific production functions.[5]

As an example, he quoted Robert Dorfman:

> businessmen determine the cost of attaining any [desired] output by choosing the combination of factors [labor, materials, or capital] with which to produce that output .... The production function incorporates all the technical data about production; it shows the greatest amount of output that can be obtained by the use of every possible

1. Bain, *Barriers to New Competition*, pp. 72-73.
2. Scherer and Ross, pp. 114-15.
3. *Ibid.*, pp. 112-13.
4. Adams and Brock, pp. 36-37; see also Murray Bookchin, *Post-Scarcity Anarchism* (Berleley, Ca.: The Ramparts Press, 1971), pp. 108-110.
5. Stein, p. 27.

the greatest amount of output that can be obtained by the use of every possible combination of input quantities.[1]

Stein continued:

> If this describes the actual situation, then questions of allocation become critical. However, there is very good reason to believe that industrial firms operate not on or near their production frontier, but well inside it, and, correspondingly, measures assuming the ideal case are likely to be misleading.
>
> There are two points to be made. The lesser is related to utilization of capacity. It is clear that what might be theoretically true with regard to the efficiency of a plant that is operating at design capacity, with all fixed assets properly contributing their share to output, will hardly be true when some fraction of the assets are, in effect, idle . . . .
>
> But excess capacity is the minor point. More important is the fact that while economists focus on problems of allocation, businessmen have always spent more time on problems of internal efficiency, in the obvious belief that it can be increased . . . .[2]

In contrast to the neoclassical assumption that the production elves were magically running things in an optimal manner inside the black box, Stein appealed to Harvey Leibenstein's key concept of "x-efficiency."

Leibenstein suggested "an approach to the theory of the firm that does not depend on the assumption of cost-minimization by all firms."

> The level of unit cost depends in some measure on the degree of x-efficiency, which in turn depends on the degree of competitive pressure, as well as on other motivational factors. The responses to such pressures, whether in the nature of effort, search, or the utilization of new information, is a significant part of the residual [unexplained increase] in economic growth.[3]
>
> . . . [F]irms and economies do not operate on an outer-bound production possibility surface consistent with their resources. Rather they actually work on a production surface that is well within that outer bound. This means that for a variety of reasons people and organizations normally work neither as hard nor as effectively as they could.[4]

As Stein commented,

> the usual assumptions about the efficient use of resources within a firm are simply not true. What is more, the extent of those inefficiencies is not small. There is significant opportunity for firms to increase their output for any given array of resources or, alternatively, to reduce their use of resources for any given level of output . . . .
>
> It is at least arguable . . . that there can be no perfect utilization of available resources. Theories concerning the firm that assume that *any* single specific parameter is responsible for observed behavior are positing an overly simplistic assumption. Corporations . . . do not act uniquely as entities, but as a composite of human subsystems, each of which is attempting to satisfy conflicting and complex needs, some personal . . . and some organizational . . . . What is clear . . . is that the larger the firm and the more complex the subsystem of interactions, the more the possibility that alternative solutions exist and the likelihood that efficiency, however measured, can be improved.
>
> Support for these views of potential loss of efficiency can also be gained from simple observation of the extent to which companies "discover" during lean times that they are perfectly capable of operating at the same level with substantially fewer

---

1. Robert Dorfman, *Prices and Markets* (Englewood Cliffs, N.J.: Prentice-Hall, 1967), pp. 67-68, in Stein pp. 27-28; Stein commented, in fn1 p. 98: "Of course, no one assumes that the production function is either known with precision or ideally followed, but the assumption is that businesses, by and large, operate sufficiently close to their production frontier so that attention can shift to the exogenous variables influencing the firm."

2. Stein, p. 28.

3. Harvey Leibenstein, "Allocative Efficiency vs. X-Efficiency," *American Economic Review* (June 1966), pp. 412-13.

4. *Ibid.*, p. 413.

are perfectly capable of operating at the same level with substantially fewer employees or, in some cases, facilities . . . .

The significance of all this is simply that computations and estimates of economies of scale . . . can be misleading or downright inaccurate, since they typically assume that firms and plants operate efficiently within their constraints. This is generally not the case; what actually is being measured, if anything, is the relative productivity of various entities, all of which are capable of increasing their efficiency by amounts and in ways that are uniquely related to that entity. In addition, such savings as might in fact be available because of the real economies of scale (ranging up to perhaps 20 or 25 percent for a substantial change in size) are capable of being overwhelmed by the continuing increases due to improvement in "x-efficiency."

It may be that these inefficiencies help explain the great lack of consistency in the many studies of economies of scale . . . .[1]

D. Increased Distribution Costs

It's also important to remember that whatever reduction in unit production cost results from internal economies of large-scale production is to some extent offset by the diseconomies of large-scale distribution.

. . . [U]nit costs of production, which up to some point decrease with scale, must be compared to unit costs of distribution, which tend to increase (other things being equal) with the size of the area served.[2]

As Ralph Borsodi observed years ago, the larger the plant needed to achieve economies of scale in production, the larger the market area it serves; hence, the longer the distances over which the product must be distributed. His observation, stated simply as Borsodi's Law: as production costs fall, distribution costs rise.

In most cases, the increased cost of distribution exceeds the reduced cost of production at a level of output far lower than would be ideal for maximizing purely internal economies of scale. The increase in unit production cost, even for significant reductions in size below the optimum for productive economy of scale, is quite modest: The 1975 study referenced earlier by Bain, surveying twelve industries in seven industrialized nations, found a remarkably shallow cost curve for plants below optimal size: in half the industries surveyed, a plant with output at a third of the optimal level suffered unit cost increases of less than 5%.[3] Compare this to the reductions in distribution cost for a market area reduced by two-thirds.

Distribution costs are increased still further by the fact that larger-scale production and greater levels of capital intensiveness increase the unit costs resulting from idle capacity, and thereby (as we saw in the last chapter) greatly increase the resources devoted to high-pressure, "push" forms of marketing. Borsodi's book *The Distribution Age* was an elaboration of the fact that, as he stated in the Preface, production costs fell by perhaps a fifth between 1870 and 1920, even as the cost of marketing and distribution nearly tripled.[4] "[E]very part of our economic structure," he wrote, was "being strained by the strenuous effort *to market profitably what modern industry can produce.*"[5]

Kirkpatrick Sale describes the high cost of advertising as an tnery barrier that "tends to keep smaller and cheaper firms out of a market . . . thus reducing the competition that might lead to lower consumer prices."

1. Stein, pp. 28-30.
2. *Ibid.*, p. 65.
3. Bain, pp. 114-15.
4. Ralph Borsodi, *The Distribution Age* (New York and London: D. Appleton and Company, 1929), p. v.
5. *Ibid.*, p. 4.

In markets that are saturated, and where Brand A is not especially different from Brand B, it is necessary to find gimmicks that make a product stand out—bigger boxes, added partitions, toys, contests—and lead to added costs.[1]

As with "x-inefficiency," the costs of the "push" distribution made necessary by large scale probably outweigh any savings in unit cost resulting from economy of scale itself. As we saw in Chapter One, the shift from bulk commodity sales to pre-packaged brand-named goods resulted in a price increase of some 300%. Barry Stein noted that the price of Consumer Value Stores' store brand was generally less than two-thirds that of the nationally branded version of the same goods—themselves underpriced by CVS, a discount store.

> . . . . the CVS products are all attractively packaged and in no obvious way inferior in appearance or presentation to the national brands (therefore, no great savings are being made by cheaper packaging) . . . . [And] it is likely, from CVS' own description of its program, that these products, by and large, are being manufactured on order by relatively small firms (such as manufacturing chemists). If this is not the case and they are, in fact, being produced by the same type of large firm as the national products, one can still clearly conclude that, at least for products of this class, whatever economies of scale exist in production, they are being dwarfed by *diseconomies* in advertising, promotion, and physical distribution.[2]

In other words, the alleged economies of large-scale production result in such expensive, high-capacity facilities that large corporations are required to take heroic measures—often more expensive than the supposed unit cost savings from large scale—to move enough of their product to keep the plants running at full capacity.

Increased unit costs from idle capacity, given the high overhead of large-scale production, are the chief motive behind the push distribution model. Even so, the restrained competition of an oligopoly market limits the competitive disadvantage resulting from idle capacity—so long as the leading firms in an industry are running at roughly comparable percentages of capacity, and can pass their overhead costs onto the customer. The oligopoly mark-up included in consumer price reflects the high costs of excess capacity.

> It is difficult to estimate how large a part of the nation's production facilities are normally in use. One particularly able observer of economic tendencies, Colonel Leonard P. Ayres, uses the number of blast furnaces in operation as a barometer of business conditions. When blast furnaces are in 60 per cent. operation, conditions are normal . . . .
> It is obvious, if 60 per cent. represents normality, that consumers of such a basic commodity as pig iron must pay dividends upon an investment capable of producing two-thirds more pig iron than the country uses in normal times.

Borsodi also found that flour mills, steel plants, shoe factories, copper smelters, lumber mills, automobiles, and rayon manufacturers were running at similar or lower percentages of total capacity.[3] Either way, it is the consumer who pays for overaccumulation: both for the high marketing costs of distributing overproduced goods when industry runs at full capacity, and for the high overhead when the firms in an oligopoly market all run at low capacity and pass their unit costs on through administered pricing.

Borsodi's law applies not only to the relative efficiencies of large versus small factories, but also to the comparative efficiencies of factory versus home production. Borsodi argued that for most light goods like food, textiles, and furniture, the overall costs were actually lower to manufacture them in one's own home. The reason was that the electric motor put small-scale production machinery in the home on the same footing as large machinery in

1. Kirkpatrick Sale, *Human Scale* (New York: Coward, McCann, & Geoghegan, 1980), pp. 315-16.

2. Stein, *Size, Efficiency, and Community Enterprise*, pp. 67-68.

3. Borsodi, *The Distribution Age*, pp. 42-43.

the factory. Although economies of large-scale machine production exist, most economies of machine production are captured with the bare adoption of the machinery itself, even with household electrical machinery. After that, the production cost curve is very shallow, while the distribution cost curve is steep.

Borsodi's study of the economics of home manufacture began with the home-grown tomatoes his wife canned. Expressing some doubts in response to Mrs. Borsodi's confidence that it "paid" to do it, he systematically examined all the costs going into the tomatoes, including the market value of the labor they put into growing them and canning them, the cost of the household electricity used, etc. Even with all these things factored in, Bordodi still found the home product cost 20-30% less than the canned tomatoes at the market. The reason? The home product, produced at the point of consumption, had zero distribution cost. The modest unit cost savings from large-scale machinery were insufficient to offset the enormous cost of distribution and marketing.[1]

Borsodi went on to experiment with home clothing production with loom and sewing machine, and building furniture in the home workshop.

> I discovered that more than two-thirds of the things which the average family now buys could be produced more economically at home than they could be brought factory made;
> —that the average man and woman could earn more by producing at home than by working for money in an office or factory and that, therefore, the less time they spent working away from home and the more time they spent working at home, the better off they would be;
> —finally, that the home itself was still capable of being made into a productive and creative institution and that an investment in a homestead equipped with efficient domestic machinery would yield larger returns per dollar of investment than investments in insurance, in mortgages, in stocks and bonds . . . .
> These discoveries led to our experimenting year after year with domestic appliances and machines. We began to experiment with the problem of bringing back into the house, and thus under our own direct control, the various machines which the textile-mill, the cannery and packing house, the flour-mill, the clothing and garment factory, had taken over from the home during the past two hundred years . . . .
> In the main the economies of factory production, which are so obvious and which have led economists so far astray, consist of three things: (1) quantity buying of materials and supplies; (2) the division of labor with each worker in industry confined to the performance of a single operation; and (3) the use of power to eliminate labor and permit the operation of automatic machinery. Of these, the use of power is unquestionably the most important. today, however, power is something which the home can use to reduce costs of production just as well as can the factory. The situation which prevailed in the days when water power and steam-engines furnished the only forms of power is at an end. As long as the only available form of power was *centralized* power, the transfer of machinery and production from the home and the individual, to the factory and the group, was inevitable. But with the development of the gas-engine and the electric motor, power became available in decentralized forms. The home, so far as power was concerned, had been put in position to compete with the factory.
> With this advantage of the factory nullified, its other advantages are in themselves insufficient to offset the burden of distribution costs on most products . . . .
> The average factory, no doubt, does produce food and clothing cheaper than we produce them even with our power-driven machinery on the Borsodi homestead. But factory costs, because of the problem of distribution, are only first costs. They cannot, therefore, be compared with home costs, which are final costs.[2]

1. Ralph Borsodi, *Flight From the City: An Experiment in Creative Living on the Land* (New York, Evanston, San Francisco, London: Harper & Row, 1933, 1972), pp. 10-15.

2. *Ibid.*, pp. 17-19.

Even the internal economies of the factory, it should be added, were offset by the overhead costs of administration, and the dividends and interest on capital.[1]

Since first reading Borsodi's account I have encountered arguments that his experience was misleading or atypical, given that he was a natural polymath and therefore perhaps a quicker study than most, and therefore failed to include learning time in his estimate of costs. These objections cannot be entirely dismissed. Still, Borsodi's case studies are a useful counter to claims that economies of scale are inherent in the greater technical efficiency of large-scale machinery. And the savings in unit cost Borsodi demonstrated, if true, would be sufficient to compensate a fair amount of learning time. Besides, a relatively modest degree of division of labor would be sufficient to overcome a great deal of the learning curve for craft production in the informal and barter economies. Most neighborhoods probably have a skilled home seamstress, a baker famous for his homemade bread, someone with a well-equipped woodworking shop, or the like. Present-day home hobbyists, producing for barter, could make use of their existing skills. What's more, in so doing they would optimize efficiency even over Borsodi's model: they would fully utilize the spare capacity of household equipment that would have been idle much of the time with mere hobby production, and spread the costs of such capital equipment over a number of households (rather than, as in Borsodi's model, duplicating it in each household).

The internal economies resulting from division of labor, specifically, are also greatly exaggerated. Stephen Marglin argued that the economies in question resulted, not from division of labor as such, but from the separation and sequencing of tasks. Nearly the same economies could be achieved by a single workman or group of workmen in a small shop, by such separation and sequencing. To illustrate, he took Adam Smith's famous example of the pin factory and stood it on its head. An individual cottage workman, instead of painstakingly making one pin at a time, might draw out and straighten the wire for an entire run of production, then cut all the wire, then sharpen it all, etc., dividing the total operation into the very same subtasks as in Smith's pin factory.[2]

One alleged reason for economies of large-scale production is that large scale permits ever more specialized production machinery. But as Adam Smith pointed out, the profitability of division of labor is determined by market size; and when transportation ceases to be subsidized, so that the savings from maximal automation with highly specialized machines are offset by the true cost of long-distance distribution, the spurious economies of excessive division of labor disappear. Without artificially large market areas resulting from artificially cheap distribution, the demand in the smaller market areas would be insufficient in most cases to operate expensive specialized machinery at full capacity. It would be more efficient overall to produce most goods in short production runs, for local markets, on general purpose machinery.

And even in the case of the largest existing corporations under state capitalism, with artificially large market areas resulting from subsidized transportation, their attachment to the largest-scale machinery is often misguided. While individual machines may be "superefficient" from the standpoint of minimizing unit costs *of that particular stage of production*, they are often quite disruptive and inefficient from the standpoint of the overall flow of production. Their adoption is typically associated with the "batch-and-queue" operation of American Sloanist industry, which (as the authors of *Natural Capitalism* put it) optimizes the efficiency of individual steps in the production process by pessimizing the overall flow of production. Their excessive "efficiency," from the perspective of the overall production process, means that they generate excess inventories and buffer stocks that raise costs and

1. Ralph Borsodi, *This Ugly Civilization* (Philadelphia: Porcupine Press, 1929, 1975), pp. 34, 37.
2. Steven A. Marglin, "What Do Bosses Do? The Origins and Functions of Hierarchy in Capitalist Production—Part I" *Review of Radical Political Economics* (Summer 1974).

disrupt flow. On the other hand, a smaller and less "efficient" machine that is compatible with the other stages of production may result in improved flow and greatly reduced overall cost, despite the higher unit costs of that particular stage. Consider the case of Pratt & Whitney:

> The world's largest maker of jet engines for aircraft had paid $80 million for a "monument"—state-of-the-art German robotic grinders to make turbine blades. The grinders were wonderfully fast, but their complex computer controls required about as many technicians as the old manual production system had required machinists. Moreover, the fast grinders required supporting processes that were costly and polluting. Since the fast grinders were meant to produce big, uniform batches of product, but Pratt & Whitney needed agile production of small, diverse batches, the twelve fancy grinders were replaced with eight simple ones costing one-fourth as much. Grinding time increased from 3 to 75 minutes, but the throughput time for the entire process decreased from 10 days to 75 minutes because the nasty supporting processes were eliminated. Viewed from the whole-system perspective of the complete production process, not just the grinding step, the big machines had been so fast that they slowed down the process too much, and so automated that they required too many workers. The revised production system, using a high-wage traditional workforce and simple machines, produced $1 billion of annual value in a single room easily surveyable from a doorway. It cost half as much, worked 100 times faster, cut changeover time from 8 hours to 100 seconds, and would have repaid its conversion costs in a year even if the sophisticated grinders were simply scrapped.

When entire processes are taken into account, "excessive scale or speed at any stage of production turns the smooth flow of materials into turbulent eddies and undertows that suck down earnings and submerge entire industries."[1]

Another example comes from the cola industry, where the most "efficient" large-scale machine creates enormous batches that are out of scale with the distribution system, and result in higher unit costs overall than would modest-sized local machines that could immediately scale production to demand-pull. The reason is the excess inventories that glut the system, and the "pervasive costs and losses of handling, transport, and storage between all the elephantine parts of the production process."[2]

E. The Link Between Size and Innovation

The superior innovativeness of the large corporation, baldly asserted by Schumpeter and Galbraith, is also questionable at best.

T.K. Quinn, a former Vice President of GE (writing in the heyday of managerialist liberalism), viewed the oligopoly firm's role in the innovation process as largely parasitic:

> I know of no original product invention, not even electric shavers or heating pads, made by any of the giant laboratories or corporations, with the exception of the household garbage grinder . . . . The record of the giants is one of moving in, buying out, and absorbing the smaller creators.[3]

Paul Baran and Paul Sweezy, commenting on Quinn's observation, added that "[w]hen a new industry or field of operation is being opened up,

1. Paul Hawken, Amory Lovins, and L. Hunter Lovins. *Natural Capitalism: Creating the Next Industrial Revolution* (Boston, New York, London: Little, Brown, and Company, 1999), pp. 128-29.

2. *Ibid.*, p. 129.

3. *Giant Business: Threat to Democracy: The Autobiography of an Insider* (New York, 1953), p. 117, cited in Paul Baran and Paul Sweezy. *Monopoly Capitalism: An Essay in the American Economic and Social Order* (New York: Monthly Review Press, 1966), p. 49.

the big corporation tends to hold back deliberately and to allow individual entrepreneurs or small businesses to do the vital pioneering work. Many fail and drop out of the picture, but those which succeed trace out the most promising lines of development for the future.[1]

John Jewkes, surveying the period from 1900 to 1958, found that comparatively few major inventions in the 20th century had come from large organizations. Out of 61 of the most important inventions, 33 were individual efforts, seven were of mixed or unclear origins, and only 21 the product of corporate research labs. In even the latter group, five of the inventions came from smaller corporations. And the inventions coming out of the large corporations often involved research teams that were quite small,[2] what today might be called "skunk works." To take a more recent example:

> At a $5 billion survey company, three of the last five new-product introductions have come from a classic skunk works. It consists at any one time of eight to ten people, and is located in a dingy second-floor loft six miles from the corporate headquarters. The technical genius is a fellow whose highest degree is a high-school equivalency diploma . . . (although the company has literally thousands of Ph.D. scientists and engineers on its payroll) . . . .
>
> The group's first product, now a $300 million per year sales item, was fully developed (prototyped) in twenty-eight days. Last year a major corporate product bombed. A skunk works member asked for and got permission to take two samples home and set them up in his basement. He used one as a benchmark. He tinkered with the other for about three weeks and corrected virtually all of its flaws (with nickel and dime items), actually improving performance over original design specs by a factor of three. The president visited his basement and approved design changes on the spot. The latest of the group's successes was designed in (covert) competition with a corporate engineering "team" of almost 700 people.[3]

Arnold Cooper found that the small firm made better use of its R&D dollars, and that its technical workers were on average more capable.[4] And Jacob Schmookler, testifying before Congress in 1965, found an inverse relationship between firm size and productivity per research dollar:

> . . . [B]eyond a certain not very large size, the bigger the firm, the less efficient its knowledge-producing activities are likely to be. Evidently, as the size of the firm increases, there is a decrease per dollar of R&D in (a) the number of patented inventions, (b) the percentage of patented inventions used commercially, and (c) the number of significant inventions.[5]

A National Science Foundation study of technical innovation between 1953 and 1973 found that the smallest firms produced "about 4 times" as many major innovations per R&D dollar as did the mid-sized firms, and 24 times as many as the largest firms.[6]

Adams and Brock contrast the innovativeness of the pre-WWII auto industry, with its many modest-sized firms, with the stagnation under the Big Three during the first decades of the postwar era.

> . . . [W]ith the demise of the independents and the concentration of industry control in the hands of three giant firms, the pace of product innovation slackened significantly. Innovations like front-wheel drive, disc brakes, fuel injection, fuel-efficient subcompacts,

1. *Ibid.*, p. 49.
2. John Jewkes, David Sawers, and Richard Stillerman, *The Sources of Invention* (London: MacMillan & Co Ltd, 1958), pp. 72-88.
3. Thomas J. Peters and Robert S. Waters, *In Search of Excellence: Lessons from America's Best-Run Companies* (New York: Warner Books, 1982), pp. 211-212.
4. "R&D is More Efficient in Small Companies," *Harvard Business Review* (May-June 1964), in Stein, *Size, Efficiency, and Community Enterprise*, p. 35.
5. Quoted in Stein, p. 34.
6. Walter Adams and James Brock, *The Bigness Complex*. First Edition (New York: Pantheon Books, 1986), p. 52.

novations like front-wheel drive, disc brakes, fuel injection, fuel-efficient subcompacts, and utilitarian minivans languished in the hands of the Big Three .... "The major features of today's automobiles—V-8 engines, automatic transmissions, power steering, and power brakes—are all prewar innovations. These have been considerably improved and refined over the past twenty-five years," [economist Lawrence J. White] concluded in 1971, "but still the industry has been uninterested in pursuing alternatives. The suspension, ignition, carburetion, and exhaust systems are fundamentally the same."[1]

Paul Goodman also viewed the automobile industry as a typical example of this aspect of oligopoly behavior: "Three or four manufacturers control the automobile market, competing with fixed prices and slowly spooned-out improvements."[2] As evidence, consider the way the Big Four automakers colluded to suppress antipollution devices. They agreed that no company would announce or install any innovation in antipollution exhaust devices without an agreement of the other three. They exchanged patents and agreed on a formula for sharing the costs of patents acquired from third parties.[3]

In the computer field, Intel saw the main market for its micro-processors as giant institutional clients, and IBM dismissed the idea of small computers for the home. The desktop computer was created by members of the Homebrew Computer Club who, "playing with electronic junk ..., combined Intel's microprocessor with spare parts," and built the first cheap computers able to "run on the kitchen table."[4] Apple produced its first desktop computers for the commercial market in Steve Jobs' garage.[5]

Harvey Leibenstein noted that the adoption of even known technologies and best practices, even when known to result in astronomical increases in productivity, occurs at a glacial pace in concentrated industries with little competitive pressure.

> ... there is a great deal of evidence that the delay time between invention and innovation is often exceedingly long (sometimes more than 50 years), and the lag time between the use of new methods in the "best practice" firms in an industry and other firms is often a matter of years. Salter in his study on *Productivity and Technical Change* ... points to the following striking example: "In the United States copper mines, electric locomotives allow a cost saving of 67 per cent yet although first used in the mid-twenties, by 1940 less than a third of locomotives in use were electric."[6]

The drug industry's massive R&D spending is almost entirely directed toward gaming the patent system, rather than genuine innovation. A majority of R&D spending goes toward tweaking existing drugs on the verge of going generic just enough to justify a new patent for the "me, too" version of the old cash cow, rather than to developing fundamentally new drugs ("new molecular entities").[7] Even when fundamentally new drugs are developed, a majority of the total cost is not for developing the drug itself, but for testing all the possible variants of the drug in order to secure patent lockdown against competition. "Quasibill," a frequent commenter at my blog with a background in engineering, is quite informative on the subject:

> In the rare instances that big pharma produces and markets such medicines [cancer medications], it has purchased them from small start-ups that themselves are the result normally of a university laboratory's work. When big pharma cites to billions of research

1. Adams and Brock, *The Bigness Complex*, 2nd ed., pp. 48-49.

2. Paul Goodman, *People or Personnel*, p. 58, in *People or Personnel* and *Like a Conquered Province* (New York: Vintage Books, 1963, 1965), p. 58.

3. Green, *et al.*, *The Closed Enterprise System*, pp. 254-256.

4. Johan Soderberg, *Hacking Capitalism: The Free and Open Source Software Movement* (New York and London: Routledge, 2008), p. 17.

5. Adams and Brock, 2nd edition, pp. 52-56.

6. Leibenstein, "Allocative Efficiency vs. 'X-Efficeincy,'" p. 403.

7. *Ibid.*, pp. 57-58.

costs, what it is talking about is the process whereby they literally test millions of very closely related compounds to find out if they have a solid therapeutic window. This type of research is directly related to the patent system, as changing one functional group can get you around most patents, eventually. So you like to bulk up your catalogue and patent all closely related compounds . . . .

This work is incredibly data intensive, and requires many Ph.D's, assistants, and high powered computers and testing equipment to achieve. But it is hardly necessary in the absence of a patent regime. In the absence of patents, (and of course the FDA), you could just focus on finding a sufficient therapeutic window, and cut out the remaining tests. It would be an issue of marginal costs to determine whether someone would go to the effort to find a "better" therapeutic window, or related parameter.[1]

He noted elsewhere that Big Pharma displayed the general cultural atmosphere of waste that we normally identify with the Land of Cost-Plus Pricing, usually found in military contractors and the like.

Have you ever been to a Merck campus (yes, they are campuses, not buildings or sites)? If you look at the structure of the business, the first thing that strikes you is that it looks like Detroit, circa 1980. And there's only one reason for that—government protection of their profit margin . . . . And yet while Detroit has suffered and is still paying for employing such a business model, Pharma's been posting huge profits. Why's that?[2]

In addition, a great deal of Big Pharma's drug R&D is conducted at taxpayer expense, either through subsidies to the drug giants, or through research actually carried out in university and government agency labs.[3]

The one thing massive organizational size and expenditure *aren't* very good for, according to Michael Perelman, is innovation. They attempt to compensate for their mediocre performance in developing new drugs "by more intensive marketing, taking over smaller, more innovative companies, and laying off workers."[4] He quotes a *Wall Street Journal* article:

The rise of generics wouldn't matter so much if research labs were creating a stream of new hits. But that isn't happening. During the five years from 2002 through 2006, the industry brought to market 43% fewer new chemical-based drugs than in the last five years of the 1990s, despite more than doubling research-and-development spending . . .

The dearth of new products has led the industry to invest heavily in marketing and legal tactics that squeeze as much revenue as possible out of existing products. Companies have raised prices; the average price per pill has risen 63% since 2002, according to Michael Krensavage, Raymond James analyst. Companies raised advertising spending to $5.3 billion in 2006 from $2.5 billion in 2001 and since 1995 have nearly tripled the number of industry sales representatives to 100,000 . . . .

The industry spent $155 million on lobbying from January 2005 to June 2006, according to the Center for Public Integrity, on "a variety of issues ranging from protecting lucrative drug patents to keeping lower-priced Canadian drugs from being imported." The industry also successfully lobbied against allowing the federal government to negotiate Medicare drug prices, the center said. The lobbying has drawn fire from politicians, doctors and payers, and damaged the industry's public image.[5]

1. Comment on Kevin Carson, "Intellectual Property Stifles Innovation," Mutualist Blog, May 21, 2006 <http://mutualist.blogspot.com/2006/05/intellectual-property-stifles.html>.
2. Comment on Ronald Bailey, "This Is One Reason People Hate Drug Companies," *Reason* Magazine Hit&Run blog, February 24, 2006 <http://www.reason.com/blog/show/112756.html>.
3. Adams and Brock, 2nd edition, p. 58.
4. "Pharmaceutical Crackup?" *EconoSpeak*, December 8, 2007 <http://econospeak.blogspot.com/2007/12/pharmaceutical-crackup.html>.
5. Barbara Martinez and Jacob Goldstein, "Big Pharma Faces Grim Prognosis: Industry Fails to Find New Drugs to Replace Wonders Like Lipitor," *Wall Street Journal*, December 6, 2007, in *Ibid*.

After a decade or so of relative fluidity caused by the disruptive onset of globalization, global capital has settled back (with joint ventures and strategic alliances) into the same oligopoly pattern as the old American economy. That's especially true of the auto industry. After a brief period of admittedly traumatic shock, when they first encountered vigorous Japanese and European competition,

> the Big Three began to spin a far-reaching web of joint ventures and alliances with their major foreign competitors. Thus, General Motors . . . has joined with Toyota . . . to jointly produce compact cars in California. GM also has acquired sizable ownership in Japanese carmakers Isuzu and Suzuki, built a jointly owned production plant with Suzuki in Canada, and acquired half-ownership of Swedish manufacturer SAAB. Ford, for its part, acquired a 25 percent ownership stake in Mazda (later expanded); joined with Mazda to acquire an ownership stake in the Korean car firm Kia; joined with Mazda to build a production facility in Flat Rock, Michigan; combined its Latin American operations with Volkswagen (subsequently dissolved); and engaged in partnerships with Nissan to jointly produce vehicles (in addition to more recently acquiring outright control of Jaguar, Volvo, and rolls Royce). Chrysler joined with Mitsubishi to build the Diamond Star Motors assembly facility in Bloomington, Illinois, while spawning a variety of partnership pacts with other global car firms.

The major American and European auto manufacturers also participate in their respective R&D consortia.[1] So thanks to joint ventures, foreign automakers have reason to view themselves more as partners than as competitors to the American firms in this country. Lawrence Wilkinson brilliantly described the way in which corporations regulate innovation, as oligopoly reasserts itself:

> We're headed to a world that's more oligopolylike, a transition from a period of robust change to a period of lock in . . . . All over, there's a settling down, a slowing of the pace of change. Companies aren't really killing innovation—they're rationalizing it to manage its pace. The definition of oligopolistic economics is three or so players behaving in lockstep with the marketplace. They don't necessarily collude, but they develop ways of signaling pricing and containing innovation.[2]

F. ECONOMY OF SCALE IN AGRICULTURE

If there is one industry in which the triumphalist rhetoric of "superior efficiency" of large size is unjustified by reality, it is large-scale agribusiness. The reader has surely heard the rhetoric: claims that without "Green Revolution" techniques "the world would starve," ADM's boasts that "we feed the world," etc.

But the claimed "superior efficiency" of the large-scale agribusiness operation over the family farm is illusory. Likewise unfounded is the claimed superiority of mechanized, chemical agriculture, whether family or corporate, over more labor- and soil-intensive forms of production. The large agribusiness operation, with mechanized row-cropping and monocultures, is the most efficient "solution" to an artificial problem. The techniques of the so-called Green Revolution are only more efficient if one assumes from the outset the goals of the latifundistas and other state-privileged landed oligarchs in the Third World, and of the giant agribusiness interests in the West.

According to a 1973 USDA pamphlet (of all things), even mechanized farming reaches peak efficiency at a fairly small scale. Like all other internal economies of scale, economy of scale in mechanized farming relies mainly on making full use of equipment:

> The fully mechanized one-man farm, producing the maximum acreage of crops of which the man and his machines are capable, is generally a technically efficient farm.

1. Adams and Brock, 2nd edition, pp. 160–61.
2. Quoted in Harriet Rubin, "Power," Fast Company No. 65 (November 2002), p. 76.

From the standpoint of costs per unit of production, this size farm captures most of the economies associated with size . . . . Beyond that range there may be diseconomies due to the increasing burden of supervision and communication between supervisor and workers . . . . The incentive for increasing farm size beyond the technically optimum one-man form is not to reduce costs per unit of production, but to increase the volume of business, output, and total income.[1]

More specifically, USDA studies have found that the optimal size farm for raising vegetables (using conventional mechanized techniques) is around 200 acres, while the optimal cereal farm in the Midwest tops out at 800 acres.[2]

The secret to the success of large-scale agribusiness is not greater internal efficiency, but its greater efficiency at manipulating the state for benefits. The real difference in profitability comes from the channeling of state-subsidized inputs to large-scale agribusiness. As California family farmer Berge Bulbulian testified to Congress,

> . . . Probably the biggest obstacle we face in our struggle to save the family farm is the attitude . . . that the family farm is obsolete, it is inefficient, and therefore unable to compete with the efficient and well-financed conglomerates. Well-financed they are, but efficient they are not. I challenge any giant agribusiness corporation to match my efficiency. There is no way a large concern with various levels of bureaucracy and managed by absentee owners can compete in terms of true efficiency with a small, owner-operated concern . . . .
>
> . . . . No, I can't sell for a loss and make it up in taxes, nor can I lose on the farming end of the business and make it up at another level as a vertically integrated operation can . . . .
>
> I have no political clout and lobbying to me means writing a letter to my Congressman or Senator. But that is not what efficiency is all about.
>
> Efficiency has to do with the relation between input and output. No, the big agribusiness firms are not efficient except in farming the government.[3]

The family farm is more efficient than the large agribusiness operation (what Mason Gaffney calls "latifundia") in terms of output per acre. Gaffney found that while big corporate farms have somewhat higher output per man-hour, their output per acre is actually *less* than that of small farms.

> One may at least firmly conclude that large farm units are less improved and less peopled than small and medium-sized farms. There are two possible interpretations. One is that big farms are more efficient, getting more from less, but that is refuted by their getting less output per $L. The other is that Veblen was right, many of them are oversized stores of value, held first to park slack money and only secondly to produce food and fiber, and complement the owner's workmanship. The Florida 9 may represent a home grown rural "third world" of large, underutilized landholdings that preempt the best land and force median farmers onto small farms on low-grade land.[4]

According to Frances Moore Lappé, large landowners—both in the U.S. and in the Third World—are not only least productive in terms of output per acre, but they hold huge tracts of arable land out of cultivation. In Colombia, for example, a 1960 study found that

---

1. W.R. Bailey, *The One-Man Farm* (Washington, D.C.: USDA Agriculture Economic Research Service, 1973), pp. v, 3. Quoted in L.S. Stavrianos, *The Promise of the Coming Dark Age* (San Francisco: W.H. Freeman and Company, 1976), p. 38.

2. Kirkpatrick Sale, *Human Scale* (New York: Coward, McCann, & Geoghegan, 1980), p. 233.

3. *Farmworkers in Rural America 1971-1972*. Hearings before the Subcommittee on Children and Youth of the Committee on Labor and Public Welfare, United States Senate, 92nd Congress, 11 January 1972, Part 3A, p. 1156. In Stavrianos, *The Promise of the Coming Dark Age*, pp. 38-39.

4. Mason Gaffney, from Chapter 10 of *Ownership, Tenure, and Taxation of Agricultural Land*, edited by Gene Wunderlich (Westview Press), excerpted in Dan Sullivan's seminar on "The Myth of Corporate Efficiency" at SavingCommunities.Org <http://savingcommunities.org/seminars/corpefficiency.html>.

the largest landowners, who controlled 70% of the land, planted only 6% of it.[1] The best land, belonging to the large landholders, was often used for grazing cattle instead of growing staple crops.[2] In Guatemala, Del Monte planted only 9,000 of its 57,000 acres.[3] Small cultivators are consistently found to produce greater outputs per acre. In India, the smallest farms produce per-acre outputs a third higher than the larger ones. In Thailand, farms of 2-4 acres produce 60% more rice per acre than farms of over 140 acres. A World Bank study in Latin America found a three- to fourteen-fold difference in yield per acre between small and large farms.[4]

In the modern Green Revolution, Michael Perelman argues, "the really revolutionary changes in American agriculture have not been directed toward increasing yields . . . . Actually, the unique achievement of U.S. agriculture is not the production of maximum crop yields [per acre] but the harnessing of fossil fuel energy to replace human energy in agriculture.[5]

And bear in mind that these comparative figures on optimal economy of scale apply only when the large- and small-scale operations are both engaged in conventional mechanized row-cropping. The use of intensive raised-bed techniques for vegetables (the biointensive method of John Jeavons, for example) is far more productive than conventional commercial agriculture in terms of output per acre. Jeavons, as we shall see in Chapter Fourteen, has managed to reduce to four or five thousand square feet the space needed to meet the bare subsistence requirements of the average person.

It's especially important to remember that there's no such thing as generic or immaculate "technology," independent of the purposes of those who design it. The decision to develop one technology, rather than another, is made from the perspective of someone's interest. The choice of a particular technology is an answer to a question—so we should always be aware of who's asking the question. The avenues of technological development taken by the Green Revolution reflect a conscious political decision to develop technologies of use primarily to large-scale agribusiness with access to government-subsidized irrigation water and other inputs, rather than technologies that would increase the productivity of the peasant smallholder without subsidized water.

Large-scale plantation agribusiness, typically, flourishes only when supported by government-subsidized irrigation projects. For example, a large share of American produce comes from rain-poor areas of the West: vegetables are actually imported by rain-rich regions like New England, because subsidized irrigation water makes the Western operations artificially competitive. It is far more cost-effective in semi-arid regions, when irrigation is not subsidized, to use cisterns to save water from the limited rainy seasons for use through the dry period. For a subsistence farmer making intensive use of small spaces, runoff from the rainy season may well be sufficient to provide irrigation water during the dry spell. The main technical problem is providing enough storage tanks. The ITDG was quite successful in designing cheap water tanks made from local materials.[6] And biointensive horticulture,

1. Frances Moore Lappé, *Food First: Beyond the Myth of Scarcity* (New York: Ballantine Books, 1977), p. 14.

2. *Ibid.*, p. 42.

3. *Ibid.*, p. 107.

4. *Ibid.*, pp. 183-84.

5. "Farming for Profit in a Hungry World: The Myth of Agricultural Efficiency." Louis Junker, ed., *The Political Economy of Food and Energy* (Ann Arbor: University of Michigan, 1977), pp. 40-41.

6. George McRobie. *Small is Possible: A factual account of who is doing what, where, to put into practice the ideas expressed in E. F. Schumacher's SMALL IS BEAUTIFUL* (New York: Harper & Row, 1981)., p. 45.

which minimizes plant spacings and maximizes soil cover, requires up to 88% less water than conventional large-scale farming.[1]

The so-called "Green Revolution" in the Third World, particularly, occurred in the context of a colonial history where peasant cultivators were pushed off of the best land and onto marginal land, and the most fertile, level land was used for plantation farming of cash crops. It is a myth that Third World hunger results mainly from primitive farming techniques, or that the solution is a technocratic fix. Hunger results from the fact that land once used to grow staple foods for the people working it is now used to grow cash crops for urban elites or for the export markets, while the former peasant proprietors are without a livelihood.

Native farming techniques, often derided by colonizers as primitive or backward, were in fact well-suited to local tradition as the result of generations of experience. Lappé cites A. J. Voelker, a British agricultural scientist in India during the 1890s:

> Nowhere would one find better instances of keeping land scrupulously clean from weeds, of ingenuity in device of water-raising appliances, of knowledge of soils and their capabilities, as well as of the exact time to sow and reap, as one would find in Indian agriculture. It is wonderful, too, how much is known of rotation, the system of "mixed crops" and of fallowing . . . . I, at least, have never seen a more perfect picture of cultivation.[2]

Colonial agricultural policy focused all subsidies to research and innovation on export crops, leaving subsistence techniques to stagnate. Slaves and hired farm laborers had no incentive for preserving traditional knowledge, let alone refining technique. To the contrary, farm laborers had every incentive to do the bare minimum, reduce output, and even sabotage production. (I believe Adam Smith had similar observations about the incentive effects of absentee land ownership in England.) The African peasant "went into colonialism with a hoe and came out with a hoe." The most important effect of plantation culture, perhaps, was a "narrowing of the experience of agriculture to plantation work . . . [which] over generations robbed entire populations of basic peasant farming skills."[3] Lappé cited the observations of Pascal de Pury, a WCC agronomist, that

> often [appropriate] technology turns out to be rediscoveries of a people's traditional practices that Western arrogance caused them to be ashamed of. Over and over again he finds peasant cultures that had refined and adopted techniques over centuries to be losing them in our time. What stands to be irretrievably lost is . . . successful, productive techniques uniquely suited to local conditions . . . .[4]

It is impossible to understand the so-called Green Revolution as it occurred in the Third World, unless one first understands the political context in which it took place. The central facet of that context was the process by which the land of subsistence farmers was expropriated and turned over to cash crop cultivation, native populations were reduced to dependency, and formerly independent peasants were often forced to engage in cash crop production. The best land was often taken over by the colonial powers and handed over to settlers, and the former subsistence cultivators transformed into farm laborers.

> . . . Throughout the colonies, it became standard practice to declare all "uncultivated" land to be the property of the colonial administration. At a stroke, local communities were denied legal title to lands they had traditionally set aside as fallow and to the forests, grazing lands and streams they relied upon for hunting, gathering, fishing and herding.

1. Hawken *et al.*, *Natural Capitalism*, p. 210.
2. Lappé, *Food First*, pp. 101–02.
3. *Ibid.*, p. 113.
4. *Ibid.*, p. 173.

Where, as was frequently the case, the colonial authorities found that the lands they sought to exploit were already "cultivated", the problem was remedied by restricting the indigenous population to tracts of low quality land deemed unsuitable for European settlement. In Kenya, such "reserves" were "structured to allow the Europeans, who accounted for less than one per cent of the population, to have full access to the agriculturally rich uplands that constituted 20 per cent of the country. In Southern Rhodesia, white colonists, who constituted just five per cent of the population, became the new owners of two-thirds of the land . . . . Once secured, the commons appropriated by the colonial administration were typically leased out to commercial concerns for plantations, mining and logging, or sold to white settlers.[1]

Sometimes the labor of the dispossessed was secured by slavery and other forms of forced labor, although the colonial powers usually preferred to use direct taxation on people, land and houses to compel the native population to enter the wage labor market.

Lappé presents some instances of her own. For example, in 1815, following the British conquest of the Kandyan Kingdom (present day Sri Lanka), all central parts of the island were designated as crown land and sold for nominal prices to coffee planters, with government funding of surveying and road-building costs. In Java, the Dutch administration "authorized" village headmen (usually under the influence of bribes) to lease communal land to Dutch plantation companies. Often entire villages were thus "sold" to foreign planters, without the consent of the rightful owners of the land.[2] Colonial authorities worldwide similarly abrogated the traditional status of land, when it was the inalienable property of a village commune or clan, by making it—in violation of native law—usable as a pledge for debt. Likewise, such communally-owned land was often made seizable for non-payment of taxes by the individual cultivator.[3] We see the same phenomenon in our own day, with the Chinese state expropriating villages' common land for use as industrial parks.

In addition, colonial authorities simultaneously granted protectionist privileges to settler plantations and imposed legal disabilities on independent native producers, through the mercantilist policies of shipping companies and produce marketing boards.[4]

Given this maldistribution of land through state-abetted land theft (either by colonial regimes or by landed oligarchies in collusion with Western agribusiness interests), the logical next step is for the state to divert inputs like subsidized irrigation systems, roads, and so forth, disproportionately to the large plantations while denying them to subsistence farmers. The state's direct subsidies and loan programs are set up so that only large holdings, with access to preferential benefits like state-subsidized irrigation, can qualify. Heavily state-subsidized agricultural R&D, likewise, is channelled in directions geared to increasing the profits of cash crop agriculture on the big plantations, rather than to increasing the productivity of small peasant holdings.

The "high-yielding variety" (HYV) seeds associated with the so-called Green Revolution are normally productive only under the most favorable conditions, like those prevailing on the big agribusiness plantations. The Green Revolution was a state-subsidized research project to develop plant varieties tailored to the prevailing conditions in the state-subsidized agri-

1. "Development as Enclosure: The Establishment of the Global Economy," *The Ecologist* (July/August 1992) 133.

2. Lappé, *Food First*, pp. 103–06.

3. *Ibid.*, pp. 114–15.

4. Walter Rodney, "Chapter Five. Africa's Contribution to the Capitalist Development of Europe: The Colonial Period," in *How Europe Underdeveloped Africa* (Dar-Es-Salaam: Bogle-L'Overture Publications, London and Tanzanian Publishing House, 1973) Transcribed by Joaquin Arriola <http://www.marxists.org/subject/africa/rodney-walter/how-europe/index.htm>.

business sector. They are deliberately designed to be productive, in other words, under precisely the conditions provided by corporate agribusiness operating on stolen land.

> . . . [T]he term "high-yielding varieties" is a misnomer because it implies that the new seeds are high-yielding *in and of themselves*. The distinguishing feature of the seeds, however, is that they are highly *responsive* to certain key inputs such as irrigation and fertilizer . . . . [W]e have chosen to use the term "high-response varieties" (HRV's) as much more revealing of the true character of the seeds . . . . Unless the poor farmers can afford to ensure the ideal conditions that will make these new seeds respond . . . , their new seeds are just not going to grow as well as the ones planted by better-off farmers . . . .
>
> Just as significant for the majority of the world's farmers is that the new seeds show a greater yield variability than the seeds they replace. The HRV's are more sensitive to drought and flood than their traditional predecessors . . . .
>
> HRV's are often less resistant to disease and pests. [They supplant] varieties that had evolved over centuries in response to natural threats in that environment.[1]

They are, in other words, "highly responsive" to plentiful water from subsidized irrigation projects, large-scale inputs of chemical fertilizer and pesticides, and monocultural growing conditions. And they are also most responsive on the kind of especially fertile, well-watered land that just happened to be stolen by landed elites under the colonial or post-colonial regimes.

Under the conditions of peasant subsistence farming, the traditional drought- and pest-resistant varieties are far more productive. Locally adapted varieties tend to be drought-resistant and hardy, and to produce steady yields under harsh conditions.[2]

Locally adapted varieties are also highly responsive to the kinds of inputs that are more likely to be within the means of the small subsistence farmer: for example, better plowing and harrowing techniques and weed elimination, crop rotation, green manuring, better soil conservation, and better moisture retention in the soil.[3]

"Green Revolution" seeds are like a genetically engineered superman who will die outside of his plastic bubble.

In Mexico, 97.7% of land devoted to corn and most land devoted to wheat lacked irrigation. The Institute for Agricultural Investigation, a Mexican research organization, set out to develop varieties of corn and wheat that would produce greater yields on small non-irrigated farms. But the Rockefeller Foundation concentrated on developing varieties that produced high yields in response to high levels of irrigation and synthetic fertilizer.

> . . . The resulting new "miracle" strains enabled Mexico to become self-sufficient in wheat, but the beneficiaries were the wealthy landowners, who could afford the fertilizers and irrigation. The mass of the Mexican peasants have experienced increased unemployment or underemployment with the growing mechanization of the large estates.

The same pattern prevailed in India, Pakistan and the Philippines, where research went to developing seed varieties primarily of benefit to large landowners with access to subsidized irrigation water and fertilizer, rather than to the 70-90% farming non-irrigated land. At the same time, the resulting land hunger on the part of the great subsidized farmers has led to pressure to expropriate smallholders by abrogating traditional rights of land tenure, and to evict tenant farmers paying rent on land that is rightfully theirs. The landless and the underemployed rural proletariat, in turn, swell the urban slums with people who once fed themselves.[4] In addition, as Lappé observed (or perhaps, rather, recycled an observation at least as old as Henry George), the increased productivity from Green Revolution

---

1. Lappé, pp. 130-31.
2. *Ibid.* p. 130.
3. *Ibid.* pp. 150-51.
4. Stavrianos, *The Promise of the Coming Dark Age*, pp. 42-44.

seeds drives up rents, with crop share rents increasing from the traditional 50% to 70%.[1]
Naturally, this further increases the tendency toward eviction of small holders and the consolidation of the large estates.

It is a widespread observation that the large plantations benefiting from Green Revolution techniques are likely to receive highly preferential access to subsidized inputs like irrigation water. According to Michael Perelman,

> . . . It is true that the Green Revolution has increased the amount of wheat and rice pro-
> duced in Asia. But it is also true that the adoption of this technology requires heavy gov-
> ernment subsidies in the form of cheap credit, favorable foreign exchange rates, and high
> government support prices . . . . Much of the increase comes from the use of irrigation
> for prime agricultural lands. Extending irrigation is expensive and some observers even
> question whether it is possible to continue irrigating without depleting the ground wa-
> ter.[2]

As a good example of the big landed interests' privileged access to subsidized irrigation water, consider the case of Pakistan. The big landowners seek new dams to provide
more subsidized water for their agribusiness plantations—and since they don't pay for it
themselves, they're not very careful about how they use it:

> We, as a nation, tend to build, neglect and throw away, only to build again. There is
> no concept of maintenance. Pakistan has the largest contiguous irrigation system in the
> world. It is supposed to be a miracle of engineering that has helped increase our food
> production. But we don't maintain it. Operation, maintenance, and replacement costs a
> lot of money . . . .
>
> Some of the data in the recent World Bank report, "Pakistan's water economy run-
> ning dry," is quite frightening. When comparing Pakistan with Australia, the report
> shows that in Australia, the entire cost of efficient operation, maintenance and replace-
> ment is paid by the actual users, whereas taxpayers pay the interest on any loans that may
> have been accrued in putting that water system into place.
>
> *In Pakistan, taxpayers—not users—are paying most of the operation and maintenance costs,
> no one is paying for replacement . . . . When we can't even look after our existing infrastructure, is
> there even a case for building new infrastructure? . . . .*
>
> *Water rights in Pakistan is tied to ownership of land, so in spite of so many reforms, we still
> have very big farms owned by very powerful people, (rather than smaller farm owners) and landless
> peoples who actually work the land . . . .* Where we have bigger landlords with their rent-
> seeking behaviour on the land, their payment for water is not a major consideration.
> Where sharecropping arrangements have been perpetuated, there isn't much impetus to
> change because the system suits the landowners.
>
> So all we hear about is a demand for more water. The entire world is going on to
> use less water and grow more crops but here we are shouting for more water to maintain
> some of the lowest productivity not only in the world, but also in the subcontinent.
> There are so many cheap technologies available—drip and sprinkler irrigation and there
> are already people here producing this equipment.[3]

The same resources currently put into subsidizing the needs of agribusiness, if put
into research efforts in the interest of small-scale farmers, would have meant a fundamentally different direction of technical development. L.S. Stavrianos wrote:

> Large corporations are . . . virtually the sole beneficiaries of agriculture research financed
> by the federal, state, and county governments. Research oriented toward benefiting fam-
> ily farms would devise cooperative-ownership systems and credit schemes; develop low-
> cost simple machinery; provide information on the purchase, operation, and maintenance

1. Lappé, *Food First,* pp. 136.
2. "Farming for Profit in a Hungry World," p. 34.
3. "Interview—Simi Kamal" *Newsline* (Pakistan) February 2006 <http://www.newsline.com.pk/
NewsFeb2006/interviewfeb2006.htm>.

of machinery; and promote biological control of insect pests. Instead, scientists with research grants develop complicated and tremendously expensive machines. They breed new food varieties better adapted to mechanical cultivation . . . . Paramount has been the vision of rural America as a factory producing food, fiber, and profits for vertical monopolies extending from the fields to the supermarket checkout counter.[1]

The administration of Lazaro Cardenas in Mexico, during the 1930s, is a good example of the result when state policy is less one-sided. His agrarian reform, starting in a country where two percent of the population owned 97% of the land, resulted in 42% of the agricultural population owning 47% of the land and producing 52% of agricultural output. Under Cardenas, state loans and technical support were aimed primarily at the needs of small-scale agriculture. The result was an explosive increase in the rural standard of living. As for state-funded agricultural R&D,

> . . . The purpose . . . was not to "modernize" agriculture in imitation of United States agriculture but to improve on traditional farming methods. Researchers began to develop improved varieties of wheat and especially corn, the main staple of the rural population, always concentrating on what could be utilized by small farmers who had little money and less than ideal farm conditions.
>
> Social and economic progress was being achieved not through dependence on foreign expertise or costly imported agricultural inputs but rather with the abundant, underutilized resources of local peasants . . . . Freed from the fear of landlords, bosses, and moneylenders, peasants were motivated to produce, knowing that at last they would benefit from their own labor.[2]

The groups alienated by Cardenas—the great rural landowners, the urban commercial elites, and (as you might expect) the U.S. government—reasserted their political control under Cardenas' post-1940 successor, Avila Camacho. Rather than small farms and cooperatives, development spending was directed, on the American model, toward

> electric power, highways, dams, airports, telecommunications, and urban services that would serve privately owned, commercial agriculture and urban industrialization . . . .[3]

The Camacho administration, naturally, was heavily involved in the postwar Green Revolution. The direction of the new big research program was diametrically opposite to that under Cardenas.

> . . . Policy choices systematically discarded research alternatives oriented toward the nonirrigated, subsistence sector of Mexican agriculture. Instead, all effort went to the development of a capital-intensive technology applicable only to the relatively best-endowed areas or those that could be created by massive irrigation projects.[4]

Under Camacho, huge irrigation projects were developed for favorably situated land owned by big landed elites, and massive state subsidies were provided for the importation of mechanized equipment.

As Lappé writes, the Camacho approach could not coexist with that of Cardenas. The Cardenas agenda of increasing the productivity of peasant proprietors would have increased their standard of living; in so doing, it would have reduced the surplus going to urban and export markets rather than domestic consumption, and also reduced the flow of landless refugees to the cities. In other words, the Cardenas policies threatened the supply of cheap wage labor for industrialization, and the supply of cheap food to feed it.

The point to all this is not that Cardenas' version of state intervention was desirable, but 1) that the present system touted by neoliberals as the "free market" involves at least as

1. Stavrianos, *The Promise of the Coming Dark Age*, p. 35.
2. Lappé, *Food First,* pp. 123-24.
3. *Ibid.*, p. 124.
4. *Ibid.*, pp. 125-26.

much state intervention; and 2) that there is no such thing as neutral, politically immaculate technology that can be divorced from questions of power relationships. Criteria of technical "efficiency" depend on the nature of the organizational structures which will be adopting a technology. And the forms of state R&D subsidy and other development aid entailed in the Green Revolution artificially promoted capital-intensive plantation agriculture, despite

> overwhelming evidence from around the world that small, carefully farmed plots are more productive per acre than large estates and use fewer costly inputs . . .[1]

What's more, the high-response varieties developed by the Green Revolution crowded out equally viable alternatives that were more appropriate to traditional smallholder agriculture. Any just assessment of the Green Revolution must take into consideration the path not taken (or Bastiat's "unseen"). The Green Revolution, coming as it did on the heels of land expropriation, channelled innovation in the directions most favoring the land-grabbers. It was a subsidy to the richest growers, artificially increasing their competitiveness against the subsistence sector.

> . . . Historically, the Green Revolution represented a choice to breed seed varieties that produce high yields under optimum conditions. It was a choice not to start by developing seeds better able to withstand drought or pests. It was a choice not to concentrate first on improving traditional methods of increasing yields, such as mixed cropping. It was a choice not to develop technology that was productive, labor-intensive, and independent of foreign input supply. It was a choice not to concentrate on reinforcing the balanced, traditional diets of grains plus legumes.[2]

HRVs are actually less hardy and durable under the conditions prevailing on subsistence farms—less drought-resistant, for example. Locally improved varieties are specifically adapted to be productive under conditions of low rainfall, and more resistant to insects and fungi without costly chemical inputs. Local seed varieties, combined with intensive techniques and the creative use of biological processes, result in levels of output comparable in many cases to that of Green Revolution seed varieties combined with heavy chemical inputs and subsidized irrigation. Even setting aside the long-term costs of soil depletion, good husbandry with local varieties of seed produce almost as much corn and sorghum output per acre. An experiment in Bangladesh—ceasing pesticide use in order to raise fish in rice paddies—resulted in a 25% increase in rice production, along with the high quality protein from the fish. The fish controlled insects more efficiently than chemical pesticides, and fertilized the rice.[3]

A rural development agenda geared toward the interests of peasant proprietors would have emphasized, not increasing the yield of seeds in response to expensive irrigation and chemical inputs, but improving the soil.

This brings us back to our earlier consideration of the concept of "efficiency." The discussion above gives the lie to vulgar Coasean arguments that justice in holdings doesn't matter, as long as they wind up in the "most efficient" hands. For one thing, it matters a great deal to the person who was robbed; it matters a great deal whether you're producing enough staple crops on your own land to feed your family, or instead holding a begging bowl in the streets of Calcutta or living in some tin-roofed shantytown on the outskirts of Mexico, while your stolen land is being used to grow export crops for those with the purchasing power to buy them. But more importantly, the Green Revolution and the alternatives it crowded out demonstrate—again—that *there's no such thing as generic "efficiency" in the*

1. *Ibid.*, p. 127.
2. *Ibid.*, p. 153.
3. *Ibid.*, p. 127.

use of resources. The "most efficient" use of a piece of land depends mightily on who owns it, and what their needs are. An "efficient" technique for the land thief is entirely different from what would have been efficient for the land's rightful owner.

One can afford to be a lot less efficient in the use of inputs that he gets for free. Capital-intensive techniques that increase output per man-hour, but reduce output per acre, are suited to the interests of American-style agribusiness. They're perfect for large landowners who, as a historical legacy, have preferential access to large tracts of land (to the extent that they can even afford to hold significant parts of it out of use), but want to reduce the agency costs of labor by capital substitution. In areas with underutilized land and unemployed population, on the other hand, where millions of unemployed people would *rather* be working the land than squatting in the streets of Calcutta or the shantytowns of Mexico City, it makes a lot more sense to increase output per acre by adding labor inputs. And this is exactly the pattern that prevails in small-scale agriculture. Lappé found, in a survey of studies from around the world, that small farms were universally more productive—far more productive—per acre than large plantations. Depending on the region and the crop, small farms were from one-third to fourteen times more productive. The efficiency of small proprietors working their own land, compared to plantation agribusiness using wage or tenant labor, is analogous to that of the small family plots in the old USSR compared to the state farms. Plantation agriculture is able to outcompete the peasant proprietor only through "preferential access to credit and government-subsidized technology . . . ."[1]

Green Revolution techniques are very "efficient" indeed—but only given the artificial objectives of those who stole the land.

CONCLUSION

Overall, the importance of economy of scale was summed up very well by Barry Stein, in his concluding remarks on a survey of the empirical literature:

> Such uncertainty and variability suggest that technical economies of scale are not the primary determinant of either competitive ability or true efficiency. Available data indicate first, that in most industries the penalties for operating plants well below the apparent optimal scale are not great; second, the presence of substantial relatively constant costs (added to those directly associated with production) dilutes even those clear advantages of greater productive scale; and third, there is no strong case to be made for significant economies of firm (as against plant) size.[2]

So why are giant corporations able to survive, despite such manifest violation of all the laws of efficiency? The reason is twofold.

First, they are protected, by state intervention, from the competitive disadvantages resulting from inefficiency. A state-cartelized oligopoly firm can operate at higher costs and pass its costs on to the consumer, because it is protected from the full vigor of competition from smaller and more efficient producers.

Second, as we already mentioned at the outset of this chapter, the figures above for optimal economy of scale assume the existing input costs, without considering the extent to which the state subsidizes inputs and externalizes a wide range of operating costs on the taxpayer.

In the next chapter, we will consider the whole range of measures by which the state restricts competition and subsidizes inefficiency costs.

1. Lappé, *Food First,* p. 189.
2. *Size, Efficiency, and Community Enterprise,* pp. 24-25.

3

State Policies Promoting Centralization and Large Organizational Size

apitalism, if we take it in R.A. Wilson's sense of a political and economic system in which the state is controlled by capitalists and intervenes in the market on their behalf, has been exploitative since the beginning. It was established at the outset by massive acts of state robbery and restrictions on liberty: the so-called "primitive accumulation" by which the peasantry's property in the land was expropriated, the Laws of Settlement which acted as an internal passport system restricting movement of the working class, the Combination Laws which restricted the bargaining power of labor, and the mercantilism and imperial aggression by which the so-called world market was created. These matters fall too far outside of our focus for detailed examination. A summary of all the uses of force involved in the establishment of capitalism can be found in Chapter Four of *Studies in Mutualist Political Economy.*[1]

Once established on this basis, the system was maintained through various state-enforced legal privileges. This, also, is too far outside the scope of the present chapter to examine in depth. The main forms of privilege that existed before the rise of corporate capitalism in the nineteenth century were the "Four Monopolies" summarized by Benjamin Tucker in "State Socialism and Anarchism," and will be considered in greater depth in our examination of privilege in Chapter Eleven.

Our main concern here is with the state's later role under monopoly capitalism: in the creation and development of the corporate economy, the concentration of capital, and the centralization of production. Specifically: what state policies have promoted the domination of the economy by corporations grown far beyond the point of maximum efficiency?

I. The Corporate Transformation of Capitalism in the Nineteenth Century

The regime of legal privilege described by Tucker and the individualist anarchists, referred to above, predated the corporate transformation of capitalism. It took the form primarily of unequal exchange on the individual level, whether it was the sale of labor-power on disadvantageous terms in an unequal labor market, or the purchase of goods on unequal terms because of patents, copyrights and tariffs. The individualists, habituated to view exchange in such individualistic terms, neglected the structural changes in the American economy—the tendency toward the concentration of capital and the centralization of production—and the ways that the tariff and intellectual property monopolies promoted these structural changes. In addition, Tucker and the other individualists largely ignored the organizational ties between the corporation and the state, the state's increasing assumption

1. Kevin A. Carson, *Studies in Mutualist Political Economy.* Self-published via Blitzprint (Fayetteville, Ark., 2004).

nizational ties between the corporation and the state, the state's increasing assumption of the corporation's operating expenses through direct subsidies, and the state's limitation of competition between large corporations through its cartelizing regulations.

Later in life, when Tucker took note of the trusts, he became pessimistic about the potential for reversing the concentration of economic power by merely eliminating privilege. He feared the great trusts had grown so large, and the concentration of wealth so great, that they might be self-perpetuating even without further state intervention.

> Forty years ago ..., the denial of competition had not yet effected the enormous concentration of wealth that now so gravely threatens social order. It was not yet too late to stem the current of accumulation by a reversal of the policy of monopoly. The Anarchistic remedy was still applicable.
>
> Today the way is not so clear. The four monopolies, unhindered, have made possible the modern development of the trust, and the trust is now a monster which I fear, even the freest banking, could it be instituted, would be unable to destroy .... Were all restrictions upon banking to be removed, concentrated capital could meet successfully the new situation by setting aside annually for sacrifice a sum that would remove every competitor from the field.
>
> If this be true, then monopoly, which can be controlled permanently only by economic forces, has passed for the moment beyond their reach, and must be grappled with for a time solely by forces political or revolutionary.[1]

But even then, he seemingly viewed such concentration of wealth only as the result of the prior operation of the Four Monopolies, working on an individual level. So his pessimism, arguably, reflected a neglect of the extent to which the power of large corporations depended on ongoing state intervention on a *structural* level, operating on them as organizations. Perhaps, then, we need not be so pessimistic.

As we shall see later in this chapter, Gabriel Kolko showed that the large trusts at the turn of the twentieth century were unable to maintain their market share against more efficient smaller firms. The stabilization of most industries on an oligopoly pattern was possible, in the end, only with the additional help of the Progressive Era's anti-competitive regulations. The fact that the trusts were so unstable, despite the cartelizing effects of tariffs and patents, speaks volumes about the level of state intervention necessary to maintain monopoly capitalism. But without the combined influence of tariffs, patents, and railroad subsidies in creating the centralized corporate economy, there would not have been any large corporations even to *attempt* trusts in the first place. The corporate transformation of the economy in the late 19th century—made possible by the government's role in railroad subsidies, protectionism, and patents—was a necessary precondition for the full-blown state capitalism of the 20th century.

A. THE NINETEENTH CENTURY CORPORATE LEGAL REVOLUTION

The American legal framework was transformed in the mid-nineteenth century in ways that made a more hospitable environment for large corporations. Among the changes were the rise of a general federal commercial law, general incorporation laws, and the status of the corporation as a person under the Fourteenth Amendment. The cumulative effect of these changes on a national scale was comparable to the later effect, on a global scale, of the Bretton Woods agencies and the GATT process: a centralized legal order was created, prerequisite for their stable functioning, coextensive with the market areas of large corporations.

---

1. "Postscript to State Socialism and Anarchism" (1926), in *Individual Liberty:* Selections From the Writings of Benjamin R. Tucker (New York: Vanguard Press, 1926). Reproduced online at Flag.Blackened.Net <http://flag.blackened.net/daver/anarchism/tucker/tucker.html>.

The federalization of the legal regime is associated with the recognition of a general body of federal commercial law in *Swift v. Tyson* (1842), and with the application of the Fourteenth Amendment to corporate persons in *Santa Clara County v. Southern Pacific Railroad Company* (1886).

It was originally held under American constitutional law that there was no general body of federal commercial law—only case law developed pursuant to the specific and limited delegated powers of Congress. The diversity of citizenship jurisdiction of the federal courts—their jurisdiction over disputes between citizens of different states—was not pursuant to the federal government's power to regulate commerce, but simply served to promote comity between the states. Cases in diversity jurisdiction were to be decided, not on the basis of any general federal commercial law, but on the basis of the law of the state in which the tort or contract took place. Until *Swift v. Tyson*, this state law was taken to include the case law which explicated it. *Swift v. Tyson* held, instead, that the law of the state consisted only of statute law; as Justice Story argued,

> in the ordinary use of language, it will hardly be contended that the decision of courts constituted laws. They are, at most, only evidence of what the laws are, and are not, of themselves law.

The federal judiciary, therefore, was governed in its diversity jurisdiction only by state statutes, and not state case law. The federal judiciary was free to develop its own body of judge-made common law—to judge according to "the general principles of commercial law"—in deciding diversity cases.[1] As Horwitz argued, Story's opinion was a throwback to the understanding of the common law as "found, not made," a general body of principles accessible to reason, which had almost entirely collapsed by that time in the face of the modern understanding of positive law.[2]

The Santa Clara decision[3] was followed by an era of federal judicial activism, in which state laws were overturned on the basis of "substantive due process." The role of the federal courts in the national economy was similar to the global role of the contemporary World Trade Organization, with higher tribunals empowered to override the laws of local jurisdictions which were injurious to corporate interests.

In the federal courts, the "due process" and "equal protection" rights of corporations as "juristic persons" have been made the basis of protections against legal action aimed at protecting the older common law rights of flesh and blood persons. For example local ordinances to protect groundwater and local populations against toxic pollution and contagion from hog farms, to protect property owners from undermining and land subsidence caused by coal extraction—surely indistinguishable in practice from the tort liability provisions of any just market anarchy's libertarian law code—have been overturned as violations of the "equal protection" rights of hog factory farms and mining companies. Barry Yeoman recounts a Pennsylvania community's passage of an anti-sludge ordinance based on health and safety concerns,

> only to be sued by a sludge hauler called Synagro, which argued that the township had infringed on its rights under the 14th Amendment, passed after the Civil War to guarantee "equal protection" to all . . . .
>
> After *Santa Clara*, federal judges began granting more and more rights to nonliving "persons." In 1922, the Supreme Court ruled that the Pennsylvania Coal Co. was entitled to "just compensation" under the Fifth Amendment because a state law, designed to

---

1. In Morton Horwitz, *The Transformation of American Law 1780-1860* (Cambridge and London: Harvard University Press, 1977), p. 245.

2. *Ibid.* p. 246.

3. 118 U.S. 394 (1886) <http://caselaw.lp.findlaw.com/scripts/getcase.pl?navby=CASE&court=US&vol=118&page=394>.

keep houses from collapsing as mining companies tunneled under them, limited how much coal it could extract . . . .

Local regulation of toxic sludge prompted lawsuits on the grounds that such restrictions violated corporate rights with regard to "equal protection, due process, taking without just compensation, and rights guaranteed under the commerce clause." Agribusiness took the fight to the state Legislature, supporting a law under which the state attorney general could sue any local government for passing an ordinance that "prohibits or limits a normal agricultural operation."[1]

The phrase "normal agricultural operation," by the way, foreshadows a later theme in this chapter: the ways in which the federal regulatory state has preempted and overriden older common law standards of liability, replacing the potentially harsh damages imposed by local juries with a least common denominator of regulatory standards based on "sound science" (as determined by industry, of course).

More important than either of the above changes, however, is the general change in corporate law: a move toward general incorporation laws at the state level, and the rise of corporate entity status[2] under both state and federal law.

Robert Hessen has argued that general incorporation statutes provide no benefits that could not be achieved by simple private contract.[3] Piet-Hein Van Eeghen, however, raises the question of whether the entity status of the corporation, distinct from any or all of the individual stockholders, could be established solely by private contract.

> Entity status means that certain legal rights and duties are held by the corporation as a separate, impersonal legal entity. In the case of the private business corporation, entity status implies that title to the firm's assets is held by the corporation in its own right, separate from its shareholders.
>
> Illustrative of the fact that the corporate form of private enterprise deviates from traditional forms of private property, entity status renders the legal position of both corporate shareholders and managers (directors) awkward and ambiguous. As for corporate shareholders, they are commonly regarded as the owners of the corporation, but they are owners only in a limited sense. Shareholders do not have title to the assets of the corporate firm, but merely possess the right to appoint management and to receive dividends as and when these are declared; title to the firm's assets reverts back to shareholders only when its corporate status is terminated. The lack of ownership rights over assets is illustrated by the fact that, in contrast to partners in an unincorporated partnership, corporate shareholders cannot lay claim to their share of the assets of the corporate firm nor do they have the right to force their co-partners to buy them out. Corporate shareholders can liquidate their investment only by selling their shares to third parties . . . .
>
> As for corporate management, their legal position is equally ambiguous. Managers are appointed by directors who are the representatives of shareholders . . . . This, however, is only part of the picture. While management is the agent for shareholders in the sense of being ultimately appointed by and accountable to them, it is also the agent for the corporation itself. After all, in order to manage the corporation's assets, management must legally represent the corporation as the titleholder to these assets. And because the corporation is an impersonal legal entity, agency for the corporation lends a significant degree of autonomy to the position of management, which is precisely why it has proved so difficult to make shareholder control over management more effective . . . .

1. Barry Yeoman, "When Is a Corporation Like a Freed Slave?" *Mother Jones,* November-December 2006 <http://www.motherjones.com/news/feature/2006/11/when_is_a_corporation_like_a_freed_slave.html>.

2. The evolution of legal theory regarding the corporate entity status is discussed at length by Morton Horwitz in *The Transformation of American Law, 1870-1960: The Crisis of Legal Orthodoxy* (New York and Oxford: Oxford University Press, 1992), pp. 65-107.

3. *In Defense of the Corporation* (Stanford, Calif.: Hoover Institution, 1979).

Other typical features of the corporation like limited liability and perpetuity are not independent, original attributes, but are derived from its entity status.

Shareholders possess limited liability because they do not own the corporation's assets and are, consequently, also not liable for claims against these assets. Responsibility for corporate debt rests with the corporation in its own right rather than with them . . . .

The corporate feature of perpetuity can also be traced back to the corporation's entity status. It is because assets are owned by the corporation in its own right rather than by shareholders that the death or departure of shareholders does not affect its continued existence . . . .[1]

Van Eeghen argues that general incorporation under statute law is a source of special privilege, insofar as it confers what were previously considered the incidents of statehood, and is therefore impermissible from a libertarian standpoint:

It has, in fact, always been foreign to common law principles to allow private persons the unrestricted freedom to assign their assets to the ownership of impersonal, and thus state-like, legal entities . . . .[2]

Originally only state institutions (central, regional, and local government) possessed corporate status, which seems entirely natural and appropriate. If we wish to escape Louis XIV's infamous dictum "l'état c'est moi" ("I am the state") . . . , the state should indeed be given a legal entity separate from its officials. Only if such a separation exists can state power be vested in the office rather than the person; and only when state power is vested in the office can it be circumscribed by law . . . .

If it is agreed that entity status is indeed a typical attribute of the state, then anarchocapitalists who advocate a stateless society have even more reason to oppose private firms taking on state-like attributes such as happens when they acquire corporate status.[3]

Further, Van Eeghen argues, corporate entity status and all its incidents have had the practical effect of enabling all the negative features commonly identified in critiques of corporate power:

(a) Increased Speculative Instability

Because incorporation separates ownership from control, shares in a modern corporation can be traded without necessarily affecting the management nor the capital position of the firm. As a result, an active market in such shares develops more easily . . . . Moreover, partners normally have the right to consultation in ownership transfers, which also reduces the marketability of ownership stakes in unincorporated businesses.

. . . . Since incorporation significantly increases the marketability of ownership stakes, it thereby also enhances the opportunities for speculative activity in share markets. In addition, many of the participants in speculative markets are corporations themselves and thus enjoy a degree of risk protection in the form of limited liability. Because the balance between risk and reward is tampered with, speculative activity is artificially stimulated . . . .

(b) Increased Market Concentration and Concentration of Control

Because the corporate form increases the average firm size, it will also *ceteris paribus* increase the degree of concentration in any given market. Furthermore, because incorporation enhances the marketability of shares as well as the ease with which capital can

1. Piet-Hein van Eeghen. "The Corporation at Issue, Part I: The Clash of Classical Liberal Values and the Negative Consequences for Capitalist Practice" *Journal of Libertarian Studies* Vol. 19 Num. 3 (Fall 2005), pp. 52–54 <http://www.mises.org/journals/jls/19_3/19_3_3.pdf>.

2. Piet-Hein van Eeghen. "The Corporation at Issue, Part II: A Critique of Robert Hesson's In Defense of the Corporation and Proposed Conditions for Private Incorporation" *Journal of Libertarian Studies* Vol. 19 Num. 4 (Fall 2005), p. 39 <http://www.mises.org/journals/jls/19_4/19_4_3.pdf>.

3. Van Eeghen, "The Corporation at Issue, Part I," pp. 54, 56.

be raised, it also creates better opportunities to gain market share by mergers and take-overs.[1]

Although Hessen argued that entity status could be established solely by contract, van Eeghen takes issue with that claim. Hessen, he argues, "confuse[s] the joint-stock principle with corporate status." Entity status does not consist merely of the shareholders acting "as a unified collective in a court of law"; rather, entity status refers to the corporation as "a legal entity separate from shareholders."

> If it is agreed that the corporation is a legal entity separate from shareholders, then Hessen's claim that it can be the product of private contracting is obviously severely weakened if not dismissed. It is clear that private contracting can achieve only *joint ownership* of the contractors' assets (a partnership); it cannot establish a legal entity separate from the natural persons of the contractors themselves to which they assign their assets . . . .[2]

I confess the argument that separate entity status could be established by private contract is not entirely implausible. Van Eeghen's argument from the nonexistence of such private contracts is not, in itself, very convincing. One might argue that the general idea of free contract is quite recent, that it has been given even comparatively free rein only in the past few centuries, and that, even so, the form it has taken in that time has reflected the path dependencies created by a far more statist society. A great many contractual arrangements might be conceivable without the state that have never yet come into existence simply because the state still casts such a huge shadow. Arguably, the very availability of statutory provisions for general incorporation has had the effect of crowding out private contractual arrangements. I can see nothing inherently nonsensical or repugnant in the idea of a number of private individuals contracting to create a permanent corporate entity separate from any or all of themselves as individuals, or of local free juries choosing to recognize the standing of such entities under the body of libertarian law.

Whether the corporation, as distinguished by its entity status from an ordinary partnership, could come about through private contracting alone, is in my opinion a question involving so much counterfactual speculation as to be unanswerable. But even stipulating that it could won't get Hessen very far. He misses the point entirely:

> The actual procedure for creating a corporation consists of filing a registration document with a state official . . . , and the state's role is purely formal and automatic. Moreover, to call incorporation a "privilege" implies that individuals have no right to create a corporation. But why is governmental permission needed? Who would be wronged if businesses adopted corporate features by contract? . . . . If potential creditors find any of these features objectionable, they can negotiate to exclude or modify them.[3]

But they could negotiate to exclude or modify them a lot more effectively in a system where corporations *had* to be established entirely by private contract, than they can under a system where incorporation is "automatic," and where the potentially objectionable features are the default version. The fact that the state makes establishing entity status and all its accidents so much easier, by providing a ready-made and *automatic* venue for incorporation, surely results in a considerable distortion of the market. General incorporation legislation creates a standard procedure for setting up a corporation with entity status, with standard forms to file and automatic recognition to anyone following the prescribed procedure. Thus, the state intervenes to make the corporation the standard form of business organization, and essentially removes the transaction costs of organizing it.

1. *Ibid.*, pp. 60–64.
2. "The Corporation at Issue, Part II," p. 46.
3. Robert Hessen, "Corporations," *The Concise Encyclopedia of Economics* (Library of Economics and Liberty) <http://www.econlib.org/library/Enc/Corporations.html>.

Leaving aside the broader question of entity status, both Murray Rothbard and Stephan Kinsella have argued that the narrower principle of limited liability for debt could be established by contract, simply by announcing ahead of time that individual shareholders in a firm would be liable only for the amount of their investment. In that case, it would be entirely the voluntary decision of creditors whether or not to accept such terms, and if most creditors found such terms objectionable, the market would punish firms attempting to limit liability by prior announcement in this way.[1] But the very fact that limited liability can be had, not by negotiating it in a private contract on a case by case basis and persuading each group of creditors separately to accept such terms, but merely by filing some standard papers under the general terms of the corporate form provided by statute, distorts the market away from the voluntary nature of limited liability as it would exist under a purely contractual regime. If, under the auspices of the state's code of laws, the limited liability corporation becomes the dominant form of organization, how "voluntary" can the choice of alternatives be from the standpoint of a creditor? As Gregory White, a commenter on Kinsella's article, asked, "if you can get a large immunity from debts just by the relatively smaller cost of incorporating, why wouldn't a self-interested investor/owner do so?"

> So once every firm of any substantial size is incorporated, what real 'agreement' (really choice) is there? . . . .
>
> With limited liability to debts granted by government charter, the "right of a free individual" to *effectively* choose the contract is destroyed by implication. In practice they have little choice but to accept the limited liability condition, since it is a government granted privilege that any business person would quickly seize on.
>
> . . . The legislation distorts the market by destroying some measure of bargaining power on the part of creditors.

In response to Kinsella's claim that the government merely duplicates the effect of private contract ("The government only helps hang a bright neon sign *recognizing that* the shareholders are broadcasting to all third parties: if you deal with us, you can't come after our personal assets"), White responded:

> . . . [The "sign hanging"] guarantees an immunity, destroying possible terms of negotiation. Without government, the corporation can do no more than ask for agreement . . . .
> The government distorts the market here . . . . And that distortion plays into natural rights. Some will not be able to recover their own property, where without the distortion, they could have otherwise formed a different contract. It will distort bargaining power in some circumstances.[2]

Whether or not it could be established by mere contract in a hypothetical scenario, the understanding of the corporate entity status that emerged from the late nineteenth century on was a radical departure from the earlier understanding of the property rights of individual shareholders in a joint-stock corporation. To that extent, the modern corporation with separate entity status really is fundamentally different from the earlier joint-stock corporation. As understood under the earlier doctrine, the property rights of the individual shareholder really were analogous to those of a partner. The understanding is exemplified by the majority opinion in the Dartmouth College case, in which any amendment to a corporate charter, or indeed "any fundamental corporate change," was considered a breach of the shareholder's contract, a "taking" of his property. All such changes had to be consented to unanimously by shareholders, in exactly the same manner as members would consent to the change in terms of a partnership. Under the modern understanding, on the

---

1. Stephan Kinsella "In Defense of the Corporation," Mises Economics Blog, October 27, 2005 <http://blog.mises.org/archives/004269.asp>.
2. *Ibid.*

other hand, the corporation is an entity separate entirely from any or all individual share-holders, and governed by a simple majority vote.[1]

In addition, many critics of the corporate form argue that the "corporate veil" dilutes legal responsibility. It is true, as Kinsella argued, that officers and shareholders are techni-cally liable for criminal acts, and not legally exempt for criminal behavior under the corpo-rate form.[2] And as Joshua Holmes pointed out:

> Limited Liability is not at all absolute . . . . In cases of fraud, or where the corporate [sic] does not have sufficient independence from its shareholders, courts will "pierce the veil". When courts pierce the veil, plaintiffs against a corporation can indeed hold the share-holders directly liable. This often happens when the corporation is undercapitalised, that is, when the corporation obviously doesn't have enough assets to cover its liabilities. This happens surprisingly frequently, and more often in torts cases than contracts cases.[3]

But the legal status of the modern corporation starts from the presumption against le-gal responsibility, as opposed to the common law presumption in the case of sole proprietorships and partnerships that the burden of monitoring one's property and avoiding the criminal or tortious use of it by one's hired agents lay with the owner. Sheldon Richman made a similar observation, raising the issue of

> whether one is at all responsible for what happens with one's property . . . . If one has no liability, one has no incentive to pay attention to how "one's property" is being used.[4]

The corporate veil seems deliberately designed to dilute or obscure personal respon-sibility. The corporate form provides shareholders with some of the benefits of ownership, while freeing them from the normal responsibilities associated with property ownership under the common law. An ordinary property owner is expected to take reasonable care in overseeing it, and exercise reasonable supervision over his hired overseers, or risk being charged with negligence if the property is misused to someone else's harm. The corporate form not only absolves the "owners" of such responsibility, but makes the exercise of re-sponsible control impossible. It functions, in effect, as a form of "plausible deniability," in-creasing the difficulty of assigning blame for malfeasance.

Corporate officers, under pressure from "the market for corporate control" to in-crease profit margins (without overmuch scrupulosity on the investors' part as to what means management uses to achieve the result), are put in a double bind. As "quasibill," an astute commenter on my blog, remarked on my review of van Eeghen's articles:

> The reality is that management *does* get directives from the shareholders, in the form of a demand for greater dividends/share prices. Management does respond to this directive, sometimes at the expense of innocent third parties. And management does present this situation as a defense—"I would've been fired had I paid for a proper truck driver for that route!" and often juries/factfinders will buy that defense—implicitly finding that it was the shareholder's demands that caused the negligence.[5]

"Who will rid me of this turbulent priest?" If anyone considers the expression "plausible deniability" overblown, consider this bit of legal advice:

> First, the corporate veil is always disregarded by courts for criminal acts of the offi-cers, shareholders, or directors of a corporation. Further, federal and state tax laws gener-ally impose personal liability on those individuals responsible for filing sales and income tax returns for the corporation.

----

1. Horwitz, *Transformation of American Law (1870-1960)*, pp. 87-89.
2. *Ibid.*
3. Comment under Kevin Carson, "Corporate Personhood" April 24, 2006 <http://mutualist.blogspot.com/ 2006/04/corporate-personhood.html>.
4. *Ibid.*
5. *Ibid.*

For most other matters, the corporate veil is most often pierced by courts in situations where the shareholders of a corporation disregard the legal separateness of the corporation and the corporation acts as nothing more than an alter ego for the shareholders' own dealings . . .

It is essential that minutes be maintained of board and shareholder actions. Corporate minutes are the first line of defense against the IRS, creditors, and other parties making claims against the corporation, particularly if a claim is based on a theory that the corporation should not be taxed as a corporation or afforded limited liability (piercing the corporate veil) . . . . Many closely-held corporations fail to keep even annual minutes, which greatly weakens the position of the corporation and its shareholders, directors, and officers in many circumstances. Regular minutes can also:

- Prevent IRS claims of unreasonable compensation of executives who are shareholders
- Protect against IRS claims of excess accumulated earnings
- Create defenses against lawsuits attempting to establish personal liability of directors or officers, by evidencing board business judgment and specific authorization
- Protect against spurious lawsuits of minority shareholders
- Establish authority for corporate actions for the benefit of outside parties

Minutes of a meeting should be prepared by the Secretary of the Corporation, signed, and then approved by the Board or shareholders, as the case may be, at the next meeting or in the next action. This will minimize any claim that the written minutes do not accurately reflect the action taken. Minutes should always reflect that proper notice was given or waived, who was present and who was absent, and that a quorum was present. Any abstentions or dissents on a vote should be noted for the protection of the director abstaining or dissenting. In a closely-held corporation, meetings are often held to create minutes rather than to make decisions, but holding formal meetings with parliamentary procedures tends to result in more deliberate and organized decision- making and is recommended if practical.

It is equally important that minutes be limited to material which helps and not hurts the corporation. Resolutions should be set forth. The fact that a report was given or a discussion held on a subject should be noted. Statements made by a director or the actual content of a report or discussion, however, should generally not be included, since these references tend to be damaging more often than not. Claimants of a corporation will many times establish their case on the basis of minutes which were too detailed . . . . Generally, only formal resolutions adopted by the Board should be set forth in minutes.[1]

In other words, cover your ass with the minimal amount of documentation to pay homage to the corporate form, but avoid potentially incriminating specific details as much as possible, so you can distance yourself from the decision-making process after the fact.

Although shareholders and corporate officers are liable in theory for malfeasance, in practice the standard is applied far differently to the corporation, and the sole proprietorship, respectively. As "quasibill" points out,

agency law is a major source of liability for sole proprietors, but is arbitrarily cut off in the case of shareholders merely by invoking the statutory grant of incorporation. One can argue that the corporate veil can be pierced, but the standards are not the same; in essence, so long as the shareholder is extremely negligent in how the business is run, he's insulated from responsibility. In contrast, agency law places a burden on a sole proprietor to be responsible about his choice of agents.

[The shareholder is protected], so long as [he] can demonstrate that he "respected the corporate identity." So, as long as he didn't mix and mingle assets, or fail to hold corporate meetings, he's protected from liability. In fact, so long as he colludes with his

1. "How to Avoid Piercing of Your Corporate Veil." Click&Inc. The Internet's *Only* Customized Incorporation Service for Home & Small Business Owners <http://www.clickandinc.com/corporate_veil.asp>.

fellow shareholders, he can make it airtight by demonstrating that after all corporate formalities were followed, they all voted for the same result . . . .

In contrast, a sole proprietor who turned the day to day operation of his business over to a hired manager would be bound by the acts of his agent that were taken in the scope of the agency, period. The sole proprietor is responsible for choosing that person and imbuing him with authority. Especially if he didn't supervise the manager very well and the manager uses the business to defraud customers . . . . In contrast, the shareholders are actually encouraged to take LESS care in how the day to day manager is operating the business. The less care he takes, the more he can claim he respected the corporate personality.[1]

In countering the argument from the shareholders' moral responsibility, Kinsella is put in the awkward position of repudiating much of what Mises said about the entrepreneurial corporation, and thereby conceding ground to Berle and Means on the divorce of ownership from control. As we shall see in Chapter Seven, Mises repudiated the theory of the managerial corporation, and clearly distinguished the bureaucratic from the entrepreneurial organization. The entrepreneurial corporation, no matter how large, he said, is simply an agent of the owner's will, enforced by the magic of double-entry bookkeeping.

Kinsella, on the other hand, was obliged to attenuate the shareholder's theoretical ownership relationship as much as possible:

It is bizarre that there is this notion that owners of property are automatically liable for crimes done with their property . . . Moreover, property just means the right to control. This right to control can be divided in varied and complex ways. If you think shareholders are "owners" of corporate property just like they own their homes or cars—well, just buy a share of Exxon stock and try to walk into the boardroom without permission . . . .[2]

In correspondence with Sean Gabb, Kinsella "raise[d] doubts about the effective control that shareholders have over their companies, and wonder[ed] if they should not rather be placed in the same category as employees or lenders or contractors." The answer, Gabb said, is that shareholders are "the natural owners of their companies. They have not lent money to them. They are not providing paid services. They are the owners."[3]

In a subsequent article, Kinsella argued that "the default libertarian position is that an individual is responsible for torts he commits."

If you want to hold others liable for this too, you need to show some kind of causal connection between something done by the third person, and the tort committed by the direct tortfeasor. You seem to assume that this connection is present in the case of a shareholder because he is the "true" or "natural" owner of the company's assets. This I think is what troubles me the most—it seems too much of an assertion to me.[4]

Of course this is a complete departure from the traditional distinction between residual and contractual claimants. The shareholder is the residual claimant, owner and principal; the management are his agents. The creditor's entitlement is to a "contractually defined absolute return";[5] the residual claimant is entitled to the net revenue after contractual claims are paid. It was of great importance to Mises to demonstrate that the owner's control of the corporation was real, and that the management were entirely his agents. Kinsella, on the other hand, is apparently so dead set on helping the shareholder to evade the responsibilities of owner-

1. Comment under Stephan Kinsella, "Sean Gabb's Thoughts on Limited Liability," Mises Economics Blog, September 26, 2006 <http://blog.mises.org/archives/005679.asp>.

2. Comment under Carson, "Corporate Personhood."

3. Sean Gabb "Thoughts on Limited Liability" *Free Life Commentary*, Issue Number 152, 26th September 2006 <http://www.seangabb.co.uk/flcomm/flc152.htm>.

4. Stephan Kinsella, "Sean Gabb's Thoughts on Limited Liability."

5. Quasibill comment under *Ibid*.

ship, as to identify ownership with "control," and to argue on that basis that the *de jure* "ownership" of the shareholders is ambiguous at best.

> . . . .You conceive of a shareholder as the "natural" owner of the enterprise. I am skepti-
> cal of relying on the conceptual classifications imposed by positive law. To me a share-
> holder's nature or identity depends on what rights it has. What are the basic rights of a
> shareholder? What is he "buying" when he buys the "share"? Well, he has the right to
> vote—to elect directors, basically. He has the right to attend shareholder meetings. He
> has the right to a certain share of the net remaining assets of the company in the event it
> winds up or dissolves, after it pays off creditors etc. He has the right to receive a certain
> share of dividends paid *if* the company decides to pay dividends—that is, he has a right
> to be treated on some kind of equal footing with other shareholders—he has no absolute
> right to get a dividend (even if the company has profits), but only a conditional, relative
> one. He has (usually) the right to sell his shares to someone else. Why assume this bundle
> of rights is tantamount to "natural ownership"—of what? Of the company's assets? But
> he has no right to (directly) control the assets . . . . Surely the right to attend meetings is
> not all that relevant. Nor the right to receive part of the company's assets upon winding
> up or upon payment of dividends—this could be characterized as the right a type of
> lender or creditor has.[1]

Kinsella has come a long way from his initial argument that the corporation was simply a contractual device for property owners to pool their property and appoint managers
for it as they saw fit, and there is little left of his trail of breadcrumbs. He winds up, as quasibill comments, "intimat[ing] that there is no real owner of corporate property—that an
abstraction . . . [has] property rights."[2]

Kinsella does not seem clearly to grasp just how much baby he is throwing out with
the bathwater. He concedes much ground to those who argue that the "private" ownership is a legal fiction, and that the corporation is a quasi-state institution controlled by
managers with only certain contractually defined obligations—mostly usufructory—to
shareholders. Mises' arguments regarding calculation all assume an "entrepreneurial" corporation that is really an extension of the owner's will and judgment; he saw the
Berle/Means argument as a challenge to be overcome, and his distinction between the bureaucratic and the entrepreneurial organization was central to his attempt to refute them.
Kinsella is forced to abandon this project.

He makes this retreat explicit, in defending the shareholder from liability based on his
lack of control:

> . . . [A] sole proprietor is liable because he directs the actions of the negligent em-
> ployee, and actually runs the company—sets policies, controls it, manages it. In a joint
> stock company, the shareholders don't do any of this. They elect the board, which ap-
> points managers. In my view, the managers are more analogous to the sole proprietor
> than the shareholders are.
> . . . . Merely being a shareholder is not sufficient. It's having control. I believe most
> of the corporation opponents have some view that inherently connects liability to prop-
> erty. I think this is confused and wrong. Liability flows from one's actions—from con-
> trol—from causing the harm to occur . . . .[3]

In addition, he misses the point: claiming the absence of control is not a defense, because it begs the question of whether they *should* have exercised *more* control. The proper
question is whether property ownership *ought* to entail some minimal level of oversight
and responsibility, and whether one of the benefits of the corporate form (from the owners' perspective) is that it enables the evasion of that responsibility. Arguably, doesn't the

---

1. *Ibid.*
2. Comment under *Ibid.*
3. Comment under *Ibid.*

very act of delegating control of property in a way that makes one's own direct oversight less feasible, in itself make one liable for any resulting malfeasance by one's agent? Isn't the absentee owner negligent precisely *because* he put himself in a position in which he exercised little or no control over how his agents used his property? In short: isn't one of the virtues of the corporate form, from the shareholders' perspective, that it creates plausible deniability?

So there is an irresolvable contradiction in the Hessen-Kinsella understanding of property rights in the corporation. Such defenders of the corporation start out by defending it as a normal outgrowth of private property rights and the right, by free contract, to make arrangements for governing one's property. But before they're done, they wind up minimizing the property relations between individual shareholders and the corporation. The overall effect is one of deliberate ambiguity, in which the corporation is treated as property in the ordinary sense, or as an instrument of the shareholders' exercise of property rights, only when convenient. There is a contradiction in saying the corporation is merely a contractual arrangement for arranging property, like a partnership, and then minimizing the property relationship or responsibility of any particular property holder. Either the corporation is just another form of partnership, in which case shareholders are the real legal actors, or the corporation is a state-created entity for privatizing profit while attenuating responsibility. It can't be both ways.

Interestingly, some defenders of the corporation have been quite aware of the contradiction. For example, Dwight Jones wrote:

> . . . . The main value of a corporate charter arises from the fact that powers and privileges are thereby acquired which individuals do not possess. It is this that makes the difference between a business corporation and a partnership. In the former there is no individual liability . . . . There is no death . . . . It is not policy therefore for a corporation to break down its own independent existence by burying its original character in the common place privileges of the individual . . . . Any mingling of corporate existence with the existence of the shareholders will weaken corporate rights.[1]

Jones defended the attenuation of shareholder liability under the entity form, in terms quite similar to Kinsella. But he perceived much more acutely than Kinsella that this defense comes at a price: it completely rules out any defense of the corporation in which the latter is an ordinary contractual expression of the property rights of the shareholders, in the same sense as a partnership.

Even those defending entity status, like Hessen and Kinsella, as an outgrowth of ordinary private contracting akin to the partnership, faced difficulties. The most notable proponent of the "natural entity" doctrine (favored also by Hessen and Kinsella) was Ernst Freund, author of *The Legal Nature of Corporations* (1897). Freund attempted to reconcile the status of the corporation as a representative entity governed by corporate rule, with an individualist understanding of it as the sum of its parts in the same sense as a partnership. Nevertheless, he was somewhat put off by the fact that corporate powers were vested directly in the board of directors. The practical effect, he was forced to admit, was that

> corporate capacity [was] thereby shifted from the members at large to the governing body . . . . Such an organization reduces the personal cohesion between the [shareholders] to a minimum, and allows us to see in a large railroad, banking or insurance corporation rather an aggregation of capital than an association of persons.[2]

Henry Williams argued, in an 1899 *American Law Register* article, that shareholders "possess[ed] no actual existing legal interest . . . whatever" in the corporation . . . . Their

1. Dwight A. Jones, "A Corporation as 'A Distinct Entity,'" 2 Couns. 78, 81 (1892), in Horwitz, *The Transformation of American Law 1870-1960*, p. 91.
2. Quoted in Horwitz, *The Transformation of American Law 1870-1960*, pp. 102-103.

legal rights accrued only at dissolution, and even then their rights were "entirely subsidiary" to those of creditors.[1]

In the same regard, almost directly contrary to Mises' perception, the market for corporate control, far from an instrument of the absolute property rights of the entrepreneur, has been associated with the attenuation of shareholder property rights in the corporation. As we saw above, the modern corporate entity status required a shift to majority shareholder control of the corporation, and an end to the earlier understanding (reflected in *Dartmouth*) of the shareholder as possessing absolute property rights analogous to those in a partnership. The result, by the early twentieth century, was a common legal understanding in which "the modern stockholder is a negligible factor in … management," and in which a sharp distinction was made between the status of "investor" and "proprietor."[2] The shift was encouraged by the rise of public securities markets. Until the 1890s, public issues of stock were rare and public trading (outside of railroad stock) almost unheard of. In an environment in which the issuance of stock was still largely private and associated with the formation of joint-stock companies, it was more plausible to regard investment in a corporation as equivalent to buying into a partnership. The creation of public equity markets, in which shares were commonly acquired by those with no direct role in the formation or governance of the firm, and bought on an anonymous market rather than issued directly to the shareholder by the firm, made the cultural holdover far less tenable. It became virtually impossible to maintain with a straight face the earlier "trust fund" doctrine of *Dartmouth* and other decisions, in which the shareholder was a partner with absolute property rights in the governance of the corporation.[3] By the turn of the century, the board of directors was clearly coming to be seen as the agent, not of shareholders, but of the corporation as a separate entity.[4]

To sum up, it may be true, as Hessen argued, that something like the corporate form—with entity status and limited liability—could be established by purely private contract. But it's also true, as Gregory White said, that the state artificially lowered the transaction costs of the corporate form compared to alternative models of firm organization, by providing an established and virtually automatic mechanism to facilitate adoption of the corporate form. What's more, it has promoted a particular model of the corporation out of a number of possible alternative corporate models that might have been established by contract. The standard corporate form, established under general incorporation laws, is based on an amalgamation of capital which hires workers. The state artificially privileges this form against, and crowds out, alternative corporate organizational models: for instance, a model in which associated labor is the residual claimant and pays only fixed contractual returns on borrowed capital.

As I will argue in Chapter Eight, the management of a corporation is a self-perpetuating oligarchy, in control of a free-floating mass of unowned capital, and its alleged representation of the shareholders serves merely as a legitimizing ideology to insulate it from internal stakeholder control.

B. Subsidies to Transportation and Communication Infrastructure

"Internal improvements" were a controversial issue throughout the nineteenth century, and were a central part of the mercantilist agenda of the Whigs and the Gilded Age

1. *Ibid.* p. 103.
2. *Ibid.* p. 93.
3. *Ibid.* pp. 96–98.
4. *Ibid.* p. 99.

GOP. But the government's role in promoting a national railroad system effected a revolution several orders of magnitude greater than anything that had occurred before.

As we shall see below, the failure of the trust movement at the turn of the 20th century reflected the insufficiency of railroad subsidies, tariffs and patents alone to maintain stable monopoly power. But without the government-subsidized "internal improvements" of the nineteenth century, it is doubtful that most national-scale industrial firms would have *existed*. If the neo–Hamiltonianism of the 19th century was not a sufficient condition for the state capitalism of the 20th, it was certainly a necessary one.

As Coase pointed out, "[i]nventions which tend to bring factors of production nearer together, by lessening spatial distribution, tend to increase the size of the firm."[1] This applies as well to inventions that lessen the cost of spatial distribution by making transportation cheaper over longer distances. The effect of transportation subsidies is to artificially enlarge market areas, and hence to artificially increase firm size.

Adam Smith argued over two hundred years ago for the fairness of internalizing the costs of transportation infrastructure through user fees.

> It does not seem necessary that the expense of those public works should be defrayed from that public revenue, as it is commonly called, of which the collection and application is in most countries assigned to the executive power. The greater part of such public works may easily be so managed as to afford a particular revenue sufficient for defraying their own expense, without bringing any burden upon the general revenue of society . . . .
>
> When the carriages which pass over a highway or a bridge, and the lighters which sail upon a navigable canal, pay toll in proportion to their weight or their tonnage, they pay for the maintenance of those public works exactly in proportion to the wear and tear which they occasion of them . . . .
>
> It seems not unreasonable that the extraordinary expense which the protection of any particular branch of commerce may occasion should be defrayed by a moderate tax upon that particular branch; by a moderate fine, for example, to be paid by the traders when they first enter into it, or, what is more equal, by a particular duty of so much percent upon the goods which they either import into, or export out of, the particular countries with which it is carried on.[2]

But that's not the way things work under what the neoliberals like to call "free market capitalism." Spending on transportation and communications networks from general revenues, rather than from taxes and user fees, allows big business to externalize its costs on the public, and conceal its true operating expenses. Chomsky described this state capitalist underwriting of shipping costs quite accurately:

> One well-known fact about trade is that it's highly subsidized with huge market-distorting factors . . . . The most obvious is that every form of transport is highly subsidized . . . . Since trade naturally requires transport, the costs of transport enter into the calculation of the efficiency of trade. But there are huge subsidies to reduce the costs of transport, through manipulation of energy costs and all sorts of market-distorting functions.[3]

Every wave of concentration of capital in the United States has followed a publicly subsidized infrastructure system of some sort. The national railroad system, built largely on free or below-cost land donated by the government, was followed by concentration in heavy industry, petrochemicals, and finance. Albert Nock ridiculed the corporate liberals of

---

1. "The Nature of the Firm," *Economica*, November 1937, p. 397.
2. *Wealth of Nations* pp. 315, 319.
3. Noam Chomsky, "How Free is the Free Market?" *Resurgence* no. 173 <http://www.oneworld.org/second_opinion/chomsky.html>.

his time, who held up the corruption of the railroad companies as examples of the failure of "rugged individualism" and "laissez-faire."

> The fact is that our railways, with few exceptions, did not grow up in response to any actual economic demand. They were speculative enterprises enabled by State intervention, by allotment of the political means in the form of land-grants and subsidies; and of all the evils alleged against our railway-practice, there is not one but what is directly traceable to this primary intervention.[1]

The federal railroad land grants, as Murray Rothbard described them, included not only the rights-of-way for the actual railroads, "but fifteen-mile tracts on either side of the line." As the lines were completed, this adjoining land became prime real estate and sky-rocketed in value. As new communities sprang up along the routes, every house and business in town was built on land acquired from the railroads. The tracts also frequently included valuable timber land.[2]

And Michael Piore and Charles Sabel consider it quite unlikely the railroads would have been built as quickly or on as large a scale, absent massive subsidies. The initial capital outlays (securing rights of way, preparing roadbeds, laying track) were simply too costly.[3]

As we saw in Chapter One, it was the creation of the national railroad system which made possible first national wholesale and retail markets, and then large manufacturing firms serving the national market.

The next major transportation projects were the national highway system and the civil aviation system. From the earliest days of the automobile-highway complex, when the Model-T met the "good roads" movement in the state legislatures, a modern highway network was synonymous in the public mind with "progress."

And the "good roads" movement had had the backing of mercantilist interests from the turn of the century.

> One of the major barriers to the fledgling automobile industry at the turn of the century was the poor state of the roads. One of the first highway lobbying groups was the League of American Wheelmen, which founded "good roads" associations around the country and, in 1891, began lobbying state legislatures . . . .
> The Federal Aid Roads Act of 1916 encouraged coast-to-coast construction of paved roads, usually financed by gasoline taxes (a symbiotic relationship if ever there was one). By 1930, the annual budget for federal road projects was $750 million. After 1939, with a push from President Franklin Roosevelt, limited-access interstates began to make rural areas accessible.[4]

It was this last, in the 1930s, that signified the most revolutionary change. From its beginning, the movement for a national superhighway network was identified, first of all, with the fascist industrial policy of Hitler, and second with the American automotive industry.

> The "most powerful pressure group in Washington" began in June, 1932, when GM President, Alfred P. Sloan, created the National Highway Users Conference, inviting oil and

1. Albert Jay Nock, *Our Enemy, the State* (Delavan, Wisc.: Hallberg Publishing Corporation, 1983), p. 102.

2. Murray N. Rothbard, *Power & Market: Government and the Economy* (Menlo Park, Calif.: Institute for Humane Studies, Inc., 1970), p. 70.

3. Michael J. Piore and Charles F. Sabel, *The Second Industrial Divide: Possibilities for Prosperity* (New York: HarperCollins, 1984), p. 66.

4. Jim Motavalli, "Getting Out of Gridlock: Thanks to the Highway Lobby, Now We're Stuck in Traffic. How Do We Escape?" *E Magazine*, March/April 2002 <http://www.emagazine.com/view/?534>.

rubber firms to help GM bankroll a propaganda and lobbying effort that continues to this day.[1]

One of the earliest depictions of the modern superhighway in America was the Futurama exhibit at the 1939 World's Fair in New York, sponsored by (who else?) GM.

> The exhibit . . . provided a nation emerging from its darkest decade since the Civil War a mesmerizing glimpse of the future—a future that involved lots and lots of roads. Big roads. Fourteen-lane superhighways on which cars would travel at 100 mph. Roads on which, a recorded narrator promised, Americans would eventually be able to cross the nation in a day.[2]

The Interstate's association with General Motors didn't end there, of course. Its actual construction took place under the supervision of DOD Secretary Charles Wilson, formerly the company's CEO. During his 1953 confirmation hearings, when asked whether "he could make a decision in the country's interest that was contrary to GM's interest,"

> Wilson shot back with his famous comment, "I cannot conceive of one because for years I thought what was good for our country was good for General Motors, and vice versa. The difference did not exist. Our company is too big."[3]

Wilson's role in the Interstate program was hardly that of a mere disinterested technocrat. From the time of his appointment to DOD, he "pushed relentlessly" for it. And the chief administrator of the program was "Francis DuPont, whose family owned the largest share of GM stock . . . ."[4] Corporate propaganda, as so often in the twentieth century, played an active role in attempts to reshape the popular culture.

> Helping to keep the driving spirit alive, Dow Chemical, producer of asphalt, entered the PR campaign with a film featuring a staged testimonial from a grade school teacher standing up to her anti-highway neighbors with quiet indignation. "Can't you see this highway means a whole new way of life for the children?"[5]

Whatever the political motivation behind it, the economic effect of the Interstate system should hardly be controversial. Virtually 100% of the roadbed damage to highways is caused by heavy trucks. And despite repeated liberalization of maximum weight restrictions, far beyond the heaviest conceivable weight the Interstate roadbeds were originally designed to support,

> fuel taxes fail miserably at capturing from big-rig operators the cost of exponential pavement damage caused by higher axle loads. Only weight-distance user charges are efficient, but truckers have been successful at scrapping them in all but a few western states where the push for repeal continues.[6]

So only about half the revenue of the highway trust fund comes from fees or fuel taxes on the trucking industry, and the rest is externalized on private automobiles. Even David S. Lawyer, a skeptic on the general issue of highway subsidies, only questions whether highways receive a net subsidy from general revenues over and above total user

---

1. Mike Ferner, "Taken for a Ride on the Interstate Highway System," MRZine (*Monthly Review*) June 28, 2006 <http://mrzine.monthlyreview.org/ferner280606.html>.

2. Justin Fox, "The Great Paving How the Interstate Highway System helped create the modern economy—and reshaped the FORTUNE 500." Reprinted from Fortune. CNNMoney.Com, January 26, 2004 <http://money.cnn.com/magazines/fortune/fortune_archive/2004/01/26/358835/index.htm>.

3. Edwin Black, "Hitler's Carmaker: How Will Posterity Remember General Motors' Conduct? (Part 4)" History News Network, May 14, 2007 <http://hnn.us/articles/38829.html>.

4. Ferner, "Taken for a Ride."

5. *Ibid.*

6. Frank N. Wilner, "Give truckers an inch, they'll take a ton-mile: every liberalization has been a launching pad for further increases—trucking wants long combination vehicle restrictions dropped,"*Railway Age*, May 1997 <http://findarticles.com/p/articles/mi_m1215/is_n5_v198/ ai_19460645>.

fees on both trucks and cars; he effectively concedes the subsidy of heavy trucking by the gasoline tax.[1]

As for the civil aviation system, from the beginning it was a creature of the state. The whole physical infrastructure was built, in its early decades, with tax money.

> Since 1946, the federal government has *poured billions of dollars into airport development.* In 1992, Prof. Stephen Paul Dempsey of the University of Denver estimated that the current replacement value of the U.S. commercial airport system—virtually all of it developed with federal grants and tax-free municipal bonds—at $1 trillion.
>
> Not until 1971 did the federal government begin collecting *user fees* from airline passengers and freight shippers to recoup this investment. In 1988 the Congressional Budget Office found that *in spite of user fees paid into the Airport and Airways Trust Fund, the taxpayers still had to transfer $3 billion in subsidies per year to the FAA* to maintain its network of more than 400 control towers, 22 air traffic control centers, 1,000 radar-navigation aids, 250 long-range and terminal radar systems and its staff of 55,000 traffic controllers, technicians and bureaucrats.[2]

(And even aside from the inadequacy of user fees, eminent domain remains central to the building of new airports and expansion of existing airports.)

Subsidies to the airport and air traffic control infrastructure of the civil aviation system are only part of the picture. Equally important, as we shall see below, were the direct role of the state in creating the heavy aircraft industry, whose heavy cargo and passenger jets revolutionized civil aviation after WWII. The civil aviation system is, many times over, a creature of the state.

The result of the government-sponsored highway and civil aviation systems, taken together, was massive concentration in retail, agriculture, and food processing. The centralized corporate economy depends for its existence on a shipping price system which is artificially distorted by government intervention. To fully grasp how dependent the corporate economy is on socializing transportation costs, imagine what would happen if truck and aircraft fuel were taxed enough to pay the full cost of maintenance and new building costs on highways and airports; and if fossil fuels depletion allowances were removed. The result would be a massive increase in shipping costs. Does anyone seriously believe that Wal-Mart's national "warehouses on wheels" distribution system would be feasible, or corporate agribusiness could outcompete the local farm?

It is fallacious to say that state-subsidized infrastructure "creates efficiencies" by making possible large-scale production for a national market. If production on the scale promoted by infrastructure subsidies were actually efficient enough to compensate for *real* distribution costs, the manufacturers would have presented enough effective demand for such long-distance shipping at actual costs to pay for it without government intervention. On the other hand, an apparent "efficiency" that presents a positive ledger balance only by shifting and concealing real costs, is really no "efficiency" at all. Costs can be shifted, but they cannot be destroyed.

Intellectually honest free market advocates freely admit as much. For example, Tibor Machan wrote in *The Freeman* that

> Some people will say that stringent protection of rights [against eminent domain] would lead to small airports, at best, and many constraints on construction. Of course— but what's so wrong with that?
>
> Perhaps the worst thing about modern industrial life has been the power of political authorities to grant special privileges to some enterprises to violate the rights of third

---

1. David S. Lawyer, "Are Roads and Highways Subsidized?" March 2004 <http://www.lafn.org/~dave/trans/econ/highway_subsidy.html>.

2. James Coston, Amtrak Reform Council, 2001, in "America's long history of subsidizing transportation" <http://www.trainweb.org/moksrail/advocacy/resources/subsidies/transport.htm>.

parties whose permission would be too expensive to obtain. The need to obtain that permission would indeed seriously impede what most environmentalists see as rampant—indeed reckless—industrialization.

The system of private property rights—in which . . . all . . . kinds of . . . human activity must be conducted within one's own realm except where cooperation from others has been gained voluntarily—is the greatest moderator of human aspirations . . . . In short, people may reach goals they aren't able to reach with their own resources only by convincing others, through arguments and fair exchanges, to cooperate.[1]

The state played a pivotal role in creating the centralized communications infrastructure of the twentieth century. The modern telecommunications system goes back to the Bell Patent association, organized in 1875, which controlled a huge arsenal of government-enforced patents on virtually every aspect of telephony.[2] Meanwhile, as the Bell patents began to expire in the 1890s, AT&T turned to the "progressive" expedient of becoming a regulated utility to protect itself from competition. Here's Mary Ruwart's account:

> Before 1894, Bell Telephone's patents protected it from competition by other firms. Its growth averaged 16% per year; annual profits approached 40% of its capital. Bell catered primarily to the business sector and the wealthy. When the patents expired, other companies began providing affordable telephone service to the middle class and rural areas. The independents charged less since customers could call only those serviced by the same company. Consumers were evidently pleased to make such a tradeoff; by 1907, some 20,000 independents controlled half of all the new telephone installations. The number of phones zoomed from 266,000 in 1893 to 6.1 million in 1907. The independents matched Bell's monopoly market share in 14 short years.
>
> Competition from the independents had caused annual Bell profits to plummet from 40% to 8% as many consumers chose the independents who served them best . . . .
>
> As telephones went from a curiosity to a standard household utility, the independents began developing a plan for sharing each other's lines to avoid duplication and to increase the number of phones each customer could call . . . .
>
> Theodore Vail, Bell's new chairman, was determined to regain a monopoly market. He asked Americans to use the aggression of exclusive licensing against the independents that had served them so well. He claimed that competition caused duplication and penalized the customer (i.e., telephone service was a "natural" monopoly) . . . .
>
> . . . [B]y 1910, Americans were persuaded to accept Bell's proposal. The government of each local community would allow only one telephone company to operate in that region . . . . Since Bell was the largest single company, it was in the best position to lobby the state utility commissions effectively and was almost always chosen over the independents . . . .[3]

It's hard to say what form a national telephone network would have taken absent the AT&T monopoly for most of the twentieth century, but it seems unlikely that the pattern of local cooperation and bottom-up federation Ruwart describes before 1910 would have led to a centralized system of high capacity trunk lines on anything like the present scale. Mumford's contrast of a loose network of locally oriented light rail systems, as against the centralized national network created by the federal land grant program, is probably a useful model for comparison.

On a global scale, the physical backbone of the telecom network until the 1960s was the transoceanic cable system, largely a creature of the British state. And as Herbert Schiller

1. Tibor S. Machan, "On Airports and Individual Rights," *The Freeman: Ideas on Liberty* (February 1999), p. 11.

2. David F. Noble: *Science, Technology, and the Rise of Corporate Capitalism* (New York: Alfred A. Knopf, 1977), *America by Design*, pp. 91-2.

3. Mary Ruwart, *Healing Our World: The Other Piece of the Puzzle* (Kalamazoo, Michigan: SunStar Press, 1992, 1993). "Chapter 7. Creating Monopolies that Control Us" <http://www.ruwart.com/Healing/chap7.html>.

describes it, its successor—the communications satellite network—was an even larger state capitalist project by the U.S. government:

> . . . the research and development funds that led to the conception and production of [the communications satellite network] were provided by an American military-commercial alliance with very clear objectives in mind . . . . Satellite development, *from the beginning*, represented the successful drive of private communications corporations in the United States to dislodge the British from their domination of international communications, exercised through their . . . control of intercontinental submarine cables. In this effort monopolistic business acted closely with the U.S. Armed Forces, whose interest in instantaneous global communications was extraordinarily high . . . . In fact, the first communications satellite system in operation was a military-controlled operation.
>
> A decade later, in the early 1970s, an international consortium (called INTELSAT) of . . . 91 nations uses the United States-developed satellite system. The system has, from the start, been controlled by American Big Business . . . working with the U.S. State Department at the intergovernmental level.[1]

The most recent such project was the infrastructure of the Internet, originally built by the Pentagon.

> The internet owes its very *existence* to the state and to state funding. The story begins with ARPA, created in 1957 in response to the Soviets' launch of Sputnik and established to research the efficient use of computers for civilian and military applications.
>
> During the 1960s, the RAND Corporation had begun to think about how to design a military communications network that would be invulnerable to a nuclear attack. Paul Baran, a RAND researcher whose work was financed by the Air Force, produced a classified report in 1964 proposing a radical solution to this communication problem. Baran envisioned a decentralized network of different types of "host" computers, without any central switchboard, designed to operate even if parts of it were destroyed. The network would consist of several "nodes," each equal in authority, each capable of sending and receiving pieces of data.
>
> Each data fragment could thus travel one of several routes to its destination, such that no one part of the network would be completely dependent on the existence of another part. An experimental network of this type, funded by ARPA and thus known as ARPANET, was established at four universities in 1969.
>
> Researchers at any one of the four nodes could share information, and could operate any one of the other machines remotely, over the new network. (Actually, former ARPA head Charles Herzfeld says that distributing computing power over a network, rather than creating a secure military command-and-control system, was the ARPANET's original goal, though this is a minority view.)
>
> By 1972, the number of host computers connected to the ARPANET had increased to 37. Because it was so easy to send and retrieve data, within a few years the ARPANET became less a network for shared computing than a high-speed, federally subsidized, electronic post office. The main traffic on the ARPANET was not long-distance computing, but news and personal messages.
>
> As parts of the ARPANET were declassified, commercial networks began to be connected to it. Any type of computer using a particular communications standard, or "protocol," was capable of sending and receiving information across the network. The design of these protocols was contracted out to private universities such as Stanford and the University of London, and was financed by a variety of federal agencies. The major thoroughfares or "trunk lines" continued to be financed by the Department of Defense.
>
> By the early 1980s, private use of the ARPA communications protocol . . . far exceeded military use. In 1984 the National Science Foundation assumed the responsibility of building and maintaining the trunk lines or "backbones." (ARPANET formally ex-

1. *Communications and Cultural Domination* (White Plains, N.Y.: M.E. Sharpe, Inc., 1976), p. 59. Schiller discusses the history this project at length in *Mass Communications and American Empire* (N.Y.: Augustus M. Kelley, 1969), pp. 127-146.

pired in 1989; by that time hardly anybody noticed). The NSF's Office of Advanced Computing financed the internet's infrastructure from 1984 until 1994, when the backbones were privatized.

In short, both the design and implementation of the internet have relied almost exclusively on government dollars . . . .

We must be very careful not to describe the internet as a "private" technology, a spontaneous order, or a shining example of capitalistic ingenuity. It is none of these. Of course, almost all of the internet's current applications—unforeseen by its original designers—have been developed in the private sector.

(Unfortunately, the original web and the web browser are not among them, having been designed by the state-funded European Laboratory for Particle Physics (CERN) and the University of Illinois's NCSA.)

And today's internet would be impossible without the heroic efforts at Xerox PARC and Apple to develop a useable graphical user interface (GUI), a lightweight and durable mouse, and the Ethernet protocol. Still, none of these would have been viable without the huge investment of public dollars that brought the network into existence in the first place . . . .

What kind of global computer network would the market have selected [absent ARPANET]? We can only guess. Maybe it would be more like the commercial online networks such as Comcast or MSN, or the private bulletin boards of the 1980s. Most likely, it would use some kind of pricing schedule, where different charges would be assessed for different types of transmissions.[1]

Johan Soderberg provides some more detail for one of the items Klein mentions, the Bulletin Board System (BBS):

The Internet was predated by a grassroots network, the Bulletin Board System (BBS). The software and the hardware devices necessary to hike on to the telephone lines and to send electronic text and code through it were largely developed by phone phreaks.[2]

As Klein's reference to private bulletin boards suggests, it is quite plausible that some sort of Internet would have come about through voluntary interaction and free contributions. Universities and private firms might have built a less ambitious system of interconnected servers, and community bulletin boards might have linked together from the bottom up. It would almost certainly have been more decentralized and lower in capacity than the Internet we know today. Once again, a suggestive analogy is Lewis Mumford's speculation on the local light rail networks that might have developed in a decentralized eotechnic economy, with the "national" system consisting largely of a loosely networked, low capacity amalgamation of local systems, as opposed to the centralized system of trunk lines actually created by the state. The Internet might, in that case, be a loose network of community Internets, with the process of patching through to a distant community bulletin board being comparable to that of making a long-distance call in the days before direct dialing.

The telecommunications revolution of the past two decades or so permits, for the first time, direction of global operations in real time from a single corporate headquarters, and is accelerating the concentration of capital on a global scale.

C. Patents and Copyrights

Although free market libertarians of all stripes are commonly stereotyped as apologists for big business, it is hard to imagine a position more at odds with the interests of big business than the dominant libertarian view on patents. Certainly that is true of Murray Roth-

---

1. Peter G. Klein, "Government Did Invent the Internet, But the Market Made It Glorious," Mises.Org, June 12, 2006 <http://www.mises.org/story/2211>.

2. *Hacking Capitalism: The Free and Open Source Software Movement* (New York and London: Routledge, 2008), p. 96.

bard, who was not shy about denouncing patents as a fundamental violation of free market principles:

> Patents prevent a man from using his invention even though all the property is his and he has not stolen the invention, either explicitly or implicitly, from the first inventor. Patents, therefore, are grants of exclusive monopoly privilege by the State and are invasions of property rights on the market.[1]

It is sometimes argued, in response to attacks on patents as monopolies, that "all property is a monopoly." True, as far as it goes; but tangible property is a monopoly by the nature of the case. A parcel of land can only be occupied and used by one owner at a time, because it is finite. By nature, two people cannot occupy the same physical space at the same time. "Intellectual property," in contrast, is an artificial monopoly where scarcity would not otherwise exist. And unlike property in tangible goods and land, the defense of which is a necessary outgrowth of the attempt to maintain possession, enforcement of "property rights" in ideas requires the invasion of *someone else's* space. "Patents . . . invade rather than defend property rights."[2]

Patents make an astronomical price difference. Until the early 1970s, for example, Italy did not recognize drug patents. As a result, Roche Products charged the British national health a price over 40 times greater for patented components of Librium and Valium than charged by competitors in Italy.[3]

Patents suppress innovation as much as they encourage it. Chakravarthi Raghavan pointed out that patents and industrial security programs prevent sharing of information, and suppress competition in further improvement of patented inventions.[4] Rothbard likewise argued that patents eliminate "the competitive spur for further research" because incremental innovation based on others' patents is hindered, and because the holder can "rest on his laurels for the entire period of the patent," with no fear of a competitor improving his invention. And they hamper technical progress because "mechanical inventions are discoveries of natural law rather than individual creations, and hence similar independent inventions occur all the time. The simultaneity of inventions is a familiar historical fact."[5]

Patents are a hindrance to progress because of the "shoulders of giants" effect. Any new invention presupposes a wide variety of existing technologies that are combined and reworked into a new configuration. Patents on existing technologies may or may not marginally increase the incentives to new invention, but they also increase the cost of doing so by levying a tariff on the aggregation of existing knowledge to serve as building blocks of a new invention.[6] James Watt's refusal to license his patent on the steam engine, for example, prevented others from improving the design until the patent expired in 1800. This delayed the introduction of locomotives and steamboats.[7]

And patents are not necessary as an incentive to innovate, which means that their main practical effect is to cause economic inefficiency by levying a monopoly charge on the use of existing technology without significantly promoting innovation. According to Rothbard, invention is motivated not only by the quasi-rents accruing to the first firm to introduce an innovation, but by the threat of being surpassed in product features or pro-

1. *Man, Economy, and State: A Treatise on Economic Principles* (Auburn, Ala.: The Ludwig von Mises Institute, 1962, 1970, 1993), p. 655.

2. Rothbard, *Power and Market*, p. 71.

3. Chakravarthi Raghavan, *Recolonization: GATT, the Uruguay Round & the Third World* (Penang, Malaysia: Third World Network, 1990), p. 124.

4. *Ibid*, p. 118.

5. *Man, Economy, and State*, pp. 655, 658-9.

6. Yochai Benkler, *The Wealth of Networks*, pp. 36-37.

7. Soderberg, *Hacking Capitalism*, p. 116.

ductivity by its competitors. He cites Arnold Plant: "In active competition . . . no business can afford to lag behind its competitors. The reputation of a firm depends upon its ability to keep ahead, to be the first in the market with new improvements in its products and new reductions in their prices."[1]

This is borne out by F. M. Scherer's testimony before the Federal Trade Commission in 1995.[2] Scherer spoke of a survey of 91 companies in which only seven "accorded high significance to patent protection as a factor in their R & D investments." Most of them described patents as "the least important of considerations." Most companies considered their chief motivation in R & D decisions to be "the necessity of remaining competitive, the desire for efficient production, and the desire to expand and diversify their sales." In another study, Scherer found no negative effect on R & D spending as a result of compulsory licensing of patents. A survey of U.S. firms found that 86% of inventions would have been developed without patents. In the case of automobiles, office equipment, rubber products, and textiles, the figure was 100%.

The one exception was drugs, of which 60% supposedly would not have been invented. Even this is doubtful, though. For one thing, drug companies get an unusually high portion of their R & D funding from the government, and many of their most lucrative products were developed entirely at government expense. And Scherer himself cited evidence to the contrary. The reputation advantage for being the first into a market is considerable. For example in the late 1970s, the structure of the industry and pricing behavior was found to be very similar between drugs with and those without patents. Being the first mover with a non-patented drug allowed a company to maintain a 30% market share and to charge premium prices. We have already seen, in the previous chapter, the extent to which the direction of innovation of skewed by considerations of gaming the patent system and patent trolling the competition. The majority of R & D expenditure is geared toward developing "me, too" drugs: in essence slightly different versions of existing drugs, tweaked just enough to justify repatenting. And of the enormous R & D expenditures which patents are allegedly necessary to allow the drug companies to recoup, a majority goes not to developing the actual drug that goes to market, but to securing patent lockdown on all the possible major variations of that drug.

The injustice of patent monopolies is exacerbated by government funding of research and innovation, with private industry reaping monopoly profits from technology it spent little or nothing to develop. In 1999, extending the research and experimentation tax credit was, along with extensions of a number of other corporate tax preferences, considered the most urgent business of the Congressional leadership. Hastert, when asked if any elements of the tax bill were essential, said: "I think the [tax preference] extenders are something we're going to have to work on." Ways and Means Chair Bill Archer added, "before the year is out . . . we will do the extenders in a very stripped down bill that doesn't include anything else." A five-year extension of the research and experimentation credit (retroactive to 1 July 1999) was expected to cost $13.1 billion. (That credit makes the effective tax rate on R & D spending less than zero).[3]

The Government Patent Policy Act of 1980, with 1984 and 1986 amendments, allowed private industry to keep patents on products developed with government R & D money—and then to charge ten, twenty, or forty times the cost of production. For exam-

1. Rothbard, *Power and Market*, p. 74.
2. Scherer testimony, *Hearings on Global and Innovation-Based Competition*. FTC, 29 November 1995 <http://www.ftc.gov/opp/gc112195.pdf>.
3. Citizens for Tax Justice. "GOP Leaders Distill Essence of Tax Plan: Surprise! It's Corporate Welfare" 14 September 1999 <http://www.ctj.org/pdf/corp0999.pdf>.

ple, AZT was developed with government money and in the public domain since 1964. The patent was given away to Burroughs Wellcome Corp.[1]

As if the deck were not sufficiently stacked already, Congress has more than once extended drug companies' patents beyond the expiration of their normal term under patent law; as just one example, the pharmaceutical companies in 1999 lobbied Congress to extend certain patents by two years by a special act of private law.[2]

So far we have considered patents mainly insofar as they resulted in unequal exchange and higher prices at the individual level—essentially from Tucker's standpoint of the nineteenth century. We have not yet examined their structural effects on the economy—the ways in which they promoted the corporate transformation of capitalism.

The patent privilege has been used on a massive scale to promote concentration of capital, erect entry barriers, and maintain a monopoly of advanced technology in the hands of western corporations. It is hard even to imagine how much more decentralized the economy would be without it.

Patents played a large role in the creation of the corporate economy from the late nineteenth century on. According to David Noble, they were "bought up in large numbers to suppress competition," which also resulted in "the suppression of invention itself."[3] According to Edwin Prindle, a corporate patent lawyer, "Patents are the best and most effective means of controlling competition."[4]

The exchange or pooling of patents between competitors, historically, has been a key method for cartelizing industries. This was true especially of the electrical appliance, communications, and chemical industries. G. E. and Westinghouse expanded to dominate the electrical manufacturing market at the turn of the century largely through patent control. In 1906 they curtailed the patent litigation between them by pooling their patents. G.E., in turn, had been formed in 1892 by consolidating the patents of the Edison and Thomson-Houston interests.[5] AT&T also expanded "primarily through strategies of patent monopoly." The American chemical industry was marginal until 1917, when Attorney-General Mitchell Palmer seized German patents and distributed them among the major American chemical companies. Du Pont got licenses on 300 of the 735 patents.[6]

As Yale undergrad Benjamin Darrington points out, "intellectual property" promotes large scale organization in another way. It

> promotes time and investment intensive forms of development and research with high potential payoffs at the expense of the incremental, tinkering sort of innovation that would prevail in the absence of these "rights," which tilts the market for the development of new technology and techniques in favor of centralized institutions and high-tech solutions.[7]

The rise of the global economy in recent decades has been associated with a severe upward ratcheting of copyright protections. In the contemporary global economy, "intellectual property" plays the same protectionist role for TNCs that tariffs performed in the old

1. Chris Lewis, "Public Assets, Private Profits," *Multinational Monitor*, in *Project Censored Yearbook 1994* (New York: Seven Stories Press, 1994).

2. Benjamin Grove, "Gibbons Backs Drug Monopoly Bill," *Las Vegas Sun* 18 February 2000 <http://www.ahc.umn.edu/NewsAlert/Feb00/022100NewsAlert/44500.htm>.

3. *America by Design: Science, Technology, and the Rise of Corporate Capitalism* (New York: Alfred A. Knopf, 1977), pp. 84-109.

4. *Ibid.*, p. 90.

5. *Ibid.*, p. 92.

6. *Ibid.*, pp. 10, 16.

7. "Government Created Economies of Scale and Capital Specificity" (2007) <http://agorism.info/_media/government_created_economies_of_scale_and_capital_specificity.pdf>, pp. 7-8. Paper presented at Austrian student conference, p. 18.

national economies. Michael Perelman argues that the upsurge in "intellectual property" protection since the late 1960s has been an integral part of the neoliberal revolution.

> Although many old line industries could no longer compete effectively in world markets, exports of intellectual property in the form of royalties and copyright fees soared.
> I have not seen hard data regarding the effect of intellectual property rights on the rate of profit, but I am convinced that it is substantial. Just think about Microsoft and the pharmaceutical industry with their low marginal costs relative to their market prices. For example, Microsoft reported that it makes 85 percent margin on its Windows system . . . .[1]

Elsewhere he cites figures showing that revenues on "intellectual property" rose, between 1947 and the early 1990s, from ten percent to over half of all American exports. In 1999 export revenues from royalties and licensing revenue reached $37 billion, exceeding the revenue from aircraft export ($29 billion).[2]

As an indication of IP's central importance to global corporate profits, and its threat to the owners of proprietary content, consider the discussion in Microsoft's "Halloween Memo" of the threat from open-source software.[3] Darl McBride, of the software company SCO, warned Congress in even more dramatic terms that "the unchecked spread of Open Source software, under the GPL, is a much more serious threat to the spread of our capitalist system than U.S. corporations realize."[4]

The new digital copyright regime has done away with many traditional limitations on copyright from the days when it affected mainly the print medium, like the fair use exception. We can thank the traditional exceptions to copyright, for example, for the public library and for free access to photocopiers.

Charles Johnson gives, as an example of the fair use exception, the common university practice of making course reserves available for photocopying, rather than expecting every student to buy a scholarly book at the academic publishing houses' steep rates. (I myself have numerous photocopies of books ordered through Interlibrary Loan, which would otherwise have cost me $70 or more, often for slim volumes of under two hundred pages.) But, he says,

> as soon as the University eliminates the paper medium, and facilitates *exactly the same thing* through an non-commercial, internal University course pack website—which does nothing at all more than what the xerox packets did, except that it delivers the information to pixels on a monitor instead of toner on a page—the publishers' racket can run to court, throw up its arms, and start hollering Computers! Internet!, send their lawyers to try to shake down have a discussion with the University administration for new tribute to their monopoly business model, and then, failing that, *utterly uncontroversial* decades-old practices of sharing knowledge among colleagues and students suddenly become a legal case raising core issues like the future of the business model for academic publishers, while even the most absurd protectionist arguments are dutifully repeated by legal flacks on behalf of sustaining the racket . . . .[5]

---

1. "Intellectual Property Rights and the Commodity Form: New Dimensions in the Legislative Transfer of Surplus Value," *Review of Radical Political Economics* 35:3 (Summer 2003), pp. 307-308.

2. Michael Perelman, *Steal This Idea: Intellectual Property Rights and the Corporate Confiscation of Creativity* (New York: Palgrave, 2002), p. 36.

3. "Open Source Software: A (New?) Development Methodology" (Halloween Document), Version 1.17 (Version 1.00 August 11, 1998). Hosted online, with commentary, by Eric S. Raymond <http://www.catb.org/~esr/halloween/halloween1.html>.

4. <http://www.osaia.org/letters/sco_hill.pdf>, in Johan Soderberg, *Hacking Capitalism: The Free and Open Source Software Movement* (New York and London: Routledge, 2008), p. 31.

5. Charles Johnson, "How Intellectual Protectionism promotes the progress of science and the useful arts," *Rad Geek People's Daily*, May 28, 2008 <http://radgeek.com/gt/2008/05/28/how_intellectual/>.

D. TARIFFS

As with patents, we are interested here in the aspects of tariffs that Tucker neglected: their effect in promoting the cartelization of industry. In the next chapter, on the rise of monopoly capitalism, we will see the full-blown effects of what Schumpeter called "export-dependent monopoly capitalism." That term refers to an economic system in which industry cartelizes behind the protection of tariff barriers; sells its output domestically for a monopoly price significantly higher than market-clearing level, in order to obtain super-profits at the consumer's expense; and disposes of its unsellable product abroad, by dumping it below cost if necessary.

Brandeis referred to the tariff as "the mother of trusts" because of the way it facilitated collusion between large domestic producers and the creation of oligopolies. Mises, in *Human Action*, described the dependence of cartels on tariff barriers (especially interacting with other state-enforced monopolies like patents). Of course, in keeping with his usual "pro-business" emphasis, Mises treated the large industrial firms, at worst, as passive beneficiaries of a state protectionist policy aimed primarily at raising the wages of labor. This parallels his view of the early industrial capitalists, and their non-implication in the primitive accumulation process, in the previous chapter.

II. Twentieth Century State Capitalism

The state capitalism of the twentieth century differed fundamentally from the misnamed "laissez-faire" capitalism of the nineteenth century in two regards: 1) the growth of direct organizational ties between corporations and the state, and the circulation of managerial personnel between them; and 2) the eclipse of surplus value extraction from the worker through the production process (as described by classical Marxism), by the extraction of "super-profits" a) from the consumer through the exchange process and b) from the taxpayer through the fiscal process.

Although microeconomics texts generally describe the functioning of supply and demand curves as though the nature of market actors were unchanged since Adam Smith's day, in fact the rise of the large corporation as the dominant economic actor was a revolution as profound as any in history. It occurred parallel to the rise of the centralized regulatory state in the nineteenth and early twentieth century. And, vitally important to remember, the two phenomena were mutually reinforcing. The state's subsidies, privileges and other interventions in the market were the major force behind the centralization of the economy and the concentration of productive power. In turn, the corporate economy's need for stability and rationality, and for state-guaranteed profits, has been the central force behind the continuing growth of the leviathan state.

The rise of the centralized state and the centralized corporation has created a system in which the two are organizationally connected, and run by essentially the same recirculating elites (a study of the careers of David Rockefeller, Averell Harriman, and Robert McNamara should be instructive on the last point). This phenomenon has been most ably described by the "power elite" school of sociologists, particularly C. Wright Mills and G. William Domhoff.

The identification of state ownership and central planning, as such, with "socialism" is a twentieth century anachronism. Even state socialists like Friedrich Engels considered state ownership of industry only a necessary, not a sufficient, condition of establishing socialism. The central defining characteristic of socialism was the political and economic power of the working class. Depending on who held the reins of power, state control of the economy could be a characteristic either of socialism or monopoly capitalism:

At a further stage of evolution this form [the joint-stock company] also becomes insufficient: the official representative of capitalist society—the state—will ultimately have to
undertake the direction of production. This necessity for conversion into state property is
felt first in the great institutions for intercourse and communication—the post office, the
telegraphs, the railways.[1]

The *International Socialist Review* in 1912 warned workers not to be fooled into identifying social insurance or the nationalization of industry with "socialism." Such state programs as workers' compensation, old age and health insurance, were only measures to
strengthen and stabilize capitalism. And nationalization simply reflected the capitalist's realization "that he can carry on certain portions of the production process more efficiently
through his government than through private corporations .... Some muddleheads find
that will be Socialism, but the capitalist knows better."[2]

It's interesting in this regard to compare the effect of antitrust legislation in the U.S.
to that of nationalization in European "social democracies." In most cases, the firms affected by both policies tend to involve centrally important infrastructures or resources, on
which the corporate economy as a whole depends. Nationalization in the Old World is
used primarily in the case of energy, transportation and communication. In the U.S., the
most famous antitrust cases have been against Standard Oil, AT&T, and Microsoft: all cases
in which excessive prices in one firm were perceived as a threat to the interests of monopoly capital as a whole. And recent "deregulation," as it has been applied to the trucking
and airline industries, has likewise been in the service of those general corporate interests
harmed by monopoly transportation prices. In all these cases, the state has on occasion
acted as an executive committee on behalf of the entire corporate economy, by thwarting
the mendacity of a few powerful corporations.

And the mixed economy that emerged in 20th century America was, indeed, created
to serve the interests of monopoly capital. Rothbard treated the "war collectivism" of
World War I as a prototype for twentieth century state capitalism. He described it as

a new order marked by strong government, and extensive and pervasive government intervention and planning, for the purpose of providing a network of subsidies and mo-
nopolistic privileges to business, and especially to large business, interests. In particular,
the economy could be cartelized under the aegis of government, with prices raised and
production fixed and restricted, in the classic pattern of monopoly; and military and
other government contracts could be channeled into the hands of favored corporate
producers. Labor, which had been becoming increasingly rambunctious, could be tamed
and bridled into the service of this new, state monopoly-capitalist order, through the device of promoting a suitably cooperative trade unionism, and by bringing the willing union leaders into the planning system as junior partners.[3]

Gabriel Kolko used the term "political capitalism" to describe the general objectives
big business pursued through the "Progressive" state:

Political capitalism is the utilization of political outlets to attain conditions of stability, predictability, and security—to attain rationalization—in the economy. *Stability* is the elimination of internecine competition and erratic fluctuations in the economy. *Predictability* is
the ability, on the basis of politically stabilized and secured means, to plan future economic action on the basis of fairly calculable expectations. By *security* I mean protection

1. *Anti-Dühring*, vol. 25 of Marx and Engels *Collected Works* (New York: International Publishers, 1987) 265.
2. Robert Rives La Monte, "You and Your Vote," *International Socialist Review* XIII, No. 2
(August 1912); "Editorial," *International Socialist Review* XIII, No. 6 (December 1912).
3. "War Collectivism in World War I," in Murray Rothbard and Ronald Radosh, eds., *A
New History of Leviathan: Essays on the Rise of the American Corporate State* (New York: E. P. Dutton
& Co., Inc., 1972), pp. 66-7.

from the political attacks latent in any formally democratic political structure. I do not give to *rationalization* its frequent definition as the improvement of efficiency, output, or internal organization of a company; I mean by the term, rather, the organization of the economy and the larger political and social spheres in a manner that will allow corporations to function in a predictable and secure environment permitting reasonable profits over the long run.[1]

A. CARTELIZING REGULATIONS

From the turn of the twentieth century on, there was a series of attempts by corporate leaders to create some institutional structure by which price competition could be regulated and their respective market shares stabilized. "It was then," Paul Sweezy wrote,

> that U.S. businessmen learned the self-defeating nature of price-cutting as a competitive weapon and started the process of banning it through a complex network of laws (corporate and regulatory), institutions (e.g., trade associations), and conventions (e.g., price leadership) from normal business practice.[2]

But merely private attempts at cartelization (i.e., collusive price stabilization) before the Progressive Era—namely the so-called "trusts"—were miserable failures, according to Kolko. The dominant trend at the turn of the century—despite the effects of tariffs, patents, railroad subsidies, and other existing forms of statism—was competition. The trust movement was an attempt to cartelize the economy through such voluntary and private means as mergers, acquisitions, and price collusion. But the over-leveraged and over-capitalized trusts were even less efficient than before, and steadily lost market share to their smaller, more efficient competitors. Standard Oil and U.S. Steel, immediately after their formation, began a process of eroding market share. In the face of this resounding failure, big business acted through the state to cartelize itself—hence, the Progressive regulatory agenda. "Ironically, contrary to the consensus of historians, it was not the existence of monopoly that caused the federal government to intervene in the economy, but the lack of it."[3]

The FTC and Clayton Acts reversed this long trend toward competition and loss of market share and made stability possible.

> The provisions of the new laws attacking unfair competitors and price discrimination meant that the government would now make it possible for many trade associations to stabilize, for the first time, prices within their industries, and to make effective oligopoly a new phase of the economy.[4]

The Federal Trade Commission created a hospitable atmosphere for trade associations and their efforts to prevent price cutting.[5] Butler Shaffer, in *In Restraint of Trade*, provides a detailed account of the functioning of these trade associations, and their attempts to stabilize prices and restrict "predatory price cutting," through assorted codes of ethics.[6] Specifically, the trade associations established codes of ethics directly under FTC auspices that had the force of law: "[A]s early as 1919 the FTC began inviting members of specific industries to participate in conferences designed to identify trade practices that were felt by "the practically unanimous opinion" of industry members to be unfair." The standard procedure,

1. *The Triumph of Conservatism: A Reinterpretation of American History 1900-1916* (New York: The Free Press of Glencoe, 1963) 3.
2. "Competition and Monopoly," *Monthly Review* (May 1981), pp. 1-16.
3. Kolko, *Triumph of Conservatism*, p. 5.
4. *Ibid.*, p. 268.
5. *Ibid.*, p. 275.
6. *In Restraint of Trade: The Business Campaign Against Competition, 1918-1938* (Lewisburg: Bucknell University Press, 1997).

through the 1920s, was for the FTC to invite members of a particular industry to a conference, and solicit their opinions on trade practice problems and recommended solutions.

> The rules that came out of the conferences and were approved by the FTC fell into
> two categories: Group I rules and Group II rules. Group I rules were considered by the
> commission as expressions of the prevailing law for the industry developing them, and a
> violation of such rules by any member of that industry—whether that member had
> agreed to the rules or not—would subject the offender to prosecution under Section 5
> of the Federal Trade Commission Act as an "unfair method of competition." . . .
>
> Contained within Group I were rules that dealt with practices considered by most
> business organizations to be the more "disruptive" of stable economic conditions. Gener-
> ally included were prohibitions against inducing "breach of contract; . . . commercial brib-
> ery; . . . price discrimination by secret rebates, excessive adjustments, or unearned discounts;
> . . . *selling of goods below cost or below published list of prices for purpose of injuring competitor,* mis-
> representation of goods; . . . use of inferior materials or deviation from standards; [and]
> falsification of weights, tests, or certificates of manufacture [emphasis added]."[1]

The two pieces of legislation accomplished what the trusts had been unable to: they
enabled a handful of firms in each industry to stabilize their market share and to maintain
an oligopoly structure between them.

> It was during the war that effective, working oligopoly and price and market agreements
> became operational in the dominant sectors of the American economy. The rapid diffu-
> sion of power in the economy and relatively easy entry virtually ceased. Despite the ces-
> sation of important new legislative enactments, the unity of business and the federal gov-
> ernment continued throughout the 1920s and thereafter, using the foundations laid in
> the Progressive Era to stabilize and consolidate conditions within various industries. And,
> on the same progressive foundations and exploiting the experience with the war agen-
> cies, Herbert Hoover and Franklin Roosevelt later formulated programs for saving
> American capitalism. The principle of utilizing the federal government to stabilize the
> economy, established in the context of modern industrialism during the Progressive Era,
> became the basis of political capitalism in its many later ramifications.[2]

The various safety and quality regulations introduced during this period also worked
to cartelize the market. They served essentially the same purpose as attempts in the Wilson
war economy to reduce the variety of styles and features available in product lines, in the
name of "efficiency." Any action by the state to impose a uniform standard of quality (e.g.
safety), across the board, necessarily eliminates that feature as a competitive issue between
firms. As Shaffer put it, the purpose of "wage, working condition, or product standards" is
to "universalize cost factors and thus restrict price competition."[3] Thus, the industry is par-
tially cartelized, to the very same extent that would have happened had all the firms in it
adopted a uniform quality standard, and agreed to stop competing in that area. A regulation, in essence, is a state-enforced cartel in which the members agree to cease competing
in a particular area of quality or safety, and instead agree on a uniform standard which they
establish through the state. And unlike private cartels, which are unstable, no member can
seek an advantage by defecting.

Although theoretically the regulations might simply put a floor on quality competition and leave firms free to compete by exceeding the standard, corporations often take a
harsh view of competitors that exceed regulatory safety or quality requirements:

> The Bush administration said Tuesday it will fight to keep meatpackers from testing
> all their animals for mad cow disease.

---

1. *Ibid.*, pp. 82–84.
2. Kolko, *Triumph of Conservatism,* p. 287.
3. *Calculated Chaos: Institutional Threats to Peace and Human Survival* (San Francisco: Alchemy
Books, 1985), p. 143.

The Agriculture Department tests fewer than 1 percent of slaughtered cows for the disease, which can be fatal to humans who eat tainted beef. A beef producer in the western state of Kansas, Creekstone Farms Premium Beef, wants to test all of its cows.

Larger meat companies feared that move because, if Creekstone should test its meat and advertised it as safe, they might have to perform the expensive tests on their larger herds as well.

The Agriculture Department regulates the test and argued that widespread testing could lead to a false positive that would harm the meat industry.[1]

Exceeding government safety standards, it seems, unfairly implies that products which merely meet the ordinary USDA standard are less than adequate. Likewise, government minimum labeling requirements sometimes become a de facto maximum, with restrictions on the voluntary provision of additional information not required by law: e.g. Monsanto's legal thuggery against competitors that label their products as free from growth hormones, and similar use of "food libel" laws to constrain commercial free speech:

Federal Agencies Advised of Misleading Milk Labels and Advertising . . . .

ST LOUIS (April 3, 2007)—Monsanto Company announced today that letters from more than 500 concerned individuals and Monsanto have been submitted to the U.S. Food and Drug Administration (FDA) and Federal Trade Commission (FTC) requesting action to stop deceptive milk labeling and advertising. The two letters outline how certain milk labels and promotions that differentiate milk based on farmer use of POSILAC bovine somatotropin (bST) are misleading to consumers and do not meet the standards set by laws and regulations for either the Federal Trade Commission or the Food and Drug Administration.

"The people who signed these letters are dairy producers, industry professionals and consumers from across the country who have expressed concerns about specific labels they find to be false or misleading," said Kevin Holloway, president of Monsanto Dairy Business. "In many cases, they came to Monsanto to find out what could be done about milk marketing tactics that disparage milk and deny farmers a choice in using approved technologies. We believe FDA and FTC are the correct agencies to address the matter with the companies who employ misleading labels or promotions."

The letter to the FDA highlights deceptive milk labels and calls for clear guidance and enforcement by FDA to address labeling that disparages milk from cows supplemented with POSILAC . . . .

"This is of great concern to dairy producers" said Dennis Areias, a Los Banos, Calif., dairy producer who signed the letters. "Deceptive labels suggest to consumers that there is something wrong with the milk they have been drinking for the past 13 years. Even though the companies that print these labels know this is not true, they choose to mislead consumers in an effort to charge more money for the same milk . . . ."[2]

So once the FDA approves POSILAC, it is forbidden to advertise any product differentiation based on a more stringent safety standard than that of the FDA. Merely telling the consumer whether or not you choose to use FDA-approved additives, by implying that the government-established industry standard is insufficient, amounts to (in Aerias' words) "disparaging the image of milk that we have invested heavily in promoting as a safe, healthy product."

In one jurisdiction, the issue is no longer in doubt. Pennsylvania, in November 2007, officially prohibited dairies from labeling their milk growth hormone-free.

1. Associated Press, "U.S. government fights to keep meatpackers from testing all slaughtered cattle for mad cow," *International Herald-Tribune*, May 29, 2007 <http://www.iht.com/articles/ap/2007/05/29/america/NA-GEN-US-Mad-Cow.php>.

2. "Monsanto Declares War on 'rBGH-free' Dairies," April 3, 2007 (reprint of Monsanto press release by Organic Consumers Association) <http://www.organicconsumers.org/articles/article_4698.cfm>.

State Agriculture Secretary Dennis C. Wolff said advertising one brand of milk as free from artificial hormones implies that competitors' milk is not safe, and it often comes with what he said is an unjustified higher price.

"It's kind of like a nuclear arms race," Wolff said. "One dairy does it and the next tries to outdo them. It's absolutely crazy." . . .

Monsanto spokesman Michael Doane said the hormone-free label "implies to consumers, who may or may not be informed on these issues, that there's a health-and-safety difference between these two milks, that there's 'good' milk and 'bad' milk, and we know that's not the case." . . .

Acting on a recommendation of an advisory panel, the Pennsylvania Agriculture Department has notified 16 dairies in Pennsylvania, New York, New Jersey, Connecticut and Massachusetts that their labels were false or misleading and had to be changed by the end of December.[1]

Every time I think the morally repellant filth at Monsanto have gone as far as humanly possible in trampling normal standards of decency underfoot, they manage to outdo themselves.

Nobody who's read the material above should be surprised to learn that Monsanto actually lobbied to preserve the regulatory state. When Congressman James Walsh, a New York Republican, tried in 1995 to repeal GMO regulations, Monsanto and other leaders in the industry lobbied against the repeal.[2]

Similarly, the provision of services by the state (R&D funding, for example) removes them as components of price in cost competition between firms, and places them in the realm of guaranteed income to all firms in a market alike. Whether through regulations or direct state subsidies to various forms of accumulation, the corporations act through the state to carry out some activities jointly, and to restrict competition to selected areas.

Kolko provided abundant evidence that the main force behind this entire legislative agenda was big business. The Meat Inspection Act, for instance, was passed primarily at the behest of the big meat packers. In the 1880s, repeated scandals involving tainted meat had resulted in U.S. firms being shut out of several European markets. The big packers had turned to the government to inspect exported meat. By organizing this function jointly, through the state, they removed quality inspection as a competitive issue between them, and the government provided a seal of approval in much the same way a trade association would. The problem with this early inspection regime was that only the largest packers were involved in the export trade, which gave a competitive advantage to the small firms that supplied only the domestic market. The main effect of Roosevelt's Meat Inspection Act was to bring the small packers into the inspection regime, and thereby end the competitive disability it imposed on large firms. Upton Sinclair simply served as an unwitting shill for the meat-packing industry.[3] This pattern was repeated, in its essential form, in virtually every component of the "Progressive" regulatory agenda.

Within the cartelizing framework of the regulatory state, it's a stretch to call the relationship between industries in an oligopoly market "competitive."

The corporate web of today is a byzantine mix of interlocking board directorships, strategic alliances, and contracting networks that link virtually every Fortune 500 corporation with every other. John Malone, CEO of TCI, one of the great cable and media gi-

---

1. "Pa. bars hormone-free milk labels," *USA Today*, November 13, 2007 <http://www.usatoday.com/news/nation/2007-11-13-milk-labels_N.htm>.

2. Charlers Derber, *Corporation Nation: How Corporations are Taking Over Our Lives and What We Can Do About It* (New York: St. Martin's Griffin, 1998), p. 150.

3. Kolko, *Triumph of Conservatism*, pp. 98-108.

ants, describes his relationship to Rupert Murdoch as that of variously "competitors or partners or co-schemers."[1]

B. Tax Policy

Coase argued that the differential treatment, for sales tax purposes, of transactions organized through the market and transactions organized internally, gave a competitive advantage to the firm over the market: " . . . it is clear that [the sales tax] is a tax on market transactions and not on the same transactions organized within the firm." The sales tax, therefore, would not only "furnish a reason for the emergence of a firm in a specialized exchange economy," but "tend to make [firms] larger than they would otherwise be."[2]

Double taxation of dividends is a powerful force for concentration, arguably, encouraging corporations to reinvest earnings rather than issue them as dividends. Martin Hellwig argues that, far from leading to a rationing of credit, the tendency of large corporations to fund capital investments primarily from retained earnings leads to overinvestment. Were the profits issued as dividends, they might be reinvested by shareholders in new enterprises. Instead, firms in the monopoly capital sector frequently find that their retained earnings exceed available opportunities for rational investment, so that reinvestment promotes overaccumulation; meanwhile, firms in the competitive sector will be starved for investment funds.[3]

Other tax policies also encourage the concentration of capital. Stock transactions involved in mergers and acquisitions are exempted from the capital gains tax, for example (Henry Manne referred to stock swaps as "one of the most important 'get-rich-quick' opportunities in our economy today").[4] And the interest on corporate debt is a significant deduction from the corporate income tax. A study of hostile takeovers in the '80s found that the tax savings from increased indebtedness was one of the chief benefits.[5]

Tax credits and deductions for research and development and for capital depreciation, along with state-subsidized technical education, tend to increase the capital- and technology-intensiveness of the predominant firm—thereby increasing the firm size and capitalization necessary to enter the market, and promoting cartelization.

I am familiar, by the way, with Austrian objections to the treatment of differential tax exemptions as equivalent to subsidies. It is wrong, they say, because letting the taxpayer keep more of his money is an entirely different thing from subsidizing him out of the public treasury. That's true enough, technically. But the practical effect of a differential tax exemption is exactly the same as a subsidy. For example, offering tax deductions for accelerated depreciation, R&D, interest on corporate debt, etc., has exactly the same competitive effects, mathematically as if we started with a corporate income tax rate of zero, and then imposed a punitive tax only on those firms *not* heavily engaged in capital-intensive production, mergers and acquisitions, etc

1. Derber, *Corporation Nation*, p. 18.

2. Coase, "The Nature of the Firm," p. 393.

3. Martin Hellwig, "On the Economics and Politics of Corporate Finance and Corporate Control," in Xavier Vives, ed., *Corporate Governance: Theoretical and Empirical Perspectives* (Cambridge: Cambridge University Press, 2000), p. 117.

4. Henry Manne, "Mergers and the Market for Corporate Control," *Journal of Political Economy* 73 (April 1965), p. 113.

5. Sanjai Bhagat, Andrei Shleifer and Robert W. Vishny, "Hostile Takeovers in the 1980s: The Return to Corporate Specialization," *Brookings Papers on Economic Activity: Microeconomics* (1990), pp. 1-85. Quoted in Doug Henwood, *Wall Street: How it Works and for Whom* (London and New York: Verso, 1997), p. 280.

Finally, while they don't technically fall under the heading of tax policy, SEC security registration restrictions play a significant role in starving small startup firms of capital and artificially skewing investment toward established firms. Small, "unaccredited" investors (i.e., everyone outside the top 2% of income) are prohibited from buying stock in small, local businesses.[1]

C. THE CORPORATE LIBERAL PACT WITH LABOR

The old Progressive leitmotif of Big Business-Big Government collusion reappeared in the New Deal, along with another Crolyite theme: coopting labor into the corporatist system. The core of business support for the New Deal was, in Ronald Radosh's words, "leading moderate big businessmen and liberal-minded lawyers from large corporate enterprises."[2] Thomas Ferguson and Joel Rogers described them more specifically as "a new power bloc of capital-intensive industries, investment banks, and internationally oriented commercial banks."[3]

Labor was a relatively minor part of the total cost package of such businesses; at the same time, capital-intensive industry, as Galbraith pointed out in his analysis of the "technostructure," depended on long-term stability and predictability for planning. Therefore, this segment of big business was willing to trade higher wages for social peace in the workplace.[4] The roots of this faction can be traced to the relatively "progressive" employers described by James Weinstein in his account of the National Civic Federation at the turn of the century, who were willing to engage in collective bargaining over wages and working conditions in return for uncontested management control of the workplace.[5]

This attitude was at the root of the Fordist social contract, in which labor agreed to let management manage, in return for a bigger share of the pie.[6] Such an understanding was most emphatically in the interests of large corporations. The sitdown movement in the auto industry and the organizing strikes among West coast longshoremen were virtual revolutions among rank and file workers on the shop floor. In many cases, they were turning into regional general strikes. The Wagner Act domesticated this revolution and brought it under the control of professional labor bureaucrats.

Industrial unionism, from the employer's viewpoint, had the advantage over craft unionism of providing a single bargaining agent with which management could deal. One of the reasons for the popularity of "company unions" among large corporations, besides the obvious advantages in pliability, was the fact that they were an alternative to the host of separate craft unions of the AFL. Even in terms of pliability, the industrial unions of the Thirties had some of the advantages of company unions.

Gerard Swope of GE, in particular, experimented during the heyday of welfare capitalism with company unions that offered a grievance procedure, along with a measure of due process provided by binding arbitration on disciplinary matters. The purpose of such unions

---

1. Michael S. Shuman, "Legalize Localization: Post-Meltdown Thoughts (Part I)," Small-Mart.Org, Nov. 11, 2008 <http://www.small-mart.org/legalize_localization>.

2. Ronald Radosh, "The Myth of the New Deal," in Rothbard and Radosh, eds., *A New History of Leviathan*, pp. 154-5.

3. Thomas Ferguson and Joel Rogers. *Right Turn* (New York: Hill and Wang, 1986), p. 46; this line of analysis is pursued more intensively in Thomas Ferguson, *Golden Rule: The Investment Theory of Party Competition and the Logic of Money-Driven Political Systems* (Chicago: University of Chicago Press, 1995).

4. Ferguson, *Golden Rule* pp. 117 et seq.; John Kenneth Galbraith, *The New Industrial State* (New York: Signet Books, 1967), pp. 25-37, 258-9, 274, 287-9.

5. Weinstein, *Corporate Ideal in the Liberal State*, esp. the first two chapters.

6. Montgomery, *Workers' Control in America*, pp. 49-57.

was to secure workplace peace and stability while reserving questions of work organization and compensation to management. At one point, in 1926, Swope made an (unsuccessful) secret proposal to William Green of the AFL to bypass the Balkanized craft jurisdictions and organize GE by "winning control of the works-council system."[1] The industrial unions of the Wagner regime, as it turned out, did not reserve pay and benefits to management prerogative. But they did reserve questions of work organization ("let management manage") and secure long-term stability through the enforcement of contracts.

By bringing collective bargaining under the aegis of federal labor law, management was able to use union leadership to discipline its own rank and file, and to use federal courts as a mechanism of enforcement.

> The New Dealers devised . . . a means to integrate big labor into the corporate state. But only unions that were industrially organized, and which paralleled in their structure the organization of industry itself, could play the appropriate role. A successful corporate state required a safe industrial-union movement to work. It also required a union leadership that shared the desire to operate the economy from the top in formal conferences with the leaders of the other functional economic groups, particularly the corporate leaders. The CIO unions . . . provided such a union leadership.[2]

Moderate members of the corporate elite were reassured by the earlier British experience in accepting collective bargaining. Collective bargaining did not affect the distribution of wealth, because firms in an oligopoly position, with a relatively inelastic demand, were able to pass increased labor costs on to the consumer at virtually no cost to themselves.[3]

The Wagner Act served the central purposes of the corporate elite. To some extent it was a response to mass pressure from below. But the decision on whether and how to respond, the form of the response, and the implementation of the response, were all firmly in the hands of the corporate elite. According to Domhoff (writing in *The Higher Circles*), "The benefits to capital were several: greater efficiency and productivity from labor, less labor turnover, the disciplining of the labor force by labor unions, the possibility of planning labor costs over the long run, and the dampening of radical doctrines."[4] James O'Connor described it this way: "From the standpoint of monopoly capital the main function of unions was . . . to inhibit disruptive, spontaneous rank-and-file activity (e.g., wildcat strikes and slowdowns) and to maintain labor discipline in general. In other words, unions were . . . the guarantors of 'managerial prerogatives.'"[5] The objectives of stability and productivity were more compatible with such a limited social compact than with a return to the labor violence of the late nineteenth century.

In *The Power Elite and the State*, Domhoff put forth a slightly more nuanced thesis.[6] It was true, he admitted, that a majority of large corporations opposed the Wagner Act in its final form. But the basic principles of collective bargaining embodied in it had been the outcome of decades of corporate liberal theory and practice, worked out through policy networks in which "progressive" large corporations had played a leading role; the National Civic Federation, as Weinstein described its career, was a typical example of such networks. The motives of those in the Roosevelt administration who framed the Wagner Act were

1. Michael J. Piore and Charles F. Sabel, *The Second Industrial Divide: Possibilities for Prosperity* (New York: HarperCollins, 1984), p. 132. See also Richard Edwards, *Contested Terrain: The Transformation of the Workplace in the Twentieth Century* (New York: Basic Books, 1979), p. 106.

2. Radosh, "The Myth of the New Deal," pp. 178-9, 181.

3. G. William Domhoff, *The Higher Circles: The Governing Class in America* (New York: Vintage Books, 1971), p. 223.

4. *Ibid*, p. 225.

5. *The Fiscal Crisis of the State* (New York: St. Martin's Press, 1973).

6. *The Power Elite and the State: How Policy is Made in America* (New York: Aldine de Gruyter, 1990), pp. 65-105.

very much in the corporate liberal mainstream. Although they may have been ambivalent about the specific form of Wagner, Swope and his corporate fellow travelers had played the major role in formulating the principles behind it. Wagner was drafted by mainstream corporate lawyers who were products of the intellectual climate created by those same business leaders; and it was drafted with a view to their interests. Although it was not accepted by big business as a whole, Wagner was crafted by representatives of big business interests whose understanding of its purpose was largely the same as those outlined in Domhoff's quote above from *The Higher Circles*. At the same time, although it was intended to contain the threat of working class power, it enjoyed broad working class support as the best deal they were likely to get. The class nature of the legislation was further complicated by the fact that the southern segment of the Democratic Party establishment used its veto power to limit the corporate liberal agenda of the big industrialists: the southern wing was willing to go along with Wagner because it specifically exempted agricultural laborers.

Another major aspect of American labor policy, which perhaps began with Cleveland's response to the Pullman strike, was continued in the Railway Labor Relations Act and Taft–Hartley (which, in James O'Connor's words, "included a ban on secondary boycotts and hence tried to 'illegalize' class solidarity . . ."),[1] and Truman's and Bush's threats to use soldiers as scabs in, respectively, the steelworkers' and longshoremen's strikes. Taft–Hartley's "cooling off" and arbitration provisions enable the government to intervene in any case where transport workers threaten to turn a local dispute into a general strike; they can be used for similar purposes in other strategic sectors, as demonstrated by Bush's invocation of it against the longshoremen's union.

Wagner and Taft–Hartley greatly reduced the effectiveness of strikes at individual plants by transforming them into declared wars fought by management rules, and likewise reduced their effectiveness by prohibiting the coordination of actions across multiple firms or industries. Taft–Hartley's cooling off periods, in addition, gave employers time to prepare for such disruptions and greatly reduced the informational rents embodied in the training of the existing workforce. Were not such restrictions in place, today's "just-in-time" economy would be far more vulnerable to such disruption than that of the 1930s.

The federal labor law regime criminalizes many forms of resistance, like sympathy and boycott strikes up and down the production chain from raw materials to retail, that made the mass and general strikes of the early 1930s so formidable.

D. The Socialization of Corporate Cost

The common thread in all these lines of analysis is that an ever-growing portion of the functions of the capitalist economy have been carried out through the state. According to James O'Connor, state expenditures under monopoly capitalism can be divided into "social capital" and "social expenses."

> *Social capital* is expenditures required for profitable private accumulation; it is indirectly productive (in Marxist terms, social capital indirectly expands surplus value). There are two kinds of social capital: social investment and social consumption (in Marxist terms, social constant capital and social variable capital) . . . . *Social investment* consist of projects and services that increase the productivity of a given amount of laborpower and, other factors being equal, increase the rate of profit . . . . *Social consumption* consists of projects and services that lower the reproduction costs of labor and, other factors being equal, increase the rate of profit. An example of this is social insurance, which expands the productive powers of the work force while simultaneously lowering labor costs. The second category, *social expenses*, consists of projects and services which are required to maintain social harmony—

---

1. James O'Connor, *Accumulation Crisis* (Oxford: Basil Blackwell Ltd, 1984) p. 75.

to fulfill the state's "legitimization" function . . . . The best example is the welfare system, which is designed chiefly to keep social peace among unemployed workers.[1]

According to O'Connor, such state expenditures counteract the falling direct rate of profit that Marx predicted. Monopoly capital is able to externalize many of its operating expenses on the state; and since the state's expenditures indirectly increase the productivity of labor and capital at taxpayer expense, the apparent rate of profit is increased. "In short, monopoly capital socializes more and more costs of production."[2]

O'Connor listed several ways in which monopoly capital externalizes its operating costs on the political system:

> Capitalist production has become more interdependent—more dependent on science and technology, labor functions more specialized, and the division of labor more extensive. Consequently, the monopoly sector (and to a much lesser degree the competitive sector) requires increasing numbers of technical and administrative workers. It also requires increasing amounts of infrastructure (physical overhead capital)—transportation, communication, R&D, education, and other facilities. In short, the monopoly sector requires more and more social investment in relation to private capital . . . . The costs of social investment (or social constant capital) are not borne by monopoly capital but rather are socialized and fall on the state.[3]

These forms of state expenditure exemplify several of the "counteracting influences" to the declining rate of profit that Marx described in Volume 3 of *Capital*. The second such influence Marx listed, for example, was the "depression of wages below the value of labor power." Through welfare, taxpayer-funded education, and other means of subsidizing the reproduction cost of labor-power, the state reduces the minimum sustainable cost of labor-power that must be paid by employers. The state educational system, in particular, the Austrian economists Walter Grinder and John Hagel commented,

> supplies the economy with a highly skilled and literate labor force inculcated with "technocratic" values. The evolution of the state-financed educational system has been profoundly influenced by the changing needs of the corporate economy and this . . . relationship has been a prominent characteristic of state capitalist societies. Compulsory education also inculcates a value system encouraging subservience and docility among unskilled labor and the lower strata of society.[4]

This is true also of Marx's third influence: the "cheapening of the elements of constant capital." The state, by subsidizing many of the operating costs of large corporations, artificially shifts their balance sheet further into the black. The fourth influence listed, "relative overpopulation," is promoted by state subsidies to the capital substitution, and to the education of technically skilled manpower at government expense—with the effect of artificially increasing the supply of labor relative to demand, and thus reducing its bargaining power in the labor market.[5] According to Samuel Bowles and Herbert Gintis, the formal right of the employer to hire and fire

> is effective . . . only when the cost to workers is high; that is, when there is a large pool of labor with the appropriate skills available in the larger society, into which workers are

---

1. O'Connor, *Fiscal Crisis of the State*, pp. 6-7.
2. *Ibid.*, p. 24.
3. *Ibid.*, p. 24.
4. "Toward a Theory of State Capitalism: Ultimate Decision-Making and Class Structure," *Journal of Libertarian Studies* 1:1 (Spring 1977), p. 73 <http://www.mises.org/journals/jls/1_1/1_1_7.pdf>.
5. Karl Marx and Friedrich Engels, *Capital* vol. 3, vol. 37 of Marx and Engels *Collected Works* (New York: International Publishers, 1998), pp. 234-235.

threatened to be pushed. Indeed, . . . the maintenance of such a "reserve army" of skilled labor has been a major, and not unintended, effect of U.S. education through the years.[1]

We should briefly recall here our examination above of how such socialization of expenditures serves to cartelize industry. By externalizing such costs on the state, through the general tax system, monopoly capital removes these expenditures as an issue of cost competition between individual firms. The costs and benefits are applied uniformly to the entire industry, removing it as a competitive disadvantage for some firms.

Although it flies in the face of "progressive" myth, big business is by no means uniformly opposed to national health insurance. Currently, corporations in the monopoly capital sector are the most likely to provide insurance to their employees; and such insurance is one of the fastest-rising components of labor costs. Consequently, firms that already provide this service at their own expense are the logical beneficiaries of a nationalized system. The effect of national health insurance would be to remove the cost of insurance as a competitive disadvantage for the companies that provided it. Even if the state only requires large corporations to provide health insurance across the board, it is an improvement of the current situation, from capital's point of view: health insurance ceases to be a component of price competition among the largest firms. A national health system provides a competitive advantage to a nation's firms at the expense of their foreign competitors, who have to fund their own employee health benefits—hence, American capital's hostility to the Canadian system, and its repeated attempts to combat it through the WTO.

Daniel Gross, although erroneously viewing it as a departure from big business's supposed hostility to the welfare state, has made the same point about corporate support of government health insurance.[2] Large American corporations, by shouldering the burden of health insurance and other employee benefits borne by the state in Europe and Japan, is at a competitive disadvantage both against companies there and against smaller firms here.

Democratic presidential candidate Dick Gephart, or rather his spokesman Jim English, admitted to a corporate liberal motivation for state-funded health insurance in his 2003 Labor Day address. Gephart's proposed mandatory employer coverage, with a 60% tax credit for the cost, would (he said) eliminate competition from companies that don't currently provide health insurance as an employee benefit. It would also reduce competition from firms in countries with a single-payer system.[3]

The level of technical training necessary to keep the existing corporate system running, the current level of capital intensiveness of production, and the current level of R&D efforts on which it depends, are all heavily subsidized. The state's education system provides a technical labor force at public expense, and whenever possible overproduces technical specialists on the level needed to ensure that technical workers are willing to take work on the employers' terms. On this count, O'Connor quoted Veblen: the state answers capital's "need of a free supply of trained subordinates at reasonable wages . . . ."[4] Starting with the Morrill Act of 1862, which subsidized agricultural and mechanical colleges, the federal government has underwritten a major part of the reproduction cost of technical labor.[5] In research and development, likewise, federal support goes back at least to the agricultural

1. *Schooling in Capitalist America: Educational Reform and the Contradictions of Economic Life* (New York: Basic Books, Inc., Publishers, 1976), p. 55.

2. "Socialism, American Style: Why American CEOs covet a massive European-style social-welfare state" *Slate* Aug. 1, 2003 <http://slate.msn.com/id/2086511/>.

3. C-SPAN, September 1, 2003.

4. O'Connor, *Fiscal Crisis of the State*, p. 111.

5. Noble, *America by Design*, pp. 24 et seq.

and experiment stations of the late nineteenth century, created under the Hatch Act of 1887.[1]

The state's socialization of the cost of reproducing a technically sophisticated labor force, and its subsidies to R&D, make possible a far higher technical level of production than would support itself in a free market. The G.I. Bill was an integral part of the upward ratcheting of state capitalism during and after WWII.

> Technical-administrative knowledge and skills, unlike other forms of capital over which private capitalists claim ownership, cannot be monopolized by any one or a few indus-trial-finance interests . . . . In the context of a free market for laborpower . . . no one corporation or industry or industrial-finance interest group can afford to train its own labor force or channel profits into the requisite amount of R&D . . . . Thus, on-the-job training (OJT) is little used not because it is technically inefficient . . . but because it does not pay.

Nor can any one corporation or industrial-finance interest afford to fund its own R&D. In the last analysis, R&D is coordinated through the state because of the high costs and uncertainty of getting usable results.[2]

At best, from the point of view of the employer, state-funded education creates a "re-serve army" of scientific and technical labor—as William Appleman Williams put it, it en-sures that "experts are a glut on the market."[3] At worst, when there is a shortage of such labor-power, the state at least absorbs the cost of reproducing it and removes it as a com-ponent of private industry's operating costs. In either case, "the greater the socialization of the costs of variable capital, the lower will be the level of money wages, and . . . the higher the rate of profit in the monopoly sector."[4] And since the monopoly capital sector is able to pass its taxes onto the consumer or to the competitive capital sector, the effect is that "the costs of training technical laborpower are met by taxes paid by competitive sector capital and labor."[5]

Even welfare expenses, although O'Connor classed them as completely unproductive, are really another example of the state underwriting variable capital costs. Some socialists speculate that, if they could, capitalists would lower the prevailing rate of subsistence pay to that required to keep workers alive only when they were employed. But since that would entail starvation during periods of unemployment, the prevailing wage must cover contin-gencies of unemployment; otherwise, wages would fall below the minimum cost of repro-ducing labor. Under the welfare state, however, the state itself absorbs the cost of providing for such contingencies, so that the uncertainty premium is removed as a component of wages.

And leaving this aside, even as a pure "social expense," the welfare system acts pri-marily (in O'Connor's words) to "control the surplus population politically."[6] The state's subsidies to the accumulation of constant capital and to the reproduction of scientific-technical labor provide an incentive for much more capital-intensive forms of production than would have come about in a free market, and thus contribute to the growth of a permanent underclass of surplus labor;[7] the state steps in and undertakes the minimum cost necessary to prevent large-scale homelessness and starvation, which would destabilize the

1. *Ibid.*, p. 132.

2. O'Connor, *Fiscal Crisis of the State*, p. 112.

3. "A Profile of the Corporate Elite," in Rothbard and Radosh, eds., *New History of Levia-than*, p. 5.

4. O'Connor, *Fiscal Crisis of the State*, p. 124.

5. *Ibid.*, p. 160.

6. *Ibid.*, p. 69.

7. *Ibid.*, p. 161.

system, and to maintain close supervision of the underclass through the human services bureaucracy.[1]

The general effect of the state's intervention in the economy, then, is to remove ever
increasing spheres of economic activity from the realm of competition in price or quality,
and to organize them collectively through organized capital as a whole.

Through the military-industrial complex, the state has socialized a major share—
probably the majority—of the cost of "private" business's research and development. If
anything the role of the state as purchaser of surplus economic output is eclipsed by its role
as subsidizer of research cost, as Charles Nathanson pointed out. Research and development was heavily militarized by the Cold War "military-R&D complex." Military R&D
often results in basic, general use technologies with broad civilian applications. Technologies originally developed for the Pentagon have often become the basis for entire categories of consumer goods.[2] The general effect has been to "substantially [eliminate] the major
risk area of capitalism: the development of and experimentation with new processes of
production and new products."[3]

This is the case in electronics especially, where many products originally developed by
military R&D "have become the new commercial growth areas of the economy."[4] Transis-
tors and other miniaturized circuitry were developed primarily with Pentagon research
money. The federal government was the primary market for large mainframe computers in
the early days of the industry; without government contracts, the industry might never
have had sufficient production runs to adopt mass production and reduce unit costs low
enough to enter the private market.

Overall, Nathanson estimated, industry depended on military funding for around 60%
of its research and development spending; but this figure is considerably understated by the
fact that a significant part of nominally civilian R&D spending is aimed at developing civilian applications for military technology.[5] It is also understated by the fact that military
R&D is often used for developing production technologies (like automated control systems in the machine tool industry) that become the basis for production methods
throughout the civilian sector.

E. STATE ACTION TO ABSORB SURPLUS OUTPUT

The roots of the corporate state in the U.S., more than anything else, lie in the crisis
of overproduction as perceived by corporate and state elites—especially the traumatic Depression of the 1890s—and the requirement, also as perceived by them, for state intervention to absorb surplus output or otherwise deal with the problems of overproduction, underconsumption, and overaccumulation.

According to William Appleman Williams, "the Crisis of the 1890's raised in many
sections of American society the specter of chaos and revolution."[6] Economic elites saw it
as the result of overproduction and surplus capital, and believed it could be resolved only
through access to a "new frontier." Without state-guaranteed access to foreign markets,

1. Frances Fox Piven and Richard A. Cloward. *Regulating the Poor: The Functions of Public
Welfare.* Updated edition (New York: Vintage Books, 1971, 1993).

2. "The Militarization of the American Economy," in David Horowitz, ed., *Corporations and
the Cold War* (New York and London: Monthly Review Press, 1969), p. 208.

3. *Ibid.*, p. 230.

4. *Ibid.*, p. 230. See also David F. Noble, *Forces of Production*, for the primary role of military
industry in developing cybernetics, robotics, automated control systems, etc.

5. *Ibid.*, pp. 222–25.

6. William Appleman Williams, *The Tragedy of American Diplomacy* (New York: Dell Publishing Company, 1959, 1962) 21-2.

output would fall below capacity, unit costs would go up, and unemployment would reach dangerous levels.

The seriousness of the last threat was underscored by the radicalism of the Nineties. The Pullman Strike, Homestead, and the formation of the Western Federation of Miners (in many ways the precursor organization to the IWW) were signs of dangerous levels of labor unrest and class consciousness. Coxey's army of the unemployed marched on Washington. The People's Party seemed poised to take the White House. At one point Jay Gould, mouthpiece of the robber barons, threatened a capital strike if the populists came to power. In 1894 businessman F. L. Stetson warned, "We are on the edge of a very dark night, unless a return of commercial prosperity relieves popular discontent."[1] Both business and government resounded with claims that U.S. productive capacity had outstripped the domestic market's ability to consume, and that the government had to take active measures to obtain outlets.

This perception is often ridiculed by Austrians on the grounds that overproduction and underconsumption simply cannot happen." They ignore the fact that Say's law only applies to a free market. One might just as well airily dismiss Mises' theories of malinvestment and the crackup boom on the grounds that "such things cannot happen in the free market." What we have is not a free market, but a corporatist system in which the state subsidizes overaccumulation and the cartelization of industry, so that overbuilt industry cannot dispose of its entire product when operating at full capacity—especially not at cartel prices. Neo-Marxist theories of overproduction and imperialism, and New Left revisionist treatments of American foreign policy, both lend themselves quite well to thoughful free market analysis. Joseph Stromberg's essay, "The Role of State Monopoly Capitalism in the American Empire,"[2] is an excellent example of such an approach.

The abortive NIRA was an attempt to solve the problem of overproduction by government-sponsored industrial cartels: by that means, corporations would be able to set prices and apportion shares of output among themselves so as to maximize income through monopoly pricing, thus guaranteeing them a minimum rate of profit even while operating far below capacity. Besides this unsuccessful attempt, thwarted by the Supreme Court, FDR also attempted to mobilize idle manpower and spending power through deficit-funded spending programs, with mixed results at best.

The crowning achievement of FDR's state capitalism, of course, was the military-industrial complex which arose from World War II, and has continued ever since. It has since been described, variously, as "military Keynesianism," or a "perpetual war economy." A first step in realizing the monumental scale of the war economy's effect is to consider that the total value of plant and equipment in the United States increased by about two-thirds (from $40 to $66 billion) between 1939 and 1945, most of it a taxpayer "gift" of forced investment funds provided to the country's largest corporations.[3] Profit was virtually guaranteed on war production through "cost-plus" contracts.[4] In addition, some two-thirds of federal R&D spending was channeled through the 68 largest private laboratories (40% of it to the ten largest), and the resulting patents given away to the companies that carried out the research under government contract.[5]

1. *Ibid.*, p. 26.
2. *Journal of Libertarian Studies* Volume 15, no. 3 (Summer 2001) <http://www.mises.org/journals/jls/15_3/15_3_3.pdf>.
3. C. Wright Mills, *The Power Elite* (Oxford and New York: Oxford University Press, 1956, 2000), p. 101.
4. David W. Eakins, "Business Planners and America's Postwar Expansion," in David Horowitz, ed., *Corporations and the Cold War* (New York and London: Monthly Review Press, 1969), p. 148.
5. G. William Domhoff, *Who Rules America?* (Englewood Cliffs, N.J.: Prentice-Hall, 1967), p. 121.

World War II went a long way toward postponing America's crises of overproduction and overaccumulation for a generation, by blowing up most of the capital in the world outside the United States and creating a permanent war economy to absorb surplus output.

Nevertheless, demobilization of the war economy after 1945 very nearly threw the overbuilt and government-dependent industrial sector into a renewed depression. For example, in *Harry Truman and the War Scare of 1948,* Frank Kofsky described the aircraft industry as spiraling into red ink after the end of the war, and on the verge of bankruptcy when it was rescued by Truman's new bout of Cold War spending on heavy bombers.[1]

The Cold War restored the corporate economy's heavy reliance on the state as a source of guaranteed sales. Charles Nathanson argued that "one conclusion is inescapable: major firms with huge aggregations of corporate capital owe their survival after World War II to the Cold War . . . ."[2] For example, David Noble pointed out that civilian jumbo jets would never have existed without the government's heavy bomber contracts. The production runs for the civilian market alone were too small to pay for the complex and expensive machinery. The 747 is essentially a spinoff of military production.[3]

The heavy industrial and high tech sectors were given a virtually guaranteed outlet, not only by U.S. military procurement, but by grants and loan guarantees for foreign military sales under the Military Assistance Program. Although apologists for the military-industrial complex have tried to stress the relatively small fraction of total production represented by military goods, it makes more sense to compare the volume of military procurement to the amount of idle capacity. Military production runs amounting to a minor percentage of total production might absorb a major part of total excess production capacity, and have a huge effect on reducing unit costs. Besides, the rate of profit on military contracts tends to be quite a bit higher, given the fact that military goods have no "standard" market price, and the fact that prices are set by political means (as periodic Pentagon budget scandals should tell us).[4] So military contracts, small though they might be as a portion of a firm's total output, might well make the difference between profit and loss.

Seymour Melman described the "permanent war economy" as a privately-owned, centrally-planned economy that included most heavy manufacturing and high tech industry. This "*state-controlled economy*" was based on the principles of "maximization of costs and of government subsidies."[5]

> It can draw on the federal budget for virtually unlimited capital. It operates in an insulated, monopoly market that makes the state-capitalist firms, singly and jointly, impervious to inflation, to poor productivity performance, to poor product design and poor production managing. The subsidy pattern has made the state-capitalist firms failure-proof. That is the state-capitalist replacement for the classic self-correcting mechanisms of the competitive, cost-minimizing, profit-maximizing firm.[6]

The chief virtue of the military economy is its utter unproductivity. That is, it does not compete with private industry to supply any good for which there is consumer demand. But military production is not the only such area of unproductive government spending. Neo-Marxist Paul Mattick elaborated on the theme in a 1956 article. The overbuilt corporate economy, he wrote, ran up against the problem that "[p]rivate capital formation . . . finds its limitation in diminishing market-demand." The State had to absorb

1. (New York: St. Martin's Press, 1993).
2. Nathanson, "The Militarization of the American Economy," p. 214.
3. Noble, *America by Design,* pp. 6-7.
4. Nathanson, "The Militarization of the American Economy," p. 208.
5. *The Permanent War Economy: American Capitalism in Decline* (New York: Simon and Schuster, 1974), p. 11.
6. *Ibid.,* p. 21.

part of the surplus output; but it had to do so without competing with corporations in the private market. Instead, "[g]overnment-induced production is channeled into non-market fields—the production of non-competitive public-works, armaments, superfluities and waste.[1] As a necessary result of this state of affairs,

> so long as the principle of competitive capital production prevails, steadily growing production will in increasing measure be a "production for the sake of production," benefiting neither private capital nor the population at large.
>
> This process is somewhat obscured, it is true, by the apparent profitability of capital and the lack of large-scale unemployment. Like the state of prosperity, profitability, too, is now largely government manipulated. Government spending and taxation are managed so as to strengthen big business at the expense of the economy as a whole . . . .
>
> In order to increase the scale of production and to accummulate [sic] capital, government creates "demand" by ordering the production of non-marketable goods, financed by government borrowings. This means that the government avails itself of productive resources belonging to private capital which would otherwise be idle.[2]

Such consumption of output, while not always directly profitable to private industry, serves a function analogous to foreign "dumping" below cost, in enabling industry to operate at full capacity despite the insufficiency of private demand to absorb the entire product at the cost of production.

It's interesting to consider how many segments of the economy have a guaranteed market for their output, or a "conscript clientele" in place of willing consumers. The "military-industrial complex" is well known. But how about the state's education and penal systems? How about the automobile-trucking-highway complex, or the civil aviation complex? Foreign surplus disposal ("export dependant monopoly capitalism") and domestic surplus disposal (government purchases) are different forms of the same phenomenon.

Finally, as Marx pointed out in Volume Three of *Capital*, the rise of major new forms of industry could absorb surplus capital and counteract the falling direct rate of profit." Baran and Sweezy, likewise, considered "epoch-making inventions" as partial counterbalances to the ever-increasing surplus. Their chief example was the rise of the automobile industry in the 1920s, which (along with the highway program) was to define the American economy for most of the mid-20th century.[3] The high tech boom of the 1990s was a similarly revolutionary event. It is revealing to consider the extent to which both the automobile and computer industries, far more than most industries, were direct products of state capitalism.

The destruction of capital postponed the crisis of overaccumulation until around 1970, when the industrial capacity of Europe and Japan had been rebuilt. By the late 1960s, according to Piore and Sabel, American domestic markets for industrial goods had become saturated.[4] According to Walden Bello, the capitalist state attempted to address the resumed crisis of overproduction with a new series of expedients, including a combination of neo-liberal restructuring and globalization, and financialization. The former sought new outlets for surplus capital in havens like China, while the latter used derivatives and debt-based securities to soak up investment capital for which no outlet existed in productive industry. Unfortunately for the state capitalists, China itself has become saturated with industrial investment, and we're currently seeing (as of November 2008) the results of financialization.[5] State capitalism seems to be running out of safety valves.

1. "The Economics of War and Peace," *Dissent* (Fall 1956), p. 377.

2. *Ibid.*, pp. 378–379.

3. Paul Baran and Paul Sweezy, *Monopoly Capitalism: An Essay in the American Economic and Social Order* (New York: Monthly Review Press, 1966), p. 220.

4. Piore and Sabel, *The Second Industrial Divide*, p. 184.

5. Walden Bello, "A Primer on Wall Street Meltdown," *MR Zine*, October 3, 2008 <http://mrzine.monthlyreview.org/bello031008.html>.

F. NEOLIBERAL FOREIGN POLICY

Neoliberal foreign policy, in large measure, is a subset of the broader category of state action to absorb surplus output and surplus capital.

The central theme of American foreign policy, from the 1890s until today, was what William Appleman Williams called "Open Door imperialism";[1] it consisted of using U.S. political power to guarantee access to foreign markets and resources on terms favorable to American corporate interests, without relying on direct political rule. Its central goal was to obtain for U.S. merchandise, in each national market, treatment equal to that afforded any other industrial nation. Most importantly, this entailed active engagement by the U.S. government in breaking down the imperial powers' existing spheres of economic influence or preference. The result, in most cases, was to treat as hostile to U.S. security interests any large-scale attempt at autarky, or any other policy whose effect was to withdraw major areas of the world from the disposal of the U.S. corporate economy. When the power attempting such policies was an equal, like the British Empire, the U.S. reaction was merely one of measured coolness. When it was perceived as an inferior, like Japan, the U.S. resorted to more forceful measures, as events of the late 1930s indicate. And whatever the degree of equality between advanced nations in their access to Third World markets, it was clear that Third World nations were still to be subordinated to the industrialized West in a collective sense.

Open Door Empire was the direct ancestor of today's neoliberal system, which is falsely called "free trade" in the apologetics of court intellectuals. It depended on active management of the world economy by dominant states, and continuing intervention to police the international economic order and enforce sanctions against states which did not cooperate.

The Bretton Woods System, created on the initiative of FDR and Truman in the latter part of World War II, was the culmination of the Open Door. FDR saw the guarantee of American access to foreign markets as vital to ending the Depression and the threat of internal upheaval that went along with it. His ongoing policy of Open Door Empire, faced with the withdrawal of major areas from the world market by the autarkic policies of the Greater East Asia Co-Prosperity Sphere and Fortress Europe, led to American entry into World War II, and culminated in the postwar establishment of what Samuel Huntington called a "system of world order" guaranteed both by global institutions of economic governance like the IMF, and by a hegemonic political and military superpower.

In the summer of 1940, the CFR and State Department undertook a joint study to determine the minimum portion of the world the U.S. would have to integrate with its own economy, in order to provide sufficient resources and markets for economic stability; it also explored policy options for reconstructing the postwar world. They found that the U.S. economy could not survive in its existing form without access to the resources and markets not only of the Western Hemisphere, but of the British Empire and the Far East (together called the Grand Area). But the western Pacific was rapidly being incorporated into Japan's economic sphere of influence. And the fall of France and the Low Countries, and the ongoing Battle of Britain, raised the possibility that Germany might capture much of the Royal Navy (and with it some portion of the Empire). FDR resolved to contest Japanese power in the Far East, and if necessary to initiate war.[2] In the end, however, he successfully maneuvered Japan into firing the first shot.

1. *The Contours of American History* (Cleveland and New York: The World Publishing Company, 1961).

2. Laurence H. Shoup and William Minter, "Shaping a New World Order: The Council on Foreign Relations' Blueprint for World Hegemony, 1939-1945," in Holly Sklar, ed., *Trilateralism: The Trilateral Commission and Elite Planning for World Management* (Boston: South End Press, 1980), pp. 135-56

The American policy that emerged from these struggles was to secure control over the markets and resources of the global "Grand Area" through institutions of global economic governance, as created by the postwar Bretton Woods system.

The problem of access to foreign markets and resources was central to U.S. postwar planning. Given the structural imperatives of "export dependent monopoly capitalism,"[1] the possibility of a postwar depression was real. The original drive toward foreign expansion at the end of the nineteenth century reflected the fact that industry, with state capitalist encouragement, had expanded far beyond the ability of the domestic market to consume its output. Even before World War II, the state capitalist economy had serious trouble operating at the level of output needed for full utilization of capacity and cost control. Military-industrial policy during the war exacerbated the problem of over-accumulation, greatly increasing the value of plant and equipment at taxpayer expense. The end of the war, if followed by the traditional pattern of demobilization, would result in a drastic reduction in orders to that same overbuilt industry just as over ten million workers were being dumped back into the civilian labor force.

A central facet of postwar economic policy, as reflected in the Bretton Woods agencies, was state intervention to guarantee markets for the full output of U.S. industry and profitable outlets for surplus capital. The World Bank was designed to subsidize the export of capital to the Third World, by financing the infrastructure without which Western-owned production facilities could not be established there. According to Gabriel Kolko's 1988 estimate, almost two thirds of the World Bank's loans since its inception had gone to transportation and power infrastructure.[2] A laudatory Treasury Department report referred to such infrastructure projects (comprising some 48% of lending in FY 1980) as "externalities" to business, and spoke glowingly of the benefits of such projects in promoting the expansion of business into large market areas and the consolidation and commercialization of agriculture.[3] The Volta River power project, for example, was built with American loans (at high interest) to provide Kaiser aluminum with electricity at very low rates.[4]

More recently, companies engaged in the supposedly "free market" activity of offshoring work notified host governments of their requirements for corporate welfare:

> SUNIL RAMAN, BBC—The Indian city of Bangalore must improve its infrastructure if it wants to hold on to vital IT business, company executives have warned. The heads of some of the biggest companies in India's IT industry have asked the government of the southern Indian state of Karnataka to improve infrastructure in Bangalore, or they will move their businesses to other states. The high-profile delegation included bosses of top Indian IT companies Wipro and Infosys, as well as representatives from Dell, IBM, Intel, and Texas Instruments among others.[5]

1. "Now the price that brings the maximum monopoly profit is generally far above the price that would be fixed by fluctuating competitive costs, and the volume that can be marketed at that maximum price is generally far below the output that would be technically and economically feasible . . . . [The trust] extricates itself from this dilemma by producing the full output that is economically feasible, thus securing low costs, and offering in the protected domestic market only the quantity corresponding to the monopoly price—insofar as the tariff permits; while the rest is sold, or 'dumped,' abroad at a lower price . . . ."—Joseph Schumpeter, "Imperialism," in *Imperialism, Social Classes: Two Essays by Joseph Schumpeter.* Translated by Heinz Norden. Introduction by Hert Hoselitz (New York: Meridian Books, 1955) 79-80.

2. Gabriel Kolko, *Confronting the Third World: United States Foreign Policy 1945-1980* (New York: Pantheon Books, 1988), p. 120.

3. *United States Participation in the Multilateral Development Banks in the 1980s.* Department of the Treasury (Washington, DC: 1982), p. 9.

4. Stavrianos, *Promise of the Coming Dark Age*, p. 42.

5. Sunil Rahman, "India's silicon valley faces IT exodus," BBC News, August 10, 2004 <http://news.bbc.co.uk/1/low/business/3553156.stm>.

Besides the benefit of building "an internal infrastructure which is a vital prerequisite for the development of resources and direct United States private investments," such banks (because they must be repaid in U.S. dollars) require the borrowing nations "to export goods capable of earning them, which is to say, raw materials . . . ."[1]

The International Monetary Fund was created to facilitate the purchase of American goods abroad, by preventing temporary lapses in purchasing power as a result of foreign exchange shortages. It was "a very large international currency exchange and credit-granting institution that could be drawn upon relatively easily by any country that was temporarily short of any given foreign currency due to trade imbalances."[2]

The Bretton Woods system by itself, however, was insufficient to ensure the levels of output needed to keep production facilities running at full capacity, or to absorb excess investment funds. First the Marshall Plan, and then the permanent war economy of the Cold War, came to the rescue.

The Marshall Plan was devised in reaction to the impending economic slump predicted by the Council of Economic advisers in early 1947 and the failure of Western Europe "to recover from the war and take its place in the American scheme of things." Undersecretary of State for Economic Affairs Clayton declared that the central problem confronting the United States was the disposal of its "great surplus."[3]

The permanent war economy had an advantage over projects like the TVA that produced use-value for the civilian population: since it did not produce consumer goods, it didn't add to the undisposable surplus or compete with the output of private capital in consumer markets. In the apt words of Emanuel Goldstein: "Even when weapons of war are not actually destroyed, their manufacture is still a convenient way of expending labor power without producing anything that can be consumed." War is a way of "shattering to pieces, or pouring into the stratosphere, or sinking in the depths of the sea," excess output and capital.[4]

Besides facilitating the export of goods and capital, the Bretton Woods agencies play a central role in the discipline of recalcitrant regimes. There is a considerable body of radical literature on the Left on the use of debt as a political weapon to impose pro-corporate policies (e.g., the infamous "structural adjustment program") on Third World governments, analogous to the historic function of debt in keeping miners and sharecroppers in their place.[5] As David Korten argued,

> The very process of the borrowing that created the indebtedness that gave the World Bank and the IMF the power to dictate the policies of borrowing countries represented an egregious assault on the principles of democratic accountability. Loan agreements, whether with the World Bank, the IMF, other official lending institutions, or commercial banks, are routinely negotiated in secret between banking officials and a handful of government officials—who in many instances are themselves unelected and unaccountable to the people on whose behalf they are obligating the national treasury to foreign lenders. Even in democracies, the borrowing procedures generally bypass the normal appro-

1. Gabriel Kolko, *The Roots of American Foreign Policy: An Analysis of Power and Purpose* (Boston: Beacon Press, 1969), p. 72.

2. G. William Domhoff, *The Power Elite and the State: How Policy is Made in America* (New York: Aldine de Gruyter, 1990), p. 166.

3. Williams, *Tragedy of American Diplomacy*, p. 271.

4. George Orwell, *1984*. Signet Classics reprint (New York: Harcourt Brace Jovanovich, 1949, 1981), p. 157.

5. Cheryl Payer, *The Debt Trap: The International Monetary Fund and the Third World* (New York: Monthly Review Press, 1974); Walden Bello, "Structural Adjustment Programs: 'Success' for Whom?" in Jerry Mander and Edward Goldsmith, eds., *The Case Against the Global Economy* (San Francisco: Sierra Club Books, 1996); Bruce Franklin. "Debt Peonage: The Highest Form of Imperialism?" *Monthly Review* 33:10 (March 1982).

priation processes of democratically elected legislative bodies. Thus, government agencies are able to increase their own budgets without legislative approval, even though the legislative body will have to come up with the revenues to cover repayment. Foreign loans also enable governments to increase current expenditures without the need to raise current taxes . . . . The system creates a powerful incentive to over-borrow.[1]

Another way the Bretton Woods agencies punish disobedient regimes is by withholding aid. This powerful political weapon has been used at times to undermine elective democracies whose policies fell afoul of corporate interests, and to reward compliant dictatorships. For example, the World Bank refused to lend to the Goulart government in Brazil; but following the installation of a military dictatorship in 1964, the Bank's lending averaged $73 million a year for the rest of the decade, and reached almost a half-billion by the mid-70s. Chile, before and after Pinochet's coup, followed a similar pattern.[2] As Ambassador Korry warned, in the latter-day equivalent of a papal interdict, "Not a nut or bolt shall reach Chile under Allende. Once Allende comes to power we shall do all within our power to condemn Chile and all Chileans to utmost deprivation and poverty."[3]

Cheryl Payer's *The Debt Trap* is an excellent historical survey of the use of debt crises to force countries into standby arrangements, precipitate coups, or provoke military crackdowns. In addition to their use against Goulart and Allende, as mentioned above, she provides case studies of the Suharto coup in Indonesia and Marcos' declaration of martial law in the Philippines.

Among the many features of the so-called structural adjustment program, mentioned above, the policy of "privatization" (by selling state assets to "latter-day Reconstructionists," as Sean Corrigan says below) stands out. Joseph Stromberg described the process, as it has been used by the Iraq Provisional Authority, as "funny auctions, that amounted to new expropriations by domestic and foreign investors . . . ." Such auctions of state properties will "likely lead . . . to a massive alienation of resources into the hands of select foreign interests."[4]

The promotion of unaccountable, technocratic Third World governments, insulated from popular pressure and closely tied to international financial elites, has been a central goal of Bretton Woods agencies since World War II.

> From the 1950s onwards, a primary focus of Bank policy was "institution-building", most often . . . promoting the creation of autonomous agencies within governments that would be continual World Bank borrowers. Such agencies were intentionally established to be independent financially from their host governments, as well as minimally accountable politically—except, of course, to the Bank.[5]

The World Bank created the Economic Development Institute in 1956 to enculture Third World elites into the values of the Bretton Woods system. Its six-month course in "the theory and practice of development," by 1971 had produced some 1300 alumni, including prime ministers and ministers of planning and finance.[6]

> The creation of such patronage networks has been one of the World Bank's most important strategies for inserting itself in the political economies of Third World countries. Operating according to their own charters and rules (frequently drafted in response to

1. David Korten, *When Corporations Rule the World* (West Hartford, Conn.: Kumarian Press, 1995; San Francisco, Calif.: Berrett-Koehler, Publishers, Inc., 1995), p. 166.

2. Bruce Rich, "The Cuckoo in the Nest: Fifty Years of Political Meddling by the World Bank," *The Ecologist* (January/February 1994), p. 10.

3. Holly Sklar, "Overview," in Holly Sklar, ed., *Trilateralism: The Trilateral Commission and Elite Planning for World Management* (Boston: South End Press, 1980), pp. 28–29.

4. "Experimental Economics, Indeed" Ludwig von Mises Institute, January 6, 2004 <http://www.mises.org/fullstory.asp?control=1409>.

5. Rich, "Cuckoo in the Nest," p. 9.

6. *Ibid.*, pp. 9–10.

Bank suggestions), and staffed with rising technocrats sympathetic, even beholden, to the Bank, the agencies it has funded have served to create a steady, reliable source of what the Bank needs most—bankable loan proposals. They have also provided the Bank with critical power bases through which it has been able to transform national economies, indeed whole societies, without the bothersome procedures of democratic review and discussion of the alternatives.[1]

Despite the vast body of scholarly literature on the issues discussed in this passage, perhaps the most apt description of it was a pithy comment by a free market libertarian, Sean Corrigan:

Does he [Treasury Secretary O'Neill] not know that the whole IMF-US Treasury carpet-bagging strategy of full-spectrum dominance is based on promoting unproductive government-led indebtedness abroad, at increasingly usurious rates of interest, and then—either before or, more often these days, after, the point of default—bailing out the Western banks who have been the agents provocateurs of this financial Operation Overlord, with newly-minted dollars, to the detriment of the citizenry at home?

Is he not aware that, subsequent to the collapse, these latter-day Reconstructionists must be allowed to swoop and to buy controlling ownership stakes in resources and productive capital made ludicrously cheap by devaluation, or outright monetary collapse?

Does he not understand that he must simultaneously coerce the target nation into sweating its people to churn out export goods in order to service the newly refinanced debt . . . ?[2]

What American elites mean by "free markets" and "free trade" was ably stated by Thomas Friedman in one of his lapses into frankness:

For globalism to work, America can't be afraid to act like the almighty superpower it is . . . . The hidden hand of the market will never work without a hidden fist—McDonald's cannot flourish without McDonnell Douglas, the designer of the F-15. And the hidden fist that keeps the world safe for Silicon Valley's technologies is called the United States Army, Air Force, Navy and Marine Corps.[3]

The "system of world order" enforced by the U.S. since World War II, and so celebrated by Friedman, is nearly the reverse of the classical liberal notion of free trade. This new version of "free trade" is aptly characterized in a passage by Christopher Layne and Benjamin Schwarz:

The view that economic interdependence compels American global strategic engagement puts an ironic twist on liberal internationalist arguments about the virtues of free trade, which held that removing the state from international transactions would be an antidote to war and imperialism . . . .

. . . . Instead of subscribing to the classical liberal view that free trade leads to peace, the foreign policy community looks to American military power to impose harmony so that free trade can take place. Thus, U.S. security commitments are viewed as the indispensable precondition for economic interdependence.[4]

Oliver MacDonagh pointed out that the modern neoliberal conception, far from agreeing with Cobden's view of free trade, resembled the "Palmerstonian system" that the Cobdenites so despised. Cobden objected, among other things, to the "dispatch of a fleet 'to protect British interests' in Portugal," to the "loan-mongering and debt-collecting operations in which our Government engaged either as principal or agent," and generally, all

1. *Ibid.*, p. 10.
2. Sean Corrigan, "You Can't Say That!" August 6, 2002, *LewRockwell.Com* <http://www.lewrockwell.com/corrigan/corrigan13.html>.
3. Thomas Friedman, "What the World Needs Now," *New York Times*, March 28, 1999.
4. Christopher Layne and Benjamin Shwartz, "American Hegemony Without an Enemy," *Foreign Policy* (Fall 1993), pp. 12-3.

"intervention on behalf of British creditors overseas." Cobden favored the "natural" growth of free trade, as opposed to the forcible opening of markets. Genuine free traders opposed the confusion of "free trade" with "mere increases of commerce or with the forcible 'opening up' of markets."[1]

The neoliberal understanding of "How to Have Free Trade" was lampooned quite effectively by Joseph Stromberg:

> For many in the US political and foreign policy Establishment, the formula for having free trade would go something like this: 1) Find yourself a global superpower; 2) have this superpower knock together the heads of all opponents and skeptics until everyone is playing by the same rules; 3) refer to this new imperial order as "free trade;" 4) talk quite a bit about "democracy." This is the end of the story except for such possible corollaries as 1) never allow rival claimants to arise which might aspire to co-manage the system of "free trade"; 2) the global superpower rightfully in charge of world order must also control the world monetary system . . . .
>
> . . . . [W]hen, from 1932 on, the Democratic Party— with its traditional rhetoric about free trade in the older sense—took over the Republicans project of neo-mercantilism and economic empire, it was natural for them to carry it forward under the "free trade" slogan. They were not wedded to tariffs, which, in their view, got in the way of implementing Open Door Empire. Like an 18th-century Spanish Bourbon government, they stood for freer trade within an existing or projected mercantilist system. They would have agreed, as well, with Lord Palmerston, who said in 1841, "It is the business of Government to open and secure the roads of the merchant." . . . .
>
> Here, John A. Hobson . . . was directly in the line of real free-trade thought. Hobson wrote that businessmen ought to take their own risks in investing overseas. They had no right to call on their home governments to "open and secure" their markets.[2]

And by the way, it's doubtful that superpower competition with the Soviets had much to do with the role of the U.S. in shaping the postwar "system of world order," or in acting as "hegemonic power" in maintaining that system of order. Layne and Schwarz cited NSC-68 to the effect that the policy of "attempting to develop a healthy international community" was "a policy which we would probably pursue even if there were no Soviet threat."

> Underpinning U.S. world order strategy is the belief that America must maintain what is in essence a military protectorate in economically critical regions to ensure that America's vital trade and financial relations will not be disrupted by political upheaval. This kind of economically determined strategy articulated by the foreign policy elite ironically (perhaps unwittingly) embraces a quasi-Marxist or, more correctly, a Leninist interpretation of American foreign relations.[3]

The planners who designed the Bretton Woods system and the rest of the postwar framework of world order, apparently, paid little or no mind to the issue of Soviet Russia's role in the world. The record that appears, rather, in Shoup and Minter's heavily documented account, is full of references to the U.S. as a successor to Great Britain as guarantor of a global political and economic order, and to U.S. global hegemony as a war aim (even before the U.S. entered the war). As early as 1942, when Russia's very survival was doubtful, U.S. policy makers were referring to "domination after the war," "Pax Americana," and "world control." To quote G. William Domhoff, "the definition of the national interest that led to these interventions was conceived in the years 1940-42 by corporate planners in

1. Oliver MacDonough, "The Anti-Imperialism of Free Trade," *The Economic History Review* (Second Series) 14:3 (1962).

2. Joseph R. Stromberg, "Free Trade, Mercantilism and Empire," February 28, 2000 <http://www.antiwar.com/stromberg/s022800.html>.

3. Layne and Shwartz, "American Hegemony Without an Enemy," pp. 5, 12.

terms of what they saw as the needs of the American capitalist system, well before commu-nism was their primary concern."[1]

The central feature of the post-Axis world, as envisioned by American planners, was the replacement of a world order under British by one under American hegemony. If anything, the Cold War with the Soviet Union appears almost as an afterthought to American plan-ning. Far from being the cause of the U.S. role as guarantor of a system of world order, the USSR acted as a spoiler to preexisting U.S. plans for acting as sole global superpower.

Historically, any rival power which has refused to be incorporated into the Grand Area, or which has encouraged other countries (by "defection from within") to withdraw from it, has been viewed as an "aggressor." Quoting Domhoff once again,

> . . . . I believe that anticommunism became a key aspect of foreign policy only after the Soviet Union, China, and their Communist party allies became the challengers to the Grand Area conception of the national interest. In a certain sense . . . , they merely re-placed the fascists of Germany and Japan as the enemies of the international economic and political system regarded as essential by American leaders.[2]

Likewise, as Domhoff's last sentence in the above quote suggests, any country which has interfered with U.S. attempts to integrate the markets and resources of any region of the world into its international economic order has been viewed as a "threat." The Economic and Financial Group of the CFR/State Department postwar planning project, produced, on July 24, 1941, a document (E-B34), warning of the need for the United States to "defend the Grand Area," not only against external attack by Germany, but against "defection from within" . . . .[3] The centrality of this consideration is illustrated by the report of a 1955 study group of the Woodrow Wilson Center, which pointed to the threat of "a serious reduction in the potential resource base and market opportunities of the West owing to the subtraction of the communist areas and their economic transformation in ways that reduce their willingness and ability to complement the industrial economies of the West."[4]

One way of defending against "defection from within" is to ensure that Third World countries have the right kind of government. That can be done either by supporting authoritarian regimes, or what neoconservatives call "democracy." The key quality for na-tive elites, in either case, is an orientation toward what Thomas Barnett calls "connec-tivity." The chief danger presented by "outlaw regimes" lies in their being disconnected "from the globalizing world, from its rule sets, its norms . . . ."[5]

The neoconservative version of democracy is more or less what Chomsky means by "spectator democracy": a system in which the public engages in periodic legitimation ritu-als called "elections," choosing from a narrow range of candidates all representing the same elite. Having thus done its democratic duty, the public returns to bowling leagues and church socials, and other praiseworthy manifestations of "civil society," and leaves the me-chanics of policy to its technocratic betters—who immediately proceed to take orders from the World Bank. This form of democracy is equivalent to what neocons call "the Rule of Law," which entails a healthy dose of Weberian bureaucratic rationality. The stabil-ity and predictability associated with such "democracies" is, from the business standpoint, greatly preferable to the messiness of dictatorship or death squads.

---

1. Domhoff, *The Power Elite and the State*, p. 113.

2. *Ibid.*, p. 145.

3. *Ibid.*, pp. 160-1.

4. William Yandell Elliot, ed., *The Political Economy of American Foreign Policy* (Holt, Rinehart & Winston, 1955), p. 42.

5. Thomas Barnett, "The Pentagon's New Map," *Esquire* March 2003 <http://www.thomaspmbarnett.com/published/pentagonsnewmap.htm>.

American "pro-democratic" policy in the Third World, traditionally, has identified "democracy" with electoralism, and little else. In Central America, for example, a country is a "democracy" if its government "came to power through free and fair elections." But this policy ignores the vital dimension of popular participation, "including the free expression of opinions, day-to-day interaction between the government and the citizenry, the mobilization of interest groups," etc. The "underlying objective" of pro-democracy policies is "to maintain the basic order of what . . . are quite undemocratic societies." Democracy is a means of "relieving pressure for more radical change," but only through "limited, top-down forms of democratic change that [do] not risk upsetting the traditional structures of power with which the United States has been allied."[1] Democracy policy through the Duarte regime in El Salvador, more specifically, did not touch the power of the military or landed oligarchies.[2]

American elites prefer "democracy" whenever possible, but will resort to dictatorship in a pinch. The many, many cases in which the U.S. Assistance Program, the School of the Americas, the CIA, the World Bank and IMF, and others from the list of usual suspects have collaborated in just this expedient are recounted, in brutal detail, by William Blum in *Killing Hope*.[3]

Had anti-Sovietism or anti-communism been the U.S. government's main preoccupation, its policy would have been much different.

> While there were many varieties of capitalism consistent with the anti-Communist politics the United States . . . sought to advance, what was axiomatic in the American credo was that the form of capitalism it advocated for the world was to be integrated in such a way that *its* businessmen played an essential part in it. Time and again it was ready to sacrifice the most effective way of opposing Communism in order to advance its own national interests . . . .
>
> . . . . [I]t was its clash with nationalist elements, as diverse as they were, that revealed most about the U.S. global crusade, for had fear of Communism alone been the motivation of its behavior, the number of obstacles to its goals would have been immeasurably smaller.[4]

This postwar global system suffered a series of perceived challenges in the 1970s. The fall of Saigon, the increasing ability of the Soviet Union to act as spoiler against American intervention, the nonaligned movement, the New International Economic Order, etc., were taken as signs that the corporate world order was losing control.

Reagan's escalating intervention in Central America, the military buildup, and the partial resumption of Cold War were all responses to this perception. In addition, the collapse of the rival Soviet superpower, the Uruguay Round of GATT, NAFTA, and similar "free trade" [sic] agreements (particularly their draconian "intellectual property" provisions, symbiotically related to domestic counterparts like the Digital Millennium Copyright Act), together achieved a total end run against the perceived challenges of the 1970s. The neoliberal revolution of the '80s and '90s, coming as it did directly on the heels of diminished American power in the '70s, snatched total victory from the jaws of defeat; it ended all barriers to TNCs buying up entire economies, locked the west into monopoly control of modern technology, and created a "de facto world government" on behalf of global corporations. The '90s were the era of the G8, Davos, and Tom Friedman.

1. Thomas Carothers, "The Reagan Years: The 1980s," in Abraham F. Lowenthal, ed., *Exporting Democracy* (Baltimore: Johns Hopkins, 1991), pp. 117-8.
2. Ibid., pp. 96-7.
3. *Killing Hope: U.S. Military and CIA Interventions Since World War II* (Monroe, Maine: Common Courage Press, 1995).
4. Kolko, *Confronting the Third World*, pp. 117, 123.

The draconian "intellectual property" lockdown we've experienced since the 1980s is mind-boggling in its extent. Patents are being used on a global scale to lock transnational corporations into a permanent monopoly of productive technology. The first brick in the wall was the intellectual property regime under the Uruguay Round of GATT. It extended protection to trade secrets, thus absolving corporations of the traditional obligation to publish patented technologies.[1] Naturally, it abandons traditional requirements that required a holder to work the invention in a country in order to receive patent protection, with compulsory licensing required if an invention was not being worked, or being worked fully, and demand was instead being met by importation; or where the export market was not being supplied because of the patentee's refusal to grant licenses on reasonable terms.[2] But its single most totalitarian provision is probably the Trade-Related aspects of Intellectual Property rights (TRIPS) agreement. It has extended both the scope and duration (fifty years! of patents far beyond anything ever envisioned in original patent law.[3] Patents have also been expanded to biological processes.[4] The provisions for biotech apply patents to genetically-modified organisms, effectively pirating the work of generations of Third World breeders by isolating beneficial genes in traditional varieties and incorporating them in new GMOs.

Another key escalation of international "intellectual property" law was the World Intellectual Property Organization (WIPO) Copyright Treaty of 1996. The Digital Millennium Copyright Act (DMCA), was passed in 1998 pursuant to the U.S. government's obligations under that treaty. The DMCA is a fundamental departure from traditional copyright doctrines, like fair use and first sale. The legislation does not only punish strictly defined copyright violations after the fact. It prohibits the production of any hardware features which can circumvent digital locks, even when the purchaser is simply attempting what would have been considered fair use under the old regime. Jon Johanssen was prosecuted for distributing DeCSS, which circumvents the content scrambling system on DVDs.[5] The Sonny Bono Copyright Term Extension Act of 1998 extended copyright to seventy years after the death of the author. Similar legal mandates against DRM circumvention were introduced in the EU by the EU Copyright Directive in 2001 and the EU Directive on the Enforcement of Intellectual Property Rights in 2004.[6]

Still another radical innovation is the extension of patent law into areas traditionally covered by copyright. This is especially true of software. Copyright law only protects an actual work, not the general idea behind it. Patents, on the other hand, cover the idea itself. In the case of software, this means that rather than simply copyrighting the actual code, a software proprietor can charge competitors with patent violations for even attempting to write code to deal with the same problem. Software patents are a powerful weapon against open-source software, since it is a roadblock to open-source development of software to perform the same functions as existing proprietary software.[7]

Another prospective treaty in its planning stages in the WIPO is a Broadcasting Treaty which will give "cable networks, broadcasters, and, possibly, Internet portals, a fifty year monopoly over the material which they are transmitting."[8]

1. Raghavan, *Recolonization*, p. 122.
2. Raghavan, *Recolonizatinon*, pp. 120, 138
3. *Ibid.*, pp. 119-20.
4. Martin Khor Kok Peng, *The Uruguay Round and Third World Sovereignty* (Penang, Malaysia: Third World Network, 1990), p. 28.
5. Soderberg, *Hacking Capitalism*, p. 87.
6. *Ibid.*, p. 83.
7. *Ibid.*, pp. 83-84.
8. *Ibid.*, p. 84.

The developed world has pushed particularly hard to protect industries relying on or producing "generic technologies," and to restrict diffusion of "dual use" technologies. The U. S.–Japanese trade agreement on semi-conductors, for example, is a "cartel-like, 'managed trade' agreement."[1] The central motivation in the GATT intellectual property regime is to permanently lock in the collective monopoly of advanced technology by TNCs, and prevent independent competition from ever arising in the Third World. It would, as Martin Khor Kok Peng writes, "effectively prevent the diffusion of technology to the Third World, and would tremendously increase monopoly royalties of the TNCs whilst curbing the potential development of Third World technology." Only one percent of patents worldwide are owned in the Third World. Of patents granted in the 1970s by Third World countries, 84% were foreign-owned. But fewer than 5% of foreign-owned patents were actually used in production. As we have already seen, the purpose of owning a patent is not necessarily to use it, but to prevent anyone else from using it.[2]

The Western consumer corporations that tend to thrive in the global economy, as we already saw, are those in the sectors most heavily dependent on the international "intellectual property" regime: entertainment, software, and biotech.

Raghavan summed up nicely the effect on the Third World: "Given the vast outlays in R and D and investments, as well as the short life cycle of some of these products,"

> the leading Industrial Nations are trying to prevent emergence of competition by controlling . . . the flows of technology to others. The Uruguay round is being sought to be used to create export monopolies for the products of Industrial Nations, and block or slow down the rise of competitive rivals, particularly in the newly industrializing Third World countries. At the same time the technologies of senescent industries of the north are sought to be exported to the South under conditions of assured rentier income.[3]

1. Dieter Ernst, *Technology, Economic Security and Latecomer Industrialization*, in Raghavan, *Recolonization*, pp. 39-40.

2. Martin Khor Kok Peng, *The Uruguay Round and Third World Sovereignty*, pp. 29-30.

3. Raghavan, *Recolonization*, p. 96.

Part Two
Systemic Effects of Centralization and Excessive Organizational Size

4

Systemic Effects of State-Induced Economic Centralization and Large Organizational Size

In Part One, we examined the ways in which the state intervenes to promote economic centralization and organizational size beyond the levels that would prevail in a free market. In Part Two, we will examine the effects, on a systemic level, of such predominantly large organizational size.

At an individual level, the state's promotion of hierarchy and centralizing technology increases the average person's depencency on credentialed elites for meeting his basic needs, and transforms him into a client of "professional" bureaucracies. It erects barriers to comfortable subsistence: i.e., it exacts tolls on all attempts to transform personal labor and skill into use value.

Organizationally, there are two effects. The first is a simple crowding out: society is dominated by large organizations, which proliferate at the expense of small ones; thus, the predominant organizational size is far larger than considerations of efficiency would justify in a free market.

The second is even more insidious. Quantity, as the Marxists say, is transformed into quality. The internal culture of the large corporation and the large government agency is not limited to the actual large organization. It doesn't just crowd out the small, decentralized alternative, but coopts and contaminates it. It becomes a hegemonic norm, so that its culture of bureaucracy and hierarchy pervades all organizations within society; the cultural style of the large organization becomes the standard to be imitated by all other organizations—including small firms, nonprofits, and cooperatives.

The total effect was summed up quite well by Robert Jackall and Henry Levin. The "processes of centralization and bureaucratization," they write,

> have transformed our demographic patterns, refashioned our class structure, altered our communities, and shaped the very tone and tempo of our society. Unlike a century ago, we are today an urban people, largely propertyless (in the productive sense), and dependent on big organizations—in short, a society of employees coordinated by bureaucratic elites and experts of every sort. At the ideological level, of course, all of these developments—and the entire social fabric woven on this warp—come to assume a taken-for-granted status, an aura of inevitability; it becomes difficult for most people to conceive of other ways of arranging the world . . . .[1]

Our analysis relies heavily on Ivan Illich's concept of counter-productivity (also called "net social disutility," the "second threshold," or "second watershed"). These terms all refer

1. "The Prospects for Worker Cooperatives in the United States" in Robert Jackall and Henry M. Levin, eds., *Worker Cooperatives in America* (Berkeley, Los Angeles, London: University of California Press, 1984), pp. 277-278.

to the adoption of a technology past the point of negative net returns. Each major sector of the economy "necessarily effects the opposite of that for which it was structured."[1]

> When an enterprise grows beyond a certain point . . . , it frustrates the end for which it was originally designed, and then rapidly becomes a threat to society itself.[2]

Beyond a certain point medicine generates disease, transportation spending generates congestion and stagnation, and "education turns into the major generator of a disabling division of labor" in which basic subsistence becomes impossible without paying tolls to the credentialing gatekeepers.[3]

The first threshold of a technology results in net social benefit. Beyond a certain point, which Illich calls the second threshold, increasing reliance on technology results in net social costs and increased dependency and disempowerment to those relying on it. The technology or tool, rather than being a service to the individual, reduces him to an accessory to a machine or bureaucracy.

> There are two ranges in the growth of tools . . . . In the first, man as an individual can exercise authority on his own behalf and therefore assume responsibility. In the second, the machine takes over—first reducing the range of choice and motivation in both the operator and the client, and second imposing its own logic and demand on both.[4]
> . . . [T]he progress demonstrated in a previous achievement is used as a rationale for the exploitation of society as a whole in the service of a value which is determined and constantly revised by an element of society, by one of its self-certifying professional elites.[5]

In the case of medicine, the first watershed involved improvements like clean water, sanitation, rat control, and basic aseptic techniques and antibiotics in medicine—all of which together dramatically reduced mortality from infectious disease at comparatively low cost.[6] At the second watershed,

> costly treatment became increasingly the privilege of those individuals who through previous consumption of medical services had established a claim to more of it. Access to specialists, prestige hospitals, and life-machines goes preferentially to those people who live in large cities, where the cost of basic disease prevention . . . is already exceptionally high . . . .
> The second watershed was approached when the marginal utility of further professionalization declined, at least insofar as it can be expressed in terms of the physical well-being of the largest numbers of people.[7]

An infinitesimal fraction of the total patient population, the very richest of them, had access to the newest and most advanced procedures, while the costs of basic care were driven up for everyone else.

Although Illich failed to use it himself, the root concept of Pareto optimality is central to properly understanding the cause of counter-productivity:

> Given a set of alternative allocations and a set of individuals, a movement from one allocation to another that can make at least one individual better off, without making any other individual worse off, is called a Pareto improvement or **Pareto optimization**. An

1. "The Three Dimensions of Public Option," in *The Mirror of the Past: Lectures and Addresses, 1978-1990* (New York and London: Marion Boyars, 1992), p. 84.

2. Illich, *Tools for Conviviality* (New York, Evanston, San Francisco, London: Harper & Row, 1973), pp. xxii-xxiii.

3. Illich, *Disabling Professions* (New York and London: Marion Boyars, 1977), p. 28.

4. Illich, *Tools for Conviviality*, pp. 84-85.

5. *Ibid.*, p. 7.

6. *Ibid.*, pp. 1-2.

7. *Ibid.*, pp. 3, 6-7.

allocation of resources is **Pareto efficient** or **Pareto optimal** when no further Pareto improvements can be made.[1]

The distinction between Pareto optimal and non-optimal coincides with that Oppenheimer made between the economic and political means.[2] The dividing line, in either case, is privilege. Pareto non optimal outcomes, or net social disutility, can occur only when those who personally benefit from the introduction of new technologies beyond the second threshold, are able to force others to bear the disutilities. Were those who benefited from a technology forced to internalize all the costs, it would not be introduced beyond the point where overall disutilities equal overall utilities. Coercion, or use of the "political means," is the only way in which one person can impose disutility on another.

A technology will not normally be adopted by an unconstrained individual, of his own free choice, beyond the point at which the disutilities exceed the utilities. He will adopt a machine or tool for his own ends, when he fully internalizes the costs and benefits, only because he judges his individual utility to outweigh the disutility. The second watershed is the point beyond which the marginal utility of further adoption is zero when all costs and benefits are internalized. Without state-enforced privilege to shift the costs of a technology away from the primary beneficiary, the sum total of such free decisions by individuals will be net social utility. A technology or form of organization will be adopted beyond the point where the negative effects outweigh the positive, only when those making the decision to adopt it are able to collect the benefits while shifting the costs to others.

Illich mistakenly contrasted counterproductivity with the traditional economic concept of externality, treating them as "negative internalities" entailed *within* the act of consumption.[3] But counter-productivity is *very much* an externality. The presence of disutility in consumption is nothing new: all actions, all consumption, normally involve both utilities and disutilities intrinsic to the act of consumption. When the consumer internalizes all the costs and benefits, he makes a rational decision to stop consuming at the point where the disutilities of the marginal unit of consumption exceed its utilities. In the case of counter-productivity, the net social disutility occurs precisely because the *real* consumer's benefit is not leavened with any of the cost.

Illich's mistake lies in his confusion over who the actual consumer is. Counterproductivity is not a "negative internality," but the negative externality of *others'* subsidized consumption. The real "consumer" is the party who profits from the adoption of a technology beyond the second watershed—as opposed to the ostensible consumer, who may have no choice but to make physical use of the technology in his daily life. The real consumer is the party for whose sake the system exists; the ostensible consumer who is forced to adjust to the technology is simply a means to an end. In the case of all of the "modern institutions" Illich discusses, the actual consumer is the institutions themselves, not their conscript clienteles. In the case of the car culture, the primary consumer is the real estate industry and the big box stores, and the negative externality is suffered by the person whose feet, bicycle, etc., are rendered useless as a source of access to shopping and work. Rather than saying that "society" suffers a net cost or is enslaved to a new technology, it is more accurate to say that the non-privileged portion of society becomes enslaved to the privileged portion and pays increased costs for their benefit.

1. "Pareto efficiency," Wikipedia, the free encyclopedia (captured June 19, 2007) <http://en.wikipedia.org/wiki/Pareto_efficiency>.

2. Franz Oppenheimer, *The State: Its History and Development Viewed Sociologically.* 2nd revised edition, with Introduction by Paul Gottfried (Edison, N.J.: Transaction Publishers, 1999).

3. Illich, *In the Mirror of the Past: Lectures and Addresses, 1978-1990* (New York: M. Boyars, 1992), p. 84.

"John Gall," in his satirical book on organization theory, half-facetiously suggested the same thing in his discussion of the inversion of inputs:

> A giant program to conquer cancer is begun. At the end of five years, cancer has not been conquered, but one thousand research papers have been published. In addition, one million copies of a pamphlet entitled "You and the War Against Cancer" have been distributed. These publications will absolutely be regarded as Output rather than Input.[1]

Likewise, his distinction between "the stated purpose of the system" and "what the system really does" (the latter defined by the "blind, instinctive urge to *maintain itself*") This imperative is reflected in the dictum: "What's good for General Motors is good for the Country."[2] The purpose of the system has nothing to do with serving the needs of its alleged clients. The actual things that individual human beings want cannot be delivered by large, centralized systems.

> . . . . *most of the things we human beings desire are nonsystems things.* We want a fresh apple picked dead ripe off the tree. But this is precisely what a large system can never supply. No one is going to set up a large system in order to supply one person with a fresh apple picked right off the tree. The system has other goals and other people in mind.

Apparent exceptions, in which the system appears to be actually supplying what people want, turn out on closer examination to be cases in which the system has adjusted people's desires to what the system is prepared to supply:

> *Example* . . . . Doesn't the universal availability of cheap, fresh, enriched white bread represent a great systems achievement in terms of nourishing the American population?
> *Answer.* The short answer is that it is not bread. The French peasant eats fresher bread than we do, and it tastes better. The Egyptian fellah, one of the poorest farmers in the world, eats bread that is still hot from the oven at a price he can easily afford. Most of the cost of our bread is middleman costs . . . which would not be incurred if it were produced by local bakers rather than by a giant system.[3]

In short, the people running the system are the consumers, and it's working just fine for them. The objection that it doesn't work so well for us is as irrelevant as the fact that slavery wasn't such a hot deal for the people picking the cotton.

By failing to grasp the central role of the state coercion in promoting counterproductivity, Illich produced an analysis that we must stand on its head. Rather than simply eliminating the basic engine of counterproductivity—state intervention, which externalizes the costs of counterproductive technology on parties other than the direct beneficiaries—he advocated new *prohibitions* on the adoption of the technology.

> I will argue that we can no longer live and work effectively without public controls over tools and institutions that curtail and negate any person's right to the creative use of his or her energy. For this purpose we need procedures to ensure that controls over the tools of society are established and governed by political process rather than decisions by experts.

As if that were not sweeping enough, he called for "politically defined limits on all types of industrial growth . . . ."[4]

At times, Illich seemed on the edge of conceptual clarity. For example, he noted that "queues will sooner or later stop the operation of any system that produces needs faster than the corresponding commodity . . . ."[5] And elsewhere: "[I]nstitutions create needs

1. John Gall, *Systemantics: How Systems Work and Especially How They Fail* (New York: Pocket Books, 1975), p. 74.
2. *Ibid.*, pp. 88–89.
3. *Ibid.* pp. 62–64.
4. Illich, *Tools for Conviviality*, pp. 12, 17.
5. Illich, *Disabling Professions*, p. 30.

faster than they can create satisfaction, and in the process of trying to meet the needs they generate, they consume the Earth."[1] But he failed to take the next step: discerning the *reason* that needs are generated faster than they can be met. And it's a glaring omission, because his language could be a textbook description of the effects of subsidy: when the state provides a good at subsidized prices, demand at the artificially low price will grow faster than the state can meet it. A classic example is subsidized transportation which, as Illich observed, "created more distances than they helped to bridge; more time was used by the entire society for the sake of traffic than was 'saved.'"[2]

A. RADICAL MONOPOLY AND ITS EFFECTS ON THE INDIVIDUAL

The counterproductive adoption of technology results in what Illich calls a "radical monopoly":

> I speak about radical monopoly when one industrial production process exercises an exclusive control over the satisfaction of a pressing need, and excludes nonindustrial activities from competition . . . .
> Radical monopoly exists where a major tool rules out natural competence. Radical monopoly imposes compulsory consumption and thereby restricts personal autonomy. It constitutes a special kind of social control because it is enforced by means of the imposed consumption of a standard product that only large institutions can provide.[3]
> Radical monopoly is first established by a rearrangement of society for the benefit of those who have access to the larger quanta; then it is enforced by compelling all to consume the minimum quantum in which the output is currently produced . . . .[4]

This quote from Marilyn Frye, in "Oppression," is a good statement of how radical monopoly feels from the inside:

> The experience of oppressed people is that the living of one's life is confined and shaped by forces and barriers which are not accidental or occasional and hence avoidable, but are systematically related to each other in such a way as to catch one between and among them and restrict or penalize motion in any direction.[5]

In addition, the goods supplied by a radical monopoly can only be obtained at comparably high expense, requiring the sale of wage labor to pay for them, rather than direct use of one's own labor to supply one's own needs.

The effect of radical monopoly is that capital-, credential- and tech-intensive ways of doing things crowd out cheaper and more user-friendly, more libertarian and decentralist, technologies. The individual becomes increasingly dependent on credentialed professionals, and on unnecessarily complex and expensive gadgets, for all the needs of daily life. Closely related is Leopold Kohr's concept of "density commodities," consumption dictated by "the technological difficulties caused by the scale and density of modern life."[6]

---

1. Illich, *Deschooling Society* (1970), Chapter Seven (online edition at Reactor Core courtesy of Paul Knatz) <http://reactor-core.org/deschooling.html>.

2. Illich, *Tools for Conviviality*, pp. 7-8.

3. *Ibid*, pp. 52-53.

4. Illich, *Energy and Equity* (1973), Chapter Six (online edition courtesy of Ira Woodhead and Frank Keller) <http://www.cogsci.ed.ac.uk/~ira/illich/texts/energy_and_equity/energy_and_equity.html>.

5. Quoted in Charles Johnson, "Scratching By: How Government Creates Poverty as We Know It," *The Freeman: Ideas on Liberty* 57:10 (December 2007) <http://www.fee.org/publications/the-freeman/article.asp?aid=8204>.

6. Kohr, *The Overdeveloped Nations: The Diseconomies of Scale* (New York: Schocken Books, 1978, 1979), p. 39.

Subsidized fuel, freeways, and automobiles mean that "[a] city built around wheels becomes inappropriate for feet."[1] A subsidized and state-established educational bureaucracy leads to "the universal schoolhouse, hospital ward, or prison."[2]

In car culture-dominated cities like Los Angeles and Houston, to say that the environment has become "inappropriate for feet" is a considerable understatement. The mere fact of traveling on foot stands out as a cause for alarm, and can invite police harrassment.[3]

In healthcare, subsidies to the most costly and high-tech forms of medicine crowd out cheaper and decentralized alternatives, so that cheaper forms of treatment—even when perfectly adequate from the consumer's standpoint—become less and less available.

There are powerful institutional pressures for ever more radical monopoly. At the commanding heights of the centralized state and centralized corporate economy—so interlocked as to be barely distinguishable—problems are analyzed and solutions prescribed from the perspective of those who benefit from radical monopoly. So we see elites calling for "more of the same" as a cure for the existing problems of technology.

> It has become fashionable to say that where science and technology have created problems, it is only more scientific understanding and better technology that can carry us past them. The cure for bad management is more management.

Illich described it as an "attempt to solve a crisis by escalation."[4] It's what Einstein referred to as trying to solve problems "at the same level of thinking we were at when we created them." Or as E. F. Schumacher says of intellectuals, technocrats "always tend to try and cure a disease by intensifying its causes."[5] More recently, Butler Shaffer put it this way:

> In our carefully nourished innocence, we believe that institutions exist for the purposes they have taught us, namely, to provide us with goods and services, protection, security, and order. But in fact, institutions exist for no other purpose than their self-perpetuation, an objective requiring a continuing demand for their services . . . . If institutions are to sustain themselves and grow, they require an escalation of the problems that will cause us to turn to them for solutions.[6]

A classic local example is the standard approach, among the unholy alliance of traffic engineers, planners, and real estate developers, to "relieving congestion." Here in Northwest Arkansas, the new US 471 (locally called "the bypass") was built to the west of existing city limits to "relieve congestion" on the older highway passing through the major towns. But, as anyone might predict based on the lessons of Micro-Econ 101, when the marginal cost of a unit of consumption bears no relation to the marginal benefit, consumption increases long past the point of diminishing social returns. So the bypass, instead of relieving congestion in the city, quickly filled up with *new* congestion generated by the subdivisions and strip malls that mushroomed at every exit. And now the traffic engineers, the chambers of commerce, and the current highway money pimp representing the Third Congressional District, are all prescribing *yet another* new bypass a few miles further to the west, outside the new, expanded city limits, to "relieve congestion" on the *old* bypass.

1. Illich, *Disabling Professions*, p. 28.
2. Illich, *Tools for Conviviality*, p. xxiv.
3. Langdon Winner, *The Whale and the Reactor: A Search for Limits in an Age of High Technology* (Chicago and London: University of Chicago Press, 1986), p.9; Jane Jacobs, *The Death and Life of Great American Cities* (New York: Vintage Books, 1961, 1992), p. 46.
4. Illich, *Tools for Conviviality*, p. 9.
5. E. F. Schumacher, *Small is Beautiful: Economics as if People Mattered* (New York, Hagerstown, San Francisco, London: Harper & Row, Publishers, 1973), p. 38.
6. Butler Shaffer, *Calculated Chaos: Institutional Threats to Peace and Human Survival* (San Francisco: Alchemy Books, 1985), pp. 46-47.

Likewise, voters in the city of Fayetteville levied a one cent sales tax on themselves to pay for a major expansion of sewage processing facilities, in order to deal with the "increasing burden" of recent years. Of course, the "increasing burden" resulted mainly from the new subdivisions built by the local real estate industry. The "progressive," "smart growth" mayor announced that the "only alternatives" were to increase the sales tax, or to increase sewer rates by 30%. Of course, one "alternative" completely left off the table was increasing sewer hookup fees for new subdivisions enough to cover the costs they imposed on the system. But the mayor pushed it through by appealing to voters' greed: the 30% rate increase would apply only to townies, while the sales tax would shake down visitors who spent money in Fayetteville. So the new subdivisions get subsidized sewer service at the expense of working people paying increased sales tax on their groceries—but the voters think they pulled a fast one on those rubes from out of town. As the saying goes, it's a lot easier to con a greedy man. But do you really think the burden on Fayetteville's sewer system will *decrease* now?

It's not necessary to be overly cynical about the motivations of policymakers. They have no doubt absorbed the same conventional wisdom as the public, which is rooted in their institutional mindset. As Paul Goodman wrote,

> I have been trying to show that some of these historical conditions are not inevitable at all but are the working-out of willful policies that aggrandize certain styles and prohibit others. But of course *historically*, if almost everybody believes the conditions are inevitable, including the policy-makers who produce them, then they are inevitable. For to cope with emergencies does not mean, then, to support alternative conditions, but further to support and institutionalize the same conditions. Thus, if there are too many cars, we build new highways; if administration is too cumbersome, we build in new levels of administration . . . .[1]

Radical monopoly also tends to perpetuate itself because large organizations select for new technologies adapted to their own needs and amenable to control by large organizations. "The left hand of society seems to wither, not because technology is less capable of increasing the range of human action . . . , but because such use of technology does not increase the power of an elite which administers it."[2] As Kirkpatrick Sale put it:

> Political and economic systems select out of the range of current technology those artifacts that will best satisfy their particular needs, with very little regard to whether those artifacts are the most efficient or sophisticated in terms of pure technology . . . . The particular technological variation that becomes developed is always the one that goes to support the various keepers of power. Hence in an age of high authoritarianism and bureaucratic control in both governmental and corporate realms, the technology tends to reinforce those characteristics—ours is not an age of the assembly line and the nuclear plant by accident. Nonetheless, it must be recognized that there are always many other technological variations of roughly equal sophistication that are created but *not* developed, that lie ignored at the patent office or unfinished in the backyard because there are no special reasons for the dominant system to pick them up . . . .[3]

The main effect of radical monopoly on the individual is an increased cost of subsistence, owing to the barriers that mandatory credentialing erects against transforming one's labor directly into use-value (Illich's "convivial" production), and the increasing tolls levied by the licensing cartels and other gatekeeper groups.

> People have a native capacity for healing, consoling, moving, learning, building their houses, and burying their dead. Each of these capacities meets a need. The means for the

1. Paul Goodman. *Like a Conquered Province*, in *People or Personnel* and *Like a Conquered Province* (New York: Vintage Books, 1965, 1967, 1968), p. 337.
2. Ivan Illich, *Deschooling Society*, Chapter Four.
3. Kirkpatrick Sale, *Human Scale* (New York: Coward, McCann & Geoghegan, 1980), pp. 161–62.

satisfaction of these needs are abundant so long as they depend on what people can do for themselves, with only marginal dependence on commodities . . . .

These basic satisfactions become scarce when the social environment is transformed in such a manner that basic needs can no longer be met by abundant competence. The establishment of a radical monopoly happens when people give up their native ability to do what they can do for themselves and each other, in exchange for something "better" that can be done for them only by a major tool. Radical monopoly reflects the industrial institutionalization of values . . . . It introduces new classes of scarcity and a new device to classify people according to the level of their consumption. This redefinition raises the unit cost of valuable services, differentially rations privileges, restricts access to resources, and makes people dependent.[1]

The overall process is characterized by

the replacement of general competence and satisfying subsistence activities by the use and consumption of commodities; the monopoly of wage-labor over all kinds of work; redefinition of needs in terms of goods and services mass-produced according to expert design; finally, the arrangement of the environment . . . [to] favor production and consumption while they degrade or paralyze use-value oriented activities that satisfy needs directly.[2]

Some major causes of these phenomena include state-mandated credentialing to provide particular services, legally mandated product design standards (ostensibly for "safety") which outlaw more user-friendly alternative technologies, and subsidized education which unnecessarily inflates the minimal levels of education required for a particular job.

A good example is the building trades, where the entry barrier enjoyed by licensed contractors "reduces and cancels opportunities for the otherwise much more efficient self-builder." Construction codes prevent most self-building, and drive the cost of professionally built housing to excessive levels.[3] So-called "safety" regulations prohibit simpler and more user-friendly technologies that might be safely managed by an intelligent layman, instead mandating more complex technologies that can only be safely handled by licensed professionals. The system selects against simple technologies that can be safely controlled, and in favor of complex technologies that can only be safely wielded by a priesthood. For example, self-built housing in Massachusetts fell from around a third of all single-family houses to 11%, between 1945 and 1970. But by 1970 the feasible self-building technologies could have been far safer and more user-friendly than in 1940, had not the building trades actively suppressed them.[4]

Illich elaborated in greater detail on both the potentially feasible convivial building technologies, and the measures taken to suppress them, in the case of the "vast tracts of self-built *favelas*, *barriadas*, or *poblaciones*" surrounding major Latin American cities.

Components for new houses and utilities could be made very cheaply and designed for self-assembly. People could build more durable, more comfortable, and more sanitary dwellings, as well as learn about new materials and options . . . . [But the government instead] defines the professionally built house as the functional unit, and stamps the self-built house a shanty. The law establishes this definition by refusing a building permit to people who cannot submit a plan signed by an architect. People are deprived of the abil-

---

1. Illich, *Tools for Conviviality*, p. 54.
2. Illich, *Vernacular Values* (1980), "Part One: The Three Dimensions of Social Choice," online edition courtesy of The Preservation Institute <http://www.preservenet.com/theory/Illich/Vernacular.html>.
3. Illich, *Tools for Conviviality*, p. 39.
4. Illich, *Ibid.*, p. 40.

ity to invest their own time with the power to produce use-value, and are compelled to work for wages and to exchange their earnings for industrially defined rented space.[1]

Colin Ward's account of the Laindon and Pitsea communities in Essex parallels the Latin American favelas. Following a depression in agricultural land prices in the 1880s, some of the farmers in the area sold out to developers, who divided it up into cheap plots but did little in the way of development. In succeeding decades, many of those plots were sold (often for as little as 3 per 20-ft. frontage), and used not only for cheap bungalows but for every imaginable kind of self-built housing ("converted buses or railway coaches, with a range of army huts, beach huts and every kind of timber-framed shed, shack or shanty"), as working class people painstakingly hauled odds and ends of building material to the sites and gradually built up homes. During the WWII bombing of the East End of London, many working class families were bombed out or fled to plots in Pitsea and Laindon, increasing the area's population to 25,000 at the end of the war. Two thousand of the 8500 dwellings were conventionally built brick and tile, and another thousand lighter dwellings which met Housing Act standards. The rest included five thousand "chalets and shacks," and 500 "derelict" dwellings which were probably occupied. The range of self-built housing Ward describes is fascinating. For example, one wooden cabin is "a first world war army hut which grew." The street on which it sits was paved by the neighborhood, with residents pooling their own money to buy sand and cement. In general, the sort of people who resorted to such self-built expedients "would never have qualified as building society mortgagees," owing to their low incomes.

> What in fact those Pitsea-Laindon dwellers had was the ability to turn their labour into capital over time, just like the Latin American squatters. The poor in the third-world cities—with some obvious exceptions—have a freedom that the poor in the rich world have lost . . . .
>
> You might observe of course that some of the New Town and developing towns have—more than most local authorities have—provided sites and encouragement to self-build housing societies. But a self-build housing association has to provide a fully-finished product right from the start, otherwise no consent under the building regulations, no planning consent, no loan. No-one takes into account the growth and improvement and enlargement of the building over time, so that people can invest out of income and out of their own time, in the structure.[2]

Another example Ward provides is Walter Southgate, a former street corner agitator and founding member of the Labour Party. Southgate first built himself a carpenter's bench, and then constructed an 8-by-16 ft. two-room hut, finally hiring a Model-T to move it in sections to the concrete foundation he and his wife had laid on their 2.5 acre site. They taught themselves brickwork in the process of building the chimney. They bought the land after the First World War, began construction during the General Strike of 1926, and completed the home in 1928. During the almost thirty years the Southgates lived in their home, they "produced every kind of fruit and vegetable, kept poultry, rabbits and geese, grew a variety of trees including a coppice of 650 saplings and in fact made their holding more productive than any farmer could."

---

1. Illich, *Ibid.*, pp. 62–63. For a discussion of parallel developments in the UK, a good source is the article "Shanty Settlements in Britain" in *Radical Technology*. The self-built houses, not only far cheaper but often quite beautiful and elegantly designed, all predate the 1947 Planning Acts "which changed the nature of building permission and made it a much tighter financial game." Godfrey Boyle and Peter Harper, eds. *Radical Technology*. From the editors of *Undercurrents* (New York: Pantheon Books, 1976). p. 107.

2. Colin Ward, "The Do It Yourself New Town," *Talking Houses: Ten Lectures by Colin Ward* (London: Freedom Press, 1990), pp. 25-31.

Ward considered the Southgates typical of dozens of people he investigated who, "with no capital and no access to mortgage loans, had changed their lives for the better." For example Fred Nichols, who bought a 40-by-100 ft. plot of land for ten pounds in 1934, and—starting from a tent where his family was housed on weekends—"gradually accumulated tools, timber and glass which he brought to the site strapped to his back as he cycled down from London." He sank his own well in the garden. Elizabeth Granger and her husband, who bought two adjoining 20-by-150 ft. plots for ten pounds (borrowing a pound to pay the deposit); like Nichols, they stayed in a tent there on days off, gradually building a bungalow with second-hand bricks. They raised chickens, geese and goats.[1]

Ward quotes Anthony King, in *The Bungalow*, on conditions in the first half of the twentieth century:

> A combination of cheap land and transport, pre-fabricated materials, and the owner's labour and skills had given back to the ordinary people of the land, the opportunity denied to them for over two hundred years, an opportunity which, at the time, was still available to almost half of the world's non-industrialized populations: the freedom for a man to build his own house. It was a freedom that was to be very short-lived.[2]

This kind of non-standard construction, "that gives the underprivileged a place of their own," has been stamped out by urban planners of the very cultural type who profess the most concern about the needs of the poor.[3] Such legislation amounts to "a highly regressive form of indirect taxation."[4]

The situation is doubly unfortunate, because urban areas are full of vacant lots which would be ideal for such self-build projects, but which are seen as uneconomical by conventional developers. Two architects, at a time when the London borough of Newham claimed to be running out of building sites, surveyed the borough for sites of less than a half-acre, excluding sites which were claimed for local authority housing proposals, or lay in exclusively industrial areas. They found sufficient land to house three to five thousand people in single-family dwellings. The council, however, told them that "all these small and scattered plots were useless . . . . Given the local authority's procedures, it would be uneconomic to develop them."[5] They would, however, have been found quite "economic" by Southgate *et al.*

Amory Lovins describes one instance of a would-be radical monopoly by the suppliers of conventional energy:

> In 1975 . . . some U.S. officials were speculating that they might have to seek central regulation of domestic solar technologies, lest mass defection from utility grids damage utility cash flow and the state and municipal budgets dependent on utility tax revenues.[6]

Harry Boyte reports that utilities in Columbia, Missouri managed to secure the imposition of a monthly penalty on new buildings that used solar power.[7]

Subsidies to highways and urban sprawl also erect barriers to cheap subsistence. Under the old pattern of mixed-use development, when people lived within easy walking or bicycle distance of businesses and streetcar systems served compact population centers, the minimum requirements for locomotion could be met by the working poor at little or no

1. *Ibid*, pp. 70–71.
2. Ward, "The Do It Yourself New Town," pp. 90–91.
3. *Ibid.*, p. 30.
4. *Ibid.*, p. 72.
5. *Ibid.*, pp. 73–74.
6. *Soft Energy Paths: Toward a Durable Peace* (New York, Cambridge, Hagerstown, Philadelphia, San Francisco, London, Mexico City, Sao Paolo, Sydney: Harper & Row, Publishers, 1977), p. 154.
7. *The Backyard Revolution: Understanding the New Citizen Movement* (Philadelphia: Temple University Press, 1980), p. 143.

expense. As subsidies to transportation generate greater distances between the bedroom community and places of work and shopping, the car becomes an expensive necessity; feet and bicycle are rendered virtually useless, and the working poor are forced to earn the additional wages to own and maintain a car just to be *able* to work at all.

Approaches that attack the car culture at the level of individual voluntarism and feel-good activity will be of little benefit, so long as they fail to address the structural incentives resulting from the radical monopoly of the car culture. With such an approach, car-free living is an expensive consumer good that requires people to swim upstream against the incentives of the market, for purely psychic rewards.

> ... [G]iven the spatial arrangements of America created by the predominant use of the car, the car is the most sensible instrument to use to get around them. Since the car has created suburbs and scattered-site housing and low-density cities, the car is just about the only way to travel in and between them.[1]

State-subsidized (and state-mandated) education also has the effect of inflating the minimal level of education necessary for any particular job. As Leopold Kohr argued,

> And what does the worker gain by the higher education of which we are so proud? Almost nothing. With so many workers going to school, higher education, already intellectually sterile, seems even materially without added benefit, having become the competitive minimum requirement for almost any job . . . .
> As a result, what has actually risen under the impact of the enormously increased production of our time is not so much the standard of living as the level of subsistence.[2]

Or as Paul Goodman put it, "decent poverty is almost impossible."[3] Illich, similarly, observed that in New York those with less than twelve years' schooling were "treated like cripples":

> ... they tend to be unemployable, and are controlled by social workers who decide for them how to live. The radical monopoly of overefficient tools exacts from society the increasing and costly conditioning of clients. Ford produces cars that can be repaired only by trained mechanics. Agriculture departments turn out high-yield crops that can be used only with the assistance of farm managers who have survived an expensive school race . . . . The real cost of these doubtful benefits is hidden by unloading much of them on the schools that produce social control.[4]

Joe Bageant made quick work of the meritocratic ideology, with its treatment of "more education" as a panacea:

> Look at it this way: The empire needs only about 20-25% of its population at the very most to administrate and perpetuate itself—through lawyers, insurance managers, financial managers, college teachers, media managers, scientists, bureaucrats, managers of all types and many other professions and semi-professions.
> What happens to the rest? They are the production machinery of the empire and they are the consumers upon whom the empire depends to turn profits. If every one of them earned a college degree it would not change their status, but only drive down wages of the management class, who are essentially caterers to the corporate financial elites who govern most things simply by controlling the availability of money at all levels, top to bottom . . . .
> Clawing down basic things like an education in such a competitive, reptilian environment makes people hard. And that's what the empire wants, hardassed people in the degreed classes managing the dumbed down, over-fed proles whose mental activity consists of plugging their brains into their television sets so they can absorb the message to buy more . . . .

1. Sale, *Human Scale*, p. 255.
2. Kohr, *The Overdeveloped Nations*, pp. 27-28.
3. *Compulsory Miseducation*, in *Compulsory Miseducation* and *The Community of Scholars* (New York: Vintage books, 1964, 1966), p. 108.
4. Illich, *Tools for Conviviality*, p. 63.

. . . . Right now we are seeing the proletarianization of college graduates, as increasingly more of them are forced to take service and labor jobs. (Remember that it only takes a limited number to directly or indirectly manage the working masses, which these days includes workers like hospital technicians, and a thousand other occupations we have not traditionally thought of as working class.).[1]

The system also creates scarcity by erecting barriers to the transfer of skill, requiring proper credentials to pass them on.

A demand for scarce skills can be quickly filled even if there are only small numbers of people to demonstrate them; but such people must be easily available . . . .

Converging self-interests now conspire to stop a man from sharing his skill. The man who has the skill profits from its scarcity and not from its reproduction . . . . The public is indoctrinated to believe that skills are valuable and reliable only if they are the result of formal schooling. The job market depends on making skills scarce and on keeping them scarce, either by prosecuting their unauthorized use and transmission or by making things which can be operated and repaired only by those who have access to tools or information which are kept scarce.

Schools thus produce shortages of skilled persons.[2]

Credentialing, like "intellectual property," is a toll on the free transfer of information. For that matter, "intellectual property" can itself be used to make technology less convivial, as when planned obsolescence is reinforced by the use of patents to restrict or eliminate the supply of spare parts, or drive up their price (thus increasing the expense of repair compared to replacement).

The state in some cases taxes scarce resources to fund radical monopoly, and in others legally restricts the alternatives; the very act of subsidizing the favored version artificially increases its competitive advantage against alternatives operating on their own dime, so that they are either marginalized or completely driven out of the market.

These changes are reinforced by a shift in cultural attitudes, by which the individual comes to see services as naturally the product of institutions:

Many students . . . intuitively know what the schools do for them. They school them to confuse process and substance. Once these become blurred, a new logic is assumed: the more treatment there is, the better are the results . . . . The pupil is thereby "schooled" to confuse teaching with learning, grade advancement with education, a diploma with competence, and fluency with the ability to say something new. His imagination is "schooled" to accept service in place of value . . . . Health, learning, dignity, independence, and creative endeavor are defined as little more than the performance of the institutions which claim to serve these ends, and their improvement is made to depend on allocating more resources to the management of hospitals, schools, and other agencies in question . . . .

[Schools teach the student to] view doctoring oneself as irresponsible, learning on one's own as unreliable and community organization, when not paid for by those in authority, as a form of aggression or subversion . . . . [R]eliance on institutional treatment renders independent accomplishment suspect . . . .[3]

The hidden curriculum teaches all children that economically valuable knowledge is the result of professional teaching and that social entitlements depend on the rank achieved in a bureaucratic process.[4]

---

1. Joe Bageant, "The masses have become fat, lazy, and stupid," December 11, 2006 <http://www.joebageant.com/joe/2006/12/the_masses_have.html>.

2. Illich, *Deschooling Society*, Chapter Six.

3. *Ibid.*, Chapter One.

4. Illich, "After Deschooling, What?", in Alan Gartner, Colin Greer, Frank Riessman, eds., *After Deschooling, What?* (N.Y., Evanston, San Francisco, London: Harper & Row, 1973), p. 9.

B. Systemic Effects on Institutional Culture

As radical as these changes are at the individual level, even more significant from the standpoint of our study is the application of Illich's concept of radical monopoly in the institutional realm. In an economy where the size of the dominant institutions is determined by state intervention, even non-capitalist entities will be infected by the pathological institutional culture. The effects of radical monopoly on the institutional level were described in much more detail, albeit in different terminology, by Paul Goodman.

The large corporation and centralized government agency do not exist just as discrete individual organizations. Beyond a certain level of proliferation, such large organizations crystalize into an interlocking and mutually supporting system. Even the small and medium-sized firm, the cooperative, the non-profit, must function within an overall structure defined by large organizations. As Paul Goodman put it,

> A system destroys its competitors by pre-empting the means and channels, and then proves that it is the only conceivable mode of operating.[1]
> ... [T]he genius of our centralized bureaucracies has been, as they interlock, to form a mutually accrediting establishment of decision-makers, with common interests and a common style that nullify the diversity of pluralism.[2]

The interlocking network of giant organizations includes not only the oligopoly corporation and government agency, but as Goodman pointed out, the large institutional non-profit: large universities, think tanks, and charities like the Red Cross and United Way. The so-called "non-profit" sector underwent a managerial transformation at the same time as the corporation, remade in the image of the professional New Class around the turn of the twentieth century. The professionalized charitable foundation largely replaced not only the individual philanthropy of the rich, but more importantly the vibrant network of self-organized associations for mutual aid among the working class. In the years before World War I, as Guy Alchon recounted, the major foundations funded projects to enable social workers to survey the cities comprehensively and obtain statistics about working conditions, unemployment, and social ills. They funded educational, research, and public health institutions aimed at attacking the root causes of social problems.

> This reorientation encouraged and was in part the product of a general movement toward the professional administration of philanthropy . . . .
> This widely hailed movement toward professional administration was a reflection in the philanthropic sphere of the tendency of large organizations to come under the direction of professional managers.[3]

At any rate Goodman's typology of organizations clearly "cuts across the usual division of profit and non-profit," as shown by the prevalence in the latter of "status salaries and expense accounts ..., [and] excessive administration and overhead ...."[4] Indeed, Goodman defines the typical culture of the large organization largely in terms of those qualities, which stem largely from the nature of hierarchy, with work being divorced from responsibility, power or intrinsic motivation (as suggested by the contrasting spontaneous and frugal style of bottom-up organizations):

> To sum up: what swell the costs in enterprises carried on in the interlocking centralized systems of society, whether commercial, official, or non-profit institutional, are all the factors of organization, procedure, and motivation that are not directly determined to

1. Paul Goodman, *People or Personnel*, p. 70.
2. Goodman, *Like a Conquered Province*, p. 357.
3. Guy Alchon, *The Invisible Hand of Planning: Capitalism, Social Science, and the State in the 1920s* (Princeton, N.J.: Princeton University Press, 1985), p. 11.
4. Goodman, *People or Personnel*, pp. 114-15.

the function and the desire to perform it. Their patents and rents, fixed prices, union scales, featherbedding, fringe benefits, status salaries, expense accounts, proliferating administration, paper work, permanent overhead, public relations and promotions, waste of time and skill by departmentalizing task-roles, bureaucratic thinking that is penny-wise pound-foolish, inflexible procedure and tight scheduling that exaggerate congingencies and overtime.

But when enterprises can be carried on autonomously by professionals, artists, and workmen intrinsically committed to the job, there are economies all along the line. People make do on means. They spend on value, not convention. They flexibly improvise procedures as opportunity presents and they step in in emergencies. They do not watch the clock. The available skills of each person are put to use. They eschew status and in a pinch accept subsistence wages. Administration and overhead are *ad hoc*. The task is likely to be seen in its essence rather than abstractly.[1]

A good illustration of this latter principle occurred locally a few years ago. Voters in the neighboring town of Siloam Springs, Arkansas refused to increase the property tax millage to fund the allegedly urgent needs of the school system. Shortly afterward, the school administration announced that, instead of purchasing new computers as originally planned, they would simply upgrade existing computers, which would result in almost the same improvement in performance at a fraction of the cost. So it occurred to the school system to add $100 dollars worth of RAM per computer, as opposed to buying a new PC for close to $1000, only when the lack of "free" money forced them to think in such terms. As Milton Friedman said, people tend to be much more careful spending their own money than other people's money, and more careful spending money on themselves than on other people.

In the case of education,

> there is an immense increase in the number of administrators themselves. With centralization, standardization, and "efficiency," the ratio of teachers to students may fall. But the ratio of administrators in the population will rise perhaps *even more than proportionately* . . . .
>
> My guess is that the more "efficiently" the academic machine is run, the more expensive it is per unit of net value . . . .[2]

Goodman, taking the example of Columbia University, estimated the cost per capita if students hired instructors directly and paid market rents on the buildings, and found that actual tuition charges were "four times as much as is needed to directly pay the teachers and the rent! This seems to be an extraordinary mark-up for administration and overhead."[3]

At any rate, far from the system of "countervailing power" hypothesized by Galbraith, the large for-profit corporation, large government agency, and large non-profit in fact cluster together into coalitions: "the industrial-military complex, the alliance of promoters, contractors, and government in Urban Renewal; the alliance of universities, corporations, and government in research and development. This is the great domain of cost-plus."[4]

The inflexibility of bureaucratic rules is not just the result of especially bad mismanagement within the large organization. It is the inevitable result of large size as such. The inflexibility itself, far from being an example of irrationality, is the only rational way of dealing with the agency and information problems inherent in a large organization.

> . . . the centralized and bureaucratic style has important moral advantages. We have seen that pedantic due process and red tape often make for fairness. Workmen who are not

1. *Ibid.*, p. 113.
2. Goodman, *The Community of Scholars*, in *Compulsory Miseducation* and *The Community of Scholars*, p. 242.
3. *Ibid.*, pp. 241-242.
4. Goodman, *People or Personnel*, p. 115.

engaged in their own intrinsic enterprises . . . must protect themselves by union scales and even featherbedding.[1]

In other words, the "advantages" of "the central and bureaucratic style" are actually *cures* for the *disease* created by the large organization in the first place.

The great overhead cost of the large hierarchical organization, compared to the small self-managed organization, also tends to reinforce the earlier-mentioned tendency toward radical monopoly on an individual level: the increased cost of basic subsistence and the barriers to decent poverty. The transfer of activities from the informal economy and from small, self-managed organizations to the control of large bureaucracies is associated with, probably, an order of magnitude increase in overhead costs.

> We seem to put an inordinate expense into maintaining the structure. Everywhere one turns . . . there seems to be a markup of 300 and 400 per cent, to do anything or make anything . . . .
>
> Consider it simply this way: One visits a country where the per capita income is one quarter of the American, but, lo and behold, these unaffluent people do *not* seem four times "worse off" than we, or hardly worse off at all.[2]

It's important, again, to keep in mind that the importance of large organizations—corporations, government agencies, universities, think tanks, and charitable foundations—goes far beyond the total quantitative portion of economic activity they control. Together they constitute a system greater than the sum of its parts. They interlock organizationally, with some organizations providing inputs, support, or coordination to others. They also tend to share a common rotating pool of personnel, as observed by the power elite sociologists C. Wright Mills and G. William Domhoff, in effect becoming an interlocking directorate of large profit and nonprofit, corporate and government organizations.

William Dugger has observed that non-corporate institutions are increasingly "hollowed out," as they either become adjuncts of the corporate economy or take on a corporate internal culture.

> At the institutional level, the core value of corporate life—corporate success—corrodes away the values of noncorporate institutions. The main change here is an accelerated weakening of family and community and a growing distortion of church, state, and school. These noncorporate institutions used to provide a rough balance of different values and meanings. But with their corrosion, a social vacuum has opened up. The social space they once occupied is being filled by the corporation . . . . [The corporation] is becoming a total institution.[3]

Under the systemic pressures of the larger corporate environment, even institutions founded on avowedly anti-capitalist or decentralist principles take on the character of the capitalist corporation. Perhaps the best illustration of this is the general phenomenon of "demutualization," as consumer cooperatives on the Rochedale model (and producer cooperatives as well) are either outright sold to absentee investors, gradually introduce such absentee ownership on a creeping basis, or simply adopt the same conventional forms of hierarchy and "professionalism" as the large corporation. As an example of the last, the natural foods cooperative to which I belong has for the past several years had a mission statement hanging on the wall: surely a sign that our society is on the path to hell.

Given the starting foundations of expropriation of much of the general population's small-scale wealth in early modern times, and the ongoing money monopoly which makes mobilization of capital artificially difficult even from the property the working classes do possess, we wind up with a financial system geared to the needs of large-scale absentee in-

1. Goodman, *Ibid.*, p. 124.
2. Goodman, *Ibid.*, p. 120.
3. William M. Dugger. *Corporate Hegemony* (New York: Greenwood Press, 1989), p. xv.

vestors. From the standpoint of this system, the consumer- or worker-owned firm is an alien body. The pressures of such a financial system are one of the central forces for demutualization.

For cooperative enterprises with low enough levels of capital-intensiveness to be funded solely from the savings of the membership, this isn't a problem. The problem starts at the point at which such internally generated investment becomes insufficient.

Katherine Newman's study of work collectives found that they often succeeded in turning the collective into a source of livelihood and thereby reducing their need for outside income at a "regular" job.

> The only solution to the problem [to the time pressure of outside work] was to find some source of funding so that collective members could rely upon the collective organizations themselves for their financial needs . . . .
>
> For two of the collectives concerned this dilemma was easily solved. The members of the organization were able to invest their own capital in order to provide for operating expenses and minimally adequate salaries. Both of these were what we have termed "business collectives." The fact that they were able to generate enough cash from their own pockets to stay in business was significant. This was possible mainly because the business itself, if successful, would eventually pay its own way. The cash intake from either wholesale or retail trade provided enough to keep these two colletives going once they had a sufficient amount of start-up capital.
>
> The "bureaucratization" story ends here for these two collectives, for they never did develop any form of organization other than the egalitarian collectivity they began with . . . .
>
> For the other ten collectives, however, the process of bureaucratization began at the point where they had to solicit outside support . . . . The type of financial aid available to the collectives varied somewhat . . . . Business collectives could apply to banking institutions for loan funds, while service and information collectives could not . . . . Service and information collectives tended to solicit grants from community agencies . . . .
>
> In all cases, these collectives had to convince outsiders that they warranted financial assistance . . . . [I]n both situations the collectives were under pressure to persuade standard, highly bureaucratized institutions of their viability . . . .
>
> . . . . One of the most compelling reasons for their initial failure was the fact that the organizational format of the collectives was simply unacceptable to the tradition-bound agencies to which they had applied for help . . . . Banks were unwilling to take twenty cosigners on a loan form, and county supervisors were not about to turn over federal grant monies to organizations without formal hierarchies. After all, who was to be held responsible for the use of funds? In general, these collectives which sought external assistance discovered that they would have to play by the rules of these large bureaucratic agencies . . . . [1]

Leaving aside the pressures toward both bureaucratic decay of mutuals and their demutualization into capitalist enterprises altogether, the system also exerts strong structural pressures against the formation of cooperative enterprise in the first place. P.M. Lawrence, a polymath and heterodox economist who comments frequently on my blog, compared systems of political economy to ecosystems in their tendency to exclude alien elements:

> You'd better have a good think about just how ground cover plants work. They cooperate to make a network externality to dominate a local ecology to exclude other plants, usually by outshading them but sometimes like Eucalyptus by poisoning the earth against other root types (e.g. with leaf litter). The thing is, while the analogy applies to one sort of economy, that doesn't make the alternative on offer exempt from the same

---

1. Katherine Newman, "Incipient Bureaucracy: The Development of Hierarchies in Egalitarian Organizations," in Gerald M. Britan and Ronald Cohen, eds., *Hierarchy and Society: Anthropological Perspectives on Bureaucracy* (Philadelphia: Institute for the Study of Human Issues, Inc., 1980), pp. 148-50.

flaws. Almost *any* approach that worked as a system would inherently tend to exclude other approaches.[1]

This is quite relevant in the case of cooperatives, as islands in a corporate capitalist sea. Winfried Vogt, after discussing the superior internal efficiencies and reduced agency costs of "liberal firms" (i.e., non-hierarchical and largely self-managed), raised the question of why their superior efficiency didn't result in their taking over the economy.

> If [liberal firms] were more efficient than capitalist ones, shouldn't they have invaded capitalist economies and made their way in history? Apparently, efficient liberal firms should be able to enter a capitalist economy, receive higher profits than comparable capitalist firms and thereby take over the economy and transform it to a liberal one . . . .
>
> However, there is no proof that evolution always leads to optimal solutions . . . . If there are multiple solutions, like those of a capitalist and a liberal economy, real development may be path-dependent, i.e. the pattern which it follows may be determined by initial conditions and not by overall optimality conditions . . . .[2]

The comparative success rate of cooperatives is distorted by several factors. Historically, producer cooperatives have tended to be formed by employee buyouts of foundering enterprises, in order to prevent unemployment. And given the discriminatory nature of credit markets, cooperatives also tend to be formed in relatively non-capital-intensive fields with low entry barriers, like restaurants, bookstores, and groceries; and industries with low entry barriers tend for that reason to have high failure rates.[3]

> It is a commonplace of social analysis that every society promotes, both explicitly and tacitly, certain forms of productive organization by reinforcing the conditions for growth and survival of some types of enterprise while ignoring or even opposing other possibilities. Specifically, in the United States, the very forms of legal structure, access to capital, entrepreneurship, management, the remuneration of workers, and education all favor and reinforce the establishment and expansion of hierarchical corporate forms of enterprise and simultaneously create barriers to cooperative ones. Worker cooperatives are anomalies to these mainstream trends.[4]

One example of such structural forces is the capitalist credit market, which tend to be hostile because the cooperative form precludes lender representation on the board of directors, and seriously limits the use of firm equity as collateral. Dealing as equals with managers who can be replaced by their workers also presents cultural difficulties for conventional banks.[5]

In addition, the hegemony of interlocking large organizations affects civil society in another way: formerly autonomous institutions like the informal and household economies, that once defined the overall character of the system, are instead integrated into the corporate framework, serving its needs.

Large organizations also tend to turn the surrounding communities into sterile monocultures whose entire economy is geared toward serving them. Consider the growth

1. P.M. Lawrence comment on Kevin Carson, "Dan Swinney Article on the High Road," *Mutualist Blog*, August 5, 2005 <http://mutualist.blogspot.com/2005/08/dan-swinney-article-on-high-road.html>.

2. Winfried Vogt, "Capitalist Versus Liberal Firm and Economy: Outline of a theory," in Ugo Pagano and Robert Rowthorn, eds., *Democracy and Efficiency in the Economic Enterprise*. A study prepared for the World Institute for Development Economics Research (WIDER) of the United Nations University (London and New York: Routledge, 1994, 1996), p. 53.

3. Robert Jackall and Henry M. Levin, "Work in America and the Cooperative Movement" in Jackall and Levin, ed., *Worker Cooperatives in America*, p. 9.

4. *Ibid.*, p. 10.

5. *Ibid.*, p. 10

of Columbia University, reflected in Jane Jacobs' quote from a 1964 student newspaper editorial:

> In the original quadrangle of the campus . . . the University constituted a dead center of academic buildings, separated from the neighborhood and lacking its total life. But this center was small . . . . As Columbia has expanded, the central area has grown. The policy has been to build new structures as close to the old ones as possible. The justification has been the convenience of adjacent classrooms and offices. But with expansion . . . stores and services have begun to disappear . . . . The disappearance of variety saps the life of the community.

Jacobs commented:

> Just by being present and in the way, other enterprises thus conflict with the efficiency of the university—not, to be sure, the university as a body of students and faculty, but the university as an administrative enterprise.[1]

C. THE LARGE ORGANIZATION AND CONSCRIPT CLIENTELES

We already saw, in Chapter Three, the ways in which the state apparatus is tied organizationally to the corporate economy, either providing direct inputs (training technical personnel, funding R&D, and subsidizing other input costs) or acting as an executive committee for the corporate economy to prevent destructive competition from lowering the rate of profit.

One way in which they interlock functionally is by the common management of what Edward Friedenberg called "conscript (or reified) clienteles":

> A large proportion of the gross national product of every industrialized nation consists of activities which provide no satisfaction to, and may be intended to humiliate, coerce, or destroy, those who are most affected by them; and of public services in which the taxpayer pays to have something very expensive done to other persons who have no opportunity to reject the service. This process is a large-scale economic development which I call the *reification of clienteles* . . . .
>
> Although they are called "clients," members of conscript clienteles are not regarded as customers by the bureaucracies that service them, since they are not free to withdraw or withhold their custom or to look elsewhere for service. They are treated as raw material that the service organization needs to perform its social function and continue in existence.[2]
>
> . . . Taken together, a large proportion of the labor force [he estimated about a third] employed in modern society is engaged in processing people according to other people's regulations and instructions. They are not accountable to the people they operate on, and ignore or overlook any feedback they may receive from them . . . .[3]

Friedenberg limited his use of the term largely to bureaucracies directly funded with taxpayer money, and those whose "clients" were literally unable to refuse service. He drastically underestimated, in my opinion, the numerical significance of the institutions managing conscript clienteles. He neglected, for one thing, those in the private sector whose clients are nominally free to refuse their services, but likely won't because competition is legally suppressed: the legal and medical licensing cartels, for example. Likewise, firms that sell mainly to the procurement offices of large corporations, providing poorly-designed institutional goods that are essentially the same in any large institution, and whose quality or user-friendliness is entirely irrelevant because they're being produced mainly for corporate pro-

---

1. Jane Jacobs, *The Economy of Cities* (New York: Vintage Books, 1969, 1970), p. 101.
2. Edgar Z. Friedenberg, *The Disposal of Liberty and Other Industrial Wastes* (Garden City, New York: Anchor Books, 1976), pp. 1-2.
3. *Ibid.*, p. 18.

curement officers who won't use them, buying them on behalf of clients who have no choice but to use them (e.g. those awful toilet paper dispensers in the plastic housings, which seem painstakingly designed to perform their basic function of supplying toilet paper as poorly as possible, and to break your wrist in the process, while costing about twenty times as much as a simple spool from Lowe's). Likewise, again, goods under patent and copyright monopoly, or in which competition in basic design is limited by a regulatory cartel (e.g., the "broadcast flag" restrictions that have essentially frozen the market in DVD players), or when planned obsolescence is reinforced by intellectual property restrictions on the manufacture of cheap replacement parts.

One of Friedenberg's favorite specific cases is the so-called "public" schools, an industry that costs the taxpayer as much as the Vietnam War at its height:

> It does not take many hours of observation—or attendance—in a public school to learn, from the way the place is actually run, that the pupils are there for the sake of the school, not the other way round.[1]
>
> This, too, is money spent providing goods and services to people who have no voice in determining what those goods and services shall be or how they shall be administered; and who have no lawful power to withhold their custom by refusing to attend even if they and their parents feel that what the schools provide is distasteful or injurious. They are provided with textbooks that, unlike any other work, from the Bible to the sleaziest pornography, no man would buy for his personal satisfaction. They are, precisely, not "trade books"; rather, they are adopted for the compulsory use of hundreds of thousands of other people by committees, no member of which would have bought a single copy for his own library.[2]
>
> School children certainly fulfill the principal criterion for membership in a reified clientele: being there by compulsion. It is less immediately obvious that they serve as raw material to be processed for the purposes of others, since this processing has come to be defined by the society as preparing the pupil for advancement within it .... Whatever the needs of young people might have been, no public school system developed in response to them until an industrial society arose to demand the creation of holding pens from which a steady and carefully monitored supply of people trained to be punctual, literate, orderly and compliant and graded according to qualities determining employability from the employer's point of view could be released into the economy as needed.[3]

This raw material processing function is central from the standpoint of our systemic focus: "bureaucracies with conscript clienteles become clients of one another, mutually dependent for referral of cases."[4] Friedenberg called this an "institutional symbiosis,"

> by which institutions with reified clienteles become dependent on one another for referrals, so that a person who has been enrolled as a client of one such institution finds himself being batted from one to another like a Ping-pong ball.[5]

One example of such logrolling between managers of conscript clienteles is the way the "public" schools supply processed human raw material to corporate departments of "human resources":

> We do not have an open economy; even when jobs are scarce, the corporations and state dictate the possibilities of enterprise. General Electric swoops down on the high schools, or IBM on the colleges, and skims off the youth who have been pre-trained for them at public or private expense .... Even a department store requires a diploma for its sales-

1. *Ibid.*, p. 2.
2. *Ibid.*, p. 6.
3. *Ibid.*, p. 16.
4. *Ibid.*, p. 2.
5. *Ibid.*, p. 18.

people, not so much because of the skills they have learned as that it guarantees the right character: punctual and with a smooth record.[1]

The primary function of the schools, even over and above the technical training of skilled labor-power, is—as William Dugger put it—the installation of buttons and strings:

> The artisan . . . is a problem to the organization. She lacks buttons and strings. She must have them installed before she is fully operational. Installation . . . can be time-consuming and expensive; better that it be done at school and at public expense than at work and at corporate expense. So the process of contamination usually begins in school where youthful explorers who learn for the fun of it are turned into obedient students who learn for the external rewards of grades.[2]

One of the central lessons of the public school system is that the important tasks are those assigned by an authority figure behind a desk, and that the way to advance in life is to find out what that authority figure wants and do it, so as to get a gold star on one's paper or another line on one's resume. For the typical college student, Paul Goodman said, ever since first grade

> schooling has been the serious part of his life, and it has consisted of listening to some grown-up talking and of doing assigned lessons. The young man has almost never seriously assigned himself a task. Sometimes, as a child, he thought he was doing something earnest on his own, but the adults interrupted him and he became discouraged.[3]

That's the corollary of the central lesson: any task chosen for oneself is trivialized as a "hobby," to be subordinated to the serious business of carrying out tasks assigned by the organization.

The mutually supporting relationship between the state schools and corporate personnel departments is suggested by their common affinity for personality, intelligence, and aptitude testing. And as with so many other corporate practices—among them deskilling automated control technologies and quality control—the military arguably played a significant role in their early promotion and adoption. For example Binet's IQ test, originally developed in France, owed much of its rapid spread in the U.S. to the military's interest in the grading and sorting of human resources. As the managerial classes caught on to its "the potential use of the tests for achieving a more efficient and rationally ordered society," it and other classification systems were heavily promoted by the large foundations. After WWI, the Carnegie Corporation and Ford Foundation threw their weight behind the adaptation of intelligence testing to public education and the tracking of pupils into proper employment.[4]

If not for an entire population inculcated, at taxpayer expense, with the character traits desirable in a waged or salaried employee, the structural nature of employment would have developed in a far different manner in the first place. The massive subsidy involved in the public schools' reproduction of labor-power has influenced the nature of the employment relation. Without such tax-funded social engineering, corporate America would likely be confronted with an entire population of job applicants expressing such attitudes as "Pee in a cup? Screw you, Jack!" or "Carry a pager when I'm off the clock? You know any other funny jokes like that?" Samuel Bowles and Herbert Gintis remarked on the central importance of this social engineering function: "Since its inception in the United States,

1. Goodman, *Compulsory Miseducation*, pp. 20–21.
2. Dugger, *Corporate Hegemony*, p. 41.
3. Goodman, *Compulsory Miseducation*, p. 131.
4. Samuel Bowles and Herbert Gintis, *Schooling in Capitalist America: Educational Reform and the Contradictions of Economic Life* (New York: Basic Books, Publishers, Inc., 1976), pp. 196–197.

the public-school system has been seen as a method of disciplining children in the interest of producing a properly subordinate adult population."[1]

And much of the mandated credentialling, under meritocracy, is far in excess of the actual requirements of a particular task.

> To get a good job requires more degress [sic] than we needed. What used to take a high school degree now takes a college degree. What once took a college degree now requires an M.B.A. All these degrees do not really get them ahead; the extra degrees just keep them up with the competition—which is the essence of the speedup.[2]

In a society without taxpayer subsidized technical and engineering education, most of the deskilling and most of the shift of power over production into white collar hierarchies that occurred in the twentieth century would never have happened.

Ideally, as much of the educational industry's processed material will pass directly into corporate human resources departments. For the management of those not suited for corporate employment, however, we have the welfare state and the "helping professions" (which, Friedenberg suggested, "often have to catch their clients before they can administer help to them.").[3]

And, to repeat, this interlocking directorate of large organizations determines the basic character of the overall system in which even small organizations operate, and permeates their internal cultures.

From the perspective of these captive clienteles, to the extent that they are ostensible consumers of the "services" of large institutions, the large institutions often function as a package deal in which the "services" of one institution lock the captive client into dependence on the services of other allied institutions.

> Auto manufacturers, we have already observed, produce simultaneously both cars and the demand for cars. They also produce the demand for multilane highways, bridges, and oil-fields. The private car is the focus of a cluster of right-wing institutions. The high cost of each element is dictated by elaboration of the basic product, and to sell the basic product is to hook society on the entire package.[4]

Perhaps a better example is the way in which expensive radical monopolies over a wide range of consumer goods reinforce the control of the consumer credit industry, and the two together reinforce the average person's dependence on wage labor.

D. The New Middle Class and the Professional-Managerial Revolution

To a large extent the systemic effects of large organizations on society, both on individuals and on organizational culture, have been mediated by the professional and managerial classes: what C. Wright Mills called the New Middle Class.[5] Unlike the old middle class, whose livelihood was based on the ownership of small property and the control of independent business enterprise, the New Middle Class made its living as the salaried employees of large organizations.

> The organizational reason for the expansion of the white collar occupations is the rise of big business and big government, and the consequent trend of modern social structure,

1. *Ibid.*, p. 37.
2. Dugger, *Corporate Hegemony*, p. 70.
3. Friedenberg, p.
4. Illich, *Deschooling Society*, Chapter Four.
5. C. Wright Mills, *White Collar: The American Middle Classes* (New York: Oxford University Press, 1953), p. 63.

the steady growth of bureaucracy. In every branch of the economy, as firms merge and corporations become dominant, free entrepreneurs become employees, and the calculations of accountant, statistician, bookkeeper, and clerk in these corporations replace the free "movement of prices as the coordinating agent of the economic system. The rise of big and little bureaucracies and the elaborate specialization of the system as a whole create the need for many men and women to plan, co-ordinate, and administer new routines for others. In moving from smaller to larger and more elaborate units of economic activity, increased proportions of employees are drawn into co-ordinating and managing. Managerial and professional employees and office workers of various sorts . . . are needed; people to whom subordinates report, and who in turn report to superiors, are links in chains of power and obedience, co-ordinating and supervising other occupational experiences, functions, and skills.[1]

The coalescence of large organizations into a single interlocking system has been promoted by the development of a common professional culture, which is largely that of the professional and managerial classes. The corporate revolution of the post-Civil War period and the associated rise of the centralized regulatory state, followed by the large charitable and educational organizations dominating civil society, gave rise before the turn of the twentieth to the New Middle Class (or New Class) which administered the new large organizations. It has been described variously as a "managerial transformation" (C. Wright Mills[2]) and "corporate reconstruction of capitalism" (Martin Sklar[3]). The early twentieth century saw not only the hegemony of the large organization extended into civil society, but the transformation of large organizations of all kinds by a common managerialist culture.

The process was drastically accelerated and consolidated during what Murray Rothbard called the "War Collectivism" of WWI:

. . . the war mobilization introduced the technocratic approach and world view to a broad range of government, labor, and business leaders, thus creating a network of personal and professional associations that could become a planning constituency.[4]

As suggested by our discussion of conscript clienteles, the new large organizations dominating civil society sprang up largely to service the needs of the corporate economy: public schools and higher vocational-technical education to supply properly processed "human resources" to corporate employers; and the charitable non-profits and the welfare state to manage the surplus population not suited to the needs of the corporate economy, to keep their disorder and squalor from spilling over or reaching politically destabilizing levels, and to keep their purchasing power from collapsing to catastrophically low levels and worsening the problems of overproduction and overaccumulation.

The groups making up the managerial-professional New Middle Class that arose in the new state capitalist economy were the same ones described by Emmanuel Goldstein, in *The Book*, as the base of the totalitarian Ingsoc movement in Oceania:

The new aristocracy was made up for the most part of bureaucrats, scientists, technicians, trade-union organizers, publicity experts, sociologists, teachers, journalists, and professional politicians. These people, whose origins lay in the salaried middle class and the upper grades of the working class, had been shaped and brought together by the barren world of monopoly industry and centralized government.

Twentieth century politics was dominated by the ideology of the professional and managerial classes that sprang up to run the new large organizations. "Progressivism," es-

1. *Ibid.*, pp. 68-69.
2. C. Wright Mills, *The Power Elite* (Oxford and New York: Oxford University Press, 1956, 2000), p. 147
3. Martin Sklar, *The Corporate Reconstruction of American Capitalism, 1890-1916: The Market, the Law, and Politics* (Cambridge, New York and Melbourne: Cambridge University Press, 1988), p. 27
4. Guy Alchon, p. 22.

pecially—the direct ancestor of 20th century liberalism (also called corporate liberalism by New Left critics)—was the ideology of the New Middle Class. As Christopher Lasch put it, it was the ideology of the "intellectual caste," in a future which "belonged to the manager, the technician, the bureaucrat, the expert."[1]

Especially as exemplified by Ralph Easley's National Civic Federation,[2] and by Herbert Croly and his associates in the *New Republic* circle, Progressivism sought to organize and manage society as a whole by the same principles that governed the large organization. The classic expression of this ideology was Croly's "New Nationalist" manifesto, *The Promise of American Life*. Here's how Rakesh Khurana describes it:

> The disruption of the social order occasioned by the rise of the large corporation in America and the attempt to construct a new social order for this profoundly altered social context stand as defining events of the modern era. Industrialization, coupled with urbanization, increased mobility, and the absorption of local economies into what was increasingly a single national economy dominated by large corporations, had facilitated the deinstitutionalization of traditional authority structures. The reconstitution of the institutions of science, professions, and the university in the course of the late nineteenth century offered alternative structures and rationales that could serve as the foundation for a new social order that, its proponents argued, was more suited to changed social conditions . . . . Amid the sometimes violent clashes of interests attending the rise of the new industrial society, science, the professions, and the university presented themselves as disinterested communities possessing both expertise and commitment to the common good. The combination made these three institutions, built on rational principles and widely shared, even quasi-sacred values, appear to be ideal instruments to address pressing social needs. In each case, a vanguard of institutional entrepreneurs led efforts to define (or redefine) their institutions, frame societal problems, and mobilize constituencies in ways that won credibility for these institutions in the nascent social order.[3]

The New Class's general attitudes, its culture of managerialism, and its predilection for "professionalizing" all areas of life, were described well by Robert H. Wiebe:

> . . . . Most of [the Progressive reformers] lived and worked in the midst of modern society and, accepting its major thrust, drew both their inspiration and their programs from its peculiar traits. Where their predecessors would have destroyed many of urban-industrial America's outstanding characteristics, the new reformers wanted to adapt an existing order to their own ends. They prized their organizations not merely as reflections of an ideal but as sources of everyday strength, and generally they also accepted the organizations that were multiplying about them . . . . The heart of progressivism was the ambition of the new middle class to fulfill its destiny through bureaucratic means.[4]

The managerial revolution carried out by the New Class, in the large corporation, was in its essence an attempt to apply the engineer's approach (standardizing and rationalizing tools, processes, and systems) to the rationalization of the organization.[5] These Weberian/Taylorist ideas of scientific management and bureaucratic rationality, first applied in the large corporation, quickly spread to all large organizations. And from there, they extended to attempts at "social engineering" on the level of society as a whole.

---

1. Christopher Lasch, *The New Radicalism in America (1889-1963): The Intellectual as a Social Type* (New York: Vintage Books, 1965), p. 174

2. See James Weinstein, *The Corporate Ideal in the Liberal State, 1900-1918* (Boston: Beacon Press, 1968).

3. Rakesh Khurana, *From Higher Aims to Hired Hands: The Social Transformation of American Business Schools and the Unfulfilled Promise of Management as a Profession* (Princeton and Oxford: Princeton University Press, 2007), p. 87.

4. Robert H. Wiebe, *The Search for Order, 1877-1920* (New York: Hill and Wang, 1967), pp. 165-166, in Khurana, p. 38.

5. Khurana, p. 56.

The transfer of mechanical and industrial engineers' understanding of production processes to the management of organizations, and of the managers' understanding of organizations to society as a whole, is the subject of Yehouda Shenhav's excellent book *Manufacturing Rationality: The Engineering Foundations of the Managerial Revolution.*[1]

> Since the difference between the physical, social, and human realms was blurred by acts of translation, society itself was conceptualized and treated as a technical system. As such, society and organizations could, and should, be engineered as machines that are constantly being perfected. Hence, the management of organizations (and society at large) was seen to fall within the province of engineers. Social, cultural, and political issues . . . could be framed and analyzed as "systems" and "subsystems" to be solved by technical means.[2]

It's no coincidence, as Shenhav points out, that Progressivism was "also known as the golden age of professionalism . . ."[3]

> During this period, "only the professional administrator, the doctor, the social worker, the architect, the economist, could show the way." In turn, professional control became more elaborate. It involved measurement and prediction and the development of professional techniques for guiding events to predictable outcomes. The experts "devised rudimentary government budgets, introduced central, audited purchasing, and rationalized the structure of offices." This type of control was not only characteristic of professionals in large corporate systems. It characterized social movements, the management of schools, roads, towns, and political systems.[4]

Progressivism was primarily a movement of "middle-class, well-to-do intellectuals and professionals," which "provided legitimization for the roles of professionals in the public sphere."

> Progressive culture and big systems supported each other, slouching toward an economic coherence that would replace the ambiguity of the robber barons' capitalism through bureaucratization and rationalization.[5]

It's also probably no coincidence that there is so much overlap between the engineers' and managers' choice of value-terms as described by Shenhav, the values of corporate liberalism described by James Weinstein, and the objectives of Gabriel Kolko's "political capitalism" reflected in the Progressive regulatory agenda. In every case, the same language was used: "system," "standardization," "rationality," "efficiency," "predictability." For example, in the field of labor relations:

> Labor unrest and other political disagreements of the period were treated by mechanical engineers as simply a particular case of machine uncertainty to be dealt with in much the same manner as they had so successfully dealt with technical uncertainty. Whatever disrupted the smooth running of the organizational machine was viewed and constructed as a problem of uncertainty.[6]

That might be taken as a mission statement of corporate liberalism, and specifically of the National Civic Federation which Weinstein treated as the prototype of corporate liberalism.[7]

---

1. Yehouda Shenhav, *Manufacturing Rationality: The Engineering Foundations of the Managerial Revolution* (Oxford and New York: Oxford University Press, 1999).

2. *Ibid.*, p. 74

3. *Ibid.*, p. 35.

4. *Ibid.*, p. 35. Quoted material is from Robert Wiebe, *In Search of Order*.

5. *Ibid.*, p. 162.

6. *Ibid.*, p. 174.

7. The influence of engineering culture on Progressivism and corporate liberalism is also discussed, quite engagingly, in John M. Jordan, *Machine-Age Ideology: Social Engineering and American Liberalism, 1911-1939,* pp. 33-67.

The agenda of the Progressives (and of their British Fabian counterparts) initially had some anti-capitalist elements, and inclined in some cases toward a paternalistic model of state socialism. But they quickly became useful idiots for corporate capitalism, and their "socialism" was relegated to the same support role for the corporate economy that Bismarck's "Junker socialism" played in Germany. The New Class tended to expand its activities into areas of least resistance, which meant that its "progressive" inclinations were satisfied mainly in those areas where they tended to ameliorate the crisis tendencies and instabilities of corporate capitalism, and thereby to serve its long-term interests. And since genuine working class socialism wasn't all that friendly to a privileged position for the New Middle Class, whatever form of "socialism" the latter supported tended toward an extremely managerialist model that left the old centralized corporate economic structure in place with "progressive" white collar managers running it "for the workers' good."

As guild socialist G.D.H. Cole explained it,[1] genuine socialism (in the sense of direct worker control of production) wasn't a very hospitable environment for managerialism. So the Progressive and Fabian types chose, instead, a model where production continued to be organized by giant corporate organizations, with a "progressive" New Middle Class running things and redistributing part of those organizations' income in lieu of redistributing property itself.

But the practical limit on redistribution was on what the great capitalists themselves saw as necessary to overcome the tendencies toward overproduction, underconsumption, and political instability. So the New Class was able to promote "progressive" ends, for the most part, only to the extent that they were doing what the plutocracy needed for its own ends anyway. The New Class satiated its managerial instincts, instead, by regimenting the workers themselves (to "progressive" ends, of course, and for the workers' own good).

The distributist Hilaire Belloc believed Fabian collectivism to be less dedicated to state or workers' ownership as such than to the idea of control by "efficient" centralized organizations. It would be politically impossible to expropriate the large capitalists. Therefore, attempts to regulate industry to make labor more bearable, and to create a minimal welfare state, would lead instead to a system in which employers would provide a minimum level of comfort and economic security for their employees, in return for guaranteed profits. The working class would be reduced to a state of near-serfdom, with legally-defined status replacing the right of free contract, and the state fitting the individual into a lifetime niche in the industrial machine. Such a society would appeal to the authoritarian kind of socialist, whose chief values were efficiency and control.

> Let laws exist which make the proper housing, feeding, clothing, and recreation of the proletarian mass be incumbent upon the possessing class, and the observance of such rules be imposed, by inspection and punishment, upon those whom he pretends to benefit, and all that he really cares for will be achieved.[2]

Lest this be dismissed as overstatement, consider the actual proposals of the early Fabians (the British counterpart of America's Crolyite Progressives), and the extent to which they were taken up by the Margaret Sanger eugenicist wing of American liberalism. H.G. Wells favored a minimum safety net of aid to the children of the destitute, in return for making parents responsible to the state (on pain of rehabilitation in "celibate labor establishments"). Minimum wages and housing standards would be designed, not to guarantee subsistence to poor families, but to end the availability of cheap housing and low-paying jobs on which the destitute subsisted. The goal was to cease perpetuating "the educationally and technically unadaptable elements in the population" and to breed "a more effi-

---

1. G. D. H. Cole, "Socialism and the Welfare State," *Dissent* 1:4 (Autumn 1954), pp. 315-331.
2. Hilaire Belloc, *The Servile State* (Indianapolis: Liberty Classics, 1913, 1977), pp. 146-147.

cient race by increased state supervision"—in Wells's words to "convince these people that to bear children into such an unfavorable atmosphere is an extremely inconvenient and undesirable thing."

Sidney and Beatrice Webb wanted relief conditioned on "treatment and disciplinary supervision," with local government councils imposing compulsory vaccination and determining who was "mentally defective or an excessive drinker" (these things became a reality in the Swedish "social democracy"). Those too unemployable even for the "compulsory labor exchanges" would be required to attend training camps, with "their whole time mapped out in a continuous and properly varied program of physical and mental work, all of it being made of the utmost educational value." Those refusing to cooperate would be sent to "Reformatory Detention Colonies."[1]

To repeat, the central theme for the New Middle Class was managerialism. This meant, especially, minimizing conflict, and transcending class and ideological divisions through the application of disinterested expertise.

> For the new radicals, conflict itself, rather than injustice or inequality, was the evil to be eradicated. Accordingly, they proposed to reform society . . . by means of social engineering on the part of disinterested experts who could see the problem whole and who could see it essentially as a problem of resources . . . the proper application and conservation of which were the work of enlightened administration.[2]

In Yehouda Shenhav's account, this apolitical ethos goes back to engineers' self-perception, which subsequently influenced the managerial ideology in the large organization and the Progressive movement at the level of society as a whole: "American management theory was presented as a scientific technique administered for the good of society as a whole without relation to politics."[3] Taylor saw bureaucracy as "a solution to ideological cleavages, as an engineering remedy to the war between the classes."[4] At the level of state policy, the Progressives' professionalized approach to politics was "perceived to be objective and rational, above the give-and-take of political conflict." It reflected "a pragmatic culture in which conflicts were diffused and ideological differences resolved."[5] Both Progressives and industrial engineers "were horrified at the possibility of 'class warfare,'" and saw "efficiency" as a means to "social harmony, making each workman's interest the same as that of his employers."[6]

The problem was that this simplistic view of a "common interest" in increased productivity ignored the question (as we will see in our discussion of privilege in Chapter Eleven) of who appropriated the productivity gains, or how they were divided between labor and capital. It begged the question as to whether there was an objective basis in principle on how the surplus was to be divided. If, in fact, management took advantage of its power to appropriate the results of increased labor productivity, the "soldiering" that Taylor complained of was entirely rational.

The tendency in all aspects of life was to treat policy as a matter of expertise rather than politics: to remove as many questions as possible from the realm of public debate to the realm of administration by properly qualified authorities.

1. H. G. Wells, *Mankind in the Making* (New York: Scribner's Sons, 1909); Sidney and Beatrice Webb, *The Prevention of Destitution* (London, New York: Longmans, Green and Co., 1911); John P. McCarthy, *Hilaire Belloc, Edwardian Radical* (Indianapolis: Liberty Press, 1970).

2. Lasch, *The New Radicalism in America*, p. 162.

3. Shenhav, p. 5.

4. *Ibid.*, p. 8.

5. *Ibid.*, p. 35.

6. *Ibid.*, p. 96.

Social problems were thus allowed to enter the organizational realm only after being dressed in technical terms. Pragmatic solutions were to replace ideological controversies.[1]

As a *New Republic* editorial put it, "the business of politics has become too complex to be left to the pretentious misunderstandings of the benevolent amateur."[2] JFK, in similar terms, announced that

> most of the problems . . . that we now face are technical problems, are administrative problems. They are very sophisticated judgments, which do not lend themselves to the great sort of passionate movements which have stirred this country so often in the past. [They] deal with questions which are now beyond the comprehension of most men . . . .[3]

The "end of ideology" thesis, obviously, was very much an ideology of the New Middle Class, as is interest group pluralism.

Central to the Progressive mindset was the concept of "disinterestedness," by which the "professional" was a sort of philosopher-king qualified to decide all sorts of contentious issues on the basis of immaculate expertise, without any intrusion of ideology or sordid politics.[4] I quote at length from Christopher Lasch, in *The Revolt of the Elites*:

> The drive to clean up politics gained momentum in the progressive era . . . . [T]he progressives preached "efficiency," "good government," [the origin of the term "goo-goo"] "bipartisanship," and the "scientific management" of public affairs and declared war on "bossism." They attacked the seniority system in Congress, limited the powers of the Speaker of the House, replaced mayors with city managers, and delegated important governmental functions to appointive commissions staffed with trained administrators . . . . They took the position that government was a science, not an art. They forged links between government and the university so as to assure a steady supply of experts and expert knowledge. But they had little use for public debate. Most political questions were too complex, in their view, to be submitted to popular judgment . . . .
>
> Professionalism in politics meant professionalism in journalism. The connection between them was spelled out by Walter Lippmann . . . . [His books] provided a founding charter for modern journalism, the most elaborate rationale for a journalism guided by the new ideal of professional objectivity.[5]

This distrust of controversy and debate—of politics—is exemplified in the Gradgrindian vision of Horace Mann, the founder of education. Mann, as a precursor of the New Class, contrasted the realm of "fact," administered by qualified and disinterested experts, with that of opinion. In practice this meant he distrusted not only controversy and debate, but "pedagogically unmediated experience."

> Like many other educators, Mann wanted children to receive their impressions of the world from those who were professionally qualified to decide what was proper for them to know, instead of picking up impressions haphazardly from narratives (both written and oral) not expressly designed for children. Anyone who has spent much time with children knows that they acquire much of their understanding of the adult world by listening to what adults do not necessarily want them to hear—by eavesdropping, in effect, and just by keeping their eyes and ears open. Information acquired in this way . . . enables children to put themselves imaginatively in the place of adults instead of being treated simply as objects of adult solicitude and didacticism. It was precisely this imagina-

---

1. *Ibid.*, p. 189.
2. Quoted by John M. Jordan in *Machine Age Ideology: Social Engineering and American Liberalism, 1911-1939* (Chapel Hill, University of North Carolina Press, 1994), p. 76.
3. Christopher Lasch, *The Culture of Narcissism: American Life in an Age of Diminishing Expectations* (New York: Warner Books, 1979), p. 145.
4. Khurana, p. 69.
5. Christopher Lasch, *The Revolt of the Elites and the Betrayal of Democracy* (New York and London: W.W. Norton & Co., 1995), pp. 167-168.

tive experience of the adult world, however—this unsupervised play of young imagina-
tions—that Mann hoped to replace with formal instruction . . . .

The great weakness in Mann's educational philosophy was the assumption that
education takes place only in schools . . . . It simply did not occur to him that activities
like politics, war, and love—the staple themes of the [fiction] books he deplored—were
educative in their own right. He believed that partisan politics, in particular, was the bane
of American life.[1]

. . . Nothing of educational value . . . could issue from the clash of opinion, the
noise and heat of political and religious debate. Education could take place only in institutions deliberately contrived for that purpose, in which children were exposed exclusively to knowledge professional educators considered appropriate.[2]

This last belief is a foreshadowing of the general disapproval of politics which became
central to the later political agenda of the New Middle Class:

> . . . Mann wanted to keep politics out of the school . . . because he distrusted political
> activity as such . . . . It generated controversy— . . . in Mann's eyes, a waste of time and
> energy . . . . [Political history] could not be ignored entirely; otherwise children
> would gain only "such knowledge as they may pick up from angry political discussions,
> or from party newspapers." But instruction in the "nature of a republican government"
> was to be conducted so as to emphasize only "those articles in the creed of republican-
> ism, which are accepted by all, believed in by all, and which form the common basis of
> our political faith."[3]

The same principle is reflected in the cult of "objectivity" in the Lippmann model of
professional journalism. Lippmann's view of society and government in general was that
"[s]ubstantive questions could be safely left to experts, whose access to scientific knowledge immunized them against the emotional 'symbols' and 'stereotypes' that dominated
public debate." His influence on twentieth century journalism, in particular, was to destroy
the earlier function of newspapers in the nineteenth century as the center of democratic
debate. "Newspapers might have served as extensions of the town meeting. Instead they
embraced a misguided ideal of objectivity and defined their goal as the circulation of reliable information . . . ."[4] This was the basis of the modern model of "journalism as stenography," with reporters simply repeating what "he said" and "she said," and viewing any direct recourse by the reporter to the realm of fact as a violation of his neutrality (see Appendix on Journalism as Stenography).

In both journalism and education, this prejudice is fundamentally wrong-headed. As
Lasch so pointedly observed, controversy "is educative in its own right."[5]

> . . . Since the public no longer participates in debates on national issues, it has no
> reason to inform itself about civic affairs. It is the decay of public debate, not the school
> system (bad as it is), that makes the public ill informed, notwithstanding the wonders of
> the age of information. When debate becomes a lost art, information, even though it
> may be readily available, makes no impression.
>
> What democracy requires is vigorous public debate, not information. Of course, it
> needs information too, but the kind of information it needs can be generated only by
> debate. We do not know what we need to know until we ask the right questions, and we
> can identify the right questions only by subjecting our own ideas about the world to the
> test of public controversy. Information, usually seen as the precondition of debate, is bet-
> ter understood as its byproduct. When we get into arguments that focus and fully engage

1. *Ibid*, p. 151.
2. *Ibid*., p. 158.
3. *Ibid*., p. 153.
4. *Ibid*., p. 11.
5. *Ibid*., p. 10.

our attention, we become avid seekers of relevant information. Otherwise we take in information passively—if we take it in at all.[1]

    .... Lippmann had forgotten what he learned (or should have learned) from William James and John Dewey: that our search for reliable information is itself guided by the questions that arise during arguments about a given course of action. It is only by subjecting our preferences and projects to the test of debate that we come to understand what we know and what we still need to learn .... It is the act of articulating and defending our views that lifts them out of the category of "opinions" .... In short, we come to know our own minds only by explaining ourselves to others.[2]

The partisan press of the nineteenth century is the classic example of the emergence of truth through dialectic, or the adversarial process. "Their [Greeley's, Godkin's, etc.] papers were journals of opinion in which the reader expected to find a definite point of view, together with unrelenting criticism of opposing points of view."[3] Lippmann's view of the world, on the other hand, amounted to a "spectator theory of knowledge."[4]

The meritocratic ideal described earlier is a vitally important legitimizing ideology for the New Middle Class. Although meritocracy and "upward mobility" are now commonly equated to the American democratic ideology, the meritocratic ideal is in fact a complete departure from the earlier Jeffersonian democratic ideal. Lasch described very astutely the differences between them. Under the old, populist conception, what mattered was the class structure at any given time. The ideal was the wide diffusion of property ownership, with the great majority in the producing classes having a material base for economic independence. The advocates of the democratic ideal, as it existed through the first half of the nineteenth century,

> understood that extremes of wealth and poverty would be fatal to the democratic experiment .... Democratic habits, they thought—self-reliance, responsibility, initiative— were best acquired in the exercise of a trade or the management of a small holding of property. A "competence," as they called it, referred both to property itself and to the intelligence and enterprise required by its management. It stood to reason, therefore, that democracy worked best when democracy was distributed as widely as possible among the citizens.
>
>   The point can be stated more broadly: Democracy works best when men and women do things for themselves, with the help of their friends and neighbors, instead of depending on the state.[5]

The average member of the producing classes should rest secure in the knowledge that he would be able to support himself in the future, without depending on the whims of an employer. The purpose of education was to produce a well-rounded individual. It aimed at the wide diffusion of the general competence needed by ordinary people for managing their own affairs, on the assumption that they retained control over the main forces affecting their daily lives.

> When Lincoln argued that advocates of free labor "insisted on universal education," he did not mean that education served as a means of upward mobility. He meant that citizens of a free country were expected to work with their heads as well as their hand.... Advocates of free labor took the position ... that "heads and hands should cooperate as friends; and that [each] particular head, should direct and control that particular pair of hands.[6]

1. *Ibid.*, p. 163.
2. *Ibid.*, p. 170.
3. *Ibid.*, p. 163.
4. *Ibid.*, p. 171.
5. *Ibid.*, pp. 7–8.
6. *Ibid.*, p. 69.

The meritocratic philosophy, on the other hand, holds that the functions of "hands" and "head" should be exercised by distinct classes of people, with the "head" class managing the "hands" class. "Social mobility" means simply that members of the "hands" class should have the opportunity to advance into the "head" class if they're willing to go to school for twenty years and abase themselves before enough desk jockeys.

The meritocratic philosophy, as Lasch described it, called not for rough equality of condition, but only for social mobility (defined as the rate of "promotion of non-elites into the professional-managerial class").[1]

> The new managerial and professional elites . . . have a heavy investment in the notion of social mobility—the only kind of equality they understand. They would like to believe that Americans have always equated opportunity with upward mobility . . . . But a careful look at the historical record shows that the promise of American life came to be identified as social mobility only when more hopeful interpretations of opportunity had become to fade.[2]

Through most of the nineteenth century, Americans viewed as abnormal both a large class of propertyless wage laborers, and the ownership of economic enterprise by an absentee rentier class that lived entirely off the returns on accumulated wealth. Such things were associated with the decadence and corruption of the Old World.

Lincoln denounced as the "mud-sill theory" the idea "that nobody labors unless someone else, owning capital, somehow, by the use of that capital, induces him to it." He contrasted to this the small-r republican ideal, that "a large majority are neither *hirers* nor *hired*."

One of Lasch's most telling comments on meritocracy was that "[s]ocial mobility does not undermine the influence of elites; if anything, it helps to solidify their influence by supporting the illusion that it rests solely on merit."[3]

Meritocracy also has a powerful legitimizing effect on the concentration of wealth and power.

> High rates of mobility are by no means inconsistent with a system of stratification that concentrates power and privilege in a ruling elite. Indeed, the circulation of elites strengthens the principle of hierarchy, furnishing elites with fresh talent and legitimizing their ascendancy as a function of merit rather than of birth.[4]

It's hard to get much closer to a pure meritocracy than the Inner Party of *1984*.

We already saw, in the section of this chapter on radical monopoly, how credentialling and professionalization erect entry barriers or toll gates against comfortable subsistence. These things, more fundamentally, are the result of the New Middle Class's hegemony. Lasch, in his introduction to David Noble's *America by Design*, described Taylorism as an expropriation of the worker's skill, following directly on the expropriation of his land and capital in the so-called primitive accumulation process.

> The capitalist, having expropriated the worker's property, gradually expropriated his technical knowledge as well, asserting his own mastery over production . . . .
> The expropriation of the worker's technical knowledge had as a logical consequence the growth of modern management, in which technical knowledge came to be concentrated. As the scientific management movement split up production into its component procedures, reducing the worker to an appendage of the machine, a great expan-

1. *Ibid.*, p. 5.
2. *Ibid.*, p. 50.
3. *Ibid.*, p. 41.
4. *Ibid.*, p. 77.

sion of technical and supervisory personnel took place in order to oversee the productive process as a whole.[1]

The same was true of the "helping professions" that governed so many aspects of the worker's life outside of work. If Taylorism expropriated the worker's skill on the job, then the "helping professions" alienated him from his own common sense in the realms of consumption and family life.

> . . . [C]areerism tends to undermine democracy by divorcing knowledge from practical experience, devaluing the kind of knowledge that is gained from experience, and generating social conditions in which ordinary people are not expected to know anything at all.[2]
> . . . The conversion of popular traditions of self-reliance into esoteric knowledge administered by experts encourages a belief that ordinary competence in almost any field, even the art of self-government, lies beyond reach of the layman.[3]

The average person was transformed into a client of professional bureaucracies, as Barton Bledstein described it in *The Culture of Professionalism: The Middle Class and the Development of Higher Education in America*:

> The citizen became a client whose obligation was to trust the professional. Legitimate authority now resided in special places like the courtroom, the classroom, and the hospital; and it resided in special words shared only by experts.[4]

Lasch referred to "a consensus among 'helping professions' that the family could no longer provide for its own needs."

> Ellen Richards, founder of the modern profession of social work, argued: "In the social republic the child as a future citizen is an asset of the state, not the property of its parents. Hence its welfare is a direct concern of the state."[5]

Social workers lamented their inability to "instill . . . principles of mental health" in parents, and the "inaccessibility" of the home as a barrier to their promoting high levels of mental health in the new generation of assets of the state. Especially of concern, among all the recalcitrant attitudes displayed by atavistic parents, was a "warped view of authority" (for which refusal to cooperate cheerfully with the authorities was, of course, prima facie evidence).[6]

One aspect of the therapeutic culture, in particular, is seldom remarked on. Although the mental health approach to crime is often celebrated as an advance in humanity, it also erodes all the traditional due process protections of the accused under criminal law. After all, why would you need protection against someone who's acting for your own good? While the convicted felon is absolutely free and beholden to no one when his sentence is complete, the "patient" isn't free until his "helpers" decide he's cured. That's a theme developed by C.S. Lewis in both fiction (*That Hideous Strength*) and non-fiction (*The Abolition of Man*) venues, and by Anthony Burgess in *A Clockwork Orange*.

John McKnight described the ways the "helping professions" infantilize ordinary citizens:

1. Lasch, "Introduction," David F. Noble. *America By Design: Science, Technology, and the Rise of Corporate Capitalism* (New York: Alfred A. Knopf, 1977), pp. xi–xii.
2. Lasch, *The Revolt of the Elites*, p. 79.
3. Lasch, *The Culture of Narcissism*, p. 226.
4. Quoted in Harry Boyte, *The Backyard Revolution: Understanding the New Citizen Movement* (Philadelphia: Temple University Press, 1980).
5. Lasch, *The Culture of Narcissism*, pp. 268–269.
6. *Ibid.*, pp. 269–270.

When the capacity to define the problem becomes a professional prerogative, citizens no longer exist. The prerogative removes the citizen as problem definer, much less problem solver. It translates political functions into technical and technological problems.[1]

This is true not just of the "helping professions," although Lasch focused mainly on them. On a more general level, the dominance of so many areas of economic life by professional license cartels has had the same effect (as we saw earlier in this chapter—e.g. Ivan Illich's discussion of self-built housing) of alienating the individual from his own competency. To quote Lasch again, there was a general phenomenon of

> the erosion of self-reliance and ordinary competence by the growth of giant corporations and of the bureaucratic state that serves them. The corporations and the state now control so much of the necessary know-how that Durkheim's mage of society as the "nourishing mother" . . . more and more coincides with the citizen's everyday experience.[2]

The hegemony of the New Class over the large organization was matched by the escalating importance of professionalism even in services performed at an individual level. Through most of the nineteenth century, admissions to the legal and medical professions were governed by an informal and largely unregulated apprenticeship system. Formal training at legal or medical schools was not required; and the professions, collegially, had no formal licensing power.[3] "By the 1890s," however (Rakesh Khurana writes), "the traditional professions were strongly reasserting themselves, while many new ones were arising to stake their own claims to professional authority and privilege."[4]

From 1886 to 1909, the number of legal and medical schools in the United States mushroomed. After that time their numbers fell significantly; but this reflected the increasing power of the professions, collegially organized, to suppress professional schools that failed to meet either the professions' standards of quality or their institutional culture. The Carnegie Foundation's 1910 report on medical education, and its 1914 report on legal education, were the entering wedge of the licensing cartels' power to regulate professional education and to suppress competing models of practice.[5] From around this time on, for example, the medical field came to be regulated according to strictures set by formal associations of allopathic physicians, and competing medical schools reflecting other models of practice—chiropractic, osteopathic, naturopathic, etc.—were either shut down or severely restricted.

The phenomenon was manifested, locally, in the movement to "professionalize" municipal government. According to Samuel Hays, it was primarily the upper class that favored "reform" in local government.

> The drama of reform lay in the competition for supremacy between two systems of decision-making. One system based on ward representation . . . involved wide latitude for the expression of grass roots impulses . . . . [In] the other . . . decisions arose from expert analysis and flowed from fewer and smaller centers outward to the rest of society.[6]

1. John McKnight "Are the Helping Systems Doing More Harm Than Good?" (Speech to the 1976 retreat of the Brainerd, Minn. Community Planning Organization), quoted in Boyte pp. 173-174.
2. Lasch, *The Culture of Narcissism*, p. 386.
3. Khurana, p. 65.
4. *Ibid.*, p. 67.
5. *Ibid.*, p. 67.
6. Samuel P. Hays, "The Politics of Reform in Municipal Government in the Progressive Era," *Pacific Northwest Quarterly*, October 1964, pp. 152, 170. In Samuel Bowles and Herbert Gintis, *Schooling in Capitalist America: Educational Reform and the Contradictions of Economic Life* (New York: Basic Books, Inc., 1976),

The purpose of school administration "reform," as of the whole municipal "good government" agenda, was

> to centralize control of urban education in the hands of experts. They sought to replace ward elections for school boards by citywide at-large elections, to grant autonomy to the superintendent, and to develop a more specialized and well-defined hierarchical bureaucratic order for the improvement and control of the schools. Schools were to be as far removed as possible from the sordid world of politics.
>
> . . . Proponents of reform tended to be lawyers, businessmen—particularly the new and rising corporate elite—upper-class women's groups, school superintendents, university professors, and presidents . . . . Though locally based, these reformers used the National Education Association, the Chambers of Commerce, newspapers, professional journals, and businessmen's clubs to forge what one of their foremost historians termed a "nationwide interlocking directorate."[1]

The "reformers" were quite explicit on what they viewed as overrepresentation of blue collar workers on school boards, and the need to elevate the quality of their membership. For example, consider the 1911 Statement of the Voters' League of Pittsburgh:

> Employment as ordinary laborer and in the lowest class of mill worker would naturally lead to the conclusion that such men did not have sufficient education or business training to act as school directors . . . . Objection might also be made to small shopkeepers, clerks, workmen at many trades, who by lack of educational advantages and business training, could not, no matter how honest, be expected to administer properly the affairs of an educational system, requiring special knowledge, and where millions are spent each year.[2]

In the twenty-eight largest cities in the U.S. from 1893 to 1913, the average number of seats on central school boards was cut in half and most ward school boards were eliminated altogether. In the meantime, business and professional representation drastically increased on school boards, and clerical and wage workers fell below ten percent of the membership.[3]

A central preoccupation of the professional and managerial New Middle Class was social control. As one might guess, they served as shock troops of the revolution in "manufacturing consent" or engineering public consciousness: a series of related fields including state propaganda, psychological warfare, public relations, and mass advertising. St. Woodrow's crusade, for which the Creel Commission "manufactured consent," may or may not have been a war to make the world "safe for democracy." But the science of molding public consciousness, pioneered by the Creel Commission and such figures as Edward Bernays and Harold Lasswell, most definitely made democracy safe for the giant corporation and the authoritarian state.

> The new industry of advertising . . . appeared to the social engineers of an earlier time as an exciting exercise in mass education. Even before the First World War showed that it was possible to mobilize public opinion in overwhelming support of predetermined policies—showed, in the words of that super-salesman, George Creel, "how we advertised America"—the more advanced planners had glimpsed the implications of advertising for the science of social control. Ellen H. Richards, in her book *Euthenics: The Science of Controllable Environment*, argued that advertising could even take the place of religion as a stimulus to good behavior.[4]

As we already saw in Chapter One, mass advertising was developed as a way of internalizing the kind of mass consumption behavior that was necessary for economic stability in an economy of mass production and push distribution. More generally, the science of

---

1. Bowles and Gintis, p. 187.
2. Quoted in *Ibid.*, pp. 188–189.
3. *Ibid.*, p. 189
4. Lasch, *The New Radicalism in America*, p. 167.

"manufacturing consent" came about to serve the need of giant corporate and government organizations to shape the kind of public consciousness and behavior suited to their own needs.

As Noam Chomsky has observed in numerous places, the appearance of majority literacy, universal suffrage and formal democracy occurred at roughly the same time that society was falling under the control of large, centralized organizations that required insulation from instability and outside political interference by the masses. Galbraith's "technostructure," with its enormous capital investments, large-scale organization of technical manpower, and long planning horizons, is a good example: it needed a stable and predictable economic environment, and in particular a public conditioned to consume what it produced. The same is true of the corporate state's apparatus for global political and economic management: as described by Samuel Huntington in *The Crisis of Democracy*, the United States was able to function as "the hegemonic power in a system of world order" only because of a domestic structure of political authority in which the country, for the first twenty-five blessed years after WWII,

> was governed by the president acting with the support and cooperation of key individuals and groups in the Executive office, the federal bureaucracy, Congress, and the more important businesses, banks, law firms, foundations, and media, which constitute the private establishment.[1]

The dominance of such institutions over society can only survive when the public is conditioned to define political "moderation" and "centrism" in terms of the range of policy alternatives compatible with the existence of those institutions, and to limit "reform" to those measures which can be implemented by the elites running those institutions.

It's interesting to consider, just as a side note, how the New Middle Class has been treated by different segments of contemporary American politics. It has, to be sure, featured in the thought of such prominent conservatives as Peggy Noonan and David Brooks. The odd thing, though, is that their discussion of the "New Class" focuses entirely on the helping professions, journalism, and so forth: in other words, what I call the *soft* New Class. They neglect almost entirely the *hard* New Class of managers and engineers in the corporate economy. They ignore the obvious parallels between Taylorism and Fordism in industry, and the dominance of professionals in education and mental health. But as Lasch pointed out, all are manifestations of exactly the same phenomenom: the rise of monopoly capitalism, with the attendant bureaucratization of business, government, *and* society.[2]

> It is true that a professional elite of doctors, psychiatrists, social scientists, technicians, welfare workers, and civil servants now plays a leading part in the administration of the state and of the "knowledge industry." But the state and the knowledge industry overlap at so many points with the business corporation ..., and the new professionals share so many characteristics of the managers of industry, that the professional elite must be regarded not as an independent class but as a branch of modern management.[3]
> ... Both the growth of management and the proliferation of professions represent new forms of capitalist control, which first established themselves in the factory and then spread throughout society. The struggle against bureaucracy therefore requires a struggle against capitalism itself. Ordinary citizens cannot resist professional dominance without also asserting control over production and over the technical knowledge on which modern production rests.[4]

---

1. Samuel P. Huntington, Michael J. Crozier, Joji Watanuki. *The Crisis of Democracy*. Report on the Governability of Democracies to the Trilateral Commission: Triangle Paper 8 (New York: New York University Press, 1975), p. 92.

2. Lasch, *The Culture of Narcissism*, pp. 290n, 392.

3. *Ibid.*, p. 394.

4. *Ibid.*, p. 396.

POSTSCRIPT: CRISIS TENDENCIES

Through the twentieth century, ever larger portions of the operating costs of big business were externalized on the taxpayer. Indeed, it is quite plausible that a positive rate of profit, under twentieth century state capitalism, was possible only because the state underwrote so much of the cost of reproduction of constant and variable capital, and undertook "social investment" which increased the efficiency of labor and capital and consequently the rate of profit on capital.

And the demands of monopoly capital on the state, for more and subsidized inputs to maintain the illusion of profit, only increased through the century. As James O'Connor described it in *Fiscal Crisis of the State*,

> . . . the increases over time and increasingly is needed for profitable accumulation by monopoly capital. The general reason is that the increase in the social character of production (specialization, division of labor, interdependency, the growth of new social forms of capital such as education, etc.) either prohibits or renders unprofitable the private accumulation of constant and variable capital.[1] socialization of the costs of social investment and social consumption capital

O'Connor did not adequately deal with a primary reason for the fiscal crisis: the increasing role of the state in performing functions of capital reproduction removes an ever-growing segment of the economy from the market price system. But the effect of such economic irrationality has already been suggested by Ivan Illich:

> . . . . queues will sooner or later stop the operation of any system that produces needs faster than the corresponding commodity . . . .[2]
> . . . institutions create needs faster than they can create satisfaction, and in the process of trying to meet the needs they generate, they consume the Earth.[3]

The distortion of the price system, which in a free market ties quantity demanded to quantity supplied, leads to ever-increasing demands on state services. Normally price functions as a form of feedback, a homeostatic mechanism much like a thermostat. David Boyer, an Austrian economist,

> All human action has ends and means. All human action also has consequences determined objectively (and unsubjectively) by reality. The consequences for actions are the feedback mechanism by which a human being controls his behavior. No matter how complex the human social institution you end up with individuals acting and controlling their actions based on the feedback they get from reality based on the consequences of their actions.
> The natural market has the feedback mechanisms built-in . . . .
> . . . . All human action (in order to achieve it's intended aims) must be accompanied by objective feedback data . . . .
> . . . . [The state] uses it's "legitimate" monopoly on force to externalize (fancy word for avoiding consequences, or what I'm calling the feedback loop) the costs of its actions.[4]

(and those of the privileged ruling class elements that sit at the helm of the state, as well).

Putting a candle under a thermostat will result in an ice-cold house. When the consumption of some factor is subsidized by the state, the consumer is protected from the real cost of providing it, and unable to make a rational decision about how much to use. So the state capitalist sector tends to add factor inputs extensively, rather than intensively; that is, it uses the factors in larger amounts, rather than using existing amounts more efficiently. The

1. James O'Connor, *The Fiscal Crisis of the State* (New York: St. Martin's Press, 1973), p. 8.
2. Illich, *Disabling Professions*, p. 30.
3. Illich, *Deschooling Society*, p. 58.
4. David Boyer posts to Austrian School of Economics YahooGroup, January 29 and 30, 2004.

state capitalist system generates demands for new inputs from the state geometrically, while the state's ability to provide new inputs increases only arithmetically. The result is a process of snowballing irrationality, in which the state's interventions further destabilize the system, requiring yet further state intervention, until the system's requirements for stabilizing inputs finally exceed the state's resources. At that point, the state capitalist system reaches a breaking point.

As we argued earlier, policymaking elites tend to solve problems of input shortage or overburdened infrastructure by more of the same—i.e., even more subsidized inputs—thus pushing the system even more rapidly toward collapse.

> The total collapse of the industrial monopoly on production will be the result of synergy in the failure of multiple systems that fed its expansion. This expansion is maintained by the illusion that careful systems engineering can stabilize and harmonize present growth, while in fact it pushes all institutions simultaneously toward their second watershed.[1]

Two of the early lessons learned by Jay Forrester, the founder of Systems Dynamics, were that "the actions that people know they are taking, usually in the belief that the actions are a solution to difficulties, are often the cause of the problems being experienced," and "the very nature of the dynamic feed-back structure of a social system tends to mislead people into taking ineffective and even counterproductive action."[2]

Probably the best example of this phenomenon is the transportation system. State subsidies to highways, airports, and railroads, by distorting the cost feedback to users, destroy the link between the amount provided and the amount demanded. The result, among other things, is an interstate highway system that generates congestion faster than it can build or expand the system to accommodate congestion. The transportation system continues to expand out of control, and yet is bottlenecked at any given time.

The cost of repairing the most urgent deteriorating roadbeds and bridges is several times greater than the amount appropriated for that purpose. The problem is exacerbated by the fact that the price of asphalt used in road construction and repair is tied pretty closely to the price of petroleum. So the fiscal crisis of the state is further exacerbated in the face of subsidized demand. And there's no easy way out, because—as James Kunstler points out—the interstate highway system is extremely high-maintenance. A given stretch of highway is either well-maintained, or it quickly becomes unusable altogether as the constant pounding from heavy trucks compounds initial wear and tear, in just a few years reaching a level of pulverization at which the axles of those heavy trucks are likely to break.

> If the "level of service" . . . is not maintained at the highest degree, problems multiply and escalate quickly . . . . The system does not tolerate partial failure. The interstates are either in excellent condition, or they quickly fall apart . . . .
>
> I believe that the interstate highway system will reach a point of becoming unfixable and unmaintainable not far into the twenty-first century. The resources will not be there to keep up the level of service at the minimum necessary to prevent cascading failure. I think we will be shocked by how rapidly its deterioration proceeds.[3]

As the government finds its resources stretched, it will be able to fund smaller and smaller portions of the most urgent repair work, with highway after highway abandoned as unusable and the surviving portion of motor freight on those routes switching to lighter trucks on older, barely passable two-lane state highways.

1. Illich, *Tools for Conviviality*, p. 103.

2. Jay Forrester, "System Dynamics and the Lessons of 35 Years" (a chapter for *The Systemic Basis of Policy Making in the 1990s*, edited by Kenyon B. De Greene), April 29, 1991.

3. James Howard Kunstler, *The Long Emergency: Surviving the Converging Catastrophes of the Twenty-First Century* (New York: Atlantic Monthly Press, 2005), pp. 264-265.

Remember the discussion of that proposed "western bypass" the local growth machine has been pushing for in Northwest Arkansas? Despite the fact that even the new suburban developments under construction are likely to become unfinished ghost towns, and that gas prices next summer are likely to be even higher than $4/gallon, despite the fact that the current housing market collapse and the recent fuel crisis were the direct result of subsidies to highways and the car culture, the project is still on their Christmas list. When speculation began after Obama's election that a stimulus package might include a large amount of infrastructure spending, the immediate reaction of the Northwest Arkansas Council and its media sycophants was "Great! Now we can get our pork after all!" It is impossible, as Einstein said, to solve a problem with the same level of thinking that caused it.

In civil aviation, at least before the September 11 attacks, the result was planes stacked up six high over O'Hare airport. There is simply no way to solve these crises by building more highways or airports. The only solution is to fund transportation with cost-based user fees, so that the user perceives the true cost of providing the services he consumes. But this solution would entail the destruction of the existing centralized corporate economy.

The same law of excess consumption and shortages manifests itself in the case of energy. When the state subsidizes the consumption of resources like fossil fuels, business tends to add inputs extensively, instead of using existing inputs more intensively. Since the incentives for conservation and economy are artificially distorted, demand outstrips supply. But the energy problem is further complicated by finite reserves of fossil fuels. "Peak Oil," for example, has been a highly visible issue for the past couple of years—i.e., the contention that oil production has peaked or will do so shortly, and that a dwindling supply of ever more expensive petroleum will be available for allocation among competing global needs. It seems likely that such steep increases in fuel prices would lead, through market forces, to a radical decentralization of the economy and a resurgence of small-scale production for local markets—as Warren Johnson suggested during the shortages of the 1970s. It's interesting, by the way, that the only time in the twentieth century that absolute levels of fuel consumption actually declined was during the historic peak in oil prices of the early 1980s, which were high enough to encourage energy efficiency in earnest. Like every other kind of state intervention, subsidies to transportation and energy lead to ever greater irrationality, culminating in collapse.

Other centralized offshoots of the state capitalist system produce similar results. Corporate agribusiness, for example, requires several times as much synthetic pesticide application per acre to produce the same results as in 1950—partly because of insect resistance, and partly because pesticides kill not only insect pests but their natural enemies up the food chain. At the same time, giant monoculture plantations typical of the agribusiness system are especially prone to insects and blights which specialize in particular crops. The use of chemical fertilizers, at least the most common simple N-P-K varieties, strips the soil of trace elements—a phenomenon noted long ago by Max Gerson. The chemical fillers in these fertilizers, as they accumulate, alter the osmotic quality of the soil—or even render it toxic. Reliance on such fertilizers instead of traditional green manures and composts severely degrades the quality of the soil as a living biological system: for example, the depletion of mycorrhizae which function symbiotically with root systems to aid absorption of nutrients. The cumulative effect of all these practices is to push soil to the point of biological collapse. The hardpan clay on many agribusiness plantations is virtually sterile biologically, often with less than a single earthworm per cubic yard of soil. The result, as with chemical pesticides, is ever increasing inputs of fertilizer to produce diminishing results: to put the same thing in two slightly different ways, U.S. fertilizer use increased 900% from

1940 to 1975 while farm output increased only 90%, and in 1975 it took five times as much nitrogen fertilizer to produce the same crop as in 1947.[1]

Hazel Henderson, in "The Great Economic Transition," added another significant example of diminishing returns: the effect of decreasing supplies and increased extraction costs of natural resources (of which Peak Oil is only one example).[2] Henry George observed over a century ago that, as the increased productivity of labor from technological advancement led to increased social wealth, an ever larger share of the total social product would be eaten up by the sinkhole of rent to landlords, because increased personal income would simply increase the amount individuals would be prepared to bid for the virtually inelastic supply of land. Indeed, the overall measure of social wealth might be inflated by the rising rent component of GDP. Similarly, an ever-larger overall portion of the GDP today is taken up not only by land-rent, but by the rising costs of progressively depleted resources.

In general, the overall cost of infrastructure, support, and administration rise faster than the GDP, until further economic growth produces negative returns. According to Illich, " . . . beyond a certain level of per capita GNP, the cost of social control must rise faster than the total output and become the major institutional activity within an economy."[3] Or as Hazel Henderson described her "Entropy State": " . . . the stage when complexity and independence have reached the point where the transaction costs that re generated equal or exceed the society's productive capabilities."[4]

> Because advanced industrial societies develop such unmanageable complexity, they naturally generate a bewildering increase in unanticipated social costs: in human maladjustment, community disruption, and environmental depletion . . . . The cost of cleaning up the mess and caring for the human casualties . . . mounts ever higher. The proportion of the GNP that must be spent in mediating conflicts, controlling crime, protecting consumers and the environment, providing ever-more comprehensive bureaucratic coordination . . . begins to grow exponentially . . . .[5]

Externalities—costs of production and consumption not factored into prices—also increase, as "individuals, firms and institutions simply attempt to 'externalize' costs from their own balance sheets and push them onto each other or, around the system, onto the environment or future generations."[6] (and they continue to increase exponentially *because* they are not factored into prices).

Leopold Kohr made a similar observation about the tendency of secondary costs to increase geometrically with increased political and economic scale, as actual consumption goods increased only arithmetically:

> . . . [W]e must distinguish between two general categories of goods: *social* and *personal* consumer goods. Social consumer goods—goods consumed by society to maintain its political and economic apparatus . . . —may . . . be largely discounted . . . since they measure not personal but social standards. In addition, being largely paid for by taxes,

1. Kirkpatrick Sale, *Human Scale*, p. 229; Barry Commoner, "Energy and Rural People: Address before the National Conferance on Rural America, Washington, D.C., April 17, 1975," in *Center for the Biology of Natural Systems* (St. Louis: Washington University, 1975), p. 11, in L.S. Stavrianos, *The Promise of the Coming Dark Age* (San Francisco: W.H. Freeman and Company, 1976), p. 40.

2. Henderson, "The Great Economic Transition," in *Creating Alternative Futures: The End of Economics* (New York: G.P. Putnam's Sons, 1978), pp. 126-27.

3. Illich, *Energy and Equity*, p. 3.

4. Hazel Henderson, "The Entropy State," in *Creating Alternative Futures*, pp. 83-84.

5. *Ibid*, pp. 84-85

6. Henderson, "The Great Economic Transition," pp. 126-127; "Inflation: The Viewpoint from Beyond Economcs," in *Creating Alternative Futures*, p. 138.

they are so clearly identifiable as not the fruit but the cost of existence that there is no danger of having their greater availability confused with greater welfare. Nevertheless they are indirectly of significance since their seemingly geometric rise with every arithmetic increase in the size of a state is responsible for the declining proportion of increasing output that can be diverted into personal channels . . . . Their hallmark is that their production does not improve the status of the individuals producing them.

One telling example cited by Kohr: of the "much advertised" $25 billion increase in GNP, $18 billion (or 72%) of it was taken up by such support and administrative costs.[1] (See also his earlier cited example of the skyscraper, in which the portion of each floor taken up by ducts and elevator shafts increases with each added story, until increased height finally results in *reduced* total floor space).

Another useful idea that parallels Kohr's analysis is Kenneth Boulding's "non-proportional change" principle of structural development:

As any structure grows, the proportions of the parts and of its significant variables *cannot* remain constant . . . . This is because a uniform increase in the linear dimensions of a structure will increase all its areas as the square, and its volume as the cube, of the increase in the linear dimension . . . .[2]

It follows, as a corollary, that

the size of the structure itself is limited by its ultimate inability to compensate for the non-proportional changes. This is the basic principle which underlies the "law of eventually diminishing returns to scale" familiar to economists. Thus as institutions grow they have to maintain larger and larger specialized administrative structures in order to overcome the increasing difficulties of communication between the "edges" or outside surfaces of the organization . . . and the central executive. Eventually the cost of these administrative structures begins to outweigh any of the other possible benefits of large scale, such as increasing specialization of the more directly productive parts of the organization, and these structural limitations bring the growth of the organization to an end. One can visualize, for instance, a university of a hundred thousand students in which the entire organization is made up of administrators, leaving no room at all for faculty.

. . . . [T]he critical problem of large-scale organization is that of the communications system . . . . This being a "linear" function tends to become inadequate relative to the "surface" functions of interaction as the organization grows.[3]

In every case, the basic rule is that, whenever the economy deviates from market price as an allocating principle, it deviates to that extent from rationality. In a long series of indices, the state capitalist economy uses resources or factors much more intensively than would be possible if large corporations were paying the cost themselves. The economy is much more transportation-intensive than a free market could support, as we have seen. It is likewise more capital-intensive, and more intensively dependent on scientific-technical labor, than would be economical if all costs were borne by the beneficiaries. The economy is far more centralized, capital intensive, and high-tech than it would otherwise be. Had large corporate firms paid for these inputs themselves, they would have reached the point of zero marginal utility from additional inputs much earlier.

At the same time as the demand for state economic inputs increases, state capitalism also produces all kinds of social pathologies that require "social expenditures" to contain or correct. By subsidizing the most capital-intensive forms of production, it promotes unemployment and the growth of an underclass. But just as important, it undermines the very social structures—family, church, neighborhood, etc.—on which it depends for the reproduction of a healthy social order.

1. Kohr, *The Overdeveloped* Nations, pp. 36–37.
2. Kenneth Boulding, *Beyond Economics* (Ann Arbor: University of Michigan Press, 1968), p. 75.
3. *Ibid.*, pp. 76–77.

As mentioned above in the main body of the chapter, the corporate economy integrates formerly autonomous spheres of civil society, like the informal and household economies, into itself. But by atomizing them, it undermines the conditions of its own existence. Under state capitalism, the state is driven into ever new realms in order to stabilize the corporate system. State intervention in the process of reproducing human capital (i.e., public education and tax-supported vocational-technical education), and state aid to forms of economic centralization that atomize society, result in the destruction of civil society and the replacement by direct state intervention of activities previously carried out by autonomous institutions. The destruction of civil society, in turn, leads to still further state intervention to deal with the resulting social pathologies.

Lewis Mumford, for example, described the dependence of the "megamachine" on the socializing functions of precapitalist institutions:

> [A]n . . . important factor in protecting the power system from internal assault was the presence of many surviving historic institutions whose customs and folkways and active beliefs supplied an essential structure of values . . . .
>
> With the erosion of this traditional heritage, megatechnics lost a social ingredient essential for its full working efficiency: self-respect, loyalty to a common moral code, a readiness to sacrifice immediate rewards to a more desirable future. As long as this basic morality . . . remained "second nature" in the community, the power complex had a stability and continuity that it no longer possesses. This means . . . that in order to remain in effective operation, the dominant minority must, as in Soviet Russia and China, resort to the same system of ruthless coercion their predecessors established back in the Fourth Millennium B.C. Otherwise, in order to ensure obedience and subdue counter-aggression, they must use more "scientific" modes of control . . . .[1]

Some useful commentary on this latter phenomenon includes C.S. Lewis (*The Abolition of Man*), and Huxley's *Brave New World*. Neoconservatism is an alternative approach to the same general problem, attempting to put new wine in old bottles by artificially reengineering "traditional social mores" through the state.

Immanuel Wallerstein, likewise, pointed to the role of the non-monetized informal and household sectors of the economy in reproducing human labor power. If those precapitalist institutions disappeared and their functions could only be procured in the cash economy, the level of subsistence income would rise considerably. A good example is the predominance of the nuclear family with two wage-earners, in which the services previously supplied by a full-time mother, or by a grandmother or aunt, must be hired from a babysitter or daycare center.

The state capitalist system thus demands ever greater state inputs in the form of subsidies to accumulation, and ever greater intervention to contain the ill social effects of state capitalism. Coupled with political pressures to restrain the growth of taxation, these demands lead to (as O'Connor's title indicates) a "fiscal crisis of the state," or "a tendency for state expenditures to increase faster than the means of financing them."[2] The "'structural gap' . . . between state expenditures and state revenue" is met by chronic deficit finance, with the inevitable inflationary results. Under state capitalism "crisis tendencies shift, of course, from the economic into the administrative system . . ." This displaced crisis is expressed through "inflation and a permanent crisis in public finance."[3]

The problem is intensified by the disproportionate financing of State expenditures by taxes on the competitive sector (including the taxes on the monopoly capital sector which

---

1. Lewis Mumford, *The Myth of the Machine: The Pentagon of Power* (New York: Harcourt Brace Jovanovich, Inc., 1964, 1974), pp. 351-352.

2. O'Connor, *Fiscal Crisis of the State*, p. 9.

3. Jürgen Habermas, *Legitimation Crisis*. Trans. by Thomas McCarthy (United Kingdom: Polity Press, 1973, 1976) 61, 68.

are passed on to the competitive sector), and the promotion of monopoly capital profits at the expense of the competitive sector. This depression of the competitive sector simultaneously reduces its purchasing power and its strength as a tax base, and exacerbates the crises of both state finance and demand shortfall.

Most importantly, the crises are not isolated; they are systemic and interlocking; they all result from the same structural problems of state capitalism (i.e., subsidized inputs), and they develop exponentially, as subsidized inputs generate demand for more inputs faster than they can be met.

> Now it can be fairly objected here that every age has had its crises . . . .
>
> But that lesson from the past disguises one important fact of the present: our crises proceed, like the very growth of our system, *exponentially* . . . .
>
> The crises of the present . . . have grown so large, so interlocked, so exponential, that they threat unlike that ever known. [check original wording] It has come to the point where we cannot solve one problem, or try to, without causing some other problem, or a score of problems, usually unanticipated.[1]

As much as many modern Misesians would disassociate themselves from such an analysis (a good many, George Reisman chief among them, congregate at Mises.Org), most of it was implied by Mises himself in *Interventionist Government*.

The cumulative effect of all these interlocking crises, as already stated, will be that the system eventually reaches a breaking point, when the chickens of rationality come home to roost, and the state can no longer subsidize sufficient inputs for the hypertrophied corporate economy to operate at a profit.

> Another emerging fact of complex societies is the newly perceived vulnerability of their massive, centralized technologies and institutions, whether manifested in the loss of corporate flexibility, urban decline, power blackouts, skyjacking, or the many frightening scenarios of sabotage and violence now occurring daily.
>
> Meanwhile expectations are continually inflated by business and government leaders, and it becomes more difficult to satisfy demands of private mass consumption while trying to meet demands for more and better public consumption, whether for housing, mass transit, health, education, welfare benefits, parks and beaches, or merely to keep the water potable and the air breathable.[2]

---

1. Sale, *Human Scale*, pp. 25-26.
2. Henderson, "The Entropy State," pp. 84-85.

Appendix
Journalism as Stenography

1. Scott Cutlip

According to Scott Cutlip of the University of Georgia, some 40% of the "news" in newspapers consists of material generated by press agencies and PR departments, copied almost word for word by "objective" professional journalists.[1]

2. Justin Lewis

The norms of "objective reporting" thus involve presenting "both sides" of an issue with very little in the way of independent forms of verification . . . [A] journalist who systematically attempts to verify facts—to say which set of facts is more accurate—runs the risk of being accused of abandoning their objectivity by favoring one side over another . . . .

. . . . [J]ournalists who try to be faithful to an objective model of reporting are simultaneously distancing themselves from the notion of independently verifiable truth . . . .

The "two sides" model of journalistic objectivity makes news reporting a great deal easier since it requires no recourse to a factual realm. There are no facts to check, no archives of unspoken information to sort through . . . . If Tweedledum fails to challenge a point made by Tweedledee, the point remains unchallenged.[2]

3. Sam Smith

. . . I find myself increasingly covering Washington's most ignored beat: the written word. The culture of deceit is primarily an oral one. The soundbite, the spin, and the political product placement depend on no one spending too much time on the matter under consideration.

Over and over again, however, I find that the real story still lies barely hidden and may be reached by nothing more complicated than turning the page, checking the small type in the appendix, charging into the typographical jungle beyond the executive summary, doing a Web search, and, for the bravest, actually looking at the figures on the charts.[3]

4. Harry Jaffe

In his more than two decades covering the military, Ricks has developed many sources, from brass to grunts. This, according to the current Pentagon, is a problem.

The Pentagon's letter of complaint to Post executive editor Leonard Downie had language charging that Ricks casts his net as widely as possible and e-mails many people.

Details of the complaints were hard to come by. One Pentagon official said in private that Ricks did not give enough credence to official, on-the-record comments that ran counter to the angle of his stories.[4]

1. Cited by Lasch in *The Revolt of the Elites*, p. 174.

2. Justin Lewis, "Objectivity and the Limits of Press Freedom," in Peter Phillips & Project Censored, *Censored 2000: The Year's Top 25 Censored Stories* (New York, London, Sydney, and Toronto: Seven Stories Press, 2000), pp. 173-74.

3. Sam Smith, in *Censored 2000*, p. 60.

4. Harry Jaffe, "Pentagon to Washington Post Reporter Ricks: Get Lost," *The Washingtonian*, December 29, 2003 <http://washingtonian.com/inwashington/buzz/tomricks.html>.

5. *The Daily Show*

STEWART: Here's what puzzles me most, Rob. John Kerry's record in Vietnam is pretty much right there in the official records of the US military, and haven't been disputed for 35 years?

CORDDRY: That's right, Jon, and that's certainly the spin you'll be hearing coming from the Kerry campaign over the next few days.

STEWART: Th-that's not a spin thing, that's a fact. That's established.

CORDDRY: Exactly, Jon, and that established, incontravertible fact is one side of the story.

STEWART: But that should be—isn't that the end of the story? I mean, you've seen the records, haven't you? What's your opinion?

CORDDRY: I'm sorry, my *opinion*? No, I don't have 'o-pin-i-ons'. I'm a reporter, Jon, and my job is to spend half the time repeating what one side says, and half the time repeating the other. Little thing called 'objectivity'—might wanna look it up some day.

STEWART: Doesn't objectivity mean objectively weighing the evidence, and calling out what's credible and what isn't?

CORDDRY: Whoa-ho! Well, well, well—sounds like someone wants the media to act as a filter! [high-pitched, effeminate] 'Ooh, this allegation is spurious! Upon investigation this claim lacks any basis in reality! Mmm, mmm, mmm.' Listen buddy: not my job to stand between the people talking to me and the people listening to me.[1]

6. *Brent Cunningham*

It exacerbates our tendency to rely on official sources, which is the easiest, quickest way to get both the "he said" and the "she said," and, thus, "balance." According to numbers from the media analyst Andrew Tyndall, of the 414 stories on Iraq broadcast on NBC, ABC, and CBS from last September to February, all but thirty-four originated at the White House, Pentagon, and State Department. So we end up with too much of the "official" truth.

More important, objectivity makes us wary of seeming to argue with the president—or the governor, or the CEO—and risk losing our access . . . .

The Republicans were saying only what was convenient, thus the "he said." The Democratic leadership was saying little, so there was no "she said." "Journalists are never going to fill the vacuum left by a weak political opposition," says The New York Times's Steven R. Weisman.[2]

7. *Avedon Carol*

Hm, let's see . . . I can go to whitehouse.gov and read everything administration officials have to say on the record, or I can spend money to buy a newspaper and read a repetition of selected quotes from that said material. What should I do?

If that's all newspapers are good for, what are newspapers good for?[3]

1. Eschaton blog, August 22, 2004 <http://atrios.blogspot.com/2004_08_22_atrios_archive.html #109335851226026749>.

2. Brent Cunningham, "Rethinking Objective Journalism Columbia Journalism Review." Alternet, July 9, 2003 <http://www.alternet.org/mediaculture/16348/>.

3. Avedon Carol, "Pilloried Post," August 12, 2004 <http://slacktivist.typepad.com/slacktivist/2004/08/pilloried_post.html>.

Part Three
Internal Effects of Organizational Size Above That Required for Optimum Efficiency

5

Knowledge and Information Problems in the Large Organization

Although the analysis of information problems in large organizations has been refined in many constructive ways, little special insight is required to recognize their bare existence. They have been acknowledged even by corporate managers:

> One of the executive vice-presidents of the Union Carbide Corporation . . . remarked in a private conversation that he and his colleagues "had no idea how to manage a large corporation." He said they simply did not know enough of the corporate workings, nor did they know what to do even if a clear problem was identified.[1]

A. THE VOLUME OF DATA

From the beginning of organization theory as a distinct discipline, numerous writers have remarked on the central feature of information problems: the sheer volume of data to be processed within organizations, and their inadequacy for doing so.

Herbert Simon introduced the concept of "bounded rationality."

> The limits of rationality have been seen to derive from the inability of the human mind to bring to bear upon a single decision all the aspects of value, knowledge, and behavior that would be relevant.[2]

The *"principle of bounded rationality,"* stated in so many words, was that

> The capacity of the human mind for formulating and solving complex problems is very small compared with the size of the problems whose solutions is required for objectively rational behavior in the real world—or even for a reasonable approximation to such rationality.[3]

Friedrich Hayek's groundbreaking article on distributed knowledge, "The Use of Knowledge in Society," was written in the context of the ongoing socialist calculation debate, and directed primarily at the inability of state central planners to replace the price mechanism as a system for processing information. But it is also highly applicable to similar attempts by central planners within the corporation to replace the market with hierarchy.

> *If* we possess all the relevant information, *if* we can start out from a given system of preferences and *if* we command complete knowledge of available means, the problem which remains is purely one of logic. That is, the answer to the question of what is the best use of the available means is implicit in our assumptions. The conditions which the solu-

---

1. Barry Stein, *Size, Efficiency, and Community Enterprise* (Cambridge: Center for Community Economic Development, 1974), p. 49.

2. Herbert Simon, *Administrative Behavior* (New York: The Free Press; London: Collier-Macmillan Limited, 1945, 1947, 1957), pp. xxiii–xxiv, 39, 108.

3. Simon, "Rationality and Administrative Decision-Making," in Simon, *Models of Man: Social and Rational* (New York, London, Sydney: John Wiley & Sons, Inc., 1957) p. 198.

tion of this optimum problem must satisfy have been fully worked out and can be stated best in mathematical form: put at their briefest, they are that the marginal rates of substitution between any two commodities or factors must be the same in all their different uses.

This, however, is emphatically *not* the economic problem which society faces . . . .

The peculiar character of the problem of a rational economic order is determined precisely by the fact that the knowledge of the circumstances of which we must make use never exists in concentrated or integrated form, but solely as the dispersed bits of incomplete and frequently contradictory knowledge which all the separate individuals possess. The economic problem of society is thus not merely a problem of how to allocate "given" resources—if "given" is taken to mean given to a single mind which deliberately solves the problem set by these "data." It is rather a problem of how to secure the best use of resources known to any of the members of society, for ends whose relative importance only these individuals know. Or, to put it briefly, it is a problem of the utilization of knowledge not given to anyone in its totality.[1]

Hayek's list of assumptions in the first paragraph, by the way, sound remarkably like the neoclassical model of the firm as a simple "production function," with the most efficient combination of factors determined by technical considerations. His allocation of "given" resources, likewise, foreshadows the concept of "allocative efficiency," as opposed to "x-efficiency," which we examined in Chapter Two.

He went on to apply his concept of distributed knowledge more specifically to the production process, coming up something much like Michael Polanyi's "tacit knowledge." Of course, Hayek in turn was anticipated by Chester Barnard, who wrote about the "know-how" or "behavioral knowledge" which was "necessary to doing things in concrete situations" but was "not susceptible of verbal statement."[2] At any rate, Hayek wrote:

. . . a little reflection will show that there is beyond question a body of very important but unorganized knowledge which cannot possibly be called scientific in the sense of knowledge of general rules: the knowledge of the particular circumstances of time and place. It is with respect to this that practically every individual has some advantage over all others in that he possesses unique information of which beneficial use might be made, but of which use can be made only if the decisions depending on it are left to him or are made with his active cooperation. We need to remember only how much we have to learn in any occupation after we have completed our theoretical training, how big a part of our working life we spend in learning particular jobs, and how valuable an asset in all walks of life is knowledge of people, of local conditions, and special circumstances . . . .

If we can agree that the economic problem of society is mainly one of rapid adaptation to changes in the particular circumstances of time and place, it would seem to follow that the ultimate decisions must be left to the people who are familiar with these circumstances, who know directly of the relevant changes and of the resources immediately available to meet them.[3]

Polanyi described "tacit knowledge" in quite similar terms. The basic rules of an art, he said, are useful only when integrated into a practical knowledge of the art which is gained by experience; otherwise, they are mere maxims.[4] The practical knowledge, in many cases, cannot be reduced to a verbal formula for transmission.

An art which cannot be specified in detail cannot be transmitted by prescription, since no prescription for it exists. It can be passed on only by example from master to ap-

1. Friedrich A. Hayek, "The Use of Knowledge in Society," *The American Economic Review*, Vol. 35, No. 4. (Sept. 1945), pp. 519-20.

2. Chester Barnard, *The Functions of the Executive* (Cambridge: Harvard University Press, 1938), p. 291.

3. Hayek, "The Use of Knowledge in Society," pp. 521-22, 524.

4. Michael Polanyi, *Personal Knowledge: Towards a Post-Critical Philosophy* (New York and Evanston: Harper & Row, Publishers, 1958, 1962), p. 50.

prentice. This restricts the range of diffusion to that of personal contacts, and we find accordingly that craftsmanship tends to survive in closely circumscribed local traditions . . . It follows that an art which has fallen into disuse for the period of a generation is altogether lost. There are hundreds of examples of this to which the process of mechanization is continuously adding new ones. These losses are usually irretrievable. it is pathetic to watch the endless efforts—equipped with microscopy and chemistry, with mathematics and electronics—to reproduce a single violin of the kind the half-literate Stradivarius turned out as a matter of routine more than 200 years ago.[1]

A great deal of technique cannot be reduced to a verbal formula because it is unconscious, based on an acquired feel for the tools in one's hand, and built into one's muscular memory like the technique for riding a bicycle.[2]

This is of real practical importance for industry. The great technical research laboratories of modern industry, seeking to apply scientific method to the analysis of production techniques, first faced the daunting task of reducing the knowledge of traditional craft production into a form they could understand—i.e., "of discovering what actually was going on there and how it was that it produced the goods." In the case of the study of cotton spinning in the 1920s, "most of the initial decade's work on the part of the scientist will have to be spent merely in defining what the spinner knows."

If it makes sense to keep production decisions as close as possible to direct knowledge of the production process, then the worker cooperative would seem to be the ideal form of organization for aggregating knowledge. Top-down systems of authority present inherent knowledge problems because those with direct experience of the matter under consideration must follow policies made by those without such direct experience; and those making the policies must base their decisions on information which has been distorted by several rungs of hierarchy between those with the process-knowledge and those with the power.

Continuing in his last-quoted passage, Hayek elaborated further on the kinds of idiosyncratic knowledge involved in the production process:

> To know of and put to use a machine not fully employed, or somebody's skill which could be better utilized, or to be aware of a surplus stock which can be drawn upon during an interruption of supplies, is socially quite as useful as the knowledge of better alternative techniques . . . .
>
> . . . . Is it true that, once a plant has been built, the rest is all more or less mechanical, determined by the character of the plant, and leaving little to be changed in adapting to the ever-changing circumstances of the moment?
>
> . . . . In a competitive industry at any rate—and such an industry alone can serve as a test—the task of keeping cost from rising requires constant struggle, absorbing a great part of the energy of the manager. How easy it is for an inefficient manager to dissipate the differentials on which profitability rests, and that it is possible, with the same technical facilities, to produce with a great variety of costs, are among the commonplaces of business experience which do not seem to be equally familiar in the study of the economist.[3]

This is quite close to what Barry Stein wrote on the importance, cumulatively, of incremental changes in the production process, which might well have a greater effect on productivity than simply building a new factory with the latest generation of equipment. And as Stein pointed out, in largely the same terms as Hayek, the workers directly engaged in the production process are, more than anyone else, possessed of the specialized knowledge of how to tweak the process in order to improve productivity.

Such specialized distributed knowledge is also, in the hands of labor, a source of enormous agency problems. The possession of idiosyncratic knowledge can be parlayed into

1. *Ibid.*, p. 53.
2. *Ibid.*, pp. 61–62.
3. Hayek, "The Use of Knowledge in Society," p. 522.

into considerable information rents. As we shall see in Chapter Nine, the special knowledge of workers can be used by workers to slow down work or hamper the profitability of
the enterprise, in ways which it is almost impossible for management to adequately monitor or assign blame. Likewise, such idiosyncratic knowledge drastically degrades (in its lack)
the performance of "replacement workers," and involves enormous costs of replacing and
training a new labor force in the event of a strike or lockout.

Of course, the fact remains that the individual with idiosyncratic information is himself ignorant of much of the larger environment within which he operates. The price system, Hayek wrote, is ideally suited to coordinating the information dispersed among many
such individuals.

> Fundamentally, in a system where the knowledge of the relevant facts is dispersed among
> many people, prices can act to coordinate the separate actions of different people in the
> same way as subjective values help the individual to coordinate the parts of his plan.[1]

If this is a point for the market system against state planning, it is also a point for the
market system against the internal hierarchy of the corporation. Everything Hayek says
about the ability of planners to do an adequate job of aggregating distributed information
in the economy at large applies to the ability of management to aggregate distributed information within the large corporation. Everything Hayek says about the calculation problems attending the replacement of the market by administrative decisionmaking in a centrally planned economy applies, equally, to reliance on administrative decisionmaking
within the centrally planned corporation (about which more in Chapter Seven).

Oliver Williamson described the worker's power over the production process resulting
from distributed knowledge in terms much like Hayek's and Polanyi's:

> Almost every job involves some specific skills. Even the simplest custodial tasks are facili-
> tated by familiarity with the physical environment specific to the workplace in which
> they are being performed. The apparently routine operation of standard machines can be
> importantly aided by familiarity with the particular piece of operating equipment . . . .
> In some cases workers are able to anticipate the trouble and diagnose its source by subtle
> changes in the sound or smell of the equipment. Moreover, performance in some pro-
> duction or managerial jobs involves a team element, and a critical skill is the ability to
> operate effectively with the given members of the team . . . .[2]

But he used this, believe it or not, as an argument for hierarchy. Idiosyncratic knowledge (or "task idiosyncrasies"), he said, were a kind of asset specificity which led to small
numbers bargaining problems in the market, which in turn could be solved by replacing
the market with hierarchy. That's rather odd, considering that hierarchy tends to make
idiosyncratic knowledge *less usable* by reducing the control by any one individual over matters under his direct observation.

It's odd, as well, because Williamson admits elsewhere that the very same task idiosyncrasies that result in small-numbers exchanges in the market persist as information rents
from impacted knowledge *within* an organization. For example, the process of on-the-job
training, by which incumbents in possession of idiosyncratic knowledge are expected to
pass it on to new employees. The danger, Williamson says, is that the incumbent employees
"will hoard information to their personal advantage and engage in a series of bilateral mo-
nopolistic exchanges with the management . . . ."[3] And this is not always just the moral
equivalent of price-gouging—it can also be legitimate self-defense, in an environment

1. *Ibid.*, p. 526.
2. Oliver Williamson, *Markets and Hierarchies, Analysis and Antitrust Implications: A Study on the
Economics of Internal Organization* (New York: Free Press, 1975), pp. 5, 62-63.
3. *Ibid.*, p. 63.

where the interests of workers and management are often diametrically opposed, and workers' knowledge can be used against them. As Dave Pollard points out:

> Employees hoard rather than sharing knowledge, including knowledge that could yield innovation, to protect their position and rank in the company.
> Employees rarely volunteer new ideas, fearing ridicule, retribution, being ignored, or having credit for the idea stolen by their boss if it succeeds.[1]

Although Williamson doesn't mention it, the same phenomenon occurs even when a plant is fully staffed, to the advantages of an incumbent workforce against a management that might attempt to replace it during a strike. One of the information rents of idiosyncratic knowledge, in the case of collective bargaining, is the costs of training replacement workers without the cooperation of the striking incumbents, and the long learning curve during which productivity will be seriously degraded by the lack of the incumbents' idiosyncratic knowledge. We will examine this problem at greater length in Chapter Nine.

B. THE DISTORTION OF INFORMATION FLOW BY POWER

Our consideration of Williamson's treatment of information rents in a hierarchy, immediately above, suggests another problem with information in the large organization. In addition to the basic problems caused by the sheer volume of data and the inability of hierarchical organizations to process it, information problems are complicated by power relations within the bureaucracy.

As early as 1932, F. C. Bartlett published a study of serial reproduction of information that had a strong bearing on the transmission of information in a hierarchy. The experiment was a fancy version of the child's game "telephone," where a bit of information is repeated around a circle from person to person and comes out unrecognizable at the end. In this case, a line drawing of an owl was transformed by serial reproduction into "a recognizable cat." Bartlett drew the conclusion:

> It is now perfectly clear that serial reproduction normally brings about startling and radical alterations in the material dealt with . . . . At the same time the subjects may be very well satisfied with their efforts, believing themselves to have passed on all important features with little or no change, and merely, perhaps to have omitted unessential matters.[2]

Oliver Williamson saw the experiment as a lesson on the distortion of information within a hierarchy. On that subject, he wrote:

> Communications distortions can take either assertive or defensive forms. Defensively, subordinates may tell their supervisor what he wants to hear; assertively, they will report those things they want him to know . . . . Distortion to please the receiver is especially likely when the recipient has access to extensive rewards and sanctions in his relations with the transmitter, as in up-the-line communication in an administrative hierarchy . . . . The cumulative effects across successive hierarchical levels of . . . adjustments to the data easily result in gross image distortions . . . and contribute to a limitation of firm size . . . .[3]

(Or rather, under state capitalism, because of limits to the competitive ill effects of such distortions, they contribute to the low levels of efficiency typical of the dominant firms.)

1. David Pollard, "A Prescription for Business Innovation: Creating the Technologies that Solve Basic Human Needs (Part Two)" *How to Save the World*, April 20, 2004 <http://blogs.salon.com/0002007/2004/04/20.html>.

2. F.C. Bartlett, *Remembering* (New York: Cambridge University Press, 1932), quoted in Oliver Williamson, *Economic Organization: Firms, Markets, and Policy Control* (New York: NYU Press, 1986), p. 35.

3. Williamson, *Markets and Hierarchies*, pp. 122-23.

Other thinkers have made similar observations, but drawn more radical conclusions from them. For example, Kenneth Boulding wrote:

> Another profitable line of study lies . . . in the analysis of the way in which organizational structure affects the flow of information, hence affects the information input into the decision-maker, hence affects his image of the future and his decisions . . . . There is a great deal of evidence that almost all organizational structures tend to produce false images in the decision-maker, and that the larger and more authoritarian the organization, the better the chance that its top decision-makers will be operating in purely imaginary worlds. This is perhaps the most fundamental reason for supposing that there are ultimately diminishing returns to scale.[1]

R. A. Wilson also remarked on the informational problems of hierarchies. For Wilson, the distortions that occur as information is filtered through a hierarchy result not just from errors of replication, but from systematic distortion in a particular direction. Information is distorted by power relationships within a hierarchy.

> . . . . in a rigid hierarchy, nobody questions orders that seem to come from above, and those at the very top are so isolated from the actual work situation that they never see what is going on below . . . .[2]
>
> . . . [A] man with a gun is told only that which people assume will not provoke him to pull the trigger. Since all authority and government are based on force, the master class, with its burden of omniscience, faces the servile class, with its burden of nescience, precisely as a highwayman faces his victim. Communication is possible only between equals. The master class never abstracts enough information from the servile class to know what is actually going on in the world where the actual productivity of society occurs . . . . The result can only be progressive disorientation among the rulers.[3]
>
> A civilization based on authority-and-submission is a civilization without the means of self-correction. Effective communication flows only one way: from master-group to servile-group. Any cyberneticist knows that such a one-way communication channel lacks feedback and cannot behave "intelligently."
>
> The epitome of authority-and-submission is the Army, and the control-and-communication network of the Army has every defect a cyberneticist's nightmare could conjure. Its typical patterns of behavior are immortalized in folklore as SNAFU (situation normal—all fucked-up), FUBAR (fucked-up beyond all redemption) and TARFU (Things are really fucked-up) . . . .
>
> Proudhon was a great communication analyst, born 100 years too soon to be understood. His system of voluntary association (anarchy) is based on the simple communication principles that an authoritarian system means one-way communication, or stupidity, and a libertarian system means two-way communication, or rationality.
>
> The essence of authority, as he saw, was Law—that is, fiat—that is, effective communication running one way only. The essence of a libertarian system, as he also saw, was Contract—that is, mutual agreement—that is, effective communication running both ways. ("Redundancy of control" is the technical cybernetic phrase.)[4]
>
> You know I think I began to realize the danger of hierarchy and developed the snafu principal about communication when I was working for the second largest engineering firm in the United States. I listened to the engineers bitching all the time about how the financial interests wouldn't let them do any of the work that seemed really important for them to improve their output. And I was reading William Faulkner's *Go*

1. Kenneth Boulding, "The Economics of Knowledge and the Knowledge of Economics," *American Economic Review* 56: 1/2 (March 1966), p. 8

2. Robert Shea and Robert Anton Wilson, *The Illuminatus! Trilogy* (New York: Dell Publishing, 1975), p. 388.

3. *Ibid.*, p. 498.

4. Robert Anton Wilson, "Thirteen Choruses For the Divine Marquis," from *Coincidance— A Head Test*. <http://www.deepleafproductions.com/wilsonlibrary/texts/raw-marquis.html> Originally published in *The Realist*.

Down Moses, which is still one of my favorite novels, and there was a sentence in there which was like a mini satori for me. And the sentence goes: "To the sheriff, Lucas was just another nigger and they both knew that; to Lucas the sheriff was an ignorant redneck with no cause for pride in his ancestors, nor any hope for it in his prosperity. But only one of them knew that." And I suddenly realized, yeah, every power situation means the people on top are not being told what the people on the bottom are really noticing. Then I could see how this applied to this engineering firm. And then how it applied to corporations in general and so on.[1]

Or as Hazel Henderson quoted Bertram Gross, "organizations are devices for screening out reality in order to focus attention on their own specific goals."

> . . . . they regularly intercept, distort, impound, or amplify information, structuring it for their own needs and channeling employees' efforts toward their own goals . . .
>   A person with great power gets no valid information at all.[2]

Hierarchy, by impeding the exchange of information, works against the very purposes for which cooperative, group production is undertaken in the first place. According to Peter Blau and Richard Scott, the superiority of group over individual production results from three factors:

(1) the sifting of suggestions in social interactions serves as an error-correction mechanism;
(2) the social support furnished in interaction facilitates thinking; and
(3) the competition among workers for respect mobilizes their energies for contributing to the task.[3]

Hierarchy interferes with these tendencies. It reduces social interaction and support. It also sets up barriers to mutual respect by reducing the lower-ranked individual's potential for acquiring respect, and the higher-ranked individual's respect for the performance of those at lower rungs of the hierarchy. The inflated importance of recognition by superiors also weakens the importance of mutual esteem among peers.[4] Finally, hierarchy distorts the error-correcting function of interaction, by increasing the perceived costs of correcting the errors of a superior.[5]

These interferences by hierarchy in the information-aggregating process are affirmed by Melville Dalton's case studies of corporate management. He cites the social insularity of engineers and other staff officers, at a factory he studied, and their coolness toward the foremen and line supervisors. Some foremen, in interviews with the author, stated their habit of avoiding the management cafeteria, despite an interest in the work problems being discussed there, because of the aloof attitude of the engineers. Such differences in status, Dalton observed, "discourage easy informal ties between staffs and many middle and lower line supervisors," and "prevent staff people from getting close to situations . . . ."[6]

Information is also distorted by the fact that the end-user of the information relies on information sorters so far removed from him as to have little idea of what will be useful and what will not. Lester Thurow, for example, observed:

1. Lance Bauscher, *Utopia USA* interview with Robert Anton Wilson. 22 Feb 2001 <http://www.deepleafproductions.com/utopialibrary/text/raw-inter-utopia.html>.

2. Hazel Henderson, "Coping With Organizational Future Shock," *Creating Alternative Futures: The End of Economics* (New York: G.P. Putnam's Sons, 1978), p. 225.

3. Peter M. Blau and W. Richard Scott. *Formal Organizations: A Comparative Approach* (San Francisco: Chandler Publishing Co., 1962), p. 121.

4. *Ibid.*, p. 122.

5. *Ibid.*, p. 123.

6. Melville Dalton, *Men Who Manage* (New York: John Wiley & Sons, Inc., 1959), p. 94.

[W]ith the onset of the new information technologies, ordinary bosses could implement what extraordinary bosses had always preached. Bosses could do a lot more bossing
. . . .

To do so, however, one had to build up enormous information bureaucracies. Information could be gotten, but only at the cost of adding a lot of white-collar workers
to the system . . . .

To the boss, more information seems like a free good. He orders it from subordinates, and the cost of acquiring it appears on the budgets of his subordinates. Subordinates in turn can neither refuse to provide the requested information nor know if the information is valuable enough to justify the costs of its acquisition . . . . Essentially, both
bosses and subordinates are imprisoned in standard operating procedures that create an
institutional set of blinders.[1]

Not surprisingly, this leads to a huge glut of useless information, as bureaucracies generate the maximum level of information input to make themselves appear useful and to insure themselves against blame, with little idea of what is useful and what is not. At the same
time, management makes decisions to suit its own interests, but justifies them by genuflect-
ing toward the information. Thus information becomes a legitimizing ideology.

Martha Feldman and James March found little relationship between the gathering of
information and the policies that were ostensibly based on it. In corporate legitimizing
rhetoric, of course, management decisions are always based on a rational assessment of the
best available information. And in the neoclassical view of the firm as production function,

information is gathered and used because it helps to make a choice. Investments in information are made up to the point at which marginal expected cost equals marginal
expected return.[2]
. . . . This [conventional] perspective on decision making leads to some simple expectations for information utilization. For example, relevant information gathered for use
in a decision will be examined before more examination is requested or gathered; needs
for information will be determined prior to requesting information; information that is
irrelevant to a decision will not be gathered.
Studies of the uses of information in organizations, however, reveal a somewhat different picture. Organizations seem to deal with information in a different way from that
anticipated from a simple reading of decision theory.[3]

Feldman and March did case studies of three organizations, and found an almost total
disconnect between policies and the information they were supposedly based on:

The literature reports phenomena that can be summarized by six observations about the
gathering and use of information in organizations . . . . : (1) Much of the information
that is gathered and communicated by individuals and organizations has little decision
relevance. (2) Much of the information that is used to justify a decision is collected and
interpreted after the decision has been made, or substantially made. (3) Much of the information gathered in response to requests for information is not considered in the making of decisions for which it was requested. (4) Regardless of the information available at
the time a decision is first considered, more information is requested. (5) Complaints that
an organization does not have enough information to make a decision occur while available information is ignored. (6) The relevance of the information provided in the decision-making process to the decision being made is less conspicuous than is the insistence
on information. In short, most organizations and individuals often collect more information than they use or can reasonably expect to use in the making of decisions. At the

    1. Lester Thurow, *Head to Head: The Coming Economic Battle among Japan, Europe, and America*
(New York: William Morrow, 1972), pp. 171-72, in David M. Gordon, *Fat and Mean: The Myth of
Managerial Downsizing*, p. 76.
    2. Martha S. Feldman and James G. March, "Information in Organizations as Signal and
Symbol," Administrative Science Quarterly 26 (April 1981), p. 182
    3. *Ibid.*, p. 172

same time, they appear to be constantly needing or requesting more information, or complaining about inadequacies in information.[1]

Feldman and March did their best to provide a charitable explanation—an explanation, that is, other than "organizations are systematically stupid."[2] "Systematically stupid" probably comes closest to satisfying Occam's Razor, and I'd have happily stuck with that explanation. But Feldman and March struggled to find some adaptive purpose in the observed use of information.

They began by surveying more conventional assessments of organizational inefficiency as an explanation for the observed pattern. First, organizations are "unable . . . to process the information they have. They experience an explanation glut as a shortage. Indeed, it is possible that the overload contributes to the breakdown in processing capabilities . . . ." Second, " . . . the information available to organizations is systematically the wrong kind of information. Limits of analytical skill or coordination lead decision makers to collect information that cannot be used."[3]

Then they made three observations of their own on how organizational structure affects the use of information:

> First, ordinary organizational procedures provide positive incentives for underestimating the costs of information relative to its benefits. Second, much of the information in an organization is gathered in a surveillance mode rather than in a decision mode. Third, much of the information used in organizational life is subject to strategic misrepresentations.
>
> Organizations provide incentives for gathering more information than is optimal from a strict decision perspective . . . . First, the costs and benefits of information are not all incurred at the same place in the organization. Decisions about information are often made in parts of the organization that can transfer the costs to other parts of the organization while retaining the benefits . . . .
>
> Second, post hoc accountability is often required of both individual decision makers and organizations . . . .
>
> Most information that is generated and processed in an organization is subject to misrepresentation . . . .

The decision maker, in other words, must gather excess information in anticipated defense against the possibility that his decision will be second-guessed.[4] By "surveillance mode," the authors mean that the organization seeks out information not for any specific decision, but rather to monitor the environment for surprises. The lead time for information gathering is longer than the lead time for decisions. Information must therefore be gathered and processed without clear regard to the specific decisions that may be made.[5]

The incentives Feldman and March discussed so far all seem to result mainly from large size and hierarchy. The problem of non-internalization of the costs and benefits of information-gathering by the same actor, of course, falls into the inefficiency costs of large size. The problem of post hoc accountability results from hierarchy. At least part of the problem of surveillance mode is another example of poor internalization: the people gathering the information are different from the ones using it, and are therefore gathering it with a second-hand set of goals which does not coincide with their own intrinsic motives.

The strategic distortion of information, as an agency problem, is (again) the result of hierarchy and the poor internalization of costs and benefits in the same responsible actors. In other words, the large, hierarchical organization *is* "systematically stupid."

1. *Ibid.*, p. 174.
2. *Ibid.*, p. 174.
3. *Ibid.*, p. 175.
4. *Ibid.*, pp. 175-76.
5. *Ibid.*, p. 176.

The authors' most significant contribution in this article is their fourth observation: that the gathering of information serves a legitimizing function in the organization.

> Bureaucratic organizations are edifices built on ideas of rationality. The cornerstones of rationality are values regarding decision making . . . .
>
> The gathering of information provides a ritualistic assurance that appropriate attitudes about decision making exist . . . . The belief that more information characterizes better decisions engenders a belief that having information, in itself, is good and that a person or organization with more information is better than a person or organization with less . . . .
>
> Observable features of information use become particularly important in this scenario. When there is no reliable alternative for asserting a decision maker's knowledge, visible aspects of information gathering and storage are used as implicit measures of the quality and quantity of information possessed and used . . . .[1]

In other words, when an organization gets too big to have any clear idea how well it is performing the function for which it officially exists, it creates a metric for "success" defined in terms of the processing of inputs.

This adoption of extrinsic measures as proxies for real productivity, when the organization is incapable of measuring productive work, extends far beyond the specific task of information-gathering. When (as Paul Goodman put it in a quote below) management is incapable of knowing "what a good job of work is," a proxy measure must be found. One such false metric is "face time," as opposed to actual work, as blogger Atrios observed:

> During my summers doing temp office work I was always astounded by the culture of "face time"—the need to be at your desk early and stay late even when there was no work to be done and doing so in no way furthered any company goals. Doing your work and doing it adequately was entirely secondary to looking like you were working hard as demonstrated by your desire to stay at work longer than strictly necessary.[2]

One of Atrios' commenters, in considerably more pointed language, elaborated:

> If you are a manager who is too stupid to figure out that what you should actually measure is real output then the next best thing is to measure how much time people spend pretending to produce that output. Of course you really should know what the output you should measure really consists of. If you don't know that then you are sort of forced into using the time spent measurement.

But in fairness to management, it's not the stupidity of the individual; it's the stupidity of the *organization*. All large, hierarchical organizations are stupid. (The problem may also result from management being *too* smart. In many cases, management adopts an irrelevant metric because maximizing it has the incidental effect of promoting their own bureaucratic interests, whereas maximizing a more relevant measure might require the diversion of resources that management would prefer to devote to empire building and self-dealing.

More importantly, though, the gathering of information provides ritual reassurance that management decisions are rational and based on the best possible information, and therefore secures acquiescence to management authority.[3]

The way that information-gathering, in Feldman and March's analysis, serves to engineer the acceptance of decisions as "legitimate," bears a striking resemblance to the tendency in American political culture for citizens to rally around the government even (or especially) in catastrophic wars, on the assumption that "they have access to information that we don't." I've witnessed it myself in the workplace, unfortunately. A coworker of

---

1. *Ibid.*, pp. 177-178.
2. "Face Time," *Eschaton* blog, July 9, 2005 <http://atrios.blogspot.com/2005_07_03_atrios_ archive.html#112049256079118503>.
3. Feldman and March, pp. 177-178.

mine in a VA hospital where I used to work frequently rallied to the defense of the MBA types' clueless decisions, on the grounds that "they went to school and took special classes to make decisions."

It's remarkable how often professional decision-making bureaucracies, supposedly privy to almost unlimited information, are blinded by groupthink and institutional cultures, while those outside the decision loop with far more modest amounts of information are able to get a clearer picture of reality simply by subjecting the bureaucracy's unquestioned assumptions to the test of common sense. The tendency of insular decision-making circles toward over-optimism, and refusing to take possible negative or unintended consequences into consideration, was the subject of Irving Janis' *Group Think*.

Robert Jackall, in *Moral Mazes*, described the legitimization of management decisions in terms similar to those of Feldman and March, albeit from a much more jaded perspective. "Vocabularies of rationality are always invoked to cloak decisions, particularly those that might seem impulsive when judged by other standards."[1] Such vocabularies of rationality are invoked, especially, in the face of management policies that an outside observer might perceive as examples of cynical self-dealing:

> . . . just after the CEO of Covenant Corporation announced one of his many purges, legitimated by "a comprehensive assessment of the hard choices facing us" by a major consulting firm, he purchased a new Sabre jet for executives and a new 31-foot company limousine for his own use . . . . He then flew the entire board of directors to Europe on a Concorde for a regular meeting to review, it was said, his most recent cost-cutting strategies.[2]

The management at the hospital where I work, similarly, announced the cancellation of PTO (paid time off) hours because of their allegedly dire financial circumstances—and then announced three months later that they'd leased a corporate suite at the local baseball stadium.

Feldman and March sum up their attempt to rescue the corporation from charges of "systematic stupidity":

> It is possible, in considering these phenomena, to conclude that organizations and the people in them lack intelligence. We prefer to be somewhat more cautious. We have argued that the information behavior observed in organizations is not, in general, perverse. We have suggested four broad explanations for the conspicuous over-consumption of information. First, organizations provide incentives for gathering extra information . . . . Second, much of the information in organizations is gathered and treated in a surveillance mode rather than a decision mode . . . . Third, much of the information in organizations is subject to strategic misrepresentation . . . . Fourth, information use symbolizes a commitment to rational choice.[3]

But in fact, their own argument proves that the organization *is* systematically stupid, *in terms of its own official rationale for existing in the first place*. We have already argued that the first three explanations all involve excessive size and hierarchy, poor internalization of the positive and negative results of decisions by decision-makers, and the separation of knowledge from authority. As for the fourth, organizations elevate the collection of useless information into a legitimizing ideology, and substitute a symbolic metric for genuine rationality, *because* they are systematically stupid. The health of the organizational apparatus (in the same sense as Bourne's "war is the health of the state") supplants the organization's original purpose for existing. The consumption of inputs is redefined as an output of the organization.

1. Robert Jackall, *Moral Mazes: The World of Corporate Managers* (New York: Oxford University Press, 1988), p. 75.

    2. *Ibid*. p. 144.

    3. Feldman and March, p. 182.

And it is hardly necessary to attribute stupidity to individuals in order to explain the functional stupidity of the organization. Because of the pathologies of large size and excessive hierarchy, the organization in effect provides a sort of invisible hand mechanism by which individuals, by maximizing their utility in a rational manner given the environment of incentives, collectively promote inefficiency and irrationality. That, to my thinking, is the very definition of "perverse."

As if to verify this assessment, Feldman and March go on to describe the circumstances in which conspicuous over-consumption of information is likely to occur:

> The kinds of information behavior noted here should be more common in situations in which decision criteria are ambiguous than in situations where they are clear, more common where performance measures are vague than where they are precise, more common when decision quality requires a long period to establish than when there is quick feedback, more common where the success of a decision depends on other decisions that cannot be predicted or controlled than where a decision can be evaluated autonomously.[1]

In other words, it is more common in situations where the organization is so large that nobody has any clear idea of what's going on, what other people are doing, or what the purpose of action even is. It is more common in situations where decisionmaking authority is removed from those in direct contact with the problem, who are most capable of directly assessing what needs to be done and monitoring the results of action, and given to those separated from such knowledge by several rungs of authority. It is more common in situations where authority flows downward, with each rung of hierarchy interfering with those below who are better informed, and receiving orders from those above who are even more clueless, until one reaches Boulding's "completely imaginary world" at the apex of the pyramid.

But I repeat, the systematic stupidity of the large, hierarchical organization is perfectly compatible with the individual competence of those making it up. The inefficiencies of size and hierarchy are such, as Paul Goodman wrote, that *nobody* could do an effective job of running it:

> Assume, for the sake of analysis, that the top-direction of a very large centralized corporation is very wise and devoted to the goal of the organization. Nevertheless, being one man or a small group, top-management does not have enough *mind* to do an adequate job . . . .
> Top management cannot be departmentalized. A manager cannot restrict himself to policy, but must be the final judge of application to doubtful and new cases as well. If because of pressure of time unique cases are treated as routine, a manager's expert judgment is useless.
> . . . .A policy is decided, and to make sure that it is understood and correctly executed, it is simplified and a procedure is standardized. In a large organization such standardization is essential . . . . But of course the standard misfits every actual instance . . . . It is almost impossible for the best procedure to be used except clandestinely, or for the best man to be employed unless he goes through unusual channels . . . .
> Subordinates tend to become stupider more rapidly and directly, simply because they cannot learn anything by exercising initiative and taking responsibility. Stultification occurs acutely when a man is bright and sees a better way to do something, but must follow a worse directive.[2]

1. *Ibid.*, p. 183.
2. Paul Goodman, *People or Personnel*, in *People or Personnel* and *Like a Conquered Province* (New York: Vintage Books, 1963, 1965), pp. 76-79.

Although the organization may contain a great deal of expertise and skill, severally, the individual's expertise is useless when nobody has authority to apply it directly to a problem on his own initiative. The whole is less than the sum of its parts. To quote Goodman again:

> When the social means are tied up in such complicated organizations, it becomes extraordinarily difficult and sometimes impossible to do a simple thing directly, even though the doing is common sense and would meet with universal approval, as when neither the child, nor the parent, nor the janitor, nor the principal of the school can remove the offending door catch . . . .
>
> . . . . [A]s the feeling of powerlessness spreads, there is a deep conviction that "Nothing Can Be Done" because of the machinery that has to be set in motion, even when the problem or the abuse is simple and something can easily be done.[1] (For an example of this, see the Appendix to Chapter Six, "Toilet Paper as Paradigm.")

One reason the individual skills and competencies of the organization's members are unusable is that idiosyncratic knowledge is poorly, or not at all, transferable. The production worker is second-guessed by management who are not only less qualified than he to judge competence in his line of work, but less qualified to make the framework of rules within which he practices his specialty.

> In my opinion, the salient cause of ineptitude in promotion and in all hiring practices is that, under centralized conditions, fewer and fewer know what *is* a good job of work . . . . Just as there is reliance on extrinsic motives, there is heavy reliance [in the large university] on extrinsic earmarks of competence: testing, profiles, publications, hearsay among wives, flashy *curricula vitae*. Yet there is no alternative method of selection. In decentralized conditions, where a man knows what goes on and engages in the whole enterprise, an applicant can present a masterpiece for examination and he has functional peers who can decide whether they want him in the guild . . . .
>
> There is no test for performing a highly departmentalized role except evidence of playing a role and of ability at routine skills. Inevitably, the negative criteria for selection become preponderant . . . and so the whole enterprise becomes still stupider . . . .
>
> In brief, as those who judge—colleagues, consumers, the electorate—become stupid, management also becomes stupid. So after a while we cannot maintain the assumption that in established firms top-management *can* be wise and capable.[2]

As increased division of labor within the organization leads to functions being stovepiped, it takes a progressively longer time for those in one department to receive the knowledge they need for their own functioning, and progressively more overhead and time are consumed in aggregating inputs from the different departments for making an organization-wide policy. And because the knowledge of one specialty is poorly reducible or summarizable, the person in one department is a poor judge of exactly what information or other inputs another department needs, and a generalist senior manager is a poor judge of the inputs he is aggregating from the departments below.

As we saw in Part One, the large corporation survives, in spite of internal diseconomies from information problems, because it is insulated from the competitive ill effects of inefficiency. Because of the greater inefficiency costs of hierarchy, as R. Preston McAffee and John McMillan argue, the hierarchical firm can only exist in a monopoly market, and the length of hierarchies varies inversely with the competitiveness of markets. The firm must be a net beneficiary of monopoly, so that the inefficiency costs of hierarchy can be subsidized by rents drawn from the rest of the economy.[3]

1. *Ibid.*, pp. 88, 91.
2. Goodman, *People or Personnel*, pp. 83–84.
3. R. Preston McAffee and John McMillan, "Organizational Diseconomies of Scale," *Journal of Economics & Management Strategy*, Vol. 4, No. 3 (Fall 1995): 399–426.

Private information creates a cost of operating a hierarchy, which becomes larger as the hierarchical distance between the information source and the decision maker increases. When information about a firm's capabilities is dispersed among the individuals in the firm, production is inefficient even though everyone behaves rationally. Because hierarchies need rents in order to function, a firm with a long hierarchy may not be viable in a competitive industry.[1]

Rents ... are the lubricants that make it possible for a hierarchy to function .... [I]f larger firms mean longer hierarchies, then potential rents must be present for a large firm to be viable. Thus firms are small because the industry is competitive.[2]

Do monopolies produce above minimum cost, causing a welfare loss beyond the thoroughly explored allocative inefficiencies? Conversely, does competition force minimum-cost production? Generations of economists have believed that competition provides the discipline needed to induce managers to make relatively efficient production decisions. Adam Smith said that monopoly is "a great enemy to good management, which can never be universally established but in consequence of that free and universal competition which forces everybody to have recourse to it for the sake of self-defense."[3]

In an oligopoly market, the typical firm can afford to be inefficient and bureaucratic because all the firms in the market share the same institutional cultures, the same management assumptions, and the same conventional patterns of organization. Indeed, when the state's subsidies and protections for large size cause large size to be typical in a given market, the typical firm cannot be otherwise than inefficient.

The proliferation of useless information, described by Feldman and March above, has a synergistic relationship to the expansion of bureaucracy. Lloyd Dumas argues that the proliferation of paperwork and new forms within a bureaucracy leads to the creation of new managerial positions to take the burden off of existing managers; but these new managers simply generate even more paperwork. And this paperwork, in turn, is used to justify the hiring of more administrative personnel—and so on.[4] This, Dumas says, is the basis of Parkinson's Law.[5]

CONCLUSION AND SEGUE TO CHAPTER SIX

In addition to all this, information problems are a necessary precondition for agency problems. The information problems of the large organization are such that those lower in the hierarchy are usually desperate to make those at the top aware of how things really are; nevertheless, as we have already seen Williamson suggest, the strategic withholding or monopoly of information by agents is a source of rents against the principal.

As Oliver Williamson showed, neither bounded rationality nor opportunism, taken alone, would present a significant problem. Each is a problem only in the presence of the other. In the absence of opportunism, for example, bounded rationality could be solved by a simple "general clause," by which the parties to a contract agree in good faith to deal with problems arising from contractual incompleteness by disclosing all relevant information and to acting cooperatively to adjust to new information or new circumstances. And without bounded rationality, opportunism could be overcome by comprehensive contracting.[6]

1. *Ibid.*, p. 399.

2. *Ibid.*, p. 402.

3. *Ibid.*, pp. 414.

4. Lloyd Dumas, *The Overburdened Economy: Uncovering the Causes of Chronic Unemployment, Inflation, and National Decline.* (Berkeley, Los Angeles, London: University of California Press, 1986), pp. 65–66.

5. C.N. Parkinson, *Parkinson's Law, or the Pursuit of Progress* (London: John Murray, 1958).

6. Williamson, *The Economic Institutions of Capitalism : Firms, Markets, Relational Contracting* (New York: Free Press; London: Collier Macmillan, 1985), p. 48, 50, 67.

We have already seen this, in the discussion above of the information rents attending idiosyncratic knowledge. The "assertive distortions" that Williamson referred to fall on the indistinct boundary line between information and agency problems. Self-dealing from information rents is a form of opportunism. And more generally, asymmetrical information is central to most agency problems. As we quoted Williamson in the Introduction to Part III, opportunism wouldn't be a problem without bounded rationality; otherwise it would be possible to rule it out ahead of time with comprehensive contracting covering every possible contingency.

The basic agency problem as resulting from information asymmetries, as Paul Milgrom and John Roberts described:

> . . . some of the information that is important for the organization to make good decisions is not directly available to those charged with making the decisions. Instead, it is lodged with or producible only by other individuals or groups that are not empowered to make the decisions but may have a direct interest in the resulting outcome.[1]

Or to put it the other way around, what Williamson calls "information impactedness" is more a problem of opportunism than of bounded rationality. It is

> mainly attributable to the pairing of uncertainty with opportunism. It exists in circumstances in which one of the parties to an exchange is much better informed than is the other regarding underlying conditions germane to the trade, and the second party cannot achieve information parity except at great cost—because he cannot rely on the first party to disclose the information in a fully candid manner.[2]
>
> The reason why outsiders are not at a parity with insiders is usually because outsiders lack firm-specific, task-specific, or transaction-specific experience.[3]

This results, as we shall see in our chapter on managerialism, in rents accruing to corporate management at the expense of outside investors. But the same principle, inside the corporation, limits the managerial hierarchy's effective control over the productive labor force.

---

1. Paul Milgrom and John Roberts, "An Economic Approach to Influence Activities in Organizations," *American Journal of Sociology*, Supplement to vol. 94 (1988), p. S156.
2. Williamson, *Markets and Hierarchies*, p. 14.
3. *Ibid.*, p. 31.

APPENDIX

THE NHS's IT PROGRAM AS AN EXAMPLE OF SYSTEMATIC STUPIDITY[1]

[From Alex at *Yorkshire Ranter.*]

"The inspiration to digitize this far-flung bureaucracy first surfaced in late 2001, when Microsoft's Bill Gates paid a visit to British Prime Minister Tony Blair at No. 10 Downing St. The subject of the meeting, as reported by The Guardian, was what could be done to improve the National Health Service. At the time, much of the service was paper-based and severely lagging in its use of technology. A long-term review of NHS funding that was issued just before the Blair-Gates meeting had concluded: "The U.K. health service has a poor record on the use of information and communications technology—the result of many years of serious under-investment."

Coming off a landslide victory in the 2001 general election, Blair was eager to move Britain's health services out of technology's dark ages. Gates, who had come to England to tell the CEOs of the NHS trusts how to develop integrated systems that could enhance health care, was happy to point the way. "Blair was dazzled by what he saw as the success of Microsoft," says Black Sheep Research's Brampton. Their meeting gave rise to what would become the NPfIT."

[Alex helpfully comments, "Couldn't they have introduced him to Richard Stallman?" And remaining helpful, he adds boldface to the project's key failures:]

After a February 2002 meeting at 10 Downing St. chaired by Blair and attended by U.K. health-care and Treasury officials as well as Microsoft executives, the NPfIT program was launched.

In quick order, a unit was established to purchase and deliver I.T. systems centrally. To run the entire show, NHS tapped Richard Granger, a former Deloitte and Andersen management consultant. Granger signed on in October 2002 at close to $500,000 a year, making him the highest-paid civil servant in the U.K., according to The Guardian.

In one of his first acts, Granger commissioned the management consulting company McKinsey to do a study of the massive health-care system in England. Though the study was never published, it concluded, according to The Guardian, that no single existing vendor was big enough to act as prime contractor on the countrywide, multibillion-dollar initiative the NHS was proposing. Still, Granger wanted to attract global players to the project, which meant he needed to offer up sizable pieces of the overall effort as incentives . . . .

The process for selecting vendors began in the late fall of 2002. It was centralized and standardized, and was conducted, Brennan and others say, in great secrecy. To avoid negative publicity, NHS insisted that contractors not reveal any details about contracts, a May 2005 story in ComputerWeekly noted. As a byproduct of these hush-hush negotiations, front-line clinicians, except at the most senior levels, were largely excluded from the selection and early planning process, according to Brennan.

[Alex summarizes the failures:]

First of all, letting the producer interest poison the well. Microsoft execs, eh? The big centralised-bureaucratic proprietary system vendor Microsoft was permitted to influence the whole process towards a big centralised-bureaucratic proprietary system from the very beginning. This occurred at a time when Health Secretary Alan Milburn was constantly railing against "producer interests" blocking his "modernising reforms". This was code for the trade unions that represented low-waged nurses and cleaners, and the British Medical Association that represented doctors. Can anyone spot the difference between the two groups of producer interests? *One of these things is not like the other.*

---

1. Alex Harrowell, "HOW NOT TO Build a Computer System," *Yorkshire Ranter*, November 19, 2006 <http://yorkshire-ranter.blogspot.com/2006/11/hownotto-build-computer-system.html>. The quotes are from "UK Dept of Health: Prescription for Disaster," *Baseline Magazine*, November 13, 2006 <http://www.baselinemag.com/c/a/Projects-Management/UK-Dept-of-Health-Prescription-for-Disaster>.

The managerialists inevitably called on a management consultant to run the show—as we all know, we are living in a new world, and the status quo is not an option, so nobody who actually knew anything about the NHS, hospitals, or for that matter computers could be considered. (Granger failed his CS degree.) With equal inevitability, he called on management consultants to tell him what to do. The great global consulting firm McKinsey duly concluded that only great, global consulting firms could do the job.

Choosing which ones was clearly a job only central authority could undertake, and the intervention of the press, the unions, competitors or elected representatives would only get in the way, so the whole thing vanished behind a cloud of secrecy. Secrecy enhances power. It does this by *exclusion*. The groups excluded included the doctors, nurses, technicians and administrators of the NHS—which means that the canonical mistake, the original sin of systems design was predetermined before the first requirements document was drawn up or the first line of code written. *Secrecy specifically excluded the end users from the design process.* There are two kinds of technologies—the ones that benefit the end-user directly, and the ones that are designed by people who think they know what they want. They can also be described as the ones that succeed and the ones that fail. Ignore the users, and you're heading for Lysenkoism.

Among the "problems" of the NHS system was that most hospitals had their own computer systems, developed either by small IT firms or in-house. The contracts stated that each of the five new regional service providers and the "spine" (BT) would have to replace them, design a single regional system, but also maintain "common standards" nationally. The sharp will spot the contradiction. If you have common standards for information exchange, why can't you have them within the region as well as between regions? Why do you need the regional system at all? Why do you need the big global consulting firm—standards, after all, are for everyone, from Google to the hobby programmer cranking out a few lines of Python or such. In fact, almost all developments in computing in the last 10 years have been in the direction of separating levels of abstraction. It doesn't matter if the web server runs Linux and the database Windows Server if they both speak XML at the application layer.

This was actually recognised for some purposes. The NHS bought 900,000 desktop licences for MS Windows and further commissioned Microsoft to develop a common interface for the NPfIT, thus ensuring that any common interface would be proprietary and unalterable except by Microsoft. But no-one seems to have thought through the implications of common standards. Instead, the contracts specified that the old systems must be torn out and the data transferred to the new, thus adding a huge sysadmin nightmare to the costs.

Trying to keep down the costs, iSoft outsourced the development to India. But the Thomas Friedman dream of hordes of crack coders as cheap as chips showed some flaws—specifically:

> the programmers, systems developers and architects involved didn't comprehend some of the terminology used by the British health system and, more important, how the system actually operated, the CfH conceded.

Neither did IDX's developers working with Microsoft in Seattle know anything about the NHS. This choice, like the secrecy, ensured that no NHS institutional memory would be available to the developers. So, 100 medics were shipped off to the coder farm to explain. Naturally, this effort to fix fundamental architecture problems by tinkering just added complexity and cost, as Pareto's theory of the second best bit. Eventually, one of the regional systems contractors decided to take iSoft's off-the-shelf product and hack it into something vaguely suitable, and another walked away. IDX and GE Healthcare's product was so dire that even BT couldn't make more than one implementation work in two and a half years, and then sacked them.

But, there is no sign any of this will affect policy whatsoever. Instead, the managers content themselves with intermediate statistical targets (apparently they are installing 600 N3 lines a month, a rather poor performance for any normal ISP), rigged definitions (the deal with Microsoft is said to have saved £1.5 billion—compared to what? certainly not open-source) and bully rhetoric about feeding the slower huskies to the faster ones (I am not joking). The inevitable signs of failure, meanwhile, emerge—it doesn't work.

As an example, in July, mission–critical computer services such as patient admini-stration systems, holding millions of patient records being provided by the CSC alliance across the Northwest and West Midlands region, were disrupted because of a network equipment failure, according to the CfH. As a result, some 80 trusts in the region were unable to access patient records stored at what was supposed to be either a foolproof data center or a disaster recovery facility with a full backup system. Every NPfIT system in the area was down for three days or longer. Service was fully restored and no patient data was lost, the CfH says.

That was not the first such failure. In fact, in the past five months more than 110 major incident failures having to do with NHS systems and the network have been re-ported to the CfH, according to *ComputerWeekly*.

But, of course, the users are lying and everything is wonderful.

"The CfH responded in an e-mail to Baseline: "It is easy to misinterpret the ex-pression 'major incident.' Some of these could have been, for example, individual users experiencing "slow running." We encourage reporting of incidents, and we are open and transparent about service availability levels, which we publish on our Web site."

Perhaps they'll put the chocolate ration up there too.

6

Agency and Incentive Problems within the Large Organization

INTRODUCTION

Most of our discussion of information problems in the previous chapter assumed, for the sake of simplicity, the absence of opportunism (i.e., it neglected the possibility that individual subgoals might conflict with maximizing the organization's goals). We considered mainly the costs of transferring and aggregating information that result from human conceptual limitations, and not those that result from strategic concealment of information in order to derive rents from private knowledge.

In this chapter, we will examine the agency problems resulting from opportunism: the deliberate pursuit of private goals at the expense of the organization, self-dealing by management at the expense of productive efficiency, shirking by production workers, and similar problems. The problem of inefficiency resulting from knowledge problems is compounded when those engaged in productive work try to influence policy in a more rational direction, and find that it is blocked by the self-interest of management (but justified, of course, by reference to the organization's official values). And misalignment of incentives and open differences in legitimate self-interest are themselves a problem, even without opportunism.

Before we go further, it might be a good idea to quote Oliver Williamson's definition of opportunism:

> By opportunism I mean self-interest seeking with guile. This includes but is scarcely limited to more blatant forms, such as lying, stealing, and cheating. Opportunism more often involves subtle forms of deceit . . . .
>
> More generally, opportunism refers to the incomplete or distorted disclosure of information, especially to calculated efforts to mislead, distort, disguise, obfuscate, or otherwise confuse. It is responsible for real or contrived conditions of information asymmetry, which vastly complicate problems of economic organization.[1]

The basic agency problem, as stated by Paul Milgrom and John Roberts, results from the fact that the agent has "an informational advantage":

> . . . only the agent knows what action he has taken in pursuit of his or the principal's goals, or only the agent has access to the specialized knowledge on which his action is based. The principal's problem is to design a compensation and control (monitoring) system that attracts and retains good agents and motivates them to behave appropriately (in the principal's interest). The asymmetry of information prevents easy determination of

---

1. Oliver Williamson, *The Economic Institutions of Capitalism: Firms, Markets, Relational Contracting* (New York: Free Press; London: Collier Macmillan, 1985), pp. 47-48.

whether a particular observed action or outcome corresponds to desirable behavior and thus renders the problem nontrivial.[1]

The general subject matter and subtopics of the agency and incentive field was ably described, also, by Laffont and Martimort in their general introduction to agency theory:

> The starting point of incentive theory corresponds to the problem of delegating a task to an agent with private information. This private information can be of two types: either the agent can take an action unobserved by the principal, the case of *moral hazard* or *hidden action*; or the agent has some private knowledge about his cost or valuation that is ignored by the principal, the case of *adverse selection* or *hidden knowledge* . . . . Another type of information problem that has been raised in the literature is the case of *nonverifiability*, which occurs when the principal and the agent share ex post the same information but no third party and, in particular, no court of law can observe this information.[2]

A. Mainstream Agency Theory

The effect of incentive structures and the distribution of rewards on performance, and the agency problems attending the shift of part of the reward of labor to rentier classes, was a matter of common sense observation long before the rise of formal organization theory. Adam Smith compared the incentive effects of various systems of agricultural labor in Book Three, Chapter Two of *The Wealth of Nations*.

> . . . [I]f great improvements are seldom to be expected from great proprietors, they are least of all to be expected when they employ slaves for their workmen. The experience of all ages and nations, I believe, demonstrates that the work done by slaves, though it appears to cost only their maintenance, is in the end the dearest of any. A person who can acquire no property, can have no other interest but to eat as much, and to labour as little as possible. Whatever work he does beyond what is sufficient to purchase his own maintenance can be squeezed out of him by violence only, and not by any interest of his own . . . .

> To the slave cultivators of ancient times gradually succeeded a species of farmers known at present in France by the name of metayers . . . . The proprietor furnished them with the seed, cattle, and instruments of husbandry, the whole stock, in short, necessary for cultivating the farm. The produce was divided equally between the proprietor and the farmer, after setting aside what was judged necessary for keeping up the stock, which was restored to the proprietor when the farmer either quitted, or was turned out of the farm . . . .

> Land occupied by such tenants is properly cultivated at the expense of the proprietor as much as that occupied by slaves. There is, however, one very essential difference between them. Such tenants, being freemen, are capable of acquiring property, and having a certain proportion of the produce of the land, they have a plain interest that the whole produce should be as great as possible, in order that their own proportion may be so . . . .

> It could never, however, be the interest even of this last species of cultivators to lay out, in the further improvement of the land, any part of the little stock which they might save from their own share of the produce, because the lord, who laid out nothing, was to get one half of whatever it produced. The tithe, which is but a tenth of the produce, is found to be a very great hindrance to improvement. A tax, therefore, which amounted to one half must have been an effectual bar to it. It might be the interest of a metayer to make the land produce as much as could be brought out of it by means of the stock furnished by the proprietor; but it could never be his interest to mix any part of his own with it. In France, where five parts out of six of the whole kingdom are said to be still occupied by this species of cultivators, the proprietors complain that their metayers take

1. Paul Milgrom and John Roberts, "An Economic Approach to Influence Activities in Organizations," *American Journal of Sociology*, supplement to vol. 94 (1988), p. S155.

2. Jean-Jacques Laffont and David Martimort, *The Theory of Incentives: The Principal-Agent Model* (Princeton and Oxford: Princeton University Press, 2002), p. 3.

every opportunity of employing the master's cattle rather in carriage than in cultivation; because in the one case they get the whole profits to themselves, in the other they share them with their landlord . . . .

To this species of tenancy succeeded, though by very slow degrees, farmers properly so called, who cultivated the land with their own stock, paying a rent certain to the landlord. When such farmers have a lease for a term of years, they may sometimes find it for their interest to lay out part of their capital in the further improvement of the farm; because they may sometimes expect to recover it, with a large profit, before the expiration of the lease.[1]

Frank Knight's 1921 work *Risk, Uncertainty and Profit* treated the firm as a mechanism for assumption of risk by the entrepreneur. Knight contrasted the "handicraft stage," or "production for the market," with "free enterprise." Under the former, a large number of individuals were independent producers who bore uncertainty for themselves. Under the latter, the great majority of small producers became contractual suppliers of productive services to the entrepreneur, who specialized in uncertainty-bearing and in return received the residual income of the firm.[2]

Of course this is grossly misleading, since there is no reason risks cannot be pooled and spread among small producers as joint residual claimants of a larger producer-owned firm, through cooperative ventures in auxialliary services like marketing, and through mutual insurance. The location of the entrepreneurial function in a small handful of large-scale owners is a historical accident. In fact Knight himself admitted as much shortly thereafter:

It matters not at all whether the persons liable to a given contingency organize among themselves into a fraternal or mutual society or whether they separately contract with an outside party to bear their losses as they fall in. Under competitive conditions and assuming that the probabilities involved are accurately known, an outside insurer will make no clear profit and the premiums will under either system be equal to the administrative costs of carrying on the business.[3]

The actual causal relationship is just the reverse of Knight's portrayal: the particular form of uncertainty-bearing that Knight associates with "free enterprise"—large-scale absentee ownership—is the outcome of large-scale, concentrated absentee ownership in the first place, and the attendant necessity of mitigating the risk for absentee owners.

Knight's discussion of "free enterprise" is the source of the distinction, widely relied upon in organization theory, between contractual and residual claimancy. Contractual income is a defined rent for productive services, while residual income (or profit, in the accounting sense) is what goes to the firm owner when all contractual expenses are paid.[4]

But Knight treated the firm as a mechanism for *managing* risk, as well as assuming it. He argued that organization was substituted for markets, and higher forms of organization like the corporation for lower forms like the partnership, in order to minimize the form of risk he called "moral hazard" (a term he borrowed from the insurance industry to include the broader category of "assumption by one person of the consequences of another person's decisions").[5]

Unfortunately, as Knight himself recognized, these risk-managing benefits were offset to some extent by the generation of *new* risks—agency risks—*within* the firm:

1. Adam Smith, *An Inquiry into the Nature and Causes of The Wealth of Nations*. Great Books edition (Chicago, London, Toronto: Encyclopedia Britannica, Inc., 1952), pp. 167-169.

2. Frank Knight, *Risk, Uncertainty, and Profit* (Boston and New York: Houghton Mifflin Company, 1921), p. 244.

3. *Ibid.*, p. 247.

4. *Ibid.* p. 271.

5. *Ibid.*, pp. 252-253.

Those in control of the policies of a business are almost inevitably in a better position to foresee its future earnings than are outsiders, and it is difficult to prevent their taking advantage of this position to the detriment of their efficiency as managers of productive operations. The "corporation problem" arises largely out of this situation.

Matters become still worse when the managers of productive property begin to manipulate their industrial and financial policies with a view to *producing* changes in capital values, of which they inevitably know in advance of outsiders and of which they take advantage with corresponding ease . . . . Perhaps as bad as manipulating policies for the sake of quick gains on the securities market is the corruption of sources of information for the same purpose.[1]

Chester Barnard, in *The Functions of the Executive*, distinguished between "effectiveness" and "efficiency," which was an early way of considering the ways in which individual pursuit of sub-goals may detract from the performance of the organization's goals.

Although effectiveness of cooperative effort relates to accomplishment of an objective of the system and is determined with a view to the system's requirements, efficiency relates to the satisfaction of individual motives.[2]

Of course the term "organization's goals" is misleading, since the organization is not a conscious entity with a will of its own. In fact, the goals of the organization are the goals of a particular group of individuals, whether it be the shareholders or the senior management. In the end, the "goals of the organization," or the "purpose" or "requirements" of the "system," are really the goals, purpose, and requirements of those who hold power within the organization or system.

The problem, therefore, is how to structure incentives so as to bring the individual's efforts in line with the purposes of those who run the organization. The most efficient form this takes is moral suasion:

In the words of Butler Shaffer, "institutions are . . . anxious to have us identify with them."

Because they have purposes of their own that transcend any conflicting personal interests, and because they can accomplish their purposes only through us, institutions have an incentive to promote those attitudes and conditions that will get us to subordinate our wants to theirs and submit to their authority . . .

In an effort to strengthen our attachments to them, institutions endeavor to persuade us that their interests and ours are entirely compatible . . .[3]

Much, if not most, of this function is carried out at the level of society as a whole, and the cost of much of it is underwritten by the state. Perhaps the single most important propaganda function, for shaping of the average employee's mindset, is carried out by the state schools. It's hardly coincidental that the first centralized state school systems were created, in the early middle decades of the nineteenth century, when the factory system needed a work force trained in the virtues of punctuality and obedience.

On a broader societal level, the extent to which the state and the corporate media together act as a propaganda apparatus has been described by Edward Herman and Noam Chomsky in *Manufacturing Consent*.[4]

As suggested by our snarky comment above, one essential component of the prevailing belief system that's especially important in the workplace is the ideology of "professionalism" (which will be discussed at length in Chapter Eight).

1. *Ibid.*, pp. 334–335.
2. *Ibid.*, p. 56.
3. Butler Shaffer, *Calculated Chaos: Institutional Threats to Peace and Human Survival* (San Francisco: Alchemy Books, 1985), pp. 40–41.
4. Edward S. Herman and Noam Chomsky, *Manufacturing Consent: The Political Economy of the Mass Media* (New York: Pantheon Books, 1988).

Barnard was well aware of the dangers presented by the employee who was not successfully socialized by any of these methods—especially the disgruntled employee who quietly remained within the belly of the beast:

> . . . If a communication is believed to involve a burden that destroys the net advantage of connection with the organization, there no longer would remain a net inducement to the individual to contribute to it. The existence of a net inducement is the only reason for accepting *any* order as having authority. Hence, if such an order is received it must be disobeyed (evaded in the more usual cases) as utterly inconsistent with personal motives that are the basis of accepting any orders at all. Cases of voluntary resignation from all sorts of organizations are common for this sole reason. Malingering and intentional lack of dependability are the more usual methods . . . .
>
> . . . [T]he determination of authority remains with the individual. Let these "positions" of authority in fact show ineptness, ignorance of conditions, failure to communicate what ought to be said, or let leadership fail . . . to recognize implicitly its dependence on the essential character of the relationship of the individual to the organization, and the authority if tested disappears.[1]

The "evasion" of orders, "malingering and intentional lack of dependability," all fall within the definition of sabotage as the "willful withdrawal of efficiency from the production process." Oliver Williamson described it as

> the possibility that disaffected members of the organization may, rather than quit the organization, choose to subvert it . . . . The disaffected employee whose estrangement is unknown may deliberately plant misinformation or disclose sensitive information to outsiders in ways that impair the performance of the firm.[2]

A large portion of the present-day workforce, having in fact seen corporate management demonstrate its "ineptness, ignorance of conditions, failure to communicate what ought to be said," or to show respect to the workforce commensurate with its dependence on them, is quietly engaged in just that sort of passive-aggressive rebellion. And as the official ideology fails to counteract the effects of what workers see with their own eyes, as more workers become disgruntled by stagnant wages, downsizings, and speedups, we can expect to see more and more such quiet rebellion driving up operating costs.

Philip Selznick, in a 1948 article, echoed Barnard's themes of the dependency of authority on consent, and the existence of private sub-goals at odds with the goals of the organization:

> . . . [I]t is recognized that control and consent cannot be divorced even within formally authoritarian structures . . . .
>
> Unfortunately for the adequacy of formal systems of coordination, the needs of individuals do not permit a single-minded attention to the stated goals of the system within which they have been assigned. The hazard inherent in the act of delegation derives essentially from this fact. Delegation is an organizational act, having to do with formal assignments of functions and powers. Theoretically, these assignments are made to roles or official positions, not to individuals as such. In fact, however, delegation necessarily involves concrete individuals who have interests and goals which do not always coincide with the goals of the formal system. As a consequence, individual personalities may offer resistance to the demands made upon them by the official conditions of delegation.[3]

1. Barnard, *Functions of the Executive*, pp. 166, 174.

2. Oliver Williamson, *Markets and Hierarchies, Analysis and Antitrust Implications: A Study in the Economics of Internal Organization* (New York: Free Press, 1975), pp. 122-123.

3. Philip Selznick, "Foundations of the Theory of Organization," *American Sociological Review*, Vol. 13, No. 1 (Feb. 1948), pp. 26-27.

Kenneth Arrow was one of the first thinkers to raise the issue[1] of monitoring costs in measuring an employee's productive output, as well as in verifying obedience. He divided the problem of "organizational control" into two parts:

> the choice of operating rules instructing the members of the organization how to act, and the choice of enforcement rules to persuade or compel them to act in accordance with the operating rules.[2]

Enforcement rules, in turn, raised problems of incentive and monitoring systems. Arrow named two:

> . . . (1) An effective incentive system creates new demands for information; the reward is a function of performance, so top management must have a way of measuring performance. This may be the objective function itself, or it may be some other, more easily measurable, index. If the index is something other than the objective itself, the manager's incentives may not be directed optimally from the viewpoint of the corporation; for example, if the index of the manager's performance is based primarily on output rather than profits, he will be tempted to be wasteful of inputs . . . . (2) Even if the index is thoroughly appropriate, the relation between the reward and the index remains to be determined.

Specifically, the agent's reward must reflect his contribution to an extent sufficient to secure his effort, without violating the purpose of the organization: namely, the appropriation of most of his productivity contributions. "The corporation of course intends to share in the profits attributable to the skill of its managers and not to give them all away to him . . . ."[3]

Arrow fails to mention one method by which such high-powered incentives could be achieved: residual claimancy by those engaged in productive effort. Of course he assumes, as a given, the absentee owned corporation worked by wage-laborers. But this is precisely the reason for most of the agency and information problems in the corporate economy: it starts from the premise of absentee ownership, and then resorts to hierarchy and extrinsic incentives to simulate the kind of employee behavior that would arise naturally in an economy of producer cooperatives. The hierarchical corporation is a sort of Rube Goldberg contraption for carrying out tasks as efficiently as possible given an utterly irrational foundation.

Michael Reich and James Devine criticized Arrow for his assumption of "implicit contract" rather than conflictual power relations between labor and capital. He presumed the existence of a harmony of interests, with hierarchy as an instrument for joint utility maximization by labor and capital.[4] If this was a failing on Arrow's part, then Armen Alchian and Harold Demsetz were guilty of it in spades.

Alchian and Demsetz made the next major contribution to the literature on the effort metering problem.[5] Their article, "Production, Information Costs, and Economic Organization," includes some extremely useful analysis. Much of their concrete discussion of the incentives for shirking, and the relative cost of monitoring compared to the savings is very much on the mark. Unfortunately, it's embedded in a larger context with so many Looking-Glass World ideological assumptions, that extracting the genuine insights and incorporating them into a more realistic general framework is a considerable operation.

1. Kenneth J. Arrow, "Control in Large Organizations," *Management Science (pre-1986)* 10:3 (April 1964), pp. 397-408.

2. *Ibid.* p. 398.

3. *Ibid.*, pp. 400-401.

4. Michael Reich and James Devine, "The Microeconomics of Conflict and Hierarchy in Capitalist Production," *The Review of Radical Political Economics* vol. 12 no. 4 (Winter 1981), p. 28.

5. Armen A. Alchian and Harold Demsetz, "Production, Information Costs, and Economic Organization," *The American Economic Review*, pp. 777-795.

They go entirely too far, for example, in asserting the nature of the corporation as a nexus of voluntary contracts. They deny, in fact, that authority relations are involved any more in employment in a corporate hierarchy than in self-employment in the market; the employment relation is a mere contractual relationship between equals, exactly comparable to the relation between a grocer and his customer.[1] First of all, on an existential level, it should be a matter of simple common sense to compare the feeling of being "a man set under authority" when one's continued livelihood depends on not offending a single employer, as opposed to offending one out of a hundred regular customers. But even on a purely theoretical level, Alchian and Demsetz implicitly assume, and unwarrantedly so, that labor relations take place in the environment of a free market. In such a free market, there would indeed be a common interest among employees of an organization to structuring the rules so as to minimize shirking and maximize output, because any increase in output would be shared by employees according to their marginal contributions to production. In the real world of state capitalism, however, the employment relation exists in the broader environment of a rigged market. The employment relationship takes on a considerable zero-sum character, in which the worker is apt to keep little if any of any increase in output, and any increase in productivity is likely to result only in speedups and downsizing. In the real world, the motives for what Taylor called "soldiering" are quite rational. In the real world, shirking and consumption on the job result not just from the prisoner dilemma created by imperfect metering, but from adversarial power relations within the corporation. Jeffrey Nielsen put it aptly:

> With rank-based logic, people see work as a burden and organization as a necessary evil. We only grudgingly join up with organizations and then find life within them to be nasty, boring, and deadening to the spirit. When the organization encounters hardships, the assumption is that those below should be sacrificed to protect the privilege of those above. All too frequently we read in the financial section of the paper about this type of logic in action: another CEO who laid off hundreds of workers is awarded with a fat bonus at the end of the year.[2]

A good illustration is Charles Johnson's critique of the predominant anti-union position among libertarians, as stated by Karen DeCoster:

> De Coster, like lots of other anti-union libertarians, claims that unions are economically harmful because they're toxic to efficiency and flexibility. The idea is that organized workers will tend to use their organization to oppose advances like automation, technological upgrades, flexible job duties, and reorganization of processes for greater efficiency. Partly because union contracts tend to preserve old job descriptions in amber, to better mark off each worker's turf, and partly because organized workers will use their coordinated bargaining power to oppose anything that reduces organized workers' hours or introduces new, not-yet-unionized (or differently-unionized) jobs into the shop. I don't necessarily find this complaint very persuasive. But. hell, let's grant most of it, for the sake of argument. Suppose that a union like the UAW *does* tend to block upgrades for greater efficiency and flexibility. If that's true, why is it true? *Because the unionized workers don't own the means of production.*
>
> It's no surprise that there would be conflicts between the interests of the workers and the interests of the boss and board when it comes to innovation in shop-floor technology or processes. For a wage laborer, sometimes new technology and new processes mean easier and better work to do; often they mean that your hours will be cut or you'll lose your job entirely. In any case they will be deployed and integrated into the flow of work according to what the *boss* finds most useful; they may very well result in you, as a wage laborer, getting stuck with speed-ups or harder work.

1. *Ibid.*, pp. 777-778.
2. Jeffrey Nielsen, *The Myth of Leadership: Creating Leaderless Organizations* (Palo Alto Calif.: Davies-Black Publishing, 2004), p. 53.

None of this is a decisive argument *against* innovations in shop-floor technology or processes; sometimes things have to change, and change can be hard. But it *is* a natural source of conflicts between labor and capital. Why should workers *want* to do more work faster, or to take on more flexible job descriptions, if they only stand to lose hours or subjected to speed-ups for their trouble? Both workers' livelihoods and process efficiency get caught in the crossfire.[1]

Alchian's and Demsetz's analysis of metering problems begins with the very useful recognition that metering problems might be reduced significantly by relying on market relations between separate firms, instead of on internal hierarchies.

> Metering problems sometimes can be resolved well through the exchange of products across competitive markets, because in many situations markets yield a high correlation between rewards and productivity. If a farmer increases his output of wheat by 10 percent at the prevailing market price, his receipts also increase by 10 percent. This method of organizing economic activity meters the *output directly*, reveals the marginal product and apportions the *rewards* to resource owners in accord with that direct measurement of their outputs. The success of this decentralized, market exchange in promoting productive specialization requires that changes in market rewards fall on those responsible for changes in *output*.[2]

If anything, the authors don't go far enough in making this argument. If the ideal contract is MacNeil's sharp ins and outs, then the market contract between separate firms or individuals is the ideal way to achieve it. Market contracting, as opposed to vertical integration, makes a virtue of treating the production process as a black box. When a firm decides to buy rather than make an input, all that matters is the contractually defined inputs and outputs; all questions of the efficiency with which inputs are used are "outsourced" to the firm. And a contracting firm with its functions limited to one or a few stages of the production process, will have most production decisions made close to the shop floor—thereby greatly reducing its internal agency and information problems. As for changes in rewards falling on those responsible for changes in output, this is not just a requirement—it's a virtue. From the standpoints of metering, internal efficiency, and high-powered rewards, the optimum is to integrate stages of production through market relations rather than hierarchy, and for each stage to be organized not merely as a firm, but as a worker cooperative in which those engaged in production, as residual claimants, reap all the rewards of increased output.

In the case of large organizations, metering is complicated by the fact that most production is what Alchian and Demsetz call "team production," so that no individual's marginal productivity is clearly identifiable, and it is difficult to determine the individual's share of the joint output. The authors argue that team production increases, by an order of magnitude, the cost of measuring individual productivity. As a result, the prevention of shirking becomes a problem.

> Clues to each input's productivity can be secured by observing behavior of individual inputs. When lifting cargo into the truck, how rapidly does a man move to the next piece to be loaded, how many cigarette breaks does he take, does the item being lifted tilt downward toward his side?
> If detecting such behavior were costless, neither party would have an incentive to shirk, because neither could impose the cost of his shirking on the other (if their cooperation was agreed to voluntarily). But since costs must be incurred to monitor each other, each input owner will have more incentive to shirk when he works as part of a team, than if his performance could be monitored easily or if he did not work as a team . . . .

1. Charles Johnson, "King Ludd's throne," *Rad Geek People's Daily*, May 23, 2008 <http://radgeek.com/gt/2008/05/23/king_ludds/>.
2. Alchian and Demsetz, p. 778.

Both leisure and higher income enter a person's utility function. Hence each person should adjust his work and realized reward so as to equate the marginal rate of substitution between leisure and production of real output to his marginal rate of substitution in consumption. That is, he would adjust his rate of work to bring his demand prices of leisure and output to equality with their true costs. However, with detection, policing, monitoring, measuring or metering costs, each person will be induced to take more leisure, because the effect of relaxing on *his realized* (reward) rate of substitution between output and leisure will be less than the effect on his *true* rate of substitution. His realized cost of leisure will fall more than the true cost of leisure, so he "buys" more leisure . . . .

If his relaxation cannot be detected perfectly at zero cost, part of its effects will be borne by others in the team . . . .[1]

Alchian and Demsetz, for the sake of accuracy, point out that by "leisure" they refer to all "non-pecuniary income." In this they include, in addition to shirking, what McManus (below) calls "consumption on the job":

In a university, the faculty use office telephones, paper, and mail for personal uses beyond strict university productivity. The university administrators could stop such practices by identifying *the* responsible person in each case, but they can do so only at higher costs than administrators are willing to incur. The extra costs of identifying each party (rather than merely identifying the presence of such activity) would exceed the savings . . . .[2]

The authors, with their unwarranted assumption of a non-zero-sum situation, assert that such shirking and consumption on the job result in lower pecuniary income for the faculty.[3] This ignores the possibility that such "non-pecuniary income" on the job will come in fact at the expense of rents that would otherwise accrue to management or to the owners, as a result of unequal exchange on the labor market.

But leaving aside their apologetic bias, the importance of their example in the block quote above cannot be overstated. In the vast majority of cases, any management attempt, through internal surveillance and authoritarianism, to prevent shirking, consumption on the job, or deliberate imposition of increased production costs (i.e., sabotage) by disgruntled workers, can be circumvented at less cost and difficulty by workers. In the offensive-defensive arms race between workers and employers, the workers will always be several steps ahead. Oliver Williamson's commentary on the above example sheds additional light on this problem. Referring to Alchian's and Demsetz's assertion that if detection of such pilfering were costless, it would be eliminated, he responded:

But is this really so? Does it assume, implicitly, that metering intensively, where this is easy (costless), has no effect on the attitudes of workers with regard to transactions that are costly to meter?

The distinction between perfunctory and consumate [sic] cooperation . . . is relevant in this connection. It seems at least plausible that extending metering with respect to such peccadilloes as appear to be of concern to Alchian and Demsetz . . . will be regarded as picayune and will elicit resentment. Cooperative attitudes will be impaired with the result that tasks such as teaching effectiveness—which can be metered only with difficulty, because information is deeply impacted, but for which consummate cooperation is important—will be discharged in a more perfunctory way.[4]

A disgruntled work force is quite adept at shifting its non-compliance to areas in which accurate metering is impossible, and thereby raising overall costs for the employer.

1. *Ibid.*, p. 780.
2. *Ibid.*, p. 780.
3. *Ibid.*, p. 780.
4. Oliver Williamson, *Markets and Hierarchies,* pp. 55-56.

Williamson's distinction between perfunctory and consummate cooperation will figure prominently in our discussion, in a later chapter, of the agency problems of labor.

Williamson argues that it's impossible, "for information impactedness reasons, [to] determine whether workers put their energies and inventiveness into the job in a way which permits task-specific cost-savings to be fully realized . . . ." Workers are able to thwart management policy by "withholding effort."[1] (It's odd, given such admissions, that Williamson elsewhere argues that opportunism poses less of a problem in organizations than in markets ("because . . . the internal incentive and control machinery is much more extensive and refined than that which obtains in market exchanges").[2] This is the logic of Chapter Nine.

Alchian's and Demsetz's "team production" focus is at the heart of the ideological difficulties in their articles. Their first example involves an actual work team and the problem of team members shirking at the expense of their coworkers. But their use of the term "team production" blurs (perhaps deliberately) the distinction between the team in the sense of a primary production unit of actual workers, and a "team" consisting of the owners of all production inputs—capital owners alongside workers. And it's understandable, given their ideological assumptions; they deny that there *is* a difference. For them the one is a "team," a nexus of contracts between equals, in the same sense as the other.

Their ideological agenda emerges even more clearly as they propose solutions to metering problems. It becomes increasingly clear that the image of the team as actual work unit has outlived its usefulness, and that their hypothetical "team" refers henceforward to the capitalist firm.

Alchian and Demsetz propose that the residual claimant in the firm should be assigned the monitoring function, and reap the productivity gains of monitoring, as a way of maximizing incentives to monitor accurately. The monitor's functions include

> measuring output performance, apportioning rewards, observing the input behavior of inputs as means of detecting or estimating their marginal productivity and giving assignments or instructions in what to do and how to do it. (It also includes . . . authority to terminate or revise contracts.)[3]

They portray this as a joint, voluntary contractual arrangement between the members of the "team" to give the capital-owning "team member" residual claimancy, in order to promote their common interests as co-equal members of the "team." The authors' idea of a "team" is reminiscent of the kind of "democracy" in which the sheep and the wolf, as equals, vote on what to have for dinner. What emerges from this agreement of equals, they continue, is an

> entire bundle of rights: 1) to be a residual claimant; 2) to observe input behavior; 3) to be the central party common to all contracts with inputs; 4) to alter the membership of the team; and 5) to sell these rights, that defines the *ownership* (or the employer) of the *classical* (capitalist, free-enterprise) firm. The coalescing of these rights has arisen, our analysis asserts, because it resolves the shirking information problem of team production better than does the noncentralized contractual arrangement.[4]

So, it finally emerges, what started out promising to be an examination of the problem of monitoring costs arising within the conventional, hierarchically managed corporate form, and possible solutions for it, has at long last shown itself instead to be a paean to hierarchical management as a *solution* to the monitoring problem. It does not examine monitoring costs as a problem of the capitalist firm, but explains the capitalist firm as the *solution*

1. Williamson, *Markets and Hierarchies*, p. 69.
2. *Ibid.*, p. 10.
3. Alchian and Demsetz, op. cit., p. 782.
4. *Ibid.*, p. 783.

to monitoring costs. It treats residual claimancy by the capitalist owner as a response to *team* needs, with workers relying on the helpful employer to provide some solution to their prisoner's dilemma problem of shirking. It is, more specifically, an edifying account of how, in a society of free and equal people, some small number of whom just happen to own most of the means of production, and some of whom just happen to have only their labor-power to sell, everyone jointly agrees—as a matter of common interest, of course—to organize production in absentee-owned, hierarchical, capitalist firms. It seems that we have a new companion fable to share an honored place beside Marx's "bourgeois nursery-tale" of primitive accumulation.

Unfortunately, it ignores the extent to which monitoring problems *arise* from the separation of ownership from labor, the divorce of decision-making power from knowledge, and the dissociation of effort from reward, in the hierarchical and absentee-owned firm. The truth is that hierarchy comes into existence only to "solve" problems *created* by structural barriers to the most efficient form of production: the worker-owned and worker-managed firm.

In other words, to paraphrase a bumper sticker, if the hierarchical, absentee-owned, capitalist firm is the answer, it must be a real stupid question.

But on reflection, it is possible that much of Alchian's and Demsetz's overall argument can be salvaged. Their treatment of monitoring costs and shirking is quite useful, if one mentally translates their "team" perspective to a "hierachy" perspective. For example, their insight that efficiency requires a close correlation of productivity and rewards:

If the economic organization meters poorly, with rewards and productivity only loosely correlated, then productivity will be smaller; but if the economic organization meters well productivity will be greater.[1]

Again, to take the commonsense implication of what they actually say, as opposed to their ideological assumptions about what it means, this principle can be taken as a fairly straightforward argument for the greatest possible amount of 1) worker equity in the firm; and 2) worker self-management.

Although Alchian and Demsetz clearly have capitalist ownership in mind, their explicit statements equating employer, firm owner, and residual claimant, and arguing for the assignment of the monitoring function to the residual claimant, do not *technically* require these roles to be filled by the owner of capital inputs. Their argument for a monitoring function of the residual claimant, conceivably, could be applied to a situation in which the workers possessed residual claimancy and hired capital from an absentee input-owner; certainly, at least, it is fully consistent with that possibility, however little they have it in mind and however hostile they may be to it.

Their argument for assigning the monitoring function to the residual claimant, in itself, makes perfect sense. Stripped of all their cultural biases and pro-capitalist apologetics, the essential core of the argument is that monitoring power should be vested in the residual claimant: a principle that makes sense in the case of any kind of ownership, including worker ownership.

What does not make sense is their assumption that residual claimancy will rest with the owners of capital inputs.[2] In fact, the efficiencies resulting from assigning the monitor-

1. *Ibid.* p. 779.

2. In fact, at one point toward the end of their article, they further undermine the basis for this assumption by suggesting that stockholder "ownership" of the corporation might be a myth, and arguing that the difference between ownership of equity and debt, and more specifically between preferred stock and other securities of all kinds, is at most a matter of degree. In so doing, intentionally or not, they abandon the idea that residual claimancy is vested in capital ownership, and instead put forth ownership of the firm itself rather than ownership of capital (a distinction that will be familiar to readers of David Ellerman) as the basis of residual claimancy. In so doing, they

ing function to the residual claimant are maximized in the producer cooperative. Monitoring is more expensive for the capital-owning member of the "team" because it requires a paid specialist, like a foreman or other front-line supervisor. On the other hand, if the monitoring of effort is a good method for approximating the member's marginal contribution, then production workers are ideally situated to monitor each other's efforts in the normal course of their work.

> "What is meant by performance? Input energy, initiative, work attitude, perspiration, rate of exhaustion? Or output? It is the latter that is sought—the *effect* or output. But performance is nicely ambiguous because it suggests both input and output. It is *nicely* ambiguous because as we shall see, sometimes by inspecting a team member's input activity we can better judge his output effect, perhaps not with complete accuracy but better than by watching the output of the *team*."[1]

Savings on monitoring costs are maximized when workers are monitoring themselves, because they are the most effective and cheapest monitors—when, that is, they have a rational interest in maximizing output. That's why producer cooperatives typically have about a quarter as many foremen as capitalist-owned firms in the same industry.

Their blurring of the distinction between the capitalist firm with its managerial hierarchy, and the actual production team, is quite unfortunate. First, while the members of a production team may have a common interest in preventing one member from shirking at the expense of the others, they may also (in the real world of adversarial employment relations) have a common interest in reducing their effort as a group (i.e., the slowdown or "going canny"); there is, therefore, a real difference between shirking at the expense of one's coworkers and shirking at the expense of the company. Second, the costs and difficulty of monitoring individual workers by higher levels of authority within a managerial hierarchy—to which Alchian and Demsetz devote little attention—are probably an order of magnitude greater than the costs and difficulty of mutual monitoring among members of a work team.

John McManus also contributed greatly, in an article written not long afterward, to the literature on metering problems. He argued that the choice between the hierarchical firm and the price system reflected the comparative transaction costs of metering between one and the other.

> A centralized organization, such as a firm, can improve on the allocative results of a price system only by effecting changes in the behaviour of the individuals within the group we are considering, given the costs of enforcing constraints on the activities of the individuals. The establishment of a firm leads to changes in the behaviour of individuals by changing the nature of constraints on their activities. In the place of market prices are substituted the directives of a central authority.[2]

The problem is that McManus (and other leading New Institutionalist figures like Oliver Williamson) tend to exaggerate the transaction costs of markets compared to hierarchy. McManus, in particular, was so focused on countering the neoclassical assumption that market prices were "costlessly enforceable behavior,"[3] that he neglected the contrary case. Defining enforcement cost as "the resource cost incurred to detect violations of behavior constraints," he continued:

abandon whatever moral basis they may have had for vesting residual claimancy in the managerial hierarchy as representatives of the "owners," and leave the choice between control by a self-perpetuating managerial oligarchy and control by production teams as an arbitrary choice, based in mere legal convention, between two groups of employees.

1. *Ibid.*, pp. 781–782n.
2. McManus, "The Costs of Alternative Economic Organizations," op. cit., p. 342.
3. *Ibid.*, p. 337.

When we count our change, weigh meat, punch time clocks, inspect a used car, or su-pervise labourers, we are incurring costs to enforce behaviour constraints by monitoring or measuring the activity of another individual.[1]

The difference is that when a butcher weighs meat and gives back change, verifying the weight of the meat and counting the change are quite straightforward, compared to the me-tering problems inside an organization—where there is often no easily quantifiable "meat" and no "change" to count. The time clock may verify when a warm body was present—the theme, once again, of Chapter Nine—but the level of effort expended is another matter en-tirely. In most normal conditions, it is less expensive to measure product outputs than process inputs, which makes market trading across firm boundaries preferable in achieving the clear ins and outs that MacNeil treated as the defining feature of the ideal contract.

One reason for the inferiority of hierarchies to markets is that administrative con-straints are less powerful than the "pecuniary behaviour constraints" (or high-powered in-centives) of the market. McManus is entirely correct that this substitution is necessary within a hierarchy.

> Although one never observes a firm in which pecuniary incentives are completely ab-sent, because it is costly to enforce centralized control, it remains true that the firm "su-percedes" . . . a price system.[2]

The substitution of administrative for high-powered market incentives does, in some cases, make the individual employee more indifferent between the alternative assignments he may receive, and hence more cooperative and more compliant to authority:

> Centralized organization normally make [sic] some efforts to prevent members from ex-changing among themselves, often called bribery . . . . In a centralized organization some forms of exchange . . . would reduce the total output of the members of the organization by creating an incentive for an individual to impose damages on others and/or by mak-ing it more costly for the members to enforce the directives of the central authority.

The prohibited forms of internal trade include, among others, the sale or cherry-picking of assignments, and attempts to sabotage others, if high-powered rewards are tied to the value-added of the particular assignment.[3]

Oliver Williamson argues, on similar grounds that "hierarchy uses flat incentives be-cause these elicit greater cooperation and because unwanted side effects are checked by added internal controls."

> Not only, therefore, will workers be more willing to accommodate because their com-pensation is the same whether they "do this" or "do that," but an unwillingness to ac-commodate is interpreted not as an excess of zeal but as a predilection to behave in a non-cooperative way.[4]

But it's questionable how effectively the side-effects are checked by internal controls. As we will see in a later chapter, the agency problems of the incomplete contract, coupled with imperfect monitoring and the tendency toward perfunctory cooperation, probably make the internal transaction costs of hierarchy at least as high, *ceteris paribus*, as those of the market.

Williamson himself admits there is a tradeoff involved in "the bureaucratized reward structure in the large firm which relies on salary and promotion rather than direct partici-

---

1. *Ibid.*, p. 336.
2. *Ibid.*, p. 342.
3. *Ibid.*, pp. 342-343.
4. Oliver Williamson, "Comparative Economic Organization: The Analysis of Discrete Structural Alternatives," *Administrative Science Quarterly*, 36 (1991), p. 275.

pation in the earnings associated with successful innovation."[1] Such low-powered incentives (i.e., lacking a strong correlation between changes in effort and changes in reward)[2] do not elicit much in the way of enthusiastic contribution.

In fact, contrary to Williamson's assumption, low-powered incentives may actually make workers *less* indifferent between assignments. Paul Milgrom and John Roberts argue that low-powered incentives are themselves an incentive for gaming the system, or "influence activities," as they call it. Were the remuneration for each job closely tied to its pleasantness or unpleasantness, as is the case in a free labor market, compensation would adjust automatically "to insulate employees against any non-monetary effects of the organization's decisions." In that case, employees would be "indifferent among the various decisions the organization might take, and . . . would have no reason not to cooperate fully in promoting the organization's objectives."[3] But since the central principle of hierarchy is the downward shifting of unpleasantness and the upward shifting of perks, this correspondence of reward to disutility is ruled out by the nature of things.

Although the substitution of administrative for market incentives is necessary within an employment relationship, that is really only another reason for the greater overall efficiencies of market contracting compared to hierarchy. The hierarchy is more "efficient" only in cases when a market simply can't do the job (Williamson admitted as much, as we saw in Chapter One, treating markets as superior to hierarchies aside from the exceptional case of asset specificity). Even in a majority of the latter cases, the calculus takes place in an environment of artificially high asset specificity, so that state capitalism promotes higher levels of asset specificity (and hence of hierarchy) than would prevail in a free market. And in a much larger majority of cases, the choice of hierarchy reflects power considerations: the usefulness of the organization as a base for exercising power in the outside society, or as a machine for internal control of a labor-force largely devoid of intrinsic motivation, given the structural forces that promote absentee ownership and the wage system.

It's odd, therefore, that Williamson persists in treating hierarchy as a solution to the problem of opportunism under incomplete contracting.

> Not every transaction fits comfortably into the classical contracting scheme. In particular, for long-term contracts executed under conditions of uncertainty complete presentiation [i.e., anticipation of future contingencies in the terms of the contract] is apt to be prohibitively costly if not impossible. Problems of several kinds arise. First, not all future contingencies for which adaptations are required can be anticipated at the outset. Second, the appropriate adaptations will not be evident for many contingencies until the circumstances materialize. Third, except as changes in states of the world are unambiguous, hard contracting between autonomous parties may well give rise to veridical disputes when state-contingent claims are made. In a world where (at least some) parties are inclined to be opportunistic, whose representations are to be believed?
>
> Faced with the prospective breakdown of classical contracting in such circumstances . . . [one alternative] would be to remove those transactions from the market and organize them internally instead. Adaptive, sequential decision-making would then be implemented under unified ownership and with the assistance of hierarchical incentive and control systems.[4]

. . . Which would alter bounded rationality and opportunism *how*, exactly? The functioning of Williamson's "hierarchical incentive and control systems" depends on internal monitoring systems which are equally vulnerable, given information impactedness and opportunism, to "veridical disputes." The hierarchy does indeed gain increased authority, un-

---

1. Williamson, *Markets and Hierarchies*, pp. 129-30.
2. Williamson, "Comparative Economic Organization," p. 275.
3. Milgrom and Roberts, "An Economic Approach to Influence Activities in Organizations," p. S158.
4. Williamson, *The Economic Institutions of Capitalism*, p. 70.

der a "general clause," to meet new contingencies on an ad hoc basis without having to renegotiate. But compliance with management policies is as subject to monitoring problems and opportunism under hierarchy as is compliance with the terms of a contract. The general clause *itself* is as unenforceable in practical terms under hierarchy as in the market. As Williamson's own treatment of "perfunctory cooperation" suggests, passive aggression can bring any managerial hierarchy to its knees.

McManus writes a great deal on the particular agency problems resulting from the adminstrative incentives of the corporate hierarchy:

> The establishment of a centralized organization weakens the relationship between an individual's income and his actions . . . .
>
> The loss that results from the attenuation or elimination of pecuniary behaviour constraints is due to the cost of enforcing constraints against consumption "on the job" in a centralized organization. . . . [T]here are always some opportunities in any organization to direct one's activities to such non-pecuniary forms of consumption. In watching pretty girls, the enjoyment of companions and good conversations, taking pride in one's workmanship, and in countless other ways individuals "produce" output for use while on the job. With a centralized organization such as a firm, there is no immediate, direct loss of pecuniary income from consumption on the job and individuals will, therefore, tend to damage other members of the firm by shirking, thus reducing the total output . . . generated within the firm.
>
> . . . The external effects that will lower output within a price system will mainly be due to individuals' exploiting the opportunities for consumption on the job against which it is too expensive . . . to enforce constraints.[1]

In a 1976 article, Michael Jensen and William Meckling built further on this work on self-dealing and other agency costs. They started with a summary of the agency relationship and its problems:

> If both parties to the relationship are utility maximizers, there is good reason to believe that the agent will not always act in the best interests of the principal. The *principal* can limit divergences from his interest by establishing appropriate incentives for the agent and by incurring monitoring costs designed to limit the aberrant activities of the agent . . . . However, it is generally impossible for the principal or the agent at zero cost to ensure that the agent will make optimal decisions from the principal's viewpoint.
>
> Agency costs result from "[t]he problem of inducing an 'agent' to behave as if he were maximizing the 'principal's' welfare . . . ."[2]

And these agency problems, they add in a footnote, are "generated at every level of the organization."[3]

In the rest of the article they argue that the less equity an owner-manager owns in the firm, the greater his incentive toward self-dealing; the resulting reduction in overall organizational income is diluted among numerous owners, while the gain accrues entirely to him.[4] But in fact this argument applies to all agency relationships, and is an excellent ar-

---

1. McManus, op. cit., pp. 344-345.
2. Michael C. Jensen and William H. Meckling, "Theory of the Firm: Managerial Behavior, Agency Costs and Ownership Structure," *Journal of Financial* Economics, vol. 3 no. 4 (October 1976), pp. 5-6.
3. *Ibid.*, p. 6n.
4. Kenneth Arrow took a more nuanced view. It was not enough to reward a manager *proportionally* to his marginal profitability, if the absolute amount of the reward was too small a fraction of his actual marginal contribution. Nevertheless, he said, productivity rewards may still achieve a maximum return at a relatively modest level well below the value of the manager's marginal contribution. "Research in Management Controls: A Critical Synthesis," in C. Bonini, R. Jaediche, and H. Wagner, eds., *Management Controls: New Directions in Basic Research* (New York: McGraw-Hill, Inc., 1964), pp. 325-326. Of course Arrow, writing in 1964, had little idea of the

gument for vesting residual claimancy in production workers, as a way of reducing monitoring costs to a minimum and securing maximum effort.

We have already seen, in the previous chapter, that considerable transaction costs result from the distribution of idiosyncratic information among the members of an organization, and the difficulties involved in getting it to the right people. All this is true even without opportunism. When opportunism is thrown in, costs and information problems are further increased by the fact that those in possession of idiosyncratic information deliberately use it as a source of rents. Agents do their best to maintain a monopoly on information to which they are presently in sole possession, at the expense of the principal, in order to continue collecting such rents.

Hayek observed that the private information distributed among the members of an organization is vital to the successful operation of the organization. But as R. Preston McAffee and John McMillan point out,[1] those in possession of such information often see the organization's need for it as a source of bargaining power for themselves, and "[make] strategic use . . . of any special knowledge they have acquired":

> This distortion increases cumulatively as the information moves up the hierarchy, so longer hierarchies have greater informational inefficiencies.[2]

Milgrom and Roberts, likewise, refer to the perceived benefits of "suppressing or distorting information" in order to influence decisions. The cost of bureaucratic politics is one of the diseconomies of the M-form corporation, as opposed to contracting across independent firm boundaries: "The boundaries between independent firms reduce the possibilities for influence. Consequently, those boundaries reduce influence costs."[3]

Oliver Williamson saw the small-numbers exchange relations in a hierarchy, and the information rents extracted under such circumstances, as quite similar to their counterparts in the outside market economy:

> Shifting a transaction from the market to the firm is significant not because a small-numbers exchange relation is eliminated but rather because the incentives of the parties are transformed. Indeed, the typical internal transaction is really a small-numbers exchange relation writ large. Investment by a firm in fixed plant and organizational infrastructure serves to insulate internal transactions from competition in the product market—with the result that, in the short run at least, there may be no credible alternative source of supply whatsoever. Functional managers, naturally, are not unaware of this condition. Coupled with the information impactedness advantage that they enjoy, a nontrivial degree of managerial discretion obtains.
>
> Internal opportunism takes the form of subgoal pursuit where by subgoal pursuit is meant an effort to manipulate the system to promote the individual and collective interests of the affected managers. Such efforts generally involve distorting communications in a strategic manner.[4]

The rents extracted from such control of information within the organization are directly analogous to the rents on control of information (through so-called "intellectual property" laws) in the outside economy. One reason mid-level managers are so resistant to networked organization models like "Enterprise 2.0" is that they enable ordinary produc-

sheer magnitude of today's potential for managerial self-dealing within the corporation, or the comparative opportunities for feathering one's own nest at the expense of profit-maximization.

    1. R. Preston McAffee and John McMillan, "Organizational Diseconomies of Scale," *Journal of Economics & Management Strategy*, Vol. 4, No. 3 (Fall 1995): 399-426.

    2. *Ibid.*, pp. 400-401.

    3. Paul Milgrom and John Roberts, "Bargaining Costs, Influence Costs, and the Organization of Economic Activity," in James E. Alt and Kenneth A Shepsis, eds., *Perspectives in Positive Political Economy* (New York: Cambridge University Press, 1990), pp. 482-485.

    4. Williamson, *Markets and Hierarchies*, pp. 124-125.

tion workers who generate useful knowledge to bypass the manager's informational gate-keeping function. Likewise, the corporate economy's hostility to peer-production and open-source information models in the outside economy is a response to a perceived (and very real) threat to the gatekeeping role of companies that have lost the technological basis they had for that role in the old days of broadcast culture, and today depend entirely on the so-called "intellectual property" that they own.

Corporate management also extracts rents from the production workers at lower levels of the hierarchy, when enabled by non-competitive markets, in a manner parallel to their rent extraction from the outside society.

> In a firm, according to our model, (a) production efficiency falls as the hierarchy lengthens; (b) production efficiency may rise or fall, depending on the form of the cost function, when the firm's output market becomes more competitive; (c) the longer the hierarchy, the smaller the marginal rate of payment with respect to output of the workers at the bottom of the hierarchy (so small firms will pay their workers piece rates, large firms will pay closer to fixed wages); (d) the more competitive the firm's output market, the more sensitive pay is to performance (so competitive firms will pay their workers piece rates, monopolists will pay closer to fixed wages); (e) the higher an individual is up the hierarchy, the more sensitive are marginal payments to performance (so bonuses will be a bigger fraction of income for executives than for production-line workers); and (f) a firm with a long hierarchy may not be viable in a competitive industry (so a large firm might respond to an increase in competition by shortening its hierarchy).[1]

McAffee's and McMillan's argument is, obviously, a considerable departure from Oliver Williamson's approach. Williamson considers monopoly explanations of hierarchy to be overblown, and prefers to stress the increased governance efficiencies of hierarchy over market in cases of asset specificity.

Information rents are, in large part, the basis for the phenomena we will be examining in Chapters Eight and Nine, on agency problems associated with management and labor. Because of information rents, complete contracts—even when theoretically possible—are largely unenforceable. Open-ended promises by workers to accept direction from superiors, by management to pursue the interests of shareholders in preference to their own, or by the management of an acquiring firm to intervene in the affairs of the newly integrated division only in the case of clearly specified justifications—all these things are unenforceable, because the verification of compliance depends on information to which the promising party alone is privy.

We have already seen hints of a recurring theme in the preceding material: the need to internalize effort and reward in the same actor, if incentives are to operate with maximum efficiency. This was a matter of special importance for Alchian and Demsetz, although in their formulation it required the counter-intuitive mechanism of vesting the monitoring function in the managerial hierarchy as residual claimants, in order to maximize the incentive of the monitor to extract maximum effort from workers through administrative incentives. They took the rather perverse stance that sharing profits with those actually engaged in production would reduce the incentive to produce, by reducing the incentive of the overseer to wield the whip effectively over the producers.

Holmstrom and Milgrom showed some awareness of the principle, arguing for asset ownership as the source of high-powered incentives: "When an agent owns a set of productive assets, she maintains those assets more effectively. She also reaps the many implicit returns that accrue through such ownership, notably those stemming from an enhanced

---

1. McAfee and McMillan, op. cit., p. 401.

bargaining position."[1] The implication in favor of producer cooperatives would seem fairly obvious, but perhaps not in this crowd.

In fact, it's remarkable just how little the question of internalizing rewards among production workers enters into the mainstream discussion of agency and incentives. Workers are often presented as the only participants in the firm whose main motivation is, as a matter of course, the fear of detection and punishment rather than the hope of reward for greater output.

A good example is the disconnect between Michael Jensen's perception of motivational issues for senior corporate management, and his perception of motivational issues for production workers. In the 1970s and '80s, Jensen was the apostle of the "entrepreneurial corporation." The central focus of his thought was how to structure incentives, through stock options and bonuses, to tighten the shareholder reins on management. Meanwhile, he decried the obstacles to economic progress posed by "striking Eastern Air Lines pilots, Pittston Coal miners, [and] New York Telephone employees, who seem perfectly content to destroy or damage their employer's organization while attempting to serve their own interests." The idea that his principles of management motivation might be applied to workers, attempting to align their interests with those of the firm by transforming them into stakeholders with some degree of residual claimancy, apparently never occurred to him.[2]

More generally, the corporate culture's view of how to structure incentives to overcome agency problems is completely different for management than it is for the productive work force. The corporate CEO's drive to loot the company, it seems, is so overwhelming and fundamental that a Welch or Nardelli must be given a salary and stock options, each worth tens of millions of dollars, to dissuade him from taking off for Costa Rica with several suitcases full of embezzled cash—and even then, it often doesn't work. For the production worker, on the other hand, the threat of termination and a bit of Fish! Philosophy are enough to elicit maximum effort and get him to view the employer's interests as identical to his own.

B. RADICAL AGENCY THEORY

While mainstream organization theory tends to take hierarchy for granted, many of its findings dovetail with the work of more radical thinkers. For example Paul Goodman and Ursula LeGuin, two of the most insightful of them, elaborate principles that are implicit but undeveloped in the orthodox discipline.

Especiallty relevant Goodman's distinction between intrinsic and extrinsic motivation: "subordinates are restricted in both initiative and self-expression and their motivation is likely to be merely extrinsic, rise in status and salary."[3]

Extrinsic motivation comes into play in exploitative situations, where the work process is subjected to control from above and the expenditure of effort is for goals imposed from outside. Extrinsic is substituted for intrinsic motivation as a matter of necessity, when the institutional structure (absentee ownership or an administrative hierarchy) precludes production workers from internalizing the fruits of their labor:

1. Holmstrom and Milgrom, p. 972.

2. Michael C. Jensen, "The Evidence Speaks Loud and Clear," *Harvard Business* Review 89 (November-December), pp. 12-14. Quoted in Doug Henwood, *Wall Street: How it Works and for Whom* (London and New York: Verso, 1997), p. 272.

3. Paul Goodman, *People or Personnel*, in *People or Personnel* and *Like a Conquered Province* (New York: Vintage Books, 1963, 1965), p. 81.

The conqueror is originally a pirate; he and his band do not share in the commonwealth, they have interests apart from the community preyed on. Subsequently, however, piracy becomes government, the process of getting people to perform by extrinsic motivators, of penalty and blackmail, and later bribery and training .... Necessarily, such directed and extrinsically motivated performance is not so strong, efficient, spontaneous, inventive, well-structured, or lovely as the normal functioning of a free community of interests. Very soon society becomes lifeless. The means of community action, initiative, decision, have been preempted by the powerful .... Inevitably, as people become stupider and more careless, administration increases in size and power; and conversely.[1]

In such cases, the goals of the owners or the administrators are substituted for the intrinsic motivation of those directly engaged in work, and enforced with administrative penalties. In the case of higher education,

it makes an enormous difference if it is directly society that uses the schools to train youth for its needs, or if it is directly the scholars that use the schools to learn or teach what they practically want to know or profess. When seminaries are founded to train ministers or our present universities are heavily subsidized to train military engineers, the social needs exist in the school as "goals of the administration" and this adds many complications: the scholars must be motivated, disciplined, evaluated. But when students who want to be lawyers or doctors find themselves a faculty, or masters with something important to profess attract disciples, the case is simpler: the goals are implicit and there is no problem of motivation.[2]

One does not have to equate pecuniary motivation, as such, to extrinsic motivation, to appreciate the usefulness of Goodman's distinction. To use the language of mainstream organization theory, the substitution of administrative incentives for the "high-powered incentives" of the market is a substitution of extrinsic for intrinsic motivation: effort is divorced from reward, so that the two are no longer internalized in the same actor. But the substitution of entirely pecuniary motivation as a compensation for loss of control of one's work (the Taylorist bargain) is also a substitution of extrinsic for intrinsic motivation. One of the defining features of extrinsically motivated work is the loss of control over the pace and organization of one's own work, and the satisfaction that come from it, as well as the stress that comes from such loss of control:

It is not so much that the pace is fast . . . but that it is someone else's pace or schedule. One is continually interrupted. And the tension cannot be normally discharged by decisive action and doing things one's own way. There is competitive pressure to act a role, yet paradoxically one is rarely allowed to do one's best or use one's best judgment. Proofs of success or failure are not tangibly given in the task, but always in some superior's judgment.[3]

Indeed, as we saw in Chapter Four, one of the central purposes of the state's school system is to train people from early childhood to understand that the tasks assigned by others, by authority figures, and motivated extrinsically, are the important ones. Self-selected tasks done for intrinsic motivation are trivialized as "play" or "hobbies." The school is almost diabolically designed to make children identify "learning" with the execution of tasks imposed by authority, and thus to impart utter loathing of the very idea of learning. As a result, like Huxley's Deltas who as infants learned to associate books with painful electrical shocks, the majority of people can be safely trusted not to engage in any form of learning not directly associated with service to the corporate state. The school perverts and destroys all joy in learning in exactly the same way that the job perverts and destroys all joy in productive labor. The school, finally, is designed to habituate the young person to a life in

1. *Ibid.*, pp. 182-183.
2. Goodman, *The Community of Scholars*, in *Compulsory Miseducation* and *The Community of Scholars* (New York: Vintage books, 1964, 1966), pp. 212-213.
3. Goodman, *Like a Conquered Province*, in *People or Personnel* and *Like a Conquered Province*, p. 351.

which, for eight hour chunks of the day, five days a week, he walks through the doors of an institutional building into a life that is not his own and accepts tasks that are not his own; the relevance as a preparation for working life should be obvious.

In the typical large corporation, a major part of the work of Human Resources cheerleaders is devoted to the pretense that workers' main motivation is intrinsic. This is especially true in my field, healthcare. The HR cheerleaders pretend that the mission, vision, and values statements actually mean something to the worker (or to anybody, for that matter). But why should they, when senior management cares only about career advancement, white collar featherbedding, and bureaucratic empire building? Workers who really *are* dedicated to patient care are cynically manipulated and squeezed dry of every drop of compassion, their every minute at work a hell of short-staffing and stress. The typical hospital's management manufactures burnouts like Carter manufactures liver pills.

Goodman's contrast of extrinsic to intrinsic motivation was illustrated, in a fictional venue, by Ursula LeGuin in *The Dispossessed*. Her protagonist Shevek, a traveller from the libertarian communist world of Anarres, recalls his conversation with an elderly conservative (Atro) on the authoritarian and capitalist world of Urras. Shevek looks back on the conversation from his later perspective, hiding out in a warehouse after the suppression of a workers' insurrection in the leading imperialist state on Urras:

> Atro had once explained to him how this was managed, how the sergeants could give the privates orders, how the lieutenants could give the privates and the sergeants orders, how the captains . . . and so on and so on up to the generals, who could give everyone else orders and need take them from none, except the commander in chief. Shevek had listened with incredulous disgust. "You call that organization?" he had inquired. "You even call it discipline? But it is neither. It is a coercive mechanism of extraordinary inefficiency—a kind of seventh-millennium steam engine! With such a rigid and fragile structure what could be done that was worth doing?" This had given Atro a chance to argue the worth of warfare as the breeder of courage and manliness and weeder-out of the unfit, but the very line of his argument had forced him to concede the effectiveness of guerrillas, organized from below, self-disciplined. "But that only works when the people think they're fighting for something of their own—you know, their homes, or some notion or other," the old man had said. Shevek had dropped the argument. He now continued it, in the darkening basement among the stacked crates of unlabeled chemicals. He explained to Atro that he now understood why the Army was organized as it was. It was indeed quite necessary. No rational form of organization would serve the purpose. He simply had not understood that the purpose was to enable men with machine guns to kill unarmed men and women easily and in great quantities when told to do so.[1]

The hierarchical corporation, likewise, is a clumsy Rube Goldberg device for eliciting effort from people with absolutely no rational cause to be willing to expend unnecessary effort or increase output or productivity.

Douglas McGregor, the father of "Theory Y" management, made a similar observation about work incentives:

> Theory Y assumes that people will exercise self-direction and self-control in the achievement of organizational objectives *to the degree that they are committed to those objectives*. If that commitment is small, only a slight degree of self-direction and self-control will be likely, and a substantial amount of external influence will be necessary. If it is large, many conventional external controls will be relatively superfluous, and to some extent self-defeating. Managerial policies and practices materially affect this degree of commitment.[2]

1. Ursula LeGuin, *The Dispossessed* (New York: Harper Paperbacks, 1974), pp. 305–306.
2. Douglas McGregor, *The Human Side of Enterprise* (New Work, London, Toronto: McGraw-Hill Book Company, Inc., 1960), p. 56.

Management policy affects commitment by creating (or most likely *not* creating) an environment "in which the individual can achieve his goals *best* by directing his efforts toward the success of the organization."

> ... ["Best"] means that he will continuously be encouraged to develop and utilize voluntarily his capacities, his knowledge, his skill, his ingenuity in ways which contribute to the success of the enterprise.[1]

Of course this seldom happens. Wage labor (and most salaried work) is defined by the substitution of the organization's alien goals for one's own during the time one has alienated to the organization. As C. Wright Mills wrote,

> Alienation in work means that the most alert hours of one's life are sacrificed to the making of money with which to "live" .... It means that while men must seek all values that matter to them outside of work, they must be serious during work .... In short, they must be serious and steady about something that does not mean anything to them ....
>
> Each day men sell little pieces of themselves, in order to try to buy them back each night and week end with the coin of "fun."[2]

In short, what McGregor called "Theory X" assumptions about human nature are an accurate description of the subordinate in a hierarchy. So long as the organization exists for purposes other than those of the people doing the work, and operates under leadership unaccountable to them, there's a *need* for LeGuin's "steam engine."

Although Oliver Williamson is hardly a radical of the same order as Goodman or LeGuin, his discussion of the "atmospheric consequences" of large size echoes their treatment of incentives. The "atmospheric advantages" of a firm, as opposed to market contracting, include "associational relations that may be valued," and "involvements of a continuing sort in which members are more sensitive to part-whole relations." But increasing organizational size negates these advantages, and promotes instead directly contrary atmospheric *dis*advantages:

> ... large size and hierarchical structure favor impersonality among the parties, which is more characteristic of a calculative orientation. This is partly attributable to the specialization of information gathering and the more limited disclosure of information ... as firm size and hierarchical structure are extended ... The corresponding assignment of decision-making to what are perceived by lower-level participants to be remote parts of the enterprise also contributes to this result .... To the extent that nonknowledgeability and nonparticipation impair involvement and larger-size results in role incompatibility, ... a more calculative orientation is to be expected .... Put differently, attitudes of voluntary cooperation are supplanted by a *quid pro quo* orientation. Since, moreover, each individual in the large organization is small in relation to the whole, so that the percentage effects of individual behavior are perceived to be insubstantial, the large organization may be thought to be better able to tolerate perfunctory performance or even deviant conduct.
>
> A reduction in group disciplinary pressures ... thus obtains .... Indeed, should alienation from the enterprise develop among individual components of the firm, small-group powers may even be turned against the enterprise in subtle but significant respects. The disaffected group may allocate rewards and sanctions in a perverse fashion. Industrial sabotage is an extreme manifestation of this condition.[3]

It's also important to bear in mind that perfunctory compliance and passivity do not occur just in special cases, when workers react to especially authoritarian hierarchies or

---

1. *Ibid.*, p. 55.
2. C. Wright Mills, *White Collar: The American Middle Classes* (London, Oxford, New York: Oxford University Press, 1951), pp. 236–237.
3. Williamson, *Markets and Hierarchies*, pp. 128–129.

abusive superiors. To a large extent, they are inculcated by hierarchy and the superior-subordinate relationship themselves.

> We all know what it feels like to be told how to do something by someone else, particularly when that person does not do it every day. This is not a problem of ineffective individuals but of management as a system. Whenever someone in a superior position gives us orders, our natural responses are either:
>
> - Blind, robotic obedience, not caring whether it is done well
> - Unspoken, passive-aggressive resistance, or what employees sometimes call "public compliance and private defiance"
> - Hostility, opposition, and rebellion
>
> Through years of experience, employees learn that it is safer to suppress their innate capacity to solve problems and wait instead for commands from above.[1]

Still another important consideration about perfunctory cooperation to bear in mind: it operates as a positive feedback system. The internal "crisis of governability" of the hierarchical organization is subject to the same kind of exponential growth and escalation we saw on a systemic level in Chapter Four. Authoritarianism breeds passive resistance and active hostility, which necessitates still harsher authoritarianism and surveillance, which inspires still more resentment and makes the workforce even harder to govern, which forces management to devote even more resources to internal control, etc., etc. To quote Cloke and Goldsmith again:

> The intrinsic emphasis in hierarchies on unquestioning conformity and strict enforcement of rules encourages managers to coerce and manipulate employees into obedience. It equally encourages employees to obey rules blindly, resist responsibility for outcomes, and shelve their creativity, reinforcing the need for managers to watch over them. This makes the system self-reinforcing, turning it in a circle. Because bureaucracy mandates conformity to a single standard, it produces apathy, cynicism and irresponsibility at the bottom and autocracy, privilege, and unilateral action at the top. These dynamics make management even more immune to change, thereby reinforcing the need for bureaucracy.[2]

In addition to all the foregoing agency and incentive problems, finally, additional agency problems are created by incomplete contracting.[3] This is especially true of the incomplete nature of the labor contract, which will be the topic of Chapter Nine. But it is true of other internal contracting within the firm, as well:

> The problem is that none of the following is costlessly enforceable: promises by division managers to utilize assets with "due care"; promises by owners to reset transfer prices and exercise accounting discretion "responsibly"; promises to reward innovation in "full measure"; promises to preserve promotion prospects "without change"; and agreements by managers to "eschew politics."[4]

In theory, the advantage of an incomplete contract is that it provides the management of the firm with a "general clause" allowing them to adjust the terms by fiat as the situation changes: "One advantage of hierarchy . . . with respect to bilateral adaptation is that internal contracts can be more incomplete."[5] In practice, however, the terms emerging from the "general clause" result from the de facto bargaining power of the different interest groups

---

1. Kenneth Cloke and Joan Goldsmith, *The End of Management and the Rise of Organizational Democracy* (New York: John Wiley & Sons, 2002), p. 10.

2. *Ibid.*, p. 94.

3. Williamson, *The Economic Institutions of Capitalism*, p. 29

4. Williamson, *The Economic Institutions of Capitalism*, p. 161.

5. Williamson, Oliver Williamson. "Comparative Economic Organization: The Analysis of Discrete Structural Alternatives" *Administrative Science Quarterly* 36:2 (June 1991), p. 280.

within the firm. Enforcement of the management prerogative is limited by agents' rents from impacted information, and the difficulty of monitoring compliance.

> ... [P]arties that bear a long-term bilateral dependency relation to one another must recognize that incomplete contracts require gapfilling and sometimes get out of alignment. Although it is always in the collective interest of autonomous parties to fill gaps, correct errors, and effect efficient realignments, it is also the case that the distribution of the resulting gains is indeterminate. Self-interested bargaining predictably obtains. Such bargaining is itself costly.[1]

There is a major difference in the contractual enforcement tools available in markets and hierarchies. Exogenous enforcement through official legal action in the courts is far more feasible in markets; courts are more likely to refuse to intervene in the internal disputes of a firm, and leave it to resolution by endogenous enforcement mechanisms.

> There is a logic to classical market contracting and there is a logic for forbearance law, and the choice of one regime precludes the other. Whether a transaction is organized as make or buy—internal procurement or market procurement, respectively—thus matters greatly in dispute-resolution respects: the courts will hear disputes of the one kind and will refuse to be drawn into the resolution of disputes of the other. Internal disputes between one division and another regarding the appropriate transfer prices, the damages to be ascribed to delays, failures of quality, and the like, are thus denied a court hearing . . .
>
> The underlying rationale for forbearance law is twofold: (1) parties to an internal dispute have deep knowledge—both about the circumstances surrounding a dispute as well as the efficiency properties of alternative solutions—that can be communicated to the court only at great cost, and (2) permitting internal disputes to be appealed to the court would undermine the efficacy and integrity of hierarchy.[2]

SUMMARY

Individual human beings make optimal decisions only when they internalize the costs and benefits of their own decisions. The larger the organization, the more the authority to make decisions is separated both from the negative consequences, and from direct knowledge of the results. And in a hierarchy, the consequences of the irrational and misinformed decisions of those at the top are borne by the people who are actually doing the work. The direct producers, who know what's going on and experience directly the consequences of the decisions, have no direct control over those decisions.

An institution, according to Butler Shaffer, is by definition an organization which is unaccountable to those making it up.

> By "institution," I mean to refer to *any permanent social organization with purposes of its own, having formalized and structured machinery for pursuing those purposes, and making and enforcing rules of conduct in order to control those within it.* An institution is an independent, self-justifying, self-perpetuating organization that is, for all practical purposes, no longer accountable to nor under the control of its members.[3]

Conflict of interest is built into a hierarchy. The relationship between any higher and lower levels in a hierarchy is, by definition, zero-sum. Those in authority benefit by shifting work downward while appropriating rewards for themselves. Since they do not appropriate the fruits of increased effort, subordinates benefit by perfunctory cooperation, and exploiting their private information to reduce effort.

1. *Ibid.*, p. 278.
2. *Ibid.*, p. 275-276.
3. Butler Shaffer, *Calculated Chaos: Institutional Threats to Peace and Human Survival* (San Francisco: Alchemy Books, 1985), p. 9.

APPENDIX
TOILET PAPER AS PARADIGM

I like to use toilet paper dispensers as a paradigm for the systematic stupidity of organizations. One thing that large institutions seem to have in common is public restrooms with completely unusable toilet paper dispensers. The typical public restroom in a large organization of any kind has one of those Georgia Pacific monstrosities (or something similar), encased in a plastic housing that makes the toilet paper roll difficult to reach and often almost impossible to turn. The housing is locked, so that an empty roll can be changed only by a housekeeper with a key, and it's impossible to just take the roll out for easy use. The worst part of it is, these toilet paper dispensers probably cost $20 or more each. I wouldn't be surprised, in the case of some government institutions, if their paper dispensers were custom designed (at great expense) to an elaborate set of specs, worked out in painstaking detail, for the individual institution. And what's really sickening is that you can probably go to Home Depot and get a toilet paper spool that actually works for less than a dollar.

I'm at an utter loss to understand what rational purpose this serves. Maybe they're afraid vandals will piss all over the toilet paper if it isn't properly shielded. Or maybe someone will try to make a fortune selling it on the black market. But you'd probably break your back stealing enough gross of cheap scratch-ass paper to equal the money wasted on a single one of those over-designed dispensers (not to mention the labor wasted in getting a housekeeper to make a special trip to the supply closet and unlock the dispenser every time the roll is empty).

So why do we find so many examples of this sort of thing? Why does just about any large institutional building have toilet paper dispensers that seem deliberately designed, at enormous cost, to perform their function as badly as possible? The answer lies in the nature of large organizations.

For one thing, the dispenser is produced for a "customer" who is not the actual user of the toilet paper, but some government or corporate procurement officer. And the procurement officer himself probably doesn't even set the product specifications. There are so many layers of bureaucracy between the producer of the crappy dispensers, and the ultimate user, that a company can specialize in producing such hardware for institutional customers without ever worrying that anybody will ever refuse to accept it on grounds of quality. Matthew Parris, by the way, announced his "new theory"

> that the free market doesn't work properly when the real customers are those who commission a product rather than those who use it. It is, for example, businesses, not the householder, that choose the courier service that makes you stay in all day in case it calls; it is insurance companies, not patients, that are are private medicine's real customers.[1]

Just about anyone who comes into contact with the dispensers on a daily basis (in a hospital that would be patients, nursing staff, and housekeepers) could tell the central supply department: "Just mass-order the $1 dollar kind from Home Depot, increase patient

1. Matthew Parris, "I love boring old mobiles," *The Times* (London), December 20, 2007 <http://www.timesonline.co.uk/tol/comment/columnists/matthew_parris/article3075580.ece>. Chris Dillow, of *Stumbling and Mumbling* blog, expressed some surprise that a ten-year figure in the British Conservative Party, a party which talked endlessly about the wonders of "free markets," could have reinvented the agency problem without ever having heard of it in his political circles. Dillow suggested it might be because "his Tory colleagues were just never really interested in market economics, and only talked about 'free markets' as an ideological cover for what was really just class hatred and union bashing?" Dillow, "Parris blurts out the truth," *Stumbling and Mumbling*, December 20, 2007 <http://stumblingandmumbling.typepad.com/stumbling_and_mumbling/2007/12/parris-blurts-o. html>.

satisfaction, and save yourselves umpteen hundred bucks." But, again, there are so many layers of hierarchy that the cost of tracking such things would be greater than the cost of the irrationality itself. Worse yet, nobody knows which decisions are rational and which are irrational, because the information required to assess that is divided among so many individuals that the transaction costs of aggregating it are prohibitive. And (as we will see in the next chapter on agency and incentive problems) the people most apt to observe the problem and most competent to suggest a remedy have absolutely no reason to take the trouble to pass it along to their employer; if anything, they're more likely to view the money lost as a form of psychic consumption on the job, partial compensation for their low wages and increased work loads.

7

Economic Calculation in the Corporate Commonwealth (the Corporation as Planned Economy)

The general lines of Mises' rational calculation argument are well-known. A market in factors of production is necessary for pricing production inputs, so that a planner may allocate them rationally.[1] The problem has nothing to do either with the volume of data, or with agency problems. The question, rather, is how is the data generated in the first place? Roderick Long:

> The problem is not, and never was, lack of adequate means of processing "given data." (If that were the problem, computers might indeed help.) The problem is, first, that the data cannot be *obtained* apart from market choices.[2]

And Peter Klein: "How does the principal know *what* to tell the agent to do?"[3] Without market valuation, there is no basis for price. As Murray Rothbard put it, "there can be no implicit estimates without an explicit market!"[4]

But the Austrian critique of central planning can be applied more widely than to mere state planning. From the standpoint of a Martian observer, what goes on inside the large firm would probably look a lot like a planned economy. The neoclassical description of an economy coordinated by the price mechanism and with no central planning authority, Ronald Coase said,

> gives a very incomplete picture of our economic system. Within a firm, the description does not fit at all. For instance, in economic theory we find that the allocation of factors of production between different uses is determined by the price mechanism. The price of factor *A* becomes higher in X than in Y. As a result, *A* moves from Y to X until the difference between the prices in X and Y, except in so far as it compensates for other differential advantages, disappears. Yet in the real world, we find that there are many areas where this does not apply. If a workman moves from department Y to department X, he does not go because of a change in relative prices, but because he is ordered to do so. Those who object to economic planning on the grounds that the problem is solved by price movements can be answered by pointing out that there is planning within our economic system which is . . . akin to what is normally called economic planning . . .

---

1. Ludwig von Mises, *Human Action: A Treatise on Economics*. Third Revised Edition (Chicago: Henry Regnery Company, 1949, 1963, 1966)., pp. 698-701.

2. Roderick Long, "Re: Is leftlibertarianism compatible with support for the market system?" Message #14168, December 25, 2006, LeftLibertarian yahoogroup <http://groups.yahoo.com/group/LeftLibertarian/message/14168>.

3. Peter Klein, "Economic Calculation and the Limits of Organization," *The Review of Austrian Economics* Vol. 9 No. 2 (1996).

4. *Man, Economy, and State: A Treatise on Economic Principles* (Auburn, Ala.: The Ludwig von Mises Institute, 1962, 1970, 1993), p. 543.

It can, I think, be assumed that the distinguishing mark of the firm is the supersession of the price mechanism.[1]

A. The Divorce of Entrepreneurial from Technical Knowledge

The question of whether market price is the only feasible method of making rational decisions about factor inputs (and this was the central question at issue) is far less important, from my standpoint, than what Mises had to say on the relation between technological and entrepreneurial judgments. "Technology," Mises wrote,

> shows what could be achieved if one wanted to achieve it, and how it could be achieved provided people were prepared to employ the means indicated . . . .
> . . . . [Technology] ignores the economic problem: to employ the available means in such a way that no want more urgently felt should remain unsatisfied because the means suitable for its attainment were employed—wasted—for the attainment of a want less urgently felt . . . . Technology tells how a given end could be attained by the employment of various means which can be used together in various combinations . . . . But it is at a loss to tell man which procedures he should choose out of the infinite variety of imaginable and possible modes of production . . . .
> Technology and the considerations derived from it would be of little use for acting man if it were impossible to introduce into their schemes the money prices of goods and services. The projects and designs of engineers would be purely academic if they could not compare input and output on a common basis.[2]

Technology, Mises argues, describes the different technical possibilities for organizing production. At the same time, knowledge of the relative values of inputs is necessary to judge which technical process is most appropriate. Knowledge of technical possibilities, without knowledge of the relative value of production inputs to each other and to the finished product, is empty. But although Mises neglected to mention it, the opposite is true as well. Knowledge of the money prices of production inputs, and of finished goods, would be purely academic without the knowledge of how to organize production so as to economize on the most valuable inputs and to organize means properly in relation to ends.

Knowledge of the value of inputs without knowledge of their concrete use in the production process results in calculational chaos, to the very same extent as the reverse state of affairs. What Mises regarded as the "entrepreneurial" realm (whether the function be exercised by finance capitalists or corporate management), to the extent that it is isolated from knowledge of the production process, is an island of calculational chaos.

Fully rational decisions are possible only if the knowledge of the relative value of inputs is combined with knowledge of how those inputs are to be used internally. The separation of ownership of capital from the knowledge of the production process leads to decisions divorced from reality. The same is true of the separation of management from direct involvement in the production process, and the accountability of management to absentee owners rather than to workers.

This is true regardless of whether Mises was right, or Lange and Schumpeter were right, on the issues in dispute in the calculation debate. The question of whether *non-price* calculation of the relative value of production inputs is feasible is irrelevant to this problem. Under *any* system, *whatever* the method of calculating the relative value of producer goods, price or non-price, knowledge of the value of producer goods must be integrated with knowledge of the technical possibilities for using them. In *any* system, price or non-price, in which organizational size goes beyond the possibility of such integration, decisions will become irrational. So the management of a large corporation is operating in the same island of calculational

---

1. Ronald H. Coase, "The Nature of the Firm," *Economica* (November 1937), pp. 387-388.
2. Mises, *Human Action*, pp. 206-08 (emphasis added).

chaos as the management of an old Soviet industrial ministry. The problem attends *any* system in which those who control the allocation of resources lack adequate knowledge of the effect their decisions will have on the production process.

It also makes little difference whether the entrepreneurial function of large-scale allocation of investment resources is carried out by outside investors and financiers, or internally by senior management allocating resources between subdivisions of an M-form corporation. In their ignorance of the production side of things, the cluelessness of senior corporate management and the cluelessness of outside money shufflers are both of a kind. The investment bankers and rentiers simply shuffle money from one venture to another based on the expected return, while seeing the internal production process as a black box. But senior management, MBA types who focus on finance and marketing almost to the exclusion of production, likewise see the actual production operations of the firm as a black box.

This is partly the result of the Sloan model of management accounting, which (as William Waddell and Norman Bodek argue in *The Rebirth of American Industry*)[1] regards manufacturing operations purely as "cost centers," that is in terms of their expenses and revenues, and without regard to their internal functioning. Waddell and Bodek cite, as evidence of "the prevailing attitude at GM headquarters,"

> Sloan's assertion that manufacturing was a secondary concern—that cars were basically commodities—and that sales and marketing were the keys to competitiveness. Manufacturing, in their minds, was a pedestrian sort of activity, to be controlled for sure, but not one worthy of much of their time and effort.[2]

> With the implementation of the Sloan system, General Motors transitioned from being a manufacturing company with marketing and finance functions to a marketing and finance company that happened to perform manufacturing functions.[3]

It also results from the culture of the so-called "FIRE economy" (Finance, Insurance, Real Estate) spilling over into the rest of the economy. The MBAs in charge of manufacturing come to evaluate their production facilities like financial instruments and real estate investments, as a revenue stream that can be capitalized.[4]

Mises' contrast between the entrepreneur and the corporate manager, and his treatment of corporate bureaucracy, are fundamentally flawed. Mises overplayed the distinction between the entrepreneur and the mere corporate manager. He neglected the amount of investment generated internally through retention of profits, and likewise neglected the role of the senior management of an M-form corporation in allocating finance between divisions. He also ignored the extent of corporate management's discretion in *how* to spend available capital—i.e., to choose between alternative forms of production technology. At times, the entrepreneurial role of finance capital in allocating resources among firms became quite significant—as it did in the era of the hostile takeover in the early 1980s. At other times, the relative power of corporate management to make investment decisions is much greater—as it was in the postwar model of corporate capitalism that Galbraith described. But at all times, including now, the entrepreneurial leeway of corporate management is considerable. With a few brief exceptions, the main investment decisions made by corporate management involve retained earnings rather than outside finance.

Mises also erred in the sharp contrast he made between the entrepreneurial function and the "mere" organization of production.

1. William H. Waddell and Norman Bodek, *Rebirth of American Industry: A Study of Lean Management* (Vancouver, WA: PCS Press, 2005).
2. *Ibid.*, p. 77.
3. *Ibid.*, p. 83.
4. Doug Henwood, *Wall Street: How It Works and for Whom* (London and New York: Verso, 1997), p. 80.

The entrepreneur determines alone, without any managerial interference, in what lines of business to employ capital and how much capital to employ. He determines the expansion and contraction of the size of the total business and its main sections. He determines the enterprise's financial structure. These are the essential decisions which are instrumental in the conduct of business.[1]

First of all, the general environment Mises assumes is a historically determined one, in no way necessarily connected to the essential features of the market economy as such. Mises assumes a society in which most investment capital is concentrated in the hands of a relatively small plutocratic class, the dominant form of enterprise is the large corporation, and investment decisions involve mainly the movement of large blocks of capital between those enormous enterprises. As an indication of his culturally bound conception of entrepreneurship, consider his equation of that function to the existence of "the stock and commodity exchanges, the trading in futures, and the bankers and moneylenders . . . ."[2] In fact, he actually considered the existence of a stock market—which assumes both the absentee-owned corporation as the dominant form of enterprise and corporate equity as the dominant form of property—to be the defining feature of a market society. As Murray Rothbard recounted:

> One time, during Mises' seminar at New York University, I asked him whether, considering the broad spectrum of economies from a purely free market economy to pure totalitarianism, he could single out one criterion according to which he could say that an economy was essentially "socialist" or whether it was a market economy. Somewhat to my surprise, he replied readily: "Yes, the key is whether the economy has a stock market." That is, if the economy has a full-scale market in titles to land and capital goods. In short: Is the allocation of capital basically determined by government or by private owners?[3]

Actually, the significance of a stock market is that the economy has a full-scale market in equity in *firms*, not in "titles to land and capital goods." Rothbard was almost as prone as Mises to confuse the historical accidents of corporate capitalism with the essence of markets, property and entrepreneurship.

Consider: if what the radical economists call primitive accumulation—the expropriation of the laboring classes in early modern times—had not taken place, a market society of small-scale property and worker-ownership might have evolved. Had the state not subsidized the corporate revolution and economic centralization, the economy might have remained dominated by small factories or artisan shops, with manufacturing consisting of small-scale machine production for local markets. In such an economy, the "entrepreneurial" function would have involved mainly the decision by workers themselves as to the reinvestment of their savings from labor income, supplemented by small loans financed by the cooperative pooling of such savings. Mises' basic description of the entrepreneur's function involves not the essential functions of employing resources as such, but the particular historical form that those functions have taken under state capitalism.

Mises' argument that an economy of worker cooperatives would result in calculational chaos, are sheer nonsense.[4] As Post-Objectivist Bryan Register argued, the entrepreneurial function simply requires markets; it presupposes no particular form of ownership.

1. Mises, *Human Action*, p. 307.

2. *Ibid.*, pp. 708–09.

3. "The End of Socialism and the Calculation Debate Revisited," *The Review of Austrian Economics*, Vol. 5, No. 2 (1991), p. 59.

4. In arguing that "Syndicalism" would not allow a market in factors of production, Mises made the mistake of confusing a market in producer goods with a market in equity in firms. Rothbard, in assuming that an economy of producer cooperatives would rule out markets in credit or capital goods, likewise erred. *Man, Economy, and State*, p. 544.

The individual business concern produces goods of some kind which are sold on a market. The owner of that concern must design the concern to maximize her profit. She does this by arranging to produce goods for which there is a relatively high demand relative to supply, and for which cost is low relative to expected income. However, she cannot arrange things in this way without knowing the social relations of supply and demand, and the expected costs and income to be expended and derived from a given arrangement of the productive forces. This information exists in the form of prices: current prices of the good to be produced, as well as the capital and labor required to produce those goods. Without prices, the owner of an individual business concern could make no decisions at all; no investment decision could be any more rational than any other.

If we were to, through some form of social action, eliminate the distinction between Marx's classes, such that the owners of the business concern are identical with those who work at it, the problem to be solved would not disappear (nor need it be exacerbated). The owners of a worker-owned business concern would have as their goal (*ceteris paribus*, of course—*homo economicus* is a myth) the maximization of their wealth, which would be derived in the form of a portion of the profits gained by their business concern. They would thus benefit from the social information carried by prices, just as the bourgeois owner of the business would have benefited.[1]

Entrepreneurship, in fact, is inseparable from decisions involving the direct organization of production. The "minor" decisions of which Mises was so dismissive, and the "great" decisions he regarded as truly entrepreneurial, are the same in kind: both involve the most effective allocation of resources. Shuffling great blocks of money around between enterprises, or between the divisions of an M-form corporation, is not different in kind from decisions as to what kind of machinery to buy, how to link it together, and how to organize the human tasks of production around the machinery.

There is a wide range of possible ratios of input to output possible, depending on minute changes in the technical process of production. According to Barry Stein,[2] a series of seemingly minor and incremental changes in the production process in an older factory with older machinery, "tweaking" things a bit here or there, often has a greater cumulative effect on productivity than building an entirely new factory with the latest generation of production machinery. In these cases, such technical decisions have a larger effect on the total allocation of resources among ends than the decisions of investment bankers. In the words of Hayek:

> To know of and put to use a machine not fully employed, or somebody's skill which could be better utilized, or to be aware of a surplus stock which can be drawn upon during an interruption of supplies, is socially quite as useful as the knowledge of better alternative techniques . . . .
> . . . [I]t is possible, with the same technical facilities, to produce with a great variety of costs, are among the commonplaces of business experience which do not seem to be equally familiar in the study of the economist.[3]

This is essentially what Harvey Leibenstein meant by "x-efficiency": not the most efficient combination of gross inputs, but the most efficient use of those inputs within the production process. Mises' conception of "entrepreneurship" as the shifting around of great blocks of investment capital, and of the "merely" technical aspects of production as a near-automatic response to the objective constraints of science, is—much as it may pain the ostensibly contrarian Austrians for me to say so—quite *neoclassical*, in its own way. Neo-

1. Bryan Register, "Class, Hegemony, and Ideology: A Libertarian Approach" (2001) <http://folk.uio.no/thomas/po/class-hegemony-ideology-lib.html>.
2. Barry Stein. *Size, Effiency, and Community Enterprise* (Cambridge, Mass.: Center for Community Economic Development, 1974).
3. F.A. Hayek, "The Use of Knowledge in Society," *The American Economic Review*, vol. 35, no. 4 (September 1945), pp. 522-523.

classical economics assumes, as Leibenstein put it, "that every firm *purchases and utilizes* all of its inputs 'efficiently.'" Firms "are presumed to exist as entities that make optimal input decisions,"[1] based on production functions which can be obviously induced from technical constraints.

If "entrepreneurship" is the adaptation of means to ends, then surely the "technical" judgments Hayek and Leibenstein describe are—at least—as entrepreneurial as large-scale investment decisions. Interestingly, the ILO study Leibenstein cited found that

> low productivity is frequently caused by top management's concern with the commercial and financial affairs of the firm rather than with the running of the factory. The latter was frequently treated as a very subordinate task.[2]

Sound familiar?

A decision on the shop floor as to which technical means to choose and how to organize them is very much an entrepreneurial calculation that must take into account the relative costs of all the production inputs.

Mises at times came close to admitting as much, mentioning in passing that "[t]he function of the entrepreneur cannot be separated from the direction of the employment of factors of production for the accomplishment of definite tasks."[3] Or as he wrote at greater length elsewhere:

> The entrepreneurs are not omnipresent. They cannot themselves attend to the manifold tasks which are incumbent upon them. Adjustment of production to the best possible supplying of the consumers with the goods they are asking for most urgently does not merely consist in determining the general plan for the utilization of resources. There is, of course, no doubt that this is the main function of the promoter and speculator. But besides the great adjustments, many small adjustments are necessary too. Each of them may seem trifling and of little bearing upon the total result. But the cumulative effect of shortcomings in many of these minor matters can be such as to frustrate entirely the success of a correct solution of the great problems. At any rate, it is certain that every failure to handle the smaller problems results in a squandering of scarce factors of production and consequently in impairing the best possible satisfaction of the consumers.[4]

The problem seems to lie in his obstinate relegation of the "technician," as such, to a "purely technological point of view," and his dichotomy between the "entrepreneur, as such" and the technician, when the actual function of entrepreneurship is so closely intertwined with technical decisions. Mises' teachable moment having seemingly come and gone, he continued in the same passage:

> It is important to conceive in what respects the problem we have in mind differs from the technological tasks of the technicians. The execution of every project upon which the entrepreneur has embarked in making his decision with regard to the general plan of action requires a multiplicity of minute decisions. Each of these decisions must be effected in such a way as to prefer that solution of the problem which—without interfering with the designs of the general plan for the whole project—is the most economical one. It must avoid superfluous costs in the same way as does the general plan. The technician from his purely technological point of view either may not see any difference in the alternatives offered by various methods for the solution of such a detail or may give preference to one of these methods on account of its greater output in physical quantities. But the entrepreneur is actuated by the profit motive. This enjoins upon him the urge to prefer the most economical solution, i.e., that solution which avoids employing

---

1. Harvey Leibenstein, "Allocative Efficiency vs. 'X-Efficiency,'" *The American Economic Review* 56 (June 1966), p. 397.

2. *Ibid.*, p. 406.

3. *Human Action*, p. 306.

4. *Ibid.*, pp. 303–04.

factors of production whose employment would impair the satisfaction of the more intensely felt wants of the consumers. He will prefer among the various methods with regard to which the technicians are neutral, the one the application of which requires the smallest cost. He may reject the technicians' suggestion to choose a more costly method securing a greater physical output if his action shows that the increase in output would not outweigh the increase in cost required. Not only in the great decisions and plans but no less in the daily decisions of small problems as they turn up in the current conduct of affairs, the entrepreneur must perform his task of adjusting production to the demand of the consumers as reflected in the prices of the market.[1]

The actual person making such technical decisions may have a far better knowledge of the relative money costs of alternative inputs, and of the money cost ratios of inputs and outputs under alternative methods of organizing production, than the "entrepreneur" has of the way that such technical decisions affect his money calculations of cost and benefit. Either way, it's a mistake to separate (even with the magical words "as such") the purely entrepreneurial from the purely technical function. The functions may be separated as a matter of definition. But as Rothbard said, "In the real world, each *function* is not necessarily performed by a different person."[2] The entrepreneurial and the technical are not so much two different bodies of knowledge, as two different ways of thinking about knowledge. It is possible to consider technical data with entrepreneurial considerations of factor and product prices in mind, as well as the reverse.

In addition, I've seen it argued quite convincingly that the distinction between purely "technical," as opposed to "economic" standards of efficiency, is a strawman; and that the cost of inputs is a basic efficiency consideration for engineers in developing a product or process. Max Chiz, in a comment to a *Mises Economics Blog* post by Peter Klein, wrote:

> It is a general misconception, shared by Dr. Klein, that "technological value is not the same as economic value". The entire job of an engineer, and what you spend years in college learning how to do, is to combine the data of the market (in the form of prices for materials, components, land, buildings, labor, assembly equipment, etc) with knowledge of science to better meet the needs of the customer. Engineers try to find the optimal tradeoff between quality, cost, and time to market. It is true that engineers often describe products in terms of "elegance", "beauty", etc., but these terms would have no meaning if it weren't for the market. A device is "elegant" precisely because of the ingenuity that went into satisfying customers—it uses less parts (and hence costs less), it fits in less space (and hence has higher quality in the eyes of the customer), it will let you get your product out the door in half the time (and meet consumer desires sooner). I am especially embarrassed that an Austrian blog can't get this simple point—as it is a critical part of the calculation problem. After all, if I don't have prices for all of those factors, the combination of things I can build is effectively infinite.[3]

In response to a private email, in which I asked Chiz to clarify his position on entrepreneurship in relation to that of Mises, he added:

> Engineers do two things:
> 1. They make technology using science.
> 2. They design goods using technology.
> #2 requires prices in order to correctly make the trade-offs between time-to-market, quality, and cost.
> I don't consider this to be the entrepreneurial function because the uses of the inputs are almost always not marginal (and hence their price will be determined in broader factor markets.)

1. *Ibid.* p. 304.
2. *Man, Economy, and State*, p. 542.
3. Peter Klein, "Government Did Invent the Internet, But the Market Made It Glorious," *Mises Economic Blog*, June 12, 2006 <http://blog.mises.org/archives/005174.asp>.

Both the technician and the entrepreneur possess what Hayek called idiosyncratic knowledge, and neither one can exercise his own art effectively without incorporating the other's art into his own immediate considerations. Knowledge cannot be entirely delegated, because it's impossible to judge someone else's use of his own art without possessing some general knowledge of that art for oneself. Neither specialty's considerations are conducive to being distilled into an executive summary, to be considered by the other specialty as an afterthought after it has already set priorities in terms of its own considerations.

The technical possibilities of production have a direct bearing on questions of factor productivity compared to cost, and must be borne in mind continuously as entrepreneurial questions are being considered. The costs of inputs and of the finished product, likewise, have a direct bearing on which technical solution is the most efficient, and must be continuously borne in mind by one considering technical matters. If, as some neurologists suspect, the brain functions as a Bayesian calculating device ("taking various bits of probability information, weighing their relative worth, and coming to a good conclusion quickly," to quote Professor Alex Pouget), this is especially true.

> . . . [I]f we want to do something, such as jump over a stream, we need to extract data that is not inherently part of that information. We need to process all the variables we see, including how wide the stream appears, what the consequences of falling in might be, and how far we know we can jump. Each neuron responds to a particular variable and the brain will decide on a conclusion about the whole set of variables using Bayesian inference.
>
> As you reach your decision, you'd have a lot of trouble articulating most of the variables your brain just processed for you. Similarly, intuition may be less a burst of insight than a rough consensus among your neurons.[1]

If so, the whole relevant body of knowledge must be in the original mix.

Under state capitalism, however, corporate size is promoted to the point that technical and entrepreneurial judgments are "stovepiped," with specialists making decisions with regard largely to their own field in isolation, and then trying to splice in the considerations of other fields as an afterthought.

When the organization reaches a sufficiently large size, the moneyed "entrepreneur" lacks any direct knowledge of the "various methods" or "minor matters," and hence is likely to be operating in an atmosphere of calculational chaos.

In short, coherent decisions cannot be made unless the relevant "technical" and "entrepreneurial" knowledge are aggregated by the same decision-makers. And state capitalism has caused to predominate organizations of such size and complexity that the relevant information cannot be encompassed by any such unified decision-maker, and there are insurmountable agency problems involved in getting the necessary knowledge of the production process to the people making the grand "entrepreneurial" decisions. If anything, the "technician" and the production worker are probably more qualified to add the entrepreneur's legitimate knowledge to their own and take over the functions of ownership and management efficiently for themselves, than the entrepreneur and manager are to obtain adequate knowledge of the production process.

Joseph Juran made a similar observation in regard to quality control. In suggesting process improvements for reducing waste or defects, he wrote, engineers had to quantify the savings in economic terms that management could understand. Engineers have to speak the "language of money . . . the universal language of upper management" in order to bridge the gap and get their ideas across to management. Juran wrote at length on the practical issues involved in selling a quality improvement measure to management, by

1. Alex Pouget "Mysterious 'neural noise' actually primes brain for peak performance," *EurekAlert*, November 10, 2006 <http://www.eurekalert.org/pub_releases/2006-11/uor-mn111006.php>.

translating the cost of poor quality into economic terms that they could understand: i.e., quantifying quality costs as a percent of sales, compared to profit, compared to the magnitude of current problems, as a percentage of share value, as a percent of cost of goods sold, as a percent of total manufacturing cost, and the effect of quality costs on the breakeven point.[1] In firms with a large number of statistically significant non-conformances, engineers must prioritize sources of deficiency in order of their economic significance.[2] In other words it's usually the quality control and engineering staff who work out the *entrepreneurial* significance of Mises' "purely technical" questions, and then distill their findings into an idiot version for management.

The great investors are almost entirely clueless as to what their supposed "employees," the corporation managers are doing. The CEOs are almost entirely clueless as to what the branch and facility managers are doing. And the management of each facility are almost entirely clueless as to what is going on within the black box of the actual production process. In the light of this reality, Mises' "entrepreneur"—so carefully and closely involved in the minutiae of choosing between technical possibilities of production, a brooding omnipresence guiding the efforts of every employee—is largely a construction of fantasy. It's quite ironic, in fact, considering that Mises starts out the block quote above with the announcement that the entrepreneur is not omnipresent.

B. Hayek vs. Mises on Distributed Knowledge

Hayek's treatment of distributed knowledge[3] is commonly viewed as opening a second Austrian front against the collectivists in Mises' ongoing "socialist calculation" war. And it certainly was that—but it was also more. It was an assault not just on the collectivists' view of central planning, but on Mises' managerial "planned economy" under the direction of the omniscient entrepreneur. The calculation debate, especially on the Hayekian front, results in as many casualties on the side of large-scale corporate capitalism as on that of centrally planned state socialism. To a large extent, the real calculation debate is not Mises and Hayek vs. Lange and Schumpeter, but Hayek vs. Mises.[4]

Matthew Yglesias explains just why the cult of the cowboy CEO is so asinine, in Hayekian terms:

> . . . it's noteworthy that the business class, as a set, has a curious and somewhat incoherent view of capitalism and why it's a good thing. Indeed, it's in most respects a backwards view that strongly contrasts with the economic or political science take on why markets work.
>
> The basic business outlook is very focused on the key role of the *executive*. Good, profitable, growing firms are run by brilliant executives. And the ability of the firm to grow and be profitable is evidence of its executives' brilliance. And profit ultimately stems from executive brilliance. This is part of the reason that CEO salaries need to keep escalating—recruiting the best is integral to success. The leaders of large firms become revered figures . . . .
>
> The thing about this is that if this were generally true—if the CEOs of the Fortune 500 were brilliant economic seers—then it would really make a lot of sense to imple-

1. J.M. Juran and Frank M Gryna, *Juran's Quality Control Handbook*. Fourth edition (New York: McGraw-Hill Book Company, 1951, 1988), 4.3-4, 4.15
2. *Ibid.*, 6.38.
3. "The Use of Knowledge in Society," op. cit.
4. Indeed there seems to be considerable hostility for Hayek's calculation argument among the more ardent followers of Mises. This is not the place to recapitulate the entire "dehomogenization debate." But it seems that for some Misesians, any suggestion that entrepreneurial decisions are based on market data is in some way a detraction from the reverential awe due the mystical function of entrepreneu rship

ment socialism. Real socialism. Not progressive taxation to finance a mildly redistributive welfare state. But "let's let Vikram Pandit and Jeff Immelt centrally plan the economy—after all, they're really brilliant!"

But in the real world, the point of markets isn't that executives are clever and bureaucrats are dimwitted. The point is that *nobody* is all that brilliant.[1]

The neoclassical convention was to treat the internal workings of the firm as a "black box." As Peter Klein described it,

> The "firm" is a production function or production possibilities set, a means of transforming inputs into outputs. Given the available technology, a vector of input prices, and a demand schedule, the firm maximizes money profits subject to the constraint that its production plans must be technologically feasible . . . . The firm is modeled as a single actor, facing a series of relatively uncomplicated decisions: what level of output to produce, how much of each factor to hire, and so on . . . . In the long run, the firm may also choose an optimal size and output mix, but even these are determined by the characteristics of the production function (economies of scale, scope and sequence). In short: the firm is a set of cost curves, and the "theory of the firm" is a calculus problem.[2]

Or again, Reich and Devine: " In go inputs—'capital,' 'labor,' and so forth—and out come outputs, connected only by the engineering relation called the production function."[3]

Of course, Mises gave his entrepreneur a much more creative role than the neoclassical firm in relation to the outside world: the entrepreneur who guided the firm did not merely react automatically to a series of uncomplicated situations, but made active assessments and exercised foresight in the light of dynamic conditions, much like a commander in the fog of war. Still, as far as the internal workings of the firm were concerned, Mises essentially agreed with the neoclassicals: the firm was a unitary actor, its internal functions mere extensions of the entrepreneur's will.

Mises denied any correlation between bureaucratization and large size in and of itself. Bureaucracy as such, he argued, was a rules-based approach to policy-making, as opposed to the profit-driven behavior of the entrepreneur. But Mises neglected the extent to which rational profit-driven entrepreneurial behavior becomes *impossible* because of the information and coordination problems inherent in large size. The large corporation, necessarily, distributes the knowledge relevant to informed entrepreneurial decisions among many departments and sub-departments, until the cost of aggregating them outweighs the benefits of doing so.

Try as he might, Mises could not exempt the capitalist corporation from the problem of bureaucracy. One cannot define bureaucracy out of existence, or overcome the problem of distributed knowledge, simply by using the word "entrepreneur." Mises tried to make the bureaucratic or entrepreneurial character of an organization a simple matter of its organizational goals, rather than its functioning. The motivation of the corporate employee, from CEO down to production worker, would be profit-seeking, his will in harmony with that of the stockholder because he belonged to the stockholder's organization.

By defining organizational goals as "profit-seeking," Mises—like the neoclassicals—treated the internal workings of the organization as a black box. In treating the internal policies of the capitalist corporation as inherently profit-driven, Mises simultaneously treated the entrepreneur as an indivisible actor whose will and perception permeated the entire organization. Although (as we saw above) Mises at one point explicitly denied that the entrepreneur

---

1. Matthew Yglesias, "Two Views of Capitalism," *Matthew Yglesias*, Nov. 22, 2008 <http://yglesias.thinkprogress.org/archives/2008/11/two_views_of_capitalism.php>.

2. "Economic Calculation and the Limits of Organization," p. 5.

3. Michael Reich and James Devine. "The Microeconomics of Conflict and Hierarchy in Capitalist Production," *The Review of Radical Political Economics* vol. 12 no. 4 (Winter 1981), p. 27.

was omnipresent, in practice he viewed his entrepreneur as a brooding omnipresence whose influence guided the action of every employee from CEO to janitor.

Mises viewed the separation of ownership from control, and the agency problems resulting from it, as largely non-existent. The invention of double-entry bookkeeping, which made possible the separate calculation of profit and loss in each division of an enterprise, "reliev[ed] the entrepreneur of involvement in too much detail." The only thing necessary to transform every single employee of a corporation, from CEO on down, into a perfect instrument of his will was the ability to monitor the balance sheet of any division or office and fire the functionary responsible for red ink.

> It is the system of double-entry bookkeeping that makes the functioning of the managerial system possible. Thanks to it, the entrepreneur is in a position to separate the calculation of each part of his total enterprise in such a way that he can determine the role it plays within his whole enterprise. Thus he can look at each section as if it were a separate entity and can appraise it according to the share it contributes to the success of the total enterprise .... Thus the entrepreneur can assign to each section's management a great deal of independence. The only directive he gives to a man whom he entrusts with the management of a circumscribed job is to make as much profit as possible. An examination of the accounts shows how successful or unsuccessful the managers were in executing this directive.[1]

Mises also identified outside capital markets as a control mechanism limiting managerial discretion. Of the popular conception of stockholders as passive rentiers, and of managerial control, he wrote:

> This doctrine disregards entirely the role that the capital and money market, the stock and bond exchange, which a pertinent idiom simply calls the "market," plays in the direction of corporate business .... In fact, the changes in the prices of common and preferred stock and of corporate bonds are the means applied by the capitalists for the supreme control of the flow of capital. The price structure as determined by the speculations on the capital and money markets and on the big commodity exchanges not only

---

1. *Human Action*, p. 305. Nicolai Foss made a valiant effort to extricate Mises from this morass of absurdity. However, it involved putting an extremely generous spin on what Mises actually said, to the extent of rewriting it for all intents and purposes: As Mises (1949: 309) emphasized, '... entrepreneurs are not omnipresent. They cannot themselves attend to the manifold tasks which are incumbent upon them.' Mises ((1949: 305) clearly recognized that in many firms decision rights are allocated by the entrepreneur (and the board of directors) to lower levels, presumably in irder to better cope with distributed knowledge, an insight that is not present in Coase (1937). He perceptively recognized that delegation leads to agency problems, but argued that the system of double-entry bookkeeping and other double control measures may partly cope with such problems. ... In the Misesian scheme, an organizational equilibrium obtains when decision rights are delegated in such a way that the benefits of delegation in terms of better utilizing local knowledge are balanced against the costs of delegation in terms of agency losses. ... [Nicolai J. Foss. "Misesian Ownership and Coasean Authority in Hayekian Settings: The Case of the Knowledge Economy" (Frederiksberg, Denmark: Department of Industrial Economics and Strategy, Copenhagen Business School, 2000 [revised draft, July 2, 2001]), pp. 10-11.]But any fair reading of the Mises material quoted in this section should indicate that there was no "may partly cope" about it. That is entirely Foss's qualification. I challenge anyone reading the extended passages quoted to find any indication in Mises that a tradeoff was involved, or that the entrepreneurial control and the entrepreneurial character of the organization made possible by double-entry bookkeeping were anything less than total. In addition, Foss takes "the very fact that firms exist" as "*prima facie* evidence that they can somehow cope with the problems implied by Hayekian settings." Sure. And the very fact that turtles sit atop fenceposts is *prima facie* evidence that turtles can climb.

decides how much capital is available for the conduct of each corporation's business; it creates a state of affairs to which the managers must adjust their operations in detail.[1]

Mises' naiveté is almost breathtaking. One can hardly imagine the most hubristic of state socialist central planners taking a more optimistic view of the utopian potential of numbers-crunching.

Peter Klein, in his excellent study of economic calculation arguments as they affect firm size,[2] argues that Mises first scenario foreshadowed Henry Manne's treatment of the mechanism by which entrepreneurs maintain control of corporate management. So long as there is a market for control of corporations, the discretion of management will be limited by the threat of hostile takeover. Although management possesses a fair degree of administrative autonomy, any significant deviation from profit-maximization will lower stock prices and bring the corporation into danger of outside takeover.[3]

Oliver Williamson demolished such arguments quite effectively. They require

> that a *mechanism* exist whereby control over monopoly power can actually ... be transferred through the capital market. It requires that control ... reside with the stockholders rather than the managers and that this control be transferable through financial (capital market) rather than political (managerial ascension) processes.[4]

As we shall see in Chapter Eight, whether these requirements are met in the real world is doubtful. Corporate management tends to rely as much as possible on retained earnings for new investment, for example, and is also very good at gaming internal governance rules so as to protect itself from hostile takeover.

A more fundamental question, though, is whether those making investment decisions (whether they be senior management allocating capital among divisions of a corporation, or outside finance capitalists) even possess the information needed to assess the internal workings of the firm, sufficient to make appropriate decisions.

How far the real-world process of internal allocation of finance differs from Mises' picture, is suggested by Robert Jackall's account of the actual workings of a corporation[5] (especially the notorious practices of "starving" or "milking" an organization in order to inflate its apparent profit in the short-term). Whether an apparent profit is sustainable, or an illusory side-effect of eating the seed corn, is often a judgment best made by those directly involved in production. The purely money calculations of those at the top do not suffice for a valid assessment of such questions.

One big problem with Mises' model of entrepreneurial central planning by double-entry bookkeeping: it is often the constraints of the "general plan," as refined at each level of the hierarchy, that *result* in red ink at lower levels. Those at lower levels have their hands tied by irrational constraints from above. But those above them in the hierarchy refuse to acknowledge the double-bind they put their subordinates in. "Plausible deniability," the

1. *Ibid.,* pp. 306-07.
2. "Economic Calculation and the Limits of Organization," *The Review of Austrian Economics* Vol. 9, No. 2 (1996): 3-28.
3. "Mergers and the Market for Corporate Control," *Journal of Political Economy* 73 (April 1965) 110-20; however, Klein cites the argument by Williamson, in *Markets and Hierarchies*, that the internal structure of the M-form corporation is more effective than external control devices like the capital market; see also Roberta Romano's "A Guide to Takeovers: Theory, Evidence, and Regulation," *Yale Journal on Regulation* 9 (1992): 119-80, for a survey of the debate on the effectiveness of the takeover threat.
4. Oliver Williamson, *The Economics of Discretionary Behavior: Managerial Objectives in a Theory of the Firm* (Englewood Cliffs, N.J.: Prentice-Hall, Inc., 1964) p. 22.
5. Robert Jackall, *Moral Mazes: The World of Corporate Managers* (New York: Oxford University Press, 1988).

downward flow of responsibility and upward flow of credit, and the practice of shooting the messenger for bad news, are what lubricate the wheels of any large organization.

As for outside investors, participants in the capital markets are even further removed than corporate management from the data needed to evaluate the efficiency of factor use within the "black box." In practice, hostile takeovers tend to gravitate toward firms with low debt loads and apparently low short-term profit margins. The corporate raiders are more likely to "smell blood" when there is the possibility of loading up an acquisition with new debt and stripping it of assets for short-term returns. The best way to avoid a hostile takeover is to load an organization with debt, and inflate the short-term returns by milking its long-term productivity.

A good illustration is a recent story on hedge fund managers and investment bank CEOs, which describes how the financial system rewards short-term at the expense of long-term profit maximization. Payment at the end of a year based on a percentage of gains creates an incentive to maximize gains in that year, even if they are followed by a loss. As a result, finance capital gravitates toward short-term profit and toward volatile, high-risk investments with potential high payoffs.[1]

Another problem, from the perspective of those at the top, is determining the *significance* of red or black ink. How does the large-scale investor distinguish red ink that results from senior management's gaming of the system in its own interest at the expense of the productivity of the organization, from red ink that results from the normal effects of the business cycle? And the "gaming" might be purely defensive, a way of deflecting pressure from those above whose only concern is to maximize apparent profits without regard to long-term productivity. The practices of "starving" and "milking" organizations that Jackall made so much of—downsizing human capital, deferring needed maintenance costs, letting plant and equipment run down, and the like, in order to inflate the quarterly balance sheet—resulted from just such pressure.

The problem is complicated when the same organizational culture—determined by the needs of the managerial system itself—is shared by all the corporations in an oligopoly industry, so that the same pattern of red ink appears industry-wide. It's complicated still further when the general atmosphere of state capitalism enables the corporations in a cartelized industry to operate in the black, despite excessive size and dysfunctional internal culture (as Leibenstein put it, "for an industry to have a nonminimal cost equilibrium").[2] It becomes impossible to make a valid assessment of why the corporation is profitable at all: does the black ink result from efficiency, or from some degree of protection against the competitive penalty for inefficiency?

If the decisions of MBA types to engage in asset-stripping and milking, in the interest of short-term profitability, result in long-term harm to the health of the enterprise, they are more apt to be reinforced than censured by investors and higher-ups. After all, they acted according to the conventional wisdom in the *Big MBA Handbook*, so it couldn't have been *that* that caused them to go in the tank. Must've been sunspots or something.

This managerial culture was a "success" in corporate America because, when all the major firms in an oligopoly market share the same approach to management, nobody suffers competitive harm from it.

> The theory was that a good manager could run any business. It was all done by the numbers, and knowledge of the product or the manufacturing process was not important. The theory was correct, because it was self-fulfilling. Every one of the big, public companies was managed exactly the same way, although they all spun their systems with

1. James Surowiecki, "Performance Perplexes," *The New Yorker*, November 12, 2007 <http://www.newyorker.com/talk/financial/2007/11/12/071112ta_talk_surowiecki>.

2. Leibenstein, "Allocative Efficiency vs. 'X-Efficiency,'" p. 409.

slightly different lingo . . . . As it turns out he would not have been doing much good at any of them, but no one knew that at the time. They all managed by the numbers, and they all calculated the numbers the same way.

With all of the money being made, it was very easy to believe that we were, in fact, managerial geniuses. The American corporations ruled the world. The great business schools . . . cranked out people thoroughly steeped in the DuPont ROI way, and the money continued to roll in.[1]

Far from *punishing* inefficiency, the conventional wisdom in the financial community is more likely to punish transgressions against the norms of corporate culture, even when they are quite successful by conventional measures. Costco's stock actually fell in value, in response to adverse publicity in the business community about its above-average wages. The *New York Times* quoted Costco's CEO: "Good wages and benefits are why Costco has extremely low rates of turnover and theft by employees . . . ." Despite Costco's having outperformed Wal-Mart in profit, Deutsche Bank analyst Bill Dreher snidely remarked: "At Costco, it's better to be an employee or a customer than a shareholder." In the world of faith-based investment, Wal-Mart "remains the darling of the Street, which, like Wal-Mart and many other companies, believes that shareholders are best served if employers do all they can to hold down costs, including the cost of labor."[2] The lesson Alex Kjerulf draws from this:

> Executives who believe in treating employees well are faced with pressure from analysts and the stock market to stop doing so and start being more like anyone else— regardless of the results their strategy has been getting them so far.[3]

(Dreher's remark, by the way, should come across as odd to any free market thinker in the habit of arguing that market relations are positive-sum and based on equal exchange. Why *should* it be better to be a shareholder than an employee or customer?)

On the other hand, senior management may be handsomely rewarded for running a corporation into the ground, so long as they are perceived to be doing everything right according to the norms of corporate culture. In a story which Digg aptly titled "Home Depot CEO Gets $210M Severance for Sucking at Job,"[4] departing Home Depot CEO Robert Nardelli received an enormous severance package despite abysmal performance. It's a good thing he didn't raise employee wages too high, though, or he'd probably be eating in a soup kitchen by now.

As you might expect, the usual suspects stepped in to defend Mr. Nardelli's honor. An Allan Murray article at The Wall Street Journal noted that he had "more than doubled [Home Depot's] earnings."

But Tom Blumer of BizzyBlog pointed out some inconvenient facts about how Nardelli achieved those increased earnings:

> * His consolidation of purchasing and many other functions to Atlanta from several regions caused buyers to lose touch with their vendors . . . .

1. Waddell and Bodek, op. cit., p. 96.

2. Stanley Holmes and Wendy Zellner, "The Costco Way: Higher wages mean higher profits. But try telling Wall Street" *Business Week Online* April 12, 2004 <http://www.businessweek.com/magazine/content/04_15/b3878084_mz021.htm>; Steven Greenhouse, "How Costco Became the Anti-Wal-Mart," New York Times, July 17, 2005 <http://www.nytimes.com/2005/07/17/business/yourmoney/17costco.html? ex=1279252800&en=8b31033c5b6a6d68&ei=5088>.

3. Alex Kjerulf, "Analysts to Costco: Stop treating your employees so well," *Chief Happiness Officer*, July 17, 2007 <http://positivesharing.com/2007/07/analysts-to-costco-stop-treating-your-employees-so-well/>.

4. The original, more prosaicly titled article appeared in the *New York Times*, January 3, 2007.

> ★ Firing knowledgeable and experienced people in favor of uninformed newbies and part-timers greatly reduced payroll and benefits costs, but has eventually driven customers away, and given the company a richly-deserved reputation for mediocre service.[1]

> ★ Nardelli and his minions played every accounting, acquisition, and quick-fix angle they could to keep the numbers looking good, while letting the business deteriorate.[2]

Blumer followed up with a comment on my blog, in response to a blog post in which I quoted the above:

> I have since learned that Nardelli, in the last months before he walked, took the entire purchasing function out of Atlanta and moved it to . . . . India—Of all the things to pick for foreign outsourcing.
>
> I am told that "out of touch" doesn't even begin to describe how bad it is now between HD stores and Purchasing, and between HD Purchasing and suppliers.
>
> Not only is there a language dialect barrier, but the purchasing people in India don't know the "language" of American hardware—or even what half the stuff the stores and suppliers are describing even is.
>
> I am told that an incredible amount of time, money, and energy is being wasted—all in the name of what was in all likelihood a bonus-driven goal for cutting headcount and making G&A expenses look low ("look" low because the expenses have been pushed down to the stores and suppliers).[3]

Nardelli has since been punished for his mismanagement by being appointed CEO of Chrysler, by the way.

And as the example of "Chainsaw Al" Dunlap (a corporate hit man who made a career of downsizing corporations) shows, Mises' celebrated double-entry bookkeeping isn't much of a panacea for principal-agent problems when the agent is keeping the books. Except in the rare cases where the founding family of a corporation retains a controlling block of stock and has its own members on the board, insider control of the books is the norm. Dunlap was a master at figuring out how to make a company appear profitable on paper. Dunlap left Nitec Paper Corporation with an enormous severance package, in the face of a threatened walkout by the rest of the management team, after he gutted that company of its human capital. After he left, it turned out he'd used "creative accounting" ("expenses, inventory, and cash on hand had all been adjusted") to transform a $5.5 million deficit into a $5 million increase in profit. He did the same at Sunbeam, with the help of the magicians of Arthur Andersen.[4]

In fact, under the DuPont/Sloan/Brown accounting method, which treats inventory as an asset, fooling the market with such jugglery is (to a lesser degree) a normal part of management operating procedure. A major feature of the Sloan management accounting system is "overhead absorption," which means fully incorporating overhead costs into the price of goods "sold" to inventory, so that it shows up as a positive figure on the balance sheet.[5] In colorful language, it amounts to "goosing the numbers by sweeping overhead under the rug and into inventory."[6]

---

1. *BizzyBlog*, January 8, 2007 <http://www.bizzyblog.com/2007/01/08/disarming-nardellis-defenders-part-1/>.

2. *Ibid.*, January 8, 2007 <http://www.bizzyblog.com/2007/01/08/disarming-nardellis-defenders-part-3/>.

3. Blumer comment under Kevin Carson, "Economic Calculation in the Corporate Commonwealth: Part II: Hayek vs. Mises on Distributed Knowledge (Excerpt)," *Mutualist Blog*, Friday, March 16, 2007 <http://mutualist.blogspot.com/2007/03/economic-calculation-in-corporate.html>.

4. Arianna Huffington, *Pigs at the Trough: How Corporate Greed and Political Corruption are Undermining America* (New York: Crown Publishers, 2003), pp. 62-65.

5. Waddell and Bodek, op. cit., pp. 135-140.

6. *Ibid.*, p. 143.

By defining the creation of inventory, including work-in-process, as a money-making endeavor, any incentive to encourage flow went out the window. The 1950s saw the emergence of warehouses as a logical and necessary adjunct to manufacturing. Prior to that, the manufacturing warehouse was typically a small shed out behind the plant . . . . By the 1960s warehouse space often equaled, or exceeded, production space in many plants . . . .[1]

The whole point of overhead and inventory jugglery is concealment: "Every dollar of overhead that is added to the cost of a product for inventory valuation purposes increases the incentive to produce in volume rather than eliminate waste . . . ."[2]

On the other hand, the first stages of implementing lean production (the real thing, not the Jack Welch crap) show up as bad numbers.

When a plant has a Kaizen Blitz, and makes substantial improvements in cycle time, the short term financial numbers can get clobbered. Converting inventory to cash makes book profit look worse.[3]

If things aren't already opaque enough for Mises' entrepreneur, we can throw in the investment banks, who have a vested interest (in collusion with corporate management) in using stock analysis to drive up share prices and promote sales.[4]

Dennis May remarked on the general tendency of the large corporation, in response to the perverse incentives that motivated Nardelli and Dunlap, to engage in counter-productive "cost cutting" measures:

I have noticed with increasing frequency—from direct experience and from contact with other companies—that common sense is going out the window in favor of easily quanti-fiable cost savings masking difficult to quantify losses. It amounts to cost shifting and hid-ing losses while claiming a savings. This has become more common as bean counters with no manufacturing knowledge or experience implement incorrect approaches to cost savings. The feedback process to correct the problem involves too much effort be-cause the obvious losses are difficult to quantify and those in a position to point out the errors will not be rewarded for informing their superiors of the error they have commit-ted.[5]

Doug Henwood, in *Wall Street*, makes essentially the same point about communica-tion between managers and shareholders:

Even if participants are aware of an upward bias to earnings estimates, and even if they correct for it, managers would still have an incentive to try to fool the market. If you tell the truth, your accurate estimate will be marked down by a skeptical market. So, it's entirely rational for managers to boost profits in the short term, either through ac-counting gimmickry or by making only investments with quick paybacks.

If the markets see high costs as bad, and low costs as good, then firms may shun ex-pensive investments because they will be taken as signs of managerial incompetence. Throughout the late 1980s and early 1990s, the stock market rewarded firms announcing write-offs and mass firings—a bulimic strategy of management—since the cost-cutting was seen as contributing rather quickly to profits. Firms and economies can't get richer by starving themselves, but stock market investors can get richer when the companies

1. *Ibid.*, p. 97. Huffington provides illustrations of the popular practice of "earnings restate-ments," typically coming out after the usual suspects have fully profited from earlier glowing reports of outstanding performance (pp. 173-176).
2. Waddell and Bodek, p. 233.
3. *Ibid.*, p. 130.
4. Huffington, pp. 154-169. Doug Henwood, *Wall Street*, pp. 100-102.
5. Mays' comment originally appeared as a post to the Atlantis II yahoogroup. It was quoted by the late Christopher Tame, Director of the Libertarian Alliance, in "An Intersting Observation—A Common Economic Error Becoming More Common," Message #45728, July 6, 2005 <http://groups.yahoo.com/group/libertarian-alliance-forum/message/45728>.

they own go hungry—at least in the short term. As for the long term, well, that's someone else's problem the week after next.[1]

Iain McKay, in the Anarchist FAQ, noted the resemblance of such perverse incentives
to those faced by plant managers in the old Soviet economy.

> Ironically, this situation has a parallel with Stalinist central planning. Under that system
> managers of State workplaces had an incentive to lie about their capacity to the planning
> bureaucracy. The planner would, in turn, assume higher capacity, so harming honest
> managers and encouraging them to lie. This, of course, had a seriously bad impact on the
> economy. Unsurprisingly, the similar effects caused by capital markets on economies sub-
> ject to them are just as bad, downplaying long term issues and investment.[2]

(For an entertaining illustration of Corporate America's resemblance to the Soviet economy, by the way, look at Waddell's and Bodek's account of the "end of the quarter shuffle"
in Appendix 7A. Anyone who's familiar with accounts of the internal doings of a Soviet
factory at the end of a plan period should get a good chuckle.)

Corporate management is enabled to engage in such gamesmanship at all levels of the
hierarchy, to the prejudice of any would-be omniscient entrepreneur cum double-entry
bookkeeper, in part because of the information rents entailed in their positions. For example Michael Schiff and Arie Lewin, in a 1968 study, challenged the traditional approach to
management accounting, which treats individuals as "passive members of the system." In
its place they substituted a model based on modern organization theory, which emphasizes
limited information-processing capability and individual sub-goals. In the real world, they
said, the budget preparation process involves management bargaining "about the performance criteria by which they will be judged throughout the year and for resource allocations. The outcome is a bargained budget incorporating varying degrees of slack." Slack is
defined as the difference between "minimum necessary costs and the actual costs of the
firm." They hypothesized that

> [m]anagers are motivated to achieve two sets of goals—the firm's goals and their per-
> sonal goals. Personal goals are directly related to income . . . , size of staff, and control
> over allocation of resources. To maximize personal goals while achieving the goals of the
> firm requires a slack environment. This suggests that managers intentionally create slack.[3]

In their study of three divisions of Fortune 100 corporations, they found that "slack
may account for as much as 20 to 25 per cent of divisional budgeted operating expenses."
And although senior management is aware of such padding at lower levels, it lacks the information to prevent it.[4]

Corporations in an oligopoly market are quite tolerant of slack, when they can pass
costs on to the customer with little pressure from price competition. Under those circumstances, they are entirely comfortable with the "cost-plus" culture.

> Where the pressure of competition does not force prices down to costs, costs themselves
> tend to rise: internal management checks alone cannot overcome the tendency to be sat-
> isfied with costs when the overall level of profit is satisfactory.[5]

1. Henwood, *Wall Street*, p. 171.

2. "I.4.8. What About Investment Decisions?" *An Anarchist FAQ* Webpage Version 12.2
(February 27, 2008) <http://www.infoshop.org/faq/>.

3. Michael Schiff and Arie Lewin, "Where Traditional Budgeting Fails," *Financial Executive*
36 (May 1968), p. 51.

4. *Ibid.*, p. 62.

5. Carl Kaysen, "The Corporation: How Much Power? What Scope?" in Edward S. Mason,
ed., *The Corporation in Modern Society* (Cambridge, Mass.: Harvard University Press, 1966), p. 92.

In other words, they pursue the same kind of cost-maximization Seymour Melman describes in military industry—a pathology inevitably associated with administered pricing and "cost plus."

R. Preston McAffee and John McMillan pointed to similar behavior in the Soviet planned economy:

> Misreporting was rife in the pre-reform Soviet firm, according to Berliner's 1957 study, based on interviews with expatriate former managers. One of Berliner's informants said there is "An enormous amount of falsification in all branches of production and in their accounting systems . . . everywhere there is evasion, false figures, untrue reports." . . . . Enterprise managers misrepresented their firms' costs in their reports to the ministries. They exaggerated their needs for labor, materials, and equipment; failed to report improvements in techniques; concealed the productivity of new machines; understated the number of engineers on hand; and overstated the time needed for a task . . . . The misinformation caused the Soviet planer . . . [sic] to order inefficient output quantities . . . . The misreporting was not unknown to the ministry/principal, but the manager/agent understood incentive compatibility: "Although the purchasing organizations sometimes make attempts to check up on the statements of requirements presented to them, they have no dat for this purpose, and therefore they simply adopt the method of indiscriminate cutting, which in turn causes some enterprises to present even more greatly inflated statements of requirements." . . . . The ministry/principal did not, however, appear to design incentive contracts . . . , but rather simply asked what the enterprise's technical possibilities were. The manager/agent was not rewarded for revealing production capacity to be large . . . .
>
> . . . [M]isreporting within the Soviet enterprise "is not confined to one level of management but permeates the whole system. Within the enterprise each official seeks to maintain a little factor of safety unknown to his immediate superior. The consequence is a cumulative discrepancy between actual capacity and plan targets." . . . . The cumulative increase in misreporting did not even end at the enterprise level. The ministry officials in charge of the enterprise overstated its costs to the State Planning Commission . . . .[1]

Corporate management is also very good at manipulating data to confuse outside investors. For example, according to Martin Hellwig incumbent management tends to buttress its security with company resources, accumulating and decumulating hidden reserves (like real estate investments) that can be used to smooth out cash flow.[2]

Mises' argument for the restraint of management by capital markets has been revived in a much more sophisticated form by Jeffrey Friedman, who has incorporated into it a partial defense against criticisms like those above. According to Friedman, the cognitive capacity of the entrepreneur, and his ability to interpret data, *don't matter.* The capital market, acting by an invisible hand mechanism, directs capital to successful investors even when they stumble onto success by blind luck—thereby simulating rationality independently of conscious human direction.[3]

The problem with Friedman's argument is that the market, as an information processor, is subject to the GIGO ("garbage in, garbage out") rule: operating as it does within the limits of a state capitalist framework, the market system answers the wrong questions be-

1. R. Preston McAffee and John McMillan, "Organizational Diseconomies of Scale," Journal of Economics & Management Strategy, Vol. 4, No. 3 (Fall 1995), pp. 402-403; the Soviet material comes from Joseph S. Berliner, *Factory and Manager in the USSR* (Cambridge: Harvard University Press, 1957).

2. Martin Hellwig, "On the Economics and Politics of Corporate Finance and Corporate Control," in Xavier Vives, ed., *Corporate Governance: Theoretical and Empirical Perspectives* (Cambridge: Cambridge University Press, 2000), p. 119.

3. Jeffrey Friedman, "Taking Ignorance Seriously: Rejoinder to Critics," *Critical Review* 18:4 (2006), p. 474.

cause the wrong data are being fed into it. Therefore, given the pervasive pattern of subsidies to inefficient activity, the identification of "success" as what the market rewards with more resources is likely to be circular.

The irony is that the institutional forms entrepreneurship has taken under state capitalism—the forms which the culture-bound Mises himself identified with entrepreneurship as such—concentrate entrepreneurial decision-making in a class so far removed from the relevant information. Mises' version of the "market" economy, in which investment capital is concentrated in the hands of billionaire stockholders and investment bankers, rather than worker-owners reinvesting their surplus in their own enterprises, is largely a historical accident ("accidental" in the sense of having no necessary connection to the essence of a free market—but you'd better believe it was on purpose).

Beyond a certain corporate size, the "entrepreneur" is as clueless about the doings within the corporation whose stock he holds, and the CEO about the doings within his own organization, as was their counterpart in a Soviet industrial ministry. The problem, separation of knowledge of goals from knowledge of process, and of finance from production, is inherent in large size and administrative differentiation.

It's worth noting that Mises, in his sweeping assertions of double-entry bookkeeping's potential for solving all the informational and motivational problems of agency, inadvertently makes a large concession to Lange and Schumpeter. If Mises' claims for double-entry bookkeeping as a mechanism for "central planning" at corporate headquarters are correct, then factor pricing is the *only* constraint on calculation by a central planner, and Hayek's problems of distributed knowledge are non-existent. In fact, it's quite difficult to distinguish Mises' quote above on the potential for double-entry bookkeeping in the internal planned economy of an M-form corporation, by itself, from Lange's and Schumpeter's vision of a collectivized economy planned by bookkeepers. The only difference between Mises and the collectivists is over the extent to which private property and markets are necessary to establish the general goals of large organizations. Their views on the internal functioning of large organizations themselves, and their amenability to central planning, are identical.

C. Rothbard's Application of the Calculation Argument to the Private Sector

Mises argued that socialist governments directing nationalized economies were able to more or less approach economic rationality by setting their internal input prices with reference to foreign prices in countries where markets still prevailed. They would be able to function to some degree, despite the absence of market prices for producer goods, because

> these were not isolated socialist systems. They were operating in an environment in which the price system still worked. They could resort to economic calculation on the ground of the prices established abroad.[1]

In *Man, Economy, and State*, Rothbard applied the calculation argument to the private sector firm in a market economy, raising the question of "the role of implicit earnings and calculation in a vertically integrated firm."[2]

> The firm buys labor and land factors at both the fifth and the fourth stages; it also makes the fourth-stage capital goods itself and uses them in another plant to make a lower-stage good . . . .

---

1. *Human Action*, p. 703.
2. *Man, Economy, and State*, p. 545.

Does such a firm employ calculation within itself, and if so, how? Yes. The firm assumes that it *sells itself* the fourth-rank capital good. It separates its net income as a producer of fourth-rank capital from its role as producer of third-rank capital. It calculates the net income for each separate division of its enterprise and allocates resources according to the profit or loss made in each division. *It is able to make such an internal calculation only because it can refer to an existing explicit market price for the fourth-stage capital good.* In other words, a firm can accurately estimate the profit or loss it makes in a stage of its enterprise only by finding out the *implicit* price of its internal product, and it can do this only if an *external* market price for that product is established elsewhere.

On the other hand, suppose that there is no external market, i.e., that the Jones Company is the only producer of the intermediate good. In that case, it would have no way of knowing which stage was being conducted profitably and which not. It would therefore have no way of knowing how to allocate factors to the various stages. There would be no way for it to estimate any implicit price or opportunity cost for the capital good at that particular stage. Any estimate would be completely arbitrary and have no meaningful relation to economic conditions.

In short, if there were no market for a product, and all of its exchanges were internal, there would be no way for a firm or for anyone else to determine a price for the good .... Not being able to calculate a price, the firm could not rationally allocate factors and resources from one stage to another.

Since the free market always tends to establish the most efficient and profitable type of production (whether for type of good, method of production, allocation of factors, or size of firm), we must conclude that complete vertical integration for a capital-good product can never be established on the free market (above the primitive level). *For every capital good, there must be a definite market in which firms buy and sell that good.* It is obvious that this economic law *sets a definite maximum to the relative size of any particular firm on the free market* .... Because of this law, there can never be One Big Cartel over the whole economy or mergers until One Big Firm owns all the productive assets in the economy. The force of this law multiplies as the area of the economy increases and as islands of noncalculable chaos swell to the proportions of masses and continents. As the area of incalculability increases, the degrees of irrationality, misallocation, loss, impoverishment, etc., become greater ....

... Mises ... has demonstrated irrefutably that a socialist economic system cannot calculate, since it lacks a market, and hence lacks prices for producers' and especially for capital goods. Now we see that, paradoxically, the reason why a socialist economy cannot calculate is *not* specifically because it is socialist! ... The reason for the impossibility of calculation under socialism is that *one agent* owns or directs the use of all the resources in the economy. It should be clear that it does not make any difference whether that one agent is the State or one private individual or private cartel.[1]

... [T]he free market places definite limits on the size of the firm, i.e., the limits of *calculability* on the market. In order to calculate the profits and losses of each branch, a firm must be able to refer its internal operations to *external markets* for *each* of the various factors and intermediate products. When any of these external markets disappears, because all are absorbed *within* the province of a single firm, calculability disappears, and there is no way for the firm rationally to allocate factors to that specific area. The more these limits are encroached upon, the greater and greater will be the sphere of irrationality ....[2]

He further elaborated on this argument in "Ludwig von Mises and Economic Calculation Under Socialism":

... [T]he theory is not about socialism at all! Instead, it applies to *any* situation where one group has acquired control of the means of production over a large area—or, in a strict sense, throughout the world .... For what the Mises theory focuses on is ... the fact that a market for capital goods has disappeared. This means that, just as Socialist

1. *Ibid.*, pp. 545–49.
2. *Ibid.*, p. 585.

central planning could not calculate economically, no One Big Firm could own or control the entire economy.

. . . One Big Firm would soon find itself suffering severe losses and would therefore disintegrate under this pressure. . . . [I]t seems to follow that, as we *approach* One Big Firm on the market, as mergers begin to eliminate capital goods markets in industry after industry, these calculation problems will begin to appear, albeit not as catastrophically as under full monopoly . . . . If, then, calculation problems begin to arise as markets disappear, this places a free-market limit, not simply on One Big Firm, but even on partial monopolies that eradicate markets. Hence, the free market contains within itself a built-in mechanism limiting the relative size of firms in order to preserve markets throughout the economy.[1]

The main shortcoming of Rothbard's analysis is that, as Peter Klein characterized it, "Rothbard is making a claim only about the upper bound of the firm, not the incremental cost of expanding the firm's activities (as long as external market references are available)."[2]

But (as the Soviet analogy suggests) the larger and more vertically integrated the corporation, even when outside markets continue to exist for all its inputs, the further removed are its internal conditions from the immediate conditions under which prices are formed moment to moment in the outside market. The external market prices are to some extent arbitrary, reflecting the situation of market actors outside the firm rather than the situation within the firm. Pricing based on the available supply and the valuation of purchasers under the spot conditions of the market may lead to irrational allocations given different conditions of supply and valuation within the firm. If nothing else, the fact that the firm is "exchanging" factors internally, rather than bidding in the outside market, distorts the price in the outside market so that it is different from what it would be if the firm were a participant in it. The outside market's prices are atypical or misleading precisely to the extent that they do not incorporate the valuations of the firm in question. Rothbard himself admitted as much, in a footnote to *Man, Economy and State:*.

The implicit price, or opportunity cost of selling to oneself, might be less than the existing market price, since the entry of the Jones Company on the market might have lowered the price of the good, say to 102 ounces.[3]

In Rothbard's view, Peter Klein comments, external markets do not have to be perfectly competitive. "For Rothbard, 'thin' markets are adequate: all that is necessary to have a genuine 'external market' is the existence of at least one other producer (seller) of the intermediate good."[4]

But this is unsatisfactory. The whole purpose of a price system is for price to fluctuate so as to equalize the quantities demanded and supplied in a specific environment. The conditions of supply and demand by which spot prices are set in an outside market are highly unlikely to duplicate the exact conditions of supply and demand within a firm, and will therefore be highly inefficient for regulating the flow of inputs within the firm. They will be average, not marginal prices. The outside market price is as approximate and distorted, from the standpoint of the firm's internal planners, as market prices in the West were to Soviet state planners. Or at least, the unsatisfactoriness and approximateness are similar in kind, if not degree. If all that matters is that some external market continue to exist, no matter how unrepresentative of conditions within the firm, then a state-planned economy ought also to work just fine with implicit pricing based on foreign markets, so long as some market continued to exist anywhere in the world.

1. "Ludwig von Mises and Economic Calculation under Socialism," pp. 75-76.
2. "Economic Calculation and the Limits of Organization," p. 15.
3. *Man, Economy, and State*, pp. 900-01, n56.
4. "Economic Calculation and the Limits of Organization," p. 14 n. 13; reference is to Jack Hirshleifer, "On the Economics of Transfer Pricing," *Journal of Business* 29 (1956): 172-89

In any case, the practical effect even of Rothbard's argument as stated results in a size threshold for calculational problems far lower than Rothbard himself would likely have been comfortable with. He explicitly stated that the requirement for "factor markets" applies to intermediate components or unfinished goods as well as basic raw materials. If many or most of the component parts of a complex consumer good are unique and differentiated from the components of competing versions of that good, in ways that prevent generic pricing of the components, the firm must set an internal transfer price for the component that is estimated on some cost-plus basis. In this case, Rothbard seemed to argue, the more indirectly the transfer price is derived from the actual market prices of higher order producer goods, the further removed from reality are the firm's attempts at calculation. If this is taken as Rothbard's explicit doctrine, then most oligopoly manufacturing corporations probably exceed Rothbard's threshold; the majority of firms would fall within his threshold only where the predominant model of organization was to organize each stage of production as a separate firm and coordinate them by contract.

When no external market exists for intermediate products or components, the usual practice is to estimate the transfer price on a cost-plus basis, or perhaps to allow the buying and selling divisions to bargain in an internal "market." Rothbard dismissed such a transfer price as "only an arbitrary symbol."[1] Peter Klein adds:

> At the very least, any artificial or substitute transfer prices will contain less information than actual market prices . . . .[2]

John Menge's 1961 account of transfer pricing seems to bear out my speculations on the pricing of intermediate goods unique to a particular firm.[3] In his case study of the automobile industry, intermediate goods were assigned to three categories for the sake of transfer pricing: Class X (goods for which no outside market exists—"integral, non-substitutable, components of the finished product"); Class Z (goods which are readily available in the outside market); and Class Y goods, which are both produced internally and available on the market. In the case of Class Y and Z goods, management is in roughly the same situation as state socialist planners relying on outside prices. If they are bought on the outside and then traded between units, the price in outside markets will not fully reflect the supply and demand for the goods inside the firm from one day to the next. If they are produced internally, but also available in outside markets, the outside price may be a very poor reflection of the internal costs of producing it.

In the case of Class X goods, intermediate goods unique to the firm, transfer pricing is far more arbitrary. Transfer prices "are to be established on the basis of the estimated costs of an efficient producer plus a markup equal to the divisional profit objective on the assets utilized."[4]

> The principal determinants of this price are estimates of material costs, direct labor costs, overhead costs, starting or tooling costs, unanticipated program acceleration costs, return on assets employed and standard volume.[5]

At the time he wrote, Menge observed that the portion of intermediate goods in Class X had fallen from 75% to 65% in the previous five years; but the process seemed to have reached a saturation point beyond which little further reduction was feasible. He speculated

1. Rothbard, *Man, Economy, and State*, p. 547.
2. "Economic Calculation and the Limits of Organization," p. 14.
3. John A. Menge, "The Backward Art of Interdivisional Transfer Pricing," *The Journal of Industrial Economics*, vol. 9, no. 3 (July 1961), pp. 215-32.
4. *Ibid.*, p. 220.
5. *Ibid.*, p. 225.

that Class X goods would always represent a majority of intermediate goods in the indus-try.[1]

The problem is exacerbated by interdivisional politics, because, as Gary Miller points out, "the executives in each division are normally compensated on the basis of their own division's book profits."

> Therefore, the user division has every incentive to try to obtain the other division's product for as little as possible . . . . Similarly, the supplier division has every incentive to charge the other division as much as possible for its product . . . .
> Thus, the divisions often end up engaging in hostilities around the set of issues known as "transfer pricing."[2]

As an amusing aside, in considering the parallel application of the calculation argument to the state and corporate planned economies, Kenneth Arrow suggested an expedient for corporate transfer pricing much like Oskar Lange's proposal for simulating the market in a planned economy: let each manager set initial transfer prices based on guess-work, observe the relative inputs and outputs, and then adjust them to internal "market" clearing levels.[3] So there's some justification for Roderick Long's dismissal of "market-based management": "as far as I can tell, MBM is just a way of simulating markets à la market socialism . . ."[4]

The difference between transfer pricing of intermediate goods for which there is no external market, and reliance on outside spot prices for establishing transfer prices within the firm, is really only a difference in degree. In both cases, they rely on estimates based on outside prices. The difference is that establishing transfer prices of unique intermediate goods relies on indirect cost-plus calculations from the prices of even more basic components. But both are indirect to a large extent, and involve relying on spot market information that is removed from the immediate conditions prevailing inside the firm. If the cost-plus pricing of intermediate goods is unacceptable to Rothbard, then so also should be the reliance on "thin" outside markets for pricing generic intermediate goods.

Rothbard's assertion that "[f]ar lesser evils prevent entrepreneurs from establishing even islands of incalculability," under corporate capitalism, is quite doubtful. He neglects the extent to which the large corporation, as an island of incalculability, is insulated from the market penalties for calculational chaos.

The existing state capitalist system has promoted economic centralization and large scale to the extent that it is impossible for any decision-maker to aggregate the distributed knowledge necessary to take both entrepreneurial and technical questions into account in making a rational decision. But the large corporate firm operates in an environment of re-straints on competition, shared cultures of inefficiency with other firms in the same indus-

---

1. *Ibid.*, p. 218.

2. Gary J. Miller, *Managerial Dilemmas: The Political Economy of Hierarchy* (New York: Cambridge University Press, 1992), p. 131.

3. Kenneth Arrow, "Control in Large Organizations," *Management Science* (pre-1986), Vol. 10, No. 3 (April 1964), p. 405.

4. Roderick Long, "Shadow of the Kochtopus," *Austro-Athenian Empire*, May 5, 2008 <http://praxeology.net/blog/2008/05/05/shadow-of-the-kochtopus/>. And while we're on the subject, there's another parallel between the Lange model of market socialism and the incentive system within the corporation: the lack of symmetry between management's rewards for profit, and management's risk from losses, that results from their lack of real ownership of the capital assets at risk. This lack of real ownership by enterprise managers under market socialism, Mises argued, was a major flaw: because they would not be risking their own assets, their incentive would be to take risks with a very large potential payoffs, in situations where the risk aversion of a real owner would probably lead him to reject them.

try, and push distribution models, so that it is insulated to a considerable degree from the consequences of irrational decisions.

In fact, the parallels between the kinds of uneven development and misallocation that exist under state socialism, and the equivalent phenomena under state capitalism, are striking. The corporate economy, as a whole, operates in nearly the same atmosphere of calculational chaos as the Soviet planned economy. Like the Soviet planned economy, it is able to stagger on because it does at least translate production inputs into real use-value. But like the Soviet planned economy, its managers have little idea whether the use-value produced came at the expense of some other, greater use-value that might otherwise have resulted from the same inputs. Like the Soviet economy, it has little idea of the comparative efficiency or inefficiency with which productive inputs have been used. Like the Soviet planned economy, although to a lesser extent, it is insulated from competition by those who might more accurately assess the needs of consumers or organize resources more efficiently in meeting those needs.

And like the Soviet and other state-planned economies, it sometimes results in comical examples of inefficient, ass-backward planning:

> Remember when the Airbus A380 was delayed and it was an example of the *total bankruptcy of socialist Europe's way of life*? Look what's happening with Boeing's 787 Dreamliner (and B[ritish] A[irways]'s fleet) . . .
>
> Boeing blamed the delivery delay on continuing problems with flight control software, being produced by Honeywell International, and integrating other systems on the plane, which it did not detail.
>
> It said it now expects the first test flight of the 787 to take place "around the end of the first quarter" next year, suggesting it could be as late as March or even April 2008.
>
> That is a drastic extension to its original plan to start airborne tests in August 2007. In early September, Boeing scheduled the first test flight for mid-November to mid-December as it wrestled with software problems and a shortage of bolts.
>
> Bolts? Boeing has run out of *bolts*? That's positively Soviet. Call GOSPLAN and get a brigade of shock workers on the bolts right now! There's probably one huge bolt on a low loader in the yard at Boeing Field . . . Snark aside . . . actually, fuck putting the snark aside. Let's get the snark out of the shed and give it a damn good snarking. There's something about the Reuters report that makes me think the software actually uses bolts; it's made in Seattle, after all.
>
> I suppose they called it the Dreamliner because unlike the A380 it's, well, still a dream.[1]

Alex Harrowell's reference to "one huge bolt on a low loader" is an allusion to the old Soviet-era joke about the nail factory that filled its entire quota for the Five Year Plan by producing a single sixteen-ton nail. He links to a post at *Three-Toed Sloth* blog which uses the joke to illustrate "a broader problem with using quantitative performance targets, namely that people will tend to meet the quantitative criteria, which can be only very poorly related to the real job they are supposed to be doing."[2]

The problem with a state economy, as Mises pictured it, was not that it would be incapable of technical sophistication. A state socialist economy might produce use-value. The problem is that the planners would have absolutely no idea whether the use-value created was worth the cost: did it absorb inputs that might have been used for some greater use value? "All economic change . . . would involve operations the value of which could nei-

---

1. Alex Harrowell, " 0x05B7Y: Out of Bolts Error," *The Yorkshire Ranter*, October 10, 2007 <http://yorkshire-ranter.blogspot.com/2007/10/0x05b7y-out-of-bolts-error.html>.

2. Cosma Shalizi, "Eigenfactor (Why Oh Why Can't We Have a Better Academic Publishing System? Dept.)," *Three-Toed Sloth*, March 20, 2007 <http://www.cscs.umich.edu/~crshalizi/weblog/479.html>.

ther be predicted beforehand nor ascertained after they had taken place. Everything would be a leap in the dark."[1]

Richard Ericson remarked on the ability of communist systems to achieve great feats of engineering without regard to cost:

> When the system pursues a few priority objectives, regardless of sacrifices or losses in lower priority areas, those ultimately responsible cannot know whether the success was worth achieving."[2]

Consider also Hayek's prediction of the uneven development, irrationality, and misallocation of resources within a planned economy:

> There is no reason to expect that production would stop, or that the authorities would find difficulty in using all the available resources somehow, or even that output would be permanently lower than it had been before planning started . . . . [We should expect] the excessive development of some lines of production at the expense of others and the use of methods which are inappropriate under the circumstances. We should expect to find overdevelopment of some industries at a cost which was not justified by the importance of their increased output and see unchecked the ambition of the engineer to apply the latest development elsewhere, without considering whether they were economically suited in the situation. In many cases the use of the latest methods of production, which could not have been applied without central planning, would then be a symptom of a misuse of resources rather than a proof of success.

As an example he cited "the excellence, from a technological point of view, of some parts of the Russian industrial equipment, which often strikes the casual observer and which is commonly regarded as evidence of success . . . ."[3]

To anyone observing the uneven development of the corporate economy under state capitalism, this should inspire a sense of *deja vu*. Entire categories of goods and production methods have been developed at enormous expense, either within military industry or by state-subsidized R&D in the civilian economy, without regard to cost.[4] Subsidies to capital accumulation, R&D, and technical education radically distort the forms taken by production. Blockbuster factories and economic centralization become artificially profitable, thanks to the Interstate Highway System and other means of externalizing distribution costs.

These quotes on communist central planning also describe quite well the environment of pervasive irrationality *within* the large corporation: management featherbedding and self-dealing; "cost-cutting" measures that decimate productive resources while leaving management's petty empires intact; and the tendency to extend bureaucratic domain while cutting maintenance and support for existing obligations. Management's allocation of resources no doubt creates use value of a sort—but with no reliable way to assess opportunity cost or determine whether the benefit was worth it.

1. Mises, *Socialism: An Economic and Sociological Analysis*. Translated by J. Kahane. New edition, enlarged with an Epilogue (New Haven: Yale University Press, 1951).

2. "The Classical Soviet-Type Economy: Nature of the System and Implications for Reform." *Journal of Economic Perspectives* 5:4 (1991), p. 21.

3. F. A. Hayek. "Socialist Calculation II: The State of the Debate (1935)," in Hayek, *Individualism and Economic Order* (Chicago: University of Chicago Press, 1948), pp. 149-50.

4. Two of David Noble's works, *Forces of Production: A Social History of Industrial Automation* (New York: Alfred A. Knopf, 1984), and *America by Design: Science, Technology, and the Rise of Corporate Capitalism* (New York: Alfred A. Knopf, 1977) are a good starting point on this subject. Miniaturized circuitry, digital control systems for machine tools, cybernetics, and quality control systems—just to name a few examples—were all direct spillovers from the military economy.

CONCLUSION

In this chapter we have examined the inefficiencies of the large corporation, resulting directly from the internal diseconomies of scale: the separation of economic from technical knowledge; the informational problems of aggregating distributed knowledge in a hierarchy; the agency problems of divorcing the benefits of increased productivity from the knowledge of how to improve the process; and the calculational chaos created by removing internal transfer pricing from its proper basis in the market.

The solution is to avoid hierarchy as much as possible, and to internalize the costs and benefits of organizing production in the same decision-makers. Insofar as the production process involves a series of discrete, severable steps, the best way of circumventing informational and incentive problems may be to relate the separate steps to one another by contract—especially if each step, organized under a separate firm, takes the internal form of a producer cooperative.

Each step, although a black box to those outside, from an inside perspective is ideally suited to aggregating all relevant information for consideration by a single group of decision-makers. In a self-managed enterprise, the same people who consider the relative prices of different productive inputs, and the price of the finished product, are also experienced in the actual production process in which the inputs are used. They are most qualified, of all people, to decide both the relative priority by which productive inputs ought to be economized, and the most effective technical methods of organizing production in order to economize those inputs.

From an outside perspective, on the other hand, other contracting firms are able to make a virtue of necessity in treating a particular stage of production—organized as a separate firm—as a black box. The outside contractor and the internal hierarchy are equally ignorant of goings-on inside the black box. The difference is that an outside contractor, unlike a hierarchy, has no *need* to know what's happening in the internal production process, and no *power* to interfere with what he doesn't understand. So long as the inputs (likely in money terms) are specified by contract, and the outputs are verifiable and enforceable, what goes on inside the box isn't the outside contractor's problem.

If the ideal contract is MacNeil's "sharp ins by clear agreement, sharp outs by clear performance," then it is far simpler and less costly to simply monitor the contractually specified "ins" and "outs" going to and from a contracting firm, than to monitor the internal use of inputs within the production process: the "in" usually consisting simply of an amount of money established by contract, perhaps along with some intermediate goods for processing, and the "out" a finished product of specified quality and quantity. So long as the ins and outs (the money price and the quality and quantity of finished goods) can be effectively monitored, the contracting party has no need to worry about the internal efficiency of the production process. It has effectively outsourced the responsibility for decisions on how best to organize production to those *engaged* in production.

And the contracting firm, if cooperatively owned by self-managed workers, is uniquely qualified to organize production most efficiently given the specified ins and outs. Just as important, unlike a production unit within a corporate hierarchy, the production workers within the contracting producers' co-op fully internalize all the costs and benefits of their production decisions. There is no conflict of interests resulting from the making of decisions by managers who stand to reap the benefits of increased productivity while workers suffer only the costs.

William Ouchi's distinction between "output control" and "behavior control" is quite useful here.[1] Behavior control (the monitoring of effort and input use within the production process) requires much more intensive supervision than does the simple monitoring of outputs. Behavior control requires a considerable staff of supervisors with enough independent knowledge of the production process to overcome knowledge rents among production workers, and it requires that all significant parts of the production process itself be amenable to monitoring and measurement.[2] As we saw already regarding Williamson's treatment of "consummate" and "perfunctory" cooperation, if some parts of the process are less amenable to monitoring, workers will maximize output in the areas being monitored and cooperate only perfunctorily in the areas not subject to effective monitoring.

The main shortcoming of Ouchi's argument is that he focuses entirely on output control *within* the organization. As he himself observes, subordinates within a hierarchy will game an output control system to maximize the quantities being measured, at the expense of things less measurable.[3]

But in the case of a contract with an *outside* firm, particular with a worker-owned cooperative, this is not a problem. The contractee firm, as a unit, is unable to maximize selected measures while externalizing the costs of neglecting other forms of output.

1. William G. Ouchi. "The Relationship Between Organizational Structure and Organizational Control" *Administrative Science Quarterly* 22 (March 1977) pp. 95-113.

2. *Ibid.*, p. 97.

3. *Ibid.*, p. 109. See also Ouchi, "The Transmission of Control Through Organizational Hierarchy," *Academy of Management Journal* vol. 21 no. 2 ((1978), pp. 175-176.

Appendix
"The End of the Quarter Shuffle"

From Chapter Twelve, "End of the Quarter Shuffle," in *Rebirth of American Industry*, by William Waddell and Norman Bodek.[1]

During those last few days of the quarter, all of the stops are pulled out to make the numbers. Some of what is done is downright illegal. Much of it is unethical. Just about all of it is senseless. However, management salaries and promotions are driven by numbers . . . .

Most plants have been through the drill so many times that the people need very little coaching. All the way down to the operators on the production floor, the people know how to rig the numbers.

Every machine and every production employee will run all-out if there is anything in the plant for them to work on. Supervisors who are normally lenient concerning breaks will become frenzied taskmasters. Of course, there will be no employee or safety meetings. Nothing will keep production people from their machines in the last few work days of the quarter.

There will be a steady stream of shop supervisors to the production control office demanding that production orders be written to machine, assemble, paint, or pack whatever parts they have been able to find in the plants. If there were a demand for those parts they would already have production orders, but they are not producing for demand. They are producing for the sole purpose of earning credit for direct labor hours, which, in term, earns credit for overhead on their budgets.

Quality inspection will virtually shut down. If anything produced is bad, no one wants to know about it until next week—after the books are closed on this quarter . . . .

Every shipping and receiving manager and employee worth his or her salt is a master of the game. Product not scheduled to ship for days or even weeks will be pulled, skidded, wrapped, labeled and entered into the system as gone—then stacked off to the side . . . .

. . . [The plant manager] can be found behind an overflowing in-basket, because plant spending was shut down days before. Requisitions for maintenance supplies, training materials, and anything else deemed not critical to production will not be approved until the next quarter . . . .

This scenario, to varying degrees, happens at every plant every quarter.

1. Waddell and Bodek, pp. 127-130

8

Managerialism, Irrationality and Authoritarianism in the Large Organization

A. THE CORPORATE FORM AND MANAGERIALISM

We already saw, in Chapter Three, that defenders of the corporate legal form like Stephan Kinsella have been forced to abandon much of Mises' "entrepreneurial corporation" doctrine, and concede ground to the proponents of the managerial revolution.

As I said in Chapter Three, this was a long step for Kinsella, considering that he initially argued that the corporation was simply a contractual device for property owners to pool their property and appoint managers for it as they saw fit. In order to absolve shareholders of liability for the actions of their alleged "servants," he was eventually forced to concede most of the ground claimed by such theorists of the "managerial corporation" as Berle and Means.

Along the same lines Alchian and Demsetz suggested (as mentioned in passing in Chapter Six) that the "ownership" role of the stockholder might be largely a myth, and that the only real difference between stockholders' ownership of equity and bondholders ownership of debt (or more specifically the difference between preferred stockholders, and common stockholders and bondholders) was one of degree.

> If we treat bondholders, preferred and convertible preferred stockholders, and common stockholders and warrant holders as simply different classes of investors ... why should stockholders be regarded as "owners" in any sense distinct from the other financial investors?[1]

In our discussion of the corporation's internal calculation problem in Chapter Seven, we saw that the "entrepreneurial corporation" theory assumes one of two alternative mechanisms: Mises' entrepreneur with double-entry bookkeeping, or Mises' and Manne's market for control. The interesting part is that the second mechanism allows entrepreneurial "control" short of direct control of the corporation hierarchy itself: the ability of the investor to shift funds away from firms that do not perform to his satisfaction, and to firms that meet his standards of profits, in search of the investment vehicles with the highest rates of return. This mechanism implicitly treats the corporation as an autonomous, self-owned entity, with the capitalist rentier classes in the position of customers whose main instrument of control is the ability to take their business elsewhere. As we will see below, both mechanisms are considerably less effective than their proponents believe: the "entrepreneurial" investor's direct control over the board of directors and senior management is largely a legal fiction; the threat of hostile takeover, although real at times, tends to arise at widely separated intervals and to be subject to mitigating responses by management; the threat of capital flight is

---

1. Armen A. Alchian and Harold Demsetz, "Production, Information Costs, and Economic Organization," *The American Economic Review*, p. 789n.

limited by the corporation's reliance on retained earnings for the majority of finance and by minimal reliance on new share issues.

The arguments of Kinsella, and of Alchian and Demsetz, taken together, suggest that capitalist ownership of the individual corporation is a myth, in the sense that a particular corporation is the property of its stockholders (or preferred stockholders with voting rights) in any real sense.

Instead, the corporation is an agglomeration of unowned capital, under the control of a self-perpetuating managerial oligarchy. To quote John Kay: " . . . if we asked a visitor from another planet to guess who were the owners of a firm . . . by observing behaviour rather than by reading text books in law or economics, there can be little doubt that he would point to the company's senior managers."[1] This is the starting assumption of Eugene Fama, who "set[s] aside the typical presumption that a corporation has owners in any meaningful sense," and assigns the entrepreneur's functions of risk bearing and management as factors "within the set of contracts called a firm." The entrepreneurial role is filled by management, in an environment in which the corporation is "disciplined by competition from other firms . . . ."[2]

The mythical nature of shareholder sovereignty is borne out by Martin Hellwig's analysis, which shows that Manne's "market for corporate control" is more myth than reality. Hellwig argues that the concept of residual claimancy applies not so much to the shareholders as to management, which has the power "to disfranchise outside shareholders . . . , [and] that in all circumstances not otherwise provided for, . . . has the effective power to set the rules of decision making so as to immunize itself against unwanted interference from outsiders."[3]

The theory that management is controlled by outside capital markets assumes a high degree of dependence on outside finance. But in fact management's first line of defense is to *minimize* its reliance on outside finance. Management tends to finance new investments as much as possible with retained earnings, followed by debt, with new issues of shares only as a last resort.[4] Issues of stock are important sources of investment capital only for startups and small firms undertaking major expansions.[5] Most corporations finance a majority of their new investment from retained earnings, and tend to limit investment to the highest priorities when retained earnings are scarce.[6] As Doug Henwood says, in the long run "almost all corporate capital expenditures are internally financed, through profits and depreciation allowances." Between 1952 and 1995, almost 90% of investment was funded from retained earnings.[7]

The threat of shareholder intervention is also diluted by stock buy-backs. According to Henwood, U.S. nonfinancial corporations from 1981-96 retired some $700 billion more stock than they issued.[8]

1. John Kay, The Business of Economics (Oxford: Oxford University Press, 1996), p. 111, in Luigi Zingales, "In Search of New Foundations," *The Journal of Finance*, vol. lv, no. 4 (August 2000), p. 1638.

2. Eugene F. Fama, "Agency Problems and the Theory of the Firm," *Journal of Political Economy* 88:2 (1980), p. 289.

3. Martin Hellwig, "On the Economics and Politics of Corporate Finance and Corporate Control," in Xavier Vives, ed., *Corporate Governance: Theoretical and Empirical Perspectives* (Cambridge: Cambridge University Press, 2000), p. 98.

4. *Ibid.*, pp. 100-101.

5. Ralph Estes, *Tyranny of the Bottom Line: Why Corporations Make Good People Do Bad Things* (San Francisco: Berrett-Koehler Publishers, 1996), p. 51.

6. Hellwig, pp. 101-102, 113.

7. Doug Henwood, *Wall Street: How it Works and for Whom* (London and New York: Verso, 1997), p. 3.

8. *Ibid.*, pp. 3, 72-73.

Hellwig makes one especially intriguing observation, in particular, about financing from retained earnings. He denies that reliance primarily on retained earnings necessarily leads to a "rationing" of investment, in the sense of underinvestment; internal financing, he says, can just as easily result in overinvestment, if the amount of retained earnings exceeds available opportunities for rational capital investment.[1] This confirms Schumpeter's argument, cited in Chapter Three, that double taxation of corporate profits promoted excessive size and centralization, by encouraging reinvestment in preference to the issue of dividends. Of course it may result in structural misallocations and irrationality, to the extent that retention of earnings prevents dividends from returning to the household sector to be invested in other firms, so that overaccumulation in the sectors with excessive retained earnings comes at the expense of a capital shortage in other sectors.[2] Henwood contrasts the glut of retained earnings, under the control of corporate bureaucracies with a shortage of investment opportunities, to the constraints the capital markets place on small, innovative firms that need capital the most.[3]

The high debt to equity ratio might seem to cast some doubt on the primacy of internal financing. For example "newson," a commenter at Mises Blog, challenged my claims on the insignificance of outside finance:

> i find this hard to square with the fact that the debt-to-equity ratio on the sp500 averaged at about one over 2007. the tax deductibility of interest makes debt financing particularly attractive vis-a-vis equity. look at the numbers on equity buy-backs in the past years. management certainly have had an interest in raising share prices, and maintaining eps in order to maximize their option-rich remuneration packages.[4]

But the overwhelming bulk of corporate borrowing goes to finance takeovers or stock buybacks, not new investment. The mergers and acquisitions of the 80s and 90s were the source of $1.9 trillion in debt.[5] So to repeat, the corporate economy finances new investment almost entirely independently of the capital markets.

Hellwig's thesis that management is the real "residual claimant" is reinforced by management's role in making the very rules by which the corporation is governed, including the rules by which shareholders exercise whatever power they have. Management, as the primary influence on the internal bylaws of the corporation, has considerable power to dilute the power of shareholders.[6]

Likewise, the board of directors, which theoretically represents shareholders and oversees management in their interests, is in fact likely composed mostly of inside directors who take their positions at the invitation of management and are controlled by management's proxy votes. As a result, they are likely to engage in mutual logrolling, with management supporting the directors' continued tenure, the directors rubber-stamping large salary increases for the CEO, and the oligarchy perpetuating itself through cooptation rather than outside election.[7]

> CEO pay in the United States has exploded for the simple reason that CEOs largely get to write their own checks. CEO pay is determined by corporate compensation boards, most of the members of which are put there with the blessing of the CEOs themselves. Usually the CEOs have a large voice in determining who sits on the corporate boards

1. Hellwig, pp. 114-115.
2. *Ibid.*, p. 117.
3. Henwood, *Wall Street*, pp. 154-155.
4. Newson comment under Ben O'Neill, "How to Bureaucratize the Corporate World," *Mises Economics Blog*, January 23, 2008 <http://blog.mises.org/archives/007691.asp>.
5. Henwood, pp. 73-76.
6. Hellwig, pp. 109, 112.
7. Myles L. Mace, *Directors: Myth and Reality*. Revised ed. (Boston: Harvard Business School Press, 1986), in Estes, op. cit., pp. 64-67.

that ultimately have responsibility for the operation of the corporation. These corporate boards then appoint a committee that determines CEO pay. In effect, we allow the CEO to pick a group of friends to decide how much money he should earn.[1]

Proxy contests are almost always lost by dissident stockholders, because management rigs the rules against them.[2]

Of course this still leaves the threat of hostile takeover, of which entrepreneurial theories of the corporation make so much. But it is overrated for the same reason as other alleged instruments of entrepreneurial control: management controls the rules. Hostile takeovers tend to occur in waves every few decades, and to run their course in a few years as management devises new strategies for deflecting the threat. That is very much the case with the much-ballyhooed wave of hostile takeovers of the '80s, which supposedly rendered the managerial corporation obsolete. In fact, as Hellwig argued, the rise in hostile takeovers in the '80s was the immediate result of some very specific innovations, like junk bond financing, and quickly ran its course as management developed new techniques like the "poison pill" and "shark repellent" to limit the threat of hostile takeover—i.e., they took advantage of their control, as incumbents, over the internal governance rules of the corporation. There were a significant number of takeovers and mergers in the '90s, but they were for the most part friendly takeovers: strategic attempts to increase market shares and take advantage of alleged synergies, rather than hostile takeovers motivated by governance issues.[3] And in friendly takeovers, of course, the management of the acquired firm is much more likely to be in collusion than in opposition.

In addition, in the case of mergers and acquisitions, the "market for corporate control" argument used by Mises and Manne makes an unwarranted assumption: that the acquisition is motivated by the interest of the acquiring firm's stockholders, and not that of its senior management. In fact Ben Branch argued, not long after Manne wrote on the market for corporate control, that most mergers did not "work to the advantage of the acquiring fund's stockholders":

> Thus, either corporate officials are consistently misjudging merger opportunities, or a great deal of merger activity is motivated by managerial interests.[4]

Henwood backs this up. Surveying the literature on post-merger corporate performance, in mergers and acquisitions from the turn of the 20th century through the '80s, he found that both acquiring and acquired firms tended to do worse, in terms of profits and stock performance, after a merger. The active parties in hostile takeovers were not, as Mises and Manne would have us think, "entrepreneurial" stockholders. They were empire-building managers.

> Managers feel richer and more powerful if their firm is growing, and if the business can't grow quickly on its own, then they can gobble up others. Related to this is the idea that while mergers may not result in a higher rater of return (profits divided by invested capital), they may result in a higher quantity of profits, that is more zeroes on the bottom line.[5]

The threats of hostile takeover and capital flight are also limited, in practical terms, by the cognitive problems we considered in Chapter Seven: the inability of investors to accurately assess the meaning of market data on share value and returns. Even when the threat

1. Dean Baker, *The Conservative Nanny State: How the Wealthy Use the Government to Stay Rich and Get Richer* (Washington, D.C.: Center for Economic and Policy Research, 2000), pp. 42–43.

2. Mace, *Directors*, p. 69.

3. Hellwig, op. cit., p.111.

4. Ben Branch, "Corporate Objectives and Market Performance," *Financial Management* vol. 2 no. 2 (Summer 1973), p. 26.

5. Henwood, *Wall Street*, pp. 278–281.

of hostile takeover is real, it is limited by the ability of outsiders to assess the meaning of performance data. Their basis for comparison is conditioned by the existence of a "normal" rate of profit for each industry, which in turn reflects the average level of managerialism. So given restraints on competition, and given the small number of oligopoly firms sharing a common institutional culture, the "good" profit-maximizing corporations that avoid takeover are pretty atrocious in terms of any absolute standard of efficiency. As Ben Branch argues,

> By not doing as well as they might, managers widen the gap between actual and potential market value. This encourages takeover bids and proxy fights . . . .
> [But s]ince it is often quite difficult for outsiders to evaluate management, there may be considerable sacrifice of shareholders' interests before management's position is threatened.[1]

For that matter, as we also saw in Chapter Seven, to the extent that pressure to maximize profits *is* effective, it is precisely the *effectiveness* of such pressure that may result in destructive behaviors that cripple long-term productivity.

Another possible instrument of shareholder control sometimes put forward is the concerted influence of institutional investors. But institutional stock ownership is often nearly as dispersed as ownership by individual shareholders. Henry Hansmann gives the example of General Motors, whose top five institutional shareholders together own only six percent of stock.[2]

Rakesh Khurana, one of the ablest historians of corporate managerialism, nevertheless buys largely into the conventional view that changes in corporate governance and managerial incentives amounted to a revival of the entrepreneurial corporation, and the reassertion of shareholder control at the expense of management. He portrays the changes in executive incentives (executive stock options and performance-based pay) and the alleged resurgence of the "market for corporate control" (the hostile takeover wave of the '80s) as part of a fundamental power shift from managerial to investor capitalism.[3]

In this, I believe he is fundamentally mistaken. With the exception of a relatively brief period of hostile takeovers, which (as Hellwig explains) was soon thwarted by management counter-measures, there was no real loss of managerial autonomy or shift of power.

Managerial behavior did indeed change in response to the change in incentives; but it was a voluntary change in behavior by autonomous management, acting to maximize its own self-interest in an environment of altered incentive structures. The discretion was still management's. And it is questionable, at the very least, whether these changed incentives elicited behavior in the real interest of shareholders. As already described in Chapter Seven, such "performance-based" incentives have, in fact, encouraged management to maximize apparent short-term profit at the expense of long-term profitability, in order to inflate their own bonuses and stock options and leave a gutted shell to the "owners."

It's hard to deny, though, that the change in incentives led to a change in managerial culture. In place of the old organization man, the responsible and disinterested Weberian/Taylorist technocrat, arose the new entrepreneurial model of senior management, with superstar-CEOs like Jack Welch celebrated in the media. In the old days, CEOs tended to see themselves as being at the apex of the technostructure, rather than as entrepreneurs gaming the market to maximize their own compensation. After Iacocca, the focus of business culture shifted, in quite distasteful ways, to a cult of "leadership" and "vision,"[4] reflected both in the business press, and in the proliferation of wretched (see "Ken Blanch-

1. Branch, "Corporate Objectives aand Market Performance," p. 24.
2. Henry Hansman, *The Ownership of Enterprise* (Cambridge and London: The Belknap Press of Harvard University Press, 1996), p. 57.
3. Khurana, pp. 302, 318.
4. *Ibid.*, pp. 355-362.

ard") management theory and motivational books in the 1990s. But this new kind of cow-boy CEO, arguably, was in his own way even more of a maximizer of self-interest at the expense of shareholder value than his managerialist predecessor. Arianna Huffington, in *Pigs at the Trough*, provides many examples of corporate CEOs collecting enormous com-pensation packages for running their companies into the ground.[1]

In light of all these considerations, the arguments of C. Wright Mills and Martin Sklar on the "corporate reorganization of the capitalist class" and the "corporate transformation of capitalism" (that the interlocked corporate economy, rather than being directly "owned" by capitalist shareholders, is largely an instrument of indirect, collective control by the capi-talist class, whose power is conditioned by the managers it has incorporated as junior part-ners) make much more sense.[2] The capitalist hegemony over the economy is conditioned by the managerial instrument through which it must work.

So the corporate economy as a whole is capitalist. But the real, direct capitalist owner-ship is over investment funds only, and is exercised over the corporate organization only through the power to withdraw money from one investment and move it to another with higher yields. And that power itself, remember, is limited by management's tendency to rely whenever possible on retained earnings in preference to outside finance.

The managerialist corporation is profit-maximizing in some regards, but not in oth-ers. As seen in Chapter Seven, it indeed promotes short-term profit at the expense of long-term productivity, because of the perverse incentives to even the most destructive forms of profit maximization presented by the capital markets (including management stock op-tions). As I argued in Chapter Three, the corporate form provides a convenient form of plausible deniability, by which investors are able to use the threat of withdrawal of funds to pressure corporate management to maximize profits "by any means necessary," while be-ing able to maintain a plausible pose of ignorance and irresponsibility regarding the means actually taken by corporate management. And corporate management is able to hide be-hind the corporate veil in order to avoid personal responsibility for any harmful actions the corporation takes to maximize profits. That veil becomes a travesty, especially, when man-agement is able to pump up its own stock options by ethically and legally shady actions taken under cover of the corporate form.

Outside pressures to maximize profits are quite effective in matters of cost-externalization. The most decent corporate manager, as an individual, will engage in the most anti-social acts as a manager, in the name of "shareholder value."

The threat of capital flight is an effective disciplinary tool in cases of profit lowering policies like "corporate social responsibility" and the like, precisely because such policies are not a part of the normal corporate culture. There is, therefore, the potential for real competition between corporations based on whether they do or do not follow such prac-tices. As a result, "socially responsible" corporations are largely limited to a niche market appealing to the psychic returns of Bobos and limousine liberals. Outside of this niche market, "social responsibility" consists largely of greenwashed rhetoric that involves little if any cost to the bottom line.

Profit maximization is far less operative, however, when it comes to the interests of management itself. There is much less chance of competition between corporations based on the degree of internal management self-dealing, because the overwhelming majority of corporations operate with a shared managerialist culture that takes self-dealing for granted

1. Arianna Huffington, *Pigs at the Trough: How Corporate Greed and Political Corruption are Undermining America* (New York: Crown Publishers, 2003), pp. 43-55.

2. C. Wright Mills, *The Power Elite*. Revised edition (Oxford University Press, 1956, 2000); Martin Sklar, *The Corporate Reconstruction of American Capitalism, 1890-1916: The Market, the Law, and Politics* (Cambridge: Cambridge University Press, 1988).

as a normal part of business. At the same time, the prevalence in most industries of oligopoly firms that derive large rents from consumers means that the inefficiency costs of managerialism cause little competitive harm; as a result, shareholders can afford to pay the high rents going to management.

As a result, the capitalists' control over outside investment funds, and their threat of capital flight, is only able to spur profit maximization in areas that do not directly affect the managerialists' class interests. The collective interests of the managers as a class are the limit to capitalists' control over the corporate economy.

In many cases, the interests of stockholders would be better served if management ranks were drastically cut, resources were shifted into more production workers and higher wages, and workers had more control over the production process. But that would be a death blow to the managerial culture in the average large American corporation. Management has a great deal of autonomy in promoting its own interests within the corporation, along with the power to thwart outside interference. Any reform that management perceives as contrary to its self-interest will be killed. What's more, part of it is not so much mendacity as genuine cluelessness: they can't think of any way to improve how workers are doing things except to increase the number of managers swarming around and poking into everything they do.

None of this is to deny—far from it—the extent to which rentier incomes on land and capital reflect special privilege, or the fact that labor is exploited by the propertied classes under the present system. Certainly in the past few decades, the income of the very top reaches of the plutocracy has exploded upward. But on the whole, I suspect that the average worker suffers as much from managerialism and the resources eaten up by bureaucratic overhead as from the income of rentiers. That is suggested by the statistics below on the compensation of supervisory employees now compared to thirty years ago—an increase whose value rivals the average rate of profit.

The rentier classes, to a large extent, are held hostage by their dependence on the managerial stratum. The monopoly profits of big business depend on cartelization by the state; and given this situation, even at bare minimum a considerable power is entailed for the managerial bureaucracy. The large corporate size promoted by state intervention increases the leverage of managers against shareholders. According to Khurana,

> "Really big" organizations required large numbers of managers, which in turn created more leverage for management vis-à-vis owners. The political and legal decisions that removed constraints on corporate growth thus aided managers in their struggle with owners for control of the corporation.[1]

The owners are also held hostage, somewhat counterintuitively, by the way the corporate form treats capital as the ostensible source of control rights. Management's freedom to promote its interests at the expense of workers leads, simultaneously, to the promotion of management interests at the expense of productivity, which reduces overall returns. To a large extent the shareholders and workers have a common interest, versus management, in dividing the additional productivity gains that might result from the elimination of management self-dealing. A comment by John Micklethwait is interesting, in this light. After a survey of arguments for stakeholder capitalism, and his own dismissive comments about its performance in countries like Germany where it's been tried, he argued that stakeholder interests would be best served by strengthening shareholder interests at the expense of management:

> This defense of shareholding may sound horribly complacent. What about all those fat cats paying themselves gigantic salaries? And what about the golden parachutes that allow

---

1. Khurana, *From Higher Aims to Hired Hands*, pp. 29-30.

these weighty felines to get rich on failure? In fact, the best way to deal with the anxieties that have given rise to the recent stakeholder debate is to give more power to shareholders, not less. Study almost any corporate disaster . . . and you find a board acting without anybody looking over its shoulder.[1]

Micklethwait got it completely backward. He might have forgotten that the gigantic salaries and golden parachutes came about in the '80s, in the cowboy management culture that *resulted* from attempts to strengthen shareholder control. As those attempts (stock options, bonuses, hostile takeovers, etc.) have demonstrated, genuine shareholder control over management is as much a pipe dream as genuine citizen control over a continent-sized "representative democracy." But management *could* be effectively checked by others *on the inside*. Ironically, it's the myth of management responsibility to shareholders, as a legitimating ideology of managerial control, that insulates management from control by internal stakeholders. As a result, we get the problem we see described by Luigi Zingales in Chapter Nine: the portion of firm value created by human capital is expropriated by management, creating a zero-sum relationship in which it is in the interest of internal stakeholders to minimize personal investment of effort and skill in the firm. The firm runs far below optimal efficiency, because the system of ownership denies its main source of value-added a proportional share in the value they create.

Michels' Iron Law applies very much to the corporation: regardless of the ostensible aims of an organization and the formal accountability of its leadership to some constituency, it ossifies over time into a power structure whose primary purpose is to serve those directing the organization.

> Thus, from a means, organization becomes an end . . . .[2]
> . . . . By a universally applicable social law, every organ of the collectivity, brought into existence through the need for the division of labor, creates for itself, as soon as it becomes consolidated, interests peculiar to itself. The existence of these special interests involves a necessary conflict with the interests of the collectivity. Nay, more, social strata fulfilling peculiar functions tend to become isolated, to produce organs fitted for the defense of their own peculiar interests. In the long run they tend to undergo transformation into distinct classes.[3]
> . . . . "It is organization which gives birth to the dominion of the elected over the electors, of the mandatories over the mandators, of the delegates over the delegators. Who says organization, says oligarchy."[4]

Robert Shea, in his aptly titled article "Empire of the Rising Scum," argued that any organization—regardless of its ostensible external mission—would eventually be dominated by those whose primary skill was the acquisition and maintenance of power.

> . . . [T]he better an organization is at fulfilling its purpose, the more it attracts people who see the organization as an opportunity to advance themselves . . . .
> Whatever the original aim of the organization, to publish books, to heal the sick, to share information about computers, once it has been taken over by apparatchiks, it will acquire a new aim—to get bigger. It doesn't matter whether a bigger organization will fulfill its purpose as well, serve its customers or constituents as well, or be as good a place for people to work. It will get bigger simply because those at the top want it to get big-

---

1. John Micklethwait and Adrian Wooldridge, *The Witch Doctors: Making Sense of the Management Gurus* (New York: Times Books, 1996), p. 184.

2. Robert Michels, *Political Parties: A Sociological Study of the Oligarchical Tendencies of Modern Democracy*. Translated by Eden and Cedar Paul (New York: The Free Press, 1962), p. 338.

3. *Ibid.*, p. 353.

4. *Ibid.*, p. 365.

ger. Apparatchiks do to organizations what cancer viruses do to cells; they promote pur-
poseless growth . . . .[1]

B. Self-Serving Policies for "Cost-Cutting," "Quality" and "Efficiency"

We already saw, in Chapter Six, Jensen's and Meckling's argument that management has
an incentive to shift capital investment from allocations that maximize productivity, to allocations that feather their own nests.[2] If management is relatively free to choose its level of per-
quisites, subject only to the diluted loss of returns from ownership of a small fraction of corporate stock, "[its] welfare will be maximized by increasing [its] consumption of non-
pecuniary benefits."[3] Oliver Williamson, in *The Economics of Discretionary Behavior* (originally
his PhD dissertation), anticipated the Meckling-Jensen argument and elaborated on it at great
length.[4] One term he coined, "expense preference," is especially useful:

> . . . [M]anagers do not have a neutral attitude toward all classes of expenses. Instead, some
> types of expenses have positive values attached to them: they are incurred not merely for
> their contributions to productivity (if any) but, in addition, for the manner in which they
> enhance the individual and collective objectives of managers.[5]

Further, as we already saw in Chapter Seven, the market's perverse incentives to
maximize short-term profit by gutting long-term productivity will mean that even the
profit-maximization incentive presented by management's stock options will likely cause
them to game the system to maximize their options at the expense of the organization's
long-term welfare.

As one might guess, given all these considerations, any time it is left to management
to find new ways of improving "quality," their solution is likely to be everything *but* increasing the resources and autonomy of production workers; again, as you might expect, it
will rather involve expanding the power of management with even more committees,
meetings, tracking forms, etc., so that production workers have even more interference and
paperwork to deal with, and less time to get their real work done.

This is true even when management pays lip service to a management theory fad that
calls for empowering workers, and eliminating process inefficiencies resulting from bureaucratic interference. The problem is that any such theory is implemented by *bosses* —which
means that any theory, no matter how empowering its rhetoric, will translate in practice
into rewarmed Taylorism. If corporate management adopted Jeffersonianism as a management philosophy, it would ignore the part about inalienable human rights and local self-
government, and just keep the part about screwing your slaves.

We also saw, in Chapter Seven, that each level of a hierarchy creates slack. Whenever
possible managers, like all bureaucrats, like to increase the size of their domain and the number of staff under their control. The number of "direct reports" is a mark of prestige. They
will increase the size of their domain even when it interferes with the efficient running of
their existing domain. A good example of this is the behavior of Pentagon apparatchiks who

---

1. Robert Shea, "Empire of the Rising Scum" (1990). The article originally appeared in the
now-defunct Loompanics catalog, and is now preserved on Carol Moore's website
<http://www.carolmoore.net/articles/empirerisingscum.html>.
2. Michael C. Jensen and William H. Meckling. "Theory of the Firm: Managerial Behavior,
Agency Costs and Ownership Structure" *Journal of Financial Economics* 3:4 (October 1976).
3. *Ibid.*, p. 18.
4. Oliver Williamson. *The Economics of Discretionary Behavior: Managerial Objectives in a Theory
of the Firm* (Englewood Cliffs, N.J.: Prentice-Hall, Inc., 1964).
5. *Ibid.*, p. 33.

divert funds to new weapons programs, at the expense of providing adequate pay, training, fuel, ammunition, and maintenance for existing personnel and equipment. Anthony Downs describes the phenomenon, as it appears in the public sector bureaucracy:

> An official can more easily add to his power by obtaining more subordinates than by increasing his degree of control over his existing subordinates.
> . . . Officials tend to react to change by attempting to increase their overall appropriations rather than by reallocating their existing appropriations.[1]

But when absolute cuts in a firm, division or department are necessary, managers will direct them primarily to production workers, while preserving as much as possible of the staff attached to their offices. Management's approach to "increasing productivity" and "cutting costs" will mean decimating productive resources while leaving their own petty empires intact. As the downsizing of production workers and increased workloads lead to the proliferation of errors, management will respond by devoting still more resources to what Deming called "exhortations," "slogans," and "revival meetings," and Drucker called "management by drives." Any "reform" carried out by management will serve mainly to increase the power of managers.

Cost-cutting in corporate bureaucracies closely resembles its counterpart in government bureaucracies. Lacking any explicit budget line-item for "waste, fraud, and abuse," senior management simply sets arbitrary figures to cut, say 20 or 30%, and leaves the details to subordinates in the bureaucracy. In private industry, this takes the form of cutting out entire categories of production workers and consolidating their job descriptions, or reducing entire categories of workers by some arbitrary percentage. Of course, the last thing to be cut is management—and management itself is cut only from the bottom up. Their petty bureaucratic empires, the *real purpose* of the organization from the perspective of those actually running it, remain intact.

Robert Jackall, in *Moral Mazes*, recounts just such a process after the new CEO of "Covenant" corporation took over. He ordered the presidents of its subsidiaries to carry out thorough reorganizations with "census reduction," but left the details entirely up to them (aside from setting aside some top management posts for his cronies). In the "Alchemy" subsidiary, the new president ("Smith") carried out a series of firings Jackall refers to as "the purge," and promoted his personal clients from his former division of the company to leadership positions.

Smith met the Covenant CEO's financial targets in 1980, but the company entered a period of falling profits during the 1981 recession. Alchemy met only 60% of the profit target, and even then only with considerable accounting sleight-of-hand. In the ensuing period, the atmosphere of fear and paranoia resembled that of the Stalinist purge era, with rumors of Smith's disfavor flying wildly and everyone attempting to divert any potential disfavor from himself by betraying his colleagues. Senior management people positioned themselves for advancement in the event of Smith's fall, and betrayed him and each other. One senior management figure, notorious as an amoral "troubleshooter," publicly accused everyone who missed a staff meeting held during a record blizzard of disloyalty to the company.

As the recession worsened in 1982, the Covenant CEO pressured Smith to "aggressively cut staff" and "streamline operations" in order to "emerge lean and poised" for the recovery. Later that year, the CEO demanded a 30% reduction in staff at Alchemy. In a second wave of downsizings, Smith fired 200 people, *mostly technical support people rather than management.*

1. Anthony Downs, *Inside Bureaucracy*. A RAND Corporation Research Study (Boston: Little, Brown and Company, 1967), p. 267.

Interestingly, when Smith's successor ("Brown") carried out a third downsizing, he fired another 150—this time however mainly from management. The surviving managers saw this as a violation of the unwritten management code, and management became increasingly hostile. (In the meantime, the CEO began an aggressive campaign of acquisitions—mostly mature companies, which belied his claim to be focusing on tech startups with high growth potential.)[1]

This concurrent gutting of productive assets (especially staff) and irrational capital investments is a common pattern in the corporate world.

For reasons we examined in Chapter Seven, what large capital expenditures are made in the large corporation are typically made in an environment of calculational chaos, with little idea of their opportunity cost and no realistic estimate as to their likely effect on the organization's productivity. Management's choice of which productive resources to decimate, and to leave largely untouched, reflects no discernable criterion of efficiency. In fact the calculation problems in the corporation make any such efficiency judgments largely arbitrary, so that management has little idea of the opportunity costs of the capital investments it does make.

As Daniel Gross points out, this irrational cost-cutting approach is especially prone to focus on downsizing human capital:

> This type of self-defeating cost-cutting often occurs at knowledge businesses whose only real asset is smart, motivated employees . . . .
>
> To be sure, if companies were indifferent to costs across the board, they wouldn't be in business. But the penny-pinching is aimed squarely at the vast productive middle. Top executives are generally unaffected.[2]

Also, as we shall see in our discussion of Waddell's and Bodek's work below, the management accounting system encourages this confusion, by treating inventory as an asset and management as a fixed cost, and human capital as a variable cost. After all, an MBA is someone who would break up every stick of furniture in his house and throw it in the furnace, and then brag about how good the numbers look this month without the fuel bill.

One of my favorite writers on corporate culture, Jerome Alexander, puts it in appropriately jaundiced terms. Alexander, of *Corporate Cynic* blog, is an MBA and accountant who's spent his entire career in one middle management hell after another. He writes of the "leaders" and "heroes" who "see the big picture," and possess "expertise"

> at closing down operations, disposing of assets, etc . . . .
>
> I wonder when the garage sale will occur? Maybe they'll sell the forklifts and office equipment to help fund their exit packages. It's a shame but predictable because they have no shame.[3]

And when management makes large capital investments, they are apt to resemble Hayek's predictions for a planned economy: uneven development, with productive resources underfunded or gutted in some sectors and overbuilt in others, and no clear idea of the comparative cost or likely productive returns of spending anywhere.

A survey by *McKinsey Quarterly* found that, on average, corporate-level executives considered many of their firms' capital investment decisions to be bad ideas in retrospect:

> corporate-level executives responding to the survey with an opinion indicate that 17 percent of the capital invested by their companies went toward underperforming invest-

---

1. Robert Jackall, *Moral Mazes: The World of Corporate Managers* (New York: Oxford University Press, 1988), pp. 25-32.

2. "Pinching the Penny-Pinchers: idiotic examples of corporate cost-cutting," *Slate*, September 25, 2006 <http://www.slate.com/id/2150340/>.

3. Jerome Alexander, "Honey, We've Shrunk the Company!" *The Corporate Cynic*, July 20, 2007 <http://thecorporatecynic.wordpress.com/2007/07/20/honey-we%e2%80%99ve-shrunk-the- company/>.

ments that should be terminated and that 16 percent of their investments were a mistake to have financed in the first place. Business unit heads and frontline managers say 21 percent of investments should not have been approved and indicate another 21 percent should be terminated.

. . . [A] sizable number of survey respondents also indicate that a significant number of investments should have been made but were not. Corporate-level executives who have an opinion say it was a mistake not to provide funding for 21 percent of all rejected investments even though the forecast rate of return for the projects met or exceeded their companies' benchmarks. Business unit heads and frontline managers say nearly twice as many should have received funding.

It's worth noting that these figures exclude a significant number of survey respondents: roughly 40 percent, for example, don't have a point of view on how many investments should be terminated. This figure could be a warning sign that postmortem analysis is infrequent at many companies . . . .

. . . [W]hen asked what best explains the approval of the company's least successful project in recent memory, 45 percent of executives at all levels say it was approved because "a senior leader advocated the project."[1]

This strongly suggests that capital investment decisions are made in a prevailing atmosphere of groupthink and bureaucratic toadyism in which critical analysis is unwelcome.

. . . [T]he less-than-ideal combination of optimism, risk aversion, and one-off decision making is perhaps exacerbated by the prominence of corporate politics. Respondents say that behind-the-scenes lobbying and logrolling—and sometimes outright deception—are fairly frequent and seem to inhibit constructive debate and dissent throughout the resource allocation process.

Corporate politics interferes not only with the free expression of opinion on the wisdom of courses of action being considered, but with the availability of information needed for assessment:

Beyond simple politicking, 36 percent of respondents say managers hide, restrict, or misrepresent information at least "somewhat" frequently when submitting capital-investment proposals. (On this measure there is almost no difference in the views of respondents from public and private companies.)

As executives maneuver for position behind the scenes and sometimes even deceive one another, constructive debate and dissent appear to suffer. Only about a third of respondents, for instance, say executives frequently disagree about the attractiveness of future growth opportunities—hardly a topic that would seem to lend itself to unanimity. What's more, a majority of respondents say it's at least "somewhat" important to avoid contradicting superiors.

Corporate capital investments are also apt to be made in "an environment in which it's common for estimates of project duration and sales to be excessively optimistic . . ."

Another indication of executive optimism comes from the responses of a subset of executives who were asked to estimate a single project's rate of return compared with other similar projects approved in the past. Roughly half say the new investment would have a return greater than 25 percent—a figure hard to reach in competitive market economies. Such findings are consistent with a strong tendency toward managerial optimism highlighted in other research.

Management is especially prone, as Oliver Williamson writes, to persistent refusal to abandon sunk costs. He quotes Drucker's quip that "[n]o institution likes to abandon any-

1. "How Companies Spend Their Money: A McKinsey Global Survey," *McKinsey Quarterly*, June 2007 <http://www.mckinseyquarterly.com/article_page.aspx?ar=2019&L2=21>.

thing," and elaborates that "budget based institutions are more prone to persist with unproductive or obsolete projects than are revenue based institutions . . . ."[1]

Most personnel downsizing is counterproductive in terms of its stated rationale. According to Richard Sennett, downsizings typically lower the productivity of the organization and result in lower profits. Early '90s studies by the American Management Association and the Wyatt Companies found that repeated downsizings resulted in "lower profits and declining worker productivity . . ." Less than half of the companies carrying out downsizings actually achieved their expense reduction goals, less than a third increased profitability, and less than a fourth increased productivity. Worker morale and motivation fell sharply after downsizing.[2]

One reason, in addition to the degrading of productivity through understaffing and poor morale, is that savings from staffing cuts often go to subsidize increased management self-dealing and featherbedding, rather than to improve the bottom line. For example, Jackall refers to Covenant's expenditure of $100,000 on paint alone to repaint a plant whenever the CEO visited, and spending $10,000 to produce a single copy of a lavishly illustrated book on the plant's history and operations as a gift to the visiting CEO.[3] Another example:

> . . . just after the CEO of Covenant Corporation announced one of his many purges, legitimated by "a comprehensive assessment of the hard choices facing us" by a major consulting firm, he purchased a new Sabre jet for executives and a new 31-foot company limousine for his own use . . . . He then flew the entire board of directors to Europe on a Concorde for a regular meeting to review, it was said, his most recent cost-cutting strategies.[4]

Another reason is that downsizing undoes the long-term and painstaking process of building human capital. It amounts to hollowing out a company, the moral equivalent of eating the seed corn.

> Impressive short-term results can frequently be produced by hard-hitting managers who are generating a long-term catastrophe. Such conduct, says [Rensis] Likert, is encouraged by company reward systems that "enable a manager who is a 'pressure artist' to achieve high earnings over a few years, while destroying the loyalties, favorable attitudes, cooperative motivations, etc., among the supervisory and non-supervisory members of the organization." Such steamroller managers are frequently even promoted in recognition of their talents after, say, two or three years, which is just about the period that elapses before the damage begins to show up in the figures, leaving someone else to clean up (and no doubt take the blame for) the wreckage . . . .
>
> What is happening, in effect, is that valuable resources are being disposed of and earnings given a short-term, artificial boost. No management would stand for such cavalier treatment of physical assets, and even if management were willing, the auditors would not be. Since human resources do not appear on the balance sheet, they can be liquidated at will by managers oriented to "the bottom line" (where net profit appears), in order to give a spurious injection to earnings.[5]

A good example is Jerome Alexander's account of "Ann," "an AP clerk whose position was eliminated last month due to co-sourcing."

1. Oliver Williamson, *Markets and Hierarchies, Analysis and Antitrust Implications: A Study in the Economics of Internal Organization* (New York: Free Press, 1975), p. 122.
2. Richard Sennett, *The Corrosion of Character: The Personal Consequences of Work in the New Capitalism*, p. 50.
3. Jackall, *Moral Mazes*, pp. 22-23.
4. *Ibid.* p. 144.
5. David Jenkins, *Job Power: Blue and White Collar Democracy* (Garden City, New York: Doubleday & Company, Inc., 1973), p. 237.

Prior to making the decision to let her go, no one bothered to ask Ann what she actually did or how she did it. It wouldn't have mattered anyway because the new brainiacs at corporate HQ mandated that her position be eliminated on a date certain. Ann is gone.

Poor Marie! Her misfortune was geography. She just happened to occupy the cubicle that was next to Ann's . . . . Now Marie is being inundated with piles of mail, requests for emergency checks and investigations into why suppliers are not being paid. The operating and purchasing folks could care less about the co-sourcing project. They need things done . . . . Although Marie protests and tells them that she has nothing to do with accounts payable, they pester her incessantly anyway. Some will even wait for her to vacate her cubicle and then secretly swoop in to drop requests on her desk or chair. Marie's voicemail and E-mail inbox are now full to overflowing. Marie is overwhelmed.

Marie's boss, Jim, is in the same boat. He's only been with company for six months. Jim was initially told about the co-sourcing project and the fact that Ann would be leaving. Coming to work for a large corporation, Jim assumed that that the project had been well thought out. Get real Jim! Jim is now being attacked by even higher level operating and purchasing folks over the same issues. In Jim's case, however, the frenzy goes beyond simply dealing with the needs of that constituency. It seems that Ann performed a lot of other accounting related tasks that were not exactly of an accounts payable nature. Ann had been with the company for over ten years and had survived a variety of previous reorganizations and downsizings . . . . Over the years and through necessity, Ann had taken on a variety of different tasks, all of which were mundane but no less essential. No disrespect to Ann, but in a lot of cases, she was really unaware of how important some of these duties were. She just performed them with aplomb. Now Jim is finding out exactly how deep in the hole he is.

. . . Now Jim and Marie are stuck "holding the bag". They are frantic, frazzled, and overwhelmed. Marie is actively seeking employment elsewhere . . . .

Instead of analyzing the workload first to eliminate the arbitrary, superfluous and redundant tasks and requirements, *the focus is always on cutting the resources* [emphasis added]. What a back-asswards approach to problem solving! Even after reducing staff, they will continuously come up with new requirements and even more compressed timetables—turning the arbitrary, the goofy, and superfluous into the essential.[1]

Or again:

Last week, I watched as the company that I used to work for chopped another 35 administrative and technical positions. The "non-surprise" for the survivors was that none of the work was eliminated and none of the deadlines were changed. Those who remain will just have to do more. But the few keep getting fewer, more tired, cranky and scared to death of what could be next. What a great way to work and live! To top it all off, the corporation has embarked upon one of those "Help us define the 'values' of our company" programs. Talk about adding insult to injury![2]

Or again:

When the consultant asks, "Tell me what you do?" The accounts receivable clerk answers, "I post cash receipts to open invoices." The consultant then responds with the infamous set up question," And how long does that take you every day?" "Oh, I can get that done in an hour or so," beams the clerk trying to impress the consultant with their prowess and efficiency. I cringe every time I hear this because I can see the wheels turning behind the consultant's beady little eyes. "Hmmm, an hour a day! What are they doing for the other seven . . . ? . . . . The report back to the executive suite will be devastating. It will reinforce the notion that the function is easy and equally unimportant . . . .

1. Jerome Alexander, "'Outing' Some of the Downsides of Outsourcing," *The Corporate Cynic*, April 3, 2008 <http://thecorporatecynic.wordpress.com/2008/04/03/%e2%80%9couting%e2%80%9d-some-of-the-downsides-of-outsourcing/>.

2. Alexander, "Distressed about Job Stress? Don't Worry, Your Employer Isn't!" *The Corporate Cynic*, March 25, 2008 <http://thecorporatecynic.wordpress.com/2008/03/25/ distressed-about-job-stress-don%e2 %80%99t-worry-your-employer-isn%e2%80%99t/>.

What's never asked about is the time and effort spent on supplier account maintenance and customer account housekeeping, collection calls, straightening out paychecks or payroll tax issues, inventory cycle counting and correcting bills of material issues. These are the items that take the time and require the experience of the employees. This is the tender loving care that will be lost when the positions are cut or consolidated. The effects won't surface immediately, but when they do—look out below.[1]

What Alexander describes, the job-specific experience of employees, is human capital. Management has little idea just how much of their organization's productivity and book value depends on such human capital. To MBAs, schooled in the orthodoxy of the Sloan accounting system, human capital is not a productive asset, but a cost. It follows naturally from such cluelessness, Harold Oaklander (a specialist on workforce reductions at Pace University) argues, that "many 'cost-cutting' layoffs are actually counterproductive," because they interfere with "the firm's knowledge system."[2]

What this means, in specific terms, is suggested by Kim S. Cameron's list of the problems typically resulting from downsizing:

> . . . (1) loss of personal relationships between employees and customers; (2) destruction of employee and customer trust and loyalty; (3) disruption of smooth, predictable routines in the firm; (4) increases in formalization (reliance on rules), standardization, and rigidity; (5) loss of cross-unit and cross-level knowledge that comes from longevity and interactions over time; (6) loss of knowledge about how to respond to nonroutine aberrations faced by the firm; (7) decrease in documentation and therefore less sharing of information about changes; (8) loss of employee productivity; and (9) loss of a common organizational culture.[3]

Alex Markels and Matt Murray, at *The Wall Street Journal* (in an article appropriately titled "Call it Dumbsizing"), describe the long-term effects of ill-advised and indiscriminate downsizings, as practiced by most corporations:

> Eastman Kodak Co. expected to save thousands of dollars a year when it laid off Maryellen Ford in March in a companywide downsizing. But within weeks, Kodak was paying more for the same work.
> Ms. Ford, a computer-aided designer and 17-year Kodak veteran, was snapped up by a local contractor that gets much of its work from Kodak. "I took the project I was working on and finished it here," she says. But instead of paying her $15 an hour plus benefits, Kodak now pays the contractor $65 an hour, and Ms. Ford earns $20 an hour (but gets no benefits).
> Kodak's layoffs have left its engineering group in Rochester, N.Y., overworked and demoralized, Ms. Ford contends. "They're burned out and they don't even care. When they send a job over here and we say, 'It's going to cost you X,' they just say 'Go ahead,'" she says . . . .

At my own employer, a hospital, management has imposed several waves of drastic downsizing: of nursing staff, physical/occupational therapists, and respiratory techs, among other job categories. And guess what? First of all, they've suffered horribly from bad word of mouth in the surrounding community, thanks to the deterioration of quality in patient care. Second, exactly as with Kodak, they wound up actually paying more in staffing costs than they were before. The hospital routinely pays staffing agencies over $100 and hour for travel RNs and respiratory techs. In December 2007, half the physical and occupational

1. Alexander, "What would "The Duke" say about the Trivialization of Non-executive Functions?" *The Corporate Cynic*, April 10, 2008 <http://thecorporatecynic.wordpress.com/2008/04/10/what-would-%e2%80%9cthe-duke%e2%80%9d-say-about-the-trivialization-of-non-executive-functions/>.

2. Alvin Toffler, *Powershift: Knowledge, Wealth and Power at the Edge of the 21st Century* (New York: Bantam, 1991), p. 222.

3. Kim S. Cameron, "Downsizing, Quality and Performance," in Robert E. Cole, ed., *The Death and Life of the American Quality Movement* (New York: Oxford University Press, 1995), p. 97.

therapists on the rehab ward where I work gave notice, because a local nursing home paid therapists several bucks an hour more and had better working conditions. As a result, the hospital was forced to cap the ward's census at twelve patients for several months, and to run it at even that capacity had to hire several therapists from staffing agencies (again, at premium rates *at least* three times the wage paid in-house). So much for management's brilliant attempt to "cut costs" through understaffing and skimping on pay. This doesn't even touch on the costs from abysmal employee morale, on wards where one orderly often has twenty or thirty patients, from the skyrocketing rates of absenteeism among nursing staff who dread coming to work under such conditions, and the very high rates of turnover and costs of training replacements. Not to mention the costs of disgruntled employees deliberately throwing expensive supplies away or giving them away for free to patients without billing them.

But the damage to an organization's human capital goes far beyond the mere cost of replacing staff:

Despite warnings about downsizing becoming dumbsizing, many companies continue to make flawed decisions—hasty, across-the-board cuts—that come back to haunt them, on the bottom line, in public relations, in strained relationships with customers and suppliers, and in demoralized employees. Sweeping early-retirement and buyout programs sometimes eliminate not only the deadwood but the talented, many of whom head straight to competitors. Meanwhile, many replacements arrive knowing little about the company and soon repeat their predecessors' mistakes.

"Cost-cutting has become the holy grail of corporate management," says Rick Maurer, an Arlington, Va., management consultant. "But what helps the financial statement up front can end up hurting it down the road."

In Digital Equipment Corp.'s 1994 reorganization, its second in as many years, the company eliminated hundreds of sales and marketing jobs in its health-industries group, which had been bringing in $800 million of annual revenue by selling computers to hospitals and other health-care providers world-wide . . . .

But in the health-industries group, the cutbacks imposed unexpected costs. Digital disrupted longstanding ties between its veteran salespeople and major customers by transferring their accounts to new sales divisions. It also switched hundreds of smaller accounts to outside distributors without notifying the customers.

At the industry's annual conference, "I had customers coming up to me and saying, `I haven't seen a Digital sales rep in nine months. Whom do I talk to now?'" recalls Joseph Lesica, a former marketing manager in the group who resigned last year. "That really hurt our credibility. I was embarrassed."

Resellers of Digital computers, who account for most of its health-care sales, also complained about diminished technology and sales support. "There were months when you couldn't find anybody with a Digital badge," complains an official at one former reseller who had been accustomed to Digital sales reps accompanying him on some customer calls. "They walked away from large numbers of clients." . . .

Many Digital customers turned to International Business Machines Corp. and Hewlett-Packard Co., and so did some employees of Digital's downsized healthcare group. Mr. Lesica says some laid-off workers went to Hewlett-Packard and quickly set about bringing Digital clients with them. "That's another way DEC shot itself in the foot," he says.

Such wounds aren't unusual when longtime sales relationships are disrupted. "Nobody sits down and asks, `What's going to be the impact on our customers?'" says D. Quinn Mills, a Harvard Business School professor. "It falls between the cracks all the time." . . .

The question is, to what extent are [payroll] savings offset by the new hires' lack of experience? Ms. Shapiro, the consultant, contends that a company is set back severely by the loss of "knowledge and judgment earned over the years. That's the stuff that gives you a real competitive advantage in the long run." Human-resources experts estimate that it typically costs $50,000 to recruit and train a managerial or technical worker . . . .

Others try to reduce employment costs by replacing experienced veterans with less expensive contract workers. But that can heighten a company's chances of being represented by people who perform poorly—or worse . . . .

Nynex's early-out programs for managers and craft-level employees, which have trimmed about 12,000 jobs since 1993, have caused labor shortages as well. Nynex has hired back hundreds of former employees, including managers already receiving pensions . . . .

Even greater than the rehiring expense is the blight on Nynex's reputation for customer service—right when its core market is opening up to competition for the first time. "Their past reputation for customer service is their key competitive advantage," says Joe Kraemer, a management consultant at the A.T. Kearney subsidiary of Electronic Data Systems Inc. in Rosslyn, Va. "But they've put all that at risk, just to gain a few cents per share in a given quarter. It's just plain dumb."[1]

As Charles Derber put it, "[c]ontract workers are usually clueless about inside knowledge specific to the firm, and lack key social ties in and out of the company necessary to close deals and maintain relations to customers.[2]

Self-serving management policies undermine the trust which is required for workers to invest their human capital in the enterprise. Gary Miller, in *The Political Economy of Hierarchy*, argues that trust is the main distinguishing feature of firms that make the most productive use of human capital. He cites work in behavioral economics and game theory on how relationships of trust are built up through repeated interactions, when the parties know they will be dealing with each other in the future. The lesson for the firm, in particular, is illustrated by piece rates. In the short run, management may have a rational incentive to elicit greater effort through piecework pay, and then cutting piece rates. But in the long run, it will only be possible to elicit greater effort if workers are confident that management will not change the rules of the game to screw them over; otherwise, the rational strategy for workers is deliberate shirking. Management can elicit greater effort through prolonged confidence-building measures to demonstrate, in a credible manner, their lack of intent to expropriate the productivity gains of greater effort. Management can only elicit workers' investment of their effort in the productivity of the enterprise by giving them long-term property rights in their share of productivity gains, with credible safeguards against expropriation.[3]

Unfortunately, Miller continues, because such cooperative cultures are established by "mutually reinforcing expectations," they are highly dependent on "the beliefs of the various players about the likely responses of other players." That means that they are extremely fragile when one party acts to undermine trust.

Miller illustrates the lesson with a case study of an Indiana gypsum mine in the 1950s. The management had an informal and egalitarian relationship with the workers, and generally showed up in work clothes. The management style was extremely lax about things like clocking in late or clocking out early, sick days, etc., and relied heavily on employee initiative and motivation in solving problems without micromanagement. The work force was willing to pull long hours of overtime in emergencies; rather than hoarding their tacit knowledge, they were willing to invest it in increasing productivity.

A new Pharaoh arose, however, who knew not Joseph. When the old plant manager died, his replacement was a Barney Fife type who was horrified at the lax enforcement of rules. He strictly enforced clock-in and clock-out times, hired foremen who would

1. Alex Markels and Matt Murray, "Call It Dumbsizing: Why Some Companies Regret Cost-Cutting," *Wall Street Journal*, May 14, 1996 <http://www.markels.com/management.htm>.

2. Charlers Derber, *Corporation Nation: How Corporations are Taking Over Our Lives and What We Can Do About It* (New York: St. Martin's Griffin, 1998), pp. 111-112.

3. Gary J. Miller, *Managerial Dilemmas: The Political Economy of Hierarchy* (New York: Cambridge University Press, 1992), pp. 201-202.

micromanage production and treat thinking as a management prerogative, and generally instituted an adversarial culture.

Of course, the workers responded in kind. They decided that, if management was going to stand on the rules, they would do the same. Remarking on the new "zero tolerance" time clock policy, one worker said:

> Well, if that's the way he wants it, that's the way he wants it. But I'll be damned if I put in any overtime when things get rough and they'd like us to.
>
> O.K., I'll punch in just so, and I'll punch out on the nose. But you know you can lead a horse to water and you can lead him away, but it's awful hard to tell how much water he drinks while he's at it.[1]

All this is closely related to human capital and "dumbsizing." An organizational culture of cooperation and mutual trust is a very important form of human capital—one that takes a great deal of time and effort to build up, and can be destroyed overnight by the typical idiot MBA who thinks he can goose his stock options by laying off half the work force.

One of the most important ways to safeguard a culture of trust is through confidence-building measures, which make it more costly for management to defect and reassure the workforce that the increased value they produce will not be expropriated. This coincides with the observations of Rajan and Zingales (which we will see in Chapter Nine) on the importance of stakeholder equity rights in the corporation.

> Many firms that are most successful at encouraging high levels of commitment and non-monitored effort from subordinates have effectively reallocated to employees some of the property rights to the assets owned by the firm, creating a sense of what is significantly called "employee ownership," or long-term control over those aspects of the workplace that are most important to employees.[2]

This quote from Jeffrey Nielsen, which we already saw in Chapter Six, is worth another look:

> With rank-based logic, people see work as a burden and organization as a necessary evil. We only grudgingly join up with organizations and then find life within them to be nasty, boring, and deadening to the spirit. When the organization encounters hardships, the assumption is that those below should be sacrificed to protect the privilege of those above. All too frequently we read in the financial section of the paper about this type of logic in action: another CEO who laid off hundreds of workers is awarded with a fat bonus at the end of the year.

Nielsen continued to write, directly after the material quoted above:

> Author Jason Jennings, in a *USA Today* (2002) editorial, said that many leaders believe downsizing in tough economic times is the right leadership thing to do. Citing a major 2002 research project of the Business Roundtable on the relationship between layoffs and productivity, Jennings challenges this conventional wisdom. The research revealed that the world's most productive firms make an explicit promise never to balance the books through layoffs.[3]

But we must always keep in mind that "the right leadership thing to do," from the perspective of "leaders," is tacitly defined in terms of the private *interest* of those leaders. I have no doubt that Jennings' preferred course of action is more effective by *his* standards of productivity: increased sales, lower costs, and more profit per employee. But for corporate

---

1. *Ibid.*, pp. 207-210.

2. Raghuram Rajan and Luigi Zingales, "The Governance of the New Enterprise," in Xavier Vives, ed., *Corporate Governance: Theoretical and Empirical Perspectives* (Cambridge: Cambridge University Press, 2000), p. 226.

3. Jeffrey Nielsen, *The Myth of Leadership: Creating Leaderless Organizations* (Palo Alto Calif.: Davies-Black Publishing, 2004), p. 53.

management, the "productivity" of an organization means something entirely different: the support of management in the lifestyle to which it is entitled. For management, getting most of a small pie is usually preferable to a small piece of a bigger pie; their goal is to maximize the size, not of the pie, but of their piece. We must never forget that the real goal of the organization, from the perspective of management, is to serve management; all that smarmy rhetoric in the mission statement is for outside consumption. From management's perspective, it's hard to imagine an organization being more "productive" than GE was for Welch or Home Depot was for Nardelli. While Nielsen's peer-based organizations may be more productive for "everyone" (probably not for Welch and Nardelli), the hierarchical organization is more productive for the people who count.

Asset-stripping is quite common in the managerialist culture. As Robert Jackall said, making correct decisions for long-term productivity may be politically disastrous; the effects will not be seen until long after the decision-maker is no longer around to take credit.[1]

General Motors is a good example of the tendency to hollow out productive capabilities. As Eric Husman observed,[2] GM has become, increasingly, a company that brands, markets, and finances cars, rather than building them. Their main source of profit is now GMAC, the auto sale finance arm of the company. And if they turn a large profit in a given year, there's a good chance it's the result of selling off another couple of plants.

As already suggested by several anticipatory remarks in this chapter, all these tendencies are reinforced in American corporate culture by the Sloan management accounting system, which is described in clinical detail by William Waddell and Norman Bodek in *Rebirth of American Industry*.[3]

Waddell and Bodek contrast the Sloan system to Taichi Ohno's Toyota Production System, or lean manufacturing, which measures profitability by revenue stream. If there's more money coming in this week than going out, the operation is profitable. Assets are of interest only when applying for a loan or liquidating the enterprise. Inventory that isn't bringing in real cash from outside is a cost, not an asset. The best way to reduce costs is to fully utilize equipment and reduce cycle time through increased flow, to avoid waste and rework through designing defects out of the production process rather than inspecting for quality after the fact, and to minimize inventory through just-in-time production. And these things are all achieved mainly with the help of the company's chief asset, its human capital.

The Sloan system (or DuPont/Sloan/Brown system), on the other hand, attempts to maximize Return on Investment (ROI), which translates into share value: i.e., the book value of the company divided by the number of shares. The larger the sum that could be raised by auctioning off the company's assets in the event of bankruptcy, the better managed it was.[4]

> Pierre DuPont devised a system to be sure that the salvage value of the companies in which he invested was high. From one end of the country to another, GE and GM plants can be had for salvage value.[5]

And corporate management's primary activity for the last twenty years has been living off the salvage value of the organizations whose assets it has gutted.

Perversely, the Sloan system counts inventory toward this book value (a metric that works directly at cross-purposes to the lean system, which treats inventory as a cost).

1. Jackall, *Moral Mazes*, p. 84.
2. See Chapter Ten.
3. William H. Waddell and Norman Bodek, *Rebirth of American Industry: A Study of Lean Management* (Vancouver, WA: PCS Press, 2005).
4. *Ibid.*, pp. 68-69.
5. *Ibid.*, p. 108.

With inventory declared to be an asset with the same liquidity as cash, it did not really matter whether the next "cost center," department, plant, or division actually needed the production output right away in order to consummate one of these paper sales. The producing department put the output into inventory and took credit.[1]

This is referred to as "overhead absorption," which means fully incorporating all production costs into the price of goods "sold" to inventory, at which point they count as an asset on the balance sheet.[2] American factories frequently have warehouse shelves filled with millions of dollars worth of obsolete inventory, which is still there "to avoid having to reduce profits this quarter by writing it off."[3]

At the same time, it defines production labor as the primary "variable cost," so that all "cost-cutting" and "efficiency" measures focus almost entirely on downsizing the labor force. This, despite the ways that human capital increases both the productivity and book value of an organization. Yet other intangibles, like "goodwill" and "intellectual property," are treated, oddly, as assets, on the grounds that they contribute to book value. Since inventory is as good as cash, and management salaries are a fixed rather than variable expense, management understandably filters out overhead when it comes to finding ways to cut costs; the overall effect is that corporate management automatically thinks of downsizing production workers as the first and only cost-cutting alternative.

> Brown's contribution was primarily that he could take this definition of ROI, look out over General Motors operations and envision islands of cost awash in a sea of assets. Those islands of cost were basically people. Well-supervised, they could turn one form of inventory into another with little of their time left over to detract from profits. Left uncontrolled, however, they could waste a lot of money with nothing to show for it . . . .[4]

> . . . While Sloan, Brown and the rest may have looked out over the plants and seen islands of cost in a sea of assets, they knew that around the edges and lurking beneath the surface there were other costs in the form of overhead. The problem was that these costs, such as the costs of moving things around, fixing machines, inspecting parts, and supervising, were awfully hard to assign to a specific operation. They went along with everything in general, but nothing in particular. Without any means of directly assigning and controlling them, these costs were simply assigned percentages in the hope that they would stay reasonably in proportion to the direct labor costs which could be controlled, and that was good enough.

> Without any direct link, all that could be measured with great confidence was the direct, easy to correlate part of the job: labor. It did not take much of a mathematician to figure out that, if all you really care about is the cost of performing one operation to a part, and you were allowed to make money by doing that single operation as cheaply as possible and then calling the partially complete product an asset, it would be cheaper to make them a bunch at a time.

> It stood to reason that spreading set-up costs over many parts was cheaper than having to set-up for just a few even if it meant making more parts than you needed for a long time. It also made sense, if you could make enough parts all at once, to just make them cheaply, and then sort out the bad ones later.

> Across the board, batches became the norm because the direct cost of batches was cheap and they could be immediately turned into money—at least as far as Mr. DuPont was concerned—by classifying them as work-in-process inventory.[5]

The obsession with lowering direct labor costs, and direct labor costs only, caused costs from correcting defects and storing inventory to skyrocket. Not to mention recalls, which frequently run around half of total production.[1]

1. *Ibid.*, p. 75.
2. *Ibid.*, pp. 135–141.
3. *Ibid.*, p. 132.
4. *Ibid.*, p. 68
5. *Ibid.*, p. 98.

H. Thomas Johnson and Robert S. Kaplan, in *Relevance Lost*, also discussed the perverse effects of treating direct labor as the main source of cost. If a production manager achieves savings in overhead costs, the savings are diluted over all the cost centers in the factory because of the allocation procedure. "Therefore, rational managers focus their attention where it does the most 'good'": direct labor. "Consequently, less attention is devoted to escalating overhead costs than to small increments in labor costs." This also creates a perverse incentive to outsource or offshore production of components to take advantage of cheap labor, even though it only affects the cost of direct labor which may be relatively minor compared to the part of factory overhead not driven by direct labor, and therefore "saves only a relatively small fraction of the component's costs." In fact, the transaction costs involved in subcontracting tend to increase overhead costs. "But these newly added costs are not traced to the purchased component because it has zero direct labor content. Instead, the higher overhead costs are shifted to the labor-intense products and processes still remaining in the plant."[2]

David F. Noble discussed the same phenomenon in *Progress Without People*, referring to the standard accounting practice of measuring productivity in terms of "output per person-hour":

> An overriding assumption of almost all discussion about automation is that productivity increases result from the substitution of machines for hourly production workers. That is, a reduction in factory jobs is *ipso facto* understood to mean a gain in productivity . . . . [But], as Thomas Gunn argued in 1982, "Direct labor accounts for only ten to twenty-five percent of the total cost of manufacturing . . . .
>
> John Simpson, Director of Manufacturing Engineering at the National Bureau of Standards, took this same message a bit further: "In metalworking manufacture, direct labor amounts to roughly 10 percent of total cost, as opposed to materials at 55 percent and overhead another 35 percent. Yet, as of 1982, management was expending roughly 75 percent of managerial and engineering effort on labor costs reduction, as compared to 15 percent on material cost reduction and 10 percent on overhead cost reduction. This is a striking disparity."
>
> It certainly is. As *Business Week* discovered in its 1982 survey of executives, few managers anticipated much use of the new equipment to displace management, even though such reduction in overhead, as Simpson suggests, would no doubt serve the goal of increased productivity.[3]

In my own experience, the obsession with cutting patient care staff as a "variable cost" in most hospitals leads to the phenomena described in Appendix 8A of this chapter. Costs from patient falls, hospital-acquired infections, and errors, as a direct result of understaffing, rise until they more than offset the ostensible labor cost savings. The gutting of human capital described earlier drastically reduces the quality of care. Hospitals are even forced to turn away patients (what is called "diversion mode") for want of sufficient staff to care for them. As a result, they suffer catastrophic losses to their reputations and lose business. This is the direct, inevitable result of treating human capital, which takes years to build up and years to acquire its network of social relationships and distributed knowledge, as a "variable cost" to be fired and rehired as often as demand shifts—and meanwhile treating management as a fixed expense to be paid in both fat times and lean.

As we will see in the next chapter, human and organizational capital—the human relationships, trust, and tacit knowledge of processes that take years to build up, and cannot

1. Langdon Winner, *The Whale and the Reactor: A Search for Limits in an Age of High Technology* (Chicago and London: University of Chicago Press, 1986), p. 77.

2. H. Thomas Johnson and Robert S. Kaplan, *Relevance Lost: The Rise and Fall of Management Accounting* (Boston: Harvard Business School Press, 1987), pp. 188-189.

3. David F. Noble, *Progress Without People: New Technology, Unemployment, and the Message of Resistance* (Toronto: Between the Lines, 1995), p. 105.

be rebuilt in a short time at any cost—are the reason a firm's equity is greater than the book value of its tangible assets. It really is capital, and a productive asset. "Dumbsizing" disrupts and mutilates this human capital, and guts an organization's long-term productive capability. But the Sloan system treats labor as "the biggest profit detractor [a] company [has] . . ."[1] The Sloan system's "arrogant and demeaning" approach to people "assured that employee involvement in production would not happen."[2]

> Direct labor is not a variable cost as a result of some mystic truth or a law of either nature or physics. It is a variable cost because management decided it would be so. Calling inventory an asset, while people are not an asset is also a distortion of the truth.[3]

For this reason, the right-wingers and corporate apologists in this country who spend so much time tisk-tisking about Japanese "lifetime employment guarantees" miss the point. The irony is that the people who are quickest to observe that "nobody washes a rental car," in regard to the benefits of and "ownership society" outside the workplace, are the same idiots who complain the most about the evils of job security *inside* the workplace.

"Lifetime employment" is just another way of saying the Japanese treat human capital as an asset rather than a direct cost, which is precisely the lesson we learned above from Waddell and Bodek. Employment security builds trust, and hence human capital, by reassuring workers that they have a secure property right in their contributions to productivity, that the productivity gains they create won't be expropriated by management, and that their increased effort and productivity won't be used against them through rate-busting, speedups and downsizing. It elicits the kind of behavior that Rajan and Zingales describe: workers investing in the productivity of the enterprise. To quote William Ouchi,

> The first lesson of Theory Z is trust. Productivity and trust go hand in hand, strange as it may seem . . . .
> . . . [T]he central feature of the [Japanese] trading firm is an extensive management system that maintains a sense of trust between employees in the trading company. . . . [The employees] work in an environment of tremendous uncertainty, buying and selling copper ore, crude oil, wheat and televisions. . . . Often, the firm's overall profitability will be maximized if an office takes a loss, which will be more than made up in another office so that the company benefits overall. The success of the trading company depends critically upon the willingness of individual offices and employees to make these sacrifices. That willingness exists because the Japanese trading firm uses managerial practices that foster trust through the knowledge that such sacrifices will always be repaid in the future . . . .
> One American company that has a definite uniqueness but at the same time resembles the Japanese management style is Hewlett-Packard [Ouchi wrote before Carly Fiorina, obviously].[4]

The problem, for the right-wingers, is probably that "increasing productivity" is something the John Galts do, while workers are passive dullards who contribute nothing to the production process. An extreme example of this is George Reisman, who continually rewrites the same article at Mises.Org: the only way to increase the worker's standard of living is to increase the wealth of the capitalist, who invests his capital in increasing the worker's productivity, which drives up wages. The concept of human capital, or the possibility (as we saw in Chapters Two, Five and Seven) that the worker's unique knowledge of how best to *employ* existing physical capital matters more to productivity than the *amount*

---

1. Waddell and Bodek, p. 152.
2. *Ibid.*, p. 153.
3. *Ibid.*, p. 207.
4. William Ouchi, *Theory Z: How American Business Can Meet the Japanese Challenge* (New York: Avon Books, 1981), pp.5-6. Ouchi wrote, obviously, before Carly Fiorina destroyed "the HP Way."

of capital employed, is lost on such people. If the reader suspects me of exaggeration, consider these quotes, first from Mises himself and then from Reisman:

> You have the courage to tell the masses what no politician told them: you are inferior and all the improvements in your conditions which you simply take for granted you owe to the effort of men who are better than you.[1]
>
> Carson is simply unaware that innovation is the product of exceptional, dedicated individuals who must overcome the uncomprehending dullness of most of their fellows, and often their hostility as well.[2]

One of the most interesting proposals for countering this perverse treatment of human capital as a cost is the idea of "human resource accounting." It came out of a research project which Rensis Likert (mentioned above) inspired, at the University of Michigan's Institute for Social Research, aimed at correlating management styles to profitability. The idea is to transform the management bromide that "employees are our most valuable asset" from a mere hypocritical slogan into reality, and develop a metric for counting the actual equity value of human capital toward the bottom line.

> The Michigan team has laid out three basic approaches to the problem, by computing figures for (1) the value of investments in human resources (approximately corresponding to book value for physical assets); (2) replacement values; and (3) economic values, that is, the capitalized value of earnings directly attributable to these resources.
>
> A good start has been made on the first two, which include "expenditures in recruiting, hiring, training, developing, and organizing employees into effective work groups . . . ." Since 1966, the R. G. Barry Corp . . . . has been developing, with the help of the Michigan team, methods of calculating these figures. By 1970, "book value" figures had been computed for all 147 managers in the company and 425 factory and clerical personnel . . . .
>
> In 1969, Barry drew up, for internal use, a "capital budget for human resources," believed to be the first of its kind, which can answer questions in such areas as new expenditures for training programs, the real costs of employee turnover, and whether the human resources in any particular department are rising or falling. In this way, if any manager attempts to juice up short-term profits at the expense of company resources, top management will be alerted immediately . . . . [The 1969 annual report showed] that, because of heavy employee-development costs (which, logically, might be better capitalized than expensed), reported earnings were understated by about 10 percent, and that when "net investments in human resources" were added to the asset side of the balance sheet, total assets rose by some 15 percent.[3]

Unfortunately human resource accounting has remained largely a fringe movement, at most something to which lip service is paid while human capital continues to be treated in practice as a variable cost.

The Sloan system is at the heart of the American MBA curriculum, and the ruling paradigm in American corporate governance.

Sloan cost metrics, which focus almost entirely on reducing the "direct cost" of labor involved in every operation, have seriously skewed the direction of production technology.

> . . . [M]anufacturing engineers . . . were directed more and more to focus only on direct labor savings. Machines that were more accurate or flexible could not be justified in a batch environment. Where Ford's engineers built machines to speed flow and assure quality,

1. Mises' letter to Ayn Rand, quoted in Bettina Bien Greaves, "To What Extent Was Rand a Misesian?" *Mises.Org*, April 11, 2005 <http://mises.org/story/1790>.

2. George Reisman, "Freedom is Slavery: Laissez-Faire Capitalism is Government Invasion: A Critique of Kevin Carson's *Studies in Mutualist Political Economy*," *The Journal of Libertarian Studies* 20:1 (Winter 2006), p. 55.

3. Jenkins, *Job Power*, pp. 238–240.

American engineers were pushed more and more into focusing on labor elimination technology.[1]

And between the accounting people Ernie Breech brought in from GM, and the "whiz kids" Bob McNamara brought in from the war department, Ford was eventually cured of that nonsense.[2]

Interestingly, the mostly uneducated workers of recuperated enterprises in Argentina, forced to use their own common sense after the managers and accountants abandoned the plants, spontaneously reinvented Ford's system of cash flow accounting on their own.

> How did these men (none of whom have a university degree and most of whom do not even have a high school diploma) administer, manage, market, and run nothing less than an entire factory in the complex reality of today's market, economy, and finances?
> We wanted to go with a very small-time economy. Nothing complicated. Buy this, sell that, this much is left, and that's it.[3]

The Sloan system focuses, exclusively, on labor savings "perceived to be attainable only through faster machines. Never mind that faster machines build inventory faster, as well."[4] As the authors of *Natural Capitalism* argue, batch production results from attempts to optimize each separate step of the production process in isolation ("optimizing one element in isolation from others and thereby pessimizing the entire system"), without regard to its effect on the flow of the overall production process. A machine can reduce the labor cost of one step, by running at enormous speeds, and yet be out of sync with the overall process, so that it simply produces excess inventory that waits to be used by the next step in the process.[5] The giant cola-canning machine and Pratt & Whitney's robotic grinders, which we saw in Chapter Two, are good examples. The Toyota Production System, on the other hand, emphasizes *takt*: pacing the output of each stage of production to meet the needs of the next stage, and coordinating all of the stages in accordance with current orders.[6]

As Waddell and Bodek argue, lean production isn't primarily a matter of shop floor organization. Shop floor organization, rather, tends to follow automatically from the incentives the management accounting system puts in place.

> However the accounting system is set up, it defines "making money" for the company and becomes the basis for all decision making. The quality system, production and inventory control systems and policies, people policies and so forth are all structured to enable the company to make the most money. How these systems are structured is a direct result of how the management of the company defines making money.
> . . . . Early Ford and later Toyota defined money in a lean accounting manner and lean practices resulted. General Motors defined making money as optimizing ROI and we all know the practices that arose as a result. Henry Ford and the Toyoda family did not personally go out and implement assembly lines or kanbans any more than Alfred Sloan went out and personally created batch production. These men defined 'profitability' for their companies, then urged and pushed their organizations to aggressively and creatively attain that version of profitability.[7]

1. Waddell and Bodek, p. 106.
2. *Ibid.*, pp. 89-90.
3. The Lavaca Collective, *Sin Patron: Stories from Argentina's Worker-Run Factories*. Translated by Katherine Kohlstedt (Chicago: Haymarket Books, 2007), p. 190
4. Waddell and Bodek, p. 119.
5. Hawken, Paul, Amory Lovins, and L. Hunter Lovins, *Natural Capitalism: Creating the Next Industrial Revolution* (Boston, New York, London: Little, Brown, and Company, 1999), pp. 129-30.
6. Waddell and Bodek, pp. 122-123.
7. *Ibid.*, pp. 92-93.

Success, in lean terms, barely shows up as such by Sloan metrics. Of the United Defense plant in Aberdeen, South Dakota (one of the few American lean experiments that actually "got" the Toyota system), Waddell and Bodek write:

> A balance sheet prepared according to DuPont would miss the value of the plant in Aberdeen entirely. According to the statistics in the most recent Best Manufacturing Practices award from the Navy, inventory is down 78% from where it was just a few years ago, and it was low by industry standards to begin with. A balance sheet, however, would not reflect that as much of an accomplishment. The same balance sheet would assign no value to the 150 cross-trained, self-directed, customer-focused employees who generate very profitable, sustained manufacturing results.[1]

Indeed, most American companies would lay half of them whenever business slowed down, warn the remaining workers to work hard to pick up the slack (with a little Fish! Philosophy and a catchy new core values statement thrown in to jolly them into enjoying being screwed), and figure they could hire more help from a temp agency when things picked up.

But "imagine," Waddell and Bodek write, a software or tech company declaring that "computer science is a commodity—"

> basically any warm body from the local temp agency can do it—and that the key to success in running these technology companies is not technology, but finance and marketing. Imagine further that they all but declare war on their programmers and system design folks, classifying them as variable costs and devising a management system aimed directly at cutting their numbers and minimizing their pay.[2]
>
> Sloan and Brown were dead wrong. People are not interchangeable commodities, to be fired and laid off every time the wind blows from a different direction. Manufacturing is too complicated; there are far too many variables. There is no computer big enough or fast enough to plan and control it. Toyota knows this. It takes a factory full of trained, focused, committed people to get all of the details right in the midst of so many dynamic events. They are not commodities.
>
> A new accountant can be hired and pretty much become as effective as he or she is going to get within a month or two. A production employee is more likely to take six months or more—a year according to the self-directed teams at United Defense. Yet the accountant is a fixed expense with a fair amount of job security, while the production worker is a commodity.
>
> . . . . The best way to develop the work force quickly and increase balance sheet accuracy for the sake of the investor is to capitalize the cost of training and educating people . . . .
>
> Only in the world of F. W. Taylor, Pierre DuPont, Alfred Sloan and Donaldson Brown can kicking trained, experienced, capable people out of a company be seen as a positive move. There is nothing positive about it. It is proof of a basic failure of management. To do so within months of paying the top manager better than $10 million in performance bonuses ought to be proof enough that the system is broken.

To anticipated objections, from those steeped in the Sloan management culture, to capitalizing an intangible like human capital, Waddell and Bodek respond, "[t]hat has never stopped the Sloan companies from capitalizing goodwill and intellectual property, often on far shakier ground than capitalizing people."[3]

One thing Waddell and Bodek fail to pick up on, perhaps being more charitable than I am, is how incredibly well the Sloan system's cost and profit metrics dovetail with the class interests of management. If management is simply a fixed cost to be paid in both lean times and bad, but production work is a "direct cost" to be minimized and constantly adjusted—by layoffs and firings—to the current level of demand, management (not surprisingly) are the last to lose their jobs or suffer pay cuts. The metrics of the Sloan system co-

1. *Ibid.*, p. 159.
2. *Ibid.*, p. 223.
3. *Ibid.*, pp. 240-242.

incide so closely with management's pecuniary and careerist motives, in fact, that it's a bit of a chicken and egg problem figuring out whether American managerialism as it currently exists results from the Sloan system's incentives, or the Sloan system was adopted because American management found it so conducive to their interests. There's probably a mutual synergy involved.

Waddell and Bodek do see the implications of the system very clearly, however, even if they don't see how well it reinforces management venality.

> It is so commonly accepted in the United States that direct labor is a variable cost that the consequences of this arbitrary decision are rarely appreciated. At the top of the hierarchy are the policy makers, strategists and those charged with controlling the factories. Their salaries are a fixed cost, which means their jobs are relatively safe regardless of business results, within a broad reasonable range. In the middle are manufacturing management whose jobs have been, as a result of refinements to the cost accounting system, categorized as semi-fixed or step function costs. Their jobs are only secure to a point. At the bottom are Taylor's workers who should have no input to how things are made. They should be expected to simply produce to the maximum efficiency. Their jobs are purely variable, meaning their job security is purely a function of sales volume.
>
> Those variable cost people—the ones Taichi Ohno points out are not even whole people in American cost accounting—are not people at all. They are "headcount". That simple fact makes lean manufacturing virtually impossible in Sloan companies. Lifetime employment, such as that at Toyota, is nothing more than changing the system to categorize production labor as a fixed expense.[1]
>
> Just about every company says they want their people to work smarter not harder . . . . [But people] will not work harder if management has defined the ultimate goal to be a lights out factory, while they soar like hawks over the plant hunting for jobs to eliminate and people to lay off. People everywhere will work smarter and harder for the customer, but people will not work harder for someone who has defined them as a variable cost.[2]

Contrast this to the Japanese approach, as described by W. Edwards Deming based on his experiences in Japanese industry.

> In Japan, when a company has to absorb a sudden economic hardship such as a 25 per cent decline in sales, the sacrificial pecking order is firmly set. First the corporate dividends are cut. Then the salaries and the bonuses of top management are reduced. Next, management salaries are trimmed from the top to the middle of the hierarchy. Lastly, the rank and file are asked to accept pay cuts or a reduction in the work force through attrition or voluntary discharge. In the United States, a typical firm would probably do the opposite under similar circumstances [except for the relative priority of dividends and management pay, of course—KC]."[3]

To the usual suspects at the *Wall Street Journal* and on *CNBC* money programs, it goes without saying that the Toyota approach is wrong-headed. It makes perfect sense to pay Bob "Sucks at Job" Nardelli or "Chainsaw Al" Dunlap a multi-million salary for all that "productivity." But guaranteeing lifetime employment to production workers is *just plain wrong*. As the analyst community's reaction to Costco demonstrates, even if you can afford to pay good wages and provide job security, it falls into the same moral category—vaguely decadent things that just don't seem right—as putting a diamond collar on a dog. Such pampering makes companies "bloated," "fat," and "lazy," don't you know!

Never mind that the Toyota approach to lifetime employment is perfectly consistent with their understanding of the importance of painstakingly acquired human capital as a source of organizational value. And never mind that it works. For example, John Mickleth-

1. *Ibid.*, p. 153.
2. *Ibid.*, p. 158.
3. W. Edwards Deming, *Out of the Crisis* (Cambridge, Mass.: M.I.T., Center for Advanced Engineering Study, 1986), p. 147.

waite reports, before a Range Rover factory made a lifetime employment pledge in the early '90s, only 11% of employees entered the annual employee suggestions competition, "because they were worried that increased efficiency might cost them their jobs; afterward the proportion rose to 84 percent." And a single one of those proposals saved the company 100 million pounds.[1]

> When employees are a fixed cost, the source of their job security is plant profitability. When employees are a variable cost, they find job security by assuring that the work is never complete. Lean companies outperform Sloan companies because profits are in the best interests of the production employees in lean companies. It is hard to imagine how Sloan and Brown could have expected a system to work that polarized workers and management so thoroughly.[2]

But again, never mind. What matters is that no decent person puts a diamond collar on a dog, and no decent company (despite all the Official Happy Talk about "teamwork" and "our most valuable asset") actually *treats* its production workers like valuable assets. You don't take money from starving kids to pamper a dog, and you don't take money from Nardelli or Welch to pay production workers a living wage. It doesn't matter whether it's profitable; it's a matter of *decency*. And in any case, when management is the de facto owner of the corporation and runs it in its own interests, it's obviously not going to hurt its own interests for the sake of productivity.

Blogger Richard Posner once argued that Lawrence Summers should not be accountable to the faculty for his conduct as President of Harvard University. The reason, he said:

> They [the faculty] should not be the owners. The economic literature on worker cooperatives identifies decisive objections to that form of organization that are fully applicable to university governance. The workers have a shorter horizon than the institution. Their interest is in getting as much from the institution as they can before they retire; what happens afterwards has no direct effect on them unless their pensions are dependent on the institution's continued prosperity. That consideration aside (it has no application to most professors' pensions), their incentive is to play a short-run game, to the disadvantage of the institution—and for the further reason that while the faculty as a group might be able to destroy the institution and if so hurt themselves, an individual professor who slacks off or otherwise acts against the best interests of the institution is unlikely to have much effect on the institution.[3]

Given the material so far in this section, Posner's bizarro-world description sounds like a clinically accurate description of corporate management—but with the word "workers" substituted for "management." If anything, a trained chicken would probably have a longer time-horizon than the average corporation's senior management.

The short time-horizons involved in hierarchy mean that making correct decisions from the long-term perspective will result in someone else taking credit. On the other hand, living off of seed corn to inflate short-term returns (at the cost of long-term disaster) may pay off spectacularly, by enabling a careerist to outrun the consequences of his bad decisions.[4]

At the plant level, this means neglecting necessary maintenance and upgrades to inflate short-term earnings. The manager who does this can be sure that he will get a bump

---

1. John Micklethwait and Adrian Wooldridge, *The Witch Doctors: Making Sense of the Management Gurus* (New York: Times Books, 1996), p. 209.

2. Waddell and Bodek, p. 169.

3. Richard Posner, "Summers' Resignation and Organization Theory," The Becker-Posner Blog, February 26, 2006 <http://www.becker-posner-blog.com/archives/2006/02/summers_resigna_1.html>.

4. Jackall, *Moral Mazes*, pp. 86, 90–91.

up the career ladder for the immediate returns of his short-sighted policy, and the career of a successor will be ruined instead of his own when the bills come due.[1]

Indeed, corporations' internal policies are often designed to facilitate such strategies. Top management deliberately avoids any long-term tracking of the consequences of individual decisions because it would threaten *them* with accountability.[2]

The overall effect is pressure on managers to "hit desired numbers . . . by squeezing the resources under one's control . . ." Deferring capital expenditures, including maintenance as well as new investment in improving the production process—referred to as "starving" or "milking" a plant.[3] Jackall quoted an upper-middle manager from the chemical subdivision in a corporate case study:

> We're judged on the short-term because everybody changes their jobs so frequently. As long as we have a system where I'm told that I am not going to be in a job for the long term, you're going to have this pressure. And you're not tracked from one job to the next, so you can milk your present situation and never have it pinned on you in the future . . . . If a piece of fairly large capital equipment needs to be replaced—well almost anything can be fixed and you can just keep patching things up, just putting absolutely no money at all into the business. Or you can just make an edict that will cut supplies by 25 percent, [things like] pumps, motors, tools, and so on . . . . My favorite things are not to replace my stores inventory and that shows up as direct profit on your balance sheet; not replace people who retire, and stretch everybody else out . . . . In the chemical business, another way to do it is to let waste accumulate, shutting off any capital expenditures and anything that is an expense. And you know what happens when you do that? The guy who comes into that mess is the one who gets blamed, not the guy who milked it."[4]

Jackall comments:

> Some managers become very adept at milking businesses and showing a consistent record of high returns. They move from one job to another in a company, always upward, rarely staying more than two years in any post. They may leave behind them deteriorating plants and unsafe working conditions . . . , but they know that if they move quickly enough, the blame will fall on others . . . .
> In fact, the manager who "takes the money and runs" is usually not penalized but rewarded and indeed given a license to move on to bigger mistakes.[5]

In one case, a manager in the chemical division Jackall studied was notorious for having "milked and milked thoroughly every plant he ever supervised." When challenged in a meeting for this practice, by a vice president who was his superior, he responded: " . . . [H]ow can you sit there and say that to me? How in the hell do you think you got to where you are . . . ?"[6]

Jackall adds that milking is more prevalent among policymakers at corporate headquarters than at the individual plant level, because the former are more insulated from the consequences when things go bad:

> Of course, the closer one is in the hierarchy to a business being milked, the greater the potential danger of being caught in a catastrophe and the more sure one has to be that one gets out in time. For this reason, managers feel that most milking, though not all, is done by those at the top of the hierarchy who are well removed and insulated from a local situation.[7]

1. *Ibid.*, p. 87.
2. *Ibid.*, p. 88.
3. *Ibid.*, p. 91.
4. *Ibid.*, pp. 91–92.
5. *Ibid.*, p. 94.
6. *Ibid.*, p. 96.
7. *Ibid.*, p. 93.

Jackall also gives a specific example of milking leading to a catastrophe. A large coking plant in the same chemical subdivision was under pressure from the CEO to defer "unnecessary" capital expenditures, in order to use the subdivision as a cash cow to finance new investments. As a result, a decaying battery was patched up for four years in lieu of the needed replacement. When it finally collapsed, the consequences to the company were disastrous (including breach of contract with a steel producer and costly pollution lawsuits)—total costs running from $100-150 million, compared to $6 million for simply replacing the battery.[1]

The CEO's interference, and its consequences, remind me of an anecdote from Russia's Great Patriotic War with the Nazis. The political officer of an artillery unit forbade the commander to withdraw a short distance, despite the commander's frantic attempts to explain that the apparent "retreat" was necessary to get proper range on the main road along which a German column was moving. (Another, more facetious anecdote claims that the Egyptians lost the 1967 war by literally adhering to the advice of Soviet military manuals: "Retreat into the heartland and wait for the first snowfall.")

Another author gives a less dramatic example, in which pennywise pound-foolish cost cutting policies severely degraded the customer service capability of a privatized utility:

> Management attempted to "sell" the new structure to the staff by claiming that its sole purpose was to improve standards of service for the customer. However, the fact that management was perceived as wishing to introduce the Beta structure "on the cheap" (minimizing on staff training and keeping staffing levels low, pressing on with inadequate systems because of the expense involved in correcting them quickly and so on) undermined the claim that change was primarily intended to improve service . . . . This was of enormous significance for workers who dealt constantly and directly with the customer. Management was forcing them to provide an unsatisfactory service . . . .[2]

Of course, management engages in asset-stripping, or starving or milking an operation, not just because of pressure from outside. It also does so, as we remarked above, because the funding of the organization's productive resources comes at the expense of management self-dealing.

Management may pay lip service to quality, but any subordinate who reduces short-term income for the sake of a long-term improvement in quality is taking his life in his own hands.

Besides pure venality, the irrationalities of management policy are exacerbated by the information problems discussed in Chapter Five.

Some of the knowledge problems are no doubt deliberate, exemplifying the principle variously known as "CYA" or "plausible deniability." If a written policy is in place, management can blame systemic problems on subordinates who disregard policy. For example, consider Tyson's response when an undercover PETA activist working in a Tyson facility filmed inhumane slaughter of poultry:

> [Tyson] said the man had signed a document confirming he had completed the company's animal-welfare training "and was responsible for ensuring that no birds remained alive. His job gave him the responsibility to process any live birds, stop the line or sound an alarm if there was a problem." . . . .

---

1. *Ibid.*, pp. 81-82.
2. Julia O'Connell Davidson, "The Sources and Limits of Resistance in a Privatized Utility," in J. Jermier and D. Knights, editors, *Resistance and Power in Organizations* (London: Routledge, 1994), p. 85.

Responding to the company's statement, PETA said its investigator had been "taught to rip the animals' heads off by a plant supervisor, for when there are too many who miss the neck slicer."[1]

Auschwitz and Treblinka no doubt had a "written policy" against killing Jews.

Corporate hierarchies, as Robert Jackall describes them, have a strong tendency to "push down detail." One purpose is to avoid responsibility for failure. By setting general objectives and leaving subordinates responsible for the details, those at the top retain the right to shift the blame for failure—even if the general objective assigned was unrealistic given the resources senior management was willing to allocate.

> . . . [P]ushing down details relieves superiors of the burden of too much knowledge, paticularly guilty knowledge.
> . . . [B]ecause they are unfamiliar with—indeed distance themselves from— entangling details, corporate higher echelons tend to expect successful results without messy complications. This is central to executives' well-known aversion to bad news and to the resulting tendency to kill the messenger who bears the news.[2]

But some of it is surely genuine. A great deal of the "management mentality" results from the psychotically distorted and isolated world in which management operates, thanks to the informational filtering mechanisms described by R.A. Wilson and Kenneth Boulding in Chapter Five.

Management is under the illusion that its policies are actually carried into effect, at the bottom end of the hierarchical filtering mechanism, in a fashion even remotely resembling their intentions. And they refuse to perceive the obstacles that their own rigidly enforced policies put in the way of their stated values. For example, here's how Peters and Waterman describe the "manager's mentality":

> We behave as if the proclamation of policy and its execution were synonymous. "But I made quality our number one goal years ago," goes the lament . . . . [The] president's subordinate clarified the message, "Of course, he's for quality. That is, he's never said, 'I don't care about quality.' It's just that he's for everything. He says, 'I'm for quality,' twice a year and he acts, 'I'm for shipping product,' twice a day."[3]

Management is prone to a sort of magical thinking: the belief that to put something into writing has a corresponding effect on reality. As Paul Goodman said,

> It is to will to be in control, without adjusting to the realities . . . . In this fantasy they employ a rhetoric of astounding dissociation between idea and reality . . . . For example, they claim that they are depolluting streams, but they allot no money; . . . the depressed area of Appalachia has been reclaimed, but the method is an old highway bill under another name; poor people will run their own programs, but any administrator is fired if he tries to let them; . . . this seems to be just lying, but to my ear it is nearer to magic thinking.[4]

This has been true of management thinking since it first emerged as a separate discipline, as Yehouda Shenhav describes it:

> The systematizers' emphasis on formalization through systems was promoted as rational, but it was a particular type of rationality, labeled by economist Friedrich Hayek as "constructive rationality" or "plan rationality" . . . .

1. "Tyson Foods Under Fine for Inhumane Slaughter of Poultry," *Agribusiness Examiner*, June 6, 2005 #408 <http://www.organicconsumers.org/OFGU/tyson060605.cfm>.

2. Jackall, *Moral Mazes*, pp. 20-21.

3. Thomas J. Peters and Robert H. Waterman, *In Search of Excellence: Lessons from America's Best-Run Companies* (New York: Warner Books, 1982), p. 73.

4. Paul Goodman, *Like a Conquered Province*, in *People or Personnel* and *Like a Conquered Province* (New York: Vintage Books, 1963, 1965), p. 339.

Formalization was also to include the company rules. Some suggested the company rules and policy should be posted in industrial bulletins . . . . For example . . . , "The rate of pay is a personal matter between the individual employee and employer, and must not become the business of other persons." It was suggested that each bulletin "established harmony at once". Furthermore, "everyone seemed to be infused with a desire to make a good record" and with "loyalty".[1]

Cut off almost completely from an understanding of the production process and the prerequisites for real efficiency, management puts production workers in a double bind by officially demanding particular results while systematically stripping them of all the resources needed to achieve those results. In boss-think, when one says something in a mission statement or in "educational" handouts, the effect is like reciting a spell: a verbal formula "makes it so" without the expenditure of any money (and especially without the diversion of resources from management featherbedding to production).

The information filtering mechanisms described by Wilson and Boulding don't just work automatically. They're actively enforced from above. It's true, as Wilson said, that people tend to self-censor based on what they think those in authority want to hear. But those at the top of the pyramid also *suppress* negative feedback on the effects of their policies. According to Joyce Rothschild and Terance Miethe, whistleblowers usually start out attempting to work within the system, naively expecting that management wants to improve the system and will welcome their feedback in good faith. Only when management responds by trying to destroy them do they air their message to the outside world, in self-defense.

> . . . [W]e find that whistleblowers start out expecting a constructive or at least modest organizational response to their disclosures. In our interviews, whistleblowers told us time and again that they started out believing that because they were respected and valued employees, their information presented to "higher-ups" would be taken seriously and would be the catalyst for the constructive organizational change they sought. As a result, few were prepared for what was about to happen to them . . . .
>
> Often, what we find is that once employees reveal they possess and might use information that challenges management's judgment, the full resources of the organization will be brought to bear against them . . . . In cases we studied, upon learning that an individual had a concern and information that could be used against them, management *immediately* fired the individual, or if that was not possible, then they set up the process by which they could be later fired, by abruptly downgrading their job performance. If the claims of "incompetence" could not be sustained, then we found that managers sometimes resorted to a tactic that we had not anticipated: they would endeavour to get the whistleblower labeled "crazy". Towards this end, management would direct the whistleblower to see an agency or company psychologist and would inform the psychologist that the person was being sent because they appeared to be "out of their mind" or a "paranoid schizophrenic" . . . .
>
> It is important to understand that as soon as management first hears of the concerns and information of the whistleblower, they often act immediately to downgrade the individual's job performance and begin explicitly to build a case for firing the individual. In other words, management reprisals begin as soon as management becomes aware that the individual *might* become a whistleblower.[2]

More generally, the same corporations that slavishly professed Kwality as the management fad du jour in the '90s blatantly ignored one of Deming's central principles: "Drive out fear." Fear systematically shapes and distorts the information that moves up the

---

1. Yehouda Shenhav, *Manufacturing Rationality: The Engineering Foundations of the Managerial Revolution* (New York and Oxford: Oxford University Press, 1999), pp. 87-88. Quotes are from *American Machinist*, Oct. 22, 1914.

2. Joyce Rothschild and Terance D. Miethe, "Whistleblowing as Resistance in Modern Work Organizations: The Politics of Revealing Organizational Deception and Abuse," in A. Baum and J.E. Singer, eds., *Advances in Environmental Psychology* (Hillsdale, N.J.: Earlbaum, 1980), pp. 264-266.

hierarchy, while reaffirming the official picture of reality is a test of loyalty. For example, a survey at a number of companies attempted to discover what issues employees considered "undiscussable," and found the number one answer was "management practices."[1] Thus, management suppresses exactly the kind of feedback from subordinates that is most needed to assess the effectiveness of company policy.

> Most employees are reluctant to discuss morale-reducing behaviors openly with their managers, primarily because of management's superior power, causing employee morale to decline even further due to a lack of open, honest, authentic, timely communication or genuine efforts at resolution. In nearly all organizational cultures, employees speak more freely with each other than they do with managers, and monitor their communications with managers to make sure they do not risk termination . . . .[2]

At Jackall's "Covenant" corporation, managers stated the importance of, variously, "aligning oneself with the dominant ideology of the moment," or "bowing to whichever god currently holds sway."

> . . . [T]he belief of insiders in abstract goals is not a prerequisite for personal success; belief in and subordination to individuals who articulate organizational goals is. One must, however, be able to act, at a moment's notice, as if official reality is the only reality . . . . The knowledgeable practitioners of corporate politics, whether patrons or leaders of cliques and networks, value nothing more highly than at least the appearance of unanimity of opinion among their clients and allies, especially during times of turmoil.[3]

For the most part those at or near the top of a hierarchy will suffer few moral qualms in adapting to its requirements for suppressing the truth. As Gordon Tullock said, the greater the extent to which advancement in a hierarchy demands the sacrifice of ordinary personal morality, the greater the advantage the amoral climber will have over his more scrupulous colleagues; as a result, the hierarchy selects against morality and that undesirable trait has been effectively weeded out at the top.[4]

Given all these phenomena, it's not surprising that career advancement within the corporate hierarchy is generally perceived to have little to do with genuine achievement. Robert Jackall writes:

> Managers rarely speak of objective criteria for achieving success because once certain crucial points in one's career are passed, success and failure seem to have little to do with one's accomplishments.

The corporate hierarchy relies, instead, on credentialing for the presumption of competence, and on a culture of obedience and careerism to guarantee the correct attitude toward the values of the hierarchy.[5]

> Profits and other kinds of results matter, but managers see no *necessary* connections between performance and reward. Although meritocratic ideologies are constantly invoked in the corporate world to explain or justify promotions, demotions, or other organizational changes, such rationales are always viewed by managers with a measure of skepticism . . . .
> . . . . Merit pay systems, for instance, are widely considered to be used simply as sophisticated, highly rational legitimations for what is in practice a complicated political patronage system . . . .

1. Kenneth Cloke and Joan Goldsmith. *The End of Management and the Rise of Organizational Democracy* (New York: John Wiley & Sons, 2002), p. 49.

2. *Ibid.*, p. 55.

3. Jackall, *Moral Mazes*, pp. 52–53.

4. Gordon Tullock, *The Politics of Bureaucracy* (Washington, D.C.: Public Affairs Press, 1965), p. 22.

5. Jackall, *Moral Mazes*, p. 41.

There is, for example, often a built-in inequity between the classes of management which are included or excluded from bonus programs. At Covenant Corporation, "even during the . . . rocky red-ink years [of the 1981 recession] . . . , generous bonuses were regularly passed out to the chosen few."[1]

As a result, there is an understandable fear of showing initiative or sticking one's neck out. Those at the top either seek plausible deniability, or seek "buy–in" from subordinates in order to implicate as many people as possible in the shared blame if a decision leads to bad results. Those at the bottom, on the other hand, keep their heads down and avoid making commitments, and wait for those at the top to take the initiative. One manager at Covenant said:

> People try to cover themselves. They avoid putting things clearly in writing. They try to make group decisions so that responsibility is not always clearly defined . . . .
>
> [These tendencies are] rooted in the pervasive social uncertainty of the organization . . . , [*i.e.*] management's sense of organizational contingency, of authoritarian capriciousness, and of the lack of firm connections between risk and reward.[2]

Management's approach to corporate governance was ably summed up by Preston Glidden, a frequent commenter at my blog with a fifteen year background in corporate quality control and quality assurance:

> Modern management's goal is to squeeze the last drop of blood out of a company's quarterly numbers, while fooling customers and investors about the actual long–term health of the company. If it kills the company in the long term, so be it. The golden parachute awaits senior management, and employees pay the price.[3]

C. The Authoritarian Workplace:
Increased Hierarchy and Surveillance

The elites who run our state capitalist economy made a strategic decision, in the 1970s, to cap real wages and transfer all productivity increases into reinvestment, dividends, or CEO salaries. So while real wages have remained stagnant for thirty years, the wealth of the top few percent of the population has exploded astronomically. The percentage of wealth owned by the top 1%, which as of the mid–70s had held steady at around 25% for decades, is now close to 40%. To impose this policy on society, obviously, required increasing authoritarianism in all aspects of social life. I quote at length from my account, in *Studies in Mutualist Political Economy*, of the considerations that went into that elite policy[4]:

> The American corporate elite reacted in the 1970s to the combination of fiscal, accumulation and legitimation crises by adopting a neoliberal agenda of curtailing consumption and subsidizing new accumulation. Along with these new policies, it adopted the forms of political control necessary to force them on a recalcitrant population.
>
> Until the late 1960s, the elite perspective was governed by the New Deal social compact. The corporate state would buy stability and popular acquiescence in imperialist exploitation abroad by guaranteeing a level of prosperity and security to the middle class. In return for higher wages, unions would enforce management control of the workplace. As Richard K. Moore put it, prosperity would guarantee public passivity. But starting in the Vietnam era, the elite's thinking underwent a profound change.

1. *Ibid.*, pp. 62–64.
2. *Ibid.*, p. 79.
3. Preston Glidden comment under Kevin Carson, "Liberation Management, or Management by Stress?" Mutualist Blog: Free Market Anticapitalism, August 28, 2006 <http://mutualist.blogspot.com/2006/08/liberation-management-or-management-by.html>.
4. Kevin Carson, *Studies in Mutualist Political Economy*. Self-published via Blitzprint (Fayetteville, Ark., 2004), pp. 328–334.

They concluded from the 1960s experience that the social contract had failed. Besides unprecedented levels of activism in the civil rights and antiwar movements, and the general turn toward radicalism among youth, the citizenry at large also became less manageable. There was a proliferation of activist organizations, alternative media, welfare-rights organizations, community activism, etc.

Elite intellectuals like Samuel P. Huntington lamented the drastic decrease in the level of trust of government and other leading institutions among the general public. In *The Crisis of Democracy*, written by Huntington and others as an inaugural paper for the Trilateral Institution (an excellent barometer of elite thinking), the authors argued that the system was collapsing from demand overload, because of an excess of democracy . . .

For Huntington, America's role in maintaining the global state capitalist system depended on a domestic system of power; this system of power, variously referred to in this work as corporate liberalism, Cold War liberalism, and the welfare-warfare state, assumed a general public willingness to stay out of government affairs. For the first two decades or so after WWII, the U.S. had functioned as *"the hegemonic power in a system of world order."* And this was only possible because of a domestic structure of political authority in which the country *"was governed by the president acting with the support and cooperation of key individuals and groups in the Executive office, the federal bureaucracy, Congress, and the more important businesses, banks, law firms, foundations, and media, which constitute the private establishment."*

America's position as defender of global capitalism required that its government have the ability *"to mobilize its citizens for the achievement of social and political goals and to impose discipline and sacrifice upon its citizens in order to achieve these goals."* Most importantly, this ability required that democracy be largely nominal, and that citizens be willing to leave major substantive decisions about the nature of American society to qualified authorities. It required, in other words, "some measure of apathy and non-involvement on the part of some individuals and groups."

Unfortunately, these requirements were being gravely undermined by *"a breakdown of traditional means of social control, a delegitimation of political and other means of authority, and an overload of demands on government, exceeding its capacity to respond."*

. . . . The task of traditional state capitalist elites, in the face of this crisis of democracy, was to restore that "measure of apathy and noninvolvement," and thus to render the system once again "governable."

In response to the antiwar protests and race riots, LBJ and Nixon began to create an institutional framework for coordination of police state policy at the highest levels, to make sure that any such disorder in the future could be dealt with differently. This process culminated in *Department of Defense Civil Disturbance Plan 55-2, Garden Plot*, which involved domestic surveillance by the military, contingency plans for military cooperation with local police in suppressing disorder in all fifty states, plans for mass preventive detention, and joint exercises of police and the regular military . . . .

The New Deal social compact with organized labor was reassessed in the light of new events. The country was swept by a wave of wildcat strikes in the early 1970s . . . . These disruptions indicated that the business unions could no longer keep their rank and file under control, and that the Fordist system was no longer serving its purpose of maintaining social control in the workplace.

At the same time, the business press was flooded with articles on the impending "capital shortage," and calls for shifting resources from consumption to capital accumulation, by radically scaling back the welfare state and hamstringing organized labor. This shift was reflected in traditionally corporate liberal think tanks like Brookings and the CED, which both produced studies acknowledging the need to impose limits on consumption in the interest of accumulation; for example, the Brookings Institution's 1976 study *Setting National Priorities: The Next Ten Years.*

Business journals predicted frankly that a cap on real wages would be hard to force on the public in the existing political environment. For example, an article in the October 12, 1974 issue of *Business Week* warned that

Some people will obviously have to do with less . . . . [I]ndeed, cities and states, the home mortgage market, small business and the consumer will all get less than they want . . . . [I]t will be a hard pill for many Americans to swallow—the idea of doing with less so that big business can

*have more . . . . Nothing that this nation, or any other nation has done in modern history compares
in difficulty with the selling job that must now be done to make people accept the new reality.*

This only heightened the imperative to curb the excess of democracy and make the
state less vulnerable to popular pressure.

Corporations embraced the full range of union-busting possibilities in Taft-Hartley,
risking only token fines from the NLRB. They drastically increased management resources devoted to workplace surveillance and control, a necessity because of discontent
from stagnant wages and mounting workloads (aka increased "productivity").

. . . . Wages as a percentage of value added have declined drastically since the 1970s,
and real wages have been virtually flat. Virtually all increases in labor productivity have
been channeled into profit and investment, rather than wages . . . .

As policy elites attempted to transform the country into a two-tier society, a kinder
and gentler version of the Third World pattern, the threat of public discontent forced the
government to greater and greater levels of authoritarianism.

*The most obvious means of social control, in a discontented society, is a strong, semi-
militarized police force. Most of the periphery has been managed by such means for centuries. This
was obvious to elite planners in the West, was adopted as policy, and has now been largely implemented . . . .*

*So that the beefed-up police force could maintain control in conditions of mass unrest, elite
planners also realized that much of the Bill of Rights would need to be neutralized . . . . The
rights-neutralization project has been largely implemented, as exemplified by armed midnight raids,
outrageous search-and-seizure practices, overly broad conspiracy laws, wholesale invasion of privacy,
massive incarceration, and the rise of prison slave labor.*

"The Rubicon," Moore concludes, "has been *crossed—the techniques of oppression long
common in the empire's periphery are being imported to the core."*

With the help of the Drug War, and assorted Wars on Gangs, Terrorism, etc., the apparatus of repression continued to grow . . . .

This authoritarianism, in response to perceived disgruntlement over the clampdown,
has been reflected to an especially strong degree in the workplace. This was the theme of
David M. Gordon's *Fat and Mean: The Corporate Squeezing of Working Americans and the Myth
of Managerial Downsizing.* As the title suggests, management downsizing in the 80s and 90s
was largely a myth. In fact, the proportion of employees in supervisory positions has
grown, along with the proportion of total compensation going to management salaries.
Hierarchy, authoritarianism, and internal surveillance have increased, largely from their perceived necessity for dealing with a workforce disgruntled over stagnant wages and rising
work loads.

As Gordon observes, real hourly take home pay for production and non-supervisory
workers fell over ten percent from the mid-70s to the mid-90s, reaching roughly the same
levels as in the late '60s—this, despite the fact that per capita GDP in constant dollars was
53% higher.[1] Average non-supervisory wages skyrocketed, in 1994 dollars, from $6.40 in
1948 to $10.50 in 1972. Then from 1972 to 1992 they fell to $9.40.[2] During the 1980s,
while productivity growth averaged 12% a year, real wages actually *fell* by 0.6% a year.[3]

Meanwhile, despite the conventional view to the contrary, the proportion of managers and supervisors actually *grew* during the 1990s.[4] Executive, administrative and managerial employees in private, nonfarm employment rose from 12.6% to 13.2% of the labor
force. Managers made up 26.6% of nonfarm job growth from 1991-95.[5] In 1995, the Wall
Street Journal debunked the myth of management downsizing: the "corporate giants," as-

1. David M. Gordon, *Fat and Mean: The Corporate Squeeze of Working Americans and the Myth
of Management "Downsizing"* (New York: The Free Press, 1996), p. 4.
2. *Ibid.*, p. 19.
3. *Ibid.*, pp. 68-69.
4. *Ibid.*, p. 5.
5. *Ibid.*, pp. 52-54.

sociated with the most dramatic stories of managerial layoffs, had "more managers per 100 employees today than . . . in 1993."[1] What's more, the percentage of national income going to management was increased drastically. In 1973 40.4% of national income went to production workers, and 16.2% to supervisory employees. In 1993 the figures were 34.5% and 24.1%, respectively.[2] In other words, over twenty years management salaries rose from 28.6% to 41.1% of total employee compensation. The difference would have been enough to increase the hourly pay of production workers by almost 25%.

Cross-national comparisons are equally informative. Compared to 13% of the U.S. nonfarm private sector workforce, management was a much smaller proportion in Europe and Japan. On the European continent, the percentage ranged from 2.6% in Sweden to 6.8% in Norway; in Japan, it was 4.2%.

And bear in mind, as Seymour Melman points out, that the proportional increase in management was almost entirely for the sake of control, not efficiency:

> Within firms, managerial activity and costs proliferate independently of their effects on production. Studies of the relation between the costs of managing and the volume of industrial production have found either a negative correlation or the absence of any significant linkage at all. From 1977 to 1980, for example, the value of goods and services produced in the United States rose 7.9 percent, while employment of blue-collar and white-collar workers grew 2 and 12 percent respectively. The jobs of the blue-collar people were clearly linked to output; the tasks of the much-enlarged white-collar group were mainly undertaken for control rather than production . . . . Evidently the extension of such control has been given priority, even over profitability, in the mores of management . . . .
>
> . . . [T]he largest part of the growth [in administrative employees] has been in the functions that enhance control, not in those that increase production.[3]

Gordon's thesis is that the two trends, "the wage squeeze" and "the bureaucratic burden," are directly connected:

> In one direction, stagnant or falling wages create the need for intensive management supervision of frontline employees. If workers do not share in the fruits of the enterprise, if they are not provided a promise of job security and steady wage growth, what incentive do they have to work as hard as their bosses would like? So the corporations need to monitor the workers' effort and be able to threaten credibly to punish them if they do not perform. The corporations must wield the Stick. Eventually the stick requires millions of Stick-wielders.
>
> In the other direction, once top-heavy corporate bureaucracies emerge, they acquire their own, virtually ineluctable expansionary dynamic. They push for more numbers in their ranks and higher salaries for their members. Where does the money come from? . . . One of the most obvious targets is frontline workers' compensation. The more powerful the corporate bureaucracy becomes, and the weaker the pressure with which employees can counter, the greater the downward pressure on production workers' wages.[4]

As the cross-national statistics on the management burden above suggest, the facts tend to bear out this correlation. Gordon observes that high bureaucratic burdens tend to be associated with "conflictual" labor-management relations:

> "The United States has the highest amount of conflict between business and labor of any democratic nation," concludes MIT labor expert Thomas Cochran . . . .

1. Alex Markels, "Restructuring Alters Middle-Management Role But Leaves It Robust," *Wall Street Journal*, Sept. 25, 1995, in *Ibid.*, p. 58.

2. Gordon, *Fat and Mean*, p. 82.

3. Seymour Melman, *Profits Without Production* (New York: Alfred A. Knopf, 1985), pp. 70–71.

4. Gordon, *Fat and Mean.*, pp. 5–6.

In short, "fat" and "mean" go together like the proverbial horse and carriage. In our economy, it would appear, you can't have one without the other. The international data certainly feed such a suspicion, since the United States has recently featured *both* the slowest real wage growth *and* the top-heaviest corporate bureaucracies among the leading advanced economies.[1]

When workers have a high degree of job security and expectations of steady wage increases corresponding to productivity growth, they can be trusted "to coordinate many of their own activities in production, relieving their corporate owners of the need for intensive and continuous monitoring and supervision."

> With a coercive approach, by contrast, a much more fundamental conflict between owners and workers is likely to persist over workers' labor effort. Corporations are naturally interested in their employees working as hard as possible. In the absence of strong wage benefits and employment security, however, what provides the worker with the incentive to work anywhere nearly as intensively as the corporation would prefer? . . .
>
> The solution to such motivational problems . . . is a combination of intensive supervision of employees and the threat of job dismissal . . . .
>
> And so in the absence of the carrot, conflictual systems are likely to display legions of stick-wielders as one of their central features, armies of supervisors and managers saddled with the principal direct or indirect responsibility for ensuring that production and nonsupervisory workers don't shirk on the job . . . .
>
> Increasingly intensive supervision grew more and more necessary after the early 1970s because, far from sharing productivity dividends with employees as a way of spurring their effort, corporations on balance have been driving down wages and taking away other employee benefits and protections as well.[2]

The important thing to note about all these trends described by Gordon is that management doesn't just have a zero-sum relationship with workers. It has, to almost the same extent, a zero-sum relationship with stockholders. Gordon cites a meeting of twenty-one experts on corporate management in the late '70s; all of them agreed or agreed strongly with the statement that "In many cases control and power are more important to managers than profits or productivity." The management hierarchy possesses a great deal of autonomy, and tends to promote its own expansion at the expense of both wages and profits. Management tends to engage in featherbedding at the expense both of worker compensation *and* returns on equity.[3]

Note, especially, some indicators in Gordon's account—you might miss them if you don't look closely—of corporate management's veto-power over organized capital. For one thing, note that the policy elites of the early '70s did not see high *management* compensation as competing for the resources needed for capital investment. Although the compensation of hourly workers declined drastically from 1973 to 1993, according to Gordon's figures above, they were *more than offset* by the rise in management salaries. In fact, the total compensation of production workers and management together *rose* from 56.6% to 58.6% of national income during that period. So if there were a zero-sum relationship between employee compensation and investment, then the workplace policies of the past thirty years have increased, not reduced, total employee compensation at the expense of funds available for investment. On the other hand, once the decision was made to discipline production workers, the increased levels of hierarchy and supervision required made capital even more dependent on management and more vulnerable to management self-dealing and other agency problems.

1. *Ibid.*, p. 62.
2. *Ibid.*, pp. 65–66, 68.
3. *Ibid.*, pp. 75–78.

Work monitoring has become much more intensive. Peter Skott and Frederick Guy suggest that the introduction of automation and monitoring capability is responsible for the stagnation of wages in service industry over the past generation. "Power-biased technological change," by enabling management to monitor unskilled and semi-skilled labor more closely, has reduced the bargaining power of labor—thus simultaneously increasing work intensity and exerting a downward pressure on wages.[1] With such technology, management can control the pace of work in service industry in the same way that an automated production line does in manufacturing.

Of course, as we will see in the next chapter, such a strategy has built-in limits. While management may be able to monitor selected aspects of effort expenditure, there are always some aspects of the workplace environment that are not amenable to effective monitoring. As Oliver Williamson showed, workers are apt to maintain adequate levels of effort in areas of job performance that are monitored, while shifting to perfunctory cooperation (or worse) in areas that are not effectively monitored. And if workers become disgruntled enough over the pace of work, they can probably find ways to impose astronomical cost increases in the areas not amenable to monitoring, with little or no chance of getting caught. I can testify from personal experience, in an increasingly downsized and sped-up hospital, that this is no mere theoretical possibility. The costs from employee disgruntlement—deliberate waste and destruction, and supplies given away free to patients rather than being charged to their accounts—probably exceed by far what would have been the cost of hiring adequate levels of staff and raising their pay to acceptable levels.

The need for monitoring and surveillance probably has a lot to do with the failure of telecommuting to live up to the early hype. Chris Dillow, of *Stumbling and Mumbling* blog, writes on the culture of "presenteeism":

> [A]n often overlooked feature of the new economy . . . [is] that many workers now have more and better capital equipment at home than they do at work.
>
> This destroys the traditional reason for going out to work; in industrial societies we had to go to factories because that was where the machinery was.
>
> With this reason no longer applying for many of us, one would expect to have seen an explosion in the numbers of people working from home. After all, there are enormous costs to having workplaces separate from our homes; commuting and rent to name but two.
>
> However, teleworking is still rare . . . .
>
> . . . I suspect the main obstacle to the growth of teleworking is not technology but power. Offices (and maybe factories too) exist not because they are technically efficient but because they provide easy ways for the boss class to supervise and control workers.

In the course of his argument, he cited Stephen Marglin's excellent article "What Do Bosses Do?"[2] which argued that the advantage of the factory lay less in its superior technical efficiencies over home production, than in its superior efficiency at securing effort and extracting surplus value from the laborer. As evidence that the surprising failure of telecommuting to take off reflected similar interests, he cites the fact "that teleworkers contain disproportionate numbers of self-employed," which he takes as evidence "that working for others means subordination, which means working in offices even when it is not technically necessary to do so?"[3]

---

1. Peter Skott and Frederick Guy, "A Model of Power-Biased Technological Change," September 14, 2006 <http://www.people.umass.edu/pskott/SkottGuyFinalVersion13Sept2006.pdf>.

2. Steven A. Marglin. "What Do Bosses Do? The Origins and Functions of Hierarchy in Capitalist Production—Part I" *Review of Radical Political Economics* 6:2 (Summer 1974).

3. Chris Dillow, "Capitalism and Presenteeism," *Stumbling and Mumbling* blog, June 21, 2005 <http://stumblingandmumbling.typepad.com/stumbling_and_mumbling/2005/06/capitalism_and_.html>.

Claire Wolfe also noted the conspicuous absence of telecommuting, at least on the scale predicted fifteen years ago:

> Although computer-based "knowledge work" hasn't enabled millions of us to leave the corporate world and work at home (as, again, it was supposed to), that's more a problem of corporate power psychology than of technology. Our bosses fear to "let" us work permanently at home; after all, we might take 20-minute coffee breaks, instead of 10![1]

Personality profiling and testing are also becoming much more intrusive. Increasingly paranoid about employee disgruntlement (probably in part because of their own bad consciences), management tries ever more obsessively to root out any evidence their workers may be concealing non-Stepford Wife opinions behind a facade of obedience.

For example, Barbara Ehrenreich mentions an interview with Wal-Mart at a job fair, of which the centerpiece was a four-page "opinion survey" ("no right or wrong answers," according to the rather dubious assurance of the interviewer). Among other things, it asks "whether management is to blame if things go wrong . . . ."[2] Well, I guess that depends on whether the guy who cuts you off at the knees is responsible for you falling down.

> What these tests tell employers about potential employees is hard to imagine, since the "right" answers should be obvious to anyone who has ever encountered the principle of hierarchy and domination. Do I work well with others? You bet, but never to the point where I would hesitate to inform on them for the slightest infraction. Am I capable of independent decision making? Oh yes, but I know better than to let this capacity interfere with a slavish obedience to others . . . . Naturally, I "never" find it hard "to stop moods of self-pity," nor do I imagine that others are talking about me behind my back or believe that "management and employees will always be in conflict because they have totally different sets of goals." The real function of these tests, I decide, is to convey information not to the employer but to the potential employee, and the information being conveyed is always: You will have no secrets from us. We don't just want your muscles and that part of your brain that is directly connected to them, we want your innermost self.[3]

> Now, my approach to preemployment personality tests has been zero tolerance vis-a-vis the obvious "crimes"—drug use and theft—but to leave a little wriggle room elsewhere, just so it doesn't look like I'm faking out the test. When presenting yourself as a potential employee, you can never be too much of a suck-up. Take the test proposition that "rules have to be followed to the letter at all times": I had agreed to this only "strongly" rather than "very strongly" or "totally" and now Roberta wants to know why.[4]

D. AUTHORITARIANISM: CONTRACT FEUDALISM

The term "contract feudalism" was coined by Elizabeth Anderson in a post at *Left2Right* blog:

> . . . Under feudalism, wealthy landlords employed hundreds of retainers, servants, and tenants who depended on them for subsistence. The price of dependence was servility: the duty to obey any arbitrary whim, however humiliating, called out as an order to them by their lord. Commerce and manufactures liberated individuals from such abject servility, by enabling people to live off sales to thousands of customers instead of one

---

1. Claire Wolfe, "Dark Satanic Cubicles," *Loompanics 1995 Catalog* <http://www.loompanics.com/cgi-local/SoftCart.exe/Articles/darksatanic.html> (Loompanics site now defunct; link no longer active).
2. Barbara Ehrenreich, *Nickel and Dimed: On (Not) Getting By in America* (New York: Henry Holt and Co., 2001), p. 58.
3. *Ibid.*, p. 59.
4. *Ibid.*, p. 124.

master. It enabled large numbers of people to enjoy personal independence for the first time . . . .

Of course, matters were different for wage laborers than for independent shopkeepers and craftsmen. Wage laborers *did* have to obey an arbitrary master on the factory floor.

But their subjection to this authority was mitigated, and their personal dependence from the employer secured, by

the separation of work from the home. However arbitrary and abusive the boss may have been on the factory floor, when work was over the workers could at least escape *his* tyranny . . . . Again, in the early phase of industrialization, this was small comfort, given that nearly every waking hour was spent at work. But as workers gained the right to a shortened workday—due to legislation as well as economic growth—the separation of work from home made a big difference to workers' liberty from their employers' wills.

Nevertheless, to the extent that this liberty is secured by competition for workers and convention alone, rather than by legal right, it is vulnerable to invasion.[1]

And sure enough, as the bargaining power of labor has decreased over the past thirty years, the separation of work from the home has undergone steady erosion. A growing portion of the workforce finds itself subject to management whims even away from the job, and personal time subject to intrusion from work, in a way quite reminiscent of the feudal vassal's 24/7 subjection to his master's whims. Hence Anderson's term "contract feudalism": the contractual alienation of personal independence by propertyless people, whose lack of bargaining power renders them vulnerable, in return for subsistence, and the corresponding conversion of the propertied classes' ownership into dominion over people.[2]

Contract feudalism covers a wide range of events that have been in the news lately. One is described by Anderson in her blog post. According to the New York Times,[3] Howard Weyers, president of Michigan-based Weyco, in early 2005 forbade his workers to smoke—"not just at work but anywhere else." The policy, taken in response to the rising cost of health coverage, requires workers to submit to nicotine tests.

Guardsmark, a security company, forbids its workers to socialize with each other off the job—a policy upheld by an NLRB ruling. The *Washington Post*'s Harold Meyerson compares the employer's power to issue such arbitrary commands to the power of—you guessed it—a feudal lord:

There's a word for the kind of employer-employee relationship that the NLRB has just sanctioned. It's "feudal." The brave new world that emerges from this ruling looks a lot like the bad old world where earls and dukes had the power to control the lives of their serfs—not just when the serfs were out tilling the fields but when they retired in the evening to the comfort of their hovels. But then the Bill of Rights in America has never reached very far into the workplace. And now, the strictures on workers' rights within the workplace are being extended without.[4]

An especially alarming trend is "Doocing," i.e. the firing of bloggers for public comments written on their own time: for example, Joe Gordon, editor of the Woolamaloo Gazette[5] blog, who was fired from Waterstone's (a UK chain bookstore roughly comparable to

1. Elizabeth Anderson, "Adventures in Contract Feudalism," Left2Right blog, Feb. 10, 2005 <http://left2right.typepad.com/main/2005/02/adventures_in_c.html>.

2. Elizabeth Anderson, "How Not to Complain About Taxes (II): Against Natural Property Rights," Left2Right blog, Jan. 20, 2005 <http://left2right.typepad.com/main/2005/01/why_i_reject_na.html>.

3. *NYT*, Feb. 8, 2005 <http://www.nytimes.com/2005/02/08/business/08smoking.html>.

4. Harold Meyerson, "Big Brother on and Off the Job," *Washington Post*, Aug. 10, 2005 <http://www.washingtonpost.com/wp-dyn/content/article/2005/08/09/AR2005080901162.html>.

5. <http://www.woolamaloo.org.uk/>

B&N) when it came to his bosses' attention that he'd made the occasional venting post (quite mild, from my perspective) after a particularly bad day at work.[1]

Blogger B.K Marcus, in discussing his experiences with libertarian writers who later attempt to remove their writings from the Web, hints that some of them might be motivated by the fear of what a prospective employer might stumble upon.[2] The danger is a very real one. As someone who was hunting a job myself only three years ago, and as a prolific writer with a large body of online material on radical political and economic themes, I well remember my paranoia that HR Nazis might Google my name during the application process.

Workers are increasingly required to be on-call for extended periods, or reachable at all times, during what used to be called "their own time." Consider, for example, the "open availability" policy of some Wal-Mart stores, which regional management also tried to make official company policy:

> Wal-Mart officials in Cross Lanes told employees on Tuesday they have to start working practically any shift, any day they're asked, even if they've built up years of seniority and can't arrange child care . . . .
>
> "We have many people with set schedules who aren't here when we need them for our customers," said John Knuckles, a manager at the store, which is located in the Nitro Marketplace shopping center and employs more than 400.
>
> "It is to take care of the customers, that's the only reason," he said.
>
> Workers who have had regular shifts at the store for years now have to commit to being available for any shift from 7 a.m. to 11 p.m., seven days a week. If they can't make the commitment by the end of this week, they'll be fired.
>
> "It shouldn't cause any problem, if they [store employees] are concerned about their customers," Knuckles said.
>
> Several single mothers working at the store have no choice now but to quit, said one employee, who would not give her name for fear of retribution . . . .
>
> Along with the "open-availability" policy, the store is requiring all floor employees to learn how to run cash registers, several employees said. They suspect this is an attempt to brace for the departure of many of the employees who now work as cashiers.
>
> When announcing the new policies, store managers said they expected to lose about 60 people, according to another employee who asked not to be named.
>
> "They said sales were down so much, they had to make a change," the worker said. "The past year they've really been nitpicking" longer-term employees, who are paid more.[3]

Although the Wal-Mart stores involved in the story beat a hasty retreat in the face of intense public criticism, there is some indication similar policies have since been implemented on a store-wide level.

> . . . . Sally Wright, 67, an $11-an-hour greeter at the Wal-Mart in Ponca City, Okla., said she quit in August after 22 years with the company when managers pressed her to make herself available to work any time, day or night.
>
> . . . . The company says it gives employees three weeks' notice of their schedules and takes their preferences into account, but that description differs from those of many workers interviewed. Workers said that their preferences were often ignored and that they were often given only a few days' notice of scheduling changes . . . .

1. Patrick Barkham, "Blogger sacked for sounding off," *The Guardian*, Jan. 12, 2005 <http://www.guardian.co.uk/online/weblogs/story/0,14024,1388466,00.html> (link defunct); Ken Macleod, "The Case of the Blogging Bookseller," *The Early Days of a Better Nation*, Jan. 12. 2005 <http://kenmacleod.blogspot.com/2005_01_01_kenmacleod_archive.html#110551826393727206>.

2. B. K. Marcus, "The Memory Hole," *lowercase liberty* blog, Jan. 19, 2005 <http://www.bkmarcus.com/blog/2005/01/memory-hole.html>.

3. Joe Morris, "Wal-Mart institutes availability requirement," *The Charleston Gazette*, June 15, 2005, in *Wake Up Wal-Mart* blog <http://www.wakeupwalmart.com/news/20050615-cg.html>.

A big area of discrepancy between what Wal-Mart says and what the workers say is whether the company has a policy of "open availability," requiring employees to make themselves available around the clock. Ms. Clark, the Wal-Mart spokeswoman, said the company had no such a policy, adding, "Our main goal is to match the ratio of associates to customers shopping in our stores resulting in better customer service hour by hour." Wal-Mart says it pays higher wages to night-shift workers.

But in March, workers from a Wal-Mart in Nitro, W.Va., held a small protest rally in the center of town after Wal-Mart managers demanded 24-hour availability and cut the hours of workers who balked. And workers from other stores around the country said in interviews that similar demands had been made on them.

Houston Turcott, the former overnight stocking manager at the Wal-Mart in Yakima, Wash., said that managers had told workers, "Either they had full, open availability so we can schedule them when we would like or we would cut their hours."

Tracie Sandin, who worked in the Yakima store's over-the-counter drug department until last February, said, "They said, if you don't have open availability, you're put on the bottom of the list for hours."[1]

The use of "concern about the customers" to justify such policies is especially telling. A major aspect of contract feudalism is the extension of the "professionalist" ideology into even unskilled service jobs. The minimum wage housekeeper, retail or restaurant worker is now expected to have the same sense of "calling," of dedication to customer service, and of career as a source of identity, as members of the traditional professions—but without the pay or the autonomy.

E. AUTHORITARIANISM: THE HEGEMONY OF "PROFESSIONALISM"

The professionalist ideology is closely linked to contract feudalism. Consider, again, our discussion above of the level of single-minded dedication to "customer service," the 24/7 availability, and the identification with one's job as a career, required even from un-skilled service workers.

The only area of the job market where such things were expected, before the 1970s, was the white collar salariat of "professional" employees. For a good fictional example, take a look at Darren Stevens on the TV series *Bewitched*, a white collar "professional" in the advertising industry. Most of the comic situations on the show hinged on frequent "visits" to Stevens' house by his boss, Larry Tate, a partner in the advertising firm, and Stevens' need to entertain clients at home. Stevens was constantly having to explain his unusual life-style to Larry, who obviously felt entitled to an explanation. And that intrusion in itself, remember, wasn't meant to be viewed as especially comical by the audience; it was just a set-up for all the wacky comic situations resulting from Samantha's witchcraft. The back-ground itself was just based on the common understanding of what life was like for the "organization man."

As a comedy of "how the other half lives," it was especially humorous to the blue-collar manufacturing worker just because it was so unlike his own way of life. Imagine a master machinist in the IAM tolerating constant drop-in visits from a foreman, who felt entitled to demand explanations for odd happenings in the machinist's home! At the time, such intrusion of the "career" into one's homelife was associated entirely with white collar work. As Orwell's character George Bowling put it in *Coming Up for Air*,

> There's a lot of rot talked about the sufferings of the working class. I'm not so sorry for the proles myself . . . . The prole suffers physically, but he's a free man when he isn't working. But in every one of those little stucco boxes there's some poor bastard who's

---

1. Steven Greenhouse and Michael Barbaro, "Wal-Mart to Add Wage Caps and Part-Timers," *The New York Times*, October 2, 2006 <http://www.nytimes.com/2006/10/02/business/02walmart.html>.

NEVER free except when he's fast asleep and dreaming that he's got the boss down the bottom of a well and is bunging lumps of coal at him.

But except for a very small and shrinking remnant of unionized manufacturing workers, "we're all organization men now." The ethos of white collar "professionalism" has contaminated a major part of wage labor.

The concept of professionalism has achieved an unprecedented hegemony in society at large. For a very large part of the population, one's identity as "a professional" is the main source of reference. People commonly, in situations where they are required to sum themselves up, simply identify themselves as professionals. In the 1950s, it was common for someone to refer to himself, in situations completely removed from politics or government, as "just an ordinary citizen," or the like. Today, for many in the white collar middle class, it's "a professional." Professionalism has acquired the same ideological significance once held by civic culture and citizenship. In either case, the individual was defined in terms of some particular authority relation in which he existed.

Letters to advice columnists commonly begin with some phrase like this: "Dear Abby, my husband and I are both professionals in our 40s . . . ." The implied subtext, of course, is " . . . so obviously this isn't something we caused by our own stupidity," or " . . . so this is a legitimate problem, unlike those of most of the beer-swilling yahoos who read your column."

The concept of the profession has also largely supplanted that of the skilled trade in the occupational realm. The adjective "professional" is used almost exclusively to describe work or behavior that once would have been described as "businesslike," or characterized by a sense of craftsmanship. "Professional" and "unprofessional" are used as words of praise and blame, respectively, in occupations that were never regarded as professions back when the term had any meaning. People in virtually all white collar or service jobs, regardless of the level of training associated with them, are expected to display "professionalism" in their work attitudes and dress.

The ideology of "professionalism" has spread like a cancer and contaminated most occupations. Originally, the culture of the professions grew out of the skilled trades. A master of arts, for example, was analogous to a master of any other trade, with bachelors and undergraduates corresponding to journeymen and apprentices; a university was a place where one apprenticed to a master scholar. As we saw in Chapter Four, in the nineteenth century even the professions of medicine and law were generally perpetuated by some sort of informal apprenticeship system, rather than standardized education and occupational licensing. But I'd gladly compromise on the original five professions—letters, medicine, law, holy orders, and arms—if we could only reclaim the concept of the skilled trade for everything else.

So why has professionalism so successfully colonized the entire realm of work? Who benefits from promoting it as an ideology? What functions does it serve?

The fundamental purpose of professionalism, like that of any other ideology, is to get people's minds right—in this case, workers.

Professionalism fosters a house-slave mentality by getting large categories of workers to identify with management (Good ole Massa knows we're really like him, not like those shiftless old field slaves), setting white collar against blue collar workers, and enabling management to rule through a divide-and-conquer strategy. There's a saying that a dishonest man is the easiest target for a con artist. Likewise, it's a lot easier to exploit a status-insecure snob, as long as he can be a notch or two above someone else who's exploited worse.

Professionalism undermines the separation of work and home. Throughout the entire service sector, increasingly, low-paid wage workers are expected to think of their job as a calling, and of customer service as something to sacrifice "ownlife" for. In nursing, a trade that fell under the spell of professionalism long ago, this is old news. For all of living memory, hospital managements have cynically manipulated nurses' concern for their patients to guilt them into working unwanted overtime. This is often done, deliberately, in preference to hiring enough staff to avoid overtime, because it economizes on the costs of benefits.

But the phenomenon has spread far beyond licensed nurses. As we saw in the reference in the section above to Wal–Mart's 24/7 availability policy, the same kind of selfless "professional" dedication is now required in the lowest levels of the two-tier economy.

Ken Blanchard has expressed great dissatisfaction with the TGIF mentality, speaking for many managers who resent their workers' view of the job as a means to an end, and of their life in the outside world as the end their job serves. As Blanchard put it in his introduction to the *Fish! Philosophy* book, "too many people are trading time on the job to satisfy needs elsewhere . . ." Imagine that! People view going to a place where they're treated like a disposable resource, worked like dogs, and required to take orders, as a necessary evil, rather than looking forward to it as the central source of meaning in their lives.

Finally, management tries to identify "professionalism" with obedience and docility. This means, in concrete terms, that talking back to management and fighting for one's rights are forms of conduct unbecoming "a professional." Pressuring management to improve working conditions, reduce hours, increase staffing or pay, and the like, are the kinds of "low-class" behavior that slobs like Ralph Kramden engage in—not for respectable wannabes like us.

In the old days, before the metastatic spread of professionalism diluted its meaning, professions tended to maintain a collegial mentality, an internal solidarity, against the demands of authority—much like the master craftsmen who resisted the watering down of quality in the industrial revolution. A professional might resist unreasonable demands from outside, like a demand to do substandard work or cut corners to compensate for understaffing, because of professional pride. Today, outside the old-line professions, professionalism has ceased to be a moral basis for resistance to authority, and instead become another force for promoting obedience and identification with authority.

This aspect of professionalism gets back to the divide and conquer function I mentioned above: "professionalism" means seeing oneself in the same social category as management (albeit at a lower rung), and as part of the same "team." It's the vicarious self-esteem acquired by a house slave who identifies with the owner rather than with the field slaves. Professionalism, along with the rest of the meritocratic ideology of which it is a part, is used to legitimize job segmentation and hierarchy within the enterprise. The effect is to set blue and white collar workers in competition against each other, and to coopt white collar workers into identification with management rather than labor.

> In U.S. economic life, legitimation has been intimately bound up with the techno-cratic-meritocratic ideology . . . .
>
> This legitimation of capitalism as a social system has its counterpart in the individual's personal life. Then, just as individuals must come to accept the overall social relations of production, so workers must respect the authority and competence of their own "supervisors" to direct their activities, and justify their own authority . . . over others . . . .
>
> This meritocratic ideology has remained a dominant theme of the mainstream of social science since the rise of the factory system in the United States. The robustness of this perspective . . . is due, in no small part, to its incorporation in major social institutions—factories, offices, government bureaus, and schools. For the technocratic justification of the hierarchical division of labor leads smoothly to a meritocratic view of the process by which individuals are matched to jobs. An efficient and impersonal bureaucracy, so the story goes, assesses the individual purely in terms of his or her expected contribution to production. And the main determinants of job fitness are seen to be those cognitive and psychomotor capacities relevant to the worker's technical ability to do the job . . . .

The linking of technical skills to economic success indirectly via the educational system strengthens . . . the legitimation process. First, the day-to-day contact of parents and children with the competitive, cognitively oriented school environment, with clear connections to the economy, buttresses, in a very immediate and concrete way, the technocratic perspective on economic organization . . . . Second, by rendering the outcome (educational attainment) dependent not only on ability but also on motivation, drive to achieve, perseverance, and sacrifice, the status allocation mechanism acquires heightened legitimacy. Moreover, such personal attributes are tested and developed over a long period of time, underlining the apparent objectivity and achievement orientation of the stratification system.[1]

The talking head commentariat of the corporate center (the New Deal liberal, New Democrat, and neoconservative strands of mainstream politics are almost equally managerialist) are decidedly meritocratic in their view of contemporary economic issues. For all of them, the main cause for the ill fortunes of the bottom tier of the labor force under globalization is the lack of adequate education to get with the program, and the solution for everybody is education and more education. Stern but avuncular figures ranging from Dr. Phil to Bill Cosby solemnly remind teenagers that the only way to success is to "get an education." Neoconservative practitioners of "tough love" stridently assert that the solution to all our educational ills is more "discipline," hierarchy, school uniforms, along with a greater homework burden and the dedication of every waking hour to drilling for the SATS or testing mandated by "No Child Left Behind." Correspondence school commercials show grousing workers confronted by a boss who says "I used to have a 'dead end job' just like you, until I went back to school to become a boss—and you can too!"

This is a classic example of the fallacy of composition, as we saw Joe Bageant argue in Chapter Four. The state capitalist system can only use so many managerial and technical workers. The effect of expanded managerial and technical education is merely to overproduce white collar workers, so that the educational requirements for menial labor are inflated and those who manage to win the musical chairs competition for white collar jobs wind up adopting a dog-eat-dog mentality toward those whom they beat out.

The managerialist-meritocratic perspective also ignores several central, salient facts: 1) in most cases the education and credentialing imposed by professionalism are far in excess of any level that could be justified by the objective requirements of any actual tasks to be performed; 2) the system selects for the most hierarchical and technocratic ways of organizing production, even when the same quality of output could be achieved by less deskilling technology, for the sake of rendering the workforce more amenable to control; and 3) for most tasks involved in coordinating and organizing production, the most important source of qualification is direct experience in the process, and the typical pointy-haired boss is often clueless as to the real effect of his decisions on the production process.

F. MOTIVATIONAL PROPAGANDA AS A SUBSTITUTE FOR REAL INCENTIVES

Ever since social science was applied to the workplace in the early 20th century, there has been no dearth of humanistic theories of employee relations; the Human Relations movement and Theory Y management are the most prominent early examples. Unfortunately, their implementation has been limited almost entirely to lip service. More than one commentator has observed that they amount, in practice, to sugar-coated Taylorism or Theory X management. Tom Peters, for example, dismissed the great majority of corporate motivational programs, despite all the "respect for others" and "golden rule" rhetoric, as either

1. Samuel Bowles and Herbert Gintis, *Schooling in Capitalist America: Educational Reform and the Contradictions of Economic Life* (New York: Basic Books, Inc., Publishers, 1976), pp. 104-106.

"lip service" or "gimmicks," intended mainly to "serve as a smoke-screen while management continues to get away with not doing its job of real people involvement."[1]

The reason isn't hard to find: it's because all such management theory fads, no matter
how humanistic and empowering their rhetoric, are implemented by bosses. And the primary interest of management is in cementing its control of the workplace and its ability to
derive status and perks from that position of control. So the main thing adopted from fashionable theories of worker empowerment is the jargon. The jargon of "empowerment" is
used as motivational propaganda to elicit more effort from workers who have no real share
in decisionmaking, no real control over the work process, and no real share in the productivity gains from working more efficiently.

And from the start, the empowering part of humanistic theories of management was
largely superficial. As Thomas Frank said, "Whether Taylorist or humanist, theories of management were sold as a way of defusing class conflict while keeping control of the shop
floor firmly in the hands of the owners."[2] That's especially true of the fads of the '90s:
Deming, quality circles, Six Sigma, and the like. While Deming himself was a brilliant observer of the production process, the managers who have ostensibly adopted his ideas have
in fact adopted only the rhetoric. The very workplaces that most energetically used Kwality rhetoric were also most likely to try fixing process problems with slogans and exhortations, and to take behavioral approaches to solving problems caused by management (see
Appendix, "Blaming Workers for the Results of Mismanagement").

Thomas Frank noted the contrast between the empowering rhetoric, the talk about
"openness" and "flattening hierarchies," and the actual practice of tightening control:

> Plenty of average Americans, having considerable personal experience with the way
> the corporation worked, could easily have made their own contributions to the national
> conversation about the nature of the "business revolution." They could have pointed out
> that the most noticeable change that swept through the workplaces of the late eighties
> and nineties was the diverging fortunes of top management and everyone else; that the
> workplace was becoming ever more arbitrary; that they increasingly worked under an
> omnipresent threat of instant termination; that regardless of how they toiled they seemed
> always to be losing ground . . . .[3]

> Talk to many of those blue-collar workers and you will discover that they are quite
> right to fear the "new openness." Great displays of soulfulness by top management, they
> find, often go hand in hand with a species of shop-floor Taylorism so advanced and con-
> centrated as to be almost inhuman. Management talks of the liberating power of "crazi-
> ness"; workers get a life so regimented and rationalized that I have even heard rumors,
> from blue-collar workers whose sensitive managers put them on twelve-hour rotating
> shifts, of deliberate corporate plans to wear them out, shave a year or two off their lives,
> and thus save millions in pension outlays. In this experience, talk of empowerment, par-
> ticipation, and reengineering is followed automatically by intensification of management
> demands.[4]

> . . . Every new theory, new buzzword, new movement, new consultant seems . . .
> merely to offer another means to the same goal: fewer workers, more output . . . . What
> is an intellectual playground for an entire class of consultants and gurus is, for the vast
> majority of working Americans, a living hell of surveillance and degradation in which
> every emotion is faked and every response is anticipated.[5]

1. Thomas J. Peters and Robert H. Waterman, *In Search of Excellence: Lessons from America's
Best-Run Companies* (New York: Warner Books, 1982), p. 241.

2. Thomas Frank, *One Market Under God: Extreme Capitalism, Market Populism, and the End of
Economic Democracy* (New York: Anchor Books, 2001), p.227.

3. *Ibid.*, p. 171.

4. *Ibid.*, p. 246.

5. *Ibid.*, p. 248.

We will reserve for Chapter Ten most discussion of management fads like reeingi-neering, as they affect the actual organization of production. Our main concern here is with programs aimed at motivating workers.

Probably the most notorious such programs in recent years have been *Who Moved My Cheese?* and Fish! Philosophy. *Who Moved My Cheese?* was the premier motivational fad of the '90s, and Fish! essentially recycled the very same themes for this decade.

Many of the themes of *WWMC?* were foreshadowed in Tom Lagana's *Chicken Soup* series. Lagana and his *Chicken Soup* books were described in this way by the—unfortunately now defunct—Molotov Cocktail for the Soul site:

> Snatching hypocritical victory from the jaws of defeat, this electrical engineer turned mind engineer is now complicit with his old "redundancy eliminators." He now helps "organizations who want to get the most out of people;" and those people would, of course, be the Prozac-plied personnel now doing twice the work they would have at the same position twenty years ago and are too sedated to feel the boss's whip cracking across their backs. "[Lagana] put a smile on my face and it stayed there even after I went back to work," gushes one successfully sheered sheep, her organization now getting the most out of her. "I already feel less stress as I apply some of the techniques," bleated an-other after scampering from a Lagana seminar payed for by the Firm.[1]

Lagana repeatedly asked that this "hateful" review be taken down, so apparently it must have struck home.

Who Moved My Cheese?, by Spencer Johnson, was created as a management tool for dealing with "change resisters." So naturally, it's a big favorite of HR departments every-where, who order it by the gross for employee consumption.

In Spencer Johnson's world, change, like cheese, is something that "just happens." Much like Tom Friedman's version of globalization, it's not the product of human action, but an inevitable and impersonal force of nature. We're expected to accept "change" as it comes, and deal with it within whatever framework is established by the anonymous gods in white coats who structure the maze.

In fact, Johnson's recipe for "dealing with change in your work and in your life" is a lot like the medieval peasant's fatalistic acceptance of one ruler after another, washing over him in succession like a series of tidal waves. "Keep your head down, do your work, pay your rent, don't look beyond your station in life—and don't, above all, meddle in the af-fairs of the great lords." It's also a bit like Parsons' enthusiastic embrace of "change" in 1984: "The choco-ration's been increased to 20 grammes. Doubleplusgood, eh?"

The fundamental, unquestioned assumption of *Who Moved My Cheese?* is that "change" is the prerogative of management, and that it's our job to adjust to it. As Thomas Frank pointedly observes, there's one question we're never to ask:

> While most of us must "adapt to change," others get to make change; while most of us are expected to smilingly internalize management theory, to learn our place in the world from vapid fairy tales, others buy the insulting stuff in bulk in order to cram it down the throats of thousands who have the misfortune to work in the bigperson's in-surance agency or box factory.
>
> Will the time ever come, Americans might well ask, when *we* get to move *manage-ment's* cheese?

This assessment of *WMMC?* is fairly common. Consider these excerpts from my fa-vorite Amazon reviews of it:

1. Rejuvenal, "Molotov Cocktail for Tom Lagana's Soul," July 1998. *Molotov Cocktail for the Soul* site <http://www.connect.ab.ca/~mctsoul/lagana.htm> (defunct—available only through In-ternet Archive).

If you are a manager who wants to be excused for his/her bad decisions by disguising them as "change" that "just happens," this is the book you should make mandatory reading for your employees.

That's how a lot of corporate America works, after all: companies do not make mistakes, it's the employees who cannot adapt to "change."

★ ★ ★

This book is wrong. It teaches that you must accept change without regard to whether it is appropriate it not. It teaches that you must not struggle, you must not fight. You must simply accept whatever change happens. This is the perfect book to distribute when a company is going through reorganization . . . .

I found it especially interesting that so many employees have come to recognize their employer's distribution, promotion, and forced reading of *Who Moved My Cheese?* as a prelude to layoffs.

That's the common perception of the book, and if Spencer Johnson's comment in an endpaper blurb is any indication, he resents the hell out of it:

> Some even fear it suggests all change is good and that people should mindlessly conform to unnecessary changes imposed by others, although that is not in the story.[1]

No, it's just implicit in *every single page* of this wretched little turd of a book. The real question is, how could a reader *not* make such an interpretation?

First of all, Johnson's pissing and moaning is directly across from a facing page full of enthusiastic endorsements from "organizations" that used the book to get their employees' minds right. This is our first clue that there might be a hidden agenda. The fact that WMMC?'s website is geared toward corporate clients might also raise some eyebrows. Like both the earlier *Chicken Soup for the Soul* series and the later Fish!, the book's prime customer is HR departments.

As more than one Amazon reviewer noted, the "book" is a heavily marked up piece of fluff, specifically designed to be marketed in bulk to HR departments, who in turn pass it on to a captive audience of wage-serfs. And a lot of those employees, mindful of Haw's slogan "Noticing Small Changes Early Helps You Adapt To The Bigger Changes That Are To Come,"[2] see the distribution of this book as a prelude to downsizing or a general tightening of the screws on the "littlepeople." If your employers start passing out *WWMC?*, just remember what Victor said in that *Ren and Stimpy* cartoon: "Relax and think happy thoughts, because this is really . . . gonna . . . HURT!"

Just about every page of *Who Moved My Cheese?* has something to bear out the interpretation that Johnson finds so objectionable. It is full of examples of people wisely adapting to "change" and being rewarded, and obstinate "change resisters" who suffer the consequences of their folly. The leading character, Haw, at first questions change and then discovers the error of his ways. But there is not one single, solitary example of a character questioning change, deciding that it was unjustified, and turning out to be right. The only character in the book who even raises the question of who is responsible for change and whether it is justified, Hem, is portrayed as unattractively as possible.

> "What? No Cheese?" Hem yelled. He continued yelling, "No Cheese? No Cheese?" as though if he shouted loud enough someone would put it back.
> "Who moved my Cheese?" he hollered.
> Finally, he put his hands on his hips, his face turned red, and he screamed at the top of his voice, "It's not fair!"[3]

---

1. Spencer Johnson, *Who Moved My Cheese? An A-Mazing Way To Deal With Change In Your Work And In Your Life* (New York: G.P. Putnam's Sons, 1998, 2002), p. iv.
2. *Ibid.*, p. 68.
3. *Ibid.*, p. 33.

When Hem even raises the question of who moved the cheese, and why, it's portrayed as the moral equivalent of a toddler's temper tantrum.

"Why should we change?" Hem asked. "We're littlepeople. We're special. This sort of thing should not happen to us. Or if it does, we should at least get some benefits."

"Why should we get benefits?" Haw asked.

"Because we're entitled," Hem claimed . . . .

"Why?" Haw asked.

"Because we didn't cause this problem," Hem said. "Somebody else did this and we should get something out of it."

Haw suggested, "Maybe we should simply stop analyzing the situation and go find some New Cheese?"[1]

It's kind of hard to make a reasoned evaluation of whether change is "unnecessary" when it's out of bounds even to raise the question of who's responsible for it. For that matter, Spencer makes his "change" the work of anonymous forces which are never identified, conveniently making the question of who moved the cheese impossible to answer. No scientist in a white lab coat ever reaches in to move the cheese. "Change" is not the product of human agency—it's just "there." I'm surprised Johnson didn't name his "littlepeople" Spit and Swallow, since those seem to be the only possible responses to what's done to them.

It's also hard to imagine, in Johnson's little world, just what the identifying features of unnecessary or unjustified change would be, although in his indignant endpaper blurb he appears to recognize it as a theoretical possibility (like antimatter or wormholes, or something).

In fact, Barbara Ehrenreich reads *WMMC?* in light of another book, *QBQ! The Question Behind the Question,* in which "we are told that questions beginning with 'who' or 'why' are symptoms of 'victim thinking.'"[2] In every concrete example in this sorry excuse for a book, the very act of questioning whether a change is necessary puts one squarely in the camp of Hem. For example, consider this anecdote from Ken Blanchard's introduction:

> One of the many real-life examples comes from Charlie Jones, a well-respected broadcaster for NBC-TV, who revealed that hearing the story of "Who Moved My Cheese?" saved his career . . . .
> . . . Charlie had worked hard and had done a great job of broadcasting Track and Field events at an earlier Olympic Games, so he was surprised and upset when his boss told him he'd been removed from these showcase events for the next Olympics and assigned to Swimming and Diving.
> Not knowing these sports as well, he was frustrated. He felt unappreciated and he became angry. He said he felt it wasn't fair! His anger began to affect everything he did.
> Then, he heard the story of "Who Moved My Cheese?"
> After that he said he laughed at himself and changed his attitude. He realized his boss had just "moved his Cheese." So he adapted. He learned the two new sports, and in the process, found that doing something new made him feel young.
> It wasn't long before his boss recognized his new attitude and energy, and he soon got better assignments. He went on to enjoy more success than ever and was later inducted into Pro Football's Hall of Fame—Broadcaster's Alley.[3]

So Job, though sorely tempted to doubt, finally recognized that the Lord moves in mysterious ways, his wonders to perform. And "the LORD blessed the latter end of Job more than his beginning . . ." For Charlie to question his boss was like Job questioning the voice from the whirlwind. "My boss decided it, I accept it, that settles it."

1. *Ibid.*, p. 38.
2. Barbara Ehrenreich, "Who Moved My Ability to Reason?" *The New York Times,* August 14, 2005 <http://www.nytimes.com/2005/08/14/books/review/14EHRENRE.html>.
3. *Ibid.*, pp. 14-16.

And Johnson's own book, apparently, has itself become a form of cheese-moving to be accepted without question. As Blanchard put it in his introduction,

> it stimulated their [his employees'] thinking about how they might apply what they'd learned to their own situation.[1]

See, whether or not they agreed with what they read wasn't even an issue—just how to "apply" what "they'd learned."

The fictionalized Discussion in the last part of the book, between the class reunion attendees, includes an extended anecdote by "Michael," the meta-story's fictionalized author of the "little story," who invented it to deal with "change resisters" in his own "organization." At one point, he actually appears to be about to address the question of resisting change imposed from above:

> Well, the further we went into our organization, the more people we found who felt they had less power. They were understandably more afraid of what the change imposed from above might do to them. So they resisted change.
> In short, a change imposed is a change opposed.

But having skirted the edge of heresy by raising this question, he apparently dismisses it as unworthy of serious consideration. The book helped all these recalcitrants to improve their attitude toward change, and the issue of its legitimacy was set aside with no further mention:

> But when the Cheese Story was shared with literally everyone in our organization, it helped us change the way we looked at change. It helped everyone laugh, or at least smile, at their old fears and want to move on.[2]

There it is again: management assigns (er, excuse me, "shares") this shitty little book to "literally everyone in [the] organization," and they all stop asking about who's imposing this change from above, who it benefits, and whether it's a good idea. They get their minds right.

> . . . practically everyone, those who left and those who stayed, said the Cheese story helped them see things differently and cope better.
> Those who had to go out and look for a new job said it was hard at first but recalling the story was a great help to them . . . .
> . . . [I]nstead of complaining about the changes that were happening, people now said, "They just moved our Cheese. Let's look for the New Cheese." It saved a lot of time and reduced stress . . . .[3]

I'll just *bet* it did, at least for management. "They just moved our Cheese. Let's look for the New Cheese" is certainly less stressful to hear than "They ran the company into the ground, cashed in their stock options just before the earnings report came out, and flushed our pension fund down the toilet! Let's lynch the bastards!"

> Before long, the people who had been resisting saw the advantage of changing. They even helped bring about change.
> Michael was then asked why he thought this happened. The answer: people naturally have a good attitude about getting screwed, in the absence of "peer pressure."
> "I think a lot of it had to do with the kind of peer pressure that can exist in a company.
> "What happens in most organizations you've been in when a change is announced by top management? Do most people say the change is a great idea or a bad idea?"
> "A bad idea," Frank answered.
> "Yes," Michael agreed. "Why?"

1. *Ibid.*, p. 18.
2. *Ibid.*, p. 91.
3. *Ibid.*, p. 92.

Carlos said, "Because people want things to stay the same and they think the change will be bad for them. When one smart person says the change is a bad idea, others say the same."

"Yes, they may not really feel that way," Michael said, "but they agreed in order to look smart as well. That's the sort of peer pressure that fights change in any organization . . . ."

"People changed because no one wanted to look like Hem!"[1]

Workers who question a "change . . . announced by top management" (a change that may involve downsizings, a freeze in pay, or a hike in the health insurance deductible), are just like Davey in an episode of *Davey and Goliath*, where he's pressured to smoke so he can fit in with the cool kids. He would have been just fine if he'd only listened to Mom and Dad, instead of being led into trouble by those bad influences.

But there were, alas, still a few Hems who failed to respond to the glorious visions of change presented by the Dear Leader. Pay attention, because this is really important:

"Unfortunately, the Hems were the anchors that slowed us down . . . . They were either too comfortable or too afraid to change. Some of our Hems changed only when they saw the sensible [by definition] vision we painted that showed them how changing would work to their advantage . . . ."

"What did you do with the Hems who didn't change?" Frank wanted to know.

"We had to let them go," Michael said sadly.[2]

Again, I've scoured this narrative for the slightest hint that the changes imposed by "leaders" could ever be unnecessary or a bad idea. Nothing. In every example in this book, the pattern is: Leader imposes change, the Haws get with the program, and the Hems get the door. In Laura Lemay's words,

You will read the cheese book, and you will like the cheese book. It will change your life. Or we will fire your ass.[3]

Or as Spencer Johnson himself helpfully put it, "all change is good and . . . people should mindlessly conform to unnecessary changes imposed by others."

While we're on the subject of that Discussion: it probably says a great deal about Johnson. Outside of the Bible in a Sunday School class, or *Quotations from Chairman Mao* in a Red Guard study circle, it's hard to imagine any book getting such a relentlessly positive and uncritical reception from a group of readers. One almost expects somebody to stand up and ask "Mr. Johnson: Your book's sales have the momentum of a runaway freight train. How do you explain its popularity?"

The only conclusion I can draw from all this is that Spencer Johnson is a dishonest, cowardly weasel. His book was obviously written, with deliberate intent, to impart the very message that he so strenuously disavows: "all change is good and . . . people should mindlessly conform to unnecessary changes imposed by others." He just doesn't have the guts to own up to it.

If anything, Fish! is more vile than *WMMC?*. The aim of the latter fad was simply to secure worker acquiescence to the downsizings and increased workloads of the '90s. Fish!, on the other hand, seeks to elicit positive *enthusiasm* from the employee whose work conditions have deteriorated so much; in fact, it explicitly stresses the fact that the worker is working up positivity and enthusiasm *despite* his lack of control over working conditions. Fish! is an attempt to manufacture intrinsic motivation where there is no rational cause for it whatsoever. Its basic purpose was described by C. Wright Mills several decades ago:

1. *Ibid.*, pp. 92–93.
2. *Ibid.*, p. 86.
3. Laura Lemay, "The Cheese Stands Alone" (2001), lauralemay.com <http://www.lauralemay.com/essays/cheese.html>.

To secure and increase the will to work, a new ethic that endows work with more than an economic incentive is needed. During war, managers have appealed to nationalism; they have appealed in the name of the firm or branch of the office or factory . . . . They have repeatedly writtten that . . . "job enthusiasm is a hallmark of the American Way." But they have not yet found a really sound ideology.

What they are after is "something in the employee," outwardly manifested in a "mail must go through" attitude, "the 'we' attitude," "spontaneous discipline," "employees smiling and cheerful."[1]

Any clear idea of "morale" requires that the values used as criteria be stated. Two relevant values would seem to be the cheerfulness or satisfaction of the worker, and the extent of his power to determine the course of his work life . . . .

In contrast . . . the "morale" of the human relations expert is the morale of a worker who is powerless but nevertheless cheerful . . . . Assuming that the existing framework of industry is unalterable and that the aims of the managers are the aims of everyone, the experts of "human relations" do not examine the authoritarian structure of modern industry and the role of the worker in it. They define the problem of morale in very limited terms, and by their techniques seek to reveal to their managerial clients how they can improve employee morale within the existing framework of power. Their endeavor is manipulative.[2]

In Fish! Philosophy, unlike *WMMC?*, mere acquiescence to power is not enough. "It's not enough to obey Big Brother, Winston. You must *love* him." To repeat, its purpose is to manufacture intrinsic motivation where there is no objective reason for it. It is to evoke, in people with no control over their work and whose wages have been stagnant for thirty years, intense feelings of commitment to a vocation.

Far beyond even the mere substitution of extrinsic for intrinsic motivation, Fish! is a way to save management the cost of providing even *extrinsic* motivation, by manipulating the worker into liking whatever he gets: "learning to love what we [sic] do, even if at the moment we may not be doing exactly what we [sic] love."[3] Chester Barnard's discussion of coercion as a way to adjust the worker to make previously insufficient levels of motivation sufficient (see Chapter Six) is relevant here.

The theme of powerlessness is central to Fish!. The theme is repeatedly stated, not only in the book itself: . . .

There is always a choice about the way you do your work, even if there is not a choice about the work itself.[4]

We don't have a lot to do with selecting the work that needs to be done, but we can choose how we approach that work.[5]

. . . ut in the even more dumbed-down literature of institutional Fish! programs:

We can either give in to external events and pressures, *few of which we can control*, or we can take control of our own happiness. Our choices are, after all, the only things that no one can take from us in this world.[6]

Many of us believe our attitudes are caused directly by outside influences like unpleasant experiences or negative people. While these things may act as triggers for our feelings, we can choose to either be subservient to these events, *few of which we can control*, or we can take charge of our own responses.[7]

1. C. Wright Mills, *White Collar: The American Middle Classes* (London, Oxford, New York: Oxford University Press, 1951), p. 234.

2. Mills, *The Sociological Imagination* (New York: Grove Press, Inc., 1959), p.

3. *Ibid.*, p. 11.

4. *Ibid.*, p. 36.

5. *Ibid.*, p. 58.

6. Fish Philosophy official site <http://www.charthouse.com/ffc/goods_collegiateCapsule_choose.asp?whoenter=>.

7. "The Fish Philosophy," New South Wales Country Areas Program <http://www.cap.nsw.edu.au/QI/TOOLS/def/fishphil.html>.

We can't control what happens to us, but we do have a choice about how we respond.[1]
You can't always control what happens, but you can control how you respond.[2]
You can't always control circumstances, but you can control your own thoughts.[3]

Powerful people control *events*. Powerless people control their *attitudes* about those events. It's that simple.

Fish! Philosophy is a lesson from the powerful to the powerless. It involves an enormous sleight of hand, carried out through that ubiquitous word "we." One of the Fish! reviewers at Amazon.Com drew, as the central message of the book: "since you're being raped, you might as well enjoy it."

Fish!, by sleight of hand, conceals the elephant in the living room: "we" are not all equally powerless in the face of circumstances. Some people *make* circumstances, and some people *adjust* to circumstances.

Take, for example, the godawful "Third Floor" in the Fish! narrative, which the protagonist is brought in to turn around. The bank's management, as the book repeatedly stresses, is horrified at the negative atmosphere on that floor.

> Words like *unresponsive, entitlement, zombie, unpleasant, slow, wasteland,* and *negative* were used frequently to describe this group . . . .
> Supervisors swapped stories about the latest fiasco on the third floor.[4]

But golly, why is management being so negative about the atmosphere on the Third Floor? Isn't the whole lesson of Fish! that they're supposed to learn to love it? They can't control what employees on the Third Floor do, but they can *choose their attitude* about it. Oh, wait . . . . that's right. It's only those on the *bottom* who must adjust their attitudes to circumstances imposed on them by others; those at the *top*, on the other hand, get to do the imposing.

To grasp just how presumptuous Fish! really is, just try a thought experiment: imagine management's reaction if the circumstances were reversed. Imagine the bosses' reaction if you and your coworkers matter-of-factly announced that, henceforth, you would be working at a slower pace for the same amount of money, or that you would be receiving a higher hourly wage. Imagine telling the boss "you can't do anything about these changes, but you can choose to have a good attitude about them!" My guess is your boss would demonstrate in short order that he *does* have control over events, and that it's not *his* attitude that has to be adjusted. That's because, while *you* may be powerless, your bosses most certainly are *not*.

This asymmetrical power relationship is implicit in Fish! Philosophy. And you'd better believe that the people who push it are fully aware of their agenda. If you have any doubts of what the agenda is, and who's pushing it, just Google "Fish! Philosophy"+"your organization." As with *Who Moved My Cheese?*, the people who control organizations are the primary market for Fish!, and the audiences they buy it for are the "human resources" they manage.

They are the ones who *do* things. We are the ones that things are done *to*. Learn to enjoy it, or else. That's the message of Fish! Philosophy.

---

1. "Fish Philosophy," Mr. Stepien's Science Page, Buffalo Academy of the Sacred Heart <http://www.myteacherpages.com/webpages/RStepien/fish.cfm>.

2. "Create a Great Work Environment," *A Special Report* (Council of State Governments— West) <http://www.csgwest.org/Publications/s_rep_work.pdf>.

3. "Appreciative Inquiry: Application and Celebration. Two WLA Sessions presented at Wisconsin Dells Conference, 2006" (Wisconsin Library Association) <http://www.wla.lib.wi.us/conferences/2006/documents/wlahandouts2006.pdf>.

4. Lundin *et al., Fish!*, p. 18.

We saw the common theme, on the left side of the comma in all those snippets quoted above, that we "can't control" what happens to us. But there's a second part to the slogan: we can "control how we respond," or "control our own thoughts." In short, we can "*Choose Our Attitude.*" And what "attitude" is it we are to "choose"? The Fish! authors, quoting John Gardner, unwittingly give a glimpse of the man behind the curtain:

> There is something I know about you that you may not even know about yourself. You have within you more resources of energy than have ever been tapped, more talent than has ever been exploited, more strength than has ever been tested, and more to give than you have ever given.[1]

And we will take, and take, and take, until you have given every last drop you have to give, and then we will replace you. Reading the quote above, I can't help thinking of the human batteries in *The Matrix.*

The reason for burnout in most workplaces is that management has deliberately and systematically downsized staffing levels, trying to get more and more work out of fewer and fewer people. The management of the average corporation manufactures burned out employees like Carter manufactures liver pills. Through Fish! Philosophy, management attempts to deal with burnout entirely through cheerleading and slogans—Stakhanovism—without having to increase staffing levels or pay, or otherwise alter its own contribution to the problem. Fish! Philosophy, at its core, is an attempt to get something for nothing.

Burnout is the natural reaction to prolonged stress: a survival mechanism that involves shutting down, withdrawing, and breaking connections to the sources of stressful stimuli. It's what happens when people are doing their own work plus that of the downsized, often with no time for meal breaks, with less and less control over the structure and pacing of their jobs. Fish! Philosophy reminds me a lot of the military's attempts at creating pharmacologically engineered super-soldiers, robocops who can go 72 hours without sleep and never feel guilt or develop PTSD. In both cases, it's an artificial attempt to squeeze more out of people who've been pushed to the breaking point, rather than doing anything about the stresses they're subjected to.

In such an environment, all the motivational appeals to serving internal and external customers, and viewing coworkers in other departments as part of the same team, is a sick joke. A cooperative social order breaks down in an atmosphere of scarcity. Understaffing and increased workloads inevitably pit workers against each other and against the customer. When the workers in every department are systematically deprived of the staffing levels needed to do an adequate job, they naturally come to see any source of additional work as the enemy. Every request from an external or internal customer is another weight added to an unbearable load. Workers see increased business as nothing but an increase in their already intolerable workload, from which management or shareholders will appropriate all the increased income for themselves, and workers will never see a dime of increased income. Therefore, they are increasingly hostile to the customer. Different departments see each other as sources of additional work, much like one drowning man pulling another down, and attempt to push off their insupportable workloads off on each other. Under those conditions, management's cynical exhortations to "teamwork" are about as effective as throwing a bone into a yard full of hungry dogs and then saying "y'all play nice now, y'hear?"

Here's the thing: management doesn't care about what they've done to people, or whether it's right or wrong. And they don't care about internal or external customers, or their mission statements (and vision and values statements, either). What they care about is their petty empires of direct reports and the value of their stock options. All their oleagi-

---

1. *Ibid.,* p. 51.

nous Hallmark Cards rhetoric notwithstanding, both the production worker and the customer are means to an end for them. They're riding the gravy train, and they want to keep right on riding it. To keep the things that matter to them, they have to keep us running on the treadmill. And when they notice we're not putting out like we used to, they need to figure out what buttons to push to get their human resources back to producing value-added. Fish! Philosophy is a way of pushing those buttons.

That's what it's all about: squeezing more effort out of fewer people, without increasing their pay. Management helpfully informed us, in the monthly official happy talk newsletter at the hospital where I work, that "if we [sic] choose to provide extraordinary patient care" we could do so, "regardless of our [sic] abundance or lack of resources." This is reminiscent of Pharaoh, decreeing that the Hebrew slaves continue to make as many bricks as before, "regardless of their abundance or lack of straw." This was the same management, by the way, who were high-fiving each other behind closed doors on their successful downsizing at the very same time they were churning out saccharine motivational agit-prop. While they were publicly gushing that we were their "most important asset," all of us one big happy "team," they were privately congratulating each other on how effectively they'd screwed us over and gotten away with it.

It's interesting to hear the fictionalized managers in *Fish!* complain about the sense of "entitlement" on the Third Floor. A sense of *entitlement*?! Golly, what would *that* look like? *Management's* sense of entitlement comes through loud and clear in *Fish!* Management is *entitled* to a workforce that's enthusiastic and dedicated and constantly goes the extra mile, regardless of how it gets screwed. Management is *entitled* to a workforce that greets every new steaming pile with a joyous cry of "Oh, boy! Shit again!" Management is *entitled* to something for nothing.

It's important to notice the dog that doesn't bark. A moral tale told by someone in a position of authority, with the intention of imparting some attitude in those subject to that authority, is a lot like a magic act. What's important is the part of the act that the illusionist doesn't want you to see—or the part of the story that's left out. As in *Who Moved My Cheese?*, the one subject the Fish! authors strenuously try to avert attention from is the nature and causes of this objective reality that we're supposed to adjust our attitudes to.

Issues of power, ownership and control are entirely absent from the Fish! book. Things just are the way they are, like the moving cheese, as the result of blind impersonal forces; even to ask the identity of those forces is an act of insubordination. The fact that our society has been transformed from one made up almost entirely of the self-employed, to one in which giant authoritarian hierarchies control the vast majority's access to livelihood, goes completely unremarked.

In one of the most obscene parts of the book, one character, Lonnie, actually compares the homely atavism of his grandmother's kitchen to the modern corporate workplace, as an illustration of "choosing your attitude," as if the two were remotely comparable.

> Let me tell you about my grandmother. She always brought love and a smile to her work. All of us grandkids wanted to help in the kitchen because washing dishes with Grandma was so much fun. In the process a great deal of kitchen wisdom was dispensed. Us kids were given something truly precious, a caring adult.
>
> I realize now that my grandma didn't love dishwashing. She *brought* love to dishwashing, and her spirit was infectious.[1]

There's one big difference between Grandma's kitchen and the contemporary corporate workplace: the word "her." It was *her* kitchen. It was *her* dishes. She didn't have a boss. She could control how she did the dishes, not just in the lame sense of how enthusiastic an attitude she chose to adopt, but in the real sense of how fast she washed, how many spells

1. *Ibid.*, pp. 37-38.

of work she wanted to break the job up into and how long to rest in between, what order she washed them in, whether she had separate sinks of wash water and rinse water, what kind of soap to use, whether to dry them with a towel or let them air dry, etc.—all the decisions you'd *better believe* a boss would make for her if she was on a time clock. And unlike the wage serf in the corporate workplace, she was working entirely for herself and her family: she was washing the dishes that she and her loved one's ate off of, and she and her family appropriated all the benefits from washing them.

If Grandma worked in a corporate kitchen, using a hellish institutional dishwasher; if the kitchen staff were downsized until Grandma was handling the load previously handled by three dishwashers, and the dishes just kept piling up faster than she could wash them; if there were repeated inservice meetings and "counsellings" over the kitchen staff's failure to keep up with the increased workload; if she went three years in a row without a cost-of-living raise because "these are lean times and the organization can't afford it," while the CEO's stock options went through the roof and he made a bigger bonus than she'd earn in a lifetime; and if all this time she and her coworkers were barraged with relentlessly upbeat propaganda about "choosing our attitude" and our "core values" . . . . Well, I'm guessing that Grandma would probably get through her shift about the same way I do at the hospital where I work: by god-damning the management to hell under her breath every single minute of it.

The difference between *work*, as it existed in a society of free and self-employed producers, and the *job*, is exactly the difference between self-directed *learning* and the *schooling* one receives inside a K-12 prison. The one is an expression of one's self, in a world under one's own control; the other requires internalizing a set of goals imposed by others, out of their own self-interest. To seriously equate the one with the other requires an almost superhuman feat of false consciousness.

Colin Ward quotes Nigel Balchin, a novelist who was invited to address a conference on incentives in industry.

> Industrial psychologists must stop messing about with tricky and ingenious bonus schemes and find out why a man, after a hard day's work, went home and enjoyed digging in his garden.[1]

The answer, of course, was that it was *his* garden, and he worked it to suit himself without a boss looking over his shoulder.

The good Lord may have sentenced us to earn our bread by the sweat of our brow, but he never said anything about being harassed while we were doing it by some peckerhead in a suit and tie. An anarchist whose program appeared on the local cable access channel once made a very pointed observation: it's wired into us, she said, when somebody follows us around and won't stop bugging the shit out of us, to do one of two things—either get away from them, or beat the crap out of them. A situation in which we're bugged by a boss for eight hours a day, with this "fight or flight" instinct revving our nervous and endocrine systems at 80 mph in first gear, is something we're not designed for by the evolutionary process.

For the Fish! authors, the unpleasantness of a job has absolutely nothing to do with the objective conditions created by those in authority. For example, the authors never spend a moment considering *why* the Third Floor has such abysmally low morale. There's obviously no cause or reason—it happened "just because." So obviously, the only thing needed to fix it is for the staff to get their minds right, without regard to any change in objective, external reality. And management, seemingly, are the only parties who don't have a choice. None of their decisions or policies has anything to do with whether the job is a

1. Colin Ward, *Anarchy in Action* (London: Freedom Press, 1982), p. 95.

humanly tolerable one, or whether it is an overstressed, understaffed shithole. They *have no choice* but to react negatively when they can't get more work out of people for the same pay—it's just the objective nature of things. So while management lives in a world bounded by material constraints and limited by objective conditions, workers live in a world created entirely by pure thought.

Another character in the book, Wolf, actually compares working conditions to a car wreck, and his choice of attitude during recovery to one's choice of attitude in the work-place.[1] There's one big difference, though. The race car wasn't a conscious being with a will. It wasn't "treating" him *any* way. And it especially wasn't trying to manipulate him into "choosing" to have a good attitude about being hurt, so it could hurt him again more easily in the future. "Change" isn't something that "just happens" like a car wreck. It's something *done* by conscious agents with an agenda, to promote their own perceived self-interest.

In looking at the big picture behind Fish!, we should bear in mind Barbara Ehren-reich's observation:

> Cheerfulness, upbeatness and compliance: these are the qualities of subordinates—of servants rather than masters . . . .[2]
> . . . The frequent admonitions on attitude go beyond any simple, common-sense warnings to behave pleasantly in an interview, and instead demand that positive feelings be fully internalized. One website catering to the white-collar job search culture warns that any "negative attitude"—like anger toward a former employer—will show despite your best effort to correct it.[3]

As the Bible says, "*Curse not the king*, no *not* in *thy thought*; and *curse not* the rich in *thy* bedchamber: for a bird of the air shall carry the voice . . . ."

In short, all the "flexibility" and "openness to change," all the positive attitude, are entirely one-sided. The worker is obligated to "think happy thoughts" about whatever is done to him, but is entitled to appeal to absolutely no corresponding obligation on the part of those with power. The worker's duty was ably summed up by Julia O'Connell Da-vidson: "Employers require workers to be *both* dependable *and* disposable."

Managers themselves, of course, for the most part do not take such motivational blather seriously.

> High morale is variously thought to improve productivity or, at the least, to "make for a family spirit." Only a few managers are willing to voice what a top official of Weft Corporation thinks is actually a widespread managerial sentiment about workers' happiness: "Let them be happy on their own time."[4]

More than a few workers see through all the official happy talk, as well. For example, one worker's reaction to a "corporate culture" campaign at a heavy vehicle manufacturing company in Lancashire: "They give the impression we work together when it suits them, but when it gets rough, we're the ones who get it."[5]

A good example is Robert Jackall's "Covenant" corporation, the locus of the great downsizing described earlier in this chapter. Immediately after the purge of 600 Covenant

---

1. *Fish!*, p. 80.

2. Barbara Ehrenreich, *Bait and Switch: The (Futile) Pursuit of the American Dream* (New York: Metropolitan Books, Henry Holt and Company, 2005), p. 230.

3. *Ibid.*, p. 220.

4. Robert Jackall, *Moral Mazes: The World of Corporate Managers* (New York: Oxford University Press, 1988), p. 138.

5. David Collinson, "Strategies of Resistance: Power, Knowledge, and Subjectivity in the Workplace," in J. Jermier and D. Knights, eds., *Resistance and Power in Organizations* (London: routledge, 1994), p. 33.

employees, and in the midst of all the Byzantine maneuverings, betrayals, and other bureaucratic warfare fought to avoid responsibility for losses during the 1982 recession, the company held a "Family Day." Afterward, the CEO bloviated:

> I think Family Day made a very strong statement about the [Covenant] "family" of employees at [Corporate Headquarters]. And that is that we can accomplish whatever we set out to do if we work together; if we share the effort, we will share the rewards. The "New World of [Covenant]" has no boundaries only frontiers, and each and everyone can play a role, for we need what *you* have to contribute.[1]

Management's real attitude toward employee relations and motivation is probably best summed up by this little anecdote:

> At the Manhattan offices of Steelcase, Inc., an office furniture-maker, workers and visitors are greeted in the lobby by a 6-by-4-foot ant farm: . . . [I]t was chosen by the company to make a statement about work. In an article in the *Wall Street Journal* . . . , the company said it was looking for a metaphor to describe how people live and work. "Work is dramatically different than it used to be," Steelcase manager Dave Lathrop told the *Journal*. "For more people, work and nonwork are blending." He explained that the company liked that the ants were able to "silently represent that, simply by doing what they do."[2]

---

1. Jackall, *Moral Mazes*, p. 37.
2. Daniel S. Levine, *Disgruntled: The Darker Side of the World of Work* (New York: Berkley Boulevard Books, 1998), p. 237.

APPENDIX A
BLAMING WORKERS FOR THE RESULTS OF MISMANAGEMENT

"Employee error," increasingly, is scapegoated for whatever goes wrong in today's downsized, understaffed, sped-up workplace. Four items on the same theme:

1. Senators Were Warned of Lexington Air Controller Understaffing[1]

JEFFREY MCMURRAY, ABC NEWS—Months before the Comair jet crash that killed 49 people, air traffic controllers at the Lexington airport wrote to federal officials complaining about a hostile working environment in the tower and short-staffing on the overnight shift, according to letters obtained by The Associated Press. In identical letters sent April 4 to Kentucky's senators, Republicans Mitch McConnell and Jim Bunning, a control tower worker said the overnight shift, or "mid," is staffed with two people "only when convenient to management."

The Federal Aviation Administration's guidelines called for two people to be there the morning of the Aug. 27 crash, but only one was present. "We had a controller retire last month and now we are back to single man mids," wrote Faron Collins, a union leader for the Lexington control tower workers. "I ask you one simple question. Are two people needed on the mids for safety or not? If they are, why are they not scheduled?" . . . .

2. Dian Hardison. "I F-ing Warned Them!"[2]

I told them that the technicians and engineers were overworked. I told them that there were too many managers and too many meetings and "dog-and-pony" shows. I told them that their senior "face time" play games, while they spent all their time plotting how to give each other pay raises, and left the guys on the floor to struggle day to day with obsolete and overpriced and unqualified equipment, was going to result in another Challenger.

I was there for Challenger.

I saw the same exact conditions happening again. Overpaid, lazy, irresponsible managers concerned solely with their climbing up their ladders.

I told them they were skimping on inspections. I told them that the ground crews were asleep on their feet from exhaustion. I made as much noise as I knew how to make about the top-heavy bureaucracy sitting around in their fancy panelled offices, giving whorish press interviews in their smugness, while they did not have a clue what was going on in the real world where I was working . . . .

Like Challenger, those who are most guilty are the ones who will attempt to make the most political capital out of it. But the blame for Columbia lies entirely and totally with the NASA administrators. They should all be investigated for their criminal negligence. They should all serve time in jail.

3. MSHA Makes The "Wrong Decision" To Blame Workers For Accidents[3]

That management likes to blame worker behavior for accidents will come as no surprise to American workers. That this "blame the worker" theory is not consistent with the

1. ABC News <http://abcnews.go.com/US/wireStory?id=2427312&CMP=OTC-RSSFeeds 0312>. Link now dead. Originally linked in Progressive Review; quotes are from originally quoted text preserved in blog post: Kevin Carson, "Blaming Workers for the Results of Mismanagement," Mutualist Blog, Sept. 17, 2006 <http://mutualist.blogspot.com/2006/09/blaming-workers-for-results-of.html>.

2. Dian Hardison, "Shuttle Crash & Smug NASA Managers 'I F-ing Warned Them!'" Counterpunch, Feb. 1, 2003 <http://www.counterpunch.org/hardison02012003.html>.

3. "MSHA Makes The 'Wrong Decision' To Blame Workers For Accidents," Labor Blog, July 28, 2005 <http://www.nathannewman.org/laborblog/archive/003252.shtml>.

facts, that it doesn't get to the root causes of workplace incidents is also not a surprise to American workers.

So this new Mine Safety and Health Administration program comes as a great surprise to all of us.

MSHA Launches New Safety and Health Initiative[1]

ARLINGTON, Va.—The U.S. Department of Labor's Mine Safety and Health Administration (MSHA) today launched "Make the Right Decision," a safety and health initiative that helps miners and mine operators focus on human factors, such as decision-making, when at work. The campaign encourages miners and mine management to work together on safety and health issues.

"MSHA will increase its focus on safety decisions during this campaign, which is not a limited-time initiative," said David G. Dye, deputy assistant secretary of labor for mine safety and health. "We want miners and management to make the right decisions to ensure the safety and health of America's miners."

So what's the problem with encouraging workers to make the right decision?

First, the assumption of this program is that most accident happen because workers make the wrong decisions. In other words, all you need is a little education, training and enlightenment and all will be well. If accidents continue to happen, they're caused by worker carelessness, incompetence, stupidity, suicidal tendencies—and just plain dumb decisions.

In other words, "Make the Right Decision" is just your same old "behavioral safety" program under a new name. Behavioral safety theories say that worker carelessness or misconduct is the cause of most accidents, and disciplining workers is the answer. But behavioral theories don't hold up to a closer look at the root causes of most workplace accidents: generally management system and organizational problems that lead to unsafe conditions . . . .

It is somewhat ironic that this program is starting now. Clearly acting Assistant Secretary Dye hasn't read the June 2005 issue of *Occupational Health & Safety* which contains an article by Fred Manuele entitled "Serious Injury Prevention."

Manuele cites experts who point out that what may look like "human error" are actually system errors:

R. B. Whittingham, in his book *The Blame Machine: Why Human Error Causes Accidents*, describes how disasters and serious accidents result from recurring, but potentially avoidable, human errors. He shows that such errors are preventable because they result from defective systems within a company.

Whittingham identifies the common causes of human error and the typical system deficiencies that lead to those errors. They are principally organizational, cultural, and management system deficiencies. Whittingham says that in some organizations, a "blame culture" exists whereby the focus in incident investigation is on individual human error, and the corrective action is limited to that level. He writes: "Organizations, and sometimes whole industries, become unwilling to look too closely at the system faults which caused the error"

He notes that although humans may be involved in the errors that lead to accidents, James Reason and Alan Hobbs, in *Managing Maintenance Error: A Practical Guide* point out that one needs to look deeper:

> Errors are consequences not just causes. They are shaped by local circumstances: by the task, the tools and equipment and the workplace in general. If we are to understand the significance of these factors, we have to stand back from what went on in the error maker's head and consider the nature of the system as a whole . . . this book has a constant theme . . . that situations and systems are easier to change than the human condition.

    1. Department of Labor press release, "MSHA Launches New Safety and Health Initiative," July 13, 2005 <http://www.msha.gov/MEDIA/PRESS/2005/NR050713.asp>.

In other words, look at the safety systems and find the root causes. If managers (and MSHA) continue to attempt to prevent accidents by focusing on human errors and "wrong decisions," the same accidents, injuries and deaths will continue to happen.

4. Labor Relations in the Health Care Industry for Nurses[1]

More Nurses Needed

* Understaffing: There are not enough nurses to do what needs to be done on any given shift and the nurses who are on duty are exhausted and stressed. A 2003 study by the Institute of Medicine (IOM) found the environment in which nurses work a breeding ground for medical errors which will continue to threaten patient safety until substantially reformed. The IOM points to numerous studies showing that increased infections, bleeding and cardiac and respiratory failure are associated with inadequate numbers of nurses. A 2002 report by the Joint Commission on Accreditation of Healthcare Organizations called the nursing shortage "a prescription for danger" and found that a shortage of nurses contributed to nearly a quarter of the anticipated problems that result in death or injury to hospital patients.

* Low Nurse-to-Patient Ratios: With managed care restructuring the health care industry in the 1990s, hospitals reduced staffing levels to lower costs. Nurses care for more patients and patients who are more acutely ill due to shorter hospital stays. One study of hospital staffing found that decreases in the number of LPN/LVNs added to RNs' patient load. Studies have linked low nurse-to-patient ratios to medical errors and to poorer patient outcomes, as well as to nurses leaving patient care. A 2002 study by Linda Aiken, et al., found that for each additional patient over four in an RN's workload, the risk of death increases by 7% for hospital patients. Patients in hospitals with eight patients per nurse have a 31% higher risk of dying than those in hospitals with four patients per nurse. The IOM study recommends that nurse staffing levels be raised in all health care facilities.

* Mandatory Overtime and Floating: Because of the nursing shortage, many hospitals routinely require nurses to work unplanned or mandatory overtime and to "float" to departments outside their expertise. On average, RNs work 8.5 weeks of overtime per year according to a recent union survey. Mandatory overtime was an issue in several recent strikes and 77% of RNs favor a law banning it except when an emergency is declared.

* Burnout: Among nurses there are high rates of emotional exhaustion and job dissatisfaction which are strongly associated with inadequate staffing and low nurse-to-patient ratios. The Aiken study found each additional patient per nurse corresponds to a 23% increased risk of burnout, as well as a 15% increase in the risk of job dissatisfaction.

What's even worse, management's penny-wise, pound-foolish policies, which attempt to cut costs by deliberate understaffing, don't really even save money:

Statistical model shows [sic] that when nursing units are understaffed the additional costs associated with patients who develop complications are greater than the labor savings due to understaffing . . . .

While immediate personnel costs are less with short staffing, long term costs were higher because patients with complications often stay longer in the hospital and require other expensive treatments . . . .

Institutions attempting to decrease costs through health care worker reductions may, in the final analysis, incur higher costs as a result of higher rates of nosocomial infection, longer hospital stays and use of expensive antimicrobials and increased mortality.[2]

1. Michigan State University, School of Labor and Industrial Relations, "Labor Relations in the Health Care Industry for Nurses: Online Credit Program" <http://www.lir.msu.edu/distance_learning/MNAArticleandWebPage.htm>.

2. Wisconsin Federation of Nurses and Health Professionals, "A Summary of Recent Research Supporting the Need for Staffing Ratios and Workload Limitations in Healthcare" <http://www.wfnhp.org/setlimits/researchsummary.html>. The link no longer active, but is available through Internet Archive.

By the way: the healthcare industry has its very own "behavioral safety" approach to hospital-acquired infections, directly analogous to the "human error" approach described above in the mining industry. The spread of MRSA and other infections in hospitals is the direct result of downsizing and understaffing—also the primary cause of patient falls, medication errors, wrong site surgery, etc., etc., etc., etc., ad nauseam. Healthcare workers know they need to wash their hands—but *knowing* and *being able to do* are two different things when the only orderly on the floor is literally running from one call light to another, and he's got three patients sitting on bedside commodes at the same time as two other fall-risk patients are setting off their bed alarms. Rather than deal with the root cause—the dangerous levels of understaffing that have resulted from the downsizings of the past decade—hospital administrators resort to asinine gimmicks like the "Partners in Your Care" program (designed by a manufacturer of hand disinfectants):

> Patients and families are asked to be Partners in Your Care by asking all healthcare workers that have direct contact with their family member patient "Did You Wash Your Hands?" or "Did You Sanitize Your Hands?"[1]

Dilbert effectively parodied a similar program: the company response to on-the-job accidents was a "safety dog" who admonished "Woof, woof! Don't use scissors!"

Attempts to deal with safety issues through such behavioral approaches, rather than by addressing the structural and process causes, are what Peter Drucker called "management by drives" and Deming dismissed as "slogans, exhortations, and revival meetings." But in the modern workplace, such slogans and gimmicks are likely to appear on the very same bulletin board as kwality jargon from Six Sigma or ISO-9000.

1. Official Steris corporate website. <http://www.steris.com/aic/partners.cfm>.

APPENDIX B

CORPORATE RHETORIC VS. CORPORATE REALITY:
THE CASE OF "CHAINSAW AL" DUNLAP

In a 1995 *Wall Street Journal* article by Alex Markels and Joann S. Lublin,[1] I saw one Albert J. Dunlap, referred to as simply a "turnaround specialist" and CEO of Scott Paper, quoted on the wisdom of eliminating employee longevity awards.

> To some managers, rewarding long service reinforces the very attitude of entitlement they are trying to stamp out.
>
> Last year, Scott Paper dropped its entire service-award program as part of a broad restructuring. "We [were] rewarding longevity and the status quo; the status quo had been an abysmal failure," says Albert J. Dunlap, a turnaround specialist hired as chairman and chief executive last year to revive Scott's sagging fortunes. Mr. Dunlap concedes that he "got some grief" over the move, but he wasn't swayed.
>
> Like other companies cutting awards, Scott also cited a desire to cut costs. "Everybody likes to go to big dinners and get nice awards," Mr. Dunlap says. "But it's not right. You're using shareholders' money," he adds.

When I read that quote, my only immediate reaction was to wonder just how enormous an executive compensation package Mr. Dunlap received, whether he felt "entitled" to it, and whether he thought it came from shareholders' money. But the name seemed to ring a bell, for some reason. Having read Arianna Huffington's *Pigs at the Trough* a few weeks earlier, I checked to see if I might have seen Dunlap mentioned in there. And boy, howdy, was he![2] Contrasting his pious rhetoric above to his swinish behavior is a lesson in hypocrisy.

I mentioned Dunlap, in Chapter Seven, as evidence that Mises' much-vaunted double-entry bookkeeping, which he promoted as a panacea for the agency problems resulting from the separation of ownership from control, is of little avail when the agent is keeping the books. Dunlap was a master of the game when it came to massaging the numbers, gaming the short-term profits and maximize his stock options and bonuses, taking off with the loot, and leaving a gutted shell behind.

Dunlap didn't just massage the numbers. He gave them a thorough rolfing. And the scale of downsizing he practiced, which earned him the nickname "Chainsaw Al," make Bob Nardelli look positively prodigal.

His final downfall resulted from his performance at Sunbeam, a Boca Raton appliance maker. His approach to "turning around" that underperforming company was to fire half the workforce, close 18 of 26 plants, and eliminate 80% of the product line. That, in itself, wouldn't be so remarkable. That's just an extreme version of the typical MBA playbook these days.

What's really remarkable is the appalling lengths he went to, in using accounting jugglery to deceive shareholders. His gutting of productive capability didn't make the company profitable, or increase the value of the shares. So, as Huffington said, "[i]f he couldn't actually make the company profitable, Dunlap decided, he could at least make it look profitable on paper."

> With a little help from the corporate criminal's best friend, the master chefs of book-cooking at Arthur Andersen, Dunlap used illegal accounting tricks to shift revenue around,

1. Alex Markels and Joann S. Lublin, "Management: Longevity-Reward Programs Get Short Shrift," *The Wall Street Journal*, April 27, 1995 <http://www.markels.com/management.htm>.

2. Arianna Huffington, *Pigs at the Trough: How Corporate Greed and Political Corruption are Undermining America* (New York: Crown Publishers, 2003), pp. 62-65.

which had the effect of increasing Sunbeam's reported losses under previous management. Millions of dollars of expenses incurred in 1997, his first full year at Sunbeam, were charged to 1996 instead. Dunlap then dipped into the artificial reserve to inflate accounts and "increase" earnings. Here's how an SEC spokesman later described Dunlap's scam: "You load up the cookie jar with improper reserves and then when you need a sugar jolt, which in this example is positive earnings, you reach into the cookie jar."

We've already seen, in Chapter Seven, Martin Hellwig's reference to the standard corporate practice of accumulating large reserves of real estate and other investments, in order to smooth out cash flow in bad years.

It's especially comical to read the *WSJ*'s reference to Dunlap above as exemplifying opposition to ordinary production workers' "attitude of entitlement," and his pious words about "the shareholders' money," in light of his performance at Sunbeam. The extent of his respect for "the shareholders' money" should be pretty clear from the account above.

As for "attitudes of entitlement," how's this: When called to account before the Sunbeam board of directors, he shouted, "I'm much too rich and much too powerful to have to take this shit from you!"

9

Special Agency Problems of Labor (Internal Crisis Tendencies of the Large Organization)

Introduction

We already examined, in Chapter Four, the *systemic* crises that result from state promotion of economic centralization and excessive organizational size: the growth of demand for subsidized inputs, faster than it can be met by the state, ultimately leads to input and fiscal crises that make state capitalism unsustainable. In this chapter, we examine the parallel *internal* crises of the large organization.

As Barry Stein observed, the larger the organization, the greater the levels of absenteeism, disgruntlement, and sabotage.[1] We have already seen that the larger the organization, the more senior management's authority is constrained by agency and information problems. And as we saw in Chapter Eight, unique agency problems result from incomplete contracting and endogenous enforcement and from asymmetric information about the work process. The situation is exacerbated by stagnant pay and increasing authoritarianism, and an increasingly adversarial relationship between management and labor. Putting all this together, we find that as the organization grows larger, it becomes increasingly vulnerable to asymmetric warfare from within at the very same time the workforce is becoming increasingly disgruntled.

A. The Special Agency Problems of Labor

It's a common observation among institutional economists that the best way to minimize agency costs is to vest residual claimancy (or ownership) in the "limiting" factor—the factor whose control presents the most agency problems for another party. Ugo Pagano and Robert Rowthorn, for example, argue that

> if governance arises to save on agency costs, organizations should be controlled by the most specific or difficult-to-monitor factors: they will be able to save the most on the risk-premium due to resource specificity or on the monitoring expenses that would have to be paid if they were employed in other people's organizations.

On the other hand, if ownership is not vested in the hardest to monitor factor, the owning factors will have to resort to special expedients to overcome the monitoring problem:

> . . . each type of owner will tend to develop a technology that saves on the agency costs of employing the remaining non-owning factors . . . .
> . . . Owning factors have to pay high agency costs in order to employ difficult-to-monitor and specific factors. Thus they will try to replace these factors by easy to moni-

---

1. Barry Stein, *Size, Efficiency, and Community Enterprise* (Cambridge: Center for Community Economic Development, 1974), p. 47.

tor or non-specific factors: an attempt will be made to change the nature of the non-owning factors and to make them "easy to monitor" and "general purpose."[1]

And in fact, as we shall see below, this latter unsatisfactory expedient *has* generally been chosen as a substitute for vesting firm ownership in the factor with the highest monitoring costs: labor.

It's hard to imagine circumstances under which the agency and monitoring problems of any other factor could exceed those of labor. As "Lenin," of Lenin's Tomb blog, observed:

> Henry Ford once asked "how come, when I just want a pair of hands, I get a human being too?" . . . . [W]]hat Ford was looking for [was] a disposable commodity that wouldn't have needs, grudges or grievances, one that wouldn't answer back, try to change the terms of its use or renegotiate its price. The problem with purchasing labour is that it is a distinctly unusual commodity, imbued with intentionality.[2]

Labor-power is the one factor of production that is not subject to ownership by anyone other than the worker.

Murray Rothbard argued against even voluntary, contractual slavery on the grounds that human will and moral agency are inalienable: "the only valid transfer of title of ownership in the free society" involves property which is, "in fact and in the nature of man, *alienable* by man."

> All physical property owned by a person is alienable, i.e., in natural fact it can be given or transferred to the ownership and control of another party . . . . But there are certain vital things which, in natural fact and in the nature of man, are inalienable, i.e., they *cannot* in fact be alienated, even voluntarily. Specifically, a person cannot alienate his *will*, more particularly his control over his own mind and body . . . . Since his will and control over his own person are inalienable, then so also are his *rights* to control that person and will . . . .
>
> Hence, the unenforceability, in libertarian theory, of voluntary slave contracts. Suppose that Smith makes the following agreement with the Jones Corporation: Smith, for the rest of his life, will obey all orders, under whatever conditions, that the Jones Corporation wishes to lay down . . . . Our contention . . . is that Smith's promise was not a valid (i.e., not an enforceable) contract. There is no transfer of title in Smith's agreement, because Smith's control over his own body and will are *inalienable*. Since that control *cannot* be alienated, the agreement was not a valid contract, and therefore should not be enforceable. Smith's agreement was a *mere* promise, which it might be held he is morally obligated to keep, but which should not be legally obligatory.[3]
>
> . . . [A] man may not agree to permanent bondage by contracting to work for another man for the rest of his life. He might change his mind at a later date, and then he cannot, in a free market, be compelled to continue an arrangement whereby he submits his will to the orders of another, even though he might have agreed to this arrangement previously.[4]

"Voluntarily" selling oneself into slavery, as a commenter on the LeftLibertarian2 yahoogroup put it, is a lot like selling a car and then remaining in the driver's seat. It is impossible to alienate moral agency.

But the same is true of the wage labor contract. The agency problems embedded in the sale of labor-power are similar in kind to those entailed in selling oneself into perma-

---

1. Ugo Pagano and Robert Rowthorn, "The Competitive Selection of Democratic Firms in a World of Self-Sustaining Institutions," in Pagano and Rowthorn, eds., *Democracy and Efficiency in the Economic Enterprise*. A study prepared for the World Institute for Development Economics Research (WIDER) of the United Nations University (London and New York: Routledge, 1996), pp. 117-118.

2. "Lenin", "Dead Zone Revisited," Lenin's Tomb blog, June 7, 2005 <http://leninology.blogspot.com/2005/06/dead-zone-revisited.html>.

3. Murray N. Rothbard, *The Ethics of Liberty* (New York and London: New York University Press, 1998), pp. 134-136.

4. Rothbard, *Man, Economy, and State: A Treatise on Economic Principles* (Auburn, Ala.: The Ludwig von Mises Institute, 1962, 1970, 1993), p. 142.

nent slavery. Unlike sellers of capital equipment and land, the seller of labor-power remains in the driver's seat at all times.

David Ellerman took Rothbard's moral agency argument a step further, arguing that moral agency was inalienable even in the case of selling labor-power for short periods of time. It was, he said, a "rather implausible assertion that a person can vacate his or her will for eight or so hours a day for weeks, months, or years on end but cannot do so for a working lifetime."[1] He argued that, like the voluntary slavery contract,

> the contract to voluntarily rent oneself out . . . should also be considered . . . juridically invalid . . . . The immediate retort is that the abolition of renting people would violate the "freedom of contract." When one thus hears the rhetoric of liberal capitalism, it is important to remember the invalidity of the self-sale contract.[2]
>
> In general, any contract to take on the legal role of a thing or non-person is inherently invalid because a person cannot in fact voluntarily give up and alienate his or her factual status as a person. I can in fact give up and transfer my use of this pen (or computer) to another person, but I cannot do the same with my own human actions—not for a lifetime and not for eight hours a day.[3]

I don't go as far as Ellerman in denying the legitimacy of wage labor contracts. But the practical difficulties he raises concerning the inalienability of moral agency are genuine, and make labor—by the very nature of the case—a unique source of agency problems. Because labor is the only factor with a mind of its own, and whose employment cannot be separated from its ownership and moral agency, it is necessarily the factor with the highest agency costs from idiosyncratic knowledge and opportunism.

The agency problems of labor follow directly from the incompleteness of the labor contract, and its enforcement by "endogenous" means (or "private ordering"). Michael Reich and James Devine describe it this way:

> Conflict is inherent in the employment relation because the employer does not purchase a specified quantity of performed labor, but rather control over the worker's capacity to work over a given time period, and because the workers' goals differ from those of the employer. The amount of labor actually done is determined by a struggle between workers and capitalists.[4]

Richard Edwards, in *Contested Terrain*, writes that "the capacity to do work is useful to the capitalist only if the work actually gets done . . . ."

> One the wages-for-time exchange has been made, the capitalist cannot rest content. He has purchased a given quantity of labor power, but he must now "stride ahead" and strive to extract actual labor from the labor power he now legally owns.
>
> Workers must provide labor power in order to receive their wages; that is, they must show up for work; but they need not necessarily provide *labor*, much less the amount of labor that the capitalist desires to extract from the labor power they have sold. In a situation where workers do not control their own labor process . . . , any exertion beyond the minimum needed to avert boredom will not be in the workers' interest. On the other side, for the capitalist it is true *without limit* that the more work he can wring out of the labor power he has purchased, the more goods will be produced; and they will be produced without any increased wage costs . . . .
>
> . . . . Conflict exists because the interests of workers and those of employers collide, and what is good for one is frequently costly for the other. Control is rendered problematic because, unlike the other commodities involved in production, labor power is always

1. David Ellerman, *Property and Contract in Economics: The Case for Economic Democracy* (pdf version online), p. 37.

2. *Ibid.*, p. 63.

3. *Ibid.*, p. 84.

4. Michael Reich and James Devine, "The Microeconomics of Conflict and Hierarchy in Capitalist Production," *The Review of Radical Political Economics* vol. 12 no. 4 (Winter 1981), pp. 27-28.

embodied in people, who have their own interests and needs and who retain their power to resist being treated like a commodity.[1]

Harvey Leibenstein, the father of "X-Efficiency," had anticipated a considerable part of these lines of argument, in criticizing the neoclassical treatment of labor:

> .... Human capital, the source of human inputs, cannot be purchased outright by firms. Usually what is purchased are units of labor time. But these are not the units critical for production. What is critical is directed effort, at or beyond some level of skill. Directed effort, however, involves choice and motivation ....
>
> Since the labor contract is almost always incomplete, and since occupational roles have to be interpreted from various behavioral acts and incomplete information, the dimensions of these are rarely completely specified.[2]

From the incompleteness of the contract, Samuel Bowles and Herbert Gintis argue, endogenous bargaining necessarily follows:

> The classical theory of contract implicit in most of neo-classical economics holds that the enforcement of claims is performed by the judicial system at negligible cost to the exchanging parties. We refer to this ... as *exogenous enforcement*. Where, by contrast, enforcement of claims arising from an exchange by third parties is infeasible or excessively costly, the exchanging agents must themselves seek to enforce their claims. Endogenous enforcement in labour markets was analysed by Marx—he termed it the extraction of labour from labour power—and has recently become the more or less standard model among microeconomic theorists.

Because exogenous enforcement is unavailable for many issues under the labor contract, employers must rely on private ordering for enforcement:

> ... when there is no relevant third party ..., when the contested attribute can be measured only imperfectly or at considerable cost (work effort, for example ...), when the relevant evidence is not admissible in a court of law ... [,] when there is no possible means of redress ..., or when the nature of the contingencies concerning future states of the world relevant to the exchange precludes writing a fully specified contract.
>
> In such cases the *ex post* terms of exchange are determined by the structure of the interaction between A and B, and in particular on the strategies A is able to adopt to induce B to provide the desired level of the contested attribute, and the counter strategies available to B
> ....
>
> An employment relationship is established when, in return for a wage, the worker B agrees to submit to the authority of the employer A for a specified period of time in return for a wage w. While the employer's promise to pay the wage is legally enforceable, the worker's promise to bestow an adequate level of effort and care upon the tasks assigned, even if offered, is not. Work is subjectively costly for the worker to provide, valuable to the employer, and costly to measure. The manager-worker relationship is thus a contested exchange.[3]

In other words, the labor contract is an *incomplete contract*. That means that all its terms cannot be established *ex ante*, or ahead of time. From this, Oliver Williamson puts argues,

1. Richard Edwards, *Contested Terrain: The Transformation of the Workplace in the Twentieth Century* (New York: Basic Books, 1979), p. 12.

2. Harvey Leibenstein, "Organizational or Frictional Equilibria, X-Efficiency, and the Rate of Innovation," *Quarterly Journal of Economics* pp. 601, 603.

3. "Is the Demand for Workplace Democracy Redundant in a Liberal Economy?" in Ugo Pagano and Robert Rowthorn, eds., *Democracy and Efficiency in the Economic Enterprise*. A study prepared for the World Institute for Development Economics Research (WIDER) of the United Nations University (London and New York: Routledge, 1994, 1996), pp. 69-70.

"bargaining is pervasive" in hierarchies, "on which account the institutions of private ordering . . . take on critical economic significance."[1]

It is ordinarily in the interest of employers to avoid defining workers' duties too
closely by contract, because it runs contrary to their need for a free hand in safeguarding
authority (under a "general clause") to redefine duties as the need arises, and to take advantage of management authority to extract the maximum value from labor-power. But
the converse problem is, in Oliver Williamson's phrase, "the unenforceability of general
clauses"[2] when opportunism is present.

We saw in Chapter Six that idiosyncratic knowledge is a source of agency problems,
and that the possessors of such knowledge are able to extract rents from it. This is especially
true of workers' knowledge of the production process. A good example is management's
dependence on call center workers' specialized knowledge in a privatized utility:

> As successive problems with the systems emerged, it became clear to the staff that
> the people who had designed the systems had an inadequate knowledge of the content
> of clerical work, and assumed it to be far less complex than it was in reality. Somewhat
> ironically, the introduction of systems intended to simplify and standardize clerical work
> actually drew the clerks' attention to the fact that they provided the company with a
> kind of expertise that cannot easily be written into a computer programme. As one clerk
> noted, "Each section involves knowledge that has to be picked up, that can't be built
> into the systems" . . . . A supply clerk explained:
>
> > . . . I don't think we realized before just how much management depends on
> > us knowing about the job . . . . They thought they knew all what we did, they
> > said, "We know the procedures, we've got it written down." I think it's been
> > a bit of a shock to them to find out they didn't know, that procedure is not
> > necessarily how you do the job, job descriptions can't cover everything.[3]

This is often true even in cases of "deskilling" technology, when management's objective was to reduce its dependence on workers' idiosyncratic knowledge of the work
process, and thereby also to reduce worker rents resulting from the cost of replacing a
skilled workforce.

Given these special agency problems, there are two alternative ways of dealing with them:

1) Increase hierarchy and substitute factors with lower agency costs (like capital) for
labor as much as possible. The problem is that administrative overhead and capital outlays
are likely to be very high, with unit costs higher than would be the case if organization and
production methods were chosen with regard solely to productive efficiency.

2) Make labor, the factor with the highest agency costs, the residual claimant, thereby reducing conflict of interest and internalizing the costs and benefits of decisions in the same actors.

The latter would normally be the most efficient form of organization. But the very
structure of the system, the legacy of a primitive accumulation process by which labor was
separated from the means of production and investment capital was concentrated in the
hands of a small number of absentee owners, rules out such an approach at the outset.
Therefore it is necessary to resort to second-best expedients to make absentee ownership
as efficient as possible: hierarchy, deskilling, and capital-substitution.

All the various forms of hierarchy, and the management fads for coping with its inherent inefficiencies, are intended to cope with the workforce's lack of intrinsic motivation
to share knowledge or to maximize efficiency or output. Hierarchy is a primitive mecha-

---

1. Oliver Williamson, *The Economic Institutions of Capitalism* (New York: The Free Press,
1985), p. 29.
2. *Ibid.*, p. 63.
3. Julia O'Connell Davidson., "The Sources and Limits of Resistance in a Privatized Utility,"
in J. Jermier and D. Knight, eds., *Resistance and Power in Organizations* (London: Routledge, 1994),
pp. 82–83.

nism for getting people to perform tasks which they have no rational interest in perform-ing. At the risk of bowdlerizing Ursula LeGuin and Peter Drucker, hierarchy is the most efficient means for carrying out an inherently inefficient task.

The strategy of substituting capital for labor is not nearly as effective as it sounds. Consider, for example, one of the most expensive experiments in labor discipline ever made, the introduction of automated control systems for machine tools (described by David Noble in *Forces of Production*). The roots of numeric control systems lay in manage-ment's reaction to the labor disputes of the 1930s and 1940s. During WWII and the early Cold War, military contractors using USAAC/USAAF/USAF money carried out intensive R&D in cybernetics, servomechanisms and remote control. Digital control systems for ma-chine tools were one of the civilian spin-offs, first introduced in the Air Force's civilian contractors. Management adopted the new technology, with encouragement from the Pen-tagon, as a way of deskilling labor—that is, reducing the control of master machinists over the production process, and shifting control upward to white collar engineers and manag-ers. The goal was to reduce labor's asset specificity and its rents from idiosyncratic knowl-edge of the production process, so that it could be easily replaced—thus ultimately reduc-ing the bargaining power of labor. The problem was, it didn't pan out quite as expected. As it turned out, management was heavily dependent on the "consummate cooperation" of labor to keep the extremely expensive machines from breaking down. It required consider-able worker initiative and interest just to keep the machines from breaking down, let alone keep the scrap rate to manageable levels. But management attempted to treat workers as extensions of the machines, and lowered the skill ratings on which their pay was based. Predictably,

> . . . [t]he workers increasingly refused to take any initiative—to do minor maintenance (like cleaning lint out of the tape reader), help in diagnosing malfunctions, repair broken tools, or even prevent a smash-up. The scrap rate soared . . . along with machine down-time, and low morale produced the highest absenteeism and turnover rates in the plant. Walkouts were common and, under constant harassment from supervisors, the operators developed ingenious covert methods of retaining some measure of control over their work, including clever use of the machine overrides.
> . . . . The part of the plant with the most sophisticated equipment had become the part of the plant with the highest scrap rate, highest turnover, and lowest productivity . . . .[1]

So the workers were much better at reasserting their control over the production process than management was at circumventing it. The agency costs of labor are virtually insurmountable, even with capital-substitution and deskilling. These latter methods may deprive workers of direct positive control of the production process; but under any circum-stances they are likely to maintain a negative veto power, the ability to impose costs on the job with virtually no risk or inconvenience to themselves.

And hierarchy and monitoring are unsatisfactory solutions. It stands to reason that, if hierarchy is adopted because of the difficulty of verifying the specified levels of work per-formance in a contract, workers in a hierarchy must be more susceptible to the monitoring of their efforts and quality of work. But if so, then why is it necessary to use work incen-tives to overcome the costs of monitoring? And doesn't the effectiveness of work incen-tives depend on management's ability to assess individual performance accurately? And if there are limits to management's monitoring capability *within* a hierarchy, then don't monitoring and incentives have the same practical problems within the hierarchy as with-out? New institutionalists like Williamson, who tend to underestimate agency costs within a hierarchy, provide no satisfactory answer.

1. David F. Noble, *Forces of Production: A Social History of Industrial Automation* (New York: Alfred A. Knopf, 1984), p. 277.

The internal governance of the corporation on the American model, with the firm controlled by management that claims to represent shareholders to the exclusion of internal stakeholder interests, presents special difficulties. Luigi Zingales argues.

> If we accept the view that decision rights should be allocated to the party that can benefit and lose the most from these decisions, then this view of the firm has very sharp implications for the allocation of voting rights. Looking just at explicit contracts, the only residual claim is equity. Thus, shareholders deserve the right to make decisions. Hence, we have the basis for shareholder supremacy.
>
> To accept this view at face value, one has to take a very legalistic view of contracts.[1]

It requires, specifically, the assumption that the particular explicit contracts included in the corporate nexus of contracts effectively protects the rights of *all* contractual claimants. If, in fact, there is a conflict of interest by which the party in power can adversely affect the interests of contractual claimants in ways that they are not protected against, and "other contracting parties besides equity holders are not fully protected by the explicit contracts," then the basic premise of shareholder supremacy is undermined.[2]

Arguably the management and workers are both de facto residual claimants, but with rights not protected by explicit contract, so that management has the power to expropriate the de facto residual claimancy rights of the rest of the human capital in the organization.

Zingales writes that "a firm is not simply the sum of components readily available on the market but rather is a unique combination, which can be worth more or less than the sum of its parts." The difference reflects the value of organizational and human capital.[3] This means that a significant portion of shareholder equity may in fact be a positive externality of the firm's organizational capital, which has not been appropriated by the rightful parties because property rights are so poorly defined under the standard corporate form.[4]

As John Kay argues, the principal-agent model of corporate governance, which treats salaried executives as hired agents of the shareholders, is a fiction: "You cannot own a structure of relationships between people, or own their shared knowledge, or own the routines and modes of behaviour they have established."[5]

Zingales identifies the human capital of the firm as owners of "growth options." Because ownership of such growth options is not effectively represented by property rights and exercises no effective influence on the governance of the firm, a conflict of interest is created in which management benefits from foregoing opportunities for growth and instead starving the organization of resources that might increase its long-term productivity.[6] To repeat our earlier analogy, management prefers a big piece of a smaller pie to making the pie bigger.

So to recapitulate, the structural biases of the present system rule out the most efficient solution to the agency problem—worker ownership—from the outset. As a result, hierarchy must be adopted as a sort of Rube Goldberg contraption to extract effort from those with no intrinsic motivation.

But this second-best expedient is becoming less and less effective over time, as the agency problems of labor and the costs of monitoring it increase.

1. Luigi Zingales, "In Search of New Foundations," *The Journal of Finance*, vol. lv, no. 4 (August 2000), p. 1631.

2. *Ibid.*, p. 1632.

3. *Ibid.*, pp. 1633–1634.

4. *Ibid.*, p. 1634.

5. John Kay, *The Business of Economics* (Oxford: Oxford University Press, 1996), p. 81.

6. Zingales, "In Search of New Foundations," p. 1636.

B. Labor Struggle as Asymmetric Warfare

Vulgar libertarian critiques of organized labor commonly assert that unions depend entirely on force (or the implicit threat of force), backed by the state, against non-union laborers; they assume, in so arguing, that the strike as it is known today has always been the primary method of labor struggle. Jeffrey Tucker, in commenting on the Hollywood writers' strike, displays the prevailing view at Mises.Org:

> . . . [Unions] are large groups of workers seeking to cartelize themselves against competition from other workers. Exclusion is their goal . . . .
>
> . . . [O]rganizing the form of a union, and extracting money through what is essentially a forced blackmail, is incompatible with the peaceful and contractual relations that characterize market relations . . . .
>
> The peak [in union membership] was 1945, a result of wartime economic planning that had followed a New Deal policy giving unions special privileges in law. It was not lost on people after the war that the unions were wrecking the prospects for economic recovery, so a few rights were granted back to companies, though unions retained the upper hand. The decline has been steady ever since, falling to a mere 7.5 percent in the private sector (the public sector is a different animal entirely), which is almost but not quite as low as it was in the pre-New Deal period of free markets. [sic]
>
> . . . [U]nions only benefit themselves at others' expense.[1]

Thomas DiLorenzo, also of Mises.Org, is their most prominent writer on labor issues. His work can be taken as a proxy for the vulgar libertarian view. I quote the following as an example:

> Historically, the main "weapon" that unions have employed to try to push wages above the levels that employees could get by bargaining for themselves on the free market without a union has been the strike. But in order for the strike to work, and for unions to have any significance at all, some form of coercion or violence must be used to keep competing workers out of the labor market.[2]

Such writers extrapolate from the functioning of unions under state capitalism to the fundamental nature of organized labor *as such*. Charles Johnson remarked on this:

> General Motors has benefited *at least* as much from government patronage as the UAW, yet libertarian criticism of the magnates of state capitalism is hardly extended to business as such in the way that criticism of existing unions is routinely extended to any form of organized labor.[3]

In any case, DiLorenzo's comments betray both a profound ignorance of the history of the labor movement outside the sterile bubble of the Wagner Act, and of the purposes of the Wagner Act itself.[4]

First of all, when the strike *was* chosen as a weapon, it relied more on the threat of imposing costs on the employer than on the forcible exclusion of scabs. You wouldn't think it so hard for the Misoids to understand that the replacement of a major portion of the

1. Jeffrey Tucker, "Hollywood's Workers and Peasants," *InsideCatholic.Com*, November 3, 2007 <http://insidecatholic.com/Joomla/index.php?option=com_content&task=view&id=1354&Itemid=48>.

2. Thomas DiLorenzo, "The Myth of Voluntary Unions," Mises.Org, September 14, 2004 <http://www.mises.org/story/1604>.

3. Charles Johnson, "Liberty, Equality, Solidarity: Toward a Dialectical Anarchism," in Roderick T. Long and Tibor R. Machan, eds., *Anarchism/Minarchism: Is a Government Part of a Free Country?* (Hampshire, UK, and Burlington, Vt.: Ashgate Publishing Limited, 2008). Quotes are from a textfile provided by the author.

4. It also displays, as much as it would pain Dilorenzo to admit it, a neoclassical understanding of unions, to the extent that it matches Oliver Williamson's description of the neoclassical approach: "Labor union organization was treated almost entirely as a matter of monopoly, there being little or no reference to efficient governance and the attenuation of opportunism." Williamson, *The Economic Institutions of Capitalism* (New York: Free Press, 1985), p. 65.

workforce, especially when the supply of replacement workers is limited by moral sympathy with the strike, might entail considerable transaction costs and disruption of production. The idiosyncratic knowledge of the existing workforce, the time and cost of bringing replacement workers to an equivalent level of productivity, and the damage short-term disruption of production may do to customer relations, together constitute a rent that invests the threat of walking out with a considerable deterrent value.

And the cost and disruption is greatly intensified when the strike is backed by sympathy strikes at other stages of production. Wagner and Taft-Hartley greatly reduced the effectiveness of strikes at individual plants by transforming them into declared wars fought by Queensbury rules, and likewise reduced their effectiveness by prohibiting the coordination of actions across multiple plants or industries. Taft-Hartley's cooling off periods, in addition, gave employers time to prepare ahead of time for such disruptions and greatly reduced the informational rents embodied in the training of the existing workforce. Were not such restrictions in place, today's "just-in-time" economy would likely be far more vulnerable to such disruption than that of the 1930s. Jane Slaughter argued as much:

> "Just-in-time" . . . has made the union potentially more powerful than ever. The lack of
> buffer stocks makes quickie stoppages or slowdowns in support of an immediate demand
> extremely effective. The same is true with labor power—if workers in a department re-
> fuse to work, management has no extras to replace them. Action by even a few members
> could affect production drastically.[1]

A British management consultant warned, in similar terms, about the vulnerability of just-in-time to disruption:

> Without buffer stocks between production each process is entirely dependent on
> the upstream one to deliver. Hence JIT bestows upon those who work it the capacity to
> create disruptions which, intentionally or otherwise are likely to be extremely pervasive
> . . . .
> A mere refusal to work overtime or to be flexible about tea breaks and working
> practices could cause severe problems, and a work-to-rule or stoppage could be disas-
> trous . . . .
> The ideal JIT system has no inventories, no buffer stock, and no stocks of finished
> goods. If the supplier fails to deliver, production stops; if any one process fails to deliver,
> production stops; and if transport fails, production stops.[2]

More importantly, though, unionism was historically less about strikes or excluding non-union workers from the workplace than about what workers did *inside* the workplace to strengthen their bargaining power against the boss. For example, P.J. Passmore, London organizer for the Industrial Syndicalist Education League, addressed a branch meeting of the Amalgamated Society of Railroad Servants: "How foolish it is to go on strike, thus placing ourselves in the power of the companies, who can starve us into subjection, when, by a little intelligent use of sabotage, &c., on the job, we could obtain our ends."[3] A radical British workers' daily, the *Daily Herald*, coined the apt phrase "Staying in on Strike" as an alternative to going out on strike to be starved.[4]

The Wagner Act, like the rest of the corporate liberal legal regime, aimed to divert labor resistance away from the successful asymmetric warfare model, and toward a formal-

---

1. Jane Slaughter, "Management by Stress," *The Multinational Monitor*, January/February 1990 <http://www.multinationalmonitor.org/hyper/issues/1990/01/slaughter.html>.
2. Barry Wilkinson and Nick Oliver, "Power, Control and the Kanban," *New Manufacturing* No. 3. (1989), in "Management Schemes—Part 1 (UE's Information for Workers)" <http://www.ranknfile-ue.org/stwd_mgtsch.html>.
3. Quoted in Geoff Brown, *Sabotage: A Study of Industrial Conflict* (Nottingham, England: Spokesman Books, 1977), p. 28.
4. *Ibid.*, p. 36. Here "sabotage" is used in the broad sense of "deliberate withdrawal of efficiency."

ized, bureaucratic system centered on labor contracts enforced by the state and the union hierarchies. As Karl Hess suggested,

> one crucial similarity between those two fascists [Hitler and FDR] is that both successfully destroyed the trade unions. Roosevelt did it by passing exactly the reforms [sic] that would ensure the creation of a trade-union bureaucracy. Since F.D.R., the unions have become the protectors of contracts rather than the spearhead of worker demands. And the Roosevelt era brought the "no strike" clause, the notion that your rights are limited by the needs of the state.[1]

Incidentally, one of the recurring themes in the early part of Geoff Brown's book on sabotage, which we cited a few paragraphs up, is the hostility of much of the union leadership to direct action on the job—particularly "going canny"—as early as the turn of the twentieth century. Even then, the nascent labor establishment favored a regime in which the primary function of unions was collective bargaining and the enforcement of contracts, with the workers as a passive clientele, and with bargaining power centralized in the labor establishment. The most important service of the Wagner regime, to the leadership of both big business and big labor, was to strengthen the labor establishment at the expense of the rank and file. The effect, desired by both, was to transform unions from instruments of struggle by the rank and file into hierarchical organizations whose leaders could make comfortable backroom deals with the corporate bosses, without any disruptive interference from below.

If this seems like an exaggeration for rhetorical effect, consider Sam Dolgoff's account:

> In 1937 Lewis assured the employers that " . . . a CIO contract is adequate protection against sit-downs, lie-downs, or any other kind of strike . . . . " . . . .
>
> According to the organ of big business (*Business Week*—June 7, 1958) the corporations accepted the CIO brand of "industrial unionism" because as a matter of policy, the mass-production industries prefer to bargain with a strong international union able to dominate its locals and keep them from disrupting production.
>
> As far back as 1926, Gerald Swope, President of General Electric Corporation, tried to persuade the AFL to organize a nation-wide union of electrical workers on an industrial basis. Swope believed than an industrial union " . . . would mean the difference between an organization which we can work with on a business basis, and one that was an endless source of difficulties . . . . " The difficulties Swope had in mind were negotiating separate contracts with different local unions in the same plant or vicinity, whose contracts expire and must be renegotiated at different times which could prolong strikes and halt production indefinitely.
>
> The implementation of the CIO brand of "industrial unionism" necessitated the creation of a highly centralized bureaucratic organizational structure which practically emasculated control of the union by the membership.[2]

Before Wagner, industrial unions saw even conventional strikes as requiring strategic depth. But the federal labor law regime criminalizes many forms of resistance, like sympathy and boycott strikes up and down the production chain from raw materials to retail, that made the mass and general strikes of the early 1930s so formidable. The Railway Labor Relations Act was specifically designed to prevent transport workers from turning local strikes into general strikes. Taft-Hartley's cooling off period can be used for similar purposes in other strategic sectors, as demonstrated by Bush's invocation of it against the longshoremen's union.

---

1. "More From Hess," *freeman, libertarian critter*, June 9, 2005 <http://freemanlc.blogspot.com/2005/06/more-from-hess.html>.

2. Sam Dolgoff, "Ethics and the Unions—Part 2," in *The American Labor Movement: A New Beginning*. Originally published in 1980 in *Resurgence*. <http://www.iww.org/culture/library/dolgoff/labor2.shtml>

The extent to which state labor policy serves the interests of employers is suggested by the old (pre-Milsted) Libertarian Party Platform, a considerable deviation from the stereotypical libertarian position on organized labor. It expressly called for a repeal, not only of Wagner, but also of Taft-Hartley's prohibitions on sympathy and boycott strikes and of state right-to-work prohibitions on union shop contracts. It also condemned any federal right to impose "cooling off" periods or issue back-to-work orders.[1]

Wagner was originally passed, as Alexis Buss suggests below, because the *bosses* were begging for a regime of enforceable contract, with the unions as enforcers. This only confirms Adam Smith's observation that when the state regulates relations between workmen and masters, it usually has the masters for its counselors.

Far from being a labor charter that empowered unions for the first time, FDR's labor regime had the same practical effect as telling the irregulars of Lexington and Concord "Look, you guys come out from behind those rocks, put on these bright red uniforms, and march in parade ground formation, and in return we'll set up a system of arbitration to guarantee you don't lose *all* the time." Unfortunately, the Wagner regime left organized labor massively vulnerable to liquidation in the event that ruling elites decided they *wanted* labor to lose all the time, after all. And Taft-Hartley was passed because they decided, in fact, that unions *were* still winning too much of the time. Since the late '60s, corporate America has moved to exploit the full union-busting potential of Taft-Hartley. And guess what? Labor is prevented by law, for the most part, from abandoning the limits of Wagner and Taft-Hartley and returning to the successful unilateral techniques of the early '30s.

Admittedly, Wagner wasn't all bad for workers, so long as big business saw organized labor as a useful tool for imposing order on the workplace. If workers lost control of how their job was performed, at least their pay increased with productivity and they had the security of a union contract. Life as a wage-slave was certainly better under the corporate liberal variant of state capitalism than under the kind of right-to-work banana republic Reagan and Thatcher replaced it with.

Note well: I'm far from defending the statism of the FDR labor regime in principle. I'd prefer not to have my face stamped by a jackboot in Oceania, *or* be smothered with kindness by Huxley's World Controller. I'd prefer a legal regime where labor is free to obtain its full product by bargaining in a free labor market, without the state's thumb on the scale on behalf of the owning classes. But if I'm forced to choose between forms of statism, there's no doubt which one I'll pick: the one whose yoke weighs less heavily on my own shoulders.

In any event, the Wagner regime worked for labor only so long as capital *wanted* it to work for labor. It was originally intended as one of the "humane" measures like those the kindly farmer provided for his cattle in Tolstoy's parable (the better to milk them, of course).[2] Of course, if we're going to be livestock, that beats the hell out of the kind of "farmer" we've had since the neoliberal reaction: one who decides it's more profitable to work us to death and then replace us.

But that's all moot now; the corporate elite decided in the 1970s that the "labor accord" had outlived its usefulness, and labor began its long retreat. Whatever value the Wagner regime had for us in the past, it has outlived. We are getting kicked in the teeth under the old rules. If labor is to fight a successful counteroffensive, it has to stop playing by the bosses' rules. We need to fight completely outside of Wagner's structure of NLRB certifi-

---

1. The original plank, "Unions and Collective Bargaining," is preserved by the Web Archive at <http://web.archive.org/web/20050305053450/http://www.lp.org/issues/platform/uniocoll.html>. Nothing resembling it is included in the new LP platform.

2. Leo Tolstoy, " Parable," reproduced at <www.geocities.com/glasgowbranch/parable.html>.

cation and contracts, or at least treat them as a secondary tactic in a strategy based on direct action.

In the neoliberal age, they bosses have apparently decided that we need the contracts more than they do, and that "at-will" is the best thing for them. But I think if we took off the gloves, *they* might be the ones begging for a return to contracts.

That may seem counterintuitive. The technofascists, with Echelon, RFID chips, public surveillance cameras, and the like, have us under tighter surveillance at home than we could have imagined a generation ago; they also have the globe under the closest thing to an unchallenged hegemony that's ever existed in history. In their wildest dreams for the near future, the PNAC types probably imagine something like Ken Macleod's US/UN Hegemony in *The Star Fraction*, enforced by a network of orbital laser battle stations capable of incinerating ships and armored formations anywhere on the Earth's surface.[1]

Nevertheless, I suspect that all these high-tech lines of defense, against would-be military rivals and against subversion at home, are a modern-day version of the Maginot Line. In Macleod's story, that Hegemony was overthrown in the end by asymmetric warfare, fought by a loose coalition of insurgencies around the world. Their fluid guerrilla tactics never presented a target for the orbital lasers; and they kept coming back with one offensive after another against the New World Order, until the cost of the constant counterinsurgency wars bled the U.S. economy dry and a general strike finally broke the back of the corporate state.

Bin Laden, murderous bastard though he is, has a pretty good sense of strategy. Expensive, high tech weapons are great for winning battles, he says, but not for winning wars. The destitute hill people of Afghanistan already brought one superpower to its knees. Perhaps the remaining superpower will be similarly humbled by its own people right here at home.

In the military realm, the age-old methods of decentralized and networked resistance have most recently appeared in public discussion under the buzzword "Fourth Generation Warfare."[2]

But networked resistance against the Empire goes far beyond guerrilla warfare in the military realm. The same advantages of asymmetric warfare accrue equally to domestic political opposition. Consider this passage in Harry Boyte's *The Backyard Revolution*, written almost thirty years ago:

> Citizen activists in the 1970s often developed sophisticated understanding of the importance of organizational space, the need to form networks among the different spaces, and the process of transformation involved within them . . . . Ralph Nader saw the development of different citizen groups as, potentially, "an alternative communications system to the main public information systems which are so corporate dominated. If you're dealing with nuclear power, for example, you can't rely on the news to get the real facts. You have to have direct citizen contact between groups. And eventually citizen groups have to get access to satellite systems, to the new technologies."[3]

That sounds almost like the design specs for the Internet, doesn't it? It's directly analogous to Illich's vision of decentralized learning networks in *Deschooling Society*, at a time when the only technology available for supporting such networks was telephones and tape recorders. The Internet couldn't have been better suited to the organizational needs

---

1. Ken Macleod, *The Star Fraction* (Tor Books, 2001).
2. William S. Lind's archives on the subject at LewRockwell.Com <http://www.lewrockwell.com/ lind/lind-arch.html> are a good starting place for study, along with John Robb's *Global Guerrillas* blog <http://globalguerrillas.typepad.com/>.
3. Harry C. Boyte, *The Backyard Revolution: Understanding the New Citizen Movement* (Philadelphia: Temple University Press, 1980), pp. 37-38.

Nader (or Illich) described if it had been specifically designed for it. And in fact, the Internet resulted in a quantum leap in the potential for networked resistance.

There is a wide range of ruling elite literature on the dangers of "netwar" to the existing system of power, along with an equal volume of literature by the Empire's enemies celebrating it. Most notable among the former are probably the Rand studies, from the late 1990s on, by David Ronfeldt et al. In The Zapatista "Social Netwar" in Mexico[1], those authors expressed grave concern over the possibilities of decentralized "netwar" techniques for undermining elite control. They saw ominous signs of such a movement in the global political support network for the Zapatistas. Loose, ad hoc coalitions of affinity groups, organizing through the Internet, could throw together large demonstrations at short notice, and "swarm" the government and mainstream media with phone calls, letters, and emails far beyond their capacity to absorb. Ronfeldt noted a parallel between such techniques and the "leaderless resistance" advocated by right-wing white supremacist Louis Beam, circulating in some Constitutionalist/militia circles. These were, in fact, the very methods later used at Seattle and afterward. Decentralized "netwar" was essentially the "crisis of governability" Samuel Huntington had warned of in the 1970s—but potentially several orders of magnitude greater.

The post-Seattle movement confirmed such elite fears, and resulted in a full-scale backlash. Paul Rosenberg recounted in horrifying detail the illegal repression and political dirty tricks used by local police forces against anti-globalization activists at protests in 1999 and 2000.[2] There have even been some reports that Garden Plot[3] was activated on a local basis at Seattle, and that Delta Force units provided intelligence and advice to local police.[4] The U.S. government also seems to have taken advantage of the upward ratcheting of the police state after the 9-11 attacks to pursue its preexisting war on the anti-globalization movement. The intersection of the career of onetime Philadelphia Police Commissioner John Timoney, a fanatical enemy of the post-Seattle movement, with the highest levels of Homeland Security (in the meantime supervising the police riot against the FTAA protesters in Miami) is especially interesting in this regard.[5]

Jeff Vail discusses netwar techniques in his A Theory of Power blog, in a much more sympathetic manner, as "Rhizome."[6] Vail predicts that the political struggles of the 21st century will be defined by the structural conflict between rhizome and hierarchy.

1. David Ronfeldt, John Arquilla, Graham Fuller, Melissa Fuller. The Zapatista "Social Netwar" in Mexico MR-994-A (Santa Monica: Rand, 1998) <http://www.rand.org/ pubs/ monograph_ reports/MR994/index.html>.

2. "The Empire Strikes Back: Police Repression of Protest from Seattle to L.A." (L.A. Independent Media Center, August 13, 2000). The original online file is now defunct, unfortunately, but is preserved for the time being at <http://web.archive.org/web/20030803220613/ http://www.r2kphilly.org/pdf/empire-strikes.pdf>.

3. Frank Morales, "U.S. Military Civil Disturbance Planning: The War at Home" Covert Action Quarterly, Spring-Summer 2000; this article, likewise, is no longer available on the Web, but is preserved at <http://web.archive.org/web/20000818175231/http://infowar.net/warathome/warathome.html>.

4. Alexander Cockburn, "The Jackboot State: The War Came Home and We're Losing It" Counterpunch May 10, 2000 <http://www.counterpunch.org/jackboot.html>; "US Army Intel Units Spying on Activists" Intelligence Newsletter #381 April 5, 2000 <http://web.archive.org/ web/20000816182951/http://www.infoshop.org/news5/army_intel.html>.

5. I put together much of the relevant information in these blog posts: "Fighting the Domestic Enemy: You," Mutualist Blog, August 11, 2005 <http://mutualist.blogspot.com/2005/08/fighting-domestic-enemy-you.html>; and "Filthy Pig Timoney in the News," Mutualist Blog, December 2, 2005 <http://mutualist.blogspot.com/2005/12/filthy-pig-timoney-in-news.html>.

6. <http://www.jeffvail.net/> The book A Theory of Power is available as a free pdf file at <http://www.jeffvail.net/atheoryofpower.pdf>.

Rhizome structures, media and asymmetric politics will not be a means to support
or improve a centralized, hierarchical democracy—they will be an alternative to it.

Many groups that seek change have yet to identify hierarchy itself as the root cause
of their problem . . . , but are already beginning to realize that rhizome is the solution.

As an example of rhizome politics, he gives the examples of the antiglobalization protests beginning in Seattle in 1999, along with similarly organized protests like the 2004
RNC convention in Philadelphia. The network of political blogs is organized on the same
principle.

. . . Rhizome networks are better able to process information than hierarchies, with
their numerous layers that information must relay between, . . . [resulting] in an information processing burden that significantly slows the ability of hierarchy to execute the
OODA [Observe, Orient, Decide, Act[1]] loop . . . .

[Rhizome action is] beginning to coalesce into an effective system . . . , founded
upon the information processing capability of rhizome . . .

The comparative performance in 2004 of Democratic bloggers and of the Kerry campaign was definitive evidence of the superiority of rhizome techniques. Had Kerry fired his
opposition research staff and put Kos or Atrios in charge of his war room, he'd probably be
president today. For example, consider the humorous ad the Bush campaign ran, with rag-
time music and footage of jalopies, about Kerry's "funny ideas" on energy (it concerned
his proposal for increasing the fuel tax to discourage consumption). Within a couple of
days, the liberal bloggers had links to Congressman Dick Cheney's bill, in a time of historic
low petroleum prices, to impose a tax on imported petroleum whenever the price fell
below a certain level; it was, pure and simple, a price support tax for the domestic oil
industry. Another example was the so-called Swiftboat campaign to smear Kerry's war
record. The leading figure in that group, as the Democratic bloggers pointed out, had also
smeared George Bush's own father, accusing him of personal malfeasance during his plane
crash in the Pacific Theater during WWII. Had Kerry simply led with such talking points
at a few press conferences, he'd have wiped the floor with Bush.

Vail, of course, also applies rhizome to national security (Open Source Warfare), with
Al Qaeda as the leading example of a distributed warfare network.:

Without the centralized command structure of hierarchy, actions and tactics are proposed
by the network and adapted by constituent nodes via a process similar in many ways to a
clinical trial. Some node devises a tactic or selects a target and makes this theory publicly
available—Open Source. One or several trials of this theory are conducted, and the tactic
is then adopted and improved upon by the network as a whole based on its success.

Vail speculates that many groups engaged in rhizome political or military action will
come to see the conflict with hierarchy as the root of their various causes, and consciously
adopt a rhizome structure.

The interconnectivity between anti-globalization, economic localization, human rights,
freedoms, environmental concerns, and equal opportunity policies will become clear, and
the combined power of each of these policies will, working together, be far greater than
the sum of their parts.[2]

One question that's been less looked into is the extent to which the ideas of networked resistance and asymmetric warfare are applicable to labor relations. It's rather odd
labor relations aren't considered more in this context, since the Wobbly idea of "direct action on the job" is a classic example of asymmetric warfare.

1. The concept originated with Col. Frank Boyd, USAF.
2. Jeff Vail, "Rhizome: Guerrilla Media, Swarming and Asymmetric Politics in the 21st
Century," *A Theory of Power: Jeff Vail's Critique of Hierarchy and Empire*, July 21, 2005
<http://www.jeffvail.net/2005/07/rhizome-guerrilla-media-swarming-and.html>.

An alternative model of labor struggle, and one much closer to the overall spirit of organized labor before Wagner, would include the kinds of activity mentioned in the old Wobbly pamphlet "How to Fire Your Boss," and discussed by the I.W.W.'s Alexis Buss in her articles on "minority unionism" for *Industrial Worker.*

If labor is to return to a pre-Wagner way of doing things, what Buss calls "minority unionism" will be the new organizing principle.

> . . . [W]e need to break out of the current model, one that has come to rely on a recipe increasingly difficult to prepare: a majority of workers vote a union in, a contract is bargained. We need to return to the sort of rank-and-file on-the-job agitating that won the 8-hour day and built unions as a vital force . . . .
>
> Minority unionism happens on our own terms, regardless of legal recognition . . . .
> The labor movement was not built through majority unionism-it couldn't have been.[1]
> How are we going to get off of this road? We must stop making gaining legal recognition and a contract the point of our organizing . . . .
> We have to bring about a situation where the bosses, not the union, want the contract. We need to create situations where bosses will offer us concessions to get our cooperation. Make them beg for It.[2]

As a matter of fact, a strike may well be as effective when carried out by an unofficial union without government certification. Workers without officially recognized unions have successfully won strikes, walking off the job and attracting negative press by picketing with signs. For example, immigrant workers at the Cygnus soap factory in Chicago persuaded teamsters not to cross their picket line, despite the fact that their walkout was a spontaneous action and they belonged to no NLRB-sanctioned union. It took two or three untrained replacement workers to do the work of the strikers, and with many more accidents. Corporate management sent a negotiator and quickly caved in to their demands, owing in part to the negative publicity.[3]

Sam Dolgoff quoted *Black Cat,* a periodical of the Boston I.W.W. branch, from April 1980:

> . . . The nurses should say: "To hell with the election, to hell with Board certification, to hell with the whole NLRB union-busting trap." They should begin to act union on the job. If they have enough support to win a representation election, they have enough support to go ahead and make their demands to management and get them. This would require a different kind of unionism than the one that relies on the NLRB procedure. This would require direct action and solidarity . . . .[4]

As the Wobbly pamphlet "How to Fire Your Boss" argues, the conventional strike in its current form is about the least effective form of action available to organized labor.

> The bosses, with their large financial reserves, are better able to withstand a long drawn-out strike than the workers . . . . And worst of all, a long walk-out only gives the boss a chance to replace striking workers with a scab (replacement) workforce.
> Workers are far more effective when they take direct action while still on the job. By deliberately reducing the boss' profits while continuing to collect wages, you can cripple the boss without giving some scab the opportunity to take your job. Direct ac-

1. "Minority Report," *Industrial Worker,* October 2002 <http://www.iww.org/organize/strategy/AlexisBuss102002.shtml>.
2. "Minority Report," *Industrial Worker,* December 2002 <http://www.iww.org/organize/strategy/AlexisBuss122002.shtml>.
3. Kari Lydersen, "On Strike Without a Union," *In These Times,* September 12, 2007 <http://www.inthesetimes.com/article/3327/on_strike_without_a_union/>.
4. Dolgoff, "Discussion on Regeneration of the American Labor Movement," in *The American Labor Movement: A New Beginning.* <http://www.iww.org/culture/library/dolgoff/labor6.shtml>

tion, by definition, means those tactics workers can undertake themselves, without the help of government agencies, union bureaucrats, or high-priced lawyers.[1]

Instead of conventional strikes, "How to Fire Your Boss" recommends such forms of direct action as the slowdown, the "work to rule" strike, the "good work" strike, selective strikes (brief, unannounced strikes at random intervals), whisteblowing, and sick-ins. These are all ways of raising costs on the job, without giving the boss a chance to hire scabs.

The pamphlet also recommends two other tactics that are likely to be problematic for many free market libertarians: the sitdown and monkey-wrenching (more about which later).

It was probably easier to build unions by means of organizing strikes, getting workers to "down tools" and strike in hot blood when a flying squadron entered the shop, than it is today to get workers to jump through the NLRB's hoops (and likely resign themselves to punitive action) in cold blood. And it certainly was easier to win a strike before Taft-Hartley outlawed secondary and boycott strikes. The classic CIO strikes of the early '30s involved multiple steps in the chain—not only production plants, but also their suppliers of raw materials, their retail outlets, and the teamsters who hauled finished and unfinished goods. They were planned strategically, as a general staff might plan a campaign. Some strikes turned into what amounted to regional general strikes. Even a minority of workers striking, at each step in the chain, can be far more disruptive than a conventional strike limited to one plant.

If nothing else, all of this should demonstrate the sheer nonsensicality of the Misoid claims that strikes are ineffectual unless they involve 100% of the workforce and are backed up by the threat of violence against scabs. Even a sizeable minority of workers walking off the job, if they're backed up by similar minorities at other stages of the production and distribution process on early CIO lines, could utterly paralyze a company.

It seems clear, from a common sense standpoint, that the Wobbly approach is potentially far more effective than the current business union model of collective bargaining under the Wagner regime. The question remains, though, what should be the libertarian ethical stance on such tactics.

As I already mentioned, sitdowns and monkey-wrenching would appear at first glance to be obvious transgressions of libertarian principle. Regarding these, I can only say that the morality of trespassing and vandalism against someone else's property hinges on the just character of their property rights.

Murray Rothbard raised the question, at the height of his attempted alliance with the New Left, of what ought to be done with state property. According to Rothbard, since state ownership of property is in principle illegitimate, all property currently "owned" by the government is really unowned. And since the rightful owner of any piece of unowned property is, in keeping with radical Lockean principles, the first person to occupy and mix his labor with it, it follows that government property is generally the rightful property of whoever is currently occupying and using it. That means, for example, that state universities are the rightful property of either students or faculty, and should be organized either as producer or consumer cooperatives. More provocative still, Rothbard tentatively applied the same principle to the (theatrical gasp) private sector! First he raised the question of nominally "private" universities that got most of their funding from the state. Columbia,

1. "How to Fire Your Boss: A Worker's Guide to Direct Action" <http://home.interlog.com/~gilgames/boss.htm>. It should be noted that the I.W.W. no longer endorses this pamphlet in its original form, and reproduces only a heavily toned down version at its website. It has disavowed portions of the pamphlet—particularly, perhaps understandably given the potential use of "counter-terrorism" powers against radical unions, the section on industrial sabotage—in recent years.

surely a "private" college only "in the most ironic sense," deserved "a similar fate of virtu-ous homesteading confiscation."

But if Columbia University, what of General Dynamics? What of the myriad of corporations which are integral parts of the military-industrial complex, which not only get over half or sometimes virtually all their revenue from the government but also par-ticipate in mass murder? What are their credentials to "private" property? Surely less than zero. As eager lobbyists for these contracts and subsidies, as co-founders of the garri-son stare, they deserve confiscation and reversion of their property to the genuine private sector as rapidly as possible. To say that their "private" property must be respected is to say that the property stolen by the horsethief and the murderer must be "respected."

But how then do we go about destatizing the entire mass of government property, as well as the "private property" of General Dynamics? . . . One method would be to turn over ownership to the homesteading workers in the particular plants; another to turn over pro-rata ownership to the individual taxpayers. But we must face the fact that it might prove the most practical route to first nationalize the property as a prelude to redistribution. Thus, how could the ownership of General Dynamics be transferred to the deserving taxpayers without first being nationalized enroute? And, further more, even if the government should decide to nationalize General Dynamics—without compensa-tion, of course— per se and not as a prelude to redistribution to the taxpayers, this is not immoral or something to be combatted. For it would only mean that one gang of thieves—the government—would be confiscating property from another previously co-operating gang, the corporation that has lived off the government. I do not often agree with John Kenneth Galbraith, but his recent suggestion to nationalize businesses which get more than 75% of their revenue from government, or from the military, has consider-able merit. Certainly it does not mean aggression against private property . . . . But why stop at 75%? Fifty per cent seems to be a reasonable cutoff point on whether an organi-zation is largely public or largely private.[1]

In my opinion, it is a mistake to use direct state subsidies alone as a criterion for "public" status. If a corporation gets the bulk of its profits from state intervention of any kind (including patents, copyrights, and other forms of anti-competitive privilege), it is an arm of the state. And also in my opinion, the Fortune 500 is a pretty good proxy for the sector of the economy whose profits come almost entirely from state intervention—what James O'Connor called the "monopoly capital sector."

Brad Spangler observed that when a man is robbed, it's a mistake to limit the term "robber" to the man holding the gun. The bagman who collects the loot is just as much a robber, if he's a willing part of the team. Likewise, a corporation whose profits result mainly from state action, and whose CEOs, directors, and vice presidents constantly rotate back and forth from the "private sector" to political appointments in the regulatory state, is in reality a part of the state.[2] Big Business is as much a part of the state as the great land-lords were under the Old Regime.

At any rate, if corporations that get the bulk of their profits from state intervention are essentially part of the state, rightfully subject to being treated as the property of the workers actually occupying them, then sitdowns and sabotage should certainly be legiti-mate means for bringing this about.

As for the other, less extreme tactics, those who object morally to such on-the-job di-rect action fail to consider the logical implications of a free contract in labor that we de-scribed above. The very term "adequate effort" is meaningless, aside from whatever way its definition is worked out in practice based on the comparative bargaining power of worker

1. "Confiscation and the Homestead Principle," *The Libertarian Forum*, June 15, 1969 <http://www.mises.org/ journals/lf/1969/1969_06_15.pdf>.

2. Brad Spangler, "Recognizing faux private interests that are actually part of the state," *Brad-Spangler.Com*, April 29, 2005 <http://www.bradspangler.com/blog/archives/54>.

and employer. Since it's impossible to design a contract that specifies exact levels of effort and standards of performance ahead of time, or for employers to reliably monitor performance after the fact, the workplace is contested terrain. Workers are justified entirely as much as employers in attempting to maximize their own interests within the leeway left by an incomplete contract. How much effort is "normal" to expend is determined by the informal outcome of the social contest within the workplace, given the de facto balance of power at any given time. And that includes slowdowns, "going canny," and the like. The "normal" effort that an employer is entitled to, when he buys labor-power, is entirely a matter of convention. If libertarians like to think of "a fair day's wage" as an open-ended concept, they should bear in mind that "a fair day's work" is equally open-ended.[1]

Oliver Williamson quotes Arthur Okun to the effect that what "the firm wants when it hires an employee is productive performance . . . . It wishes to buy quality of work rather than merely time on the job." Williamson continues:

> . . . Accordingly, exploited incumbent employees are not totally without recourse. Incumbent employees who are "forced" to accept inferior terms can adjust quality to the disadvantage of a predatory employer. The issues here have been addressed previously in distinguishing between consummate and perfunctory cooperation . . . . Of necessity, the employment contract is an incomplete agreement, and performance varies with the way in which it is executed.[2]

Williamson's distinction between "consummate" and "perfunctory" cooperation originally appeared in *Markets and Hierarchies*:

> Consummate cooperation is an affirmative job attitude—to include the use of judgment, filling gaps, and taking initiative in an instrumental way. Perfunctory cooperation, by contrast, involves job performance of a minimally acceptable sort . . . . The upshot is that workers, by shifting to a perfunctory performance mode, are in a position to "destroy" idiosyncratic efficiency gains.[3]

He also quotes Peter Blau and Richard Scott on the difficulty of contractually enforcing anything beyond perfunctory cooperation:

> . . . [T]he contract obligates employees to perform only a set of duties in accordance with minimum standards and does not assure their striving to achieve optimum performance . . . . [L]egal authority does not and cannot command the employee's willingness to devote his ingenuity and energy to performing his tasks to the best of his ability . . . . It promotes compliance with directives and discipline, but does not encourage employees to exert effort, to accept responsibilities, or to exercise initiative.[4]

Williamson suggests elsewhere that disgruntled workers will follow a passive-aggressive strategy of compliance in areas where effective metering is possible, while shifting their perfunctory compliance (or worse) into areas where it is impossible.[5] Williamson also argues that it's impossible, "for information impactedness reasons, [to] determine whether workers put their energies and inventiveness into the job in a way which permits

---

    1. In reading Richard Edwards' *Contested Terrain* a few weeks before this final writing, when the chapter was in something close to its final form, I found that in writing this passage I had reinvented the wheel: "Thus, in the slogan, 'A fair day's work for a fair day's pay,' *both* elements become matters of conflict. 'A fair day's work' is as much an issue for bargaining, as is the 'fair day's pay.'" Edwards, op. cit., p. 15.

    2. Oliver Williamson, *The Economic Institutions of Capitalism* (New York: The Free Press, 1985), p. 262.

    3. Oliver Williamson, *Markets and Hierarchies, Analysis and Antitrust Implications: A Study in the Economics of Internal Organization* (New York: Free Press, 1975), p. 69.

    4. Peter Blau and Richard Scott, *Formal Organizations* (San Francisco: Chandler, 1962), p. 140, in Williamson, *The Economic Institutions of Capitalism*, p. 263.

    5. Williamson, *Markets and Hierarchies*, pp. 55–56.

task-specific cost-savings to be fully realized . . . ." Workers are able to thwart management policy by "withholding effort."[1]

A classic example is the quote from a worker at the Indiana gypsum mine we saw in Chapter Eight:

> O.K., I'll punch in just so, and I'll punch out on the nose. But you know you can lead a horse to water and you can lead him away, but it's awful hard to tell how much water he drinks while he's at it.[2]

The organization's dependence on workers' idiosyncratic knowledge, and their active "use of judgment, filling gaps, and taking initiative," by the way, should make it clear just why the passive-aggressive technique of "working to rule" is so diabolically effective. Since the CEOs get paid the big bucks to think, and our job is to shut up and do what we're told, we'll do just that—and see what happens. It's pretty hard for a boss to fire a worker for *not* disregarding policy, eh?

> We may go so far as to say that some factories are only kept going by the workers disregarding the instructions they are given for doing their jobs . . . .
> . . . .The workers are the "underground" of industrial efficiency, breaking the company's regulations to get the job done. This can be demonstrated . . . by the effect of "working to rule" . . . .
> Medical officers and ergonomics experts have constantly pointed out that between 50 and 80 per cent of all working behavior departs from the official norms . . . . [E]ven assembly work is not purely automatic . . . . Even in the most repetitive jobs . . . , workers are far from being robots, if the desired production level is to be achieved they have to show continual initiative for the benefit of their firm. Were they to rest content with obeying orders to the letter, their factory would grind to a halt.[3]

At the "softest" end of the spectrum, direct action methods fade into the general category of moral hazard or opportunism. (For that matter, the whole Austrian concept of "entrepreneurship" arguably presupposes to a large extent rents from asymmetrical information).

The average worker can probably think of hundreds of ways to raise costs on the job, with little or no risk of getting caught, if he puts his mind to it. The giant corporation, arguably, has become so hypertrophied and centralized under the influence of state subsidies that it's vulnerable to the very same kinds of "asymmetrical warfare" from within that threaten the world's sole remaining superpower from without. In Jeremy Weiland's words,

> Their need for us to behave in an orderly, predictable manner is a vulnerability of theirs; it can be exploited. *You have the ability to transform from a replaceable part into a monkey wrench.*[4]

Now, it's almost impossible to outlaw these things *ex ante* through a legally enforceable contract. Every time I go to work it strikes me even more how much of what the Wobblies considered "direct action" couldn't possibly be defined by any feasible contractual or legal regime, and are therefore restrained entirely by the workers' perception of what they can get away with in the contested social space of the job. What constitutes a fair level of effort is entirely a subjective cultural norm, that can only be determined by the real-world bargaining strength of owners and workers in a particular workplace.

1. *Ibid.*, p. 69.
2. Gary J. Miller, *Managerial Dilemmas: The Political Economy of Hierarchy* (New York: Cambridge University Press, 1992), pp. 207-210.
3. P. Dubois, *Sabotage in Industry* (Hammondsworth, England: Penguin Books, 1979), pp. 14-16.
4. Jeremy Weiland, "You are the monkey wrench," *Social Memory Complex*, March 7, 2008 <http://blog.6thdensity.net/?p=918>.

Further, as downsizing, speedups and stress continue, workers' definitions of a fair level of effort and of the legitimate ways to slow down are likely to undergo a drastic shift. Kevin Depew writes:

- Productivity, like most "financial virtues," is the products of positive social mood trends.
- As social mood transitions to negative, we can expect to see less and less "virtue" in hard work.
- Think about it: real wages are virtually stagnant, so it's not as if people have experienced real reward for their work . . . .
- If social mood has, in fact, peaked, we can expect to see a different attitude toward work and productivity emerge.[1]

Rick, at *Flip Chart Fairy Tales*, finds disengagement and perfunctory performance to be a normal reaction from a work force with no financial stake in increased profit and no control over their work:

Pay consultants Towers Perrin have just published some research which found that 38% of employees around the world feel partly to fully disengaged from their companies—engagement being defined as 'willing to go the extra mile'. In plain English, then, that means that 38% go to work to do their jobs and nothing much more . . . .

Could lack of engagement be due to alienation? Given that a person's lack of control over his or her work is one of the major causes of stress, there's a pretty good chance that alienation and disengagement are linked.

What I find interesting, though, is that so many managers are surprised by this general level of disengagement among their workforces . . . .

Bosses tend to assume that everyone in the company has, or should have, the same levels of motivation and commitment as the management. They forget that, without the position power and the share options, most workers are, as [Harry] Braverman would have put it, alienated from the means of production. This lack of awareness explains why managers can impose a minor cost-cutting exercise, such as taking away free coffee and newspapers in the staff canteen, then be completely surprised that this causes uproar. However, if those managers had understood that employees lack a sense of control over their working environment, they could have predicted that stopping free newspapers would simply emphasise that lack of control and cause an inevitable backlash.

The number of times that executives are caught out by the negative reaction to their crass initiatives never ceases to amaze me. If they stopped to think about it, though, it should not come as a great surprise that people with less of a financial stake in the company might just be that bit less willing to go along with every company initiative.[2]

The slowdown, or "going canny," has a venerable place in the history of labor struggle. It's usually noted as a component of organized struggle, but as an uncoordinated individual practice it fades into what Williamson called "perfunctory cooperation." As Dubois pointed out, "working without enthusiasm," absenteeism and high turnover are forms of "sabotage" that probably do more damage than strikes.[3]

Apparently there is serious concern, in management circles, with perfunctory compliance and passive-aggressive "change resistance."

In addition to overt sabotage, there's other misconduct that's just as deadly to a company's operations. "In today's workplace, there's a lot of covert, subtle sabotage that's happening daily," says Nancy Probst, manager and organizational development consult-

---

1. Kevin Depew, "Five Things You Need to Know," *Minyanville Financial Infotainment*, September 13, 2007 <http://www.minyanville.com/articles/KKR-FDC-Bernanke-Credit+Suisse-CFC/index/a/14090>.

2. Rick, "Is a Bit of Marxism Good for Managers?" *Flip Chart Fairy Tales*, October 31, 2007 <http://flipchartfairytales.wordpress.com/2007/10/31/is-a-bit-of-marxism-good-for-managers/>.

3. Dubois, *Sabotage in Industry*, pp. 51–59.

ant of management advisory services for Dixon Odom PLLC, a certified public account-ing and management advisory firm based in High Point, North Carolina. Examples in-clude intentional reductions in productivity, especially at large organizations in which management has flattened and spans of control have greatly expended. Then there are managers who agree to whatever is being planned, but have no intention of actually do-ing it and sabotage those final plans in subtle ways. Employees who actively resist change efforts also could be considered saboteurs.[1]

The popularity of *Fish!* in management circles may in part be a response to perceived employee disgruntlement, an attempt to counter perfunctory cooperation and other forms of "deliberate withdrawals of efficiency" through motivational propaganda. Consider this passage:

> She had overheard Martha describing how she handled those in the company who "has-sled" her to do her processing faster—she put their file under the out-basket "by mistake."[2]

It's telling that there's absolutely no consideration of whether Martha might in fact be burdened by an increasingly heavy workload, as a result of a conscious management policy of squeezing more work out of fewer people. Slowing down, going canny, and sol-diering are perfectly rational strategies, on the part of workers in an asymmetric power re-lationship and suffering deteriorating work conditions, to pressure management to change *its* attitude. Management's goal, as evidenced by the frantic promotion of Fish! Philosophy, is to stamp out worker perceptions of self-interest and motivate them to adopt manage-ment's interests as their own.

The potential for one form of direct action in particular, "open mouth sabotage," has grown enormously in the Internet era. As described in "How to Fire Your Boss":

> Sometimes simply telling people the truth about what goes on at work can put a lot of pressure on the boss. Consumer industries like restaurants and packing plants are the most vulnerable. And again, as in the case of the Good Work Strike, you'll be gaining the support of the public, whose patronage can make or break a business.
>
> Whistle Blowing can be as simple as a face-to-face conversation with a customer, or it can be as dramatic as the P.G.&E. engineer who revealed that the blueprints to the Diablo Canyon nuclear reactor had been reversed. . . .
>
> Waiters can tell their restaurant clients about the various shortcuts and substitutions that go into creating the faux-haute cuisine being served to them. Just as Work to Rule puts an end to the usual relaxation of standards, Whistle Blowing reveals it for all to know.

The authors of *The Cluetrain Manifesto* are quite expansive on the potential for frank, unmediated conversations between employees and customers as a way of building cus-tomer relationships and circumventing the consumer's ingrained habit of blocking out canned corporate messages.[3] They characterize the typical corporate voice as "sterile hap-pytalk that insults the intelligence," "the soothing, humorless monotone of the mission statement, marketing brochure, and your-call-is-important-to-us busy signal."[4]

When employees engage customers frankly about the problems they experience with the company's product, and offer useful information, customers usually respond positively.

1. Jennifer Kock, "Employee Sabotage: Don't Be a Target!" <http://www.workforce.com/archive/features/22/20/88/mdex-printer.php>.

2. Stephen C. Lundin, Harry Paul, and John Christensen. *Fish! A Remarkable Way to Boost Morale and Improve Results* (New York: Hyperion, 2000).

3. "Markets are Conversations," in Rick Levine, Christopher Locke, Doc Searls and David Weinberger, *The Cluetrain Manifesto: The End of Business as Usual* (Perseus Books Group, 2001) <http://www.cluetrain.com/book/index.html>.

4. "95 theses," in *Ibid.*

85. When we have questions we turn to each other for answers. If you didn't have such a tight rein on "your people" maybe they'd be among the people we'd turn to.

86. When we're not busy being your "target market," many of us *are* your people. We'd rather be talking to friends online than watching the clock. That would get your name around better than your entire million dollar web site. But you tell us speaking to the market is Marketing's job.[1]

Christopher Locke recounts his experiences as "director of communications" for a software firm. He soon figured out that that the press perceived PR people as thinly disguised hucksters. Locke didn't have much taste for that role, so he started engaging in unscripted, off-message conversations with editors and reporters.

We talked about software . . . —what it could and couldn't do. We talked about the foibles of the industry itself, laughed about empty buzzwords and pompous posturing, swapped war stories about trade shows and writing on deadline. We talked about our own work. But these conversations weren't work. They were interesting and engaging. They were exciting. They were fun . . . .

Then something even more amazing happened. The company started "getting ink." Lots of it. And not in the lowly trade rags it had been used to, but in places like The New York Times and The Wall Street Journal and Business Week. One day the CEO called the VP of Marketing into my office.

"What has Chris been doing for you lately?" the CEO asked him.

"I'm glad you brought that up," said the marketing veep. "In the whole time he's been here, he hasn't done a single thing I've asked him to."

"Well . . ." said the CEO looking down at his shoes—here it comes, I thought, this is what it feels like to get sacked—"whatever it is he's doing, leave him alone. From now on, he reports to me."

That's how I discovered PR doesn't work and that markets are conversations.[2]

A Saturn mechanic joined a conversation in a newsgroup sparked by a customer who posted a message titled "Am I Getting F-'ed By My Saturn Dealer???" Eventually the mechanic showed up who, rather than robotically spouting official happy talk with a permasmile (as an official spokesman would do), provided frank and useful information about company policy and what the customer's options were for handling the situation.

The Saturn mechanic was speaking for his company in a new way: honestly, openly, probably without his boss's explicit sanction—and he greatly served the interests of Saturn. He and others like him are changing the way Saturn supports its customers. And Saturn corporate might not even know it's happening.[3]

Symantec officially encouraged a similar approach when it launched CafE, "a suite of programming tools for Java developers."

They had one person virtually living in the public support newsgroups. He responded to questions, fielded tech support requests, and generally got himself known as a very straight shooter about Symantec's products. He was only one person, but he was almost single-handedly responsible for the developer community's positive take on Symantec. He wasn't there to promote, but strictly to assist. He gave honest answers to hard questions, acknowledged product shortcomings, and painted an honest, open picture of the product's strengths and weaknesses. The developer community's collective opinion of Symantec soared.

Another anecdote from the public relations history of Sun's Java team paints an anti-example. In the first year and a half that Sun's Java group existed, members of the engineering team spoke directly with customers and the press. Java grew from a glimmer, a possibility, to a platform with thousands of curious, turned-on early adopters. There

1. "95 theses."
2. "Chapter One. Internet Apocalypso," in *The Cluetrain Manifesto*.
3. "Chapter Three. Talk is Cheap," in *The Cluetrain Manifesto*.

was a general perception that Sun's Java team listened, answered questions, and was actively engaged with the community of Java developers.

After about eighteen months, the workload grew to such a point that we started shutting down our channels to the outside world. PR and marketing took over much of our contact with the outside world . . . . As we went underground, the perception of the Java group in the marketplace changed from "a small team of great engineers producing neat stuff" to "a hype engine to push Sun's stock."[1]

What the *Cluetrain* authors *don't* mention is the potential for disaster, from the company's perspective, when disgruntled workers see the customer as a potential ally against a common enemy. What would have happened if Locke, the Saturn mechanic, or the Symantec rep had decided, not that their company's management was somewhat clueless and needed to be gently pushed to do a better job for its own good, not that they wanted to help *their* company by rescuing it from the tyranny of PR and the official line and winning over customers with a little straight talk—but that they hated the company and that its management was evil? What if, rather than simply responding to a specific problem with what the customer had needed to know, they'd aired all the dirty laundry about management's asset stripping, gutting of human capital, hollowing out of long-term productive capability, gaming of its own bonuses and stock options, self-dealing on the job, and logrolling with directors?

Corporate America, for the most part, still views the Internet as "just an extension of preceding mass media, primarily television." Corporate websites are designed on the same model as the old broadcast media: a one-to-many, one-directional communications flow, in which the audience couldn't talk back. But now the audience *can* talk back.

Imagine for a moment: millions of people sitting in their shuttered homes at night, bathed in that ghostly blue television aura. They're passive, yeah, but more than that: they're isolated from each other.

Now imagine another magic wire strung from house to house, hooking all these poor bastards up. They're still watching the same old crap. Then, during the touching love scene, some joker lobs an off-color aside—and everybody hears it. Whoa! What was that? . . . The audience is suddenly connected to itself.

What was once The Show, the hypnotic focus and tee-vee advertising carrier wave, becomes . . . an excuse to get together . . . . Think of Joel and the 'bots on Mystery Science Theater 3000. The point is not to watch the film, but to outdo each other making fun of it.

And for such radically realigned purposes, some bloated corporate Web site can serve as a target every bit as well as Godzilla, King of the Monsters . . . .

So here's a little story problem for ya, class. If the Internet has 50 million people on it, and they're not all as dumb as they look, but the corporations trying to make a fast buck off their asses are as dumb as they look, how long before Joe is laughing as hard as everyone else?

The correct answer of course: not long at all. And as soon as he starts laughing, he's not Joe Six-Pack anymore. He's no longer part of some passive couch-potato target demographic. Because the Net connects people to each other, and impassions and empowers through those connections, the media dream of the Web as another acquiescent mass-consumer market is a figment and a fantasy.

The Internet is inherently seditious. It undermines unthinking respect for centralized authority, whether that "authority" is the neatly homogenized voice of broadcast advertising or the smarmy rhetoric of the corporate annual report.[2]

. . . . Look at how this already works in today's Web conversation. You want to buy a new camera. You go to the sites of the three camera makers you're considering. You hastily click through the brochureware the vendors paid thousands to have designed, and you finally find a page that actually gives straightforward factual information. Now you go to a

1. *Ibid.*
2. "Chapter One. Internet Apocalypso," in Locke, *et al., Cluetrain Manifesto.*

Usenet discussion group, or you find an e-mail list on the topic. You read what real customers have to say. You see what questions are being asked and you're impressed with how
well other buyers—strangers from around the world—have answered them . . . .

Compare that to the feeble sputtering of an ad. "SuperDooper Glue—Holds Anything!" says your ad. "Unless you flick it sideways—as I found out with the handle of my
favorite cup," says a little voice in the market. "BigDisk Hard Drives—Lifetime Guarantee!" says the ad. "As long as you can prove you oiled it three times a week," says another little voice in the market. What these little voices used to say to a single friend is
now accessible to the world. No number of ads will undo the words of the market. How
long does it take until the market conversation punctures the exaggerations made in an
ad? An hour? A day? The speed of word of mouth is now limited only by how fast people can type . . . .[1]

. . . Marketing has been training its practitioners for decades in the art of impersonat-
ing sincerity and warmth. But marketing can no longer keep up appearances. People talk.[2]

Even more important for our purposes, employees talk. It's just as feasible for the corporation's workers to talk directly to its customers, and for workers and customers together
to engage in joint mockery of the company.

In an age when unions have virtually disappeared from the private sector workforce,
and downsizings and speedups have become a normal expectation of working life, the vulnerability of employer's public image may be the one bit of real leverage the worker has
over him—and it's a doozy. If they go after that image relentlessly and systematically,
they've got the boss by the short hairs. Given the ease of setting up anonymous blogs and
websites (just think of any company and then look up the URL employernamesucks.com),
the potential for other features of the writeable web like comment threads and message
boards, the possibility of anonymous saturation emailing of the company's major suppliers
and customers and advocacy groups concerned with that industry . . . . well, let's just say
the potential for "swarming" and "netwar" is corporate management's worst nightmare.
Graham Meikle examined something very much like Ronfeldt's "swarming," in the more
recent form he called the "virtual sit-in": campaigns to shut down official government and
corporate websites with excessive traffic.[3]

It's already become apparent that corporations are quite vulnerable to bad publicity
from dissident shareholders and consumers. For example, Luigi Zingales writes,

shareholders' activist Robert Monks succeeded [in 1995] in initiating some major
changes at Sears, not by means of the norms of the corporate code (his proxy fight failed
miserably) but through the pressure of public opinion. He paid for a full-page announcement in the *Wall Street Journal* where he exposed the identities of Sears' directors,
labeling them the "non-performing assets" of Sears . . . . The embarrassment for the directors was so great that they implemented all the changes proposed by Monks.[4]

There's no reason to doubt that management would be equally vulnerable to embarrassment by such tactics from disgruntled production workers, in today's networked world.

The corporate world is beginning to perceive the danger of open-mouth sabotage, as
well. For example, one Pinkerton thug almost directly equates sabotage to the open mouth,
to the near exclusion of all other forms of direct action. According to Darren Donovan, a
vice president of Pinkerton's eastern consulting and investigations division,

[w]ith sabotage, there's definitely an attempt to undermine or disrupt the operation in
some way or slander the company . . . . There's a special nature to sabotage because of

1. "Chapter Four. Markets Are Conversations," *The Cluetrain Manifesto*.
2. *Ibid.*
3. Graham Meikle, "Electronic civil disobedience and symbolic power," in Athina Karatzogianni, ed., *Cyber Conflict and Global Politics* (London and New York: Routledge, 2009).
4. Zingales, "In Search of New Foundations," pp. 1627-1628.

the overtness of it—and it can be violent .... Companies can replace windows and equipment, but it's harder to replace their reputation .... I think that's what HR execs need to be aware of because it *is* a crime, but it can be different from stealing or fraud.[1]

As suggested by both the interest of a Pinkerton thug and his references to "crime," there is a major focus in the corporate world on identifying whistleblowers and leakers through surveillance technology, and on the criminalization of free speech to combat negative publicity.

But the problem with such authoritarianism, from the standpoint of the bosses and their state, is that before you can waterboard open-mouth saboteurs at Gitmo you've got to *catch them* first. If the litigation over Diebold's corporate files and emails teaches anything, it's that court injunctions and similar expedients are virtually useless against guerrilla netwar. The era of the SLAPP lawsuit is over, except for those cases where the offender is considerate enough to volunteer his home address to the target. Even in the early days of the Internet, the McLibel case (a McDonald's SLAPP suit against some small-time pamphleteers) turned into "the most expensive and most disastrous public-relations exercise ever mounted by a multinational company."[2] As we already noted, the easy availability of web anonymity, the "writeable web" in its various forms, the feasibility of mirroring shut-down websites, and the ability to replicate, transfer, and store huge volumes of digital information at zero marginal cost, means that it is simply impossible to shut people up. The would-be corporate information police will just wear themselves out playing whack-a-mole. They will be exhausted and destroyed in exactly the same way that the most technically advanced army in the world was defeated by a guerrilla force in black pajamas.

The last section of Naomi Klein's *No Logo* discusses in depth the vulnerability of large corporations and brand name images to netwar campaigns.[3] She pays special attention to "culture jamming," which involves riffing off of corporate logos and thereby "tapping into the vast resources spent to make [a] logo meaningful."[4] A good example is the anti-sweatshop campaign by the National Labor Committee, headed by Charles Kernaghan.

> Kernaghan's formula is simple enough. First, select America's most cartoonish icons, from literal ones like Mickey Mouse to virtual ones like Kathie Lee Gifford. Next, create head-on collisions between image and reality. "They live by their image," Kernaghan says of his corporate adversaries. "That gives you a certain power over them . . . these companies are sitting ducks."[5]

For example, although Wal-Mart workers are not represented by NLRB-certified unions, in any bargaining unit in the United States, the "associates" have been quite successful at organized open-mouth sabotage through Wake Up Wal-Mart and similar activist organizations.

Consider the public relations battle over Wal-Mart "open availability" policy, discussed in Chapter Eight. Corporate headquarters in Bentonville quickly moved, in the face of organized public criticism, to overturn the harsher local policy announced by management in Nitro, West Virginia.

> A corporate spokesperson says the company reversed the store's decision because Wal-Mart has no policy that calls for the termination of employees who are unable to work certain shifts, the Gazette reports.

---

1. Jennifer Kock, "Employee Sabotage: Don't Be a Target!"
2. "270-day libel case goes on and on . . . ," 28th June 1996, Daily Telegraph (UK) <http://www.mcspotlight.org/media/thisweek/jul3.html>.
3. Naomi Klein, *No Logo* (New York: Picador, 2000, 2002), pp. 279-437.
4. *Ibid.*, p. 281.
5. *Ibid.*, p. 351.

"It is unfortunate that our store manager incorrectly communicated a message that was not only inaccurate but also disruptive to our associates at the store," Dan Fogleman tells the Gazette. "We do not have any policy that mandates termination."[1]

The Wal-Mart Workers' Association acts as an unofficial union, and has repeatedly obtained concessions from store management teams in several publicity campaigns designed to embarrass and pressure the company.[2] As Ezra Klein noted,

> This is, of course, entirely a function of the pressure unions have exerted on Wal-Mart—pressure exerted despite the unions having almost no hope of actually unionizing Wal-Mart. Organized Labor has expended tens of millions of dollars over the past few years on this campaign, and while it hasn't increased union density one iota, it has given a hundred thousand Wal-Mart workers health insurance, spurred Wal-Mart to launch an effort to drive down prescription drug prices, drove them into the "Divided We Fail" health reform coalition, and contributed to the company's focus on greening their stores (they needed good press to counteract all the bad).[3]

Another example is the IWW-affiliated Starbucks union, which publicly embarrassed Starbucks Chairman Howard Schultz. It organized a mass email campaign, notifying the Co-op Board of a co-op apartment he was seeking to buy into of his union-busting activities.[4]

Charles Johnson points to the Coalition of Imolakee Workers as an example of an organizing campaign outside the Wagner framework, relying heavily on the open mouth:

> They are mostly immigrants from Mexico, Central America, and the Caribbean; many of them have no legal immigration papers; they are pretty near all mestizo, Indian, or Black; they have to speak at least four different languages amongst themselves; they are often heavily in debt to coyotes or labor sharks for the cost of their travel to the U.S.; they get no benefits and no overtime; they have no fixed place of employment and get work from day to day only at the pleasure of the growers; they work at many different sites spread out anywhere from 10–100 miles from their homes; they often have to move to follow work over the course of the year; and they are extremely poor (most tomato pickers live on about $7,500–$10,000 per year, and spend months with little or no work when the harvesting season ends). But in the face of all that, and across lines of race, culture, nationality, and language, the C.I.W. have organized themselves anyway, through efforts that are nothing short of heroic, and *they have done it as a wildcat union with no recognition from the federal labor bureaucracy and little outside help from the organized labor establishment.* By using creative nonviolent tactics that would be *completely illegal* if they were subject to the bureaucratic discipline of the Taft-Hartley Act, the C.I.W. has won major victories on wages and conditions over the past two years. They have bypassed the approved channels of collective bargaining between select union reps and the boss, and gone up the supply chain to pressure the tomato buyers, because they realized that they can exercise a lot more leverage against highly visible corporations with brands to protect than they can in dealing with a cartel of government-subsidized vegetable growers that most people outside of southern Florida wouldn't know from Adam.
>
> The C.I.W.'s creative use of moral suasion and secondary boycott tactics have already won them agreements with Taco Bell (in 2005) and then McDonald's (this past spring), which almost doubled the effective piece rate for tomatoes picked for these res-

1. "Wal-Mart Nixes 'Open Availability' Policy," *Business & Labor Reports* (Human Resources section), June 16, 2005 <http://hr.blr.com/news.aspx?id=15666>.

2. Nick Robinson, "Even Without a Union, Florida Wal-Mart Workers Use Collective Action to Enforce Rights," *Labor Notes*, January 2006. Reproduced at Infoshop, January 3, 2006 <http://www.infoshop.org/inews/article.php?story=20060103065054461>.

3. Ezra Klein, "Why Labor Matters," *The American Prospect*, November 14, 2007 <http://www.prospect.org/csnc/blogs/ezraklein_archive?month=11&year=2007&base_name=why_labor_matters>.

4. "Say No to Schultz Mansion Purchase," Starbucks Union <http://www.starbucksunion.org/node/1903>.

taurants. They established a system for pass-through payments, under which participating restaurants agreed to pay a bonus of an additional penny per pound of tomatoes bought, which an independent accountant distributed to the pickers at the farm that the restaurant bought from. Each individual agreement makes a significant but relatively small increase in the worker's effective wages . . . [,] but each victory won means a concrete increase in wages, and an easier road to getting the pass-through system adopted industry-wide, which would in the end nearly *double* tomato-pickers' annual income.

Burger King held out for a while after this, following Taco Bell's earlier successive strategies of ignoring, stonewalling, slick PR, slander (denouncing farm workers as "richer than most minimum-wage workers," consumer boycotts as extortion, and C.I.W. as scam artists), and finally even attempt at federal prosecution for racketeering.[1]

As Johnson predicted, the dirty tricks were of no avail. He followed up on this story in May 2008, when Burger King caved in. Especially entertaining, after the smear campaign and other dirty tricks carried out by the Burger King management team, was this public statement by BK CEO John Chidsey:

> We are pleased to now be working together with the CIW to further the common goal of improving Florida tomato farmworkers' wages, working conditions and lives. The CIW has been at the forefront of efforts to improve farm labor conditions, exposing abuses and driving socially responsible purchasing and work practices in the Florida tomato fields. We apologize for any negative statements about the CIW or its motives previously attributed to BKC or its employees and now realize that those statements were wrong.[2]

Jon Husband, of *Wirearchy* blog, writes of the potential threat network culture and the free flow of information pose to traditional hierarchies.

> Smart, interested, engaged and articulate people exchange information with each other via the Web, using hyperlinks and web services. Often this information . . . is about something that someone in a position of power would prefer that other people (citizens, constituents, clients, colleagues) not know . . . .
> The exchanged-via-hyperlinks-and-web-services information is retrievable, reusable and when combined with other information (let's play connect-the-dots here) often shows the person in a position of power to be a liar or a spinner, or irresponsible in ways that are not appropriate. This is the basic notion of transparency (which describes a key facet of the growing awareness of the power of the Web) . . . .
> Hyperlinks, the digital infrastructure of the Web, the lasting retrievability of the information posted to the Web, and the pervasive use of the Web to publish, distribute and transport information combine to suggest that there are large shifts in power ahead of us. We have already seen some of that .. we will see much more unless the powers that be manage to find ways to control the toings-and-froings on the Web.
> . . . . [T]he hoarding and protection of sensitive information by hierarchical institutions and powerful people in those institutions is under siege . . . .[3]

Chris Dillow, of *Stumbling and Mumbling* blog, argues we're now at the stage where the leadership of large, hierarchical organizations has achieved "negative credibility." The public, in response to a public statement by Gordon Brown, seemingly acted on the assumption that the truth was the direct opposite.

1. Charles Johnson, "Coalition of Imolakee Workers marches in Miami," *Rad Geek People's Daily*, November 30, 2007 <http://radgeek.com/gt/2007/11/30/coalition_of/>.
2. Coalition of Immokalee Workers. "Burger King Corp. and Coalition of Immokalee Workers to Work Together," May 23, 2008 <http://www.ciw-online.org/BK_CIW_joint_release.html>. Charles Johnson, "¡Sí, Se Puede! Victory for the Coalition of Imolakee Workers in the Burger King penny-per-pound campaign," *Rad Geek People's Daily*, May 23, 2008 <http://radgeek.com/gt/ 2008/05/23/si_se/>.
3. Jon Husband, "How Hard is This to Understand?" *Wirearchy*, June 22, 2007 <http://blog.wirearchy.com/ blog/_archives/2007/6/22/3040833.html>.

Could it be that the ruling class now has *negative* credibility? Maybe people are now taking seriously the old *Yes, Minister* joke—that one should never believe anything until it's officially denied.

If so, doesn't this have serious implications? It means not merely that the managerial class has lost one of the weapons it can use to control us, but that the weapon, when used, actually fires upon its user.

Ah, "negative credibility"—what a beautiful expression! Every shift I finish at the hospital where I work, if I've managed to reduce the credibility of management (whether in the eyes of patients or of my coworkers), I feel I've accomplished my mission. My ultimate goal is for the hospital's senior management to feel engulfed by an almost tangible wave of hatred every time they enter the building. I want them to look into a sea of sullen, expressionless faces, afraid to turn their backs on any of them—like an American G.I. in Saigon ca. 1968.

We have probably already passed a "singularity," a point of no return, in the use of networked information warfare. It took some time for employers to reach a consensus that the old corporate liberal labor regime no longer served their interests, and to take note of and fully exploit the union-busting potential of Taft-Hartley. But once they began to do so, the implosion of Wagner-style unionism was preordained. Likewise, it will take time for the realization to dawn on workers that things are only getting worse, that there's no hope in traditional unionism, and that in a networked world they have the power to bring the employer to his knees by their own direct action. But when they do, the outcome is also probably preordained. The twentieth century was the era of the giant organization. By the end of the twenty-first, there probably won't be enough of them left to bury.

Even if there were some way of objectively specifying expected levels of effort by *ex ante* contract, the costs of monitoring would likely be very high in practice. I suspect most market anarchists would reject, in principle, exogenous systems to enforce intra-workplace contract that are not paid for entirely by those who rely on the service: in a market anarchy, those contractual arrangements which cost more to enforce than the benefits would justify would simply "wither away," regardless of whether the contractual violations incurred the moral disapproval of some.

As long ago as the 1930s, Douglas McGregor concluded that internal authoritarianism was counter-productive: any "efficiency" gains from greater work discipline were outweighed by costs resulting from passive sabotage.

> The assumptions of Theory Y imply that unless integration [of goals] is achieved *the organization will suffer.* The objectives of the organization are *not* achieved best by the unilateral administration of promotions, because this form of management by direction and control will not create the commitment which would make available the full resources of those affected. The lesser motivation, the lesser resulting degree of self-direction and self-control are costs which, when added up for many instances over time, will more than offset the gains obtained by unilateral decisions for the good of the organization.[1]

If things ever progress to the point where most workers see themselves as engaged in a zero-sum contest with management, the war will be over before it is fairly begun—because the comparative costs of monitoring and evasion are heavily stacked against management. Assuming a workforce that is bent on evading monitoring, I would venture to guess that there is no internal monitoring or surveillance system in existence that cannot be circumvented at a fraction of the cost of putting it in place. In the offensive-defensive arms race between management and labor, labor will always have the edge. As McGregor

---

1. Douglas McGregor, *The Human Side of Enterprise* (New York, London, Toronto: McGraw-Hill Book Company, Inc., 1960), p. 52.

put it, "The ingenuity of the average worker is sufficient to outwit *any* system of controls devised by management."[1]

The cumulative effect of these kinds of worker resistance, even when practiced only on an uncoordinated individual basis, can be overwhelming. J.C. Scott refers to "the small arsenal of relatively powerless groups," including among other things "such acts as foot dragging, dissimulation, false compliance, feigned ignorance, desertion, pilfering," and the like.

> These techniques, for the most part quite prosaic, are the ordinary means of class struggle
> . . . . When they are practiced widely by members of an entire class against elites or the state, they may have aggregate consequences out of all proportion to their banality when considered singly.[2]

We already saw, in Chapter Eight, the ways in which corporate hierarchies have turned to increasing internal authoritarianism in response to the perceived rise in worker disgruntlement and the associated threat of sabotage. There is a wide array of evidence that this perception on management's part is entirely accurate. The stagnant wages, downsizings, and speedups of the past thirty years have been associated with a dramatic increase in sabotage.

> Jeff Zakaryan, president of Global Strategies, an executive coaching firm based in Dana Point, California, says he's seen a dramatic increase in bitterness from people in many types of workplaces over the past decade. He adds: "Sabotage seems to be just one more way for [workers] to kick the big corporation in the shins.[3]

In 1998 there was an estimated $400 billion loss, or 6% of annual corporate revenue, from "employee fraud and abuse" (for some reason, I doubt the management practices described in Chapter Eight are included in this category). But such sabotage is actually under-reported, because negative publicity compounds the cost of the original sabotage. The news media, in effect, do our open-mouth sabotage for us: "Companies fear public scrutiny about what they did to cause an employee to get so angry or feel so desperate."[4] According to Naomi Klein, rates of employee theft have risen dramatically in retail, and management has become much more frankly adversarial in searching the bags and purses of their "associates" at the end of the shift.[5]

The perceived disconnect between management's rhetoric of "empowerment" and the reality of downsizing, speedups and stagnant pay, probably adds fuel to the fire. Workers are not stupid, after all.

> . . . [C]ompanies that continue to assault their workers with degradation, poor wages and mistreatment run the risk of finding themselves the victims of the workplace equivalent of guerrilla warfare. At a time when management gurus like to talk about "empowering" employees by flattening out the organizational chart, introducing total quality management and team workgroups, employees embrace sabotage as a way to accomplish instant empowerment without the hefty consulting fees and nauseating jargon. Certainly there is nothing more empowering than pouring a cup of coffee into the back of a computer, intentionally misfiling an important document or putting a little Krazy Glue into the back of a critical file cabinet. Only the boss might be able to crack the whip, but anyone can pull a plug.[6]

---

1. *Ibid.*, p. 9.
2. J.C. Scott, "Everyday Forms of Resistance," in F.D. Colburn, ed., *Everyday Forms of Peasant Resistance* (Armonk, N.Y. M.E. Sharpe, 1989), p. 5.
3. Jennifer Kock, "Employee Sabotage: Don't Be a Target!"
4. *Ibid.*
5. Naomi Klein, *No Logo*, pp. 268-69.
6. Daniel S. Levine, *Disgruntled: The Darker Side of the World of Work* (New York: Berkley Boulevard Books, 1998), p. 192.

The perception of powerlessness and the resort to destructive behavior are intimately connected. As workers feel increasingly powerless (and Fish!'s mantra that "we can't control what happens to us" doesn't exactly help, does it?), the cumulative cost from petty and sporadic acts of destruction will continue to climb. One study, for example, found a close correlation between "employee deviance" (theft or destruction of property, or deviance from expected quantity or quality of production) and dissatisfaction with the work environment.[1] Another correlated destruction directly to perceived lack of control. One high school student who smashed a locker "recalled passing it for the next three years and each time thinking proudly, 'there's my little destruction to this brand new school.'"[2] This, apparently, was one student who didn't fully internalize all the administration agitprop about "school spirit." And I suspect very few workers are stupid or brainwashed enough to buy into management's official happy talk about "our workplace," either.

The HR Nazis' reactions to the threat are almost comical—especially their hamhanded attempts at personality profiling to identify potential saboteurs (any worker who can't figure out what answers HR is looking for probably shouldn't be around heavy machinery anyway). One example of the genre refers to "negative attitudes toward authority" and a sense of being "alienated from authority" as self-evidently pathological. The possibility that negative attitudes toward authority might be a reasonable and justified response to objective changes in the environment, it seems, never occurs to these people. In an incredible display of mirror-imaging, the authors identify these feelings with a "sense of entitlement."[3]

Getting back to the issue of moral legitimacy, it's difficult to see how a wing of libertarianism that agrees with Walter Block on the moral defensibility of blackmail can consistently get all squeamish when workers pursue the exact same interest-maximizing behavior. That's no exaggeration, by the way. Contrast libertarian commentary on the virtuous function of price gouging after Katrina with this message board reaction at Libertarian Underground to the idea of workers doing *exactly the same thing*:

> *Fisticuffs*: Economically speaking, why should [workers] do more than the minimum possible for their pay?
> *Charles M.*: Why not just rob people if you can get away with it? Economically speaking?
> *Fisticuffs*: If a person does a certain amount of work and gets paid for that amount of work, is the person really pricing himself efficiently if he does more work without getting paid more??[4]

Here's a little thought experiment: try imagining Charles M.'s reaction if Fisticuffs had complained that *employers* are "robbing people" when they try to get the most work they can for an hour's wages. You can also do an experiment in real life: go to any mainstream libertarian discussion forum and complain about the bad behavior of the typical worker. The responses will range from commiseration over "how hard it is to get good help nowadays," to visceral outrage at the ingratitude and perversity of such uppity workers. Then go to a comparable forum and complain in exactly the same tone about your boss's behavior. The predictable response will be a terse and pissy "if you don't like it, look for another job." Try it for yourself.

1. R. C. Hollinger and J. P. Clark, "Employee Deviance: a Perceived Quality of the Work Experience," *Work and Occupations* Vol. 9 No. 1 (February 1982).
2. V. L. Allen and D. B. Greenberger, "Destruction and Perceived Control," in A. Baum and J.E. Singer, eds., *Advances in Environmental Psychology* (Hillsdale, N.J.: Earlbaum, 1980).
3. Eric D. Shaw, Jerold M. Post, Keven G. Ruby, "Inside the Mind of the Insider" <http://www.securitymanagement.com/library/000762.html>.
4. "Proud to be a Replacement Worker," *Libertarian Underground*, March 2, 2004 <http://www.libertarianunderground.com/Forum/index.php/topic,865.0.html>.

I also recall seeing a lot of tsk-tsking from Paul Birch and others of like mind in some discussion forum several months back, about what blackguards union workers were for demanding higher wages when their labor was most needed. Golly, aren't these the same people who defend "price gouging" by the oil companies? It's not very consistent to go from "caveat emptor" and "fooled me twice, shame on me!" in every realm *except* labor relations, to spelling "God" E-M-P-L-O-Y-E-R within the workplace. The hostility is quite odd, assuming the person feeling it is motivated by free market principle rather than a zeal for the aggrieved interests of big business. Their implicit model of employer-employee relations, in fact, seems to be a cultural holdover from the old master-servant relationship.

Brad Spangler, in the comment thread to a Mises Blog post linking Jeffrey Tucker's article on the Hollywood writers' strike, pointed out this double standard when it comes to collective bargaining:

> Negotiation of terms is part of the transaction process and, hence, the market.
>
> Are you implying that sellers ought only passively accept or decline deals and never assertively negotiate with a potential buyer, merely so long as more than one potential buyer exists? . . .
>
> 1) If so, do you apply that dictum universally, or just in the case of labor deals?
>
> 2) If so, AND if you limit that view solely to the labor market, then I must ask what (in economic terms) is so special about labor?
>
> If so, AND if you apply it universally, then I must say you're really doing yourself a disservice when it comes to selling a home or car . . . .
>
> That statement [that there is no way to sell anything for a higher price than the highest bidder is willing to pay] sort of misses the point—namely, that rhetorical efforts to systematically discourage assertive negotiation by one subset of transaction participants (under color of economic thought) are a misguided effort to cripple the market's own discovery process for determining what "the highest bidder is willing to pay".[1]

Despite all the libertarian rhetoric of "free contract," (as Paul Graham put it) "[o]ur employer-employee relationship still retains a big chunk of master-servant DNA."[2] This was recognized by no less of a free market libertarian than Herbert Spencer.

> . . . . So long as the worker remains a wage-earner, the marks of *status* do not wholly disappear. For so many hours daily he makes over his faculties to a master . . . , and is for the time owned by him . . . . He is temporarily in the position of a slave, and his overlooker stands in the position of a slave-driver. Further, a remnant of the *régime* of *status* is seen in the fact that he and other workers are placed in ranks, receiving different rates of pay . . . .

David Ellerman pointed out that the modern terms "employer" and "employee" were coined to avoid the awkwardness of the previous terms, which are still used in employment law: master and servant. To avoid the unpleasant fact that human beings are rented, it is necessary to resort to "the usual linguistic sugar-coating involved in saying employees are 'hired,' 'employed,' 'given a job,' or 'invited to join the firm.'"[3]

> "Employer-employee" is not the traditional name; it is newspeak which has only come into English usage within the last century. Society seems to have "covered up" in the popular consciousness the fact that the traditional name is "master and servant" . . . .
>
> The master-servant language was used by the 18th century Blackstone, but in the 19th century it had acquired such negative connotations that it had passed out of common usage . . . .

1. Comments under Jeffrey Tucker, "Hollywood's Workers and Peasants," Mises Blog, November 3, 2007 <http://blog.mises.org/archives/007391.asp>.

2. Paul Graham, "What Business Can Learn from Open-Source," August 2005 <http://www.paulgraham.com/opensource.html>.

3. Ellerman, op. cit., p. 64.

Modern labor legislation uses the newspeak of "employer-employee." The continuing use of the traditional "master-servant" language in agency law is not without controversy. Some writers consider the "master-servant" language to be so archaic that it can be used as technical terminology without any undue negative connotations . . . .

The etymology of the word "servant" is of interest. Western history has seen three general types of economic systems: slavery in ancient times, feudalism in the Middle Ages, and capitalism (private and public) in modern times. The worker's role in this evolution can be traced in the evolution of his name. The Latin word for slave "servus" evolved into the French "serf" (and Italian "servo") under feudalism, which in turn became "servant" under capitalism. If the three word version of Economics is "Supply and Demand," the three word version of Labor History is "Servus, Serf, Servant." . . .

In the course of its career, the word "servant" has denoted workers from the slave to the modern employee as if its own ontogeny had to recapitulate the servus-serf-servant phylogeny. Although servants are never called "slaves" (except as hyperbole), slaves were often called "servants" in premodern times. Even within recent decades, some dictionaries such as the 1959 *Webster's New Collegiate* lists "A slave" as a second definition of "servant." At the same time, lawbooks use "servant" as the technical legal term for the modern employee. Thus the three word version of Labor History could be shortened to one word, "Servant." . . .

Most people who work, work as employees. Yet they do not know employment is the rental relation applied to persons and they do not know the traditional name of the relationship. The system of social indoctrination has been so successful that the employer-employee relation is not even perceived as something that could be different. "To be employed" has become synonymous with "having a job," to be "unemployed" is to be without work so "employment" has become the same as work. The employment relationship is accepted as part of the furniture of the social universe. We have even described the opposite system without the employment relationship as "universal self-employment" [which is akin to describing the opposite of the slavery system as universal self-ownership] . . . .[1]

Returning to Spencer: he also, by the way, pointed out a weakness in the Misoid position that unions accomplish nothing that would not be accomplished by the market price system raising wages along with productivity. Even if the market produces that effect in the long run, the organized bargaining power of a union is itself a market actor that speeds up the process. And even when wages are fully equal to the marginal productivity of labor, a union reduces the uncertainty of employment for an individual.

Judging from their harsh and cruel conduct in the past, it is tolerably certain that employers are now prevented from doing unfair things which they would else do. Conscious that trade-unions are ever ready to act, they are more prompt to raise wages when trade is flourishing than they would otherwise be; and when there come times of depression, they lower wages only when they cannot otherwise carry on their businesses.

Knowing the power which unions can exert, masters are led to treat the individual members of them with more respect than they would otherwise do: the *status* of the workman is almost necessarily raised. Moreover, having a strong motive for keeping on good terms with the union, a master is more likely than he would else be to study the general convenience of his men, and to carry on his works in ways conducive to their health. There is an ultimate gain in moral and physical treatment if there is no ultimate gain in wages.[2]

1. *Ibid.*, pp. 66-68. Kenneth Cloke and Joan Goldsmith present a similar historical perspective in *The End of Management and the Rise of Organizational Democracy* (New York: John Wiley & Sons, 2002), pp. 21-30.

2. Herbert Spencer, *Principles of Sociology* Book VIII Chapter 20. I first read this passage thanks to Roderick Long, in "Herbert Spencer, Labortarian," Austro-Athenian Empire, April 10, 2007 <http://praxeology.net/blog/2007/04/10/herbert-spencer-labortarian/>.

And before we put the sainted "employer" on too high a pedestal, let's consider this quote from a vice president of PR at General Motors (in David M. Gordon's *Fat and Mean*):

> . . . . We are not yet a classless society . . . . [F]undamentally the mission of [workers'] elected representatives is to get the most compensation for the least amount of labor. Our responsibility to our shareholders is to get the most production for the least amount of compensation.[1]

And here, from the same source, is an advertising blurb from a union-busting consulting firm:

> We will show you how to screw your employees (before they screw you)—how to keep them smiling on low pay—how to maneuver them into low-pay jobs they are afraid to walk away from—how to hire and fire so you always make money.[2]

That kind of honesty is quite refreshing, after all the smarmy Fish! Philosophy shit I've been wading through lately.

The AFL-CIO's Lane Kirkland, at one point, half-heartedly suggested that things would be easier if Congress repealed all labor laws, and let labor and management go at it "mano a mano."[3]

It's time to take up Kirkland's half-hearted suggestion, not just as a throwaway line, but as a challenge to the bosses. We'll gladly forego legal protections against punitive firing of union organizers, and federal certification of unions, if you'll forego the court injunctions and cooling-off periods and arbitration. We'll leave you free to fire organizers at will, to bring back the yellow dog contract, if you leave us free to engage in sympathy and boycott strikes all the way up and down the production chain, to boycott retailers, and to strike against the hauling of scab cargo, etc., effectively turning every strike into a general strike. We give up Wagner (such as it is), and you give up Taft-Hartley and the Railway Labor Relations Act. And then we'll mop the floor with your ass.

According to David M. Gordon, the percentage of "discouraged union workers" (workers who say they would join a union in their workplace if one were available) is around a third of private sector, non-union workers—that's the same percentage who actually belong to unions in Canada, where union membership is based on a simple card-check system.[4] So the number of people looking for a way to fight back is about the same as it always was. The avenues of fighting back just seem to have been closed off, from their perspective. We need to show them they're wrong.

Another useful change in strategic direction might be toward the French model of unions, which are at least as much socially-based as workplace-based. Charles Derber wrote, ten years ago:

> The real constituency of the new labor movement Sweeney envisions is the American public as a whole, as well as workers throughout the world. As the old social contract unravels, the great majority of those in jeopardy are not American union members but unrepresented American workers, as well as workers in the third world. Beyond organizing new members, labor must transform itself into a voice speaking mainly for these expansive constituencies who are not already American union members. Ironically, this will be the most effective way to service its own dues-paying members. In France, for example, less than 10 percent of the workforce is in unions, but the French people as a whole support union work stoppages to protect wages or benefits. In 1997, a majority of the

---

1. David M. Gordon, *Fat and Mean: The Corporate Squeeze of Working Americans and the Myth of Management "Downsizing"* (New York: The Free Press, 1996).
2. *Ibid.*
3. Tom Geoghegan, *Which Side Are You On?* (New York: Farrar, Strauss & Giroux, 1991), p. 251.
4. David M. Gordon, *Fat and Mean*, p. 243.

French population virtually closed down the country in support of transportation workers' efforts to protect retirement and vacation benefits.[1]

Since Derber wrote this, we've seen the developments mentioned above, like the unofficial unionism of Wal-Mart workers and Imolakee farm laborers, aimed more at creating pressure through negative publicity and boycotts than at conventional collective bargaining in the Wagner framework. We've seen the exponential growth of open mouth sabotage on the web, still nowhere near its full flowering. The model of socially-based organizing Derber talked about has already succeeded as well as he could have imagined ten years ago, and it's barely getting started.

In addition, a socially-based union movement might take a page from the Owenites' book, offering cheap mutual health insurance not only to job-based union members, but to society-based members in non-union workplaces. It might try organizing production for exchange by unemployed workers, as well as setting up worker cooperatives on the model attempted by the Knights of Labor. During the great CIO organizing strikes of the early 1930s, one of A. L. Muste's great innovations was to ally the industrial unions with local organizations of the unemployed, to involve the latter in support of the strikes and weaken the social base for scabbing. A broad-based union movement, involved in creating social solidarity both in and out of the workplace, a self-organized workers' welfare state including not only job-based union members but non-union workers and the unemployed, would create a social base of support much like what Derber described in France, and undermine the bosses' divide-and-rule strategy.

And if we're considering ways the labor movement might regain some of its strength, how's this for one small step in the right direction: start sending a big box of "How to Fire Your Boss" pamphlets to the headquarters of every union local that's just lost a conventional strike. The pamphlet describes a Wobbly cell in one restaurant that had lost a strike. Once back on the job, the workers agreed on a strategy of "piling the customer's plates high, and figuring the bill on the low side." Within a short time, the boss was asking for terms. Unions that have just got their teeth kicked in playing by the bosses' rules might well be open to making the bosses fight by *their* rules for a change.

C. THE GROWING IMPORTANCE OF HUMAN CAPITAL: PEER PRODUCTION VS. THE CORPORATE GATEKEEPERS

There's also another, much newer, possibility for labor organizing. Luigi Zingales argues that as the importance of implicit contracts relative to explicit contracts increases, the rationale for shareholder residual claimancy is further weakened. In developing this argument, Zingales puts special emphasis on human capital. He builds his case on prior an article by Sanford Grossman and Oliver Hart: "The Costs and Benefits of Ownership."[2]

Grossman and Hart argue that the firm's assignment of property rights affects productivity, because vesting residual claimancy in one party reduces the incentive of the other to invest in the firm. The party with residual claimancy will "use [its] residual rights of control to obtain a larger share of the ex post surplus," which will cause the party without residual claimancy to underinvest. The optimal allocation of property rights, therefore, is for the party whose investment is most crucial to the enterprise to own the firm.[3] The clear implication is that as human capital becomes decisive to the firm, residual claimancy of labor is

1. Charlers Derber, *Corporation Nation: How Corporations are Taking Over Our Lives and What We Can Do About It* (New York: St. Martin's Griffin, 1998), p. 291.

2. Sanford J. Grossman and Oliver D. Hart. "The Costs and Benefits of Ownership: A Theory of Vertical and Lateral Integration" *Journal of Political Economy* vol. 94 no. 4 (1986).

3. Grossman and Hart, pp. 716-717.

necessary to secure a proper level of worker "investment" of their human capital in the firm.

Gary Miller's discussion of incentive systems in *Managerial Dilemmas* reinforces this lesson. Proper compensation not only serves as an efficiency wage for reducing turnover in human capital, but elicits hidden knowledge that otherwise might be exploited for information rents. The problem, he points out:

> Since wages for subordinates are costs for the owner of residual profits, profit maximization by the center is an obstacle to the efficient resolution of both the hidden information and hidden action problem. The desire of owners to maximize revenues less payoffs for team members constantly tempts them to choose incentive schemes that encourage strategic misrepresentation and inefficient production methods by subordinates . . . .

> The central dilemma in a hierarchy is thus how to constrain the self-interest of those with a stake in the inevitable residual generated by an efficient incentive system . . . . There will be a set of managerial alternatives available to the owner that will decrease the overall size of the pie, while increasing the owner's share of that pie.[1]

> . . . A firm will be better off if it can guarantee its subordinates a secure "property right" in a given incentive plan and a right to control certain aspects of their work environment and work pace . . . . Security in these property rights can give employees reason to make investments of time, energy, and social relationships that produce economic growth.[2]

Unfortunately, the temptation for the owner (whether shareholders or management) to expropriate the net productivity gains and destroy employee trust in the long run is ever-present. For this reason, once again, the only stable solution to this built-in conflict of interest is to vest residual rights in the workforce itself.

Zingales, writing with Raghuram Rajan, first built on the work of Grossman and Hart in a 1998 article: "Power in a Theory of the Firm."[3] They examined the ways in which firms might, by allowing access to their productive resources, encourage investment in human capital by employees. However, they stopped short of arguing for residual claimancy for workers.

It was only in "In Search of New Foundations" (2000) that Zingales developed this line of thought to its logical conclusion. In that article, he argued that as human capital becomes the decisive factor for growth inside the firm, the existing model of shareholder supremacy becomes more and more of an impediment to increasing productivity. Workers' investments in human capital, along with their ability to reduce the value of the firm by withholding it, is a form of equity not represented in the formal ownership mechanism.

Marjorie Kelly argues, in similar terms, that the formal ownership of the corporation (for her the shareholders, but for us the senior management) involves an expropriation of the value created by human capital.

> Let us assume, for the sake of argument, that all profits legitimately belong to stockholders. Let's assume they own all tangible corporate assets, so the book value of the corporation is theirs. (Book value means everything you own minus everything you owe.) Even granted this, stockholders are still running off with 75 percent of corporate value that's arguably not theirs.

> Consider: At year-end 1995, book value of the S&P 500 accounted for only 26 percent of market value. "Intangibles" were worth three times the value of tangible assets.

> Thus, even if S&P stockholders owned the companies' tangible assets, they got off scot-free with other airy stuff worth three times as much.

1. Gary J. Miller, *Managerial Dilemmas: The Political Economy of Hierarchy* (New York: Cambridge University Press, 1992), pp. 154-155.

2. *Ibid.*, p. 157.

3. Raghuram Rajan and Luigi Zingales. "Power in a Theory of the Firm" *Quarterly Journal of Economics* (May 1998) pp. 387-432.

Included in intangibles are a lot of things, like discounted future value, patents, and reputation. But also included is a company's knowledge base, its living presence. Or to call it by a simpler name: employees.[1]

Labor has the ability to exploit its skills and idiosyncratic knowledge in ways not subject to effective control. Rents from information impactedness and from the ineffectiveness of monitoring systems, and the potential of worker opportunism to impede the production process, mean that representation of human capital as residual claimant is becoming an absolute necessity for the organization to function effectively. To state it even more strongly, the increasing value of human capital relative to physical capital, and the increasing status of human capital as limiting factor because of agency problems, creates a set of problems that can only be solved by vesting residual claimancy *primarily* in the labor force.

But the really revolutionary implication is that, as the value of human capital increases, and the cost of physical capital investments needed for independent production by human capital decreases, the power of corporate hierarchies becomes less and less relevant. As the value of human relative to physical capital increases, the entry barriers become progressively lower for workers to take their human capital outside the firm and start new firms under their own control. Zingales gives the example of the Saatchi and Saatchi advertising agency. The largest block of shareholders, U.S. fund managers who controlled 30% of stock, thought that gave them effective control of the firm. They attempted to exercise this perceived control by voting down Maurice Saatchi's proposed increased option package for himself. In response, the Saatchi brothers took their human capital (in actuality the lion's share of the firm's value) elsewhere to start a new firm, and left a hollow shell owned by the shareholders.[2]

Interestingly, in 1994 a firm like Saatchi and Saatchi, with few physical assets and a lot of human capital, could have been considered an exception. Not any more. The wave of initial public offerings of purely human capital firms, such as consultant firms, and even technology firms whose main assets are the key employees, is changing the very nature of the firm. Employees are not merely automata in charge of operating valuable assets but valuable assets themselves, operating with commodity-like physical assets.[3]

In another, similar example, the former head of Salomon Brothers' bond trading group formed a new group with former Salomon traders responsible for 87% of the firm's profits.

. . . if we take the standpoint that the boundary of the firm is the point up to which top management has the ability to exercise power . . . , the group was not an integral part of Salomon. It merely rented space, Salomon's name, and capital, and turned over some share of its profits as rent.[4]

Marjorie Kelly gave the breakup of the Chiat/Day ad agency, in 1995, as an example of the same phenomenon.

. . . What is a corporation worth without its employees?
This question was acted out . . . in London, with the revolutionary birth of St. Luke's ad agency, which was formerly the London office of Chiat/Day. In 1995, the owners of Chiat/Day decided to sell the company to Omnicon—which meant layoffs were looming and Andy Law in the London office wanted none of it. He and his fellow

1. Marjorie Kelly, "The Corporation as Feudal Estate" (an excerpt from *The Divine Right of Capital*) *Business Ethics*, Summer 2001. Quoted in GreenMoney Journal, Fall 2008 <http://greenmoneyjournal.com/article.mpl?articleid=60&newsletterid=15>.

2. Zingales, "In Search of New Foundations," p. 1641.

3. *Ibid.*, p. 1641.

4. Raghuram Rajan and Luigi Zingales, "The Governance of the New Enterprise," in Xavier Vives, ed., *Corporate Governance: Theoretical and Empirical Perspectives* (Cambridge: Cambridge University Press, 2000), pp. 211-212.

employees decided to rebel. They phoned clients and found them happy to join the rebellion. And so at one blow, London employees and clients were leaving.

Thus arose a fascinating question: What exactly did the "owners" of the London
office now own? A few desks and files? Without employees and clients, what was the
London branch worth? One dollar, it turned out. That was the purchase price—plus a
percentage of profits for seven years—when Omnicon sold the London branch to Law
and his cohorts after the merger. They renamed it St. Luke's . . . . All employees became
equal owners . . . Every year now the company is re-valued, with new shares awarded
equally to all.[1]

David Prychitko remarked on the same phenomenon in the tech industry, as far back
as 1991:

> Consider . . . the recent wave of "break-away" firms in the computer industry. Old
> firms act as embryos for new firms. If a worker or group of workers is not satisfied with
> the existing firm, each has a skill which he or she controls, and can leave the firm with
> those skills and establish a new one. In the information age it is becoming more evident
> that a boss cannot control the workers as one did in the days when the assembly line was
> dominant. People cannot be treated as workhorses any longer, for the value of the pro-
> duction process is becoming increasingly embodied in the intellectual skills of the
> worker. This poses a new threat to the traditional firm if it denies participatory organiza-
> tion.
>
> The appearance of break-away computer firms leads one to question the extent to
> which our existing system of property rights in ideas and information actually protects
> bosses in other industries against the countervailing power of workers. Perhaps our cur-
> rent system of patents, copyrights, and other intellectual property rights not only im-
> pedes competition and fosters monopoly, as some Austrians argue. Intellectual property
> rights may also reduce the likelihood of break-away firms in general, and discourage the
> shift to more participatory, cooperative formats.[2]

The enormously reduced capitalization cost of enterprise, in so many sectors of the
economy, also undermines much of the rationale for divorcing ownership and control. For
one thing, as the examples of Saatchi and Salomon show, production units in capital-
intensive industry need not share a common ownership to function within a firm; therefore "the enterprise need not be commonly owned." Although they don't specifically
mention it, this clearly has implications for the networked model of production. And given
the far lower levels of investment required to enter the market, "there is no need to have a
large number of investors. Thus ownership and operational control in the enterprise can be
much more closely associated than in the past."[3]

Rajan's and Zingales' work quoted above predates much of the writing on peer network production by thinkers like Yochai Benkler, so aside from one throwaway line ("even
technology") they largely ignore the entertainment and software industries, to which the
same principle applies far more forcefully.

Zingales writes at length on the ways in which the new-model firms comprising
much of the contemporary economy differ from the traditional capital-intensive firm.

> First, the traditional firm, which according to Chandler . . . emerged during the second
> industrial revolution to exploit economies of scale and scope, was very asset intensive and
> highly vertically integrated . . . . As a result, the realm of transactions governed by power
> rather than by prices tended to coincide with the legal boundaries of the corporation.

1. Kelly, op. cit.
2. David L Prychitko, *Marxism and Workers' Self-Management: The Essential Tension* (New York;
London; Westport, Conn.: Greenwood Press, 1991), p. 121n.
3. Rajan and Zingales, "The Governance of the New Enterprise," p. 219.

Today, in contrast, it tends to coincide with intangible property rights of various sorts (e.g., the music and software industry's reliance on "intellectual property") that act as artificial barriers restricting human capital's independent access to the market.

> Second, the traditional firm had a high degree of control over its employees . . . . The scarcity of competitors, both in the intermediate and in the output market, implied a thin outside labor market able to use (and pay for) the skills that employees acquired on the job. Through its control of the firm's assets, the headquarters effectively controlled the main source of employment open to its specialized employees, giving to top management enormous power.

> Third, the size and the asset specificity of the traditional firm required more investment and more risk taking than were within the capacity of the management. The control conferred by the ownership of crucial assets, however, made outside ownership feasible. Therefore, the traditional firm came to be owned by dispersed investors.

> Finally, the concentration of power at the top of the organizational pyramid, together with the separation between ownership and control, made the agency problem between top managers and shareholders the problem . . . .[1]

Thorstein Veblen described this power based on ownership of capital assets from the standpoint of a contemporary. Intangible assets, he wrote, arise from the fact that ownership of the community's physical equipment makes the capitalist the "*de facto* owner of the community's aggregate knowledge of ways and means," particularly the capabilities of engineers and workers—and hence the right to restrict the use of such knowledge and capabilities, and thereby draw monopoly rents from them.[2] But, as Zingales observes, the declining importance of physical assets relative to human capital has changed this. Physical assets, "which used to be the major source of rents, have become less unique and are not commanding large rents anymore." And "the demand for process innovation and quality improvement . . . can only be generated by talented employees," which increases the importance of human capital.[3] This is even more true since Zingales wrote, with the rise of what has been variously called the Wikified firm, the hyperlinked organization, Enterprise 2.0, etc.

Tom Peters remarked in quite similar language, some six years earlier in *The Tom Peters Seminar*, on the changing balance of physical and human capital. Of *Inc.* magazine's 500 top-growth companies, which include a good number of information, computer technology and biotech firms, 34% were launched on initial capital of less than $10,000, 59% on less than $50,000, and 75% on less than $100,000.[4] Clearly, in such an environment, established firms' ownership of copyrights and patents is the main entry barrier for competing firms.

As often as not, "intellectual property" serves as a tollgate to prevent existing technical knowledge from being built and improved on by competing firms in the same industry—as a barrier to progress through the free flow of information—rather than as a spur to progress. In a free market, the normal pattern would be a brief period of entrepreneurial profits from being the first to innovate, with marginal profits falling to zero as competitors adopted the same innovation; after a brief period of entrepreneurial profit, the benefits of increased productivity are quickly transferred to the consumer, and price falls to the newly reduced production cost. But under the kind of corporate capitalism which is built on "intellectual property," the typical pattern is rather companies living off the rents of past innovation—"one hit wonders"—and collecting tribute from anyone who wants to further

1. Zingales, "In Search of New Foundations," pp. 1641-1642.
2. Veblen, *The Theory of Business Enterprise*, in Commons, *Institutional Economics* pp. 663-664.
3. Zingales, pp. 1641-1642.
4. Tom Peters. *The Tom Peters Seminar: Crazy Times Call for Crazy Organizations* (New York: Vintage Books, 1994), p. 35.

improve on existing proprietary technology. Peters said, "there's a surplus of everything," and success comes only from adding value through quality, service, and innovation.[1] What he failed to add was that success can also come through using the state's "intellectual property" monopoly to *stop* competitors from doing so. "Intellectual property" is as much a barrier to technical progress, as the tolls of assorted German principalities and feudal baronies were a barrier to commerce.

Peters cited former 3M strategic planner George Hegg on the increasing portion of product "value" made up of "intellectual property" (i.e., the amount of final price consisting of tribute to the owners of "intellectual property"): "We are trying to sell more and more intellect and less and less materials." Peters produces a long string of such examples (my comments follow):

> . . . My new Minolta 9xi is a lumpy object, but I suspect I paid about $10 for its plastic casing, another $50 for the fine-ground optical glass, and the rest, about $640, for its intellect . . .[2]
>
> It is a soft world . . . . Nike contracts for the production of its spiffy footwear in factories around the globe, but it creates the enormous stock value via superb design and, above all, marketing skills. Tom Silverman, founder of upstart Tommy Boy Records, says Nike was the first company to understand that it was in the lifestyle business . . . . Shoes? Lumps? Forget it! Lifestyle. Image. Speed. Value via intellect and pizazz.[3]
>
> "Microsoft's only factory asset is the human imagination," observed *The New York Times Magazine* writer Fred Moody. In seminars I've used the slide on which those words appear at least a hundred times, yet every time that simple sentence comes into view on the screen I feel the hairs on the back of my neck bristle.[4]
>
> . . . "Does anyone here know what it means to 'manage the human imagination?'"[5]
>
> A few years back, Philip Morris purchased Kraft for $12.9 billion, a fair price in view of its subsequent performance. When the accountants finished their work, it turned out that Philip Morris had bought $1.3 billion worth of "stuff" (tangible assets) and $11.6 billion of "Other." What's the other, the 116/129?
>
> . . . . Call it intangibles, good-will (the U.S. accountants' term), brand equity, or the ideas in the heads of thousands of Kraft employees around the world.[6]

Regarding Peters' Minolta example, as Benkler points out the marginal cost of reproducing "its intellect" is virtually zero. So about 90% of the price of that new Minolta comes from tolls to corporate gatekeepers, who have been granted control of that "intellect." In an economy where software and product design were the product of peer networks, unrestricted by the "intellectual property" of old corporate dinosaurs, 90% of the product's price would evaporate overnight. To quote Michael Perelman,

> the so-called weightless economy has more to do with the legislated powers of intellectual property that the government granted to powerful corporations.[14] For example, companies such as Nike, Microsoft, and Pfizer sell stuff that has high value relative to its weight only because their intellectual property rights insulate them from competition.[7]

We are working ten times as many hours as necessary, in order to pay tribute to the grantees of special privilege. If product design and software were produced on an open source model by peer networks, so that that the main source of product cost were the actual physical inputs, and there were no patent or brand-name markups, we could probably

1. *Ibid.*, p. 37.
2. *Ibid.*, p. 10.
3. *Ibid.*, pp. 10-11.
4. *Ibid.*, p. 11.
5. *Ibid.* p. 12.
6. *Ibid.* p. 12.
7. Michael Perelman, "The Political Economy of Intellectual Property," *Monthly Review*, January 2003 <http://www.monthlyreview.org/0103perelman.htm>.

earn enough to pay for our present standard of living in an average workweek of less than twenty hours. The rest of it is tribute to the owners of the human imagination.

The same goes for Nike's sneakers. I suspect the amortization cost of the physical capital used to manufacture the shoes in those Asian sweatshops, plus the cost of the sweatshop labor, is less than 10% of the price of the shoes. The wages of the workers could be tripled or quadrupled with negligible impact on the retail price. One of these days the actual producers of Nike sneakers will realize that they can disregard Nike's ownership of the swoosh, and dispense with the lifestyle, image, speed and pizazz along with it, and sell just the "lumps" at one-tenth the price to a virtually unlimited domestic market in their own country—while giving themselves a 300% payraise.

Johan Soderberg suggests that the current model of outsourcing and networked production makes capital vulnerable to being cut out of the production process by labor. He begins with an anecdote that seems to cast doubt on our earlier remarks on the vulnerability of just-in-time production to disruption by strikes. He refers to Toyota subcontractor Aisin Seiki, "the only manufacturer of a component critical to the whole Toyota network," whose factory was destroyed in a fire:

> The whole conglomerate was in jeopardy of grinding to a halt. In two months Toyota would run out of supplies of the parts produced by Aisin Seiki [and, note, it would have been far sooner had the supply chain been leaner]. Faced with looming disaster, the network of subcontractors fervently cooperated and created provisory means for substituting the factory. In a stunningly short time, Toyota subsidiaries had restructured themselves and could carry on unaffected by the incident. Duncan Watt attributes the swift response by the Toyota conglomerate to its networked mode of organisation. The relevance of this story for labour theory becomes apparent if we stipulate that the factory was not destroyed in an accident but was held-up in a labour conflict. Networked capital turns every point of production, from the firm down to the individual work assignment, into a node subject to circumvention. . . . [I]t is capital's ambition to route around labour strongholds that has brought capitalism into network production . . . . Nations, factories, natural resources, and positions within the social and technical division of labour, are all made subject to redundancy. Thus has capital annulled the threat of blockages against necks in the capitalist production chain, upon which the negotiating power of unions is based.

Of course, I would take issue with Soderberg on the significance of this phenomenon as an end-run around labor. No doubt the cost of rerouting around the blockage caused by the Aisin Seiki fire, and retooling other suppliers to produce the component, was considerable, and involved considerable inconvenience. And it is within the power of workers, simply by walking out for a few days at unannounced intervals at a tiny fraction of the nodes in the network, to force capital to resort constantly to such expensive emergency responses.

Nevertheless, Soderberg himself goes on to describe how this redundancy created by capital, as a way of routing around blockages, threatens to make capital itself redundant:

> The fading strength of unions will continue for as long as organised labour is entrenched in past victories and outdated forms of resistance. But the networked mode of production opens up a "window of opportunity" for a renewed cycle of struggle, this time, however, of a different kind. *Since all points of production have been transformed into potentially redundant nodes of a network, capital as a factor of production in the network has itself become a node subject to redundancy.*[1]

Soderberg sees the growing importance of human relative to physical capital, and the rise of peer production in the informational realm, as reason for hope that independent and self-managed networks of laborers can route around capital. Hence the importance he at-

---

1. Soderberg, *Hacking Capitalism*, pp. 141-142.

taches to the increasingly draconian "intellectual property" regime as a way of suppressing the open-source movement and maintaining control over the conditions of production.[1]

Dave Pollard, writing from the imaginary perspective of 2015, made a similar observation about the vulnerability of corporations that follow the Nike model of hollowing themselves out and outsourcing everything:

> In the early 2000s, large corporations that were once hierarchical end-to-end business enterprises began shedding everything that was not deemed 'core competency', in some cases to the point where the only things left were business acumen, market knowledge, experience, decision-making ability, brand name, and aggregation skills. This 'hollowing out' allowed multinationals to achieve enormous leverage and margin. It also made them enormously vulnerable and potentially dispensable.

> As outsourcing accelerated, some small companies discovered how to exploit this very vulnerability. When, for example, they identified North American manufacturers outsourcing domestic production to third world plants in the interest of 'increasing productivity', they went directly to the third world manufacturers, offered them a bit more, and then went directly to the North American retailers, and offered to charge them less. The expensive outsourcers quickly found themselves unnecessary middlemen . . . . The large corporations, having shed everything they thought was non 'core competency', learned to their chagrin that in the connected, information economy, the value of their core competency was much less than the inflated value of their stock, and they have lost much of their market share to new federations of small entrepreneurial businesses.[2]

Returning to Peters and his exalted reaction to Moody's Microsoft quip, it's a bit odd to hear the "human imagination" described as a "factory asset" in a country that celebrates the abolition of slavery. It may raise Peters' neck hairs, but it makes my stomach turn. Unfortunately, most of the profitable sectors in the corporate economy (software, entertainment, biotech, pharma) are built on the assumption that the human imagination is subject to corporate ownership. And to answer Peters' question about managing the human imagination, Microsoft's Internet Explorer web browser is getting a run for its money from a browser, Firefox, produced entirely by *self-managed* human imagination, and distributed without copyright. Microsoft is able to manage the "human imagination" working on its products because of its artificial property rights. The human networks writing code for Microsoft are quite similar to the human networks outside in the free software movement. The main difference between them is the corporate boundaries enforced by Microsoft's artificial property on "intellect."

The *Cluetrain Manifesto* makes a similar observation. Today the networked public knows more about the company's product than its own officers do, getting "far better information and support from one another" than from the company's official representatives. The internal workforce of the corporation, in the age of the "hyperlinked organization," is similarly networked through the intranet; although corporations initially install intranets "top-down to distribute HR policies . . . that workers are doing their best to ignore, before long people are "talking to each other inside the company—and not just about rules and regulations, boardroom directives, bottom lines." Both the work force and the public are networked and engaged in conversations that corporate management can't control. And "[a] metaphysical construct called 'The Company' is the only thing standing between the two."

1. *Ibid.*, pp. 142-142
2. David Pollard, "The Future of Business," *How to Save the World*, January 14, 2004 <http://blogs.salon.com/0002007/2004/01/14.html>.

However subliminally at the moment, millions of people now online perceive companies as little more than quaint legal fictions that are actively impeding these conversations from intersecting.[1]

To the outside, the company begins to look like a set of hyperlinked clusters who select themselves based on trust and respect and even their sense of fun . . . .

The business now consists of a shifting set of hyperlinked groups, self-organizing . . . , regardless of where—and whether—they are on the org chart. Management is simply an impediment to these groups. In fact, rather than employees feeling that they must constantly justify themselves to management, management now needs to give workers a single reason why it should be involved in the life of the business it used to believe it ran.[2]

The difference between Benkler and Peters is that, while Peters perceives the decisive shift from physical to human capital just as clearly as Benkler, Peters envisions the shift as occurring in the context of a corporate economy in which a handful of firms continue to *own* the "human imagination" and "intellect," with the help of the Digital Millennium Copyright Act and TRIPS accords. And while Peters perceives the importance of "assembled brainpower" and "ad hoc networks" just as clearly as Benkler, he envisions corporate ownership of "intellectual property" as the basis for their control over these human networks. The worst nightmare of the corporate dinosaurs is that, in an economy where imagination is the main source of value, the people who actually possess the "imagination" might figure out they no longer need the company's permission, and realize its "intellectual property" is unenforceable in an age of encryption and bittorrent.

For example, Peters gives the example of Oticon, which got rid of "the entire formal organization" and abolished departments, secretaries, and formal management titles. Employees put their personal belongings in "caddies, or personal carts, moving them to appropriate spots in the completely open space as their work with various colleagues requires."[3] The danger for the corporate gatekeepers, in sectors where outlays for physical capital cease to present significant entry barriers, is that one of these days knowledge workers may push their "personal carts" out of the organization altogether, and decide they can do everything just as well without the company.

The same is true of Zingales' emphasis, albeit in a much less egregious way. His primary focus is on finding ways to effectively utilize human capital *within* the firm, to overcome agency problems by giving effective property rights in the firm to human capital. The problem, in the case of employees, is "to create a situation where employees know that their rewards will be greater if they make firm-specific investments."[4] More generally,

The deintegration of the firm and the growing purpose of human capital are changing the terms of the problem. Power and rents are not concentrated at the top of a steep pyramid; they are sprinkled throughout the organization, even outside the legal boundaries of the firm, as is the case for crucial independent suppliers. Now that power is diffused, the major corporate governance problem becomes how to prevent conflicts among stakeholders from paralyzing or destroying the firm.[5]

This emphasis on the stability of the firm is the chief shortcoming of Zingales' article. At the time he wrote, in 2000, discussion of the possibilities for peer production was confined to far more marginal circles than today. But in the case of forms of production that center almost entirely on human capital and where outlays on physical capital are low, the firm itself (in the conventional sense) is arguably an anachronism that serves no useful purpose. In the absence of high-value physical assets to which the managers and workers are

1. "95 Theses, " in Locke, *et al.*, *The Cluetrain Manifesto*.
2. "Chapter Five. The Hyperlinked Organization," *The Cluetrain Manifesto*.
3. Peters, *The Tom Peters Seminar*, pp. 29-30.
4. Zingales, pp. 1645-1646.
5. *Ibid.*, pp. 1647-1648.

held hostage, the main rationale for the firm structure—to govern those assets—is gone. The real solution may be simply to *dissolve* the firm's boundaries, in industries with low capital outlays, and replace the formal organization with loose peer networks. The abolition of the artificial property rights (copyrights, patents, and trademarks) which are currently the main bulwark of the corporation as locus of control, will cause most firms to wither away in industries centered on human capital. For many industries, an organizational model similar to that of the construction and movie industries, based on projects rather than firms, may make more sense: rather than discrete firms being started and going out of business, individuals will move freely between projects; peer groups with extremely porous boundaries will constantly federate and divide, gaining and losing members, for specific projects.

In industries like manufacturing, which even with general-purpose technologies for decentralized production may require comparatively large capital outlays, Zingales' solution—residual claimancy by labor—may be more relevant. In that sector, cooperative ownership, relying either on internal financing or debt as a source of investment capital, may well be the most suitable model. Even if capital outlays per capita become small enough to be within workers' reach, the aggregate outlay will be sufficient to require some organizational structure for managing it.

The increasing agency problems of human capital within the corporation, and the resulting change in perceived self-interest of capital as it affects firm ownership, may serve to promote cooperative ownership even of capital-intensive industry. For over a century, the principle of shareholder supremacy has reflected the perceived self-interests of large-scale absentee owners of investment capital. But with the increased agency problems entailed in wage labor and absentee ownership, they may well decide that the dangers of expropriation are less when the capitalist is a contractual claimant collecting a fixed payment on debt.

As described in Benkler in *The Wealth of Networks*, the networked digital world has created an unprecedented state of affairs. In many industries, the initial outlay for entering the market was in the hundreds of thousands of dollars or more. The old electronic mass media, for instance, were "typified by high-cost hubs and cheap, ubiquitous, reception-only systems at the end. This led to a limited range of organizational models for production: those that could collect sufficient funds to set up a hub."[1] The same was true of print periodicals, with the increasing cost of printing equipment from the mid-nineteenth century on serving as the main entry barrier for organizing the hubs. Between 1835 and 1850, the typical startup cost of a newspaper increased from $500 to $100,000—or from roughly $10,000 to $2.38 million in 2005 dollars.[2]

The networked economy, in contrast, is distinguished by "network architecture and the [low] cost of becoming a speaker."

> The first element is the shift from a hub-and-spoke architecture with unidirectional links to the end points in the mass media, to distributed architecture with multidirectional connections among all nodes in the networked information environment. The second is the practical elimination of communications costs as a barrier to speaking across associational boundaries. Together, these characteristics have fundamentally altered the capacity of individuals, acting alone or with others, to be active participants in the public sphere as opposed to its passive readers, listeners, or viewers.[3]

The central change that makes this possible is that "the basic physical capital necessary to express and communicate human meaning is the connected personal computer."

1. Yochai Benkler, *The Wealth of Networks: How Social Production Transforms Markets and Freedom* (New Haven and London: Yale University Press, 2006), p. 179.

2. *Ibid.*, p. 188.

3. *Ibid.*, pp. 212–13.

The core functionalities of processing, storage, and communications are widely owned throughout the population of users . . . . The high capital costs that were a prerequisite to gathering, working, and communicating information, knowledge, and culture, have now been widely distributed in the society. The entry barrier they posed no longer offers a condensation point for the large organizations that once dominated the information environment.[1]

The desktop revolution and the Internet mean that the minimum capital outlay for entering most of the entertainment and information industry has fallen to a few thousand dollars, and the marginal cost of reproduction is zero. If anything that overstates the cost of entry in many cases, considering how rapidly computer value depreciates and the relatively miniscule cost of buying a five-year-old computer and adding RAM. The networked environment, combined with endless varieties of cheap software for creating and editing content, makes it possible for the amateur to produce output of a quality once associated with giant publishing houses and recording companies.[2] That is true of the software industry, the music industry (thanks to cheap equipment and software for high quality recording and sound editing), desktop publishing, and to a certain extent even to film (as witnessed by affordable editing technology and the success of *Sky Captain*). Podcasting makes it possible to distribute "radio" and "television" programming, at virtually no cost, to anyone with a broadband connection. A network of amateur contributors have peer-produced an encyclopedia, Wikipedia, which Britannica sees as a rival. As Tom Coates put it, "the gap between what can be accomplished at home and what can be accomplished in a work environment has narrowed dramatically over the last ten to fifteen years."[3]

It's also true of news, with ever-expanding networks of amateurs in venues like Indymedia, alternative new operations like Robert Parry's and Greg Palast's, and natives and American troops blogging news firsthand from Iraq, at the very same time the traditional broadcasting networks are shutting down foreign news operations because of the high cost. "With a digital camera ready-at-hand and an Internet connection close by, the anarchistic mode of news reporting turns any passer-by into a potential journalist for a moment . . . ."[4]

The central characteristic of information and culture production, in the networked digital age, is "nonrivalry" and zero marginal reproduction cost. "Nonrival" means that possession of an information good does not make it less available for consumption by others. And digitized information can be reproduced indefinitely at virtually no cost whatever.[5]

James Bennett describes this as "the end of capitalism" (in the sense of absentee ownership and wage labor) "and the triumph of the market economy."

> . . . [F[or the first time since the beginning of the Industrial Revolution, the ownership of the most critical tool of production of the most critical industry of the worlds leading economy [is] readily affordable by the individual worker. Throughout the first three decades of the Information Age, the individual worker was still as dependent on his employer for his means of production as was any textile worker in Manchester or Lawrence in 1840. Suddenly, this changed. Now, it is as if a steelworker could afford his own blast-furnace or rolling-mill; an automobile worker his own assembly line . . . .
>
> The second thing which has changed is the rise of the Internet. This is taking the control of the communication networks, and ultimately of the communications media, out of the hands of the large corporations which have always controlled them . . . . Just as the individually-owned computer capable of producing first-rate software is revolutionizing the work relations of software, the individually-owned Webcasting

---

1. *Ibid.*, pp. 32–33.
2. *Ibid.*, p. 54.
3. Tom Coates, "(Weblogs and) The Mass Amateurisation of (Nearly) Everything . . ." *Plasticbag.org*, September 3, 2003 <http://www.plasticbag.org/archives/2003/09/weblogs_and_the_mass_amateurisation_of_nearly_everything>.
4. Johan Soderberg, *Hacking Capitalism*, p. 126.
5. Benkler, pp. 35–36.

tionizing the work relations of software, the individually-owned Webcasting facility will change the nature of the media.

It is also changing the dynamics of production. Even though the tools of production can now be owned by the workers, individually and severally, there still seemed to be a need to bring programmers together in one place and put them under the control of management. Although this is still the case in most instances, the rise of Linux and other open-source products has provided another paradigm, and one which will soon grow to become the principal model of production in the principal industry of the leading economies of the planet.[1]

In this environment, the only thing standing between the old information and media dinosaurs and their total collapse is their so-called "intellectual property" rights—at least to the extent they're still enforceable. In any such industry, where the basic production equipment is affordable to all, and bottom-up networking renders management obsolete, it is likely that self-managed, cooperative production will replace the old managerial hierarchies. The network revolution, if its full potential is realized,

> will lead to substantial redistribution of power and money from the twentieth century industrial producers of information, culture, and communications—like Hollywood, the recording industry, and perhaps the broadcasters and some of the telecommunications giants—to a combination of widely diffuse populations around the globe, and the market actors that will build the tools that make this population better able to produce its own information environment rather than buying it ready-made."[2]

And the same model of organization can be extended to fields of employment outside the information and entertainment industries—particularly labor-intensive service industries, where human capital likewise outweighs physical capital in importance. The basic model is applicable in any industry with low requirements for initial capitalization and low or non-existent overhead. Perhaps the most revolutionary possibilities are in the temp industry. In my own work experience, I've seen that hospitals using agency nursing staff typically pay the staffing agency about three times what the agency nurse receives in pay. Cutting out the middleman, perhaps with some sort of cross between a workers' co-op and a longshoremen's union hiring hall, seems like a no-brainer. An AFL-CIO organizer in the San Francisco Bay area has attempted just such a project, as recounted by Daniel Levine.[3]

The chief obstacle to such "break-away firms" (to use Prychitko's term) is non-competition agreements signed by temp workers at their previous places of employment. Typically, a temp worker signs an agreement not to work independently for any of the firm's clients, or work for them through another agency, for some period (usually three to six months) after quitting. Of course, this can be evaded fairly easily, if the new cooperative firm has enough workers to direct particular assignments to those who aren't covered by the non-competition clause in relation to that particular client.

One important implication of these phenomena is that the traditional association of capitalization with productivity (especially notable among Austrians) has become obsolete. Even the mainstream marginalist tradition, in its Austrian and neoclassical variants, professes to believe that capital is just one factor of production among many; it is therefore a bit odd, as "Jed" notes at Anomalous Presumptions blog, to name the market system for one factor in particular ("capitalism"). And, Jed also argued, technological advances are simultaneously reducing by orders of magnitude the capital outlays needed to set up in many industries, even as human capital replaces physical capital as the critical factor. Given this shift in the

---

1. James C. Bennett, "The End of Capitalism and the Triumph of the Market Economy," from *Network Commonwealth: The Future of Nations in the Internet Era* (1998, 1999) <http://www.pattern.com/bennettj-endcap.html>.

2. *Ibid.*, p. 23.

3. Levine, *Disgruntled.*, p. 160.

relative importance of capital and labor, it makes less sense than ever to treat capital as the primary factor.[1]

D. AUSTRIAN CRITICISM OF THE USEFULNESS OF UNIONS

Finally, I want to address the common contention of right-wing libertarians that unions are useless. I've read *Economics in One Lesson*. I'm familiar with the argument that "in a free market" wages are determined by productivity. I'm familiar with Rothbard's argument that unions can't do anything for workers, in a free market, that isn't already accomplished by the operation of the market on an individual basis.

I've also seen, in the real world, real wages that have remained stagnant or even fallen slightly since the 1970s, as labor productivity soared and the real GDP nearly doubled. Labor is far more productive than it was thirty years ago; yet virtually the entire increase in GDP in that time has gone to corporate profits, CEO salaries, and exploding land rents. The entire growth of economic output over the past thirty years has gone into mushrooming incomes for the rentier classes, while the majority have kept up their purchasing power by cashing out home equity at Ditech. These facts, seemingly so at odds with Hazlitt's dictum, bring to mind a quote from Mises:

> If a contradiction appears between a theory and experience, we always have to assume that a condition presupposed by the theory was not present, or else that there is some error in our observation . . . . The disagreement between the theory and the facts of experience consequently forces us to think through the problems of the theory again. But so long as a re-examination of the theory uncovers no errors in our thinking, we are not entitled to doubt its truth.[2]

When the theory predicts that in a free market wages will be determined by the productivity of labor, and we see that they aren't, what's the obvious conclusion? That this isn't a free market. That we're dealing with power relations, not market relations.

In a state capitalist market, where some component of employer profits are rents extracted from the employee because of state-enforced unequal exchange, organized labor action may provide the bargaining leverage to reduce those ill-gotten gains.

It's also odd that the Rothbardians see so little advantage in contracts, from a worker's perspective. Thomas L. Knapp, a left-Rothbardian who joined the Wobblies, remarked on the contrast between mainstream libertarians' attitudes toward labor contracts and their attitudes toward contracts in all other economic realms:

> Contract is the basis of the free market; yet the non-union laborer's "contract" is an unenforceable, malleable verbal agreement which can be rescinded or modified at any time, called "at will employment." There's nothing philosophically repugnant about "at will employment," but I find it odd that Pacificus does not likewise decry written, enforceable, binding contracts between other entities—suppliers and purchasers, for example.
>
> Far from putting employers and employees at odds with each other, dealing on the basis of explicit contract minimizes misunderstandings. Each party knows what he or she is required to do to execute the contract, and each party knows what he or she can expect as a benefit under it.[3]

---

1. Jed, "Capital is Just Another Factor," *Anomalous Presumptions*, March 8, 2007 <http://jed.jive.com/?p=28>.

2. Ludwig von Mises, *Epistemological Problems of Economics*. Translated by George Reisman (Princeton, New York, Toronto, London: D. Van Nostrand, Inc., 1960), p. 30.

3. The original exchange between Knapp and Pacificus has disappeared, unfortunately. The quote above is taken from a post of mine, "Thomas L. Knapp Joins the One Big Union," *Mutualist Blog*, April 6, 2005 <http://mutualist.blogspot.com/2005/04/thomas-l-knapp-joins-one-big-union. html>.

Contracts introduce long-term stability and predictability for everyone: something free-market libertarians consider to be a fairly non-controversial benefit, when anything but labor supply is involved. Had Rothbard held down a blue collar job, he might have understood the incredible feeling of relief in knowing you're protected by a union contract against arbitrary dismissal and all the associated uncertainty and insecurity, that comes with being an "at-will" employee.

Any time you see a right-wing libertarian throwing a hissy fit over something they approve in principle under other circumstances, it's a pretty safe bet it must be benefiting workers.

Another point, on the same subject: Rothbard's hostility toward the "economic illiteracy" of workers who voluntarily refrained from crossing picket lines, and consumers who boycott scab goods, is quite uncharacteristic for a subjectivist. It's certainly odd, for adherents of an ideology that normally accepts no second-guessing of "revealed preference," to get their noses so out of joint when that preference is for respecting a picket line or buying "fair trade" coffee.

More importantly, in acknowledging that enough potential "replacement workers" so honored picket lines as to constitute a "problem," from his perspective, he also gave the lie to arguments by DiLorenzo and his ilk that the success of strikes depends on forcible exclusion of scabs. A strike does not have to achieve 100% participation of the workforce, or exclude 100% of potential replacements. It only has to *persuade* enough of both groups to inconvenience the employer beyond his threshold of tolerance. And that a general moral culture which encourages labor solidarity and respect for picket lines, alone, may be enough to achieve this, is suggested by the very fact that Rothbard and his right-wing followers regard that kind of moral culture as such a threat.

APPENDIX A

SABOTAGE IN A LONDON NIGHTCLUB: A CASE STUDY

From *Sabotage*, by Farhad Analoui and Andrew Kakabadse.

The authors document, from Analoui's personal observations during an undercover stint as a worker at a large London nightclub, many examples of workers imposing costs or reducing efficiency in response to perceived unfairness by the employer. Worker disgruntlement was expressed actively through wastage of supplies, deliberate destruction, and over-generosity toward the customer (i.e., the "good work strike"); it was also expressed through more passive measures, like withdrawal of enthusiasm and working to rule. As mild as "withdrawal of enthusiasm" may sound, the simple refusal to show initiative or to take timely action based on direct observations in the work process may result in massive losses to the employer. Consider this for example:

> In the early hours of one Saturday morning, the staff discovered that a high voltage electrical transformer had started to smoulder. However, they did not disconnect the appliance from the mains, or inform the managers. It was only when a small, but potentially destructive, fire broke out that one of the group members went to find a manager.
>
> The comments which the staff used to explain away their behaviour on this occasion were typical of those which would follow a case of inaction. For example, Ali said, 'I couldn't give a damn, let the bloody place burn down. It's nothing to do with me.' Sandra's reaction was: 'Oh to hell with it. I'm not going to go running to tell them every time something goes wrong, every time I see a little fire. It's their problem. If the place is really going to burn down, they'll find out soon enough and they can sort it out.'[1]

A disgruntled worker, through deliberate wastage, can cost an employer large sums of money with virtually no chance of getting caught. For example one member of the bar staff, Joe, asked to leave work upon hearing that his wife had checked their son to the hospital. The Catering Manager's response: "If you want to go, go but don't bother coming back if you do. You lot get paid to do a job. I couldn't care less, it's the business I am interested in not your kids. Don't waste my time again." Joe subsequently ruined several hundred pounds worth of spirits by contaminating them with Pernod.[2]

Another worker, Chris, described a "nightmare" shift of loud, abusive customers swearing at her. The management response, predictably: " . . . you're not being chirpy enough. You've got to smile!" After that manager left her station, she dropped a full bottle of Tia Maria in the trash bin.[3]

Even when the overall bargaining power of labor is seemingly too weak to permit significant resistance, it's possible to make one's will felt by timing the strategic refusal of cooperation to coincide with the employer's greatest vulnerability. Analoui and Kabadse recount one example at an engineering firm in northeastern England, where union demands for a 9.6% raise were met with a counter-offer of only a 7.6% raise, along with the warning to consider the high rate of unemployment before rejecting it. Not long afterward, the firm received an order for five hundred water pumps, enormously profitable to the firm, but which would require acceptance of overtime to complete by deadline. The shop steward, not surprisingly, announced that the workers weren't in the mood to work the overtime.[4]

---

1. Farhad Analoui and Andrew Kakabadse. *Sabotage: How to Recognize and Manage Employee Defiance* (Management Books 2000 Ltd, 2000), pp. 84-85.

2. *Ibid.*, p. 87.

3. *Ibid.*, p. 88.

4. *Ibid.*, p. 94.

In another example, the bar at which Analoui worked undercover was selected for a surprise visit by the parent company's directors, with little advance notice. The General Manager, who had recently fired several cleaners, announced to the overworked bar staff (in a lengthy late-night meeting after a long, hellish shift) that they would be expected to come in early the next day to get the place shipshape for the visiting dignitaries. As you might expect, the General Manager wound up being humiliated in front of his own bosses.[1]

That last is an especially effective form of "open-mouth sabotage," by the way: exposing the boss's dirt to *his* bosses.

1. *Ibid.*, pp. 96–98.

Appendix B

Yochai Benkler on Open-Mouth Sabotage: Diebold and Sinclair Media as Case Studies in Media Swarming

On October 9, 2004, the *Los Angeles Times* broke the story of Sinclair Media's plans to air *Stolen Honor*. The official response by the Kerry campaign over the next few days was tepid at best, consisting of a perfunctory FCC complaint that produced no results during the period in question. After MyDD.com, Daily Kos and Talking Points Memo picked up the story on October 9, however, it was a matter of hours before several Sinclair boycott websites had been set up, with links was quickly circulated throughout the Democratic blogosphere. The next day, Daily Kos posted a list of Sinclair sponsors, also widely circulated. In the ensuing boycott campaign, advertisers were deluged with more mail and phone calls than they could handle. By October 13, some sponsors were threatening litigation, viewing unsolicited boycott emails as illegal SPAM. Nick Davis, creator of one of the boycott sites, posted legal information explaining that anti-SPAM legislation applied only to commercial messages, and directed threatening sponsors to that information. At the same time, some Sinclair affiliates threatened litigation against sponsors who withdrew support in response to the boycott. Davis organized a legal support effort for those sponsors. By October 15, sponsors were pulling ads in droves. The price of Sinclair stock crashed, recovering only after Sinclair reversed its decision to air the documentary.[1]

In January 2003, Bev Harris of blackboxvoting.com discovered Diebold's online archive of over 40,000 files, including specs and code for the voting machines and vote-tallying systems. In February she posted them on her website and invited technical commentary. In July, she published an analysis of the files in Scoop.com, based on discussions on her site, claiming that access to the Diebold open archives could have been used to affect tightly contested races in 2002. The attached Scoop.com editorial included this statement:

> We can now reveal for the first time the location of a complete online copy of the original data set. As we anticipate attempts to prevent the distribution of this information we encourage supporters of democracy to make copies of these files and to make them available on websites and file sharing networks . . . At this stage in this inquiry we do not believe that we have come even remotely close to investigating all aspects of this data; i.e., there is no reason to believe that the security flaws discovered so far are the only ones. Therefore we expect many more discoveries to be made. We want the assistance of the online computing community in this enterprise and we encourage you to file your findings at the forum HERE [providing link to forum].

This declaration of war displayed "a genuinely different mind-set . . . about how censorship and power are circumvented." Anticipating Diebold's attempt to suppress the information, Scoop.com relied on "widespread distribution of information—about where the files could be found, and about where tools to crack the passwords and repair bad files could be found—matched with a call for action: get these files, copy them, and store them in many places so they cannot be squelched."

Also in July, a group of computer scientists at the Information Security Institute, Johns Hopkins University, released an analysis of Harris' collection of documents, known as the [Aviel] Rubin Report. The ensuing debate among computer scientists had considerable influence on public policy concerning electronic voting machines, including measures requiring some modifications.

---

1. Benkler, *The Wealth of Networks*, pp. 220-223.

In August, someone provided a cache of thousands of Diebold internal emails to *Wired* magazine and to Bev Harris. Harris posted the emails on her site. Diebold threatened litigation, demanding that Harris, her ISP, and other sites reproducing the emails take them down. Although the threatened parties complied, the emails had been so widely replicated and stored in so many varied settings that Diebold was unable to suppress them. Among others, university students at numerous campuses around the U.S. stored the emails and scrutinized them for evidence. Threatened by Diebold with provisions of the DMCA that required Web-hosting companies to remove infringing materials, the universities ordered the students to remove the materials from their sites. The students responded with a campaign of civil disobedience, moving files between students' machines, duplicating them on FreeNet (an "anti-censorship peer-to-peer publication network") and other peer-to-peer file-sharing systems . . . . They remained publicly available at all times.[1]

1. *Ibid.*, pp. 227–231.

Appendix C
DeCSS as an Example of Media Swarming

Journalist Eric Corley—better known as Emmanuel Goldstein, a nom de plume borrowed from Orwell's *1984*—posted the code for DeCSS (so called because it decrypts the Content Scrambling System that encrypts DVDs) as a part of a story he wrote in November for the well-known hacker journal 2600. The Motion Picture Association of America (MPAA) claims that Corley defied anticircumvention provisions of the Digital Millennium Copyright Act (DMCA) by posting the offending code . . . .

The whole affair began when teenager Jon Johansen wrote DeCSS in order to view DVDs on a Linux machine. The MPAA has since brought suit against him in his native Norway as well. Johansen testified on Thursday that he announced the successful reverse engineering of a DVD on the mailing list of the Linux Video and DVD Project (LiViD), a user resource center for video- and DVD-related work for Linux . . . .

The judge in the case, the honorable Lewis Kaplan of the US District Court in southern New York, issued a preliminary injunction against posting DeCSS. Corley duly took down the code, but did not help his defense by defiantly linking to myriad sites which post DeCSS . . . .

True to their hacker beliefs, Corley supporters came to the trial wearing the DeCSS code on t-shirts. There are also over 300 Websites that still link to the decryption code, many beyond the reach of the MPAA.[1]

---

1. Deborah Durham-Vichr, "Focus on the DeCSS trial," CNN.Com, July 27, 2000 <http://archives.cnn.com/2000/TECH/computing/07/27/decss.trial.p1.idg/index.html>.

APPENDIX D
OPEN–MOUTH SABOTAGE, CONT.: ALISHER USMANOV AS A CASE STUDY IN MEDIA SWARMING

> *The Register*, UK: Political websites have lined up in defence of a former diplomat whose blog was deleted by hosting firm Fasthosts after threats from lawyers acting for billionaire Arsenal investor Alisher Usmanov.
>
> Four days after Fasthosts pulled the plug on the website run by former UK ambassador to Uzbekistan Craig Murray it remains offline. Several other political and freedom of speech blogs in the UK and abroad have picked up the gauntlet however, and reposted the article that originally drew the takedown demand.
>
> The complaints against Murray's site arose after a series of allegations he made against Usmanov . . . .
>
> After being released from prison, and pardoned, Usmanov became one of a small group of oligarchs to make hay in the former USSR's post-communist asset carve-up . . . .
>
> On his behalf, libel law firm Schillings has moved against a number of Arsenal fan sites and political bloggers repeating the allegations . . . .[1]

That reference to "[s]everal other political and freedom of speech blogs," by the way, is like saying the ocean is "a bit wet." An article at *Chicken Yogurt* blog provides a list of all the venues that have republished Murray's original allegations, recovered from Google's cache of the site or from the Internet Archive. It is a very, very long list[2]—so long, in fact, that *Chicken Yoghurt* helpfully provides the html code with URLs already embedded in the text, so it can be easily cut and pasted into a blog post. In addition, *Chicken Yoghurt* provided the IP addresses of Usmanov's lawyers as a heads-up to all bloggers who might have been visited by those august personages.

---

1. Chris Williams, "Blogosphere shouts 'I'm Spartacus' in Usmanov-Murray case: Uzbek billionaire prompts Blog solidarity," *The Register*, September 24, 2007 <http://www.theregister.co.uk/2007/09/24/usmanov_vs_the_internet/>.

2. "Public Service Announcement—Craig Murray, Tim Ireland, Boris Johnson, Bob Piper and Alisher Usmanov . . . ," Chicken Yoghurt, September 20, 2007 <http://www.chickyog.net/2007/09/20/public-service-announcement/>.

Appendix E
Open Mouth Sabotage, Cont.:
Wikileaks as a Case Study in Media Swarming

Remember McLibel? There Are Echoes of It in the Following Case . . .

Associated Press (via the first amendment center) reports that "an effort at (online) damage control has snowballed into a public relations disaster for a Swiss bank seeking to crack down on Wikileaks for posting classified information about some of its wealthy clients. While Bank Julius Baer claimed it just wanted stolen and forged documents removed from the site (rather than close it down), instead of the information disappearing, it rocketed through cyberspace, landing on other Web sites and Wikileaks' own "mirror" sites outside the U.S . . . .

The digerati call the online phenomenon of a censorship attempt backfiring into more unwanted publicity the "Streisand effect." Techdirt Inc. chief executive Mike Masnick coined the term on his popular technology blog after the actress Barbra Streisand's 2003 lawsuit seeking to remove satellite photos of her Malibu house. Those photos are now easily accessible, just like the bank documents. "It's a perfect example of the Streisand effect," Masnick said. "This was a really small thing that no one heard about and now it's everywhere and everyone's talking about it."[1]

1. "PR disaster, Wikileaks and the Streisand Effect," PRdisasters.com, March 3, 2007 <http://prdisasters.com/pr-disaster-via-wikileaks-and-the-streisand-effect/>.

Appendix F

Stupid White Men as a Case Study in Media Swarming

According to Michael Moore, the first 50,000 copies of his book *Stupid White Men* were printed and ready to ship on September 11, 2001. Following the 9-11 attacks, Harper-Collins, an imprint controlled by Rupert Murdoch and headed by Fox News' Judith Regan, attempted to suppress the book because it was considered inappropriate for the national mood at the time. Moore was told the book wouldn't be published unless he rewrote half of it—particularly the passages insufficiently respectful to that beady-eyed little turd, the utterly worthless George W. Bush. The publishers said it would be "intellectually dishonest" not to admit that Bush, at least since 9-11, had done "a good job."

> . . . we're now known as the "9-11 publishers"—we've got a couple of quickie books on the Twin Towers heroes in the works, we're publishing the autobiography of the police chief, and we're doing a photo book of the tragedy. Your book no longer fits with our new image.

Moore, apparently, gave little thought to the possibility of public protest. He did, however, mention his treatment at the hands of Harper-Collins at a public appearance, where he read a couple of chapters from the suppressed book. Unbeknownst to him, a librarian in the audience was sufficiently outraged to email a large number of her fellow librarians, which quickly led in turn to a public pressure campaign against Harper-Collins. The campaign first came to Moore's attention via an angry phone call from someone in near-hysterics at the publisher:

> WHAT DID YOU TELL THE LIBRARIANS? . . .
> You were out in New Jersey and you told the librarians everything! . . .
> Some librarian is spreading the whole story. AND NOW WE'RE GETTING HATE MAIL FROM LIBRARIANS!"

Under the pressure of public embarrassment, Harper-Collins decided, grudgingly, to publish the book without alteration. They tried to kill it, however, with a minimal promotion campaign: absolutely no print advertisements, and a book tour of only three cities. Nevertheless, the generation of publicity on the Internet (starting with Moore's announcement to his own mailing list) led to the printing being sold out the first day. The book quickly moved to No. 1 on the *New York Times*, Amazon, and every other bestseller list in the country.[1]

---

1. Michael Moore, "Introduction," *Stupid White Men . . . and Other Sorry Excuses for the State of the Nation!* (New York, London, Toronto: Penguin Books, 2002), pp. xi-xix.

10

Attempts at Reform from Within:
Management Fads

We have seen, in previous chapters, the numerous information and agency problems of the hierarchical, absentee-owned enterprise, and the benefits of increased worker participation in reducing those problems. Why do we therefore see so little genuine profit-sharing, and so little genuine self-management, in Western corporate economies?

The answer is suggested by Leo Tolstoy's parable of the humane farmer, who experiments with larger stalls, better hay, piped-in music, and other expedients to make his cattle happier. When asked why he doesn't take the simpler route of setting free, he replies "But then I couldn't milk them."

From the perspective of management and shareholders, worker empowerment—no matter how much of an improvement in efficiency—has one seeming disadvantage: it requires increasing the worker's share of his labor-product. Full internalization by the worker of the fruits of his productivity may result in major efficiency gains, but only by violating the whole purpose of capitalism.

So corporate management resorts to all sorts of fads to simulate worker empowerment, without being able to try the real thing.

A. New Wine in Old Bottles

From my first reading of Tom Peters' work (and much of the other management literature of the 1990s) my overwhelming impression was of the ambivalent or dialectical character of the "revolutionary" trends he championed. Depending on the system of power into which such ideas are incorporated, they could make life either heaven or hell for those doing the actual work. The rhetoric of management literature closely resembled that of the libertarian left on things like worker self-management, flattening hierarchies, and the like. Superficially, Peters' work comes across as a survey of the seeds of a potentially decentralized and human-scale economic order of worker-managed production, seeds that might actually sprout if the state stopped propping up the current corporate system. But the reality of most of it—as practiced—is an attempt to put new wine in old bottles.

The same generalization applies to most other organizational and management theory trends (quality, reengineering, lean production, and the like), all of which celebrate the dissolution of corporate hierarchies and the organization of production along decentralized, consumer-driven, and (allegedly) bottom-up lines. A lot of it, to repeat, sounds like what might be the seeds of a libertarian, self-managed, decentralized economy—if the structural bulwarks to authoritarianism were removed. But the same practices, when integrated into the existing structure of state capitalism, become what Mike Parker and Jane Slaughter call "management-by-stress."[1]

Many of the stated principles, as such, might be good, if they were applied by workers for themselves, in a libertarian environment of worker ownership and self-management. But when they are done *to* workers by management, they become management-by-stress.

The striking thing is that ideas like demand-pull, self-directed teams, and flexible manufacturing are discussed both by corporate management gurus like Peters, and by left-wing economic decentralists, in language that is sometimes virtually indistinguishable from one group to the other. The difference is that Peters, despite his revolutionary rhetoric, largely envisions integrating such ideas into the existing corporate economy, while the left-wingers imagine a post-corporate economy of producer and consumer cooperatives built around the new practices.

Reading Peters brought another, seemingly obvious, question to mind. In his work of the late '80s and early '90s, he wrote of the dissolution of corporate walls, the elimination of middle management, and the rise of team self-management as inevitable revolutionary trends that the Fortune 500 would inevitably adopt ("must dos") if they were to survive into the near future. If the large corporation were not revolutionized along such lines, he wrote, it would go the way of Gosplan. Michael Hammer and James Champy, in *Reeingineering the Corporation*, described the imperative for reengineering in similar terms:

> The alternative is for Corporate America to close its doors and go out of business. The choice is that simple and that stark.[2]

Yet, fifteen or twenty years later, those revolutionary predictions read a bit like one of those 1950s magazine features on the City of the Future, with its giant hanging gardens, moving sidewalks, and flying cars. The corporate dinosaurs are still thrashing quite vigorously in those tarpits, with no sign of going under. And the bosses are just as pointy-haired as ever; in fact, the gurus' "revolutionary" rhetoric of fifteen years ago is now lampooned as a symbol of the status quo: mission/vision/values statements, Kwality jargon, and all the rest of it.

So why didn't the old hierarchical corporation disintegrate to anywhere near the extent Peters predicted, and why isn't the flattened network of self-directed teams anywhere near as prevalent? One partial answer is that Peters greatly exaggerated the competitive disadvantages of inefficiency in a cartelized, state capitalist market, and underestimated the inertia of the existing system. When a market is dominated by a handful of corporate "Gosplans" that share the same pathological organizational culture and follow the same "industry trends," Gosplan can be pretty profitable.

But another part of the answer may be that the stuff Peters talked about actually *was* adopted to a large extent; it's just that the contrast between the new and old ways of doing things wasn't nearly as great as he imagined, and that what's called the "self-directed team" can be integrated quite nicely into the old hierarchy without anywhere near the revolutionary upheaval he expected.

Peters himself made it clear that he wasn't opposed to bigness, as such; he just wanted to simulate the advantages of smallness in the context of a large organization. Virtually every radical management reform advocated by Peters is an attempt to artificially simulate, in the hostile environment of the giant corporation, what would naturally exist in a small enterprise

---

1. Mike Parker and Jane Slaughter *Working Smart: A Union Guide to Participation Programs and Reengineering* (Detroit: Labor Notes, 1994).

2. Michael Hammer and James Champy, *Reengineering the Corporation: A Manifesto For Business Revolution* (N.Y.: HarperCollins Publishers, Inc., 1993), p. 1.

Production itself would be decentralized considerably, middle management radically streamlined, and the corporation transformed into a loose network of self-directed teams, with the buzzword of "outsourcing everything"; but it would all take place within a conventional corporate framework in which corporate headquarters retained central control of "intellectual property," branding, and finance. Additional advantages of bigness, for such an organization, would include market power—particularly the price-setting power that comes from coordinated buying and selling, sufficient stability and deep pockets to ride out market fluctuations, and sufficient size to attract investment.[1] Or, in the words of James O'Tool whom Peters quotes, "the 'big power' of an imposing market presence."[2] (Interestingly, Peters himself admits that "'Network big' could easily become sluggish and anti-competitive," using alliances to stifle competition.[3] Whew! Good thing that didn't happen.)

Hammer and Champy, in *Reengineering the Corporation*, also wrote of the benefits of combining centralization and decentralization.[4] The main benefit is the ability to regulate competition, and to externalize diseconomies of scale on others.

The vertical de-integration that has resulted from Peters' "organization as rolodex," from his "outsourcing of everything," was described in more realistic terms by John Micklethwait, who pointed out that "even if such small firms count as separate entities, their workers are in fact no less reliant on these corporate hubs than their peers working at the big firms."[5]

Nike (as described by Naomi Klein) has taken the principle to its logical conclusion, outsourcing all the production to an archipelago of "independent" sweatshops, while retaining control of corporate finance and the Nike brand-name.

> . . . [D]espite the fact that they have no local physical holdings—they don't own the buildings, land or equipment—brands like Nike, the GAP and IBM are omnipresent, irresistibly pulling all the strings. They are so powerful as buyers that the hands-on involvement owning the factories would entail has come to look, from their perspective, like needless micromanagement . . . .
>
> If anything, the multinationals have more power over production by not owning the factories. Like most committed shoppers, they see no need to concern themselves with how their bargains were produced—they simply pounce on them, keeping the suppliers on their toes by taking bids from slews of other contractors.[6]

Johan Soderberg elaborates on the same theme: "Product diversification, rapid turnovers and short life-cycles have made the management of physical assets risky. The burden of ownership is pushed down onto smaller entities while corporations stay in control by gate-keeping finances, marketing, distribution channels, and intellectual property."[7]

It's pretty hard to miss the fact that the world in which Peters saw his ideas being implemented was the world described by Tom Friedman, upheld not by the invisible hand but by the fist of the World Bank, IMF and WTO, and the U.S. armed forces. So while the boundaries between the corporation and the outside market may seem to blur from some perspectives, the corporation as an entity will continue to be very real as a beneficiary of state privilege and an extractor of profits.

1. Tom Peters, *Liberation Management: Necessary Disorganization for the Nanosecond Nineties* (New York: Fawcett Columbine, 1992), pp. 289-91.

2. *Ibid.*, p. 554.

3. *Ibid.*, p. 555.

4. Hammer and Champy, *Reengineering the Corporation*, p. 63.

5. John Micklethwait and Adrian Wooldridge, *The Witch Doctors: Making Sense of the Management Gurus* (New York: Times Books, 1996), p. 103.

6. Naomi Klein, *No Logo* (New York: Picador USA, 1999), p. 226.

7. Johan Soderberg, *Hacking Capitalism: The Free and Open Source Software Movement* (New York and London: Routledge, 2008), p. 141.

One of Peters' subheadings in *Thriving on Chaos* was "Act Small/Start Small/Break Into Small Units Or Teams: A Solution For Big Firms."

> . . . acting small, if you are big, is much easier said than done. A new-product team in a big company has a tough time achieving true independence.[1]

This Peters theme first appeared in *In Search of Excellence*, where he coined the revealing term "simulated entrepreneurship" to describe it.[2]

> Perhaps the most important element of their enviable track record is an ability to be big and yet to act small at the same time. A concomitant essential apparently is that they encourage the entrepreneurial spirit among their people, because they push autonomy remarkably far down the line . . . .[3]

Elsewhere in the same book, he refers to "chunking," or the performance of most specific tasks by small, ad hoc groups within a large organization.

> . . . . That simply means breaking things up to facilitate organizational fluidity and to encourage action. The action-oriented bits and pieces come under many labels—champions, teams, task forces, czars, project centers, skunk works, and quality circles—but they have one thing in common. They never show up in the formal organization chart and seldom in the corporate phone directory . . . .

The small group is the most visible of the chunking devices. Small groups are, quite simply, the basic organizational blocks of excellent companies.[4]

In *The Tom Peters Seminar*, he refers to the "gotta unit," a business unit of modest size in a larger body,

> which routinely does the impossible . . . for precisely the reason the mom-and-pop grocery store will do almost anything . . . to serve its neighbors in the surrounding seven-block area. Without that effort, it goes out of business . . . . In other words, they do it 'cause they gotta.

As an example, he mentions Zurich Insurance's reorganization into "moderate-sized specialist companies," with "[s]mall-company soul and speed in a big company body . . ."[5]

Other examples are Random House (organized with "more than two dozen feisty small-business units, or imprints" within the corporate framework),[6] and Shoebox Greetings ("a small, creative, entrepreneurial part of Hallmark").[7] Since then, we've also seen Anheuser-Busch marketing "craft beers" under quasi-independent labels which (understandably) avoid any reference to Anheuser-Busch.

As Peters describes it, this corporate strategy is essentially that of Nike, as described by Klein. "Nintendo keeps most of the crucial design and marketing management functions to itself, but lets just about everything else go to partners and licensees."[8]

Eric Husman considers GM to be moving toward a similar business model, in which the corporation makes money primarily by financing and branding rather than actually

1. Tom Peters, *Thriving on Chaos: Handbook for a Management Revolution* (New York: Alfred A. Knopf, 1988), pp. 199, 201.

2. Robert Waterman and Tom Peters, *In Search of Excellence: Lessons from America's Best-Run Companies* (New York: Warner Books, 1982), pp. 112-113.

3. *Ibid.*, p. 201.

4. Waterman and Peters, *In Search of Excellence*, p. 126.

5. *The Tom Peters Seminar*, p. 45.

6. *Ibid.*, p. 47.

7. *Ibid.*, p. 49.

8. Tom Peters, *The Tom Peters Seminar: Crazy Times Call for Crazy Organizations* (New York: Vintage Books, 1994), p. 123.

making cars.[1] GM's main source of profit is now its auto finance arm, GMAC. And in the years when GM turns a profit, there's a pretty good chance it did so by selling off a couple more plants.

For that matter, as Husman writes elsewhere, Peters' "outsource everything" model, as actually applied in most of corporate model, could be drawn directly from the original Sloan paradigm. Most of the objectionable features of rule by MBAs that I commented on in Chapter Eight have their origins in "the imposition of the DuPont definition of profit, the Sloan management method, and the Brown accounting method onto American industry."

> The Sloan system (the common, short-form name) essentially transformed manufacturers into marketing companies with a manufacturing function. [Bill Waddell and Norman Bodek, in *Rebirth of American Industry*] argue that the definition of profit is the most important aspect to consider: for DuPont, profit meant Return on Investment (ROI). The accounting system that counted inventory as an asset and people as a cost followed from that principle. No wonder GM treated its workers and suppliers (and suppliers' workers) so poorly, no wonder the UAW felt so strongly, and no wonder they are both so screwed up today. In fact, you can clearly see why GM would push problems (what most would call business risk and employees) out the door to suppliers. Once you have decided on that strategy, you have declared that you are no longer a manufacturer with a sales office, you are a marketing firm for product manufactured by someone (you are indifferent as to who manufactures).[2]

Consider also Peters' discussion of the music industry, which he uses as an illustration of his "craziness" and "revolution" leitmotifs. He cites Lewis Perlman's description of a recording process in which "recordings are assembled from component parts created all over the world," with guitar tracks recorded in London, drum tracks in New Orleans, etc., and all put together "anywhere from a Hollywood studio to a barn in the Berkshires."[3] What he doesn't mention is that the same corporate media dinosaur, with the help of ham-handed legislation like the Digital Millennium Copyright Act to prevent this "revolution" from carrying over into the ownership and distribution of music, still owns the copyright on the product.

The Tom Peters Seminar, as we mentioned in Chapter Nine, constantly harps on the theme of how much product value consists of intangibles, with ten percent of the price of his Minolta 9xi coming from labor and materials, and the other ninety percent from "intellect." Or on Nike sneakers, whose value consists mostly of "lifestyle" and "image." Or Kraft, most of whose equity derived from "intangibles" rather than physical assets. Or Microsoft, whose "only factory asset is the human imagination."

The difference is, Peters' "revolution" assumes that the intangible component of value will continue to be the property of powerful corporations. And in this context, Peters' faux Silicon Valley "libertarian" bravado about telling the government to get out of the way falls especially flat. The entire business model he describes depends on legislation passed under Reagan and Clinton, drastically ratcheting up trademark protections, on the Uruguay Round's radical extension of patent rights, and on the virtual outlawing of fair use under the terms of the Digital Millennium Copyright Act.[4]

His discussion of networked organization, with separate firms carrying out design, engineering, and various stages of production, and linked together, also bears a superficial

1. Eric Husman, "GM vs. Toyota Again," GrimReader, April 7, 2007 <http://www.zianet.com/ehusman/weblog/2007/04/gm-v-toyota-again.html>.
2. Eric Husman, "The Accounting Chains on American Industry," Grim Reader, March 3, 2006 <http://www.zianet.com/ehusman/weblog/2006/03/accounting-chains-on-american-industry.html>.
3. Peters, *The Tom Peters Seminar*, p. 8.
4. See, for example, Naomi Klein, *No Logo*, p. 177.

resemblance to the ideas of peer production enthusiasts. The difference is that Peters sees the networking taking place largely under corporate strategic supervision:

> A piece of ice hockey equipment, designed in Scandinavia, engineered in the U.S. to meet the requirements of the large U.S. and Canadian market, manufactured in Korea and distributed through a multinational market network with initial distribution from Japan. *The question is: Where is, what is the organization?* Instead of a simple organization with design, engineering, manufacturing, distribution and sales under one corporate roof, the example shows several organizations hooked together for perhaps only one product "event." . . ."[1]

And the coordination of all these separate stages assumes, as Peters put it, that a "certain minimum size" is necessary for effectiveness "as a global marketer."[2]

In a networked economy based on genuinely decentralist ideas, on the other hand, just for starters there wouldn't even *be* a "large U.S. and Canadian market." Rather, goods might be designed by a peer network of engineers working on linked home computers, and physical production carried out by a small factory (or a number of small factories or machine shops carrying out the separate stages of production, organized by a peer-production network), and then sold in the same county-sized market where all the networked design and manufacture had taken place. Incidentally, in discussing the benefit of "networks," Peters gives as much attention to Henry Clay Whig stuff like canals, railroads and the Interstate Highway System as to the Internet.[3] His networked economy is not one based on moving information instead of stuff, as envisioned by genuine decentralists. It is one based on the subsidized movement of physical goods over long distances.

Peters' self-managed teams and incentive pay, obviously, are just a half-assed corporate imitation of the self-management that naturally occurs in producer cooperatives.[4] His close contact between customer, marketing, research and production, and the resulting turnaround time, are also attempts to duplicate within the hostile environment of a corporation what would naturally occur in a small enterprise using general-purpose machine tools. In the latter case, product design and market research would be carried out by pretty much the same people setting up the machines, based on their direct conduct with the market in their community. Peters' systems of worker incentives are just a weak version of what would exist in a self-managed cooperative, where the workers directly engaged in the production process would have the power to put their ideas for process improvement into immediate practice, and reap the full rewards for any increased efficiency.

The same principle applies to Peters' ideas on close ties and responsiveness to one's customers. As much as the rhetoric sounds superficially like the demand-pull model of marketing, in substance (with his emphasis on "fashion" and the "entertainizing of everything") it's a lot closer to the old supply-push model than you might think. The old ideas of thinking up stuff to produce and then persuading people that they need it, central to the American mass-production and mass-consumption economy since the 1920s, is still very much a part of Peters' postmodern version of the Push economy.

The function of product design and marketing in an "entertainized" and "fashionized" economy is to create "needs" for product features completely irrelevant to the product's primary purpose, so that the consumer will pay a markup of several hundred percent for the increased status attached to a particular trademark or other identifying cosmetic feature. The whole purpose, as we saw in Chapter One, is to create artificial differentiation

---

1. *Liberation Management*, p. 149.
2. *Ibid.*, p. 559.
3. *Ibid.*, p. 112.
4. Peters, *Thriving on Chaos*, pp. 332-342.

between products, so as to prevent competition from driving price down to production cost (the normal pattern in price competition between commodities).

So even in the minority of cases where management theory fads were implemented with some faithfulness to the libertarian rhetoric of their authors, their implementation was still in marked contrast to the approach of the libertarian left. For the left-wing economic decentralists, such ideas are expected to reach their full flourishing only when intellectual property, centralized finance, and corporate headquarters themselves have gone the way of T. Rex. Peters' prescription, as it is actually being implemented, is a way to integrate the Goths into the framework of the old Roman imperial structure and give the Empire a new lease on life.

And this is only when such ideas have been implemented *at their best*. The more frequent practice, as we shall see below, is to pay lip service to the ideas or dumb them down.

B. LIP SERVICE AND BUSINESS AS USUAL

In a second, larger class of cases, either the implementation of the ideas consisted of little more than lip-service (management more often than not has only the vaguest ideas of what all the Kwality jargon on the coffee mugs even means), or Tom Peters' vision itself was far less radical in concrete terms than his rhetoric implied. Self-directed teams have been introduced here and there, "quality circles" were a popular management fad for a while, and there are always outliers like Semco and W. L. Gore. But for the most part, the average corporation as seen from the bottom by one of its employees is at least as authoritarian as ever.

Peters' personality is part of the problem, along with the fact that he has gotten worse as his career progressed (eventually degenerating into a total embarrassment, with the occasional genuinely libertarian insights buried in a mountain of Gingrichoid crap). His work probably reached its peak in quality with the genuinely exciting *Thriving on Chaos*. After that, it went downhill; *Liberation Management* and *The Tom Peters Seminar* could have been written by an automated Tom Peters Hyperbole Generator.

In his later work, in the 90s, he tended to throw around words like "revolution" and "radical" and "crazy" and "extreme" to the point of self-parody. A good example is the self-indulgent *Tom Peters Seminar*, which must use the term "revolution" several hundred times from cover to cover—but whose assertions are backed up mainly by quotes from Fortune 500 CEOs. By the time I finished reading that book, I felt like he'd quoted all five hundred of them, about twenty times each; he's a worse name-dropper than Tom Friedman. The overall effect is like a version of *State and Revolution* in which Lenin manages to insert three quotes from the Tsar and his ministers on every page. His celebration, in *Liberation Management*, of "Ted Turner as Hero" (along with Jack Welch and Al Neuharth), speaks volumes about the kind of "revolution" he has in mind: one with its own Thermidorean reaction already built in.

The rhetoric goes to the edge of silliness—and then far, far beyond. Consider the following examples:

> Change? Change! Yes, we've almost all, finally, embraced the notion that "change is the only constant." Well, sorry. Forget change! The word is feeble. Keep saying "revolution." If it doesn't roll easily off your tongue, then I suggest you have a perception problem—and, more to the point, a business or a career problem.[1]
>
> Do you and your colleagues routinely use "hot" words: "revolution," "zany," "weird," "freaky," "nuts," "crazy," "apeshit," "Holy Toledo" ...? ....
>
> Are you prepared to forswear the word "change" for "revolution"? If not, why not? Because I'm an extremist? Or because you aren't?

1. Peters, *The Tom Peters Seminar*, p. 8.

> On a scale of 1 to 10, how "crazy" (a) are you? (b) is your unit? (c) your company? (d) your most innovative competitor?[1]

Reading such passages, I was suddenly struck by Peters' resemblance to "Poochie," the "edgy" cartoon character introduced on *Itchy & Scratchy*. When challenged to give him more "more attitude," the writers finally added sunglasses. Wow, just like Huey Lewis! Ten years ago, when the Fox Family Network premiered, a Fox corporate PR woman gushed about the "edginess" and "quirkiness" of the new network's programming. When questioned on exactly what she meant by those terms, she was unable to define them without reusing the words "quirky" and "edgy": e.g. by reference to the network's "quirky" and "edgy" demographic, sensibilities, etc. I suspect that "quirky" and "edgy," like Peters' "crazy" and "zany," amounted in substance to little more than a pair of sunglasses. Tom Peters may not have sunglasses like Poochie's, but he demonstrates his own "attitude" by wearing Hawaiian beach trunks with a suit jacket in the back cover photo of *The Tom Peters Seminar*. Whoa, *radical*, dude!

Just how much he exaggerated the radicalism of prospective change and the pressure for such change, Peters himself sometimes lets slip. Just as a basis for comparison, first consider this rather hyperbolic quote:

> Change and constant improvement (*kaizen*, per the Japanese), the watchwords of the '80s, are no longer enough. Not even close. Only revolution, and perpetual revolution at that, will do.
>
> Leaders at all levels must accept what the transformational leaders tell us: that the organization can "take it" (enormous change), that only a bias for constant action and a bold embrace of failure, big as well as amall, will move companies forward. The point is to compress 10 years' worth of "change," by yesterday's standard, into one year, if not months. Then draw a deep breath and start again. Forget the calm at the end of the storm. If you sense calm, it's only because you're in the eye of the hurricane.[2]

Or this one:

> Ah, how sad it is, in these turbulent times, to watch the average company, small or large, trying to succeed in the herd by moving maybe "a little bit faster than yesterday" or "delivering a little better quality or service than yesterday." Forget it. It'll be trampled.[3]

Then contrast the above rhetoric in Commandante Peters' *Revolutionary Communique No. 1* to the following passages, in which he lets slip some hints that perhaps the marketplace isn't quite as revolutionary, nor the creative destruction quite so frenzied, as he depicts it. For example, he quotes Wal-Mart CEO David Glass on the "absolute dearth of new and exciting fashion-forward products," and adds:

> He's right. Among all the new products hitting Wal-Mart's shelves, where is the equivalent of the early microwave oven, the video cassette recorder, or the Walkman— the kind of products, as Glass put it, that sucked people off their couches by the millions and propelled them into his stores?
>
> New soft and hard products alike are coming at us in increasing numbers from every corner of the global economy, but are they exciting, magical, special? Do they pass the Wow Test . . . ? . . . [A]s former Apple Computer chairman John Sculley said, "What's the new capability? . . . . It's like Rocky IV and Godfather V."[4]

Shortly thereafter, he writes:

1. *Ibid.*, p. 22.
2. *Ibid.*, p. 271.
3. *Ibid.*, p. 283.
4. *Ibid.*, p. 18.

Look through a sample of 25 catalogs, from pet supplies to personal computers. They're thick, but are they interesting? How many new offerings take your breath away . . . ?[1]

Peters, in such passages, inadvertently tells a tale on himself. To someone who hasn't been successfully reeducated to Peters' New Capitalist Man values, all those "revolutionary" corporations seem to be still following something that bears a suspicious resemblance to the traditional oligopoly strategy of spooning out carefully rationed improvements. And come to think of it, if there's such a dearth of innovative products, there can't really be all *that* much "revolutionary" pressure to compete with a bunch of companies producing mediocre crap, can there? He challenges his readers, at the end of the same chapter:

> How many processes and products have been tossed overboard (not "changed") in the last 12 months? If none or only a handful, why?[2]

Um . . . maybe because there's a dearth of new and exciting products from our competitors, and none of their catalogs contain products that take our breath away, so we figure we can probably get filthy rich making the same kind of crap they do? *Duh.*

In the roughly thirteen years since Peters wrote all that bovine scatology about the absolute necessity for continuous revolution in quality and service, if a corporation was to survive, we've seen virtually every corporation in the country adopt the universally despised "automated customer service menu." Martha Giminez calls it "self-sourcing":

> Consumption increasingly requires the performance of tasks previously done by paid workers. Jobs are not disappearing just because of automation, downsizing, and outsourcing; they disappear because they are increasingly done without pay by millions of consumers while the people who previously held those low-paid service and clerical jobs find themselves unemployed and perhaps unemployable.[3]

In that thirteen years, we've seen Home Depot, Lowe's, and Wal-Mart adopt a common model parodied by *King of the Hill*'s Mega-lo-Mart, in which most service jobs are held by pimply high school kids in smocks who know little about the store's products and care less. I've seen it for myself at Lowe's, where the "associates" in the garden supply department know absolutely nothing about plants or soil additives, and the stock answer to any question is "I dunno. I guess if you don't see it, we ain't got it." I've talked to veterans of numerous Fortune 500 companies who all tell versions of the same story: career sales employees who knew the product lines and customer needs inside and out, replaced by high school kids working for minimum wage. As we saw in Chapter Seven, that's pretty much what Bob Nardelli did to Home Depot to get himself a $200 million-and-change severance package. (Nardelli was an avowed Six Sigma enthusiast, by the way; his idea of "process improvement" was to downsize the service staff and nearly double the number of customers each "associate" had to serve in an hour.) Some friggin' revolution.

Joseph Juran compared the widespread Kwality rhetoric to the reality of its implementation, in much more sober tones, in an interview with *Quality Digest Magazine*.[4] There are two parallel dynamics at work. First, contra Peters, "mediocre quality is still saleable" (as Peters himself inadvertently let slip in some of the material quoted above. At the same time, paying lip-service to Kwality is a useful marketing gimmick, even without any of the substance of quality. A good example Juran points to is ISO 9000, whose standards are usually considerably below what a company is already doing:

1. *Ibid.*, p. 21.

2. *Ibid.*, p. 22.

3. Martha Giminez, "Self-Sourcing: How Corporations Get Us to Work Without Pay," *Monthly Review* 59:7 (December 2007).

4. "Juran: A Lifetime of Quality," *Quality Digest Magazine*, August 2002 <http://www.qualitydigest.com/aug02/articles/01_article.shtml>.

We've been taken in by the standardization people coming up with a standard that's not at the excellence level but at the mediocre level. We've been taken in by the standardization people coming up with a standard that's not at the excellence level but at the mediocre level. That's inherent in the way standards are set. There has to be a consensus. The different members from companies of different standardization bodies are not going to agree to standards that their companies are not able to meet. They are starting to change the standards, but that's at a glacial pace. It takes a long time to change an international standard.

ISO 9000 standards amount, in practice, to a ratification of the least common denominator standards in an industry—or the setting of common quality standards by a cartel. To the extent that ISO 9000 is promoted by governments, it falls into the category of state measures for cartelizing industry, discussed in Chapter Three.

> QD: Do you think that ISO 9000 has actually hindered the quality movement?
> Juran: Of course it has. Instead of going after improvement at a revolutionary rate, people were stampeded into going after ISO 9000, and they locked themselves into a mediocre standard. A lot of damage was, and is, being done.

ISO 9000 is therefore just a way of throwing away good money on consultants. But what matters is the market's perception of ISO 9000 as an imprimatur of superior quality. When Juran pointed out to corporate management the worthlessness of ISO 9000 certification, the response was "We know that. But we don't think, from a marketing standpoint, that we can be in a position where our competitor is certified and we are not. We'd be at a marketing disadvantage."

Consider the examples of radically "reengineered" corporations showcased in Hammer's and Champy's *Reengineering the Corporation*. The reengineered corporation streamlines certain complicated processes that exist at that level of complexity *in the first place* only because the corporation has hypertrophied several orders of magnitude far beyond maximum economy of scale. The new, streamlined process is a considerable improvement, but the benchmark for measuring that improvement is the typical centralized, hierarchical corporation. The reengineered corporation is *relatively* more flexible and efficient, in the *context* of an economy dominated by large, bureaucratic corporations. Or as Hammer and Champy put it, management wants an organization "lean *enough* to beat any competitor's price . . . . [emphasis added]"[1]

C. MANAGEMENT BY STRESS

So far we have considered the cases in which ideas like those of Peters and of Hammer and Champy have been adopted with genuine benefit (albeit within the limitations of the corporate framework), or in which their implementation was only superficial and rhetorical or had far less radical significance than their authors' rhetoric implied. Had this been the sole extent of their influence, it wouldn't have been so bad.

But there's a third case, arguably the most significant: the use of libertarian-sounding management theory, with its talk of "flattening hierarchies" and "self-directed teams," as a rhetorical smokescreen for tightening the screws on labor. This is the phenomenon described by Parker and Slaughter as "management by stress."[2] In practice, as actually implemented in the corporate capitalist workplace, the team concept and assorted Kwality fads translate into relentless downsizing and speedups, and a nightmare of overwork and job insecurity. As Parker and Slaughter describe it, these fashionable management practices can

1. Hammer and Champy, *Reengineering the Corporation*, p. 7.
2. Mike Parker and Jane Slaughter. *Working Smart: A Union Guide to Participation Programs and Reengineering* (Detroit: Labor Notes, 1994).

be broken down into several key components (they focus especially on the NUMMI joint-venture of Toyota and GM).

The first is the speedup. Lean production, they say, systematically isolates and removes all the buffers against bottlenecks, like stockpiled parts or extra workers to fill in for absentees. The system is deliberately stressed to identify not only the weak parts, but those that are too strong.

A good example is the use of the "andon board," representing every work station. The green light means the station is keeping up. Yellow means it is falling behind. Red is a problem that requires stopping the line. Under management-by-stress, all green is not good. The idea is to stress the system, removing staffing and other resources from green areas, until a satisfactory number of yellow lights indicates that the system is operating near its absolute limits.[1]

A second key aspect of management-by-stress is the just-in-time, or demand-pull approach to production. This is another idea that, if developed in the directions described by left-wing decentralists like Barry Stein, Dave Pollard, and Michel Bauwens, would be a good thing. But adapted to the capitalist workplace, the dark side of its dialectical nature is revealed. The idea is to reduce inventories of finished and unfinished goods to an absolute minimum. The lack of a cushion helps to stress the system, pressuring those in weak spots to superhuman efforts to catch up. Those causing bottlenecks are isolated and identified, and subjected to hellish pressure.[2] The peer pressure to avoid stopping the line and attracting unwanted attention from one's coworkers or supervisor is so intense that some workers, who have trouble keeping up, will come in early or use breaks to build stocks to avoid falling in the hole.[3]

The removal of staffing buffers also results in peer pressure for keeping up and against absenteeism. The worker who cannot keep up with the pace of the sped-up line creates more work and stress for those down the line. And since the work group is just barely large enough to handle its work load, there is absolutely no margin for absenteeism. The team passes on its collective stress to the recalcitrant worker. The pressure is overwhelming to work through all but the most incapacitating illnesses.[4] This is reminiscent, albeit to a lesser degree, of the colorful stories veterans tell about the practice of collective punishment in the military, and the "blanket parties" organized for the individuals who made a unit suffer.

In short, the system is not bufferless at all. The workers themselves are the buffers, at little or no cost to the company.[5]

> Glitches are inevitable, anywhere. Could a system that really had no buffers to deal with these glitches be as productive as this system is? Lean production does remove or sharply curtail those buffers that add significant cost—a stock of work-in-progress, back-up machinery, extra workers, or spare time—but it replaces these with an alternative. The real buffers in bufferless production are the workers, who are expected to put out extra effort to maintain production despite the unavoidable glitches.
>
> If the just-in-time system makes a part shipment late and the team leader has to run to get it, that's the job. If overtime is required and workers have to forego personal plans, that's the job too. Using workers as the shock absorbers of the system costs management little (except for workers compensation claims), but it can be very unhealthy for the human element.[6]

1. *Ibid.*, pp. 24–25.
2. *Ibid.*, pp. 25–27.
3. *Ibid.*, p. 29.
4. *Ibid.*, p. 29.
5. *Ibid.*, p. 69.
6. *Ibid.*, p. 80.

At least as practiced in the dumbed-down version that predominates in America, *kaizen* usually means reducing staffing, not individual effort. It's a way to get more work out of fewer people. The object is to reduce man-hours enough to eliminate an entire person. As Parker and Slaughter say, "Reducing effort is not the issue, reducing jobs is."

The team concept, in practice, is far less democratic and bottom-up than Peters pictures it:

> In the actual operation of the plant—as opposed to the ideological hype—the main significance of teams is that they are simply the name management gives to administrative units. For the most part, if we substituted "supervisor's sub-group" for team . . . , understanding of management-by-stress would not suffer at all.

> There is, however, some reality to the widespread notions about teams. Some teams meet and discuss real problems. When the lines move slowly enough, workers can and do help each other out. But this is most likely during initial start-up, when the "teams" often consist mainly of supervisors, engineers, and team leaders. Once the line is up to speed, jobs are specified in detail and each worker can barely keep up with his or her own job, let alone help someone else out . . . .

> When the system is running at regular production speed, team meetings tend to drop in frequency . . . . In other cases, team meetings are nothing more than shape-up sessions where quality or overtime information is transmitted to the workers or a supervisor announces changes in assignments.

> When management talks to itself about what makes the system work, teams, in the sense of teamwork or team meetings, are rarely mentioned. In his description of Toyota, considered the reference by many NUMMI managers, Yasuhiro Monden does not use the term "team" at all. He does describe the mandatory Quality Control Circles made up of "a foreman and his subordinate workers." In the entire 230-page book explaining the production system, discussion of these circles totals seven pages, and much of this discussion covers the suggestion system and its rewards.

> Similarly, John Krafcik, an MIT researcher and a former quality control engineer at NUMMI, lists teams as one of the reasons for NUMMI's success. But in describing them, Krafcik discusses only the supervisory duties of team leaders . . . and the peer pressure against absenteeism, not any supposed team powers or problem-solving functions.[1]

And even when the teams are fully functioning as in theory, their decision-making domain is heavily circumscribed:

> NUMMI management tries to guide its Problem Solving Circles by placing boundaries on what the circles may address. Included in the untouchables list are: Company Operating Principles, Human Resources Policy and Rules, Supplier Selection, New Model Design, Sales and Marketing Policies. The message is that creativity means finding ways to meet targets established by management . . . .

> If workers may not address those areas—the ones that would actually give them some say over what happens in and to the company—what's left of workers' power? Well, the Problem Solving Circles have the power to kaizen. If "company operating principles"—i.e., leanness—are off limits, how are circles to address problems of workload or understaffing?[2]

The answer, clearly is that they are not. As Preston Glidden, a frequent commenter at my blog with fifteen years experience in quality control and quality assurance put it,

> I find that so-called 'worker empowerment' in practice translates into making a worker responsible for failures, without giving him/her any real power to fix the problem.[3]

1. *Ibid.*, p. 35.
2. *Ibid.*, pp. 70, 77.
3. Preston Glidden comment under Kevin Carson, "Liberation Management, or Management by Stress?" Mutualist Blog: Free Market Anticapitalism, August 28, 2006 <http://mutualist.blogspot.com/2006/08/liberation-management-or-management-by.html>.

David M. Gordon, in *Fat and Mean*, similarly observed that "[m]any firms . . . hope to have their cake and eat it too":

> They announce programs to encourage higher employee productivity but often fail to support other programs that provide strong worker rewards or cut substantially into managerial power or prerequisites.[1]

So why does the reality described above differ so sharply from the gushing, quasi-syndicalist rhetoric of management theory gurus like Peters? Two words: "Potemkin village."

> This chapter points to an unlovely picture of life in a management-by-stress plant. It contradicts most of what is said in the glowing accounts of the team concept in the popular media. Where do these accounts come from?
>
> Many stories about how workers feel about life in management-by-stress plants are based on reports of company officials, union officers, or consultants who have some vested interest in the programs' being declared a success. Some very positive descriptions are based on interviews at the time the plant was starting up. As we have described earlier, the conditions, the role of teams and teamwork during the start-up period are transformed by the time the lines reach full production speed. Some reports are based on testimony by workers specially selected by the company to meet reporters. The distortions are then compounded by authors who know little about what life is like in a factory.[2]

So the lesson here seems to be that, at least in some aspects of the workplace, a revolutionary change really did take place in the '90s and the first years of the 21st century. Judged against Peters' liberatory rhetoric, the team concept has meant little practical change. But judged in terms of "management-by-stress," a great deal of change—mostly for the worse—has occurred. Radically downsized workforces have been pushed to their limits, with greatly increased stress and turnover and diminished morale. Peters' radical rhetoric, implemented within the framework of a corporate economy, is in practice a system for tightening management control.

Interestingly, even some consultants in the field of *kaizen* or lean production admit the same, in a backhanded manner. Consider, for example, the reaction of Jon Miller at Panta Rei (a lean blog) to an article critical of kaizen by Christian Berggren.[3] Berggren noted that even in the auto industry itself (kaizen got its start as "the Toyota system"), even in Japanese ventures, there was great variation in working conditions. As an example of "starkly opposing views on Japan and the Toyota Production System (nowadays denominated 'lean production')," he cited a Saab consultant who

> at Honda he had seen the light: this was a 'total new work experience, egalitarian, creative, dynamic, uniquely productive' . . . . But other Saab managers and technicians had also been visiting Honda plants in North America. They had seen very different things: a frantic work pace, relentless attendance demands, substandard production equipment creating a lot of work hazards, and heavy indoctrination in a quasi-totalitarian culture.

He also quoted a contrasting pair of evaluations, one from the enthusiastic MIT study of lean production, the other from the head of a UAW local at a Japanese-owned American plant.

> Lean production combines the best features of both craft production and mass production . . . lean production offers a creative tension in which workers have many ways to address challenges. This creative tension involved in solving complex problems is precisely

---

1. David M. Gordon, *Fat and Mean*, p. 93.
2. Parker and Slaughter, p. 37.
3. Christian Berggren, "Lean Production: The End of History?" Expanded version of paper presented for a seminar at the Science and Technology Analysis Research Programme, University of Wollongong (September 1991) <http://www.uow.edu.au/arts/sts/research/STPPapers/LeanProduction-10.html>.

what has separated manual factory work from professional 'think' work in the age of mass production. (Daniel Jones *et al.* in *The Machine that Changed the World*, MIT, 1990.)

They promised us a rose garden. They gave us a desert. (Phil Keeling, UAW President at Mazda's Flat Rock plant.)

In fact, Berggren points out that the character of lean production is mixed, at least as practiced in Japanese "transplants" in North America. Job security is greater, along with a greater degree of egalitarianism within the hierarchy. And American workers in such plants are generally proud of the genuinely superior quality of the cars they build.

Nevertheless, the system is not only lean but *mean*—in ways that corroborate Parker's and Slaughter's analysis of management by stress.

> But there is another side of the sword: unlimited performance demands and working hours, recurrent health and safety complaints, and an utterly rigorous factory regime.
>
> 1. *Unlimited performance demands.* Transplants do not recognize any union regulations of performance demands or other limitations on management's discretion to organize work. With the help of *kaizen* all slack is eliminated. In the GM car factories, even those that have achieved high productivity and quality like Buick City, the work pace is relatively relaxed. People have time to talk to visitors and do some reading at their work stations. These things are unthinkable at Japanese transplants . . . .
>
> 2. *Unlimited working hours.* In a fundamental sense, lean production is not free of buffers. Long and flexible working hours are the hidden buffer that is utilized if necessary. The amount of overtime work, often ordered at very short notice, was high in all transplants. The far-reaching management discretion to determine working hours means that, in principle, production quotas will be reached irrespective of what happened during the day or on the shift . . . . The 8-hour day has been a goal for more than a century in the West, but it is very hard to fit into the logic of the transplants . . . .
>
> 4. *Growing health and safety complaints.* Japanese plants place considerable emphasis on safety and the avoidance of accidents which can interrupt production. The products are designed for easy manufacture, with great precision in the making of parts. But the sheer repetitiveness of the jobs, which are designed according to very Taylorist principles, combined with the intense pace and long working hours, nevertheless lead to significant health risks, above all cumulative trauma disorders (CTD) or repetitive strain injuries (RSI). Incidentally these are not recognized as an occupational injury in Japan.
>
> 5. At Mazda, for instance, there were early reports of an unusually high incidence of carpal tunnel syndrome, damage to nerves and tendons in the hands and wrists. The total number of work-related injuries was three times higher at Mazda in than in comparable American plants.
>
> 6. There seems to be very little tolerance of such injuries. When we visited Honda's auto plant in Anna, management did not even admit that this was a problem in any way related to conditions of production, but maintained it was entirely dependent on individuals. 'There are weak and strong people. And there are right and wrong attitudes.'
>
> 7. *A rigorous factory regime.* By eliminating buffers, lean production increases management's dependence on employees and their contribution. In the *Machine* . . . book the MIT authors emphasize that the elimination of all kind [sic] of buffers and reserves makes the system much more dependent on the dedication of the workforce. 'Trust and feelings of reciprocity' are represented as the basis of the system. But the elimination of traditional safety nets (buffers, etc.) is more than compensated for by the strict personnel selection and scrupulous factory regime, replete with compulsory uniforms, detailed conduct and discipline codes, absolute demands for attendance, minute regulation of the workplace and elimination of all personal attributes. In many respects the transplants involve a militarization of the plant regime . . . .

Berggren also presents evidence to confirm the allegation of Parker and Slaughter that the team concept becomes more authoritarian over time. At the Canadian CAMI plant (a Ford-Suzuki joint venture), researchers found:

On the one hand, the researchers found a consistently high level of participation in sugges-tion activities (71% of the respondents in the second study) and a majority of workers sup-porting QC activities. On the other hand there was a deeply ambiguous assessment of the team concept. The social qualities were appreciated, but in the second round 41% of the in-terviewees thought teams were a way to get people to pressure one another, up from only 19% in the first field study. Also in the second round of observation, the research team dis-cerned a growing overall disillusionment with CAMI philosophy: 78% of the interviewed workers argued that CAMI was a factory where management still had all the power.

At the NUMMI plant, likewise, there has been "strong opposition, criticizing the intensive line speed and the constant pressure to work harder and faster, not just smarter."

Berggren also suggests that lean production is only questionably applicable outside the auto industry, especially in industries where an obsessive focus on reducing labor-hours per unit of output may be inappropriate.

When I first reviewed Parker's and Slaughter's book on my blog, an anonymous reader "eyeball-deep in a developing Lean work environment" confirmed their analysis, and that of Berggren, from personal experience:

> In the past year that my company has jumped on the Lean bandwagon and Kaizen has become our reality, I have watched the majority of our most skilled and intelligent workers break down and leave. I myself am at the breaking point. This system does noth-ing but remove management responsibility from the management and place it on the shoulders of the employees. We have watched management recieve large raises and bo-nuses as a result of *us* doing *their* jobs for them. As we have worked harder and faster and profits have gone up, our health (both mental and physical) has declined day by day. Meanwhile managers wander around on their "Gemba" rounds and do basically nothing all day.[1]

As I mentioned in introducing Berggren's analysis, Jon Miller, a lean proponent at Panta Rei blog, was forced to concede some of his criticisms, however grudgingly.

> It is very easy to implement "display Lean" with all of the surface similarities but not the supporting human resource development and management problem solving disci-plines built in. Even when it does have these things, a Lean workplace is fraught with ten-sion. Ideally it should be a healthy tension that focuses the mind on solving problems and serving the customer. When people lack respect between one another, or when working conditions do not meet the basic needs of people this tension becomes unhealthy . . . .
>
> Lean production does not respect people. Of course it doesn't. Production systems do not have feelings or the ability to respect human beings. Production systems are a set of rules and principles that describe effective ways to make money based on following certain laws of physics and economics.
>
> But Lean is not capable of being mean either, unlike people are. When people criti-cize Lean production as "lean and mean" what they are really saying is that the people in charge of implementing Lean care less about the livelihoods of the workers as they do for themselves. This is one side of human nature. Lean production used by people who care less about people can be brutal while Lean production used by people who care about people can be a wonderful thing.[2]

Allowing for its focus on mere differences in the personal style of management, as opposed to structural issues of power, Miller seems to be saying (albeit in much milder form) something very much like my point: that management systems like *kaizen* and qual-ity can be either empowering or hellish for workers, depending on the institutional con-text in which they are adopted.

---

1. Anonymous comment under Carson, "Liberation Management or Management by Stress?"
2. Jon Miller, "Lean Production Does Not Respect People," Panta Rei, May 10, 2006 <http://www.gembapantarei.com/2006/05/lean_production_does_not_respect_people.html>.

A good example is the treatment of downtime on the job as *muda*, or waste, as mentioned by Berggren. Traditionally, one way workers have made their jobs bearable (especially jobs intermittently requiring strenuous effort) is by regulating the pace of work, and interspersing downtime with bursts of effort. This is sometimes referred to as "one on, one off," as workers engaged in some physically exhausting activity take alternate staggered periods of effort and rest, despite being on the clock. The wage paid for the time takes into account the pace of work set by workers. Employers, on the other hand, have always sought to substitute regulation of the pace of work by machine, in order to extract maximum continuous effort from workers. When management succeeds in reducing downtime to a minimum and extracting maximum effort with a minimum of interruption, the result is the kinds of stress, burnout and repetitive motion injuries described by Berggren.

Michael Yates, in a *Monthly Review* article, relies on worker accounts to illustrate the physical demands of lean production (at least what passes under that name in the U.S.) in extremely vivid terms.

> . . . Not only are [auto workers] facing rapidly rising insecurity, they are also confronted every day with a work regimen so Taylorized that they must work fifty-seven of every sixty seconds. What must this be like? What does it do to mind and body? . . . In her book, *On the Line at Subaru-Isuzu* (1995), sociologist Laurie Graham tells us about her work routine in one of these gulags. Below, I have skipped a lot of the steps, because I just want to give readers a sense of the work. Remember as you read it that the line is relentlessly moving while she is working:
> 1. Go to the car and take the token card off a wire on the front of the car.
> 2. Pick up the 2 VIN (vehicle identification number) plates from the embosser and check the plates to see that they have the same number.
> 3. Insert the token card into the token card reader.
> 4. While waiting for the computer output, break down the key kit for the car by pulling the 3 lock cylinders and the lock code from the bag.
> 5. Copy the vehicle control number and color number onto the appearance check sheet . . . .
> 8. Lift the hood and put the hood jig in place so it will hold the hood open while installing the hood stay . . . .
> 22. Rivet the large VIN plate to the left-hand center pillar.
> 23. Begin with step one on the next car.
> This work is so intense that it is not possible to steal a break much less learn your workmate's job so that you can double-up, then rest while she does both jobs. Within six months of the plant's start-up, a majority of the workers had to wear wrist splints for incipient carpal tunnel. Necks and backs ache from bodies being twisted into unnatural positions for eight hours a day. Supervisors recommend exercises and suggest that workers who cannot deal with the pain are sissies.
> What is true for auto workers is true for all who do this type of labor—whether it be in beef processing plants or on chicken disassembly lines where workers labor with slippery blood and gore on the floor and on their bodies. And where cuts lead to infections and disease.[1]

Charlie Post and Jane Slaughter quoted one autoworker who described lean production as "eight hours of aerobic activity each day."[2]

There's nothing illegitimate about downtime on the job. It's as legitimate a perk as the CEO's mahogany desk, his enormous salary, his bonuses, and his severance package. Such control over the pace of work was a normal part of life under the older self-

1. Michael Yates, "The Injuries of Class," *Monthly Review* 59:8 (January 2008), pp. 6–7 <http://www.monthlyreview.org/080101yates.php>.
2. Charlie Post and Jane Slaughter, "Lean Production: Why Work is Worse Than Ever, and What's the Alternative" A Solidarity Working Paper (2000) <http://www.solidarity-us.org/Lean Production.html>.

employment regime. Since he self-employed worker appropriated his full product, any particular choice of exertion was a straightforward exchange of effort for consumption. And as radical economic historians like Stephen Marglin have pointed out, a chief motive of the factory system was to put capitalists in control of the pace of work, in order to reduce downtime and increase the effort extracted for a given payment. The history of industrial relations since then, from Ure and Taylor on, from the deskilling described by Katharine Stone in the steel industry to the introduction of automated machine tools described by David Noble, has been a struggle over whether the pace of work will be set by workers on the shop floor, or by machines controlled by management.

As we noted earlier, whether the alternation of exertion and rest is considered "waste," or a worker's normal exchange of total effort for total consumption, depends on who holds the power. The definition of "waste" depends on one's understanding of efficiency; this means entirely different things, from the respective standpoints of labor and capital. For labor, efficiency means maximizing the ratio of consumption outputs to labor inputs (optimizing returns on labor); for capital, it means optimizing returns on capital.

Something like lean production could be practiced in a worker-controlled setting to eliminate *real* waste, like unnecessary use of materials or misdirected efforts, without treating the wage of labor itself as a cost of business rather than the purpose of the business. The workers, rather, would see the payment of labor as the rationale for their enterprise, and treat the mixture of exertion and rest undertaken in earning that payment as a matter to be decided by those who know where the shoe pinches.

> In a worker-run economy, the introduction of new technology could bring more free time, more jobs, more interesting work and less stress, rather than unemployment, deskilling and speed-up.[1]

The fundamental problem is the conflict of interest involved in the power differential, by which one party reaps the benefits of its policies, while imposing the costs on the other party. Lean, as actually practiced, treats labor as the main "cost" to be economized on.

Eric Husman, although generally hostile to the Parker and Slaughter book, in reviewing it makes some points that coincide with my own analysis.[2] Most of his major objections involve their inconsistent cultural and ideological attitudes, rooted in the old corporate liberal model of unionism. For example, despite their identification of lean production with "super-Taylorism," they actually share more values in common with actual Taylorism than does lean production. Parker and Slaughter equate "Taylorism," in simplistic fashion, to time-and-motion study and the identification of the "best way," when—as Husman points out—its central feature was actually the strict separation of management from labor functions, and of thinking from doing. In this, with their affinity for "rigid work rules, rigid work classifications, bureaucratization," Parker and Slaughter are actually quite close to Taylor.

In fairness to those authors, I should point out that the issue of bureaucratic work rules arguably has a dialectical character. Parker and Slaughter themselves sometimes concede, in passing, that many of the techniques of TQM or *kaizen*, in and of themselves, might be useful in the context of a production system owned and controlled by workers. On the other hand, in a workplace organized on the principles of absentee ownership and managerialism, such work rules can be a necessary evil; giving management the discretion it needs to implement more flexible systems would result in those systems being turned against the workers. So in a sense, union interference with the most efficient ways of or-

---

1. Post and Slaughter, "Lean Production."
2. Eric Husman, "Working Smart? Or Rather Neither, Really," Grim Reader, October 10, 2006 <http://www.zianet.com/ehusman/weblog/2006/10/working-smart-or-rather-neither-really.html>.

ganizing production are a necessary result of the agency problems inherent in wage labor. Labor's preference for rigid work rules is quite rational, despite their interference with efficiency, given management's real propensity to abuse the discretion and flexibility needed to run things more efficiently.

Nevertheless, despite all of Husman's objections, Parker and Slaughter are correct in their central contention: that most of what is *called* "lean manufacturing" by American employers (and what is called TQM and Six Sigma as well) amounts, as actually practiced, to downsizing and speedup, and an attempt to squeeze more work out of fewer people for less money. They are mistaken only in taking the "lean" label at face value in most cases.

For example, take Judith Biewener's case study of the Regional Bell companies, where cross-functional training and teams were combined with downsizing, speedups and reduced job security.

> At the company I studied, downsizing has generated widespread resentment and a sense of insecurity among employees, leaving them cynical and suspicious of management initiatives. In general, workers are positive about the idea of bringing this particular set of jobs together; they consider it helpful to be able to immediately resolve problems with their coworkers in other job titles that before would require phone calls to other offices and, very often, a great deal of waiting. For the most part, however, cross-functional teaming is closely associated with the pain and disruption of consolidation and downsizing . . . .
>
> Because job reductions have outpaced the work redesign in many cases, stress from work speedup in the centers is at high levels . . . . Meanwhile, frequent failure to meet service levels because of the extra work offends workers' strong service ethic . . . .
>
> Since this company has introduced cross-functional groups and cross-training in a way that is effectively divorced from employee involvement, such ill feeling may not seem to pose a significant problem for management. However, to the extent that workers resist or even undercut the new cross-functional arrangements being introduced—by holding back information to coworkers about their jobs, for example—such sentiment among workers is problematic even for the abbreviated high performance work system being implemented by this company.
>
> In addition, the ability of the company to proceed with multiskilling and job rotation has been severely hampered by the dramatic extent of the downsizing. For instance, in certain cases functional and geographic specializations are being *reinforced* as the pressure to "just get the work done" squeezes out time for workers to learn new tasks and procedures or to teach others about their jobs. And despite management hopes that cross-training will lessen the skill loss associated with downsizing, when cuts are made so deeply and swiftly, skill transfer can be undercut by the departure of experienced workers.[1]

And this Husman does not directly contest. His most important point, in my opinion, is that most of the American firms treated as case studies by Parker and Slaugher were only superficially adherents of lean or *kaizen*. Only NUMMI, of all the American plants they mentioned, even came close. The authors' main shortcoming, aside from all the cultural attitudes to which Husman objects, is that they uncritically identify "lean" manufacturers mainly by taking lean slogans at face value. But the Berggren article, which Husman takes far more seriously than the Parker and Slaughter book (indeed, he recommended it to me in the first place), has some areas of overlap with Parker and Slaughter in its treatment of lean production in plants where it is seriously applied (e.g., NUMMI, the original Toyota Production System, and Japanese transplants in North America). Namely, according to Berggren, lean production has an ambivalent character that can sometimes be expressed in speedups and constantly increasing extraction of effort even when it is genuinely practiced.

1. Judith Biewener, "Downsizing and the New American Workplace," *Review of Radical Political Economics* 29:4 (December 1997), pp. 16-17.

Husman's main objection, together with the aspects of Parker and Slaughter that are backed up by Berggren, give us what amounts to a restatement of two of my central themes in this chapter: 1) corporate America in more cases than not only pays lip-service to management theory fads, with little or no understanding of what the slogans even mean; and 2) when they really are seriously applied, rather than living up to their libertarian potential they tend to take on an authoritarian character as they are adapted to the structural imperatives of absentee ownership, managerialism and hierarchy. Despite their sloppiness and other shortcomings, I found Parker and Slaughter a source of much useful information. Nevertheless, I believe that Husman and I are largely in agreement. As he said in response to my own review,

> I believe that lean is amoral: it can be used for good or bad, e.g. GM probably has found a system for eliminating more jobs. And we certainly have seen lots of people use the slogans without getting the message. But I also believe that it is potentially valuable, especially as lean is exactly the type of system Kirkpatrick Sale tries to describe as a means for producing goods locally from generalized machinery . . . and it is exactly what Amory Lovins and Paul Hawken see as the productive mechanism in *Natural Capitalism* . . . .

I agree with every word of that.

D. DUMBING DOWN

Interestingly, those directly involved in developing such practices as TQM and the Toyota Production System, etc. (and just about anyone who takes the ideas seriously), tend to be contemptuous of most dumbed-down corporate attempts to put them into practice. The writers who show the most enthusiasm for some such practice's "revolutionary" application in a long string of Fortune 500 corporations, generally, are superficial popularizers and cheerleaders like Peters. The serious Quality people I've met, with industrial engineering backgrounds, tend to contrast Deming's thought with today's corporate Kwality programs in terms very like Nietzsche's dictum: "There was only one Christian, and he died on the cross."

The one seeming exception is Six Sigma, for which I've been able to find nothing *but* popularized descriptions. If Six Sigma has anything comparable to Deming's *Out of the Crisis* as a serious and authoritative exposition, it must be some in-house work for Motorola engineers. That impression is confirmed by my discussions with people from industrial engineering backgrounds, and who have had direct experience with assorted lean and quality programs. I also get the impression, from discussion with such people, that there *is* no "serious" version of Six Sigma in the same sense as with Deming or Juran, whose work was subsequently dumbed down for consumption by the corporate suits: Six Sigma is *itself* the pop version of Quality, dumbed down for the corporate suits.

One correspondent (who wishes to remain anonymous) humorously compares it to "a branch of Scientology, what with the belts and the toolkits and the specific minimum project sizes and meaningless acronyms," and treats the Black Belts as equivalent to Operating Thetans. In substance, he says, Six Sigma has little or nothing to offer in addition to Walter Shewhart's 1930s work on statistical quality control at Western Electric; any substantive refinements to Shewhart's work were already made by Juran and Deming back in the 1950s, and further improved on by Ohno. Everything substantive in Six Sigma is cribbed from those earlier versions of quality control, with a new brand name (McQuality) put on it. As Juran said, "From what I've seen of it, it's a basic version of quality improvement. There is nothing new there."[1]

---

1. "Juran: A Lifetime of Quality."

In the case of lean manufacturing, as Eric Husman pointed out above, Bill Waddell refuses to work with American corporations in the GM-DuPont tradition, which focus on the kind of short-sighted, pennywise-pound foolish approach to cost cutting mandated by GAAP accounting practices.

> [Parker and Slaughter] talk repeatedly of how management uses lean processes and reengineering to make it easier to outsource and introduce automation, yet these are the diametric opposite of what Toyota does. Toyota is famously conservative about the introduction of technology. By outsourcing, Parker and Slaughter mean forcing single supplier systems to stock parts for Just-In-Time pull, but Toyota keeps dual suppliers and works with them to introduce real JIT methods into their operations. As a result, many Toyota First-Tier suppliers have expanded their business by supplying to Toyota's competitors, while GM, Ford, Delphi, and all the rest of the Sloanist, GAAP, Taylorist producers keep laying off, outsourcing, and automating their way to oblivion . . . .
>
> Waddell and Bodek persuasively argue in *Rebirth of American Industry* that GM and companies based on its management principles will never fully grasp or be able to apply lean management theories because of the accounting rules they use . . . .
>
> To put it in perspective, it is valuable to compare the original Ford and the Toyoda family values to the GM values. Henry Ford and Kiichiro Toyoda both owned a manufacturing concern and made money by manufacturing things. DuPont owned a group of companies that manufactured things, but he had two options for making money: he could manufacture things or he could break the organization up and sell it off by piece. Therefore, he and Brown devised a system designed always to be ready to sell off . . . .
>
> So it should be no surprise that when union activists look at GM's application of lean theories they find a facade and little else. The accounting system in place in almost all public companies will force them to the same conclusion: eliminate labor because it is a cost, don't worry about inventory because it is an asset. GE took this to its logical limit: keep the name, sell off the manufacturing capability, put all of your effort into marketing and financing. The result today is that GMAC and GE Capital are the most profitable divisions of those companies. The MBAs in charge were baptized in the GAAP and Sloanist M-Form corporation theory; they eliminate variable costs (labor) by investing in specialized automation or by outsourcing it.
>
> And Toyota is beating the crap out of them with people and relatively low-tech, general application machinery.[1]

Sam Smith, in *Progressive Review*, described the general phenomenon in more jaundiced terms:

> We have created an economy based not on actually doing anything, but on facilitating, supervising, planning, managing, analyzing, tax advising, marketing, consulting or defending in court what might be done if we had time to do it. The few remaining truly productive companies become immediate targets for another entropic activity, the leveraged buyout.[2]

As Husman said, it's utterly pointless even to try implementing lean production in a company with Sloan accounting. Every day, Waddell and Bodek write, a Sloanist factory holds a "production meeting" which demands two figures: the value of output (i.e. by DuPont standards that include the value of goods "sold" to inventory), and the labor-hours expended to produce it.[3]

American corporate culture has always paid lip-service to the latest management theory fads, while remaining oblivious both as to what any of the buzzwords actually mean, and utterly uncaring, and the inconsistency of their practice with the basic principles of

1. Husman, "The Accounting Chains on American Industry."
2. Sam Smith, "The Corporate Curse," *Undernews*, May 7, 2008 <http://prorev.com/2008/05/corporate-curse.html>.
3. William H. Waddell and Norman Bodek, *Rebirth of American Industry: A Study of Lean Management* (Vancouver, WA: PCS Press, 2005), pp. 132-133.

their professed theory. Despite all their lip-service, the typical management approach to "solving" any problem is the direct opposite of the substantive ideas of Drucker, Juran or Deming.

Both Peter Drucker and W. Edwards Deming opposed attempts to solve problems and reduce costs through sloganeering. They rejected the "behavioral" approach to solving problems (see Appendix 8A, "Blaming Workers for the Results of Mismanagement"), and saw genuine solutions as possible only by means of structural changes in the production process. Deming, for instance, wrote:

> Eliminate targets, slogans, exhortations, posters, for the work force that urge them to increase productivity. "Your work is your self-portrait. Would you sign it?" *No*—not when you give me defective canvas to work with, canvas not suited to the job, brushes worn out, so that I can not call it my work. Posters and slogans like these never helped anyone to do a better job . . . .
>
> "Do it right the first time." A lofty ring it has. But how could a man make it right the first time when the incoming material is off-gauge, off-color, or otherwise defective, or if his machine is not in good order, or the measuring instruments not trustworthy? This is just another meaningless slogan, a cousin of zero defects.
>
> "Getting better together." Production workers have told me that this slogan makes them furious. Together! What is that when no one will listen to our problems and suggestions?[1]

Drucker, likewise, dismissed "management by drives," with pennywise/pound-foolish "economies" that degrade long-term productivity. To focus on individual effort rather than process only produces, at best, a short-term bump in productivity that quickly evaporates.[2]

This fundamental conflict between American management culture and the requirements for genuine quality are the reason attempts at lean, Quality, TPS, or whatever other name you choose always wind up being dumbed down. As Waddell and Bodek put it, that management culture inevitably resulted in the way General Electric "turned Six Sigma into the strategy to outsource and offshore everything."

> They value streamed the corporation and came to the conclusion that just about everyone except headquarters (of course) added insufficient value and needed to go.

Lean manufacturing got "Sloaned."[3]

The implementation of quality and kaizen in most American corporations makes the efforts of GM and General Electric look positively wonkish by comparison. As I mentioned earlier, senior management more often than not has little or no idea of what the Kwality jargon they're paying lip service to even means.

Jerome Alexander (an MBA and CPA with a career background in middle management, who blogs on management issues at *The Corporate Cynic*) describes the superficial management approach to TQM at one of his past employers[4]. He prefaces his comments by noting that he had initially supported the TQM concept, until turned off by his experience with management's actual implementation of it. At the time, the height of TQM popularity in the '90s, he was a division operations manager for a national corporation, and

1. W. Edwards Deming. *Out of the Crisis* (Cambridge, Mass.: M.I.T., Center for Advanced Engineering Study, 1986), pp. 65-66.
2. Peter F. Drucker, *The Practice of Management* (New York: Harper & Brothers Publishers, 1954), pp. 127-128.
3. Waddell and Bodek, pp. 201-202.
4. Jerome Alexander, "Requiem for TQM of Total Quality Mismanagement," The Corporate Cynic, April 1, 2007 <http://thecorporatecynic.wordpress.com/2007/04/01/tqm-mayhem-or-total-quality-mismanagement/>. Alexander wrote this post in response to a request from Jon Miller of Panta Rei blog for his opinion on TQM.

his division faced serious customer dissatisfaction as a result of quality problems with a line of capital equipment that it had introduced.

> The company spared no expense getting us on fast track to TQM. They picked one of the more expensive TQM program providers and flew us all over country. I was chosen to be an instructor because I managed a large region and my operations were far flung . . . .
>
> I will admit that I was skeptical about the TQM concept from the outset. How could such a culture change take place at an extremely conservative firm like ours? I did not like the gimmicky "Fru-Fru" (you know –the silly exercises, role playing, campaign buttons, etc.) that was associated with the training. I've never liked that stuff. I really didn't think that TQM would work in our kind of operations either. But I was committed to learning the methods and as long as I was chosen to be an instructor, I dug into the materials like I would study for any other academic course. It took me a while to intellectualize the concepts but over a cocktail one night at the program sponsored "happy hour", it clicked. The whole thing was unbelievably simple. It made sense logically and I felt that the concepts could be easily communicated to the employees – with or without the "Fru-Fru." I actually began believe that this could work . . . .
>
> We got down to the business of setting up training at the division level in accordance with the schedule and format set out by the program. It was a step-by-step process that rolled out in a series of stages. But while we in the field were diligently at work laying the groundwork, things were already going awry at corporate headquarters. Part of the implementation protocol required a show of support by top management. This included a visit by one of the TQM program consultants to meet with CEO. Ron informed me that the CEO had refused to meet with them. After a plethora of pleadings by the consultants, he relented but had assigned the whole program to a lower level vice president.

At the "big corporate 'kick off' meeting" at headquarters, the CEO gave himself away in his keynote address.

> Two of his comments were telling: " . . . I hope that no one thinks that we're getting into this program because I happened to pick up Business Week and read an article about it. We need this." and his final comment with which we were sent off to go and do TQM, "I really want this program to work but I don't want people wasting their time attending a lot of meetings."

The significance of the latter comment becomes clear, from Alexander's account of senior management's actual training in TQM:

> 1. The key corporate executives only participated in the "executive summary" overview session (held at a resort in Florida). Some did not even consider it worthwhile to attend.
>
> 2. Due to the CEO's statement about "too many meetings", corporate employees received mandatory but abridged training. They did get all of the "Fru-Fru." . . . .

And those engaged in production, the heart of any real TQM process, were never truly engaged:

> . . . [T]he events were always confined to corporate headquarters and never found their way down to the production worker level. Everything that occurred at our company was always centered on corporate headquarters. That's where the CEO and the power base were located. Everything revolved around them. Even though the production facilities were the areas deemed as needing the program, only their top managers were called into headquarters to participate. Production workers only read about it in the company newsletters.
>
> Over the next twelve months, the program peaked and then began to degenerate as the novelty wore off and company priorities began to change. The training schedules, formats, and overall protocol that the program consultants had laid out began to be modified and reprioritized by corporate officials.

Unfortunately, the implementation of the basic concept was hamstrung by management's superficial understanding of TQM, and its simultaneous exclusion of production workers from the substance of the quality improvement process. Senior management, whose knowledge of TQM was about as substantial as the TQM mugs they received at their half-day "Executive Summary for Clueless Bosses" seminar, interfered with the proper operation of the process (imagine *Dilbert*'s pointy-haired boss interfering with the engineers' work based on some half-digested article in *Business Week*, and you'll get the idea). And the paucity of worker suggestions for process improvement, resulting from the lack of initial involvement and buy-in, resulted in management attempts to artificially generate suggestions (Opportunities for Improvement, or OFIs). Alexander went into considerable detail about what this meant in concrete terms:

> These were to be grassroots ideas for improving the processes performed by the employees themselves, i.e. "If my area had better lighting, I could more easily . . . . and the work that I pass on work would contain less defects." "If the parts were degreased before I got them, I could . . . ." "If I had a different tool, I could . . . ." You get the picture. The intent was to improve the process.

One of the corporate AVPs, "who had only attended an 'Executive Summary' session," dug up an old idea that had nothing to do with process improvement. Worse, he "decided that this example should be used as the model for all OFI's." From there, it went downhill:

> Besides, the company had just made a considerable monetary investment in TQM training and, by God; they wanted to see something for it. The entire OFI program deteriorated into a numbers game and a contest. You can guess the rest. If you can't imagine the undue pressure placed on line management, the nonproductive shenanigans, infighting and poor morale that resulted, I can write an entire post about them.

If you think things couldn't be dumbed down and bastardized any further, prepare to be disillusioned. Alexander's description has to be read to be believed:

> . . . Corporate headquarters, of course, held a massive affair combining several of the benchmarking events into one. Sparing no expense, a hotel ballroom was transformed into a genuine three-ring circus arena complete with clowns, prize booths and even a dunk tank. The office staff was dressed in "zero defect" tee shirts and played ring toss games to win giant yardsticks for "measurement." Banners and balloons carried the words "All work is a Process" and "Quality is Free." The tab for all of it sure couldn't have been. The food was great. But other than for the fun and games, no one really seemed to know why they were there. It was all kind of surreal . . . .
>
> Three years later it was all over. The company received a spiffy "Quality Statement" like all large corporations have today. New employees received a booklet describing the TQM process that they were to memorize. They might also have been shown a videotape. The OFI process had stopped (thank God). The entire administration of the TQM program had been remanded to the Quality Assurance Department. Their focus went back [to] inspecting finished goods and reviewing production processes. The relationship with original program consultants reverted to receiving a monthly newsletter. Nothing else changed.
>
> The banners were sagging on the walls and the balloons were all but deflated and hanging limp, sad reminders of an extremely expensive foray into the TQM fad of the '90's.

Following his lengthy and rather painful account of the TQM trainwreck, Alexander eloquently summarized what went wrong in these brief words:

> Enacted for the wrong reasons. Afforded only lip service support by a disinterested top management. Continuously modified by ill-informed senior officials."

That could be the epitaph for most large corporate ventures in Kwality. But the interesting part, from a perverse stopping-to-look-at-an-accident perspective, is the sheer catharsis involved in reading all the excruciating details of just *how* it was screwed up in a particular case, and thereby receiving the gratifying reassurance that, yep, while the specific details may differ, those pointy-haired bosses are equally stupid everywhere. As Tolstoy might have put it, every incompetently managed corporation is incompetently managed in its own way.

Juran remarked on the corporate tendency to pay lip service to quality, referring to general policy statements on the subject as "Motherhood policies":

> . . . . Virtually all published statements of corporate quality policy contain a brief declaration which summarizes the company's position. For example:
>> It is the policy of the company to provide products and services of a quality that meet the initial and continuing needs and expectations of customers in relation to the price paid and to the nature of competitive offerings, and in doing so, to be the leader in product quality reputation.
>> To achieve and sustain a reputation for quality at competitive prices in the National and International markets for our entire product range.
>> To provide a product which satisfies performance, quality, reliability, and safety requirements of our customers at a fair market price.
>> To provide products and services which consistently meet the needs and expectations of our customers and of users within the company.
> No one quarrels with such statements. However, they are regarded by most managers as too vague to provide guides for conduct. (Hence the name "motherhood" policies; i.e., everyone is in favor of motherhood.)[1]

Or as Peters quoted some anonymous employee about his manager, in Chapter Eight: He's all for quality, in the sense that he never says he's against it—the problem is he's for everything. And although he occasionally speaks in favor of quality, he acts a hundred times a day in favor of shipping product.

One common feature in most dumbed-down versions of lean production and quality, as opposed to the real thing, is that management takes the costs of genuine quality improvement in isolation, rather than in the context of the *far greater* cost of poor quality. This idea, the "Cost of Non-Compliance," is especially central to the thought of Philip Crosby[2] (who also noted that it's typically disregarded by most management quality initiatives).

For example, as Husman points out in his critique of Parker and Slaughter, genuine advocates of lean production consider injury to workers as itself a cost of doing business.

Dumbed-down lean production also differs from the real thing in what it identifies as *muda*, or waste. For Ohno, the primary target in eliminating waste was activity that did not contribute directly to value-added: one-off activities removed from the production process. On his frequent visits to Detroit after WWII, judged the American system as "rife with *muda*."

> He reasoned that none of the specialists beyond the assembly workers was actually adding any value to the car. What's more, Ohno thought that assembly workers could probably do most of the functions of the specialists and do them much better because of their direct acquaintance with conditions on the line . . . . Yet, the role of the assembly worker had the lowest status in the factory.[3]

I wonder how Ohno would classify those in management ranks whose jobs involve mainly writing mission, vision and values statements, inventing new "employee recognition" gimmicks, or schmoozing with the revolving door of expensive consultants from Fish! or whatever other "motivational" program is the flavor of the week.

Ohno's approach, as described by Womack *et al.*, dovetails with Deming's account (already quoted in Chapter Eight) of the typical pattern of Japanese cost-cutting priorities:

1. J.M. Juran, *Juran's Quality Control Handbook*, 5.4-5.
2. Philip Crosby, *Quality is Free: The Art of Making Quality Certain* (New York: McGraw-Hill Book Company, 1979). See also Juran, 4.4-5.
3. James P. Womack, Daniel T. Jones, Daniel Roos. *The Machine That Changed the World* (New York: Macmillan Publishing Company, 1990), p. 56.

start with cutting dividends, and then management salaries and bonuses, with wage cuts and layoffs an absolute last resort.[1]

This is borne out by the example of Toyota Corporation in the late 1940s, when company president and founding family member Eiji Toyoda regarded a layoff of 25% of workers as so blameworthy as to call for his own resignation. In so doing, he treated the layoffs as a unique, one-time event, coupled with a corporate social compact in which life-time employment for core workers would be the norm and layoffs would be governed by the list of priorities Deming described.[2]

Most dumbed-down American lean manufacturing systems, on the other hand, target the productive workforce as their first priority in eliminating "waste," and try to squeeze as much effort as possible out of the smallest possible number of people. And their overall priority list is exactly the opposite of Deming's: first cut the total productive workforce, or their pay, benefits, or work hours; then cut back on middle management; and only in the direst emergency, cut back on the perks of senior management.

Management almost never compares the direct cost (or indirect cost in lost production time) of scrap and rework, or of replacing defective customer orders, or of lost good-will, etc., to the cost of the resources needed to produce a quality product in the first place. In hospitals, this cost of poor quality includes nosocomial (hospital-acquired) infections, medication errors, patient falls, and general patient dissatisfaction and bad word-of-mouth resulting from the poor quality of service.

Another way in which dumbed-down Kwality programs differ from the original idea was the importance of "driving out fear" in Deming's original program, so that workers felt safe discussing the causes of waste among themselves. Contrast this to the paranoid atmosphere at NBC News, when Jack Welch's infatuation with Six Sigma was the party line at parent company GE:

> Six Sigma—the methodology for the improvement of business processes that strives for 3.4 defects or fewer per million opportunities—was a somewhat mysterious symbol of management authority at every GE division. Six Sigma messages popped up on the screens of computers or in e-mail in-boxes every day. Six Sigma was out there, coming, unstoppable, like a comet or rural electrification. It was going to make everything better, and slowly it would claim employees in glazed-eyed conversions. Suddenly in the office down the hall a coworker would no longer laugh at the same old jokes. A grim smile suggested that he was on the lookout for snarky critics of the company. It was better to talk about the weather.[3]

As Parker and Slaughter point out, most TQM programs do just the opposite of "driving out fear." The organizations continue to rely heavily on what Deming called the "deadly diseases" of performance evaluations, merit ratings, and annual reviews[4]—all predicated on a behavioral approach to increasing productivity by increasing individual pressure to perform, rather than properly structuring the process.

Perhaps the most significant discrepancy between the original principles of quality, and Kwality as it is practiced in Corporate America, is the tendency to substitute increased employee effort for genuine process improvement. At the hospital where I work, for example, I looked (just for fun) into the *Quality Improvement Handbook*, a binder with inserts go-

1. W. Edwards Deming, *Out of the Crisis* (Cambridge, Mass.: M.I.T., Center for Advanced Engineering Study, 1986), p. 147.

2. Womack *et al.*, *The Machine That Changed the World*, p. ?

3. John Hockenberry, "You Don't Understand Our Audience: What I learned about network television at Dateline NBC," *Technology Review* (MIT), January/February 2008 <www.technologyreview.com/Infotech/19845/>.

4. Mike Parker and Jane Slaughter, "Beware! TQM is coming to Your Campus," *NEA Higher Ed*, Spring 1994 <http://www2.nea.org/he/tqm.html>.

ing back as far as the mid-90s, and found an astonishing geological cross-section of fossil-ized, abandoned management theory fads. The ghost of Deming appeared in both his TQM and Six-Sigma incarnations, not to mention Deming's distant cousin ISO-9000. What's really funny is to see all the "Plan, Do, Check, Act" jargon in the posters on bulle-tin boards, along with impressive-looking charts of adverse events over time. But right next to them, on the very same bulletin boards, are all sorts of "slogans and exhortations" (big Deming no-nos, examples of the very behavioral approach he regarded as anathema to Quality), to get people to minimize adverse events by working harder and being more en-thusiastic. They parrot all the jargon of Kwality while missing the central point of Dem-ing's Red Bead Experiment: process variation occurs because *the process* is badly designed (i.e., designed to produce a given level of variation), and it can be corrected only by *chang-ing the process* so that reduced variation is its normal output.—not by slogans and exhorta-tions aimed at eliciting greater levels of effort, motivation, or attention from workers. De-spite all the lip service to Deming, their substantive approach amounts to what Drucker called "management by drives."

In contrast, Juran treated "Perfectionism" as a deviation from orthodox quality, and identified one of its central characteristics as the "Belief that humans can be motivated to make no errors."[1]

He wrote at great length on the idiocy of the behavioral approach to "quality" through drives:

> . . . The kind of management thinking that seeks remedy in short-term programs is usually the kind of thinking that brought about the poor quality performance in the first place. When a campaign is sought, what is actually needed is a change in management systems that will enable people to consistently produce high levels of quality . . . .
>
> Some grievous errors have been made in quality campaigns which have left the or-ganization in worse shape, with less performance capability than before the campaign, even when the stated objectives of the campaign were met and short-term results ob-tained. The major assumption underlying most short-term programs is that deficient quality performance (errors, defects, etc.) results from an unwillingness of workers to pay attention to the necessary details necessary for quality. Hence, the thrust of the campaign is to convince workers to take greater care and pride in their work without providing a method to improve . . . .
>
> . . . The majority of defects are inherent in the system and, therefore, only manage-ment can create the conditions for improvement.[2]
>
> . . . Many upper managers have opted for a road which can properly be called "ex-hortation only." This road consists of using skillful propaganda to arouse awareness among subordinates that quality is important. This is an important first step in a program, but it does not provide organizational machinery to tackle the long-standing complex quality problems. Further, it does not provide a specific answer to the questions "What do you want me to do differently?"[3]
>
> Many managers harbor deep-seated beliefs that most defects are caused during manufacture and specifically are due to worker errors, i.e., that defects are mainly worker-controllable. The facts seldom bear this out, but the belief persists.[4]

The majority of defects, as Juran puts it elsewhere, are "management-controllable," and therefore cannot be addressed by "motivational and disciplinary measures."[5] And many of those which are apparently "worker-controllable" (e.g. defects resulting from lack of at-

1. J.M. Juran and Frank M Gryna, *Juran's Quality Control Handbook*. Fourth edition (New York: McGraw-Hill Book Company, 1951, 1988), 3.29.

2. *Ibid.*, 10.48.

3. *Ibid.*, 22.11.

4. *Ibid.*, 22.32.

5. *Ibid.*, 22.35.

tention, etc.) are in fact management controllable defects in disguise: i.e., they result from a production process that requires unreasonable levels of sustained effort and vigilance, and thus inevitably leads to error when management finds it cannot sloganize away human nature:

> . . . Inadvertent errors are those which workers are unable to avoid because of human inability to pay attention. Centuries of experience have demonstrated that human beings are simply unable to maintain continuing attention . . . .
> Remedies for inadvertent errors involve two approaches:
> 1. Reducing the extent of dependence on human attention [i.e., fail-safe systems] . . . .
> 2. Making it easier for the human beings to remain attentive. Reorganization of work to reduce fatigue and monotony, job rotation, sense multipliers, templates, masks, and overlays are examples of remedies.[1]

In addition to inadvertent errors, there are deliberate errors caused by the double bind in which subordinates are sometimes put by impossible management demands, or by an "atmosphere of blame." When the time and resources available to do a job are simply inadequate (especially because of understaffing), but the pressure to "get it done" is relentless, production workers will cut corners and falsify the upward flow of data, and each subsequently level of the hierarchy will behave similarly toward its higher-ups.[2]

A classic example is the approach to patient satisfaction in hospitals. When satisfaction surveys reveal dissatisfaction over the time it takes to answer a call light, for example, management doesn't see the problem as insufficient staffing to keep up with the workload, or the solution as (say) eliminating some staff positions in the nursing office and reducing the size of "quality" committees in order to provide more nursing staff—heaven forfend! Management's solution is to issue pagers to orderlies so they can listen to its constant squawking that "Assistance is needed in Rm. 17!" The problem, you see, isn't that the orderly is up to his elbows in shit or soaked to the skin giving somebody a shower, and that most of the lights in his group of a dozen patients have gone off before he can get away from what he's doing. It isn't that none of his coworkers is able to answer the light for him, because they're all similarly up to their elbows in shit and unable to even answer their own call lights that are stacking up on the intercom. Oh, no! It's that the worker doesn't hear the constant ringing out in the hall (believe me, he does—most of us hear the hellish things in our sleep after a shift in one of those understaffed shitholes), or that he's too lazy or incompetent to get to them in time. So what's needed is a new form of electronic torture, combined with harassment and progressive penalties if he doesn't reduce his time-to-answer to management specifications.

CONCLUSION AND SEGUE TO PART FOUR

To reiterate, all of the previous analysis is not to say that these fashionable management theories are inherently worthless. Depending on whose power framework they're incorporated into, the resulting world can be either an iron-heeled cyberpunk dystopia, or as humanly appealing as the 21st century England of William Morris. Either "all will be well, and all manner of things will be well," or the future will be a boot stamping on a human face forever. Or maybe we'll just muddle through somewhere in between, with them trying to enslave us but not quite getting off with everything they want.

But I don't think our corporate masters can keep their grip on the world, and I don't think they can even just muddle through for many more decades. Their state-subsidized economy is generating costs faster than they can externalize them on the rest of us, and it's

1. *Ibid.*, 22.55-56.
2. *Ibid.*, 22.59.

headed for the breaking point: Peak Oil, the debt crisis, overbuilt highway infrastructure crumbling several times faster than money can be appropriated for repairs, etc. To borrow Stavrianos' imagery from *The Promise of the Coming Dark Age*, the seeds of a genuinely new economy are there, waiting to sprout up through the cracks in the ruins of state capitalism. And when it happens, rather than new wine being poured into old bottles, we'll be using the new ideas as the fundamental organizing principles of a new economy—not to keep the old one on life support.

We have seen, in Parts Two and Three, the crisis tendencies, both at a systemic level and within the large organization, which render the present system unsustainable. In Part Four, we'll examine some of the building blocks of the successor society we might end up with after these crises run their course.

As hard as it is to prophesy the specifics of a post-state (or at least a much more genuinely free) society, the general direction of change should be fairly easy to guess. Looking at a man with acromegaly, it's hard to say just what his face would look like without the distorting effects of his hormonal imbalance. But it's a safe guess that his jaw and forehead would be smaller, not larger. We saw, in Parts One through Three, the general tendencies encouraged by state intervention in the present system: centralization, large size, hierarchy, authority, rents on artificial property, capital-intensiveness, push distribution, credentialism, unconvivial technology, etc. Treating each of these qualities as one pole of an axis, we can expect a society with drastically reduced state intervention to shift significantly toward the opposite poles on all the axes.

When it comes to more specific guesses, all bets are off. The biggest unknown is the speed and time-compression of the transition. Will it be a "long emergency" of a few decades, with time to make a stable transition from one society to another? Or will it be a total collapse scenario, with all the crises together creating a "perfect storm," and the new society (maybe) coalescing in tiny islands out of the post-apocalyptic chaos?

The former is clearly preferable. But in either case, there are three main tendencies currently at work that will determine the form society takes after the crises have passed.

The first is the unsustainability of centralism and large scale. The state's subsidies to the corporate economy create an exponential growth in demand for subsidized inputs, far faster than the state can provide the inputs. The state nears a fiscal crisis beyond which it cannot increase subsidized inputs at all; and some subsidized inputs, being non-renewable resources, become available in diminishing quantities. As a result the state capitalist system, which requires extensive increases in inputs and constant expansion for its health, hits a wall. What must emerge in its place is an economy based on decentralized, small-scale production for local markets, in which "growth" results from more efficient use of existing inputs rather than the extensive addition of new ones.

The second is the increasing unenforceability of "intellectual property" and the untenability of business models based on it, and the rise of an open-source model of product design and technical innovation. As a result, the portion of product price which currently derives from rents on "intellectual property" will implode, with price falling to reflect the actual costs of material and labor—a fraction of its present value in most cases.

The third is what amounts to a singularity, both in terms of our capability for internal resistance within the corporate economy, and of the availability of high-quality attractive alternatives for subsistence outside the corporate economy. These include networked resistance (or asymmetric warfare) capabilities that increase the bargaining power of labor and reduce the ability of capital to extract a profit, social lending and other forms of networked mobilization of capital, and technological advances (on a trajectory comparable to Moore's Law) toward increasing the quality of life and lowering the capital outlay costs for supporting an "unplugged" subsistence lifestyle.

So far in this book, we have discussed three issues that, together, imply our direction of inquiry in Part IV—the shape of a future libertarian economy. Those issues were: the extent to which economic centralization, large firm size, capital- and skill-intensive production methods, and so forth, have been promoted by state intervention in the market; the ways in which potentially decentralizing and liberatory forms of organization have been distorted by the state capitalist framework of the economy; and the assortment of input and other crises that are tending toward the exhaustion and collapse of that state capitalist framework.

So what do we propose to replace the present state capitalist system with? And how do we intend to get there?

To a large extent, the alternative can be defined in negative terms. If state intervention currently promotes economic centralization and hierarchy, we can expect a free market to promote a decentralized and distributively owned economy of small-scale production for local use.

In the following part of the book, I will attempt to sketch the basic building blocks, or suggest a contrasting set of rules, for organizing society organized along genuinely free market lines: with no special privileges guaranteeing monopoly returns to land or capital, or protecting favored firms from competition, and no subsidies externalizing the inefficiencies of particular forms of production on others. The central organizing principles of such a free market economy are non-coercive, voluntary interaction, and what the individualist anarchists called the cost principle.

Those building blocks are already in existence, but distorted by the existing state capitalist framework. Earlier in this chapter, I suggested that the "revolutionary" ideas of Peters and other management gurus, although ideally suited to a genuinely libertarian economic order, had been distorted by implementation within a statist framework, and served only to give corporate power a new lease on life.

The decentralist production technologies we are about to consider, likewise, are ideally suited to a fundamentally different kind of society, but have so far been integrated into the framework of mass production industry. Lewis Mumford argued that the neotechnic technologies developed since the late nineteenth century on, based on the decentraliing potential of small-scale electrically powered machinery, have not been used to their full potential as the basis for a new kind of economy; they have, rather, been incorporated into a paleotechnic framework. He observed that neotechnic had not "displaced the older regime" with "speed and decisiveness," and had not yet "developed its own form and organization."

> Emerging from the paleotechnic order, the neotechnic institutions have nevertheless in many cases compromised with it, given way before it, lost their identity by reason of the weight of vested interests that continued to support the obsolete instruments and the anti-social aims of the middle industrial era. *Paleotechnic ideals still largely dominate the industry and the politics of the Western World . . . .* To the extent that neotechnic industry has failed to transform the coal-and-iron complex, to the extent that it has failed to secure an adequate foundation for its humaner technology in the community as a whole, to the extent that it has lent its heightened powers to the miner, the financier, the militarist, the possibilities of disruption and chaos have increased.[1]
>
> The new machines followed, not their own pattern, but the pattern laid down by previous economic and technical structures.[2]
>
> We have merely used our new machines and energies to further processes which were begun under the auspices of capitalist and military enterprise: we have not yet util-

---

1. Lewis Mumford. *Technics and Civilization* (New York: Harcourt, Brace, and Company, 1934), pp. 212-13.

2. *Ibid.*, p. 236.

ized them to conquer these forms of enterprise and subdue them to more vital and humane purposes . . . .

Not alone have the older forms of technics served to constrain the development of the neotechnic economy: but the new inventions and devices have been frequently used to maintain, renew, stabilize the structure of the old social order . . . .[1]

This also sums up the actual use so far of management theory fads like "self-directed work teams," etc.

The present pseudomorph is, socially and technically, third-rate. It has only a fraction of the efficiency that the neotechnic civilization as a whole may possess, provided it finally produces its own institutional forms and controls and directions and patterns. At present, instead of finding these forms, we have applied our skill and invention in such a manner as to give a fresh lease of life to many of the obsolete capitalist and militarist institutions of the older period. Paleotechnic purposes with neotechnic means: that is the most obvious characteristic of the present order.[2]

Mumford cited Spengler's idea of the "cultural pseudomorph" to illustrate the process:

. . . in geology . . . a rock may retain its structure after certain elements have been leached out of it and been replaced by an entirely different kind of material. Since the apparent structure of the old rock remains, the new product is called a pseudomorph. A similar metamorphosis is possible in culture: new forces, activities, institutions, instead of crystallizing independently into their own appropriate forms, may creep into the structure of an existing civilization . . . . As a civilization, we have not yet entered the neotechnic phase . . . . [W]e are still living, in Matthew Arnold's words, between two worlds, one dead, the other powerless to be born.[3]

But the second, current stage of the pseudomorph is much weaker, and shows signs of its final downfall. In the first stage, as Mumford observed, neotechnic methods (the integration of general-purpose electrical machinery into local craft production as envisioned by Kropotkin and Borsodi) have were integrated into a mass-production framework fundamentally opposed to the the technology's real potential. But this stage reached its limit by the 1970s. In the second stage, mass production on the Taylor-Sloan model is being replaced by flexible, networked production with general-purpose machinery, with the production process organized along lines much closer to the neotechnic ideal. But the neotechnic, even though it has finally begun to emerge as the basis of a new, coherent production model governed by its own laws, is still distorted by the pseudomorph in a weaker form: the persistence of the corporate framework of marketing, finance and "intellectual property."

So long as the state successfully manages to prop up the centralized corporate economic order, libertarian and decentralist technologies and organizational forms will be incorporated into the old corporate framework. As the system approaches its limits of sustainability, those elements become increasingly destabilizing forces within the present system, and prefigure the successor system. When the system finally reaches that limit, those elements will (to paraphrase Marx) break out of their state capitalist integument and become the building blocks of a fundamentally different society. We are, in short, building the foundations of the new society within the shell of the old.

A great deal of practice that is currently limited to cranky homesteaders and intentional communities, when the distorting effects of state policy are removed and the costs of waste and centralization are fully felt, will become not only feasible but a pressing need in the rest of society. Consider, for example, Paul and Percival Goodman's discussion of the

1. *Ibid.*, p. 266.
2. *Ibid.* p. 267.
3. *Ibid.*, p. 265.

small-scale and diversified production in the kibbutzim in *Communitas*, or the illustrations of independent settlements in *Radical Technology*. The material and economic basis for self-sufficiency in these communities is applicable to any similarly-sized community (as shown by the illustrated plans for adapting existing urban row-houses, also in *Radical Technology*), even if the community chose less communal social arrangements. And in a society where centralization was no longer subsidized, these technologies would cease to be relegated to self-ghettoized communes, and be diffused to the city flatblocks and suburban cul-de-sacs. The market pressures to conservation and small-scale production would dissolve the boundaries between the intentional community and the rest of society.

APPENDIX
THE MILITARY ORIGINS OF QUALITY CONTROL

As a matter of historical interest, industrial quality control is yet another example of industrial practices adopted largely under military influence. We already saw, in Chapter Three, references to David Noble's historical work on the role of the state in creating the military-university-industrial-R&D complex, on automated control systems as an offshoot of military technology, and on the central role of military R&D in the development of the modern electronics industry. Industrial quality control falls into the same category.

In "The Military Origins of Quality Control,"[1] Eric Husman starts with the historical background on the origins of many of the organizing principles of the factory itself in the military hierarchy, and more specifically of standardized production in military industry. The principle of interchangeable parts, for example, started with the Napoleonic army's requirements for arms producers, and was transplanted to American industry by Eli Whitney (it was not successfully implemented by Whitney himself, but in the 1820s by a machinist named John Hall).

> Drawing on the work of his predecessors, especially Simeon North and his use of a master model, Hall worked out a system of gauges and jigs or "rational fixtures". The real trick was to keep close watch on those gauges to make sure they are still in specification or tolerance. We can see in this the basic science of statistical quality control, the science of figuring out how much error is acceptable.

It was also the direct ancestor of Henry Ford's mass production system.

But for our purposes, Husman's most important material begins with the military origins of the modern form of statistical Quality Control in the 1930s and of continuous improvement in WWII, and the adoption of both postwar Japan.

> The other side of this story begins when W. Edwards Deming learned of statistical process control from Walter Shewhart. After applying the methods to the 1940 census, Deming was brought to Japan by Gen. Douglass Macarthur's Japanese Occupational Force to help with the 1951 census. While there, he was invited to teach statistical process control methods to the war torn economy there. What is little appreciated, however, is that Macarthur also had access to legions of instructors from the Training Within Industry (TWI) service to help teach modern methods to the Japanese.
>
> TWI was a program created by the War Manpower Commission of the War Department for the purpose of helping manufacturers cope with the fact that they were being asked to ramp up production at the same time many of their employees were being enlisted or drafted into the Armed Forces. TWI consisted of 4 programs: Job Instruction, Job Methods, Job Relations (and another version of this for union officials), and Program Development. Together, these taught what would be recognizable today as standard work and continuous improvement or kaizen. That the Japanese programs brought back into vogue in the US had an American origin is not well known, but also beyond dispute. Maazaki Isai says in *Kaizen: The Key to Japan's Competitive Success*, "It is well known that the initial concepts of statistical quality control and its managerial implications were brought to Japan by such pioneers as Deming and Juran in the postwar years. Less well known is the fact that the suggestion system was brought to Japan about the same time by TWI (Training Within Industries [sic]) and the U. S. Air Force. In addition, many Japanese executives who visited the United States right after the war learned about the suggestion system and started it at their companies." In the intro to Donald Dinero's *Training Within Industry: The Foundation of Lean*, John Shook writes about a time when he was working for Toyota when he "protested to my Japanese colleague, declaring that the

---

1. Eric Husman, "The Military Origins of Quality Control," Grim Reader, September 4, 2006 <http://www.zianet.com/ehusman/weblog/2006/09/military-origins-of-quality-control.html>.

program as configured just wouldn't do and required radical revision before being unleashed on the NUMMI workforce." His colleague, Toyota Master Trainer Iaso Kato, "stormed out and fetched from a back room file a yellowed, dog-eared, coffee-stained copy of the English-language original training manual, just as he had received it . . . . To my absolute amazement, the program that Toyota was going to great expense (including retranslating from Japanese to English) to "transfer" to NUMMI was exactly what the Americans had taught the Japanese decades earlier. Of course, it was JI, the Job Instruction module of TWI. Toyota still used it in 1984 and continues to use it today. . . ." These same points are made in Jim Huntzinger's article, "The Roots of Lean; Training Within Industry: The Origin of Kaizen ". To bring it full circle, the American Society for Quality says that the term "Total Quality Management" was first used by the U.S. Naval Air Systems Command around 1984 "to describe its Japanese-style management approach to quality improvement."

As for ISO 9000, it had its origins in the U.S. Army's standardization requirements which, via NATO, influenced European industry:

> The final promised tale is that of the evolution of Army quality specification MIL-Q-9858 (1958). This standard was soon adopted by NATO as AQAP-1 (1969). That in turn was adopted by the British Standards Institute as BS 5750 in 1979, which in turn became the basis of the original ISO 9000 standard in 1987. Thus we have a direct line of descendancy from an American military standard to a protectionist European an international industrial standard in about 30 years. From my understanding, it is just about impossible to fail a certification inspection because they are done by for-profit consultants. As a result, the automotive industry has established their own variant, QS 9000, because they need actual standardization and not lots of paperwork and paper tiger certifications.

ISO 9000, in other words, seems to be a management gimmick *deliberately designed* for the sake of lip service. (Perhaps not coincidentally, it is one of the many abortive ventures preserved in the *Continuous Process Improvement* handbook at the hospital where I work, along with CQI, reengineering, Six Sigma, and generic Kwality jargon from no specified system.)

Interestingly, Juran claims that published statements of company quality policy were rare until the 1950s, and occurred mainly in firms engaged in government contracting, in response to "requirements by government agencies that their contractors prepare written manuals for review and approval."[1] In Arkansas, and probably many other states, it is a statutory requirement that every department have a quality improvement committee in place (in addition to being a JCAHO requirement).

"quasibill," another astute commenter at my blog with considerable direct experience with the idiocy of management in the corporate world, confirmed Husman's analysis:

> Every single management consultant we had at my old company was ex-military or ex-military contractor. In fact, when we switched to project teams (with much fanfare and investment), we brought in a guy from a big military contractor to "implement" the teams.

---

1. J.M. Juran, *Juran's Quality Control Handbook*, 5.2.

Part Four
Conjectures on Decentralist
Free Market Alternatives

11

The Abolition of Privilege

A. RECIPROCITY

The norm of reciprocity seems to be very deeply and universally ingrained in human nature.[1] Alvin Gouldner identifies the universal concept of exploitation with deviation from reciprocity. Human relations normally involve the mutual conferring of benefits, with both parties participating in a relationship because they see them as beneficial. Exploitation results from the intrusion of power relations, so that the party with superior power is able to derive a lopsided benefit from the relationship, receiving benefits from the other party while providing a smaller quantity of benefits in return. Exploitation is unequal exchange resulting from an inequality of power. Gouldner even suggests "reciprocity imbalance" as a less emotionally charged alternative to "exploitation."[2]

Reciprocity was at the heart of the medieval idea of the just price. And contrary to condescending dismissals by modern economists who treat it as a quaint notion akin to the number of angels on the head of a pin, in fact the just price was rooted in a common sense understanding of human nature. Just price was based on the principle of reciprocity underpinning the popular understanding of equity in exchange. As Aquinas explained,

> . . . . buying and selling seems to have been entered into for the common advantage of both parties, since, indeed, one lacks what the other has, and the reverse . . . . But what is entered into for common advantage ought not to be more burdensome to one party concerned than to the other. Therefore an agreement ought to be arranged between them in accordance with an equality of advantage.[3]

"Just price," as conceived by Church authorities, was based on reciprocity of cost and effort, with cost of production including a remuneration for labor consistent with one's station. Albertus Magnus identified equality of value with "equal amounts of labour and expense" in production, and Aquinas adopted this doctrine without alteration.[4]

> . . . . No man must ask more than the price fixed, either by public authorities, or, failing that, by common estimation. True, prices even so will vary with scarcity, for, with all their rigor, theologians are not so impracticable as to rule out the effect of changing supplies. But they will not vary with individual necessity or individual opportunity. The bugbear is the man who uses, or even creates, a temporary shortage . . . .

1. See, for example, Alvin Gouldner, "The Norm of Reciprocity," *American Sociological Review,*" 25 (May 1961): 161-179. See also Michael Shermer's extensive discussions of the evolutionary roots of reciprocity, in *The Mind of the Market: Compassionate Apes, Competitive Humans, and Other Tales from Evolutionary Economics* (New York: Henry Holt and Company, 2008).

2. Gouldner, pp. 165-167.

3. Hannah Robie Sewall, *The Theory of Value Before Adam Smith. Publications of the American Economic Association,* vol. II, no. 3 (August, 1901), p. 14.

4. Rudolf Kaulla, *Theory of the Just Price: A Historical and Critical Study of the Problem of Economic Value.* Translated by Robert D. Hogg (London: George Allen and Unwin Ltd, 1940), pp. 37-38.

. . . . The dominant conception of Aquinas [was] that prices, though they will vary with the varying conditions of different markets, should correspond with the labor and costs of the producer, as the proper basis of the *communis estimatio* . . . .[1]

The basis of the just price was also transparent, tending as it did to coincide with a community's "common estimation" of a reasonable price to recoup production cost and make a living, and reflecting the common understanding of justice in exchange in a society where, as Ronald Meek argued, commodity exchange between self-employed producers predominated:

. . . [F]or the major part of the period of commodity production as a whole, *supply prices* have . . . been directly or indirectly determined by "values" in Marx's sense. And these supply prices are by no means hypothetical: for most of the period of commodity production they have been firmly rooted in the consciousness of the producers them- selves. Even in primitive societies one can see the beginnings of the idea that the ex- change of commodities "at their values" in the Marxian sense is "the rational way, the natural law of their equilibrium". In quite a few cases, apparently, the prices asked and received for commodities in primitive markets are based on production costs. The intro- duction of money, which "materially simplifies the determination of equivalence", and the gradual extension of commodity production and exchange within the community, contribute substantially to the growth of this idea in the consciousness of the producers. After a while, the producers of commodities come quite naturally to think of the actual price they happen to receive for their commodity in terms of the extent to which this price deviates from the supply price—i.e., roughly, from the *value* of the commodity in Marx's sense. The value of the commodity, although the market price may not often "tend" to conform to it at any particular stage of development owing to the existence of certain specific forms of monopoly, state interference, etc., characteristic of that stage, is regarded by the producers themselves as a sort of basis from which the deviations caused by these factors may legitimately be measured.

The idea that the exchange of commodities "at their values" represents the "natu- ral" way of exchanging them was of course often expressed in ethical terms . . . . But ideas as to what constitutes a "fair" exchange come into men's minds in the first in- stance from earth and not from heaven. When the small capitalist who is faced with the competition of a powerful monopolist says that he has the right to receive a "fair" profit on his capital, or when the peasant who exchanges his produce for that of a guildsman on disadvantageous terms says that he has a right to receive a "fair" return for his labour, the standard of "fairness" erected by each of the complainants actually has reference to the way in which exchanges *would in fact be conducted in the real world* if the particular form of monopoly to which he is objecting did not exist. In pre-capitalist times, there must always have been some commodities which were exchanged more or less at their values, and some times and localities in which deviations of price from value were rela- tively small, so that the "natural" method of exchanging commodities could actually be seen in operation. For obvious reasons, this "natural" method was regarded as the only really "fair" one. Thus the persistence of the concept of a "just price" throughout the major part of the precapitalist period . . .[2]

This suggests that there was a great deal of overlap between the medieval conception of the just price and the "natural price" of the political economists (the latter being the normal value toward which the prices of reproducible goods gravitate "in a regime of free

1. R. H. Tawney, *Religion and the Rise of Capitalism* (New York: Mentor Books, 1926, 1954), p. 42.

2. Ronald L. Meek, *Studies in the Labor Theory of Value* (New York and London: Monthly Review Press, 1956), pp. 294-296. (As we shall see in the next section, the medieval concept of usury was in fact closely associated with the idea of unequal exchange resulting from extra-econo- mic power, in exactly the way Meek describes here.)

competition"). The common estimation of the "just price" was based on "the prices actu-ally paid over a period of time when there was no disturbing cause."[1]

And as Meek also suggested, there was good reason for that overlap: both conceptions are rooted in the same common-sense understanding of human nature. This understanding underlay Adam Smith's idea of a "natural value" toward which price normally fluctuated in a competitive market, exemplified by his famous illustration of the exchange of deer and beaver. As James Buchanan argued, it was based on an implicit understanding of man as a rational utility-maximizer.

> Even in so simple a model, why should relative costs determine normal exchange values? They do so because hunters are assumed to be rational utility-maximizing indi-viduals *and* because the positively valued "goods" and the negatively valued "bads" in their utility functions can be identified. If, for any reason, exchange values should settle in some ratio different from that of cost values, behavior will be modified. If the individ-ual hunter knows that he is able, on an outlay of one day's labor, to kill two deer or one beaver, he will not choose to kill deer if the price of a beaver is three deer, even should he be a demander or final purchaser of deer alone. He can "produce" deer more cheaply through exchange under these circumstances . . . . Since all hunters can be expected to behave in the same way, no deer will be produced until and unless the expected ex-change value returns to equality with the cost ratio. Any divergence between *expected* ex-change value and *expected* cost value in this model would reflect irrational behavior on the part of the hunters.
>
> . . . Labor time, the standard for measurement, is the common denominator in which the opportunity costs are computed.[2]

When the market is free from obstructions and privilege, the tendency is for embod-ied effort to equalize itself through the free movement of labor into those occupations that command the highest returns in terms of others' labor—the same mechanism described by Buchanan. That is, by what Smith and his radical disciple Hodgskin called "the higgling of the market":

> *Smith*: It is often difficult to ascertain the proportion between two different quanti-ties of labour. The time spent in two different sorts of work will not always alone deter-mine this proportion. The different degrees of hardship endured, and of ingenuity exer-cised, must likewise be taken into account. There may be more labour in an hour's hard work than in two hour's easy business; or in an hour's application to a trade which it cost ten years' labour to learn, than in a month's industry at an ordinary and obvious employment. But it is not easy to find any accurate measure either of hardship or inge-nuity. In exchanging, indeed, the different productions of different sorts of labour for one another, some allowance is commonly made for both. It is adjusted, however, not by any accurate measure, but by the higgling and bargaining of the market, according to that sort of rough equality which, though not exact, is sufficient to carry on the business of common life.[3]
>
> *Hodgskin*: . . . . There is no principle or rule, as far as I know, for dividing the pro-duce of joint labour among the different individuals who concur in production, but the judgment of the individuals themselves . . . .

1. W. Cunningham, *The Growth of English Industry and Commerce*. Vol. 1 (The Early Middle Ages) . Fourth Edition (Cambridge: Cambridge University Press, 1905), p. 253.

2. James Buchanan, *Cost and Choice: An Inquiry in Economic Theory*, vol. 6 of *Collected Works* (Indianapolis: Liberty Fund, 1999) 4.

3. Adam Smith, *An Inquiry Into the Nature and Causes of the Wealth of Nations* (Chicago, Lon-don, Toronto: Encyclopedia Britannica, Inc., 1952), p. 13.

.... If all kinds of labour were perfectly free ..., there would be no difficulty on this point, and the wages of individual labour would be justly settled by what Dr Smith calls the "higgling of the market."[1]

Franz Oppenheimer expounded, at greater length, on the actual process by which this would be done: under the inducements of a truly free labor market, labor would distribute itself among employments until incomes became "equal"—in our terms, equal in relation to given quantities of subjectively perceived effort.[2] Oppenheimer, in "A Post-Mortem on Cambridge Economics," quoted with approval Adam Smith's claim that "[t]he whole of the advantages and disadvantages of the different employments of labour and stock must, in the same neighbourhood, be either perfectly equal or continually tending to equality." He also quoted, with like approval, Johann Henirich von Thuenen's posited equilibrium at which "labor of equal quality is equally rewarded in all branches of production . . . ."[3]

Reciprocity (or mutuality, or commutative justice) was central to Proudhon's economic thought. In a passage in Volume II of *System of Economical Contradictions* (with a phrase at the end that ought to be good for a yelp from the Randroids), he wrote

> The theory of *mutuality*, or *mutuum*, that is to say exchange in kind, of which the simplest form is the loan for consumption, where the collective body is concerned, is the synthesis of the notions of private property and collective ownership. This synthesis is as old as its constituent parts since it merely means that society is returning through a maze of inventions and systems, to its primitive practices as a result of a six-thousand-year-long meditation on the fundamental proposition that A=A.[4]

And in *Political Capacity of the Working Class*:

> .... [The mutualist principle] is service for service, product for product, loan for loan, insurance for insurance, credit for credit, security for security, guarantee for guarantee. It is the ancient law of retaliation, *an eye for an eye, a tooth for a tooth, a life for a life*, as it were turned upside down and transferred from criminal law and the vile practices of the vendetta to economic law, to the tasks of labor and to the good offices of free fraternity. On it depend all the mutualist institutions: mutual insurance, mutual credit, mutual aid, mutual education; reciprocal guarantees of openings, exchanges and labor for good quality and fairly priced goods, etc.[5]

The "synthesis . . . of private property and collective ownership" anticipates Tucker's argument that market competition, in the absence of privilege and artificial scarcity, causes the benefits of private property to be socialized. As Stephen Pearl Andrews commented:

> One side of the truth of the subject, the individualistic side, Warren, more fortunate than Proudhon, did discover and formulate; the other side, the opposite and counterparting side, is communism, best represented as yet, on any large scale, by the Oneida Perfection-

---

1. Thomas Hodgskin, *Labour Defended Against the Claims of Capital* (New York: Augustus M. Kelley, 1963 (1823)), pp. 83–86.

2. Eduard Heimann, "Franz Oppenheimer's Economic Ideas," *Social Research* (February 1949), p. 34.

3. Franz Oppenheimer, "A Post Mortem on Cambridge Economics (Part I)," *The American Journal of Economics and Sociology* 1942/43 pp. 373–374.

4. *System of Economical Contradictions*, vol. II, quoted in Stewart Edwards, ed., *Selected Writings of P.J. Proudhon* (Garden City, N.Y.: Anchor Books, 1969), pp. 57–59. Edwards mistakenly attributes it to the first volume; but it is, in fact, from the second. Although vol. II was never translated in its entirety, the passage appeared, in English translation, in *The Spirit of the Age* I, 7 (August 18, 1849). The translation here is a different one; like most of the material in Edwards' collection, it was translated by Elizabeth Frazer. The version that appeared in *Spirit of the Age*, in its entirety, can be found at Shawn Wilbur's *In the Libertarian Labyrinth* archive site (I'm indebted for his help in clearing up the source of the material) <http://libertarian-labyrinth.blogspot.com/2007/ 03/proudhon-coming-era-of-mutualism.html>.

5. *Political Capacity of the Working Class*, in Edwards, ed., pp. 59–60.

ists. These two opposite ideas and types of life are to be reconciled and united, not merely despite of their appositeness, but *because of their oppositeness*. Everything that approximates perfection is made up, primarily, of two opposite factors.[1]

The perfect expression of mutuality was the contract between equals, both "synallagmatic" (bilateral) and "commutative" (reciprocal, based on an exchange of equal values).[2]

For Proudhon, unequal exchange was the defining characteristic of exploitation:

> . . . If . . . the tailor, for rendering the value of a day's work, consumes ten times the product of the day's work of the weaver, it is as if the weaver gave ten days of his life for one day of the tailor's. This is exactly what happens when a peasant pays twelve francs to a lawyer for a document which it takes him an hour to prepare . . . .
>
> Every error in commutative justice is an immolation of the laborer, a transfusion of the blood of one man into the body of another . . . .[3]

The principle of reciprocity is built into the normal functioning of a free market. When exchange is free and uncoerced, it is impossible for one party to benefit at another's expense. The ratio at goods and services are exchanged will move toward a value that reflects the respective costs of the parties, including the disutility of their labor. If one party is able to find another exchange that provides a higher degree of utility, he will choose it in preference to the lesser utility. And if one party receives a producer surplus or rent above his costs, and market entry is free from barriers, others will find it profitable to offer a better deal. The normal pattern of free exchange is cost for cost, effort for effort, disutility for disutility, so that things equal out through the "higgling of the market." Or as Proudhon described it,

> Whoever says commerce says exchange of equal values, for if the values are not equal and the injured party perceives it, he will not consent to the exchange, and there will be no commerce.[4]
>
> . . . . What characterizes the contract is the agreement for equal exchange; and it is by virtue of this agreement that liberty and well-being increase; while by the establishment of authority, both of these necessarily diminish . . . .
>
> Between contracting parties there is necessarily for each one a real personal interest; it implies that a man bargains with the aim of securing his liberty and the loss of revenue at the same time, without any possible loss. Between governing and governed, on the contrary, no matter how the system of representation or of delegation of the governmental function is arranged, there is *necessarily* alienation of a part of the liberty and of the means of the citizen . . . .
>
> The contract therefore is essentially reciprocal: it imposes no obligation upon the parties, except that which results from their personal promise of reciprocal delivery . . . .
>
> The social contract should increase the well-being and liberty of every citizen.—If any one-sided conditions should slip in; if one part of the citizens should find themselves, by the contract, subordinated or exploited by the others, it would no longer be a contract; it would be a fraud, against which annulment might at any time be invoked justly.[5]

1. Stephen Pearl Andrews, "Proudhon and His Translator," *The Index*, June 22, 1876. Formatted by Shawn Wilbur at *Libertarian Labyrinth* <http://libertarian-labyrinth.org/theindex/1876-tucker-andrews.pdf>.

2. Proudhon, *The Principle of Federation*. Translated by Richard Vernon (Toronto, Buffalo, London: University of Toronto Press, 1979), p. 36.

3. Pierre-Joseph Proudhon, *System of Economical Contradictions, or, The Philosophy of Misery*, translated by Benjamin R. Tucker (Boston: Benjamin R. Tucker, 1888), p. 123.

4. Pierre-Joseph Proudhon, *What is Property?* Edited and translated by Donald R. Kelley and Bonnie G. Smith (Cambridge and New York: Cambridge University Press, 1994), p. 103.

5. Pierre-Joseph Proudhon, *General Idea of the Revolution in the Nineteenth Century*. Trans. by John Beverley Robinson (New York: Haskell House Publishers, Inc., 1923, 1969), pp. 113-114.

. . . . For no one has a right to impose his own merchandise upon another: the sole judge of utility, or in other words the want, is the buyer . . . . Take away reciprocal liberty, and exchange is no longer the expression of industrial solidarity: it is robbery.[1]

Coercive intervention, on the other hand, forces one party to a contract to accept a lower-ranking preference than he otherwise would, in order to provide the other party with his preference at a lower cost. Murray Rothbard described the principle in *Man, Economy, and State*. Although he wrote of slavery in particular, his description applied to all forms of compulsory exchange or coercive state intervention:

. . . . In this form of compulsory exchange . . . only the ruler benefits from the exchange, since he is the only one who makes it of his own free choice. Since he must impose the threat of violence in order to induce the subject to make the exchange, it is clear that the latter loses by the exchange. The master uses the subject as a factor of production for his own profit at the latter's expense, and this hegemonic relationship may be called *exploitation*. Under hegemonic exchange, the ruler exploits the subject for the ruler's benefit.[2]

. . . . [W]hen the society is free and there is no intervention, everyone will always act in the way that he believes will maximize his utility, i.e., will raise him to the highest possible position on his value scale. In short, everyone's utility *ex ante* will be "maximized" . . . . Any exchange on the free market, indeed any action in the free society, occurs because it is expected to benefit each party concerned. If we may use the term "society" to depict the pattern, the array, of all individual exchanges, then we may say that the free market maximizes social utility, since everyone gains in utility from his free actions.

Coercive intervention, on the other hand, signifies *per se* that the individual or individuals coerced *would not have voluntarily done what they are now being forced to do by the intervener* . . . . The man being coerced, therefore, *always loses in utility as a result of the intervention,* for his action has been forcibly changed by its impact . . . .

. . . In contrast to the free market, therefore, all cases of intervention supply one set of men with gains *at the expense* of another set . . . .

. . . . Voluntary exchanges, in any given period, will increase the utility of everyone and will therefore maximize social utility.[3]

B. Privilege and Inequality

In the real world, the law of reciprocity is often honored in the breach; coercive intervention in the market, as we saw in the previous section, violates the principle of reciprocity and in so doing benefits some at the expense of others. We also see a high degree of inequality. As R. A. Wilson suggested, the two phenomena just might be related:

Privilege implies exclusion from privilege, just as advantage implies disadvantage . . . . "In the same mathematically reciprocal way, profit implies loss. If you and I exchange equal goods, that is trade: neither of us profits and neither of us loses. But if we exchange unequal goods, one of us profits and the other loses. Mathematically. Certainly. Now, such mathematically unequal exchanges will always occur because some traders will be shrewder than others. But in total freedom— in anarchy— such unequal exchanges will be sporadic and irregular. A phenomenon of unpredictable periodicity, mathematically speaking. Now look about you, professor— raise your nose from your great books and survey the actual world as it is— and you will not observe such unpredictable functions. You will observe, instead, a mathematically smooth function, a steady profit accruing to one group and an equally steady loss accumulating for all others. Why is this, professor? Because the system is not free or random, any mathematician would tell you a priori . . . . When A meets B in the marketplace, they do not bargain as equals. A bargains from

1. Proudhon, *System of Economical Contradictions*, pp. 80-81.
2. Murray Rothbard, *Man, Economy, and State: A Treatise on Economic Principles* (Auburn University, Alabama: Ludwig von Mises Institute, 1962, 1970, 1993), p. 71.
3. *Ibid.*, pp. 768-770.

a position of privilege; hence, he always profits and B always loses. There is no more Free Market here than there is on the other side of the Iron Curtain . . . .[1]

Anna Morgenstern, of *Tranarchy* blog, described the phenomenon in terms quite similar to Wilson's:

> Once a pocket of unmet demand is discovered, under anarchy, capital will flow in that direction and will arbitrage out the profit opportunity pretty rapidly.
>
> So while there will always be profit making going on somewhere in the economy, it will never consistently flow to the same people. If it does, that is prima facie evidence of violent intervention or fraud, IMO.
>
> This is just one reason why I don't think anarchy will have a large inequality of wealth.[2]

Thus the so-called "Matthew Effect": "To him that hath, more shall be given." In somewhat more scientific terms, it is sometimes referred to as "Pareto's law."

> It is well known that wealth is shared out unfairly. "People on the whole have normally distributed attributes, talents and motivations, yet we finish up with wealth distributions that are much more unequal than that," says Robin Marris, emeritus professor of economics at Birkbeck, University of London . . . .
>
> In 1897, a Paris-born engineer named Vilfredo Pareto showed that the distribution of wealth in Europe followed a simple power-law pattern, which essentially meant that the extremely rich hogged most of a nation's wealth (*New Scientist* print edition, 19 August 2000). Economists later realised that this law applied to just the very rich, and not necessarily to how wealth was distributed among the rest.
>
> Now it seems that while the rich have Pareto's law to thank, the vast majority of people are governed by a completely different law. Physicist Victor Yakovenko of the University of Maryland in College Park, US, and his colleagues analysed income data from the US Internal Revenue Service from 1983 to 2001.
>
> They found that while the income distribution among the super-wealthy—about 3% of the population—does follow Pareto's law, incomes for the remaining 97% fitted a different curve—one that also describes the spread of energies of atoms in a gas . . .[3]

The reason, as we saw at the close of the previous section, is that privilege—coercion—creates a zero-sum situation in which one party benefits at the expense of the other. There is a symmetrical relationship between one party's gain and the other party's loss.

As Ricardo described the relationship of landlords to capitalists and laborers, "The dealings between the landlord and the public are not like dealings in trade, whereby both the seller and the buyer may equally be said to gain, but the loss is wholly on one side, and the gain wholly on the other . . . ."[4]

A monopoly creates artificial scarcity, so that the holder of the monopoly privilege benefits at the expense of the public who, forced to pay for something that is not naturally scarce, are absolute losers in the transaction. Stephen Pearl Andrews divided society into opposing classes of net exploiters and net exploited:

> The whole community may be divided . . . into those who receive more than equivalents for their labor and those who receive less than equivalents . . . .
>
> It is clear, if this exchange is not equal, if one party gives more of his own labor . . . than he *gets* of the labor of the other, . . . that he is oppressed, and becomes so far as this

1. Robert Shea and Robert Anton Wilson, *The Illuminatus! Trilogy* (New York: Dell Publishing, 1975), pp. 553-554.

2. Comment under Kevin Carson, "Chapter Seven Draft," *Mutualist Blog: Free Market Anti-Capitalism*, November 12, 2007 <http://mutualist.blogspot.com/2007/11/chapter-seven-draft.html>.

3. Jenny Hogan, "Why it's hard to share the wealth," *New Scientist*, March 12, 2005. <http://www.newscientist.com/article.ns?id=dn7107>.

4. David Ricardo, *The Principles of Political Economy and Taxation*. Everyman's Library edition (London: J. M. Dent & Sons, Ltd, 1965), p. 225.

inequality goes, the slave or subject of the other. He has, just so far, to expend his labor, not for his own benefit, but for the benefit of another.[1]

Benjamin Tucker, who inherited this tradition, treated state intervention as a zero-sum game:

> To-day (pardon the paradox!) society is fundamentally anti-social. The whole so-called social fabric rests on privilege and power, and is disordered and strained in every direction by the inequalities that necessarily result therefrom. The welfare of each, instead of contributing to that of all, as it naturally should and would, almost invariably detracts from that of all. Wealth is made by legal privilege a hook with which to filch from labor's pockets. Every man who gets rich thereby makes his neighbor poor. The better off one is, the worse off the rest are. As Ruskin says, every grain of calculated Increment to the rich is balanced by its mathematical equivalent of Decrement to the poor. The Laborer's Deficit is precisely equal to the Capitalist's Efficit.[2]

Or as Big Bill Haywood said, for every man who gets a dollar he didn't work for, there's another man who worked for a dollar he didn't get.

Perhaps the best summary of the nature of privilege is that of William Batchelder Greene: "It is right that all persons should be equal before the law; but when we have established equality before the law, our work is but half done. We ought to have EQUAL LAWS also. Of what avail is it that we are all equal before the law, if the law is itself unequal."[3]

The social and organizational pathologies we examined in the second and third parts of this book all result from coercive interference with the natural expression of the principle of reciprocity in voluntary market exchange. Coercion benefits one party at the other's expense by forcing the other to accept a lesser utility. It creates an externality by forcing one party to bear the other's costs. When exchange is uncoerced, the outcome is Pareto optimal. Every party enters the exchange because it offers the highest utility of all available alternatives—and there is no artificial limitation on the availability of alternatives. Government, on the other hand, is in the *business* of limiting alternatives.

This limitation of alternatives by government coercion, in order that owners of the remaining alternatives may collect rent on them, is what Franz Oppenheimer meant by defining privilege as the "political means" to wealth ("unrequited appropriation of the labor of others"), as opposed to the "economic means" ("one's own labor and the equivalent exchange of one's own labor for the labor of others").[4] The political means is to collect tribute through artificial scarcity: political action to limit the available alternatives (especially through the political appropriation of land).

Oppenheimer approved, conditionally, the contention of "bourgeois economics" that the division of society into an exploited and exploiting class took place only after all land had been appropriated and vacant land was no longer freely available for homesteading:

> All teachers of natural law, etc., have unanimously declared that the differentiation into income-receiving classes and propertyless classes can only take place when all fertile lands have been occupied. For so long as man has ample opportunity to take up unoccupied land, "no one," says Turgot, "would think of entering the service of another . . . ."[5]

1. Stephen Pearl Andrews, *Science of Society*, Part II, Chapter II ("Equity and the Labor Note"):54, 57. Online edition provided courtesy of the late Ken Gregg, at *CLASSical Liberalism* blog <http://classicalliberalism.blogspot.com/2006/04/science-of-society-no_10.html>.

2. Benjamin R. Tucker, "Socialism: What it Is," in Tucker, *Instead of a Book, By a Man Too Busy to Write One*. Gordon Press facsimile (New York: 1973 [1897]), pp. 361-362.

3. William Batchelder Greene, *Equality, No. 1* (1849). Online text edited by Shawn Wilbur at *Libertarian Labyrinth*. <http://libertarian-labyrinth.org/mutual/wbg-equality.html>.

4. Franz Oppenheimer, *The State*, Free Life Edition, translated by John Gitterman (San Francisco: Fox & Wilkes, 1914, 1997), p. 14.

5. Oppehneimer, *The State*, p. 6.

... This equality remained unshaken as long as there was still free land available for everyone who wanted it; for, evidently, in Turgot's phrase, "No well man will be willing to work for another, as long as he can take for himself as much land as he wants to cultivate."[1]

Where he differed was in his understanding of *how* the land had come to be completely appropriated:

> Now it is true that the class State can only arise where all fertile acreage has been *occupied* completely; and since I have shown that even at the present time, all the ground is not occupied economically,[2] this must mean that it has been preempted politically. Since land could not have acquired "natural scarcity," the scarcity must have been "legal." This means that the land has been preempted by a ruling class against its subject class, and settlement prevented.[3]
>
> .... Nowhere in the world has the land been appropriated by small and medium free peasants, "until the holdings," as Rousseau remarked "couching one another, covered the whole country." Even in the most densely populated countries, at the present time when the population has increased beyond all former experience, many more holdings of that size could exist than the number that would be needed to provide for their whole agrarian population, family operating owners, tenants and landless laborers combined.
>
> Of course, the differentiation into classes proves that the whole land is covered by holdings. But this has not occurred only because peasants have taken up small and medium-sized farms in gradual, peaceful settlement.[4]

Rather, the land has been universally appropriated by political means: the entire supply of vacant land has been engrossed by one landed aristocracy or another, and their artificial titles used either to exclude laborers who might otherwise cultivate vacant land as an alternative to wage employment, or to collect tribute from those who have rightfully appropriated the land through cultivation. The result is that, as Mill said, "The population of each country may be considered as composed, in unequal proportions, of two distinct nations or races: the first the proprietors of the land, the latter the tillers of it."[5] Henry George, Jr., made a similar observation in *The Menace of Privilege*, contrasting the high wages and lack of either severe poverty or great riches in eighteenth century America, when "easy access to land made it a comparatively simple matter for all men to get subsistence,"[6] to the appearance of great disparities in wealth when most land had been politically appropriated in the nineteenth century.[7]

> Not that all this vast territory is settled and in use. Far from it. There are thousands upon thousands of square miles of productive, accessible land that would yield bountifully to labor .... But it is not used. It is preempted and belongs to this or that individual, who chooses to hold it, not for use, but for what it will bring its owners when the increasing

1. Oppenheimer, "A Post Mortem on Cambridge Economics (Part Two)," *The American Journal of Economics and Sociology*, vol. 2, no. 4 ((a943), p. 534.

2. In the United States, Nock observed in the 1930s, if the settlement of land had occurred "in a natural way . . . , our western frontier would not be anywhere near the Mississippi River." In Rhode Island, the most densely populated state at that time, it was possible to drive across the state on a major highway and see almost no sign of human occupancy. "All discussions of 'over-population' from Malthus down, are based on the premise of legal occupancy instead of actual occupancy, and are therefore utterly incompetent and worthless." Albert Jay Nock, *Our Enemy, the State* (Delavan, Wisc.: Hallberg Publishing Corporation, 1983), p. 67n.

3. Oppenheimer, *The State*, p. 8.

4. Oppenheimer, "A Post Mortem on Cambridge Economics (Part Two)," p. 534.

5. *Ibid.*, p. 535.

6. Henry George, Jr., *The Menace of Privilege*, Chapter One (part one), <http://www.progress.org/archive/hgjr1a.htm>; Chapter One (conclusion), <http://www.progress.org/archive/hgjr1b.htm>

7. *Ibid.*, Chapter Two (part one), <http://www.progress.org/archive/hgjr2a.htm>

population has made a greater demand for it. *The owners ask for its present use a price based upon their expectation of its value for the future.* Vast quantities of unused land can be had, but not from the Government, and free, as of yore. It is to be had only from private owners and on the payment of a price . . . .[1]

George *fils* explained the derivation of the term "privilege" as private law, or class legislation benefiting one group of individuals at the expense of another:

> Now the word "privilege" means not a natural, but an artificial condition. Even its derivation shows that. It comes from the Latin *privilegium*, meaning an ordinance in favor of a person; and *privilegium* comes from *privus*, private, and *lex* or *legem*, a law. Hence, in its essence, the word "privilege" means a private law, a special ordinance or a usage equivalent to a grant or an immunity in favor of a particular person.[2]

And the primary effect of privilege, as we have already seen, is to "empower their holders to appropriate, without compensation or adequate compensation, a large or small share of the produce of labor."[3]

Although Oppenheimer's primary focus (like that of all Georgists) was on the political appropriation of land as a form of artificial scarcity, the same principle of artificial scarcity applies to all form of privilege. The present global corporate economy, for instance, depends primarily on the enforcement of artificial scarcity by so-called "intellectual property" (although old-fashioned land theft and eviction of peasant subsistence farmers still deserves honorable mention for its role in promoting sweatshop labor and reducing the bargaining power of those engaged in it).

The general distinction between the political and economic means was developed independently by a wide range of thinkers: by Saint-Simon and Comte in France, and by Enlightenment radicals like Paine and Godwin and Ricardian socialists like Thomas Hodgskin in England, among many others.[4] Samuel Edward Konkin III made it the basis of his agorist class theory, which he erected as an alternative to Marxian class theory:

> 1. The State is the main means by which people live by plunder; the Market, in contradistinction, is the sum of human action of the productive.
>
> 2. The State, by its existence, divides society into a plundered class and a plundering class.[5]

According to R.H. Tawney, the broad concept of usury in the middle ages roughly corresponded to unequal exchange, extortion, or "taking advantage." It included "the raising of prices by a monopolist" and rack-renting of land, among other things. Although the term was not carefully defined, it generally applied to "any bargain, in which one party obviously gained more advantage than the other, and used his power to the full."[6]

For Adam Smith, as John Commons observed, the disutility of labor was the cause and regulator of value (this was also the basis, as we saw in the first section, of medieval notions of justice in exchange). Labor's disutility created value by restricting output of reproducible goods, when the worker considered the income to be too low relative to the labor-pain entailed in production. It regulated value by shifting labor from employments where income was low relative to pain to employments where it was high relative to pain, and thus equal-

---

1. *Ibid.*, Chapter Eight (part one), <http://www.progress.org/archive/hgjr8a.htm>

2. *Ibid.*, Chapter Two (part one).

3. *Ibid.*, Chapter Two (conclusion), <http://www.progress.org/archive/hgjr2b.htm>

4. This is the theme of an excellent historical survey by David M. Hart and Walter E. Grinder, "The Basic Tenets of Real Liberalism. Part IV Continued: Interventionism, Social Conflict and War," *Humane Studies Review* vol. 3 no. 1 (1986), pp. 1-7

5. Samuel Edward Konkin III, *"Cui Bono?* Introduction to Libertarian Class Theory," *New Libertarian Notes* no. 28 (December 1973), reproduced in Wally Conger, *Agorist Class Theory: A Left Libertarian Approach to Class Conflict Analysis* (Movement of the Libertarian Left, 2006).

6. Tawney, *Religion and the Rise of Capitalism* pp. 130-131.

izing pain per unit of income. This was also the basis of Smith's critique of mercantilism and other forms of privilege. Privilege resulted in an unequal distribution of labor-pain per unit of income, and imposed pain on some for the benefit of others:

> Man was condemned to labor—that was true on account of the original sin. He was compelled to lay down a portion of his ease, liberty, and happiness, in order that goods might be produced. But this should be done fairly. No individual should be compelled to suffer more than any other individual in his capacity of producing, accumulating, and exchanging use-values for the good of his fellow men.[1]

> Having identified his automatic regulator of scarcity-value with the quantity of labor-pain, Smith proceeds to inquire why it is that, upon the labor-market, the price . . . of labor does not, under existing conditions, coincide with the quantity of labor-pain delivered in exchange for the produce. All of these discrepancies we shall find to be various aspects of artificial scarcity controlled by custom, sovereignty, or other collective action, instead of regulated automatically by quantity of labor-pain. . . . Among these restrictions were exclusive privileges of corporations (guilds), long apprenticeship, understandings between competitors, free education at public expense, state regulation of wages, price fixing, tariffs, bounties levied in order to maintain a favorable balance of trade, and obstructing the free circulation of labor and stock [capital] by poor laws.

> But even if these mercantilist interferences with liberty were eliminated, there were still two other proprietary claimants, the landlords and the capitalist employers, who, even under conditions of perfect liberty, prevented the accurate proportionment between labor-pain and wages. These other two claimants, who introduced the factor of proprietary scarcity, were examples of the Common Law of Private Property. "As soon as the land of any country has all become private property, the landlords, like all other men, love to reap where they never sowed, and demand a rent even for its natural produce."[2]

Profits on capital, likewise, were regulated both by the value of the capital employed and by combination among masters to keep down wages.[3] As most of the radical classical liberals argued, much if not most nominal "private property" in land is artificial, and thus a form of artificial scarcity created by privilege. And as we shall see later, much of the value of capital results from artificial scarcity created by the state's banking laws.

Thomas Hodgskin, writing in regard to the illegitimate "property" rights of England's landed oligarchy, made the crucial distinction between natural and artificial rights of property. Natural property rights are simply "a man's right to the free use of his own mind and limbs, and to appropriate whatever he creates by his own labour . . . ."[4] Artificial rights, he said, are "the power of throwing the necessity to labour off [one's] own shoulders . . . by the appropriation of other men's produce," and "[t]he power . . . possessed by idle men to appropriate the produce of labourers . . . ."[5]

1. John R. Commons, *Institutional Economics* (New York: Macmillan, 1934), pp. 203-204. The radical Thomas Hodgskin in Great Britain, as well as some of the American individualists, were influenced by Smith in their understanding of the labor theory of value. Hodgskin, like Smith, saw labor's repugnance as the basis of its value-creating capacity. In the United States, Stephen Pearl Andrews wrote that "by cost is meant the amount of *labor* bestowed on [a good's] production, that measure being again measured by the *painfulness* or *repugnance* of the labor itself" (*Science of Society* Pt. II:20), and identified cost with "the amount of repugnance overcome." (*Ibid.*, Pt. II:79); Benjamin Tucker argued that absent monopoly there would be "no price where there is no burden . . ." And elsewhere, "Is there any just basis of price except cost? And is there anything that costs except labor or suffering (another name for labor)?" (*Instead of a Book, By a Man Too Busy to Write One*, pp. 214, 403).

2. *Ibid.*, pp. 207-208.
3. *Ibid.*, p. 208.
4. Thomas Hodgskin, *Popular Political Economy: Four Lectures Delivered at the London Mechanics' Institution* (London: Printed for Charles and William Tait, Edinburgh, 1827), pp. 236-237.
5. Hodgskin, *Popular Political Economy*, pp. 30, 237.

... [C]ertain classes, it may be said, do not labour .... The receivers of rent and profit subsist on the produce of other men's labour; so do those who live on taxes .... Social laws may compel some classes to labour for other classes, or may even give the whole annual produce to those who never labour. If we admit that the members of the government, and the ministers of the church, are labourers, ... we cannot say the same for the slave-owners of the West Indies ... : we cannot say the same for the landlords and fund holders of England, and for other similar classes. They are all subsisted and supported, supplied with all their wealth, by the labour of the slaves in the West Indies, or of the toil-worn and half-starved slave-descended labourers of Europe.[1]

Social regulations and commercial prohibitions, he said, "compel us to employ more labour than is necessary to obtain the prohibited commodity," or "to give a greater quantity of labour to obtain it than nature requires," and put the difference into the pockets of privileged classes.[2]

While Hodgskin defended the natural right of property without hesitation, he ridiculed those who wanted to "preserve ... inviolate" the "existing right of property" or to hold it "sacred against the claims of the labourer to own whatever and all which he produces."

Hodgskin's distinction between natural and artificial property rights overlaps considerably with similar distinctions made by other thinkers. Oppenheimer distinguished political appropriation of the land from economic appropriation, and Albert Jay Nock distinguished "labour-made" from "law-made" property.[3]

As our treatment of Proudhon suggests, artificial property rights in land are paradigmatic of artificial property rights in general. The same distinction in principle between natural and artificial property rights in land is made, in analogous manner, between natural and artificial property rights in all other areas. The same principle applies to patents and copyrights, business and occupational licenses, and every other form of privilege: natural property rights *reflect* scarcity, while artificial property rights *create* it; natural property rights secure the individual's right to his *own* labor-product, while artificial property rights entitle the holder to collect tribute on the labor-product of *others*; natural property rights entitle the holder to a return for his *contributions* to production, while artificial property rights entitle the holder to collect a toll for *not impeding* production.

Thus, in response to the proprietor's claim not only to have labored but to have provided employment to those otherwise without means of support, Proudhon challenged:

> You have laboured! Have you never made others labour? Why, then, have they lost in labouring for you what you have gained in not labouring for them?
> You have laboured! Very well, but let us see your creations. We will count, weigh, and measure them. It will be the judgment of Balthasar; for I swear by this balance, level, and square, that if you have appropriated another's labour in any way whatsoever, you shall restore it to the last iota.[4]

Like the children of Israel in Canaan, the proprietor reaps where he did not sow.[5]

Because of the near-universal appropriation of land, most of it vacant and unimproved land held out of use, labor's ability to create wealth for the laborer is impeded, and instead becomes a means of creating wealth for the proprietor. Artificial property rights in land give the proprietor, as a result, property rights in the labor of others. Privilege enables the holder of property rights to appropriate the productivity of nature or society for himself, and to stand in for "society" or "nature" in charging users according to their benefit—despite having done nothing to provide that benefit. The "value" of the service, i.e. the

1. Hodgskin, *Popular Political Economy*, pp. 29-30.
2. Hodgskin, *Popular Political Economy*, pp. 33-34.
3. Nock, *Our Enemy, the State*, p. 80.
4. Proudhon, *What is Property?*, p. 69.
5. *Ibid.*, p. 119.

price he is able to charge for access, depends entirely on its positive utility to the buyer; so he is able to follow the standard method of monopoly pricing and target his price to the buyer's ability to pay.

> According to Carey and Bastiat, and contrary to Ricardo and the communists and anarchists, the landlord or capitalist rendered a service to the community as much as did the laborer. The value of this service was the alternative price which the employer or laborer would be compelled to pay if he did not pay rent to the landlord, or profit and interest to the capitalist. He was better off by paying rent for superior land than he would be by going to the margin of cultivation where no rent was paid, and better off by paying profits and interest to capitalists than b working for marginal capitalists who made no profits.[1]

But Bastiat and Carey did not distinguish "productivity" and "service" from rents on artificial scarcity. For Bastiat, the landlord and capitalist contributed a "service" equivalent to the alternative cost if his land or capital were not available. The "unearned accrual of social value," in the form of improved land and technology, is provided by "society" to the laborer at far below its value to him. If the rent on land and the profit on capital are less than the utility the laborer receives from access to them compared to what his utility would be in the days before improved land and modern production technology were available, that is actually an unearned rent accruing to *labor*.

> . . . all this social accrual of value was freely available to present laborers who did not own it, and thereby "saved" them from the labor they would otherwise be compelled to perform, as individuals repeating the past history of society, in order to obtain the present necessaries and luxuries.

But for some reason the landlord and the capitalist are allowed to stand in for "society" in taking credit for the improved land and technology that make increased productivity possible. Although the laborer did not earn the increased powers of productivity, which he did not himself produce, the landlord and capitalist apparently *did*.[2] Actually Bastiat's landlord was in a position, thanks to privilege, to collect tribute for the productivity gains created by society.

Railroad apologists argued in the nineteenth century that the cost of transporting wheat by horse over dirt roads was 50 cents per ton-mile; the railroads, therefore, were doing the farmer a favor by charging only 3 cents per ton-mile, in effect giving the farmer a consumer surplus of 47 cents. But as Commons pointed out, the proper comparison is not between the cost of railroad transportation and the cost of transportation by dirt road fifty years earlier. It is between railroad transportation and the best available alternative *today*. And if the best available alternative is rendered worse than it might otherwise have been, or access to it is restricted, by the railroads' privileges and artificial property rights, then the 3 cents per mile is an unjust form of tribute.[3]

Reason magazine's Ron Bailey has updated the railroaders' argument for the 21st century. Citing a study that compared the overall economic value to consumers from increased life expectancy to the cost paid for drugs, he argued that "drug companies don't get enough money . . . for the life-saving benefits they give us . . . ."[4]

Ahem. There's a word for a firm that's able to price a good according to the consumer's benefit from it: a monopolist. One of the commenters under Bailey's post summed it up quite eloquently:

1. Commons, *Institutional Economics*, p. 114.
2. *Ibid.*, pp. 319-320.
3. *Ibid.*, pp. 317-318.
4. Bailey, "Drug Companies Don't Get Enough Money . . . ," *Reason Hit&Run* blog, February 22, 2006 <http://www.reason.com/blog/show/112727.html#012727>.

Many products generate massive "consumer surplus"—benefit to their purchasers vastly in excess of their cost—because competition among suppliers drives the cost down to near the cost of production, rather than up to the level of benefit to the purchasers.

Proudhon illustrated the same principle with regard to the landlord's alleged "service" or "contribution" to production, in merely not impeding access to land he was not working himself.

> The blacksmith who makes farming equipment for the farmer, the wheelright who makes him a cart, the mason who builds his barn, the carpenter, the basket-maker, etc., all of whom contribute to agricultural production by the tools they provide, are producers of utility; and to this extent they have a right to a part of the products.
>
> "Without any doubt," Say says, "but the land is also an instrument whose service must be paid for, and so . . ."
>
> I agree that the land is an instrument, but who made it? The proprietor? Did he, by the efficacious virtue of the right of property, by this moral quality infused into the soil, endow it with vigour and fertility? The monopoly of the proprietor lies just in the fact that, though he did not make the implement, he requires payment for its use.[1]

The land is productive; but its productive forces are freely given by nature. They can contribute to exchange value only when the free gift of nature is monopolized. The landlord's only "contribution" to value is that he sits atop the free gift without using it himself, and charges tribute for access to it. His rent, in its essence, is the toll collected by one of Dobb's gatekeepers (mentioned below). Or as Marx had put it in volume 3 of Capital,

> land becomes personified in the landlord and . . . gets on its hind legs to demand, as an independent force, its share of the product created with its help. Thus, not the land receives its due portion of the product for the restoration and improvement of its productivity, but instead the landlord takes a share of this product to chaffer away or squander.[2]

The "trinitarian formula" of labor-wages, capital-profit, and land-rent is

> an enchanted, perverted, topsy-turvy world, in which Monsieur le Capital and Madame la Terre do their ghost-walking as social characters and at the same time directly as mere things.[3]

Benjamin Tucker, ridiculing claims that "whatever contributes to production is entitled to an equitable share in the distribution," countered: "Wrong! *Whoever* contributes to production is alone so entitled. *What* has no claims that *Who* is bound to respect. *What* is a thing. *Who* is a person. Things have no claims . . . . The possession of a right cannot be predicated of dead material . . . ."[4]

Tucker criticized, in similar terms, Henry George's "Hodge and Podge" justification for interest based on the productivity of nature.[5] The illustration George used was of one party, Hodge, charging for the productivity of natural forces: Hodge sold Podge a pail of boiling water, not merely for the labor cost of fetching it from the stream and building the fire to heat it, but also for the contribution of a natural force—fire. Profit, Tucker paraphrased George as saying, is "the capitalist's share of the results of the increased power which Capital gives the laborer," with "Hodge's boiling water . . . made a type of all those products of labor which afterwards increase in utility purely by natural force." Nevertheless, George argued that this share was not a deduction from the laborer's earnings.

As Tucker pointed out, this is economic nonsense: "Where there is free competition in the manufacture and sale of spades, the price of a spade will be governed by the cost of

1. Proudhon, *What is Property?*, pp. 124-126.
2. Karl Marx and Friedrich Engels, *Capital* vol. 3, vol. 37 of Marx and Engels *Collected Works* (New York: International Publishers, 1998), p. 811.
3. *Ibid.*, p. 817.
4. Benjamin R. Tucker, "Capital's Claim to Increase," *Instead of a Book*, p. 184.
5. Tucker, "Economic Hodge-Podge," *Instead of a Book*, pp. 202-205.

its production, and not by the value of the extra potatoes which the spade will enable its purchaser to dig." Only when someone has a monopoly on the supply of spades, can he charge according to utility to the user rather than cost of production. In that case, he can pocket most of the proceeds of increased productivity, and leave the purchaser just enough of the net increase in potatoes to persuade him to buy the spade. And the monopolist's price is clearly a deduction from the wages of labor:

> What are the normal earnings of other men? Evidently what they can produce with all the tools and advantages which they can procure *in a free market* without force or fraud. If, then, the capitalist, by abolishing the free market, compels other men to procure their tools and advantages of him on less favorable terms than they could get before, while it may be better for them to come to his terms than to go without the capital, does he not deduct from their earnings?

Hodge, therefore, will be able to charge Podge according to what the natural process of combustion contributes to the boiling of water, only if he can monopolize the boiling of water. Otherwise, competitors will drive the price down to the actual cost of performing the service, which does not include services provided free of charge by nature.

It is ironic that George should have failed to grasp this principle in the case of capital, because it was the basis for his criticism of land monopoly: the injustice of monopolizing natural opportunities in order to collect tribute from the labor of others.

> He does not see that capital in the hands of labor is but the utilization of a natural force or opportunity, just as land is in the hands of labor, and that it is as proper in the one case as in the other that the, benefits of such utilization of natural forces should be enjoyed by the whole body of consumers . . . .
>
> The truth in both cases is just this,—that nature furnishes man immense forces with which to work in the shape of land and capital, that in a state of freedom these forces benefit each individual to the extent that he avails himself of them, and that any man or class getting a monopoly of either or both will put all other men in subjection and live in luxury on the products of their labor. But to justify a monopoly of either of these forces by the existence of the force itself, or to argue that without a monopoly of it any individual could get an income by lending it instead of by working with it, is equally absurd whether the argument be resorted to in the case of land or in the case of capital, in the case of rent or in the case of interest. If any one chooses to call the advantages of these forces to mankind rent in one case and interest in the other, I do not know that there is any serious objection to his doing so, provided he will remember that in practical economic discussion rent stands for the absorption of the advantages of land by the landlord, and interest for the absorption of the advantages of capital by the usurer.

It is privilege that enables a class of absentee owners to appropriate the productivity gains of social labor. As Proudhon pointed out, the increase in productivity from collective labor is appropriated entirely by the owning classes.

> "The capitalist," they say, "has paid the labourers their 'daily wages'"; at a rate agreed upon; more precisely, it should be said that the capitalist has paid as many times "one day's wage" as he has employed labourers each day, which is not at all the same thing. For he has paid nothing for that immense power which results from the union and harmony of laborers and the convergence and simultaneity of their efforts. Two hundred grenadiers set the obelisk of Luxor upon its base in a few hours; do you suppose that one man could have accomplished the same task in two hundred days? Yet according to the calculation of the capitalist, the amount of wages would have been the same.
>
> . . . A force of a thousand men working for twenty days has been paid the same as a force of one working fifty-five years; but this force of one thousand has done in twenty days what a single man, working continuously for a million centuries, could not accomplish: is this exchange equitable? Once more, no; for when you have paid all the individ-

ual forces, you have still not paid the collective force. Consequently, there always remains a right of collective property which you have not acquired and which you enjoy unjustly.[1]

Privilege is enforced by a monopoly on the supply of credit, which prevents associated labor from appropriating the productivity gains from association in the form of increased wages. Since the rentier classes maintain a monopoly on the supply of credit, they maintain a monopoly on the function of advancing the capital necessary to organize collective production, and supplying the labor fund. They are able, therefore, to appropriate the net product to themselves as profit. The worker, whose wage is based on the productivity of one solitary man's labor rather than of his share in the productivity of collective labor, is unable to buy back the product.

> . . . It is in consequence of monopoly that in society, net product being figured over and above gross product, the collective laborer must repurchase his own product at a price higher than that which this product costs him . . . ; that the natural balance between production and consumption is destroyed . . . .[2]

The purpose of Proudhon's credit schemes was to enable the worker, rather than the absentee owner and the merchant-capitalist, to profit from collective force: "the collective force, which is a product of the community, ceases to be a source of profit to a small number of managers and speculators: it becomes the property of all the workers."[3]

This issue was at the heart of our discussion of lean production in Chapter Ten. The central question, in evaluating lean production, is the context of class power in which it takes place: who is in a position to appropriate the benefits of increased efficiency? If it is the worker, then lean production and labor-saving production technology are simply ways to make his own work easier, and to reduce the ratio of effort to consumption. If it is the absentee owner or manager, then the purpose of lean production becomes to eliminate jobs, not effort, and "increased efficiency" takes the form of downsizing and speedup.

The normal effect of market competition is for the productivity benefits of new technology to translate directly into lower consumer prices. It is only through artificial property rights that privileged sellers can charge the consumer in proportion to his increased utility, regardless of the cost of supplying the good. As Proudhon described it, the natural process of competition is that

> . . . . a mechanical invention, notwithstanding the privilege which it temporarily creates and the disturbances which it occasions, always produces in the end a general amelioration; . . . the value of an economical process to its discoverer can never equal the profit which it realizes for society . . . .[4]

Patents impede the normal process of market competition by which technological innovation translates directly into lower consumer cost. Benjamin Tucker, in "State Socialism and Anarchism," argued that opening up the supply of capital and land to free competition would result in their benefits being socialized. Likewise, eliminating patents and other barriers to the free adoption of innovations will result in the socialization of the fruits of increased productivity.

So artificial property rights enable the privileged to appropriate productivity gains for themselves, rather than allowing their benefits to be socialized through market competition. But they do more than that: they make possible the privilege to collect tribute for the "service" of *not* obstructing production. As Commons observed, the alleged "service" performed by the holder of artificial property rights, in "contributing" some factor to produc-

1. Proudhon, *What is Property?*, pp. 91, 93.
2. Proudhon, *System of Economical Contradictions*, p. 303.
3. Proudhon, *General Idea of the Revolution*, pp. 221, 223.
4. Proudhon, *System of Economical Contradictions*, p. 126.

tion, is defined entirely by his ability to obstruct access to it. And as I wrote in *Studies in Mutualist Political Economy*, marginalist economics

> treated the existing structure of property rights over "factors" as a given, and proceeded to show how the product would be distributed among these "factors" according to their marginal contribution. By this method, if slavery were still extant, a marginalist might with a straight face write of the marginal contribution of the slave to the product (imputed, of course, to the slave-owner), and of the "opportunity cost" involved in committing the slave to one or another use.[1]

Such privileges, Maurice Dobb argued, were analogous to a grant of authority to collect tolls:

> Suppose that toll-gates were a general institution, rooted in custom or ancient legal right. Could it reasonably be denied that there would be an important sense in which the income of the toll-owning class represented "an appropriation of goods produced by others" and not payment for an "activity directed to the production or transformation of economic goods?" Yet toll-charges would be fixed in competition with alternative roadways, and hence would, presumably, represent prices fixed "in an open market . . . ." Would not the opening and shutting of toll-gates become an essential factor of production, according to most current definitions of a factor of production, with as much reason at any rate as many of the functions of the capitalist entrepreneur are so classed today? This factor, like others, could then be said to have a "marginal productivity" and its price be regarded as the measure and equivalent of the service it rendered.[2]

Veblen made a similar distinction between property as capitalized serviceability, and capitalized disserviceability. The latter consisted of power advantages over rivals and the public which enabled owners to withhold supply, and constituted the bulk of tangible assets.[3]

The circular reasoning of marginalist economics, by which forbearing to impede production is a "contribution" to production, for which "service" the holder of an artificial property right is entitled to compensation from the productive labor which he helpfully refrained from impeding, is beautifully illustrated by Peter Schiff in the context of the global economy. It's hilarious—until you consider it's dead-on accurate:

> Suppose six castaways are stranded on a deserted island, five Asians and one American. Further, suppose that the castaways decide to divide the work load among them in the following manner: (for the purpose of simplicity, the only desire the castaways work to satisfy is hunger) one Asian is put in charge of hunting, an other in charge of fishing, and a third in charge of finding vegetation. A fourth is put in charge of preparing the meal, while a fifth is given the task of gathering firewood and tending to the fire. The American is given the job of eating.
>
> So, on our island five Asians work all day to feed one American, who spends his day sunning himself of the beach. He is employed in the equivalent of the service sector, operating a tanning salon which none of the Asians on the island utilize. At the end of the day, the five Asians present a painstakingly prepared feast to the American, who sits at the head of a special table, built by the Asians specifically for this purpose.
>
> Realizing that subsequent banquets will only be forthcoming if the Asians are alive to provide them, he allows them just enough scraps from his table to sustain their labor for the following day.
>
> Modern day economists would say that this American is the lone engine of growth driving the island's economy and that without his ravenous appetite, the Asians on the island would be unemployed.[1]

---

1. Kevin Carson, *Studies in Mutualist Political Economy*. Self-published via Blitzprint (Fayetteville, Ark., 2004), p. 73.

2. Dobb, *Political Economy and Capitalism: Some Essays in Economic Tradition*, 2nd rev. ed. (London: Routledge & Kegan Paul Ltd, 1940, 1960), p. 66.

3. Veblen, *The Place of Science in Modern Civilization and other Essays*, p. 352, in Commons, p. 664.

In a sense that's true—if you accept the premise that the land the Asians are working belongs to the American, or that he has a legitimate "intellectual property" right in the seeds or techniques they use to grow food. It's always technically true that a ruling class "provides" jobs, if you take at face value its claimed right to rope off the means of production and charge admission.

These considerations are fundamental to a correct resolution of the debate on profit between Bastiat and Proudhon. What Bastiat fails to recognize, in his illustration of the plane, is the role of monopoly in enabling the maker of the plane not only to rent it out at a price that amortizes his actual cost and effort in producing it, but in addition to appropriate the plane's contribution to productivity. Wakefield and Oppenheimer both observed that the level of wages is set by the competing terms offered by self-employment. The maker of the plane is able to rent it out for such high monopoly rents, likewise, only when the alternative of acquiring one's own plane is artificially expensive. One of Tucker's correspondents, "Apex" (in a discussion that anticipates our treatment of mutual banking later in this chapter), explained the principle:

> The question is this: "Is a man who loans a plough entitled in equity to compensation for its use?" My answer is, "Yes." Now, then, what of it? Does that make something for nothing right? Let us see. We must take it for granted that the loaning of the plough was a good business transaction. Such being the case, the man who borrows the plough must give good security that he will return the plough and pay for what he wears out. He must have the wealth or the credit to make the owner of the plough whole in case he should break or lose the plough. Now, I claim that this man, having the wealth or credit to secure a borrowed plough, could transmute that same credit or security into money, *without cost*, and with the money buy a plough, were it not for a monopoly of money. For a monopoly of money implies a monopoly of everything that money will buy.[2]
>
> Let us remember that no man can borrow money, as a good business transaction, under any system, unless he has the required security to make the lender whole in case he should lose the money. What a stupendous wrong is this—that a man having credit cannot use it, but must exchange it and pay a monopoly price, which is really for the privilege of using his own credit![3]

Tucker, immediately following the series of exchanges between Apex and the defenders of interest, added his comment:

> But under the system of organized credit contemplated by Apex no capable and deserving person would borrow even a title to capital. The so-called borrower would simply so change the face of his own title as to make it recognizable by the world at large, and at no other expense than the mere cost of the alteration. That is to say, the man having capital or good credit, who, under the system advocated by Apex, should go to a credit-shop—in other words, a bank—and procure a certain amount of its notes by the ordinary process of mortgaging property or getting endorsed commercial credit discounted, would only exchange his own personal credit . . . for the bank's credit, known and receivable for products delivered throughout the State, or the nation, or perhaps the world. And for this convenience the bank would charge him only the labor-cost of its service in effecting the exchange of credits, instead of the ruinous rates of discount by which, under the present system of monopoly, privileged banks tax the producers of unprivileged property out of house and home.[4]

Regarding Bastiat's example of the plane, Tucker pointed out that price in a free market is governed by cost of production rather than utility to the purchaser, and "that James

1. Peter Schiff, "Even Stephen Roach Has It Wrong," *Safe Haven*, March 29, 2005 <http://www.safehaven.com/article-2810.htm>.
2. Tucker, "Another Answer to Mr. Babcock," *Instead of a Book*, p. 189.
3. "Usury," *Ibid.*, p. 191.
4. Tucker, "Apex or Basis," *Ibid.*, p. 194.

consequently, though his plane should enable William to make a million planks, could not sell or lend it for more than it cost him to make it, except he enjoyed a monopoly of the plane-making industry."[1]

Capitalism, as opposed to the free market, could not exist without artificial property rights—as its most honest defenders admit. This is the theme, for example, of a post by Elizabeth Anderson of *Left2Right* blog, one of the better liberal bloggers.[2] She rejects natural property rights because they are "incompatible with capitalism"—particularly with the form of "advanced capitalism" she so admires. Advanced capitalism, she argues, depends on artificial forms of property like the limited liability corporation and "intellectual property rights" (which are both "indispensable to capitalism and deeply artificial). On first reading the post, in fact, I mistakenly read Anderson's defense of artificial property rights as written in the spirit of Swift's "modest proposal": a brilliant satiric *attack* on capitalism.

Anderson's judgment in placing the divide between "natural" and "artificial" strikes me as oddly counterintuitive in some cases. For example, she identifies "natural" property in land as a hypersteroidal form of Lockeanism, in which the absolute power of transfer is limited by no requirement of possession. I would tend, rather, to measure the artificiality of property rights by the distance of their remove from simple possession and transfer of possession. She quotes De Soto as an authority on the importance of government in transforming customary property rights into artificial (and enforceable) ones, but neglects the present role of government in suppressing more egalitarian forms of possessory ownership in favor of the artificial property rights of latifundistas and other landed oligarchs. Likewise, she regards bankruptcy as an artificial limitation on the "natural" property rights of creditors, whereas Spooner's position limiting the creditor's right of collection to the debtor's property currently in hand strikes me as far more natural.

Thomas Hodgskin, almost a hundred years before J.A. Hobson or John Maynard Keynes, remarked on the effect of privilege in the maldistribution of purchasing power.

> . . . . The peasant, who produces so much corn, that his master is ruined by its reduced price, has not wherewithal to eat and cover himself. The weaver, who supplies the world with clothing, whose master undertakes perilous adventures to tempt savages to use his productions, is perishing with hunger and nakedness in the midst of an inclement season . . . . The established right of property,—that *right* which denies bread and raiment to the labourer, in order to pamper those who do not labour with luscious viands and clothe them in purple and fine linen, [is threatened with] total subversion by violence . . . .[3]

Privilege results in distorting and destabilizing effects that, in turn, lead to corrective government intervention. A central problem of the advanced economies, from the late 19th century on, has been the crisis of overproduction, overaccumulation and underconsumption. They all result from the maldistribution of purchasing power that occurs when privilege breaks the direct connection between effort and reward. To quote Hodgskin again,

> The wants of individuals which labour is intended to gratify, are the natural guide to their exertions. The instant they are compelled to labour for others, this guide forsakes them, and their exertions are dictated by the greed and avarice, and false hopes of their masters . . . . By this system the hand is dissevered from the mouth, and labour is put in motion to gratify vanity and ambition, not the natural wants of animal existence. When we look at the commercial history of our country, and see the false hopes of our merchants and manufacturers leading to periodical commercial convulsions, we are compelled to conclude, that they have not the same source as the regular and harmonious ex-

1. Tucker, "The Position of William," *Ibid.*, p. 200.
2. Elizabeth Anderson, "How Not to Complain Against Taxes (II): Against Natural Property Rights" <*Left2Right*, January 20, 2005. http://left2right.typepad.com/main/2005/01/why_i_reject_na.html>.
3. Hodgskin, *Popular Political Economy*, p. 264.

ternal world. Capitalists have no guide to their exertions, because nature rejects and opposes their dominion over labour. Starts of national prosperity, followed by bankruptcy and ruin, have the same source then as fraud and forgery.[1]

The major function of the interventionist state from the early 20th century on, as we saw in Chapter Three, has been to guarantee a market for overproduction, either through foreign imperialism (as J.A. Hobson described), through government spending to use up the surplus product, or through Keynesian policies of increasing aggregate demand.

C. Specific Forms of Privilege, and the Effect of Their Abolition

The central area of disagreement between individualist anarchists and state socialists (along with all other "progressive" ideologies that see state intervention as the solution to the evils of capitalism) is over the relationship between the interventionist state and economic exploitation. The statists see exploitation as the natural outcome of an unregulated market, and see state intervention as necessary to counteract this outcome. Individualist anarchists see exploitation as the result of privilege created by state intervention in the market, and propose opening up all the forms of artificial scarcity created by such privilege to the revolutionary force of market competition. As Tucker put it, we are consistent Manchester liberals.

Tucker described the functioning of privilege in the ostensibly "free market" economy:

When Warren and Proudhon, in prosecuting their search for justice to labor, came face to face with the obstacle of class monopolies, they saw that these monopolies rested upon Authority, and concluded that the thing to be done was ... to utterly uproot Authority and give full sway to the opposite principle, Liberty, by making competition, the antithesis of monopoly, universal. They saw in competition the great leveler of prices to the labor cost of production. In this they agreed with the political economists. The query then naturally presented itself why all prices do not fall to labor cost; where there is any room for incomes acquired otherwise than by labor; in a word, why the usurer, the receiver of interest, rent, and profit, exists. The answer was found in the present one-sidedness of competition. It was discovered that capital had so manipulated legislation that unlimited competition is allowed in supplying productive labor, thus keeping wages down to the starvation point, or as near it as practicable ...; but that almost no competition at all is allowed in supplying capital, upon the aid of which both productive and distributive labor are dependent for their power of achievement, thus keeping the rate of interest on money and of house-rent and ground-rent at as high a point as the necessities of the people will bear.

On discovering this, Warren and Proudhon charged the political economists with being afraid of their own doctrine. The Manchester men were accused of being inconsistent. The believed in liberty to compete with the laborer in order to reduce his wages, but not in liberty to compete with the capitalist in order to reduce his usury ....

.... So they raised the banner of Absolute Free Trade; free trade at home, as well as with foreign countries; the logical carrying out of the Manchester doctrine; *laissez faire* the universal rule. Under this banner they began their fight upon monopolies, whether the all-inclusive monopoly of the State Socialists, or the various class monopolies that now prevail.

Of the latter they distinguished four of principal importance: the money monopoly, the land monopoly, the tariff monopoly, and the patent monopoly.[2]

1. Hodgskin, *The Natural and Artificial Right of Property Contrasted. A Series of Letters,* addressed without permission to H. Brougham, Esq. M.P. F.R.S. (London: B. Steil, 1832). Online Library of Liberty <http://oll.libertyfund.org/index.php?option=com_staticxt&staticfile=show.php%3Ftitle=323&layout=html>. "Letter the Eighth: Evils of the Artificial Right of Property"
2. Tucker, "State Socialism and Anarchism: How Far They Agree, and Wherein They Differ," *Instead of a Book,* pp. 9-11.

The phenomenon Tucker described, the coexistence of almost unlimited competition in the supply of labor with greatly circumscribed competition in the supply of capital, has been remarked upon by many thinkers over the years. The general principle is described by Noam Chomsky as "socialism for the rich, free market discipline for the poor." Or as Geoff Olson describes it, at greater length:

> For several decades, middle-class North Americans have been coached on the virtues of beating out the other guy or gal for a grade, contract, job or home. "Competition" and "competitiveness" have become magical spells for warding off the last remaining gremlins of socialism . . . .
>
> If we seem to be working more than our parents ever did, and receiving less for the effort, that may offer a bit of a clue. It's intriguing that mainstream media always trots out competitiveness whenever the indefensible needs defending. Whether it's an argument for the minimum wage, a celebration of corporate merger, or applause for a super-star CEO's golden parachute, we're told it's really about us being more competitive as a city, province, nation, trading bloc, etc.
>
> But hang on a moment. If this is the case, why do we find relatively little direct competition at the highest levels of business? What of the interlocking boards of major corporations, in which the same names crop up over and over?
>
> Once you get past mom and pop businesses, the North American economic landscape is mostly an "oligopoly" . . . . Hence, the comfortable push/pull between remaining monopolies—the Coke/Pepsi dynamic. This mirrors the monopolies in the political realm, summed up in the comic battles between the Democrats and Republicans . . . .
>
> Those at the top have little to gain from direct competition. They and their parents hail from the same prep schools, head for the same golf courses, and subscribe to the same journals. Their interactions are usually more country club than cutthroat. With a multigenerational game this good, the plutocrats have plenty of reason to convince everyone else to keep fighting among themselves, by pushing the glorious virtues of competition through foundations and media outlets. In fact, their continuing comfort depends on it.[1]

The central function of privilege being the extraction unearned wealth by impeding production, and by obstructing access to unused productive resources by those who could put them to productive use, it follows that the general effect of abolishing privilege will be the opposite: to increase production and wealth, both through the allocation of productive resources without impediment to their most productive use, and through the full reward of productive labor.

1. The Credit Monopoly

Tucker listed the credit monopoly first among the forms of legal privilege that robbed labor of its product. That monopoly consists of state-enforced entry barriers, like licensing and capitalization requirements (even for secured loans) that restrict competition in the supply of credit, and enable banks to charge a monopoly price.

The form such restrictions take in recent times was described by Karl Hess and David Morris:

> First, one gets a certificate which gives permission to raise capital for the bank and outlines what conditions need to be met in order to receive a charter. Step two is getting the charter after having met the conditions. The conditions are numerous, but the most important one is that a given amount of deposit capital must be raised in a specific period of time. In order to get permission to raise capital a group must prove that there is a

1. Geoff Olson, "Social Darwinist competition leads to Ik-y mess," *The Vancouver Courier*, July 20, 2007 <http://www.canada.com/vancouvercourier/news/opinion/story.html>.

reason to have another bank, that it can serve a necessary function, and that it has a viable chance of succeeding.[1]

Capitalization requirements for institutions providing secured loans, over and above the security provided for the loans themselves, amount to unnecessarily mandating a double guarantee. Their only real function is to raise the entry cost for the credit industry so that a monopoly price can be charged for issuing currency against property.

> BANK-BILLS are doubly guaranteed. On one side, there is the capital of the bank, which is liable for the redemption of the bills in circulation: on the other side are the notes of the debtors of the bank, which notes are . . . a sufficient guaranty for all the bills; for no bills are issued by any bank, except upon notes whereby some responsible person is bound to restore to the bank. after a certain lapse of time, money to the amount borne on the face of the bills. If the notes given by the receivers of the bills are good, then the bills themselves are also good.[2]

Privilege, or its lack, has a powerful effect on the bargaining power of labor. The very term "employment" (with "self-employment" an anomaly comparable to a freed slave or an unowned horse), and the idea of work as something that someone must be *given* rather than something one *does*, assumes a lack of direct access to means of production and subsistence:

> Our natural resources, while much depleted, are still great; our population is very thin, running something like twenty or twenty-five to the square mile; and some millions of this population are at this moment "unemployed," and likely to remain so because no one will or can "give them work." The point is not that men generally submit to this state of things, or that they accept it as inevitable, but that they see nothing irregular or anomalous about it because of their fixed idea that work is something to be *given*.[3]

Defenders of the status quo often argue that employers are competing for labor as much as workers are competing for employment. But this is not entirely true. The competition between employers, although it exists, is artificially constrained by privilege, so that there are fewer employers competing in the labor market than would be the case in a genuinely free market.

Oliver Williamson refers, for example, to the "reputation effects" of bad employer practices: workers in the job market will evaluate prospective employers on past performance.[4] That's true, as far as it goes. But the more the number of competing employers is reduced, the worse reputation the worst employer can afford to have and still find help. To put it in terms of Böhm-Bawerk's marginal pairs, if the number of competing employers is artificially constrained, there is likely to be a disappointed worker left over at the end rather than a disappointed employer.

Vulgar libertarians like to stress that, "in a free market," workers are free to take their labor elsewhere if they don't like their working conditions. And many libertarians respond with just that advice—frequently in quite indignant terms—in response to workers' complaints about their employers. Complaints about employer restrictions on employees' free-

---

    1. Karl Hess and David Morris, *Neighborhood Power: The New Localism* (Boston: Beacon Press, 1975), p. 81.

    2. William B. Greene, *The Radical Deficiency of the Existing Circulating Medium, and the Advantages of a Mutual Currency* (1857). Online text scanned by Shawn Wilbur <http://libertarian-labyrinth.org/mutual/wbg-mb1857.html >. This work, with minor alterations, was the basis of the 1870 edition of *Mutual Banking*.

    3. Nock, *Our Enemy, the State*, p. 82n.

    4. Oliver Williamson, *The Economic Institutions of Capitalism* (New York: The Free Press, 1985), p. 259.

dom of speech and association outside of work are generally met with the response: "Nobody's forcing you to work there."

Well, yes and no. We left-wing market anarchists do not advocate imposing external constraints on an employer's freedom to set conditions of employment. The question is not whether the *state* should permit employers to set such conditions, but *what kind of a market allows it?*

Just how godawful do the other " options" have to be before somebody's desperate enough to take a job, and hold onto it like grim death, under conditions of stagnant pay, where (thanks to downsizing and speedups) they're doing their own work plus that of a former coworker? How do things get to the point where people are lined up to compete for jobs where they can be forbidden to associate with coworkers away from work, where even squalid, low-paying retail jobs can involve being on-call 24/7, where employees can't attend political meetings without keeping an eye out for an informer, or can't blog under their own names without living in fear that they're a web-search away from termination?

To grasp the extent of the state's role in such exploitation, just consider the likely effect of abundant, low-interest credit on the bargaining power of labor. Tucker's remedy of free mutual credit ("free" as in "free speech," not "free beer") was based on the mutual banking proposals of William B. Greene.

Here is how a mutual bank would function, as described by Greene in *The Radical Deficiency of the Circulating Medium*:

> Any person or company, by pledging real estate to the MUTUAL B ANK , may become a member of the Banking Company . . .
>
> Said Mutual Bank shall have power to issue paper-money to circulate *as currency* among parties willing to use it as such.
>
> Any member may borrow the paper-money of said bank, on his own notes running to maturity, to an amount not to exceed three-fourths (or such other fixed proportion as your honorable body may determine) of the value of the property by himself pledged.
>
> Each member shall be bound to receive the bills issued by said bank, at the full value borne on their face, in payment of debt, and in all the transactions of trade . . . .
>
> The rate of interest at which said money shall be loaned shall be determined by— and shall, if possible, just meet and cover—the average losses and necessary expenses of the institution.
>
> No money shall be loaned by said bank to any person who does not become, by a pledge of real estate, a member of the company . . . .
>
> Your petitioners humbly conceive that a bank is an insurance company that insures and guarantees the business-paper of individuals. Individuals give their promissory notes to the bank, which notes bear interest; and receive from the bank, in exchange for their notes, other promissory notes not bearing interest . . . .
>
> According to the estimate of your petitioners, one per cent on the amount borrowed, would more than cover the average cost of insurance . . . .Your petitioners believe that a Mutual Bank, through the simple process of legitimate competition . . . would furnish them with an instrument by which they might enable the members of the community generally to mutually insure each other's business-paper; thus providing a currency for the people at less than one-sixth of the present cost.[1]

Greene expected such free competition in the issue of secured loans to exercise a powerful downward pressure on interest rates, and to increase the independence of labor:

> Let it be assumed that the Mutual Bank has been established and offers credit at the cost of operating the bank, which is about one per cent. This will be the full rate charged on all loans. This rate comes into competition with the rate charged by all other banks and all other money lenders. The effect on the other banks will be felt very soon, because no one is going to pay six or eight per cent for money when he can get it for one

---

1. Greene, *The Radical Deficiency of the Existing Circulating Medium*.

per cent or less. One of two things must happen. The old banks must either meet the cut and also lend money at that rate, or else lose their customers who will go to the new bank, the new bank needs no capital, as it does business entirely on the capital of its customers, who are also its members; for every member virtually brings his own capital to the Mutual Bank when he joins it.

The business the Mutual Bank can do is unlimited, and each new member joining the Bank in creases the number of people who can do business with each other on this new basis. The circle of exchange becomes wider arid wider and it cannot be long before the whole communities is impelled by self interest to do business on this plan.

Once the Mutual Bank is operating, money will be available practically without interest to any responsible producer, so that his independence will no longer depend upon the whim of the usurer, but upon his determination and his ability in his line of work. There will be big factories and small shops, and the demand for wage labor will be greater than the supply, with the result that wages will soar until they approach the full value of the work done. Due to the elimination of interest, rent, and privileged profits, under Mutualism the cost of commodities will be much lower and money therefore will have more buying power, in addition to wages being higher.[1]

This was, in all its essentials, the mutual banking system that Tucker later tirelessly advocated in the pages of *Liberty*. For example:

Does the law of England allow citizens to form a bank for the issue of paper money against any property that they may see fit to accept as security; the paper money not redeemable in specie except at the option of the bank; the customers of the bank mutually pledging themselves to accept the bank's paper in lieu of gold or silver coin of the same face value; the paper being redeemable only at the maturity of the mortgage notes, and then simply by a return of said notes and a release of the mortgaged property,—is such an institution, I ask, allowed by the law of England?[2]

The ability mobilize their own credit through such a free credit system would open up an enormous source of capital for workers. As Alexander Cairncross observed, "the American worker has at his disposal a larger stock of capital at home than in the factory where he is employed . . . ."[3]

Here's how Tucker envisioned the resulting worker-friendly market, with jobs competing for workers instead of the reverse:

...[T]he thousands of people who are now deterred from going into business by the ruinously high rates which they must pay for capital with which to start and carry on business will find their difficulties removed . . . Then will be seen an exemplification of the words of Richard Cobden that, when two laborers are after one employer, wages fall, but when two employers are after one laborer, wages rise. Labor will then be in a position to dictate its wages, and will thus secure its natural wage, its entire product . . .[4]

John Beverley Robinson, a member of Tucker's circle, in *The Economics of Liberty* described the effects of such free credit on the bargaining power of labor:

With free banking, interest upon bonds of all kinds and dividends upon stock would fall to the minimum bank interest charge. The so-called rent of houses . . . would fall to the cost of maintenance and replacement.

All that part of the product which is now taken by interest would belong to the producer. Capital, however . . . defined, would practically cease to exist as an income

---

1. Greene, *Mutual Banking* (1870). Online edition scanned by Saren Calvert <http://www.the-portal.org/mutual_banking.htm>.

2. Tucker, "The Power of Government over Values," *Instead of a Book*, p. 226.

3. Alexander Cairncross, "Economic Schizophrenia," *Scottish Journal of Political Economy* (February 1950), quoted. in Michael Perelman, *Classical Political Economy: Primitive Accumulation and the Social Division of Labor* (Totowa, N.J.: Rowman & Allanheld; London: F. Pinter, 1984, c 1983), p. 27.

4. "State Socialism and Anarchism," *Instead of a Book*, p. 11.

producing fund, for the simple reason that if money, wherewith to buy capital, could be obtained for one-half of one per cent, capital itself could command no higher price.[1]

High interest rates are used by the Federal Reserve at present as a form of labor-discipline, increasing unemployment when the bargaining power of labor is too great. According to Dean Baker:

> In periods of low unemployment, workers don't only gain from higher wages. Employers must make efforts to accommodate workers' various needs, such as child care or flexible work schedules, because they know that workers have other employment options. The Fed is well aware of the difficulties that employers face in periods of low unemployment. It compiles a regular survey, called the "Beige Book," of attitudes from around the country about the state of the economy. Most of the people interviewed for the Beige Book are employers. From 1997 to 2000, when the unemployment rate was at its lowest levels in 30 years, the Beige Book was filled with complaints that some companies were pulling workers from other companies with offers of higher wages and better benefits. Some Beige Books reported that firms had to offer such nonwage benefits as flexible work hours, child care, or training in order to retain workers. The Beige Books give accounts of firms having to send buses into inner cities to bring workers out to the suburbs to work in hotels and restaurants. It even reported that some employers were forced to hire workers with handicaps in order to meet their needs for labor.
>
> From the standpoint of employers, life is much easier when the workers are lined up at the door clamoring for jobs than when workers have the option to shop around for better opportunities. Employers can count on a sympathetic ear from the Fed.[2]

In the Clinton administration, interestingly, Alan Greenspan departed from traditional practice. As unemployment threatened to drop below the four per cent mark, a minority of the Federal Reserve agitated to raise interest rates and take off the "inflationary" pressure by throwing a few million workers on the street. But as Greenspan testified before the Senate Banking Committee, the situation was unique. Given the degree of job insecurity in the high-tech economy, there was "[a]typical restraint on compensation increases." In 1996, even with a tight labor market, 46% of workers at large firms were fearful of layoffs—compared to only 25% in 1991, when unemployment was much higher.

> The reluctance of workers to leave their jobs to seek other employment as the labor market tightened has provided further evidence of such concern, as has the tendency toward longer labor union contracts . . . . The low level of work stoppages of recent years also attests to concern about job security.[3]

Near-zero interest rates would increase the independence of labor in all sorts of interesting ways. Mortgages would be paid off far more quickly, with most people in their 30s likely owning their houses free and clear. Between this and the disappearance of high-interest credit card debt, two of the greatest sources of anxiety to keep one's job at any cost would disappear. In addition, many workers would have large savings ("go to hell money"). In Doug Henwood's words,

> mortgaged workers are more pliable—less likely to strike or make political trouble. And they need money to live; nearly everyone below the upper middle class is just a few paychecks from insolvency.[4]

1. John Beverley Robinson, *The Economics of Liberty* (Minneapolis: Herman Kuehn, 1916), pp. 80–81.

2. Dean Baker, *The Conservative Nanny State: How the Wealthy Use the Government to Stay Rich and Get Richer* (Washington, D.C.: Center for Economic and Policy Research, 2000), pp. 32–33.

3. "Testimony of Chairman Alan Greenspan." U. S. Senate Committee on Banking, Housing, and Urban Affairs. 26 February 1997.

4. Doug Henwood, *Wall Street: How It Works and for Whom* (London and New York: Verso, 1997), p. 232.

Significant numbers would retire in their forties or fifties, cut back to part–time, or start businesses; with jobs competing for workers, the effect on bargaining power would be revolutionary.

The authors of *An Anarchist FAQ* elaborated on the libertarian socialist implications of Benjamin Tucker's free market in credit:

> It's important to note that because of Tucker's proposal to increase the bargaining power of workers through access to mutual credit, his individualist anarchism is not only compatible with workers' control but would in fact promote it (as well as logically requiring it). For if access to mutual credit were to increase the bargaining power of workers to the extent that Tucker claimed it would, they would then be able to: (1) demand and get workplace democracy; and (2) pool their credit to buy and own companies collectively. This would eliminate the top-down structure of the firm and the ability of owners to pay themselves unfairly large salaries as well as reducing capitalist profits to zero by ensuring that workers received the full value of their labour. Tucker himself pointed this out when he argued that Proudhon (like himself) "would individualise and associate" workplaces by mutualism, which would "place the means of production within the reach of all."[1]

The worker would become a de facto co–owner of his workplace, even if it remained nominally capitalist-owned.

In addition, the availability (or unavailability) of capital to working class people has a significant effect on the rate of self-employment and small business formation. The capitalist credit system, in particular, is biased toward large-scale, conventional, absentee-owned firms. David Blanchflower and Andrew Oswald[2] found that childhood personality traits and test scores had almost no value in predicting adult entrepreneurship. On the other hand, access to startup capital was the single biggest factor in predicting self-employment. There is a strong correlation between self-employment and having received an inheritance or a gift.[3] NSS data indicate that most small businesses were begun not with bank loans but with own or family money . . . ."[4] The clear implication is that there are "undesirable impediments to the market supply of entrepreneurship."[5] In short, the bias of the capitalist credit system toward large-scale capitalist enterprise means that the rate of wage employment is higher, and self-employment is lower, than their likely free market values.

So it follows that we have no need for state intervention to secure to labor its full product. As Tucker argued over a century ago,

> These employers have a perfect right to hire men on whatever conditions the men will accept. If the latter accept cruel conditions, it is only because they are obliged to do so. What thus obliges them? Law-sustained monopolies. Their relief lies, then, not in depriving employers of the right of contract, but in giving employees the same right of contract without crippling them in advance.[6]

I attempted to make the same point in "Contract Feudalism," a pamphlet for the Libertarian Alliance:

> We shouldn't need federal regulations to stop [the setting of onerous conditions of employment by employers] from happening. In a free market where land and capital

1. "Benjamin Tucker: Capitalist or Anarchist?" *Anarchist FAQ*, G.5 <http://www.infoshop.org/faq/secG5. html>.

2. David G. Blanchflower and Andrew J. Oswald, "What Makes an Entrepreneur?" <http://www2.warwick.ac.uk/fac/soc/economics/staff/faculty/oswald/entrepre.pdf>. Later appeared in *Journal of Labor Economics*, 16:1 (1998), pp. 26-60.

3. *Ibid.*, p. 2.

4. *Ibid.*, p. 28.

5. *Ibid.*, p. 3.

6. Tucker, "On Picket Duty," *Instead of a Book*, p. 163.

weren't artificially scarce and expensive compared to labor, jobs should be competing for workers. What's remarkable is not that contract feudalism is technically "legal," but that the job market is so abysmal that it could become an issue in the first place.[1]

In addition to the primary form of exploitation described above, the monopoly has some other ill effects.

The absentee ownership of capital also skews investment in a different direction from what it would be in an economy of labor-owned capital, and reduces investment to lower levels. Investments that would be justified by the bare fact of making labor less onerous and increasing productivity, in an economy of worker-owned capital,[2] must produce an additional return on the capital to be considered worth making in an economy of rentiers. It is directly analogous to the holding of vacant land out of use that might enable laborers to subsist comfortably, because it will not in addition produce a rent over and above the laborer's subsistence.

> It is maintained . . . that labour is not productive, and, in fact, the labourer is not allowed to work, unless, in addition to replacing whatever he uses or consumes, and comfortably subsisting himself, his labour also gives a profit to the capitalist . . . ; or unless his labour produces a great deal more . . . than will suffice for his own comfortable subsistence. Capitalists becoming the proprietors of all the wealth of the society . . . act on this principle, and never . . . will they suffer labourers to have the means of subsistence, unless they have a confident expectation that their labour will produce a profit over and above their own subsistence. This . . . is so completely the principle of slavery, to starve the labourer, unless his labour will feed his master as well as himself, that we must not be surprised if we should find it one of the chief causes . . . of the poverty and wretchedness of the labouring classes.[3]

Perhaps not coincidentally, there is a wide array of literature finding an inverse correlation between inequality of wealth and economic growth.[4]

When capital equipment is owned by the same people who make and use it, or made and used by different groups of people who divide the entire product according to their respective labor and costs, it is productive. But when capital equipment is owned by a class of rentiers separate from those who make it or use it, the owners may be said more accurately to impede production rather than "contribute" to it.[5]

> If there were only the makers and users of capital to share between them the produce of their co-operating labour, the only limit to productive labour would be, that it should obtain for them and their families a comfortable subsistence. But when in addition to this . . . , they must also produce as much more as satisfies the capitalist, this limit is much sooner reached. When the capitalist . . . will allow labourers neither to make nor use instruments, unless *he* obtains a profit over and above the subsistence of the labourer, it is plain that bounds are set to productive labour much within what Nature prescribes. In proportion as capital in the hands of a third party is accumulated, so the whole amount of profit required by the capitalist increases, and so there arises an artificial check to production and population. The impossibility of the labourer producing all which the capitalist requires prevents numberless operations, such as draining marshes, and clearing and cultivating waste lands; to do which would amply repay the labourer, by providing him with

1. "Contract Feudalism"
2. Hodgskin, *Popular Political Economy*, pp. 255-256.
3. *Ibid.*, pp. 51-52.
4. Klaus Deininger and Lyn Squire, "Economic Growth and Income Inequality: Reexamining the Links," *Finance & Development*, March 1997, pp. 38-41<http://www.worldbank.org/fandd/ english/0397/articles/0140397.htm>. Philippe Aghion, Eve Caroli, Cecilia Garcia-Penalosa, *Inequality and Economic Growth: The perspective of the new growth theories* N 9908 (June 1999) <http://www.cepremap.cnrs.fr/couv_orange/co9908.pdf>.
5. Hodgskin, *Popular Political Economy*, pp. 243-244.

the means of subsistence, though they will not, in addition, give a large profit to the capitalist. In the present state of society, the labourers being in no case the owners of capital, every accumulation of it adds to the amount of profit demanded from them, and extinguishes all that labour which would only procure the labourer his comfortable subsistence.

He developed this same theme, as it applied to land, in *The Natural and Artificial Right of Property Contrasted*:

> It is, however, evident, that the labour which would be amply rewarded in cultivating all our waste lands, till every foot of the country became like the garden grounds about London, were all the produce of labour on those lands to be the reward of the labourer, cannot obtain from them a sufficiency to pay profit, tithes, rent, and taxes . . . .
>
> In the same manner as the cultivation of waste lands is checked, so are commercial enterprise and manufacturing industry arrested. Infinite are the undertakings which would amply reward the labour necessary for their success, but which will not pay the additional sums required for rent, profits, tithes, and taxes.[1]

This resembles the argument made by some Radical Keynesians that, at zero real interest, any investment project will be undertaken that increases the net efficiency of production.

On the other hand, the availability of credit (and land) without the monopolist's surcharge will increase the producers' motivation to invest in their own production. Apologists for capitalism see the present system, in which capital investment is carried out primarily by the absentee owners of large concentrations of investment capital, as the only possible one. So any suggestion that the rates of return on absentee investment might be lowered result in cries of "but what will be the motive for investment?" In an economy of predominantly worker-owned production, the primary motive for investment will be to reduce future effort by making one's labor more productive. And the abolition of monopoly rates of interest (and rent) will increase the present-day earnings of labor from which such investments can be made. As Charles-François Chevé put it in response to Bastiat:

> "The law," you say, "will rob us of the prospect of laying by a little property, because it will prevent us from gaining any advantage from it." Quite to the contrary, the law will assure to everyone the prospect of laying by as much wealth as they have produced through their labour, by forbidding anybody to plunder his neighbour of the fruits of his labours, and by decreeing that services exchanged shall be equivalent: use for use and property for property. "It will deprive us," you add, "of all stimulus to save at the present time, and of all hope of repose for the future. It is useless to exhaust ourselves with fatigue; we must abandon the idea of leaving our sons and daughters a little property, since modern science renders it useless, for we should become traffickers in men if we were to lend it on interest." Quite to the contrary, the abolition of interest revives in you the stimulus to save at the present time and assures you the hope of repose for the future, because it prevents you, the labourers, from being plundered, by means of rent, of the greater part of the fruits of your labour, and because by obliging you to spend no more than the exact sum you have earned, it renders saving all the more indispensable to everybody, be they rich or poor. Not only will you be able to leave your sons and daughters a little property without becoming traffickers in men, but you will b able to obtain this property with a good deal less effort than today; because if, while you earn 10 francs a day and spend 5, you are deprived, as nowadays, of the other 5 by all the forms of rent and of interest on

1. Thomas Hodgskin, "Letter the Eighth: Evils of the Artificial Right of Property," *The Natural and Artificial Right of Property Contrasted. A Series of Letters, addressed without permission to H. Brougham, Esq. M.P. F.R.S.* (London: B. Steil, 1832) <http://oll.libertyfund.org/index.php? op­tion=com_staticxt&staticfile=show.php%3Ftitle=323&layout=html>

capital, after forty years you won't have a farthing to leave to your children; whereas once rent is abolished you will have more than 60,000 francs to bequeath to them.[1]

Most of the objections raised against Greene's and Tucker's radical theory of credit are strawmen, and have been debunked quite effectively.

For example, Rothbard dismissed the Greene-Tucker propsals as just another form of "money crankery," an attempt at creating prosperity by inflating the money supply with fiat currency.[2] But this objection was answered by no less an authority than Rothbard himself, as I have pointed out:

> On money and banking issues, Rothbard made the mistake of interpreting the Greene-Tucker system of mutual banking as an attempt at inflationary expansion of the money supply. Although the Greene-Tucker doctrine is often casually lumped together (in a broader category of "money cranks") with social crediters, bimetallists, etc., it is actually quite different. Greene and Tucker did not propose inflating the money supply, but rather eliminating the monopoly price of credit made possible by the state's entry barriers: licensing of banks, and large capitalization requirements for institutions engaged in providing only secured loans. Most libertarians are familiar with such criticisms of professional licensing as a way of ensuring monopoly income for the providers of medical, legal and other services. Licensing and capitalization requirements, likewise, enable providers of credit to charge a monopoly price for their services.
>
> In fact, Rothbard himself made a similar analysis of the life insurance industry, in which state reserve requirements served as market entry barriers and thus inflated the cost of insurance far above the levels necessary for purely actuarial requirements.[3]

The notions that present capital investment comes from past abstention, and that it is necessary to advance a "labor fund" from past savings, have been repeatedly attacked. Thomas Hodgskin, for example, made this point in both *Labour Defended Against the Claims of Capital* and *Popular Political Economy*:

> The only advantage of circulating capital is that by it the labourer is enabled, he being assured of his present subsistence, to direct his power to the greatest advantage . . . . Unless there were this assurance there could be no continuous thought, no invention, and no knowledge but that which would be necessary for the supply of our immediate animal wants . . . .
>
> The labourer, the real maker of any commodity, derives this assurance from a knowledge he has that the person who set him to work will pay him, and that with the money he will be able to buy what he requires. He is not in possession of any stock of commodities. Has the person who employs and pays him such a stock? Clearly not . . . .
>
> A great cotton manufacturer . . . employs a thousand persons, whom he pays weekly: does he possess the food and clothing ready prepared which these persons purchase and consume daily? Does he even know whether the food and clothing they receive are prepared and created? In fact, are the food and clothing which his labourers will consume prepared beforehand, or are other labourers busily employed in preparing food and clothing while his labourers are making cotton yarn? . . .
>
> . . . As far as food, drink and clothing are concerned, it is quite plain, then, that no species of labourer depends on any previously prepared stock, for in fact no such stock

---

1. F. C. Chevé [Charles-François Chevé (1813-1875)], one of the editors of the *Voix du Peuple*, to Frédéric Bastiat. Translation by Roderick T. Long. *The Bastiat-Proudhon Debate on Interest (1849-1850)* <http://praxeology.net/FB-PJP-DOI-IV-1.htm>.

2. Murray Rothbard, "The Tucker-Spooner Doctrine: An Economist's View," *Egalitarianism as a Revolt Against Nature and Other Essays* (Auburn, Ala.: Ludwig von Mises Institute, 2000), reproduced in *Journal of Libertarian Studies*, vol. 20, no. 1 (Winter 2006), pp. 10-12.

3. Kevin Carson, "Carson's Rejoinders," *Journal of Libertarian Studies*, vol. 20, no. 1 (Winter 2006), pp. 97-98. Rothbard's comments on the life insurance industry are found in *Power and Market: Government and the Economy* (Kansas City: Sheed, Andrews and McMeel, 1997), p. 59.

exists; but every species of labourer does constantly, and at all times, depend for his supplies on the co-existing labour of some other labourers.[1]

...When a capitalist therefore, who owns a brew-house and all the instruments and materials requisite for making porter, pays the actual brewers with the coin he has received for his beer, and they buy bread, while the journeymen bakers buy porter with their money wages, which is afterwards paid to the owner of the brew-house, is it not plain that the real wages of both these parties consist of the produce of the other; or that the bread made by the journeyman baker pays for the porter made by the journeyman brewer? But the same is the case with all other commodities, and labour, not capital, pays all wages . . . .

In fact it is a miserable delusion to call capital something saved. Much of it is not calculated for consumption, and never is made to be enjoyed. When a savage wants food, he picks up what nature spontaneously offers. After a time he discovers that a bow or a sling will enable him to kill wild animals at a distance, and he resolves to make it, subsisting himself, as he must do, while the work is in progress. He saves nothing, for the instrument never was made to be consumed, though in its own nature it is more durable than deer's flesh. This example represents what occurs at every stage of society, except that the different labours are performed by different persons—one making the bow, or the plough, and another killing the animal or tilling the ground, to provide subsistence for the makers of instruments and machines. To store up or save commodities, except for short periods, and in some particular cases, can only be done by more labour, and in general their utility is lessened by being kept. The savings, as they are called, of the capitalist, are consumed by the labourer, and there is no such thing as an actual hoarding up of commodities.[2]

In short, what political economy conventionally referred to as the "labor fund," and attributed to past abstention and accumulation, in fact resulted from the *present* division of labor and the cooperative distribution of its product. "Capital" is a term for a right of property in organizing and disposing of this present labor. The same basic cooperative functions could be carried out just as easily by the workers themselves, through mutual credit. Under the present system, the capitalist monopolizes these cooperative functions, and thus appropriates the productivity gains from the social division of labor.

Betwixt him who produces food and him who produces clothing, betwixt him who makes instruments and him who uses them, in steps the capitalist, who neither makes nor uses them, and appropriates to himself the produce of both. With as niggard a hand as possible he transfers to each a part of the produce of the other, keeping to himself the large share. Gradually and successively has he insinuated himself betwixt them, expanding in bulk as he has been nourished by their increasingly productive labours, and separating them so widely from each other that neither can see whence that supply is drawn which each receives through the capitalist. While he despoils both, so completely does he exclude one from the view of the other that both believe they are indebted him for subsistence.[3]

Franz Oppenheimer made a similar argument in "A Post Mortem on Cambridge Economics":

THE JUSTIFICATION OF PROFIT, to repeat, rests on the claim that the entire stock of instruments of production must be "saved" during one period by private individuals in order to serve during a later period. This proof, it has been asserted, is achieved by a chain of equivocations. In short, the material instruments, for the most part, are not saved in a former period, but are manufactured in the same period in which they are employed. What is saved is capital in the other sense, which may be called for present purposes "money capital." But this capital is not necessary for developed production.

1. Hodgskin, "Labour Defended Against the Claims of Capital."
2. Hodskin, *Popular Political Economy.*
3. Hodgskin, "Labour Defended."

Rodbertus, about a century ago, proved beyond doubt that almost all the "capital goods" required in production are created in the same period . . . . A modern producer provides himself with capital goods which other producers manufacture simultaneously . . . .

On the other hand, money capital must be saved, but it is not absolutely necessary for developed technique. It can be supplanted by co-operation and credit, as Marshall correctly states . . . . The initial money capital of a private entrepreneur plays, as has been aptly pointed out, merely the rôle of the air chamber in the fire engine; it turns the irregular inflow of capital goods into a regular outflow.[1]

The Greene-Tucker argument for the interest-lowering effect of mutual banking, say its critics, ignores the nature of interest as a reward for "waiting" or "abstention." They themselves ignore the basic fact that, in the case of secured loans, no abstention takes place. Or rather, the saving or abstention was carried out by the very person whose property is mortgaged. The mortgaged property is itself the accumulated savings of the borrower, and the bank only issues currency against the borrower's note:

> . . . [T]he banker, who invests little or no capital of his own, and, therefore, lends none to his customers, since the security which they furnish him constitutes the capital upon which he operates . . .[2]
> . . . Mr. Fisher seems to think it inherently impossible to use one's property and at the same time pledge it. But what else happens when a man, after mortgaging his house, continues to live in it? This is an actual every-day occurrence, and mutual banking only seeks to make it possible on easier terms,—the terms that will prevail under competition instead of the terms that do prevail under monopoly.[3]
> . . . [T]he establishment of a mutual bank does not require the investment of capital, inasmuch as the customers of the bank furnish all the capital upon which the bank's notes are based, and . . . therefore the rate of discount charged by the bank for the service of exchanging its notes for those of its customers is governed, under competition, by the cost of that service, and not by the rate of interest that capital commands.[4]

2. Artificial Property Rights in Land

We have already mentioned, in passing, the general issue of artificial property rights in land. Of the specific points of contention between the different systems of property rules for land, I wrote in Chapter Five of Studies in Mutualist Political Economy (and hope someday to revise into more satisfactory form). Here I wish only to examine the parallels between them, in the analogous distinctions they make between natural and artificial, legitimate and illegitimate, rights. As we have already seen, all major property theorists make some such distinction, despite major differences on the specifics of determining legitimacy, using quite similar language.

The possessory theories of Proudhon and the American individualist anarchists made occupancy and use the standard not only for just acquisition, but for continued ownership; all land titles not grounded in ongoing occupancy and use were to be treated as void. Among the American individualists, the general principle was stated by Tucker, who defined the land monopoly as

> the enforcement by government of land titles which do not rest upon personal occupancy and cultivation. It was obvious to Warren and Proudhon that, as soon as individualists should no longer be protected by their fellows in anything but personal occupancy and cultivation of land, ground-rent would disappear, and so usury have one less leg to stand on. Their followers of today are disposed to modify this claim to the extent of ad-

1. Franz Oppenheimer, "A Post Mortem on Cambridge Economics (Part Three)," *The American Journal of Economics and Sociology*, vol. 3, no. 1 (1944), pp, 122-123, [115-124]
2. Tucker, "Economic Hodge-Podge," *Instead of a Book*, p. 206.
3. Tucker, "Free Trade in Banking," *Instead of a Book*, p. 231.
4. Tucker, "Free Money and the Cost Principle," *Ibid.*, pp. 286-287.

mitting that the very small fraction of ground-rent which rests, not on monopoly, but on superiority of soil or site, will continue to exist for a time and perhaps forever, though tending constantly to a minimum under conditions of freedom . . . .[1]

Our earlier distinction between natural and artificial property rights applies very much to land. It was central to classical liberalism from the beginning. Thomas Hodgskin used this distinction as the title of a book: *The Natural and Artificial Right of Property Contrasted.* By natural right of property, he meant "the right of individuals, to have and to own, for their own separate and selfish use and enjoyment, the produce of their own industry, with power freely to dispose of the whole of that in the manner most agreeable to themselves . . ." This right, established by the "continual possession and use by one person of any one thing," was founded in nature. It resulted from the need of labor to satisfy human wants in the natural order of things, and on the extension of individuality to the creations of the individual's labor.[2]

Although Hodgskin cited Locke as his primary authority, his radical interpretation of Locke put an emphasis on ongoing use as the basis for continued appropriation of land in a way that would probably cause Rothbard's followers and other modern Lockeans to look askance:

> The field that has been once cleared and ploughed, is soon overrun with useless weeds, if it be not continually cultivated. There is no other wealth in the world but what is created by labour, and by it continually renewed. This principle, now universally acknowledged, makes the right of property appear more absolute and definite than it was in Mr. Locke's comprehension, because the right to own land is in fact only the right to own what agricultural or other labour produces. The natural law of appropriation, therefore, exists in full force at all times and places; and at this moment constitutes a rule for appropriating every part of the wealth which is continually created. The wants which can only be gratified by labour always exist, or are always renewed, the necessity to gratify them by labour is never suspended; and now, as at the beginning, nature bestows on the labour intended to gratify these wants whatever it can produce.[3]

Hodgskin suggested, in rather pointed terms, that the practical effect of the property rights established under the laws of the state was not at all to secure the individual's ownership of his labor product:

> Does legislation . . . proceed upon a study of the principles which determine the natural right of property? Is the latter—is the natural relation between labour and its produce recognised and acted on throughout society, as we acknowledge and act on the relation between seed time and sowing? Have all the laws of society said to be intended expressly to protect property, been framed with a view to preserve this relation entire and untouched? Has government, instituted, according to Mr. Locke, for no other purpose but to guarantee the enjoyment of our natural property, fulfilled its commission? Does labour now obtain and own whatever it produces? Is every man's right to have and enjoy whatever he creates or obtains by honest exertions protected by the law?[4]

He went on to state, much more explicitly, that the artificial property rights guaranteed by law served primarily to enable a parasitic exploiting class to live off the labor of producers. And this parasitic class included the "owners" of most of the land in England:

---

1. Tucker, "State Socialism and Anarchism: How Far They Agree, and Wherein They Differ"
2. Thomas Hodgskin, "Letter the Second. the Natural Right of Property Illustrated," *The Natural and Artificial Right of Property Contrasted. A Series of Letters, addressed without permission to H. Brougham, Esq. M.P. F.R.S.* (London: B. Steil, 1832) <http://oll.libertyfund.org/index.php? option=com_staticxt&staticfile=show.php%3Ftitle=323&layout=html>.
3. *Ibid.*
4. *Ibid.*

Laws being made by others than the labourer, and being always intended to preserve the power of those who make them, their great and chief aim for many ages, was,
and still is, to enable those who are not labourers to appropriate wealth to themselves. In
other words, the great object of law and of government has been and is, to establish and
protect a violation of that natural right of property they are described in theory as being
intended to guarantee . . . .

All the legislative classes, and all the classes whose possessions depend not on nature,
but on the law, perceiving that *law* alone guarantees and secures their possessions, and
perceiving that government as the instrument for enforcing obedience to the law, and
thus for preserving their power and possessions, is indispensable, unite one and all, heart
and soul to uphold it . . . .

Among the legislative classes embodied into, and constituting the government, we
must place the landed aristocracy. In fact, the landed aristocracy and the government are
one—the latter being nothing more than the organized means of preserving the power
and privileges of the former. After securing a revenue for the government . . . the laws
have been made with a view to guarantee the possessions and the wealth of the landowners . . . . His right to possess the land, not to possess the produce of his own labour,
is as admirably protected as can be effected by the law . . . Nature makes it a condition of
man having land, that he must occupy and cultivate it, or it will yield nothing. The instant he ceases his labour, she decks it with flowers, and stocks it with the birds and animals which she delights to clothe and feed; exacting no payment but their happiness. The
mere landowner is not a labourer, and he never has been even fed but by violating the
natural right of property . . . .

The law grants tithes, and enforces the payment of them. It gives the soil, and a power
to exact rent to the landlord, and a revenue to the government; but in all these, the great
and leading objects of law, I see no protection for the natural right of property. On the
contrary, not one of them can be thought of without trenching on this natural right . . . .

At present, besides the government, the aristocracy, and the church, the law also
protects, to a certain extent, the property of the capitalist, of whom there is somewhat
more difficulty to speak correctly than of the priest, the landowner, and the administerer
of the law, because the capitalist is very often also a labourer. The capitalist as such, however, whether he be a holder of East India stock, or of a part of the national debt, a dis-
counter of bills, or a buyer of annuities, has no natural right to the large share of the annual produce the law secures to him. There is sometimes a conflict between him and the
landowner, sometimes one obtains a triumph, and sometimes the other; both however
willingly support the government and the church; and both side against the labourer to
oppress him; one lending his aid to enforce combination laws, while the other upholds
game laws, and both enforce the exaction of tithes and of the revenue . . . .

. . . [L]aw and governments are intended, and always have been intended, to establish and protect a right of property, different from that which . . . is ordained by nature.
The right of property created and protected by the law, is the artificial or legal right of
property, as contra-distinguished from the natural right of property. It may be the theory
that government ought to protect the natural right; in practice, government seems to exist only to violate it. Never has the law employed any means whatever to protect the
property nature bestows on individuals; on the contrary, it is a great system of means devised to appropriate in a peculiar and unjust manner the gifts of nature. It exacts a revenue for the government,—it compels the payment of rent,—it enforces the giving of
tithes, but it does not ensure to labour its produce and its reward.[1]

Hodgskin's position anticipates Oppenheimer's distinction, which we saw earlier, between the economic and political means, and his conception of the class state. He anticipates
Oppenheimer in much else as well, setting forth a theory of political appropriation much
like Oppenheimer's. Were the natural right of property the basis of all appropriation, Oppenheimer argued, it would have been impossible for the land to become fully appropriated
to the extent that it was necessary for laborers to pay rent for access to it.

1. "Letter the Third: The Legal Right of Property," in *Ibid.*

[Mr. Locke] says accurately, "as much land as a man tills, plants, and improves, cultivates, and can use, the product of so much is his property."—"This is the measure of property in land, which nature has well set by the extent of man's labour, and the conveniences of life; no man's labour could subdue or appropriate all, nor could his enjoyment consume more than a small part, so that it would be impossible in this way to intrench on the right of another, or acquire to himself a property to the injury of his neighbours. Unfortunately, however, this admirable principle has not the smallest influence over legislators in dealing out that which, by the bye, is not theirs, the land of new colonies.[1]

Rather, the land was politically appropriated by conquest, so that even vacant and unimproved land could be held out of use by the artificial property titles of a ruling class, and the latter could charge tribute from labor for access to it.

The persons who thus appropriated the soil of Europe, did so by a right of conquest. They did not lay down the sword the instant they had overrun the land, they kept it drawn in their hand, and engraved with it laws for the conquered . . . . In appropriating the soil, they appropriated its inhabitants, reduced some to slavery, and continued the slavery of others. Power so acquired, and privileges so established, were the basis of the present *political and legal,* not social, edifice of Europe. These conquerors were the first legislators. By an almost uninterrupted succession, the power of legislation has continued in the hands of their descendants to the present day . . . .
. . . . Seeing that conquerors have always been the legislators, and knowing that they have always endeavoured to preserve their own power, I cannot avoid concluding, that the law has always been made with a view to preserve, as much as possible, that appropriation of the soil, that artificial right of property, and that system of government . . . .[2]

Oppenheimer and Nock, both Georgists of sorts, rejected the appropriation of land through state grants of title without personal occupancy or admixture of labor as, respectively, "political appropriation of the land" or "law-made property"; both of them, however, favored the socialization of rent as an alternative to a possessory criterion for subsequent transfers of property once appropriated, and saw land value taxation as an alternative to messy inquiries into the history of land appropriation. Rothbard, whose Lockeanism was less radical than the usufructory or Georgist theories, considered all subsequent transfers of justly acquired land to be valid in themselves, with no further requirement of personal occupancy as the criterion of ownership; nevertheless he repudiated as strenuously as anybody, as artificial and illegitimate, all titles to vacant and unimproved land never appropriated by admixture of labor.

Despite the differences between these property theorists as to the specifics of where they draw the line, their distinctions between natural and artificial property rights in land are motivated by essentially the same value. All the major *principled* theories of property rights (as opposed to the *utilitarian* system which governs real property law in the U.S. and most western countries, and which—although nominally based on Locke—pays little regard to questions of justice in acquisition) are imperfect attempts to maximize the value of self-ownership, and the individual's ownership of his labor-product. Specifically, all of the principled systems of property in land are intended to promote the individual's ownership of the labor he mixes in with the land, given the special difficulties presented by the immobility of land.

All of them are imperfect: each is more effective than the others in securing the individual's ownership of buildings and improvements in some cases, and less effective in doing so in other cases.

For example George Reisman, a prominent critic of my work, denounces the mutualist position on land (the occupancy-and-use tenure of J.K. Ingalls and Benjamin Tucker)

1. "Letter the Fourth: On the Right of Property in Land," in *Ibid.*
2. *Ibid.*

as a "philosophy for thieves."[1] The reason is that the mutualist system of property rights presents greater inconvenience, comparatively speaking, for the occupier and improver of land to recoup the value of his improvements by alienating the property:

> ... [L]et us imagine that our legitimate land owner—legitimate even by Carson's standards—has spent several years clearing or draining his land, pulling out stumps, removing rocks and boulders, digging a well, building a barn and a house, and putting up fences to keep in his livestock. It is this land that he agrees to rent to a tenant, or, what is not too different, sell on a thirty-year mortgage, which he himself will carry, on the understanding that every year for thirty years he will receive a payment of interest and principal.
>
> The tenant or mortgagee signs a contractual agreement promising to pay rent, or interest and principal, and takes possession of the property. Being a secret mutualist, however, he thereupon proclaims that the property is now his, on the basis of the mutualist doctrine that, in Carson's words, "occupancy and use is the only legitimate standard for establishing ownership of land."
>
> This is a clear theft not only of the land, but also of the product of labor. A worker has toiled for years and is now arbitrarily deprived of the benefit of his labor, and this in the name of the protection of the rights of workers![2]

Of course the factual assumptions of the scenario are ludicrous. Reisman assumed a broader community governed by Lockean principles, in which the "mutualist" acts as a sort of cuckoo in the nest and surprises the former owner by announcing himself only after the property has changed hands. In fact, mutualism, like any other system of land tenure, would depend on a local consensus on property rules.

Nevertheless, he has a point. It would be more difficult, under occupancy-and-use tenure, for an owner who no longer wants to occupy his property to recoup the value of his buildings and improvements by renting the property or selling it on installments. But this hardship is balanced by an equal hardship under Lockeanism:

> Here's an opposing case for you: Imagine I'm renting a house under a Lockean property system, and get permission to plant a garden on it. I invest a lot of effort in composting and green manuring, and even spend money on granite dust, greensand, rock phosphate and the like to improve the soil. When I get done with it, what was hardpan clay has been transformed into rich, black, friable soil. And when I cease renting, I lose the value of all the improvements I made. That's the sort of thing that happens all the time under Lockeanism. But I suspect that Reisman would say that I made the improvements with my eyes open, and am entitled to no sympathy because I knew what the rules were. I certainly doubt that he's shedding any tears over the invested labor that the South Central Farmers are in danger of losing.
>
> The difference is, when it happens under the system he's defending, it's just life; when it happens under the system he's demonizing, it's an outrage.[3]

Although the different principled systems of property rights theory draw the line at different point, in all of them the choice of where to draw the line reflects a similar distinction in principle. Despite all their differences, all the principled property rights systems regard admixture of labor or alteration as the only legitimate basis for appropriating unowned land; and all of them regard property titles to vacant and unimproved land as illegitimate.

This is true even of the most conservative of them, the Lockeans, whose most conservative Austrian representative—Mises—observed in *Socialism*:

1. George Reisman, "Mutualism: A Philsophy for Thieves," *Mises Economics Blog*, June 18, 2006 <http://blog.mises.org/archives/005194.asp>.

2. George Reisman, "Mutualism's Support for the Exploitation of Labor and State Coercion," *Mises Economics Blog*, June 23, 2006 <http://blog.mises.org/archives/005219.asp>.

3. Kevin Carson, "George Reisman's Double Standard," Mutualist Blog: Free Market Anti-Capitalism, June 23, 2006 <http://mutualist.blogspot.com/2006/06/george-reismans-double-standard.html>.

Nowhere and at no time has the large scale ownership of land come into being through the workings of economic forces in the market. It is the result of military and political effort . . . . The great landed fortunes did not arise through the economic superiority of large-scale ownership, but by violent annexation outside the area of trade.[1]

This was but a restatement of a widespread observation made in many times and places, and self-evident to anyone of common sense who takes time to look beneath the veil of "property rights" to the underlying reality: whenever the majority who cultivate the land, and whose ancestors have cultivated it from time out of mind, pay rent to the absentee owners of large land holdings, that state of affairs does not have its origins in the ordinary or natural process of appropriation. The use of force by the state, in upholding artificial rights of property on behalf of a usurping class, is at the root of it. As Jefferson said, "Whenever there are in any country uncultivated lands and unemployed poor, it is clear that the laws of property have been so far extended as to violate natural right."[2]

Even the most conservative of principled land theories, Lockeanism (and even without the Proviso),[3] is quite throughgoing in the radicalism of its effects, if it were consistently applied. This is demonstrated by the thought of Rothbard, whose consistent Lockean principles would undermine the majority of land titles in the United States and most of the world if they were put into effect. He denounced, in no uncertain terms, surviving feudal forms of land ownership (like the latifundia of Latin America, and its counterparts among the various landed oligarchies throughout the Third World). He denounced, likewise, the state's preemption of vacant land in settler states like the United States and Australia, and all present title to land stemming directly from the state's grants of vacant and unimproved land to speculators.

> . . . [S]uppose that centuries ago, Smith was tilling the soil and therefore legitimately owning the land; and then that Jones came along and settled down near Smith, claiming by use of coercion the title to Smith's land, and extracting payment or "rent" from Smith for the privilege of continuing to till the soil. Suppose that now, centuries later, Smith's descendants (or, for that matter, other unrelated families) are now tilling the soil, while Jones's descendants, or those who purchased their claims, still continue to exact tribute from the modern tillers. Where is the true property right in such a case? It should be clear that here, just as in the case of slavery, we have a case of continuing aggression against the true owners—the true possessors—of the land, the tillers, or peasants, by the illegitimate owner, the man whose original and continuing claim to the land and its fruits has come from coercion and violence. Just as the original Jones was a continuing aggressor against the original Smith, so the modern peasants are being aggressed against by the modern holder of the Jones-derived land title. In this case of what we might call "feudalism" or "land monopoly," the feudal or monopolist landlords have no legitimate claim to the property. The current "tenants," or peasants, should be the absolute owners of their property, and, as in the case of slavery, the land titles should be transferred to the peasants, without compensation to the monopoly landlords.[4]
>
> THUS, THERE ARE TWO types of ethically invalid land titles: "feudalism," in which there is continuing aggression by titleholders of land against peasants engaged in transforming the soil; and land-engrossing, where arbitrary claims to virgin land are used to keep first-transformers out of that land. We may call both of these aggressions "land monopoly"—not in the sense that some one person or group owns all the land in society, but in the sense that arbitrary privileges to land ownership are asserted in both cases,

1. Ludwig von Mises, *Socialism: An Economic and Sociological Analysis* (London, 1951), p. 375
2. Thomas Jefferson, *Writings*, Ford Edition, Vol. VII, p. 36, in George, Jr., *The Menace of Privilege*, Chapter Two (part one).
3. I.e., that there should be "enough and as good" land left for others after the appropriation.
4. Murray N. Rothbard. *The Ethics of Liberty* (New York and London: New York University Press, 1998), p. 66.

clashing with the libertarian rule of non-ownership of land except by actual transform-ers, their heirs, and their assigns.[1]

It's safe to say, based on these passages, that Rothbard didn't share the attitude of the usual suspects at Cato, who get their panties in a wad every time a leftist government initi-ates a land reform in Latin America. Unlike the vulgar libertarians, Rothbard didn't regard United Fruit Company as the "good guys" in Guatemala.

All the major principled theories of property rights in land, including the Lockean, are in agreement that the artificial scarcity resulting from enforcement of title to vacant and unimproved land artificially depresses the return on labor and inflates that on land. Among the Lockeans, this was stated quite forcefully by Rothbard:

> Keeping land out of use raises the marginal value product and the rents of remaining land and lowers the marginal value product of labor, thereby lowering wage rates.[2]

All the principled theories are likewise in agreement, not only that land is artificially scarce for labor, but that it is artificially plentiful for the privileged classes who have appro-priated it politically. As a result, the political appropriators have access to far more land than they can put to productive use, and therefore either use large tracts of land inefficiently, hold it out of use altogether, or both. Adam Smith remarked on the inefficient use of large estates in Europe:

> It seldom happens that a great proprietor is a great improver . . . To improve land with profit, like all other commercial projects, requires an exact attention to small savings and small gains of which a man born to a great fortune . . . is seldom capable. The situation of such a person naturally disposes him to attend to ornament which pleases his fancy than to profit for which he has so little occasion . . . . He embellishes perhaps four or five hundred acres in the neighbourhood of his house, at ten times the expense which the land is worth after all his improvements; and finds that if he was to improve his whole es-tate in the same manner, and he has little taste for any other, he would be a bankrupt be-fore he finished the tenth part of it . . . .[3]

The great latifundistas of Latin America, likewise, hold the majority of their land out of cultivation.

Alfred Marshall referred to the fact "that much good land is poorly cultivated, be-cause those who would cultivate it well have not access to it."[4]

In addition, the boundaries between the different principled rights theories are quite blurry. As Charles Johnson points out, any generally delineated principles of individual rights require arbitrary rules for their application: "the principle . . . does not fully *specify* how to *apply* individual rights in the case at hand." Principles, for their application, require more or less arbitrary *rules* that are not entailed *as such* in the principles.[5] As we shall see shortly, Nozick argued that any theory of property rights must include provisions for ex-tinction (i.e., transfer and abandonment), as well as initial appropriation. This is equally true of Lockeanism, which includes standards for constructive abandonment after some arbitrar-ily chosen lapse of time. Usufructory theories, likewise, must set some reasonable minimum threshold for abandonment so that it is possible to go on a long vacation or periodically

1. *Ibid.*, p. 68.
2. Murray Rothbard, *Power and Market: Government and the Economy* (Kansas City: Sheed An-drews and Mcmeel, Inc., 1970, 1977), pp. 132-133.
3. Smith, *Wealth of Nations*, pp. 166-167.
4. Alfred Marshall, *Principles of Economics*, Book VI Ch. XI
5. Charles Johnson, "Liberty, Equality, Solidarity: Toward a Dialectical Anarchism," in Roderick T. Long and Tibor R. Machan, eds., *Anarchism/Minarchism: Is a Government Part of a Free Country?* (Hampshire, UK, and Burlington, Vt.: Ashgate Publishing Limited, 2008), p. 166. Quotes are from textfile provided by the author.

leave land fallow. Rather than saying they rest on qualitatively different principles of transfer and abandonment, it's more accurate to say that both the usufructory and Lockean systems provide for abandonment, and differ qualitatively "over how long land must be left unused before it can be reclaimed as abandoned property."

Reisman ignored the requirement of conventional (and in large part arbitrary) rules, as an element common to all property rights systems. In fact, he used a double standard in using god terms and devil terms, respectively, to describe the functioning of objectively identical enforcement mechanisms under Lockean and mutualist property rules.

It's a mistake to judge a proposed property system on the assumption that it would be implemented as badly as possible, but that is often exactly what is done. For example, critics of occupancy and use tenure commonly ask about an owner letting a portion of land lie fallow as part of a crop rotation scheme, or taking an extended vacation, or even going into town to buy groceries, and finding his land or home stolen out from under him by a squatter. Now occupancy and use tenure would be enforced by juries of small property owners in a community where property universally distributed among such small owners, and all the members of the community are small owners. It would seem to be a matter of common sense that the law of occupancy and use would be enforced in view of its primary intent, which is to secure such small owners in their ownership with a minimum of inconvenience; and since most such small owners presumably would not care to live in fear of their land and homes being expropriated from under them the minute they leave home.

> Any rule is rigid less by the rigidity of its terms than by the rigidity of its enforcement. Now it is precisely in the tempering of the rigidity of enforcement that one of the chief excellences of Anarchism consists. Mr. Herbert must remember that under Anarchism all rules and laws will be little more than suggestions for the guidance of juries, and that all disputes, whether about land or anything else, will be submitted to juries which will judge not only the facts, but the law, the justice of the law, its applicability to the given circumstances, and the penalty or damage to be inflicted because of its infraction.[1]

The bare principle of private property in land does not carry with it, of any necessity, any particular set of rules of land tenure. Nozick pointed out that any theory of "justice in holdings" must include three major topics: 1) a theory of "the *original acquisition of holdings,* the appropriation of unheld things"; 2) "the *transfer of holdings* from one person to another"; and 3) "principles governing how a person may divest himself of a holding, passing it into an unheld state."[2] Or as Tucker put it, "The question is not whether we should be able to sell or acquire in 'the open market' anything which we rightfully possess, but how we come into rightful possession."[3] Free market libertarians are divided among themselves on how to answer this question.

Bill Orton has argued, quite convincingly in my opinion, that no particular system of property rules is self-evident. No ownership claim can be deduced logically from the principle of self-ownership alone, without the "'overlay' of a property system," or a system of "allocation rules."[4] No such system, whether Lockean, Georgist, or Mutualist, can be proved correct. Any proof requires a common set of allocation rules, and a particular set of allocation rules for property can only be established by social consensus, not by deduction from the principle of self-ownership.[5]

1. Tucker, "Property Under Anarchism," *Instead of a Book,* p. 12.
2. Robert Nozick, *Anarchy, State, and Utopia* (U.S.A.: Basic Books, 1974), pp. 150-151.
3. Benjamin Tucker, "An Alleged Flaw in Anarchy," *Instead of a Book,* p. 212.
4. Bill Orton, "Cohen's Argument," Free-Market.Net forums, January 1, 2001 <http://www.free-market.net/forums/main0012/messages/807541545.html> Captured April 30, 2004.
5. Orton, "Re: On the Question of Private Property," Anti-State.Com Forum, August 30, 2003 <http://www.antistate.com/forum/index.php?board=6;action=display;threadid=6726;start=20>. Captured April 30, 2004.

There is a great deal of practical overlap between the different systems. For one thing, the "stickiness" of property is a matter of degree:

> In both systems [i.e., "sticky" (Lockean) and "non-sticky" (socialist/usufruct)], in practice there are well-known exceptions. Sticky property systems recognize abandonment and salvage; usufruct allows for people to be absent for some grace period without surrendering property . . . . You might even see the two systems as a continuum from high to low threshold for determining what constitutes "abandonment."[1]

Or as Orton put it elsewhere, stickiness is a matter of degree, rather than a qualitative difference between capitalist and socialist property. They are "the same thing . . . with different parameters" for the length of time necessary to establish abandonment.[13]

Libertarianism, in the sense of adherence to the non-aggression principle, is consistent with any set of property rules. It is the set of property rules that determines whether a given act of violence is coercion or self-defense. Arguments for the superiority of one set of rules over another can be established only on consequentialist grounds (i.e., on the basis of prudential assessments of how they lead to results consistent with commonly accepted ideas of "fairness"), and not deduced from principle.

3. Patents and Copyrights

We already discussed, in Chapters Nine and Ten, the function of "intellectual property" in unequal exchange and the exploitation of labor. As we saw, Tom Peters likes to enthuse that most of the price of commodities consists of "intangibles" or "intellect." That is just another way of saying that most of the purchase price of what we buy amounts to rent on artificial property rights like copyright and patents, trademarks, and so forth, and that therefore the same portion of the labor we have done to earn that purchase price goes to pay rent to the holders of such artificial property, rather than to pay for the materials and labor actually involved in producing the goods. Whatever portion of the price of consumer goods, on average, is comprised of returns on "intellectual property," that same portion of our workweek consists of tribute to the owners of artificial property.

> It's funny that in the name of protecting "intellectual property," big media companies are willing to do such violence to the idea of *real* property—arguing that since everything we own, from our t-shirts to our cars to our ebooks, embody someone's copyright, patent and trademark, that we're basically just tenant farmers, living on the land of our gracious masters who've seen fit to give us a lease on our homes.[2]

In industries where physical capital outlays are negligible compared to human capital, patents and copyrights act as tollgates between labor and the consumer market, enabling the holders of "intellectual property" both to appropriate part of the laborer's product and to charge monopoly prices to the consumer.

> . . . [T]he vast majority of musical innovation happens on the streets by people who are not being paid by anyone. The machine that is the music industry then snatches a bit of that popular culture, sanitizes it, and then sells it back to us at a premium. They create a superstar or two out of cultural traditions of their choosing and to hell with the rest of them. Sometimes the musicians they promote are really good, but that's not the point. The point is that if the RIAA were truly interested in promoting good artists, they'd be doing lots of smaller record contracts with a wide variety of artists representing a broad cross-section of musical traditions. But as it is, if it were up to the RIAA we'd be listen-

1. Bill Orton, "Yet Another Variation," Anti-State.Com Forum, December 7, 2003 <http://anti-state.com/forum/index.php?board=1;action=display;threadid=7965;start=0>.
2. Cory Doctorow, "In the age of ebooks, you don't own your library," *Boing Boing*, March 23, 2008 <http://www.boingboing.net/2008/03/23/in-the-age-of-ebooks.html>.

ing to the music of a small handful of multimillionaire pop stars and the other 99.9% of musicians would starve.[1]

Intellectual property, in short, is theft. And it's instructive to consider the hypocrisy of those who rely on it as a business model. The publishing, music and software industry figures who whine the most about "piracy," and complain that "you can't compete with free," are the very same people who themselves ruthlessly downsized their workforces when new production technology made them redundant. David Noble, in *Progress Without People*, relates an incident in the early 1970s when the *Washington Post* was adopting computerized cold type technology which rendered pressmen obsolete. The pressroom was invaded after hours by pressmen who systematically took apart the machines with the clinical expertise of a Jack the Ripper.[2] So why is it bad for "Luddites" to smash machines that put them out of a job, while technology that puts capitalists out of a job violates their "property" rights? If the same newspaper publishers whose adoption of new technology rendered skilled workers obsolete, now find themselves threatened by cutting and pasting and hyperlinks—well, it couldn't happen to a nicer bunch of guys. And if the record companies' management and shareholders now find *themselves* redundant in the face of home sound editing, filesharing, and other forms of new technology, then let them eat cake. If workers don't have a property right in their jobs in the face of new technology, then neither do capitalists have a property in the accrual of profits from a business model rendered obsolete by new technology.

4. Occupational Licensing and Safety Codes

We already examined the role of these forms of artificial property, as they affect unequal exchange and exploit the worker and consumer, in Chapter Four. Like patents and copyrights, they serve as toll gates. In this case, they impede the individual's ability to transform his labor and skills directly either into subsistence production for his own use, or into marketable value.

A good example is the medallion system of licensing taxicabs, where a license to operate a cab costs into the hundreds of thousands of dollars. The effect of the medallion system is to criminalize the countless operators of gypsy cab services. For the unemployed person or unskilled laborer, driving carless retirees around on their errands for an hourly fee seems like an ideal way to transform one's labor directly into a source of income without doing obeisance to the functionaries of some corporate Human Resources department.

The primary purpose of the medallion system is not to ensure safety. That could be accomplished just as easily by mandating an annual vehicle safety inspection, a criminal background check, and a driving record check (probably all the licensed taxi firms do anyway, and with questionable results based on my casual observation of both vehicles and drivers). And it would probably cost under a hundred bucks rather than three hundred thousand. No, the primary purpose of the medallion system is to allow the owners of licenses to screw both the consumer and the driver.

Another good example is the entry barriers to employment as a surveyor today, as compared to George Washington's day. As Vin Suprynowicz points out, Washington had no formal schooling until he was eleven, only two years of it thereafter, and still was able to learn enough geometry, trigonometry and surveying to get a job paying $100,000 annually in today's terms.

1. David Rovics, "The RIAA vs. the World," *Counterpunch*, October 9, 2007 <http://www.counterpunch.org/rovics10092007.html>.

2. David F. Noble, *Progress Without People: New Technology, Unemployment, and the Message of Resistance* (Toronto: Between the Lines, 1995), p. 42.

How much government-run schooling would a youth of today be told he needs before he could contemplate making $100,000 a year as a surveyor—a job which has not changed except to get substantially easier, what with hand-held computers, GPS scanners and laser range-finders? Sixteen years, at least—18, more likely.[1]

1. Vin Suprynowicz, "Schools guarantee there can be no new Washingtons," *Review Journal*, February 10, 2008 <http://www.lvrj.com/opinion/15490456.html>.

Appendix
Reciprocity and Thick Libertarianism

Charles Johnson, in arguing for "thick" libertarianism, uses Chris Sciabarra's "dialectical libertarianism"[1] as a starting point. Johnson treats anti-state libertarianism as part of "a larger effort to understand and to challenge interlocking, mutually reinforcing systems of oppression, of which statism is an integral part—but only one part among others."[2] By "thick" libertarianism, he means promoting a relationship between narrowly anti-state ("thin") libertarianism, and "'thicker' bundles of socio-cultural commitments . . ."

Johnson lists several different kinds of "thickness": i.e., several possible ways in which anti-state libertarianism's non-aggression principle can be bundled together with related cultural values, so that "thick" libertarians may oppose forms of oppression or exploitation which are not formally coercive.[3]

The most important, for our purposes, is what he calls Grounds Thickness: "some commitments might be *consistent* with the non-aggression principle, but might undermine or contradict the *deeper reasons* that *justify* libertarian principles. Although you could *consistently* accept libertarianism without the bundle, you could not do so *reasonably*: rejecting the bundle means rejecting the *grounds* for libertarianism.[4] Anti-state libertarianism's opposition to coercion assumes an even more fundamental value of human moral equality and "*equality of authority*," which social and economic oppression can violate without formal coercion.[5] Given that the "underlying reason" for commitment to anti-state libertarianism is a belief in the equal political authority of human beings, while it may not be formally inconsistent for a libertarian to endorse voluntary forms of social authoritarianism, it is "*weird*."

The same is true of those who display hostility toward voluntary expressions of solidarity or mutual aid:

> One could in principle believe that everyone ought to be free to pursue her own ends while *also* holding that nobody's ends actually matter except her own. But again, while the position is possible, it is *weird*; one of the best reasons for being concerned about the freedom of others to pursue their own ends is a certain generalized respect for the importance of other people's lives and the integrity of their choices, which is intimately connected with the libertarian conception of Equality.[6]

In short, the value libertarians place on liberty is grounded in the value of human equality. We are entitled to equal liberty, and no one is entitled to coerce another, because of the equal dignity and value each of us possesses as an end in himself. And it is possible to violate this principle of equal dignity, by violating (as we shall see below) the principle of reciprocity, without formally violating liberty as such.

Matt MacKenzie builds on this foundation, in analyzing economic exploitation from the standpoint of Grounds Thickness.[7] MacKenzie begins with the fundamental value of anti-state libertarianism as such: that "it is morally impermissible to initiate coercion or

---

1. Chris Sciabarra, *Total Freedom: Toward a Dialectical Libertarianism* (University Park, Penn.: The Pennsylvania State University Press, 2000).

2. Charles Johnson, "Liberty, Equality, Solidarity: Toward a Dialectical Anarchism."

3. *Ibid.*

4. *Ibid.*

5. *Ibid.*

6. *Ibid.*

7. Matt MacKenzie, "Exploitation: A Dialectical Anarchist Perspective," *Upaya: Skillful Means to Liberation*, March 20, 2007 <http://upaya.blogspot.com/2007/03/exploitation.html>.

fraud against others."[1] But that statement immediately suggests the question of *why* it is impermissible: because others *are our equals*, entitled to be treated as ends rather than means.

MacKenzie provides his own supplemental definition of Grounds Thickness: "certain commitments ought to be accepted because they are based on the same grounds that justify one's commitment to libertarianism in the first place."[2] Economic exploitation deserves condemnation even when non-coercive, because it violates the fundamental norm of fairness underlying libertarianism's non-aggression principle.

In developing his argument against exploitation, MacKenzie relies heavily on Alan Wertheimer's book *Exploitation*.[3] Wertheimer defines exploitation, much like the average medieval tradesman of Meek and Tawney, as "taking unfair advantage."[4] He distinguishes between harmful and mutually advantageous exploitation. Harmful exploitation occurs when A exploits B in ways that create net harm to B. Mutually advantageous exploitation equates to the kind of situation described earlier in this chapter, in which the exploited party (B) is a net beneficiary from a transaction compared to his state had he not participated in it, but the exploiter (A) is able to assess payment based on the B's benefit, rather than on A's cost of providing the service. The key question, in distinguishing non-harmful exploitation from the coercive kind, is whether B benefits compared to "a no-transaction baseline." If the individual gives consent because he believes he benefits compared to his state without the transaction, it is both non-harmful and consensual exploitation. In this case, although the exploitation does not violate the non-aggression principle, it does violate the norm of *fairness*.

> . . . . [C]onsider the case in which B is in a lifethreatening situation and A is the only one who is in a position to rescue him. A offers to rescue B, but only if B agrees to sign over all of his current wealth as well as 50% of all future earnings. B, valuing his life, agrees. He benefits relative to the no-transaction baseline, which is death, but I think most would agree that he is not treated fairly. The broader point here is that parties to a mutually beneficial transaction are not indifferent to the distribution of costs and benefits between the two parties. And I see no reason to rule out from the start the idea that some distributions within the zone of mutual advantage could be exploitative.[5]

MacKenzie treats justice as a subset of the broader category of fairness: claims to justice entail a right to enforcement; claims to fairness which do not invoke the standard of justice may be equally valid, but are not necessarily enforceable.[6]

Unfairness is subject to what MacKenzie calls "transaction specific considerations," and to "background considerations":

> First, there are transaction specific considerations of fairness. Here the focus is on features of the transaction itself in relative abstraction from the larger social or historical context. For instance, if A employs fraud in order to take advantage of B, the unfairness here is a direct defect of the transaction itself. Also, cases of transient monopoly, such as standard rescue examples, may simply involve forms of transaction specific unfairness. Second, there are background considerations of fairness. These considerations deal with the larger social context within which the transaction occurs. For instance, if A has a legal monopoly on the production of widgets, this fact may be relevant to whether A's sale of widgets to B will count as an exploitative transaction. Obviously, these two types of considerations are interdependent. Background unfairness emerges from patterns of individual ac-

1. *Ibid.*
2. *Ibid.*
3. Alan Wertheimer, *Exploitation* (Princeton, N.J.: Princeton University Press, 1996). All references below to Wertheimer's arguments rely on their treatment in MacKenzie's article.
4. MacKenzie, "Exploitation,"
5. *Ibid.*
6. *Ibid.*

tions and these systemic forms of unfairness can make possible or facilitate cases of transaction specific unfairness. Moreover, background injustice—those forms of unfairness
that constitute rights violations—can make possible or facilitate forms of unfairness that
are not themselves unjust.[1]

MacKenzie sets aside, for the sake of argument, transaction specific considerations that
involve force and fraud. This leaves for consideration the very important general class of
transactions which are exploitative (in the sense of being unfair) without involving direct
coercion between the parties themselves, but nevertheless involve the exploiting party taking advantage of structural conditions that operate in his favor so that the "distribution of
costs and benefits" between the two parties is unequal.

MacKenzie's "distribution of costs and benefits between the parties" is, in essence, the
norm of reciprocity which we examined at the outset of this chapter. Economic rents that
result from short-term bottlenecks in the supply of reproducible commodities, or from similar transient phenonmena that involve no coercion or fraud, fall into the general category of
"unfairness" (in the sense of an inequality of benefits resulting from one party taking advantage of background conditions, so as to "charge what the market will bear").

So long as market entry is unconstrained, such unfair but non-coercive exchange may
be not only of net benefit to the individual by MacKenzie's no-transaction baseline, but
serve a greater social purpose as the mechanism by which resources are directed into those
uses where demand outstrips supply, so that price to gravitates toward cost. In such a case,
when exploitation amounts to a temporary producer surplus, the social attitude tends to
fall into the category of grudging admiration ("you lucky bastard"), rather than moral outrage.

Moral outrage occurs, on the other hand, when artificial (or even natural—e.g., differential land rent) constraints on market entry render the producer surplus permanent—
especially when the beneficiary had recourse to political power in creating such an entry
barrier for his own benefit.[2]

So what we have arrived at is a residual category of transactions in which both parties
participate willingly and no direct force is used by the exploiting party, and in which the
exploited party benefits compared to his no-transaction baseline, and yet exploitation takes
place from the standpoint of fairness (i.e., the comparative distribution of costs and benefits
between the parties). And further, in this category of transactions, the exploiting party is
taking unfair advantage, not of a transient state of affairs resulting from normal fluctuations
of supply in a competitive market, or of producer rents from being the first to introduce an
innovation when competitors are free to adopt it afterward, but of a state of affairs in
which the state sets up market entry barriers to competition with the exploiting party, and
thereby artificially constrains the range of alternatives available to the exploited party.

MacKenzie argues that libertarians ought to condemn as exploitative the rents that accrue to corporations taking advantage of this state of affairs, and reject such exploitation as unfair even when it occurs in nominally "voluntary" transactions between "private" entities.

> The picture, then, is this: the state directly exploits its citizens and intervenes in the mar-
> ket on behalf of privileged economic elites . . . creating a distorted, cartelized economy.
> The rents gained by the beneficiaries of state intervention constitute the extraction of
> social surplus from the exploited—workers, consumers, entrepreneurs, etc. Further, this
> pervasive exploitation is compatible with the continued improvement in the condition
> of the exploited through economic exchange. Relative to a no-transaction baseline, mar-
> ket exchange is mutually beneficial, even in a cartelized market economy. However, the

1. *Ibid.*
2. *Ibid.*

beneficiaries of cartelization are able to capture more of the surplus of social cooperation than they would be able to in a more just and competitive economy.[1]

At one point MacKenzie catches himself in what seems to me to be a basic contradiction:

> . . . . when it comes to voluntary market exchange, the appropriate libertarian principle of fairness is not—heaven forbid—a notion of an objective price or a notion of equal exchange, but rather a notion of the (hypothetical) competitive market price. The fair market price is the (hypothetical) free market price.[2]

This seems to me to contradict his earlier line of argument. In even a competitive market, short term imbalances of supply make it possible for a firm to receive a producer surplus or economic rent by taking advantage of such conditions. This, I think, clearly falls into the category of a transaction that is "unfair," in the sense of being an unequal "distribution of costs and benefits" between the parties, without being either unjust in a transaction-specific sense or in terms of background considerations. Like the unfairness of, say, producer rents from superior innate skill, they are an unfairness that is nobody's fault and which most sensible people will cheerfully accept, and yet which are still "unfair" for all that.

In my opinion, denying the "unfairness" of such temporary economic rents, even in a free and competitive market, undermines the central lesson of MacKenzie's article: the distinction between unfairness and injustice. The most important thing, in MacKenzie's model of state capitalism, is that unfairness is the product of background injustice, and thereby goes beyond *mere* unfairness to the point of being itself tinged with actual *injustice*, in a much larger share of cases than most libertarians are willing to recognize. The difference between the free market and the regime of privilege is that while the former permits unfairness, it is an unfairness in which the "unjust rewards" are temporary and promote the greater social good; the latter, on the other hand, enforces "unjust rewards" as its central end, while forcibly suppressing the process by which they serve the greater good.

But from the same distinction, it also follows that unfairness—even when it does not entail injustice, either directly or indirectly—it is still *unfair*. Libertarians should oppose unfairness because—according to the principle of grounds thickness—it contradicts the ethical basis of their libertarianism even when it does not involve actual coercion. The value of liberty itself has, underlying it, the value of moral equality. And the norm of reciprocity stems from that same value of moral equality. If you are just as important as I am, it follows that your right to pursue your own goals is as sacred as mine, that your right to be compensated for your labor is just as important to you as mine is to me, and that the costs (effort or pain) you experience are just as significant to you as mine are to me.

1. *Ibid.*
2. *Ibid.*

12

Structural Changes: The Cost Principle

INTRODUCTION

The cost principle, as originally stated by individualist anarchists, was "cost the limit of price." They largely neglected its corollary form: "cost the basis of price."[1] Such neglect was more understandable in the nineteenth century, although even then subsidies played an essential role in the development of capitalism. But the much greater scale of government subsidies today makes the issue impossible to ignore. The corollary form of the cost principle will be our primary focus in this chapter: all costs of providing goods and services should be internalized in market price, and borne by the consumer.

The cost principle, as stated by the early individualists, was originally understood to require some special administrative mechanism or set of bylaws to enforce, like labor-notes and other forms of voluntary currency, or Warren's time store. Warren set the value principle (setting price by what the market would bear) in opposition to the cost principle. Stephen Pearl Andrews, in his explication of Warren's thought, actually considered market competition to be a form of war by which the strong subjugated the weak, and the rich were made richer and the poor poorer; worse yet, he argued that competition "*prevent*[ed] *the possibility of a scientific Adjustment of Supply to Demand*," rather than being the means by which this was done.[2]

It was the insight of Hodgskin in England, and of Greene and Tucker in America, that no such artificial mechanism was necessary. Rather, the *natural tendency* of the competitive market was for the price of reproducible goods to move toward the cost of production. It was consistent *deviation* from the cost principle that required an artificial mechanism: namely artificial scarcity and unequal exchange resulting from state intervention. The problem was not "value" as such, but impediments to the natural process by which competition moves value toward cost.

Indeed, as Marx had recognized long before, the deviation of price from cost was the *mechanism* by which the market constantly adjusted supply to demand, and gravitating toward an equilibrium at which the quantities supplied and demanded coincided at a market-clearing price based on production cost. A price above or below the cost of production was what signaled an imbalance of supply and demand, and caused factors of production to be moved from one use to another until the imbalance was corrected. As Hodgskin described it:

---

1. Stephen Pearl Andrews came very close to stating the corollary principle in *The Science of Society*: "The truest condition of society . . . is that in which each individual is enabled and constrained to assume, to the greatest extent possible, the Cost or disagreeable consequences of his own acts." II:3. And elsewhere: "It is Equity that *every individual should sustain just as much of the common burden of life as has to be sustained BY ANY BODY on his account*." *Science of Society*, Part II, Chapter I ("The Cost Principle"). Online edition provided courtesy of the late Ken Gregg, at *CLASSical Liberalism* blog <http://classicalliberalism.blogspot.com/2006/04/science-of-society-no_10.html>.
2. *Science of Society*, Part Two, Chapter IV ("Value Distinguished from Cost").

The governments of some countries . . . , noticing the evils resulting from variations in
the seasons, have established public granaries to prevent them, and to equalize the operations of nature; but the merchant buying when and where commodities are cheap, and
only selling when and where they are dear, does, in fact perform . . . all the functions of
public granaries.[1]

The forms of exploitation Tucker remarked on in the nineteenth century resulted from
violation of the original, negative version of the cost principle: cost exceeded price as a result
of unequal exchange, with tenants, workers, and consumers paying assorted forms of scarcity
rent on land, capital, and goods subject to "intellectual property." And as we saw in Chapter
Eleven, such forms of unequal exchange continue to operate in corporate capitalism up to
the present day (e.g. "intellectual property," by which commodity rprices, mainly reflect
rents on artificial property rights rather than material and labor costs).

But many more of the ills specific to *corporate* capitalism, on the other hand, result
from violations of the positive version of the principle: the supply of transportation and
other production inputs to privileged enterprises *below* their market costs. Murray Rothbard described the effects of such subsidies:

> The first point to note, of course, is that these services are not and cannot be truly
> *free.* A free good . . . would simply exist in superabundance for all. If a good does not ex-
> ist aplenty for all, then the resource is scarce, and supplying it costs society other goods
> forgone. Hence it cannot be free. The resources needed to supply the free governmental
> service are extracted from the rest of production. Payment is made, however, not by users
> on the basis of their voluntary purchases, but by a coerced levy on the taxpayers. A basic
> split is thus effected between *payment* and *receipt of service* . . . .
> Many grave consequences follow from the split and from the "free" service as well.
> As in all cases where price is below the free-market price, an enormous and excessive
> demand is stimulated for the good, far beyond the supply of service available. Conse-
> quently, there will always be "shortages" of the free good, constant complaints of insuffi-
> ciency, overcrowding, etc. An illustration is the perpetual complaints about police insuffi-
> ciency, particularly in crime-ridden districts, about teacher and school shortages in the
> public school system, about traffic jams on government-owned streets and highways, etc
> . . . .
> Free supply not only subsidizes the users at the expense of non-using taxpayers; it
> also misallocates resources by failing to supply the service where it is most needed. The
> same is true, to a lesser extent, wherever the price is under the free-market price. On the
> free market, consumers can dictate the pricing and thereby assure the best allocation of
> productive resources to supply their wants. In a government enterprise, this cannot be
> done. Let us take again the case of the free service. Since there is no pricing, and there-
> fore no exclusion of submarginal uses, there is no way that the government, even if it
> wanted to, could allocate its services to their most important uses and to the most eager
> buyers. All buyers, all uses, are artificially kept on the same plane. As a result, the most
> important uses will be slighted. The government is faced with insuperable allocation
> problems, which it cannot solve *even to its own satisfaction.* Thus, the government will be
> confronted with the problem: Should we build a road in place A or place B? There is no
> rational way whatever by which it can make this decision . . . .[2]

The irrationality and misallocation that result from the divorce of payment from
benefit, or of cost from decision-making authority, have been a central theme of this book.
Indeed, Oppenheimer's "political means" might be *defined* as the divorce of payment from
benefit. The fundamental purpose of power is to receive benefits at others' expense,
through the exercise of unaccountable power over them. And this inevitably follows from

    1. Thomas Hodgskin, *Popular Political Economy: Four Lectures Delivered at the London Mechanics'
Institution* (London: Printed for Charles and William Tait, Edinburgh, 1827), p. 175.
    2. Murray Rothbard, *Man, Economy, and State: A Treatise on Economic Principles* (Auburn, Ala.:
Ludwig von Mises Institute, 1962, 1970, 1993), pp. 819-820.

the authority relationship and from hierarchy. Authority breeds conflict of interest wherever it is found, whether in the government sector or the nominal private sector. For example, as Lloyd Dumas described it,

> The assumption that control is exercised by the cost bearers is nontrivial, and in some cases unrealistic. For instance, taxpayers bear the cost of the salaries of government employees. Yet, though rational, taxpayers are not necessarily in control of government personnel decisions. Hence it is quite possible that individuals will be hired whose salaries exceed the value of their work output in the eyes of the taxpayers. In the opinion of the government administrators doing the hiring, the value of the salaries may far exceed the opportunity cost of that use of budgeted funds. But the administrators are not paying the salaries—the taxpayers are. This situation is not peculiar to government. Managers of private corporations, for example, may engage in bureaucratic empire-building and hire people whose work output is less valuable than its cost, in the eyes of the stockholders and/or consumers who share the salary costs. It is thus the judgment of the decision makers that holds sway when the decision makers and the cost bearers are different individuals.[1]

A major part of the economy consists of things which are paid for but produce no commensurate value, the moral equivalent of digging holes and filling them in again. This leads to the obvious question:

> Why would workers be paid identical salaries to provide services of . . . radically different inherent economic value? In fact, why would economically valueless output be associated with a nonzero money value? . . .
>
> [One possible answer]: there may be a discrepancy between the value of an activity or output to the decision maker who authorizes its purchase and its value to those who actually pay the price.[2]

One example he gives of unproductive consumption of inputs is administrative activity within an organization. The cost to managers

> of expanding the bureaucratic control apparatus is low, while the value to them of such expansion may well be substantially higher . . . . The managers have the relevant decision-making power: they are in operational control of hiring and purchasing decisions. Therefore, as long as the value of expansion exceeds its costs from *their* perspective, they will continue to expand the bureaucracy.[3]

In other words, decision makers aim at maximizing net utility, not to society as a whole, but to themselves personally. If their power enables them to shift marginal cost downward relative to benefits, they will consume an input beyond its point of diminishing social utility.

Such subsidies result in massive amounts of waste being built into the basic structure of the economy. For example, the centralization of the economy and concentration of industry result, among other things, from artificially cheap transportation and energy inputs. So do inefficiently energy-intensive forms of production. Subsidized research and development and technical education, as we saw in Chapter Three, have distorting effects on the choice of production technology: specifically, the choice of high-cost, capital-intensive forms of production that create entry barriers, promote hierarchy, and also promote capital substitution and the deskilling of labor.

1. Lloyd Dumas, *The Overburdened Economy: Uncovering the Causes of Chronic Unemployment, Inflation, and National Decline.* (Berkeley, Los Angeles, London: University of California Press, 1986), pp. 39–40.

2. *Ibid.*, pp. 42–43.

3. *Ibid.*, pp. 66–67.

A. Peak Oil and the "Long Emergency"

The application of the cost principle to the corporate economy would result in radical changes: a shift toward decentralized, small-scale production for local markets; toward energy-efficient industry and housing; toward walkable, mixed-use communities. One of the best summaries of the changes required by Peak Oil comes from Herman Koenig:

> Undoubtedly the first thing we will try to do as the real cost of energy increases and it becomes less available, is make adjustments to more efficient technologies . . . ; they are frequently called "technological fixes." We can and will put more insulation in our homes, opening windows a little more in the summer, turning down the thermostat in winter. Detroit will build a more efficient automobile for you, you'll get 45 or 50 miles per gallon instead of 16 in a few years. We will transfer some of the freight from the highways to the railroads. Such technological adjustments have been estimated to have the potential of saving thirty to forty percent of our present energy budget. Such adjustments will not affect our life style very much, but the "slack" will run out after a few years.
>
> The next large class of adjustments relate to our mobility. Fifty-four percent of our petroleum is used for transportation. As petroleum becomes less available, and the price rises significantly, our mobility will go down. How will this affect the landscape? We will undoubtedly find that what we need to re-invent are medium-sized communities built around a small electrical generating facility that heats our homes and commercial buildings with the residual heat. It is called district heating. These communities would also serve as transit terminal connections to other communities, and they will have a diversified commerce and some decentralized, light industry. Such communities are much more energy-efficient, since most of the elements of everyday living are near at hand.
>
> A third class of adjustments is to be found in the area of product durability. Just as small is beautiful, age will be beautiful. We have the technology to significantly increase the durability of most of our products. We can build a refrigerator that will outlive its human owner. Detroit is beginning to realize that it should develop cars that will last perhaps twice as long as present cars. If we increase product durability, as we must, there will be a tremendous opportunity not only for reducing energy requirements, but also the impact on our environment.[1]

Whether or not the state ceases to subsidize resource consumption and otherwise distort the market in favor of large-scale organization and centralization, input crises like Peak Oil are likely to make the cost principle felt sufficiently to result in such changes.

A common theme in the popular media today is that "human ingenuity" will find some magic formula which will allow the current American form of social organization (economic centralization, large-scale production for large market areas, suburban sprawl and the commuter society, the soccer mom SUV lifestyle, thousands of passenger jets in the air 24/7, etc.) to continue unchanged—but at lesser cost, and with reduced greenhouse emissions and dependence on foreign oil. But this is a fairy tale. State capitalism is headed for a crisis of inputs, the inevitable outcome of the internal contradictions that result from its having been built around subsidized inputs in the first place. The very act of subsidizing inputs leads to escalating demand faster than the state can subsidize them, until things reach a breaking point.

The Western industrial economies have become dependent on extensive inputs of long-distance shipping, to the point of insanity. Hedrick Smith, attempting to illustrate the irrationality of the Soviet economy, used the example of a trainload of concrete beams traveling from Leningrad to Moscow, passing a trainload of identical beams traveling from Moscow to Leningrad. E.F. Schumacher, in *Good Work*, wrote:

---

1. Herman Koenig, "Appropriate Technology and Resources," in Richard C. Dorf and Yvonne Hunter, eds., *Appropriate Visions: Technology the Environment and the Individual* (San Francisco: Boyd & Fraser Publishing Company, 1978). p. 259.

When you travel up the big motor road from London you find yourself surrounded by a huge fleet of lorries carrying biscuits from London to Glasgow. And when you look across to the other motorway, you find an equally huge fleet of lorries carrying biscuits from Glasgow to London. Any impartial observer from another planet would come to the inescapable conclusion that biscuits have to be transported at least six hundred miles before they reach their proper quality.[1]

James Kunstler explains why the American car culture and "warehouses on wheels" industrial culture are finished:

> Everywhere I go these days . . . , I hear an increasingly shrill cry for "solutions." This is just another symptom of the delusional thinking that now grips the nation . . . .
>
> . . . I detect in this strident plea the desperate wish to keep our "Happy Motoring" utopia running by means other than oil and its byproducts. But the truth is that no combination of solar, wind and nuclear power, ethanol, biodiesel, tar sands and used French-fry oil will allow us to power Wal-Mart, Disney World and the interstate highway system—or even a fraction of these things—in the future. We have to make other arrangements.
>
> The public, and especially the mainstream media, misunderstands the "peak oil" story. It's not about running out of oil. It's about the instabilities that will shake the complex systems of daily life as soon as the global demand for oil exceeds the global supply . . . .
>
> . . . . The idea that we can become "energy independent" and maintain our current lifestyle is absurd . . . .
>
> So what are intelligent responses to our predicament? First, we'll have to dramatically reorganize the everyday activities of American life. We'll have to grow our food closer to home, in a manner that will require more human attention. In fact, agriculture needs to return to the center of economic life. We'll have to restore local economic networks—the very networks that the big-box stores systematically destroyed—made of fine-grained layers of wholesalers, middlemen and retailers.
>
> We'll also have to occupy the landscape differently, in traditional towns, villages and small cities. Our giant metroplexes are not going to make it, and the successful places will be ones that encourage local farming.
>
> Fixing the U.S. passenger railroad system is probably the one project we could undertake right away that would have the greatest impact on the country's oil consumption . . . . The airline industry is disintegrating under the enormous pressure of fuel costs. Airlines cannot fire any more employees and have already offloaded their pension obligations and outsourced their repairs. At least five small airlines have filed for bankruptcy protection in the past two months. If we don't get the passenger trains running again, Americans will be going nowhere five years from now.[2]

I should note, in passing, that—even if giant metroplexes *don't* "make it"—there's no necessity for their collapse to be sudden or catastrophic. If their economies are sufficiently restructured, their present sites can probably support at least a majority of their current population. That would require, among other things, dedicating lawns and other forms of greenspace to raised-bed horticulture and edible landscaping, and heroic efforts at conserving rainwater. It would require the emergence of networked economies, the growth of commercial centers in existing monoculture suburbs, and local exchange systems and division of labor based on household production and crop specialization. One step toward a local manufacturing economy, based on the informal and household sectors, is the use of the better-equipped hobbyists' workshops to custom machine replacement parts for ma-

---

1. E. F. Schumacher, *Good Work* (New York, Hagerstown, San Fransisco, London: Harper & Row, 1979), p. 19.

2. James Kunstler, "Wake Up America. We're Driving Toward Disaster," *Washington Post*, May 25, 2008 <http://www.washingtonpost.com/wp-dyn/content/article/2008/05/23/AR2008052302456_pf.html>.

chinery, and the creation of neighborhood repair/recycling/ remanufacture shops, as discussed in Chapter Fourteen.[1]

Jeff Vail explains, in greater detail, both why there is no magic technological fix for Peak Oil, and what a healthy economic system post–Peak Oil will entail.[2] Quality of life, he observes, is a function of energy inputs and "technics" (the efficiency with which the energy is directed to work). Quality of life can be increased either by tapping new sources of concentrated energy, or by using the energy we have more efficiently.

The problem is that the greatest sources of concentrated energy are almost certainly reaching their peak. The only energy sources with a high "EROEI" (Energy Return on Energy Input—i.e., a concentrated energy source that produces a great deal more energy than is required to tap it) are fossil fuels. The only alternative energy sources with a fairly high EROEI, wind and hydro, won't be available in quantities even remotely sufficient to replace current energy consumption from fossil fuels. Simply put, there is no concentrated energy source in the world with an EROEI as high as that of fossil fuel, and energy sources with an EROEI significantly higher than one can take up only a small part of the slack.

Therefore the only solution is "improving technics—improving how we use the energy that we *do have* to create quality of life."

> It seems very likely that there is ample room to improve our technics. IF we accept this latter proposition—that we can improve our utilization of energy to create quality of life—then doesn't it make the most sense to focus our mitigation efforts there? I have great confidence in the power of human ingenuity to solve our problems. However, when human ingenuity meets the laws of physics and thermodynamics, I don't think they will bend to our will. Design of technics, on the other hand, seems to be an area where human ingenuity has unending room for advancement . . . .
>
> My hypothesis is that our quality of life . . . is more dependent on how we use our energy than on how much of it we use . . . . [W]e can better influence our quality of life through improving technics than through increasing energy consumption . . . .

Vail proposes a technics paradigm based on three principles: "decentralized, open source, and vernacular." As an example, he contrasts the Tuscan village with the American suburb:

> How is the Tuscan village decentralized? Production is localized. Admittedly, everything isn't local. Not by a long shot. But compared to American suburbia, a great percentage of food and building materials are produced and consumed in a highly local network. A high percentage of people garden and shop at local farmer's markets.
>
> How is the Tuscan village open source? Tuscan culture historically taps into a shared community pool of technics in recognition that a sustainable society is a non-zero-sum game. Most farming communities are this way—advice, knowledge, and innovation is shared, not guarded. Beyond a certain threshold of size and centralization, the motivation to protect and exploit intellectual property seems to take over (another argument for de-

---

1. Jeff Vail addresses this question in detail in a series of blog posts. In the first, he argues that there may be no viable alternative to suburbia in many cases because of the sunk costs ("A Resilient Suburbia (Part I)," JeffVail.Net, Nov. 10, 2008 <http://www.jeffvail.net/2008/11/resilient-suburbia-part-1.html>). In the second, he continues, Peak Oil is likely to serve " as a catalyst to reshape the economic structure of suburbia" rather than to abandon it ("A Resilient Suburbia 2: Cost of Commuting," JeffVail.Net, Nov. 17, 2008 <http://www.jeffvail.net/2008/11/resilient-suburbia-2-cost-of-commuting.html>). The third, and most interesting post, addresses the extent to which the suburban economy can increase its self-sufficiency. In this, he cites John Jeavons' work on the potential productivity of backyard gardens, and examines the possibilities of rainwater harvesting and storage and passive solar heat ("A Resilient Suburbia 3: Weighing the Potential for Self-Sufficiency," JeffVail.Net, Nov. 24, 2008 <http://www.jeffvail.net/2008/11/resilient-suburbia-3-weighing-potential.html>).
2. Jeff Vail, "The Design Imperative," *A Theory of Power*, April 8, 2007 <http://www.jeffvail.net/2007/04/design-imperative.html>.

centralization). There is no reason why we cannot share innovation in technics globally, while acting locally—in fact, the internet now truly makes this possible, leveraging our opportunity to use technics to improve quality of life.

How is the Tuscan village vernacular? You don't see many "Colonial-Style" houses in Tuscany. Yet strangely, in Denver I'm surrounded by them. Why? They make no more sense in Denver than in Tuscany. The difference is that the Tuscans recognize (mostly) that locally-appropriate, locally-sourced architecture improves quality of life. The architecture is suited to their climate and culture, and the materials are available locally. Same thing with their food—they celebrate what is available locally, and what is in season. Nearly every Tuscan with the space has a vegetable garden. And finally . . . their culture is vernacular. They celebrate local festivals, local harvests, and don't rely on manufactured, mass-marketed, and global trends for their culture nearly as much as disassociated suburbanites
. . . .

Brian Kaller's American equivalent of the Tuscan village is Mayberry. Or rather, a higher-tech version of the American Main Street lifestyle before the triumph of the car culture, symbolized by Mayberry. Kaller also takes issue with Kunstler's apocalyptic view of the Peak Oil transition.

In fact, peak oil will probably not be a crash, a moment when everything falls apart, but a series of small breakdowns, price hikes, and local crises . . . .

. . . The Long Emergency will be an era, not an event, and the challenge will be to see the larger trends as they unfold and to retool our habits and infrastructure . . . .

The Long Emergency could look like the Victory Garden movement during World War II, when Americans responded to a national threat by turning backyards into gardens and freeing food production for the troops. Within a couple of years, such gardens were producing almost half of Americans' vegetables. Contrary to popular myth, the movement was not a big-government initiative—the Roosevelt administration discouraged the effort at first, unsuccessfully, until it joined in and turned the White House lawn into crops . . . .

The same habits that helped us through that crisis—recycling, thrift, gardening—will help with this one . . . .

While peak-oil literature often considers the world to be at the end of a 200-year industrial era, it is only in the last few decades that we have truly binged. By some estimates, the world has used as much oil in the last 25 years as in the entire previous century. Restoring a low energy world, for many Americans, would not mean going back two centuries.

Take one of the more pessimistic projections of the future, from the Association for the Study of Peak Oil, and assume that by 2030 the world will have only two-thirds as much energy per person. Little breakdowns can feed on each other, so crudely double that estimate. Say that, for some reason, solar power, wind turbines, nuclear plants, tidal power, hydroelectric dams, biofuels, and new technologies never take off. Say that Americans make only a third as much money, cut driving by two thirds. Assume that extended families have to move in together to conserve resources and that we must cut our flying by 98 percent.

Many would consider that a fairly clear picture of collapse. But we have been there before, and recently. Those are the statistics of the 1950s—not remembered as a big time for cannibalism.[1]

B. THE SCALE OF POSSIBLE SAVINGS ON ENERGY INPUTS

Fortunately, Vail's optimism regarding the potential of technics seems to be fully warranted. Chapter Fourteen of this book, on decentralized production technology, deals with the feasibility of a decentralized economy organized around small-scale manufacturing for local markets. Vail himself links to a number of interesting initiatives.

1. Brian Kaller, "Future Perfect: Stop Worrying and Learn to Love Expensive Oil," *The American Conservative*, August 25, 2008, pp. 23-26.

The Energy Descent Action Plan (EDAP),[1] developed by students in the Practical Sustainability course at Kinsale Further Education College, is a detailed agenda for managing the Irish town of Kinsale's transition from a high-energy consumption to a low-energy consumption community. The study assumes that Kinsale's available fossil fuel inputs in 2021 will be half those available in 2005, and recommends measures for managing an orderly transition. To take one example, in the area of food, by 2021 lawns have disappeared, and landscaping consists entirely of edible plant permaculture. As we have already seen in this book—repeatedly—and will see again in Chapter Fourteen, the total labor required for growing food at the point of production is less than that required to earn the money to buy factory farmed produce. Taking into account also the savings in labor and money for lawn maintenance, and the improved quality of food, this would clearly be a net improvement in quality of life.

The Transition Town[2] movement in the UK, beginning with Totnes and now including some seventy towns, is another good example. Some of these towns have developed EDAPs of their own.[3] Finally, Vail mentions Richard Heinberg's *Powerdown*,[4] which has inspired various eco-village projects in the British Isles.

Cuba has already made—much more briefly and painfully—a transition comparable to what the West is likely to undergo with Peak Oil in the coming decades. Until the late 1980s, Cuba's agricultural economy was a Soviet wannabe, based on heavy mechanization and use of chemicals; the state-socialist model of agriculture was as if Cargill had turned the farms of an entire country into one giant agribusiness plantation, and then the state had expropriated the corporation and put it under a state ministry. But with the collapse of the Soviet bloc and the cutoff of Soviet "fraternal assistance," the Cuban economy was deprived of the inputs necessary for a Soviet-style agricultural model. There were drastic cutbacks in electric power and transportation, in fuel and spare parts for those big combines, and natural gas for chemical fertilizer. Left with an economy largely geared toward cash crops of sugar, and deprived of the Soviet-bloc markets for that sugar at subsidized prices, Cuba suffered something like a one-third reduction in average daily caloric intake. But more than a decade later, Bill McKibben noticed a difference:

> Cuba had learned to stop exporting sugar and instead started growing its own food again, growing it on small private farms and thousands of pocket-sized urban market gardens—and, lacking chemicals and fertilizers, much of that food became de facto organic . . . . Cubans have as much food as they did before the Soviet Union collapsed. They're still short of meat, and the milk supply remains a real problem, but their caloric intake has returned to normal . . . .
>
> . . . [T]hey have created what may be the world's largest working model of a semi-sustainable agriculture, one that doesn't rely nearly as heavily as the rest of the world does on oil, on chemicals, on shipping vast quantities of food back and forth.[5]

As the *Freedom Democrats* blog points out, Cuba's success resulted from the government simultaneously rejecting the Washington Consensus model of focusing on cash-crop exports, and loosening up state socialist impediments to bottom-up innovation domestically.

---

1. *Kinsale 2021: An Energy Descent Action Plan—Version.1.2005*. By Students of Kinsale Further Education College. Edited by Rob Hopkins (Kinsale, Ireland: Kinsale Further Education College, 2005) <http://transitionculture.org/?page_id=104>.

2. Transition Town Wiki <http://www.transitiontowns.org/>

3. Transition Town Totnes <http://totnes.transitionnetwork.org/>

4. Richard Heinberg, *Powerdown: Options and Actions for a Post-Carbon World* (New Society Publishers, 2004).

5. Bill McKibben, "The Cuba diet: What will you be eating when the revolution comes?" *Harpers*, April 2005. <http://www.harpers.org/archive/2005/04/0080501>.

. . . [M]any of the changes occurred from the bottom up and wouldn't have been possible if the communist government hadn't gotten out of the way. The growth in farmers markets and urban gardens, which have enabled half of the food consumed in Havana to come from small gardens in Havana, wouldn't have faced greater obstacles if the Cuban government hadn't backed down and recognized the right of the individual to buy and sell produce in a small-scale free market . . . .[1]

According to McKibben, just about every previously vacant lot in Havana is an intensely cultivated farm, averaging 5 kg of produce per square meter. The city gets "nearly its entire vegetable supply, and more than a token amount of its rice and meat," through such urban farming.[2]

Closer to home, Intervale—a 200-acre community-supported agriculture farm in Burlington, Vermont—supplies "7 or 8 percent of all the fresh food consumed in Burlington."[3]

A lot of the price premium on local, organic food stems from the fact that it is still consumed in insufficient quantities in most localities to maximize economies in distribution: rather than taking a full truckload to a single supermarket, a farmer often must distribute the load among several stores in an area. Another source of high prices is entrepreneurial profit, reflecting the fact that supply hasn't kept up with demand. When two things occur (both of which almost certainly will)—a much larger portion of the food consumed in each local market is local and organic, and sufficient food is grown locally to meet the demand—the price will be far more competitive. That's true even with the subsidies to large-scale chemical agribusiness, which simply won't begin to compensate for the exploding costs of long-distance transportation and chemical fertilizer.

Starting from where we are now, there is (as the authors of *Natural Capitalism* argue)[4] an abundance of low-hanging fruit, measures which could reduce energy consumption by half or three-quarters in industry after industry, and at the residential level, with virtually no impact on quality of life. That Americans have not found this fruit worth the bother of picking, speaks volumes about the distorting effect of subsidized energy and transportation.

The authors of *Natural Capitalism* compare subsidized energy consumption in the American "market" economy to that in the old Soviet Union, where economic planners priced energy at a third of the actual cost of providing it.[5]

Major savings could be achieved through better urban design. The main force behind urban sprawl is disregard of the cost principle. Local governments build subsidized freeway systems and ever further outlying bypasses in order to "relieve congestion," only generating *new* congestion as the new roads fill up with new traffic from the new subdivisions and strip malls that line them. Suburban developments commonly receive subsidized utility connections at the expense of ratepayers in the old, inlying parts of town. School boards close down old neighborhood schools to build new ones out by the new subdivisions. Urban congestion is promoted by the availability of free or underpriced parking downtown, subsidizing those who drive in from the suburbs at taxpayer expense. For example, "[m]ost

1. "Two Pathways," *Freedom Democrats*, February 11, 2008 <http://freedomdemocrats.org/node/2541>. Oxfam America also did a study on Cuba's agricultural transition: Minor Sinclair and Martha Thompson, "Cuba: Going Against the Grain" (Oxfam America: June 2001) <http://www.oxfamamerica.org/newsandpublications/publications/research_reports/art1164.html>.

2. Bill McKibben, *Deep Economy: The Wealth of Communities and the Durable Future* (New York: Times Books, 2007), pp. 74-75.

3. *Ibid.*, p. 80.

4. Paul Hawken, Amory Lovins, L. Hunter Lovins, *Natural Capitalism: Creating the Next Industrial Revolution* (Boston, New York, London: Little, Brown and Company, 1999).

5. *Ibid.*, p. 42.

American building regulations require developers to provide as much parking for each shop, office, or apartment as people would demand *if parking were free.*"[1]

Zoning prohibits mixed-use development, and thereby inflates the need for transportation to get from the monoculture residential pod to the monoculture pod commercial where one shops and works. The neighborhood grocer has been zoned out of existence, along with all but the most informal and unobtrusive of home businesses. Affordable housing in the downtown commercial district (e.g. walkup apartments over shops) is also prohibited.[2]

The combined effect of all these subsidies to sprawl is that there are two separate communities for each of us: a bedroom community where we live, and a different community where we work and shop—each with its own complete set of utilities, and joined by an expensive highway infrastructure for driving back and forth between them.

The present car-centered pattern of urban design is the result, not of the market, but of decades of government-imposed social engineering.

In Europe, where urban densities are several times higher, nearly half of trips are by foot or bicycle, and another 10% by public transit—compared to 87% by car in the U.S. Even something as low-tech as allowing mixed-use development would result in huge savings. For example, in the 1970s Portland officials estimated that reviving neighborhood grocers, alone, would be enough to reduce gasoline consumption by 5%.[3]

Other forms of waste, also associated with urban sprawl, likewise result from the distorting effects of government intervention in the market. For example, local regulations restrict the efficient use of gray water, so that people are forced to use drinking water to water lawns and hose off driveways.[4] Restrictions on composting toilets and enforced use of water-based sanitation systems mean that drinking water is wasted to flush wasted fertilizer downstream to the ocean.[5] According to Madhu Suri Prakash, "[m]ore than 40 percent of the water available for domestic purposes is used for transporting shit."[6] Water utilities, more often than not, deal with droughts by threatening administrative penalties for watering lawns, and the like, instead of charging scarcity rates or increasing rates for higher levels of usage. But in those areas where utilities resort to the latter cost-based incentives, consumers make drastic reductions in water consumption on their own initiative, without the need for neighborhood informers.[7] Switching to biologically, rather than chemically based sewage treatment, and decentralizing sewage systems to the neighborhood level, not only reduces cost but closes the loop by providing safe fertilizers for local use. Costs for purifying drinking water are also reduced.[8]

The same is true of building design and industrial processes. The radical effects of a thoroughgoing application of the cost principle, in these areas, are demonstrated by a wealth of material in *Natural Capitalism.* The sheer scale of potential savings in energy consumption that are feasible, from a purely technical standpoint, is astonishing. The central theme of the book, as stated by the authors, is that "90 to 95 percent reductions in material

1. *Ibid.*, p. 42.

2. See, for example, James Howard Kunstler, *The Geography of Nowhere: The Rise and Decline of America's Man-made Landscape* (New York and London: Simon & Schuster, 1993), for the effects of imposing car culture through zoning laws.

3. Hawken *et al.*, *Natural Capitalism*, p. 45.

4. *Ibid.*, p. 214.

5. *Ibid.*, p. 221.

6. Madhu Suri Prakash, "Compost Toilets and Self-Rule," *Yes!*, Winter 2008 <http://www.yesmagazine.org/article.asp?id=2102>.

7. Hawken *et al.*, *Natural Capitalism*, p. 224.

8. *Ibid.*, pp. 228-29.

and energy are possible in developed nations without diminishing the quantity or quality of the services that people want."[1]

Some critics of environmentalism and energy conservation (e.g. George Reisman, a regular commentator at Mises.Org) portray energy saving as tantamount to a catastrophic reduction in the standard of living—as though the energy input per unit of consumption were a fixed quantity. At times, Reisman writes as though the expenditure of energy were itself a measure of prosperity: a consumption good in and of itself, rather than a means to an end.

> A major demand of the environmental movement, put forward as essential to combating global warming, is the imposition of a massive rollback in global emissions of carbon dioxide accompanied by a freeze on such emissions at the sharply reduced level imposed . . . .
>
> Such pronouncements can be made openly and repeatedly only because the immense majority of people do not take the trouble to understand their implications . . . .
>
> In purely verbal terms, those implications are that environmentalism seeks the destruction of the energy base of the modern world, along with the elimination or radical reduction in the supply of all goods and services that depend on that energy base. . . . The goods and services in question are air conditioners, automobiles, airplane travel, housing, food, clothing, refrigerators, freezers, television sets, telephones, washers, dryers, books, computers—everything that depends on the production and use of oil, coal, or natural gas, which all release carbon dioxide into the atmosphere in being burned. The destruction of the energy base and the production of goods and services is implied by the fact that in order to rollback the emission of carbon dioxide, it is necessary to rollback the production and use of energy in these forms. But rolling back the production and use of energy reduces the production of goods and services.[2]

This is what Amory Lovins called "the bizarre notion that using less energy—or more often, failing to use much more energy— . . . means somehow a loss of prosperity."[3]

The authors of *Natural Capitalism* document countless innovations, many of them laughably cheap compared to the energy savings they would produce. Some of the biggest savings involve, not changes in particular technologies, but in overall design philosophy. A "whole-system engineering" or "integrated design" approach, focused on the way components are put together, can sometimes achieve large energy savings with little or no increase in up-front cost—or even reduced up-front cost. It's true that energy-saving components may, taken individually, cost more than their conventional counterparts. But when systems are taken as a whole, efficiencies in one area may lead to greater savings in another, with a cumulative effect.

One good example is green building design. Passive solar design can reduce heating and cooling costs by eighty percent or more. An office building in Amsterdam uses 92% less energy than neighboring buildings, at a construction cost per square meter no greater than the market average.[4] Similar savings can be made in water consumption—for example, a housing development with natural drainage swales for rain water which actually reduce building cost by $800 per home thanks to savings on expensive storm sewers, and at the same time cut wa-

---

1. *Ibid.*, p. 176. George Monbiot provides detailed examples of his own of the low-cost order of magnitude savings that result from picking the low-hanging fruit, in *Heat: How to Stop the Planet Burning* (London, New York, Toronto, Dublin, Victoria, New Delhi, Auckland, Johannesburg: Allen Lane, 2006).

2. George Reisman, "The Arithmetic of Environmentalist Devastation," *SOLO: Sense of Life Objectivists*, June 19, 2007 <http://www.solopassion.com/node/2667>.

3. Amory B. Lovins, *Soft Energy Paths: Toward a Durable Peace* (New York, Cambridge, Hagerstown, Philadelphia, San Francisco, London, Mexico City, Sao Paolo, Sydney: Harper & Row, Publishers, 1977), xiii.

4. Hawken *et al.*, *Natural Capitalism*, pp. 82-83.

ter consumption for landscape irrigation by up to half.[1] The Rocky Mountain Institute's headquarters, despite only fifty-two frost-free days a year, cut heating costs by 99% and uses only two small woodstoves; and despite considerable investments in energy conserving technology (like superinsulation, and superwindows that gain net heat in winter), the overall building costs are less thanks to the savings on furnace and ductwork.[2]

Passive solar design can reduce peak indoor temperature to 82 degrees even when outside temperatures are 104 and over—actually cooler than neighboring houses in which conventional air conditioning cannot keep up with the cooling burden.[3] While passive solar heating is comparatively well known, the principles of passive solar cooling are almost unknown. As Jeff Vail describes it:

> . . . while in Phoenix it may never get below 90 at night during some points in the summer, the temperature of the earth at 10' underground is always a nice 55-65 degrees F. A simple solar chimney on your home (roughly, imagine a normal chimney x 50%, with a single-glazed window on the South side and a black-painted vent pipe inside) will heat up and pull air rapidly out of your home. Now, for air intake, lay a "radiator", a network of pipes 10' underground that acts as a heat-exchanger with the thermal mass of the earth. As the solar chimney draws air out, you get nice, cool air blowing in through vents in your floor. 0 energy cost, 0 moving parts, simple technology, and it keeps your (well insulated) home at a comfortable temperature and well ventilated, even in Phoenix in August. Similar technology has been in use in vernacular architecture in the Middle East for thousands of years.
>
> Here's the catch: because it's vernacular technology, and can be easily implemented in a decentralized fashion, there isn't much money to be made off this through a centralized/industrialized economic mode. But it works . . . this is the very stuff of freedom.[4]

The conventional housing industry's tendency to ignore such low-cost alternatives applies to the choice of building materials, as well. Claude Lewenz, in *How to Build a Village*, describes the savings his organization achieved by using locally available materials and "vernacular" techniques, and substituting whitewash (ordinary garden lime with a dab of glue added, about a dollar a gallon—"so cheap there is no margin in it to pay for salesmen, advertising, marketing and middlemen") for paint. "The upshot was an outstanding, iconic compound of four major buildings for a shell cost more commonly associated with kitset garages."[5] Vernacular techniques are characterized by "locally sourced materials with limited processing steps from raw material to finished . . ."[6] Lewenz favors, in particular, use of low-cost bulk materials like ultra-lightweight concrete.[7] Another example is the use of compressed earth blocks, produced by the open-source CEB machine developed at Factor-E Farm, which we discuss in Chapter Fifteen.

On a more modest level, we can see the cost principle at work in the demise of the McMansion. Starting in 2007, KB Home in Los Angeles pared its 3400 sq. ft. homes down to 2400, and this year is selling a line of 1230 sq. ft. homes. Other builders are moving in the same direction. This is a reversal of a two-decade trend, in which median house size grew from under 1600 to over 2200 sq. ft.[8]

1. *Ibid.*, p. 83
2. *Ibid.*, p. 102.
3. *Ibid.*, p. 103.
4. Jeff Vail, "Passive Solar & Independence," *A Theory of Power*, June 28, 2005 <http://www.jeffvail.net/2005/06/passive-solar-independence.html>.
5. Claude Lewenz, *How to Build a Village* (Auckland, New Zealand: Village Forum Press and Jackson House Publishing Company, 2007), pp. 47-48.
6. *Ibid.*, p. 182.
7. *Ibid.*, p. 209.
8. Alex Veiga (Associated Press), "Homebuilders say 'less is more' with new homes," *MSNBC*, October 10, 2008 <http://www.msnbc.msn.com/id/27122696/>.

If direct solar radiation can be most cost-effectively adapted to heating space and water, grid electricity, by way of comparison, is about the least efficient method imaginable for doing so—burning fuel to generate electrical power at a large, centralized plant serving an enormous grid, transmitting it over long distances, and then converting it to heat through resistance at the point of consumption. And direct solar heat can be stored far more easily, through such means as water tanks and rock beds, than electrical power—thus reducing the storage and load-distribution problems of the electrical power grid.[1] On the other hand, electricity is ideal for providing shaft-power via motors, running electric lights and electronic radio and computer equipment, etc.[2] Simply shifting from electrical power to passive solar where it is suitable would eliminate the portion of fossil fuels currently consumed for residential and commercial heating and cooling. As for solar electricity itself, the designers at Open Source Ecology's Factor-E Farm community suggest that photovoltaics may be a comparatively inefficient means of generating electrical power, and express some skepticism as to whether its cost will be significantly reduced below that of fossil fuel competitors in the near future.[3] They're focusing, instead, on a solar turbine which uses the sun's heat to power a steam-driven generator.[4]

Immense savings in losses from long-distance power distribution can also be achieved by using electricity only for those end-uses suited to electrical power (which constitute some ten percent of end-use energy needs), and then sizing and locating electrical generators in accordance with demand.[5] With power generated close to the point of consumption, still greater efficiencies can be achieved by designing as many machines and appliances as possible to run on DC current, rather than using AC inverters.[6]

Another example is super-efficient cars: "a lighter, more aerodynamic car and a more efficient drive system work to launch a spiral of decreasing weight, complexity, and cost." While the greater cost of energy-efficient components may raise the overall cost of a moderately more efficient house or car, the whole-system effect of combining these efficiencies may result in lower overall cost for a *super*-efficient house or car.[7]

A small electric motor company in New Zealand produces motors with 85% efficiency, that last for years because the reduction in vibration and heat—in addition to saving on energy loss from such inefficiency—also greatly reduces wear. Replacing existing electric motors with the more efficient kind would reduce American electrical power consumption by 11%.[8]

The simple recycling of waste heat from power generators would by itself reduce America's total carbon emissions by 23%. Of total energy inputs into American generating plants, only a third is transformed into electricity. The other two-thirds are waste heat. Denmark gets around two-fifths of its electricity from such waste heat. The use of waste heat from industrial processes, whenever economical, would likewise reduce industrial en-

1. Lovins, *Soft Energy Paths*, pp. 44-45.

2. Amory Lovins, E. Kyle Datta, Thomas Feiler, Karl R. Rabago, Joel N. Swisher, Andre Lehmann, and ken Wicker, *Small is Profitable: The Hidden Economic Benefits of Making Electrical Resources the Right Size* (Snowmass, Colorado: Rocky Mountain Institute, 2002), p. 3.

3. Benjamin Gatti, "The Bell Tolls for PV," *Factor E Farm Weblog*, September 5, 2008 <http://openfarmtech.org/weblog/?p=322>.

4. "Solar Turbine—Open Source Ecology" <http://openfarmtech.org/index.php?title=Solar_ Turbine>.

5. Lovins, *Soft Energy Paths Soft Energy Paths: Toward a Durable Peace* (New York, Cambridge, Hagerstown, Philadelphia, San Francisco, London, Mexico City, Sao Paolo, Sydney: Harper & Row, Publishers, 1977), p. xiii.

6. *Ibid.*, p. 143.

7. Hawken *et al.*, *Natural Capitalism*, p. 114.

8. Lewenz, *How to Build a Village*, p. 113.

ergy consumption by 30% and total energy consumption by 11%.[1] Alana Herro, at *Common Dreams*, concurs:

> Recycling the heat that spews from industrial smokestacks may be one of the biggest opportunities for reducing greenhouse gas emissions, yet not many climate-savvy entrepreneurs are aware of it. When it comes to energy conservation, "[b]y and large, the world ignores the biggest, single most cost-effective, most profitable thing to do, which is recycle the energy that we're wasting," says Thomas Casten, chairman of the Illinois-based company Recycled Energy Development (RED).
>
> Of the 500,000 smokestacks in the United States, the 47,500 stacks that produce waste heat above 260 degrees Celsius (500 degrees Fahrenheit) could produce at least 50,000 megawatts of power, says Casten. That's almost half the energy produced by the U.S. nuclear fleet, he notes . . . .
>
> RED retrofits smokestacks with "waste-heat recovery boilers" that use the stack's heat to produce steam to spin a turbine and generate electricity. The company uses similar technology to develop new, localized power plants that are at least two times as efficient as the average U.S. electric utility plant. According to Sean Casten, president and CEO of RED, the United States could conceivably continue producing the same amount of energy it does now, with half the fossil fuel, by recycling the waste heat from its factories and electric generating stations . . . .
>
> It typically takes three to four years for RED's projects to make back their initial investment in the heat-recycling equipment, a roughly 35 percent return.[2]

And decentralized, distributed electrical production with small-scale community and neighborhood facilities is far better suited to waste heat recycling or cogeneration than are large plants serving a centralized grid. The smaller and more decentralized the power production, the more easily waste heat can be captured by the end-user.[3]

Sometimes great savings are a matter of simple positioning. One simple example is the laboratory fume hood, which can be altered to require 60–80% less fan power by repositioning a single louver.[4] On a larger scale, reduced friction from using larger, straighter pipes in a factory pumping system enabled designers to scale the pumps down from 95 to seven horsepower.

> . . . Schilham laid out the pipes first and then installed the equipment, in reverse order from how pumping systems are conventionally installed. Normally, equipment is put in some convenient and arbitrary spot, and the pipe fitter is then instructed to connect point A to point B. The pipe often has to go through all sorts of twists and turns to hook up equipment that's too far apart, turned the wrong way, mounted at the wrong height, and separated by other devices installed in between.

Besides the huge savings in power consumption, there was a significant reduction in capital outlays up-front, reduced complexity and lower maintenance costs.[5] Essentially, conventional factories were paying for pumps twelve times more powerful than necessary because engineers didn't even consider design efficiency at the whole-systems level.

> Much of the art of engineering for advanced resource efficiency involves harnessing helpful interactions between specific measures so that . . . the savings keep on multiplying. The most basic way to do this is to "think backward," from downstream to upstream in a system. A typical industrial pumping system, for example . . . , contains so many compounding losses that about a hundred units of fossil fuel at a typical power station

---

1. *Ibid.*, pp. 246–47.
2. Alana Herro, "Clean Energy's Best-Kept Secret: Waste-Heat Recovery," *CommonDreams.org*, November 21, 2007 <http://www.commondreams.org/archive/2007/11/ 21/5386/>.
3. Lovins *et al.*, *Small is Profitable*, pp. 284–285.
4. Hawken *et al.*, *Natural Capitalism*, p. 64.
5. *Ibid.*, pp. 115–116.

will deliver enough electricity to the controls and motor to deliver enough torque to the pump to deliver only ten units of flow out of the pipe . . . .

But turn those ten-to-one compounding losses around backward, as in the drivetrain of the Hypercar, and they generate a one-to-ten compounded *saving*. That is, saving one unit of energy furthest downstream (such as by reducing flow or friction in pipes) avoids enough compounding losses from power plant to end use to save about *ten* units of fuel, cost, and pollution back at the power plant.

. . . . This compounding effect also enables each successive component, as you go back upstream, to become smaller, simpler, and cheaper.[1]

The overall systems efficiency from reduced weight in the Hypercar is a good example. Complex systems are often like Rube Goldberg drawings, with some components existing only to handle excessive size and other side effects of inefficiency. A snowballing concatenation of increasingly costly components comes about, in the conventional large automobile, only to compensate for the greater handling difficulties of large size (e.g., power steering, which became necessary to control the heavy vehicles introduced after WWII). The decision to abandon the heavy internal combustion engine block makes possible a long series of savings in other systems down the line.

C. Path Dependency and Other Barriers
to Increased Efficiency

Although engineering schools pay lip service to elegance of systems design, actual practice is far different.

Designing a window without the building, a light without the room, or a motor without the machine it drives works as badly as designing a pelican without the fish. *Optimizing components in isolation tends to pessimize the whole system*—and hence the bottom line. You can actually make a system less efficient while making each of its parts more efficient, simply by not properly linking up these components. If they're not designed to work with one another, they'll tend to work against one another.

The new design required "not so much having a new idea as stopping having an old idea."[2]

The problem, in part, is path-dependency. "Traditionally poor designs often persist for generations, even centuries, because they're known to work, are convenient, are easily copied, and are seldom questioned."[3] The inertia of professional culture is too great to overcome in a short period of time, unless some catastrophic change (like a massive increase in energy costs) provides sufficient incentive for new kinds of thinking. Even though relatively low-cost (or even cheaper) design changes can reduce costs by an order of magnitude, the corporate dinosaur can afford to use factor inputs in the old, inefficient way because it is one of a handful of firms in an oligopoly market, all doing things the same way.

The American economy has hardly begun to pick the low-hanging fruit of energy savings, because technology is still designed by graduates of an engineering culture built on endless supplies of cheap, subsidized energy who can't be bothered to consider such matters. The entrenched design philosophy of the era of plentiful energy has yet to respond to the new age of energy scarcity.

The inertia of the corporate planned economy is compounded by misleading accounting practices, which—again—reflect the fact that restrained competition and a common corporate culture limit the consequences of being out of contact with reality. The average corporation treats the projected payback time for an investment in energy-saving

1. *Ibid.*, pp. 121-22.
2. *Ibid.*, p. 117.
3. *Ibid.*, p. 118.

technology far more stringently than the rate of return on any other capital investment. Typically, an energy-saving technology must pay for itself in less than two years to be considered—an astronomical rate of return when considered as a capital investment.[1]

The cost principle, applied consistently, is the one thing sure to result in rational consumption behavior over the long term. One good example, recounted in *Natural Capitalism*, is the period 1979-83 following the second oil shock. During that time, when the price of petroleum reached its highest level in real dollars to date, the economy grew by 19% while energy consumption actually shrank by 6%! The country got five times as much energy from increased efficiency as it got from new supply. The Swedish State Power Board estimated, in the 1980s, that fully utilizing available energy efficient technologies would by itself cut energy consumption in half—at a cost 78% lower than that of generating new energy.[2] The general principle has been verified many times over: conservation, as a source of newly available energy, is far cheaper per unit than new generation of power.

The problem is that the cost differential has to reach a certain threshold, as it did in the late '70s and early '80s, before it is noticed by the corporate dinosaurs. The oil shock of the early 1970s caused a significant cutback in the growth of energy consumption, but only the higher prices of the second oil shock were sufficient to result in an absolute decrease. The collapse of energy prices in the mid-80s led to a resumption of steep increases in energy consumption; the development of energy efficiencies, which had almost doubled 1975-85, stagnated.[3] The bureaucratic corporation, competing with equally bureaucratic corporations in a cartelized industry, takes a long time to reach the threshold at which inefficiency costs are high enough for the consequences to be felt.

Interestingly, gasoline consumption for late 2007 showed a modest decline for the first time since 1991, and the trend is expected to continue. Total miles traveled started falling below their 2006 levels in October 2007, with December miles traveled dropping 3.9% from 2006 to 2007. Total miles driven are down about 5% through February of 2008. But as Kevin Drum points out, with population growth that's a 6% reduction in miles traveled per capita, and considering the average annual growth of 1.5% in recent years, it's down about 7.5% from the trendline.[4] With every spike in the price of gasoline, the institutional barriers to telecommuting are lowered a bit as well.[5] The cost principle overrides management's instinct to keep workers where they can see them.

A number of economic analysts have seen the recent (May 2008) rise of oil prices to $130/barrel as a threshold or tipping point for the economy.

> "We may finally have crossed the line where the price of crude actually matters for most companies," said Peter Boockvar, equity strategist at New York financial firm Miller Tabak & Co . . . .
>
> Among the signs that the economy may finally be feeling the effect of rising oil prices was Ford Motor Co.'s announcement Thursday that it was abandoning any hope of making a profit this year or next now that sales of its gas-guzzling pickup trucks and Explorer sport utility vehicles have plunged.

1. *Ibid.*, pp. 266-67.
2. *Ibid.*, pp. 249-50.
3. *Ibid.*, pp. 253-54.
4. Steve Everly, "Gasoline Usage Heads Down," *Kansas City Star*, April 21, 2008 <http://www.kansascity.com/105/story/585815.html>. Judy Keen and Paul Overberg, "Gas prices rattle Americans," *USA Today*, May 8, 2008 <http://www.usatoday.com/money/industries/ energy/2008-05-08-gasprices_N.htm>. Kevin Drum, "Oil Prices and Driving Habits," *Washington Monthly*, May 9, 2008 <http://www.washingtonmonthly.com/archives/individual/2008_05/013696.php>.
5. "Telecommuting Picking Up As Gasoline Prices Soar," *CNBC.Com*, June 17, 2008 <http://www.cnbc.com/id/25189379>.

And experts said that the other two U.S. automakers, General Motors Corp. and Chrysler, may be in even greater trouble.

Ford Chief Executive Alan Mulally said the industry had "reached a tipping point" where energy costs were fundamentally changing what kind of vehicles Americans buy.

Meantime, to cope with higher energy prices, American Airlines and United Airlines both raised ticket prices, and American announced plans to impose a new baggage-handling fee. But experts say the price hikes barely begin to make up for recent losses.

"The airline industry is devastated. It can't survive $130-a-barrel oil," said industry analyst Ray Neidl at Calyon Securities in New York.

Many analysts think that unless oil prices fall back to about $100 a barrel—where they were as recently as April—the industry will have to slash 20% of its routes, the equivalent of knocking two major airlines out of business.[1]

We can probably expect oil prices significantly over $130 a barrel to have a similar effect on the trucking industry, with a comparable twenty percent of truckers simply going out of business.

The steep inflation in food prices, resulting from the increased fuel cost of long-distance distribution and from the conversion of land from food to ethanol production, has also spurred a large increase in home gardening.

At Al's Garden Center in Portland, Ore., sales of vegetable plants this season have jumped an unprecedented 43% from a year earlier, and sales of fruit-producing trees and shrubs are up 17%. Sales of flower perennials, on the other hand, are down 16%. It's much the same story at Williams Nursery, Westfield, N.J., where total sales are down 4.6% even as herb and vegetable-plant sales have risen 16%. And in Austin, Texas, Great Outdoors reports sales of flowers slightly down, while sales of vegetables have risen 20% over last year . . . .

Even before this year's food-price crunch, the vigor for veggies was already gaining momentum. An annual survey of more than 2,000 households by the National Gardening Association shows the average amount spent per household on flowers was flat in 2007 compared with a year earlier. But spending on vegetable plants rose 21% to $58 per household last year, and spending on herbs gained 45% to $32 . . . .

. . . . Burpee's sales of vegetables and herbs are up about 40% this year, twice last year's growth rate. Tomatoes, summer squash, onions, cucumbers, peas and beans continue to be top sellers.[2]

Many of these developments were anticipated by Warren Johnson during the energy crisis of the late 1970s, in a book called *Muddling Toward Frugality*.[3] Johnson argued that the long-term effect of rising energy prices would be to give a market advantage on shortened supply chains, small-scale production for smaller market areas, and diversified local economies. Although he jumped the gun by thirty years or so, his book is remarkably prescient in describing the likely effects of Peak Oil.

As of the final editing of this chapter (November 2008), gasoline prices have fallen below $2/gallon, after having reached $4 last summer. A quote from James Kunstler is relevant:

Looked at closely, the peak would resemble a kind of bumpy plateau because the price and demand data would all appear to wobble inconclusively for a while, perhaps for several years. High price, they say, "destroys" demand. As demand lessens, prices fall. Lower prices prompt demand to pick up again, and prices rise. The global peak period itself will be a period of both confusion and denial. Then, as the inexorable facts of the world peak assert themselves, and the global production line turns down while the demand line continues to rise, all the major systems that depend on oil . . . will begin to destabilize . . . .

1. Peter G. Gosselin, "$130 Oil: Is That a Tipping Point?" *The Los Angeles Times*, May 24, 2008 <http://www.latimes.com/business/la-fi-econ24-2008may24,0,6841046,full.story>.

2. Anne Marie Chaker, "The Vegetable Patch Takes Root," *Wall Street Journal*, June 5, 2008 <http://online.wsj.com/article/SB121262319456246841.html?mod=pj_main_hs_coll>.

3. Warren Johnson, *Muddling Toward Frugality: A Blueprint for Survival in the 1980s* (San Franciso: Sierra Club Books, 1978).

The peak will set into motion feedback loops of strange behavior . . . . Once the world is headed firmly down the arc of depletion, fuel supplies will be interrupted by geopolitical contests and culture clashes.[1]

Some Peak Oil skeptics argue, in the aftermath of this fall's price collapse, that the largest component of recent price rises have resulted, not from Peak Oil as such, but from speculative bubbles or from interruption of supply. That argument is based on a misunderstanding of the Peak Oil thesis. In fact, the speculative upward bidding of oil prices in futures markets, and the interruption of supply by terrorist attacks on pipelines and refineries, are manifestations of the very kinds of "feedback loops" Kunstler mentions in the quote above. Because the supply of oil has peaked, and is inelastic, its price is governed entirely by fluctuations in demand. It is directly analogous to the Georgist analysis of land, which states that the price of real estate is determined by the number of people bidding for a fixed supply. Wild fluctuations in price, and speculative bubbles as sellers decide to hold either oil or land off the market in anticipation of increased future demand, are exactly what we would expect under both Peak Oil theory and Georgist analysis of land. Because supply is inelastic, small increases in demand can lead to astronomical increases in price. The tighter the supply, the greater the value of being able to control the existing supply, and the greater the incentive to hold oil (or land) off the market now in anticipation of future price increases. Hence, the greatly increasing volatility of the market in the face of speculative bubbles. The forms of "arbitrage" promoted by scarcity include, most broadly, acts of terrorism to sabotage refineries, tankers and pipelines.

In any case, the current rate of oil extraction is as high as it will ever get, and will decline in the future. The only way the price of oil will decline is if demand continues to decline, either from conservation efforts or reduced demand as a result of the recession. As soon as demand returns to previous levels, we can expect even higher price spikes. If demand for fuel is not depressed by the economic downturn, we can expect the price of gasoline to peak at an even higher level next summer, and even higher the summer after that.

D. THE COST PRINCIPLE AND THE WORK-WEEK

One likely combined effect of reduced waste resulting from the cost principle, and from the abolition of privilege, is a drastic reduction in the workweek. As long ago as 1913, Kropotkin estimated the labor-time necessary to produce the actual food, clothing and housing that the average working family consumed at around 150 half-days' labor a year. The average worker's additional labor-time went either to waste or directly harmful production, or to supporting parasitic consumption.[2]

Absent the unnecessary production that amounts to fixing Bastiat's broken windows, and other waste (including the deliberate choice of planned obsolescence over reparability by the state's industrial cartels), and absent the portion of commodity price that reflects embedded rents on "intellectual property" and other artificial property rights like artificially scarce land and capital, we could probably produce something like our current standard of living working an average of two days a week. We're working the other three days to dig holes and fill them back in again, or to pay protection money so useless eaters won't use their artificial property rights to obstruct production.

Consider, first, the amount of total labor time that is devoted to waste production. Economists' calculation of the Gross Domestic Product is a textbook illustration of the

---

1. James Howard Kunstler, *The Long Emergency: Surviving the Converging Catastrophes of the Twenty-First Century* (New York: Atlantic Monthly Press, 2005), p. 67.
2. Peter Kropotkin, *The Conquest of Bread* (New York: Vanguard Press, 1926), pp. 87-94.

"broken window fallacy." As the authors of *Natural Capitalism* point out, anything that in-volves an expenditure of money adds to the GDP.[1] Jonathan Rowe writes:

> The GDP is simply a gross measure of market activity, of money changing hands. It makes no distinction whatsoever between the desirable and the undesirable, or costs and gain. On top of that, it looks only at the portion of reality that economists choose to ac-knowledge—the part involved in monetary transactions. The crucial economic functions performed in the household and volunteer sectors go entirely unreckoned. As a result the GDP not only masks the breakdown of the social structure and the natural habitats upon which the economy—and life itself—ultimately depend; worse, it portrays such break-down as economic gain.[2]

Everything that entails the expenditure of money adds to the GDP, even if most of the cost is waste that adds nothing to the actual production of use-value. A pileup on the expressway that totals out a dozen cars and results in several funerals or several people spending weeks on life support means millions of dollars added to the GDP. When you pay three times as much to buy food grown in another country with subsidized irrigation wa-ter and trucked to you on subsidized highways, as it would cost to buy food of identical quality grown by a local farmer and distributed in bulk without a brand-name markup, it adds three times as much to the GDP—even though you're just having to work three times as long to obtain identical (or inferior) use-values.

There is a small but significant body of literature on the portion of the national econ-omy made up of waste. Edward Wolff sees the economic surplus being absorbed, in addi-tion to capital accumulation, by surplus consumption and unproductive activity. The for-mer is "the consumption of use values by the surplus class," and the second "the absorp-tion of part of the product in activities that produce no use values themselves but instead serve to maintain an existing set of entitlements to the total product." Unproductive ac-tivities "use labor power but produce no directly usable output (use value)."

> Instead, they serve to maintain and reproduce an existing set of entitlements to the social product.[3]

Wolff's work is almost completely unusable because of his extremely arbitrary schema for classifying "productive" and "unproductive" activity. For example, he assigns the whole economy to those respective categories, piece by piece, almost entirely by broad sectors or industries. In so doing he neglects, almost completely, what is arguably the single most quantitatively significant form of waste in the modern corporate economy: the suboptimal allocation of resources or mixture of inputs *within* an industry. Many production inputs are necessary, in some quantity, for production; but they are used inefficiently because their consumption is subsidized by the state. In Wolff's schema, if a manufacturing industry pro-duces use value, the entire industry is categorized as "productive," no matter how wasteful of inputs. Questions of planned obsolescence, and the like, slip completely between the cracks of Wolff's sector-by-sector evaluation.

Much more useful, in my opinion, is Lloyd Dumas' study, already cited earlier in this chapter, *The Overburdened Economy*. We already saw Dumas' claim that much of GDP con-sists of the moral equivalent of digging holes and filling them back in again, products and activities which have no actual use value, but are assigned a monetary value.

> Ordinarily, the existence of a money price at which a good or service is actually pur-chased is by itself taken as proof that the good or service has economic value. Yet, if we

1. Hawken *et al.*, *Natural Capitalism*, pp. 59–60.
2. T. Halstead, Jonathan Rowe, and C. Cobb, "If the GDP is Up, Why is America Down?," *The Atlantic Monthly* 276(4):59–78, Oct. 1995, in Hawken *et al.*, *Natural Capitalism*, p. 60.
3. Edward N. Wolff, *Growth, Accumulation, and Unproductive Activity* (Cambridge, London, New York, New Rochelle, Melbourne, Sydney: Cambridge University Press, 1987), pp. 3–4.

define economic value functionally, it is clear that this is not true. The mere fact of a money price in no way establishes the existence, let alone the magnitude, of economic value. . . . Empirical constructs like gross national product are subject to this confusion of money value with economic value, and therefore require caution in their use—caution that has often been neglected.[1]

As I have argued, much of the GDP consists of the cost of replacing Bastiat's "broken windows." If these broken window costs, these unproductive uses of labor, were eliminated from the economy, the actual use-value consumed by the average worker could probably be produced in substantially fewer hours than he currently works. Such proposals frequently meet with the objection that something called "the economy" would be hurt, or that there wouldn't be enough "jobs." The argument, as stated by Dumas: "A society that does not generate waste in the form of planned obsolescence, or neutral or distractive activities, cannot, it is commonly argued, generate sufficient paid work opportunities to keep the labor force fully employed."[2] Or as stated by George Meany, who complained that labor-saving technologies were "rapidly becoming a curse to this society . . . in a mad rush to produce more and more with less and less labor, and without feeling [as to] what it may mean to the economy as a whole."[3]

Of course this is nonsense. Laborsaving technology is not a curse when the subsistence farmer manages to feed himself with less work. It becomes a curse only when the link between work and consumption is broken, when either work or its product becomes maldistributed, or when the gains from increased efficiency are appropriated by owners rather than passed along to workers and consumers. Dumas showed why Meany's complaint was nonsense.[4]

> The key here lies in the word "sufficient." To be sufficient the paid work opportunities need only supply enough income to satisfy the material needs and wants of the population, given the availability of goods and services for which no income is necessary. In the hypothetical purely wasteless economy, that means the workers must earn only enough income to supply them with the nondurable goods and services for which they must pay, plus any required or desired increase in their stock of durable goods. But once they have obtained access to a durable good, whether by purchase, gift, or inheritance, they need only enough income to cover the costs of its operation and maintenance . . . . So although there is less paid work *available* because durable goods are not built to become artificially obsolete or to fall apart, for exactly the same reason there is also less paid work *needed* by workers in order to achieve a given material standard of living. Accordingly, the permanence of durable goods may reduce the volume of paid activity, but it does not reduce the material well-being of the work force.[5]

The only point of a job is consumption, and what matters is the ratio of effort to consumption. The problem is that the average worker must perform the equivalent of twenty hours digging holes and filling them in, in addition to twenty hours of productive labor, to pay for the actual twenty hours' worth of use-value he consumes. And the price of that twenty hours' worth of use value has embedded in it the cost of another twenty hours of unproductive labor. These things result, as we saw in Chapter Eleven, from the divorce of effort from consumption, and the maldistribution of claims on his labor-product.

Dumas' test for what he calls a "contributive" activity (i.e., contributive to use value) is twofold:

1. Dumas, pp. 43–44.
2. *Ibid*, p. 75.
3. Jeremy Rifkin, *The Future of Work: The Decline of the Global Labor Force and the Dawn of the Post-Market Era* (New York: G. P. Putnam's Sons, 1995), pp. 84–85.
4. Dumas, pp. 46–47, 70–76.
5. *Ibid*., pp. 75–76.

(1) Is it part of a process that results in the production of a good or service that has inherent economic value? and (2) Does it perform a function necessary to the efficient operation of that process? A negative answer to either question disqualifies the activity from being considered contributive.

This second criterion is a major advance on the schema of Wolff, who completely ignores the question of how efficiently resources are used within the production process.

> The second test is necessary because even if the process results in an addition to the standard of living, redundant or unnecessary activities within that process do not contribute to that addition.

Activities which pass the first test but fail the second, Dumas calls "neutral." And those which fail both tests are "distractive."[1] Both are non-contributive.

> Freeing resources from neutral activities is simply a matter of an efficiency adjustment within an economically focuses process; freeing resources from a distractive process requires terminating the process itself and rechanneling all resources involved to contributive activities.[2]

"The preeminent contemporary example of neutral activity," Dumas writes, "is . . . the untoward expansion of administration relative to production." Although it is widely justified in terms of the alleged increase of productive efficiency which results from intensive use of management, the increased allocation of resources to administration has in fact not resulted in increased production.[3]

Another form of waste, one that Dumas pays little attention to, is the forced consumption resulting from Ivan Illich's "radical monopolies," which we discussed in Chapter Four. This consists of expenditures that are not actually necessary for a given standard of living, but which have been rendered artificially necessary by the effect of state policies that promote the crowding out of less expensive by more expensive ways of doing things. For example, someone who lives in a walkable city like Florence, within convenient distance of where he shops and works, and has access to convenient public transport for visiting other parts of the city, is likely to view a car as a luxury. The typical American suburbanite, on the other hand, has been deprived of all alternatives to car ownership by subsidies to sprawl and the car culture. Having no choice, he must treat the car as a necessity. The GDP is inflated by whatever amount he must spend on periodically buying a car, keeping it insured and in working order, and putting gas in the tank. That portion of the GDP is, essentially, the cost of a window broken by the state. And it's a huge part of GDP. According to Bill McKibben, in compact, mixed-use communities that emphasize walkability, bike-friendliness and public transit, transportation costs amount to only 4 or 5% of local economic output. In American freeway-centered communities, it's more like 17%.[4]

The cumulative waste described by another writer, Douglas Dowd, that falls essentially into Dumas' neutral or distractive activities, is immense.[5] It includes, of course, the entire military sector of the economy. But the waste in the military sector is probably dwarfed by the waste in the peacetime economy. This is especially true of the wastes associated with push distribution: planned obsolescence, excessive marketing costs, brand-name markups,

---

1. *Ibid.*, p. 53.
2. *Ibid.*, p. 54.
3. *Ibid.*, p. 57.
4. McKibben, *Deep Economy*, p. 154.
5. He estimates the U.S. GDP would have been 49% higher in 1980 without the enumerated forms of waste. Douglas Dowd, *The Waste of Nations: Dysfunction in the World Economy* (Boulder and London: Westview Press, 1989), p. 65.

etc.[1] Coupled with the unnecessary inflation of administrative expenses, described earlier by Dumas, it probably outweighs the material production cost of most of what we buy.

Dowd refers to toothpaste, ninety percent of whose price results from marketing costs. A still weightier example, based on General Motors' figures from 1939, indicates that some $150 of a chevy's $950 market price was actual production cost. This is true, he says, for almost all consumer goods.[2] Incidentally, Dowd was forced to go back to a 1940 FTC study on the automobile industry for the most recent available data, because the auto industry has been so secretive about its actual production costs.

Shoddy product design is another major source of waste. The central villain is what engineers call the "gold-plated turd": a product that, rather than being simply and elegantly designed to perform its primary task as efficiently and reliably as possible, is laden with extra features and options that reduce ease of use and lead to frequent breakdowns. Victor Papanek, an industrial designer who has made a career of denouncing gold plated turds, gives the example of a cheese grater which works only right-handed and, after several months use, wears out to the point that its own plastic coating is grated into the food. By way of comparison, a cheaper, simpler and more efficient model works both right- and left-handed, and will last virtually forever.[3]

Output restriction should also count as a form of waste. The resources devoted to excess industrial capacity, thanks to state-subsidized overaccumulation, inflate commodity prices. The standard practice, among oligopoly industries, of running at 75-80% of capacity and passing the cost of idle capacity on to the consumer, adds greatly to the price.[4] In farming, holding land out of use for price support or "conservation" subsidies is a lucrative real estate investment, which simultaneously adds to the social cost (albeit concealed in taxes) of corporate farm produce, and makes land artificially scarce and expensive for the small producer.

Planned obsolescence, as we shall see in Chapter Fourteen, often severely shortens product lifetime with no appreciable reduction in product cost. Consider, for example, product designs that are deliberately designed to thwart repair and encourage replacement, often relying on "intellectual property" to restrict access to replacement parts.

Dowd also refers to the lower productivity of labor and higher unit costs resulting from low morale and other incentive problems in the standard capitalist enterprise.[5] Dowd compares the 10.8% of the U.S. labor force in managerial and clerical positions in 1980, compared to 3% in Germany and 4.4% in Japan (a gap that has only increased since).

Unfortunately, Dowd telescopes internal waste in the production process together with other forms of waste, in a way that obscures a proper comparison. For example, he fails to separate the necessary costs of actually transporting a finished good from the point of production to the point of consumption from the rest of the general category of marketing and distribution. (Transportation can also be a form of waste, obviously, as with the subsidized replacement of economical passenger freight railroads by trucking and airline industries, or the lengthening of supply chains[6]—but it's still a separate issue from inflated marketing costs.) He also includes GM's astronomical oligopoly profit rate of 35%, which Wolff would call unproductive consumption, along with the wasted material inputs in the actual production process.

1. *Ibid.*, pp. 64-65.
2. *Ibid.*, pp. 65-66.
3. Langdon Winner, *The Whale and the Reactor: A Search for Limits in an Age of High Technology* (Chicago and London: University of Chicago Press, 1986), p. 77.
4. Dowd, pp. 67-68.
5. *Ibid.*, p. 70.
6. He deals with this in pp. 78-80.

Of course, the category of unproductive consumption by holders of artificial property right is important in its own right: whether it be GM's 35% profit, the 20–25% oligopoly price markup that the Nader Group described in American industry, or the majority of product value that Peters celebrated as resulting from "intellect" (i.e., rents on so-called "intellectual property").

One point in Wolff's favor is his attention to unproductive consumption by the privileged classes. Although this obviously falls within Boulding's category of implicit transfer ("a redistribution of income or command of the product from those who produce it to those who do not"), Dumas pays little attention to it. Boulding himself mentions the question of whether interest and rent, beyond a certain point, fall into Dumas' "neutral" category, and then dismisses it as a subject for further research. The amount of commodity price that reflects embedded rents on so-called "intellectual property" doesn't warrant even this much of a mention.

This is, in my opinion, a grave shortcoming on Dumas' part. Consider the amount of the average worker's total labor that is expended not only to pay for the above-mentioned embedded costs of intellectual property and for the oligopoly markup, but to pay artificial scarcity rents to owners of land and capital. The cumulative effect of eliminating all such forms of privilege would likely equal that of eliminating subsidized waste in the production process. If, as seems plausible as a rough approximation, waste production and rents on intangible property each result in what amounts to a 100% markup, then their cumulative effect is to quadruple the number of work hours actually necessary to produce our current levels of consumption. Three quarters of our labor goes either to waste or to tribute.

These things have a lot to do with the fact, observed by Ivan Illich, that countries with (say) a quarter of American per capita GDP usually seem to have a far better quality of life than that statistic would imply. The quality of life in Europe, for example, hardly seems to be two thirds or less than that in the U.S., as per capita GDP would seem to imply.

> . . . European workers are every bit as productive as ours; both German and French workers, for instance, produce more per hour than American workers. So why do Americans make 29 percent more money than Europeans? Because we work longer hours. *Much* longer hours—Americans average 25.1 working hours per person per week, but the Germans average 18.6; the average American works 46 weeks a year, while the French average is 40. Europeans work to live, not the reverse; they spend more time with their families, which may have something to do with why their divorce rates are much lower . . . .[1]

E. THE COST PRINCIPLE AND LOCAL AUTONOMY

Another positive effect of the cost principle, and the radical decentralization that would likely result from it, is a healthier relationship between industry and the local community. H. Thomas Johnson writes:

> If no firm had a financial incentive to grow beyond the limits of its bioregion, then any firm could focus its activities on a specific place where it knows its customers, employees, and suppliers face to face and it draws on sources of energy and materials found literally in its own backyard. By drawing the decisions of customers and owners of capital closer to the consequences for workers and their communities, those conditions would increase the visibility of, and increase pressure to eliminate, the externalities that plague today's widely-dispersed, global economy. A company that inhabits the region where it operates is more likely than one of today's global giants to see externalities . . . when and where they occur, and have an incentive to mitigate the consequences as quickly as possible.

1. McKibben, *Deep Economy*, pp. 223–224. The obnoxious writer he cites is Bruce Bawer, "We're Rich, You're Not, End of Story," *New York Times Magazine*, April 17, 2005.

Having more companies operate at smaller scale and in local regions has other beneficial consequences for achieving true sustainability in the human economy. One likely consequence of greater localization of economic activity is diminished inequality in the distribution of rewards and externalities. Extreme inequality of wealth and income such as the American economy has experienced in recent decades gives those individuals at the top of the heap increased power to act in ways that are contrary to the interest of sustainability for all. Another likely consequence of increased localization and smaller scale operations is less need for large amounts, or any amounts, of funds raised by sale of equities as opposed to funds generated internally from current earnings. With less emphasis on equity capital there presumably would be less interest in financial markets and stock trading. It is not impossible to imagine a locally oriented economic system where no publicly traded corporations exist to flaunt [sic] the cause of sustainability in the interest of maximizing shareholder wealth and top executive compensation packages.

Finally, with closer proximity of actions and consequences in a locally oriented economy there would hopefully be less need for accounting data to define and assess results and responsibilities. Just as the presence of those conditions in Toyota's operations virtually eliminated the use of production and financial controls to direct and assess operations, so might the business community and the larger public recognize the waste of complex and extensive accounting controls in a locally-oriented, "small is beautiful" economy. Increased proximity of actions and consequences might even reduce the need for taxes, subsidies, and regulations enforced from afar to encourage sustainable behavior. Results would now be visible real time in the local arena as part of local processes. As in Toyota, all the information needed would be contained in the work and the work would be the primary source of information about results and consequences.[1]

Starting from where we are, a trend toward economic decentralization and cooperative ownership would make communities more resilient and less vulnerable to corporate economic blackmail. One of the perceived weak points of decentralism, as stated by skeptics, is the ability of national corporations to play communities against each other, when they all have separate and uncoordinated policies. Angelica Oung, for example:

> . . . [W]hat's good for towns on an individual level can be harmful if everybody started doing it. For instance, if my town gives Walmart a bunch of tax breaks and get them to build a supercenter in my town, dollars starts pouring into my locality from all over. The "corrupt" town can indeed outcompete a non-corrupt town.
> My area starts doing really well. However, the next town over now offers all those superstores even better deals. Now I'm sweating. What other sweetheart deals can I offer to get that business?
> Eventually, every town is a loser.
> Same with . . . public parking lots . . . . I'm sure they make sense for the local municipality thinking from a purely local point of view. Bethesda, alone, cannot change car culture in America if it does not build that public lot. But it will lose out on $$$ that would be spent at that Barnes and Noble to a town that has adequate parking if it does not.[2]

If the typical manufacturing firm were a factory of a few dozen workers (or fewer) serving a local market, rather than a large oligopoly firm serving a national market and pushing a product marketed around national brand identification, it would be *a lot* less feasible to pick up and move to a different part of the U.S. (let alone overseas).

And that would be even more true, if local economies were diversified on the Emilia-Romagna model, with much higher levels of self-employment and cooperative ownership. If there were many small and medium-sized employers in manufacturing, instead of one

1. Johnson. "Sustainability and Lean Operations," *Cost Management.* March/April 2006, pp. 44-45.
2. Angelica Oung, "Local Externalities, or why decentralized isn't always better," *The Art of the Possible,* April 30, 2008 <http://www.theartofthepossible.net/2008/04/30/local-externalities-or-why-decentralized-isnt-always-better/>.

big corporation colonizing a locality, people would be a lot more prone to say "good rid-dance!"

On the other hand, an end to subsidized superhighways and airports would drastically reduce the total volume of freight in the national economy, and increase unit shipping costs. So the current model of economic colonization—building a large factory in a single location and trucking the output around a large market area—would be far less feasible. Factories would be much more likely to be built to serve the market where they were lo-cated. So maybe the answer to the problems of decentralism is more decentralism.

13

Dissolution of the State in Society

A. Revolution vs. Evolution

To a large extent, the distinction between "revolution" and "gradualism" is artificial, more a difference in emphasis than anything else. For example, revolutionary Marxists tend to believe a major part of the groundwork of socialism will be built within capitalism, until no further progressive development is possible. Only at that point will the revolutionary transition take place, and the new society burst out of the older shell that constrains it. On the other hand, even those who believe the transition from capitalism to socialism can be largely managed peacefully probably expect that some disruption may occur at the time of the final break with the old society, as rear guard forces make a desperate attempt to reverse the change.

Among anarchists, Brian Dominick rejects the tendency to identify "revolution" solely with the period of insurrection. At least as important, as part of the overall process, is the period *before* the final insurrection:

> The creation and existence of this second power marks the first stage of revolution, that during which there exist two social systems struggling for the support of the people; one for their blind, uncritical allegiance; the second for their active, conscious participation.[1]

Indeed, the primary process of "revolution" is building the kind of society we want here and now. The insurrection becomes necessary only when, and to the extent that, the state attempts to hinder or halt the process of construction.

> Aside from revolutionary upheaval, the very formation of a dual power system in the present is in fact one of the aims of the dual power strategy—we seek to create a situation of dual power by building alternative political, economic and other social institutions, to fulfill the needs of our communities in an essentially self-sufficient manner. Independence from the state and capital are primary goals of dual power, as is interdependence among community members. The dual power situation, in its pre-insurrectionary status, is also known as "alternative social infrastructure."
>
> . . . Since we have no way of predicting the insurrection, it is important for our own peace of mind and empowerment as activists that we create situations in the present which reflect the principles of our eventual visions. We must make for ourselves now the kinds of institutions and relationships, to the greatest extent possible, on which we'll base further activism. We should liberate space, for us and future generations, in the shadow of the dominant system, not only from which to build a new society, but within which to live freer and more peaceful lives today.[2]

The Wobblies use the phrase "building the structure of the new society within the shell of the old" to describe this process. But Proudhon anticipated them by some sixty years:

1. Brian A. Dominick, "An Introduction to Dual Power Strategy" (2002) <http://www.indymedia.org.uk/en/2002/09/41085.html>.
   2. *Ibid.*

Beneath the governmental machinery, in the shadow of political institutions, out of the sight of statesmen and priests, society is producing its own organism, slowly and silently; and constructing a new order, the expression of its vitality and autonomy ....[1]

Colin Ward, in the Preface to *Anarchy in Action*, conceptualized it as an anarchist society that exists, here and now alongside the statist one:

> The argument of this book is that an anarchist society, a society which organises itself without authority, is always in existence, like a seed beneath the snow, buried under the weight of the state and its bureaucracy, capitalism and its waste, privilege and its injustices, nationalism and its suicidal loyalties, religious differences and their superstitious separatism.
>
> ... [F]ar from being a speculative vision of a future society, it is a description of a mode of human organisation, rooted in the experience of everyday life, which operates side by side with, and in spite of, the dominant authoritarian trends of our society. This is not a new version of anarchism. Gustav Landauer saw it, not as the founding of something new, 'but as the actualisation and reconstitution of something that has always been present, which exists alongside the state, albeit buried and laid waste'. And a modern anarchist, Paul Goodman, declared that: 'A free society cannot be the substitution of a "new order" for the old order; it is the extension of spheres of free action until they make up most of social life.'[2]

B. Dialectical Libertarianism and the Order of Attack

In the meantime, of course, we can simultaneously attempt to roll back the state from outside, building broad coalitions to do so on an issue-by-issue basis. But if we start from the assumption that dismantling the state will be a gradual process, and that statelessness is a goal toward which we will move over time, then the *order* in which the state is dismantled will be crucial. As Benjamin Tucker put it, "the question before us is not ... what measures and means of interference we are justified in instituting, but which ones of those already existing we should first lop off."[3]

So which do we "lop off" first?

Chris Sciabarra's concept of "dialectical libertarianism" is relevant here. According to Sciabarra, it is a mistake to treat every proposed reduction in some facet of state activity as a step in the right direction. He considered it necessary, instead, to "grasp the nature of a part by viewing it systemically—that is, as an extension of the system within which it is embedded." Individual parts receive their character from the whole of which they are a part, and from their function within that whole.[4]

As Arthur Silber commented on this approach, "there are two basic methods of thinking that we can often see in the way people approach any given issue."

> One is what we might call a *contextual* approach: people who use this method look at any particular issue in the overall context in which it arises, or the system in which it is embedded. Liberals are often associated with this approach. They will analyze racism or the "power differential" between women and men in terms of the entire *system* in which those issues arise. And in a similar manner, their proposed solutions will often be systemic solutions, aimed at eradicating what they consider to be the ultimate causes of the particular problem that concerns them.

1. Pierre Joseph Proudhon, *General Idea of the Revolution in the Nineteenth Century*. Translated by John Beverly Robinson (New York: Haskell House Publishers, Ltd., 1923, 1969 [1851]), p. 243.

2. Colin Ward, *Anarchy in Action* (London: Freedom Press, 1982), p. 14.

3. Benjamin Tucker, "Voluntary Co-operation," *Instead of a Book, By a Man Too Busy to Write One*. Gordon Press facsimile (New York: 1973 [1897]), p. 104.

4. Chris Matthew Sciabarra, *Total Freedom: Toward a Dialectical Libertarianism* (University Park, Penn.: The Pennsylvania State University Press, 2000), p. 88.

The other fundamental approach is to focus on the basic principles involved, but with scant (or no) attention paid to the overall context in which the principles are being analyzed. In this manner, this approach treats principles like Plato's Forms . . . .[1]

In seeking to dismantle the state, we must start with a strategic picture of our own. It is not enough to oppose any and all statism, as such, without any conception of how particular occurrences of statism fit into the overall system of power. Each concrete example of statism must be grasped in its relation to the system of power as a whole, and with regard to the way in which the nature of the part is determined by the whole to which it belongs. That is, we must examine the ways in which it functions together with the totality of elements in the system, both coercive and market, to promote the interests of the class controlling the state.

In forming this strategic picture, we must use class analysis to identify the key interests and groups at the heart of the system of power.

We already saw, in Chapter Eleven, the distinction between the economic and political means to wealth, and the nature of the state as the organized political means. But there is a wide range of possible versions of libertarian class theory, differing on the relationship in which private actors stand to the political means and to the state.

One version of libertarian class analysis, heavily influenced by public choice theory, tends to dismiss the idea of a coherent structure to the coalition of class interests using the political means. As Sciabarra describes it, for example, Rothbard's view of the state might seem at first glance to superficially resemble interest group liberalism: although the state is the organized political means, it serves the exploitative interests of whatever random assortment of political factions happens to seize control of it at any given time. This picture of how the state works does not require any organic relation between the various interest groups controlling the state at any time, or between them and the state. The state might be controlled by a disparate array of interests, ranging from licensed professionals, rent-seeking corporations, farmers and regulated utilities, to big labor; the only thing they have in common is they happen to be currently the best at latching onto the state.

This is essentially what Roderick Long calls "statocratic" class theory: a class theory that emphasizes the state component of the ruling class at the expense of its plutocratic elements. Long cites David Friedman as an extreme version of the statocratic approach:

> It seems more reasonable to suppose that there is no ruling class, that we are ruled, rather, by a myriad of quarrelling gangs, constantly engaged in stealing from each other to the great impoverishment of their own members as well as the rest of us.[2]

Despite the superficial resemblance of Rothbard's theory to the statocratic approach, Long argues that Rothbard's position in fact more closely resembles what he calls the "plutocratic" class theory. Rothbard saw the state as controlled by

> a primary group that has achieved a position of structural hegemony, a group central to class consolidation and crisis in contemporary political economy. Rothbard's approach to this problem is, in fact, highly dialectical in its comprehension of the historical, political, economic, and social dynamics of class.[3]

1. Arthur Silber, "In Praise of Contextual Libertarianism," *The Light of Reason* blog (now defunct), November 2, 2003. Reprinted at *Once Upon a Time* blog, November 26, 2005 <http://powerofnarrative.blogspot.com/2003/11/in-praise-of-contextual-libertarianism.html>.

2. David Friedman, *The Machinery of Freedom*, quoted in Roderick T. Long, "Toward a Libertarian Theory of Class," *Social Philosophy & Policy* 15:2 (1998), p. 327.

3. *Ibid.*, p. 87.

Walter Grinder and John Hagel attempt, from an Austrian perspective, to describe this hegemonic group of classes in control of the state.[1] For Grinder and Hagel, the core of the state capitalist class system is 1) the finance capitalists running the state-created central banking cartel; and 2) the commanding heights of the industrial economy most closely clustered around finance capital.

Another excellent article, by John Munkirs,[2] treats the corporate economy as a privately owned central planning system, with a core of large industrial enterprises tightly linked through interlocking directorates, and clustered around a smaller inner core of large banks which control the whole system through the direction of capital flow. This becomes considerably more plausible, despite ostensible competition within the Fortune 500, when we remember how tightly competition between firms is actually regulated by such devices as "intellectual property," regulatory restraints on competition in product features, the partial supercession of price competition by brand name specification, and so forth. The reality is much closer to onetime ADM chief Dwayne Andreas' dictum "The competitor is our friend; the customer is our enemy."

Grinder and Hagel, like most Austrians, see the seizure of the state by this plutocratic class coalition as relatively recent, arising with the expansion of the regulatory-welfare state at the turn of the twentieth century (as described by Gabriel Kolko, among others), or with the rise of the central banking system.

In fact, however, the most fundamental "structural hegemony" was built into capitalism from its beginnings as a successor to the feudal/manorial system. The basic understanding was stated by Hodsgkin and by Oppenheimer, both of whom saw the existing capitalist order as a monstrous hybrid of genuine free markets and the old feudal order. The new capitalist ruling class was amalgamated with the landed aristocracy of the Old Regime, and made use of the same privilege, the same political means, as had the landed interests before it. This was described by Immanuel Wallerstein as a portion of the feudal landed classes transforming themselves into capitalists. Capitalism as a historical system still bears the birth scars of its origins in feudalism.

The overall class nature of the state was summarized by Tucker in comparatively simple terms: " . . . the State exists mainly to do the will of capital and secure it all the privileges it demands . . . ."[3]

To the extent that capitalists act in league with the state, and secure to themselves the benefits of special privilege by acting through the state, they should not be regarded merely as passive beneficiaries. They should be regarded as a component of the state:

> Here . . . is a wealthy manufacturer, who thinks of himself as a businessman and is so regarded by his peers. But this man's industry enjoys a legal privilege in the form of tariff protection against foreign steel, which enables him to command a higher domestic price for his own steel. This industrialist is not, however he may think of himself, a businessman; he is a subdivision of the State . . . . No private citizen, businessman or other, has the power to coerce unless the law grants him a license to bend the will of others forcibly in his favor. In which case he is a component of the state.[4]

Brad Spangler used the analogy of a gunman and bagman in a holdup to illustrate the principle:

1. Walter E. Grinder and John Hagel, "Toward a Theory of State Capitalism: Ultimate Decision-Making and Class Structure," *Journal of Libertarian Studies* 1:1 (Spring 1977), pp. 59-79 <http://www.mises.org/journals/jls/1_1/1_1_7.pdf>.

2. John Munkirs, "Centralized Private Sector Planning: An Institutionalist's Perspective on the Contemporary U.S. Economy," *Journal of Economic Issues (pre-1986)* , December 1983, pp. 931-967.

3. Benjamin Tucker, "Liberty and Aggression," *Instead of a Book*, p. 75.

4. Edmund Opitz, "Introduction," Albert Jay Nock, *Our Enemy, the State* (Delavan, Wisc.: Hallberg Publishing Corporation, 1983), p. 17.

Let's postulate two sorts of robbery scenarios.

In one, a lone robber points a gun at you and takes your cash. All libertarians would recognize this as a micro-example of any kind of government at work, resembling most closely State Socialism.

In the second, depicting State Capitalism, one robber (the literal apparatus of government) keeps you covered with a pistol while the second (representing State allied corporations) just holds the bag that you have to drop your wristwatch, wallet and car keys in. To say that your interaction with the bagman was a "voluntary transaction" is an absurdity . . . . Both gunman and bagman together are the true State.[1]

Evaluating the functions of the state in terms of the class purpose they serve makes it easier to understand the importance of dismantling them in the proper order. No politico-economic system has ever approximated total statism, in the sense that "everything not forbidden is compulsory." In every system, there is a mixture of compulsory and discretionary behavior. The choice of what forms of activity to leave to voluntary exchange, just as much as of what to subject to compulsory regulation, reflects the ruling class's strategic assessment of the overall mixture of coercion and voluntary exchange that will maximize the political extraction of wealth.

Likewise, any "free market reform" put forth by the corporate capitalist ruling class will reflect their judgment as to which mixture of statist and market elements will produce the highest overall rate of political extraction of wealth. As Walter Grinder and John Hagel put it,

It must be stressed that the beneficiaries of the political means in a market oriented economy are dependent on the existence of the economic means in order to survive and prosper . . . . In view of the dependence of the political means on the economic means, the optimal strategy for the political class to pursue will not be to maximize short-term returns, but rather to promote as productive a system as possible, consistent with the preservation of its exploitative position within that system.[2]

To welcome the ruling class's choice of targets for "free market reform," made in accordance with their own strategic vision, is equivalent to the Romans welcoming the withdrawal of the Punic center at Cannae as "a step in the right direction." Hannibal's decision in that case was not the first step toward Carthaginian withdrawal from Italy, but part of a general design aimed at maximizing his overall strength.

"Free market reform," in the terms generally proposed by corporate lobbyists and corporate-funded think tanks, is a mirror image of "lemon socialism." Under lemon socialism, the state generally chooses to nationalize those industries which corporate capital will most benefit from having taken off its hands, and to socialize those functions which capital would most prefer the state bear the cost of. Under neoliberalism, rather than big business selling lemons to the state, the state sells the plums to big business. Corporate capital liquidates interventionist policies after it has squeezed all the benefit out of them, and receives "privatized" government assets at bargain prices after the taxpayer has already borne the brunt of investment costs.

As Chomsky put it, "Concentrated private power strongly resists exposure to market forces, unless it's confident it can win in the competition." The legacy beneficiaries of all that statism decide it's finally safe to change the rules and compete with the non-beneficiaries on a "level playing field." That's pretty much what was involved in the British adoption of "free trade" in the nineteenth century: after they'd built a global commercial empire through mercantilism, suppressed the foreign textile trade, and exported enclosures

1. Brad Spangler, "Recognizing faux private interests that are actually part of the State," BradSpangler.Com, April 29, 2005 <http://www.bradspangler.com/blog/archives/54>.
2. Grinder and Hagel, "Toward a Theory of State Capitalism," p. 69.

to half the world, they decided it was time for the lion and the lamb to compete under a single law.

And as a corollary, corporate capital at any given time allows free competition only in the areas where it expects it can win. Chomsky described so-called "Free Trade" Agreements in the same piece as

> a mixture of liberalization and protectionism, designed—not surprisingly—in the interests of the designers: mainly MNCs, financial institutions, the investor/lender class generally, the powerful states that cater to their interests, etc.[1]

The prevailing libertarian approach of welcoming the reduction or elimination of any particular form of state activity as "a step in the right direction" is what Silber calls "atomistic libertarianism." Atomist libertarians argue "as if the society in which one lives is completely irrelevant to an analysis of any problem at all."[2]

Under state capitalism, some forms of state intervention are primary, directly serving the primary purpose of the ruling class: the exploitative extraction of wealth by the political means. Other forms are secondary, aimed at ameliorating the side effects of this primary wealth extraction and stabilizing the system. The latter include labor regulations and welfare state measures that keep destitution, homelessness, and starvation at manageable levels, so as to avoid their politically destabilizing effects. They include Keynesian measures to correct the tendencies toward overproduction and underconsumption that result from maldistribution of income in a system of privilege. A formal reduction in statism that applies only to those state measures limiting or ameliorating the exploitation enabled by the more fundamental forms of intervention, and without addressing the primary forms of intervention themselves which directly enable exploitation, will amount to an *absolute increase* in the level of actual exploitation enabled by the state.

The strategic priorities of genuine free market advocates should be the direct opposite: first to dismantle the fundamental, structural forms of intervention whose primary effect is to enable exploitation; and only then to dismantle the secondary, ameliorative forms of intervention which serve to make life bearable for the average person living under a system of state-enabled exploitation. Jim Henley described this approach as removing the shackles before removing the crutches (e.g., eliminating corporate welfare before welfare to the poor).[3]

Roderick Long discussed it at greater length in a 1995 article. In the case of deregulation, he presented the case of a corporation with a government-enforced monopoly that is, at the same time, subject to price controls. The question facing the would-be dismantler of the state is whether to abolish the monopoly and price controls at the same time, or if not, which to abolish first. If they are abolished simultaneously, the newly "deregulated" corporation will be in the position of collecting monopoly profits until sufficient time has elapsed for competitors to enter the market and undercut its price. This is an injustice to consumers. Long concluded that the most just alternative is to "Remove the monopoly privilege now, and the price controls later."

> But is it ethical to continue imposing price controls on what is now a private company, one competitor among others? Perhaps it is. Consider the fact that Amalgamated Widgets' privileged position in the marketplace is the result neither of it own efforts nor of mere chance; rather, it is the result of systematic aggression by government in its favor. It

1. Noam Chomsky, "Resistance to Neoliberal Globalization," ZNet Blog, Oct. 2005 <http://blog.zmag.org/index.php/weblog/entry/resistance_to_neo_liberal_globalization/>. (Now defunct—retrieved through Internet Archive.)

2. Silber, "In Praise of Contextual Libertarianism."

3. Jim Henley, "Ask Me What the Secret of 'L—TIMING!—ibalertarianism' Is," *Unqualified Offerings* blog, February 21, 2008 <http://www.highclearing.com/index.php/archives/2008/02/21/7909>.

might be argued, then, that a temporary cap on the company's prices could be justified in order to prevent it from taking undue advantage of a position it gained through unjust violence against the innocent.[1]

The individualist anarchists, starting as early as Tucker himself, made it clear that it matters very much what order the process of dissolution is to follow (or in his own words above, which measures of interference already existing we should first lop off). He called for the abolition of government "to take place gradually, beginning with the downfall of the money and land monopolies and extending thence into one field after another, . . . accompanied by such a . . . steady spreading of social truth," that the public would at last be prepared to accept the final stage of replacing government with free contract even in the area of police protection.[2]

Tucker's associate Clarence Swartz, in a passage that anticipated the neoliberals' sham "free market" policies of our day, wrote of the harm the working classes would suffer if the state were dismantled in an order that suited the interests of the plutocracy rather than of producers:

> Mutualism . . . would not abolish . . . [the tariff] first, since to do that and leave labor at the mercy of the money monopoly would be unwise and harmful, even though, in the meantime, all those engaged in producing commodities that are not protected against foreign competition are forced to pay tribute to those manufacturers who are so protected.[3]

Regulations which serve only to limit and constrain the exercise of privilege are not even, properly speaking, a net increase in statism at all. They are simply the statist ruling class's stabilizing restrictions on its own more fundamental forms of intervention.

A good example was raised by Silber in another article, regarding whether pharmacists should have the right to refuse to dispense prescribed medication (e.g. "morning after" pills) for religious reasons. The atomistic libertarian's reflexive position is "Yes, of course!" Anyone participating in the market should have the right to buy and sell, or not buy and sell, as he sees fit. "For many libertarians, that is in essence the totality of the argument." But the atomistic libertarian makes the implicit assumption "that this dispute arises in a society which is essentially *free*." But in fact, pharmacists are direct beneficiaries of compulsory occupational licensing, a statist racket whose central purpose is to restrict competition and enable them to charge a monopoly price for their services.

> . . . [T]he state has created a government-enforced monopoly for licensed pharmacists. Given that central fact, the least the state can do is ensure that everyone has access to the drugs they require . . . .[4]

When the government confers a special privilege, and then sets regulatory limits on how that privilege can be abused, the latter regulation is not a new intrusion of statism into the free market. It is the state's limitation and qualification of its own underlying statism. The secondary, qualifying regulation is not a net increase, but a net reduction in statism. On the other hand, the repeal of the secondary regulation, without an accompanying repeal of the primary privilege, would be a net increase in statism. As the beneficiaries of privilege are a de facto branch of the state, the elimination of regulatory constraints on their abuse of privilege is in practical terms a further extension of their privilege.

---

1. Roderick T. Long, "Dismantling Leviathan From Within," Part II: The Process of Reform. *Formulations* 3:1 (Autumn 1995) <http://www.libertariannation.org/a/f31l3.html>.

2. Tucker, "Protection and Its Relation to Rent," *Instead of a Book*, p. 329.

3. Clarence L. Swartz, *What is Mutualism?* (New York: Vanguard Press, 1927), p. 48

4. Arthur Silber, "Not So Fast, Please: Contextual Libertarianism, One More Time," *Once Upon a Time* blog, April 8, 2005 <http://powerofnarrative.blogspot.com/2005_04_ 01_archive.html>.

A good example is "Free Trade Agreements" on the pattern of NAFTA and the GATT Uruguay Round. The reduced old-fashioned protectionism of tariff barriers, coupled with a vast strengthening of the new protectionism of "intellectual property," actually increases the level of state protectionism in the global economy. The dominant actors in the global economy are transnational corporations, and patents and copyrights serve the same protectionist function for them that tariffs did in the old national industrial economies. In promoting what is conventionally called "free trade," the TNCs do not seek a genuine reduction in the overall level of statism. They seek to replace one form of statist protection that has outlived its usefulness with a new form of statist protection more conducive to their current business model. The old protectionism of tariffs is eliminated because it interferes with using the new, primary protectionism of patents and copyrights to its full advantage.

It is the typical approach of vulgar libertarianism to treat the secondary limitations in isolation and to clamor for their removal, while treating the underlying form of statism as irrelevant to the immediate issue (if not remaining completely oblivious to it).

C. The "Free Market" as Hegemonic Ideology

In the past, I've used the term "vulgar libertarianism" to describe the misappropriation of "free market" rhetoric to defend the interests of existing concentrations of wealth and power under corporate capitalism. As I wrote elsewhere,

> Vulgar libertarian apologists for capitalism use the term "free market" in an equivocal sense: they seem to have trouble remembering, from one moment to the next, whether they're defending actually existing capitalism or free market principles. So we get the standard boilerplate . . . arguing that the rich can't get rich at the expense of the poor, because "that's not how the free market works"—implicitly assuming that this *is* a free market. When prodded, they'll grudgingly admit that the present system is not a free market, and that it includes a lot of state intervention on behalf of the rich. But as soon as they think they can get away with it, they go right back to defending the wealth of existing corporations on the basis of "free market principles."[1]

In the vulgar libertarian universe, "actually existing corporate capitalism" is a pretty close approximation of a free market. All that is necessary to achieve a full-fledged free market society is to peel off the superstructure of taxes, regulations and welfare programs that impede big business's freedom of action. For such "libertarians," the ideal market was perfectly described by the topic of the 2008 Libertarian Alliance Chris R. Tame Memorial Essay Competition: "Can a libertarian society be described as Tesco minus the state?"[2] Sheldon Richman, answering this vulgar libertarian conception of the free market, wrote:

> Many self-styled defenders of the free market misunderstand the American system. They believe that under a thin layer of government intervention lies the system they cherish. All we need to do is scrape away that layer, and glorious capitalism will be restored.
>
> They couldn't be more wrong. There is no thin layer of intervention. Government has intruded deeply into economic activity from the beginning, most particularly in banking and finance, which is by nature at the center of any economy. The web of privilege and control is pervasive, touching all parts of the economy. Moreover, this intervention was never imposed on bankers, financiers, and the rest of the business elite. It was welcomed—to be more precise, it was invited and sponsored by them. Free enterprise,

---

1. Kevin Carson, *Studies in Mutualist Political Economy*. Self-published via Blitzprint (Fayetteville, Ark., 2004), p. 142.

2. The answer, in the winning essay by Keith Preston, was a resounding "No!" "Free Enterprise, The Antidote to Corporate Plutocracy" <http://libertarianalliance.wordpress.com/2008/10/25/chris-r-tame-memorial-prize-winning-essay>.

risk, and loss were for the little guy. Partnership with the state was for the elite. That partnership meant favoritism and protection from competition. It meant exemption from market discipline and exploitation of taxpayers, consumers, and workers.[1]

In the vulgar libertarian universe, in Ayn Rand's memorial phrases, big business is a "persecuted minority," and the military industrial complex is "a myth or worse." Giant corporations are the heroic figures of the market, the John Galts who keep the engine of the world running, and the bad guys—the "looters"—are welfare moms and "trial lawyers." The revolutionary slogan of the vulgar libertarian is "Them pore ole bosses need all the help they can get"—or perhaps an inversion of the sheep's chant in *Animal Farm*: "Two legs good, four legs *baaaad*!"

Of course, this is nonsense, as Bryan Register said. In regard to welfare recipients, for example,

> such persons are often victims not only of structural dislocations in the economy caused by the economic machinations of the ruling class, but of barriers to market entry maintained by those who wish not to face competition. Welfare is the means by which resentment against these effects is kept under control; welfare recipients ought not be looked at as members of a dominant class, but as enemies of the dominant class whose silence is purchased with state handouts.[2]

A vulgar libertarian, on the other hand, believes the main political force behind the food stamp program was not Cargill, but the powerful voting block of single welfare mothers. To quote Lawrence Lessig:

> There's a speech that Reagan gives in 1965, where he talks about how democracy always fails because once the people recognize they can vote themselves largess, they just vote themselves largess and the fiscal policy is destroyed. Well, Reagan had it half-right. It's not as if it's the poor out there who have figured out how to suck the money out of the rich. It's exactly the other way around.[3]

The values and symbolism of the "free market," as misappropriated by vulgar libertarians, function as a hegemonic ideology under state capitalism. Register, in the same article quoted above, brilliantly adapted the Gramscian theory of ideology to libertarian class analysis. In the democratic West, "members of the state itself are often not the primary beneficiaries of statism." The state capitalist ruling class, he said,

> exists within civil society and employs the state as a means to distort the workings of civil society, especially the market . . . .
>   . . . The libertarian analysis of contemporary society will be similar to Marx's in that it regards state action as caused by the desires of certain actors within civil society, but it will be like the classical liberal approach in that it regards classes within civil society as essentially constituted by differential relations to state power. Thus neither the class divisions between the state-banking nexus and others within civil society, nor the distortive actions of the state, are mere epiphenomena of one another: they relate, dialectically, in a mutually supporting manner.

The important thing, for our present purpose, is that "the maintenance of state power requires that the populace acquiesce in state actions. This requires the development of hegemony in civil society." As Ralph Nader put it,

1. Sheldon Richman, "The Corporate State Wins," The Future of Freedom Foundation, Oct. 3, 2008 <http://www.fff.org/comment/com0810b.asp>.

2. Bryan Register, "Class, Hegemony, and Ideology: A Libertarian Approach" (2001) <http://folk.uio.no/thomas/po/class-hegemony-ideology-lib.html>.

3. Christopher Hayes, "Mr. Lessig Goes to Washington," *The Nation*, May 29, 2008 <http://www.thenation.com/doc/20080616/hayes>.

The controlling power in any society strives to make sure that, one way or another, its dark sides are not part of the mainstream public dialogue nor are they part of the perceived explanation of that society's structural shortfalls and injustices.[1]

The fake "free market" ideology, disseminated in the schools and media and appealed to by mainstream politicians, plays a central role in this project. Corporate power defended in terms of traditional values of private property and freedom of contract; plutocratic wealth is justified as the reward for thrift, industry, ingenuity, and otherwise superior performance in the market.

Big government liberalism is a mirror-image of vulgar libertarianism, existing in partial opposition to it. I say *partial* opposition because both ideologies share, to a large extent, the same factual depiction of the world.

Register, discussing Robert Higgs' explanation of ideology, notes that "[f]or Higgs, the essential feature of the ideologies is that they are value-systems."

> Were we to present identical phenomena to persons with different ideologies, they would come away with different evaluations. But this is typically not the case, because we often cannot present identical phenomena to persons with different ideologies. Ideologies are not only value-systems, they also involve claims of fact. For this reason, different evaluations of 'identical' phenomena are not to be explained simply with reference to different values, but largely with reference to different beliefs about matters of fact.
>
> An example may clarify. Consider the Gulf War. As explained in the popular press of our semi-fascist semi-liberal welfare-warfare state, the Gulf War was *in fact* a response by western democracies to violent aggression by a dictator. Since the United States and its allies have a moral obligation to preserve democratic institutions, such as those of Kuwait, whenever possible, the Gulf War was clearly appropriate and moral. This is especially so in light of the negligible loss of civilian life caused by US surgical strikes.
>
> A socialist or libertarian capitalist critic of the Gulf War probably would not disagree that it is good to fight tyrants and defend democracy, and that there are times when this might be an appropriate action for a democratic state to take. Such a critic would, however, pay attention to other relevant facts of the matter and hence derive a very different evaluation. It's not that stopping tyrants is bad, it's that Hussein's tyranny was really US tyranny; it's not that democratic institutions are bad, it's that Kuwait doesn't have any; it's not that minimal loss of civilian life is bad, it's that US action has caused the deaths of millions of civilians.
>
> Because the two ideologies—that of the statist mass media, and those of the libertarian or socialist critic—seek different kinds of factual, explanatory accounts, they might end up giving different evaluations because of their different explanations of how the social world works. But with respect to explanations of social events, there is a matter of fact about how things are. An ideology which lays bare the actual explanations of events is different in kind from an ideology which mystifies or obscures the real world. This is the difference which the pejorative conception of ideology seeks to mark.

The relationship between vulgar libertarianism and big government liberalism—the two dominant economic ideologies in America—is just the opposite. They largely agree on the world of fact, but disagree on the significance or valuation they attach to those facts.

Both ideologies agree, for the most part, that big business arose from what amounted to laissez-faire, and that the concentration of capital among a small number of business enterprises is the natural outcome of the "free market." Both agree that this outcome can be prevented only by government intervention to thwart the natural functioning of the market. Both agree that the central motivation of the twentieth century regulatory-welfare state, as it emerged during the Progressive Era and New Deal, was to restrain big business in the

---

1. Ralph Nader, "Introduction," in Charlers Derber, *Corporation Nation: How Corporations are Taking Over Our Lives and What We Can Do About It* (New York: St. Martin's Griffin, 1998), p. viii.

public interest. This common view of the world was stated, in almost identical terms, by liberal Arthur Schlesinger, Jr., and Theodore Levitt of the *Harvard Business Review*:

> Liberalism in America has ordinarily been the movement on the part of the other sections of society to restrain the power of the business community.[1]
>
> Business has not really won or had its way in connection with even a single piece of proposed regulatory or social legislation in the last three-quarters of a century.[2]

Their only area of disagreement concerns whether the existence of unregulated big business is a good or a bad thing.

This common factual depiction of the world reflects the common power interests behind the two ideologies. Vulgar libertarianism and big government liberalism, respectively, are the ideologies of the two wings of the state capitalist ruling class. The power interests of both wings of corporate capital depend on public acceptance of this common factual depiction of the world. One side has a vested interest in the misconception that the present concentration of wealth and power in the hands of big business is the result of superior performance in the market, and that this distribution of wealth and power can be altered only through state intervention. The other side has a vested interest in promoting the belief that the regulatory-welfare state is necessary as a "countervailing power" to big business, as opposed to its actual function of propping it up. The two ideologies serve to legitimate, respectively, big business and big government, and are to a large extent mutually supportive.

D. Gradualism and the "Magic Button"

Charles Johnson has raised some challenging ethical questions about the dialectical approach. He finds himself in general agreement with my strategic focus:

> . . . Defending immediate and complete abolition on principle, and the abolition of *any* coercive program you may get the opportunity to abolish, doesn't entail any particular order of priorities in terms of the scope or order in which you might concentrate your own limited resources towards *making* opportunities for abolition that didn't previously exist. And that's where I think the interesting part comes in, and where there is a lot of room for interesting discussion about freedom, class, and strategic priorities when it comes to government interventions with distinctive class profiles.[3]
>
> . . . It's an odd form of libertarianism, and a damned foolish one, that operates by trying to pitch itself to the classes that control all the levers of power in both the market and the State, and to play off their fears and class resentment against those who have virtually no power, no access to legislators, are disproportionately likely not to even be able to vote, and who are trodden upon by the State at virtually every turn.[4]

In such questions of strategic priority, and in his understanding of the class nature of the state, Johnson's position is entirely dialectical:

> In setting strategic priorities, we have to look at which forms of government coercion do the most concrete damage, which forms of government coercion has intended victims who are most vulnerable to it, which forms have intended victims who can more easily evade or game the system on their own, *and, perhaps most importantly, which forms*

---

1. Arthur Schlesinger, Jr., *The Age of Jackson* (Boston: Houghton-Mifflin, 1946), p. 505.

2. "Why Business Always Loses," quoted in G. William Domhoff, *The Higher Circles: The Governing Class in America* (New York: Vintage Books, 1971), p. 157.

3. Charles Johnson, "On Crutches and Crowbars: Toward a Labor Radical Case Against the Minimum Wage," *Rad Geek People's Daily*, March 6, 2008 <http://radgeek.com/gt/2008/03/06/on_crutches/>.

4. Comment under Kevin Carson, "On Dissolving the State, and What to Replace it With," Mutualist Blog: Free Market Anti-Capitalism, March 3, 2008 <http://mutualist.blogspot.com/2008/03/on-dissolving-state-and-what-to-replace.html>.

serve as the real historical and ideological anchors for establishing and sustaining the distorted statist social order, and which forms are relatively superficial efforts to stabilize or ameliorate the effects of those anchors. [emphasis added] I think that on all these counts, a serious look at who calls the shots and who takes the bullets will show that the welfare state, such as it is, is a fairly small and superficial effort to ameliorate the effects of deep, pervasive, and incredibly destructive economic and institutional privilege for big, centralized, bureaucratic state capitalism, and (as much or more so) for the class power of the *State itself* over the poor folks that it beats up, locks up, institutionalizes, bombs, robs of their homes and livelihoods, and so on. Moreover, it's a fairly small and superficial effort which doesn't violate anybody's rights per se; it's the coercive *funding* of government doles, not their mere existence, that involves government violence . . . . All this tends to support strategic priorities in favor of (as Tom Knapp himself originally put it) cutting welfare from the top down and cutting taxes from the bottom up.[1]

Nevertheless, that phrase, "the abolition of *any* coercive program you may get the opportunity to abolish," is key. Libertarians, Johnson says, should welcome the opportunity to dismantle *any* form of state intervention, without regard to its structural function or the order in which it occurs, if an opportunity arises to do so:

If I had a platform, it would be three words—Smash the State—and the programme I favor for implementing that is for each and every government program to be abolished immediately, completely, and forever, whenever, wherever, in whatever order, and to whatever extent that we can, by hook, by crook, slingshot, canoe, wherever the political opportunity to do so presents itself.[2]

He justified this approach in terms of the primary libertarian ethics of self-ownership, and non-aggression:

I'm an immediatist, not because I deny that there's ever an importance difference in the likely results of repealing A-before-B as versus repealing B-before-A, but rather because I think that there are things that nobody ever has the moral right to do to another human being, no matter what results you can get from it, and one of those things is coercing her in her use of her own person and property. If both A and B are genuinely coercive, then I'd argue that there's never any justification or excuse for continuing to do either of them. Even if it would be better for A to go first and then B, rather than B to go first and then A, if the opportunity to repeal B arises before the opportunity to repeal A does, then I'd say that it's morally obligatory to repeal B anyway, because neither you nor I nor anybody else has the right to go on coercing anybody for even a second longer, whatever our considered judgment about the likely results of their freedom may be.

Of course, if there *isn't* any opportunity to repeal either A or B at the moment, then the question is what sort of strategy you ought to adopt in the effort to *make* the opportunity arise. And in that case, it's perfectly reasonable for your considered judgment about likely results to determine your strategic priorities, in terms of which forms of coercion you will first and most intensely focus on making repeal-able, given your limited time and resources.[3]

He went on to challenge me, on that basis, with something like the Leonard Read/Murray Rothbard "magic button" scenario:

So I reckon that the question is this: suppose you had a rather limited version of Rothbard's Magic Button, which would allow you to magically repeal (say) personal income tax on the top 10% of taxpayers, while leaving all other personal income tax and FICA payroll tax in place. And let's take it for granted that we all dialectically understand the role of the State, and its different functions, within the social order of power and its relationship with the dynamics of class exploitation. Still. There's the button. Would you

1. Johnson, "On Crutches and Crowbars."
2. *Ibid.*
3. Comment under Carson, "On Dissolving the State."

push it, or would you refuse to push it, on the grounds that you need to cut taxes either from the bottom–up or else not at all?[1]

With my back to the wall, and after much soul-searching, I decided I wouldn't push the magic button under those circumstances.

> . . . I think the net effect in this case, as in many hypothetical scenarios of disman-tling the state in the wrong order, would be—as counterintuitive as it may seem—to in-crease the net level of exploitation carried out with the help of the state. The increased freedom from state exploitation would fall almost entirely to those whose incomes de-rive from exploitation, and its chief practical effect would be to further increase the competitive advantage of their exploitative activities against those truly engaged in the "economic means."
>
> I'd probably even quibble as to whether it amounted to a reduction in statism even as such, since a high marginal tax rate on Bill Gates arguably amounts to the state ame-liorating or moderating its primary act of statism in guaranteeing the income to Gates in the first place through IP. A great deal of such "statism" amounts, in practice, to the state setting side-constraints on what can be done with the loot acquired by state robbery. To apply Brad Spangler's bag man analogy, a lot of it is akin to the gunman telling the bag-man, after the victim has handed his wallet over at gunpoint, to give the victim back enough to pay cab fare back home so he'll be more likely in future to earn enough to be robbed again.[2]

When the state is controlled by robbers, and every decision for or against state inter-vention in a particular circumstance reflects the robbers' strategic assessment of the ideal mixture of intervention and non-intervention, it's a mistake for a genuine anti-state movement to allow the priorities for "free market reform" to be set by the robbers' esti-mation of what forms of intervention no longer serve their purpose. If the corporate rul-ing class is proposing a particular "free market reform," you can be sure it's because they believe it will *increase* the net level of exploitation.

Most importantly, we can pretty much *count* on all the opportunities that present themselves for "free market reform," under the present system, having just that effect. An anti-state movement that leaves the initiative to the official corporate-funded "libertarian" movement will be relegated to a position of "yes, but . . .", whittling around the edges of Reaganism and Thatcherism, and the kinds of "free market reform" Milton Friedman celebrated in Pinochet's Chile.

Johnson did not, in fact, disagree with my assessment of the likely net effect of such a top-down approach to cutting taxes:

> Well, I'm not sure that that's especially counterintuitive. I'm perfectly willing to grant that there are plenty of cases where it's true. What I'm trying to stress is that, as far as I can tell, we don't disagree very much about the net consequences of different se-quences of repeal. I agree that in the hypothetical case I gave, there might very well be a net increase in the predominance of class exploitation in the markets for labor, land, etc.
>
> But, while I agree with you on that, I also think you have to keep in mind that when you make political choices you're not just making choices about which God's-eye-view net outcome you would prefer. You're acting within the world, as one mortal creature among many fellow creatures, and when you deliberate about what to do you have to deliberate about what sort of person you, personally, are going to be, and what you, personally, are or aren't willing to do to another human being. I know that I, per-sonally, couldn't live with deliberately choosing to shove around or rob another human being, or letting another human being go on being shoved around or robbed, for even a second longer . . . . Hence why I'd push the button, immediately and without reserva-tion, even though I do in fact think that the net consequences of doing so would be

1. *Ibid.*
2. *Ibid.*

substantially worse, in terms of things that I care about and which affect me personally, than the net consequences of repeal in the opposite order.

So I'm anti-gradualism not because I'm anti-dialectics, but rather because I think that there are personal obligations of justice involved in the political choices you make, and that dialectically-grounded praxis has to integrate those personal obligations into your course of action just as much as it has to integrate the general, big-picture view of class dynamics, socio-political structure, *et cetera*.

I don't entirely disagree with Johnson on this ethical point. But I think there's a legitimate ethical question as to whether the person pushing the button, as he would, would be directly complicit in enabling the increased net statism (i.e., the net exploitation resulting from the mixture of state and market that remains when the ruling class sets the priorities for "reform") that would result from doing so. My role in enabling coercion and exploitation would be almost (or at least) as direct in pushing the button, as in not pushing it. And while refraining from pushing would simply leave the status quo to change by its own internal processes as it would have anyway, pushing would make me an active agent in creating fundamental structural changes that would make an increased number of people worse off, as the result of increased exploitation.

A formal reduction in statism that applies only to those state measures limiting or ameliorating the exploitation, which itself is directly enabled by more fundamental forms of state intervention, and without addressing the more fundamental forms of statism that actually enable the exploitation, amounts to an absolute increase in the actual level of exploitation directly enabled by the state. Since once the button is put in my hand, I'm directly complicit in whatever level of statist exploitation exists, whatever decision I make, the most moral choice is the one that minimizes real—not formal—statism and exploitation.

The measure of statism inheres in the functioning of the overall system, not in the formal statism of its separate parts. A reduction in the formal statism of some separate parts, chosen in accordance with the strategic priorities of the statist exploiters, may result in a net increase in the overall level of statism.

Johnson's argument is essentially a restatement of Wendy McElroy's case against "gradualism." He agrees with McElroy that much of what is conventionally dismissed as gradualism in principle may in fact be nothing of the kind. As she put it,

> Libertarianism is the political philosophy based on the principle of nonaggression. Every human being is a self owner with inalienable rights. And gradualism is inconsistent with the moral foundation of libertarianism.
>
> Before proceeding, it is useful to distinguish gradualism as a policy from gradualism as a fact of reality. This latter form of gradualism says that, try as you may, it takes time to implement ideas. The transition to a libertarian society would not—because it could not—occur overnight. This is the nature of temporal reality in which we live. If this is all that is meant by gradualism—if it means 'as fast as possible'—then there is no quarrel between so called 'gradualists' and 'abolitionists' within the movement.
>
> This is not the formulation of gradualism with which abolitionists are concerned. When abolitionists say that unjust laws ought to be abolished immediately, the "ought" is a moral ought, and "immediately" means no more than as fast as possible.[1]

Nevertheless, some apparent grounds of principled disagreement still exist between abolitionists and gradualists. For example, McElroy (like Johnson) sees a fundamental conflict in principle between abolitionism and those who would refuse, if the opportunity presented itself, to immediately eliminate all or any random part of government by pushing Leonard Read's "magic button" (on the grounds that the result would be "calamitous").

---

1. Wendy McElroy, "Contra Gradualism" (November 1997) <http://www.fff.org/freedom/1197e.asp>.

Abolitionists do not deny reality; they simply insist that—as a political policy, individual rights must be given priority over all other moral and practical considerations. Libertarian abolitionists of the nineteenth century realized that the cessation of slavery would take time, but their message was that the deliberate continuation of slavery as a policy could not be justified. They demanded abolition—no "ifs," "ands," or "buts."

Those libertarians of the "ifs," "ands," or "buts" camp maintain that, in some cases, libertarianism ought to favor the gradual phasing out of unjust laws and agencies rather than pushing for immediate abolition, even if that immediate abolition is possible . . . .

The defining aspect of gradualism is the answer it gives to the key question: Could it ever be too soon to eliminate an unjust law or agency? The abolitionist gives an unqualified "no." If the gradualist does not answer "yes," he answers "maybe." Taxation is theft, but some people might starve if it ceases abruptly . . . .

. . . Abolition of government laws would result in social chaos; thus, we need a "transition" period during which deliberate rights violations would continue.[1]

I believe, however, that there is a principled basis for anarchists who, despite seeing the principles of self-ownership and nonaggression as moral absolutes, would still refrain from pushing the magic button. For one thing, I think the argument against gradualism, as stated by both Johnson and McElroy, treats the issue of moral agency as far simpler than it actually is.

In an article on the gradualism-abolitionism debate, Robert Capozzi referred to an earlier argument by Stephan Kinsella, in which the latter had distinguished gradualism in principle from gradualism in means in terms quite similar to those of Johnson and McElroy. Kinsella argued that while libertarians were quite realistic about what they could actually get away with at any particular time, they also had a principled objection to "normalizing theft" even for the short term.[2] In response, Capozzi described the calamitous consequences virtually certain to follow directly on the sudden abolition of government, and raised the question of the button-pusher's direct moral culpability in those consequences.[3]

Kinsella, in turn, objected to the magic button scenario on the grounds that it was so obviously fantastic as to be irrelevant to any real-world possibility:

For example, what do you mean, end gov't w/ a push of the button? how does the button do this? Turn poeple into robots? change their mind? blow up go'vt buildings? the only way to get rid of the state really is for most poeple not to believe in it. Are you saying woudl I PREFER most poeple not believe in the state's legitimacy? Or would I push a button that would make them change their minds? If so, how?[4]

He quoted another of his own statements, elsewhere, expressing dissatisfaction with the "magic button" scenario:

I will tell you I have no idea what this means. Magic makes no sense to me. I could only answer such a question if the means by which the end occurs is described. For example, if the magic button destroys all life on earth with a billion hydrogen bombs, that would be one way of achieving your proposed end result. I would not be in favor of that. Presumably you have some other meachanism in mind that achieves some defined result— could you explain the mechanism, and the result? That would allow other libertarians to evaluate whether they believe this action would be consistent with liberty or not.[5]

---

1. *Ibid.*

2. N. Stephan Kinsella, "The Trouble With Libertarian Activism," LewRockwell.Com, January 26, 2006 <http://www.lewrockwell.com/kinsella/kinsella19.html>.

3. Robert Capozzi, "Push the Button?" The FreeLiberal Blog, January 26, 2006 <http://www.freeliberal.com/blog/archives/001831.php>.

4. Kinsella comment under Capozzi.

5. Kinsella, "Defend Hoppe," Mises Economics Blog, February 6, 2005 <http://blog.mises.org/archives/003107.asp>.

Suppose, to pose another hypothetical, that state functionaries, directly funded by taxation and acting subject to the state's police power, are engaged on an ongoing basis in preventing an armed H-bomb (which would otherwise explode, and which will automatically explode upon the cessation of their activity) from exploding. Suppose, therefore, that pushing the magic button to eliminate government would result in the H-bomb exploding in a population center an instant later. Could the button-pusher argue legitimately that he simply removed the framework for continued aggression, and that the deaths were entirely the government's fault—the consequence, and only the consequence, of the government's prior statism? Or would the button-pusher be culpable in the loss of life, to the extent that he could be said to have directly engaged in aggression against those who died when he pushed the button knowing of the immediate consequences?

On the other hand, will the abolitionist concede that it might be advisable to postpone pushing the button just long enough to disarm the H-bomb (even though the government will, in the meantime, deposit another tax-funded paycheck into its functionaries' bank account, and taxes will in the meantime be deducted from paychecks to get the loot)? If so, the abolitionist concedes that he is, in principle, a gradualist. We're reduced to quibbling over the *degree* of gradualism.

In my opinion this hypothetical, as fantastic as it appears, is much more relevant to the kinds of real-world dilemmas facing libertarians. We live in a world where the economy and civil society have developed within a state-supported framework, so that many of their functions would cease to operate on the sudden disappearance of the state, as surely as a patient on a ventilator would die if the power were cut off before he could be weaned off his dependence on the machine. The state has, in effect, interposed itself between us and countless H-bombs controlled by dead-man triggers, so that we are dependent at least in the short term on its continued functioning until the bombs can be disarmed.

And in the real world, principled libertarians are faced every day with a piecemeal pushbutton scenario, of the very kind Johnson describes. Because the mainstream libertarian movement is largely corporate-funded and corporate-controlled, and the establishment politicians and think tanks that push for "free market reform" are for the most part corporate hirelings, in almost every case the practical proposals we are presented with for reducing the size of government amount to just such a catastrophic pushbutton scenario. In every case, the proposal will be to remove some secondary form of state intervention that stabilizes the system and makes it humanly tolerable for the majority, by constraining corporate power or by redistributing a small part of the income of the privileged classes. In every case, also, the proposal will leave untouched (and unmentioned) the primary forms of state intervention that support corporate power and enable privilege in the first place.

So if we always push the button on the terms that are presented to us, and welcome every proposed reduction in state power (which will, for all intents and purposes, always be selected according to the priorities of the corporate/state ruling class), we may be reducing the levels of formal statism. But we will be increasing the levels of substantive statism, in such a way that we will be directly implicated in the disastrous consequences that follow immediately from our support. And with every push of the button, we will help to make "libertarianism" and "free markets" even more of a stench in the nostrils of working people and the poor, and to reinforce the popular image of it as the doctrine of "pot-smoking Republicans" who want to turn the entire world into one big dioxin-soaked sweatshop.

To the extent that I have a difference in principle with McElroy and Johnson, it hinges on the blurring of the boundaries between abolitionism and gradualism by another, overlapping position: realism. Even though my ultimate goal is total abolition, and I consider nonaggression an ethical absolute, I would still refrain from pushing the button: first, because I don't think libertarianism will be achievable without a social consensus to bring it about; and second, because that will only occur if people understand it as not resulting in a total catastrophe.

So I view the ethical opposition to coercion primarily as a systemic goal to be achieved. On a purely individual level, the consequences of letting the neoliberals dismantle the state according to their own strategic priorities, or introducing a sudden collapse of the state via some mechanism like Rothbard's magic button, would have consequences so disastrous as to render the non-aggression principle utterly meaningless. The consequences would be so horrendous, IMO, as to make the whole discussion of coercion as academic as it would be in a lifeboat scenario, or as questions of just property rights would be to somebody stranded in a blizzard who breaks into an empty vacation cabin. If a stateless society is to be brought about, it must be done in a way that doesn't sidetrack us into a mass die-off or mass enslavement on the way there.

For this reason Gustav Landauer was a gradualist, seeing anarchy as an ideal to be approximated ever more closely over time. He advocated the abolition of the state only as quickly as something could take its place. He likewise saw anarchy as achievable on a stable basis only when popular attitudes had evolved sufficiently that the people would not simply restore the state.[1]

No less an abolitionist than Tucker also advocated gradualism and realism for the same reason: "If government should be abruptly and entirely abolished to-morrow, there would probably ensue a series of physical conflicts about land and many other things, ending in reaction and a revival of the old tyranny."[2]

Tucker assumed that dissolving the state would be a long-term process, and that it would be accompanied by a long-term educational campaign.

> A system of Anarchy in actual operation implies a previous education of the people in the principles of Anarchy, and that in turn implies such a distrust and hatred of interference that the only band of voluntary co-operators which could gain support sufficient to enforce its will would be that which either entirely refrained from interference or reduced it to a minimum. This would be my answer to Mr. Donisthorpe, were I to admit his assumption of a state of Anarchy supervening upon a sudden collapse of Archy. But I really scout this assumption as absurd. Anarchists work for the abolition of the State, but by this they mean not its overthrow, but, as Proudhon put it, its dissolution in the economic organism.[3]

So to summarize our argument so far, our approach is to scale back the state one step at a time, starting with those functions that subsidize the rich and handicap the poor, and finishing with those functions that cushion the poor against the harsh edges of privilege. Meanwhile, as we dissolve the state, we replace its functions with alternative institutions founded on free exchange and voluntary cooperation.

E. "Dissolving the State in the Economy"

Proudhon described the process as "dissolving the state in the economy" (or in the social body). In practical terms, that meant depriving state functions of their coercive nature so that relationships previously characterized by authority would take on the character of voluntary exchange:

---

1. Larry Gambone, "For Community: The Communitarian Anarchism of Gustav Landauer" (Montreal: Red Lion Press, 2000) <http://dwardmac.pitzer.edu/Anarchist_Archives/bright/ landauer/forcommunity.html>.
2. Tucker, "Protection, and Its Relation to Rent," *Instead of a Book*, p. 329.
3. Tucker, "Voluntary Co-operation," *Instead of a Book*, p. 104.

. . . . To dissolve, submerge, and cause to disappear the political or governmental system in the economic system by reducing, simplifying, decentralizing and suppressing, one after another, all the wheels of this great machine, which is called the Government or the State.[1]

. . . . The political idea, the ancient notion of distributive justice, must be contradicted through and through; and that of commutative justice must be reached, which, in the logic of history as well as of law, succeeds it.[2]

. . . The notion of Contract succeeding that of Government . . . ,

Economic criticism having shown that political institutions must be lost in industrial organization,

We may conclude without fear that the revolutionary formula cannot be *Direct Legislation*, nor *Direct Government*, nor *Simplified Government*, that it is NO GOVERNMENT.[3]

3. This Revolution consists in substituting the economic, or industrial, system, for the governmental, feudal and military system, in the same way that the present system was substituted, by a previous revolution, for a theocratic or sacerdotal system.

4. By an industrial system, we understand, not a form of government, in which men devoted to agriculture and industry, promoters, proprietors, workmen, become in their turn a dominant caste, as were formerly the nobility and clergy, but a constitution of society having for its basis the organization of economic forces, in place of the hierarchy of political powers.[4]

. . . . [The notion of *anarchy* in politics] means that once industrial functions have taken over from political functions, then business transactions and exchange alone produce the social order.[5]

Clarence Swartz, a veteran of Tucker's *Liberty* group, distinguished between the individualist anarchists (narrowly defined) and mutualists. Individualists had a mostly negative program, extending only to the abolition of the state and of all monopolies and privileges that depended on it. Individualism had little interest in a positive program beyond that. Mutualism, while in full agreement with the negative program of individualism, also took an interest in the positive forms social organization might take under liberty. Swartz, accordingly, devoted a major part of his book to speculation on how social functions might be carried out by cooperatives, mutuals, and other forms of voluntary association.

Individualist Anarchists . . . lay no claim to having a positive or constructive philosophy . . . . While Anarchists have demanded the destruction of the four great monopolies . . . , which object Mutualists share with them, their program for the accomplishment of that purpose has been the abolition of the State. That consummation is still far off; and Mutualists . . . believe in working toward the gradual elimination of the four great monopolies through a peaceful substitution of voluntary institutions for compulsory ones as an ever and ever greater measure of freedom is secured.[6]

As Martin Buber said (in Larry Gambone's paraphrase): "It is the growth of a real organic structure, for the union of persons and families into various communities and of communities into associations, and nothing else, that 'destroys' the State by displacing it."[7]

1. Pierre-Joseph Proudhon, *General Idea of the Revolution in the Nineteenth Century*. Translated by John Beverly Robinson (New York: Haskell House Publishers, Ltd., 1923, 1969 [1851]), p. 173
2. *Ibid.*, p. 110.
3. *Ibid.*, p. 126.
4. *Ibid.*, p. 170.
5. Proudhon, *The Federal Principle*, in *Selected Writings of Proudhon*. Edited by Stewart Edwards. Translated by Elizabeth Fraser (Garden City, N.Y.: Anchor, 1969), *p. 91.*
6. Clarence Swartz, *What is Mutualism?*, p. 37.
7. Gambone, "For Community."

F. COUNTER-INSTITUTIONS

Going back to Proudhon, anarchism (and especially mutualism) has emphasized the importance of (in the wonderful Wobbly phrase) "building the structure of the new society within the shell of the old."

> It is the substitution of one system for another, a new organism replacing one that is outworn. But this change does not take place in a matter of minutes . . . . It does not happen at the command of one man who has his own pre-established theory, or at the dictate of some prophet. A truly organic revolution is a product of universal life . . . . It is an idea that is at first very rudimentary and that germinates like a seed; an idea that is at first in no way remarkable since it is based on popular wisdom, but one that . . . suddenly grows in a most unexpected fashion and fills the world with its institution.[1]

Even Tucker, for all his professed agnosticism concerning the outlines of a stateless society, proposed the building of counter-institutions as part of the present-day anti-state agenda.

> . . . [I]n some large city fairly representative of the varied interests and characteristics of our heterogeneous civilization let a sufficiently large number of earnest and intelligent Anarchists, engaged in nearly all the different trades and professions, combine to carry on their production and distribution on the cost principle and to start a bank through which they can obtain a non-interest-bearing currency for the conduct of their commerce and dispose their steadily accumulating capital in new enterprises, the advantages of this system of affairs being open to all who should choose to offer their patronage,— what would be the result? Why, soon the whole . . . population . . . would become interested in what was going on under their very eyes, more and more of them would actually take part in it, and in a few years, each man reaping the fruit of his labor and no man able to live in idleness on an income from capital, the whole city would become a great hive of Anarchistic workers, prosperous and free individuals.[2]

Brian Dominick, as we have already seen, placed a great deal of emphasis on counter-institutions. He described the process of building counter-institutions, within the shadow of existing institutional framework, in considerable detail:

> Generally speaking, dual power is the revolutionary organization of society in its pre-insurrectionary form. It is the second power—the second society—operating in the shadows of the dominant establishment. It seeks to become an infrastructure in and of itself, the foundations of an alternative future . . . .
>
> The great task of grassroots dual power is to seek out and create social spaces and fill them with liberatory institutions and relationships. Where there is room for us to act for ourselves, we form institutions conducive not only to catalyzing revolution, but also to the present conditions of a fulfilling life, including economic and political self-management to the greatest degree achievable . . . .
>
> Thus, grassroots dual power is a situation wherein a self-defined community has created for itself a political/economic system which is an operating alternative to the dominant state/capitalist establishment. The dual power consists of alternative institutions which provide for the needs of the community, both material and social, including food, clothing, housing, health care, communication, energy, transportation, educational opportunities and political organization. The dual power is necessarily autonomous from, and competitive with, the dominant system, seeking to encroach upon the latter's domain, and, eventually, to replace it.[3]

Peter Staudenmeier used the term "social counter-power" to describe essentially the same concept, breaking it down further into takes the concrete expressions of "prefigurative politics" and "counterinstitutions."

---

1. Proudhon, *On the Political Capacity of the Working Classes* (1865), in *Selected Writings*, p. 177.
2. Tucker, "Colonization," *Instead of a Book*, pp. 423-424.
3. Dominick, "An Introduction to Dual Power Strategy."

Prefigurative politics is a fancy term that just means living your values today, instead of waiting until "after the revolution"—in fact it means beginning the revolution here and now to the extent possible. This might be called the everyday aspect of social counter-power. And counterinstitutions, of which co-ops are often an example, are the structural aspects of social counter-power.[1]

Jonathan Simcock, on the *Total Liberty* webpage, described a vision of Evolutionary Anarchism that included

... Worker Co-operatives, Housing Co-operatives, self-employment, LETS schemes, Alternative Currencies, Mutual Banking, Credit Unions, tenants committees, Food Co-operatives, Allotments, voluntary organizations, peaceful protest and non-violent direct action and a host of similar activities are the means by which people begin to "behave differently", to go beyond Anarchist theory, and begin to build the elements of a new society.[2]

G. COUNTER-INSTITUTIONS AND COUNTER-ECONOMICS

Samuel Edward Konkin proposed, as the primary form of revolutionary activity, "bring[ing] more and more people into the counter-economy and lower[ing] the plunder available to the State . . . ."

Slowly but steadily we will move to the free society turning more counter-economists onto libertarianism and more libertarians onto counter-economics, finally integrating theory and practice. The counter-economy will grow and spread to the next step ..., with an ever-larger agorist sub-society embedded in the statist society.[3]

As the agorist counter-society grew and coalesced, entrepreneurs would increasingly provide black market insurance, arbitration and protection services, until economic counter-institutions eventually comprised the entire necessary infrastructure for maintaining peace and order in the successor society. In time this agorist society would come to predominate in contiguous geographical areas, and be capable of organizing open defense against the state. The state, increasingly starved of economic resources and weakened by counter-economic resistance even within areas still under its control, would find its ability to suppress the agorist counter-society dwindling just as its desire to do so would become most urgent. From this point, the correlation of forces would shift until the state was relegated to pockets of control within a larger agorist society, and would suffer a continued erosion of control until its eventual collapse.[4]

Tucker anticipated counter-economics in some ways with his writing on passive resistance.

But, if individuals can do much, what shall be said of the enormous and utterly irresistible power of a large and intelligent minority, comprising say one-fifth of the population in any given locality? . . . If one-fifth of the people were to resist taxation, it would cost more to collect their taxes, or try to collect them, than the other four-fifths would consent to pay into the treasury.[5]

H. THE TWO ECONOMIES AND THE SHIFTING CORRELATION OF FORCES

Economic counter-institutions, unfortunately, work within the framework of a larger corporate capitalist economy. They compete in markets in which the institutional culture

1. Peter Staudenmaier, "Anarchism and the Cooperative Ideal," *The Communitarian Anarchist* 1:1.
2. Jonathan Simcock, "Editorial for Current Edition," *Total Liberty* 1:3 (Autumn 1998).
3. Samuel Edward Konkin III. *New Libertarian Manifesto* (Koman Publishing, 1983), p. 22. Online version at Agorism.Info <http://www.agorism.info/ NewLibertarianManifesto.pdf>.
4. This is a summary of the overall theme of Konkin's *Manifesto*, but is the focus in particular of Chapters Three "Counter-Economics: Our Means" and Four "Revolution: Our Strategy."
5. Tucker, "The Power of Passive Resistance," *Instead of a Book, pp. 412-413.*

of the dominant firms is top-down and hierarchical, and are in great danger of absorbing this institutional culture themselves. That's why you have a non-profit and cooperative sector whose management and organizational culture are often indistinguishable from its capitalist counterparts.

The solution is to promote as much consolidation as possible within the counter-economy. A great deal of production and consumption already takes place within the social or gift economy, self-employment, barter, etc. The linkages need to be increased and strengthened between those involved in consumers' and producers' co-ops, self-employment, LETS systems, home gardening and other household production, informal barter, etc. What economic counter-institutions already exist need to start functioning as a cohesive counter-economy.

That's what Moses Coady had in mind, for example, in building the Antigonish system:

> Away and beyond establishing co-operatives on a piecemeal basis, Coady looked forward to the wider vision which he and his associates referred to as 'the Big Picture'. Within the overall framework of 'the Big Picture', consumer co-operatives would source their requirements from co-operative wholesale societies. The wholesale societies in turn would be supplied by factories which were the property of the movement. Coady's ultimate objective was an integrated system of co-operatives which would comprise a 'Middle Way' or 'Third Sector' between capitalism and communism . . . .
>
> Coady saw consumer co-operation as embracing 'a vast field of business—retailing, wholesaling, manufacturing, money and credit and the wide range of services necessary to life in a modern society' . . . . 'The cooperative dream . . . is to cover the Maritimes with co-operatives and set the wheels of industry turning in our factories'.[1]

A good concrete example of Coady's vision in practice was the community of Larry's River, where in 1928 people were paying $37.00 per thousand feet of lumber.

> That year they built a community sawmill. The building and machinery cost $2,000. They began to manufacture their own rough lumber, boat timber, laths and shingles. By working during the winter months they can now bring logs to this community sawmill and obtain lumber at $7.50 per thousand. Some of them work at the mill and pay the $7.50 for their lumber with labor. The establishment of the sawmill made it possible for the residents to repair their homes and to build ten or more new houses and several co-operative plants.
>
> . . . . In 1932 they built a cooperative lobster factory; in 1933 they established a credit union and in 1934 a consumers' cooperative; in 1934, too, they organized a cooperative blueberry-canning industry; in 1938 they erected and operated a cooperative fish plant.[2]

Race Matthews sees the Mondragon system, with its own credit arm allocating capital between enterprises, as a model for cooperative integration.

> It takes no great leap of the imagination to envisage a third step forward, whereby the Desjardins credit unions would begin to give preference in their allocation of development capital to co-operatives which could count on being advantaged like those in Mondragon by a relative freedom from the basic agency dilemma. Nor is it difficult to envisage the credit union movement more generally establishing structures and acquiring skills with which to support recipients of commercial loans through [advisory and support] services such as those of the Empresarial Division of the Caja Laboral [credit union] in the Mark I phase of Mondragon.[3]

1. Race Matthews, *Jobs of Our Own: Building a Stakeholder Society—Alternatives to the Market & the State* (Annandale, NSW, Australia: Pluto Press, 1999), pp. 151-152.

2. Moses Coady, *Masters of Their Own Destiny: The Story of the Antigonish Movement of Adult Education Through Economic Cooperation* (New York, Evanston, and London: Harper & Row), p. 47.

3. Matthews, *Jobs of Our Own*, p. 242.

Euclides André Mance describes it as building "solidarity-based productive chains." The strategy

> entails that the different solidarity-based operators involved in the productive chain choose solidarity-based suppliers, if available, over other types of suppliers, replacing inputs with a view towards attaining the goal of ecological and social sustainability. If those inputs or suppliers do not exist, local networks should themselves undertake the production of such items. When the required investments are beyond the possibilities of the local networks, or the level of consumption of the local network is not enough to provide for the viability of the new undertaking, the regional networks should evaluate the best options, and thus it should be in increasingly horizontal approaches.
>
> In boosting solidarity in productive chains, the organization of final and productive consumption is fundamental. The activity of consumer cooperatives and other organized consumer groups proves that by organizing themselves, consumers are able to increase their purchasing power and improve their quality of life, while at the same time—if they belong to solidarity-based networks—making it possible to commercialize the goods produced by solidarity-based ventures . . . . Meanwhile, as the solidarity-based network boosts the productive chain, creating supply ventures, the profit that was previously accumulated in those segments of the productive chain becomes, thus, a surplus that goes back to feed the expansion of the network. In this way, a network that organizes ventures capable of generating a certain amount of surplus can grow by collectively reinvesting such surpluses, engaging in new ventures and boosting the productive chain of the final product itself. So, by selling the same amount of the final product, there can be a substantial increase in the number of workers in the network, the number of solidarity-based productive ventures, the volume of income distributed in the network as wages, the surplus generated in the network and its assets . . . .
>
> In this way it is possible to generate the conditions necessary to progressively replace the relations of capitalist accumulation and to expand production and consumption relations based on solidarity, sharing the surplus generated, creating new jobs, increasing consumption among participants and developing a great diversity of products and services that ensure the well-being of all those involved in solidarity-based labor and consumption.[1]
>
> The more the solidarity economy expands and diversifies, and its flows and connections improve, the smaller the need to relate to non-solidarity actors. The underlying logic is to progressively reduce relations with non-solidarity providers and distributors, putting in their place relations with solidarity actors who then become integrated with the networks . . . .[2]

As Hernando de Soto pointed out in *The Mystery of Capital*, the resources already available to us are enormous. If we could leverage and mobilize them sufficiently, they might be made to function as a counterweight to the capitalist economy. For example: the average residential lot, if subjected to biointensive farming methods, could supply the majority of a family's vegetable needs. And what's more important, the total labor involved in doing this would be less than it takes to earn the money to buy equivalent produce from the supermarket. The average person could increase his independence of the wage-system, improve the quality of his food, and reduce his total work hours, all at once.

A key objective should be building the secondary institutions and support framework we need to make the resources we already have more usable. Most people engage in a great deal of informal production to meet their own needs, but lack either access or awareness of the institutional framework by which they might cooperate and exchange with others involved in similar activities. Expanding LETS systems and increasing public awareness of

---

1. Euclides André Mance, "Solidarity-Based Productive Chains" (Curitiba: l'Institut de Philosophie de la Libération, November 2002) <http://www.solidarius.com.br/mance/biblioteca/cadeiaprodutiva-en.pdf>.

2. Euclides André Mance, "Solidarity Economics (Curitiba: l'Institut de Philosophie de la Libération, March 2007) <http://www.solidarius.com.br/mance/biblioteca/turbulence-en.pdf>.

them is vital. Every need that can be met by producing for oneself, or exchanging one's own produce for that of a neighbor, increases the amount of total consumption needs that can be met without depending on employment at someone else's whim. If an organic gardener lives next door to a plumber and they exchange produce for plumbing work, neither one can absorb the other's entire output. But each, at least, will have a secure source of supply for both his vegetables and plumbing needs, and an equally secure market for the portion of his own output consumed by the other. The more different trades come into the system, the larger the proportion of total needs that can be met outside the framework of a job.

Ultimately, we need a cooperative alternative to the capitalist banking system, to increase the cooperative economy's access to its own mutual credit. This is illegal, under the terms of capitalist banking law. The banking system is set up to prevent ordinary people from leveraging their own property for interest-free credit through mutual banking. Gary Elkin argued that it might be possible to slip mutual banking in through the back door, and evade the state's legal restrictions on free banking, by piggybacking a mutual bank on a LETS system. Members of a LETS system might start out by extending store credit against the future labor of other members, and expand from there.

The proliferation of architectures for Internet microlending systems, e-LETS systems, and the like, combined with increasingly powerful encryption, may be leading to a singularity beyond which independent exchange and credit systems can operate in direct defiance of the state, and support an alternative economy beyond the reach of the state's taxation and regulatory apparatus.

The capital and land of the rich is worthless to them without a supply of labor to produce surplus value. And even if they can find labor, their ability to extract profit depends on a labor market that favors buyers over sellers. Anything that marginally increases the independence of labor and reduces its dependence on wages, and marginally reduces the supply of labor available to capitalists and landlords, will also marginally reduce the rate of profit and thus make their land and capital less profitable to them. The value of land and capital to landlords and capitalists depends on the ability to hire labor on their own terms. Anything that increases the marginal price of labor will reduce the marginal returns on capital and land. Any shift in bargaining power from capital to labor will increase the share of their product that wage-workers receive even in capitalist industry. The individualist anarchists argue that a removal of special legal privileges for capital would increase the bargaining power of labor until the rate of profit was effectively zero, and capitalist enterprises took on the de facto character of workers' co-ops.

And the owning classes use less efficient forms of production precisely because the state gives them preferential access to large tracts of land and subsidizes the inefficiency costs of large-scale production. Those engaged in the alternative economy, on the other hand, will be making the most intensive and efficient use of the limited land and capital available to them. So the balance of forces between the alternative and capitalist economy will not be anywhere near as uneven as the distribution of property might indicate.

If everyone capable of benefiting from the alternative economy participates in it, and it makes full and efficient use of the resources already available, eventually we'll have a society where most of what the average person consumes is produced in a network of self-employed or worker-owned production, and the owning classes are left with large tracts of land and understaffed factories that are almost useless to them because it's so hard to hire labor except at an unprofitable price. At that point, the correlation of forces will have shifted until the capitalists and landlords are islands in a cooperative sea—and their land and factories will be the last thing to fall, just like the U.S Embassy in Saigon.

This is something like the theory behind Vinay Gupta's principle, stated in "The Unplugged," of "buying out at the bottom" (see Chapter Fifteen), and Ebenezer Howard's

plan for building his garden cities on cheap rural land and using it with maximum efficiency. The idea was that workers would take advantage of the rent differential between
city and country, make more efficient use of underused land than the great landlords and
capitalists could, and used the surplus income from production in the new cities (collected
as a single tax on the site value of land) for quickly paying off the original capital outlays.[1]
Howard also anticipated something like counter-economics: working people living within
his garden cities, working through building societies, friendly societies, mutuals, consumer
and worker cooperatives, etc., would find ways to employ themselves and each other outside the wage system.

> It is idle for working-men to complain of this self-imposed exploitation, and to talk of na-
> tionalizing the entire land and capital of this country under an executive of their own
> class, until they have first been through an apprenticeship at the humbler task of organis-
> ing men and women with their own capital in constructive work of a less ambitious char-
> acter . . . . The true remedy for capitalist oppression where it exists, is not the strike of *no*
> *work*, but the strike of *true work*, and against this last blow the oppressor has no weapon. If
> labour leaders spent half the energy in co-operative organisation that they now waste in
> co-operative disorganisation, the end of our present unjust system would be at hand.[2]

What impedes the actual jelling together of the resources we already have is not so
much the absence of technical architectures and umbrella organizations, but the overabun-
dance of them. No single framework has emerged as the standard. For example, there are
more concrete projects out there than I can account for providing encrypted electronic alternative currencies, P2P credit systems outside of the state capitalist banking system, etc.
Just about any of them, if it could come to the top through some sort of invisible hand
mechanism and become widely known among all the sub-movements out there, would be
serviceable as a structure for exchange within the alternative economy. But none of them
has. There are lots of good projects based on promising technology, that are largely unheard
of outside a small subculture of devotees. Likewise, there are lots of attempts at creating
federal organizations of worker cooperatives, intentional communities, LETS systems, and
the like, many of them self-consciously aimed at providing an umbrella organization for
the larger alternative economy. But again, they coexist as dozens of separate ghettoes.

One thing that might make a difference is the united support of some particular federal organization, by a sufficient number of major movements within the alternative economy, to trigger a power law threshold and provide an organizational core around which the
rest of the movement could coalesce. That was the significance of the founding convention
of the I.W.W., at Chicago convention in 1905—otherwise known as "The Continental
Congress of the Working Class." Big Bill Haywood of the Western Federation of Miners
(which formed the actual organizational nucleus of the I.W.W. as a labor union) was joined
by De Leon of the Socialist Labor Party and Debs of the American Socialist Party, along
with representatives of other radical unions—not to mention the charismatic figure of
Mother Jones and her moral authority.

One especially promising project, in my opinion, is the Solidarity Economy Network,[3] whose purpose is essentially what I have described in the paragraphs above: to provide an umbrella organization for networking alternative economy organizations like cooperatives, LETS systems, community supported farming, etc., and facilitate their coalescence into a single counter-economy.

---

1. Ebenezer Howard, *To-Morrow: A Peaceful Path to Real Reform*. Facsimile of original 1998
edition, with introduction and commentary by Peter Hall, Dennis Hardy and Colin Ward (London
and New York: Routledge, 2003), pp. 32, 42 [facsimile pp. 13, 20-21].
2. *Ibid.*, pp. 108, 110 [facsimile pp. 85-86].
3. <http://www.populareconomics.org/ussen/>

The Solidarity Economy Network emerged as a relatively low-visibility organizational project from a series of Solidarity Economy caucuses at the June U.S. Social Forum in Atlanta. But there's reason to hope it will emerge from its obscurity. It includes some especially prominent figures in the alternative economy movement. Its initial Coordinating Committee included Dan Swinney of the Center for Labor and Community Research,[1] Jessica Gordon Nembhard and Ethan Miller of Grassroots Economic Organizing,[2] Melissa Hoover and John Parker of the U.S. Federation of Worker Cooperatives,[3] and Cliff Rosenthal of the National Federation of Community Development Credit Unions.[4]

The most promising strategy for anyone involved in the alternative economy, who wants to promote the coalescence of alternative institutions into a coherent counter-economy, is probably to join the organization that shows the most promise as a common federal center for the movement (in my opinion, right now that's the SEN), and then work from within to promote links to and cross-communication with all the other movements. The most important thing is to do it under the auspices of some existing would-be umbrella organization that shows promise, like the SEN, and then work within that organization to promote cooperation with the rest of the alternative economy movement.

I. Privatizing State Property

One especially important question, in any agenda of dissolving the state, involves the privatization of state property. The typical "libertarian" proposal for this, of course, is simply to sell it off to private corporations—on the most favorable terms the corporations can get. This has been the universal pattern of neoliberal "free market reform" since Pinochet "liberalized" Chile's economy. It was central to the so-called "small government" agendas of Thatcher and Reagan. It is a major component of every "structural adjustment" program imposed by the World Bank and IMF. It has been the leitmotif of Naomi Klein's "disaster capitalism" wherever it has appeared—and it has been ubiquitous.

In fact, this so-called "privatization" agenda could more accurately be described as looting.

For starters, as we saw in Chapter Three, the state industry, services and infrastructure were usually built in the first place—at taxpayer expense—to provide subsidized support to the corporate capitalist economy. In Western mixed economies (e.g. Bismarck's "Junker socialism" and the UK under Labour), the nationalization of transportation and extractive industries was a sort of "lemon socialism." Its purposes (as described by Engels in *Anti-Dühring*) were to serve the coordinating needs of the capitalist class in control of the state.[5]

In the Third World, such state-subsidized infrastructure was created primarily to serve the needs of Western capital. What's more, the World Bank created what amounted to "Iron Triangles" with Western TNCs and technocratic elites in (often politically unaccountable) Third World governments, and promoted the running up of insane debts. These debts, in turn, were later used to blackmail the host governments into adopting "structural adjustment programs" which sold the infrastructure off (at fire sale prices) the very same multinational corporate interests it was created to serve in the first place. Whether in the West, the Third World, or the former Soviet bloc, the state almost always makes its "privatization" policy in cahoots with the corporate interests buying up the assets.

1. <http://www.clcr.org/index.php>
2. <http://www.geo.coop/>
3. <http://www.usworker.coop/>
4. <http://www.natfed.org/i4a/pages/index.cfm?pageid=1>
5. Friedrich Engels, *Anti-Dühring*, in Marx and Engels *Collected Works* (New York: International Publishers, 1987), v. 25, p. 265.

The connivance between the state and the corporate purchasers of its assets doesn't stop with the sweetheart deal on the price. First, in the period leading up to the sale, governments often sink more money in state assets to make them attractive to buyers than they wind up getting from the sale.

> Instead of encouraging investment, privatisation has left governments offering increased concessions to entice investors to acquire their assets . . . . For example, between 1991 and 1998 the Brazilian Government made some US$85 billion through the sale of state run enterprises. However, over the same period, it spent US$87 billion 'preparing' the companies for privatisation.
>
> Rather than being a major source of finance, private contractors are committing little of their own capital and are instead looking to municipalities, central government or donor governments/institutions to provide the money . . . .
>
> In fact, in many cases foreign companies are relying on the [government foreign aid] donor community to bail them out when they get it wrong.[1]

In short, governments are paying crony capitalists to take the assets off their hands.

And second (as "Bill," a commenter on my blog observed), after privatization the new owner's first order of business is likely to be asset-stripping:

> The true sin of nationalised industry is that the marketable value of its assets compared with its profits tend to be too high—there is no merger/bankrupcy mechanism to adjust this. When firms get privatised it's often hugely profitable to just sell off capital assets and pare back the service rather than concentrate on users needs. Over here, former British rail firms made most of their early dividends payouts from land sales, not service improvements . . . . They also cut the staff back, which left them prone to the massive pay demands of the few remaining drivers—they did well . . .[2]

The overall level of statism is not diminished by such "privatization," and may actually be increased. Some forms of activity may be formally shifted from the state budget to the nominal "private" sector. But the activities take place within a framework of increased state protections.

> While the privatisation of state industries and assets has certainly cut down the direct involvement of the state in the production and distribution of many goods and services, the process has been accompanied by new state regulations, subsidies and institutions aimed at introducing and entrenching a "favourable environment" for the newly-privatised industries . . . .
>
> Moreover, "states are still massively present in the processes of production, distribution and exchange", not least through framing taxation policy; setting interest rates (where independent central banks have not been introduced) or interest rate policy; directing subsidies to sectors of industry; farming out government procurement contracts; awarding franchises for privatised industries; setting pollution and health standards; and funding infrastructure projects.[3]

In other words the Pinochet/Thatcher/Reagan/Adam Smith Institute version of "free market reform" is, as Sean Gabb pointed out, just a new version of fascist economics. Nominally "private" business operates within a web of subsidies and protections provided

---

1. Clare Joy and Peter Hardstaff, *Dirty aid, dirty water: The UK government's push to privatise water and sanitation in poor countries* (London: World Development Movement, February 2005), p. 23 <http://www.wdm.org.uk/resources/reports/water/dadwreport01022005.pdf>.

2. Comment under Kevin Carson, "Public Services, 'Privatized' and Mutualized," Mutualist Blog: Free Market Anticapitalism, March 29, 2005 <http://mutualist.blogspot.com/2005/03/public-services-privatized-and.html>.

3. Nicholas Hildyard, "The Myth of the Minimalist State: Free Market Ambiguities," *The Corner House* Briefing No. 5 (March 1998) <http://www.thecornerhouse.org.uk/item.shtml? x=51960>.

by the state, in order to provide a secure level of profit without any interference from an unfettered market.

> As reconstructed in the 1980s—partly by the Adam Smith Institute—the new statism is different. It looks like private enterprise. It makes a profit. Those in charge of it are paid vast salaries, and smugly believe they are worth every penny . . . .
>
> But for all its external appearance, the reality is statism. And because it makes a profit, it is more stable than the old. It is also more pervasive. Look at these privatised companies, with their boards full of retired politicians, their cosy relationships with the regulators, their quick and easy ways to get whatever privileges they want . . . .
>
> As with National Socialism in Germany, the new statism is leading to the abolition of the distinction between public and private.[1]

Murray Rothbard proposed a far different kind of privatization. In a 1969 piece for *The Libertarian Forum*, he wrote:

> . . . [T]he libertarian must cheer any attempt to return stolen, governmental property to the private sector: whether it be in the cry, "The streets belong to the people", or "the parks belong to the people", or the schools belong to those who use them, i.e. the students and faculty. The libertarian believes that things not properly owned revert to the first person who uses and possesses them . . . ; similarly, the libertarian must support any attempt by campus "homesteaders," the students and faculty, to seize power in the universities from the governmental or quasi-governmental bureaucracy.[2]

Rothbard argued that "the most practical method de-statizing is simply to grant the moral right of ownership on the person or group who seizes the property from the State." This would entail treating the State's property as vacant or unowned, and recognizing the homestead rights of those actually using it. In most cases, that would mean transferring state industry to those working in it, and state services either to the workers or the clients, privatizing state property as either consumer or producer cooperatives. Larry Gambone refers to the process as "mutualization," decentralizing control of public schools, hospitals, utilities, etc., to the smallest feasible local unit (the neighborhood or community) and then placing them under the democratic control of their clientele.[3] Ultimately, of course, libertarians would seek and end to compulsory taxation and the funding of services with user fees.

During the fall of the Soviet empire in 1989-91, Rothbard advocated applying the same homestead principle to state property in post-communist societies. Rather than the corporate looting overseen by Jeffrey Sachs, he proposed a "syndicalist" solution:

> It would be far better to enshrine the venerable homesteading principle at the base of the new desocialized property system. Or, to revive the old Marxist slogan: "all land to the peasants, all factories to the workers!" This would establish the basic Lockean principle that ownership of owned property is to be acquired by "mixing one's labor with the soil" or with other unowned resources. Desocialization is a process of depriving the government of its existing "ownership" or control, and devolving it upon private individuals. In a sense, abolishing government ownership of assets puts them immediately and implicitly into an unowned status, out of which previous homesteading can quickly convert them into private ownership.[4]

---

1. Sean Gabb, "Dr Pirie Changes Trains (But Continues in the Same Direction)," *Free Life Commentary*, Issue Number 18 (July 3, 1998) <http://www.seangabb.co.uk/flcomm/flco18.htm>.

2. "The Student Revolution," *The Libertarian* (soon renamed *The Libertarian Forum*), May 1, 1969, p. 2.

3. Mutualize! website <http://www.geocities.com/vcmtalk/mutualize>.

4. Murray Rothbard, "How and How Not to Desocialize," *The Review of Austrian Economics* 6:1 (1992), pp. 65-77.

The question of genuine privatization also arises in regard to existing, nominally "private" property titles, that amount in practice to state property: i.e., "private" property acquired through statist means, and "private" enterprises built with profits derived predominantly from state intervention.

Jerome Tuccille coined the phrase "anarcho-landgrabbism" to describe the tendency of too many libertarians to take *de jure* property titles at face value.

> Free market anarchists base their theories of private property rights on the homestead principle: a person has the right to a private piece of real estate provided he mixes his labor with it and alters it in some way. Anarcho-land grabbers recognize no such restrictions. Simply climb to the highest mountain peak and claim all you can see. It then becomes morally and sacredly your own and no one else can so much as step on it.[1]

This is hardly hypothetical, given the number of existing land titles that can be traced to U.S. government grants to railroads and land speculators, Spanish crown grants to the ancestors of today's *latifundistas*, or even to a pope drawing a line across a map of the Americas.

Murray Rothbard pointed out the perils of the utilitarian approach to property rights (again, i.e., taking *de jure* property titles at face value):

> Suppose that libertarian agitation and pressure has escalated to such a point that the government and its various branches are ready to abdicate. But they engineer a cunning ruse. Just before the government of New York state abdicates it passes a law turning over the entire territorial area of New York to become the private property of the Rockefeller family. The Massachusetts legislature does the same for the Kennedy family. And so on for each state. The government could then abdicate and decree the abolition of taxes and coercive legislation. . . . The utilitarians, who have no theory of justice in property rights, would, if they were consistent with their acceptance of given property titles as decreed by government, have to accept a new social order in which fifty new satraps would be collecting taxes in the form of unilaterally imposed "rent." The point is that only natural-rights libertarians, only those libertarians who have a theory of justice in property titles that does not depend on government decree, could be in a position to scoff at the new rulers' claims to have private property in the territory of the country, and to rebuff these claims as invalid.[2]

It therefore follows, as Karl Hess said, that libertarianism does not automatically defend everything that's called "property":

> Because so many of its [the libertarian movement's] people . . . have come from the right there remains about it at least an aura or, perhaps, miasma of defensiveness, as though its interests really center in, for instance, defending private property. The truth, of course, is that libertarianism wants to advance principles of property but that it in no way wishes to defend, willy nilly, all property which now is called private.
>
> Much of that property is stolen. Much is of dubious title. All of it is deeply intertwined with an immoral, coercive state system which has condoned, built on, and profited from slavery; has expanded through and exploited a brutal and aggressive imperial and colonial foreign policy, and continues to hold the people in a roughly serf-master relationship to political-economic power concentrations.[3]

Rothbard took the line of argument further, arguing that the nominally "private" property of businesses whose profit depended on state subsidies was in reality just another form of state property, and should be treated as such.

1. Jerome Tuccille, "Bits and Pieces," *The Libertarian Forum*, November 1, 1970, p. 3.

2. Murray Rothbard, "Property and Exchange," *For a New Liberty: The Libertarian Manifesto* (1973, 1978). Online edition prepared by William Harshbarger. Ludwig von Mises Institute, 2002 <http://mises.org/rothbard/newliberty.asp>.

3. Karl Hess, "Letter From Washington: Where Are The Specifics?" *The Libertarian Forum*, June 15, 1969, p. 2.

But if Columbia University, what of General Dynamics? What of the myriad of corporations which are integral parts of the military-industrial complex, which not only get over half or sometimes virtually all their revenue from the government but also participate in mass murder? What are their credentials to private property? Surely less than zero. As eager lobbyists for these contracts and subsidies, as co-founders of the garrison state, they deserve confiscation and reversion of their property to the genuine private sector as rapidly as possible.[1]

Even this standard for confiscation is probably too modest. To treat gross revenue as the main criterion, as Rothbard did, oversimplifies things. For one thing, the state's contribution to the profit margin is probably a more meaningful indicator. The majority of a corporation's revenue stream may come from private sources, but with state procurement still making the margin of difference, in enabling a corporation to fully utilize otherwise idle capacity, between profit and loss. This is the case with much of the military economy, as we saw in Chapter Three, wherein the significant measure is not government procurement as a percentage of a firm's total output, but as a percentage of its idle capacity. And what of non-monetary benefits from the state, like the ability to charge monopoly prices thanks to State-enforced patents? or the state's role in stabilizing oligopoly markets through its regulations, and thus protecting large firms from market competition?

Taking these things together, it requires no stretch of the imagination to treat virtually the entire large manufacturing sector as a creation of the corporate state. That's especially true given the largely fictitious nature of shareholder ownership, as we saw in Chapter Eight, and the more realistic description of the large corporation as a mass of unowned capital controlled by a self-perpetuating managerial oligarchy. The shareholders, far from being "owners" in any real sense, are in practice another class of contractual claimant with even fewer rights than creditors.

Although Benjamin Tucker refused to advocate the seizure of such nominally private capitalist property, he speculated that it might be legitimate and useful under some circumstances.

> Professor Sumner also told Herr Most and his followers that their proposition to have the employee get capital by forcible seizure is the most short-sighted economic measure possible to conceive of. Here again he is entirely wise and sound. Not that there may not be circumstances when such seizure would be advisable as a political, war, or terroristic measure calculated to induce political changes that will give freedom to natural economic processes; but as a directly economic measure it must always and inevitably be, not only futile, but reactionary.[2]

Indeed, in later years he feared that the growth of the great trusts had advanced so far that it could no longer be reversed by "economic processes," and that a market free of privilege would be possible only after corporate capitalism had been destroyed by non-economic (i.e., revolutionary) means.

> monopoly, which can be controlled permanently only by economic forces, has passed for the moment beyond their reach, and must be grappled with for a time solely by forces political or revolutionary. Until measures of forcible confiscation, through the State or in defiance of it, shall have abolished the concentrations that monopoly has created, the economic solution proposed by Anarchism and outlined in the forgoing pages – *and there is no other solution* – will remain a thing to be taught to the rising generation, that conditions may be favorable to its application after the great leveling. But education is a slow process, and may not come too quickly. Anarchists who endeavor to hasten it by joining in the propaganda of State Socialism or revolution make a sad mistake indeed. They help to so force the march of events that the people will not have time to find out, by the study of

1. Rothbard, "Confiscation and the Homestead Principle," p. 3.
2. Tucker, "Will Professor Sumner Choose?" *Instead of a Book*, p. 372.

their experience, that their troubles have been due to the rejection of competition. If this lesson shall not be learned in a season, the past will be repeated in the future . . . .[1]

1. Benjamin Tucker, 1926 "Postscript to State Socialism and Anarchism," in Tucker, *Individual Liberty: Selections From the Writings of Benjamin R. Tucker* (New York: Vanguard Press, 1926). Reproduced online at Flag.Blackened.Net <http://flag.blackened.net/daver/anarchism/ tucker/tucker.html>.

Decentralized Production Technology

INTRODUCTION

E. F. Schumacher, in *Small is Beautiful*, outlined the basic principles of liberatory technology:

> What is it that we really require from the scientists and technologists? I should answer: We need methods and equipment which are
> —cheap enough so that they are accessible to virtually everyone;
> —suitable for small-scale application; and
> —compatible with man's need for creativity.[1]

Elaborating on the first criterion, he cited Gandhi's dictum that "there should be no place for machines that concentrate power in a few hands and turn the masses into mere machine minder, if indeed they do not make them unemployed."

Decentralized, small-scale technology, Schumacher quoted Aldous Huxley as saying, would provide the average person with the means of

> doing profitable and intrinsically significant work, of helping men and women to achieve independence from bosses, so that they may become their own employers, or members of a self-governing, cooperative group working for subsistence and a local market . . . [T]his differently orientated technological progress [would result in] a progressive decentralization of population, of accessibility of land, of ownership of the means of production, of political and economic power.[2]

Schumacher's criterion of affordability, formulated as a general rule of thumb, amounted to enterprise capitalization per worker equivalent to an average worker's annual income.[3]

On the benefits of the second criterion, small-scale application, he predicted that "men organized in small units will take better care of their bit of land or natural resources than anonymous companies or megalomaniacal governments . . . ."[4]

Schumacher contrasted "mass production" with "production by the masses": the latter "mobilises the priceless resources which are possessed by all human beings, their clever brains and skilful hands, and *supports them with first-class tools* . . . ."

> The technology of *production by the masses*, making use of the best modern knowledge and experience, is conducive to decentralisation, compatible with the laws of ecology, gentle in its use of scarce resources, and designed to serve the human person instead of making him the servant of machines.[5]

---

1. E. F. Schumacher, *Small is Beautiful: Economics as if People Mattered* (New York, Hagerstown, San Francisco, London: Harper & Row, Publishers, 1973), p. 34.
2. From Aldous Huxley, *Towards New Horizons* by Pyarelal (Navajivan Publishing House, Ahmedabad, India, 1959), in Schumacher, *Ibid.*, p. 35.
3. *Ibid.*, p. 35.
4. *Ibid.*, p. 36.
5. *Ibid.*, pp. 153–54.

In another attempt to articulate the principles of human scale technology, in the context of Third World development, Schumacher wrote:

> The task . . . is to bring into existence millions of new workplaces in the rural areas
> and small towns. That modern industry, as it has arisen in the developed countries, can-
> not fulfill this task should be perfectly obvious. It has arisen in societies which are rich in
> capital and short of labour and therefore cannot possibly be appropriate for societies
> short of capital and rich in labour . . . .
> The real task may be formulated in four propositions:
> *First*, that workplaces have to be created in the areas where the people are living
> now, and not primarily in metropolitan areas into which they tend to migrate.
> *Second*, that these workplaces must be, on average, cheap enough so that they can be
> created in large numbers without this calling for an unattainable level of capital forma-
> tion and imports.
> *Third*, that the production methods employed must be relatively simple, so that the
> demands for high skills are minimised, not only in the production process itself but also
> in matters of organisation, raw material supply, financing, marketing, and so forth.
> *Fourth*, that production should be mainly from local materials and mainly for local use.[1]

The good news is that the choice of such technologies would not require imposition by the state, or any heroic individual act of voluntary renunciation. In Chapter One, we have already seen that decentralized, less capital-intensive production for local markets using general-purpose machinery would likely be cheaper overall compared to large-scale, centralized, capital-intensive production using highly specialized machinery—cheaper, that is, when all costs are actually internalized in the price of finished goods, rather than footed by the taxpayer. And as we saw in Chapter Twelve, when all the subsidies to long-distance distribution costs, capital-intensiveness, research and development, and to the other costs of large-scale enterprise are eliminated—and when all the state's cartelizing regulations, entry barriers, and other protections against the competitive costs of inefficiency are likewise eliminated—it is likely that such a model of production will be the spontaneous outcome of market forces.

In this chapter, we will look at specific developments that offer the promise of achieving the above criteria of liberatory technology.

A. MULTIPLE-PURPOSE PRODUCTION TECHNOLOGY

Perhaps the most important concept for decentralized economics is the multiple-purpose production technology described by Murray Bookchin and Kirkpatrick Sale. The basic principle was stated by F. M. Scherer:

> Ball bearing manufacturing provides a good illustration of several *product-specific* econo-
> mies. If only a few bearings are to be custom-made, the ring machining will be done on
> general-purpose lathes by a skilled operator who hand-positions the stock and tools and
> makes measurements for each cut. With this method, machining a single ring requires
> from five minutes to more than an hour, depending on the part's size and complexity
> and the operator's skill. If a sizable batch is to be produced, a more specialized automatic
> screw machine will be used instead. Once it is loaded with a steel tube, it automatically
> feeds the tube, sets the tools and adjusts its speed to make the necessary cuts, and spits
> out machined parts into a hopper at a rate of from eighty to one hundred forty parts per
> hour. A substantial saving of machine running and operator attendance time per unit is
> achieved, but setting up the screw machine to perform these operations takes about eight

1. *Ibid.*, pp. 174-76.

hours. If only one hundred bearing rings are to be made, setup time greatly exceeds total running time, and it may be cheaper to do the job on an ordinary lathe.[1]

In a Ploughboy Interview with *Mother Earth News*, Ralph Borsodi spoke of the superior overall efficiency of small-scale production for most commodities, when internal economics of scale were offset by distribution costs.

> . . . . Adam Smith completely overlooked what factory production does to distribution costs. It pushes them up. Goods cannot be manufactured in a factory unless raw materials and fuel and workers and everything else are brought there. This is a distribution cost. And then, after you've put together whatever you're making in that plant, you've got to ship it out to the people who consume it. That can become expensive too. Now I've produced everything from tomato crops to suits of clothing which I've hand spun on my own homestead and I've kept very careful records of every expense that went into these experiments. And I think the evidence is pretty clear that probably half to two-thirds— and it's nearer two-thirds—of all the things we need for a good living can be produced most economically on a small scale . . . either in your own home or in the community where you live. The studies I made at Dogwoods—the "experiments in domestic production"—show conclusively that we have been misled by the doctrine of the division of labor. Of course there are some things—from my standpoint, a few things—that cannot be economically produced in a small community. You can't make electric wire or light bulbs, for example, very satisfactorily on a limited scale. Still virtually two thirds of all the things we consume are better off produced on a community basis.[2]

In fact, as Kirkpatrick Sale pointed out, even Borsodi overstated the superiority of large-scale factory production. Sale challenged the specific example of copper wire. The average lighting and wiring factory, even under present conditions, employs only around 65 workers.

> Posit an efficient plant, limited differentiation, and a market of 3,500 households, and the factory could be many times smaller; then figure that the quality could be improved by careful work on a limited number of items . . . so production quotas could be considerably reduced and the plant made even smaller; lastly, add in the effect of recycling on limiting annual production . . . , and the operation could be smaller still . . . .[3]

This would be made possible by the adoption of multiple-purpose production machinery for frequent switching from one short production run to another—as opposed to the current practice, in large-scale, capital intensive manufacturing, of using expensive, specialized production machinery that can only pay for itself with long production runs for giant market areas. Murray Bookchin, in *Post-Scarcity Anarchism*, described the concept:

> The new technology has produced not only miniaturized electronic components and smaller production facilities but also highly versatile, multi-purpose machines. For more than a century, the trend in machine design moved increasingly toward technological specialization and single purpose devices, underpinning the intensive division of labor required by the new factory system. Industrial operations were subordinated entirely to the product. In time, this narrow pragmatic approach has "led industry far from the rational line of development in production machinery," observe Eric W. Leaver and John J. Brown. "It has led to increasingly uneconomic specialization . . . . Specialization of machines in terms of end product requires that the machine be thrown away when the product is no longer needed. Yet the work the production machine does can be reduced to a set of basic functions—forming, holding, cutting, and so on—and these functions, if correctly analyzed, can be packaged and applied to operate on a part as needed."

1. F.M. Scherer and David Ross, *Industrial Market Structure and Economic Performance*. 3rd ed (Boston: Houghton Mifflin, 1990), p. 97.
2. "Plowboy Interview" (Ralph Borsodi), *Mother Earth News*, March–April 1974 <http://www.soilandhealth.org/03sov/0303critic/Brsdi.intrvw/The%20Plowboy-Borsodi%20Interview.htm>.
3. Kirkpatrick Sale, *Human Scale* (New York: Coward, McCann, & Geoghegan, 1980), p. 405.

Ideally, a drilling machine of the kind envisioned by Leaver and Brown would be able to produce a hole small enough to hold a thin wire or large enough to admit a pipe . . . .

The importance of machines with this kind of operational range can hardly be overestimated. They make it possible to produce a large variety of products in a single plant. A small or moderate-sized community using multi-purpose machines could satisfy many of its limited industrial needs without being burdened with underused industrial facilities. There would be less loss in scrapping tools and less need for single-purpose plants. The community's economy would be more compact and versatile, more rounded and self-contained, than anything we find in the communities of industrially advanced countries. The effort that goes into retooling machines for new products would be enormously reduced. Retooling would generally consist of changes in dimensioning rather than in design.[1]

As Kirkpatrick Sale described it, the same plant could (say) finish a production run of 30,000 light bulbs, and then switch to wiring or other electrical products—thus "in effect becoming a succession of electrical factories." A machine shop making electric vehicles could switch from tractors to reapers to bicycles.[2]

Some special-purpose machines, of course—Bookchin specifically mentions bottling and canning machines—would continue to be useful even in the context of a decentralized economy. At the same time, some kinds of production (like heavy engine blocks), that can only be done with large, specialized, capital-intensive facilities, would likely face drastic reductions in demand for their products—if the products continued to be used at all:

A major shift from conventional automobiles, buses and trucks to electric vehicles would undoubtedly lead to industrial facilities much smaller in size than existing automobile plants.[3]

Bookchin's specific example of bottling machines as a legitimate form of product-specific technology seems questionable, in light of a discussion in *Natural Capitalism*. The authors use that specific example to illustrate the inefficiencies created by machinery whose "efficiency" is out of scale with the overall production process:

All this results from the mismatch between a very small-scale operation—drinking a can of cola—and a very large-scale one, producing it. The production process is designed to run in enormous batches, at very high speeds, with very high changeover costs. But that logic is the result of applying to business organization precisely the same design flaw— discussed in the previous chapter at the level of components—namely, optimizing one element in isolation from others and thereby pessimizing the entire system. Buying the world's fastest canning machine to achieve the world's lowest fill cost per can presumably looks like an efficient strategy to the canner. But it doesn't create consumer value at least cost, because of such expenses as indirect labor (in such forms as technical support), the inventories throughout the value chain, and the pervasive costs and losses of handling, transport and storage between all the elephantine parts of the production process . . . . [F]rom a whole-system perspective, the giant cola-canning machine may well cost more per delivered can than a small, slow, unsophisticated machine that produces the cans of cola locally and immediately on receiving an order from the retailer.[4]

As we saw in Chapter Eight, that was a lesson in Waddell's and Bodek's study of the Sloan system. That system obsesses on minimizing the cost and optimizing the efficiency of each individual step in the production process, in isolation from the process as a whole, rather than optimizing the flow of the overall process.

1. Murray Bookchin, *Post-Scarcity Anarchism* (Berleley, Ca.: The Ramparts Press, 1971), pp. 110-111.

2. Sale, *Human Scale*, pp. 409-410.

3. Bookchin, *Post-Scarcity Anarchism*, p. 112.

4. Paul Hawken, Amory Lovins, and L. Hunter Lovins, *Natural Capitalism: Creating the Next Industrial Revolution* (Boston, New York, London: Little, Brown and Company, 1999), p. 129.

Eric Husman, commenting on Bookchin's and Sale's treatment of multiple-purpose production technology as described in the initial draft of this chapter, points out that they were to a large extent reinventing the wheel:

> *Human Scale* (1980) was written without reference to how badly the Japanese production methods . . . were beating American mass production methods at the time . . . . What Sale failed to appreciate is that the Japanese method (. . . almost diametrically opposed to the Sloan method that Sale is almost certainly thinking of as "mass production") allows the production of *higher* quality articles at *lower* prices . . . .
>
> . . . . Taichi Ohno would laugh himself silly at the thought of someone toying with the idea [of replacing large-batch production on specialized machinery with shorter runs on general-purpose machinery] 20 years after he had *perfected* it. Ohno's development of Toyota's Just-In-Time method was born exactly out of such circumstances, when Toyota was a small, intimate factory in a beaten country and could not afford the variety and number of machines used in such places as Ford and GM. Ohno pushed, and Shingo later perfected, the idea of Just-In-Time by using Single Minute Exchange of Dies (SMED), making a mockery of a month-long changeover. The idea is to use general machines (e.g. presses) in specialized ways (different dies for each stamping) and to vary the product mix on the assembly line so that you make some of every product every day.
>
> The Sale method (the slightly modified Sloan/GM method) would require extensive warehouses to store the mass-produced production runs (since you run a year's worth of production for those two months and have to store it for the remaining 10 months). If problems were discovered months later, the only recourse would be to wait for the next production run (months later). If too many light bulbs were made, or designs were changed, all those bulbs would be waste. And of course you can forget about producing perishables this way. The JIT method would be to run a few lightbulbs, a couple of irons, a stove, and a refrigerator every hour, switching between them as customer demand dictated. No warehouse needed, just take it straight to the customer. If problems are discovered, the next batch can be held until the problems are solved, and a new batch will be forthcoming later in the shift or during a later shift. If designs or tastes change, there is no waste because you only produce as customers demand.[1]

The serial production runs on multiple-purpose machinery favored by Bookchin and Sale, and the simultaneous production of different products using different dies on the same general-purpose machines favored by the Japanese, seem to be alternative approaches to solving the same problem.

The Japanese made still further inroads in this direction in the 1970s. Advances in semiconductor and computer technology made possible the application of numerical control, previously the preserve of large-scale Sloanist producers like the aerospace industry, on a small scale. Starting in the 1970s, the Japanese introduced

> a new kind of machine tool: numerically controlled general-purpose equipment that is easily programmed and suited for the thousands of small and medium-sized job shops that do much of the batch production in metalworking . . . . NC equipment could easily be programmed to perform the wide range of simple tasks that make up the majority of machining jobs. The equipment's built-in microcomputers allowed a skilled metalworker to teach the machine a sequence of cuts simply by performing them once, or by translating his or her knowledge into a program through straightforward commands entered via a keyboard located on the shop floor.[2]

Interestingly, H. Thomas Johnson, in his Foreword to Waddell's and Bodek's *The Rebirth of American Industry* (something of a bible for American devotees of the Toyota Production System) speculates along exactly those lines:

1. "Human Scale Part II—Mass Production," *Grim Reader* blog, September 26, 2006 <http://www.zianet.com/ehusman/weblog/2006/09/human-scale-part-ii-mass-production.html>.

2. Michael J. Piore and Charles F. Sabel, *The Second Industrial Divide: Possibilities for Prosperity* (New York: HarperCollins, 1984), pp. 216-218.

Some people, I am afraid, see lean as a pathway to restoring the large manufacturing giants the United States economy has been famous for in the past half century.

...The cheap fossil fuel energy sources that have always supported such production operations cannot be taken for granted any longer. One proposal that has great merit is that of rebuilding our economy around smaller scale, locally-focused organizations that provide just as high a standard living [sic] as people now enjoy, but with far less energy and resource consumption. Helping to create the sustainable local living economy may be the most exciting frontier yet for architects of lean operations. Time will tell.[1]

Johnson expanded on this theme, referring to the common perception that economic decentralism "would cause consumers' standards of living to fall because it would reduce the economies and efficiencies of large-scale production and distribution systems that we ostensibly have in the world today."

Herein lies the importance of understanding the fallacies of scale-economy thinking. In reality, production systems designed along the lines of Toyota's turn scale-economy thinking on its head: they make it possible to build manufacturing capacity on a much smaller scale than ever before thought possible, yet produce at unit costs equal to or lower than those of large-scale facilities now thought so necessary for cost-effective operations.

An example of this is found in Toyota's organization. Compare the plant that makes Camry and Avalon models in Melbourne, Australia with the plant that makes the same models in Georgetown, Kentucky. Located within or nearby each plant are complete facilities for engine build, axle build, plastic trim and bumper production, stamping, body weld, seat build, and final assembly. According to Toyota, these two vertically integrated plants are equally efficient and effective on all dimensions that matter to Toyota customers. However, the Melbourne plant currently produces about 90,000 vehicles per year, primarily for the Australian market, whereas the Georgetown plant produces about 500,000 vehicles per year.

If a fivefold difference in capacity yields no unit-cost differences between these two plants, then what is to be said on behalf of scale economies? In fact, Toyota people have said they probably will not build another plant as large as Georgetown in the future. The company currently is building new plants, smaller in scale and located as close as possible to customer markets. Carried to its logical extent, Toyota's example helps show how bioregional economies of 10 to 30 million people could support high-variety and low-cost manufacturing facilities for a wide range of products. Indeed, the relatively isolated Australian economy, with about 20 million people and a vast land area, supports several auto manufacturing operations in addition to Toyota's, as well as facilities producing a wide array of other products just for Australian consumers.

There are now ample technologies available to support efficient small-scale operation of almost every commercial activity. Some examples among many include the continuous-casting, mini-mill technology that transformed steel making in the last 30 years, small-scale refineries and chemical plants for almost all current petroleum and chemical processing, and Japanese paper-products plants that efficiently produce on a much smaller scale than American papermakers, for example, might think possible.[2]

And the market area Johnson writes of, with a population starting at ten million, is an upper-range estimate applying only to the most capital-intensive forms of production. Bear in mind that conventional auto design, with heavy internal-combustion engine blocks, is an "answer" to a manufactured need. The light electrical vehicles mentioned by Bookchin above, and the hypercar mentioned below, are examples of alternatives that can be produced on a much smaller scale for local markets. In short, the kind of heavy internal com-

1. H. Thomas Johnson, "Foreword," William H. Waddell and Norman Bodek, *Rebirth of American Industry: A Study of Lean Management* (Vancouver, WA: PCS Press, 2005), p. xxi.

2. Johnson, "Confronting the Tyranny of Management by Numbers," *Reflections: The SoL Journal*, vol. 5, no. 4 (2004), pp. 8-9.

bustion vehicle Toyota makes might end up as a latter-day buggy whip. Johnson acknowledges as much:

> Especially interesting are eco-designer Amory Lovins's paradigm-breaking examples of how the industrial economy can flourish at a much smaller scale than ever thought possible by rethinking, for example, the design of automobiles (with carbon composite bodies and hydrogen-cell power trains) . . . .[1]

Michael Shuman, in *The Small-Mart Revolution*, cites Johnson on the adaptability of lean methods to small-scale production for local markets. He also quotes Paul Kidd, author of *Agile Manufacturing*, on the use of "economies of scope" ("the principles that machines should be used to make a wide range of product lines with small batch sizes") to tailor product lines to specific markets.[2] The efficiencies of lean local production become even greater, as Shuman points out, when the high costs of large-scale distribution enter the picture.[3] That's especially true given the nature of the global distribution system which, as we will see immediately below, amounts even in large-scale lean production to the outsourcing of excess inventories to warehouses on wheels or on the ocean. And local, demand-pull, customer-driven distribution chains (for example, community-supported agriculture and other subscription-based services) can drastically reduce the marketing costs of push distribution.[4]

Husman himself is an enthusiastic advocate for the superior cost-effectiveness of localized production, and its special suitability to lean production:

> For another view of self-sufficiency—and I hate to beat this dead horse, but the parallel seems so striking—we have the lean literature on local production. In *Lean Thinking*, Womack et al discuss the travails of the simple aluminum soda can. From the mine to the smelter to the rolling mill to the can maker alone takes several months of storage and shipment time, yet there is only about 3 hours worth of processing time. A good deal of aluminum smelting is done in Norway and/or Sweden, where widely available hydroelectric power makes aluminum production from alumina very cheap and relatively clean. From there, the cans are shipped to bottlers where they sit for a few more days before being filled, shipped, stored, bought, stored, and drank. All told, it takes 319 days to go from the mine to your lips, where you spend a few minutes actually using the can. The process also produces about 24% scrap (most of which is recycled at the source) because the cans are made at one location and shipped empty to the bottler and they get damaged in transit. It's an astounding tale of how wasteful the whole process is, yet still results in a product that—externalities aside—costs very little to the end user. Could this type of thing be done locally? After all, every town is awash in a sea of used aluminum cans, and the reprocessing cost is much lower than the original processing cost (which is why Reynolds and ALCOA buy scrap aluminum).
>
> Taking this problem to the obvious conclusion, Bill Waddell and other lean consultants have been trying to convince manufacturers that if they would only fire the MBAs and actually learn to manufacture, they could do so much more cheaply locally than they can by offshoring their production. Labor costs simply aren't the deciding factor, no matter what the local Sloan school is teaching: American labor may be more expensive then [sic] foreign labor, but it is also more productive. Further, all of the (chimerical) gains to be made from going to cheaper labor are likely to be lost in shipping costs.

1. *Ibid.*, p. 9.
2. Michael H. Shuman, *The Small-Mart Revolution: How Local Businesses are Beating the Global Competition* (San Francisco: Barrett-Koehler Publications, Inc., 2006, 2007), pp. 70-71.
3. *Ibid.*, pp. 71-72.
4. *Ibid.*, p. 72.

Think of that flotilla of shipping containers on cargo ships between here and Asia as a huge warehouse on the ocean, warehouses that not only charge rent, but also for fuel.[1]

Just-in-Time methods, as they are applied in the existing global market, rely pretty intensively on such "warehouses on the ocean" or (for the domestic market) warehouses on wheels. If they are scalable to decentralized production for local markets, so as to eliminate the need for such expensive distribution pipelines, then they would seem to be a viable local production alternative to the Bookchin-Sale model.

Husman, incidentally, describes a localized "open-source production" model, with numerous small local machine shops networked to manufacture a product according to open-source design specifications and then to manufacture replacement parts and do repairs on an as-needed basis, as "almost an ideally Lean manufacturing process. Dozens of small shops located near their customers, each building one at a time."[2]

And the authors of *Natural Capitalism* see small-scale local production as the ideal embodiment of lean thinking, as well:

> The essence of the lean approach is that in almost all modern manufacturing, the combined and often synergistic benefits of the lower capital investment, greater flexibility, often higher reliability, lower inventory cost, and lower shipping cost of much smaller and more localized production equipment will far outweigh any modest decreases in its narrowly defined "efficiency" per process step. It's more efficient overall, in resources and time and money, to scale production properly, using flexible machines that can quickly shift between products. By doing so, all the different processing steps can be carried out immediately adjacent to one another with the product kept in continuous flow. The goal is to have no stops, no delays, no backflows, no inventories, no expediting, no bottlenecks, no buffer stocks, and no *muda*. Surprisingly, this is as true for small- as for large-scale production.[3]

This is, incidentally, the model that prevails in Italy's Emilia-Romagna region, which is organized on a "cluster model" of "[s]mall firms operating in cooperative networks . . . ." There is very little vertical integration, with most firms subcontracting with the minority of firms that produce finished goods. Not only is it a regional manufacturing economy built around the cooperative networking of small firms, but it has the highest rate of cooperative ownership in Italy—some eight thousand of them in the region, in fact (with cooperatives producing some 45% of the region's GDP).[4] Sebastian Brusco, an authority on the region, writes that the artisans and small entrepreneurs of Emilia-Romagna have

> created associations to provide administrative services for themselves and to coordinate purchasing and credit, thus establishing on a cooperative basis the conditions of achieving minimum scale of operation . . . .
>
> These associations also establish technical consultancy offices, consortia for marketing and the purchase of raw and semi-fabricated materials, and most importantly, cooperatives which provide guarantees for bank loans which can thus be obtained at the lowest possible rate of interest.[5]

The heart of Emilia-Romagna's economy is its "flexible manufacturing networks." Bruce Herman, another specialist on the region, describes how they came about:

1. "Human Scale Part III—Self-Sufficiency," *Grim Reader* blog, October 2, 2006 <http://www.zianet.com/ehusman/weblog/2006/10/human-scale-part-iii-self-sufficiency.html>.

2. Eric Husman, "Open Source Automobile," *GrimReader*, March 3, 2005 <http://www.zianet.com/ehusman/weblog/2005/03/open-source-automobile.html>.

3. Hawken *et al.*, *Natural Capitalism*, pp. 129-130.

4. Robert Williams, "Bologna and Emilia Romagna: A Model of Economic Democracy," paper presented at the annual meeting of the Canadian Economics Association, University of Calgary. May/June 2002, pp. 8-9, 24 <http://www.bcca.coop/pdfs/BolognaandEmilia.pdf>.

5. Sebastian Brusco, Emilian Model: Productive Decentralization and Social Integration, Cambridge Journal of Economics, 1982, 6, pages 167-184, in *Ibid.*, p. 10.

"Initially the small firms of Emilia Romagna served large enterprise as dependent subcontractors. To overcome the negative consequences of this situation, small shops learned to diversify their client base through horizontal linkages to small firms. Relationships of trust grew as firms subcontracted among themselves rather then refusing to take on contracts too large for the individual shop."

Flexible specialization evolved and this strengthened commercial linkages and these SME's then began to coordinate their respective enterprises, creating value-added partnerships and value-added goods.

This cooperation allowed these players to jointly bid on larger contracts, which led to the growth of flexible manufacturing networks.

The region's average wage is double that of Italy as a whole, and has among the highest productivity rates in Europe.[1]

Michael J. Piore and Charles F. Sabel specifically propose the Emilia-Romagna model as an alternative to the current American model of Sloanist production. They blame the chronic crises of American capitalism, in large part, on "the limits of the model of industrial development that is founded on mass production: the use of special-purpose (product-specific) machines and of semi-skilled workers to produce standardized goods."[2]

The rise of the mass production and push distribution model, the Chandler/Galbraith model we examined in Chapter One, was not the product of technological determinism, they argue. Rather, there were two alternative models by which the new electrically powered machinery could have been integrated into manufacturing at the turn of the 20th century.

One of them was the Sloanist model that actually prevailed in the 20th century, and it dictated the use of large-scale corporate organization in collusion with the state to stabilize markets and guarantee an outlet for mass-produced goods on the scale industry needed to produce them. The latter expedients for guaranteeing demand were inevitably entailed in the production model. Specialized machinery reduced the flexibility of production and its ability to respond to changes in demand, and required sufficiently large markets to dispose of the output of the specialized machines running at full capacity. The central role of the state, in the 20th century, in overcoming crises of overproduction and underconsumption, followed directly from the mass production model.[3]

The other possibility, the path not taken, was the integration of small-scale electrical machinery into craft production, in which "firms using a combination of craft skill and flexible equipment might have played a central role in modern economic life," with manufacturing firms "linked to their communities . . . ."[4] In this model, machines would be adopted "to augment the craftsman's skill, allowing the worker to embody his or her knowledge in ever more varied products: the more flexible the machine, the more widely applicable the process, the more it expanded the craftsman's capacity for productive expression."[5]

Although Sloanism came to predominate, the second model was adopted in enclaves like Emilia-Romagna. Piore and Sabel refer to "the networks of technologically sophisticated, highly flexible manufacturing firms in central and northwestern Italy."[6]

Free-standing electrical machinery, arguably, was far better suited to small-scale, flexible production than to mass production. As we shall see below, Mumford's "paleotechnic"

---

1. Bruce Herman, "Industrial Development: Targeting New and Basic Industries," NationalCouncil for Urban Economic Development, October 1988, in *Ibid.*, p. 12.
2. Piore and Sabel, *The Second Industrial Divide*, p. 4.
3. *Ibid.*, pp. 22-23.
4. *Ibid.*, pp. 5-6.
5. *Ibid.*, p. 19.
6. *Ibid.*, p. 17.

model of large-scale production was in large part a response to the centralization of power sources, and electrical power enabled production to take place at a smaller scale without dependence on a single prime mover. The problem is that existing institutional structure conditions both the choice between competing technologies, and the ways in when even potentially decentralizing technology is adopted. Electrical machinery, in areas where the paleotechnic model predominated, was adapted to large-scale factory production. The process was abetted by massive state intervention (e.g., the creation of the national railroad system, which Chandler admitted was the central prerequisite for the production methods he celebrated) to reconfigure markets to the needs of mass-production

This is a clear illustration of Mumford's "pseudomorph" principle, which we saw described in Chapter Ten:

> new forces, activities, institutions, instead of crystallizing independently into their own appropriate forms, may creep into the structure of an existing civilization . . . . As a civilization, we have not yet entered the neotechnic phase . . . . [W]e are still living, in Matthew Arnold's words, between two worlds, one dead, the other powerless to be born.[1]

In other words, the new wine of neotechnic production technology was poured into the old bottles of paleotechnic mass production. Although electrically powered machinery is ideally suited to flexible, small-scale craft production, we have experienced an interlude of a century or so in which the methods of the future libertarian economy have been distorted by the organizational framework of the old one. As late as the 1890s, Continental industrial districts like Remscheid seized on the potential for "renovation of decentralized production . . . , through the introduction of flexible machine tools, powered by small electric motors." But in the face of full-blown state capitalism centered on the model of production Chandler celebrated, the small-scale model—the model electrically powered machinery was ideally suited for—was marginalized and bypassed. " . . . [T]he mass production paradigm became self-evident truth . . ." As a result, "it took almost a century (from about 1870 to 1960) to discover how to organize an economy to reap the benefits of the new technology."

So it seems Husman was right. Bookchin's system of localized batch production, using multiple-purpose machinery and switching serially between production runs, would indeed be a step in the right direction. It would not be fair, strictly speaking, to dismiss it—as Husman does—as a "slightly modified" version of Sloanism. But while far more efficient and localized, it would still be a more efficient and localized version of Sloanism, and only a partial step toward the efficiencies that could be realized by lean production at the local level.

The need to make efficient use of small facilities (even with Single Minute Exchange of Dies) would rule out what Sale described as "the incessant and needless turnover in products, made not to be better or more useful but only to be marginally new and infinitesimally different."[2] The need for a single factory, in many cases, to switch back and forth between products another might limit the variations in style that could be made without prohibitive increases in production cost (the cost of annual model changes is roughly 40% of a car's sticker price).[3] But the shift away from the current push distribution model, which came about mainly to dispose of overproduction by overbuilt factories, would do away with the primary motivation for such dreck. It's likely, under such conditions, that product design would take on a quasi-Fordist model of finding a cheap, durable, reliable

1. Lewis Mumford, *Technics and Civilization* (New York: Harcourt, Brace, and Company, 1934), p. 265.

2. Sale, *Human Scale*, p. 90.

3. Barry Stein, *Size, Efficiency, and Community Enterprise* (Cambridge: Center for Community Economic Development, 1974), pp. 41-42.

and easy-to-repair model, and then sticking with it in between major generational changes of technology.

There are a few products, arguably, that require large-scale, capital-intensive forms of production: the automobile, the jumbo jet, and so forth. But the demand for such products, arguably, would likely be far less in the first place if they were not subsidized. Some of them most likely would simply never have come into existence in a free market, because their production would have entailed massive losses without the state making them artificially profitable. The clearest example is probably the jumbo jet which, as we saw in Chapter Three, would probably not have been profitable to produce without the government's heavy bomber program to guarantee production runs long enough to fully utilize the expensive capital equipment.

Other products, like the automobile, have taken far more capital-intensive production paths than they might otherwise have. The heavy internal combustion engine, for example, is by no means the only feasible option for powering a private automobile. The use of research funds to develop more efficient electric motors would have made possible decentralized automobile production without the huge factories needed to produce heavy engine blocks. Or consider the hypercar, which the authors of *Natural Capitalism* compare to "computers with wheels."[1]

Even internal combustion automobiles were produced at quite small levels of capitalization and output at one time, as shown by the facilities at which the first Model-Ts were produced. The unit costs were considerably higher. But in a society where the cost principle encouraged walkable communities with public transit, there was little need for long-distance shipping, and most people lived close to where they worked and shopped, the demand for private automobiles would probably be far lower, with a much smaller customer base paying the higher price only when an automobile was a practical necessity, or when they were rich enough to afford a luxury. The main demand for automobiles in such circumstances would likely come from dispersed rural populations, those who didn't live within convenient distance of a railhead, but needed frequent transportation in and out of town (truck farmers, for instance). And in such circumstances, the main deficiency of the electric vehicle—its limited range without recharging—wouldn't be a problem.

In any case, the great majority of the products we consume could be produced by small factories serving local markets. The New Towns in Britain were inspired by Ebenezer Howard's Garden City prototype, intended to be "largely self-reliant in food, services, and industry at a population of 32,000."[2] Howard, heavily influenced by Kropotkin's vision of the decentralized production made possible by small-scale electrically powered machinery,[3] wrote that "[t]own and country *must be married*, and out of this joyous union will spring a new hope, a new life, a new civilization."[4] Large markets, warehouses, and industry, would be located along a ring road on the outer edge of each town, with markets and industry serving the particular ward in which its customers and workers lived.[5] A cluster of several individual towns (the "social city" of around a quarter million population in an area of roughly ten miles square) would ultimately be linked together by "[r]apid railway transit," much like the mixed-use railroad suburbs which today's New Urbanists propose to resurrect and link together with light rail. Larger industries in each town would specialize in the

1. Hawken, *et al.*, *Natural Capitalism*, p. 39.
2. Sale, *Human Scale*, pp. 402-403.
3. Colin Ward, Commentator's introduction to Ebenezer Howard, *To-Morrow: A Peaceful Path to Real Reform*. Facsimile of original 1898 edition, with introduction and commentary by Peter Hall, Dennis Hardy and Colin Ward (London and New York: Routledge, 2003), p. 3.
4. Howard, *To-Morrow*, p. 28 [facsimile p. 10].
5. *Ibid.*, p. 14 [facsimile p. 34].

production of commodities for the entire cluster, in which greater economies of scale were necessary.[1]

The businesses included in the industrial belt of the projected City included "coal, lumber, and stone yards, furniture, clothing, boot factories, a printing press, a 'cycle works,' an engineering center, and even a 'jam factory.'" Frederick Osborn, who created the actual Garden Cities of Letchworth (1903) and Welwyn (1920), concluded that "[a] town which is designed for modern industry, employing people living on the spot," should have a population of from 30-50,000. The New Towns built from 1947-58, "mostly in the hinterlands," have been "quite self-contained" and "achieved rough degrees of independence" with populations averaging around 39,000.[2] The first Garden City, Letchworth,

> quickly attracted a variety of crafts and industries—bookbinding, printing, the Iceni Pottery, the St. Edmundsbury Weaving Works, motor car manufacturers, and a corset-company—and this first town (and later its younger sister Welwyn) proved economically self-sustaining and socially coherent in all the ways Howard had predicted.[3]

Kirkpatrick Sale observes that, even with the currently predominating scale of production, a village of 500 would be a sufficient population base to staff a few small manufacturing plants and consume their products, in addition to producing most of its own food and energy. Of course, if such small population units did not pool their markets to support more diversified production, the range of goods would be rather sparse.

> A village of, say, 500 people could probably grow its own food, operate its own energy systems, create its own handicrafts, perhaps carry on some manufactures, much as the Israeli kibbutzim do; but it would be hard-pressed to go in for much in the way of extensive manufacture or construction, would not likely have much variety in its wares, would have to keep its services quite simple, and would have to accept fairly limited opportunities of conviviality and culture. Even figuring a labor force of 250 in such a settlement, . . . there would probably be no more than 100 people or so available for manufacturing or recycling, the rest employed in agriculture, energy and transportation, services, and handicrafts. That would certainly be sufficient for a dozen small manufacturing plants, since . . . 65 percent of all the plants in this country operate with fewer than twenty people . . . , and in those *the average number of employees is only 5.5*; and it would no doubt cover such basics as lumber, paper, and textile mills, a carpentry and brick works, and a few small factories (bikes, maybe, and hardwares). But that would plainly be insufficient to create a full range of metal products, electrical equipment, medical instruments, books, rubber products, soaps, and paints, to pick only the basic categories of contemporary manufacturing.

But if these villages or neighborhoods federated to form a population base of several thousand, enough to support larger factories, these latter goods could be produced as well with the largest plants employing not much over a hundred workers. So a community of 10,000 could be self-sufficient in most forms of basic industry (Sale lists textiles, apparel, lumber and wood products, furniture and fixtures, paper and allied products, primary metal industries, fabricated metal products, machinery, electrical and electronic equipment, motorcycles and bicycles, and instruments and related products) and even have several competing plants in each industry.[4]

This model of federated small units dovetails to a considerable extent with Jeff Vail's "hamlet economy" (which he also calls "rhizome economy" or "resilient community"): a system of networked villages based on an idealized version of the historical "lattice net-

---

1. *Ibid.*, pp. 156-162 [facsimile pp. 130-133].

2. Sale, *Human Scale*, pp. 402-03.

3. Florence S. Boos, "*News From Nowhere* and 'Garden Cities': Morris's Utopia and Nineteenth-Century Town Design," *Journal of Pre-Raphaelite Studies*, Fall 1998 <http://www.morrissociety.org/agregation.boos.html>.

4. Sale, *Human Scale*, pp. 397-99.

work of Tuscan hill towns" numbering in the hundreds (which became the basis of a modern regional economy based largely on networked production). The individual communities in Vail's network must be large enough to achieve self-sufficiency by leveraging division of labor, as well as providing sufficient redundancy to absorb systemic shock. When larger-scale division of labor is required to support some industry, Vail writes, this is not to be achieved through hierarchy, with larger regional towns becoming centers of large industry. Rather, it is to be achieved by towns of roughly similar size specializing in producing of specialized surplus goods for exchange, via fairs and other horizontal exchange relationships.[1]

Although he doesn't challenge the economic statistics for the New Towns, Husman argues that Sale went too far in his last assertion about the amount of industry that could be supported in a town of 10,000:

> . . . Sale claims that a small number of people could locally manufacture all or most of the products we use today. He does so by listing 13 major industries and the number of people in an average size factory in each. He either does not realize, or does not wish the reader to realize, that each industry does not manufacture all of the products within that category in a single factory. Thus, for the electrical appliance industry, he only lists one factory, though the industry consists of washing machines, dryers, stoves, refrigerators, irons, clocks, stereos, telephones, faxes, lamps, toasters, mixers, coffee pots, food processors, grills, and so on. The metal industry includes steel mills, aluminum works, copper works, etc . . . . His calculations are surely off by an order of magnitude.[2]

I'm not sure whether his objection to listing only one factory each for industries with multiple products takes into account the possibility of switching between production runs for different kinds of appliances (either with the Bookchin or Ohno system). But even stipulating Husman's order of magnitude difference, a regional economy of 100,000 could be self-sufficient in most small- and medium-scale industrial production.

The local economies Sale describes would likely involve other changes besides the predominant use of general-purpose technology. There would be greater ingenuity in the substitution of local raw materials. There would, for that matter, be greater ingenuity in general, especially from workers tinkering with machinery in the small shops. As we will see in Chapter Fifteen, worker control of production is ideal from the standpoint of maximizing productivity and innovation.

Such local economies would also probably rely more heavily on recycling and repairing. Sale speculates that neighborhood recycling and repair centers would put back into service the almost endless supply of appliances currently sitting in closets or basements; as well as "remanufacturing centers" for (say) diesel engines and refrigerators.[3]

According to Lyman van Slyke, the Chinese achieved a considerable amount in this regard back in the 1970s, in meeting their own small machinery needs. This was part of a policy known as the "five smalls," which involved agricultural communes supplying their own needs locally (hydroelectric energy, agro-chemicals, cement, iron and steel smelting, and machinery) in order to relieve large-scale industry of the burden. In the case of machinery, specifically, van Slyke gives the example of the hand tractor:

> . . . [O]ne of the most commonly seen pieces of farm equipment is the hand tractor, which looks like a large rototiller. It is driven in the field by a person walking behind it . . . . This particular design is common in many parts of Asia, not simply in China. Now, at the small-scale level, it is impossible for these relatively small machine shops and machinery plants to manufacture all parts of the tractor. In general, they do not manufacture

1. Jeff Vail, "Re-Post: Hamlet Economy," *Rhizome*, July 28, 2008 <http://www.jeffvail.net/2008/07/re-post-hamlet-economy.html>.

2. Husman, "Human Scale Part II—Mass Production."

3. Sale, *Human Scale*, p. 406.

the engine, the headlights, or the tires, and these are imported from other parts of China. But the transmission and the sheet-metal work and many of the other components may well be manufactured at the small plants. Water pumps of a variety of types, both gasoline and electric, are often made in such plants, as are a variety of other farm implements, right down to simple hand tools. In addition, in many of these shops, a portion of plant capacity is used to build machine tools. That is, some lathes and drill presses were being used not to make the farm machinery but to make additional lathes and drill presses. These plants were thus increasing their own future capabilities at the local level. Equally important is a machinery-repair capability. It is crucial, in a country where there isn't a Ford agency just down the road, that the local unit be able to maintain and repair its own equipment. Indeed, in the busy agricultural season many small farm machinery plants close down temporarily, and the work force forms mobile repair units that go to the fields with spare parts and tools in order to repair equipment on the spot.

Finally, a very important element is the training function played in all parts of the small-scale industry spectrum, but particularly in the machinery plants. Countless times we saw two people on a machine. One was a journeyman, the regular worker, and the second was an apprentice, a younger person, often a young woman, who was learning to operate the machine.[1]

This was by no means a repeat of the disastrous Great Leap Forward, which was imposed in the late 1950s. It was, rather, an example of local ingenuity in filling a vacuum left by the centrally planned economy. If anything, in the 1970s—as opposed to the 1950s—the policy was considered a painful concession to necessity, to be abandoned as soon as possible, rather than a vision pursued for its own sake. Van Slyke was told by those responsible for small-scale industry, "over and over again," that their goals were to move "from small to large, from primitive to modern, and from here-and-there to everywhere."[2] Aimin Chen, in 2002, reported that the government was actually cracking down on local production under the "five smalls" in order to reduce idle capacity in the beleaguered state sector.[3]

Sale's treatment of planned obsolescence is another item in Husman's thoughtful critique of *Human Scale*.

> The other claim—that appliances could be made to last longer but are intentionally not—is based on two mistakes. The first is based on a misunderstanding of statistical quality control (SQC). We can, after analyzing lots of appliances over time, figure out that an appliance will fail in a predictable manner. The failure probability looks like a bell curve. From that, we can say that Refrigerator X will last on average Y years. From this, people will infer that the refrigerator was designed to fail in Y years. In a sense, it was, since the refrigerator was designed within certain constraints: existing technology, cost points, market demand, competitive expectations, cost of inputs including capital and materials, etc. The end result of those design choices is a refrigerator that lasts, on average, Y years. But the direction of causality is from the design to the durability, not from a selected goal of durability to the design. This is a misapplication of statistics, and is usually committed either out of malice or ignorance. I'll assume Sale does so out of the latter.
>
> The other mistake is the idea that people should design 50 year refrigerators (or whatever). Keep in mind that you can, right now, buy outstanding appliances from companies like Viking. They are very expensive. At the same time, keep in mind the fact that technology is changing and that the rate of change is increasing. Given both of those, why would you want to pay extra for something that will be overtaken by scientific and engineering—not design—obsolescence within a few years? The examples are mind-

1. Lyman P. van Slyke, "Rural Small-Scale Industry in China," in Richard C. Dorf and Yvonne L. Hunter, eds., *Appropriate Visions: Technology the Environment and the Individual* (San Francisco: Boyd & Fraser Publishing Company, 1978) pp. 193-194.

2. Van Slyke, p. 196.

3. Aimin Chen, "The structure of Chinese industry and the impact from China's WTO entry," *Comparative Economic Studies* (Spring 2002) <http://www.entrepreneur.com/tradejournals/article/print/86234198.html>.

boggling: a car radio of a few years ago does not have as good reception, disc capability, or perhaps even cassette playback capability; the incandescent lightbulb has been over-taken by the CFL and is about to be overtaken by the LED; a state-of-the-art computer from 1990 won't even begin to approach the capability of a modern computer for most of the modern applications (such as the internet, USB, etc.); the most economical and reliable car from 1975 won't even touch the most economical and reliable modern car for either of those measures or for safety (remember when airbags were only available on high-end Mercedes?). So why would anyone pay a premium for that which they could have in the future at a deep discount?[1]

Here I take issue with Husman's analysis. First of all, it's hard for me to understand why extended lifetime for an appliance, as a matter of design choice, should necessarily en-tail increased cost on the scale of Viking refrigerators. It's entirely plausible that for a given product, two designs with different longevities may not carry radical differences in cost—in which case the decision against longevity reflects some consideration besides the con-sumer's welfare.

Second, he seems to be defining "planned obsolescence" far too narrowly. Planned obsolescence refers not just to how soon or how frequently an appliance breaks down as a result of problems with individual parts, but also to the overall design's amenability to re-pair. Planned obsolescence, in this latter sense, includes 1) a deliberate choice among design alternatives in favor of a design that makes repair more costly, difficult, or complicated, and 2) the use of such expedients as patents to control the availability and pricing of replace-ment parts. In this case, a corporation artificially shifts the lifetime costing of repair upward, in order to make replacement artificially competitive.

In regard to this latter, Preston Glidden made an interesting observation. In a free market, he said,

> What I expect are "throwback designs", at least at first. Consider televisions. In the early days of televisions, the sets were made for easy field servicing. Most of the time, all you had to do was look for a dark vacuum tube, and replace it. Drug stores had tube test-ers that you could use to test the tube yourself. A nearby cabinet had replacements. I don't expect the return to a vacuum tube, but that kind of modular design could be re-created for easy servicing. It would have the added benefit of being more environmentally friendly, because we could stop throwing away the whole gadget when one component goes bad.
>
> The TV could be built for upgrades, as well. The currently scheduled transition of standard to digital TV is probably too much for a simple upgrade, but if some super-cool p2p digital broadcast idea came out , it could be integrated into a modular FM radio with a simple plug in card.
>
> Also, if you've ever seen the inside of a modern television, or most any electronic gadget, you'd see that the parts are machine soldered onto the surface of the circuit board. Such parts are very difficult to solder by hand, but the older design of through-hole soldering was made for hand-soldering. So I'd expect a throwback there. Most kit ham radios that are still sold today use through-hole tech . . . .
>
> . . . [The manufacturers] don't want field service, they want replacement. They make more money that way. Non-modular designs are slightly cheaper to build in the first place as well. But IMHO, the advantages of field service far outweigh the slight extra initial cost.[2]

Joseph Juran discussed "involuntary obsolescence" in similar terms, contrasting "vol-untary obsolesence" to

1. "Human Scale Part I—Planned Obsolescence," *Grim Reader* blog, September 23, 2006 <http://www.zianet.com/ehusman/weblog/2006/09/human-scale-part-i-planned-obsolesence.html>.

2. Preston Glidden, private email. June 5 and 12, 2007.

the case in which long-life products contain components which will not last for the life of the product. The life of these components is determined by the manufacturer. As a result, even though the user decides to have the failed component replaced (to keep the product in service), *the manufacturer makes the real decision* because the design determines the life of the component.

This situation is at its worst when the original manufacturer had designed the product in such a way that the supplies, spare parts, etc., are nonstandard, so that, in effect, the sole source for these needs is the original manufacturer. In such a situation, the user is locked in to a single source of supply.[1]

This is true, especially, of the prevalence of product design whose obvious purpose is to discourage or impede repair by the user.

. . . [A]n engineering culture has developed in recent years in which the object is to "hide the works," rendering the artifacts we use unintelligible to direct inspection . . . . This creeping concealedness takes various forms. The fasteners holding small appliances together now often require esoteric screwdrivers not commonly available, apparently to prevent the curious or the angry from interrogating the innards. By way of contrast, older readers will recall that until recent decades, Sears catalogues included blown-up parts diagrams and conceptual schematics for all appliances and many other mechanical goods. It was simply taken for granted that such information would be demanded by the consumer.[2]

Julian Sanchez gives the specific example of Apple's iPhone. The scenario, as he describes it:

(1) Some minor physical problem afflicts my portable device—the kind of thing that just happens sooner or later when you're carting around something meant to be used on the go. In this case, the top button on my iPhone had gotten jammed in, rendering it nonfunctional and making the phone refuse to boot normally unless plugged in.

(2) I make a *pro forma* trip to the putative "Genius Bar" at an Apple Store out in Virginia. Naturally, they inform me that since this doesn't appear to be the result of an internal defect, it's not covered. But they'll be only too happy to service/replace it for something like $250, at which price I might as well just buy a new one . . . .

(3) I ask the guy if he has any tips if I'm going to do it myself—any advice on opening it, that sort of thing. He's got no idea . . . .

(4) Pulling out a couple of tiny screwdrivers, I start in on the satanic puzzlebox casing Apple locks around all its hardware. I futz with it for at least 15 minutes before cracking the top enough to get at the inner works.

(5) Once this is done, it takes approximately five seconds to execute the necessary repair by unwedging the jammed button.

I have two main problems with this. First, you've got what's *obviously* a simple physical problem that can very probably be repaired in all of a minute flat with the right set of tools. But instead of letting their vaunted support guys give this a shot, they're encouraging customers—many of whom presumably don't know any better—to shell out a ludicrous amount of money to replace it and send the old one in. I appreciate that it's not always obvious that a problem can be this easily remedied on site, but in the instance, it really seems like a case of exploiting consumer ignorance.

Second, the iPhone itself is pointlessly designed to deter self service. Sure, the large majority of users are never going to want to crack their phone open. Then again, most users probably don't want to crack their desktops or laptops open, but we don't expect manufacturers to go out of their way to make it difficult to do.[3]

1. J.M. Juran and Frank M Gryna, *Juran's Quality Control Handbook*. Fourth edition (New York: McGraw-Hill Book Company, 1951, 1988), 3.4-5.

2. Matthew B. Crawford, "Shop Class as Soulcraft," *The New Atlantis*, Number 13, Summer 2006, pp. 7-24 <http://www.thenewatlantis.com/publications/shop-class-as-soulcraft>.

3. Julian Sanchez, "Dammit, Apple," *Notes from the Lounge*, June 2, 2008 <http://www.juliansanchez.com/2008/06/02/dammit-apple/>.

The kind of modular design that would be most amenable to cheap repair rather than replacement, interestingly, is also the most amenable to the kind of peer production we will examine in Chapter Fifteen. Modular design enables a peer network to break a physical manufacturing project down into discrete sub-projects, with many of the individual modules perhaps serving as components in more than one larger appliance. According to Christian Siefkes,

> Products that are modular, that can be broken down into smaller modules or components which can be produced independently before being assembled into a whole, fit better into the peer mode of production than complex, convoluted products, since they make the tasks to be handled by a peer project more manageable. Projects can build upon modules produced by others and they can set as their own (initial) goal the production of a specific module, especially if components can be used stand-alone as well as in combination. The Unix philosophy of providing lots of small specialized tools that can be combined in versatile ways is probably the oldest expression in software of this modular style. The stronger emphasis on modularity is another phenomenon that follows from the differences between market production and peer production. Market producers have to prevent their competitors from copying or integrating their products and methods of production so as not to lose their competitive advantage. In the peer mode, re-use by others is good and should be encouraged, since it increases your reputation and the likelihood of others giving something back to you. . . .
>
> Modularity not only facilitates decentralized innovation, but should also help to increase the longevity of products and components. Capitalism has developed a throwaway culture where things are often discarded when they break (instead of being repaired), or when one aspect of them is no longer up-to-date or in fashion. In a peer economy, the tendency in such cases will be to replace just a single component instead of the whole product, since this will generally be the most labor-efficient option (compared to getting a new product, but also to manually repairing the old one).[1]

What's more, planned obsolescence is by no means limited to the kind of electronic goods or appliances Husman mentions, that one might expect to be rendered obsolete by technical progress. The shoddily built houses in new subdivisions in recent years seem deliberately designed to disintegrate. The shoddy materials that go into commodities designed to fall apart often cost as much to produce as better, longer-lasting materials. In such cases, planned obsolescence is an increased long-term cost with little or no short-term savings. Solidly built, durable and human-friendly furniture can be manufactured at a lower cost in small shops than the push-marketed crap sold in chains.

B. THE TRANSITION TO DECENTRALIZED MANUFACTURING

The building, bottom-up, of local economies based on small-scale production with multiple-purpose machinery might well take place piecemeal, beginning with the kinds of recycling and repair operations mentioned above. In a post-Peak Oil world, with the severe degradation of the national transportation system and the centralized economy dependent on it, facilities to keep existing appliances and machinery running might well be the first step toward local industrial self-reliance. Small machine shops, even the backyard shops of hobbyists, out of sheer necessity might begin to custom-machine the spare parts needed to keep aging machinery in operation. From this, the natural progression would be to farming out the production of components among a number of such small shops, and perhaps designing and producing simple machinery from scratch. This would also, by the way, be an ideal bottom-up model for industrializing village-based economies in the Third World.

1. Christian Siefkes, *From Exchange to Contributions: Generalizing Peer Production into the Physical World* Version 1.01 (Berlin, October 2007), pp. 104-105.

This model is based on more than theoretical speculation: it is almost exactly the way the Japanese bicycle industry developed at the turn of the 20th century, as described by Jane Jacobs, starting with the production in bicycle shops of replacement parts for Western bikes:

> To replace these imports with locally made bicycles, the Japanese could have invited a big American or European bicycle manufacturer to establish a factory in Japan . . . Or the Japanese could have built a factory that was a slavish imitation of a European or American bicycle factory. They would have had to import most or all of the factory's machinery, as well as hiring foreign production managers or having Japanese production managers trained abroad . . . .
>
> . . . [Instead], shops to repair [imported bicycles] had sprung up in the big cities . . . . Imported spare parts were expensive and broken bicycles were too valuable to cannibalize the parts. Many repair shops thus found it worthwhile to make replacement parts themselves—not difficult if a man specialized in one kind of part, as many repairmen did. In this way, groups of bicycle repair shops were almost doing the work of manufacturing entire bicycles. That step was taken by bicycle assemblers, who bought parts, on contract, from repairmen: the repairmen had become "light manufacturers."[1]

A couple of observations here. First, the alternative in Jacobs' first blockquoted paragraph is not only the model of development promoted by neoliberal technocrats in the Third World; it's also the typical model of "economic development" pursued by states and localities in the U.S., building industrial parks, offering special corporate welfare subsidies to invite colonization. Second, the Japanese alternative would almost certainly be treated by the WTO today as "piracy," a violation of the "intellectual property" rights of the Western bicycle manufacturers.

C. Desktop Manufacturing Technology

Another revolutionary development, in recent years, is the invention of multiple-purpose machine tools in a price range suitable for the home workshop. As Johan Soderberg describes it:

> What is gradually taking shape within the hacker movement at this moment is an extension of the dream that was pioneered by the members of the Homebrew Computer Club [i.e., a cheap computer able to run on the kitchen table]. It is the vision of a universal factory able to run on the kitchen table . . . . [T]he desire for a 'desktop factory' amounts to the same thing as the reappropriation of the means of production.[2]

A good example is the multimachine, which "is an accurate all-purpose machine tool that can be used as a metal or wood lathe, end mill, horizontal mill, drill press, wood or metal saw or sander, surface grinder and sheet metal 'spinner'."[3] According to the Open Source Ecology design community, it "could be the central tool piece of a flexible workshop . . . eliminating thousands of dollars of expenditure requirement for similar abilities" and serving as "the centerpieces enabling the fabrication of electric motor, CEB, sawmill, OSCar, microcombine and all other items that require processes from milling to drilling to lathing."[4]

> It can be built by a semi-skilled mechanic using just common hand tools. For machine construction, electricity can be replaced with "elbow grease" and all the necessary

1. Jane Jacobs, *The Economy of Cities* (New York: Vintage Books, 1969, 1970), pp. 63–64.
2. Johan Soderberg, *Hacking Capitalism: The Free and Open Source Software Movement* (New York and London: Routledge, 2008), pp. 185–186.
3. <http://groups.yahoo.com/group/multimachine/?yguid=234361452>.
4. "Multimachine & Flex Fab—Open Source Ecology" <http://openfarmtech.org/ index.php?title=Multimachine_%26_Flex_Fab>.

material can come from discarded vehicle parts. It can be built in a closet size version or one that would weigh 4 or 5 tons.[1]

. . . . What can the MultiMachine be used for in developing countries?

AGRICULTURE:

Building and repairing irrigation pumps and farm implements.

WATER SUPPLIES:

Making and repairing water pumps and water-well drilling rigs.

FOOD SUPPLIES:

Building steel-rolling-and-bending machines for making fuel efficient cook stoves and other cooking equipment.

TRANSPORTATION:

Anything from making cart axles to rebuilding vehicle clutch, brake, and other parts . . . .

JOB CREATION:

A group of specialized but easily built MultiMachines can be combined to form a small, very low cost, metal working factory which could also serve as a trade school. Students could be taught a single skill on a specialized machine and be paid as a worker while learning other skills that they could take elsewhere.[2]

In addition, a number of firms have appeared recently which offer production of custom parts to the customer's digital design specifications, at a modest price, using small-scale, multipurpose desktop machinery. Two of the most prominent are Big Blue Saw[3] and eMachineShop.[4] The way the latter works, in particular, is described in a *Wired* article:

The concept is simple: Boot up your computer and design whatever object you can imagine, press a button to send the CAD file to Lewis' headquarters in New Jersey, and two or three weeks later he'll FedEx you the physical object. Lewis launched eMachine-Shop a year and a half ago, and customers are using his service to create engine-block parts for hot rods, gears for home-brew robots, telescope mounts—even special soles for tap dance shoes.[5]

Two other promising developments are mobile manufacturing (Factory in a Box),[6] and the microfactory and micro machine tools.[7]

Building on our earlier speculation about small machine shops and hobbyist workshops, new desktop manufacturing technology offers an order of magnitude increase in the quality of work that can be done for the most modest expense.

1. <http://groups.yahoo.com/group/multimachine/?yguid=234361452>.
2. <http://opensourcemachine.org/node/2>.
3. <http://www.bigbluesaw.com/saw/>.
4. <http://www.emachineshop.com/> (see also <www.barebonespcb.com/!BB1.asp>).
5. Clive Thompson, "The Dream Factory," *Wired*, September 2005 <http://www.wired.com/wired/archive/13.09/fablab_pr.html>.
6. Carin Stillstrom and Mats Jackson, "The Concept of Mobile Manufacturing," *Journal of Manufacturing Systems* 26:3-4 (July 2007) <http://www.sciencedirect.com/science?_ob=Article URL&_udi=B6VJD-4TK3FG8-6&_user=108429&_rdoc=1&_fmt=&_orig=search&_sort=d&view=c&_version=1&_urlVersion=0&_userid=108429&md5=bf6e603b5de29cdfd026d5d00379877c>.
7. Yuichi Okazaki, Nozomu Mishima and Kiwamu Ashida, "Microfactory and Micro Machine Tools," Fine Manufacturing System Group, Institute of Mechanical Engineering Systems, National Institute of Advanced Industrial Science and Technology. Reported in The 1st Korea-Japan Conference on Positioning Technology, Daejeon, Korea, 2002.

D. POLYTECHNIC

Another key concept is that of the "polytechnic," a term coined by Lewis Mumford to describe the coexistence of different "phases" of technology in a single "technological pool."

> Similarly [to a gene pool], one may talk of a technological pool: an accumulation of tools, machines, materials, processes, interacting with soils, climates, plants, animals, human populations, institutions, cultures. The capacity of this technological reservoir, until the third quarter of the nineteenth century, was immensely greater than ever before: what is more, it was more diversified—and possibly quantitatively larger, as well as qualitatively richer—than that which exists today. Not the least important part of this technological pool were the skilled craftsmen and work teams that transmitted the colossal accumulation of knowledge and skill. When they were eliminated from the system of production, that vast cultural resource was wiped out.
>
> This diversified technological assemblage not merely contributed to economic security: it permitted a continuous interplay between different phases of technology; and for a time this actually happened.

As an example, he mentions incorporation of new scientific advances into old technology, like "the altered cut of mainsail and jibs in modern sailing vessels: a change resulting from the closer analysis of air flow for the purpose of improving airplanes."[1] The seagoing technology of Poul Anderson's Maurai is an excellent fictional example of the same thing. A real-world example is 20th (and 21st) century organic farming, as developed by the Rodales, Louis Bromfield and John Jeavons, which involves the recovery and preservation of older technique (much of it, like raised-bed technique and crop-rotation, itself a highly refined art of the eotechnic period—about which see below), and its synthesis with the latest findings of soil science, botany and bacteriology.

> There was no reason whatever to make a wholesale choice between handicraft and machine production: between a single contemporary part of the technological pool and all the other past accumulations. But there was a genuine reason to maintain as many diverse units in this pool as possible, in order to increase the range of both human choices and technological inventiveness. Many of the machines of the nineteenth century, as Kropotkin pointed out, were admirable auxiliaries to handicraft processes, once they could be scaled, like the efficient electric motor, to the small workshop and the personally controlled operation.[2]

Ivan Illich, in *Vernacular Values*, speculated on the possibility of integrating new technology into a subsistence society: "modern tools make it possible to subsist on activities which permit a variety of evolving life styles, and relieve much of the drudgery of old time subsistence."[3]

Mumford's conception of the polytechnic, with multiple "phases" of technology existing side-by-side, was echoed by E.F. Schumacher:

> It is a strange fact that some people say that there are no technological choices. I read an article by a well-known economist from the U.S.A. who asserts that there is only one way of producing any particular commodity: the way of 1971. Had these commodities never been produced before? . . . . He says that the only machinery that can be procured is the very latest. Now that is a different point and it may well be that the only machinery that can be procured *easily* is the latest. It is true that at any one time there is only one kind of machinery that tends to dominate the market and this creates the im-

---

1. Lewis Mumford, *The Myth of the Machine: The Pentagon of Power* (New York: Harcourt Brace Jovanovich, Inc., 1964, 1974), pp. 154-55.

2. *Ibid.*, pp. 154-55.

3. Ivan Illich, *Vernacular Values* (1980). Online edition courtesy of The Preservation Institute <http://www.preservenet.com/theory/Illich/Vernacular.html>.

pression as if we had no choice and as if the amount of capital in a society determined the amount of employment it could have. Of course this is absurd. The author whom I am quoting also knows that it is absurd, and then he corrects himself and points to examples of Japan, Korea, Taiwan, etc., where people achieve a high level of employment and production with very modest capital equipment.

.... It is a fixation in the mind, that unless you can have the latest you can't do anything at all . . . .

.... We are told there is no choice of technology, as if production had started in the year 1971. We are told that it cannot be economic to use anything but the latest methods, as if anything could be more uneconomic than having people doing absolutely nothing.[1]

Mumford's polytechnic overlaps to a considerable extent with Schumacher's concept of "intermediate technology":

I have named it *intermediate technology* to signify that it is vastly superior to the primitive technology of bygone ages but at the same time much simpler, cheaper, and freer than the super-technology of the rich.[2]

Such an intermediate technology would be immensely more productive than the indigenous technology (which is often in a state of decay), but it would also be immensely cheaper than the sophisticated, highly capital-intensive technology of modern industry.[3]

Schumacher provided another example of polytechnic in *Good Work*: the adaptation of modern metallurgical knowledge to the traditional techniques of manufacturing metal rims for oxcart wheels:

In order to have efficient oxcarts, the wheels ought to have steel rims. We've forgotten how to bend steel accurately except with big machines in Pittsburgh or Sheffield. How do you do it in a small rural community? Is it beyond the wit of man to do this on a small scale? No, we remember that our forefathers knew how to do it before James Watt, and they had a most ingenious tool. We found one of those tools in a French village, more than two hundred years old—brilliantly conceived, clumsily made. We took this to the National College of Agricultural Engineering in England and said, "Come on boys, you can do better than that. Upgrade it, use your best mathematics to work out the required curvature and what have you." The upshot of it is that while hitherto in the modern world the smallest instrument to do this bending job would cost on the order of £700, and require outside power and electricity to operate, this tool upgraded to the level of knowledge of 1974 can be made by the village blacksmith. It costs £7, it doesn't require electricity, and anyone can do it. Now this is something quite different from going back into the preindustrial era. It is using our knowledge in a different way, and we know it can be done.[4]

This is a common pattern. Generally speaking, the refinement of older, small-scale technology has been abandoned in favor of a focus on further developing large-scale production technology. When the modern engineer turns his attention back to the old tools of small-scale production, he quickly finds a host of cheap and easy minor changes that promise to greatly increase their productivity. Intermediate technology often embodies the polytechnic idea of resurrecting near-lost techniques hastily abandoned (or crowded out, rather, with state help) during the industrial era, and refining them by the application of modern engineering principles. For example, Borsodi found that the small manual looms commonly available were designed from an impractical "artsy-craftsy" standpoint, rather than from an engineer's sensibility of maximizing the efficiency of hand production. As a result, the manual loom functioned as inefficiently as if it were deliberately designed to be

1. Schumacher, *Small is Beautiful*, pp. 213-14, 218-19.
2. *Ibid.*, pp. 153-54.
3. *Ibid.*, p. 180.
4. *Ibid.*, pp. 135-36.

slow and laborious. By modifying a manual loom with his own homemade flying shuttle, the work of three or four hours, Borsodi was able to achieve production costs lower than those of the factory.[1]

David Dickson describes two complementary approaches, from opposite poles, toward developing intermediate technology:

> The first is the development of traditional indigenous production and servicing techniques. Productivity is increased through the application of scientific and technical knowledge often derived from elsewhere, but continuity with prevailing social and cultural conditions is maintained. The second source, at the other end of the spectrum, is the adaptation of technologies currently in use in the advanced industrial nations, but in a way that greatly reduces the scale of activity involved. It should also make technology suitable for a different capital/labour ratio, as well as for the use of local materials and other resources. Occasionally included in this category are technologies which have been developed and subsequently outgrown by the advanced countries during the course of industrialization, but which may now be considered appropriate to the economic and social conditions prevailing in the developing countries.[2]

Schumacher's Intermediate Technology Development Group has made a wide range of innovations along the lines of Borsodi's loom: greatly improved and more efficient tools, designed to be operated by human labor in the context of a village economy. They include economical, small-scale brick and tile production; improved cisterns made from cheap local materials; entire catalogs of human- and horse-powered farming tools; pedal-powered vehicles with efficient transmissions for light hauling; and small windmills with improved sail design and transmission, designed for manufacture in small local shops, to power irrigation pumps. Water turbine generators, for use in small streams, operate at greatly reduced cost because they are specifically designed for maximum efficiency on a small scale, and are capable of powering village industry like a small sawmill or workshop.[3]

Mumford's "gene pool" analogy above is an apt one, by the way. Evolutionary economist Michael Shermer made a similar analogy between evolutionary preadaptation in the biological and technological realms. Since so much of technological innovation results from the adaptation of technologies developed for one purpose to another purpose completely unforeseen, it makes sense to have as diverse a technlogical pool as possible.[4]

If we cross-pollinate Mumford's polytechnic with Jacobs' Japanese bicycle model of industrialization, and with Sale's neighborhood repair/recycling/remanufacturing shops, we get still further intriguing possibilities. We're so used to an entire "production stream" being managed by a single, vertically-integrated corporation that we forget the process really involves a whole series of discrete subprocesses. And these subprocesses, individually, are amenable to being adapted to a wide variety of levels of technology. The post-WWII analysis of the effects of strategic bombing in Germany, in the Strategic Bombing Survey, and the analysis of industrial responses to strategic bombing in the Soviet civil defense literature, are full of anecdotes about factory production adapting to damage from strategic bombing (e.g., the substitution of human and other unconventional sources of power to fill specific gaps in the production process). Mumford draws similar conclusions from the resil-

1. Ralph Borsodi, *Flight from the City: An Experiment in Creative Living on the Land* (New York, Evanston, San Francisco, London: Harper & Row, 1933, 1972), pp. 52-53.

2. David Dickson, *The Politics of Alternative Technology* (New York: Universe Books, 1974), p. 154.

3. George McRobie, *Small is Possible: A factual account of who is doing what, where, to put into practice the ideas expressed in E. F. Schumacher's SMALL IS BEAUTIFUL* (New York: Harper & Row, 1981), pp. 39-71.

4. Michael Shermer, *The Mind of the Market: Compassionate Apes, Competitive Humans, and Other Tales from Evolutionary Economics* (New York: Henry Holt and Company, 2008), pp. 57-60.

ience of North Vietnamese production in the face of American strategic bombing.[1] If workers in such totalitarian regimes were this adaptable and capable of initiative to keep production going, then, *a fortiori*, that should say a lot about the kind of worker-initiated innovations we might expect from Barry Stein's worker-managed plants in a free society (which we will discuss in the next chapter).

E. EOTECHNIC, PALEOTECHNIC, AND NEOTECHNIC

The idea of resurrecting old technologies in a modern context is also suggested by Mumford's periodization of technological history in *Technics and Civilization*. Mumford divided late medieval and modern technological development into three considerably overlapping periods: the eotechnic, paleotechnic, and neotechnic.

The original technological revolution of the late Middle Ages, the eotechnic, was associated with the skilled craftsmen of the free towns, and eventually incorporated the fruits of investigation by the early scientists. It began with agricultural innovations like the horse collar, horseshoe and crop rotation. In mechanics, its greatest achievements were clockwork machinery and the intensive use of water and wind power. It achieved great advances in the use of wood and glass, masonry, and paper (the latter including the printing press). The agricultural advances of the early second millennium were further built on by the innovations of the sixteenth and seventeenth centuries, like raised bed horticulture and greenhouses.

The eotechnic phase was supplanted or crowded out in the early modern period by the paleotechnic revolution. Paleotechnic was associated with the new centralized state and its privileged economic clients, and centered on mining, iron, coal, and steam power. It culminated in the "dark satanic mills" of the nineteenth century and the giant corporations of the late nineteenth and early twentieth. Although the paleotechnic incorporated some contributions from the eotechnic period, it was a fundamental departure in direction, and involved the abandonment of a rival path of development. Technology was developed in the interests of the new royal absolutists, mercantilist industry and the factory system that grew out of it, and the new capitalist agriculturists (especially the Whig oligarchy of England); it incorporated only those eotechnic contributions that were compatible with the new tyrannies, and abandoned the rest.

The beginning of the neotechnic period was associated, among other things, with the invention of the prerequisites for electrical power—the dynamo, the alternator, the storage cell, the electric motor—along with the development of small-scale electric production machinery suitable for the small shop and power tools suitable for household production. Electricity made possible the use of virtually any form of energy, indirectly, as a prime mover for production: combustibles of all kinds, sun, wind, water, even temperature differentials.[2]

The typical factory, through the early 20th century, had machines lined up in long rows, "a forest of leather belts one arising from each machine, looping around a long metal shaft running the length of the shop," all dependent on the factory's central power plant. The neotechnic revolution made it possible to run free-standing machines off of small electric motors.[3]

The decentralizing potential of small-scale, electrically powered machinery was the central theme of Kropotkin's *Fields, Factories and Workshops*. Even before the introduction of electrical power, Kropotkin wrote, petty industry in small, wheel-powered workshops co-

---

1. Mumford, *The Myth of the Machine*, p. 144.
2. Mumford, *Technics and Civilization*, pp. 214, 221.
3. Waddell and Bodek, *Rebirth of American Industry*, pp. 119-121.

existed with large-scale industry. But with electricity "distributed in the houses for bringing into motion small motors of from one-quarter to twelve horse-power," workers were able to leave the small workshops to work in their houses.[1] More important, by freeing machinery up from a single prime mover, it ended all limits on where the small workshops themselves could be located. The primary basis for economy of scale, as it existed in the nineteenth century, was the need to economize on horsepower—a justification that vanished when the distribution of electrical power eliminated reliance on a single source of power.[2]

As we saw in Chapter Two, Ralph Borsodi showed that with electricity most goods could be produced in small shops and households with an efficiency at least competitive with that of the great factories, once the greatly reduced distribution costs of small-scale production were taken into account. The modest increases in unit production cost are offset not only by greatly reduced distribution costs, but by the possibility of timing production to need instead of attempting to engineer mass-consumption to the requirements of production:

> if the domestic grain grinder is less efficient, from a purely mechanical standpoint, than the huge flour mills of Minneapolis, it permits a nicer timing of production to need, so that it is no longer necessary to consume bolted white flours because whole wheat flours deteriorate more quickly and spoil if they are ground too long before they are sold and used.[3]

Again, this illustrates the principle that overall flow is more important to cost-cutting than maximizing the efficiency of any particular stage in isolation. In any case, if the object is to have the highest quality flour with bran and germ intact, at a reasonable cost, as opposed to nutritionally dead wallpaper paste, the small mill is the *most* efficient means available. The larger mills are only more "efficient" if the consumer is subordinated to the needs of large-scale production.

It was the decentralizing potential of electricity that inspired Kropotkin's vision of the merging of village and town in *Fields, Factories and Workshops*. As Colin Ward commented, in his edition of that work:

> The very technological developments which, in the hands of people with statist, centralising, authoritarian habits of mind . . . demand greater concentration of industry, are also those which could make possible a local, intimate, decentralised society. When tractors were first made, they were giants, suitable only for prairie-farming. Now you can get them scaled down to a Rotivator for a small-holding. Power tools, which were going to make all industry one big Dagenham, are commonplace for every do-it-yourself enthusiast.[4]

Paul Goodman remarked on the change from the time when "the sewing machine was the only widely distributed productive machine . . . , but now . . . the idea of thousands of small machine shops, powered by electricity, has become familiar; and small power-tools are a best-selling commodity."[5]

The neotechnic, in a sense, is a resumption of the lines of development of the original eotechnic revolution, following the paleotechnic interruption. The neotechnic

---

1. Peter Kropotkin, *Fields, Factories and Workshops: or Industry Combined with Agriculture and Brain Work with Manual Work* (New York: Greenwood Press, Publishers, 1968 [1898]), p. 154.
2. *Ibid.*, pp. 179-180.
3. Mumford, *Technics and Civilization*, p. 225.
4. Colin Ward, in *Fields, Factories and Workshops Tomorrow*, p. 164.
5. Paul and Percival Goodman, *Communitas: Means of Livelihood and Ways of Life* (New York: Vintage Books, 1947, 1960), p. 156.

differs from the paleotechnic phase almost as white differs from black. But on the other hand, it bears the same relation to the eotechnic phase as the adult form does to the baby.

. . . . The first hasty sketches of the fifteenth century were now turned into working drawings: the first guesses were now re-enforced with a technique of verification: the first crude machines were at last carried to perfection in the exquisite mechanical technology of the new age, which gave to motors and turbines properties that had but a century earlier belonged almost exclusively to the clock.[1]

It would be "poetic justice," as Borsodi put it, "if electricity drawn from the myriads of long neglected small streams of the country should provide the power for an industrial counter-revolution."[2]

Mumford suggested that, absent the abrupt break created by the new states and their clients, the eotechnic might have evolved directly into the neotechnic. A full-scale modern industrial revolution would likely have come about through such decentralized technology, as Mumford put it, "had not a ton of coal been dug in England, and had not a new iron mine been opened."[3]

The amount of work accomplished by wind and water power compared quite favorably with that of the steam-powered industrial revolution. Indeed, the great advances in textile output of the eighteenth century were made with water-powered factories; steam power was adopted only later. The Fourneyron water-turbine, perfected in 1832, was the first prime-mover to exceed the poor 5% or 10% efficiencies of the early steam engine, and was a logical development of earlier water-power technology that would likely have followed much earlier in due course, had not the evolution of water-power been interrupted by the paleotechnic revolution.[4]

Had the spoonwheel of the seventeenth century developed more rapidly into Fourneyron's efficient water-turbine, water might have remained the backbone of the power system until electricity had developed sufficiently to give it a wider area of use.[5]

In *The City in History*, Mumford mentions abortive applications of eotechnic means to decentralized organization, unfortunately forestalled by the paleotechnic revolution, and speculates at greater length on the Kropotkinian direction social evolution might have taken had the eotechnic passed directly into the neotechnic. Of the seventeenth century villages of New England and New Netherlands, he writes:

This eotechnic culture was incorporated in a multitude of small towns and villages, connected by a network of canals and dirt roads, supplemented after the middle of the nineteenth century by short line railroads, not yet connected up into a few trunk systems meant only to augment the power of the big cities. With wind and water power for local production needs, this was a balanced economy; and had its balance been maintained, had balance indeed been consciously sought, a new general pattern of urban development might have emerged . . . .

In 'Technics and Civilization' I pointed out how the earlier invention of more efficient prime movers, Fourneyron's water turbine and the turbine windmill, could perhaps have provided the coal mine and the iron mine with serious technical competitors that might have kept this decentralized regime long enough in existence to take advantage of the discovery of electricity and the production of the light metals. With the coordinate development of science, this might have led directly into the more humane integration

1. Mumford, *Technics and Civilization*, p. 212.
2. Borsodi, *This Ugly Civilization*, p. 65.
3. Mumford, *Technics and Civilization*, p. 118.
4. *Ibid.*, p. 118.
5. *Ibid.*, p. 143.

of 'Fields, Factories, and Workshops' that Peter Kropotkin was to outline, once more, in the eighteen-nineties.[1]

It's important to remember that there is no such thing as generic "superiority" of one technology over another, without reference to some purpose. The choice of paleo-technics, instead of further development of eotechnics, served the interests of the absolute state and its privileged clients, the great landowners and mercantilists.

Ralph Borsodi speculated, along lines similar to Mumford's, on the different direction things might have taken:

> It is impossible to form a sound conclusion as to the value to mankind of this institution which the Arkwrights, the Watts, and the Stephensons had brought into being if we confine ourselves to a comparison of the efficiency of the factory system of production with the efficiency of the processes of production which prevailed before the factory appeared.
>
> A very different comparison must be made.
>
> We must suppose that the inventive and scientific discoveries of the past two centuries had not been used to destroy the methods of production which prevailed before the factory.
>
> We must suppose that an amount of thought and ingenuity precisely equal to that used in developing the factory had been devoted to the development of domestic, custom, and guild production.
>
> We must suppose that the primitive domestic spinning wheel had been gradually developed into more and more efficient domestic machines; that primitive looms, churns, cheese presses, candle molds, and primitive productive apparatus of all kinds had been perfected step by step without sacrifice of the characteristic "domesticity" which they possessed.
>
> In short, we must suppose that science and invention had devoted itself to making domestic and handicraft production efficient and economical, instead of devoting itself almost exclusively to the development of factory machines and factory production.
>
> The factory-dominated civilization of today would never have developed. Factories would not have invaded those fields of manufacture where other methods of production could be utilized. Only the essential factory would have been developed. Instead of great cities, lined with factories and tenements, we should have innumerable small towns filled with the homes and workshops of neighborhood craftsmen. Cities would be political, commercial, educational, and entertainment centers . . . . Efficient domestic implements and machines developed by centuries of scientific improvement would have eliminated drudgery from the home and the farm.[2]

Likewise, as P. M. Lawrence has pointed out,[3] the proper comparison is not between agribusiness and subsistence farming as they exist, but between agribusiness and subsistence farming as it would exist had it been free to develop without enclosures, without rack-rents, and without the state's diversion of all resources for innovation into the channel of large-scale cash crop agriculture (about which more below).

Conventional histories—written by the victors, of course—give the paleotechnic phase credit for many advances of the eotechnic: schoolchildren are taught a received version of the industrial revolution in which "gentleman farmers" like Jethro Tull and inventors like Watt, Whitney, Fulton *et al.* are elevated into demigods, while the civilization of the free towns of the late Middle Ages is telescoped back into the "Dark Ages."

1. Mumford, *The City in History*, pp. 333-34.
2. Borsodi, *This Ugly Civilization*, pp. 60-61.
3. Comment under Carson, "Vulgar Libertarianism Watch, Part I," *Mutualist Blog: Free Market Anti-Capitalism*, January 11, 2005 <http://mutualist.blogspot.com/2005/01/vulgar-libertarianism-watch-part-1.html>; Lawrence quote in Carson, "Glenn Reynolds' Upside-Down Version of History," *Mutualist Blog: Free Market Anti-Capitalism*, June 20, 2005 <http://mutualist.blogspot.com/2005_06_01_archive.html>.

For a whole century the second industrial revolution . . . has received credit for many of the advances that were made during the centuries that preceded it. In contrast to the supposedly sudden and inexplicable outburst of inventions after 1760 the previous seven hundred years have often been treated as a stagnant period of small-scale petty handicraft production, feeble in power resources and barren of any significant accomplishments.

One reason for this, Mumford suggests, is that the history of the paleotechnic industrial revolution is filtered largely through an English lens. England had been a backwater of the earlier eotechnic civilization compared to the continent, and served mainly to supply raw materials for Dutch, north German and Italian industry. To English observers, the paleotechnic revolution was therefore perceived to be arising in a vacuum.[1]

But it was in equal part arrogant, willful blindness: the temporal provincialism of Nietzsche's Last Man, who smugly proclaimed that "we have invented happiness."

> At the very height of England's industrial squalor, when the houses for the working classes were frequently built beside open sewers and when rows of them were being built back to back—at that very moment complacent scholars writing in middle-class libraries could dwell upon the "filth" and "dirt" and "ignorance" of the Middle Ages, as compared with the enlightenment and cleanliness of their own.
>
> How was that belief possible? . . . .
>
> The mechanism that produced the conceit and the self-complacence of the paleotechnic period was in fact beautifully simple. In the eighteenth century the notion of Progress had been elevated into a cardinal doctrine of the educated classes. Man . . . was climbing steadily out of the mire of superstition, ignorance, savagery, into a world that was to become ever more polished, humane, and rational . . . .
>
> . . . . Assuming that progress was a reality, if the cities of the nineteenth century were dirty, the cities of the thirteenth century must have been six centuries dirtier . . . . If the hospitals of the early nineteenth century were overcrowded pest-houses, then those of the fifteenth century must have been even more deadly. If the workers of the new factory towns were ignorant and superstitious, then the workers who produced Chartres and Bamberg must have been more stupid and unenlightened. If the greater part of the population were still destitute despite the prosperity of the textile trades and the hardware trades, then the workers of the handicraft period must have been more impoverished.

In short, we're presented with a Monty Python parody of the Middle Ages in which a king is identified by the fact that "he's the only one who doesn't have shit all over him."

> The fact that the cities of the thirteenth century were far brighter and cleaner and better ordered than the new Victorian towns: the fact that medieval hospitals were more spacious and sanitary than their Victorian successors: the fact that in many parts of Europe the medieval worker had demonstrably a far higher standard of living than the paleotechnic drudge . . . —these facts did not even occur to the exponents of Progress as possibilities for investigation.[2]

If William Morris's vision of the colorful, airy and convivially designed 14th century English town, in *The Dream of John Ball*, was idealized, it was probably at least closer to the truth than were its detractors.

F. Decentralized Agriculture

There is an ironic parallel between the productivity of household gardens in the capitalist west, and the small private garden plots of collective farmers in the old USSR, compared to that of the large-scale mechanized operations in both countries. The court intellec-

1. Mumford, *Technics and Civilization*, pp. 151–52.
2. *Ibid.*, pp. 181–83.

tuals who most eagerly defend the alleged superior productivity of agribusiness as against small-scale farming are often the same ones who drew the most attention to the large percentage of Soviet food production carried out on a tiny percentage of arable land. And their false scientism in cheerleading for the so-called "Green Revolution" resembles nothing so much as the fondness for gigantism expressed by the collectivist technocrats of Soviet agriculture. But in fact, the productive superiority of the intensively cultivated small vegetable plot over the giant agribusiness operation, in the West, is directly comparable to the superiority of the small plot over the *kolkhoz* and *sovkhoz* in the old USSR.

And in the area where relatively large-scale, mechanized production makes most sense—cereal grains—it's hard to see how the hired tractor-driver on a corporate agribusiness plantation would have any more "entrepreneurial spirit" than a member of a Soviet collective farm. If large-scale Soviet agriculture had centered on the *mir* as a genuinely independent and self-managing unit, rather than on a *kolkhoz* plantation owned in practice by the state, collective farmers would have had if anything *more* of a "private," "entrepreneurial" interest in productivity than the agricultural wage-laborers of America.

As Colin Ward pointed out, in his commentary on Kropotkin's *Fields, Factories and Workshops*,

> The actual or potential contribution to food production of ordinary domestic gardens is another illustration of the productivity of domestic horticulture. The advocates of high-density housing have always cited the "loss of agricultural land" as a factor supporting their point of view. Sir Frederic Osborn, with equal persistence, has always argued that the produce of the ordinary domestic garden, even though a small area of gardens is devoted to food production, more than equaled in value the produce of the land lost to commercial food production. Surveys conducted by the government and by university departments in the 1950s proved him right.
>
> One implication of Kropotkin's line of argument is that, at present assumptions of population growth, nobody need starve. Hunger in the world today is not because of the soil's insufficiency, nor will it be in the conceivable future.[1]

Ward, in *Talking Houses*, cites John Seymour's contrast of the two styles of agriculture:

> There is a man I know of who farms ten thousand acres with three men (and the use of some contractors). Of course he can only grow one crop—barley, and of course his production *per acre* is very low and his consumption of imported fertiliser very high. He burns all his straw, put no humus on the land (he boasts there isn't a four-footed animal on it—but I have seen a hare) and he knows perfectly well his land will suffer in the end. He doesn't care—it will see him out. He is already a millionaire several times over . . . .
>
> Cut that land (exhausted as it is) up into a thousand plots of ten acres each, giving each plot to a family trained to use it, and within ten years the production coming from it would be enormous . . . . The motorist . . . wouldn't have the satisfaction of looking over a vast treeless, hedgeless prairie of indifferent barley—but he could get out of his car for a change and wander through a seemingly huge area of diverse countryside, orchards, young tree plantations, a myriad small plots of land growing a multiplicity of different crops, farm animals galore, and hundreds of happy and healthy children. Even the agricultural economist has convinced himself of one thing. He will tell you (if he is any good) that land farmed in big units has a low production of food per acre but a high production of food per man-hour, and that land farmed in small units has the opposite— a very poor production per man-hour but a high production per acre. He will then say that in a competitive world we must go for high production per man-hour and not per acre. I would disagree with him.[2]

---

1. Ward Commentary, *Fields, Factories and Workshops Tomorrow*, p. 116.

2. John Seymour, quoted in Colin Ward, "The Do It Yourself New Town," *Talking Houses: Ten Lectures by Colin Ward* (London: Freedom Press, 1990), pp. 33-34.

No doubt the reader has heard, ad nauseam, the same arguments we have from the agricultural establishment (including well-meaning agriculture professors and extension agents): without large-scale, mechanized, chemical agribusiness, with only organic methods, "the world would starve." For the most part this is learned disability. When pressed to think rather than regurgitate the received dogma, most such people quickly recognize such statements as nonsense on stilts. For example, I challenged a retired agriculture professor who made just such an assertion. "Do you mean to say sufficient food could not be produced from available land with the intensive raised-bed techniques of Jeavons, and careful building of soil through composting and green manuring with leguminous cover crops?" "You mean like in Japan? Ah, well, that might be a different matter . . . ."

But that's just the point. These techniques of efficient land-use were developed long before Liebig (or at least his vulgar followers) reduced the issue of soil building to infusions of synthetic N, P and K. The intensive methods of Chinese horticulture, built upon and improved, formed the basis of Jeavons' biointensive raised bed techniques. Kropotkin, writing as early as 1898, described the techniques of market gardeners in northwestern Europe and truck farmers in the United States, by which a family could support itself on a fraction of an acre. The new techniques, "created of late" (1898), were "as superior to modern farming as modern farming is to the old three-fields system of our ancestors."[1] The idea, according to Kropotkin, was "to cultivate a limited space well, to manure, to improve, to concentrate work, and to obtain the largest crop possible . . . . The annual consumption of a man is thus obtained from less than a quarter of an acre." Rather than "talk about good and bad soils," practitioners of the new technique "[made] the soils themselves . . . ." Besides composting and intensive development of the soil, techniques included the combination of cold frames and other season extenders with carefully timed succession planting, intercropping, and the like, to get as many as nine crops a year from a given plot.

> Market gardeners of Paris, Troyes, Rouen, Scotch and English gardeners, Flemish and Lombardian farmers, peasants of Jersey, Guernsey, and farmers in the Scilly Isles have opened up such large horizons that the mind hesitates to grasp them. While up till lately a family of peasants needed at least seventeen to twenty acres to live on the produce of the soil . . . we can no longer say what is the minimum area on which all that is necessary to a family can be grown, even including articles of luxury, if the soil is worked by means of intensive culture.[2]

According to Michael Perelman, in cereal farming the spade industry of eighteenth century peasants in Western Europe produced a twenty- to thirty-fold increase on seed-corn, compared to only six-fold by plow cultivation. As for vegetable horticulture, the market gardens of that time compare favorably in output even to the mechanized agriculture of the contemporary United States. One Paris gardener produced 44 tons of vegetables per acre; by way of comparison, in 1979 America, the average output per acre was 15 tons of onions or 8.6 tons of tomatoes (the two most productive crops in terms of weight per unit of area).[3] Kropotkin cited output figures from Florida that included 445-600 bushels of onions, 400 bushels tomatoes, 700 bushels sweet potatoes per acre.[4]

Many of the world's cities produce a majority of their own vegetables through roof-top and vacant lot gardening. The Netherlands, the most densely populated country in Europe, was reported in 1974 to have produced 25% more food (by value) than it con-

1. Kropotkin, *Fields, Factories and Workshops*, p.60.
2. Peter Kropotkin, *The Conquest of Bread* (New York: Vanguard Press, 1926 [1913]), pp. 192-197; Kropotkin, *Fields, Factories and Workshops*, pp. 60-68, 81-82.
3. Michael Perelman, *Classical Political Economy: Primitive Accumulation and the Social Division of Labour* (Totowa, N.J.: Rowman & Allanheld; London: F. Pinter, 1984, c 1983), pp. 41-2.
4. Kropotkin, *Fields, Factories and Workshops*, pp. 81-82.

sumed; Denmark was a net exporter by 79%.[1] During World War II, victory gardens planted in backyards, in vacant lots and on rooftops were estimated by the USDA to have produced 44% of the fresh vegetables consumed in the U.S.[2]

Mechanized chemical agriculture was not designed to use land more efficiently, but to increase the productivity of agricultural wage labor. And modern organic techniques are far in advance of traditional farming methods. According to Bill McKibben,

> ... [O]rganic farming techniques have steadily improved in recent decades, especially in their use of cover crops, or "green manures," which enrich the soil without needing animal waste.
>
> The best data come from an English agronomist named Jules Pretty, who has studied two hundred "sustainable agriculture" projects in fifty-two countries around the world. They might not pass the U.S. standards for organic certification, but they're all low-input, using far less energy and chemicals than industrialized farming. "We calculate that almost nine million farmers were using sustainable practices on about 29 million hectares, more than 98 percent of which emerged in the past decade," he noted in 2002. "We found that sustainable agriculture has led to an average 93 percent increase in per hectare food production."
>
> ... This is not simple peasant agriculture; in fact, it's far more complex than just following the fertilizer or spraying schedule that the nice man from the company hands you when you fork over your cash. But farmer-run schools have sprung up in country after country to spread the new techniques, and the longer that small farmers experiment with the new ideas, the more improvements they find.

Sustainable methods led to a 150% increase in average output for fourteen projects employing 146,000 farmers growing potato, sweet potato, and cassava crops, and a 73% increase in yield for 4.5 million grain farmers. Indonesian rice farmers experienced only steady yields, but with a drastic reduction in costs. And on top of all that, the quality of soil and productivity of farms improved over time, as contrasted with the "eroding soil and dying up aquifers" associated with industrial agriculture. An experiment with raised bed horticulture, involving households in twenty-six Kenyan communities, found hunger almost entirely eliminated and the proportion that had to buy supplemental vegetables falling from 85% to 11%. The adoption of nitrogen-fixing cover crops in Central America has increased corn yields two or three times.[3]

And local seed varieties, combined with intensive techniques and the creative use of biological processes, result in levels of output comparable in many cases to Green Revolution varieties combined with heavy chemical use. Even setting aside the long-term costs of soil depletion, good husbandry with local varieties of seed produces almost as much corn and sorghum output per acre. An experiment in Bangladesh—ceasing pesticide use in order to raise fish in rice paddies—resulted in a 25% increase in rice production, along with the high quality protein from the fish. The fish controlled insects more efficiently than chemical pesticides, and fertilized the rice.[4]

Many of the celebrated achievements of the Green Revolution, like genetically engineered "golden rice" with Vitamin A, are answers to artificial problems. Vitamin A deficiencies are much more likely to occur in the first place among growers of large monoculture rice crops, who don't grow anything else for household consumption because they need to maximize rice output to pay for the expensive seeds and chemical inputs. On the

1. Ward Commentary, *Fields, Factories and Workshops Tomorrow* p. 111.

2. Thomas J. Bassett, "*Reaping on the Margins*: A Century of Community Gardening in America," *Landscape*, 25:2 (1981), cited in Leslie Heimer, *History of Urban Agriculture, Sprouts in the Sidewalk* blog <http://sidewalksprouts.wordpress.com/history/>.

3. Bill McKibben, *Deep Economy: The Wealth of Communities and the Durable Future* (New York: Times Books, Henry Holt and Company, LLC, 2007), pp. 68-69.

4. Hawken *et al.*, Natural Capitalism, p. 211.

other hand, farmers who grow rice mainly for local consumption and can spare the expense of chemicals to protect vulnerable monoculture crops, can afford to grow more than enough leafy vegetables in their own kitchen gardens to supply their needs for Vitamin A.[1]

We frequently hear idiotic assertions from chemical agribusiness apologists like Norman Borlaug and Nina Federoff that "the world would" starve if organic methods were universally adopted, because organic farming is allegedly less efficient in terms of output per acre. For example, Borlaug, when asked about organic farming, replied:

> That's ridiculous. This shouldn't even be a debate. Even if you could use all the organic material that you have—the animal manures, the human waste, the plant residues—and get them back on the soil, you couldn't feed more than 4 billion people. In addition, if all agriculture were organic, you would have to increase cropland area dramatically, spreading out into marginal areas and cutting down millions of acres of forests.[2]

And Nina Federoff baldly asserted: "If everyone switched to organic farming, we couldn't support the earth's current population—maybe half."[3]

I've seen such statements many times, and invariably they turn out to be snap generalizations made, on little reflection, by people with little concrete knowledge of the most advanced organic techniques. It's one of those things the people in the agribusiness/USDA/research complex like to repeat that "just ain't so."

Such party line statements typically assume an "organic" model that amounts to continuation of the presently predominating form of American agribusiness, the same inefficient and land-wasteful row-cropping used by conventional large-scale, mechanized, chemical farming—just without the chemicals.

But when it comes to food output per acre, the organic-chemical divide is far less significant than that between mechanized row-cropping and soil-intensive cultivation. "Organic" is a catchall term that includes an entire spectrum of techniques. At one end is organic tractor farming, "a system fairly close . . . to current large-scale farming using chemical outputs. The primary difference is that no fertilizers, pesticides, or herbicides are used."[4] Like other forms of conventional mechanized agribusiness, its business model is aimed at economizing on labor at the expense of efficient use of the land. At the other end of the spectrum are intensive raised bed techniques.

At the small-scale end of the spectrum, the difference between the traditional techniques of small peasant cultivators, and the sophisticated intensive techniques of John Jeavons, is the difference between a Model-T and a Ferrari. Jeavons has managed to produce enough food to feed a single person on a tenth of an acre, relying only on the closed-loop recycling of wastes generated on-site and on the use of nitrogen-fixing crops, without any synthetic nitrogen fertilizer or animal manures from off-site. Of course, it is a very spare and monotonous diet, with the majority of the space devoted to high carbohydrate cereal grains, legumes or tubers that concentrate a great deal of caloric value on a small space. Only about 20% of the space can be spared for fruits and vegetables to supplement the diet with vitamins. Still, that's a flat-out *fact* that directly contradicts Borlaug's asinine, ignorant generalizations. Applying techniques like green manuring and companion planting to small peasant production in the Third World would result in a quantum increase in

1. McKibben, *Deep Economy*, pp. 205-206.

2. Ronald Bailey, "Billions Served: Norman Borlaug interviewed by Ronald Bailey," *Reason*, April 2000 <http://www.reason.com/news/printer/27665.html>.

3. Claudia Dreifus, "A Conversation With Nina V. Fedoroff: An Advocate for Science Diplomacy," *New York Times*, August 18, 2008 <http://www.nytimes.com/2008/08/19/science/19conv.html?ref=science>.

4. Peter Gillingham, "Appropriate Agriculture," in Dorf and Hunter, eds., *Appropriate Visions*, p. 94.

efficiency. The kinds of blanket assertions Borlaug and Federoff make are based on an intellectually lazy and dishonest comparison that assumes organic farmers *don't* adopt the best
available techniques.

Intensive techniques are actually more productive, in terms of output per acre, as Barbara Ward and Rene Dubos point out:

> [T]he small farmer working with his own labour on a family holding, has been shown in
> a wide variety of developing countries . . . to produce more per acre than big estates.
> Some of the highest yields are to be found in countries where acre limitations are strictly
> enforced. This productivity is secured not by heavy machines which drink gasolene and
> can easily damage fragile soils, but by hard work with light equipment which is by defi-
> nition less prone to generate ecological risks. Fertilizers and pesticides are less lavishly
> used, human and animal wastes are more carefully husbanded. Greater personal care
> keeps terraces in trim, shade trees planted, gullies forested. And earnings are not spent, as
> is often the case in semi-feudal economies, on acquiring more land for extensive use,
> thus pushing up land prices and driving working farmers away from the soil. Nor are
> they withdrawn altogether from the rural economy, by the development of 'Western'
> standards of consumption or an over-affection for numbered accounts in Swiss banks.[1]

And Peter Gillingham cites Sterling Wortman of the Rockefeller Foundation to the
same effect:

> Most large-scale mechanized agriculture is less productive per unit area than small-scale
> farming can be. The farmer on a small holding can engage in intensive high-yield "gar-
> dening" systems such as intercropping, multiple cropping, relay planting or other tech-
> niques that require attention to individual plants. The point is that mechanized agricul-
> ture is very productive in terms of output per man-year, but it is not as productive per
> unit of land as the highly intensive systems are.[2]

Regarding chemicals in particular, rather than making a stacked comparison of
chemical agribusiness to the most primitive traditional techniques, it would be more honest to say that chemical farming and the most advanced organic methods are two *alternative*
ways of significantly increasing productivity, and that development of the former has
tended to crowd out the latter.

Switching from monoculture farming to multiple cropping actually reduces losses to
pests more than adding chemical pesticides to monoculture farming, for example. And it
does so without the diminishing payoffs that result from insect resistance, and from killing
off insects' natural enemies higher in the food chain.[3] Gillingham cites the example of one
organic corn grower whose land yields 100-150 bushels per acre, with an average protein
content of 12%—compared to the 1971 U.S. average of 87 bushels per acre and 9% protein.[4]

In addition, the agribusiness apologists who talk about the tiny number of "farmers"
who produce America's food are guilty of creating a false dichotomy between "farmers"
and everybody else. A major part of the vegetables, and some of the poultry and other
small livestock, that are consumed in this country are produced in the household sector, by
a lot more than one percent of the population.

Worldwide, cities produce about a third of the food they consume.[5] In China, rooftop
and small lot production together supply 85% of urban vegetable consumption, along with

---

1. Barbara Ward and Rene Dubos, *Only One Earth*, in Godfrey Boyle and Peter Harper, eds.,
Radical Technology. From the editors of *Undercurrents* (New York: Pantheon Books, 1976), p. 249.

2. Gillingham, "Appropriate Agriculture," p. 96.

3. *Ibid.*, p. 98.

4. *Ibid.*, p. 105n.

5. *Ibid.*, p. 82.

significant amounts of tree crops and meat.[1] In Shanghai, specifically, 60% of vegetables and 90% of milk and eggs are produced on urban farms.[2]

A community-supported agriculture project of only 200 acres supplies 7 to 8% of the fresh food consumed in Burlington, Vt.[3]

All this is not to say that complete household sufficiency in food, or the elimination of division of labor between town and country, is either necessary or desirable. It only means that a return to agriculture based on intensive work with the spade, u-bar and fork would not mean starvation. It would mean greater output per acre than is presently the case.

G. A Soft Development Path

Vinay Gupta proposes a "soft development path" for the Third World, based on integrating intermediate-scale technology into the village economy:

> Our goal is simple—to remake the "lifestyle niche" of the smallholder organic farmers who comprise half of the human population into something which is healthy, prosperous, stable, environmentally benign, and includes health care and health maintenance, access to energy and education, and many other improvements. The bedrock of this transformation is appropriate technology deployed as whole systems, not as the stand-alone stepwise improvements of the past which have had such mixed success.
>
> History is on our side. The development of new technologies like ever-more-affordable solar panels and ICT (information and communication technologies) extends our reach every single day. Our goal, then, is to work with these underlying trends to maximize progress in the regions where it is needed most: to go to where the poverty is deepest, and stabilize and improve life there.
>
> It is our hope and belief that by improving life for the smallholders and in the villages using applied basic science and appropriate technology that the destructive and unsustainable flight to the cities can be slowed, and the destructive transformation of agriculture which clears farming households off their land can be arrested. To make smallholders economically productive enough to retain their land during agricultural transformation requires use of relatively modern organic farming know-how, like green manures and integrated pest management, but there are pockets of expertise in these techniques all over the world. The challenge is spreading the knowledge to make the smallholder's fields abundant. This is the bedrock and anchor of revolutionizing the lives of the poor, and stabilizing half of the population of the planet in their existing sustainable lifestyles.
>
> Then there is technology. Stoves which are five times as efficient as current stoves, adding as much as 15% to household income through reduced fuel spending. Simple electrical lights based on cheap LED lighting elements. Water purifiers which can end illness and death from water borne disease. Malaria nets and microfinance. The Hexayurt itself is a simple building designed for refugees, IDPs, and the very poor from any country who are unable to afford more traditional home. These systems together constitute a redefinition of the basic way of life of the very poorest in the same way that running water and sanitary toilets transformed the way of life of Europeans and Americans over the past 200 years, but in a manner which does not require the poor to vastly increase their income or ecological footprint.
>
> The poor cannot follow the development path that the current rich have taken without destroying the planet. It is not even clear that the rich can become sustainable, although new technology will help. The soft development path is an alternative approach to spreading results like those of the Kerala Miracle, in which an Indian region with an

---

1. Hawken *et al.*, *Natural Capitalism*, p. 200.
2. McKibben, *Deep Economy*, p. 82.
3. *Ibid.*, p. 80.

average income of $300 per year has attained quality of life as measured by lifespans, literacy and infant mortality very close to those of rich nations . . . .[1]

The "Kerala Miracle" Gupta refers to is indeed noteworthy. As Bill McKibben describes it, it is a textbook example of what E.F. Schumacher meant by intermediate technology:

> Instead of building huge factories, or lowering wages to grab jobs from elsewhere, or collectivizing farmers, the left has embarked on a series of "new democratic initiatives" that come as close as anything on the planet to actually incarnating "sustainable development," that buzzword beloved of environmentalists. The left has proposed, and on a small scale has begun, the People's Resource Mapping Program, an attempt to move beyond word literacy to "land literacy."
>
> Residents of local villages have begun assembling detailed maps of their area, showing topography, soil type, depth to the water table, and depth to bedrock. Information in hand, local people could sit down and see, for instance, where planting a grove of trees would prevent erosion. And the mapmakers think about local human problems, too. In one village, for instance, residents were spending scarce cash during the dry season to buy vegetables imported from elsewhere in India. Paddy owners were asked to lease their land free of charge between rice crops for market gardens, which were sited by referring to the maps of soil types and the water table. Twenty-five hundred otherwise unemployed youth tended the gardens, and the vegetables were sold at the local market for less than the cost of the imports. This is the direct opposite of a global market. It is exquisitely local—it demands democracy, literacy, participation, cooperation. The new vegetables represent "economic growth" of a sort that does much good and no harm. The number of rupees consumed, and hence the liters of oil spent packaging and shipping and advertising, go down, not up . . . .
>
> . . . . One can imagine, easily, a state that manages to put more of its people to work for livable if low wages. They would manufacture items that they need, grow their own food, and participate in the world economy in a modest way, exporting workers and some high-value foods like spices, and attracting some tourists. "Instead of urbanization, ruralization," says K. Vishwanathan, a longtime Gandhian activist who runs an orphanage and job-training center where I spent several days. At his cooperative, near the silkworm pods used to produce high-quality fabric, women learn to repair small motors and transistor radios—to make things last, to build a small-scale economy of permanence. "We don't need to become commercial agents, to always be buying and selling this and that," says Vishwanathan. He talks on into the evening, spinning a future at once humble and exceedingly pleasant, much like the airy, tree-shaded community he has built on once-abandoned land—a future as close to the one envisioned by E. F. Schumacher or Thomas Jefferson or Gandhi as is currently imaginable.[2]

A good example of the cheap, human-scale technology Gupta described can be found in Guatemala, where a cooperative has begun producing farm machinery from old bicycles.

> . . . [I]nstead of spending a week beating cobs with a stick to loosen the grains, then grinding them for meal in a hand-cranked mill, the average small farmer can now do the job in a day and a half, thanks to a machine that "resembles a primitive exercise bicycle" and is called a *bicimolino*, or bike mill. The company also has bike-driven irrigation pumps, a pedal-powered machine that produces cheap, strong roofing tiles, and bicycle trailers for taking crops to market.[3]

1. Vinay Gupta, "Soft Development Paths," *The Bucky-Gandhi Design Institute*, April 10, 2008 <http://vinay.howtolivewiki.com/blog/hexayurt/soft-development-paths-520>.

2. Bill McKibben, "What is True Development? The Kerala Model," *Utne Reader*, March 1998 <http://www.ashanet.org/library/articles/kerala.199803.html>.

3. McKibben, *Deep Economy*, p. 206.

15

Social Organization of Production: Cooperatives and Peer Production

INTRODUCTION

Privilege, in its broadest sense, is at the root of all the organizational pathologies we saw in the first three parts of this book. At the societal level, privilege divorces cost from benefit and leads to the systemic crises we examined in Part Two. Inside an organization, privilege creates a fundamental conflict of interest. It divorces effort from reward, responsibility from authority, and knowledge from power. The result is all the agency and knowledge problems of the large, hierarchical organization that we saw in Part Three.

The problem is inherent in what Butler Shaffer calls "institutionalization." As Shaffer described it, the difference between an institution and other organizations is that an institution is unaccountable to those who make it up, and has a purpose independent of those who serve it. It also has "a leadership that differentiates itself from those who make up the organization," with the leaders viewing their own function "as being to manipulate, threaten, induce, or coerce the group members into subordinating their personal interests and promoting organizational purposes."[1]

Shaffer distinguishes what he calls "member-oriented and member-controlled" organizations from institutions, "whose objectives interfere with personal purposes and generate conflict in society." Institutions predominate only when the state erects entry barriers to such self-organization, diverts resources to institutions, and otherwise crowds out self-organization, so that the range of alternatives is restricted and people are artificially dependent on institutions. In short, the large, hierarchical, managerial organization is the result of privilege.

Self-employment, whether individually or through worker cooperatives and peer production, is the answer to all the agency and knowledge problems we considered in Part Three.

The obvious response to this claim is the commonly raised question: if cooperatives are so much more efficient than hierarchical, absentee-owned enterprises, why are they so rare, and why do they struggle so hard to survive? In other words, if you're so smart, why ain't you rich?

Oliver Williamson, the leading New Institutionalist, views present ownership patterns and distribution of capital as evidence of some sort of generic "efficiency" in the market, taking the existing environment as a fair approximation of a free market. Consider, for example, the way he answers Branko Horvat's analogy of a transplant host's body rejecting alien tissue, used to explain the rate of failure of cooperative enterprise in a capitalist system:

---

1. Butler Shaffer, *Calculated Chaos: Institutional Threats to Peace and Human Survival* (San Francisco: Alchemy Books, 1985), p. 10.

I submit, however, that short-term bank and trade credit are more accurately described by a physical analogy. They are more nearly akin to iron filings in a magnetic field. The prospect of high (risk-adjusted) returns presents a well-nigh irresistible attraction to liquid reserves. To be sure, local exhortations to discriminate can be temporarily effective. But venture capitalists are unprincipled in their search for profit. Capital displays an inexorable tendency to equalize returns at the margin.[1]

Williamson here badly misconstrues Horvat's thesis. The structural issue is not simply the cultural attitudes of individual investors ("local exhortations to discriminate"). Of course, the comparative rate of return between enterprises will tend to overcome such prejudices in the long term, when it comes to the allocation of investment capital. The structural issue is, rather, what determines the comparative rates of return themselves. The state subsidizes the large, hierarchical, capitalist enterprises against which cooperatives compete, thus rendering them artificially profitable and competitive against alternative forms of organization.

Williamson also argues that the moral hazard (threat of expropriation of investors) is greater with external financing of cooperative enterprises, because debt owners are not effectively represented in the governance of the enterprise. Therefore, the cooperative is forced to rely more heavily on internally generated investment funds.[2]

What Williamson ignores here is the historical role of primitive accumulation in vesting such investment decisions in the hands of a class of large absentee owners in the first place. The very predominance of large firms, and ownership of investment capital by large absentee investors—itself to a large extent a creation of the state—marginalizes the firm with internally generated revenue. In an alternative economy—arguably the outcome of a free market—in which the predominant firm was smaller and internal financing was the rule, the competitive disadvantage of relying on internal financing would be far less.

The comparative success rate of cooperatives is distorted by several factors, with structural forces primary among them.

> It is a commonplace of social analysis that every society promotes, both explicitly and tacitly, certain forms of productive organization by reinforcing the conditions for growth and survival of some types of enterprise while ignoring or even opposing other possibilities. Specifically, in the United States, the very forms of legal structure, access to capital, entrepreneurship, management, the remuneration of workers, and education all favor and reinforce the establishment and expansion of hierarchical corporate forms of enterprise and simultaneously create barriers to cooperative ones. Worker cooperatives are anomalies to these mainstream trends.[3]

One example of such structural forces is the capitalist credit market, which tends to be hostile because the cooperative form precludes lender representation on the board of directors, and seriously limits the use of firm equity as collateral. Dealing as equals with managers who can be replaced by their workers also presents cultural difficulties for conventional banks.[4]

The grossly uneven distribution of wealth, resulting from land expropriations and other forms of "primitive accumulation," and from state-imposed unequal exchange (i.e., privilege), amounts to a "subsidy of history." The lack of wealth puts constraints on access to credit, which means that

1. Oliver Williamson, *The Economic Institutions of Capitalism: Firms, Markets, Relational Contracting* (New York: Free Press; London: Collier Macmillan, 1985), p. 266.

2. *Ibid.*, p. 267.

3. Robert Jackall and Henry M. Levin. "Work in America and the Cooperative Movement" in Jackall and Levin, ed., *Worker Cooperatives in America* (Berkeley, Los Angeles, London: University of California Press, 1984), p. 10.

4. *Ibid.*, p. 10.

the pattern of ownership and control depends on the distribution of wealth. In particular, the predominance of capitalist firms . . . is attributable to the credit constraints facing workers . . . .[1]

There is also a considerable element of "lemon socialism" involved in the history of producer cooperatives. Historically, producer cooperatives have tended to be formed by employee buyouts of foundering enterprises, in order to prevent unemployment. And given the discriminatory nature of credit markets, cooperatives also tend to be formed in relatively non–capital–intensive fields with low entry barriers, like restaurants, bookstores, and groceries; and industries with low entry barriers tend for that reason to have high failure rates.[2]

A. Self–Employment: Increased Productive Efficiency

Matthew Yglesias describes what he calls the "office illusion"—that "being in the office" is, "as such, working":

> Thus, minor questions like *am I getting any work done?* can tend to slip away. Similarly, when I came into an office every day, I felt like I couldn't just leave the office just because I didn't want to do anymore work, so I would kind of foot-drag on things to make sure whatever task I had stretched out to fill the entire working day. If I'm not in an office, by contrast, I'm acutely aware that I have a budget of *tasks* that need to be accomplished, that "working" means finishing some of those tasks, and that when the tasks are done, I can go to the gym or go see a movie or watch TV. Thus, I tend to work in a relatively focused, disciplined manner and then go do something other than work rather than slack off.[3]

The downside of telecommuting, for a wage-earning or salaried employee, is that it blurs the distinction between ownlife and time that belongs to the employer. Yglesias' experience is probably atypical: work is never really "over" for most people who telecommute for a wage. If it's a typical white collar cubicle job being done from the home office, there's most likely no magic point at which the worker can say "my work is done" and turn off the phone.

But it stands to reason that the same principle governs, even more strongly and without the drawbacks, the full integration of work and life that comes with self-employment. Under the "face time" paradigm of wage employment at a workplace away from home, there is no tradeoff between work and leisure. Anything done at work is "work," for which one gets paid. There is no opportunity cost to slacking off on the job. In home employment, on the other hand, the tradeoff between effort and consumption is clear. The self-employed worker knows how much productive labor is required to support his desired level of consumption, and gets it done so he can enjoy the rest of his life. If his work itself is a consumption good, he still balances it with the rest of his activities in a rational, utility-maximizing manner, because he is the conscious master of his time, and has no incentive to waste time because "I'm here anyway." Any "work" he does which is comparatively unproductive or unrewarding comes at the expense of more productive or enjoyable ways of spending his time.

---

1. Samuel Bowles and Herbert Gintis. "The Distribution of Wealth and the Viability of the Democratic Firm," in Ugo Pagano and Robert Rowthorn, eds., *Democracy and Efficiency in the Economic Enterprise*, a study proposal for the World Institute for Development of Economic Research (WIDER) of the United Nations University (London and New York: Routledge, 1996), pp. 83-84.

2. Jackall and Levin, "Work in America and the Cooperative Movement," p. 9.

3. Matthew Yglesias, "The Office Illusion," *Matthew Yglesias*, September 1, 2007 <http://matthewyglesias.theatlantic.com/archives/2007/09/the_office_illusion.php>.

At work, on the other hand, all time belongs to the boss. A shift of work is an eight-hour chunk of one's life, cut off and flushed down the toilet for the money it will bring. And as a general rule, people do not make very efficient use of what belongs to someone else.

J.E. Meade contrasts the utility-maximizing behavior of a self-employed individual to that of a wage employee:

> A worker hired at a given hourly wage in an Entrepreneurial firm will have to observe the minimum standard of work and effort in order to keep his job; but he will have no immediate personal financial motive . . . to behave in a way that will promote the profitability of the enterprise . . . . [A]ny extra profit due to his extra effort will in the first place accrue to the entrepreneur . . . .
>
> Let us go to the other extreme and consider a one-man Cooperative, i.e. a single self-employed worker who hires his equipment. He can balance money income against leisure and other amenities by pleasing himself over hours of work, holidays, the pace and concentration of work, tea-breaks or the choice of equipment and methods of work which will make his work more pleasant at the cost of profitability. Any innovative ideas which he has, he can apply at once and reap the whole benefit himself.[1]

The tendency to goof off results at least as much from the nature of wage employment itself as from the "office illusion." Any particular task is devoid of intrinsic motivation, whether it be the sense of craftsmanship that comes from work under one's control, or the knowledge that a discrete portion of one's livelihood depends on performing that task to the satisfaction of a particular customer. In self-employment, on the other hand, if there is not a good reason to perform a task based on one's own personal values, then it just doesn't get done.

B. Cooperatives: Increased Productive Efficiency

It's quite odd, considering all the destructive management behaviors we discussed in Chapter Eight, that so many orthodox organization theorists have negative things to say about the agency problems of worker cooperatives compared to the typical capitalist firm. Consider, for example, this quote from Richard Posner:

> The economic literature on worker cooperatives identifies objections to that form of organization that are pertinent to university governance. The workers have a shorter horizon than the institution. Their interest is to get as much from the institution as they can before they retire; what happens afterwards has no direct effect on them unless their pensions are dependent on the institution's continued prosperity. That consideration aside . . ., their incentive is to play a short-run game, to the disadvantage of the institution . . . .[2]

Posner, apparently, is living in a bearded-Spock universe where Robert Nardelli, "Chainsaw Al" Dunlap, and Carly Fiorina all died in their cradles. The typical CEO has the "time horizon" of a mayfly.

The worker cooperative is a significant improvement on the monitoring problems of the traditional, hierarchical enterprise. David Prychitko writes:

> . . . [W]hen one considers the degree to which our knowledge is embodied in tacit skills and judgment . . ., the extent to which real world monitors can technically obtain the information required for efficient metering as the models suggest becomes somewhat

---

1. J.E. Meade, "The Theory of Labour-Managed Firms and Profit Sharing," in Jaroslav Vanek, ed., *Self-Management: Economic Liberation of Man* (Hammondsworth, Middlesex, England: Penguin Education, 1975), p. 395.

2. Richard Posner, "The Summers Controversy and University Governance," *The Becker-Posner Blog*, February 27, 2005 <http://www.becker-posner-blog.com/archives/2005/02/the_summers_con_1.html>.

questionable. [Oliver] Williamson's awareness of information being "impacted" within a team of workers accords well with this view of knowledge: much of the knowledge embodied in team production may not be adequately observed by a monitor or efficiently communicated to a central metering authority. In fact, each team worker may have a better idea of what the others are doing (and are able to do) than a monitor, even though any particular worker may not be able to articulate that knowledge to a monitor. Under these cases the cooperative format may handle the monitoring problems more effectively than the traditional business organization.[1]

We saw in the previous section that, under self-employment, workers fully internalize the results of their efforts, and are therefore free to set the balance between effort and consumption on the job. The same is true of collective self-employment, in a cooperative. For that reason, a worker cooperative is unlikely to maximize productivity through the kind of "management by stress," or speedup, that we described in Chapter Ten. Jaroslav Vanek describes labor self-management as "the optimal arrangement when it comes to the finding of the utility-maximizing effort, the proper quality, duration and intensity of work, by the working collective."[2]

For example, in the Zanon tile factory, the largest recuperated enterprise in Argentina, cycle time on the ovens has been increased from 28 to 35 minutes. Describing the changed pace of production, a worker says:

> "When we had an owner, I couldn't talk the way we are right now. I couldn't even stop for a couple of minutes. Now I work calmly, with my conscience as my guide, and without a boss yelling that we have to reach the oh-so-important objective. Back then we ran very short oven cycles. It got down to twenty-eight minutes, when the recommended time is thirty-five or more, as we do it today."
>
> What's the difference? "it was really easy to burn your hands and because of the speed of the machines, you couldn't stop them to make adjustments. You had to fix them while they were running, which led to many accidents. You could easily lose two or three fingers.[3]

Even so, worker self-management is also uniquely suited to improving productive efficiency—but in the proper sense of eliminating wasted effort, rather than maximizing effort per worker.

As we saw in Chapter Five, Friedrich Hayek, in criticizing the planned economy, stressed the importance of distributed, idiosyncratic knowledge that could not be fully encompassed by state planners. The same principle applies to those at the top of the large corporation. As Paul Goodman wrote,

> A chief cause of the absurdity of industrial work is that each machine worker is acquainted with only a few processes, not the whole order of production . . . . Efficiency is organized from above by expert managers who first analyze production into its simple processes, then synthesize these into combinations built into the machines, then arrange the logistics of supplies, etc., and then assign the jobs.
>
> As against this efficiency organized from above, we must try to give this function to the workers. This is feasible only if the workers have a total grasp of all the operations.[4]

1. David L Prychitko, *Marxism and Workers' Self-Management: The Essential Tension* (New York; London; Westport, Conn.: Greenwood Press, 1991), pp. 120-121n.

2. Jaroslav Vanek, "Decentralization under Workers' Management: A Theoretical Appraisal," in Vanek, ed., *Self-Management*, p. 360.

3. The Lavaca Collective, *Sin Patron: Stories from Argentina's Worker-Run Factories*. Translated by Katherine Kohlstedt (Chicago: Haymarket Books, 2007), pp. 60-61.

4. Paul and Percival Goodman, *Communitas: Means of Livelihood and Ways of Life* (New York: Vintage Books, 1947, 1960), pp. 156-57.

The same is as true of agency and incentive problems as of information problems. Labor tends to be more productive in producer cooperatives because of reduced agency problems. As Vanek puts it, the production worker in a worker-managed enterprise is more likely to devote his mental energy to "reflection on how to improve the performance of his enterprise instead of how to minimize his effort without it being noticed by his supervisors . . . ."[1] Capitalist firms, Henry Levin adds, "hire workers under wage contracts."

> This arrangement gives employees few positive incentives to maintain high levels of productivity . . . .
>
> Producer cooperatives have two major characteristics that differentiate them from capitalist firms. And these divergences create differences between the two types of firms in the incentives to contribute to the productive effort as well as in the organization of the productive effort. First, cooperatives are owned by their workers. Thus, it is the workers who will share in the success of the cooperative or who will bear the consequences of its failure. Second, since a cooperative is managed according to democratic principles, the production can be organized to maximize the interests of the workers . . . .
>
> These differences lead to rather different individual and collective incentives for workers in the two types of firms as well as to differing abilities of workers to organize production to maximize their own interests. More specifically, there is a greater incentive for cooperative members to be productive because of the rather direct connection between the success of the cooperative and their own personal gain . . . .
>
> In addition, there are two major influences that tend to reinforce work effort and productivity in a cooperative. First, if a cooperative does well, all of the workers will be better off. Second, the workers tend to reinforce the productivity and work effort of their members through collegial support and peer pressure . . . . Further, every worker knows that if difficulties arise in his part of the productive process he will be helped by his fellow workers . . . .
>
> Although capitalist firms may set out pay structures and procedures for promotion that will reward individual productivity, the system must be administered by procedures and persons external to the work process rather than functioning as an integral part of that process, as happens in cooperative firms. Furthermore, the informational and administrative requirements for identifying and rewarding individual differences in productivity would create unduly high informational and transaction costs for a capitalist firm. Thus, for a capitalist firm the procedures for establishing pay and status preferences must be only approximate with respect to productivity differences, and will usually correspond to the nature of the worker's category and experience rather than to direct measures of productivity. Accordingly, for capitalist workers the ties between the incentive structures and productivity tend to be much less direct and more approximate than the rather direct and more accurate connections for cooperative workers.
>
> Moreover, the social enforcement from worker peers that is integral to a collective organization is antithetical to a capitalist organization, where workers are placed in direct competition with one another for employment, promotions, and pay.[2]

Regarding this last, the practice of endless downsizing also tends to promote hostility between workers in different departments, as workers understandably see demands from "internal customers" as an added burden on themselves when they are already unable to handle their existing workload. The workplace becomes a snake pit.

One big difference between the capitalist enterprise and the workers' cooperative is that in the cooperative, workers

---

1. Jaroslav Vanek, *The General Theory of Labor-Managed Market Economies* (Ithaca and London: Cornell University Press, 1970), p. 266.

2. Henry M. Levin, "Employment and Productivity of Producer Cooperatives," in Jackall and Levin, ed., *Worker Cooperatives in America*, pp. 24-26.

have a great incentive to take care of the machinery and the other capital with which they work and thus to reduce breakdowns and increase the productive life of the capital. By contrast, in capitalist firms there is often a disdain for the condition of the equipment and even an incentive to permit it to malfunction and break down to provide temporary respite from the work process.[1]

Edward Greenberg contrasts the morale and engagement with work, among the employees of a capitalist enterprise, with that of workers who own and manage their place of employment:

> Rather than seeing themselves as a group acting in mutuality to advance their collective interests and happiness, workers in conventional plants perceive their work existence, quite correctly, as one in which they are almost powerless, being used for the advancement and purposes of others, subject to the decisions of higher and more distant authority, and driven by a production process that is relentless . . . .
>
> The general mood of these two alternative types of work settings could not be more sharply contrasting. To people who find themselves in conventional, hierarchically structured work environments, the work experience is not humanly rewarding or enhancing. This seems to be a product of the all-too-familiar combination of repetitious and monotonous labor . . . and the structural position of powerlessness, one in which workers are part of the raw material that is manipulated, channeled, and directed by an only partly visible managerial hierarchy. Workers in such settings conceive of themselves, quite explicitly, as objects rather than subjects of the production process, and come to approach the entire situation, quite correctly, since they are responding to an objective situation of subordination, as one of a simple exchange of labor for wages. Work, done without a great deal of enthusiasm, is conceived of as intrinsically meaningless, yet necessary for the income that contributes to a decent life away from the workplace.[2]

Because of the greater intrinsic motivation of workers and the structure of self-management within the production unit itself, the administrative costs of monitoring and policing from above are greatly reduced in a cooperative.

> . . . [T]he fact that workers have incentives to produce a good product and to be highly productive means that cooperative firms need relatively few supervisors and quality control inspectors. Quality control and a disciplined work effort are internalized into the behavior of workers rather than enforced by external procedures. Thus, the cooperative is able to save the cost of a large cadre of unproductive middle managers which are an integral part of capitalist production where worker discipline and product quality must be ensured by external supervision.[3]

Greenberg notes a "striking" fact: "the vast difference in the number of supervisors and foremen found in conventional plants as compared with the plywood cooperatives."

> While the latter were quite easily able to manage production with no more than two per shift, and often with only one, the former often requires six or seven. Such a disparity is not uncommon. I discovered in one mill that had recently been converted from a worker-owned to a conventional, privately owned firm that the very first action taken by the new management team was to quadruple the number of line supervisors and foremen. In the words of the general manager of this mill who had also been manager of the mill prior to its conversion,
>
>> We need more foremen because, in the old days, the shareholders supervised themselves . . . . They cared for the machinery, kept their areas picked up,

1. *Ibid.*, p. 27.
2. Edward S. Greenberg. "Producer Cooperatives and Democratic Theory" in Jackall and Levin, eds., *Worker Cooperatives in America*, p. 185.
3. Levin, p. 27.

helped break up production bottlenecks all by themselves. That's not true anymore. We've got to pretty much keep on them all of the time.[1]

Workers in a cooperative enterprise put more of themselves into their work, and feel free to share their private knowledge—knowledge that would be exploited far more ruthlessly as a source of information rent in a conventional enterprise. Greenberg quotes a comment by a worker in a plywood co-op that speaks volumes on wage labor's inefficiency at aggregating distributed knowledge, compared to self-managed labor:

> If the people grading off the end of the dryer do not use reasonable prudence and they start mixing the grades too much, I get hold of somebody and I say, now look, this came over to me as face stock and it wouldn't even make decent back. What the hell's goin' on here?
>
> [Interviewer: That wouldn't happen if it were a regular mill?]
>
> That wouldn't happen. [In a regular mill] . . . he has absolutely no money invested in the product that's being manufactured . . . . He's selling nothing but his time. *Any knowledge he has on the side, he is not committed or he is not required to share that.* [emphasis added]
>
> It took me a little while to get used to this because where I worked before . . . there was a union and you did your job and you didn't go out and do something else. Here you get in and do anything to help . . . . I see somebody needs help, why you just go help them.
>
> I also tend to . . . look around and make sure things are working right a little more than . . . if I didn't have anything invested in the company . . . . I would probably never say anything when I saw something wrong.[2]

The Mondragon cooperative system has lower rates of absenteeism, lower turnover, and better maintenance and care for equipment, than capitalist enterprises.[3]

One worker in the *Union y Fuerza* recuperated enterprise in Argentina observes: "It's not the same when there is a supervisor looking over your shoulder, as when you are working for your own enterprise. There are companeros here that come to work even when they're sick. If you're lazy, your own coworkers will come and tell you to get with it."[4]

One recurring observation by workers in the recuperated enterprises of Argentina is that, as they learned, production labor as such had never been the source of high costs. The main source of high overhead costs was management salaries.[5]

> The books worked out well [in the *Union y Fuerza* enterprise]. They discovered that one of the differences from the previous management was the managerial cost (despite the fact that even they had bought into the neoliberal mantra according to which modern economies don't work because of labor costs).
>
> The company's owner . . . would take home 25,000 pesos a month during hard times, and up to 50,000 if he thought it necessary. And there was a group of managers. "The engineer earned 6,000 pesos, and there were six or seven others at about that same figure, and another fifteen people making 3,500 to 4,000 pesos."[6]

From what we saw in Chapter Eight of the standard GAAP accounting practice of treating labor as the main direct cost and management as a fixed cost, this should come as no surprise. And given the greatly increased share of total employee compensation going to management salaries over the past thirty years, likewise, it should also come as no surprise.

1. Greenberg, p. 193.
2. *Ibid.*, p. 191.
3. Levin, pp. 26-27.
4. The Lavaca Collective, p. 193.
5. *Ibid.*, pp. 185, 217.
6. *Ibid.*, p. 192.

These generalizations about increased productivity are true even of what Winfried Vogt called the "liberal firm,"[1] a capitalist-owned firm with comparatively high degrees of worker self-management and profit-sharing.

Experiments with worker self-management over the years have demonstrated clear productivity advantages. For example, the Tavistock Institute for Human Relations conducted an experiment in the British coal mining industry. Instead of breaking production down into its simplest component jobs and then assigning a worker to each job, the prevailing "longwall" practice,

> the group itself managed the entire job and assigned workers according to need and preference . . . . Instead of being paid on individual piece rates, the workers were given productivity-linked wages, based on group performance.
>
> The results were rather striking. The conventional unit registered only 78 percent of full potential productivity; the other unit registered 95 percent. Worker morale improved . . . . Sickness absenteeism was 8.9 percent on the conventional unit, 4.6 percent on the other; absenteeism with no reason given was 4.3 percent on the conventional unit, more than ten times the 0.4 percent on the other. There were also other improvements, such as the virtual disappearance of the need for supervision in the improved unit, and more regular production.

However, David Jenkins reports, "the results of the experiment were not enthusiastically received in British power circles"—in part because of "the threat to the larger social system of the implications of a thorough rational reform."[2]

Tom Peters relates the account of an MBA student who had been operations manager for the San Francisco branch of a major trucking company, the least profitable operation in the district. He began to involve drivers in the routing decisions previously made by supervisors with little or no input. He also began to involve them directly in soliciting new customers. Some salesmen, realizing the drivers were getting more new customers than they were, rode along to learn the technique. The operation became profitable. That state of affairs lasted, he said, "until my boss saw what was happening and became nervous of the leeway given the Teamsters. About that time, the company instituted a control system that required every Teamster to account for every fifteen minutes of his work day. Profitability disappeared and cutomer complaints increased."[3] As usual, an experiment in worker self-management was terminated despite skyrocketing morale and productivity, because management saw it as a threat to their control of the organization for their own purposes. In addition, in management perception, workers' power to increase productivity is also a power to destroy. Workers' direct control of their own work process may lead to increased productivity, but it also makes management more vulnerable to workers in the event of a dispute; hence the motivation for deskilling.

Profit-sharing and other incentive systems also have a significant effect on productivity. Harvey Leibenstein refers to a wide range of studies on the increased outputs resulting from improved incentive systems. In Britain, a literature review found increases ranging from 7% to 291%, with about half of them falling into the 43-76% range. Production increases ranged from 20-50% in Australia, and in the Netherlands averaged 36.5%. And these were all *sustained* increases.[4]

1. Winfried Vogt. "Capitalist Versus Liberal Firm and Economy: Outline of a theory," in Pagano and Rowthorn, eds., *Democracy and Efficiency in the Economic Enterprise*.

2. David Jenkins, *Job Power: Blue and White Collar Democracy* (Garden City, New York: Doubleday & Company, Inc., 1973), pp. 180-181.

3. Thomas J. Peters and Robert H. Waterman, *In Search of Excellence: Lessons from America's Best-Run Companies* (New York: Warner Books, 1982), pp. 237-238.

4. Harvey Leibenstein, "Allocative Efficiency vs. 'X-Efficiency'," *American Economic Review* 56 (June 1966), p. 401.

A classic example of a liberal capitalist enterprise is the Brazilian industrial equipment manufacturer Semco, which has extraordinarily high levels of self-management and profit-sharing. Levels of self-management and profit-sharing had been quite high by conventional standards since Ricardo Semler took over the family company in the '80s, with 25% of profits distributed to employees. But faced with the combination of a deep recession and a Brazilian law requiring two years severance pay for laid off employees, Semler was forced to take far more drastic measures.

> Then a worker's committee approached Semler with a proposal. They'd take a pay cut, but with three conditions. First, the profit-sharing percentage would be increased until salaries could be restored. Second, management would take a forty percent cut in salary. And, third, the workers would get the right to approve every expenditure. Semler agreed.
>
> In the plants, workers started handling multiple job duties and using their knowledge of how the factory worked to come up with new procedures that saved time and money. At one factory they divided themselves into three manufacturing units of about 150 people each. Each unit had complete responsibility for manufacturing, sales, and financial management. The new Semco was being born.
>
> The autonomous team idea was adopted throughout the company. As it evolved the teams began hiring and firing both workers and supervisors by democratic vote. Policy manuals disappeared to be replaced by a policy of common sense. There is an actual manual, though. It runs about twenty pages and is filled with cartoons and brief statements of principle . . . .
>
> Today's Semco doesn't have a traditional management hierarchy or typical organizational chart, or even a matrix or lattice management structure. The company is effectively made up of autonomous, democratically run units. The model of organization is that of concentric circles . . . .
>
> . . . . Associates set their own salaries which are publicly posted and worked into the budgets. All meetings are open to any Associate who wants to attend. Financial information is available to anyone who wants to see it and courses are available to help them understand what they see.[1]

Another liberal capitalist firm, W.L. Gore, has self-organized work teams and self-directed projects that resemble the functioning of peer production groups:

> "I came from a very traditional male-dominated business—the men's shoe business," [Diane Davidson] recalls. "When I arrived at Gore, I didn't know who did what. I wondered how anything got done here. It was driving me crazy." Like all new hires, Davidson was given a "starting sponsor" at Gore—a mentor, not a boss. But she didn't know how to work without someone telling her what to do . . . .
>
> . . . She eventually figured out that "your team is your boss, because you don't want to let them down. Everyone's your boss, and no one's your boss."
>
> What's more, Davidson saw that people didn't fit into standard job descriptions. They had all made different sets of "commitments" to their team, often combining roles that remained segregated in different fiefdoms at conventional companies, such as sales, marketing, and product design . . . .
>
> . . . [Gore's knack for innovation] springs from a culture where people feel free to pursue ideas on their own, communicate with one another, and collaborate out of self-motivation rather than a sense of duty. Gore enshrines the idea of "natural leadership." Leaders aren't designated from on high. People become leaders by actually leading, and if you want to be a leader there, you have to recruit followers. Since there's no chain of command, no one has to follow. In a sense, you become a talent magnet: You attract other talented people who want to work with you.[2]

1. Wally Bock, "Lessons from Semco," *Monday Memo*, May 12, 2003 <http://www.mondaymemo.net/030512feature.htm>.

2. Alan Deutschman, "The Fabric of Creativity," *Fast Company*, December 19, 2007 <http://www.fastcompany.com/node/51733/print>.

One of the most widely known and practiced versons of liberal capitalism is the Scanlon Plan. According to Karl Frieden,

> The Scanlon Plan utilizes a company-wide incentive system with three basic elements: (1) teamwork, with a common objective of increasing output; (2) a suggestion system that channels cost-saving ideas from the workforce through a labor-management committee structure that evaluates and activates accepted suggestions; (3) a bonus system based on a formula that measures productivity gains and establishes a procedure for sharing the gains equitably among the workers.
>
> The bonus system is directly related to productivity improvements. Seventy-five percent of all labor cost savings are given to workers as bonuses. The Scanlon Plan's bonus structure differs from profit-sharing in that the incentives are based in changes in the *value* of produced goods rather than profits derived from the *sales* of produced goods
> . . . .
>
> The Scanlon Plan indirectly utilizes two primary aspects of worker ownership—the sharing by workers in decision-making and other responsibilities of production, and sharing in the profits earned through production.[1]

The Plan was devised by Joe Scanlon, based on his experiences as president of a union local in the steel industry in the 1930s. He convinced both management and the union local at a failing plant to accept the basic ideas entailed in what later became the Plan, resulting in an enormous productivity increase. He introduced the first version of the Plan under his name, based on what he'd learned from similar experiences in a number of other plants, in 1945. The prototype Plan first appeared in the Adamson Company, a small maker of welded steel tanks in Ohio; it resulted in a 150% increase in profits the first year, and an employee bonus of 41% the first year and 54% the second. In 1946 it was adopted by the Lapointe Machine Tool Company of Hudson, Mass., and increased production 61% in twenty months.[2] A study of ten representative Scanlon plants in 1958 found productivity increases averaging 23% in the first two years after adoption.[3] By the late '60s, some 500 plants had adopted the Scanlon Plan.[4]

Even modest improvements in labor relations and the perceived sympathetic attitude of management can have enormous effects, as witnessed by the "Hawthorne effect" of production increases (ranging from 13 to 30%) associated with increased management attention. Leibenstein cites an ILO mission to a Pakistani textile mill that, following improved labor relations, increased productivity 30% and reduced turnover 20%.[5]

And even modestly improved working conditions can result in significant productivity increases. For example, the "shorter-hours" movement in Western Europe and the United States actually found, not just increased *rates* of output, but often increased *absolute* output, with reduced hours. Increased hours were associated with increased absenteeism and accidents.[6]

Even "job enrichment," liberal capitalism at its most tepid, has produced positive results. David Jenkins, in *Job Power*, devotes some fifty pages to a long series of case studies in liberal capitalist experiments with self-management and profit-sharing. All of them produced significant increases in productivity and profitability, along with decreased absentee-

1. Karl Frieden, *Workplace Democracy and Productivity* (Washington, D.C. : National Center for Economic Alternatives, 1980), pp. 27-28.
2. "The Scanlon Plan," *Time*, Sept. 26, 1955 <http://www.time.com/time/printout/0,8816,807657,00.html>; Frieden, p. 29.
3. Frieden, p. 28.
4. *Ibid.*, p. 27.
5. Leibenstein, "Allocative Efficiency vs. X-Efficiency," p. 401.
6. *Ibid.*, p. 402.

ism and turnover and increased employee contributions to innovation and process improvement.[1]

Of course, all these examples are anecdotal. The empirical literature on the performance results of employee self-management and profit sharing programs is uneven, often badly designed, and generally inconclusive.

To my knowledge, by far the single best literature survey on the subject, both in scope and thoroughness, is a 1995 article by Avner Ben-Ner, Tzu-Shian Han and Derek C. Jones.[2] The article is an impressive survey of most of the available studies on the productivity effects of worker participation in earnings and management. It is especially useful in its analysis of the flaws in previous studies. For example, studies that use the "first-difference" method, i.e. comparing performance before and after the introduction of participation programs, tend to show stronger correlation between participation and productivity than do studies making static inter-firm comparisons. The reason is that the former are better at controlling for other variables that are specific to individual firms, and isolating the effects of the participation programs themselves.

The article's meta-analysis is also an improvement in that, unlike many of the earlier studies, which consider the effects of only one variable without controlling for the other, it controls for the mutual interactive effects of employee control and return rights. The authors assign enterprises to sixteen cells in a two-axis classification grid, depending on the degree of employee control rights and return rights. The numbered cells range from OA_1 in the upper left corner (a conventional enterprise with no employee return or control rights) to OA_{16} in the lower right corner (a worker cooperative with full worker residual claimancy and control of management). The authors hypothesize that there may be week or even negative correlation between high degrees of employee control and productivity, in absence of rights to returns, as well as weak or negative productivity effects of increasing return rights without control. This means that firms in the upper right and lower left corners, with strong control rights and weak return rights (or the reverse), may have minimal productivity increases or actually suffer reductions in productivity compared to conventional firms in the upper left corner (i.e., those with no employee participation in either control or returns). On the other hand, firms in the lower right-hand corner of the grid, with moderate to high degrees of both employee control and employee claims on revenue, will tend to have the highest productivity increases from employee participation.

The authors find that meta-analysis of previous studies confirms their hypothesis, showing that,

> on average, it is PCs [producer cooperatives] in cell OA_{16} that have higher levels of productivity, compared to hybrid forms of PCs that we assign to other cells. Also, for PCs within the OA_{16} cell, typically it is those PCs which have the highest degree of participation in control and in economic returns that perform best.[3]

Generally speaking, in the liberal firm, increased worker self-management is more likely to increase productivity if it is combined with a significant amount of profit-sharing or residual claimancy. The reverse is also true: profit-sharing programs are far more effective when combined with a high degree of self-management.[4] When the two are divorced, participatory management is likely (for understandable reasons) to be seen as a way of looking

---

1. Jenkins, *Job Power*, pp. 182–235.
2. Avner Ben-Ner, Tzu-Shian Han and Derek C. Jones, "The Productivity Effects of Employee Participation in Control and in Economic Returns: A Review of Empirical Evidence," in Pagano and Rowthorn, eds., pp. 209–244.
3. *Ibid.*, p. 239.
4. Samuel Bowles and Herbert Gintis, "Is the Demand for Workplace Democracy Redundant in a Liberal Economy?" in Pagano and Rowthorn, eds., pp. 66–67.

for ways to work more efficiently for the boss's benefit and screw yourself out of a job. And things like ESOP programs with non-voting shares are likely to have limited productivity benefits if workers—who possess direct knowledge most relevant to increasing work efficiency—lack the authority to put their ideas into practice.

When liberal capitalist experiments with self-management and profit-sharing "fail," it's usually not because they don't increase productivity, but because they're seen as a threat to management interests.

A good example is the Kaiser Steel pipe manufacturing plant in Fontana, California, which management had concluded was simply unable to compete with the Japanese. The union persuaded management to agree to a labor-management committee to stop the plant from shutting down. Senior management was agreeable to the project, and ordered supervisors to cooperate with workers' suggestions. Workers enthusiastically supported the program, in part because they had secured management's agreement that no increases in productivity were to be achieved by speedups: "We don't want you to work harder. We want you to work smarter."

> Employee suggestions led to changes in equipment and the physical layout of the plant. The main saw, which was causing an inordinate amount of rejects, was fixed. The pipe straightener was also fixed. Inspection stations were rearranged so that the pipe could be examined more directly in the line of the process. The number of steps in the finishing mill that required storage of pipe was reduced in order to facilitate a more continuous operation. A few job positions were reassigned to make them more effective.
>
> Communication between labor and management and between the workers themselves improved. Better communication between hot mill teams and finishing floor teams eliminated unnecessary delays and waste. When a defective pipe came to a worker on one line, instead of letting it pass by as was the prior practice, the worker would stop what he was doing and check with the previous station in order to straighten out the problem immediately. Preventive maintenance increased as the workers sought to prevent problems before they occurred. The union relaxed its work rules in some instances to allow a better utilization of the workers' skills. In general, with little expenditure of capital for replacement or repairs, a number of small changes had a powerful, cumulative effect on productivity.

(This last confirms what we already saw from Hayek, Leibenstein, and Stein on the importance of workers' idiosyncratic knowledge in achieving large productivity gains from the cumulative effects of incremental improvements. And the reduction of inventory between steps of production, and the ability of production workers to stop the line to correct defects at the source, sounds remarkably like lean production.)

Within three months, productivity increased 32%. The pipe reprocessing rate was reduced from 29% to 9%, and the time for tool changes from thirty minutes to five.

However, after a change of management, the new management gradually withdrew support from the plan. Part of the reason was management embarrassment over headlines like "Worker Takeover—Productivity Rises" in the *Los Angeles Times*. "The managers were uncomfortable with the workers' success and autonomy and the implication that the company's industrial engineers were not capable of achieving maximum efficiency.[1]

Organizations, Jenkins observes, tend to be governed by a sort of homeostatic mechanism. Experiments in self-management and profit-sharing, even (or especially?) when they result in astonishing increases in productivity, meet with management hostility because they undermine the stability of the organization and threaten to require disruptive changes in the power structure. And such experiments, even (or especially) when successful, run against the

---

1. Frieden, pp. 33-35.

grain of management's assumptions about human nature and the rightful ordering of the workplace. Such experiments are often abandoned for being *too* successful.[1]

For example, an experiment at Polaroid in the early '60s with increasing the training and autonomy of machine operators, despite the success of getting new, complex machinery up and running far faster than would otherwise have been possible, was abandoned because it made the supervisors largely superfluous.

> "Management decided it just didn't want operators that qualified. We tried twice to reinstitute the program but had to give it up. The man who started the program quit the company." The employees' newly revealed ability to carry more responsibility was too great a threat to the established way of doing things and to established power patterns . . . . "The operators are still talking longingly about it."[2]

More generally, although (as we saw in Chapter Ten) corporate management has adopted the rhetoric of self-management along with a dumbed-down version of the substance, the overall trends toward genuine self-management and profit sharing that Jenkins described in the 1970s were mostly abandoned not long afterward. He described the growing unwillingness, at the time of his writing, of alienated labor to work under the old conditions, and the increasing pressure on management to concede ever-increasing levels of worker empowerment as a way of increasing productivity.

> The fact is that there is a swift decline in the willingness of people to work under he antiquated conditions still characteristic of most work organizations, . . . and meekly submit to the rigid discipline of the "papa knows best" system. People are no longer so impoverished that they feel compelled to put up with the prevalent structure, no longer so badly educated that they cannot see through the solemn sham that industrial-capitalist authoritarianism has become, and no longer so polite that they are willing to pretend that they do not see the fakery of it all.[3]

In the end, however, corporate elites decided instead to "solve" the problem through neoliberal reaction: downsizing, wage caps, and generally using job insecurity as a way to elicit greater effort and obedience despite the levels of disgruntlement. The idea was to *make* people so impoverished, or so indebted, that they once again felt compelled to put up with the prevalent structure, and once again became willing to stop seeing through the sham and pretend they didn't see through it, because keeping a roof over their heads depended on it.

As an a fortiori argument for the efficiency of worker ownership and self-management, consider the heroic achievements of worker self-management, in increasing output and productivity, and in product and process innovations, under some of the most adverse circumstances imaginable.

Take, for example, the work collectives in the anarchist-controlled areas of Spain. The private company which had owned the trolley systems serving Barcelona manufactured only 2% of the supplies for maintenance and repairs before the Revolution. After a year of workers' control, 98% of supplies for repair were produced in the trolley system's socialized shops. Workers in the railway repair yards of Barcelona manufactured armored cars, and produced the first ambulances only a week after returning to work.[4] The Catalonian metal workers managed to "rebuild the industry from scratch." Despite being "very poorly developed," it converted within a few days of the July 19 uprising to the manufacture of armored cars, hand grenades, machine gun carriages, and ambulances. Four hundred new

1. Jenkins, *Job Power*, p. 310.
2. *Ibid.*, pp. 314-315.
3. *Ibid.*, p. 284.
4. Sam Dolgoff, ed., *The Anarchist Collectives: Workers' Self-Management in the Spanish Revolution 1936-1939* (Montreal and New York: Black Rose Books, 1990), pp. 88-89.

metal factories were built in Barcelona during the war. The industry built two hundred hydraulic presses of up to 250 tons pressure, 178 lathes, and hundreds of milling and boring machines.[1] The optical industry, an assortment of small shops before the Revolution, created a manufacturing capability virtually from scratch; the workers' syndicate financed, from worker contributions, a new factory for optical apparatuses and instruments.[2]

A Spanish observer of the self-managed factories in Allende's Chile was astonished at the inventiveness of workers under the new conditions (for example, building new parts to keep old machinery running). Despite economic disruption (a lot of it resulting from shortages of raw materials in the face of efforts by Nixon and Kissinger to destroy the economy), most worker-managed factories either maintained or increased labor productivity.[3]

Chilean workers displayed considerable inventiveness, in coping with shortages of spare parts and special inputs resulting from the American economic blockade. At one textile factory, for example, workers invented a delay relay for a spinning machine that reduced the needs for imports by $2000; a system for recovering escaped gas from a condensor which saved $1200 worth of imported petroleum; heating apparatus which saved $5000 over five years; dyeing equipment which saved $1000 over three years; an increase in the boiler's generating capacity; an electrical system which replaced the mechanical clutch for a wreathing machine, saving $24,000 over three years; a mechanical press for dyeing which saved $6000; a mechanical transporting device for giant spools, which saved $20,000. The factory expanded its machine shop and began "producing and modifying tools and equipment for other textile factories." Another textile factory's machine shop began producing 80% of the spare parts which it had imported before the blockade.[4]

Another example is the recuperated enterprises in Argentina, as described by James Burke:

> After an economic crisis left thousands of factories and other businesses shuttered, workers suddenly found themselves unemployed and desperately poor. As many as 10,000 of them from roughly 200 enterprises eventually said to heck with loss of income, loss of occupation, loss of dignity. Through trial, error, commitment, and organizing, they retook their former places of employment . . . except this time not as peons, but as owners. Today, they continue producing on an industrial, competitive scale, manufacturing everything from sewer parts to balloons, tractors to ice cream under conditions of democracy, equity, and autonomy . . . .
>
> Getting themselves physically back into the factories involved either cutting the locks or getting permission from the courts. What workers found once they did reenter was devastating. The places had often been ransacked by the former owners, right down to the light bulbs and business records. Machines had been stripped of every valuable part. Many of the factories were without electricity, water, or gas.
>
> The workers usually spent many months hauling away debris. They cannibalized equipment and improvised with scrap to make at least one of each necessary machine. Neighbors donated what they could, be it their welding masks or their labor on a spare Sunday. As for what they faced in restarting production: They had no capital or credit lines with which to make over their former places of employment. For starters, they manufactured and sold infinitesimal amounts of whatever items they could produce with scrounged primary materials.

1. *Ibid.*, p. 96.

2. *Ibid.*, p. 98.

3. L.S. Stavrianos, *The Promise of the Coming Dark Age* (San Francisco: W. H. Freeman and Company, 1976), p. 73

4. Juan G. Espinosa and Andrew Zimbalist, *Economic Democracy: Workers' Participation in Chilean Industry 1970-1973.* Updated student edition (New York, London, Toronto, Sydney, San Francisco: Academic Press, 1981), p. 150.

But get back on their feet many of them did, and slowly profits began to trickle in, challenging the workers to decide how to deal with the surplus.[1]

The Lavaca Collective's book on the recuperated enterprises tells many such stories. In almost every case, the same themes recur. Factories were abandoned with large unpaid debts and utility bills, and stripped of much of their equipment (or vital parts were removed). Workers in the recuperated enterprises contributed their own money, or raised funds through community drives, to pay the bills and get power and phone service up again. They cannibalized machines, or used their own money to scrounge up spare parts, to get at least one production line going; in at least one case they had to buy a generator to supply power. When production lines were up and running, workers survived on minimal pay and plowed revenues back into the enterprise to restore still more production.[2]

A good example is how the Renacir cooperative (formerly the Aurora Corporation) restored production of washing machines:

> With the materials they had at the plant and plenty of ingenuity, they managed to build 120 washing machines that they sold in Ushuaia for 650 pesos. With that capital they restored several parts of the plant and have managed to put together 300 more . . . .
>
> If everything goes well, the factory will be able to revive several lines of home appliances.[3]

The recuperated Cordoba newspaper *Commercio y Justicia* (the city's second-largest newspaper), finding it impossible to restore the intranet any time soon because of the former employer's asset-stripping, resorted to hand-carrying word-processed copy on floppy disks from the newsroom to the printers.[4]

C. INNOVATION UNDER WORKER SELF-MANAGEMENT

The motivation for investment, in an economy where self-employment and worker ownership predominated, would likely be considerably different than at present. In the subsistence or household economy, where the link between effort and consumption is direct and obvious and not obscured by exchange, the producer perceives capital investment not as a way to "live off capital," but to make his own labor more efficient so that he can support himself with less effort.

Bastiat, in *Capital and Rent*, challenged the socialists to explain the motive for investment if there were no return on capital ("who would be willing to create the instruments of labor . . . ?"). Charles-François Chevé, in response, wrote:

> Is there no advantage to the ploughman in producing as much as possible, even though he exchanges its yield for no more than an equal value paid once, without rent or interest on capital? Is there no advantage to the industrialist in doubling or tripling his produce, even though he sells it for no more than an equivalent sum handed over once, without any interest on capital? . . . . —Who will be willing to create wealth? Why, anyone who wants to be wealthy. —Who will save? Why, anyone who wishes to live the next day off the labour of the previous day. —What interest will there be in forming

    1. James Burke, "Fábricas Recuperadas: crowd-storming your own just and equitable economy in Argentina," P2P Foundation blog, May 3, 2008 <http://blog.p2pfoundation.net/ category/p2p-governance>.
    2. Lavaca Collective, *Sin Patron*, pp. 74-75, 94, 126, 134, 190-191, 198-199.
    3. *Ibid.*, pp. 164-165.
    4. *Ibid.*, pp. 198-199.

capital? The interest in possessing 10,000 francs when one shall have produced 10,000 francs . . . .[1]

Although apologists for capitalism directly equate the scale of accumulation to productivity and wages, there is no necessary connection between the quantity of capital investment and the increase in productivity. If anything it is likely that the predominance, under the present system, of absentee investment and the concentration of investment capital into a few hands, artificially promotes the substitution of major generational innovations and large-scale blockbuster investments for incremental improvements. It promotes, likewise, a strategy of capital substitution and deskilling, to reduce the bargaining power of labor; this is so even when a capital investment increases unit costs, if it promises to reduce the agency problems of labor. The reason is that investors find it less important to economize on capital, a factor available to them in artificially large quantities, than to avoid the agency costs that would accompany the levels of autonomy necessary for worker-directed innovation.

The most efficient mixture of labor and capital would vary enormously, depending on whether capital was owned by labor seeking to maximize the return on labor, or by absentee capitalists seeking to maximize the return on capital. Critics of worker cooperatives frequently charge that they skimp on capital investment in order to maximize employment. But to put it in less value-laden terms, that simply means that cooperatives economize on capital at the expense of labor efficiency. Capitalist enterprises, on the other hand, do just the opposite: they pursue a strategy of capital substitution in order to maximize labor efficiency, reduce labor costs, and minimize agency problems associated with labor—even when it means relying on the relatively wasteful use of large capital and energy inputs.

> What's happened in the United States is that we have displaced those ways of producing goods which are efficient in using energy, efficient in using capital, and inefficient in using labor with the reverse, and the upshot is that we tend to waste energy, to run out of capital, and to run out of jobs.[2]

What's the difference between the two approaches? The difference is that we are conditioned to see the maximization of utility by owners of capital as the normal purpose of economic activity, but to dismiss maximization of utility by labor as "malingering."

Barry Stein, as we have already seen, argues that incremental improvements in the production process, cumulatively, have more of an effect on productivity than do generational changes in production machinery. Jaroslav Vanek makes a similar distinction between major and minor innovations.

> Probably the best way of distinguishing between what . . . major and minor innovations is that the latter generally cannot be the subject of a full-time professional occupation. Rather, they will arise as an externality . . . of an activity whose primary purpose is something else than to innovate—generally to produce or contribute to the production of some good or service. More concretely, . . . a repeated act of production will stimulate reflection on how that act could be facilitated, or done more efficiently . . . .
> Clearly . . . the situation most conducive to the application of minor innovations is one of an individual self-employed producer, provided that he is not constrained by financial limitations. As far as conduciveness—or the incentive—to innovate goes, the labor-managed firm is the second-best solution . . . . First of all, the self-management structure . . . provides an excellent channel of communication, unparalleled in any other

1. F. C. Chevé [Charles-François Chevé (1813-1875)], one of the editors of the *Voix du Peuple*, to Frédéric Bastiat. Translation by Roderick T. Long. *The Bastiat-Proudhon Debate on Interest (1849-1850)* <http://praxeology.net/FB-PJP-DOI-IV-1.htm>

2. Barry Commoner, "Freedom and the Ecological Imperative: Beyond the Poverty of Power," in Richard C. Dorf and Yvonne L. Hunter, eds., *Appropriate Visions: Technology the Environment and the Individual* (San Francisco: Boyd & Fraser Publishing Company, 1978), pp. 39-42.

firm, between those who have innovative ideas, those who decide on an procure the capital implementation, and those who incorporate the innovation into the income-distribution scheme of the firm. Second, the innovator in the labor-managed firm need not worry that the capital owner will exploit the innovation and leave him with only a small part of the gain.[1]

The reference to innovation as an externality of production is reminiscent of Jane Jacobs' theory of technical innovation as discovering new uses for the waste materials of an existing production process, or spinning off production techniques from existing products (for which the new techniques may not even be suitable) to new product lines. E.g., 3M's (originally Minnesota Mining and Manufacturing) adhesive tape products (including Scotch tape), were offshoots of an unsuccessful experiment in developing adhesive backing for sandpaper in their primary business line.

According to Stein, the cumulative effect on productivity of small, incremental innovations (i.e., Vanek's "minor innovations") is as great as that of generational leaps in technology. He cites a 1965 study of DuPont rayon plants by Samuel Hollander, which found that "'minor' technical changes—based on technology judged relatively 'simple' to develop . . . and usually representing 'evolutionary' advances . . . accounted for two-thirds of the unit-cost reductions attributable to technical change at most of the plants considered." Such incremental changes made it possible "to incorporate within a given structure sufficiently productive technology to permit an older plan to produce almost as efficiently as a newly built plant"—and "the sum total of the outlay needed to accomplish the alterations at the older plant [would be] relatively small."[2]

Stein echoes the insights of Vanek and Jacobs about innovation as the byproduct of the production process.

> It has already been noted that much of the technological progress within a firm is the result of a series of small innovations . . . . The primary source of all innovations is derived from the recognition of a need, rather than from technical opportunity, as such . . . . In one study, only 21 percent of the successful innovations stemmed from technical sources; 30 percent were a response to perception of a need/opportunity in manufacturing; and fully 45 percent were due to market factors. Such recognition of a need, whether within the firm or with respect to the outside market, becomes possible only under conditions in which workers . . . are more generally knowledgeable about the organization, its operation, and its relationship to its environment.[3]

The most successful product innovations often result from tinkering with existing products, as well. Tom Peters, in his observation of the corporate world, found numerous examples of the phenomenon:

> *Hewlett-Packard* . . . : "The company is seldom first into the market with its new products . . . . A competitor's new product comes on the market and HP engineers, when making service calls on HP equipment, ask their customers what they like or dislike about the new product, what features the customer would like to have . . . . And pretty soon HP salesmen are calling on customers again with a new product that answers their needs and wants . . . ."
>
> *IBM*: Going back to its early days, IBM has seldom put products on the market that are right in the forefront of new technology . . . . "It was rarely the first to take a new technical step, but it wasn't far behind. And time after time, its new lines were better designed and more effectively sold and serviced than those of competitors." . . . .
>
> *Caterpillar*. . . . . "Caterpillar is rarely the first to come up with a new offering in its markets . . . . It has rarely built its reputation by letting other companies go through the

1. Jaroslav Vanek, *The General Theory of Labor-Managed Market Economies*, pp. 263-264.

2. Barry Stein, *Size, Efficiency, and Community Enterprise* (Cambridge, Mass.: Center for Community Economic Development, 1974), p. 35.

3. *Ibid.*, p. 49.

trial and error process of introducing new products. Caterpillar later jumps in with the most trouble-free product on the market."[1]

Let's look again at that old quote from Hayek on the role of distributed knowledge in making incremental process and product improvements:

> To know of and put to use a machine not fully employed, or somebody's skill which could be better utilized, or to be aware of a surplus stock which can be drawn upon during an interruption of supplies, is socially quite as useful as the knowledge of better alternative techniques . . . .[2]

Innovation in an economy where self-employment and worker ownership predominates would likely include efficiencies which presently go unrealized because of the special agency problems of absentee ownership and hierarchical authority.

D. Social Benefits of Worker Empowerment

The increased bargaining power of labor and the shift to a genuine "ownership society" would have other salutary social effects. One such effect would be the restoration of the positive character and lifestyle traits commonly associated with artisan production and a self-sufficient yeomanry.

Here is Ralph Borsodi's picture of one well-rounded character typical of pre-industrial society, compiled from the diary of Thomas B. Hazard (aka Nailer Tom) in 1780s New England:

> Making bridle bits, worked a garden, dug a woodchuck out of a hole, made stone wall for cousin, planted corn, cleaned cellar, made hoe handle of bass wood, sold a kettle, brought Sister Tanner in a fish boat, made hay, went for coal, made nails at night, went huckleberrying, raked oats, plowed turnip lot, went to monthly meeting and carried Sister Tanner behind me, bought a goose, went to see town, put on new shoes, made a shingle nail tool, helped George mend a spindle for the mill, went to harbor mouth gunning, killed a Rover, hooped tubs, caught a weasel, made nails, made a shovel, went swimming, staid at home, made rudder irons, went eeling.

Borsodi remarks on the notable "admixture of work and play" in this account. "If the worker 'played' during the day,"

> he labored at nail making or something else at night. The day was not divided by the clock into mutually exclusive periods of work and non-work. Most of the play had an admixture of productive labor in it—it produced game or fish, for instance, while much of the work had elements of play in it.[3]

Borsodi's description sounds remarkably similar to Marx's idyllic picture of communism, in which it would be

> possible for me to do one thing today and another tomorrow, to hunt in the morning, fish in the afternoon, rear cattle in the evening, criticize after dinner, just as I have a mind, without ever becoming hunter, fisherman, herdsman or critic . . . .[4]

Science fiction writer Ken Macleod, discussing another example of subsistence worker-ownership (the Highland crofters), appealed explicitly to Marx.

1. Peters and Waterman, *In Search of Excellence*, pp. 178-179.

2. F. A. Hayek. "The Use of Knowledge in Society" *The American Economic Review* 35:4 (September 1945), p. 522.

3. Ralph Borsodi, *This Ugly Civilization* (Philadelphia: Porcupine Press, 1929, 1975), pp. 138-39.

4. Karl Marx and Friedrich Engels, *The German Ideology*, Marx and Engels *Collected Works* vol. 5 (New York: International Publishers, 1976), p. 47.

In *The Sky Road* in particular, the society of the far-future Scotland [organized around the single tax and mutual banking] was one based on imagining an area that I know reasonably well and the kind of people that I know quite well—not as individuals but as a social type, if you like. A lot of these highlanders are Heinlein's omnicompetent man—they can turn their hand to anything. They're also rather like Marx's doodle about the post-class society where you could hunt in the morning, fish in the afternoon and be a critic after dinner without ever being hunter, fisherman or critic. That is literally what these guys are like.

. . . . The highlanders are often people who own a croft, work for wages during the day and go poaching in the evening, and who read a lot. They are people who've never really been hammered into industrial society and therefore have a flexibility. They've got to. Even Adam Smith says how in the Highlands the division of labour is less developed because there is a smaller market. If you have people who are not mangled by the division of labour being part of a much larger market as they are now, they can do all that stuff.[1]

An economy of self-employment or cooperative employment would restore workers' control over the pace of work, resulting in the balance of work and leisure, and of effort and consumption on the job. It would be a restoration of the very kind of worker control over the pace of work that the factory system was designed to eliminate. E. P. Thompson contrasts the pace of work, and the sense of control, in the "older weaving communities" of Yorkshire and Lancashire to those of the factory towns:

There was no bell to ring them up at four or five o'clock . . . there was freedom to start and to stay away as they cared . . . . In the evenings, while still at work, at anniversary times of the Sunday schools, the young men and women would most heartily join in the hymn singing, while the musical rhythm of the shuttles would keep time . . . .

Some Weavers had fruit, vegetables, and flowers from their gardens. "My work was at the loom side, and when not winding my father taught me reading, writing, and arithmetic." A Keighley factory child, who left the mill for a handloom at the age of eighteen, informed Sadler's Committee (1832) that he preferred the loom to the mill "a great deal": "I have more relaxation; I can look about me, and go out and refresh myself a little." It was the custom in Bradford for the weavers to gather in their dinner break at noon:

. . . and have a chat with other weavers and combers on the news or gossip of the time. Some of these parties would spend an hour talking about pig-feeding, hen-raising, and bird-catching, and now and then would have very hot disputes about free grace, or whether infant baptism or adult immersion was the correct and scriptural mode of doing the thing. I have many a time seen a number of men ready to fight one another on this . . . topic.[2]

J. L. and Barbara Hammond made a similar observation about the contrast between the self-paced work of the peasant or self-employed spinner or weaver, and the regimented life of the factory:[3]

In the modern world most people have to adapt themselves to some kind of discipline, and to observe other' people's timetables, . . . or work under other people's orders, but we have to remember that the population that was flung into the brutal rhythm of the factory had earned its living in relative freedom, and that the discipline of the early factory was particularly savage . . . . No economist of the day, in estimating the gains or losses of factory employment, ever allowed for the strain and violence that a man suffered in his feelings when he passed from a life in which he could smoke or eat, or dig or sleep as he

1. Duncan Lawie interview with Ken Macleod, *The Zone* <http://www.zone-sf.com/ ken-macleod.html>.

2. E. P. Thompson, *The Making of the English Working Class* (New York: Vintage Books, 1963, 1966), pp. 290-291.

3. J. L. and Barbara Hammond, *The Town Labourer (1760-1832)* (London: Longmans, Green & Co., 1917), vol. 1, pp. 33-34.

pleased, to one in which somebody turned the key on him, and for fourteen hours he had not even the right to whistle. It was like entering the airless and laughterless life of a prison.

Yet another benefit of a worker-managed society would be a general increase in the critical intelligence which "education" has done such a good job of stamping out in our "meritocratic" society. The independent master tradesmen before the triumph of the factory system, as Thompson points out, tended toward fairly high degrees both of self-education, and of political awareness and involvement. According to one observer, for example,

> [t]he moral effects of the [Sheffield] Society were great indeed. it induced men to read books instead of spending their time at public houses. It taught them to think, to respect themselves, and to desire to educate their children. It elevated them in their own opinions.[1]

Thompson himself refers to "a leaven amongst the northern weavers of self-educated and articulate men of considerable attainments."

> Every weaving district had its weaver-poets, biologists, mathematicians, musicians, geologists, botanists . . . . There are northern museums and natural history societies which still possess records or collections of lepidoptera built up by weavers while there are accounts of weavers in isolated villages who taught themselves geometry by chalking on their flagstones, and who were eager to discuss the differential calculus. In some kinds of plain work with strong yarn a book could actually be propped on the loom and read at work.[2] . . At Barnsley as early as January 1816 a penny-a-month club of weavers was formed, for the purpose of buying Radical newspapers and periodicals. The Hampden Clubs and Political Unions took great pains to build up "Reading Societies" and in the larger centres they opened permanent newsrooms or reading-rooms, such as that at Hanley in the Potteries.[3]
>
> . . . The articulate consciousness of the self-taught was above all a *political* consciousness. For the first half of the 19th century, when the formal education of a great part of the people entailed little more than instruction in the Three R's, was by no means a period of intellectual atrophy. The towns, and even the villages, hummed with the energy of the autodidact. Given the elementary techniques of literacy, labourers, artisans, shopkeepers and clerks and schoolmasters, proceeded to instruct themselves, severally or in groups. And the books or instructors were very often those sanctioned by reforming opinion. A shoemaker, who had been taught his letters in the Old Testament, would labour through the *Age of Reason*; a schoolmaster, whose education had taken him little further than worthy religious homilies, would attempt Voltaire, Gibbon, Ricardo; here and there local Radical leaders, weavers, booksellers, tailors, would amass shelves of Radical periodicals and learn how to use parliamentary Blue Books; illiterate labourers would, nevertheless, go each week to a pub where Cobbet's editorial letter was read aloud and discussed.
>
> Thus working men formed a picture of the organisation of society, out of their own experience and with the help of their hard-won and erratic education, which was above all a political picture.[4]

Note well: this "desire to educate their children" was hardly an anticipation of today's emphasis on "getting an education" as a means of meritocratic climbing, by currying favor with those in a position to advance one's career goals. There was little chance of "getting a good job" through the equivalent of a degree in factory management. The object of their ambition, for the most part, was rather a critical understanding of the world they lived in, and the intellectual weapons needed to change it.

---

1. Thompson, *Making of the English Working Class*, p. 155.
2. *Ibid.*, pp. 291–292.
3. *Ibid.*, p. 717.
4. *Ibid.*, pp. 711–712.

. . . [T]he artisan culture nurtured the values of intellectual enquiry and of mutuality . . . .
The autodidact had often an uneven, laboured, understanding, but it was *his own*. Since
he had been forced to find his intellectual way, he took little on trust: his mind did not
move within the established ruts of a formal education. Many of his ideas challenged
authority, and authority had tried to suppress them. He was willing, therefore, to give a
hearing to any new anti-authoritarian ideas.[1]

The general effect on working class consciousness is beautifully summed up in this
collier's note to an overseer:

> Noo I naw some at wor colliery that has three or fower lads and lasses, and they live in
> won room not half as gude as yor cellar. I don't pretend to naw very much, but I naw
> there shudn't be that much difference . . . . I dinna pretend to be a profit, but I naw this,
> and lots o ma marrows na's te, that wer not tret as we owt to be, and a great filosopher
> says, to get noledge is to naw wer ignerent. But weve just begun to find that oot, and ye
> maisters and owners may luk oot, for yor not gan to get se much o yor own way, wer gan
> to hev some o wors now.[2]

For all his poor spelling, the anonymous north country author probably had more critical
intelligence than the average college graduate today.

A central theme for Thompson is the role of master craftsmen in working class radicalism—the trade union movement, Owenism, Chartism, etc. "By 1832—and on into
Chartist times—there is a Radical nucleus to be found in every county, in the smallest
market towns and even in the larger rural villages, and in nearly every case it is based on
the local artisans."[3] Hodgskin's lectures embodied in *Popular Political Economy* are an excellent illustration of working people's thirst for knowledge of political and economic affairs
at the time. Christopher Lasch's *The True and Only Heaven*, likewise, contains a considerable
amount of material on the role of skilled blue collar workers in the radical unionism (especially syndicalism) around the turn of the 20th century. One of the central goals of the factory system, arguably, was the suppression of this general social type. The artisans, as
Thompson put it, were the "intellectual elite of the [working] class";[4] prophets of deskilling, from Ure onward, not only aimed at eliminating them as an internal obstacle to
authority relations inside the factory, but feared their corrupting influence on the governability of society at large.

Still another improvement would be the erosion of the modern artificial distinction
between work and art: a return to medieval ideas of craftsmanship in work, celebrated by
Ruskin and Morris, and to amateurism in its original sense.

> The world needs amateur writers, painters, sculptors, teachers and scientists. It needs
> men and women who can appreciate the great achievements of the arts and sciences be-
> cause they are themselves engaged in contributing to them . . . .
>
> I do not mean incompetents when I speak of amateurs. The world does not need
> mere dilettantes who have neither the patience nor the stamina for the discipline which
> is necessary to the production of good work. The world needs able men who have such
> rounded personalities that they can express themselves in many fields with satisfaction to
> themselves and benefit to society generally. A Benjamin Franklin who is a printer, a
> writer, a scientist and a statesman; a Thomas Jefferson who is a farmer, a philosopher, a
> teacher, a statesman, a lawyer and a writer . . . .
>
> The versatility of these great men proves that it is possible for men to be masters of
> many trades, provided they are masters of their own time.
>
> As long as we are forced to solve our basic economic problem solely by the practice
> of our professions, we cannot afford to experiment and adventure in any field that hap-

1. *Ibid.*, p. 743.
2. *Ibid.*, p. 715.
3. *Ibid.*, p. 733.
4. *Ibid.*, p. 716.

pens to interest us. And what is even more important, we are not free to refuse to do work which does violence to our inclinations and our ideals.

To this extent we can free ourselves if only we organize our economic life so that earning the money for the material essentials of comfort ceases to be the major problem of our lives.[1]

Peer production, with decentralized distribution of music and art over the internet, has already gone a long way toward restoring the folk model of culture and undermining the great media corporations of the twentieth century. The marketing approach of Phish and Radiohead is the wave of the future. S.M. Koppelman's analysis of the situation is far too astute to be buried in the comment thread of a blog post, which is where I found it:

> Before the mid 19th century, when mass-market sheet music and piano roll sales created a "music industry" in which selling widgets and collecting royalties became sources of income, there was still plenty of music being made. People played fiddles and lutes and whistles and whatever around the kitchen table and the campfire. Some made money at it playing in party bands. Traveling musicians . . . could earn a modest income. Other professionals played in theaters and traveling shows, and still others earned money through composing pieces on commission.
>
> The music industry as we've come to know it in the last century and a half is a fairly new development . . . . It came into being because printing sheet music, producing piano rolls, and later, manufacturing cylinders and discs and tapes was expensive and required costly equipment. The only entities that could afford to do it were serious businesses, so the business models they created around copyright, publishing rights and manufacturing a physical product were viable. It was easy to use copyright to protect your interests because serious piracy required serious capital. Piracy that impacted the industry generally came from big operations run by organized crime . Cracking down was the relatively simple matter of raiding factories and warehouses and stopping big trucks full of bootlegs.
>
> Now the "music industry" is unnecessary. Anyone can produce a flawless CD for about forty cents at home. Maintaining the industry in its current state is simply propping up an old cartel out of a misguided sense that it's the rightful gatekeeper to music distribution.
>
> We're not rushing to ban or tax the hell out of digital cameras because Kodak and Polaroid are suffering. They haven't asked government to do so, and they'd be laughed out of town if they did.
>
> The record industry is obsolete. It's time for all those people to find another line of work. Musicians will keep making music. They just won't have an easy time making money from selling recordings. We had music for thousands of years before Edison's wax cylinders, and the inevitable end of the music industry . . . won't put a stop to it. It may signal an end to the top-down star system, though, and a return to local and personal musicmaking.[2]

Cory Doctorow argues, along similar lines, that "even if it turns out that P2P is the death knell for $300 million movies and artists who earn a living from recording, so what?"

> Radio was bad news for Vaudeville, too. Today's recording artists can earn a living because radio and records killed the careers of many live performers. If bands have to be more like Phish to survive, that's how it goes. Particular copyright business models aren't written into the Constitution; technology giveth and technology taketh away.
>
> P2P is enabling more filmmakers, more musicians, and more writers and other creators to produce a wider variety of works that please a wider audience than ever before.[3]

Self-employment and workers' control of production give workers a sense of control over their lives. Sad to say, many self-professed libertarians refuse to recognize this as a posi-

1. Borsodi, *This Ugly Civilization*, pp. 363-63.
2. S. M. Koppelman comment under Nick Gillespie, "The Man Can Bust Our Music," *Reason Hit & Run*, January 5, 2004 <http://www.reason.com/blog/show/103947.html>.
3. Ernest Lilley, "Interview: Cory Doctorow," *SFRevu*, January 1, 2007 <http://sfrevu.com/php/Review-id.php?id=4785>.

tive social value. If maintenance of the wage relationship does not rely on direct or indirect coercion, they say, then libertarians should be neutral about its cultural and psychological effects.

Nonsense. Although libertarians should not advocate force to abolish injustices that do not result from coercion, they should oppose on moral grounds anything that promotes a culture of obedience or impedes the individual's sense of control over his own life. Charles Johnson argues that libertarians ought to oppose culturally authoritarian social relationships, even uncoercive ones, on what he calls "grounds thickness": we should find them repugnant to the basic values that drove us to libertarianism in the first place.

> But while there's nothing logically inconsistent about a libertarian envisioning—or even championing—this sort of social order [based on deference and submission to authority, including from workers to bosses], it would certainly be *weird*. Noncoercive authoritarianism may be *consistent* with libertarian principles, but it is hard to *reasonably* reconcile the two. Whatever reasons you may have for rejecting the arrogant claims of power-hungry politicians and bureaucrats—say, for example, the Jeffersonian notion that all men and women are born equal in political authority and that no one has a natural right to rule or dominate other people's affairs—probably serve just as well for reasons to reject other kinds of authoritarian pretension, even if they are not expressed by means of coercive government action. While no one should be *forced* as a matter of policy to treat her fellows with the respect due to equals, or to cultivate independent thinking and contempt for the arrogance of power, libertarians certainly can—and should—*criticize* those who do not, and *exhort* our fellows not to rely on authoritarian social institutions, for much the same reasons that we have for endorsing libertarianism in the first place.[1]

Even though, "under laissez faire, there is nothing politically illegitimate about the employment relation," Sheldon Richman raises the question

> whether a libertarian can be comfortable being subject to someone's arbitrary will even through consent. Once in a job, withdrawal may not be feasible or easy, leaving the employee under a boss's thumb for an indefinite period. How can a libertarian put himself in that position? This leads me to believe that in an anarchist society, where all privilege has been abolished, people would look for alternatives to conventional employment.[2]

Dan Clore, a member of the LeftLibertarian2 yahoogroup, replied as follows to a conventional "the consumer is king" defense of the free market:

> If you want to promote the "free market", using a metaphor by which most people are in the position of a serf for eight hours each day probably isn't going to help your case. Even if they do get to go to the grocery store and play king once in a while.[3]

No less a libertarian than Claire Wolfe has perceived this. Wolfe sees the "job culture" as something fundamentally at odds with libertarian values:

> The Job Culture isn't just jobs, work, and business institutions. It's a comprehensive way of life in which millions of people place institutional paid employment at the center of their world.
>
> "What do you do?" is immediately understood to mean, "What kind of paid employment do you have?"
>
> In the Job Culture, family life, recreation, deep personal interests, and desires all must be structured around and subordinated to The Job.

1. Charles Johnson, "Libertarianism Through Thick and Thin," *The Freeman: Ideas on Liberty*, July/August 2008, p. 37 <http://www.fee.org/pdf/the-freeman/Johnson.pdf>.

2. Sheldon Richman comment under Kevin Carson, "The Ethics of Labor Struggle: A Free Market Perspective," *Mutualist Blog: Free Market Anti-Capitalism*, April 19, 2007 <http://mutualist.blogspot.com/2007/04/media-print-projection-embossed-body.html>.

3. Dan Clore, "Re: Reclaiming Corn & Culture," *LeftLibertarian2*, July 21, 2008 <http://groups.yahoo.com/group/LeftLibertarian2/message/20726>.

Even things like how we eat (fast foods), how we spend our leisure time (TV, shopping) and how we save for a rainy day (investing in stocks and bonds) are dictated by a culture of job holding and corporate institutions.

This is normal? No, *this* is whacko. This is not the way human beings evolved to live. This is a new and artificial lifestyle gradually imposed over the last couple of centuries—imposed for the sake of institutions, rather than individuals . . . .

The traditional case against jobs and the Job Culture comes from the left, which warns us of exploited workers, mindless consumerism, and environmental destruction . . . .

But if anybody should rail against the Job Culture and endeavor to bring it down, it should be libertarians, anarcho-capitalists, and true conservatives . . . .

The daily act of surrendering individual sovereignty—the act of becoming a mere interchangeable cog in a machine—an act we have been *conditioned* to accept and to call a part of "capitalism" and "free enterprise" when it is not—is the key reason why the present Job Culture is a disaster for freedom.

James Madison, the father of the Bill of Rights, wrote:

"The class of citizens who provide at once their own food and their own raiment, may be viewed as the most truly independent and happy. They are more: They are the best basis of public liberty, and the strongest bulwark of public safety. It follows, that the greater the proportion of this class to the whole society, the more free, the more independent, and the more happy must be the society itself" . . . .

Madison (and his like-minded friend Jefferson) knew that people who are self-sufficient in life's basics, who make their own decisions, whose livelihood relies on their own choices rather than someone else's, are less likely to march in lockstep. Independent enterprisers are far more likely to think for themselves, and far more capable of independent action than those whose first aim is to appease institutional gods.

Living in the Job Culture, on the other hand, has conditioned us to take a "someone else will deal with it" mentality. "I'm just doing my job." "The boss makes the decisions." "I'm just following orders." But if someone else is responsible for all the important choices in life, then we by definition, are not.

. . . [An attitude and work-style of true free enterprise] would leave millions free to say, "Screw you!" to institutional masters and "No thanks" to those who dangle tempting "benefits" in exchange for loss of personal autonomy. It would mean that more individuals dealt with each other on a more equal footing, with fewer corporate or political masters.[1]

In the republican ideology of the American Revolution and its aftermath, standing armies were feared as a threat to liberty. This was not merely because of the potential for a Caesar to cross the Rubicon or a Cromwell to purge the House of Commons. It was because the *internal culture* of a standing army—even a standing army made up entirely of voluntary enlistees—was a breeding ground for authoritarian values, for habits of obedience, that would carry over into civilian life and contaminate the larger culture.

Anyone who doubts this should reflect on the effect that the mass conscription of two generations in two world wars, starting in 1917, had on American political culture. The defining cultural style of the so-called "Greatest Generation" was formed in reaction against the previously dominant style, florid and sentimental, of the Victorian and Edwardian eras. The new cultural style probably had its roots in the "lost generation" of Great War veterans and those coming to maturity afterward: close-cropped, clean-shaven, with a jaded wiseguy persona and the terse demeanor of Gary Cooper. This cultural style, which the Baby Boomers in turn reacted against forty years later, was the basis of the "hardhat" culture of the "silent majority." And one of its central identifying features was authoritarian-

1. Claire Wolfe, "Insanity, the Job Culture, and Freedom," *Loompanics Unlimited* 2005 Winter Supplement <http://www.loompanics.com/Articles/insanityjobculture.html>.

ism, summed up by the frequent jibe: "Put that filthy hippie in the army—it'll make a man out of him!"

The founding generation focused its fear and aversion on standing armies because, in the American society of the time, they were virtually the only large, hierarchical institution in existence.[1] There were no such employers in the private sector. Even so, the aversion to standing armies was paralleled, in fact, by an aversion to wage employment, for the same reason: the cultural habits of obedience to authority which it bred. For example Jefferson, in *Notes on Virginia*, warned that the growth of manufacturing would replace an ethos of self-sufficiency with one of dependence. The predominance of manufacturing based on wage labor would subvert "the manners and spirit of a people which preserve a republic in vigor," and promote a "degeneracy" in them which would undermine the basis of liberty.[2]

The culture of authority and obedience associated with wage labor carries over into the rest of life because the human personality cannot be compartmentalized.

> You cannot expect men to take a responsible attitude and to display initiative in daily life when their whole working experience deprives them of the chance of initiative and responsibility. The personality cannot be successfully divided into watertight compartments . . . : if a man is taught to rely upon a paternalistic authority within the factory, he will be ready to rely upon one outside.[3]

The converse is also true. L. S. Stavrianos quotes Neil McWhinney, an academic psychologist who served as consultant to a Proctor & Gamble experiment in worker self-management:

> One of the striking features in our "pure" open systems plant is that workers have taken on more activities outside the workplace. The most visible involvements had to do with community racial troubles. Following major disturbances in the small city where they lived, a number of workers organized the black community to deal directly with the leaders of the city and of industry . . . . Blue collar workers won elections to the school board majority office and other local positions. Nearly ten percent of the work force of our plant holds elective offices currently . . . . We have noted that open systems workers join more social clubs and political organizations.[4]

This is especially impressive, I might add, because so many local government "reforms" of the so-called Progressive Era reflected a desire to "professionalize" government in response to just such "excessive" levels of blue collar representation. At-large representation, large wards, citywide school boards, all were created—despite the obligatory "good government" rhetoric—for the primary purpose of keeping the riff-raff out.

Empowered workers, whether self-employed or equal partners in self-management, tend to play an assertive role in their communities, strengthening the control of ordinary people over all the decisions that affect their lives. They become, to put it bluntly, less prone to take shit off of anybody. Peter Block writes:

---

1. Interestingly, according to Alfred Chandler, the techniques of managing a multi-unit corporation were first worked out in the railroads by salaried administrators from a military engineering background. Mechanical engineering was an outgrowth of, and heavily influenced in its development by, military engineering; the influence of mechanical engineering on the science of corporate management, in turn, we saw in Chapter Four.

2. Langdon Winner, *The Whale and the Reactor: A Search for Limits in an Age of High Technology* (Chicago and London: University of Chicago Press, 1986), p. 43.

3. Gordon Rattray Taylor, *Are Workers Human?*, quoted in Colin Ward, *Anarchy in Action* (London: Freedom Press, 1982), p. 95.

4. L. S. Stavrianos, *The Promise of the Coming Dark Age* (San Francisco: W. H. Freeman and Company, 1976), p. 63.

"If day in and day out we go to a workplace that breeds helplessness and compliance, this becomes our generalized pattern of response to the larger questions of our society and our lives", and democracy will flounder.[1]

E. PEER PRODUCTION

Peer production first emerged in information industries: software, entertainment, etc. As Johan Soderberg argues,

> [t]he universally applicable computer run on free software and connected to an open network . . . have [sic] in some respects leveled the playing field. Through the global communication network, hackers are matching the coordinating and logistic capabilities of state and capital.[2]

As with cooperatives, peer networks are more productive than the capitalist competition because of the agency and motivational benefits of self-employment. Soderberg quotes Linus Torvalds' comment that proprietary software systems are bad "because the people don't care," and adds

> To a hired programmer, the code he is writing is a means to get a pay check at the end of the month. Any shortcut when getting to the end of the month will do. For a hacker, on the other hand, writing code is an end in itself. He will always pay full attention to his endeavour, or else he will be doing something else.[3]

Peer production's transferability to the world of physical production is also a matter of great interest. Open source hardware refers, at the most basic level, to the development and improvement of designs for physical goods on an open-source basis, with no particular mode of physical production being specified. In Stallman's terms, open source hardware means the design is free as in free speech, not free beer. Although the manufacturer is not hindered by patents on the design, he must still bear the costs of physical production. Edy Ferreira defined it as

> any piece of hardware whose manufacturing information is distributed using a license that provides specific rights to users without the need to pay royalties to the original developers. These rights include freedom to use the hardware for any purpose, freedom to study and modify the design, and freedom to redistribute copies of either the original or modified manufacturing information . . . .
> In the case of open source software (OSS), the information that is shared is software code. In OSH, what is shared is hardware manufacturing information, such as . . . the diagrams and schematics that describe a piece of hardware.[4]

At the simplest level, a peer network may develop a product design make it publicly available; it may be subsequently built by any and all individuals or groups who have the necessary production machinery, without coordinating their efforts with the original designer(s). For example, Vinay Gupta has proposed a large-scale library of open-source hardware designs as an aid to international development:

> An open library of designs for refrigerators, lighting, heating, cooling, motors, and other systems will encourage manufacturers, particularly in the developing world, to leapfrog directly

---

1. Quoted in Dave Pollard, "Stewardship: Remaking Traditional Companies into Natural Enterprises," *How to Save the World*, July 3, 2006 <http://blogs.salon.com/0002007/2006/07/03.html#a1577>.

2. Johan Soderberg, *Hacking Capitalism: The Free and Open Source Software Movement* (New York and London: Routledge, 2008), p. 2.

3. Soderberg, p. 26.

4. "Open Source Hardware," P2P Foundation Wiki <http://www.p2pfoundation.net/Open_Source_Hardware>.

to the most sustainable technologies, which are much cheaper in the long run. Manufacturers will be encouraged to use the efficient designs because they are free, while inefficient designs still have to be paid for. The library could also include green chemistry and biological solutions to industry challenges . . . . This library should be free of all intellectual property restrictions and open for use by any manufacturer, in any nation, without charge.[1]

One item of his own design, the Hexayurt, is

a refugee shelter system that uses an approach based on "autonomous building" to provide not just a shelter, but a comprehensive family support unit which includes drinking water purification, composting toilets, fuel-efficient stoves and solar electric lighting."[2]

The basic construction materials for the floor, walls and roof cost about $200.[3]

One of the most ambitious attempts at such an open design project for village development is Open Source Ecology, with their experimental facility Factor E Farm.

We are actively involved in demonstrating the world's first replicable, post-industrial village. We take the word *replicable* very seriously—we do not mean a top-down funded showcase—but one that is based on ICT, open design, and digital fabrication—in harmony with its natural life support systems. As such, this community is designed to be self-reliant, highly productive, and sufficiently transparent so that it can truly be replicated in many contexts—whether it's parts of the package or the whole. Our next frontier will be education to train Village Builders—just as we're learning how to do it from the ground up.[4]

Here's a list of the design categories and individual projects being developed by OSE, from their Wiki:

HABITAT PACKAGE: CEB Press—Sawmill—Living Machines—Modular Housing Units—Modular Greenhouse Units—Solar Turbine CHP System—AGRICULTURE PACKAGE: Modular Greenhouse Units—Orchard and Nursery—Electric Garden Tractor—Organoponic Raised Bed Gardening—Agricultural Microcombine -Bakery - Dairy—Energy Food Bars—Agricultural Spader—Well Drilling Rig—Freeze Dried Fruit Powders—Hammer Mill—ENERGY PACKAGE: Solar Turbine CHP System—Compressed Fuel Gas—Inverters & Grid Intertie—Electric Motors/Generators—Fuel Alcohol—FLEXIBLE INDUSTRY PACKAGE: Multimachine & Flex Fab—Metal Casting and Extrusion—Plastic Extrusion & Molding—TRANSPORTATION: Open Source Car—Electric Motors/Generators—Electric Motor Controls—MATERIALS: Aluminum Extraction From Clays—Bioplastics[5]

One project that's reached the prototype stage, the Compressed Earth Block press, can be built for $5000—some 20% of the price of the cheapest commercial competitor.[6] In field testing, the CEB press demonstrated an ability to produce a thousand blocks in eight-hours, on a day with bad weather (the expected norm in good weather is 1500 a day).[7] An-

1. Vinay Gupta, "Facilitating International Development Through Free/Open Source," <http://guptaoption.com/5.open_source_development.php> Quoted from Beatrice Anarow, Catherine Greener, Vinay Gupta, Michael Kinsley, Joanie Henderson, Chris Page and Kate Parrot, Rocky Mountain Institute, "Whole-Systems Framework for Sustainable Consumption and Production." Environmental Project No. 807 (Danish Environmental Protection Agency, Ministry of the Environment, 2003), p. 24. <http://files.howtolivewiki.com/A%20Whole%20Systems %20Framework%20for%20 Sustainable%20Production%20and%20Consumption.pdf>.
2. <http://www.p2pfoundation.net/Hexayurt>.
3. <http://hexayurt.com/>.
4. "Clarifying OSE Vision," *Factor E Farm Weblog*, September 8, 2008 <http://openfarmtech.org/weblog/?p=325>.
5. Main Page, Open Source Ecology <http://openfarmtech.org/index.php?title=Main_Page>
6. "CEB Phase 1 Done," Factor E Farm Weblog, December 26, 2007 <http://openfarmtech.org/weblog/?p=91>.
7. Marcin, "The Thousandth Brick: CEB Field Testing Report," *Factor E Farm Weblog*, Nov. 16, 2008 <http://openfarmtech.org/weblog/?p=422>.

other project in development is the solar turbine, which uses the sun's heat to power a steam-driven generator, as an alternative to photovoltaic electricity.[1]

Karim Lakhani describes this general phenomenon, the separation of open-source design from an independent production stage, as "communities driving manufacturers out of the design space," with

> users innovating and developing products that can out compete traditional manufacturers. But this effect is not just limited to software. In physical products . . . , users have been shown to be the dominant source of functionally novel innovations. Communities can supercharge this innovation mechanism. And may ultimately force companies out of the product design space. Just think about it—for any given company—there are more people outside the company that have smarts about a particular technology or a particular use situation then all the R&D engineers combined. So a community around a product category may have more smart people working on the product then the firm it self. So in the end manufacturers may end up doing what they are supposed to— manufacture—and the design activity might move . . . into the community.[2]

Michel Bauwens, of the P2P foundation, provides a small list of some of the more prominent open-design projects:

> The Grid Beam Building System, at
>   http://www.p2pfoundation.net/Grid_Beam_Building_System
> The Hexayurt, at http://www.p2pfoundation.net/Hexayurt
> Movisi Open Design Furniture, at
>   http://www.p2pfoundation.net/Movisi_Open_Design_Furniture
> Open Cores, at http://www.p2pfoundation.net/Open_Cores and other Open
>   Computing Hardware, at http://www.p2pfoundation.net/Open_Hardware
> Open Source Green Vehicle, at
>   http://www.p2pfoundation.net/Open_Source_Green_Vehicle
> Open Source Scooter http://www.p2pfoundation.net/Open_Source_Scooter
> The Ronja Wireless Device at
>   http://www.p2pfoundation.net/Twibright_Ronja_Open_Wireless_Networking_Devic
>   e
> Open Source Sewing patterns, at
>   http://www.p2pfoundation.net/Open_Source_Sewing_Patterns
> Velomobiles
>   http://www.p2pfoundation.net/Open_Source_Velomobile_Development_Project
> Open Energy http://www.p2pfoundation.net/SHPEGS_Open_Energy_Project[3]

A more complex scenario involves the coordination of an open source design stage with the production process in a large peer organization, with the separate stages of production distributed and coordinated by the same peer network that created the design. Dave Pollard provides one example:

> Suppose I want a chair that has the attributes of an Aeron without the $1800 price tag, or one with some additional attribute (e.g. a laptop holder) the brand name doesn't offer? I could go online to a Peer Production site and create an instant market, contributing the specifications . . . , and, perhaps a maximum price I would be willing to pay. People with some of the expertise needed to produce it could indicate their capabilities

1. "Solar Turbine—Open Source Ecology" <http://openfarmtech.org/index.php?title=Solar_Turbine>.

2. Karim Lakhana, "Communities Driving Manufacturers Out of the Design Space," *The Future of Communities Blog*, March 25, 2007 <http://www.futureofcommunities.com/2007/03/25/communities-driving-manufacturers-out-of-the-design-space/>.

3. Michel Bauwens, "What kind of economy are we moving to? 3. A hierarchy of engagement between companies and communities," *P2P Foundation Blog*, October 5, 2007 <http://blog.p2pfoundation.net/what-kind-of-economy-are-we-moving-to-3-a-hierarchy-of-engagement-between-companies-and-communities/2007/10/05>.

and self-organize into a consortium that would keep talking and refining until they could meet this price .... Other potential buyers could chime in, offering more or less than my suggested price. Based on the number of 'orders' at each price, the Peer Production group could then accept orders and start manufacturing ....

As [Erick] Schonfeld suggests, the intellectual capital associated with this instant market becomes part of the market archive, available for everyone to see, stripping this intellectual capital cost, and the executive salaries, dividends and corporate overhead out of the cost of this and other similar product requests and fulfillments, so that all that is left is the lowest possible cost of material, labour and delivery to fill the order. And the order is exactly what the customer wants, not the closest thing in the mass-producer's warehouse.[1]

The most ambitious example of an open-source physical production project is the open source car.

Can open-source practices and approaches be applied to make hardware, to create tangible and physical objects, including complex ones? Say, to build a car? ...

Markus Merz believes they can. The young German is the founder and "maintainer" (that's the title on his business card) of the OScar project, whose goal is to develop and build a car according to open-source (OS) principles. Merz and his team aren't going for a super-accessorized SUV—they're aiming at designing a simple and functionally smart car. And, possibly, along the way, reinvent transportation.[2]

Well, actually there's a fictional example of an open-source project even more ambitious than the OScar: the open-source moon project, a volunteer effort of a peer network of thousands, in Craig DeLancy's "Openshot." The project's ship (the *Stallman*), built largely with Russian space agency surplus, beats a corporate-funded proprietary project to the moon.[3]

A slightly less ambitious open-source manufacturing project, and probably more relevant to the needs of most people in the world, is Open Source Ecology's open-source tractor (LifeTrac). It's designed for inexpensive manufacture, with modularity and easy disassembly, for lifetime service and low cost repair. It includes, among other things, a well-drilling module, and is designed to serve as a prime mover for machinery like the CEB Press or a saw mill.[4]

In either case, whether physical production is coordinated with the design stage or organized independently, it may take place in comparatively heavily capitalized factories (likely owned by workers' cooperatives in a post-capitalist society), by outsourcing the production of specific parts to more modestly capitalized small shops, to even cheaper emerging small-scale production facilities like the multimachine, or to a combination of some or all of the above.

Clearly, the emergence of cheap desktop technology for custom machining parts in small batches will greatly lower the overall capital outlays needed for networked physical production of light and medium consumer goods. The availability of modestly priced desktop manufacturing technology (coupled with the promise of LETS systems, mutual banks, and other forms of alternative credit) has led to a considerable shift in opinion in the peer-to-peer community, as evidenced by Michel Bauwens:

1. Dave Pollard, "Peer Production," *How to Save the World*, October 28, 2005 <http://blogs.salon.com/0002007/2005/10/28.html#a13322>.

2. Bruno Giussani, "Open Source at 90 MPH," Business Week, December 8, 2006 <http://www.businessweek.com/innovate/content/dec2006/id20061208_509041.htm?>. See also the OS Car website, <http://www.theoscarproject.org/>.

3. Craig DeLancey, "Openshot," *Analog*, December 2006, pp. 64-74.

4. "LifeTrac," Open Source Ecology wiki <http://openfarmtech.org/index.php?title=LifeTrac>.

I used to think that the model of peer production would essentially emerge in the immaterial sphere, and in those cases where the design phase could be split from the capital-intensive physical production sphere . . . .

However, as I become more familiar with the advances in Rapid Manucturing . . . and Desktop Manufacturing . . . , I'm becoming increasingly convinced of the strong trend towards the distribution of physical capital.

If we couple this with the trend towards the direct social production of money (i.e. the distribution of financial capital . . .) and the distribution of energy . . . ; and how the two latter trends are interrelated . . . , then I believe we have very strong grounds to see a strong expansion of p2p-based modalities in the physical sphere.[1]

Kevin Kelly argues that the actual costs of physical production are only a minor part of the cost of manufactured goods.

. . . material industries are finding that the costs of duplication near zero, so they too will behave like digital copies. Maps just crossed that threshold. Genetics is about to. Gadgets and small appliances (like cell phones) are sliding that way. Pharmaceuticals are already there, but they don't want anyone to know. It costs nothing to make a pill.[2]

When physical manufacturing is stripped of the cost of proprietary design and technology, and the consumer-driven, pull model of distribution strips away most of the immense marketing cost, we will find that the portion of price formerly made up of such intangibles will implode, and the remaining price based on actual production cost will be an order of magnitude lower. In a world where commodity price consists entirely of labor and material costs, without rents to the holders of privilege from the state, we can likely maintain the existing standard of living with an average work week of one or two days.

In any case, there is a common thread running through all the different theories of the interface between peer production and the material world: as technology for physical production becomes feasible on increasingly smaller scales and at less cost, or the lower the transaction costs of aggregating small units of capital into large ones, the less disconnect there will be between peer production and physical production.

- P2P can arise not only in the immaterial sphere of intellectual and software production, but wherever there is access to distributed technology: spare computing cycles, distributed telecommunications and any kind of viral communicator meshwork.
- P2P can arise wherever other forms of distributed fixed capital is available: such is the case for carpooling, which is the second mode of transportation in the U.S. . . . .
- P2P can arise wherever financial capital can be distributed. Initiatives such as the ZOPA bank point in that direction. Cooperative purchase and use of large capital goods are a possibility . . . .[3]

Franz Nahrada writes in the same vein, affirming Bauwens' distinction between cooperatives and peer production, but nevertheless arguing: "Once we really get a grasp of really efficient home production, the rules of the games will change drastically."[4]

In effect, the distinction between Stallman's "free speech" and "free beer" is eroding. To the extent that embedded rents on "intellectual property" are a significant portion of

1. Michel Bauwens post to Institute for Distributed Creativity email list, May 7, 2007. <https://lists.thing.net/pipermail/idc/2007-May/002479.html>

2. Kevin Kelly, "Better Than Free," *The Technium*, January 31, 2008 <http://www.kk.org/thetechnium/archives/2008/01/better_than_fre.php>.

3. Michel Bauwens, "The Political Economy of Peer Production," *CTheory*, December 2005 <http://www.ctheory.net/articles.aspx?id=499>.

4. Michel Bauwens, "Franz Nahrada: Can we produce for physical abundance or sufficiency?" *P2P Foundation Blog*, January 14, 2008 <http://blog.p2pfoundation.net/franz-nahrada-can-we-produce-for-physical-abundance-or-sufficiency/2008/01/14>.

commodity prices, "free speech" (in the sense of the free use of ideas) will make our "beer" (i.e., the price of manufactured commodities) at least a lot cheaper.

Although leading figures in the proprietary software (and proprietary everything) movement are fond of using alarmist language about peer producers—for example, Bill Gates' reference to the open-source movement as "communists"—peer production is in fact a case of "back to the future." It's a return to the kind of self-employment and small-scale production for consumption or local exchange that predated the Industrial Revolution and the corporate transformation of capitalism, but this time producing the kinds of high-quality manufactured outputs previously monopolized by large-scale industry. As "Jed," at *Anomalous Presumptions* blog, describes it, peer production makes it possible to produce without access to large amounts of capital:

> The problem for capitalists in peer production is that typically there is no way to get a return on ownership . . . .
>
> Historically, entrepreneurship is associated with creating a profitable enterprise . . . .
>
> The classical idea of profit is monetary and is closely associated with the rate of (monetary) return on assets . . . .
>
> The peer production equivalent of profit is creating a self-sustaining social entity that delivers value to participants. Typically the means are the same as those used by any classical entrepreneur: creating a product, publicizing the product, recruiting contributors, acquiring resources, generating support from larger organizations (legal, political, and sometimes financial), etc.
>
> Before widespread peer production, the entrepreneur's and capitalist's definitions of success were typically congruent, because growing a business required capital, and gaining access to capital required providing a competitive return. So classical profit was usually required to build a self-sustaining business entity.
>
> The change that enables widespread peer production is that today, an entity can become self-sustaining, and even grow explosively, with very small amounts of capital. As a result it doesn't need to trade ownership for capital, and so it doesn't need to provide any return on investment.[1]

But beyond that, Charles Johnson points out, because of the new possibilities the Internet provides for lowering the transaction costs entailed in networked mobilization of capital, peer production can take place even when significant capital investments are required—without relying on finance by large-scale sources of venture capital:

> it's not just a matter of projects being able to expand or sustain themselves with little capital . . . . It's also a matter of the way in which both emerging distributed technologies in general, and peer production projects in particular, facilitate *the aggregation of dispersed capital*—without it having to pass through a single capitalist chokepoint, like a commercial bank or a venture capital fund . . . . Meanwhile, because of the way that peer production projects distribute their labor, peer-production entrepreneurs can also take advantage of spare cycles on existing, widely-distributed capital goods—tools like computers, facilities like offices and houses, software, etc. which contributors own, which they still would have owned personally or professionally whether or not they were contributing to the peer production project . . . . So it's not just a matter of cutting total aggregate costs for capital goods . . . ; it's also, importantly, a matter of new models of *aggregating the capital goods* to meet whatever costs you may have, so that small bits of available capital can be rounded up without the intervention of money-men and other intermediaries.[2]

1. Jed, "Capitalists vs. Entrepreneurs," *Anomalous Presumptions*, February 26, 2007 <http://jed.jive.com/?p=23>.

2. Charles Johnson, "Dump the rentiers off your back," *Rad Geek People's Daily*, May 29, 2008 <http://radgeek.com/gt/2008/05/29/dump_the/>.

In making productive use of idle capital assets the average person owns anyway, providing a productive outlet for the surplus labor of the unemployed, and transforming the small surpluses of household production into a ready source of exchange value, the informal economy has for its cornerstone the stone which the builders rejected.

That's why one of the central functions of so-called "health" and "safety" codes, and occupational licensing is to prevent people from using idle capacity (or "spare cycles") of what they already own anyway, and thereby transforming them into capital goods for productive use.

Consider, for example, the process of running a small, informal brew pub or restaurant out of your home, under a genuine free market regime. Buying a brewing vat and a few small fermenters for your basement, using a few tables in an extra room as a public restaurant area, etc., would require a small bank loan for at most a few thousand dollars. And with that capital outlay, you could probably make payments on the debt with the margin from one customer a day. A few customers evenings and weekends, probably found mainly among your existing circle of acquaintances, would enable you to initially shift some of your working hours from wage labor to work in the restaurant, with the possibility of gradually phasing out wage labor altogether or scaling back to part time, as you built up a customer base. In this and many other lines of business (for example a part-time gypsy cab service using a car and cell phone you own anyway), the minimal entry costs and capital outlay mean that the minimum turnover required to pay the overhead and stay in business would be quite modest. In that case, a lot more people would be able to start small businesses for supplementary income and gradually shift some of their wage work to self employment, with minimal risk or sunk costs.

But that's illegal. You have to buy an extremely expensive liquor license, as well as having an industrial sized stove, dishwasher, etc. And that level of capital outlay can only be paid off with a large dining room and a large kitchen-waiting staff, which means you have to keep the place filled or the overhead costs will eat you alive–IOW, Chapter Eleven. These high entry costs and the enormous overhead are the reason you can't afford to start out really small and cheap, and the reason restaurants have such a high failure rate. It's illegal to use the surplus capacity of the ordinary household items we have to own anyway but remain idle most of the time: e.g. RFID chip requirements and bans on unpasteurized milk, high fees for organic certification, etc., which make it prohibitively expensive to sell a few hundred dollars surplus a month from the household economy. You can't do just a few thousand dollars worth of business a year, because the state mandates capital equipment on the scale required for a large-scale business if you engage in the business at all. Roderick Long asks:

> In the absence of licensure, zoning, and other regulations, how many people would start a restaurant *today* if all they needed was their living room and their kitchen? How many people would start a beauty salon *today* if all they needed was a chair and some scissors, combs, gels, and so on? How many people would start a taxi service *today* if all they needed was a car and a cell phone? How many people would start a day care service *today* if a bunch of working parents could simply get together and pool their resources to pay a few of their number to take care of the children of the rest? These are not the sorts of small businesses that receive SBIR awards; they are the sorts of small businesses that get hammered down by the full strength of the state whenever they dare to make an appearance without threading the lengthy and costly maze of the state's permission process.[1]

1. Roderick Long, "Free Market Firms: Smaller, Flatter, and More Crowded," *Cato Unbound*, Nov. 25, 2008 <http://www.cato-unbound.org/2008/11/25/roderick-long/free-market-firms-smaller-flatter-and-more-crowded>.

Employers, as well as big competitors, have a vested interest in keeping entry costs so high. It's a way of erecting an enormous toll gate between you and the possibility of self-employment, without a boss cracking the whip over you.

The social economy enables its participants to evade tribute in another way, as described by Scott Burns in *The Household Economy*. The most enthusiastic celebrations of increased efficiencies from division of labor—like those at Mises.Org—tend to rely on illustrations in which, as Burns puts it, "labor can be directly purchased," or be made the object of direct exchange between the laborers themselves. But in fact,

> [m]arketplace labor must not only bear the institutional burden of taxation, it must also carry the overhead costs of organization and the cost of distribution. Even the most direct service organizations charge two and one-half the cost of labor. The accountant who is paid ten dollars an hour is billed out to clients at twenty-five dollars an hour . . . . When both the general and the specific overhead burdens are considered, it becomes clear that any productivity that accrues to specialization is vitiated by the overhead burdens it must carry.
>
> Consider, for example, what happens when an eight-dollar-an-hour accountant hires an eight-dollar-an-hour service repairman, and vice versa. The repairman is billed out by his company at tow and one-half times his hourly wage, or twenty dollars; to earn this money, the accountant must work three hours and twenty minutes, because 25 per cent of his wages are absorbed by taxes. Thus, to be truly economically efficient, the service repairman must be at least three and one-third times as efficient as the accountant at repairing things.[1]

In other words, in the household and informal economy the division of labor is actually free to operate the way the right-wing libertarian hype says it should, without the overhead costs entailed in organizing it through corporate hierarchy and the wage system. In addition, the two kinds of tribute above interact synergistically: the main function of the regulatory and licensing cartels is to impose a high-overhead business model on what would otherwise be far more competitive operations. The privileged beneficiaries of the licensing system, obviously, don't *want* ordinary people to be able to deal directly with one another at sixty percent less cost.

Networked peer production dovetails both with Jane Jacobs' model of the Japanese bicycle factory, and with Kirkpatrick Sale's community repair, recycling, and remanufacturing shops, which we discussed in Chapter Fourteen. Along the same lines, Paul Goodman suggests

> the pooling of equipment in a neighborhood group. Suppose that each member of the group had a powerful and robust basic tool, while the group as a whole had, for example, a bench drill, lathes and a saw bench to relieve the members from the attempt to cope with work which required these machines with inadequate tools of their own, or wasted their resources on under-used individually-owned plant. This in turn demands some kind of building to house the machinery: the Community Workshop.
>
> But is the Community Workshop idea nothing more than an aspect of the leisure industry, a compensation for the tedium of work?[2]

Ward suggests, rather, that it will bridge the growing gap between the worlds of work and leisure.

> Could [the unemployed] make a livelihood for themselves today in the community workshop? If the workshop is conceived merely as a social service for 'creative leisure' the answer is that it would probably be against the rules . . . . But if the workshop were conceived on more imaginative lines than any existing venture of this kind, its potentiali-

1. Scott Burns, *The Household Economy: Its Shape, Origins, & Future* (Boston: The Beacon Press, 1975), pp. 163-164.

2. Ward, *Anarchy in Action*, p. 94.

ties could become a source of livelihood in the truest sense. In several of the New Towns in Britain, for example, it has been found necessary and desirable to build groups of small workshops for individuals and small businesses engaged in such work as repairing electrical equipment or car bodies, woodworking and the manufacture of small components. The Community Workshop would be enhanced by its cluster of separate workplaces for 'gainful' work. Couldn't the workshop become the community *factory*, providing work or a place for work for anyone in the locality who wanted to work that way, not as an optional extra to the economy of the affluent society which rejects an increasing proportion of its members, but as one of the prerequisites of the worker-controlled economy of the future?

Keith Paton . . . , in a far-sighted pamphlet addressed to members of the Claimants' Union, urged them not to compete for meaningless jobs in the economy which has thrown them out as redundant, but to use their skills to serve their own community. (One of the characteristics of the affluent world is that it denies its poor the opportunity to feed, clothe, or house *themselves*, or to meet their own and their families' needs, except from grudgingly doled-out welfare payments). He explains that:

> . . . [E]lectrical power and 'affluence' have brought a spread of *intermediate* machines, some of them very sophisticated, to ordinary working class communities. Even if they do not own them (as many claimants do not) the possibility exists of borrowing them from neighbours, relatives, ex-workmates. Knitting and sewing machines, power tools and other do-it-yourself equipment comes in this category. Garages can be converted into little workshops, home-brew kits are popular, parts and machinery can be taken from old cars and other gadgets. If they saw their opportunity, trained metallurgists and mechanics could get into advanced scrap technology, recycling the metal wastes of the consumer society for things which could be used again regardless of whether they would fetch anything in a shop. Many hobby enthusiasts could begin to see their interests in a new light.

'We do,' he affirms, '*need* each other and the enormous pool of energy and morale that lies untapped in every ghetto, city district and estate.'[1]

Karl Hess also discussed community workshops—or as he called them, "shared machine shops"—in *Community Technology*.

> The machine shop should have enough basic tools, both hand and power, to make the building of demonstration models or test facilities a practical and everyday activity . . . . [T]he shop might be . . . stocked with cast-off industrial tools, with tools bought from government surplus through the local school system . . . Work can, of course, be done as well in home shops or in commercial shops of people who like the community technology approach . . . .
>
> Thinking of such a shared workshop in an inner city, you can think of its use . . . for the maintenance of appliances and other household goods whose replacement might represent a real economic burden in the neighborhood . . . .
>
> . . . The machine shop could regularly redesign cast-off items into useful ones. Discarded refrigerators, for instance, suggest an infinity of new uses, from fish tanks, after removing doors, to numerous small parts as each discarded one is stripped for its components, which include small compressors, copper tubing, heat transfer arrays, and so on. The same goes for washing machines . . . .

This idea has appeared in the San Francisco Bay area, in a commercial form, as TechShop:[2]

> TechShop is a 15,000 square-foot membership-based workshop that provides members with access to tools and equipment, instruction, and a creative and supportive community of like-minded people so you can build the things you have always wanted to make . . . .

1. Keith Paton, *The Right to Work or the Fight to Live?* (Stoke-on-Trent, 1972), in Ward, *Anarchy in Action*, pp. 108-109.
2. <http://techshop.ws/>.

TechShop provides you with access to a wide variety of machinery and tools, including milling machines and lathes, welding stations and a CNC plasma cutter, sheet metal working equipment, drill presses and band saws, industrial sewing machines, hand tools, plastic and wood working equipment including a 4' x 8' ShopBot CNC router, electronics design and fabrication facilities, Epilog laser cutters, tubing and metal bending machines, a Dimension SST 3-D printer, electrical supplies and tools, and pretty much everything you'd ever need to make just about anything.

Karl Hess linked his idea for a shared machine shop to another idea, "[s]imilar in spirit," the shared warehouse:

> A community decision to share a space in which discarded materials can be stored, categorized, and made easily available is a decision to use an otherwise wasted resource . . . .
>
> The shared warehouse . . . should collect a trove of bits and pieces of building materials . . . . There always seems to be a bundle of wood at the end of any project that is too good to burn, too junky to sell, and too insignificant to store. Put a lot of those bundles together and the picture changes to more and more practical possibilities of building materials for the public space.
>
> Spare parts are fair game for the community warehouse. Thus it can serve as a parts cabinet for the community technology experimenter . . . .
>
> A problem common to many communities is the plight of more resources leaving than coming back in . . . . The shared work space and the shared warehouse space involve a community in taking a first look at this problem at a homely and nonideological level.[1]

This is reminiscent of Jane Jacobs' observations on the development of local, diversified economies through the discovery of creative uses for locally generated waste and by-products, and the use of such innovative technologies to replace imports.

E. F. Schumacher recounted his experiences with the Scott Bader Commonwealth, encouraging (often successfully) the worker-owners to undertake such ventures as a community auto repair shop, communally owned tools and other support for household gardening, a community woodworking shop for building and repairing furniture, and so forth. The effect of such measures was to take off some of the pressure to earn wages, so that workers might scale back their work hours.[2]

Another proposal for decentralizing manufacturing, first to the community and then to the household, is Nathan Cravens' Mutually Assured Production:

> Phase 1. Regional Production. Manufacture general store goods at regional distribution centers every few hundred square miles for local outlet distribution. This approach could be considered the mainframe computer era of material production. It will make obsolete the hundreds of factories that manufacture only a few goods. Accomplishing this would decrease waste created by hundreds of factories and will help turn what may have been wasted in specialized factories into useful material for making other items for use (cradle-to-cradle) in this phase. It will also shift global economies into local ones, providing a production method that can duplicated itself worldwide. Global information with local distribution is the theme.
>
> Phase 2. Outlet Production. In computing, we can liken these systems to mainframes that can contain themselves within an office rather than a whole floor. Manufactured resources will be produced and purchased at each outlet location . . . .

1. Karl Hess, *Community Technology* (New York, Cambridge, Hagerstown, Philadelphia, San Francisco, London, Mexico City, Sao Paulo, Sydney: Harper & Row, Publishers, 1979), pp. 96-98.

2. E. F. Schumacher, *Good Work* (New York, Hagerstown, San Fransisco, London: Harper & Row, 1979), pp. 80-83.

> Phase 3. Personal Production. It can produce anything based on the values men-
> tioned. This likens to the PC, laptop, and hand held device stage of computing . . . .[1]

Eric Hunting suggest, further, that the process of technological innovation under corporate capitalism, in a sort of "Phase 0," is laying the groundwork for this process. The high costs of technical innovation, the difficulty of capturing value from it, and the mass customization or long tail market, taken together, create pressures for common platforms that can be easily customized between products, and for modularization of components that can be used for a wide variety of products. And Hunting points out that the predominant "outsource everything" and "contract manufacturing" model increasingly renders corporate hubs obsolete, and makes it possible for contractees to circumvent the previous corporate principals and undertake independent production on their own account.

> I would like to suggest an additional intermediate stage in production evolution
> prior to regional; the industrial ecology as demonstrated by the personal computer in-
> dustry. Industrial ecologies are precipitated by situations where traditional industrial age
> product development models fail in the face of very high technology development over-
> heads or very high demassification in design driven by desire for personaliza-
> tion/customization producing Long Tail market phenomenon. A solution to these di-
> lemmas is modularization around common architectural platforms in order to compart-
> mentalize and distribute development cost risks, the result being 'ecologies' of many
> small companies independently and competitively developing intercompatible parts for
> common product platforms—such as the IBM PC.
> The more vertical the market profile for a product the more this trend penetrates
> toward production on an individual level due [to] high product sophistication coupled to
> smaller volumes . . . . Competitive contracting regulations in the defense industry (when
> they're actually respected . . .) tend to, ironically, turn many kinds of military hardware
> into open platforms by default, offering small businesses a potential to compete with
> larger companies where production volumes aren't all that large to begin with. Conse-
> quently, today we have a situation where key components of some military vehicles and
> aircraft are produced on a garage-shop production level by companies with fewer than a
> dozen employees.
> All this represents an intermediate level of industrial demassification that is
> underway today and not necessarily dependent upon open source technology or peer-
> to-peer activity but which creates a fertile ground for that in the immediate future and
> drives the complementary trend in the miniaturization of machine tools.[2]

Hunting adds, in an email to the Open Manufacturing list, that this process—"the modularization of product design, which results in the replacement of designs by platforms and the competitive commoditization of their components"—

> is the reason why computers, based on platforms for modular commodity components,
> have evolved so rapidly compared to every other kind of industrial product and why the
> single-most advanced device the human race has ever produced is now something most
> anyone can afford and which a child can assemble in minutes from parts sourced around
> the world.[3]

Michel Bauwens, in commenting on Hunting's remarks, notes among the "underlying trends . . . supporting the emergence of peer production in the physical world,"

---

1. Comment under Michel Bauwens, "Phases for implementing peer production: Towards a Manifesto for Mutually Assured Production," P2P Foundation *Forum*, August 30, 2008 <http://p2pfoundation.ning.com/forum/topic/show?id=2003008%3ATopic%3A6275&page=1&commentId=2003008%3AComment%3A6377&x=1#2003008Comment6377>. See also "MAP," P2P Foundation Wiki <http://p2pfoundation.net/Category:MAP>.

2. Comment under *Ibid*.

3. Eric Hunting, "[Open Manufacturing] Re: Why automate? and opinions on Energy Descent?" September 22, 2008 <http://groups.google.com/group/openmanufacturing?hl=en>.

the 'distribution' of production capacity, i.e. lower capital requirements and modularisation making possible more decentralized and localized production, which may eventually be realized through the free self-aggregation of producers.[1]

The strong implications of these possibilities, for a shift in economic power from large corporations to ordinary people in the social economy, are discussed at greater length in the section immediately following this one.

One potential cloud overshadowing networked peer production is the issue of whether it could survive a disruption to the Internet, in the event the infrastructure of the latter is compromised during the terminal crises of state capitalism. It's heartening, in this light, to remember that fairly extensive computer networks were built from the ground up by private users linking their own computers together over the phone lines, without any central web servers. The PC modem was developed in 1978 by Ward Christensen and Randy Suess to transfer data directly between their computers over the phone lines. In 1979 they introduced the X Modem protocol which allowed computers to transfer files directly without a host system. Based on these technologies, small computer networks sprang up outside the ARPANET. For example, in 1979 three students at Duke and UNC created a modified version of the UNIX protocol which made possible computer linkups over the phone lines. They used it as the infrastructure of Usenet. In 1983, Tom Jennings designed an interface system for posting bulletin boards on interlinked PCs, which became the basis of Fidonet. By 1990, it linked 2500 computers in the U.S. Meanwhile Bulletin Board Systems (BBS) in the 1980s linked several million users into assorted virtual communities, based on direct computer-to-computer connections over the phone lines. Along the same lines, wireless urban "mesh networks" today can use the electromagnetic spectrum to relay data directly from sender to sender, without the content ever passing through a centralized server. Unfortunately, such mesh networks can operate only over a few blocks—at most a single city.[2]

F. THE SOCIAL ECONOMY AND THE CRISIS OF CAPITALISM

As Bauwens describes it, it is becoming increasingly impossible to capture value from the ownership of ideas, designs, and technique—all the "ephemera" and "intellect" that Peters writes about as a component of commodity price—leading to a crisis of sustainability for capitalism.

> Recall the following: the thesis of cognitive capitalism says that we have entered a new phase of capitalism based on the accumulation of knowledge assets, rather than physical production tools. [McKenzie Wark's] vectoralist thesis says that a new class has arisen which controls the vectors of information, i.e. the means through which information and creative products have to pass, for them to realize their exchange value. They both describe the processes of the last 40 years, say the post-1968 period, which saw a furious competition through knowledge-based competition and for the acquisition of knowledge assets, which led to the extraordinary weakening of the scientific and technical commons. And they do this rather well.
>
> But in my opinion, both theses fail to account for the newest of the new, i.e. to take into account the emergence of peer to peer as social format. What is happening?

1. Michel Bauwens, "Contract manufacturing as distributed manufacturing," *P2P Foundation Blog*, September 11, 2008 <http://blog.p2pfoundation.net/contract-manufacturing-as-distributed-manufacturing/2008/09/11>.

2. Manuel Castels, *The Rise of the Network Society*. Second edition (Oxford and Malden, MA: Blackwell Publishers, 1996, 2000), pp. 49-50; Johan Soderberg, *Hacking Capitalism*, pp. 96-97.

In terms of knowledge creation, a vast new information commons is being created, which is increasingly out of the control of cognitive capitalism.[1]

In a later blog post for the P2P Foundation, he elaborated on the nature of cognitive capitalism as a response to the limits on accumulation in the finite physical realm, attempting a new form of accumulation based on ownership of the cognitive realm. But this attempt is doomed to fail because of the increasing untenability of property rights in the information realm.

> This system is now facing serious barriers that are a function of the finiteness of the natural resource base that is our planet, and global warming is one example of it. One of the meanings of global warming, coupled with the general trend of globalization, is that our growth-system now covers the whole planet, there is no more outside. What this means is that the limits of an extensive development are being reached . . . .
>
> This is no trivial affair, as the failure of extensive development is what brought down earlier civilizations and modes of production. For example, slavery was not only marked by low productivity, but could not extend this productivity as that would require making the slaves more autonomous, so slave-based empires had to grow in space, but at a certain point in that growth, the cost of expansion exceeded the benefits. This is why feudalism finally emerged, a system which refocused on the local, and allowed productivity growth as serfs had a self-interest in growing and ameliorating the tools of production.
>
> The alternative to extensive development is intensive development, as happened in the transition from slavery to feudalism. But notice that to do this, the system had to change, the core logic was no longer the same. The dream of our current economy is therefore one of intensive development, to grow in the immaterial field, and this is basically what the experience economy means. The hope that it expresses is that business can simply continue to grow in the immaterial field of experience.

However, Bauwens writes, this is not feasible. The emergence of the peer model of production, based on the non-rivalrous nature and virtually non-existent marginal cost of reproduction of digital information, and coupled with the increasing unenforceability of "intellectual property" laws, means that capital is incapable of realizing returns on ownership in the cognitive realm.

> 1) The creation of non-monetary value is exponential
> 2) The monetization of such value is linear
> In other words, we have a growing discrepancy between the direct creation of use value through social relationships and collective intelligence . . . , but only a fraction of that value can actually be captured by business and money. Innovation is becoming . . . an emergent property of the networks rather than an internal R & D affair within cor-

---

1. Michel Bauwens, *P2P and Human Evolution*. Draft 1.994 (Foundation for P2P Alternatives, June 15, 2005) <http://integralvisioning.org/article.php?story=p2ptheory1>. I believe he was influenced by a point Stefan Merten made in his Oekonux interview with Geert Lovink ("Oekonux: Interview with Stefan Merten," April 24, 2001 <http://www.nettime.org/Lists-Archives/nettime-l-0104/msg00127.html>): Today the material side of material production is rather unimportant even in capitalism. And information is something very different from the material world simply by the fact that you can copy it without losing the original. What is known as the new/Internet/digital economy is indeed the plain old money economy on new territories. What this economy does is to try to make profit from things which are inherently not profitable. The very basis for any profit is scarcity. Since the invention of computers and particularly the Internet, however, scarcity of digital information is difficult to keep. Once a digital information has been produced it is reproducible with extremely marginal cost. This is the reason why information industries of all kinds are making such a fuss about intellectual property rights: IPRs could make digital information a scarce good you then can make profit with. Personally I think the technical means of reproduction, which meanwhile are distributed among millions of households, opened the bottle, the ghost is out and nothing will be able to put it back in there.

porations; capital is becoming an a posteriori intervention in the realization of innovation, rather than a condition for its occurrence . . . .

What this announces is a crisis of value . . . , but also essentially a crisis of accumulation of capital. Furthermore, we lack a mechanism for the existing institutional world to
re-fund what it receives from the social world. So on top of all of that, we have a crisis of
social reproduction . . . .[1]

Thus, while markets and private ownership of physical capital will persist, "the core logic
of the emerging experience economy, operating as it does in the world of non-rival exchange, is unlikely to have capitalism as its core logic."

Soderberg relates the crisis of realization under state capitalism to capital's growing
dependence on the state to capture value from social production and redistribute it to private corporate owners. This takes the form both of "intellectual property" law, as well as
direct subsidies from the taxpayer to the corporate economy. He compares, specifically, the
way photocopiers were monitored in the old USSR to protect the power of elites in that
country, to the way the means of digital reproduction are monitored in this country to
protect corporate power.[2] James O'Connor's theme, of the ever-expanding portion of the
operating expenses of capital which come from the state, is also relevant here.[3] The important point is that this strategy of shifting the burden of realization onto the state is unten-
able. Strong encryption, coupled with the proliferation of bittorrent and episodes like the
DeCSS uprising, have shown that "intellectual property" is ultimately unenforceable. And
as we have already seen, in an economy of subsidized inputs, the demand for such inputs
grows exponentially, faster than the state can meet them. The state capitalist system will
reach a point at which, thanks to the collapse of the portion of value comprised of rents on
artificial property, the base of taxable value is imploding at the very time big business most
needs subsidies to stay afloat.

In another article, in which he develops these themes at greater length, Bauwens
writes that capitalism's successor system is likely to have a significant role for markets, but
that the two structural presuppositions of existing capitalism—artificial abundance of resources and artificial scarcity of information—will be replaced by the reverse.

We live in a political economy that has it exactly backwards. We believe that our
natural world is infinite, and therefore that we can have an economic system based on
infinite growth. But since the material world is finite, it is based on pseudo-abundance.

And then we believe that we should introduce artificial scarcities in the world of
immaterial production, impeding the free flow of culture and social innovation, which is
based on free cooperation, by creating the obstacle of permissions and intellectual property rents protected by the state.

What we need instead is a political economy based on a true notion of scarcity in
the material realm, and a realization of abundance in the immaterial realm.[4]

In the purely immaterial realm, the services of capital are becoming increasingly superfluous, as described by Michael Hardt and Antonio Negri:

. . . the cooperative aspect of immaterial labor is not imposed or organized from the outside, as it was in previous forms of labor, but rather, *cooperation is completely immanent to the
laboring activity itself.* This fact calls into question the old notion (common to classical and

1. Michel Bauwens, "Can the experience economy be capitalist?" *P2P Foundation Blog*, September 27, 2007 <http://blog.p2pfoundation.net/can-the-experience-economy-be-capitalist/ 2007/09/27>.
2. Soderberg, *Hacking Capitalism*, pp. 144-145.
3. James O'Connor, *The Fiscal Crisis of the State* (New York: St. Martin's Press, 1973).
4. Michel Bauwens, "Peer-to-Peer Governance, Democracy, and Economic Vision: P2P as a
Way of Living—Part 2," *Master New Media*, October 27, 2007 <http://www.masternewmedia.org/
information_access / p2p-peer-to-peer-economy / peer—to-peer-governance-production-property-
part-2-Michel-Bauwens-20071020.htm>.

Marxian political economics) by which labor power is conceived as "variable capital," that is, a force that is activated and made coherent only by capital . . . . Brains and bodies still need others to produce value, but the others they need are not necessarily provided by capital and its capacities to organize production. Today productivity, wealth, and the creation of social surpluses take the form of cooperative interactivity through linguistic, communicational, and affective networks.[1]

In addition, capitalism faces a crisis of realization in another regard that Bauwens does not directly address. For over two centuries, as Immanuel Wallerstein observed, the system of capitalist production based on wage labor has depended on the ability to externalize many of its reproduction functions on the non-monetized informal and household economies, and on organic social institutions like the family which were outside the cash nexus.

Historically, capital has relied upon its superior bargaining power to set the boundary between the money and social economies to its own advantage. The household and informal economies have been allowed to function to the extent that they bear reproduction costs that would otherwise have to be internalized in wages; but they have been suppressed (as in the Enclosures) when they threaten to increase in size and importance to the point of offering a basis for independence *from* wage labor.

The employing classes' fear of the subsistence economy made perfect sense. For as Kropotkin asked:

> If every peasant-farmer had a piece of land, free from rent and taxes, if he had in addition the tools and the stock necessary for farm labour—Who would plough the lands of the baron? Everyone would look after his own . . . .
>
> If all the men and women in the countryside had their daily bread assured, and their daily needs already satisfied, who would work for our capitalist at a wage of half a crown a day, while the commodities one produces in a day sell in the market for a crown or more?[2]

"The household as an income-pooling unit," Wallerstein writes, "can be seen as a fortress both of accommodation to and resistance to the patterns of labor-force allocation favored by accumulators." Capital has tended to favor severing the nuclear family household from the larger territorial community or extended kin network, and to promote an intermediate-sized income-pooling household. The reason is that too small a household falls so far short as a basis for income pooling that the capitalist is forced to commodify too large a portion of the means of subsistence, i.e. to internalize the cost in wages.[3] It is in the interest of the employer not to render the worker *totally* dependent on wage income, because without the ability to carry out some reproduction functions through the production of use value within the household subsistence economy, the worker will be "compelled to demand higher real wages . . . ."[4] On the other hand, too large a household meant that "the level of work output required to ensure survival was too low," and "diminished pressure to enter the wage-labor market."[5]

1. Michael Hardt and Antonio Negri, *Empire* (Cambridge and London: Harvard University Press, 2000), p. 294.
2. Peter Kropotkin, *The Conquest of Bread* (New York: Vanguard Press, 1926), pp. 36-37.
3. Immanuel Wallerstein, "Household Structures and Labor-Force Formation in the Capitalist World Economy," in Joan Smith, Immanuel Wallerstein, Hans-Dieter Evers, eds., *Households and the World Economy* (Beverly Hills, London, New Delhi: Sage Publications, 1984), pp. 20-21.
4. Wallerstein and Joan Smith, "Households as an institution of the world-economy," in Smith and Wallerstein, eds., *Creating and Transforming Households: The constraints of the world-economy* (Cambridge; New York; Oakleigh, Victoria; Paris: Cambridge University Press, 1992), p. 16. [3-23]
5. Wallerstein, "Household Structures," p. 20.

The use of the social economy as a base for independence from wage employment has a venerable history. According to E. P. Thompson, "[n]ot only did the benefit societies on occasion extend their activities to the building of social clubs or alms-houses; there are also a number of instances of pre-Owenite trade unions when on strike, employing their own members and marketing the product."[1] G. D. H. Cole describes the same phenomenon:

> As the Trade Unions grew after 1825, Owenism began to appeal to them, and especially to the skilled handicraftsmen . . . . Groups of workers belonging to a particular craft began to set up Co-operative Societies of a different type—societies of producers which offered their products for sale through the Co-operative Stores. Individual Craftsmen, who were Socialists, or who saw a way of escape from the exactions of the middlemen, also brought their products to the stores to sell."[2]
>
> . . . [This pattern of organization was characterized by] societies of producers, aiming at co-operative production of goods and looking to the Stores to provide them with a market. These naturally arose first in trades requiring comparatively little capital or plant. They appealed especially to craftsmen whose independence was being threatened by the rise of factory production or sub-contracting through capitalist middlemen.
>
> The most significant feature of the years we are discussing was the rapid rise of this . . . type of Co-operative Society and the direct entry of the Trades Unions into Co-operative production. Most of these Societies were based directly upon or at least very closely connected with the Unions of their trades, . . . which took up production as a part of their Union activity—especially for giving employment to their members who were out of work or involved in trade disputes . . . .[3]

The aims and overall vision of such organization was well expressed in the rules of the Ripponden Co-operative Society, formed in 1832 in a weaving village in the Pennines:

> The plan of co-operation which we are recommending to the public is not a visionary one but is acted upon in various parts of the Kingdom; we all live by the produce of the land, and exchange labour for labour, which is the object aimed at by all Co-operative societies. We labourers do all the work and produce all the comforts of life;—why then should we not labour for ourselves and strive to improve our conditions.[4]

As the reference to exchanging "labour for labour" suggests, the system of cooperative exchange grew beyond the level of the individual retail store. Cooperative producers' need for an outlet led to Labour Exchanges, where workmen and cooperatives could directly exchange their product so as "to dispense altogether with either capitalist employers or capitalist merchants." Exchange was based on labor time. "Owen's Labour Notes for a time not only passed current among members of the movement, but were widely accepted by private shopkeepers in payment for goods."[5]

The principle of labor-based exchange was employed on a large-scale. In 1830 the London Society opened an Exchange Bazaar for exchange of products between cooperative societies and individuals.[6] The Co-operative Congress, held at Liverpool in 1832, included a long list of trades among its participants (the b's alone had eleven). The National Equitable Labour Exchange, organized in 1832-33 in Birmingham and London, was a venue for the direct exchange of products between craftsmen, using labor-notes as a medium of exchange.[7]

1. Thompson, *Making of the English Working Class*, p. 790.

2. G.D.H. Cole. *A Short History of the British Working Class Movement (1789-1947)* (London: George Allen & Unwin, 1948), p. 76.

3. *Ibid.* p. 78.

4. *Ibid.* pp. 793-794.

5. *Ibid.*, pp. 78-79.

6. *Ibid.*, p. 76.

7. Thompson, *Making of the English Working Class*, p. 791.

The main difference in our day is a revolutionary shift in competitive advantage from wage labor to the informal economy. The rapid growth of technologies for home production in the twentieth century, based on small-scale electrically powered machinery and new forms of intensive cultivation, has radically altered the comparative efficiencies of large- and small-scale production. This was pointed out by Ralph Borsodi almost eighty years ago, and the trend has continued since.

As James O'Connor described the phenomenon in the 1980s, "the accumulation of stocks of means and objects of reproduction within the household and community took the edge off the need for alienated labor."

> Labor-power was hoarded through absenteeism, sick leaves, early retirement, the struggle to reduce days worked per year, among other ways. Conserved labor-power was then expended in subsistence production .... The living economy based on non- and anti-capitalist concepts of time and space went underground: in the reconstituted household; the commune; cooperatives; the single-issue organization; the self-help clinic; the solidarity group. Hurrying along the development of the alternative and underground economies was the growth of underemployment ... and mass unemployment associated with the crisis of the 1980s. "Regular" employment and union-scale work contracted, which became an incentive to develop alternative, localized modes of production ....
>
> ... New social relationships of production and alternative employment, including the informal and underground economies, threatened not only labor discipline, but also capitalist markets .... Alternative technologies threatened capital's monopoly on technological development ... Hoarding of labor-power threatened capital's domination of production. Withdrawal of labor-power undermined basic social disciplinary mechanisms ....[1]

More recently, "Eleutheros," of *How Many Miles from Babylon?* blog, described the sense of freedom that results from a capacity for independent subsistence:

> ... if we padlocked the gate to this farmstead and never had any trafficking with Babylon ever again, we could still grow corn and beans in perpetuity ....
>
> What is this low tech, low input, subsistence economy all about, what does it mean to us? It is much like Jack Sparrow's remark to Elizabeth Swann when ... he told her what the Black Pearl really was, it was freedom. Like that to us our centuries old agriculture represents for us a choice. And having a choice is the very essence and foundation of our escape from Babylon.
>
> ... To walk away from Babylon, you must have choices .... Babylon, as with any exploitative and controlling system, can only exist by limiting and eliminating your choices. After all, if you actually have choices, you may in fact choose the things that benefit and enhance you and your family rather than things that benefit Babylon.
>
> Babylon must eliminate your ability to choose .... First it will offer you false choices in order to distract you from the fact that you have no real choices at all ....
>
> The second way in which Babylon enforces its no-choice policy is when there really is a choice you might make, Babylon convinces you that you really don't have that choice at all. To be able to raise any of our own food we have to borrow money for land, right! You have to go to college, right? Gotta have wheels, gotta have a credit card, right? ...
>
> So I bring up my corn field in way of illustration of what a real choice looks like. We produce ... our staple bread with no input at all from Babylon. So we always have the choice to eat that instead of what Babylon offers. We also buy wheat in bulk and make wheat bread sometimes, but if (when, as it happened this year) the transportation cost or scarcity of wheat makes the price beyond the pale, we can look at it and say, "No, not going there, we will just go home and have our cornbread and beans." Likewise we sometimes buy food from stands and stores, and on a few occasions we eat out. But we always have the choice, and if we need to, we can enforce that choice for months on end ....

1. James O'Connor, *Accumulation Crisis* (New York: Basil Blackwell, 1984), pp. 184–186.

> Your escape from Babylon begins when you can say, "No, I have a choice. Oh, I can dine around Babylon's table if I choose, but if the Babyonian terms and conditions are odious, then I don't have to."[1]

And the payoff doesn't require a total economic implosion. This is a winning strategy even if the money economy and division of labor persist indefinitely to some extent—as I think they almost surely will—and most people continue to get a considerable portion of their consumption needs through money purchases. The end-state, after Peak Oil and the other terminal crises of state capitalism have run their course, is apt to bear a closer resemblance to Warren Johnson's *Muddling Toward Frugality* and Brian Kaller's "Return to Mayberry" than Jim Kunstler's *World Made by Hand*. The knowledge that you are debt-free and own your living space free and clear, and that you *could* keep a roof over your head and food on the table without wage labor indefinitely, if you had to, has an incalculable effect on your bargaining power here and now, even while capitalism persists. As Ralph Borsodi observed almost eighty years ago, his ability to "retire" on the household economy for prolonged periods of time—and potential employers' knowledge that he could do so—enabled him to negotiate far better terms for what outside work he did decide to accept.

Colin Ward, in "Anarchism and the informal economy," envisioned a major shift from wage labor to the household economy:

> [Jonathan Gershuny of the Science Policy Research Unit at Sussex University] sees the decline of the service economy as accompanied by the emergence of a self-service economy in the way that the automatic washing machine in the home can be said to supersede the laundry industry. His American equivalent is Scott Burns, author of *The Household Economy*, with his claim that 'America is going to be transformed by nothing more or less than the inevitable maturation and decline of the market economy. The instrument for this positive change will be the household—the family—revitalized as a powerful and relatively autonomous productive unit'.
>
> The only way to banish the spectre of unemployment is to break free from our enslavement to the idea of employment . . . .
> The first distinction we have to make then is between work and employment. The world is certainly short of jobs, but it has never been, and never will be, short of work . . . . The second distinction is between the regular, formal, visible and official economy, and the economy of work which is not employment . . . .
> . . . Victor Keegan remarks that 'the most seductive theory of all is that what we are experiencing now is nothing less than a movement back towards an informal economy after a brief flirtation of 200 years or so with a formal one'.
> We are talking about the movement of work back into the domestic economy . . . .[2]

Burns, whom Ward cited above, saw the formation of communes, the buying of rural homesteads, and other aspects of the back to the land movement, as an attempt

> to supplant the marketplace entirely. By building their own homes and constructing them to minimize energy consumption, by recycling old cars or avoiding the automobile altogether, by building their own furniture, sewing their own clothes, and growing their own food, they are minimizing their need to offer their labor in the marketplace. They pool it, instead, in the extended household . . . . [T]he new homesteader can internalize 70-80 per cent of all his needs in the household; his money work is intermittent when it can't be avoided altogether.[3]
> . . . Home-working has always been a byword for exploitation, low pay and sweated labour. This is why the trade unions are so hostile towards it. But is by no means a declining industry, and it is possible to reduce its least desirable aspects . . . . The most suggestive

---

1. Eleutheros, "Choice, the Best Sauce," *How Many Miles from Babylon*, October 15, 2008 <http://milesfrombabylon.blogspot.com/2008/10/choice-best-sauce.html>.
2. Colin Ward, "Anarchism and the informal economy," *The Raven* No. 1 (1987), pp. 27-28.
3. Burns, *The Household Economy*, p. 47.

illustration of one of the preconditions for effectively moving industrial production back into the home comes from the many studies of the informal economy in Italy. Sebastino Brusco claimed that it was only the existence of a vast informal sector of small workshops that saved the Italian economy from ruin in the 1970s. He points to the phenomenon of whole villages with power tools sub-contracting for the industrial giants of the motor industry, and when hit by recession, turning to other kinds of industrial components.

A BBC film took us to another Italian industrial village where 80 per cent of the women's tights made in Italy are produced. It illustrated two aspects of the informal economy there: the woman who, using a hand machine, earns a pittance from the contractor who brings her the unfinished goods for assembly and collects them finished, in the classic sweatshop situation; and, as a completely contrasted example, the woman who, with her mother, makes a good living assembling tights in her home, using a sophisticated machine which cost them L5,000 and is now paid for. Brusco claimed that what we were seeing was the decentralisation of manufacturing industry in a way which for him, as for Kropotkin, foreshadowed the pattern of a post-industrial society. Even Kropotkin's combination of industry and agriculture can be found, and is in fact traditional, in Italy. Philip Mattera reports: 'There are even people who have been moonlighting in agriculture. Studies of employees of the few large factories of the South, especially the huge Italsider plant in Taranto, have found that many are using their free time to resume their prior occupation as small farmers.'

The key difference between Brusco's two examples of the tights-makers was that one was trapped in the sweated labour situation and the other was freed from it by increased productivity, in just the same way as do-it-yourself users of power tools have increased theirs. It is of course a matter of access to a very modest amount of credit.[1]

Credit considerations affect the family farmer in a similar manner. The family farm still tends to predominate even in mechanized production, simply because the economies of larger-scale industrial farming under direct corporate ownership and management are so poor, compared to those of a family farm which achieves full utilization of all equipment but can be directly worked by a single family or by a family with the help of hired laborers under their direct supervision.[2] As a result, conventional agriculture is governed by the contract system, in which corporate agribusiness controls "the supply chains between farmers, their input suppliers and, especially, their market." It amounts to a kind of proletarianization on the same pattern as Brusco's first example of the home-work system in Italy, in which the farmer loses control of what and how much to plant, what methods to use, and so forth, and is paid barely enough to make ends meet.[3] As with the putting-out system for making tights in Italy, it's primarily the lack of credit and corporate control of the supply chain that constrain the small producer.

The shift from physical to human capital as the primary source of productive capacity in so many industries, along with the imploding price and widespread dispersion of ownership of capital equipment in so many industries, means that corporate employers are increasingly hollowed out and only maintain control over the physical production process through legal fictions. When so much of actual physical production is outsourced to the small sweatshop or the home shop, the corporation becomes a redundant "node" that can be bypassed; the worker can simply switch to independent production, cut out the middleman, and deal directly with suppliers and outlets. And the exponentially increasing demand for local produce, and the rise of farmers' markets and community-supported agriculture, mean increasing opportunities for family farmers, similarly, to circumvent ADM's and Cargill's control of the supply chains and produce directly for the local market.

1. Ward, "Anarchism and the informal economy," pp. 31-32.
2. Harold Brookfield, "Family Farms Are Still Around: Time to Invert the Old Agrarian Question," *Geography Compass* 2:1 (2008), pp. 114-115.
3. *Ibid.*, pp. 118-119.

We're experiencing a singularity, of sorts, in which it is becoming impossible for capital to prevent a shift in the supply of an increasing proportion of the necessities of life from mass produced goods purchased with wages, to small-scale production in the informal and household sector. The upshot is likely to be something like Vinay Gupta's "Unplugged" movement (see below), in which the possibilities for low-cost, comfortable subsistence off the grid result in exactly the same situation, the fear of which motivated the propertied classes in carrying out the Enclosures: a situation in which the majority of the public can take wage labor or leave it, if it takes it at all, the average person works only on his own terms when he needs supplemental income for luxury goods and the like, and (even if he considers supplemental income necessary in the long run for an optimal standard of living) can afford in the short run to quit work and live off his own resources for prolonged periods of time, while negotiating for employment on the most favorable terms. It will be a society in which workers, not employers, have the greater ability to walk away from the table. It will, in short, be the kind of society Wakefield lamented in the colonial world of cheap and abundant land: a society in which labor is hard to get on any terms, and almost impossible to hire at a low enough wage to produce significant profit.

The potential for defection is heightened by the greater efficiency with which the counter-economy extracts use-value from a given amount of land or capital.

> . . . [T]he owning classes use less efficient forms of production precisely because the state gives them preferential access to large tracts of land and subsidizes the inefficiency costs of large-scale production. Those engaged in the alternative economy, on the other hand, will be making the most intensive and efficient use of the land and capital available to them. So the balance of forces between the alternative and capitalist economy will not be anywhere near as uneven as the distribution of property might indicate.
>
> If everyone capable of benefiting from the alternative economy participates in it, and it makes full and efficient use of the resources already available to them, eventually we'll have a society where most of what the average person consumes is produced in a network of self-employed or worker-owned production, and the owning classes are left with large tracts of land and understaffed factories that are almost useless to them because it's so hard to hire labor except at an unprofitable price. At that point, the correlation of forces will have shifted until the capitalists and landlords are islands in a mutualist sea—and their land and factories will be the last thing to fall, just like the U.S Embassy in Saigon.[1]

Soderberg refers to the possibility that increasing numbers of workers will "defect from the labour market" and "establish means of non-waged subsistence," through efficient use of the waste products of capitalism.[2] The "freegan" lifestyle (less charitably called "dumpster diving") is one end of a spectrum of such possibilities. At the other end is low-cost recycling and upgrading of used and discarded electronic equipment: the rapid depreciation of computers makes it possible to add RAM to a model a few years old at a small fraction of the cost of a new computer, with almost identical performance.

The central barrier to garage production of computers is the microprocessor, which can only be produced on capital equipment costing nearly a billion dollars. But reprogrammable microprocessors will eliminate that barrier, with millions of discarded chips enabling garage industry to operate entirely on recycled inputs in the same way that minimills reprocess scrap steel on a small scale wherever a market exists.

Paul Goodman and Ivan Illich both remarked, in their unique ways, on the effect of radical monopolies in making comfortable poverty impossible. As the alternative economy

1. Kevin Carson, "'Building the Structure of the New Society Within the Shell of the Old,'" *Mutualist Blog: Free Market Anti-Capitalism*, March 22, 2005 <http://mutualist.blogspot.com/2005/03/building-structure-of-new-society.html>.

2. Soderberg, *Hacking Capitalism*, p. 172.

undermines the ability of artificial property rights to levy tribute on access to the means of subsistence, comfortable poverty becomes increasingly feasible.

Dave Pollard, of *How to Save the World* blog, describes his own version of the singularity in "The Virtuous Cycles of the Gift Economy." As people do the things they love and become better at them, it takes less and less money to live. People need to work less, and can devote the saved time not only to further developing production technique. People develop more skills, become more self-sufficient, and less dependent on store-bought commodities purchased with wages. They also invest a greater share of their productive energy in the gift economy and mutual aid, and a greater share of their time in building social capital. As a result, people on average are happier, healthier, and more responsible and competent; social problems and social costs decline, which further adds to the virtuous cycle of reduced cost and frees up more time from work. "These cycles are, of course, subversive. They threaten to undermine and starve the 'market' economy by freeing us, the end-customers of that economy, from the need to pay money into it."[1]

Pollard describes, as one way of bring about major global change, "incapacitation—rendering the old order unable to function by sapping what it needs to survive."[2]

> But suppose if, instead of waiting for the collapse of the market economy and the crumbling of the power elite, we brought about that collapse, guerrilla-style, by making information free, by making local communities energy self-sufficient, and by taking the lead in biotech away from government and corporatists (the power elite) by working collaboratively, using the Power of Many, Open Source, unconstrained by corporate allegiance, patents and 'shareholder expectations'?[3]

Gupta's short story "The Unplugged"[4] related his vision of how such a singularity would affect life in the West.

> To "get off at the top" requires millions and millions of dollars of stored wealth. Exactly how much depends on your lifestyle and rate of return, but it's a lot of money, and it's volatile depending on economic conditions. A crash can wipe out your capital base and leave you helpless, because all you had was shares in a machine.
>
> So we Unpluggers found a new way to unplug: an independent life-support infrastructure and financial architecture—a society within society—which allowed anybody who wanted to "buy out" to "buy out at the bottom" rather than "buying out at the top."
>
> If you are willing to live as an Unplugger does, your cost to buy out is only around three months of wages for a factory worker, the price of a used car. You never need to "work" again—that is, for money which you spend to meet your basic needs.

The idea was to combine "Gandhi's Goals" ("self-sufficiency," or "the freedom that comes from owning your own life support system") with "Fuller's Methods" (getting more from less). Such freedom

> allows us to disconnect from the national economy as a way of solving the problems of our planet one human at a time. But Gandhi's goals don't scale past the lifestyle of a peasant farmer and many westerners view that way of life as unsustainable for them personally . . . .

1. David Pollard, "The Virtuous Cycles of the Gift Economy," *How to Save the World*, December 6, 2006 <http://blogs.salon.com/0002007/2006/12/06.html>. The centerpiece of Pollard's article is a flow chart, which conveys these ideas far more coherently than I can in prose.

2. David Pollard, "All About Power and the Three Ways to Topple It (Part 1)," *How to Save the World*, February 18, 2005 <http://blogs.salon.com/0002007/2005/02/18.html>.

3. Pollard, "All About Power—Part Two," *How to Save the World*," February 21, 2005 <http://blogs.salon.com/0002007///2005/02/21.html>.

4. Vinay Gupta, "The Unplugged," How to Live Wiki, February 20, 2006 <http://howtolivewiki.com/en/The_Unplugged>.

Fuller's "do more with less" was a method we could use to attain self-sufficiency with a much lower capital cost than "buy out at the top." An integrated, whole-systems-thinking approach to a sustainable lifestyle—the houses, the gardening tools, the monitoring systems—all of that stuff was designed using inspiration from Fuller and later thinkers inspired by efficiency. The slack—the waste—in our old ways of life were consuming 90% of our productive labor to maintain.

A thousand dollar a month combined fuel bill is your life energy going down the drain because the place you live sucks your life way in waste heat, which is waste money, which is waste time. Your car, your house, the portion of your taxes which the Government spends on fuel, on electricity, on waste heat . . . all of the time you spent to earn that money is wasted to the degree those systems are inefficient systems, behind best practices!

James L. Wilson, at the Partial Observer, writes of ordinary people seceding from the wage system and meeting as many of their needs as possible locally, primarily as a response to the price increases from Peak Oil—but in so doing, also regaining control of their lives and ending their dependence on the corporation and the state.

Dad laughed. "You're lucky Gramma only lives a few blocks away. When I was your age my grandparents lived 2000 miles away!"

"2000 miles!" Milton, Rose's big brother, gasped. "Did you ever get to see them?"

"Oh, once, maybe twice a year . . . . But then flying got too expensive, and there were horrible experiences with flight delays . . . . And so we tried driving, but it was hard for my parents to both get the vacation days from their jobs at the same time . . . . And anyway, the price of gas got so high that even driving got to be too expensive . . . ."

"But why would they live so far away from you?"

"Because of my grampa's job, and also my Mom's job."

"Why didn't they live closer and have different jobs?'

"Good question. They had to stay with the companies they worked for because that's who paid for their health care."

"Were they slaves, Daddy?"

Dad laughed, "No! No, that's not what . . . nah." But he thought to himself, "Maybe they were, in a way."

★ ★ ★

"Well, you see all these people working on their gardens? They used to not be here. People had grass lawns, and would compete with each other for having the greenest, nicest grass. But your gramma came home from the supermarket one day, sat down, and said, 'That's it. We're going to grow our own food.' And the next spring, she planted a vegetable garden where the grass used to be.

"And boy, were some of the neighbors mad. The Homeowners Association sued her. They said the garden was unsightly. They said that property values would fall. But then, the next year, more people started planting their own gardens.

"And not just their lawns. People started making improvements on their homes, to make them more energy-efficient. They didn't do it to help the environment, but to save money. People in the neighborhood started sharing ideas and working together, when before they barely ever spoke to each other . . . .

"And people also started buying from farmer's markets, buying milk, meat, eggs and produce straight from nearby farmers. This was fresher and healthier than processed food. They realized they were better off if the profits stayed within the community than if they went to big corporations far away.

"This is when your gramma, my Mom, quit her job and opened started a bakery from home. It was actually in violation of the zoning laws, but the people sided with gramma against the government. When the government realized it was powerless to crack down on this new way of life, and the people realized they didn't have to fear the government, they became free. And so more and more people started working from home. Mommies and Daddies used to have different jobs in different places, but now more and more of them are in business together in their own home, where they're close to their children instead of putting them in day care." . . . .

Milton said, "Dad, it sounds like things were a lot worse back then. But some people say that the country is in decline, that we're not as wealthy as we used to be. They say we must restore our national greatness. Is that true?"

Dad said, "It depends on what you mean by wealth. No, people aren't making as much money as they used to. But they don't need to. If you make the things that money used to buy, you don't need the money. If your friends and family and work are close by, you don't need the cars and plane tickets. The people who want to define standard of living in terms of dollar value are missing the point. It's the quality of life that's important, and it's much better now than it's ever been. The people who want to restore "national greatness" don't even know what makes a nation great . . . . We didn't really become free, and this nation didn't really become great, until the government went bankrupt and fell apart."[1]

If anyone thinks Wilson's reference to the "national greatness" argument is a crude caricature, I can assure them it's not. I recall, in the early days of the Iraq War in 2003, hearing what a neoconservative talking head on one of the cable news programs regarded as an important lesson of the war. He saw the apparent success of the attack as an answer to those who touted the shorter work weeks, higher wages, and longer vacations in Europe. Americans, he said, prefer to work longer hours in order to have a more productive economy with higher output, so that "we" can afford to keep carrier groups all over the world. In other words, it's all worth it if our choco-rations get "increased" from thirty to twenty grams a week, if it pays for the vicarious thrill of another Floating Fortress on the Malabar Front. Like the English political economist who drew Coleridge's ire by dismissing a village as "of no importance" because it produced its consumption needs internally and contributed nothing to the national statistics, these people see "the economy" as some entity over and above the quality of life of actual, concrete human beings, and those human beings primarily as means to the end of serving "the economy."

If the coming singularity will enable the producing classes in the industrialized West to defect from the wage system, in the Third World it may enable them to skip that stage of development altogether. Gupta concluded "The Unplugged" with a hint about how the principle might be applied in the Third World: "We encourage the developing world to Unplug as the ultimate form of Leapfrogging: skip hypercapitalism and anarchocapitalism and democratic socialism entirely and jump directly to Unplugging."

Gupta envisions a corresponding singularity in the Third World when the cost of an Internet connection, through cell phones and other mobile devices, falls low enough to be affordable by impoverished villagers. At that point, the transaction costs which hampered previous attempts at disseminating affordable intermediate technologies in the Third World, like Village Earth's Appropriate Technology Library or Schumacher's Intermediate Technology Development Group, will finally be overcome by digital network technology.

It is inevitable that the network will spread everywhere across the planet, or very nearly so. Already the cell phone has reached 50% of the humans on the planet. As technological innovation transforms the ordinary cell phone into a little computer, and ordinary cell services into connections to the Internet, the population of the internet is going to change from being predominantly educated westerners to being mainly people in poorer countries, and shortly after that, to being predominantly people living on a few dollars a day . . . .

. . . Most people are very poor, and as the price of a connection to the Internet falls to a level they can afford, as they can afford cell phones now, we're going to get a chance to really help these people get a better life by finding them the information resources they need to grow and prosper.

---

1. James L. Wilson, "Standard of Living vs. Quality of Life," *The Partial Observer*, May 29, 2008 <http://www.partialobserver.com/article.cfm?id=2955&RSS=1>.

Imagine that you are a poor single mother in South America who lives in a village without a clean water source. Your child gets sick now and again from the dirty water, and you feel there is nothing you can do, and worry about their survival. Then one of your more prosperous neighbors gets a new telephone, and there's a video which describes how to purify water [with a solar purifier made from a two-liter soda bottle]. It's simple, in your language, and describes all the basic steps without showing anything which requires schooling to understand. After a while, you master the basic practical skills—the year or two of high school you caught before having the child and having to work helps. But then you teach your sisters, and none of the kids get sick as often as they used to . . . life has improved because of the network.

Then comes solar cookers, and improved stoves, and preventative medicine, and better agriculture [earlier Gupta mentions improved green manuring techniques], and diagnosis of conditions which require a doctor's attention, with a GPS map and calendar of when the visiting doctors will be in town again.[1]

In Gupta's story, the Unplugger movement included a significant minority of Western society, to the extent that their withdrawal from the consumer market caused economic dislocations. We have already seen, in Chapter One, the Brave New World model of push distribution that the industrial economy depends on, and in Chapter Twelve the amount of employment and economic activity that involve processing subsidized waste—the moral equivalent of digging holes and filling them back in again. It is therefore entirely reasonable to ask, as did one of E. F. Schumacher's questioners:

How do we move in a direction of intermediate technology if, in getting there, we stop growth and go through a world of social collapse and bankruptcy?

Schumacher responded that it would be largely a paper collapse: "Well, I shouldn't worry too much about it."

It's only on the money side, and that's not the real side. It's quite easy if the debtors don't pay. I'm not so terribly worried. If people have too much debt, they ought to default. And the creditors will be extremely angry and call them names, but life goes on. Now, of course, if these things are taken that seriously, then there may be just a general confusion and a depression. That can also happen . . . . It's not my interest, quite frankly. I would like to stick to real things. To the hungry people, to the work opportunities. On the whole, that has little to do with these games played in high finance.[2]

Schumacher's answer is perhaps too glib. The question of the transition period is a real one. There is a very real possibility that the material foundations of the new decentralized economy will not be sufficiently laid down before the old economy's system of circulation breaks down, so that many who are dependent on employment lose their means of support with nothing to take its place. How to manage the transition is far beyond the scope of this analysis. My main purpose has been, first, to show that such a transition is likely, whether we like it or not, as state capitalism reaches its limits and the technical and organizational means of withdrawing from it become available; and second, to show the likely outlines of a successor society based on the new technical and organizational means. My personal opinion, as I have already discussed in Chapter Twelve in regard to the crisis of centralization resulting from Peak Oil, is that the transition will be relatively long and stable, compared to (say) the catastrophic collapse scenarios of James Kunstler.

At any rate, the more widespread the means of subsistence in the informal and household economies, and the more local infrastructure exists for exchange and barter, the more closely the transition crisis will resemble the paper crisis envisioned by Schumacher. For

1. Vinay Gupta, "What's Going to Happen in the Future," *The Bucky-Gandhi Design Institution*, June 1, 2008 <http://vinay.howtolivewiki.com/blog/global/whats-going-to-happen-in-the-future-670>.

2. Discussion of E. F. Schumacher's "The Ethics of Thinking Small," in Dorf and Hunter, eds., p. 182.

someone who has avoided or paid off credit card debt, who has obtained a modest mort-gage and made paying it off as quickly as possible his top priority, and who has a large and productive vegetable garden, the possibility of unemployment is scary. But it's nowhere near as terrifying as for someone who's currently barely making the monthly interest pay-ments on his mortgage, and who's cashed out all his home equity and maxed out all his credit cards buying a Wii and a big-screen TV and getting a new model car every couple years. Even for the creditors and the unemployed described by Schumacher's questioner, having a roof over your head free and clear and a reliable source of food will reduce, to a large extent, the concrete harm from the paper collapse.

My hope, at least, is that conventional measures like GDP will suffer (if only gradually, over a generation) what appears to be a catastrophic implosion, as people simply stop buying shit, cut back on the hours of wage labor they previously worked to earn the money to pay for shit, and supply more and more of their own needs producing for themselves and ex-changing with their neighbors. My hope, at the same time, is that people will be so busy producing for themselves and their neighbors, and enjoying their control over their own lives and work and consumption, that they'll barely notice the collapse.

16

The Social Organization of Distribution, Exchange and Services

A. DEMAND–PULL DISTRIBUTION

We saw in Chapter One that the existing model of artificially expanded market areas and division of labor, overspecialized production machinery and over-capitalization, carries with it all sorts of imperatives like planned obsolescence and a "push" model of distribution—all aimed at maintaining a constant stream of output high enough to eliminate idle capacity in the overbuilt factories. Failing that, it requires the cartelization of industry to permit passing the cost of idle capacity on to the customer through administered pricing. In this environment, Paul Goodman observed,

> . . . the most efficient technical use of machinery is self-defeating: . . . once [the product] has been universally distributed, there is no more demand. (For instance, a great watch manufacturer has said, in a private remark, that in a year he could give everybody in the world a cheap durable watch and shut up shop.) One solution is to build obsolescence in the product . . .[1]

Ralph Borsodi characterized the "push" model of distribution as focused on production rather than consumption.

> With serial production . . . , man has ventured into a topsy-turvy world in which goods that wear out rapidly or that go out of style before they have a chance to be worn out seem more desirable than goods which are durable and endurable. Goods now have to be consumed quickly or discarded quickly so that the buying of goods to take their place will keep the factory busy.[2]

The push model of distribution that resulted from the new mass-production industry of the late nineteenth century was a fundamental departure from the earlier state of producer-customer relations. As Deming said,

> In the olden days, before the industrial era, the tailor, the carpenter, the shoemaker, the milkman, the blacksmith knew his customers by name. He knew whether they were satisfied, and what he should do to improve appreciation for his products.[3]

With the predominance of multiple-purpose production technologies for a variety of short production runs, coupled with worker-ownership and the gearing of production to demand on a just-in-time model, the market incentives would be almost the direct opposite. The central economic pressure for the push economy (the need to make maximum use of expensive, specialized tools) would be eliminated.

---

1. Paul and Percival Goodman. *Communitas: Means of Livelihood and Ways of Life* (New York: Vintage Books, 1947, 1960)., p. 125.
2. Ralph Borsodi. *This Ugly Civilization* (Philadelphia: Porcupine Press, 1929, 1975), pp. 64-65.
3. W. Edwards Deming, *Out of the Crisis* (Cambridge, Mass.: MIT Center for Advanced Engineering Study, 1982, 1986), p. 179.

Under the pull model of distribution, consumption will drive production. Mises' "dollar democracy," long celebrated by so many vulgar libertarians in the face of inconvenient fact, will become a reality: the consumer will really be sovereign. Production will be organized in response to real demand, and the consumer will direct the design of the product. This is especially true of peer group production, but also true of networked local production on the Emilia-Romagna model.

B. LOCAL EXCHANGE SYSTEMS: HOUSEHOLD AND INFORMAL ECONOMIES

The greater the share of consumption needs met through informal (barter, household and gift) economies, the less vulnerable individuals are to the vagaries of the business cycle, and the less dependent on wage labor as well.

Suppose, for the moment, that right-wing libertarians are correct in the exaggerated claims they make for unlimited division of labor and comparative advantage. Suppose that, despite all the evidence in Part One, it really is cheaper for most people to buy most of the things they consume at Wal-Mart, and work for the wages to pay for them. Weigh that against the uncertainty and vulnerability entailed in the quite significant chance of unemployment faced by most people.

As many right-wing libertarians like to remind us, the days of lifetime job security are long past. The "creative destruction" they celebrate means that people in most lines of work can count on downsizing and job changes at the very least several times in a working lifetime, often with prolonged periods of unemployment and debt accumulation between jobs and significant reductions in pay with each move. From the standpoint of people who work for a living, often mired in credit card debt, keeping their heads above water only by augmenting their purchasing power with the cash value of inflated home equity, a paycheck or two from homelessness or bankruptcy, the flux of the new economy is a lot less exhilarating.

And bear in mind that many of the same people who denigrate artisan or subsistence labor, most notably the Misoids, are not only the same people who celebrate the "creative destruction" that undermines economic security for so many people. They also regularly make the most apocalyptic predictions about credit inflation by central banks, the bursting of the housing bubble, and the Misesean "crackup boom." No little inconsistency when those attitudes are laid side by side.

The ability to meet one's own consumption needs with one's own labor, using one's own land and tools, is something that can't be taken away by a recession or a corporate decision to offshore production to China (or just to downsize the work force and speed up work for the survivors). The ability to trade one's surplus for other goods, with a neighbor also using his own land and tools, is also much more secure than a job in the capitalist economy.

Imagine an organic truck farmer who barters produce for plumbing services from a self-employed tradesman living nearby. Neither the farmer nor the plumber can dispose of his full output in this manner, or meet all of his subsistence needs. But both together have a secure and reliable source for all their plumbing *and* vegetable needs, and a reliable outlet for the portion of the output of each that is consumed by the other. The more trades and occupations brought into the exchange system, the greater the portion of total consumption needs of each that can be reliably met within a stable sub-economy. At the same time, the less dependent each person is on outside wage income, and the more prepared to weather a prolonged period of unemployment in the outside wage economy.

Borsodi described the cumulative effect of the concatenation of uncertainties in an economy of large-scale factory production for anonymous markets:

Surely it is plain that no man can afford to be dependent upon some other man for the bare necessities of life without running the risk of losing all that is most precious to him. Yet that is precisely and exactly what most of us are doing today. Everybody seems to be dependent upon some one else for the opportunity to acquire the essentials of life. The factory-worker is dependent upon the man who employs him; both of them are dependent upon the salesmen and retailers who sell the goods they make, and all of them are dependent upon the consuming public, which may not want, or may not be able, to buy what they may have made.[1]

Subsistence, barter, and other informal economies, by reducing the intermediate steps between production and consumption, also reduce the contingency involved in consumption. If the realization of capital follows a circuit, as described by Marx in *Capital*, the same is also true of labor. And the more steps in the circuit, the more likely the circuit is to be broken, and the realization of labor (the transformation of labor into use-value, through the indirect means of exchanging one's own labor for wages, and exchanging those wages for use-value produced by someone else's labor) is to fail. Marx, in *The Poverty of Philosophy*, pointed out long ago that the disjunction of supply from demand, which resulted in the boom–bust cycle, was inevitable given the large-scale production under industrial capitalism:

> . . . [This true proportion between supply and demand] was possible only at a time when the means of production were limited, when the movement of exchange took place within very restricted bounds. With the birth of large-scale industry this true proportion had to come to an end, and production is inevitably compelled to pass in continuous succession through vicissitudes of prosperity, depression, crisis, stagnation, renewed prosperity, and so on.
>
> Those who . . . wish to return to the true proportion of production, while preserving the present basis of society, are reactionary, since, to be consistent, they must also wish to bring back all the other conditions of industry of former times.
>
> What kept production in true, or more or less true, proportions? It was demand that dominated supply, that preceded it. Production followed close on the heels of consumption. Large-scale industry, forced by the very instruments at its disposal to produce on an ever-increasing scale, can no longer wait for demand. Production precedes consumption, supply compels demands.[2]

Where Marx went wrong was his assumption that large-scale industry, and production that preceded demand on the push model, were necessary for a high standard of living.

A decentralized economy, in which most production is small-scale and for local use, is ideal for the stable coordination of supply to demand. As Paul Goodman wrote,

> such a tight local economy is essential if there is to be a close relation between production and consumption, for it means that prices and the value of labor will not be so subject to the fluctuations of the vast general market . . . . That is, within limits, the nearer a system gets to simple household economy, the more it is an economy of specific things and services that are bartered, rather than an economy of generalized money.[3]

Leopold Kohr, in the same vein, compared local economies to harbors in a storm in their insulation from the business cycle and its extreme fluctuations of price.[4]

Ebenezer Howard, in his vision of Garden Cities, argued that the overhead costs of risk and distribution (as well as rent, given the cheap rural land on which the new towns

1. Ralph Borsodi. *Flight from the City: An Experiment in Creative Living on the Land* (New York, Evanston, San Francisco, London: Harper & Row, 1933, 1972), p. 147.

2. Karl Marx. *The Poverty of Philosophy*, Marx and Engels *Collected Works*, vol. 6 (New York: International Publishers, 1976).

3. Paul and Percival Goodman, *Communitas*, p. 170.

4. Leopold Kohr, *The Overdeveloped Nations: The Diseconomies of Scale* (New York: Schocken Books, 1977), p. 110.

would be built) would be far lower for both industry and retailers serving the less volatile local markets.

> They might even sell considerably below the ordinary rate prevailing elsewhere, but yet, having an assured trade and being able very accurately to gauge demand, they might turn their money over with remarkable frequency. Their working expenses, too, would be absurdly small. They would not have to advertise for customers, though they would doubtless make announcements to them of any novelties; but all that waste of effort and of money which is so frequently expended by tradesmen in order to secure customers or to prevent their going elsewhere, would be quite unnecessary.[1]

The importance of subsistence production as an economic cushion is illustrated by the Depression-era Homestead Unit project in the Dayton area, an experiment with household and community production in which Borsodi played a prominent organizing role. Despite some early success, it was eventually killed off by Harold Ickes, a technocratic liberal who wanted to run the homestead project along the same centralist lines as the Tennessee Valley Authority. The Homestead Units were built on cheap land in the countryside surrounding Dayton, with a combination of three-acre family homesteads and some division of labor on other community projects. The family homestead included garden, poultry and other livestock, and a small orchard and berry patch. The community provided woodlot and pasture, in addition.[2] A Unit Committee vice president in the project described the economic security resulting from subsistence production:

> There are few cities where the independence of a certain sort of citizen has not been brought into relief by the general difficulties of the depression. In the environs of all cities there is the soil-loving suburbanite. In some cases these are small farmers, market gardeners and poultry raisers who try to make their entire living from their little acres. More often and more successful there is a combination of rural and city industry. Some member of the family, while the others grow their crops, will have a job in town. A little money, where wages are joined to the produce of the soil, will go a long way . . . .
>
> When the depression came most of these members of these suburban families who held jobs in town were cut in wages and hours. In many cases they entirely lost their jobs. What, then, did they do? . . . . The soil and the industries of their home provided them . . . work and a living, however scant. Except for the comparatively few dollars required for taxes and a few other items they were able, under their own sail, to ride out the storm. The sailing was rough, perhaps; but not to be compared with that in the wreck-strewn town . . . .
>
> Farming as an exclusive business, a full means of livelihood, has collapsed . . . . Laboring as an exclusive means of livelihood has also collapsed. The city laborer, wholly dependent on a job, is of all men most precariously placed. Who, then, is for the moment safe and secure? The nearest to it is this home and acres-owning family in between, which combines the two.[3]

An interesting experiment in restoring the "circuit of labor" through barter exchange was Depression-era organizations like the Unemployed Cooperative Relief Organization and Unemployed Exchange Association:

1. Ebenezer Howard, *To-Morrow: A Peaceful Path to Real Reform.* Facsimile of original 1998 edition, with introduction and commentary by Peter Hall, Dennis Hardy and Colin Ward (London and New York: Routledge, 2003), pp. 100, 102 [facsimile pp. 77-78].

2. Ralph Borsodi, *The Nation*, April 19, 1933; reproduced in *Flight From the City*, pp. 154-59. Incidentally, the New Town project in Great Britain was similarly sabotaged, first under the centralizing social-democratic tendencies of Labour after WWII, and then by Thatcherite looting (er, "privatization") in the 1980s. Ward commentary, Howard, *To-Morrow*, p. 45.

3. Editorial by Walter Locke in *The Dayton News*, quoted by Borsodi in *Flight From the City*, pp. 170-71.

. . . The real economy was still there—paralyzed but still there. Farmers were still producing, more than they could sell. Fruit rotted on trees, vegetables in the fields. In January 1933, dairymen poured more than 12,000 gallons of milk into the Los Angeles City sewers every day.

The factories were there too. Machinery was idle. Old trucks were in side lots, needing only a little repair. All that capacity on the one hand, legions of idle men and women on the other. It was the financial casino that had failed, not the workers and machines. On street corners and around bare kitchen tables, people started to put two and two together. More precisely, they thought about new ways of putting two and two together . . . .

In the spring of 1932, in Compton, California, an unemployed World War I veteran walked out to the farms that still ringed Los Angeles. He offered his labor in return for a sack of vegetables, and that evening he returned with more than his family needed. The next day a neighbor went out with him to the fields. Within two months 500 families were members of the Unemployed Cooperative Relief Organization (UCRO).

That group became one of 45 units in an organization that served the needs of some 150,000 people.

It operated a large warehouse, a distribution center, a gas and service station, a refrigeration facility, a sewing shop, a shoe shop, even medical services, all on cooperative principles. Members were expected to work two days a week, and benefits were allocated according to need . . . .

The UCRO was just one organization in one city. Groups like it ultimately involved more than 1.3 million people, in more than 30 states. It happened spontaneously, without experts or blueprints. Most of the participants were blue collar workers whose formal schooling had stopped at high schools. Some groups evolved a kind of money to create more flexibility in exchange. An example was the Unemployed Exchange Association, or UXA, based in Oakland, California . . . . UXA began in a Hooverville . . . called "Pipe City," near the East Bay waterfront. Hundreds of homeless people were living there in sections of large sewer pipe that were never laid because the city ran out of money. Among them was Carl Rhodehamel, a musician and engineer.

Rhodehamel and others started going door to door in Oakland, offering to do home repairs in exchange for unwanted items. They repaired these and circulated them among themselves. Soon they established a commissary and sent scouts around the city and into the surrounding farms to see what they could scavenge or exchange labor for. Within six months they had 1,500 members, and a thriving sub-economy that included a foundry and machine shop, woodshop, garage, soap, factory, print shop, wood lot, ranches, and lumber mills. They rebuilt 18 trucks from scrap. At UXA's peak it distributed 40 tons of food a week.

It all worked on a time-credit system . . . . Members could use credits to buy food and other items at the commissary, medical and dental services, haircuts, and more. A council of some 45 coordinators met regularly to solve problems and discuss opportunities.

One coordinator might report that a saw needed a new motor. Another knew of a motor but the owner wanted a piano in return. A third member knew of a piano that was available. And on and on. It was an amalgam of enterprise and cooperation—the flexibility and hustle of the market, but without the encoded greed of the corporation or the stifling bureaucracy of the state . . . . The members called it a "reciprocal economy." . . . .

Today, the signs of financial and ecological collapse are mounting. We are strung out on foreign debt and foreign oil, and riding real estate inflation that won't last forever . . . . In this setting, the economics of self-help are increasingly relevant. The possibility of creating such an economy, though, might seem remote. In the 1930s, there were still farms on the outskirts of cities—family operations that could make barter deals on the spot. Factories were nearby too. Products were simple and made to last, and so could be scavenged and repaired.

All that has changed. The factories are in China, the farms are owned by corporations, and you can't walk to them from Los Angeles anymore. Products are made to break; the local repair shop is a distant memory. Hyper-sophisticated technology has put local mechanics out of business, let alone backyard tinkerers . . . .

Yet there are trends on the other side as well. Energy technology is moving back to the local level, by way of solar, wind, biodiesel and the rest. The popularity of organics has given a boost to smaller farms. There's also the quiet revival of urban agriculture. Community gardens are booming—some 6,000 of them in 38 U.S. cities. In Boston, the Food Project produces over 120,000 pounds of vegetables on just 21 acres. Then consider the unused land in U.S. cities: some 70,000 vacant parcels in Chicago, 31,000 in Philadelphia.[1]

Stewart Burgess, in a 1933 article, described a day's produce intake by the warehouse of Unit No. 1 in Compton. It included some fifteen different kinds of fruits and vegetables, including two tons of cabbage and seventy boxes of pears, all the way down to a single crate of beets—not to mention a sack of salt. The production facilities and the waste materials it used as inputs foreshadow the ideas of Colin Ward, Kirkpatrick Sale and Karl Hess on community warehouses and workshops, discussed in the last chapter:

> In this warehouse is an auto repair shop, a shoe-repair shop, a small printing shop for the necessary slips and forms, and the inevitable woodpile where cast-off railroad ties are sawed into firewood. Down the street, in another building, women are making over clothing that has been bartered in. In another they are canning vegetables and fruit—Boy Scouts of the Burbank Unit brought in empty jars by the wagon-load.[2]

Claude Lewenz's Villages are designed to generate 80% of their income internally and 20% externally, with internally generated wealth circulating five times before it leaves the community.

> The local economy is layered, built on a foundation that provides the basic needs independent of the global economy—if it melts down the Villagers will survive. The local economy is diversified . . . . The local economy must provide conditions that encourage a wide diversity of businesses and officers to operate. Then when some collapse or move away, the local economy only suffers a bit—it remains healthy.[3]

Lewenz's Village is also essentially the kind of "resilient community" John Robb and Jeff Vail have in mind:

> . . . [E]conomies can collapse and first-world people can starve if systems fail. We have now built a food system almost entirely dependent on diesel fuelled tractors, diesel delivery trucks and a long-distance supermarket delivery system. More recently, we shifted to an economic and communication system entirely dependent on computers—a system that only runs if the electrical grid supplies power. In the Great Depression in the USA, poor people say they hardly noticed—in those days they kept gardens because the USA was predominantly rural and village. The potential for economic collapse always looms, especially as the global economic system becomes more complex and vulnerable. Prudence would dictate that in planning for a local economy, it include provisions to assure the Village sustained its people, and those of the surrounding region, in such adverse conditions.
>
>   The challenge is to maintain a direct rural and farm connection for local, good food, and establish an underlying local economy that can operate independent of the larger economy and which can put unemployed people to work in hard times.[4]

Borsodi described, from his own personal experience, the greatly increased bargaining power of labor when the worker has the ability to walk away from the table:

> . . . . Eventually income began to go up as I cut down the time I devoted to earning money, or perhaps it would be more accurate to say I was able to secure more for my time as I became less and less dependent upon those to whom I sold my services . . . . This possibility of earning more, by needing to work less, is cumulative and is open to an immense number of professional workers. It is remarkable how much more appreciative

    1. Jonathan Rowe, "Entrepreneurs of Cooperation," *Yes!*, Spring 2006 <http://www.yesmagazine.org/article.asp?ID=1464>.

    2. J. Stewart Burgess, "Living on a Surplus," *The Survey* 68 (January 1933), p. 6.

    3. Claude Lewenz, *How to Build a Village* (Auckland, New Zealand: Village Forum Press and Jackson House Publishing Company, 2007), p. 73.

    4. *Ibid.*, p. 77.

of one's work employers and patrons become when they know that one is independent enough to decline unattractive commissions. And of course, if the wage-earning classes were generally to develop this sort of independence, employers would have to compete and bid up wages to secure workers instead of workers competing by cutting wages in order to get jobs.[1]

. . . . Economic independence immeasurably improves your position as a seller of services. It replaces the present "buyer's market" for your services, in which the buyer dictates terms with a "seller's market," in which you dictate terms. It enables you to pick and choose the jobs you wish to perform and to refuse to work if the terms, conditions, and the purposes do not suit you. The next time you have your services to sell, see if you cannot command a better price for them if you can make the prospective buyer believe that you are under no compulsion to deal with him.[2]

. . . [T]he terms upon which an exchange is made between two parties are determined by the relative extent to which each is free to refuse to make the exchange . . . . The one who was "free" (to refuse the exchange), dictated the terms of the sale, and the one who was "not free" to refuse, had to pay whatever price was exacted from him.[3]

At the same time, communities of locally owned small enterprises are much healthier economically than communities that are colonized by large, absentee-owned corporations. For example, a 1947 study compared two communities in California: one a community of small farms, and the other dominated by a few large agribusiness operations. The small farming community had higher living standards, more parks, more stores, and more civic, social and recreational organizations.[4]

Bill McKibben made the same point in *Deep Economy*. Most money that's spent buying stuff from a national corporation is quickly sucked out of the local economy, while money that's spent at local businesses circulates repeatedly in the local economy and leaks much more slowly to the outside. According to a study in Vermont, substituting local production for only ten percent of imported food would create $376 million in new economic output, including $69 million in wages at over 3600 new jobs. A similar study in Britain found the multiplier effect of ten pounds spent at a local business benefited the local economy to the tune of 25 pounds, compared to only 14 for the same amount spent at a chain store.

> The farmer buys a drink at the local pub; the pub owner gets a car tune-up at the local mechanic; the mechanic brings a shirt to the local tailor; the tailor buys some bread at the local bakery; the baker buys wheat for bread and fruit for muffins from the local farmer. When these businesses are not owned locally, money leaves the community at every transaction.[5]

C. CERTIFICATION, LICENSING AND TRUST

Without the current role of the state and other centralized institutions in overcoming the transaction costs of certifying quality and credit-worthiness, what is called "goodwill," or reputational effects, would likely take on much greater importance, with the patterns of exchange in local economies coalescing around social networks. This, too, would be a beneficial social effect of economic decentralization. Adem Kupi remarks on the role of the

1. Borsodi, *Flight From the City*, p. 100.
2. Borsodi, *This Ugly Civilization*, p. 335.
3. *Ibid.*, p. 403.
4. L. S. Stavrianos. *The Promise of the Coming Dark Age* (San Francisco: W. H. Freeman and Company, 1976), p. 41.
5. Bill McKibben, *Deep Economy: The Wealth of Communities and the Durable Future* (New York: Times Books, 2007), p. 165.

state in artificially lowering the transaction costs involved in establishing trust, underwriting risk, etc., in the anonymous transactions that occur in large markets:

> ... The Security State makes it too easy for people to stop thinking. In fact, it penalizes "over-thinking" by shortening time horizons. We just don't have time to think too much about anything, and we don't have enough options to weigh. They've done the thinking for us and pre-limited our options . . . .
>
> In the skeptical society, on the other hand, trust has to be earned, and people will rely on their local social networks to provide them with accurate information. Honesty, and not bullshit, will become the most valuable commodity. "Authority" as such will be scorned, unless it is backed up by a great deal of legitimate evidence. People will think more and do less, because that will be the only way to deal with risk. In the process, wealth will localize. No more vast towers of concentrated power. Production will become more interdependent, and decentralized, because no particular group will be able to sustain large-scale production, and thus no one will be denied the opportunity for small scale production . . . .
>
> The current growing ratio of noise to signal is putting pressure on the world to become more skeptical, which will put pressure on societies to shift away from guaranteeing security. They just won't be able to do it effectively. The idea of managing anything larger than a local area will become preposterous.[1]

Even in the present economy, organization theory blogger quasibill writes of the benefits of fraternal organizations in facilitating exchange between their members. Newsletters contain ads "from members who market their small businesses to each other (contracting, printing, landscaping, etc.)" Quasibill asked a friend in a fraternal organization whether such ads paid off. The answer was "yes":

> He noted that most members preferred doing business within the organization because there was a social peer enforcement mechanism at work. Specifically, he noted that while a vendor might be willing to "work to rule" with many customers, or even be willing to file bankruptcy against general creditors, the social peer pressure that could be exerted through the organization made dealings within the organization more fair and certain. You could win your case in court on a legal technicality, but if the members of the organization determined that you weren't acting fairly, you were going to be ostracized from the organization before you could turn your head.[2]

The same was true, to a large extent, in the old Main Street business culture, when local merchants and tradesmen depended on repeat business from people they knew. Eric Frank Russell's story of Idle Jack, in "And Then There Were None," is relevant here. The world in which the story takes place was founded by Gandhian refuges from the Terran Empire centuries before, and is organized more or less along the lines of market anarchy suggested by Josiah Warren. Land ownership is based on occupancy and use—no landlords—and the economy is based on a sort of labor exchange system ("obligations" or "obs"). A visitor wondered what the penalties were for running up obligations and then refusing to meet them. The answer took the form of a traditional morality lesson, the tale of Idle Jack, a "scratcher" ('One who lives by accepting obs but does nothing about wiping them out or planting any of his own.').

> 'Up to age sixteen Jack got away with it all along the line. He was only a kid, see? All kids tend to scratch to a certain extent. We expect it and allow for it. But after sixteen he was soon in the soup . . . .

1. Adem Kupi, "The Security State vs. the Skeptical Society," *A Pox on All Their Houses*, July 12, 2005 <http://poxyhouses.blogspot.com/2005/07/security-state-vs-skeptical-society.html>.

2. Quasibill, "Function Follows Form, or Vice Versa (except if either one contradicts your pre-determined outcomes)," *The Bell Tower*, June 10, 2008 <http://the-bell-tower.blogspot.com/2008/06/function-follows-form-or-vice-versa.html>.

'He loafed around the town gathering obs by the armful. Meals, clothes and all sorts for the mere asking. It wasn't a big town. There are no big ones on this planet. They are just small enough for everybody to know everybody—and everyone does plenty of gabbing. Within a few months the entire town knew that Jack was a determined and incorrigible scratcher . . . .

'Everything dried up . . . . Wherever Jack went people gave him the, "I won't." He got no meals, no clothes, no company, no entertainment, nothing. He was avoided like a leper. Soon be became terribly hungry, busted into someone's larder one night, treated himself to the first square meal in a week.'

'What did they do about that?'

'Nothing, not a thing.'

'That must have encouraged him some, mustn't it?'

'How could it?' asked Seth with a thin smile. 'It did him no good. Next day his belly was empty again. He was forced to repeat the performance. And the next day. And the next. People then became leery, locked up their stuff and kept watch on it. Circumstances grew harder and harder. They grew so unbearably hard that soon it was a lot easier to leave the town and try another one . . . .'

'To do the same again,' Harrison prompted.

'With the same results for the same reasons,' Seth threw back at him. 'On he went to a third town, a fourth, a fifth, a twentieth. He was stubborn enough to be witless.'

'But he was getting by,' Harrison insisted. 'Taking all for nothing at the cost of moving around.'

'Oh, no he wasn't. Our towns are small, as I said. And people do plenty of visiting from one to another. In the second town Jack had to risk being seen and talked about by visitors from the first town. In the third town he had to cope with talkers from both the first and second ones. As he went on it became a whole lot worse. In the twentieth he had to chance being condemned by anyone coming from any of the previous nineteen . . . . He never reached town number twenty-eight.'[1]

Social guarantees of trust become especially important if we reject the role of the state in enforcing debts on borrowers, under bankruptcy law. Dean Baker points out, in rather colorful language, the nature of strict bankruptcy laws as a form of welfare for the rich:

> In a free market economy, businesses know that investment decisions don't always work out as expected. Sometimes businesses invest in developing a product . . . that doesn't have the market they anticipated. They may invest based on trends, such as rising oil prices, that do not continue, leaving them with large losses. Or, they may extend credit to people . . . that turn out to be bad credit risks. No one expects that the government will step in and sustain the demand for a bad product. Nor do we expect the government to intervene to make sure investors' expectations about rising oil prices are realized, for example, by buying up massive amounts of petroleum. But when it comes to making bad credit decisions, the nanny state conservatives do expect the government to step in and bail them out.
>
> The nanny state conservatives think that it is the role of the government to act as a strong-arm debt collector for businesses that did not accurately assess the risks associated with their loans . . . . They want the government to chase after individual debtors, following them throughout their lives, to wring out every possible cent of debt repayment . . . .
>
> . . . [I]nstead of having the incompetent lenders go out of business . . . the conservative nanny state stepped in to bail them out with the 2005 bankruptcy law, using the force of the government to squeeze every last cent from debtors. Under the new bankruptcy laws, the government will monitor debtors for many years after they have declared bankruptcy, seizing assets or garnishing wages for debts that may have been incurred 20 or 30 years in the past . . . .
>
> . . . Historically, most loans required little involvement from the government because they were attached to physical property such as land, a house, or a car. If a debtor

1. Eric Frank Russell, "And Then There Were None," *Astounding Science Fiction*, vol. XLVII, no.4 (June 1951) <http://www.abelard.org/e-f-russell.php>.

had fallen behind on his payments, then the role of the court in the debt collection process was essentially a one-time proposition: the court would simply require the debtor to turn over ownership of the relevant asset to the creditor, and the case would be over . . . .

However, in the last two decades there has been an explosion of debt, mostly credit card debt, that is not secured by a physical asset . . . .[1]

Lysander Spooner denied that unsecured debt had any legal obligation beyond the debtor's ability to pay at the time of bankruptcy. "The law requires no impossibilities from any man. If a man contract to perform what proves to be an impossibility, the contract is valid only for so much as is possible . . . ." It was the creditor's responsibility to judge the debtor's ability to repay *before* loaning money.[2]

Murray Rothbard argued, based on the inalienability of moral agency, that promises were legally unenforceable. But he made an exception for debts, treating default on a debt as a fraud on the assumption that the borrower at the outset undertook an obligation to repay with a deliberate intent to default. In that case, his acceptance of funds or goods on false pretenses amounted to theft, and he is liable for restitution.

> We shall see that fraud may be considered as theft, because one individual receives the other's property but does not fulfill his part of the exchange bargain, thereby taking the other's property without his consent . . . . Contract must be considered as an agreed-upon exchange between two persons of two goods, present or future . . . . Failure to fulfill contracts must be considered as theft of the other's property. Thus, when a debtor purchases a good in exchange for a promise of future payment, the good cannot be considered his property until the agreed contract has been fulfilled and payment made. Until then, it remains the creditor's property, and nonpayment would be equivalent to theft of the creditor's property . . . .
>
> An important consideration here is that contract *not* be enforced because a promise has been made that is not kept. It is not the business of the enforcing agency or agencies in the free market to enforce promises merely because they are promises; its business is to enforce against theft of property, and contracts are enforced because of the implicit theft involved.
>
> Evidence of a *promise to pay property* is an enforceable claim, because the possessor of this claim is, in effect, the owner of the property involved, and failure to redeem the claim is equivalent to theft of the property.[3]

But as blogger quasibill argued, the borrower's subjective intent to defraud is a question on which the lender has the burden of proof.

> . . . Professor Rothbard . . . starts with an insight that he quickly backtracks on: "while it may well be the moral thing to keep one's promises, . . . it is not and cannot be the function of law . . . in a libertarian system to enforce morality. After providing this insight, however, Rothbard resorts to the metaphysical concept of title to transform an unenforceable promise into an enforceable condition of ownership transfer.
>
> Rothbard does not make clear just what is the fundamental distinction between a promise and a condition . . . . He merely states that a condition creates an incomplete transfer of title to another person, whereby the failure of keeping the promise, or condition, turns the breacher into a thief!
>
> This . . . stretches the definition of thief beyond anything any normal person would ever recognize. First, even Rothbard would admit that no violence has occurred in the transaction. Possession of the item was transferred voluntarily. Along the same lines, posses-

1. Dean Baker, *The Conservative Nanny State: How the Wealthy Use the Government to Stay Rich and Get Richer* (Washington, D.C.: Center for Economic and Policy Research, 2000), pp. 59-61.

2. Lysander Spooner, *Poverty: Its Illegal Causes and Legal Cure* (Boston: Bela Marsh, 1846) <http://www.lysanderspooner.org/Poverty.htm>.

3. Murray Rothbard. *Man, Economy, and State: A Treatise on Economic Principles* (Auburn, Ala.: The Ludwig von Mises Institute, 1962, 1970, 1993), pp. 152-153.

sion was given with the full knowledge of the original possessor, so it cannot be analogized to a pick-pocket or other non-violent theft. Given these conditions, Rothbard attempts to shoe-horn the circumstances into the concept of legal fraud. However . . . even this fails, as the failure to keep a promise, by itself, does not meet the legal definition of fraud.

Generally speaking, fraud requires an intentional misrepresentation of material fact, upon which a victim relies to their detriment . . . . Mere failure to perform a future condition is not, by itself, an intentional misrepresentation of material fact. The promisor may full well intend to fulfill his promise at the time he makes it. As such, it can't be said that his statement was an intentional misrepresentation. This insight is so basic that most jurisdictions have rules that require more than a mere failure to perform in order to establish an intentional misrepresentation.

Leaving aside legal formalities, it is clear that Rothbard's argument fails from a deontological viewpoint as well. If we view contract negotiation as the art of risk allotment, as most contract drafters do, we can understand the ethical standing of the parties involved. The original property owner, who transfers possession to another in return for a promise, is implicitly accepting the risk that the promise won't be performed. If he didn't accept the risk, he would retain possession until the promise was performed.

It is clear that, even under current contract law, or even Rothbard's proposed law, such risk allotment occurs regardless of any language in a contract governing the transfer. For example, if, after the transfer of a car contingent upon the future payment of a set sum, the transferee dies in a crash that wrecks the car, the transferor has, in all likelihood, lost all recourse through no act of aggression or deceit on the part of the transferee. He took this risk, whether he knew it or not. This concept of risk allocation is well detailed in the history of the legal concept of impossibility . . . .

So the answer appears to be that the best conflict avoiding contract law system is one where possession is, in effect, 9/10 of the law. The only exception is where possession was obtained through aggression, intentional deceit, or theft (of the pickpocket variety). Those parties who engage in voluntary transactions are free to write contracts detailing the terms of their agreement. However, the legal system will not employ legalized violence to enforce such promises. While it may be moral to keep such promises, and reputation for keeping promises may become a social good that is much sought after, it will not be a concern of the legal system.[1]

. . . . In actuality, a loan agreement involves a transaction whereby lender gives property in exchange for a promise of future performance. The contract is "complete" at that moment. The lender is in complete control of this, BTW—he can refuse to transfer the property until he is subjectively assured of the value of the promise. Some possibilities, including what you have mentioned, are insurance, or bonds, or co-signers . . .

The question of whether you can coercively enforce performance of a promise is one answered by Rothbard in an eminently reasonable fashion, IMHO . . . .

. . . . Don't forget that only coercion is forbidden. Boycott and shunning, especially organized forms, are absolutely justified actions that you can pursue rather than "grin and bear it". And if, as I think likely, there is some sort of moral court that helps organize these things (think credit agencies that have some sort of adversarial hearing), you will rarely have to "grin and bear it", unless you made a really foolish decision to trust someone that had nothing to lose with respect to commercial reputation . . . .

The key is that coercive remedies wouldn't be available until you proved that intentional misrepresentation. However, the commercial consequences of failing to keep your word, even if not fraudulent, would likely be tremendously severe in a society that adopted my model, even if the consequences were not coercive. Very few people would do business with you under any circumstance, and those that would would demand onerous conditions like large insurance contracts or deep-pocket co-signers who can be trusted. I would guess that even fewer people would default in such a society, because

1. Quasibill, "Property rights and contract enforcement," *The Bell Tower*, March 22, 2007 <http://the-bell-tower.blogspot.com/2007/03/property-rights-and-contract.html>.

they couldn't hide been legalistic decisions or sharp practices to defeat the plain understanding of what they promised to do.[1]

In a genuinely free market, all the licensing and certification regimes presently in
place would be replaced by voluntary alternatives. Morris and Linda Tannehill write:

> Of course, stiff competition between businesses is the consumer's best guarantee of
> getting a good product at a reasonable price—dishonest competitors are swiftly "voted"
> out of business by consumers. But, in addition to competition, the market would evolve
> means of safeguarding the consumer which would be vastly superior to the contradic-
> tory, confusing, and harassing weight of government regulations with which the bureau-
> crats claim to protect us today. One such market protection would be consumer rating
> services which would test and rate various products according to safety, effectiveness,
> cost, etc. Since the whole existence of these rating services would depend on their being
> right in their product evaluations, they would be extremely thorough in their tests, scru-
> pulously honest in their reports, and nearly impossible to bribe . . . .
>
> Businesses whose products were potentially dangerous to consumers would be es-
> pecially dependent on a good reputation. Drug manufacturers, for example, would know
> that if their products caused any illness or death through poor quality, insufficient re-
> search and preparation, or inadequate warnings on the labels they would lose customers
> by the thousands. The good reputation of a manufacturer's brand name would be its
> most precious asset . . . . Besides this, drug stores would strive for a reputation of stock-
> ing only products which were high quality, safe when properly used, and adequately la-
> beled . . . .
>
> A good reputation would also be important to doctors in the absence of govern-
> ment-required licensing. Of course, any man would be free to hang out a shingle and
> call himself a doctor, but a man whose "treatments" harmed his patients couldn't stay in
> business long. Besides, reputable physicians would probably form medical organizations
> which would only sanction competent doctors, thereby providing consumers with a
> guide. Insurance companies, who have a vested interest in keeping their policyholders
> alive and healthy, would provide another safeguard in the field of drugs and medical care.
> Insurance companies might well charge lower rates on life and health insurance to poli-
> cyholders who contracted to use only those medicines and to patronize only those doc-
> tors sanctioned by a reputable medical association.[2]

Sam Kazman, in a 1998 article written fairly early in the move toward federal standards for organic labeling, described the success of voluntary certification in the past:

> As demand for organic food has grown, private organic-certifying agencies have
> arisen. Some have stricter standards than others, and some may have standards and en-
> forcement practices so lenient that they are practically meaningless. But to the extent
> that differences between them really mean something to consumers, those consumers are
> fully capable of distinguishing between them (or of choosing retailers who do the job for
> them) . . . .
>
> The lack of any pressing necessity for [government] involvement is clear. The large
> organic-foodstore chains already have established connections with suppliers and certify-
> ing agencies; the same is true of conventional supermarket chains that carry organic
> products . . . .
>
> Organic growers themselves are also capable of doing without a cumbersome fed-
> eral definition. According to one organic-farming newsletter, "many growers say that if
> certified organic becomes too difficult, or meaningless, they will just use another word to
> market their produce." . . .

---

1. Quasibill, "A Challenge to Anti-Corporate Libertarians and Anarchists," *LeftLibertarian2*,
January 4, 2008. <http://groups.yahoo.com/group/LeftLibertarian2/message/16883> See also
"Contract enforcement consolidation," *The Bell Tower*, December 20, 2007. <http://the-bell-
tower.blogspot.com/2007/12/contract-enforcement-consolidation.html>.

2. Morris and Linda Tannehill, *The Market for Liberty* (New York: Laissez Faire Books, 1984),
pp. 49-50.

Consumers who care about such issues don't need the force of law in order to obtain the information they want about food products. USDA has already announced that its eventual definition will not allow genetically modified foods, but suppose it had ruled otherwise. Producers of organic foods that were *not* genetically modified could still communicate that fact to interested consumers—through labeling, through advertising, and even through private organic-certification systems that make a point of prohibiting bioengineered products. Information that groups of consumers want will make its way to them without legal compulsion.

In fact, as we already saw in Chapter Three, legal compulsion is used more often to *suppress* free commercial speech, in the interest of those whose products include bioengineered food, by *prohibiting* the labeling of GMO-free products. Kazman goes on to describe the free market certification regime for kosher foods:

> In a sense, this is exactly what has happened for kosher certification . . . . For [those concerned about the strictness of the standard met by the product] there are competing rabbinical inspection boards, each with a different logo. With the possible exception of guarding against outright fraud, there is little need for government involvement . . . . Consumers seem capable of sorting things out peacefully.[1]

D. Social Services

As we already saw in Chapter Thirteen, mutualists favor Proudhon's model of "dissolving the state in the economy." In practical terms, that means depriving state functions of their coercive nature so that relationships previously characterized by authority would take on the character of voluntary exchange.

Unlike state socialists, including Social Democrats, we oppose the direct provision of social services by the state. But unlike anarcho-capitalists and right-wing libertarians, we don't equate the selling off state functions to capitalist corporations with "privatization." And unlike the vulgar libertarians and neoliberals, we oppose the contracting out of taxpayer-funded functions to politically connected "private" corporations, or the kind of "privatization" that leaves the newly "private" public service dependent on taxpayer funds for its revenue and functioning in a web of statist protections against genuine market competition.

The genuine free market alternative is mutualizing government services: that is, decentralizing them to the smallest possible local unit of control, transforming them into consumer cooperatives governed by their own clientele, and ultimately removing all taxpayer funding and leaving them to provide their services only to willing clients. For example, citywide school boards should be dissolved, and neighborhood schools transformed into consumer co-ops directly controlled by some combination of the teachers and the parents of the children attending. Public non-profit hospitals should be transformed into *genuinely* public institutions: stakeholder cooperatives governed by representatives of patients, doctors and nursing staff, and other hospital staff. Publicly owned utilities should be turned over to the ratepayers.

Clarence Swartz speculated that government might survive, retaining its organizational integrity, into a post-state era. By ceasing to fund its services by coercive taxation of unwilling "consumers," and allowing competition from other providers, the government would take on the character of a consumers' cooperative:

> If the invasive activities of government were absolutely eradicated, it could still act as the protector of the individuals who compose it, or over whom it has jurisdiction. Yet, if it had no invasive powers at all, it could not forcibly provide for its own maintenance. It

---

1. Sam Kazman, "The Mother of All Food Fights," *The Freeman: Ideas on Liberty* 48:11 (November 1998) <http://www.fee.org/Publications/the-Freeman/article.asp?aid=3699>.

would therefore become a purely voluntary association, and would have to depend for its existence upon the satisfaction it gave in the service it rendered.[1]

Many anarcho-capitalists, speculating on the nature of a stateless society, envision a large number of competing "protection agencies." But it might well be the case that police and fire service are a natural monopoly, or at least approach it. It seems likely that it would be easier for dissatisfied clients of the primary mutual defense association, the inheritor of the old government's personnel and equipment, to stage a "hostile takeover" by replacing the board of selectmen, than to organize a competing security force of their own. A considerable minority of people might choose to hire competing private security services serving niche markets, participate in neighborhood watches, or even simply rely on their own home security measures combined with the general deterrent effect of an armed populace. But I imagine the majority would continue to think of the old municipal police and fire services, reorganized on a voluntary basis, as belonging to the community in some special sense. The sense of membership in a community, and the preference for organizing services through the community, predated the state—and it will likely survive it.

E. MUTUAL AID AND THE VOLUNTARY WELFARE STATE

As I wrote the original draft of this passage,[2] I had just finished watching an episode of CNN's *In the Money* on charitable giving. First came interviews with several retired senior corporate managers, including a guy from Citicorp who'd given away some $500 million in his lifetime, discussing the importance of private sector "entrepreneurialism" in charity work. And Bono was singing hosannas about Warren Buffett and Bill Gates. Another plutocratic charitable showcase was "Product Red," a trendy charitable venture by some of the biggest corporations —and guess where the money goes? Why, to buy AIDS drugs for Africa, from Big Pharma, at patent monopoly prices! Everyone involved in the discussion seemed to accept as entirely natural the existing corporate framework and the fact that charity was the preserve of giant non-profit foundations dominated by retired corporate management. As a matter of fact, Bono was followed by Ben Goldhirsch of *Good* magazine (the heir of the *Inc.* magazine fortune), gushing that "today's generation," unlike the protest generation of the Sixties, grew up accepting the existing corporate system, or "infrastructure"; they see the system as having made them well-off, and want to work through it to do good.

But as egregious as this particular example is, it's hardly new. At the local level, one can't pick up the "Society" or "Community" section of the newspaper without seeing a bunch of Rotary Club yahoos wearing pink ribbons for breast cancer, kissing pigs for diabetes, or handing over a giant check to the United Way.

In this environment, it's hard to believe that mutual aid was once dominated by self-organized associations of working people caring for their own: that unemployment, health and burial insurance, and other forms of mutual aid, were once primarily something the working class did for itself. Through most of the nineteenth century, even in the face of the economic privilege that existed then, a large portion of help for the sick and unemployed came from the laboring classes' self-organized mutual aid associations. As described by Colin Ward,

> in the nineteenth century the newly-created British working class built up from nothing
> a vast network of social and economic initiatives based on self-help and mutual aid. The
> list is endless: friendly societies, building societies, sick clubs, coffin clubs, clothing clubs,
> up to enormous federated enterprises like the trade union movement and the Co-

1. Clarence L. Swartz, *What is Mutualism?* (New York: Vanguard Press, 1927), p. 11.
2. November 25, 2006.

operative movement. The question that latter-day discoverers of that tradition ask is, 'How did we allow it to ossify?'

The answer, Ward continues, is that the statist Left used up all the "moral oxygen," and "invested all its fund of social inventiveness" in the centralized state, so that "its own traditions of self-help and mutual aid were stifled for lack of ideological oxygen."[1] The vigorous and thriving network was crowded out, in large part, by the combined effects of the corporate plutocracy's charitable establishment and the welfare state. As Ralph Borsodi wrote,

> . . . [I]t is a mistake to assume that without philanthropies of the Rockefeller type, the world would have been without the educational, medical, and religious institutions and activities which their gifts brought into being. On the contrary, it is quite probable that, had wealth not been so concentrated . . . , contributions from individuals who had been deprived of wealth by the Rockefellers, would have exceeded their relatively niggardly philanthropies to them . . . .
>
> The Rockefellers of today "give" colleges, hospitals, foundations, just as the medieval barons used to "give" monasteries, nunneries, chapels, and the Roman senators used to "give" baths and ampitheatres. But in reality they "give" nothing. They merely return a part of what they were acquisitive and powerful enough to seize.[2]

An anecdote from E. P. Thompson's *The Making of the English Working Class* is illustrative. As a group of factory workers passed by a Methodist chapel built by one of the millowners, one of them "looked towards the chapel and wished it might sink into hell, and Mr. Sutcliffe go with it."

> I said it was too bad, as Mr. Sutcliffe had built the chapel for their good. "Damn him," said another, "I know him . . . , and a corner of that chapel is mine, and it all belongs to his workpeople."[3]

Not only the wealthy, but the "alliance of bureaucrats and professionals . . . with their undisguised contempt for the way ordinary people organised anything,"[4] were complicit in killing off the voluntary welfare state. After 1945,

> [t]he great tradition of working class self-help and mutual aid was written off, not just as irrelevant, but as an actual impediment, by the political and professional architects of the welfare state, aspiring to a universal public provision of everything for everybody . . . . The nineteenth century working classes, living far below the tax threshold, taxed themselves in pennies every week for the upkeep of their innumerable friendly societies. The twentieth century employed workers, as well as its alleged National Insurance contributions, pays a large slice of its income for the support of the state. The socialist ideal was rewritten as a world in which everyone was entitled to everything, but where nobody except the provident had any actual say about anything. We have been learning for years, in the anti-welfare backlash, what a very vulnerable utopia that was.[5]

Starting with Beatrice Webb, the official version of history presented by the Fabian Society and by Labour governments patronized the working class's mutual aid institutions as at best well-meaning but shoddy and amateurish, and demonized them as at worst atavistic enemies of Progress.[6]

1. Colin Ward, "The welfare road we failed to take," in *Social Policy: An Anarchist Response* (London: Freedom Press, 1996), pp. 10-11.

2. Borsodi, *This Ugly Civilization*, pp. 235-36.

3. E. P. Thompson, *The Making of the English Working Class* (New York: Vintage Books, 1963, 1966), pp. 346-347.

4. Ward, "The welfare road we failed to take," p. 11.

5. *Ibid.*, pp. 11-12.

6. *Ibid.*, p. 12.

Ward contrasts the libertarian, bottom-up nature of the workers' self-organized welfare state with the institutionalized welfare and charitable systems overseen by professional administrators:

> On the one side the Workhouse, the Poor Law Infirmary, the National Society for the Education of the Poor in Accordance with the Principles of the Established Church; and, on the other, the *Friendly* Society, the Sick *Club*, the *Cooperative* Society, the Trade *Union*. One represents the tradition of fraternal and autonomous association springing up from below, the other that of authoritarian institutions directed from above.[1]

The chief limitation of working class mutual aid was its lack of resources. But imagine a society in which workers not only kept the full fruit of their labor, but in which small-scale machine production increased the surplus available for mutual aid far above nineteenth century levels, and shortened working hours allowed the leisure for convivial association.

As Colin Ward describes the voluntary welfare state in Great Britain, "Small tradesmen, artisans, labourers— all sought to insure themselves against sicknesss, unemployment, or funeral expenses through membership of 'box clubs' or friendly societies."[2] According to E. P. Thompson, best estimates for their membership grew from 648,000 in 1793 to 925,429 in 1815[3]; considering that the total British population in 1815 was around ten million, membership would have encompassed a majority of working class households. Friendly society membership continued to grow at an accelerating rate into the late 19th century. In 1877, registered membership was over 2.75 million. By 1910 membership was 6.6 million. "It is important to remember that these figures simply reflect the numbers known to the Government. For many societies preferred to avoid even the minimal interference of the British state, and simply 'failed' to register." The Chief Registrar of Friendly Societies estimated in 1892 that 3.8 million of 7 million industrial workers were insured against sickness through a registered friendly society, while at least another 3 million belonged to unregistered societies.[4]

The contemporary welfare state and the plutocrat-dominated charitable foundations are integrated into the larger state capitalist system, and serve its ends. They couple the relief of destitution, homelessness and starvation, to the extent necessary to prevent political threats to the power of the ruling class, with social discipline and supervision of the lower orders.

The workers' own libertarian welfare state, on the contrary, served the ends of workers themselves. David Green writes:

> The friendly societies were self-governing mutual benefit associations founded by manual workers to provide against hard times. They strongly distinguished their guiding philosophy from the philanthropy which lay at the heart of charitable work. The mutual benefit association was not run by one set of people with the intention of helping another separate group, it was an association of individuals pledged to help each other when the occasion arose. Any assistance was not a matter of largesse but of entitlement, earned by the regular contributions paid into the common fund by every member and justified by the obligation to do the same for other members if hardship came their way.[5]

The friendly societies, between 1790 and 1830 as described by Thompson, were part of a greater whole: an emerging, distinctively working class culture with its own institutions.

---

1. Colin Ward, *Anarchy in Action* (London: Freedom Press, 1982), p. 123.

2. Thompson, *Making of the English Working Class*, p. 419.

3. *Ibid*., pp. 420-421.

4. Tim Evans, "Socialism Without the State." Political Notes No. 99 (London: Libertarian Alliance, 1994) <http://www.libertarian.co.uk/lapubs/polin/polin099.pdf>.

5. David Green, *Reinventing Civil Society* (London: Institute of Economic Affairs, Health and Welfare Unit, 1993), p. 30.

> By 1832 there were strongly-based and self-conscious working-class institutions—trade unions, friendly societies, educational and religious movements, political organizations, periodicals—working-class intellectual traditions, working-class community-patterns, and a working-class structure of feeling.[1]
>
> .... In the simple cellular structure of the friendly society, with its workaday ethos of mutual aid, we can see many features which were reproduced in more sophisticated and complex forms in trade unions, co-operatives, Hampden Clubs, Political Unions, and Chartist lodges. At the same time the societies can be seen as chrystallising an ethos of mutuality .... Every kind of witness in the first half of the 19th century—clergymen, factory inspectors, Radical publicists—remarked upon the extent of mutual aid in the poorest districts. In times of emergency, unemployment, strikes, sickness, childbirth, then it was the poor who "helped every one his neighbour".[2]

Such common endeavors, combined with the need to exercise vigilance over a body to whom they had entrusted their funds, were a school in self-discipline and participatory democracy.

The importance of this cannot be overemphasized. For ten, twelve, or fourteen hours a day, six days a week, most of these men were held in absolute contempt. They were human raw material, means to an end, chattels whose values, opinions and desires were less than worthless. They worked in an environment in which prototypical "industrial engineers" like Andrew Ure looked for ways to deskill the work force, and to make the work process as independent as possible of the judgment of workers on the shop floor. But in these meetings, "the stone that the builders refused became the head cornerstone."

To a considerable extent, this building of counter-institutions was an act of conscious class warfare, an attempt to reconstruct an imagined social order of the past, in deliberate opposition to a class enemy which was believed to have overturned that order. "The factory hand or stockinger was also the inheritor of Bunyan, of remembered village rights, of notions of equality before the law, of craft traditions."[3] The Enclosures were a living memory to many in the 1830s, and for many others a real memory passed on by their parents and grandparents. And all were confronted, on a daily basis, by a reality defined by the Law of Settlements' internal passport system and the Poor Laws' slave auctions. The new revolutionary thought of Paine, and the new Owenite praxis, were assimilated into the world view of people who shared the historical sense of a world not long since stolen out from under them.

Unlike the modern welfare state, whose relief of poverty is simply another way the capitalists' state cleans up their potentially destabilizing messes, the workers' welfare state served as a basis for working class independence from capital and wage labor, and as a leverage for increased bargaining power against it.

The friendly societies often functioned as a base for political and economic resistance on a broader scale. The societies themselves were the soil out of which the trade unions later grew. With their secrecy of ritual, their organizational form naturally lent itself to covert political and economic action. Union procedural rules, as well as their often deliberate ceremonial, were a direct outgrowth of those of sick clubs, Masonic lodges, and the like.[4]

And when the friendly societies' functions extended to support for the unemployed, the distinction from an outright strike fund was hazy, to say the least. The potential of benefit societies to improve the bargaining position of workers was very real. For example the Clerk's Society (founded Newcastle, 1807) paid unemployment benefits of ten shillings

1. Thompson, *Making of the English Working Class*, p. 194.
2. *Ibid.*, p. 423.
3. *Ibid.*, p. 194.
4. *Ibid.*, p. 421.

a week for the first 26 weeks, extendable for another 26 weeks at the Society's discretion.[1] It's easy to see why the state was so zealous to suppress such activity under the Combination Acts and legislation regulating the benefit societies. By providing an alternative to the dilemma of "accept work on the terms offered, or starve," they seriously undermined labor discipline and increased the independence of working people. As a survey of the enclosure movement shows us, capitalism, despite its official ideology of free markets and freedom of association, is ever willing to resort to coercion when the property and associations of ordinary people give them too much power.

The very distinction between the trade unions and other friendly or benefit societies is an artificial one, argues Bob James.

> . . . [I]t makes much more historical sense to see the core of Labour History as a range of benefit societies, and to see what are called "trade unions" as just one culturally- determined response within a group and along a time-line . . . .
>
> What we now call "trade unions" were and are benefit societies, just like the Grand United Oddfellow and Freemason Lodges . . . . Concern about working conditions and the strategy of withdrawing labour, "going on strike", developed naturally out of the lodge habit of insuring against all sorts of other future dangers. Strike pay was just another benefit covered by contributions . . . .[2]

We have already seen, in Chapter Fifteen, the ways in which Owenite labor exchange systems were used by the trade unions to employ striking craft workers in production directly for barter.

The same pattern of interaction between the labor movement and self-organized institutions for mutual aid took place in the United States, according to Sam Dolgoff:

> The labor movement grew naturally into a vast interwoven network of local communities throughout the country, exercising a growing influence in their respective areas. And this early movement did not confine itself solely to immediate economic issues . . . . The mutual-aid functions of the unions expanded to keep abreast of the growing needs of the members . . . .
>
> They created a network of cooperative institutions of all kinds: schools, summer camps for children and adults, homes for the aged, health and cultural centers, insurance plans, technical education, housing, credit associations, et cetera. All these, and many other essential services were provided by the people themselves, long before the government monopolized social services wasting untold billions on a top-heavy bureaucratic parasitical apparatus; long before the labor movement was corrupted by "business" unionism.[3]

For this reason the friendly societies operated on the border of legality: the ruling class feared they would serve as a social and economic base for resistance, and as insulation against the immediate need for wage labor on whatever terms were offered by employers. The Combination Laws were enforced by a police state apparatus, functioning completely outside the due process protections of the ordinary common law (e.g., examination under oath by magistrate was a common procedure).

---

1. Peter Gray, "A Brief History of Friendly Societies," at *The Association of Friendly Societies* website <http://www.afs.org.uk/research/researchpgrayhistorypage.htm> (The link is now defunct, but can be retrieved through the Internet Archive).

2. Bob James, "The Tragedy of Labour History in Australia." According to Takver's Radical Tradition: An Australian History Page, where the article is hosted, the text is based on James' notes for a lecture given in several different venues. <http://www.takver.com/history/tragedy.htm>.

3. Sam Dolgoff, "Revolutionary Tendencies in American Labor—Part 1," in *The American Labor Movement: A New Beginning*. Originally published in 1980 in *Resurgence* <http://www.iww.org/ culture/library/dolgoff/labor4.shtml>.

Friendly societies existed as aboveground organizations, under the terms of the Friendly Societies Act, with severe constraints on federal organization at levels above the individual lodge—and outright prohibition of secret oaths. Their much larger underground extensions crossed the line into trade unionist activity prohibited until the repeal of the Combination Laws, into corresponding societies whose political agitation amounted to outright treason in the view of the ruling class, and into an entire range of counter-economic activity aimed either at organizing against factory employers or providing an independent basis for self-organized subsistence.

When the formal society of the illegal union overlapped with the informal society of the taproom, in settings where (as Thompson observed) no gentleman was likely to intrude, and where a new face would stand out, the legal prohibitions on collective labor action were often unenforceable.

> At work no leader or deputation need approach the employer with the men's demands; a hint would be dropped, an overlooker would be prompted, or an unsigned note be left for the master to see. If the demands were not met, there was no need—in the small workshop—for a formal strike; men would simply drop away or singly give notice.

The natural leaders in the workplace, those "who possess the confidence of their fellows," needed only to drop a hint, as one contemporary observer noted, and the entire plan of action discussed previously in a social setting would be put into action—especially, we might note, the custom of "one and all [to] support those who may be thrown out of work."[1]

As with the voluntary associations mentioned above as the institutional basis for networks of social trust, it is likely that voluntary associations would regain their old function as the primary social safety net in a restored civil society. Much as informal social networks would fill the vacuum left by the state in guaranteeing trust and creditworthiness, the social infrastructure of lodges and other communal institutions would fill the void left by the central welfare state. Charles Johnson writes:

> It's likely also that networks of voluntary aid organizations would be *strategically* important to individual flourishing in a free society, in which there would be no expropriative welfare bureaucracy for people living with poverty or precarity to fall back on. Projects reviving the bottom-up, solidaritarian spirit of the independent unions and mutual aid societies that flourished in the late 19th and early 20th centuries, before the rise of the welfare bureaucracy, may be essential for a flourishing free society, and one of the primary means by which workers could take control of their own lives, without depending on either bosses or bureaucrats.[2]

Poul Anderson, in the fictional universe of his Maurai series, envisioned a post-apocalypse society in the Pacific Northwest coalescing around the old fraternal lodges, with the Northwestern Federation centered on lodges rather than geographical subdivisions as the component units represented in its legislature. The lodge emerged as the central social institution during the social disintegration following the nuclear war, much as the villa became the basic social unit of the new feudal society in the vacuum left by the fall of Rome. It was the principal and normal means for organizing benefits to the sick and unemployed, as well as the primary base for providing public services like police and fire.[3]

One possibility is the resurrection of the guild as a basis for organizing mutual aid. Some writers on labor issues have argued that unions should shift their focus to attracting

1. Thompson, *Making of the English Working* Class, p. 514.

2. Charles Johnson, "Liberty, Equality, Solidarity: Toward a Dialectical Anarchism," in Roderick T. Long and Tibor R. Machan, eds., *Anarchism/Minarchism: Is a Government Part of a Free Country?* (Hampshire, UK, and Burlington, Vt.: Ashgate Publishing Limited, 2008). Quoted from textfile provided by author.

3. Poul Anderson, *Orion Shall Rise* (New York: Pocket Books, 1983).

memberships on an individual basis, whether it be in bargaining units with no certified union or among the unemployed; they would do so by offering insurance and other services.

Thomas Malone discusses such possibilities at considerable length in *The Future of
Work*, in exploring the implications of a free-agency economy of independent contractors.
Like many popularizing writers on networked enterprise in the new economy (Tom Peters
most notorious among them), Malone can come across as a bit glib in celebrating the new
era of freedom. But unlike Peters, he acknowledges the real problems faced by workers in
such an economy: the lack of job security and job-based benefits chief among them. And
his proposals are intriguing:

> Rather than relying on employers and governments to provide the benefits tradi-
> tionally associated with a job, a new set of organizations might emerge to provide stable
> "homes" for mobile workers and to look after their needs as they move from job to job
> and project to project.
>
> These organizations might be called societies, associations, fraternities, or clubs. But
> the word I like best is *guilds*, a term that conjures up images of the craft associations of
> the Middle Ages. Growing out of tradesmen's fraternities and mutual assistance clubs,
> medieval guilds served a number of functions. They trained apprentices and helped them
> find work . . . . They offered loans and schooling. And if misfortune struck, they provided
> an income for members' families . . . .
>
> Existing organizations already perform some of these functions today. Take the
> Screen Actors Guild. As much as 30 percent of the base pay of Screen Actors Guild
> members goes to the guild's benefits fund. In return, members get full health benefits
> (even in years when they have no work), generous pensions, and professional develop-
> ment programs.
>
> Imagine an extended version of this arrangement, in which members pay a fraction
> of their income to a guild in good times in return for a guaranteed minimum income in
> bad times. Unlike conventional unemployment insurance, provided through a distant,
> impersonal bureaucracy, the unemployment benefits provided by a guild could go well
> beyond temporary cash payments. For instance, other guild members would have an in-
> centive—and often the opportunity—to help fellow members find work. A guild would
> also have the means and the motivation to help its members gain new skills to remain
> economically productive as times change. Finally, the members would likely exert social
> pressure on unemployed colleagues who they felt weren't really trying to find work . . . .
>
> Companies have also traditionally helped their employees learn skills and, by assign-
> ing job titles and other kinds of credentials, signify to the world the capabilities of their
> workers. These kinds of services could also be provided by guilds. Lawyers and doctors,
> for instance, have professional societies that establish and monitor the credentials of prac-
> titioners and provide continuing educational opportunities. Unions have also had similar
> functions for years, helping craft workers progress from apprentice to journeyman to
> master craftsman.
>
> Finally, many people today derive much of their identity from their employer . . . .
> If you work for a different organization every week, where will you get this sense of self?
> Your self-identity could come from your membership in a guild: "I am a member of the
> Institute of Electrical and Electronic Engineers," or "I am a member of the MIT
> Alumni Guild." Arguably, the shared profession of guild members offers a stronger basis
> for personal identity than does a large and heterogeneous corporation.[1]

Malone sees the modern-day guilds arising from professional societies, labor unions, temp
agencies, and alumni associations, among other existing organizations.[2]

Of course the sense of stable identity Malone describes in the last paragraph quoted
applies outside the narrow framework of the corporate economy he envisions. It would
apply as well in an economy where the corporate walls had dissolved altogether in the in-

---

1. Thomas W. Malone, *The Future of Work: How the New Order of Business Will Shape Your Organization, Your Management Style, and Your Life* (Boston: Harvard Business School Press, 2004), pp. 84–87.

2. *Ibid.*, pp. 87–88.

formation and entertainment industries, being replaced by peer production on an open culture model. In such an economy, where musicians and software designers commonly moved from one peer network project to another, their guild membership would be a source of continuing personal identification.

As counter-institutions under existing capitalism, this side of its terminal crises, such guild organizations would also increase the independence of labor and strengthen its bargaining power in the wage market.

Another possible institutional basis for mutual aid was suggested by Chris Dillow: insurance, through "macro-markets," to pool risk on a large scale and hedge not only against unemployment, but against declining income or demand for entire professions.[1] The idea was originally proposed in a 1993 book by Robert Shiller, and elaborated in a 1999 article by Shiller, Eric van Wincoop, and Stefano Athanasoulis.[2]

> These so-called macro markets would be large international markets trading, in the form of futures contracts, long-term claims on major components of incomes shared by a large number of people or organizations . . . .
>
> This contract is attractive to a risk-averse individual because he or she will lose on the hedging contract only when the domestic economy is doing unexpectedly well. The individual will receive positive payments from the contract when the economy's [or sector's] performance is unexpectedly poor . . . .

F. EDUCATION

The nineteenth century working classes' self-organized institutions for mutual aid included significant educational efforts. Colin Ward cites Philip Gardner's *The Lost Elementary Schools of Victorian England*:

> He found that what he called working-class schools, set up by working-class people in working-class neighbourhoods, "achieved just what the customers wanted: quick results in basic skills like reading, writing and arithmetic, wasted no time on religious studies and moral uplift, and represented a genuinely alternative approach to childhood learning to that prescribed by the education experts". When the historian Paul Thompson discussed the implications of this book in *New Society* (6th December 1984) he concluded that the price of eliminating those schools had been "the suppression in countless working-class children of the very appetite for education and ability to learn independently which contemporary progressive education seeks to rekindle".[3]

As described by Gardener, there was "a powerful identifiable working-class educational culture, with its own characteristic values, goals and practices, which was quite distinct from those officially prescribed."

> Resistance to formal, institutionalized schooling was fed by the currents of this alternative culture which, more positively, also supported its own networks of independent practical educational activity. Until these were destroyed, the dominance of a provided system of elementary schooling "for" the working class could not be fully or finally completed. The depth and resilience of this alternative educational culture is demonstrated by its sustained popularity over time, and by its failure to die the natural death universally predicted for it.

1. Chris Dillow, *The End of Politics: New Labour and the folly of managerialism* (UK: Harriman House Ltd, 2007.

2. Robert Shiller, Eric van Wincoop, and Stefano Athanasoulis, "Macro Markets and Financial Security," *Economic Policy Review: Federal Reserve Bank of New York* (April 1999) <http://findarticles.com/p/articles/mi_qa5390/is_199904/ai_n21437806>.

3. Ward, "The welfare road we failed to take," p. 13. The quote is from Philip Gardner, *The Lost Elementary Schools of Victorian England* (Croom Helm, 1984).

Where was this alternative educational culture to be found? Not merely in organised movements like Owenism or Chartism, but . . . in the tradition of working-class private schooling.[1]

Such a school was "private" through the absence of any financial and or institutional
regulation beyond those of the parents who sent their children to it. And it was working
class by the distinctive background and character of its pupils and their parents, and the
majority of its teachers. But the most convenient and objective method of distinguishing a
working-class private school from other private schools . . . was the calculation of average
weekly fees. These were set at a maximum of 9d per week but were commonly considerably lower. Such schools possessed universal defining characteristics which market them
off from the alternative publicly provided or sanctioned institutions . . . . As well as being
self-financing, working-class private schools were completely beyond the reach or control
of the Inspectorate. They responded naturally to demand from below and not the dictates
of supply. The teachers . . . of such schools were generally without any kind of formal
training or certification, and were . . . wholly self employed . . . . The schools were very
rarely held in a building designed for the purpose, the majority being kept in the home of
the teachers . . . . [Weekly attendance averaged] between 10 and 30. Segregation or formal
grouping of the children on the basis of age, sex or ability was unusual, and teaching and
learning took place on an individual and informal basis.[2]

Such schools, which were prevalent from the early nineteenth century on, included
"dames' schools" and "common day schools." In most the curriculum was limited to reading and arithmetic, but some provided more diversified curricula, including geography and
history.[3] Estimates of attendance in mid–century ranged from 130,571 to 573,576.[4] As of
the Education Act of 1870, "something like a quarter" of elementary-school age children
attended working class private schools. Their numbers rapidly dwindled afterward, in the
face of crowding out effects from taxpayer funded schooling and the hostility of the educational establishment.[5]

Even with all the crowding out, the growth of networked computer technology has
still offered means that might be adapted to self-organized learning. Again, as in so many
other areas, the technologies the centralized system develops for its own ends inadvertently
manage to produce offshoots that increase the relative productivity of decentralized activity,
in ways that the centralized system cannot suppress. Even with the crowding out of decentralist technology by the state capitalist system's direction of resources, and with the skewing of technical development in a centralist direction, the greater efficiencies of self-
directed and decentralized activity are sufficient to enable the counter-economy, using only
the technological crumbs from state capitalism's table, to turn the system's own technology
against it.

Well over thirty years ago Ivan Illich wrote, in *Deschooling Society*, of the educational
possibilities of decentralized learning networks, based entirely on the telephone, photocop-
ier, and tape recorder, years before anyone had any idea of the potential of the Internet.
The development of computer networks, along with online libraries and databases, makes
it far cheaper to move information to the learning site than to transport "human resources" to a central processing factory.

Two possible models for doing this are the wiki format (a good example is Wikiver-
sity[6]) and MIT's Open Courseware project. In math and language, the best texts of all time
are in the public domain, and many of them are reproduced online through open-source

1. Philip Gardner, *The Lost Elementary Schools of Victorian England* (Croom Helm, 1984), p. 3.
2. *Ibid.*, p. 12.
3. *Ibid.*, p. 20.
4. *Ibid.*, p. 50.
5. *Ibid.*, p. 188.
6. <http://en.wikiversity.org/wiki/Wikiversity:Main_Page>.

textbook projects. The public domain texts available to home-schoolers, unschoolers, and self-taught children are incomparably better than the dumbed-down, political consensus-determined, cut and paste textbooks churned out by publishers to the lowest common denominator standards of as many local school boards as possible, and then marketed to local school systems the same way Big Pharma markets drugs to doctors' offices.

Once we abandon the idea of schools as institutions run by "educational professionals," and of learning as an activity that takes place at a designated location under the supervision of such professionals, the possibilities for linking individual learners to sources of knowledge are almost infinite.

Proudhon, writing in the mid-19th century, wrote of breaking down barriers between the rest of society in ways that anticipated Ivan Illich. His provisions for technical training, for example, relied heavily on linking the public education system with the workers' associations, the latter serving as

> both centers of production and centers for education . . . . Labor and study, which have for so long and so foolishly been kept apart, will finally emerge side-by-side in their natural state of union.[1]

The integration of education into the community can be physical, as well as functional. In Claude Lewenz's Villages, classroom space—rather than being concentrated in some centrally located specimen of Stalinist architecture and serviced by a bus system —is decentralized throughout the community. He quotes Christopher Alexander's Pattern No. 18 (from *A Pattern Language*):

> Instead of the lock-step of compulsory schooling in a fixed place, work in piecemeal ways to decentralise the process of learning and enrich it through contact with many places and people all over the city: workshops, teachers at home or walking through the city, professionals willing to take on the young as helpers, older children teaching younger children, museums, youth groups travelling, scholarly seminars, industrial workshops, old people and so on.

"The Village," Lewenz writes, "serves as a life-long classroom."

By decentralizing control of education to the primary community of a few thousand people, the Village can greatly reduce overhead. Lewenz again quotes Alexander on the elimination of expenses from overpriced, centrally located buildings and administrative salaries, and the use of the savings to reduce student-teacher ratios down to ten or so. He recommends building small schools, one at a time, located in the public part of the community (some of my readers may prefer the term Agora), "with a shopfront and three or four rooms."[2]

One thought experiment I like to do: try to figure the minimal tuition for a quality education, on the assumption that the parents of twenty or thirty kids pool their own money to form a cooperative school. Taking into account things like renting a house for class space, and hiring part-time teachers for different subject areas, the annual expense shouldn't go above $1-2,000 per pupil. That's assuming, of course, that the school abandons activities undertaken for prestige value, like participating in AAAA or AAA athletics and its counterpart in band. Heaven forbid the kids should have to organize pickup games with some balls and an empty lot, or participate in a "league" of other small independent schools in the same community. So how do existing schools manage to spend upwards of $8000? Most of the difference lies in the proliferation of parasitic bureaucrats with prestige

1. *On the Political Capacity of the Working Classes* (1865), in Selected Writings of Proudhon. Edited by Stewart Edwards. Translated by Elizabeth Fraser (Garden City, N.Y.: Anchor, 1969), pp. 86-87; General Idea of the Revolution in the Nineteenth Century. Translated by John Beverly Robinson (New York: Haskell House Publishers, Ltd., 1923, 1969 [1851]), p. 274.

2. Lewenz, *How to Build a Village*, p. 119.

salaries, and the fact that the state's aura of majesty requires specially designed buildings on the most expensive real estate in town.

This is a common pattern. When you try to figure out how much it would cost to organize a service for yourself, from the bottom up, and compare it to what you're paying now, it's stunning. Where does all the money go? It goes to support the overhead cost of bureaucracies with no incentive to economize. It's amazing how creative and thrifty ordinary people can be when they're spending their own money, instead of stolen loot.

Money is hardly the only thing wasted in the public schools. An incredible amount of available time is also wasted. Part of the reason is that, because of homework, the teacher is able to externalize learning time on the pupil at the expense of his home life and leisure, rather than maximizing use of available classroom time. One would think that six fifty minute periods (amounting to five solid hours of classroom time), five days a week, for nine months of the year, would be sufficient time to teach anyone anything—at least at the level of understanding the public schools aim at. But no—by the high school years, the average pupil may be assigned as many hours of homework as he spends in class.

The Borsodis' experiment in home schooling, at a time when such a thing was almost unheard of, demonstrated the immense waste of time involved in typical classroom learning:

> . . . [A]gain, individual production proved its superiority to mass production. Mrs. Borsodi found it possible to give the boys, in two hours' desk work, all the training which they were supposed to get, according to the state, in a whole school day plus the work which they were supposed to do at home.

They used the official school curriculum and its assigned texts, so their experiment was controlled for identical subject matter. As counterintuitive as it might seem for homeschoolers to duplicate the state's inculcation of its official ideology as taught in the approved history and social studies texts, though, at least the drastic reduction in time wasted on the standard curriculum left a great deal of extra time for the meat of a real education: self-directed learning in pursuit of one's own interest. Once these two hours were dispensed with, the boys devoted the rest of their day to reading and play.[1]

One of the few things I liked about Wesley Clark: when the press asked him if he was educated, he said "Yes; I read books."

Robert Pirsig, in the "Church of Reason" passage of *Zen and the Art of Motorcycle Maintenance*, describes the functioning of an education system when it becomes a tool for self-directed learning, rather than processing human resources for institutional consumers. Phaedrus speculated on the likely career of a good cramming, résumé-padding student who was exposed for the first time to an educational system in which grades and degrees had been eliminated.

> Such a student . . . would go to his first class, get his first assignment and probably do it out of habit. He might go to his second and third as well. But eventually the novelty of the course would wear off and, because his academic life was not his only life, the pressure of other obligations or desires would create circumstances where he just would not be able to get an assignment in.
>
> Since there was no degree or grading system he would incur no penalty for this. Subsequent lectures which presumed he'd completed the assignment might be a little more difficult to understand, however, and this difficulty, in turn, might weaken his interest to a point where the next assignment, which he would find quite hard, would also be dropped. Again no penalty.
>
> In time his weaker and weaker understanding of what the lectures were about would make it more and more difficult for him to pay attention in class. Eventually he would see he wasn't learning much; and facing the continual pressure of outside obliga-

---

1. Borsodi, *Flight From the City*, pp. 86–87.

tions, he would stop studying, feel guilty about this and stop attending class. Again, no penalty would be attached.

But what had happened? The student, with no hard feelings on anybody's part, would have flunked himself out. Good! This is what should have happened. He wasn't there for a real education in the first place and had no real business there at all. A large amount of money and effort had been saved and there would be no stigma of failure and ruin to haunt him the rest of his life. No bridges had been burned.

The student's biggest problem was a slave mentality which had been built into him by years of carrot-and- whip grading, a mule mentality which said, "If you don't whip me, I won't work." He didn't get whipped. He didn't work. And the cart of civilization, which he supposedly was being trained to pull, was just going to have to creak along a little slower without him.

This is a tragedy, however, only if you presume that the cart of civilization, "the system," is pulled by mules. This is a common, vocational, "location" point of view, but it's not the Church attitude.

The Church attitude is that civilization, or "the system" or "society" or whatever you want to call it, is best served not by mules but by free men. The purpose of abolishing grades and degrees is not to punish mules or to get rid of them but to provide an environment in which that mule can turn into a free man.

The hypothetical student, still a mule, would drift around for a while. He would get another kind of education quite as valuable as the one he'd abandoned, in what used to be called the "school of hard knocks." Instead of wasting money and time as a high-status mule, he would now have to get a job as a low-status mule, maybe as a mechanic. Actually his real status would go up. He would be making a contribution for a change. Maybe that's what he would do for the rest of his life. Maybe he'd found his level. But don't count on it.

In time . . . six months; five years, perhaps . . . a change could easily begin to take place. He would become less and less satisfied with a kind of dumb, day-to-day shop-work. His creative intelligence, stifled by too much theory and too many grades in college, would now become reawakened by the boredom of the shop. Thousands of hours of frustrating mechanical problems would have made him more interested in machine design. He would like to design machinery himself. He'd think he could do a better job. He would try modifying a few engines, meet with success, look for more success, but feel blocked because he didn't have the theoretical information. He would discover that when before he felt stupid because of his lack of interest in theoretical information, he'd now find a brand of theoretical information which he'd have a lot of respect for, namely, mechanical engineering.

So he would come back to our degreeless and gradeless school, but with a difference. He'd no longer be a grade-motivated person. He'd be a knowledge-motivated person. He would need no external pushing to learn. His push would come from inside. He'd be a free man. He wouldn't need a lot of discipline to shape him up. In fact, if the instructors assigned him were slacking on the job he would be likely to shape them up by asking rude questions. He'd be there to learn something, would be paying to learn something and they'd better come up with it.

Motivation of this sort, once it catches hold, is a ferocious force, and in the grade-less, degreeless institution where our student would find himself, he wouldn't stop with rote engineering information. Physics and mathematics were going to come within his sphere of interest because he'd see he needed them. Metallurgy and electrical engineering would come up for attention. And, in the process of intellectual maturing that these abstract studies gave him, he would he likely to branch out into other theoretical areas that weren't directly related to machines but had become a part of a newer larger goal. This larger goal wouldn't be the imitation of education in Universities today, glossed over and concealed by grades and degrees that give the appearance of something happening when, in fact, almost nothing is going on. It would be the real thing.[1]

1. Robert M. Pirsig, *Zen and the Art of Motorcycle Maintenance: An Inquiry Into Values* (New York: William Morrow Publishing Company, 1979). Online version courtesy of Quality page, Vir-

G. HEALTHCARE

Healthcare is yet another area in which self-organized alternatives have been suppressed by capital and the state. We already saw, in our general discussion above of friendly societies, Thompson's account of sick benefit societies. As Colin Ward writes history shows that "the self-organisation of patients provided a rather better degree of consumer control of medical services" than was achieved under the NHS.[1]

The Tredegar Medical Aid Society, founded in 1870, was a good example. It was funded by a subscription of "three old pennies in the pound from the wage-packets of miners and steelworkers," and at one time employed "five doctors, a dentist, a chiropodist and a physiotherapist," along with a hospital that served 25,000 people.[2]

As we saw above, Tim Evans quoted an estimate by the Chief Registrar of Friendly Societies in 1892 that 3.8 million of 7 million industrial workers were insured against sickness through a registered friendly society, while at least another 3 million belonged to unregistered societies.[3] Membership in registered friendly societies grew from 2.8 million in 1877 to 6.6 million in 1910 (in addition to those in unregistered societies), and Greene estimates total friendly society insurance coverage in 1910 at 9 to 9.5 million out of the 12 million covered by the National Insurance Act of 1911.

The first nail in the coffin of the workers' self-organized healthcare system was the National Insurance Act. Lloyd George originally envisioned it as "a way of extending the benefits of friendly society membership, already freely chosen by the vast majority of workers, to *all* citizens, and particularly those so poor they could not afford the modest weekly contributions."[4] Or as Ward put it, the goal was to create "one big Tredegar."

George's original proposal was distorted beyond recognition in the House of Commons by a coalition, "hostile to working-class mutual aid," of the British Medical Association and an insurance industry trade association known as the Combine. Amendments obtained under their influence eliminated all vestiges of democratic self-organization, and instead vested administration in "bodies heavily under the influence of the medical profession." They limited panel doctors to registered practitioners, thus greatly strengthening the licensing bodies' monopoly. They also eliminated any threat that working-class bargaining power would be used to keep physicians' fees within a range affordable to ordinary manual workers—from the physicians' standpoint, the worst outrage of the old friendly societies. Instead, doctors' incomes were doubled and financed by a regressive poll tax.[5] The organized medical profession also used the GMC, the primary licensing body, to "ban conduct which helped the consumer to differentiate between doctors," like advertising.[6]

The final blow came from the National Health Service, established in 1948, which nationalized delivery of service in addition to finance.

Although mutual provision of healthcare was not as extensive in America, it still included a considerable portion of the population. Certainly, as David Beito points out, self-help efforts organized through mutuals "dwarfed the efforts of formal social welfare agen-

tual School Distributed Learning Community <http://www.virtualschool.edu/mon/Quality/ PirsigZen/index.html>.
    1. Ward, "The welfare road we failed to take," p. 14.
    2. *Ibid.*, p. 15.
    3. Evans, "Socialism Without the State."
    4. David Green, *Working-Class Patients and the Medical Establishment: Self-Help in Britain from the Mid-Nineteenth Century to 1948* (Aldershot, UK: Gower/Temple, 1986), p. 2.
    5. *Ibid.*, pp. 2, 108.
    6. *Ibid.*, p. 132.

cies."[1] An 1891 study by the Connecticut Bureau of Labor Statistics found that membership in fraternal insurance orders was 15% of the general population. Of these, 60% were sick and funeral benefit orders, and 28% life insurance societies. But the study included only bodies specifically formed for the provision of insurance, and not other fraternal orders (like Masons, Elks, Patrons of Husbandry, etc.) which provided insurance as a standard benefit of membership. If the latter were included, the total membership was greater than the total male population.[2] Putting all the figures together, it's quite plausible that a majority of the male population belonged to organizations which provided sick benefits (although wives and children were often eligible, they did not count toward membership totals). In Chicago, a 1919 study by the Illinois Health Insurance Commission found that 38.8 percent of wage-earning families carried life insurance through fraternal organizations, which suggests—if the Connecticut ratios are taken as typical—that an even larger portion had sick benefits.[3] Black families at that time were noted for obtaining life insurance from private firms, but sick benefits from fraternal societies. In Chicago over four in ten blacks had sick benefits. Similar figures obtained for black populations in Philadelphia and Kansas City.[4]

The provision of healthcare through fraternal orders was not limited to insurance. Many lodges kept a physician on retainer for their membership, financed by a modest subscription fee: the so-called "lodge practice." This evoked strong antipathies from the medical community ("lodge practice evil" was a stock phrase in the medical journals).[5]

As with insurance through friendly societies, the United States also lagged behind the British and Australians in lodge practice. In the latter countries more than half of wage earners before World War I may have had access to physicians' services through lodge practice.[6] It was, nevertheless, quite prevalent in America. The New York City health commissioner, in 1915, observed that in many communities, lodge practice was "the chosen or established method of dealing with sickness among the relatively poor."[7] In Seattle, lodge members eligible for treatment by a lodge physician amounted to some 20% of the adult male population.[8] This was, remember, in addition to the number of people who obtained medical *insurance* through friendly societies and mutuals.

The cost of coverage through lodge practice averaged around $2 a year—roughly a day's wage—and some lodges offered coverage for family members at the same rate. And this was the typical charge for a single house call by a fee-for-service physician at the time. What's more, the competition from lodge practice probably resulted in lower fees for the services of physicians in private practice. That was, perhaps, one reason for the medical profession's strong resentment. Nevertheless, the practice appealed to many doctors, especially those starting out, by offering a large and stable patient base.[9]

The medical profession launched a full-scale assault on lodge practice, causing a "steep decline" by the 1920s. State medical societies imposed sanctions on doctors who ac-

1. David Beito, *From Mutual Aid to the Welfare State: Fraternal Societies and Social Services, 1890-1967* (Chapel Hill and London: The University of North Carolina Press, 2000), p. 19.
2. *Ibid.*, pp. 14-15.
3. *Ibid.*, p. 22.
4. *Ibid.*, p. 25.
5. This is the subject of an entire chapter in Beito's book, pp. 109-129. See also Roderick T. Long, "How Government Solved the Health Care Crisis: Medical Insurance that Worked—Until Government 'Fixed' It," *Formulations*, Winter 1993/94.
6. Beito, *From Mutual Aid to the Welfare State*, pp. 109-110.
7. *Ibid.*, p. 110.
8. *Ibid.*, p. 111.
9. *Ibid.*, pp. 117-118.

cepted lodge contracts, in some cases barring them from membership.[1] The campaign was still more strident at the county level, with pressure to sign anti-lodge practice pledges, or pledges not to charge fees less than the standard, and expulsions or boycotts of offenders. Hospitals were also pressured into boycotting those who engaged in lodge practice.[2] The profession also attacked the "problem" from the other end, remedying the perceived "oversupply" of doctors that made the terms of lodge practice so attractive to some physicians. Between 1910 and 1930, the number of physicians per 100,000 people shrank from 164 to 125, largely because of increasingly stringent state licensing requirements, and because of a reduction in the number of medical schools (by more than half between 1904 and 1922).[3] Finally, the rise of group insurance, starting with the Equitable Life Assurance Society's first large group insurance policy in 1912, was another major blow to both lodge practice and friendly society insurance. State legislation impeded the adoption of group insurance by lodges.[4]

Some fraternal organizations also organized their own clinics and hospitals. The Workmen's Circle in New York City, for example, organized district clinics into a citywide Medical Department with a wide array of specialist services. The Independent Order of Foresters had a similar venture in, among other places, California and Ontario.[5] The Women's Benefit Association (formerly Ladies of the Maccabees, a women's adjunct of the Knights of the Maccabees) established health service centers with visiting nurses (38 of them by 1934, in seventeen states and one Canadian province).

Any suggestion of returning to a reliance on friendly societies or mutuals as the primary source of healthcare funding today will likely meet with the objection that per capita costs are far higher, as a percentage of per capita income, than they were in the heyday of sick benefit societies and lodge practice. It's a valid point, but those who raise it approach the issue from the wrong direction. They use the present level of healthcare costs to argue that only government financing can meet the challenge. In fact, however, before we address the question of finance at all, we must first address the reasons why the present cost of healthcare is so inflated.

As enthusiastic as I am in support of cooperative healthcare finance, a cooperative approach to finance alone is inadequate. We must also organize alternative methods for delivery of service, and eliminate the state-supported monopolies that affect the price of medicine, medical technology and service providers.

The root of the problem is that the state, through such forms of artificial scarcity as drug patents and the licensing cartels, makes certain forms of practice artificially lucrative. In other words, it creates a honey pot. Is it any wonder that the standard model of practice gravitates toward the honey pot?

Drug patents, for example, create a pressure toward the use of new, patented drugs and the crowding out of older, generic drugs. Most drug company R&D is geared toward the production of "me, too" drugs, which involve only a minor tweaking of the same basic chemical formula as an existing drug, with at best marginal improvements. But these new drugs have the advantage of being patentable, so that they can replace what are essentially older versions of the same drugs whose patents are about to expire. The next step is for drug company reps to propagandize the delivery of service side of things. This is facilitated by the fact that most medical research is carried out in prestigious med schools, clinics and research hospitals whose boards of directors are also senior managers or directors of drug

1. *Ibid.*, p. 124.
2. *Ibid.*, p. 125.
3. *Ibid.*, p. 128.
4. *Ibid.*, pp. 211–212, 231.
5. *Ibid.*, p. 165.

companies. And the average GP's knowledge of new drugs, after he gets out of med school, comes from drug company literature handed out by the Pfizer or Merck rep who drops by now and then. Drug companies can also pressure doctors indirectly through their influence on the medical associations' standards of practice, or even legislative mandates (see Gardasil). Any doctor who departs too far from the standard "drug 'em and cut 'em" model of practice (for example, using nutritional supplements—like Co-Enzyme Q-10 for congestive heart failure—as a primary treatment) had better remember the state licensing board has its eye on him.

Defenders of drug patents point to the need for recouping the high cost of research and development. But in fact, most drug company R&D costs actually result from gaming the patent system, as we saw in Chapter Three.

The licensing cartels outlaw competition between multiple tiers of service, based on the consumer's preference and resources. A lot of free market advocates, in describing the causes of medical inflation, like to use the "food insurance" analogy to show why third party payments eliminate price competition: when your insurer only requires a small deductible for each trip to the supermarket, you'll probably buy a lot more T-bones. Unfortunately, what we have now is a system where the government, Big Pharma, and the license cartels act in collusion to make sure that only T-bones are available, and the uninsured wind up bankrupting themselves to eat. A lot of uninsured people would probably like access to less than premium service that they could actually afford.

Twenty-seven out of fifty states in the U.S. do not allow independent practice by mid-level clinicians like advanced practice nurses and physicians' assistants without a doctor's "oversight or collaboration," although most allow nurse practitioners to write prescriptions.[1] In fact, the MD's "supervision," more likely than not, will consist of sanctifying the clinic with his presence somewhere in the building for part of the day (and adding the cost of his medical education and living expenses to the clinic's overhead cost) as the nurse practitioner single-handedly examines and evaluates the patient and prescribes treatment. State medical and dental associations fight, tooth and nail, state legislation to expand the range of services that can be performed independently by mid-level clinicians. A good example is the proposal to allow dental hygienists to clean teeth in independent practices: the dental associations are death on the subject. The mid-level clinicians themselves are equally venal, however, seeking state legislatively mandated education requirements for licensing that have little to do with performing their primary services. Mid-level clinicians associations, in many states, attempt to mandate masters degree or doctorate as a prerequisite for practicing.

> For example, states increasingly require new NPs to obtain a master's degree. All states require physical therapists to have a master's degree. The American Association of Colleges of Nursing wants states to require a Doctor of Nursing Practice degree of all new advance practice nurses by 2015. A new law requires physician assistants to have a masters or higher degree to practice in Ohio. Every state has required a master's degree of occupational therapists since 2007.
>
> Starting in 2012, California will require new audiologists to have obtained a doctorate (Au.D.), raising concerns that the legislation would exacerbate a shortage of audiologists. The legislation followed a move by the American Speech-Language-Hearing Association, the organization that accredits college audiology programs, to require a doctorate for professional certification. Questioning both why California legislators rushed to comply and whether even a master's degree is necessary to test someone's hearing, the *Sacramento Bee* called the requirement for a doctorate an "extraordinary and costly mandate."[2]

---

1. Shirley Svorny, "Medical Licensing: An Obstacle to Affordable, Quality Care," Cato Policy Analysis No. 621, p. 3. <http://www.cato.org/pubs/pas/pa-621.pdf>.

2. *Ibid.*, pp. 4-5.

Part of the problem is the pecuniary interest of the professional education establishment. Nursing schools, for example, are set up on the same principle as the shadier sellers of vacation property, in which the buyer loses all his equity on default: a nursing student who drops out loses all his credits after a semester.

At any rate, all this licensing is of little avail. Licensing boards are frequently quite negligent in disciplining members of their professions.

> A study of Florida physicians with malpractice payouts over $1 million found that only 16 percent had been sanctioned by the state medical board. Among physicians who made 10 or more malpractice payments between 1990 and 2005, only *one-third* were disciplined by their state boards.
>
> Further complicating the disciplinary process, state boards are reluctant to pull a license or make public the results of an investigation due to the financial consequences for the sanctioned professional. Just issuing formal charges against a physician, which become public record, affect a doctor's reputation and potential income.
>
> As a result of these forces, formal disciplinary actions typically do not focus on improper or negligent care. Instead, the bulk of disciplinary actions involve inappropriate prescription of controlled substances, drug and alcohol abuse, mental illness, sexual improprieties and other issues . . . .
>
> The licensing system also comes up short in the area of reporting substandard care to the public. There are often long delays. California reports an average of 934 days in getting a case to judicial review. To avoid the high costs of lengthy hearings, boards routinely negotiate voluntary settlements for lesser offenses. In the Federation of State Medical Boards' database, the nature of the investigation is not recorded in more than 65 percent of cases that ended in sanctions between 1994 and 2002. In those cases, the state board and the physician entered an agreement without the physician being found guilty. These dynamics deny consumers information that would help them avoid low-quality physicians . . . .
>
> A closer look suggests that most patient protections are unrelated to state licensing. Concern over reputation and potential liability for medical malpractice creates incentives for private efforts to assess clinician knowledge, skills and competence that well exceed those associated with state licensing. Indeed, health care providers regularly review information on their clinicians that is broader and more up-to-date than information associated with licensure. At the point of care, hospitals and other institutions dictate what services each individual clinician may provide. On top of that, the structure of medical malpractice liability insurance rates creates some incentives for providers to avoid medical errors and other negligent care.[1]

The licensing cartels outlaw one of the most potent weapons against monopoly: product substitution. Much of what an MD does doesn't actually require an MD's level of training. Imagine a private system of accreditation with multiple tiers of training. An American-style "barefoot doctor" at a neighborhood cooperative clinic might, for example, be trained to set most fractures and deal with other common traumas, perform an array of basic tests, and treat most ordinary infectious diseases. He might be able listen to your symptoms and listen to your lungs, do a sputum culture, and give you a run of Zithro for your pneumonia, without having to refer you any further. And his training would also include identifying situations clearly beyond his competence that required the expertise of a nurse practitioner or physician.

Healthcare facilities must be licensed as well. Thirty-five states require a "certificate of need" before a new hospital can be built in an area—and as you might expect, existing providers have some of the loudest voices in the approval process.[2] The same is true of nursing homes, an industry in which new facilities cannot be built unless the government

1. *Ibid.*, pp. 7–8.
2. Michael F. Cannon and Michael D. Tanner, *Healthy Competition: What's Holding Back Health Care and How to Free It* (Washington, D.C.: The Cato Institute, 2005), p. 137.

recognizes a sufficient unmet need—and an industry, perhaps not coincidentally, in which there are waiting lists and patients are frequently turned away.

In my town of Springdale, Arkansas a couple of years ago, the state closed down an unlicensed adult daycare facility (Reflections Memory Care)—a small operation run out of the home of its owner, Judith Hollows. It cared for only a couple of elders a day, at a modest price, and their family members described it as a "godsend." As you might expect, the state acted on the complaint of a nursing home administrator:

> Deanna Shackelford, administrator of the Springdale Health and Rehabilitation Center, complained to city code enforcement that Hollows was operating without a permit.[1]

Although Hollows' facilities did not fall afoul of Office of Long Term Care regulations, her number of clients not exceeding three, Shackelford was able to appeal to the city's zoning ordinances. One of her neighbors, John Massey, explained: "It could potentially impact the value of the property."

Perhaps not coincidentally, one of Hollows' clients was formerly a resident of that same Springdale Health and Rehabilitation Center, under the direction of that same Deana Shackelford:

> "Daddy has improved so much under Judith's care," Ervin said. This is the first time he's felt safe and secure in seven months."
>
> Since Aug. 28, when he moved in with Hollows, Ward has regained 12 1/2 of the 40 pounds he lost at Springdale Health and Rehabilitation, Ervin said. His wheelchair is now in a closet. He is also drinking fruit juice and not a powdered concentrate.

This was yet another example of provision of goods in the informal household sector, with little or no overhead costs and little risk of going out of business, because of the fact that it operated mainly on the spare capacity of capital goods that the operator would have had to own for her own subsistence in any case. To repeat the lesson yet again, one of the central functions of licensing and regulation is to criminalize such self-organized production using the spare capacity of ordinary household capital, in order to render us dependent on the services of "professionals" purchased with the proceeds of wage labor.

The same tendency of service delivery to gravitate toward the honey pot occurs in the field of medical technology. According to a *New York Times* article by Alex Berenson and Reed Abelson, hospitals invest in extremely expensive CT scanners, despite the fact that most CT scans are unnecessary and have little or no proven benefit. "CT scans, which are typically billed at $500 to $1,500, have never been proved in large medical studies to be better than older or cheaper tests." But hospitals nationwide have invested in thousands of the million-dollar machines; and as San Francisco cardiologist Andrew Rosenblatt says, "[i]f you have ownership of the machine, . . . you're going to want to utilize the machine"— even if it means a provider has to "give scans to people who might not need them in order to pay for the equipment." This pressure to full utilization of capacity on the Sloanist model may have something to with American per capita healthcare costs being about twice the average in the developed world.

> No one knows exactly how much money is spent on unnecessary care. But a Rand Corporation study estimated that one-third or more of the care that patients in this country receive could be of little value. If that is so, hundreds of billions of dollars each year are being wasted on superfluous treatments . . . .
>
> The problem is not that newer treatments never work. It is that once they become available, they are often used indiscriminately, in the absence of studies to determine which patients they will benefit . . . .

1. Richard Massey, "Springdale: Caregiver of Senile Fights City Hall," *Arkansas Democrat-Gazette* (Northwest Arkansas edition), December 2, 2007 <http://www.nwanews.com/adg/News/ 209363/>.

Already, more than 1,000 hospitals and an estimated 100 private cardiology practices own or lease the $1 million CT scanners .... Once they have made that investment, doctors and hospitals have every incentive to use the machines as often as feasible. To pay off a scanner, doctors need to conduct about 3,000 tests, industry consultants say.

Fees from imaging have become a significant part of cardiologists' income— accounting for half or more of the $400,000 or so that cardiologists typically make in this country, said Jean M. Mitchell, an economist at Georgetown University who studies the way financial incentives influence doctors ....

Mitchell said cardiologists simply practice medicine the way the health system rewards them to. Given the opportunity to recommend a test for which they will make money, the doctors will.

"This is not greed," she said. "This is normal economic behavior."[1]

Arnold Kling observes that medical conditions which, thirty years ago, would have been treated "empirically" at low cost, now routinely rely on expensive CAT scans and MRIs. He mentions the case of a patient with an eye inflammation. Thirty years ago the low-cost empirical treatment would have been to send her home, in the absence of a firm diagnosis, with antibiotics and prednisone and see if that took care of it. Thanks to modern technology, she was put through a battery of inconclusive tests, then given a series of CAT scans (also inconclusive)—and finally sent home, in the absence of a firm diagnosis, with antibiotics and prednisone.[2] Kling also describes his own experience:

During a routine physical examination, the lab that examined my urine sample found microscopic amounts of blood. This condition, known as microhematuria, can be a symptom of a number of serious illnesses, including bladder cancer.

However, the incidence of bladder cancer is very low among nonsmoking men under the age of 50. Moreover, microhematuria is present in between 10 and 15 percent of the healthy population. Finally, I had a history of occasional microhematuria, going back to my childhood. Using Bayes' Theorem ..., I calculated that my chances of having bladder cancer were lower than that of a male age 60 *without* hematuria. Nonetheless, after much argument back and forth, my doctor insisted that I undergo a cystoscopy procedure. The results were negative.[3]

What Kling calls "premium medicine" has completely crowded out empirical treatment, and become the routine practice for everyone—even though it benefits only a very tiny minority of patients who would not have responded to empirical treatment. For example, everyone with a severe cough is likely to be subjected to a chest X-ray, despite the fact that 998 out of a thousand likely have a bronchial infection that will respond to simple treatment with antibiotics.[4] It's quite likely that the tens of millions of uninsured would love to have access to a policy that covered the low-cost, empirical options, provided at cost; but to return to our "food insurance" analogy, the system skews delivery of service so that only T-bones are available, even for those who can afford only hamburger.

These tendencies are exacerbated by the fact that the state, through regulatorily cartelized systems of insurance and delivery, breaks the direct market relationship between purchaser and supplier. The system runs on third party payments and cost-plus accounting, which means that those making the decisions regarding healthcare delivery have precious little incentive to economize.

1. Alex Berenson and Reed Abelson, "The Evidence Gap: Weighing the Costs of a CT Scan's Look Inside the Heart," *New York Times*, June 29, 2008 <http://www.nytimes.com/2008/06/29/business/29scan.html>.

2. Arnold Kling, *Crisis of Abundance: Rethinking How We Pay for Health Care* (Washington, D.C.: The Cato Institute, 2006), pp. 8-9.

3. *Ibid.*, p. 39.

4. *Ibid.*, pp. 12-13.

Michael Cannon and Michael Tanner argue that third-party payment distorts or conceals the price signals that would be sent in a free market by patients shopping for services with their own money. As "patients take less care to weigh the expected costs and benefits of medical care," providers have far less incentive to minimize costs per unit of service in order to offer a competitive price. Rather, with fixed payments for service from third-party payers, providers have an incentive to minimize quality and pocket the difference. "It should come as little surprise, then, that in practice, patients often receive substandard or unnecessary care." An *NEJM* study found that patients received "the generally accepted standard of preventive, acute, and chronic care" only 55% of the time. And third-party payments increase the incentive to pad the bill with unnecessary procedures, since patients do not bear the cost.[1] The medical ethic is replaced by a *"veterinary* ethic, which consists of caring for the sick animal not in accordance with its specific medical needs, but according to the requirements of its master and owner, the person responsible for paying any costs incurred."[2]

Anyone who's ever been in the hospital or made a trip to the ER is familiar with this phenomenon. The hospital bill will be padded with long lists of tests and procedures that the patient has no memory whatsoever of authorizing, and will be followed by a long series of bills from clinics for tests and consultations which the patient likewise never explicitly approved. And as someone who's experienced the system both as a hospital worker and as a patient, I'm quite familiar with the incentives to mutual logrolling between physicians, calling each other in on consultations on the flimsiest of pretexts; it's the same good ol' boy system by which academicians assign each other's overpriced textbooks to their classes. The fact that the U.S. healthcare system has the highest ratio of specialists to generalists in the industrialized world doesn't help matters.

The cumulative effect of all these policies is Illich's "radical monopoly." The state-sponsored crowding-out makes other, cheaper (and often more appropriate) forms of treatment less usable, and renders cheaper (but adequate) treatments artificially scarce. Centralized, high-tech, and skill-intensive ways of doing things make it harder for ordinary people to translate their own skills and knowledge into use-value.

One possibility for promoting cooperative delivery of service is to transform the public's theoretical ownership of community nonprofit hospitals, where it exists, into real ownership. A good example is the hospital where I work now. It was founded as a community nonprofit in the early 1950s. The people of the community had subscription drives, bake sales, all that other Norman Rockwell stuff, to raise funds to build a hospital. They were damn proud of it, and had every right to be. It was *their* hospital.

The problem was, it wasn't run like something that truly belonged to the community. Its board of directors was made up of the same usual suspects, the riff-raff from the City Council and Chamber of Commerce, who run everything else in town. It was organized on the typical corporate model that Paul Goodman described in *People or Personnel*: Weberian rationality, top-heavy hierarchy, high overhead costs, mission statements, "best practices," and management by résumé carpetbaggers with prestige salaries.

When mission statements were the flavor of the week, they wrote the best mission statement money could buy (and have since repeatedly attempted to address problems of patient satisfaction and employee morale by writing *new* mission statements to pay lip service to). They parroted all the Kwality and Six Sigma jargon, and jumped on the ISO-9000 bandwagon—and never had a clue what any of it meant. They couldn't tell the actual ideas of Deming or Juran from those of Taylor. Right next to their bulletin board covered with "Plan Do Check Act" jargon and "process variation" graphics, was another bulletin board filled with the behavioral approach to eliciting increased productivity through what Dem-

1. Cannon and Tanner, *Healthy Competition*, pp. 55-56.
2. *Ibid.*, p. 57

ing contemptuously dismissed as "slogans and exhortations, and revival meetings" and Drucker called "management by drives"—and they were too ass-brained stupid to understand that the two were diametrically opposed in principle.

Finally, in the 90s, one of the last CEOs of the independent hospital completely ran it into the ground, so that his successor wound up selling it to a for-profit corporate hospital chain. Since then, this hospital has passed from one corporate owner to another, like a drunken sorority chick pulling a train, with each new group of corporate pigs looking to hollow it out a bit more and line their own pockets before passing it on to the next bunch of piggies. They have taken something that the people of my town were proud of, and thought of as their own—and shit on it.

Since then, like typical pointy-haired bosses, they have gutted human capital in one downsizing after another, poured resources into ill-advised investments undertaken mainly for their prestige value, and all the other stuff straight out of the MBA Playbook. Their focus is on being the first to offer new, ultra-expensive specialties that benefit only a small percentage of the population, or to buy extremely expensive high-tech equipment of limited use (like a Da Vinci surgical robot that cost several hundred thousand dollars). The idea is that you can experience the world of the *Jetsons* in surgery—and then experience life in a Third World country on the squalid, understaffed patient care floor, where you shit the bed waiting an hour for a bedpan, and go five days without a bath or linen change because there's one orderly for twenty or thirty patients. They hire committees of high-salaried consultants to write mission statements (and vision statements and core values) about "extraordinary patient care" and "going above and beyond," while gutting the patient care staff. If a hospital could provide "extraordinary patient care" by writing about it in mission statements, without actually spending any money on patient care staff, the place where I work would be the best hospital in the history of the universe.

From the very beginning, it should have been run as a *genuine* community hospital, responsible *to the real community*. It should have been organized as a stakeholder cooperative, with the board of directors made up of representatives of the medical and nursing (and technical, housekeeping, maintenance, dietary, etc.) staff, and of the patient-members.

It should have pursued cost-cutting primarily by reducing overhead from management salaries and bureaucracy, which have at least as much of an effect on unit costs as the wages of production workers (although the MBA schools have to kill anyone who figures that out).

And it should have pursued a business model of offering the kinds of basic medical care that were needed by most people, efficiently and affordably, with a high quality of personal service. It should have branded itself as the hospital where the vast majority of people could go for most medical problems, and get their call lights answered in a timely fashion and get a bath every day, without the high rates of MRSA, falls, and med errors that result from understaffing. As the slogan on the Heinz ketchup bottle says, they should have done an ordinary thing extraordinarily well.

When community nonprofits are threatened, communities need to stage a hostile takeover and bring those "public" hospitals under the control of *the real public*.

In contrast, here's my vision of one possible alternative healthcare system, as it might exist in a genuinely free market. The lowest tier of service is a cooperative clinic at the neighborhood level, perhaps organized on a subscription basis by a fraternal order or mutual society, on the old lodge practice model. It might be staffed mainly with nurse-practitioners or the sort of "barefoot doctors" mentioned above. They could treat most traumas and ordinary infectious diseases themselves, with several neighborhood clinics together having an MD on retainer for more serious referrals. They could rely entirely on generic drugs (which is all there'd ultimately be in a free market, anyway), at least when they were virtually as good as the patented "me too" stuff; possibly with the option to buy more expensive, non-covered stuff with your own money. This would be a major reduction in cost for members of the cooperative, who wouldn't have to pay the cost of an expensive office visit to an MD for such service. Their service model might also look more like something designed by, say, Dr. Andrew Weil, with much greater emphasis on preventive medicine, nutrition, etc. One of the terms of membership in the lower tier plan, at standard rates, might be signing a waiver for most expensive, legally-driven CYA testing; as a result, the focus would be on Kling's "empirical," rather than "premium" treatment. For members of such a cooperative, the monthly subscription fee in real dollars might be as low as twenty or thirty dollars. No doubt many upper middle class people might prefer a healthcare plan with more frills, catastrophic care, etc. But for the 40 million or so who are presently uninsured, it'd be a pretty damned good deal.

The next tier would be an intermediate insurance policy. If the G.P. or nurse practitioner recommended a test or treatment that was beyond his competency, or the resources of the facility, the second tier of insurance would kick in. For example, the woman with the inflamed eye in the example above might be advised to get an MRI just in case, even if the doctor was 95% sure it would respond to antibiotics and steroids. But the insurance would have a rather high deductible—say twenty percent—so an MRI would require significant out of pocket expense. As a result, such premium medicine would be available, but rather than being viewed as an automatic part of ordinary treatment, for which the patient's insurance bill could be padded, it would be an out of the ordinary procedure, to be undergone only after serious consideration by the patient himself as to whether the out of pocket expense would be justified. Under such circumstances, a lot more patients would be likely to stick with the antibiotics and steroids, and skip the MRI. The cost of the intermediate tier of insurance would, as a result, be far lower than the present portion of insurance premiums that cover the inflated cost of premium care.

The third tier would provide coverage only against catastrophic illnesses.

And in a society where the mutuals and the associated community (the heir of the old local government, minus its invasive powers) replace the centralized state and the corporation as the expected means for organizing benefits, the provision of such health insurance plans would likely be a standard benefit of membership in a guild or a community association.

Bibliography

"270-day libel case goes on and on . . . ," June 28 1996, *Daily Telegraph* (UK) <http://www.mcspotlight.org/media/thisweek/jul3.html>.

Scott Adams. *The Joy of Work: Dilbert's Guide to Finding Happiness at the Expense of Your Co-workers* (New York: HarperCollins, 1998).

Walter Adams and James Brock. *The Bigness Complex*. First Edition (New York: Pantheon Books, 1986).

Adams and Brock. *The Bigness Complex: Industry, Labor and Government in the American Economy*. 2nd ed. (Stanford, Cal.: Stanford University Press, 2004).

Philippe Aghion, Eve Caroli, and Cecilia Garcia-Penalosa. *Inequality and Economic Growth: The perspective of the new growth theories* N 9908 (June 1999) <http://www.cepremap.cnrs.fr/couv_orange/co9908.pdf>.

Armen A. Alchian and Harold Demsetz. "Production, Information Costs, and Economic Organization" *The American Economic Review* 62:5 (December 1972) pp. 777-795.

Armen A. Alchian and R.A. Kessel. "Competition, Monopoly, and the Pursuit of Pecuniary Gain" in *Aspects of Labor Economics* (Princeton: National Bureau of Economic Research, 1962).

Guy Alchon. *The Invisible Hand of Planning: Capitalism, Social Science, and the State in the 1920s* (Princeton, N.J.: Princeton University Press, 1985).

Jerome Alexander. "Distressed about Job Stress? Don't Worry, Your Employer Isn't!" *The Corporate Cynic*, March 25, 2008 <http://thecorporatecynic.wordpress.com/2008/03/25/distressed-about-job-stress-don%e2%80%99t-worry-your-employer-isn%e2%80%99t/>.

Alexander. "Honey, We've Shrunk the Company!" *The Corporate Cynic*, July 20, 2007 <http://thecorporatecynic.wordpress.com/2007/07/20/honey-we%e2%80%99ve-shrunk-the-company/>.

Alexander. "'Outing' Some of the Downsides of Outsourcing," *The Corporate Cynic*, April 3, 2008 <http://thecorporatecynic.wordpress.com/2008/04/03/%e2%80%9couting%e2%80%9d-some-of-the-downsides-of-outsourcing/>.

Alexander. "Requiem for TQM of Total Quality Mismanagement," The Corporate Cynic, April 1, 2007 <http://thecorporatecynic.wordpress.com/2007/04/01/tqm-mayhem-or-total-quality-mismanagement/>.

Alexander. "What would "The Duke" say about the Trivialization of Non-executive Functions?" *The Corporate Cynic*, April 10, 2008 <http://thecorporatecynic.wordpress.com/2008/04/10/what-would-%e2%80%9cthe-duke%e2%80%9d-say-about-the-trivialization-of-non-executive-functions/>.

V. L. Allen and D. B. Greenberger. "Destruction and Perceived Control," in A. Baum and J.E. Singer, eds., *Advances in Environmental Psychology* (Hillsdale, N.J.: Earlbaum, 1980).

"America's long history of subsidizing transportation" <http://www.trainweb.org/moksrail/advocacy/resources/subsidies/transport.htm>.

Farhad Analoui and Andrew Kakabadse. *Sabotage: How to Recognize and Manage Employee Defiance* (Management Books 2000 Ltd, 2000).

An Anarchist FAQ Webpage Version 12.2 (February 27, 2008) <http://www.infoshop.org/faq/>.

Elizabeth Anderson. "Adventures in Contract Feudalism," *Left2Right*, Feb. 10, 2005 <http://left2right.typepad.com/main/2005/02/adventures_in_c.html>.

Anderson. "How Not to Complain About Taxes (II): Against Natural Property Rights," *Left2Right*, Jan. 20, 2005 <http://left2right.typepad.com/main/2005/01/ why_i_reject_ na.html>.

Stephen Pearl Andrews. "Proudhon and His Translator," *The Index*, June 22, 1876. Formatted by Shawn Wilbur at *Libertarian Labyrinth* <http://libertarian-labyrinth.org/ theindex/1876-tucker-andrews.pdf>.

Andrews. *Science of Society*. Online edition provided courtesy of the late Ken Gregg, at *CLASSical Liberalism* blog <http://classicalliberalism.blogspot.com/ 2006/04/ science-of-society-no_10.html>.

"Appreciative Inquiry: Application and Celebration. Two WLA Sessions presented at Wisconsin Dells Conference, 2006" (Wisconsin Library Association) <http://www.wla. lib.wi.us/conferences/2006/documents/wlahandouts2006.pdf>.

Kenneth J. Arrow. "Control in Large Organizations" *Management Science (pre-1986)* 10:3 (April 1964).

Arrow. "Research in Management Controls: A Critical Synthesis," in C. Bonini, R. Jaediche, and H. Wagner, eds., *Management Controls: New Directions in Basic Research* (New York: McGraw-Hill, Inc., 1964).

Associated Press. "U.S. government fights to keep meatpackers from testing all slaughtered cattle for mad cow," *International Herald-Tribune*, May 29, 2007 <http://www.iht.com/articles/ap/2007/05/29/america/NA-GEN-US-Mad-Cow.php>.

Joe Bageant. "The masses have become fat, lazy, and stupid," December 11, 2006 <http://www.joebageant.com/joe/2006/12/the_masses_have.html>.

Ronald Bailey. "Billions Served: Norman Borlaug interviewed by Ronald Bailey," Reason, April 2000 <http://www.reason.com/news/printer/27665.html>.

Bailey. "Drug Companies Don't Get Enough Money . . . ," *Reason Magazine Hit&Run*, February 22, 2006 <http://www.reason.com/blog/show/112727.html>.

Bailey. "This Is One Reason People Hate Drug Companies," *Reason Magazine Hit&Run*, February 24, 2006 <http://www.reason.com/blog/show/112756.html>.

Joe S. Bain. *Barriers to New Competition: Their Character and Consequences in Manufacturing Industries.* Third printing (Cambridge, MA: Harvard University Press, 1965).

Dean Baker. *The Conservative Nanny State: How the Wealthy Use the Government to Stay Rich and Get Richer* (Washington, D.C.: Center for Economic and Policy Research, 2000).

Paul Baran and Paul Sweezy. *Monopoly Capitalism: An Essay in the American Economic and Social Order* (New York: Monthly Review Press, 1966).

Patrick Barkham. "Blogger sacked for sounding off," *The Guardian*, Jan. 12, 2005 <http://www.guardian.co.uk/online/weblogs/story/0,14024,1388466,00.html> (link defunct).

Chester Barnard. *The Functions of the Executive* (Cambridge: Harvard University Press, 1938).

Thomas Barnett. "The Pentagon's New Map," *Esquire* March 2003 <http://www.thomaspmbarnett.com/ published/pentagonsnewmap.htm>.

The Bastiat-Proudhon Debate on Interest (1849-1850). Translated by Roderick Long

Lance Bauscher. *Utopia USA* interview with Robert Anton Wilson. 22 Feb 2001 <http://www.deepleafproductions.com/utopialibrary/text/raw-inter-utopia.html>.

Michel Bauwens. "Can the experience economy be capitalist?" *P2P Foundation Blog*, September 27, 2007 <http://blog.p2pfoundation.net/can-the-experience-economy-be-capitalist/2007/09/27>.

Bauwens. "Contract manufacturing as distributed manufacturing," *P2P Foundation Blog*, September 11, 2008 <http://blog.p2pfoundation.net/contract-manufacturing-as-distributed-manufacturing/2008/09/11>.

Bauwens. "Franz Nahrada: Can we produce for physical abundance or sufficiency?" *P2P Foundation Blog*, January 14, 2008 <http://blog.p2pfoundation.net/ franz-nahrada-can-we-produce-for-physical-abundance-or-sufficiency/2008/01/14>.

Bauwens. *P2P and Human Evolution*. Draft 1.994 (Foundation for P2P Alternatives, June 15, 2005) <http://integralvisioning.org/article.php?story=p2ptheory1>.

Bauwens. "Peer-to-Peer Governance, Democracy, and Economic Vision: P2P as a Way of Living—Part 2," *Master New* Media, October 27, 2007 <http://www.masternewmedia.org/ information_access/ p2p-peer-to-peer-economy/ peer-to-peer-governance-production-property-part-2-Michel-Bauwens-20071020.htm>.

Bauwens. "Phases for implementing peer production: Towards a Manifesto for Mutually Assured Production," *P2P Foundation Forum*, August 30, 2008 <http://p2pfoundation.ning.com/forum/topic/show?id=2003008%3ATopic%3A6275&page=1&commentId=2003008%3AComment%3A6377&x=1#2003008Comment6377>.

Bauwens. "The Political Economy of Peer Production," *CTheory*, December 2005 <http://www.ctheory.net/articles.aspx?id=499>.

Bauwens. "What kind of economy are we moving to? 3. A hierarchy of engagement between companies and communities," *P2P Foundation Blog*, October 5, 2007 <http://blog.p2pfoundation.net/what-kind-of-economy-are-we-moving-to-3-a-hierarchy-of-engagement-between-companies-and-communities/2007/10/05>.

David Beito. *From Mutual Aid to the Welfare State: Fraternal Societies and Social Services, 1890-1967* (Chapel Hill and London: The University of North Carolina Press, 2000).

Walden Bello. "A Primer on Wall Street Meltdown," *MR Zine*, October 3, 2008 <http://mrzine.monthlyreview.org/bello031008.html>.

Bello. "Structural Adjustment Programs: 'Success' for Whom?" in Jerry Mander and Edward Goldsmith, eds., *The Case Against the Global Economy* (San Francisco: Sierra Club Books, 1996).

Hilaire Belloc. *The Servile State* (Indianapolis: Liberty Classics, 1913, 1977).

Tom Bender. "Appropriate Technology," in Dorf and Hunter, eds.

"Benjamin Tucker: Capitalist or Anarchist?" *Anarchist FAQ*, G.5 <http://www.infoshop.org/faq/secG5. html>.

Yochai Benkler. *The Wealth of Networks: How Social Production Transforms Markets and Freedom* (New Haven and London: Yale University Press, 2006).

Avner Ben-Ner, Tzu-Shian Han and Derek C. Jones. "The Productivity Effects of Employee Participation in Control and in Economic Returns: A Review of Empirical Evidence," in Pagano and Rowthorn, eds., *Democracy and Efficiency in the Democratic Enterprise*.

James C. Bennett. "The End of Capitalism and the Triumph of the Market Economy," from *Network Commonwealth: The Future of Nations in the Internet Era* (1998, 1999) <http://www.pattern.com/bennettj-endcap.html>.

Christian Berggren. "Lean Production: The End of History?" Expanded version of paper presented for a seminar at the Science and Technology Analysis Research Programme, University of Wollongong (September 1991) <http://www.uow.edu.au/arts/sts/research/STPPapers/LeanProduction-10.html>.

Alex Berenson and Reed Abelson. "The Evidence Gap: Weighing the Costs of a CT Scan's Look Inside the Heart," *New York Times*, June 29, 2008 <http://www.nytimes.com/2008/06/29/business/29scan.html>.

Judith Biewener. "Downsizing and the New American Workplace," *Review of Radical Political Economics* 29:4 (December 1997).

Duncan Black, *Eschaton blog*, August 22, 2004 <http://atrios.blogspot.com/ 2004_08_22_atrios_archive.html#109335851226026749>.

Black. "Face Time," *Eschaton* blog, July 9, 2005 <http://atrios.blogspot.com/ 2005_07_03_atrios_archive.html#112049256079118503>.

Edwin Black. "Hitler's Carmaker: How Will Posterity Remember General Motors' Conduct? (Part 4)" History News Network, May 14, 2007 <http://hnn.us/articles/38829.html>.

David G. Blanchflower and Andrew J. Oswald. "What Makes an Entrepreneur?" <http://www2.warwick.ac.uk/fac/soc/economics/staff/faculty/oswald/entrepre.pdf>.

Peter M. Blau and W. Richard Scott. *Formal Organizations: A Comparative Approach* (San Francisco: Chandler Publishing Co., 1962).

William Blum. *Killing Hope: U.S. Military and CIA Interventions Since World War II* (Monroe, Maine: Common Courage Press, 1995).

Tom Blumer. "Disarming Nardelli's Defenders, Part 1," *BizzyBlog*, January 8, 2007 <http://www.bizzyblog.com/2007/01/08/disarming-nardellis-defenders-part-1/>.

Blumer. "Disarming Nardelli's Defenders, Part 3," *BizzyBlog*, January 8, 2007 <http://www.bizzyblog.com/2007/01/08/disarming-nardellis-defenders-part-3/>.

Wally Bock. "Lessons from Semco," *Monday Memo*, May 12, 2003 <http://www.mondaymemo.net/030512feature.htm>.

Eugen von Böhm-Bawerk. *The Positive Theory of Capital*. Translated by William Smart (London: Macmillan and Co., 1891).

Murray Bookchin. *Post-Scarcity Anarchism* (Berleley, Ca.: The Ramparts Press, 1971).

Florence S. Boos. "*News From Nowhere* and 'Garden Cities': Morris's Utopia and Nineteenth-Century Town Design," *Journal of Pre-Raphaelite Studies*, Fall 1998 <http://www.morrissociety.org/agregation.boos.html>.

Ralph Borsodi. *The Distribution Age* (New York and London: D. Appleton and Company, 1929).

Borsodi. *Flight from the City: An Experiment in Creative Living on the Land* (New York, Evanston, San Francisco, London: Harper & Row, 1933, 1972).

Borsodi. *Prosperity and Security* (New York and London: Harper & Brothers, 1938).

Borsodi. *This Ugly Civilization* (Philadelphia: Porcupine Press, 1929, 1975).

Kenneth Boulding. *Beyond Economics* (Ann Arbor: University of Michigan Press, 1968).

Boulding. "The Economics of Knowledge and the Knowledge of Economics" *American Economic Review* 56:1/2 (March 1966) pp. 1–13.

Samuel Bowles and Herbert Gintis. "Is the Demand for Workplace Democracy Redundant in a Liberal Economy?" in Ugo Pagano and Robert Rowthorn, eds., *Democracy and Efficiency in the Economic Enterprise*.

Bowles and Gintis. "The Distribution of Wealth and the Viability of the Democratic Firm," in Pagano and Rowthorn, eds., *Democracy and Efficiency in the Economic Enterprise*.

Bowles and Gintis. *Schooling in Capitalist America: Educational Reform and the Contradictions of Economic Life* (New York: Basic Books, Inc., Publishers, 1976).

Godfrey Boyle and Peter Harper, eds. *Radical Technology*. From the editors of *Undercurrents* (New York: Pantheon Books, 1976).

Harry Boyte. *The Backyard Revolution: Understanding the New Citizen Movement* (Philadelphia: Temple University Press, 1980).

Ben Branch. "Corporate Objectives and Market Performance," *Financial Management* vol. 2 no. 2 (Summer 1973).

Harold Brookfield. "Family Farms Are Still Around: Time to Invert the Old Agrarian Question," *Geography Compass* 2:1 (2008).

Geoff Brown. *Sabotage: A Study of Industrial Conflict* (Nottingham, England: Spokesman Books, 1977).

James Buchanan. *Cost and Choice: An Inquiry in Economic Theory*, vol. 6 of *Collected Works* (Indianapolis: Liberty Fund, 1999).

M. Northrup Buechner. "Roundaboutness and Productivity in Bohm-Bawerk" *Southern Economic Journal*, Vol. 56, No. 2 (Oct., 1989), pp. 499-510.

J. Stewart Burgess. "Living on a Surplus," *The Survey* 68 (January 1933).

James Burke. "Fábricas Recuperadas: crowd-storming your own just and equitable economy in Argentina," P2P Foundation blog, May 3, 2008 <http://blog.p2pfoundation.net/category/p2p-governance>.

Scott Burns. *The Household Economy: Its Shape, Origins, & Future* (Boston: The Beacon Press, 1975).

Alexis Buss. "Minority Report," *Industrial Worker*, October 2002 <http://www.iww.org/organize/strategy/AlexisBuss102002.shtml>.

Buss. "Minority Report," *Industrial Worker*, December 2002 <http://www.iww.org/organize/strategy/AlexisBuss122002.shtml>.

Kim S. Cameron. "Downsizing, Quality and Performance," in Robert E. Cole, ed., *The Death and Life of the American Quality Movement* (New York: Oxford University Press, 1995).

Michael F. Cannon and Michael D. Tanner. *Healthy Competition: What's Holding Back Health Care and How to Free It* (Washington, D.C.: The Cato Institute, 2005).

Robert Capozzi. "Push the Button?" *FreeLiberal*, January 26, 2006 <http://www.freeliberal.com/blog/archives/001831.php>.

Avedon Carol. "Pilloried Post," *Slacktivist*, August 12, 2004 <http://slacktivist.typepad.com/slacktivist/2004/08/pilloried_post.html>.

Thomas Carothers. "The Reagan Years: The 1980s," in Abraham F. Lowenthal, ed., *Exporting Democracy* (Baltimore: Johns Hopkins, 1991).

Kevin Carson. "Blaming Workers for the Results of Mismanagement," Mutualist Blog, Sept. 17, 2006 <http://mutualist.blogspot.com/2006/09/blaming-workers-for-results-of.html>.

Carson. "'Building the Structure of the New Society Within the Shell of the Old,'" *Mutualist Blog: Free Market Anti-Capitalism*, March 22, 2005 <http://mutualist.blogspot.com/2005/03/building-structure-of-new-society.html>.

Carson. "Carson's Rejoinders," *Journal of Libertarian Studies*, vol. 20, no. 1 (Winter 2006).

Carson. "Chapter Seven Draft," *Mutualist Blog: Free Market Anti-Capitalism*, November 12, 2007 <http://mutualist.blogspot.com/2007/11/chapter-seven-draft.html>.

Carson, "Corporate Personhood," Mutualist Blog, April 24, 2006 <http://mutualist.blogspot.com/2006/04/corporate-personhood.html>.

Carson. "Dan Swinney Article on the High Road," Mutualist Blog, August 5, 2005 <http://mutualist.blogspot.com/2005/08/dan-swinney-article-on-high-road.html>.

Carson. "On Dissolving the State, and What to Replace it With," Mutualist Blog: Free Market Anti-Capitalism, March 3, 2008 <http://mutualist.blogspot.com/2008/03/on-dissolving-state-and-what-to-replace.html>.

Carson. "Economic Calculation in the Corporate Commonwealth: Part II: Hayek vs. Mises on Distributed Knowledge (Excerpt)," *Mutualist Blog*, Friday, March 16, 2007 <http://mutualist.blogspot.com/2007/03/economic-calculation-in-corporate.html>.

Carson. "The Ethics of Labor Struggle: A Free Market Perspective," *Mutualist Blog: Free Market Anti-Capitalism*, April 19, 2007 <http://mutualist.blogspot.com/2007/04/media-print-projection-embossed-body.html>.

Carson. "Fighting the Domestic Enemy: You," Mutualist Blog, August 11, 2005 <http://mutualist.blogspot.com/2005/08/fighting-domestic-enemy-you.html>.

Carson. "Filthy Pig Timoney in the News," Mutualist Blog, December 2, 2005 <http://mutualist.blogspot.com/2005/12/filthy-pig-timoney-in-news.html>.

Carson. "Glenn Reynolds' Upside-Down Version of History." Mutualist Blog, June 20, 2005

Carson. "George Reisman's Double Standard," Mutualist Blog: Free Market Anti-Capitalism, June 23, 2006 <http://mutualist.blogspot.com/2006/06/george-reismans-double-standard.html>.

Carson. "'The High Cost of Developing Drugs,'" Mutualist Blog: Free Market Anti-Capitalism, May 22, 2006 <http://mutualist.blogspot.com/2006/05/high-cost-of-developing-drugs.html>.

Carson. "Intellectual Property Stifles Innovation." Mutualist Blog, May 21, 2006 <http://mutualist.blogspot.com/2006/05/intellectual-property-stifles.html>.

Carson. "Liberation Management, or Management by Stress?" Mutualist Blog: Free Market Anticapitalism, August 28, 2006 <http://mutualist.blogspot.com/2006/08/ liberation-management-or-management-by.html>.

Carson. "Public Services, 'Privatized' and Mutualized," Mutualist Blog: Free Market Anti-capitalism, March 29, 2005 <http://mutualist.blogspot.com/2005/03/public-services-privatized-and.html>.

Carson. Studies in Mutualist Political Economy. Self-published via Blitzprint (Fayetteville, Ark., 2004).

Carson. Studies in Mutualist Political Economy (Amazon BookSurge, 2007) <http://www.amazon.com/Studies-Mutualist-Political-Economy-Carson/dp/1419658697/ref=sr_1_1/103-8771270 1609454?ie=UTF8&s=books&qid=1183573650&sr=1-1>.

Carson. "Thomas L. Knapp Joins the One Big Union," Mutualist Blog, April 6, 2005 <http://mutualist.blogspot.com/2005/04/thomas-l-knapp-joins-one-big-union.html>.

Carson. "Vulgar Libertarianism Watch, Part I," Mutualist Blog: Free Market Anti-Capitalism, January 11, 2005 <http://mutualist.blogspot.com/2005/01/vulgar-libertarianism-watch-part-1.html>.

Manuel Castels. The Rise of the Network Society. Second edition (Oxford and Malden, MA: Blackwell Publishers, 1996, 2000).

"CEB Phase 1 Done," Factor E Farm Weblog, December 26, 2007 <http://openfarmtech.org/weblog/?p=91>.

Anne Marie Chaker. "The Vegetable Patch Takes Root," Wall Street Journal, June 5, 2008 <http://online.wsj.com/article/SB121262319456246841.html?mod=pj_main_hs_coll>.

Alfred D. Chandler, Jr. Inventing the Electronic Century (New York: The Free Press, 2001).

Chandler. Scale and Scope: The Dynamics of Industrial Capitalism (Cambridge and London: The Belknap Press of Harvard University Press, 1990).

Chandler. The Visible Hand: The Managerial Revolution in American Business (Cambridge and London: The Belknap Press of Harvard University Press, 1977).

Aimin Chen. "The structure of Chinese industry and the impact from China's WTO entry," Comparative Economic Studies (Spring 2002) <http://www.entrepreneur.com/tradejournals/article/print/86234198.html>.

Roy Childs. "Big Business and the Rise of American Statism." Reason, February and March 1971, reproduced at <http://praxeology.net/RC-BRS.htm>.

Chloe. "Important People," Corporate Whore, September 21, 2007 <http://www.corporatewhore.us/important-people/>.

Noam Chomsky. Class Warfare: Interviews with David Barsamian (Monroe, Maine: Common Courage Press, 1996).

Chomsky. "How Free is the Free Market?" *Resurgence* no. 173 <http://www.oneworld.org/second_opinion/chomsky.html>.

Chomsky. "Resistance to Neoliberal Globalization," ZNet Blog, Oct. 2005 <http://blog.zmag.org/index.php/weblog/entry/resistance_to_neo_liberal_globalization/>. (Now defunct—retrieved through Internet Archive.)

Citizens for Tax Justice. "GOP Leaders Distill Essence of Tax Plan: Surprise! It's Corporate Welfare." September 14 1999 <http://www.ctj.org/pdf/corpo999.pdf>.

"Clarifying OSE Vision," *Factor E Farm Weblog*, September 8, 2008 <http://openfarmtech.org/weblog/?p=325>.

Kenneth Cloke and Joan Goldsmith. *The End of Management and the Rise of Organizational Democracy* (New York: John Wiley & Sons, 2002).

Moses Coady. *Masters of Their Own Destiny: The Story of the Antigonish Movement of Adult Education Through Economic Cooperation* (New York, Evanston, and London: Harper & Row).

Coalition of Immokalee Workers. "Burger King Corp. and Coalition of Immokalee Workers to Work Together," May 23, 2008 <http://www.ciw-online.org/BK_CIW_joint_release.html>.

Ronald H. Coase. "The Nature of the Firm," *Economica* (November 1937).

Tom Coates. "(Weblogs and) The Mass Amateurisation of (Nearly) Everything . . ." *Plasticbag.org,* September 3, 2003 <http://www.plasticbag.org/archives/2003/09/ weblogs_and_the_mass_ amateurisation_of_nearly_everything>.

Alexander Cockburn. "The Jackboot State: The War Came Home and We're Losing It" *Counterpunch* May 10, 2000 <http://www.counterpunch.org/jackboot.html>.

G. D. H. Cole. *A Short History of the British Working Class Movement (1789-1947)* (London: George Allen & Unwin, 1948).

Cole. "Socialism and the Welfare State," *Dissent* 1:4 (Autumn 1954).

David Collinson. "Strategies of Resistance: Power, Knowledge, and Subjectivity in the Workplace," in J. Jermier and D. Knights, eds., *Resistance and Power in Organizations* (London: routledge, 1994).

Barry Commoner. "Freedom and the Ecological Imperative: Beyond the Poverty of Power," in Dorf and Hunter, eds., *Appropriate Visions.*

John R. Commons. *Institutional Economics* (New York: Macmillan, 1934).

Wally Conger. *Agorist Class Theory: A Left Libertarian Approach to Class Conflict Analysis* (Movement of the Libertarian Left, 2006).

Alan Cooper. *The Inmates are Running the Asylum: Why High-Tech Products Drive Us Crazy and How to Restore the Sanity* (Indianapolis: Sams, 1999).

Sean Corrigan. "You Can't Say That!" August 6, 2002, *LewRockwell.Com* <http://www.lewrockwell.com/corrigan/corrigan13.html>.

Matthew B. Crawford. "Shop Class as Soulcraft," *The New Atlantis*, Number 13, Summer 2006, pp. 7-24 <http://www.thenewatlantis.com/publications/shop-class-as-soulcraft>.

"Create a Great Work Environment," *A Special Report* (Council of State Governments—West) <http://www.csgwest.org/Publications/s_rep_work.pdf>.

Philip Crosby. *Quality is Free: The Art of Making Quality Certain* (New York: McGraw-Hill Book Company, 1979).

Brent Cunningham. "Rethinking Objective Journalism Columbia Journalism Review." Alternet, July 9, 2003 <http://www.alternet.org/mediaculture/16348/>.

W. Cunningham. *The Growth of English Industry and Commerce.* Vol. 1 (The Early Middle Ages) . Fourth Edition (Cambridge: Cambridge University Press, 1905).

Melville Dalton. *Men Who Manage* (New York: John Wiley & Sons, Inc., 1959).

Benjamin Darrington. "Government Created Economies of Scale and Capital Specificity" (2007)   <http://agorism.info/_media/government_created_economies_of_scale_and_capital_specificity.pdf>. Student paper submitted at Austrian scholars conference.

Julia O'Connell Davidson. "The Sources and Limits of Resistance in a Privatized Utility," in J. Jermier and D. Knights, editors, *Resistance and Power in Organizations* (London: Routledge, 1994).

Klaus Deininger and Lyn Squire. "Economic Growth and Income Inequality: Reexamining the Links," *Finance & Development*, March 1997   <http://www.worldbank.org/fandd/english/0397/articles/0140397.htm>.

Craig DeLancey. "Openshot," *Analog*, December 2006.

W. Edwards Deming. *Out of the Crisis* (Cambridge, Mass.: M.I.T., Center for Advanced Engineering Study, 1986).

Kevin Depew. "Five Things You Need to Know," *Minyanville Financial Infotainment*, September 13, 2007   <http://www.minyanville.com/articles/KKR-FDC-Bernanke-Credit+Suisse-CFC/index/a/14090>.

Charlers Derber. *Corporation Nation: How Corporations are Taking Over Our Lives and What We Can Do About It* (New York: St. Martin's Griffin, 1998).

"Development as Enclosure: The Establishment of the Global Economy," *The Ecologist* (July/August 1992) 133.

Alan Deutschman. "The Fabric of Creativity," *Fast Company*, December 19, 2007   <http://www.fastcompany.com/node/51733/print>.

David Dickson. *The Politics of Alternative Technology* (New York: Universe Books, 1974).

Chris Dillow. "Capitalism and Presenteeism," *Stumbling and Mumbling* blog, June 21, 2005   <http://stumblingandmumbling.typepad.com/stumbling_and_mumbling/2005/06/capitalism_and_.html>.

Dillow. *The End of Politics: New Labour and the folly of managerialism* (UK: Harriman House Ltd, 2007).

Dillow. "Parris blurts out the truth," *Stumbling and Mumbling*, December 20, 2007   <http://stumblingandmumbling.typepad.com/stumbling_and_mumbling/2007/12/parris-blurts-o.html>.

Thomas DiLorenzo. "The Myth of Voluntary Unions," Mises.Org, September 14, 2004   <http://www.mises.org/story/1604>.

Maurice Dobb. *Political Economy and Capitalism: Some Essays in Economic Tradition*, 2nd rev. ed. (London: Routledge & Kegan Paul Ltd, 1940, 1960).

Cory Doctorow. "In the age of ebooks, you don't own your library," *Boing Boing*, March 23, 2008   <http://www.boingboing.net/2008/03/23/in-the-age-of-ebooks.html>.

Sam Dolgoff (1980). *The American Labor Movement: A New Beginning*. Originally published in 1980 in *Resurgence*.

Dolgoff, ed (1990). *The Anarchist Collectives: Workers' Self-Management in the Spanish Revolution 1936-1939*. Montreal and New York: Black Rose Books, 1990.

G. William Domhoff. *The Higher Circles: The Governing Class in America* (New York: Vintage Books, 1971).

Domhoff. *The Power Elite and the State: How Policy is Made in America* (New York: Aldine de Gruyter, 1990).

Domhoff. *Who Rules America?* (Englewood Cliffs, N.J.: Prentice-Hall, 1967).

Brian A. Dominick. "An Introduction to Dual Power Strategy" (2002)   <http://www.indymedia.org.uk/en/2002/09/41085.html>.

Richard C. Dorf and Yvonne L. Hunter, eds. *Appropriate Visions: Technology the Environment and the Individual* (San Francisco: Boyd & Fraser Publishing Company, 1978).

Douglas Dowd. *The Waste of Nations: Dysfunction in the World Economy* (Boulder and London: Westview Press, 1989).

Anthony Downs. *Inside Bureaucracy*: A RAND Corporation Research Study (Boston: Little, Brown, and Company, 1967).

Claudia Dreifus. "A Conversation With Nina V. Fedoroff: An Advocate for Science Diplomacy," *New York Times*, August 18, 2008 <http://www.nytimes.com/2008/08/19/science/19conv.html?ref=science>.

Peter F. Drucker. *The Practice of Management* (New York: Harper & Brothers Publishers, 1954).

Kevin Drum. "Oil Prices and Driving Habits," *Washington Monthly*, May 9, 2008 <http://www.washingtonmonthly.com/archives/individual/2008_05/013696.php>.

B. Richard DuBoff and Edward S. Hermann, "Alfred Chandler's New Business History: A Review," *Politics and Society* 10 (1980): 87-110.

P. Dubois. *Sabotage in Industry* (Hammondsworth, England: Penguin Books, 1979).

William M. Dugger. *Corporate Hegemony* (New York: Greenwood Press, 1989).

Dugger, ed. *Underground Economics: A Decade of Institutionalist Dissent* (Armonk, New York and London, England: M.E. Sharpe, Inc., 1992).

Lloyd Dumas. *The Overburdened Economy: Uncovering the Causes of Chronic Unemployment, Inflation, and National Decline.* (Berkeley, Los Angeles, London: University of California Press, 1986).

Deborah Durham-Vichr. "Focus on the DeCSS trial," CNN.Com, July 27, 2000 <http://archives.cnn.com/2000/TECH/computing/07/27/decss.trial.p1.idg/index.html>.

David W. Eakins. "Business Planners and America's Postwar Expansion," in David Horowitz, ed., *Corporations and the Cold War* (New York and London: Monthly Review Press, 1969).

Richard Edwards. *Contested Terrain: The Transformation of the Workplace in the Twentieth Century* (New York: Basic Books, 1979).

Stewart Edwards, ed. *Selected Writings of P.J. Proudhon* (Garden City, N.Y.: Anchor Books, 1969).

Piet-Hein van Eeghen. "The Corporation at Issue, Part I: The Clash of Classical Liberal Values and the Negative Consequences for Capitalist Practice." *Journal of Libertarian Studies*, Vol. 19, Num. 3 (Fall 2005). <http://www.mises.org/journals/jls/19_3/19_3_3.pdf>

Van Eeghen. "The Corporation at Issue, Part II: A Critique of Robert Hesson's In Defense of the Corporation and Proposed Conditions for Private Incorporation." *Journal of Libertarian Studies*, Vol. 19, Num. 4 (Fall 2005). <http://www.mises.org/journals/jls/19_4/19_4_3.pdf>

Barbara Ehrenreich. *Bait and Switch: The (Futile) Pursuit of the American Dream* (New York: Metropolitan Books, Henry Holt and Company, 2005).

Ehrenreich. *Nickel and Dimed: On (Not) Getting By in America* (New York: Henry Holt and Co., 2001).

Ehrenreich. "Who Moved My Ability to Reason?" *The New York Times*, August 14, 2005 <http://www.nytimes.com/2005/08/14/books/review/14EHRENRE.html>.

David Ellerman. *Property and Contract in Economics: The Case for Economic Democracy* (pdf version online)

Ellerman. "Workers' Cooperatives: The Question of Legal Structure" in Robert Jackall and Henry M. Levin, eds., *Worker Cooperatives in America* (Berkeley, Los Angeles, London: University of California Press, 1984).

William Yandell Elliot, ed. *The Political Economy of American Foreign Policy* (Holt, Rinehart & Winston, 1955).

Friedrich Engels. *Anti-Dühring.* Vol. 25 of Marx and Engels *Collected Works* (New York: International Publishers, 1987).

Engels. "On Authority." Marx and Engels, *Collected Works*, vol. 23 (New York: International Publishers, 1988).

Richard Ericson. "The Classical Soviet-Type Economy: Nature of the System and Implications for Reform." *Journal of Economic Perspectives* 5:4 (1991).

Juan G. Espinosa and Andrew Zimbalist. *Economic Democracy: Workers' Participation in Chilean Industry 1970-1973*. Updated student edition (New York, London, Toronto, Sydney, San Francisco: Academic Press, 1981).

Ralph Estes. *Tyranny of the Bottom Line: Why Corporations Make Good People Do Bad Things* (San Francisco: Berrett-Koehler Publishers, 1996).

Steve Everly. "Gasoline Usage Heads Down," *Kansas City Star*, April 21, 2008 <http://www.kansascity.com/105/story/585815.html>.

Stuart Ewen. *Captains of Consciousness: Advertising and the Social Roots of Consumer Culture* (New York: McGraw-Hill, 1976).

Robert U. Eyres, "Lecture 5: Economic Growth (and Cheap Oil)."

Eugene Fama. "Agency Problems and the Theory of the Firm" *Journal of Political Economy* 88:2 (1980).

Martha S. Feldman and James G. March. "Information in Organizations as Signal and Symbol" *Administrative Science Quarterly* 26 (1981).

Thomas Ferguson. *Golden Rule: The Investment Theory of Party Competition and the Logic of Money-Driven Political Systems* (Chicago: University of Chicago Press, 1995).

Thomas Ferguson and Joel Rogers. *Right Turn* (New York: Hill and Wang, 1986).

Mike Ferner, "Taken for a Ride on the Interstate Highway System," MRZine (*Monthly Review*) June 28, 2006 <http://mrzine.monthlyreview.org/ferner280606.html>.

"Fish Philosophy," Mr. Stepien's Science Page, Buffalo Academy of the Sacred Heart <http://www.myteacherpages.com/webpages/RStepien/fish.cfm>.

"The Fish Philosophy," New South Wales Country Areas Program <http://www.cap.nsw.edu.au/QI/TOOLS/def/fishphil.html>.

Jay W. Forrester. "System Dynamics and the Lessons of 35 Years" (April 29, 1991) A chapter for *The Systemic Basis of Policy Making in the 1990s*, ed. by Kenyon B. De Greene.

Nicolai J. Foss. "Misesian Ownership and Coasean Authority in Hayekian Settings: The Case of the Knowledge Economy" (Frederiksberg, Denmark: Department of Industrial Economics and Strategy, Copenhagen Business School, 2000 [revised draft, July 2, 2001]).

Justin Fox, "The Great Paving How the Interstate Highway System helped create the modern economy—and reshaped the FORTUNE 500." Reprinted from Fortune. CNNMoney.Com, January 26, 2004 <http://money.cnn.com/magazines/fortune/fortune_archive/2004/01/26/358835/index.htm>.

Thomas Frank. *One Market Under God: Extreme Capitalism, Market Populism, and the End of Economic Democracy* (New York: Anchor Books, 2001).

Bruce Franklin. "Debt Peonage: The Highest Form of Imperialism?" *Monthly Review* 33:10 (March 1982), pp. 15-31.

Freeman, libertarian critter. "More From Hess," *freeman, libertarian critter*, June 9, 2005 <http://freemanlc.blogspot.com/2005/06/more-from-hess.html>.

Karl Frieden. *Workplace Democracy and Productivity* (Washington, D.C. : National Center for Economic Alternatives, 1980).

Edgar Z. Friedenberg. *The Disposal of Liberty and Other Industrial Wastes* (Garden City, New York: Anchor Books, 1976).

Jeffrey Friedman. "Taking Ignorance Seriously: Rejoinder to Critics," *Critical Review* 18:4 (2006): pp. 467-532.

Thomas Friedman. "What the World Needs Now," *New York Times*, March 28, 1999.

Sean Gabb. "Dr Pirie Changes Trains (But Continues in the Same Direction)," *Free Life Commentary*, Issue Number 18 (July 3, 1998) <http://www.seangabb.co.uk/flcomm/flco18.htm>.

Gabb. "Thoughts on Limited Liability" *Free Life Commentary*, Issue Number 152, 26th September 2006 <http://www.seangabb.co.uk/flcomm/flc152.htm>.

John Kenneth Galbraith. *American Capitalism: The Concept of Countervailing Power* (Boston: Houghton Mifflin, 1962).

Galbraith. *The New Industrial State* (New York: Signet Books, 1967).

John Gall. *Systemantics: How Systems Work and Especially How They Fail* (New York: Pocket Books, 1975).

Larry Gambone. "For Community: The Communitarian Anarchism of Gustav Landauer" (Montreal: Red Lion Press, 2000) <http://dwardmac.pitzer.edu/Anarchist_Archives/bright/landauer/forcommunity.html>.

Philip Gardner. *The Lost Elementary Schools of Victorian England* (Croom Helm, 1984).

Benjamin Gatti. "The Bell Tolls for PV," *Factor E Farm Weblog*, September 5, 2008 <http://openfarmtech.org/weblog/?p=322>.

Tom Geoghegan. *Which Side Are You On?* (New York: Farrar, Strauss & Giroux, 1991).

Henry George, Jr. *The Menace of Privilege* (1905). Available online at The School of Cooperative Individualism website <http://www.cooperativeindividualism.org/georgejr_menace_oo.html>

Nick Gillespie. "The Man Can Bust Our Music," *Reason Hit & Run*, January 5, 2004 <http://www.reason.com/blog/show/103947.html>.

Peter Gillingham. "Appropriate Agriculture," in Dorf and Hunter, eds., *Appropriate* Visions.

Martha Giminez. "Self-Sourcing: How Corporations Get Us to Work Without Pay," *Monthly Review* 59:7 (December 2007): pp. 37-41.

Bruno Giussani. "Open Source at 90 MPH," *Business Week*, December 8, 2006 <http://www.businessweek.com/innovate/content/dec2006/id20061208_509041.htm?>.

Paul and Percival Goodman. *Communitas: Means of Livelihood and Ways of Life* (New York: Vintage Books, 1947, 1960).

Paul Goodman. *Compulsory Miseducation* and *The Community of Scholars* (New York: Vintage Books, 1964, 1966).

Goodman. *People or Personnel* and *Like a Conquered Province* (New York: Vintage Books, 1963, 1965).

David M. Gordon. *Fat and Mean: The Corporate Squeeze of Working Americans and the Myth of Management "Downsizing"* (New York: The Free Press, 1996).

Peter G. Gosselin. "$130 Oil: Is That a Tipping Point?" *The Los Angeles Times*, May 24, 2008 <http://www.latimes.com/business/la-fi-econ24-2008may24,0,6841046,full.story>.

Alvin Gouldner. "The Norm of Reciprocity," *American Sociological Review*," 25 (May 1961): pp. 161-179.

Paul Graham. "What Business Can Learn from Open-Source," August 2005 <http://www.paulgraham.com/opensource.html>.

Peter Gray. "A Brief History of Friendly Societies," at *The Association of Friendly Societies* website <http://www.afs.org.uk/research/researchpgrayhistorypage.htm> (The link is now defunct, but can be retrieved through the Internet Archive).

Bettina Bien Greaves. "To What Extent Was Rand a Misesian?" *Mises.Org*, April 11, 2005 <http://mises.org/story/1790>.

David Green. *Reinventing Civil Society* (London: Institute of Economic Affairs, Health and Welfare Unit, 1993).

Green. *Working-Class Patients and the Medical Establishment: Self-Help in Britain from the Mid-Nineteenth Century to 1948* (Aldershot, UK: Gower/Temple, 1986).

Mark J. Green, with Beverly C. Moore, Jr., and Bruce Wasserstein. *The Closed Enterprise System: Ralph Nader's Study Group Report on Antitrust Enforcement* (New York: Grossman Publishers, 1972).

Edward S. Greenberg. "Producer Cooperatives and Democratic Theory" in Robert Jackall and Henry M. Levin, eds., *Worker Cooperatives in America* (Berkeley, Los Angeles, London: University of California Press, 1984).

William Batchelder Greene. *Equality, No. 1* (1849). Online text edited by Shawn Wilbur at *Libertarian Labyrinth*. <http://libertarian-labyrinth.org/mutual/wbg-equality.html>.

Greene. *Mutual Banking* (1870). Online edition scanned by Saren Calvert <http://www.the-portal.org/mutual_banking.htm>.

Greene. *The Radical Deficiency of the Existing Circulating Medium, and the Advantages of a Mutual Currency* (1857). Online text scanned by Shawn Wilbur <http://libertarian-labyrinth.org/mutual/wbg-mb1857.html >.

Steven Greenhouse. "How Costco Became the Anti-Wal-Mart," New York Times, July 17, 2005 <http://www.nytimes.com/2005/07/17/business/yourmoney/17costco.html

Steven Greenhouse and Michael Barbaro. "Wal-Mart to Add Wage Caps and Part-Timers," *The New York Times*, October 2, 2006 <http://www.nytimes.com/2006/10/02/ business/02walmart.html>.

Walter E. Grinder and John Hagel. "Toward a Theory of State Capitalism: Ultimate Decision-Making and Class Structure," *Journal of Libertarian Studies* 1:1 (Spring 1977) <http://www.mises.org/journals/jls/1_1/1_1_7.pdf>.

Daniel Gross. "Pinching the Penny-Pinchers: idiotic examples of corporate cost-cutting," *Slate*, September 25, 2006 <http://www.slate.com/id/2150340/>.

Gross. "Socialism, American Style: Why American CEOs covet a massive European-style social-welfare state" *Slate* Aug. 1, 2003 <http://slate.msn.com/id/2086511/>.

Sanford J. Grossman and Oliver D. Hart. "The Costs and Benefits of Ownership: A Theory of Vertical and Lateral Integration" *Journal of Political Economy* 94:4 (1986) pp. 691-719.

Benjamin Grove. "Gibbons Backs Drug Monopoly Bill," *Las Vegas Sun* 18 February 2000 <http://www.ahc.umn.edu/NewsAlert/Feb00/022100NewsAlert/44500.htm>.

Vinay Gupta. "Facilitating International Development Through Free/Open Source" <http://guptaoption.com/5.open_source_development.php>.

Gupta. "Soft Development Paths," *The Bucky-Gandhi Design Institute*, April 10, 2008 <http://vinay.howtolivewiki.com/blog/hexayurt/soft-development-paths-520>.

Gupta. "The Unplugged," How to Live Wiki, February 20, 2006 <http://howtolivewiki.com/en/The_Unplugged>.

Gupta. "What's Going to Happen in the Future," *The Bucky-Gandhi Design Institution*, June 1, 2008 <http://vinay.howtolivewiki.com/blog/global/whats-going-to-happen-in-the-future-670>.

Jürgen Habermas. *Legitimation Crisis.* Trans. by Thomas McCarthy (United Kingdom: Polity Press, 1973, 1976).

Michael Hammer and James Champy. *Reengineering the Corporation: A Manifesto For Business Revolution* (N.Y.: HarperCollins Publishers, Inc., 1993).

J. L. and Barbara Hammond. *The Town Labourer (1760-1832)* (London: Longmans, Green & Co., 1917).

Henry Hansman. *The Ownership of Enterprise* (Cambridge and London: The Belknap Press of Harvard University Press, 1996).

Dian Hardison. "Shuttle Crash & Smug NASA Managers 'I F-ing Warned Them!'" *Counterpunch*, Feb. 1, 2003 <http://www.counterpunch.org/hardison02012003.html>.

Michael Hardt and Antonio Negri. *Empire* (Cambridge and London: Harvard University Press, 2000).

Alex Harrowell. " 0x05B7Y: Out of Bolts Error," *The Yorkshire Ranter*, October 10, 2007 <http://yorkshire-ranter.blogspot.com/2007/10/0x05b7y-out-of-bolts-error.html>.

Harrowell. "HOW NOT TO Build a Computer System," *Yorkshire Ranter*, November 19, 2006 <http://yorkshire-ranter.blogspot.com/2006/11/hownotto-build-computer-system.html>.

David M. Hart and Walter E. Grinder. "The Basic Tenets of Real Liberalism. Part IV Continued: Interventionism, Social Conflict and War," *Humane Studies Review* vol. 3 no. 1 (1986).

Paul Hawken, Amory Lovins, and L. Hunter Lovins. *Natural Capitalism: Creating the Next Industrial Revolution* (Boston, New York, London: Little, Brown, and Company, 1999).

Friedrich A. Hayek. "Socialist Calculation II: The State of the Debate (1935)," in Hayek, *Individualism and Economic Order* (Chicago: University of Chicago Press, 1948).

Hayek. "The Use of Knowledge in Society" *The American Economic Review* 35:4 (September 1945) pp. 519-530.

Christopher Hayes. "Mr. Lessig Goes to Washington," *The Nation*, May 29, 2008 <http://www.thenation.com/doc/20080616/hayes>.

Samuel P. Hays. "The Politics of Reform in Municipal Government in the Progressive Era," *Pacific Northwest Quarterly*, October 1964.

Eduard Heimann. "Franz Oppenheimer's Economic Ideas," *Social Research* (February 1949).

Richard Heinberg. *Powerdown: Options and Actions for a Post-Carbon World* (New Society Publishers, 2004).

Martin Hellwig. "On the Economics and Politics of Corporate Finance and Corporate Control," in Xavier Vives, ed., *Corporate Governance: Theoretical and Empirical Perspectives* (Cambridge: Cambridge University Press, 2000).

David Hencke. "Firms Tag Workers to Improve Efficiency," *The Guardian*, June 7, 2005 <http://www.guardian.co.uk/supermarkets/story/0,12784,1500851,00.html>.

Hazel Henderson. *Creating Alternative Futures: The End of Economics* (New York: G.P. Putnam's Sons, 1978).

Jim Henley. "Ask Me What the Secret of 'L—TIMING!—ibalertarianism' Is," *Unqualified Offerings* blog, February 21, 2008 <http://www.highclearing.com/index.php/archives/2008/02/21/7909>.

Doug Henwood. *Wall Street: How it Works and for Whom* (London and New York: Verso, 1997).

Edward S. Herman and Noam Chomsky. *Manufacturing Consent: The Political Economy of the Mass Media* (New York: Pantheon Books, 1988).

Alana Herro. "Clean Energy's Best-Kept Secret: Waste-Heat Recovery," *CommonDreams.org*, November 21, 2007 <http://www.commondreams.org/archive/2007/11/21/5386/>.

Karl Hess. *Community Technology* (New York, Cambridge, Hagerstown, Philadelphia, San Francisco, London, Mexico City, Sao Paulo, Sydney: Harper & Row, Publishers, 1979).

Hess. "Letter From Washington: Where Are The Specifics?" *The Libertarian Forum*, June 15, 1969.

Karl Hess and David Morris. *Neighborhood Power: The New Localism* (Boston: Beacon Press, 1975).

Robert Hessen. "Corporations," *The Concise Encyclopedia of Economics* (Library of Economics and Liberty) <http://www.econlib.org/library/Enc/Corporations.html>.

Hessen. *In Defense of the Corporation* (Stanford, Calif.: Hoover Institution, 1979).

Robert Higgs. *Crisis and Leviathan* (Oxford: Oxford University Press, 1987).

Nicholas Hildyard. "The Myth of the Minimalist State: Free Market Ambiguities," *The Corner House* Briefing No. 5 (March 1998) <http://www.thecornerhouse.org.uk/item.shtml?x=51960>.

John Hockenberry. "You Don't Understand Our Audience: What I learned about network television at Dateline NBC," *Technology Review* (MIT), January/February 2008 <www.technologyreview.com/Infotech/19845/>.

Thomas Hodgskin. *Labour Defended Against the Claims of Capital* (New York: Augustus M. Kelley, 1963 (1823)).

Hodgskin, *The Natural and Artificial Right of Property Contrasted. A Series of Letters, addressed without permission to H. Brougham, Esq. M.P. F.R.S.* (London: B. Steil, 1832). Online Library of Liberty <http://oll.libertyfund.org/index.php?option=com_staticxt&staticfile=show.php%3Ftitle=323&layout=html>.

Hodgskin. *Popular Political Economy: Four Lectures Delivered at the London Mechanics' Institution* (London: Printed for Charles and William Tait, Edinburgh, 1827).

Geoffrey Hodgson. "Organizational Form and Economic Evolution," in Ugo Pagano and Robert Rowthorn, eds., *Democracy and Efficiency in the Economic Enterprise*, a study proposal for the World Institute for Development of Economic Research (WIDER) of the United Nations University (London and New York: Routledge, 1996).

Randy Hodson. *Dignity at Work* (Cambridge [England], New York, Oakleigh [Australia], Madrid, Cape Town: Cambridge University Press, 2001).

Jenny Hogan. "Why it's hard to share the wealth," *New Scientist*, March 12, 2005 <http://www.newscientist.com/article.ns?id=dn7107>.

R. C. Hollinger and J. P. Clark. "Employee Deviance: a Perceived Quality of the Work Experience," *Work and Occupations* Vol. 9 No. 1 (February 1982).

Stanley Holmes and Wendy Zellner. "The Costco Way: Higher wages mean higher profits. But try telling Wall Street" *Business Week Online* April 12, 2004 <http://www.businessweek.com/magazine/content/04_15/b3878084_mz021.htm>.

Bengt Holmstrom and Paul Milgrom. "The Firm as an Incentive System" *The American Economic Review* 84:4 pp. 972-991.

Morton Horwitz. *The Transformation of American Law 1780-1860* (Cambridge and London: Harvard University Press, 1977).

Horwitz. *The Transformation of American Law, 1870-1960: The Crisis of Legal Orthodoxy* (New York and Oxford: Oxford University Press, 1992).

"How Companies Spend Their Money: A McKinsey Global Survey," *McKinsey Quarterly*, June 2007 <http://www.mckinseyquarterly.com/article_page.aspx?ar=2019&L2=21>.

"How to Fire Your Boss: A Worker's Guide to Direct Action" <http://home.interlog.com/~gilgames/boss.htm>.

Ebenezer Howard. *To-Morrow: A Peaceful Path to Real Reform.* Facsimile of original 1998 edition, with introduction and commentary by Peter Hall, Dennis Hardy and Colin Ward (London and New York: Routledge, 2003).

Arianna Huffington. *Pigs at the Trough: How Corporate Greed and Political Corruption are Undermining America* (New York: Crown Publishers, 2003).

Samuel P. Huntington, Michael J. Crozier, Joji Watanuki. *The Crisis of Democracy.* Report on the Governability of Democracies to the Trilateral Commission: Triangle Paper 8 (New York: New York University Press, 1975).

Jon Husband. "How Hard is This to Understand?" *Wirearchy*, June 22, 2007 <http://blog.wirearchy.com/blog/_archives/2007/6/22/3040833.html>.

Eric Husman. "The Accounting Chains on American Industry," Grim Reader, March 3, 2006 <http://www.zianet.com/ehusman/weblog/2006/03/accounting-chains-on-american-industry.html>.

Husman. "GM vs. Toyota Again," GrimReader, April 7, 2007 <http://www.zianet.com/ehusman/weblog/2007/04/gm-v-toyota-again.html>.

Husman. "Human Scale Part I—Planned Obsolescence," *Grim Reader* blog, September 23, 2006 <http://www.zianet.com/ehusman/weblog/2006/09/human-scale-part-i-planned-obsolesence.html>.

Husman. "Human Scale Part II—Mass Production," *Grim Reader* blog, September 26, 2006 <http:// www.zianet.com / ehusman / weblog / 2006 / 09 / human-scale-part-ii-mass-production.html>.

Husman. "Human Scale Part III—Self-Sufficiency," *Grim Reader* blog, October 2, 2006 <http://www.zianet.com/ehusman/weblog/2006/10/human-scale-part-iii-self-sufficiency.html>.

Husman. "The Military Origins of Quality Control," Grim Reader, September 4, 2006 <http://www.zianet.com/ehusman/weblog/2006/09/military-origins-of-quality-control.html>.

Husman. "Open Source Automobile," *GrimReader*, March 3, 2005 <http://www.zianet.com/ehusman/weblog/2005/03/open-source-automobile.html>.

Husman. "Running on Glue and Tar," Grim Reader blog, June 3, 2007 <http://www.zianet.com/ehusman/weblog/2007/06/running-on-glue-and-tar.html>.

Husman. "Working Smart? Or Rather Neither, Really," Grim Reader, October 10, 2006 <http://www.zianet.com/ehusman/weblog/2006/10/working-smart-or-rather-neither-really.html>.

Aldous Huxley. *Science, Liberty, and Peace* (New York and London: Harper & Brothers Publishers, 1946).

Ivan Illich. "After Deschooling, What?", in Alan Gartner, Colin Greer, Frank Riessman, eds., *After Deschooling, What?* (N.Y., Evanston, San Francisco, London: Harper & Row, 1973).

Illich. *Deschooling Society* (1970). Online edition at Reactor Core courtesy of Paul Knatz <http://reactor-core.org/deschooling.html>.

Illich. *Disabling Professions* (New York and London: Marion Boyars, 1977).

Illich, *Energy and Equity* (1973). Online edition courtesy of Ira Woodhead and Frank Keller <http://www.cogsci.ed.ac.uk/~ira/illich/texts/energy_and_equity/energy_and_equity.html>.

Illich. *In the Mirror of the Past: Lectures and Addresses, 1978-1990* (New York: M. Boyars, 1992).

Illich. "The Three Dimensions of Public Option," in *The Mirror of the Past: Lectures and Addresses, 1978-1990* (New York and London: Marion Boyars, 1992).

Illich. *Tools for Conviviality* (New York, Evanston, San Francisco, London: Harper & Row, 1973).

Illich. *Vernacular Values* (1980). Online edition courtesy of The Preservation Institute <http://www.preservenet.com/theory/Illich/Vernacular.html>.

"Interview—Simi Kamal" *Newsline* (Pakistan) February 2006 <http://www.newsline.com.pk/NewsFeb2006/interviewfeb2006.htm>.

Robert Jackall. *Moral Mazes: The World of Corporate Managers* (New York: Oxford University Press, 1988).

Robert Jackall and Henry M. Levin. "The Prospects for Worker Cooperatives in the United States" in Jackall and Henry Levin, eds., *Worker Cooperatives in America*.

Jackall and Levin. "Work in America and the Cooperative Movement" in Jackall and Levin, eds., *Worker Cooperatives in America*

Jackall and Levin, editors. *Worker Cooperatives in America* (Berkeley, Los Angeles, London: University of California Press, 1984).

Jane Jacobs. *Cities and the Wealth of Nations*

Jacobs. *The Death and Life of Great American Cities* (New York: Vintage Books, 1961, 1992).

Jane Jacobs. *The Economy of Cities* (New York: Vintage Books, 1969, 1970).

Harry Jaffe. "Pentagon to Washington Post Reporter Ricks: Get Lost," *The Washingtonian*, December 29, 2003 <http://washingtonian.com/inwashington/buzz/ tomricks.html>.

Bob James. "The Tragedy of Labour History in Australia." According to Takver's Radical Tradition: An Australian History Page, where the article is hosted, the text is based on James' notes for a lecture given in several different venues. <http://www.takver.com/history/tragedy.htm>.

John Jeavons. *How to Grow More Vegetables* (Berkeley and Toronto: Ten Speed Press, 1974).

Jed. "Capital is Just Another Factor," *Anomalous Presumptions*, March 8, 2007 <http://jed.jive.com/?p=28>/

Jed. "Capitalists vs. Entrepreneurs," *Anomalous Presumptions*, February 26, 2007 <http://jed.jive.com/?p=23>.

David Jenkins. *Job Power: Blue and White Collar Democracy* (Garden City, New York: Doubleday & Company, Inc., 1973).

Michael C. Jensen and William H. Meckling. "Theory of the Firm: Managerial Behavior, Agency Costs and Ownership Structure" *Journal of Financial Economics* 3:4 (October 1976).

John Jewkes, David Sawers, and Richard Stillerman. *The Sources of Invention* (London: MacMillan & Co Ltd, 1958).

Charles Johnson. "Coalition of Imolakee Workers marches in Miami," *Rad Geek People's Daily*, November 30, 2007 <http://radgeek.com/gt/2007/11/30/coalition_of/>.

Johnson. "On Crutches and Crowbars: Toward a Labor Radical Case Against the Minimum Wage," *Rad Geek People's Daily*, March 6, 2008 <http://radgeek.com/gt/2008/03/06/on_crutches/>.

Johnson. "Dump the rentiers off your back," *Rad Geek People's Daily*, May 29, 2008 <http://radgeek.com/gt/2008/05/29/dump_the/>.

Johnson. "How Intellectual Protectionism promotes the progress of science and the useful arts," *Rad Geek People's Daily*, May 28, 2008 <http://radgeek.com/gt/2008/05/28/how_intellectual/>.

Johnson. "King Ludd's throne," *Rad Geek People's Daily*, May 23, 2008 <http://radgeek.com/gt/2008/05/23/king_ludds/>.

Johnson. "Liberty, Equality, Solidarity: Toward a Dialectical Anarchism," in Roderick T. Long and Tibor R. Machan, eds., *Anarchism/Minarchism: Is a Government Part of a Free Country?* (Hampshire, UK, and Burlington, Vt.: Ashgate Publishing Limited, 2008).

Johnson. "Libertarianism Through Thick and Thin," *The Freeman: Ideas on Liberty*, July/August 2008 <http://www.fee.org/pdf/the-freeman/Johnson.pdf>.

Johnson. "Scratching By: How Government Creates Poverty as We Know It," *The Freeman: Ideas on Liberty* 57:10 (December 2007) <http://www.fee.org/publications/the-freeman/article.asp?aid=8204>.

Johnson. "¡Sí, Se Puede! Victory for the Coalition of Imolakee Workers in the Burger King penny-per-pound campaign," *Rad Geek People's Daily*, May 23, 2008 <http://radgeek.com/gt/2008/05/23/si_se/>.

H. Thomas Johnson. "Confronting the Tyranny of Management by Numbers," *Reflections: The SoL Journal*, vol. 5, no. 4 (2004).

Johnson. "Sustainability and Lean Operations," *Cost Management*. March/April 2006.

H. Thomas Johnson and Robert S. Kaplan. *Relevance Lost: The Rise and Fall of Management Accounting* (Boston: Harvard Business School Press, 1987).

Spencer Johnson. *Who Moved My Cheese? An A-Mazing Way To Deal With Change In Your Work And In Your Life* (New York: G.P. Putnam's Sons, 1998, 2002).

Warren Johnson. *Muddling Toward Frugality: A Blueprint for Survival in the 1980s* (San Franciso: Sierra Club Books, 1978).

Derek C. Jones. "American Producer Cooperatives and Employee-Owned Firms: A Historical Perspective" in Robert Jackall and Henry M. Levin, eds., *Worker Cooperatives in America* (Berkeley, Los Angeles, London: University of California Press, 1984).

Derek C. Jones and Donald J. Schneider. "Self-Help Production Cooperatives: Government-Administered Cooperatives During the Depression" in Robert Jackall and

Henry M. Levin, eds., *Worker Cooperatives in America* (Berkeley, Los Angeles, London: University of California Press, 1984).

John M. Jordan. *Machine-Age Ideology: Social Engineering and American Liberalism, 1911-1939: Social Engineering and American Liberalism, 1911-1939* (Chapel Hill, University of North Carolina Press, 1994).

Clare Joy and Peter Hardstaff. *Dirty aid, dirty water: The UK government's push to privatise water and sanitation in poor countries* (London: World Development Movement, February 2005) <http://www.wdm.org.uk/resources/reports/water/dadwreport01022005.pdf>.

"Juran: A Lifetime of Quality," *Quality Digest Magazine*, August 2002 <http://www.qualitydigest.com/aug02/articles/01_article.shtml>.

J.M. Juran and Frank M Gryna. *Juran's Quality Control Handbook.* Fourth edition (New York: McGraw-Hill Book Company, 1951, 1988).

Brian Kaller. "Future Perfect: Stop Worrying and Learn to Love Expensive Oil," *The American Conservative*, August 25, 2008.

Jeffrey Kaplan. "The Gospel of Consumption: And the better future we left behind," *Orion*, May/June 2008. <http://www.orionmagazine.org/index.php/articles/article/2962>.

Rudolf Kaulla. *Theory of the Just Price: A Historical and Critical Study of the Problem of Economic Value.* Translated by Robert D. Hogg (London: George Allen and Unwin Ltd, 1940).

John Kay. *The Business of Economics* (Oxford: Oxford University Press, 1996).

Sam Kazman. "The Mother of All Food Fights," *The Freeman: Ideas on Liberty* 48:11 (November 1998) <http://www.fee.org/Publications/the-Freeman/ article.asp?aid=3699>.

Judy Keen and Paul Overberg. "Gas prices rattle Americans," *USA Today*, May 8, 2008 <http://www.usatoday.com/money/industries/energy/2008-05-08-gasprices_N.htm>.

Marjorie Kelly. "The Corporation as Feudal Estate" (an excerpt from *The Divine Right of Capital*) *Business Ethics*, Summer 2001. Quoted in GreenMoney Journal, Fall 2008 <http://greenmoneyjournal.com/article.mpl?articleid=60&newsletterid=15>.

Kevin Kelly. "Better Than Free," *The Technium*, January 31, 2008 <http://www.kk.org/thetechnium/archives/2008/01/better_than_fre.php>.

Rakesh Khurana. *From Higher Aims to Hired Hands: The Social Transformation of American Business Schools and the Unfulfilled Promise of Management as a Profession* (Princeton and Oxford: Princeton University Press, 2007).

Kinsale 2021: An Energy Descent Action Plan—Version.1.2005. By Students of Kinsale Further Education College. Edited by Rob Hopkins (Kinsale, Ireland: Kinsale Further Education College, 2005) <http://transitionculture.org/?page_id=104>.

N. Stephan Kinsella. "Defend Hoppe," Mises Economics Blog, February 6, 2005 <http://blog.mises.org/archives/003107.asp>.

Kinsella. "In Defense of the Corporation," Mises Economics Blog, October 27, 2005. <http://blog.mises.org/archives/004269.asp>.

Kinsella, "Sean Gabb's Thoughts on Limited Liability," Mises Economics Blog, September 26, 2006 <http://blog.mises.org/archives/005679.asp>.

Kinsella. "The Trouble With Libertarian Activism," LewRockwell.Com, January 26, 2006 <http://www.lewrockwell.com/kinsella/kinsella19.html>.

Alex Kjerulf, "Analysts to Costco: Stop treating your employees so well," *Chief Happiness Officer*, July 17, 2007 <http://positivesharing.com/2007/07/analysts-to-costco-stop-treating-your-employees-so-well/>.

Ezra Klein. "Why Labor Matters," *The American Prospect*, November 14, 2007 <http://www.prospect.org/csnc/blogs/ezraklein_archive?month=11&year=2007&base_name=why_labor_matters>.

Naomi Klein. *No Logo* (New York: Picador, 1999).

Peter Klein. "Economic Calculation and the Limits of Organization" *The Review of Austrian Economics* 9:2 (1996) pp. 3-28.

Klein. "Government Did Invent the Internet, But the Market Made It Glorious," Mises.Org, June 12, 2006 <http://www.mises.org/story/2211>.

Arnold Kling. *Crisis of Abundance: Rethinking How We Pay for Health Care* (Washington, D.C.: The Cato Institute, 2006).

Frank Knight. *Risk, Uncertainty, and Profit* (Boston and New York: Houghton Mifflin Company, 1921).

Jennifer Kock. "Employee Sabotage: Don't Be a Target!" <http://www.workforce.com/archive/features/22/20/88/mdex-printer.php>.

Herman Koenig. "Appropriate Technology and Resources," in Richard C. Dorf and Yvonne Hunter, eds., *Appropriate Visions: Technology the Environment and the Individual* (San Francisco: Boyd & Fraser Publishing Company, 1978).

Frank Kofsky. *Harry S. Truman and the War Scare of 1948* (New York: St. Martin's Press, 1993).

Leopold Kohr. *The Overdeveloped Nations: The Diseconomies of Scale* (New York: Schocken Books, 1978, 1979).

Gabriel Kolko. *Confronting the Third World: United States Foreign Policy 1945-1980* (New York: Pantheon Books, 1988).

Kolko. *The Roots of American Foreign Policy: An Analysis of Power and Purpose* (Boston: Beacon Press, 1969).

Kolko. *The Triumph of Conservatism: A Reinterpretation of American History, 1900-1916* (New York: The Free Press, 1963).

Samuel Edward Konkin III. *New Libertarian Manifesto* (Koman Publishing, 1983). Online version at Agorism.Info <http://www.agorism.info/ NewLibertarianManifesto.pdf>.

David Korten. *When Corporations Rule the World* (West Hartford, Conn.: Kumarian Press, 1995; San Francisco, Calif.: Berrett-Koehler, Publishers, Inc., 1995).

Peter Kropotkin. *The Conquest of Bread* (New York: Vanguard Press, 1926 (1913)).

Kropotkin. *Fields, Factories and Workshops: or Industry Combined with Agriculture and Brain Work with Manual Work* (New York: Greenwood Press, Publishers, 1968 [1898]).

Kropotkin. *Fields, Factories and Workshops Tomorrow*. Edited, introduced and with additional material by Colin Ward (New York, Evanston, San Francisco, London: Harper & Row, Publishers, 1974).

James Howard Kunstler. *The Geography of Nowhere: The Rise and Decline of America's Man-made Landscape* (New York and London: Simon & Schuster, 1993).

Kunstler. *The Long Emergency: Surviving the Converging Catastrophes of the Twenty-First Century* (New York: Atlantic Monthly Press, 2005).

Kunstler. "Wake Up America. We're Driving Toward Disaster," *Washington Post*, May 25, 2008 <http://www.washingtonpost.com/wp-dyn/content/article/2008/05/23/AR2008052302456_pf.html>.

Adem Kupi. "The Security State vs. the Skeptical Society," *A Pox on All Their Houses*, July 12, 2005 <http://poxyhouses.blogspot.com/2005/07/security-state-vs-skeptical-society.html>.

Robert Rives La Monte. "Editorial," *International Socialist Review* XIII, No. 6 (December 1912).

La Monte. "You and Your Vote," *International Socialist Review* XIII, No. 2 (August 1912).

Jean-Jacques Laffont and David Martimort. *The Theory of Incentives: The Principal-Agent Model* (Princeton and Oxford: Princeton University Press, 2002).

Karim Lakhana. "Communities Driving Manufacturers Out of the Design Space," *The Future of Communities Blog*, March 25, 2007 <http://www.futureofcommunities.com/2007/03/25/communities-driving-manufacturers-out-of-the-design-space/>.

Frances Moore Lappé. *Food First: Beyond the Myth of Scarcity* (New York: Ballantine Books, 1977).

Christopher Lasch. *The Culture of Narcissism: American Life in an Age of Diminishing Expectations* (New York: Warner Books, 1979).

Lasch. *The New Radicalism in America (1889-1963): The Intellectual as a Social Type* (New York: Vintage Books, 1965).

Lasch. *The Revolt of the Elites and the Betrayal of Democracy* (New York and London: W.W. Norton & Co., 1995).

The Lavaca Collective. *Sin Patron: Stories from Argentina's Worker-Run Factories.* Translated by Katherine Kohlstedt (Chicago: Haymarket Books, 2007).

Christopher Layne and Benjamin Shwartz. "American Hegemony Without an Enemy," *Foreign Policy* (Fall 1993).

William Lazonick. *Business Organization and the Myth of the Market Economy* (Cambridge, 1991).

David S. Lawyer, "Are Roads and Highways Subsidized ?" March 2004 <http://www.lafn.org/~dave/trans/econ/highway_subsidy.html>.

Ursula LeGuin. *The Dispossessed* (New York: Harper Paperbacks, 1974).

Harvey Leibenstein. "Allocative Efficiency vs. 'X-Efficiency'" *American Economic Review* 56 (June 1966) pp. 392-415.

Leibenstein. "Organizational or Frictional Equilibria, X-Efficiency, and the Rate of Innovation" pp. 600-623.

Laura Lemay. "The Cheese Stands Alone" (2001) <http://www.lauralemay.com/essays/cheese.html>.

"Lenin". "Dead Zone Revisited," Lenin's Tomb blog, June 7, 2005 <http://leninology.blogspot.com/2005/06/dead-zone-revisited.html>.

V. I. Lenin. *The Impending Catastrophe and How to Combat It.* V.I. Lenin, *Collected Works*, vol. 25 (Moscow: Progress Publishers, 1967).

Henry M. Levin. "Employment and Productivity of Producer Cooperatives" in Jackall and Levin, ed., *Worker Cooperatives in America* (Berkeley, Los Angeles, London: University of California Press, 1984).

Daniel S. Levine. *Disgruntled: The Darker Side of the World of Work* (New York: Berkley Boulevard Books, 1998).

Rick Levine, Christopher Locke, Doc Searls and David Weinberger. *The Cluetrain Manifesto: The End of Business as Usual* (Perseus Books Group, 2001) <http://www.cluetrain.com/book/index.html>.

Claude Lewenz. *How to Build a Village* (Auckland, New Zealand: Village Forum Press and Jackson House Publishing Company, 2007).

Bob Lewis. "Don't cut off your own head: Corporate cost-cutting as a goal is always a mistake," *InfoWorld*, September 11, 2000 <http://www.infoworld.com/articles/op/xml/00/09/11/000911oplewis.html>.

Chris Lewis. "Public Assets, Private Profits," *Multinational Monitor*, in *Project Censored Yearbook 1994* (New York: Seven Stories Press, 1994).

Justin Lewis. "Objectivity and the Limits of Press Freedom," *Project Censored Yearbook 2000.* pp. 173-74.

"LifeTrac," *Open Source Ecology* wiki <http://openfarmtech.org/ index.php?title=LifeTrac>.

Ernest Lilley. "Interview: Cory Doctorow," *SFRevu*, January 1, 2007 <http://sfrevu.com/php/Review-id.php?id=4785>.

Roderick T. Long. "Dismantling Leviathan From Within," Part II: The Process of Reform. *Formulations* 3:1 (Autumn 1995) <http://www.libertariannation.org/ a/f31l3.html>.

Long. "Free Market Firms: Smaller, Flatter, and More Crowded," *Cato Unbound*, Nov. 25, 2008 <http://www.cato-unbound.org/2008/11/25/roderick-long/free-market-firms-smaller-flatter-and-more-crowded>.

Long. "Herbert Spencer, Labortarian," Austro-Athenian Empire, April 10, 2007 <http://praxeology.net/blog/2007/04/10/herbert-spencer-labortarian/>.

Long. "How Government Solved the Health Care Crisis: Medical Insurance that Worked—Until Government 'Fixed' It," *Formulations*, Winter 1993/94.

Long. "Shadow of the Kochtopus," *Austro-Athenian Empire*, May 5, 2008 <http://praxeology.net/blog/2008/05/05/shadow-of-the-kochtopus/>.

Long. "Toward a Libertarian Theory of Class," *Social Philosophy & Policy* 15:2 (1998). On-line version Part One <http://www.praxeology.net/libclass-theory-part-1.pdf> and Part Two <http://www.praxeology.net/libclass-theory-part-2.pdf>.

Geert Lovink. "Oekonux: Interview with Stefan Merten," April 24, 2001 <http://www.nettime.org/ Lists-Archives/nettime-l-0104/msg00127.html>.

Amory B. Lovins. *Soft Energy Paths: Toward a Durable Peace* (New York, Cambridge, Hagerstown, Philadelphia, San Francisco, London, Mexico City, Sao Paolo, Sydney: Harper & Row, Publishers, 1977).

Amory Lovins, E. Kyle Datta, Thomas Feiler, Karl R. Rabago, Joel N. Swisher, Andre Lehmann, and Ken Wicker. *Small is Profitable: The Hidden Economic Benefits of Making Electrical Resources the Right Size* (Snowmass, Colorado: Rocky Mountain Institute, 2002).

Stephen C. Lundin, Harry Paul, and John Christensen. *Fish! A Remarkable Way to Boost Morale and Improve Results* (New York: Hyperion, 2000).

Kari Lydersen. "On Strike Without a Union," *In These Times*, September 12, 2007 <http://www.inthesetimes.com/article/3327/on_strike_without_a_union/>.

Oliver MacDonough. "The Anti-Imperialism of Free Trade," *The Economic History Review* (Second Series) 14:3 (1962).

Tibor S. Machan. "On Airports and Individual Rights," *The Freeman: Ideas on Liberty* (February 1999).

Matt MacKenzie. "Exploitation: A Dialectical Anarchist Perspective." *Upaya: Skillful Means to Liberation*, March 20, 2007 <http://upaya.blogspot.com/2007/03/exploitation.html>.

Ken Macleod. "The Case of the Blogging Bookseller," *The Early Days of a Better Nation*, Jan. 12. 2005 <http://kenmacleod.blogspot.com/2005_01_01_kenmacleod_archive.html#110551826393727206>.

MacLeod. *The Star Fraction* (Tor Books, 2001).

Thomas W. Malone. *The Future of Work: How the New Order of Business Will Shape Your Organization, Your Management Style, and Your Life* (Boston: Harvard Business School Press, 2004).

Euclides André Mance (Nov. 2002). "Solidarity-Based Productive Chains" (Curitiba: l'Institut de Philosophie de la Libération) <http://www.solidarius.com.br/mance/biblioteca/cadeiaprodutiva-en.pdf>.

Mance (March 2007). "Solidarity Economics (Curitiba: l'Institut de Philosophie de la Libération) <http://www.solidarius.com.br/mance/biblioteca/turbulence-en.pdf>.

Henry G. Manne. "Mergers and the Market for Corporate Control," *Journal of Political Economy* 73 (April 1965): pp. 110-119.

"MAP," *P2P Foundation Wiki* <http://p2pfoundation.net/Category:MAP>.

Marcin, "The Thousandth Brick: CEB Field Testing Report," *Factor E Farm Weblog*, Nov. 16, 2008 <http://openfarmtech.org/weblog/?p=422>.

B.K. Marcus. "The Memory Hole," *lowercase liberty* blog, Jan. 19, 2005 <http://www.bkmarcus.com/blog/2005/01/memory-hole.html>.

Steven A. Marglin. "What Do Bosses Do? The Origins and Functions of Hierarchy in Capitalist Production—Part I" *Review of Radical Political Economics* 6:2 (Summer 1974).

Alex Markels and Joann S. Lublin. "Management: Longevity-Reward Programs Get Short Shrift," *The Wall Street Journal*, April 27, 1995 <http://www.markels.com/ management.htm>.

Alex Markels and Matt Murray. "Call It Dumbsizing: Why Some Companies Regret Cost-Cutting," *Wall Street Journal*, May 14, 1996 <http://www.markels.com/ management.htm>.

Alfred Marshall. *Principles of Economics: An Introductory Volume*. Eighth edition (New York: The MacMillan Company, 1948).

Marx. *The Poverty of Philosophy. Collected Works*, vol. 6 (New York: International Publishers, 1976).

Karl Marx and Friedrich Engels. *Capital* vol. 3. Marx and Engels *Collected Works*, vol. 37 (New York: International Publishers, 1998).

Karl Marx and Friedrich Engels. *The German Ideology*. Marx and Engels *Collected Works*, vol. 5 (New York: International Publishers, 1976).

Marx and Engels. *Manifesto of the Communist Party*. Marx and Engels, *Collected Works*, vol. 6 (New York: International Publishers, 1976).

Edward S. Mason, ed. *The Corporation in Modern Society* (Cambridge, Mass.: Harvard University Press, 1966).

Richard Massey. "Springdale: Caregiver of Senile Fights City Hall," *Arkansas Democrat-Gazette* (Northwest Arkansas edition), December 2, 2007 <http://www.nwanews.com/adg/News/209363/>.

Race Matthews. *Jobs of Our Own: Building a Stakeholder Society—Alternatives to the Market & the State* (Annandale, NSW, Australia: Pluto Press, 1999).

Paul Mattick. "The Economics of War and Peace," *Dissent* (Fall 1956).

R. Preston McAffee and John McMillan. "Organizational Diseconomies of Scale" *Journal of Economics & Management Strategy* 4:3 (Fall 1995), pp. 399-426.

John P. McCarthy. *Hilaire Belloc, Edwardian Radical* (Indianapolis: Liberty Press, 1970).

Wendy McElroy. "Contra Gradualism" (November 1997) <http://www.fff.org/freedom/1197e.asp>.

Douglas McGregor. *The Human Side of Enterprise* (New Work, London, Toronto: McGraw-Hill Book Company, Inc., 1960).

Bill McKibben. "The Cuba diet: What will you be eating when the revolution comes?" *Harpers*, April 2005. <http://www.harpers.org/archive/2005/04/0080501>.

Bill McKibben. *Deep Economy: The Wealth of Communities and the Durable Future* (New York: Times Books, 2007).

McKibben. "What is True Development? The Kerala Model," *Utne Reader*, March 1998 <http://www.ashanet.org/library/articles/kerala.199803.html>.

John C. McManus. "The Costs of Alternative Economic Organizations" *Canadian Journal of Economics* 8:3 (August 1975) pp. 334-350.

George McRobie. *Small is Possible: A factual account of who is doing what, where, to put into practice the ideas expressed in E. F. Schumacher's SMALL IS BEAUTIFUL* (New York: Harper & Row, 1981).

J.E. Meade. "The Theory of Labour-Managed Firms and Profit Sharing," in Jaroslav Vanek, ed., *Self-Management: Economic Liberation of Man*.

Ronald L. Meek. *Studies in the Labor Theory of Value* (New York and London: Monthly Review Press, 1956).

Graham Meikle. "Electronic civil disobedience and symbolic power," in Athina Karatzogianni, ed., *Cyber Conflict and Global Politics* (London and New York: Routledge, 2009).

Seymour Melman. *The Permanent War Economy: American Capitalism in Decline* (New York: Simon and Schuster, 1974).

Melman. *Profits Without Production* (New York: Alfred A. Knopf, 1985).

John A. Menge. "The Backward Art of Interdivisional Transfer Pricing" *The Journal of Industrial Economics* 9:3 (July 1961) pp. 215-232.

Harold Meyerson. "Big Brother on and Off the Job," Washington Post, Aug. 10, 2005 <http://www.washingtonpost.com/wp-dyn/content/article/2005/08/09/AR2005080901162.html>.

Robert Michels. *Political Parties: A Sociological Study of the Oligarchical Tendencies of Modern Democracy*. Translated by Eden and Cedar Paul (New York: The Free Press, 1962).

Michigan State University, School of Labor and Industrial Relations. "Labor Relations in the Health Care Industry for Nurses: Online Credit Program" <http://www.lir.msu.edu/distance_learning/MNAArticleandWebPage.htm>.

John Micklethwait and Adrian Wooldridge. *The Witch Doctors: Making Sense of the Management Gurus* (New York: Times Books, 1996).

Paul Milgrom and John Roberts. "Bargaining Costs, Influence Costs, and the Organization of Economic Activity," in James E. Alt and Kenneth A Shepsis, eds., *Perspectives in Positive Political Economy* (New York: Cambridge University Press, 1990).

Milgrom and Roberts. "An Economic Approach to Influence Activities in Organizations," *American Journal of Sociology*, Supplement to vol. 94 (1988).

Gary J. Miller. *Managerial Dilemmas: The Political Economy of Hierarchy* (New York: Cambridge University Press, 1992).

Jon Miller. "Lean Production Does Not Respect People," Panta Rei, May 10, 2006 <http://www.gembapantarei.com/2006/05/lean_production_does_not_respect_people.html>.

C. Wright Mills. *The Power Elite* (Oxford and New York: Oxford University Press, 1956, 2000).

Mills. *The Sociological Imagination* (New York: Grove Press, Inc., 1959).

Mills. *White Collar: The American Middle Classes* (New York: Oxford University Press, 1953).

Ludwig von Mises. *Epistemological Problems of Economics*. Translated by George Reisman (Princeton, New York, Toronto, London: D. Van Nostrand, Inc., 1960).

Mises. *Human Action: A Treatise on Economics*. Third Revised Edition (Chicago: Henry Regnery Company, 1949, 1963, 1966).

Mises. *Socialism: An Economic and Sociological Analysis*. Translated by J. Kahane. New edition, enlarged with an Epilogue (New Haven: Yale University Press, 1951).

George Monbiot. *Heat: How to Stop the Planet Burning* (London, New York, Toronto, Dublin, Victoria, New Delhi, Auckland, Johannesburg: Allen Lane, 2006).

"Monsanto Declares War on 'rBGH-free' Dairies," April 3, 2007 (reprint of Monsanto press release by Organic Consumers Association) <http://www.organicconsumers.org/articles/article_4698.cfm>.

David Montgomery. *Workers' Control in America* (Cambridge and New York : Cambridge University Press, 1979).

Michael Moore. *Stupid White Men . . . and Other Sorry Excuses for the State of the Nation!* (New York, London, Toronto: Penguin Books, 2002).

Frank Morales. "U.S. Military Civil Disturbance Planning: The War at Home" *Covert Action Quarterly*, Spring-Summer 2000; this article is no longer available on the Web, but is preserved at <http://web.archive.org/web/20000818175231/http://infowar.net/warathome/warathome.html>.

Joe Morris. "Wal-Mart institutes availability requirement," *The Charleston Gazette*, June 15, 2005, in *Wake Up Wal-Mart* blog <http://www.wakeupwalmart.com/news/20050615-cg.html>.

William Morris. *News From Nowhere*, in *Three Works by William Morris*, with an introduction by A. L. Morton (New York: International Publishers, 1968).

Jim Motavalli. "Getting Out of Gridlock: Thanks to the Highway Lobby, Now We're Stuck in Traffic. How Do We Escape?" *E Magazine*, March/April 2002 <http://www.emagazine.com/view/?534>.

"MSHA Launches New Safety and Health Initiative," Department of Labor press release, July 13, 2005 <http://www.msha.gov/MEDIA/PRESS/2005/NR050713.asp>.

"MSHA Makes The 'Wrong Decision' To Blame Workers For Accidents," *Labor Blog*, July 28, 2005 <http://www.nathannewman.org/laborblog/archive/003252.shtml>.

"Multimachine & Flex Fab—Open Source Ecology" <http://openfarmtech.org/ in-dex.php?title=Multimachine_%26_Flex_Fab>.

Lewis Mumford. *The City in History: Its Origins, Its Transformations, and Its Prospects* (New York: Harcourt, Brace, & World, Inc., 1961).

Mumford. *The Myth of the Machine: The Pentagon of Power* (New York: Harcourt Brace Jo-vanovich, Inc., 1964, 1974).

Mumford. *Technics and Civilization* (New York: Harcourt, Brace, and Company, 1934).

John Munkirs. "Centralized Private Sector Planning: An Institutionalist's Perspective on the Contemporary U.S. Economy," *Journal of Economic Issues (pre-1986)* , December 1983.

Robert Murphy. "Capital and Interest (Lecture 9 of 32)." Posted by David Heinrich at Mises Economics Blog, June 11, 2004. <http://blog.mises.org/archives/002113.asp>

Charles E. Nathanson, "The Militarization of the American Economy," in David Horow-itz, ed., *Corporations and the Cold War* (New York and London: Monthly Review Press, 1969).

Katherine Newman. "Incipient Bureaucracy: The Development of Hierarchies in Egalitar-ian Organizations," in Gerald M. Britan and Ronald Cohen, eds., *Hierarchy and Soci-ety: Anthropological Perspectives on Bureaucracy* (Philadelphia: Institute for the Study of Human Issues, Inc., 1980).

Jeffrey Nielsen. *The Myth of Leadership: Creating Leaderless Organizations* (Palo Alto, Calif.: Davies-Black Publishing, 2004).

David F. Noble. *America by Design: Science, Technology, and the Rise of Corporate Capitalism* (New York: Alfred A. Knopf, 1977).

Noble. *Forces of Production: A Social History of Industrial Automation* (New York: Alfred A. Knopf, 1984).

Noble. *Progress Without People: New Technology, Unemployment, and the Message of Resistance* (Toronto: Between the Lines, 1995).

Albert Jay Nock. *Our Enemy, the State* (Delavan, Wisc.: Hallberg Publishing Corporation, 1983).

Robert Nozick. *Anarchy, State, and Utopia* (U.S.A.: Basic Books, 1974).

James O'Connor. *Accumulation Crisis* (Oxford: Basil Blackwell Ltd, 1984).

O'Connor. *The Fiscal Crisis of the State* (New York: St. Martin's Press, 1973).

Ben O'Neill. "How to Bureaucratize the Corporate World," *Mises Economics Blog*, January 23, 2008 <http://blog.mises.org/archives/007691.asp>.

Geoff Olson. "Social Darwinist competition leads to Ik-y mess," *The Vancouver Courier*, July 20, 2007 <http://www.canada.com/vancouvercourier/news/opinion/story.html? id= f70e98e6-8fbb-4f5c-9a25-76c038cca258&k=83345>.

"Open Source Hardware," *P2P Foundation Wiki* <http://www.p2pfoundation.net/ Open_Source_Hardware>.

"Open Source Software: A (New?) Development Methodology" (Halloween Document), Version 1.17 (Version 1.00 August 11, 1998). Hosted online, with commentary, by Eric S. Raymond <http://www.catb.org/~esr/halloween/halloween1.html>.

Franz Oppenheimer. "A Post Mortem on Cambridge Economics (Part I)," *The American Journal of Economics and Sociology* 1942/43.

Oppenheimer. "A Post Mortem on Cambridge Economics (Part Two)," *The American Jour-nal of Economics and Sociology*, vol. 2, no. 4.

Oppehneimer. *The State*, Free Life Edition, translated by John Gitterman (San Francisco: Fox & Wilkes, 1914, 1997).

Oppenheimer. *The State: Its History and Development Viewed Sociologically.* 2nd revised edi-tion, with Introduction by Paul Gottfried (Edison, N.J.: Transaction Publishers, 1999).

Bill Orton. "Cohen's Argument," Free-Market.Net forums, January 1, 2001
    <http://www.free-market.net/forums/main0012/messages/807541545.html>   Cap-
    tured April 30, 2004.

Orton. "Re: On the Question of Private Property," Anti-State.Com Forum, August 30, 2003
    <http://www.antistate.com/forum/ index.php?board=6;action=display;threadid=6726;
    start=20> Captured April 30, 2004.

Orton. "Yet Another Variation," Anti-State.Com Forum, December 7, 2003 <http://anti-
    state.com/forum/index.php?board=1;action=display;threadid=7965;start=0>   Cap-
    tured April 30, 2004.

George Orwell. *1984*. Signet Classics reprint (New York: Harcourt Brace Jovanovich, 1949,
    1981).

William G. Ouchi. "The Relationship Between Organizational Structure and Organiza-
    tional Control" *Administrative Science Quarterly* 22 (March 1977) pp. 95-113.

Ouchi. *Theory Z: How American Business Can Meet the Japanese Challenge* (New York: Avon
    Books, 1981).

Ouchi. "The Transmission of Control Through Organizational Hierarchy" *Academy of
    Management Journal* 21:2 (1978) pp. 173-192.

Angelica Oung. "Local Externalities, or why decentralized isn't always better," *The Art of
    the Possible*, April 30, 2008 <http://www.theartofthepossible.net/2008/04/30/local-
    externalities-or-why-decentralized-isnt-always-better/>.

"Pa. bars hormone-free milk labels," *USA Today*, November 13, 2007 <http://www.usatoday.com/
    news/nation/2007-11-13-milk-labels_N.htm>.

Ugo Pagano and Robert Rowthorn. "The Competitive Selection of Democratic Firms in
    a World of Self-Sustaining Institutions," in Pagano and Rowthorn, eds., *Democracy and
    Efficiency in the Economic Enterprise*.

Pagano and Rowthorn, eds. *Democracy and Efficiency in the Economic Enterprise*, a study pro-
    posal for the World Institute for Development of Economic Research (WIDER) of
    the United Nations University (London and New York: Routledge, 1996).

"Pareto efficiency," Wikipedia, the free encyclopedia (captured June 19, 2007)
    <http://en.wikipedia.org/wiki/Pareto_efficiency>.

Mike Parker and Jane Slaughter. "Beware! TQM is coming to Your Campus," *NEA Higher
    Ed*, Spring 1994 <http://www2.nea.org/he/tqm.html>.

Parker and Slaughter. *Working Smart: A Union Guide to Participation Programs and Reengineer-
    ing* (Detroit: Labor Notes, 1994).

C.N. Parkinson. *Parkinson's Law, or the Pursuit of Progress* (London: John Murray, 1958).

Matthew Parris. "I love boring old mobiles," *The Times* (London), December 20, 2007
    <http://www.timesonline.co.uk/tol/comment/columnists/matthew_parris/article3075580.ece>.

Keith Paton. *The Right to Work or the Fight to Live?* (Stoke-on-Trent, 1972).

Paton. "Work and Surplus" *Anarchy* 118 (December, 1970).

Cheryl Payer. *The Debt Trap: The International Monetary Fund and the Third World* (New York:
    Monthly Review Press, 1974).

Martin Khor Kok Peng. *The Uruguay Round and Third World Sovereignty* (Penang, Malaysia:
    Third World Network, 1990).

Michael Perelman. *Classical Political Economy: Primitive Accumulation and the Social Division of
    Labor* (Totowa, N.J.: Rowman & Allanheld; London: F. Pinter, 1984, c 1983).

Perelman. "Farming for Profit in a Hungry World: The Myth of Agricultural Efficiency."
    Louis Junker, ed., *The Political Economy of Food and Energy* (Ann Arbor: University of
    Michigan, 1977).

Perelman. "Intellectual Property Rights and the Commodity Form: New Dimensions in
    the Legislative Transfer of Surplus Value," *Review of Radical Political Economics* 35:3
    (Summer 2003).

Perelman. "Pharmaceutical Crackup?" *EconoSpeak*, December 8, 2007. <http://econospeak.blogspot.com/ 2007/12/pharmaceutical-crackup.html>

Perelman. "The Political Economy of Intellectual Property," *Monthly Review*, January 2003 <http://www.monthlyreview.org/0103perelman.htm>.

Perelman. *Steal This Idea: Intellectual Property Rights and the Corporate Confiscation of Creativity* (New York: Palgrave, 2002).

Charles Perrow. *Organizing America: Wealth, Power, and the Origins of Corporate Capitalism* (Princeton, N.J.: Princeton University Press, 2002).

Thomas J. Peters. *Liberation Management: Necessary Disorganization for the Nanosecond Nineties* (New York: Fawcett Columbine, 1992).

Peters. *Thriving on Chaos: Handbook for a Management Revolution* (New York: Alfred A. Knopf, 1988).

Peters. *The Tom Peters Seminar: Crazy Times Call for Crazy Organizations* (New York: Vintage Books, 1994).

Thomas J. Peters and Robert H. Waterman. *In Search of Excellence: Lessons from America's Best-Run Companies* (New York: Warner Books, 1982).

Peter Phillips & Project Censored. *Censored 2000: The Year's Top 25 Censored Stories* (New York, London, Sydney, and Toronto: Seven Stories Press, 2000).

Michael J. Piore and Charles F. Sabel. *The Second Industrial Divide: Possibilities for Prosperity* (New York: HarperCollins, 1984).

Robert M. Pirsig. *Zen and the Art of Motorcycle Maintenance: An Inquiry Into Values* (New York: William Morrow Publishing Company, 1979). Online version courtesy of Quality page, Virtual School Distributed Learning Community <http://www.virtualschool.edu/mon/ Quality/PirsigZen/index.html>.

Frances Fox Piven and Richard A. Cloward. *Regulating the Poor: The Functions of Public Welfare*. Updated edition (New York: Vintage Books, 1971, 1993).

"The Plowboy Interview: Dr. Ralph Borsodi" *Mother Earth News*, March–April 1974 <http://www.motherearthnews.com/Sustainable-Farming/1974-03-01/The-Plowboy-Interview-Dr-Ralph-Borsodi.aspx>.

Michael Polanyi. *Personal Knowledge: Towards a Post-Critical Philosophy* (New York and Evanston: Harper & Row, Publishers, 1958, 1962).

David Pollard. "All About Power and the Three Ways to Topple It (Part 1)," *How to Save the World*, February 18, 2005 <http://blogs.salon.com/0002007/2005/02/18.html>.

Pollard. "All About Power—Part Two," *How to Save the World*," February 21, 2005 <http://blogs.salon.com/0002007///2005/02/21.html>.

Pollard. "The Future of Business," *How to Save the World*, January 14, 2004 <http://blogs.salon.com/0002007/2004/01/14.html>.

Pollard. "Peer Production," *How to Save the World*, October 28, 2005 <http://blogs.salon.com/0002007/2005/10/28.html#a1322>.

Pollard. "A Prescription for Business Innovation: Creating the Technologies that Solve Basic Human Needs (Part Two)" *How to Save the World*, April 20, 2004 <http://blogs.salon.com/ 0002007/2004/04/20.html>.

Pollard. "Stewardship: Remaking Traditional Companies into Natural Enterprises," *How to Save the World*, July 3, 2006 <http://blogs.salon.com/0002007/2006/07/03.html#a1577>.

Pollard. "The Virtuous Cycles of the Gift Economy," *How to Save the World*, December 6, 2006 <http://blogs.salon.com/0002007/2006/12/06.html>.

Richard Posner. "The Summers Controversy and University Governance," *The Becker-Posner Blog*, February 27, 2005 <http://www.becker-posner-blog.com/archives/2005/02/the_summers_con_1.html>.

Posner. "Summers' Resignation and Organization Theory," The Becker-Posner Blog, February 26, 2006 <http://www.becker-posner-blog.com/archives/2006/02/summers_resigna_1.html>.

Charlie Post and Jane Slaughter. "Lean Production: Why Work is Worse Than Ever, and What's the Alternative" A Solidarity Working Paper (2000) <http://www.solidarity-us.org/LeanProduction.html>.

Alex Pouget. "Mysterious 'neural noise' actually primes brain for peak performance." *EurekAlert*, November 10, 2006 <http://www.eurekalert.org/pub_releases/2006-11/uor-mn111006.php>.

"PR disaster. Wikileaks and the Streisand Effect," PRdisasters.com, March 3, 2007 <http://prdisasters.com/pr-disaster-via-wikileaks-and-the-streisand-effect/>.

Madhu Suri Prakash. "Compost Toilets and Self-Rule," *Yes!*, Winter 2008 <http://www.yesmagazine.org/article.asp?id=2102>.

Keith Preston. "Free Enterprise, The Antidote to Corporate Plutocracy." Winner, 2008 Libertarian Alliance Chris R. Tame Memorial Essay Competition <http://libertarianalliance.wordpress.com/2008/10/25/chris-r-tame-memorial-prize-winning-essay>.

"Proud to be a Replacement Worker," *Libertarian Underground*, March 2, 2004. <http://www.libertarianunderground.com/Forum/index.php/topic,865.0.html>.

Pierre-Joseph Proudhon. *General Idea of the Revolution in the Nineteenth Century*. Trans. by John Beverley Robinson (New York: Haskell House Publishers, Inc., 1923, 1969).

Proudhon. *The Principle of Federation*. Translated by Richard Vernon (Toronto, Buffalo, London: University of Toronto Press, 1979).

Proudhon. *System of Economical Contradictions, or, The Philosophy of Misery*, translated by Benjamin R. Tucker (Boston: Benjamin R. Tucker, 1888).

Proudhon. *What is Property?* Edited and translated by Donald R. Kelley and Bonnie G. Smith (Cambridge and New York: Cambridge University Press, 1994).

David L Prychitko. *Marxism and Workers' Self-Management: The Essential Tension* (New York; London; Westport, Conn.: Greenwood Press, 1991).

"Public Service Announcement—Craig Murray, Tim Ireland, Boris Johnson, Bob Piper and Alisher Usmanov …," *Chicken Yoghurt*, September 20, 2007 <http://www.chickyog.net/2007/09/20/public-service-announcement/>.

Quasibill. "Contract enforcement consolidation," *The Bell Tower*, December 20, 2007. <http://the-bell-tower.blogspot.com/2007/12/contract-enforcement-consolidation.html>.

Quasibill. "Function Follows Form, or Vice Versa (except if either one contradicts your pre-determined outcomes)," *The Bell Tower*, June 10, 2008. <http://the-bell-tower.blogspot.com/2008/06/function-follows-form-or-vice-versa.html>.

Quasibill. "Property rights and contract enforcement," *The Bell Tower*, March 22, 2007 <http://the-bell-tower.blogspot.com/2007/03/property-rights-and-contract.html>.

Ronald Radosh. "The Myth of the New Deal," in Rothbard and Radosh, eds., *A New History of Leviathan: Essays on the Rise of the American Corporate State* (New York: E. P. Dutton & Co., Inc., 1972).

Chakravarthi Raghavan. *Recolonization: GATT, the Uruguay Round & the Third World* (Penang, Malaysia: Third World Network, 1990).

Sunil Rahman. "India's Silicon Valley faces IT exodus," BBC, August 10, 2004 <http://news.bbc.co.uk/1/low/business/3553156.stm>.

Raghuram G. Rajan and Luigi Zingales. "Financial Dependence and Growth" *The American Economic Review* 88:3 (June 1998) pp. 559-586.

Rajan and Zingales. "The Governance of the New Enterprise," in Xavier Vives, ed., *Corporate Governance: Theoretical and Empirical Perspectives* (Cambridge: Cambridge University Press, 2000): pp. 201–227.

Rajan and Zingales. "Power in a Theory of the Firm." *The Quarterly Journal of Economics* (May 1998) pp. 387–432.

Bryan Register. "Class, Hegemony, and Ideology: A Libertarian Approach" (2001) <http://folk.uio.no/thomas/po/class-hegemony-ideology-lib.html>.

Michael Reich and James Devine. "The Microeconomics of Conflict and Hierarchy in Capitalist Production." *The Review of Radical Political Economics* vol. 12 no. 4 (Winter 1981).

Rejuvenal, "Molotov Cocktail for Tom Lagana's Soul," July 1998. *Molotov Cocktail for the Soul* site <http://www.connect.ab.ca/~mctsoul/lagana.htm> (defunct—available only through Internet Archive).

George Reisman. "The Arithmetic of Environmentalist Devastation," *SOLO: Sense of Life Objectivists*, June 19, 2007 <http://www.solopassion.com/node/2667>.

Reisman. "For Society to Thrive, the Rich Must be Left Alone," Mises.Org, March 2, 2006 <http://mises.org/story/2073>.

Reisman. "Mutualism: A Philosophy for Thieves," *Mises Economics Blog*, June 18, 2006 <http://blog.mises.org/archives/005194.asp>.

Reisman. "Mutualism's Support for the Exploitation of Labor and State Coercion," *Mises Economics Blog*, June 23, 2006 <http://blog.mises.org/archives/005219.asp>.

Craig Rennie, Jeff Brookman, and Saeyoung Chang. "CEO Cash and Stock Based Compensation Changes, Layoff Decisions, and Shareholder Value" *The Financial Review Journal* [operating costs increase after downsizing]

David Ricardo. *The Principles of Political Economy and Taxation*. Everyman's Library edition (London: J. M. Dent & Sons, Ltd, 1965).

Bruce Rich. "The Cuckoo in the Nest: Fifty Years of Political Meddling by the World Bank," *The Ecologist* (January/February 1994).

Sheldon Richman. "The Corporate State Wins," The Future of Freedom Foundation, Oct. 3, 2008 <http://www.fff.org/comment/com0810b.asp>.

Rick. "Is a Bit of Marxism Good for Managers?" *Flip Chart Fairy Tales*, October 31, 2007. <http://flipchartfairytales.wordpress.com/2007/10/31/is-a-bit-of-marxism-good-for-managers/>.

Jeremy Rifkin. *The Future of Work: The Decline of the Global Labor Force and the Dawn of the Post-Market Era* (New York: G. P. Putnam's Sons, 1995).

rob. "Below is an example . . ." *This Century Sucks*, August 31, 2004 <http://www.thiscenturysucks.com/2004/08/below-is-example-of-why-daily-show-is.html>.

Austin Robinson. "The Problem of Management and the Size of the Firm" *The Economic Journal* 44:174 (June 1934) pp. 242–257.

John Beverley Robinson. *The Economics of Liberty* (Minneapolis: Herman Kuehn, 1916).

Nick Robinson. "Even Without a Union, Florida Wal-Mart Workers Use Collective Action to Enforce Rights," *Labor Notes*, January 2006. Reproduced at Infoshop, January 3, 2006 <http://www.infoshop.org/inews/article.php?story=20060103065054461>.

Lew Rockwell, "Imperialism: Enemy of Freedom," LewRockwell.Com, October 30, 2006. <http://www.lewrockwell.com/rockwell/bamboozle-bourgeoisie.html>

Walter Rodney. *How Europe Underdeveloped Africa* (Dar-Es-Salaam: Bogle-L'Overture Publications, London and Tanzanian Publishing House, 1973). Transcribed by Joaquin Arriola <http://www.marxists.org/subject/africa/rodney-walter/how-europe/index.htm>.

M. J. Roe. *Strong Managers, Weak Owners: The Political Roots of American Corporate Finance* (Princeton, N.J.: Princeton University Press, 1994).

Roberta Romano. "A Guide to Takeovers: Theory, Evidence, and Regulation," *Yale Journal on Regulation* 9 (1992): 119-80.

David Ronfeldt, John Arquilla, Graham Fuller, Melissa Fuller. *The Zapatista "Social Netwar" in Mexico* MR-994-A (Santa Monica: Rand, 1998) <http://www.rand.org/pubs/monograph_reports/MR994/index.html>.

Paul Rosenberg. "The Empire Strikes Back: Police Repression of Protest from Seattle to L.A." (L.A. Independent Media Center, August 13, 2000). The original online file is now defunct, unfortunately, but is preserved for the time being at <http://web.archive.org/web/20030803220613/http://www.r2kphilly.org/pdf/empire-strikes.pdf>.

Murray N. Rothbard. "Confiscation and the Homestead Principle," *The Libertarian Forum*, June 15, 1969 <http://www.mises.org/ journals/lf/1969/1969_06_15.pdf>.

Rothbard. "The End of Socialism and the Calculation Debate Revisited" *The Review of Austrian Economics* 5:2 (1991) pp. 51-76.

Rothbard. *The Ethics of Liberty* (New York and London: New York University Press, 1998).

Rothbard. *For a New Liberty: The Libertarian Manifesto* (1973, 1978). Online edition prepared by William Harshbarger. Ludwig von Mises Institute, 2002 <http://mises.org/rothbard/newliberty.asp>.

Rothbard. "How and How Not to Desocialize," *The Review of Austrian Economics* 6:1 (1992).

Rothbard. "Ludwig von Mises and Economic Calculation Under Socialism," Laurence S. Moss, ed., *The Economics of Ludwig von Mises* (Kansas City: Sheed and Ward, Inc., 1976).

Rothbard. *Man, Economy, and State: A Treatise on Economic Principles* (Auburn, Ala.: The Ludwig von Mises Institute, 1962, 1970, 1993).

Rothbard. *Power & Market: Government and the Economy* (Menlo Park, Calif.: Institute for Humane Studies, Inc., 1970).

Rothbard. "The Student Revolution," *The Libertarian* (soon renamed *The Libertarian Forum*), May 1, 1969.

Rothbard. "The Tucker-Spooner Doctrine: An Economist's View," *Egalitarianism as a Revolt Against Nature and Other Essays* (Auburn, Ala.: Ludwig von Mises Institute, 2000), reproduced in *Journal of Libertarian Studies*, vol. 20, no. 1 (Winter 2006).

Rothbard. "War Collectivism in World War I." In Rothbard and Ronald Radosh, eds., *A New History of Leviathan: Essays on the Rise of the American Corporate State* (New York: E. P. Dutton & Co., Inc., 1972).

Joyce Rothschild and Terance D. Miethe. "Whistleblowing as Resistance in Modern Work Organizations: The Politics of Revealing Organizational Deception and Abuse," in A. Baum and J.E. Singer, eds., *Advances in Environmental Psychology* (Hillsdale, N.J.: Earlbaum, 1980).

David Rovics. "The RIAA vs. the World," *Counterpunch*, October 9, 2007 <http://www.counterpunch.org/rovics10092007.html>.

Jonathan Rowe. "Entrepreneurs of Cooperation," *Yes!*, Spring 2006 <http://www.yesmagazine.org/article.asp?ID=1464>.

William G. Roy. *Socializing Capital: The Rise of the Large Industrial Corporation in America* (Princeton, N.J.: Princeton University Press, 1997).

Harriet Rubin. "Power." Fast Company No. 65 (November 2002).

Eric Rumble. "Toxic Shocker," *Up! Magazine*, January 1, 2007. <http://www.up-magazine.com/magazine/exclusives/Toxic_Shocker_3.shtml>

Eric Frank Russell. "And Then There Were None," *Astounding Science Fiction*, vol. XLVII, no.4 (June 1951) <http://www.abelard.org/e-f-russell.php>.

Mary Ruwart. *Healing Our World: The Other Piece of the Puzzle* (Kalamazoo, Michigan: Sun-Star Press, 1992, 1993).

Sim Van der Ryn. "Working with and through Institutions," in Dorf and Hunter, eds.

Kirkpatrick Sale. *Human Scale* (New York: Coward, McCann, & Geoghegan, 1980).

Julian Sanchez. "Dammit, Apple," *Notes from the Lounge*, June 2, 2008 <http://www.juliansanchez.com/2008/06/02/dammit-apple/>.

"Say No to Schultz Mansion Purchase" Starbucks Union <http://www.starbucksunion.org/node/1903>.

"The Scanlon Plan," *Time*, Sept. 26, 1955 <http://www.time.com/time/printout/0,8816,807657,00.html>.

F. M. Scherer. *Hearings on Global and Innovation-Based Competition* (FTC, 29 November 1995).

F.M. Scherer and David Ross. *Industrial Market Structure and Economic Performance*. 3rd ed (Boston: Houghton Mifflin Company, 1990).

Michael Schiff and Arie Y. Lewin. "The Impact of People on Budgets" *The Accounting Review* (April 1970) pp. 259-268.

Schiff and Lewin. "Where Traditional Budgeting Fails," *Financial Executive* 36 (May 1968).

Peter Schiff. "Even Stephen Roach Has It Wrong," *Safe Haven*, March 29, 2005 <http://www.safehaven.com/article-2810.htm>.

Herbert Schiller. *Communications and Cultural Domination* (White Plains, N.Y.: M.E. Sharpe, Inc., 1976).

Schiller. *Mass Communications and American* Empire (N.Y.: Augustus M. Kelley, 1969).

Arthur Schlesinger, Jr. *The Age of Jackson* (Boston: Houghton-Mifflin, 1946).

E. F. Schumacher. "The Ethics of Thinking Small," in Dorf and Hunter, eds., *Appropriate Visions*.

E. F. Schumacher. *Good Work* (New York, Hagerstown, San Fransisco, London: Harper & Row, 1979).

Schumacher. *Small is Beautiful: Economics as if People Mattered* (New York, Hagerstown, San Francisco, London: Harper & Row, Publishers, 1973).

Joseph A. Schumpeter. *Capitalism, Socialism, and Democracy* (New York and London: Harper & Brothers Publishers, 1942).

Schumpeter. "Imperialism," in *Imperialism, Social Classes: Two Essays by Joseph Schumpeter.* Translated by Heinz Norden. Introduction by Hert Hoselitz (New York: Meridian Books, 1955).

Chris Sciabarra. *Total Freedom: Toward a Dialectical Libertarianism* (University Park, Penn.: The Pennsylvania State University Press, 2000).

J.C. Scott. "Everyday Forms of Resistance," in F.D. Colburn, ed., *Everyday Forms of Peasant Resistance* (Armonk, N.Y. M.E. Sharpe, 1989).

Philip Selznick. "Foundations of the Theory of Organization" *American Sociological Review*, Vol. 13, No. 1 (Feb. 1948): pp. 25-35.

Richard Sennett. *The Corrosion of Character: The Personal Consequences of Work in the New Capitalism*

Hannah Robie Sewall. *The Theory of Value Before Adam Smith. Publications of the American Economic Association*, vol. II, no. 3 (August, 1901).

Butler Shaffer. *Calculated Chaos: Institutional Threats to Peace and Human Survival* (San Francisco: Alchemy Books, 1985).

Shaffer. *In Restraint of Trade: The Business Campaign Against Competition, 1918-1938* (Lewisburg: Bucknell University Press, 1997).

Cosma Shalizi. "Eigenfactor (Why Oh Why Can't We Have a Better Academic Publishing System? Dept.)," *Three-Toed Sloth*, March 20, 2007 <http://www.cscs.umich.edu/~crshalizi/weblog/479.html>.

Eric D. Shaw, Jerold M. Post, Keven G. Ruby. "Inside the Mind of the Insider" <http://www.securitymanagement.com/library/000762.html>.

Robert Shea. "Empire of the Rising Scum" (1990). The article originally appeared in the now-defunct Loompanics catalog, and is now preserved on Carol Moore's website <http://www.carolmoore.net/articles/empirerisingscum.html>.

Robert Shea and Robert Anton Wilson. *The Illuminatus! Trilogy* (New York: Dell Publishing, 1975).

Yehouda Shenhav. *Manufacturing Rationality: The Engineering Foundations of the Managerial Revolution* (Oxford and New York: Oxford University Press, 1999).

Michael Shermer. *The Mind of the Market: Compassionate Apes, Competitive Humans, and Other Tales from Evolutionary Economics* (New York: Henry Holt and Company, 2008).

Robert Shiller, Eric van Wincoop, and Stefano Athanasoulis. "Macro Markets and Financial Security," *Economic Policy Review: Federal Reserve Bank of New York* (April 1999) <http://findarticles.com/p/articles/mi_qa5390/is_199904/ai_n21437806>.

Laurence H. Shoup and William Minter. "Shaping a New World Order: The Council on Foreign Relations' Blueprint for World Hegemony, 1939-1945," in Holly Sklar, ed., *Trilateralism: The Trilateral Commission and Elite Planning for World Management* (Boston: South End Press, 1980), pp. 135-56.

Michael H. Shuman. "Legalize Localization: Post-Meltdown Thoughts (Part I)," Small-Mart.Org, Nov. 11, 2008 <http://www.small-mart.org/legalize_localization>.

Shuman. *The Small-Mart Revolution: How Local Businesses are Beating the Global Competition* (San Francisco: Barrett-Koehler Publications, Inc., 2006, 2007).

Arthur Silber. "In Praise of Contextual Libertarianism," *The Light of Reason* blog (now defunct), November 2, 2003. Reprinted at *Once Upon a Time* blog, November 26, 2005 <http://powerofnarrative.blogspot.com/2003/11/in-praise-of-contextual-libertarianism.html>.

Silber. "Not So Fast, Please: Contextual Libertarianism, One More Time," *Once Upon a Time* blog, April 8, 2005 <http://powerofnarrative.blogspot.com/2005_04_01_archive.html>.

Christian Siefkes. *From Exchange to Contributions: Generalizing Peer Production into the Physical World* Version 1.01 (Berlin, October 2007).

Jonathan Simcock. "Editorial for Current Edition," *Total Liberty* 1:3 (Autumn 1998).

Herbert Simon. *Administrative Behavior* (New York: The Free Press; London: Collier-Macmillan Limited, 1945, 1947, 1957).

Simon. *Models of Man: Social and Rational* (New York, London, Sydney: John Wiley & Sons, Inc., 1957).

Simon. "Organizations and Markets," *Journal of Economic Perspectives*, 1991.

Minor Sinclair and Martha Thompson. "Cuba: Going Against the Grain" (Oxfam America: June 2001) <http://www.oxfamamerica.org/newsandpublications/publications/ research_reports/art1164.html>.

Holly Sklar. "Overview," in Holly Sklar, ed., *Trilateralism: The Trilateral Commission and Elite Planning for World Management* (Boston: South End Press, 1980).

Martin Sklar. *The Corporate Reconstruction of American Capitalism, 1890-1916: The Market, the Law, and Politics* (Cambridge, New York and Melbourne: Cambridge University Press, 1988).

Peter Skott and Frederick Guy. "A Model of Power-Biased Technological Change," September 14, 2006 <http://www.people.umass.edu/pskott/ SkottGuyFinalVersion13Sept2006.pdf>.

Jane Slaughter. "Management by Stress," *The Multinational Monitor*, January/February 1990 <http://www.multinationalmonitor.org/hyper/issues/1990/01/ slaughter.html>.

Lyman P. van Slyke. "Rural Small-Scale Industry in China," in Richard C. Dorf and Yvonne L. Hunter, eds., *Appropriate Visions*.

Adam Smith. *An Inquiry into the Nature and Causes of The Wealth of Nations*. Great Books edition (Chicago, London, Toronto: Encyclopedia Britannica, Inc., 1952).

Sam Smith. "The Corporate Curse," *Undernews*, May 7, 2008 <http://prorev.com/2008/05/corporate-curse.html>.

Sam Smith. *Project Censored Yearbook 2000*

Johan Soderberg. *Hacking Capitalism: The Free and Open Source Software Movement* (New York and London: Routledge, 2008).

"Solar Turbine—Open Source Ecology" <http://openfarmtech.org/index.php?title=Solar_Turbine>.

Brad Spangler. "Recognizing faux private interests that are actually part of the state," *BradSpangler.Com*, April 29, 2005 <http://www.bradspangler.com/blog/archives/54>.

Joel Spolsky. "Measurement," *Joel on Software*, July 15, 2002 <http://www.joelonsoftware.com/news/20020715.html>.

Lysander Spooner. *Poverty: Its Illegal Causes and Legal Cure* (Boston: Bela Marsh, 1846) <http://www.lysanderspooner.org/Poverty.htm>.

Peter Staudenmaier. "Anarchism and the Cooperative Ideal," *The Communitarian Anarchist* 1:1.

L. S. Stavrianos. *The Promise of the Coming Dark Age* (San Francisco: W. H. Freeman and Company, 1976).

Barry Stein. *Size, Efficiency, and Community Enterprise* (Cambridge: Center for Community Economic Development, 1974).

Joseph R. Stromberg. "Experimental Economics, Indeed" Ludwig von Mises Institute, January 6, 2004 <http://www.mises.org/fullstory.asp?control=1409>.

Stromberg. "Free Trade, Mercantilism and Empire," February 28, 2000 <http://www.antiwar.com/stromberg/s022800.html>.

Stromberg. "The Role of State Monopoly Capitalism in the American Empire" *Journal of Libertarian Studies* Volume 15, no. 3 (Summer 2001), pp. 57-93. <http://www.mises.org/journals/jls/15_3/15_3_3.pdf>.

Michael Strong, "Forget the World Bank, Try Wal-Mart," Tech Central Station, August 22, 2006. <http://www.nyu.edu / fas / institute / dri/ Easterly / File / TCS%20Daily%20-%20Forget %20the%20World%20Bank,%20Try%20Wal-Mart.htm>

Students for a Democratic Society. "The Tranquil Statement," in Henry J. Silverman, ed., *American Radical Thought: The Libertarian Tradition* (Lexington, Mass.: D.C. Heath and Co., 1970).

Dan Sullivan. "The Myth of Corporate Efficiency." SavingCommunities.Org <http://savingcommunities.org/seminars/corpefficiency.html>.

Vin Suprynowicz. "Schools guarantee there can be no new Washingtons," *Review Journal*, February 10, 2008 <http://www.lvrj.com/opinion/15490456.html>.

James Surowiecki. "Performance Perplexes," *The New Yorker*, November 12, 2007 <http://www.newyorker.com/talk/financial/2007/11/12/071112ta_talk_surowiecki>.

Shirley Svorny. "Medical Licensing: An Obstacle to Affordable, Quality Care," Cato Policy Analysis No. 621. <http://www.cato.org/pubs/pas/pa-621.pdf>.

Clarence L. Swartz. *What is Mutualism?* (New York: Vanguard Press, 1927).

Paul M. Sweezy. "Competition and Monopoly," *Monthly Review* (May 1981), pp. 1-16.

Morris and Linda Tannehill. *The Market for Liberty* (New York: Laissez Faire Books, 1984).

R. H. Tawney. *Religion and the Rise of Capitalism* (New York: Mentor Books, 1926, 1954).

"Telecommuting Picking Up As Gasoline Prices Soar." CNBC.Com, June 17, 2008 <http://www.cnbc.com/id/25189379>.

E. P. Thompson. *The Making of the English Working Class* (New York: Vintage Books, 1963, 1966).

Clive Thompson. "The Dream Factory," *Wired*, September 2005 <http://www.wired.com/wired/archive/13.09/fablab_pr.html>.

John Tierney, "Shopping for a Nobel," *New York Times*, October 17, 2006. <http://select.nytimes.com / 2006 / 10/ 17/opinion / 17tierney.html?n=Top%2fOpinion%

2fEditorials%20and%20Op%2dEd% 2fOp% 2dEd% 2fColumnists% 2fJohn% 20Tierney& adxnnl=1&adxnnlx=1162847274-gRz1nECo/qcJ42kqMJltpQ>.

Alvin Toffler. *Powershift: Knowledge, Wealth and Power at the Edge of the 21st Century* (New York: Bantam, 1991).

Leo Tolstoy. " Parable." Reproduced at <http://www.geocities.com/glasgowbranch/ parable.html>.

Jerome Tuccille. "Bits and Pieces," *The Libertarian Forum*, November 1, 1970.

Benjamin R. Tucker. *Individual Liberty: Selections From the Writings of Benjamin R. Tucker* (New York: Vanguard Press, 1926). Reproduced online at Flag.Blackened.Net <http://flag.blackened.net/daver/anarchism/tucker/tucker.html>.

Tucker. *Instead of a Book, By a Man Too Busy to Write One.* Gordon Press facsimile (New York: 1973 [1897]).

Jeffrey Tucker. "Down with (parts of) the past!" Mises Blog, November 11, 2005, http://blog.mises.org/archives/004328.asp.

Tucker. "Hollywood's Workers and Peasants," *InsideCatholic.Com*, November 3, 2007 <http://insidecatholic.com/Joomla/index.php>.

Gordon Tullock. *The Politics of Bureaucracy* (Washington, D.C.: Public Affairs Press, 1965).

"Two Pathways," *Freedom Democrats*, February 11, 2008 <http://freedomdemocrats.org/ node/2541>.

"Tyson Foods Under Fine for Inhumane Slaughter of Poultry," *Agribusiness Examiner*, June 6, 2005 #408 <http://www.organicconsumers.org/OFGU/ tyson060605.cfm>.

United States Participation in the Multilateral Development Banks in the 1980s. Department of the Treasury (Washingon, DC: 1982).

"US Army Intel Units Spying on Activists" *Intelligence Newsletter* #381 April 5, 2000 <http://web.archive.org/web/20000816182951/http://www.infoshop.org/news5/ army_intel.html>.

Jeff Vail. "The Design Imperative," *A Theory of Power*, April 8, 2007 <http://www.jeffvail.net/ 2007/04/design-imperative.html>.

Vail. "Re-Post: Hamlet Economy," *Rhizome*, July 28, 2008 <http://www.jeffvail.net/ 2008/07/re-post-hamlet-economy.html>.

Vail. "A Resilient Suburbia (Part I)," JeffVail.Net, Nov. 10, 2008 <http://www.jeffvail.net/ 2008/11/resilient-suburbia-part-1.html>.

Vail. "A Resilient Suburbia 2: Cost of Commuting," JeffVail.Net, Nov. 17, 2008 <http://www.jeffvail.net/2008/11/resilient-suburbia-2-cost-of-commuting.html>.

Vail. "A Resilient Suburbia 3: Weighing the Potential for Self-Sufficiency," JeffVail.Net, Nov. 24, 2008 <http://www.jeffvail.net/2008/11/resilient-suburbia-3-weighing-potential.html>.

Vail. "Rhizome: Guerrilla Media, Swarming and Asymmetric Politics in the 21st Century," *A Theory of Power: Jeff Vail's Critique of Hierarchy and Empire*, July 21, 2005 <http://www.jeffvail.net/2005/07/rhizome-guerrilla-media-swarming-and.html>.

Vail. *A Theory of Power* <http://www.jeffvail.net/atheoryofpower.pdf>.

Vail. "Passive Solar & Independence," *A Theory of Power*, June 28, 2005 <http://www.jeffvail.net/ 2005/06/passive-solar-independence.html>.

Jaroslav Vanek. "Decentralization under Workers' Management: A Theoretical Appraisal," in Vanek, ed., *Self-Management.*

Vanek. *The General Theory of Labor-Managed Market Economies* (Ithaca and London: Cornell University Press, 1970).

Vanek, ed. *Self-Management: Economic Liberation of Man* (Hammondsworth, Middlesex, England: Penguin Education, 1975).

Alex Veiga (Associated Press). "Homebuilders say 'less is more' with new homes," *MSNBC*, October 10, 2008 <http://www.msnbc.msn.com/id/27122696/>.

Winfried Vogt. "Capitalist Versus Liberal Firm and Economy: Outline of a theory," in Ugo Pagano and Robert Rowthorn, eds., *Democracy and Efficiency in the Economic Enterprise*.

William H. Waddell and Norman Bodek. *Rebirth of American Industry: A Study of Lean Management* (Vancouver, WA: PCS Press, 2005).

Rowan A. Wakefield and Patricia Stafford. "Appropriate Technology: What It Is and Where It Is Going," *The Futurist*, XI:2 (April 1977).

Immanuel Wallerstein. "Household Structures and Labor-Force Formation in the Capitalist World Economy," in Joan Smith, Immanuel Wallerstein, Hans-Dieter Evers, eds., *Households and the World Economy* (Beverly Hills, London, New Delhi: Sage Publications, 1984).

Immanuel Wallerstein and Joan Smith. "Households as an institution of the world-economy," in Smith and Wallerstein, eds., *Creating and Transforming Households: The constraints of the world-economy* (Cambridge; New York; Oakleigh, Victoria; Paris: Cambridge University Press, 1992).

"Wal-Mart Nixes 'Open Availability' Policy," *Business & Labor Reports* (Human Resources section), June 16, 2005 <http://hr.blr.com/news.aspx?id=15666>.

Colin Ward. "Anarchism and the informal economy," *The Raven* No. 1 (1987).

Ward. *Anarchy in Action* (London: Freedom Press, 1982).

Ward. *Social Policy: An Anarchist Response* (London: Freedom Press, 1996), pp. 31-39.

Ward. *Talking Houses: Ten Lectures by Colin Ward* (London: Freedom Press, 1990).

Josiah Warren. *Equitable Commerce* (New York: Burt Franklin, 1852).

Beatrice and Sidney Webb. *The Prevention of Destitution* (London, New York: Longmans, Green and Co., 1911).

Jeremy Weiland. "You are the monkey wrench," *Social Memory Complex*, March 7, 2008. <http://blog.6thdensity.net/?p=918>

James Weinstein. *The Corporate Ideal in the Liberal State, 1900-1918* (Boston: Beacon Press, 1968).

H. G. Wells. *Mankind in the Making* (New York: Scribner's Sons, 1909).

Barry Wilkinson and Nick Oliver. "Power, Control and the Kanban," *New Manufacturing* No. 3. (1989), in "Management Schemes—Part 1 (UE's Information for Workers)" <http://www.ranknfile-ue.org/stwd_mgtsch.html>.

Chris Williams. "Blogosphere shouts 'I'm Spartacus' in Usmanov-Murray case: Uzbek billionaire prompts Blog solidarity," *The Register*, September 24, 2007 <http://www.theregister.co.uk/2007/09/24/usmanov_vs_the_internet/>.

Robert Williams. "Bologna and Emilia Romagna: A Model of Economic Democracy," paper presented to the annual meeting of the Canadian Economics Association, University of Calgary. May/June 2002 <http://www.bcca.coop/pdfs/ BolognaandEmilia.pdf.>.

William Appleman Williams. *The Contours of American History* (Cleveland and New York: The World Publishing Company, 1961).

Williams. "A Profile of the Corporate Elite," in Rothbard and Radosh, eds., *New History of Leviathan: Essays on the Rise of the American Corporate State* (New York: E. P. Dutton & Co., Inc., 1972).

Williams. *The Tragedy of American Diplomacy* (New York: Dell Publishing Company, 1959, 1962).

Oliver Williamson. "Comparative Economic Organization: The Analysis of Discrete Structural Alternatives," *Journal of Law, Economics, and Organization* IV:1 (1988).

Williamson. "Comparative Economic Organization: The Analysis of Discrete Structural Alternatives" *Administrative Science Quarterly* 36:2 (June 1991).

Williamson. *The Economic Institutions of Capitalism: Firms, Markets, Relational Contracting* (New York: Free Press; London: Collier Macmillan, 1985).

Williamson. *Economic Organization: Firms, Markets, and Policy Control* (New York: NYU Press, 1986).

Williamson. *The Economics of Discretionary Behavior: Managerial Objectives in a Theory of the Firm* (Englewood Cliffs, N.J.: Prentice-Hall, Inc., 1964).

Williamson. "The Logic of Economic Organization" *Journal of Law, Economics, and Organization* 4:1 (Spring 1988) pp. 65-93.

Williamson. *Markets and Hierarchies, Analysis and Antitrust Implications: A Study on the Economics of Internal Organization* (New York: Free Press, 1975).

Williamson. "The Organization of Work: A Comparative Institutional Assessment," *Journal of Economic Behavior and Organization*, 1(1): 35, quoted in Geoffrey Hodgson, "Organizational Form and Economic Evolution," in Ugo Pagano and Robert Rowthorn, eds., *Democracy and Efficiency in the Economic Enterprise*, a study proposal for the World Institute for Development of Economic Research (WIDER) of the United Nations University (London and New York: Routledge, 1996).

Frank N. Wilner. "Give truckers an inch, they'll take a ton-mile: every liberalization has been a launching pad for further increases—trucking wants long combination vehicle restrictions dropped," *Railway Age*, May 1997 <http://findarticles.com/p/ articles/mi_m1215/ is_n5_v198/ai_19460645>.

James L. Wilson. "Standard of Living vs. Quality of Life," *The Partial Observer*, May 29, 2008 <http://www.partialobserver.com/article.cfm?id=2955&RSS=1>.

Robert Anton Wilson, "Thirteen Choruses For the Divine Marquis," from *Coincidance—A Head Test* <http://www.deepleafproductions.com/wilsonlibrary/texts/raw-marquis.html>. Originally published in *The Realist*.

Langdon Winner. *The Whale and the Reactor: A Search for Limits in an Age of High Technology* (Chicago and London: University of Chicago Press, 1986).

Wisconsin Federation of Nurses and Health Professionals. "A Summary of Recent Research Supporting the Need for Staffing Ratios and Workload Limitations in Healthcare" <http://www.wfnhp.org/setlimits/researchsummary.html> Link no longer active, but available through Internet Archive.

Claire Wolfe. "Dark Satanic Cubicles," *Loompanics 1995 Catalog* <http://www.loompanics.com/ cgi-local/SoftCart.exe/Articles/darksatanic.html> (Loompanics site now defunct; link no longer active).

Claire Wolfe. "Insanity, the Job Culture, and Freedom," *Loompanics Unlimited* 2005 Winter Supplement <http://www.loompanics.com/Articles/insanityjobculture.html>.

Edward N. Wolff. *Growth, Accumulation, and Unproductive Activity* (Cambridge, London, New York, New Rochelle, Melbourne, Sydney: Cambridge University Press, 1987).

James P. Womack, Daniel T. Jones, Daniel Roos. *The Machine That Changed the World* (New York: Macmillan Publishing Company, 1990).

Michael Yates. "The Injuries of Class," *Monthly Review* 59:8 (January 2008): pp. 1-10 <http://www.monthlyreview.org/080101yates.php>.

Barry Yeoman. "When Is a Corporation Like a Freed Slave?" *Mother Jones*, November-December 2006. <http://www.motherjones.com/news/feature/2006/11/when_is_ a_corporation_like_a_freed_slave.html>.

Matthew Yglesias. "The Office Illusion," *Matthew Yglesias*, September 1, 2007 <http://matthewyglesias.theatlantic.com/archives/2007/09/the_office_illusion.php>.

Yglesias. "Two Views of Capitalism," *Matthew Yglesias*, Nov. 22, 2008 <http://yglesias.thinkprogress.org/ archives/2008/11/two_views_of_capitalism.php>.

Luigi Zingales. "In Search of New Foundations" *The Journal of Finance* 55:4 (August 2000) pp. 1623-1653.

Oliver Zunz. *Making America Corporate, 1870-1920* (Chicago: University of Chicago Press, 1990).

Index

About the Author

KEVIN A. CARSON is Research Associate at the Center for a Stateless Society. He is the author of *Studies in Mutualist Political Economy*—the focus of a symposium published in the *Journal of Libertarian Studies*—as well as of the pamphlets *Austrian and Marxist Theories of Monopoly-Capital* and *Contract Feudalism: A Critique of Employer Power Over Employees* (Libertarian Alliance); *The Ethics of Labor Struggle* (Alliance of the Libertarian Left); and *The Iron Fist behind the Invisible Hand: Corporate Capitalism As a State-Guaranteed System of Privilege* (Red Lion Press). His writing has also appeared in *Just Things, Any Time Now, The Freeman: Ideas on Liberty*, and *Land and Liberty*, as well as on the P2P Foundation blog. A member of the Industrial Workers of the World, the Voluntary Cooperation Movement, and the Alliance of the Libertarian Left, and a leader in the contemporary revival of Proudhonian mutualist anarchism, he maintains the "Free Market Anti-Capitalism" blog at http://Mutualist.BlogSpot.Com.